FIELD GEOLOGY

FIELD GEOLOGY

FREDERIC H. LAHEE, Ph.D.

Consulting Geologist since 1955
Geological and Research Counselor
of the Sun Oil Company 1947–1955
From 1921 to 1947
Chief Geologist of the Sun Oil Company
Formerly Assistant Professor of Geology
Massachusetts Institute of Technology

SIXTH EDITION

CBS Publishers & Distributors Pvt. Ltd.

New Delhi • Bengaluru • Chennai • Kochi • Kolkata • Mumbai
Hyderabad • Nagpur • Patna • Pune • Vijayawada

ISBN: 81-239-0887-3

First Indian Edition: 1987

This edition has been published in India by arrangement with McGraw-Hill Book Company, Inc., New York, USA

Published by **Satish Kumar Jain** and produced by **Varun Jain** for
CBS Publishers & Distributors Pvt. Ltd.,
4819/XI Prahlad Street, 24 Ansari Road, Daryaganj, New Delhi - 110002
delhi@cbspd.com, cbspubs@airtelmail.in • www.cbspd.com
Ph.: 23289259, 23266861, 23266867 • Fax: 011-23243014

Corporate Office: 204 FIE, Industrial Area, Patparganj, Delhi - 110 092
Ph: 49344934 • Fax: 011-49344935
E-mail: publishing@cbspd.com • publicity@cbspd.com

Branches:
- ***Bengaluru:*** 2975, 17th Cross, K.R. Road, Bansankari 2nd Stage, Bengaluru - 70 • Ph: +91-80-26771678/79 • Fax: +91-80-26771680 E-mail: cbsbng@gmail.com, bangalore@cbspd.com
- ***Chennai:*** No. 7, Subbaraya Street, Shenoy Nagar, Chennai - 600030 Ph: +91-44-26681266, 26680620 • Fax: +91-44-42032115 E-mail: chennai@cbspd.com
- ***Kochi:*** Ashana House, 39/1904, A.M. Thomas Road, Valanjambalam, Ernakulum, Kochi • Ph: +91-484-4059061-65 Fax: +91-484-4059065 • E-mail: cochin@cbspd.com
- ***Kolkata:*** 6-B, Ground Floor, Rameshwar Shaw Road, Kolkata - 700014 Ph: +91-33-22891126/7/8 • E-mail: kolkata@cbspd.com
- ***Mumbai:*** 83-C, Dr. E. Moses Road, Worli, Mumbai - 400018 Ph: +91-9833017933, 022-24902340/41 • E-mail: mumbai@cbspd.com

Representatives:

- Hyderabad: 0-9885175004
- Patna: 0-9334159340
- Jharkhand: 0-9811541605
- Nagpur: 0-9021734563
- Pune: 0-9623451994
- Uttarakhand: 0-9716462459

Printed at: Neekunj Print Process, Delhi (India)

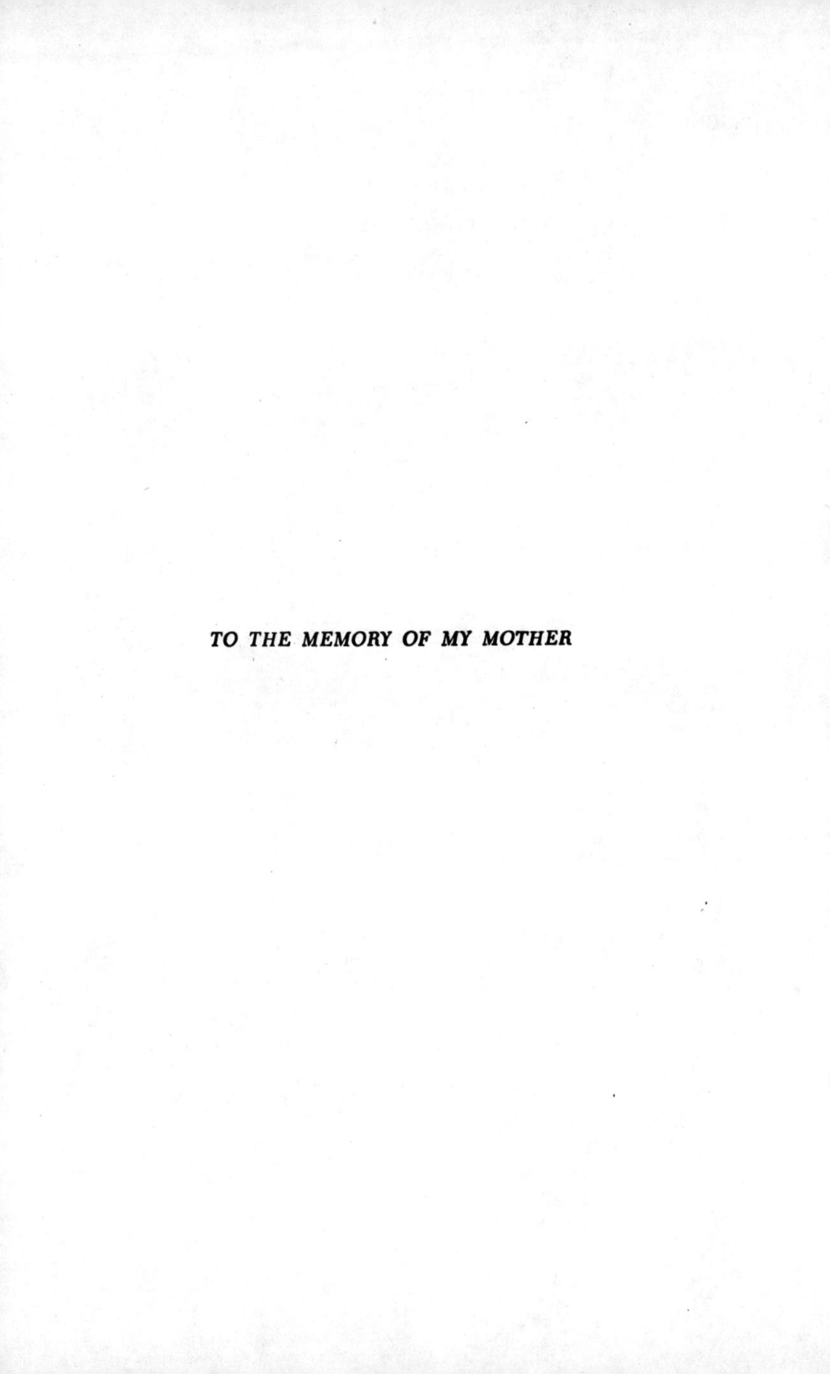

TO THE MEMORY OF MY MOTHER

PREFACE TO THE SIXTH EDITION

In preparing the sixth edition of "Field Geology," we have adhered as closely as possible to the plan of treatment maintained since the first edition was published in 1916. So appropriate is the introductory paragraph of the preface to the fifth edition to the present sixth edition that we quote it in full, as follows:

"When the first edition of this book was published, surface geology—the study of soils and outcrops, of horizontal, inclined, and vertical rock exposures, and of the relations of these phenomena to one another—served as the principal basis for interpreting the three-dimensional structure of the underground. There was some logging of drilled wells, but only of the crudest kind. Since that time tremendous advances have been made in all branches of the science. Each succeeding decade"—and this statement includes the 1950s—"has witnessed the development of new techniques and new tools in geology, all of which, with few exceptions, have been aimed at improving our understanding of that same three-dimensional structure of the underground. Some of these methods have been applied at or above the surface of the ground, as, for instance, most forms of geophysics and also air photography. Others have been applied below ground, as the several improved varieties of well logging. But in any case, whether the techniques or the tools are operated above or below ground—that is, whether they belong under surface geology or subsurface geology—both classes of geological approach are intimately interrelated. The subsurface data obtainable from well logging or from geophysical exploration greatly assist the geologist in his interpretations of surface geology, and, on the other hand, the subsurface geologist cannot adequately explain his data without a thorough knowledge of the phenomena of surface geology. Directly and indirectly *field geology* embraces many phases of both surface geology and subsurface geology."

Many new terms have been concisely defined and explained in the sixth edition, such as turbidity currents, stone tracks, patterned ground, soil profile, biologic facies, palynology, pluton, lopolith, phacolith, ringdike, cone sheet, metamorphic facies, boudin, diapir fold, wrench fault, granitization, and so on. New text has been added on contemporaneity in sedimentation, on tectonic correlation of sediments, on the "granite problem," on the terms "base level" and "grade," on the use of the Jacob staff, on distortion and displacement in air photographs, on the use of air and gas in drilling deep holes, on induction logging, on sonic (continuous velocity) logging, on dipmeter surveying, on presently used methods of electronic surveying, on refraction seismic shooting for overhang of salt domes, and so on. In view of the almost complete substitution of the gravimeter for the torsion balance in gravity surveying, this section of the chapter on geophysics has been completely rewritten.

The Bibliography contains 65 new up-to-date references. Since the older references have a historical value, we have decided not to remove them.

Two of the earlier figures have been revised, one of these being Fig. 386, the isogonic chart of the United States, brought up to 1955. Sixteen new figures have been added. Among these we are gratefully indebted to C. I. Alexander and John F. Grayson (Fig. 41); to H. R. Breck, S. W. Schoellhorn, R. B. Baum, and G. H. Westby (Fig. 536); to John L. P. Campbell and John C. Wilson (Fig. 527); to Louise Kingsley (Figs. 96 and 97); and to the Schlumberger Well Surveying Corporation (Fig. 472). The publication sources of these figures are cited in their captions.

To the following gentlemen we are grateful for advice in preparing the text for this sixth edition: Arthur A. Baker, Marland P. Billings, Laurence Brundall, L. G. Ellis, W. T. Evans, William A. Fischer, William J. Gealy, R. H. Hopkins, R. E. Rettger, C. A. Tips, Harold R. Wanless, and A. C. Winterhalter.

Frederic H. Lahee

Dallas, Texas
January, 1961

PREFACE TO THE FIRST EDITION

This book treats the subject of geology from the field standpoint. It is intended both for a textbook and for a pocket manual. As a manual, the author hopes that it will be of service not only to students of geology, but also to mining engineers, civil engineers, and others whose interests bring them in touch with geologic problems. The book has been written on the assumption that the reader has an elementary knowledge of general geology and also an acquaintance with a few common minerals and rocks.

The first twelve chapters are concerned with the recognition and interpretation of geologic structures and topographic forms as they are observed. Here the aim has been to describe together phenomena which in certain respects resemble one another, but which may be of diverse origins. Where possible the treatment has been empirical rather than genetic. In order to assist the reader in identifying various forms and structures, a number of tables or keys have been prepared. From the very nature of geology they cannot be final or complete. They are presented with the hope that they may be of some value at least in showing what features to observe in the field.

In the last six chapters[1] are described methods of geologic surveying, the nature and construction of maps, sections, and block diagrams, the interpretation of topographic and geologic maps, the solution of certain geologic computations, and the preparation of geologic reports.

An appendix containing several tables of practical value, a bibliography to which there are many footnote references throughout the text, and an index which has been made as comprehensive as possible, will be found at the end of the book.

The author wishes to express his sincere gratitude to his wife, to Professors W. M. Davis, W. Lindgren, R. A. Daly, and H. W. Shimer, and to Dr. J. D. Mackenzie, for valuable advice and criticism.

For illustrations the writer is indebted as follows, the specific sources being noted in certain cases in parentheses:[2] to Professor

[1] Expanded in later editions to the present Chaps. 13 to 22.

[2] In this paragraph the original figure numbers have been changed to agree with their present numbers in the sixth edition.

W. Lindgren for Figs. 173 and 264 ("Mineral Deposits"); to Professor R. A. Daly for Figs. 98, 110, and 123 ("Igneous Rocks and Their Origin"); to the Harvard Geological Museum for permission to photograph specimens for Figs. 14–18, 81, 245, and 251; to the University of Chicago Press and the *Journal of Geology* for Figs. 52 and 499; to the Carnegie Institute of Washington for Figs. 295, 309, and 310; to the Geological Society of America for Figs. 5A and B (modified), 171, 172 (modified), 272, and 305; to Dr. W. F. King, Chief Astronomer, Department of the Interior, Ottawa, for Fig. 76 (from R. A. Daly's "Geology of the North American Cordillera at the 49th Parallel"); to Mr. R. W. Sayles for Fig. 33; to the Geological Survey of New Jersey and the U.S. Geological Survey for Fig. 314; to the U.S. Geological Survey for Figs. 6 (*An. Rept.* 7), 44, 87, 110, 111 (*Bull.* 404), 180–182 (*An. Rept.* 13), 243 (*Bull.* 275), 248 (*Bull.* 239), 235 (*An. Rept.* 4), 268 (*Folio* 15), 286 (*Bull.* 576), 287, 289–293, 297 (*Prof. Paper* 82), 306 (*An. Rept.* 17), 312, 315, 316, and 317 (*Prof. Paper* 82), 319, 320, 322, 323, 328, 331 (*Prof. Paper* 64), 333, 336 (*Bull.* 273), 337, 338, 341, 342 (*Prof. Paper* 61), 343 (*Prof. Paper* 67), 354, 358 (*Prof. Paper* 61), 359 (*Monog.* 1), 360–362, 363 (*An. Rept.* 21), 364, 523 (*Bull.* 300), 561 and 594; to the Coast and Geodetic Survey for Fig. 386; to Professor C. K. Leith for Fig. 144, to Professors E. Blackwelder and H. H. Barrows for Fig. 247B; and to Professor W. M. Davis for Figs. 283–285, 326, 355, and 356. Figures 283 (redrawn by F. H. L.), 284, 285, 326, and 355 were taken from Professor Davis' "Geographical Essays," and Fig. 356 from "Physical Geography" by W. M. Davis and W. H. Snyder, by permission of Ginn and Company, Publishers.

To Professor H. F. Reid the author is grateful for permission to draw from his articles published in Bulletins 20 and 24 of the Geological Society of America.

The late Dr. C. W. Hayes very generously gave the writer entire freedom to borrow from his "Handbook for Field Geologists." Several mathematical tables were copied from this source.

Frederic H. Lahee

Boston, Mass.
October, 1916

CONTENTS

Chapter 1

INTRODUCTION

General Definitions

1. Processes of erosion. On the earth's surface various agents are engaged in the work of rock destruction. Rivers wear their channels; waves undermine the cliffs along shores; wind, when it has free play, scours the rocks over which it blows; and glaciers abrade their beds. These are all processes in which the agent is moving while in operation. There are other kinds of work in which the agents are essentially motionless. For instance, alternate heating and cooling in regions of wide temperature range may cause the separation of grains and chips from the surface of a rock; moisture in the cracks of a rock expands in freezing and may wedge off block after block; certain minerals may be decomposed and carried away in solution; and so on. Whether accomplished by moving or motionless agents, the various processes of rock destruction come under the head of *erosion* (*e*, off; *rodo*, gnaw). Mechanical wear by rivers, wind, etc., is *corrasion;* chemical wear is *corrosion.* Many of the processes effected by agents which are essentially motionless are included in the term, *weathering.* Weathering accomplished in a chemical way is *decomposition* and that accomplished in a mechanical way is *disintegration.*

2. Products of erosion. Through erosion a quantity of débris is formed equivalent to the amount by which the rocks are worn down. Ordinarily it is borne away from its source, part being in solution and part being handled mechanically, and is eventually accumulated as sedimentary materials.[1] Deposits of this sort are called *transported.* If products of erosion remain *in situ* they are known as *residual deposits.* Transported deposits are *chemical* if they were precipitated from solution, and they are

[1] *Sediment* and *sedimentary* are used in this book in their widest sense with reference to all rocks which originate upon the earth's surface and which are derived through the destruction of pre-existing rock.

mechanical, fragmental, or *clastic,* if they consist of detached particles and fragments of the parent rock and if their accumulation was brought about by mechanical means. Chemical and mechanical sediments may be *organic* or *inorganic,* depending either upon the nature of the materials or upon the agent of their deposition. All these deposits, including clay, mud, sand, gravel, soil, and the like, are known collectively as *mantle rock* or the *regolith.*[2]

3. Agents and modes of transportation. Particles and fragments of rock may be transported by wind, by moving water (streams, currents in lakes, seas, and oceans), or by moving ice (mountain glaciers, ice sheets, ice rafts, icebergs); also, less commonly, by other agents. Sometimes moving bodies of air or of water are so heavily charged with débris which they are carrying that they are denser than the adjoining air or water through which they flow. Such are dust storms in arid regions and mud-laden streams flowing into the clearer water of lakes or oceans. These are called *density currents* or *turbidity currents.* They may distribute rock particles (dust, mud, sand, or even some gravels) over wide areas, often far from the original source of these materials.

4. Mass movements. Processes of erosion involve not only the transportation of individual particles and fragments of rock by such agents as wind, water, and ice but also the moving of masses of rock débris. These processes are classified as *mass movements,* or *mass wasting.* They include slow flowage (rock creep, soil creep, solifluction); rapid flowage (sheetflood, mudflow, débris avalanche); landslide (slump, débris slides, rock slides); and subsidence (over mines, caverns, etc.). As suggested by these names, all these movements are due to insufficient support to prevent the settling or collapse of masses of rock material under the pull of gravity. In the different classes of mass movement, interstitial water (or ice) may be effective in lubricating or otherwise facilitating the movement.[3] On the moderately

[2] The study of mantle rock is very important in connection with scientific agriculture and also in connection with dam sites, strength of foundations, and other engineering problems. The word "soil" is sometimes used as synonymous with mantle rock, or regolith, and sometimes in the more restricted sense of earth material that will support rooted plants. Of interest here is the "soil profile," described in Art. 85.

[3] For a full discussion of this subject, see Bibliog., Sharpe, C. F. Stewart, 1938. See also Fig. 270, after Sharpe. On landslides, see Bibliog., Beaty Chester B., 1956.

sloping floors of lakes or seas, where turbidity currents (Art. 3) have deposited gravels on soft muds, movement down the slope, with commingling of pebbles and mud, may be initiated by overweighting, by earthquakes, or by other causes.[4]

5. Bedrock, outcrop, and exposure defined. Everywhere below the mantle rock, solid rock, or *bedrock*, is known to exist. When the bedrock projects through the overlying mantle of detritus, the protruding portions are called *outcrops*. Outcrops and also sections in the unconsolidated superficial mantle rock may be referred to as *exposures*.

6. Discrimination between transported and residual deposits. Transported and residual deposits can usually be distinguished in the field by their relations to the underlying bedrock. As a rule, transported materials are quite unlike the rock beneath them, whereas residual deposits commonly grade down into the subjacent rock or at least show some chemical resemblance to the latter (refer to Chap. 3 and to Arts. 84, 85).

7. Lithosphere defined. If erosion should continue long enough in any region and if the products of this erosion should be removed, at last rocks might be exposed which were once at great depth. This is just what has happened over broad areas on the continents and consequently we are able today to see and study rocks some of which have been several miles below the earth's surface. We may say, then, that we are in some degree familiar with the solid part of the earth down to a depth of several—probably well within 25—miles, at least as far as the continents are concerned. Of the ocean basins we know much less; but of this fact we can feel certain, that for some distance beneath the ocean floor, as likewise for some distance beneath the land surface, the earth consists of *rocks* of one kind or another. This outer rocky shell of the earth, of which the continental portions have been to a certain extent brought within our observation, is the *lithosphere*.

8. Field geology defined. When rocks and rock materials are investigated in their natural environment and in their natural relations to one another, the study is called *field geology*. Field geology seeks to describe and explain the surface features and underground structure of the lithosphere. Physiography and structural geology are equally important in the science of field geology. Subsurface geology, likewise very important, pertains

[4] See Bibliog., Crowell, J. C., 1957.

to the study of rock relationships by the use of data obtained underground, as in mines or from drilled wells. It is in contrast to surface geology, which is the collection and study of superficial evidences.

9. Observation and inference. Field geology is necessarily founded upon observation and inference. Only features that are superficial can be observed; all else must be inferred. We may study the surface of an outcrop, of a valley, or of a sand grain, but in attempting to explain the internal structure of the outcrop, or what underlies the valley, or how the sand grain was fashioned, we are forming inferences by interpreting certain visible facts. The ability to infer and to infer correctly is the goal of training in field geology, for one's proficiency as a geologist is measured by one's skill in drawing safe and reasonable conclusions from observed phenomena.

10. Correlation. No geologic structures and no land forms, such as hills, valleys, and the like (**265**),[5] exist as isolated phenomena. Every geologic feature is in some way dependent upon, or associated with, other geologic features, and this dependency or association the field geologist must discover. This is what is meant by *correlation*. The word signifies the description or explanation of one geologic phenomenon in relation to others. Here is an example to illustrate the case: By definition all outcrops are exposed portions of the bedrock underlying the superficial unconsolidated mantle rock. Accordingly, when the geologist examines a series of outcrops he should bear in mind that they are not single, detached forms, but that they are visible parts of a rock body which is continuous beneath the soil and that the rocks or structures which they exhibit are in some way mutually related. He will be *correlating* these outcrops when he studies them from this broad point of view and endeavors to explain these mutual relations.

11. Multiple working hypotheses. Geologic interpretation is facilitated by what is termed the method of multiple working hypotheses. Suppose, for instance, that the surface of a rock is marked by parallel grooves. In order to explain the origin of this feature, the geologist should call to mind all possible ways in which such parallel grooves might be produced. These are his working hypotheses. To determine which is the right one, he

[5] Numbers in parentheses refer to the articles in the text, denominated by the side headings.

must examine the rock surface for other phenomena which are associated with the grooves, for each hypothesis postulates a certain group of geologic features which are mutually related.

The same principle may be applied where extensive correlation is necessary. The distribution of outcrops in a small area may be such as to suggest that a certain igneous rock comes into contact with a certain sedimentary rock, but the actual junction line may be concealed beneath the mantle rock. The relation may be explained on the assumption that the two rock bodies meet in an intrusive contact, in a fault, or in a surface of unconformity. These three working hypotheses the geologist would have to keep in mind while looking for further evidence to ascertain which is the true interpretation.

12. The study of exposures. Every geologic surface has features which deserve an explanation. They may be purely superficial or they may be cross sections of structures or forms that extend below the surface. In the latter event they probably belong to the structure of the rock. To discriminate between such superficial and structural characters, break off a fragment of the bedrock, or, in the case of an unconsolidated deposit, scrape off some of the surface material. The freshly exposed surface will settle the question.

If the observed features are superficial, in respect to their origin they may be related to the surface on which they are found in one or another of these four ways: (1) They may still be in process of formation, although perhaps the agent that made them is not acting continuously. (2) They may have been made by some agent no longer working and may not yet have suffered alteration under the new conditions. This often holds for Pleistocene glacial scorings on hard, fine-grained rocks; but smoothed, striated surfaces are soon destroyed on exposed coarse granular rocks, which are much more susceptible to disintegration. (3) The surface features, if on bedrock, may have been preserved for a time under unconsolidated deposits which have recently been removed (**84, 85**). Disintegration in coarse rocks may be prevented by such a cover. On the other hand, a soil mantle may sometimes promote decomposition of the buried rock. (4) A buried surface like that just mentioned may be preserved for a much longer time by a thick cover of consolidated strata (**86**). Erosion of the overlying formation may re-expose the old surface provided the latter happens to coincide with the new erosion surface; but such instances are very rare and the exposure of the old surface cannot be complete.

If the observed features are structural, extending into the bedrock or the mantle rock, as the case may be, they should be examined with this fact constantly in mind. A line is then the cross section of a surface and an area (band or patch) is the cross section of a body that has three dimensions. The trend of the line is often indicative of the form of the surface which it represents, and the shape of the area is suggestive of the form of the body, but there are many exceptions. The geologist should always look over the outcrop or the deposit to see if he can find

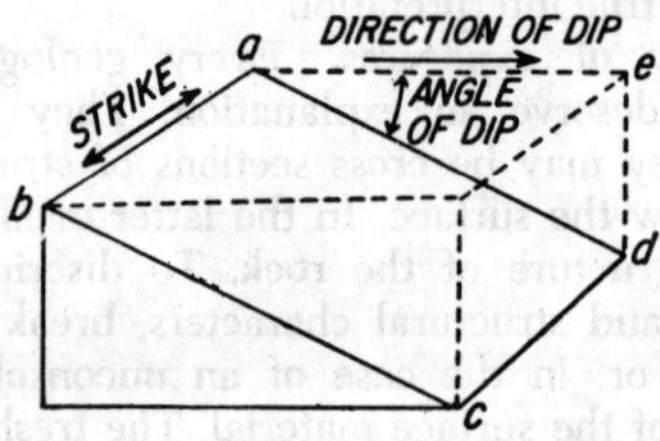

FIG. 1. Dip and strike. *bae* is a horizontal plane.

the structural surface or body exposed on two faces of this outcrop as nearly as possible at right angles to one another.

13. Primary and secondary features defined. It is sometimes convenient to refer to the features on exposures as *primary* or *secondary* according as their origin was contemporaneous with, or subsequent to, the origin of the material in which they are seen. Examples of primary structures are bedding in sedimentary rocks, ripple marks, flow structure in lava, and the like. Among secondary features may be mentioned surface stains on outcrops, glacial scratches, and fractures in rocks.

14. Dip, strike, and attitude defined. When one wishes to state the position of an inclined flat surface, two definite quantities are necessary. One must know the *dip*, that is, the maximum angle of slope of the surface, and one must know the *strike*, which is the direction of the intersection of the surface with any horizontal plane (Fig. 1). The dip is an angle in a vertical plane and must always be measured *downward* from the horizontal plane. The direction of dip is perpendicular to the strike. Dip and strike together determine the position or *attitude* of a surface with respect to horizontality and to compass directions. Obviously the attitude of a relatively thin layer of uniform thickness will be that of the layer's upper or lower surface.

15. Lineation. A term which has come into wide use by geologists is *lineation*. This word, according to the dictionary, means "an arrangement of lines." In geology it may refer to a single linear feature, or to a rectangular or polygonal distribution of linear features, or, more commonly, to a group of parallel linear features. It usually connotes relatively straight or only broadly curving parallel lines, but actually highly contorted parallel lines would fall under the geological meaning of the term. The lines, or linear features, are called ***linears***. There is another connotation, also commonly included in the case of parallel linears; that is, whether the lineation is observed in a microscopic slide, in a hand specimen, on a small or a large rock exposure, or in the photographed or mapped distribution of regional fold axes or other such structures, the spacing between the parallel "lines" is relatively much smaller than their length.

Actually lineation is a "basket word" which has been adopted to embrace a large variety of geological parallel linear features which, under various names, have long been recognized. Some of these may be of purely superficial origin, whereas others are related to rock structure in one way or another. As explained by Cloos, in his excellent survey of this subject, "Lineation is a descriptive and nongenetic term for any kind of linear structure within or on a rock."[6] It includes parallel alignment of glacial striae, grooves (**39 A, B**), and drumlin axes (**298 B**); topographic forms of marked linearity; fault striae on slickensides (**199, 207**); primary and secondary flow lines (**79, D; 81, B; 83, 84, 85**); linear parallelism of minerals (**244**) and other rock components; parallel elongate pebbles (**56**); streaks and schlieren in igneous rocks (**130**); parallel fold axes, wrinkles, and crenulations; and intersections of parallel surfaces. We wish to point out one further fact concerning the scope of the term. As suggested in the foregoing quotation from Cloos, where he says "within or on a rock," some features described under lineation may be limited in their occurrence to a surface (as striae on slickensided fault surfaces); whereas others may extend into and through a rock mass (as elongated parallel

[6] Bibliog., Cloos, Ernst, 1946. See also Bibliog., Wilson, J. Tuzo, 1948.

pebbles in a metamorphosed conglomerate). If the latter is the case, the lineation observed on a rock surface may not represent the axis of greatest elongation (see Fig. 2). Note also that, when lineation is of regional dimensions, its recognition may not be easy except on air photographs (see Art. **456**) or on small-scale maps of the terrane involved, and here the observed lineation may be (and quite frequently is) due to the exposure of the edges of parallel surfaces or layers.

A study of lineation in any region is of great value in helping to unravel problems of geologic history (see **348**). This is because the various features that come under this head were produced by movements, as, for example, the relative motion of

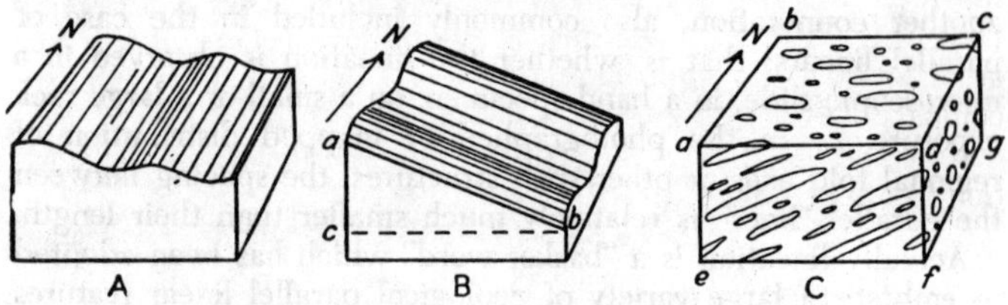

FIG. 2. Examples of lineation. In A and B the lineation (here grooves and scratches) is limited to the rock surface. In A the lineation trends north and south and is horizontal. In B it plunges east at an angle of about 30° (*abc*). In C the lineation passes into the rock. It is indicated by elongated pebbles. On surface *abcd*, it trends east and west. As seen in surface *adfe*, it plunges toward the west. On *abcd* the observed lineation is actually a horizontal component of the true lineation (*adfe*).

adjoining fault blocks in producing scratches on slickensided surfaces, the flow of igneous material in producing flow structure (**131**), and the squeezing together of sedimentary rock massifs in producing folds (and therefore fold axes), intersecting cleavage sets, and so on. With very few exceptions the movements involved in developing lineation were either parallel to or essentially perpendicular to the direction of the lineation.

16. Attitude of lineation. Because of the importance of lineation as an index of geologic history, its attitude, *i.e.*, its position in the field relative to compass directions and to horizontality, requires definition. It may be strictly a linear, or two-dimensional, feature, or it may be a surficial or layer feature which is seen and mapped edgewise, therefore appearing as lines. In the former case, if the lineation occurs on, and is limited to, a horizontal rock surface, its direction is merely referred to the points of the compass. If it occurs on an inclined surface, to which it is limited, its direction is the horizontal direction of the vertical plane in which it lies. Within this vertical plane, its inclination (which is the intersection of the vertical plane with the lineated rock surface) is its *plunge,* which like dip, is always a vertical angle measured *downward* from the horizontal. Where this kind of lineation is not restricted to a rock surface, but passes into a rock (elongated pebbles, etc.), its plunge and direction are still measured in the same way, but care must be taken to see that attention is being given to the *true* lineation, and not to a *component* of the lineation, as when the rock surface intersects the true lineation at an acute angle (see Fig. 2). In the second case, cited above (edges of surfaces or of layers), the trend of the observed lineation is referred to compass directions, but there is no plunge.

Note the lineation may occur in all azimuths and in any position from horizontal to vertical.

TABLES FOR THE IDENTIFICATION OF ROCK FEATURES

17. Use of the tables. The succeeding tables are intended for use by beginners in field geology. They require very little acquaintance with geologic structures, but they do call for an elementary knowledge of the more common mineral and rock species (Appendices 2–5). They are not to be regarded as absolutely complete. They are suggestive rather than final, indicating by references the places in the text where further information may be found. These references are to the numbered articles. Chapter and page citations are designated as such.

Among the general terms employed, the following may need definition. *Parallel banded or streaked character* refers to any structure or surface marking which may catch the eye on account of its linear appearance (**15**). *Massive character* may be regarded as the opposite of banded or streaked character. There is no linear appearance. *Inclosed areas* are superficial patches or spots scattered here and there on the surface of the exposure. *Inclosed bodies* are crystals, pebbles, rock fragments, or any other individual forms, entirely surrounded by a matrix of some kind of material. A *contact,* in general, is a surface between two contiguous rock masses. In this book the word is used to include igneous contacts (133), surfaces of conformity (83) and of unconformity (84), faults (198), and vein contacts (258). A *contact line* is the line of intersection of a contact surface with the surface of an exposure or with the surface of bedrock covered by mantle rock; *i.e.*, a contact line may be exposed or concealed. Other terms either are self-explanatory or are defined in the citations.

18. Parallel banded or streaked character.[7] The exposure has a parallel banded or streaked appearance

A. Due merely to a system of parallel fractures (see Art. 25).

B. Not due to parallel fractures. The banded or streaked appearance is

1. Purely superficial (12), being due to
   - *a.* Parallel stains which trend down a sloping surface or follow parallel grooves. Such stains may consist of iron rust (yellow, buff, brown), fine soil (brown, gray, black, etc.), moisture, or organic growth (green, yellow, pink, etc.). (Refer to Chap. 2.)
   - *b.* Parallel scratches or grooves (39).
2. Due to a structure which extends into the rock, but is viewed only in cross section, this structure being
   - *a.* A parallel arrangement of constituents which are longer than they are wide. If the rock is composed of constituents of different kinds and
     - (1) All, or most of, the constituents have parallel orientation, the rock is probably a schist; less likely, a gneiss. Mica or hornblende is usually abundant (Chap. 9).
     - (2) Only one or two kinds of constituents are distinctly orientated,
       - (*a*) The constituents with parallel arrangement being larger and more conspicuous than those not so arranged, the parallel constituents may be
         - (a_1) Flat concretions, with their flatness in the planes of the bedding of clay or mudstone, sand or sandstone.
         - (b_1) Flattish pebbles in an unmetamorphosed gravel or conglomerate (109).
         - (c_1) Flattened or somewhat spindle-shaped pebbles in a moderately sheared conglomerate. Such pebbles are generally more or less coated with mica.
         - (d_1) Broken strips (inclusions) of country rock inclosed in an igneous matrix, probably arranged in the direction in which the matrix flowed when it was molten (156).

[7] This table includes several features which come under the head of *lineation* (Art. 15).

(e_1) Phenocrysts in an igneous rock, probably arranged in the direction in which the matrix flowed when it was molten (**130**).

(f_1) Flakes of clastic mica, usually muscovite in this case, in muds, sands, mudstones, or sandstones (**110**).

(*b*) The constituents with parallel arrangement being smaller than those not so arranged, the parallel constituents probably belong to the matrix or groundmass of a schist containing metacrysts (**244**).

b. A single layer which may intersect other structures in the adjacent rock (wall rock) and may, or may not, trend parallel to some fracture system in the wall rock (refer to Art. **19**).

c. A layered structure in which the several layers differ in respect to the composition, or size, or some other character, of their constituents. If

(1) The banding is limited to a particular belt or strip of rock and

(*a*) The banding is parallel to the edges ot the strip, this banding may be due to

(a_1) Successive injections of igneous material along the same course. This feature, when seen, is most common in dikes and sills.

(b_1) Flow structure in a dike or a sill along the trend of its contact (**145**).

(c_1) Vein structure. For the distinction between veins and dikes refer to Art. **264**.

(*b*) The banding forms an acute angle with the edges of the belt or strip, the structure is probably cross-bedding (**96**).

(2) The banding is not limited to a particular belt or strip of rock. If

(*a*) The banding is simple, in one set only, and

(a_1) The rock is fine-grained or has no grain, and

(a_2) Any visible constituents are not conspicuously oriented in parallel position, the banding may be

(a_3) Flow structure in lava (rhyolite, etc.) (**130**), especially if amygdales or phenocrysts are scattered through the rock. However, some fine-grained lavas look exceedingly like rocks of (b_1).

(b_3) Lamination, or bedding, in mud, clay, fine sand, etc., and in rocks derived therefrom, provided large grains, if anywhere present, are grouped in layers parallel to the banding. Exceptionally, sand grains or pebbles may be seen scattered indiscriminately in laminated muds and shales (**106**).

(c_4) Lamination or coarser bedding in limestone and chemical precipitates for the recognition of which chemical tests are often necessary.

(b_2) Visible constituents, principally mica, have parallel orientation, the banding is probably schistosity (**244**).

(b_1) The rock is as coarse as a medium-grained sandstone, or coarser, so that the grains can be recognized, and

(a_2) The banding, as a whole, is of fairly regular and continuous character along its trend, although some layers may be lenticular, this banding may be due to

(a_3) Flow structure in an igneous rock along the trend of its contact with its country rock (cf. *c*, (1), (*a*), above).

(b_3) Stratification in transported sedimentary materials (**71**).

(c_3) Any parallel structure, answering to the description, in residual materials, such structure having been originally present in the rock from which these materials were derived. Look for the parent rock (**6, 85**).

(d_3) Gneissic structure (**244**), seen in both primary and secondary gneisses. Secondary gneisses are generally associated with mica schists and often have schistose layers and other evidences of metamorphism. For the discrimination between primary and secondary gneisses (see Art. **253**). In gneissic structure there is always a certain degree of mineral parallelism.

(e_3) Schistosity, this term always likewise implying parallel mineral arrangement (**244**).

(b_2) The bands (sometimes mere streaks) are present in igneous, usually granite-like, rock. They are generally short, and grade, especially at their ends, into the surrounding rock. They are often darker than the surrounding rock. Such bands or streaks are probably schliers (**130**).

(*b*) The banding is complex and is

(a_1) Due to differences of color or intensity of color, and is often definitely related to two or more intersecting sets of fractures (refer to Art. **20**).

(b_1) Due to differences of texture in adjacent layers, and has no necessary relation to fractures, it is probably a variety of cross-bedding (**96**).

19. Single strips or bands. The exposure exhibits a strip or band which distinctly differs in character from the rock on each side. The band may be associated with others of the same kind, but it is not one of a series of more or less similar parallel bands which together form the entire surface of the exposure. If

A. The band is purely superficial, it is probably a local stain (**12**).

B. The band is the cross section of a structure which extends into the rock, and

1. Consists of angular fragments of the rocks on both sides of it, it may be a fault breccia or a vein breccia (**243**).
2. Consists of silicate minerals such as are common in igneous rocks, or consists of rock glass, or of very dense, compact material showing no grain (felsite), it is probably
   a. A sill or a flow if it is essentially parallel to associated strata (**134, 164**).
   b. A dike if it crosses an igneous rock or the stratification of a sedimentary rock (**134, 246**).
3. Consists of vein minerals, it is probably a vein (**258, 264**).

20. Intersecting banded pattern. The exposure is marked by intersecting bands which trend in various directions. If

A. The bands are merely the result of a color variation in the rock and are always definitely associated with fractures in intersecting sets, they are probably an effect of weathering, the agents having worked inward from the fractures (**35**).

B. The bands differ in texture or composition from the adjacent rock, and

1. Consist of silicate minerals common in the igneous rocks, they are probably intersecting dikes.
2. Consist of vein minerals (**260**), they are probably veins which were deposited in intersecting fractures.
3. Consist of sandstone in shale, or of mudstone or calcareous mudstone in limestone, they may be the lithified fillings of old sun cracks viewed in plan (**65**).

21. Massive character. The exposure has a massive appearance, its constituents being neither grouped in layers nor oriented in parallel position. If

A. The rock is of very fine and uniform grain,[8] and is
   1. White, gray, or light-colored, rather soft or medium hard, and reacts for carbonates, it is probably a fine, massive limestone, marble, or dolomite.
   2. White or light-colored, highly siliceous, and very hard, it may be a fine quartzite or a siliceous replacement of massive limestone.
   3. Gray or dark gray, brownish, buff, etc., generally has a clayey odor, and may be soft or hard, it may be a dust deposit (loess), a deposit of unlaminated clay, or the consolidated rocks derived from these materials (**73**).

B. The rock is as coarse as a medium sandstone or coarser, being of relatively uniform grain, and consisting very largely of
   1. Grains of calcite or of dolomite, it is marble (**244**).
   2. Grains of quartz, it is quartzite (**244**).
   3. Grains of the silicate minerals which ordinarily constitute igneous rocks (Appendix 3), it is an igneous rock or is the residual disintegration product (often arkose) of an igneous rock (**85**).

C. The rock is not of uniform texture, but consists of a finer matrix in which are scattered relatively large grains and rock fragments, reference may be made to Art. **48** and to footnote 35 on page 103.

22. Inclosed areas or bodies. The surface of the exposure exhibits conspicuous bodies or areas (generally cross sections of bodies) surrounded by a relatively fine matrix. If

A. The areas are purely superficial (**12**), they may be color stains (**30–35**), or exfoliation scars (**37, 161**), or erosion remnants such as are described in Art. **170**.

B. The areas are cross sections or faces of inclosed bodies which are
   1. Single crystals, in part or entire, they may be
      a. Phenocrysts in igneous rocks, especially if the matrix is massive and is composed of silicate minerals (**130**). If the matrix is banded, the phenocrysts are apt to have parallel orientation.
      b. Metacrysts in a metamorphic rock, especially if the matrix is marble (test for carbonates) or is schistose (**244**). If the matrix is banded or streaked and its constituents have parallel orientation, the metacrysts are apt to have diverse orientation.
   2. Mineral aggregates, or are bodies clearly not single crystals, and if these bodies

[8] In all cases under "A" further search may prove that the rock is a thick bed interstratified with other sedimentary rocks.

a. Have well-marked outlines and
  (1) An angular form with sharp corners as if due to breaking, they are probably fragments in some kind of breccia (refer to **49, 243**).
  (2) A more or less well-rounded form, without sharp corners and without projecting knobs, and have
    (*a*) A radial or concentric arrangement of some or all of their constituents, as seen in cross section, and
      (a_1) Form the bulk of the rock, adjacent individuals being in contact, having a flattened oval shape, and usually measuring 1 to 2 or 3 ft in length, the bodies may be "pillows" in "pillow lava" (**130**).
      (b_1) Do not form the bulk of the rock, adjacent individuals, seldom in contact with one another, being
        (a_2) Inclosed within a very fine dense or glassy matrix, the bodies may be spherulites or lithophysae in lava (refer to a good textbook of petrology).
        (b_2) Inclosed within a fine-grained matrix which may have flow structure, the bodies may be amygdales, especially if they are oval in cross section, are arranged with their lengths parallel (**130**), and consist of vein minerals (**260**).
        (c_2) Inclosed within a fragmental matrix usually consisting of angular pieces of lava and volcanic dust, as in volcanic agglomerate (**243**), they are probably volcanic bombs (**130**).
        (d_2) Inclosed within a massive matrix consisting of silicate minerals characteristic of igneous rocks, are probably segregations or rounded inclusions (**158**).
    (*b*) A concentric fracture structure, most pronounced toward the periphery, but no concentric or radial arrangement of constituents, and are contained in a matrix of the same constituents, in an unconsolidated or consolidated state, the bodies are probably bowlders of disintegration still *in situ* (**55**).
    (*c*) No radial or concentric structure, and are
      (a_1) Inclosed within a fine-grained matrix which may have flow structure, etc. (continue as in (*a*) (b_2) above).

(b_1) Inclosed within a fragmental matrix, etc. (continue as in (a) (c_2) above).

(c_1) Inclosed within a massive matrix, etc. (continue as in (a), (d_2) above).

(d_1) Inclosed within a matrix of sand or sandstone of uniform texture, the bodies may be

(a_2) Concretions if they are formed of similar sand or sandstone, more compactly cemented (77), or

(b_2) Clay galls if they consist of clay (if in sand), or shale (if in sandstone) (107).

(e_1) Inclosed within a matrix of clay or argillite, the bodies may be clay concretions if they consist of similar clay or argillite, more compactly cemented (77).

(f_1) Inclosed within a matrix of sand grains and smaller pebbles, as in an ordinary gravel, the bodies are pebbles (55).

(3) A more or less well-rounded form, often with projecting knobs or excrescences, they may be

(*a*) Concretions (of clay, marcasite, flint, etc.) if they are in a sedimentary matrix (77).

(*b*) Corroded inclusions if they are in an igneous matrix (156).

(4) An elongate oval, spindle-shaped, rodlike, or lenticular form, the bodies may be

(*a*) Sheared pebbles in a schistose matrix, especially if they are clearly individual bodies (56).

(*b*) Lenses in a schistose or gneissic matrix, if they are merely lenticular areas (aggregates) which are relatively poor in mica, between wavy or winding layers relatively rich in mica (244).

b. Have indistinct or blended outlines, gradational into the surrounding matrix, and are

(1) Irregular, often wavy streaks or patches in a distinctly igneous rock refer to Art. 18.

(2) Irregular, often bent and twisted, sand or gravel layers in gravel or till, they may be "nests" (108).

(3) Roughly lenticular bands of sand or gravel (sandstone or conglomerate) in distinctly sedimentary banded materials, the body is a lens (97).

(4) Lenticular areas in schists, refer to (4) above.

23. Contact lines: mutual relations of contiguous rock masses. An exposure has two (or more) parts which meet in a fairly well defined line (contact line) and differ from one another in color, texture, composition, structure, or surface marking. Neither occurs included or surrounded by the other. If

A. The difference in character is superficial (**12**), and
  1. Is not related to any underlying difference within the rock, it may be due to the fact that
     a. The rock is stained in one place and is not stained, or is stained in a different way, in another place.
     b. The rock is wet in one place and dry in another.
     c. The rock has been affected in a different manner in two places, possibly because it was partly protected from erosion for a time (**12**).
  2. Is related to an underlying difference in the rock, it is probably due to the fact that the two kinds of rock are affected in different ways by the same erosive agents (see B, below).

B. The difference in character is due to a difference in the underlying rock, and
  1. The contact line lies between two bands, both of which are parallel to the line, and
     a. The bands are sections of adjacent laminae or beds in unmetamorphosed, or metamorphosed sediments (**252**) (refer to Art. **18**), the line may be called a line of conformity (**83**).
     b. The bands consist of igneous or of metamorphic rock, refer to Art. **18** for the banding.
  2. The contact line lies between two bands, or two banded series, which are not parallel both to one another and to the line,[9] and
     a. Both bands or banded series are sections of adjacent laminae or bends in sedimentary rocks, or in metamorphosed sediments, the line may be a line of local unconformity (**93**), or one of regional unconformity (**94**), or a fault line (**198, 335**).
     b. Both bands or banded series are not sedimentary, the line may be one of unconformity, or an igneous contact, or a fault (**335**).
  3. The contact line has any other relations, not mentioned above, to banded or massive rocks, determine the nature and classification of the rocks and then refer to Art. **335**.

24. Gradational changes in rocks. A rock exposure displays a gradational change in the texture, composition, or structure, of the materials of which it consists. If

[9] Both banded series may be parallel to one another and not to the line, or one series may be parallel to the line and not the other, or the series may be parallel neither to one another nor to the line.

A. The change appears to be directly related to a contact line, and
   1. Is present in a sedimentary rock or in a metamorphosed sediment (252), and if
      a. The contact line is a line of conformity or of unconformity (Art. 23), the variation is probably an effect of slow and uniform change of conditions during sedimentation when the rock was formed (93, 99).
      b. The contact line is an igneous contact (Art. 23), the variation is probably attributable to contact metamorphism which was induced as a result of the eruption (133, 149–152).
      c. The contact line is a fault, the variation is a result either of heat or pressure involved in the faulting, or of metamorphism accomplished by solutions or gases, which travelled along the fault (152, 257).

B. The change does not appear to be directly related to a contact line, it may be an effect of blended unconformity (85) or of blended igneous contact (133).

25. Cracks or fractures. The rock exposure is traversed by one or more cracks. Examination of such a crack shows that

A. The broken ends of structures which trend across the crack have not been separated, or have been only very slightly separated, along the crack. If
   1. The crack is one of a set of closely and rather regularly spaced, parallel fractures, the crack is a cleavage crack and the set is called a cleavage (242, 244).
   2. The crack is single, or is one of a set of fractures not very closely spaced, the crack is a joint and the set is a joint set or joint system (231).

B. The broken ends of structures which trend across the crack have been separated by displacement along the crack. Such a crack is a fault (198, 208).

26. Curvature of bands or streaks. The rock exposure has a banded appearance and the bands are curving. First determine the probable nature of the rock and the banded structure by reference to Art. 18. If

A. The rock is igneous, the curved form is probably a result of flow when this rock was molten (130, 145).

B. The rock is sedimentary, and
   1. Has a finely banded (laminated) character, and the laminae are in sets which
      a. Are not parallel to the main bedding, and if the laminae in all sets are curved, those in each set having simple and nearly

parallel curvature and being truncated by the adjacent sets, the phenomenon is probably a variety of cross-bedding (**96**).

b. Are parallel to the main bedding, and if

(1) The laminae in some or all sets are curved, those in each set having a wavy curvature in which the arches and troughs are of approximately equal size and shape, and the arches are never bent over the troughs, the phenomenon is probably ripple-mark (**96, H**). The span of the arches and troughs may be different in different sets, and any set may have its arches truncated by the overlying laminae, whether these be straight or curving.

(2) The laminae in some sets are curved and in other sets are straight or are much less curved, those in the curved sets often being of more or less irregular form or of unequal size, with associated breaks in their continuity and with the arches often bent well over the troughs, the phenomenon is probably a variety of folding such as is described in Art. **188.**

2. Is finely or coarsely bedded, and all the beds or laminae are more or less similarly curving, sometimes in a very complicated manner, the curves consisting of archlike and troughlike bends, the phenomenon is probably a result of similar folding such as is described in Arts. **176, 184.**

C. The rock is metamorphic, the curvature of the bands may be

1. An original feature (A and B, 1, above) not yet destroyed because the rock has not suffered much deformation.
2. Folding such as that described in B, 2, above, but generally of a more complex nature. This is to be expected in the mica schists.

27. Inclination of banded structure. The exposure has a banded appearance and the bands are inclined. First determine the probable nature of the rock and the banded structure by reference to Art. **18.** If

A. The rock is igneous, the inclined attitude (**14**) may have significance, as mentioned in Art. **165.**

B. The rock is sedimentary, being

1. Mud, clay, argillite, shale, or slate, and has its bedding inclined more steeply than 3° or 4° to the horizontal, this rock has probably been tilted from its original position (Art. **82**). If its bedding is inclined not over 3° or 4°, it may or may not have been tilted since its deposition.
2. Sand, sandstone, gravel, conglomerate, volcanic ash, or any other relatively coarse fragmental material, and has its bedding inclined more steeply than 35° to the horizontal, it has probably been tilted

from its original position (**82, 267**). If it dips 35° or less, it may or may not have been tilted from its original position.

C. The rock is metamorphic, the attitude of its banding is significant according as it was derived from an igneous rock or from a sedimentary rock (refer to A and B, above).

28. Sequence of steps in field work. In all field work, the outcrop to be examined, or the area to be examined, should first be rapidly looked over to form a rough, general idea of the nature of the problem and of the best mode of procedure. In regions where sedimentary rocks predominate, this preliminary reconnaissance should include an effort to outline the stratigraphic sequence (**125**). Then should follow a more careful, detailed examination of all evidence available for the solution of the problem. It is well to work from known to unknown, or from simple to complex, areas and to cross-check evidence whenever possible. For further discussion of this subject, see Arts. **349** and **350**.

Chapter 2

FEATURES SEEN ON THE SURFACES OF ROCKS

Colors of Rocks

29. Description of rock colors. The color of a rock is often one of its most conspicuous properties, but it is also one of the most difficult to define, for no two people are likely to describe a given color in exactly the same way. Therefore, in order to standardize and facilitate the naming of rock colors, a "rock-color chart" has been made available for the use of geologists, soil experts, and others, by the National Research Council.[1] On this chart 115 colors are represented, and each is assigned a number. Thus, by matching the rock sample (dry, unless otherwise stated) with a color on this chart, one can easily designate its color by name and number.[2]

In the paragraphs that follow, some of the more common rock colors are mentioned, together with their causes. The student should remember that rock colors are not only interesting as they affect scenery, but also, and geologically more important, they provide evidence of kind and degree of weathering (1) and, in the case of sediments, evidence of methods of transportation, environment or deposition, etc.

30. Black, gray, and dark brown. In igneous rocks primary gray shades are generally due to an intermixture of light and dark minerals. The more black grains (biotite, hornblende, augite, magnetite, etc.) there are, the darker gray is the rock. Gray sandstones also may owe variations in tone to variations in the content of black mineral particles, especially of magnetite. In shales, slates, and limestones, and some sandstones, grays are often caused by carbonaceous matter in the rock.

Dark brown and black incrustations of secondary origin are

[1] Published in 1948 and distributed by the Division of Geology and Geography, National Research Council, Washington, D.C.

[2] For those who are interested in a discussion of the subject of rock colors and soil colors, reference may be had to Bibliog., DeFord, Ronald K., 1944; and to Krynine, Paul D., 1948, pp. 143–145.

seen on some outcrops in arid regions. They are called *desert varnish.* These coatings consist of iron and manganese oxides believed to have been deposited from evaporating moisture which has risen to the surface by capillary action.[3]

31. Yellow and brown. Yellow and brown are nearly always secondary colors. They are caused by the rusting (oxidation and hydration) of such iron-containing minerals as biotite, hornblende, augite, garnet, pyrite, etc. Because iron-bearing minerals break down very readily, this sort of yellow staining may be found even in dry climates. Some bright yellows are due to the growth of minute organisms. Carnotite, a uranium ore, has a canary yellow color which is primary.

32. Red and pink. Some igneous rocks (notably granites and syenites) may be reddish because their constituent grains of feldspar are pink or reddish. Conglomerates, sandstones, and mudstones are sometimes red because the pebbles or grains which compose them were derived from an older red rock. The color is primary with the sedimentary rock, although it may have been either primary or secondary in the original parent rock. In this way, red feldspar may color a sedimentary rock. Some pinkish and purplish sands are tinted by garnet grains.

The red color peculiar to some extensive sedimentary formations—notably parts of the Permian and Triassic—is due to the presence of finely disseminated hematite (Fe_2O_3), which may either coat the grains of the rock or occur in the fine matrix between these grains, or both. The origin of this substance here is still imperfectly understood. It seems to have been pretty definitely associated with conditions favoring oxidation and impeding or preventing reduction. The extensive deposits of red sands and shales are believed to have been deposited mainly by stream processes at relatively low altitudes in a relatively dry climate after fluvial transportation from upland areas where a warm, moist climate prevailed. Red residual soils commonly originate only in upland areas that have a warm and moist climate. Transportation was probably not over long distances, and was comparatively rapid. The sites of deposition may have been subaerial piedmont slopes, locally having bodies of relatively saline shallow water.[4] Contrary to this view that the deposit was red when laid

[3] For a discussion of "desert varnish," see Bibliog., Engel, Celeste G., and Robert P. Sharpe, 1958.

[4] See also terra rossa and laterite, Art. **85.**

down, some geologists think that the red color of the sands may have been later derived from the associated red clays. In any case an essential condition seems to have been the absence of decaying organic matter which, if contained in sediments, acts as a reducing agent.[5]

In some places bright pinks and reds, like certain yellow tints, are produced by organisms.

33. Lighter shades and white. Many limestones, claystones, siltstones, sandstones, and evaporites (rocks like salt and anhydrite, resulting from evaporation of water) have primary colors which range from white to light gray.

Through weathering, original colors may be changed to lighter secondary shades of the same hue, or to white. This may be caused in at least five ways: (1) Feldspar grains in a rock may decompose to dull white powdery kaolin. (2) By the formation of minute solution cavities in more or less transparent soluble minerals, such as calcite, transparency is lost and the grains appear to be white. These two processes are characteristic of moist climates. (3) Organic coloring matter is sometimes "bleached" out of sedimentary rocks. (4) In dry climates, where the rainfall is slight, thin white incrustations of certain carbonates may be formed on the rock surfaces in the same way as the desert varnish, described above.[6] (What effect would a heavy shower have upon these soluble incrustations?) (5) Another phenomenon to be seen in climates where disintegration prevails is the production of minute fractures within the mineral grains, due to the action of frost or of temperature changes. Whitening of this origin, like that mentioned in (2) above, is due to the reflection of light from innumerable minute surfaces.

34. Green. Green minerals, such as chlorite, epidote, glauconite, and serpentine, may be responsible for a green or grayish-green color of the rock which contains them; and this rock may be igneous, metamorphic, or sedimentary. Glauconite is the most common green mineral in sediments. When very abundant, the rock may be called a *greensand.*

[5] For further discussion of the "red beds problem," see Bibliog., Twenhofel, W. H., 1939; and Pettijohn, F. J., 1949.

[6] Caliche is a whitish limey deposit, found in semiarid regions, where rising lime-bearing groundwater, drawn up by capillary action, has evaporated and deposited its mineral content within the soil. Caliche deposits may range from mere films to layers several feet in thickness.

Greenish or grayish spots or bands on red rocks may owe their presence to organic matter. Either the green has been produced by a reduction of the red iron oxide in proximity to the organic remains, or the rock has been reddened by oxidation except surrounding this organic matter. The action may have been caused by hydrogen sulphide gases associated with such organic matter (see **35**).

35. Relations of colors to surfaces of weakness.[7] A change of hue is sometimes associated with joints, faults, or even with igneous contacts, which are intersected by the outcrop surface. This is because such surfaces of weakness may afford access to decomposing solutions that bring about discoloration. The rock may appear to be striped or perhaps marked with a pattern of irregularly crossing bands. Since agents of discoloration always work inward, the maximum change is found at the surface of attack.

In a small joint block, a uniform inward gradation of color is not always seen. The water may enter from all sides, dissolve or decompose a little of the rock substance, carry it in, and then deposit it more or less concentric with the surface of the block. Such a joint fragment, if several times subjected to the same process, may display a number of concentric bands when it is split open.

Red sedimentary materials, colored by ferric oxide, may be bleached adjacent to faults or fissures up which hydrogen sulphide gas has ascended.[8]

Surface Features Other Than Color

36. Smoothness and polish. Smooth rock surfaces, and particularly those which are distinctly polished, have probably been rubbed by some abrasive agent which was furnished with finely divided scouring material, such as dust, rock flour, etc. Coarser particles scratch (**39**). Polish is generally limited to hard rocks, for it is not taken so well by softer varieties. Outcrops may be polished by wind carrying dust or ice crystals, by glacial ice, and by water currents or waves which are transporting sand or silt.

Polish made by wind, waves, and streams, is rather dull,

[7] Any fractures or contacts, and even the mutual contact surfaces of the grains, in rocks may be called *surfaces of weakness*.

[8] Bibliog., Moulton, Gail F., 1926.

whereas glacier-made polish may be of such perfection that objects are clearly reflected in it. Eolian dust polish is to be expected in desert regions and in other places where the prevailing winds are dry. Ice-crystal polish is seen only at high altitudes and latitudes where projecting rocks, unprotected by a snow cover, are frequently subjected to snow storms accompanied by winds of high velocity. Glacial polish is found in districts formerly overridden by ice. Another method by which rocks may be polished is by faulting, but here the smoothed surfaces cannot be seen unless the rocks on one side of the fault are gone. Fault-made polish is referred to as slickensiding (**39, H**). Polished surfaces, or slickensides, are not necessarily flat or broadly rounded. They may be hummocky, grooved, scratched, or pitted.

37. Granularity. Frost action, repeated temperature changes, and certain other processes of disintegration, cause the dislodgment of the grains of such coarse rocks as granite, diorite, gneiss, coarse marble, etc. The grains separate either in fragments along their mineral cleavages, or individually or in aggregates along their contacts with adjacent grains. Sometimes thin sheets or great slabs of rock may spall off by exfoliation (**49**). The effect of this loosening of mineral grains, singly or in groups, is to roughen the surface of the rock. So rough may the outcrops become in arid climates and at high altitudes that the sharp edges of the grains cut one's fingers. Such surfaces, if exposed to wind erosion, become more or less smoothed and polished.

Granularity of surface may be produced under water when one of the rock constituents is peculiarly susceptible to hydration. Accompanying this chemical change there is usually an increase in volume which, when affecting hundreds of grains over a rock surface, brings about strains and stresses that finally cause the dislodgment of particles. This is an example of disintegration performed by decomposition.

38. Great irregularity. The original surfaces of some kinds of lava are exceedingly irregular (**138**). The character may be observed on recent flows, on older flows that have never been covered, and on lava sheets which have been buried and subsequently re-exposed.

If a rock suffers disintegration, not by the removal of small grains or spalls, but by the detachment of joint blocks, the outcrop acquires a secondary surface which is of great irregularity. Sometimes faults, cleavage planes, or other surfaces of weakness, function instead of joints. The process by which the blocks are detached is called *natural quarrying*. It includes the bergschrund action of glaciers, the plucking of moving ice, the ordinary frost action of northern climates, and the maintenance of cliffs undermined by rivers and waves (**271**). In the last case the blocks fall because their support has been eroded away by the undermining, but their loosening is often assisted by frost action or by root growth.

On some irregular secondary rock surfaces corners and edges are sharp (Fig. 3) whereas on others they are more or less rounded. Rounding may be the result of concentric weathering (**55**) or of some sort of abrasion. Evidently, if in a given region

FIG. 3. Profile section of an outcrop which is undergoing erosion through the removal of joint blocks. There are two prominent joint sets inclined in opposite directions.

rock exposures continue highly irregular with all edges and corners sharp, the dislodgment of blocks must be more rapid than any rounding process. On ordinary surfaces of low inclination concentric weathering or scouring, as the case may be, can generally keep pace with natural quarrying. It follows that sharp edges and corners are found typically on vertical or steeply inclined surfaces. They are present on the roofs of erosion caves (**293**) and overhanging cliffs. They are more common in fine-grained and homogeneous rocks, for disintegration is often too rapid in the coarser varieties.

Rock exposures of the kind just described may subsequently undergo abrasion. If ice is the abrading agent, it is apt to destroy all traces of the original surface; but wind and water merely round off corners and scour out the hollows. They smooth over the ruggedness of the old exposure and produce a hummocky surface. The lee sides of roches moutonnées (**300, E**) may show this kind of rounding performed by the later current action of glacial waters. Rocky coasts which are not very steep display hummocky, wave-worn erosion surfaces (Fig. 4), for, since the joint blocks are wedged out one at a time at long intervals, the waves are able to keep pace with the quarrying.

It is easy to distinguish between those hummocky surfaces which originate by abrasion and those that originate by disintegration. The former are more or less smooth, while the latter are granular and rough.

39. Scratches, grooves, and ribs. Under the head of primary grooves and ribs may be mentioned the ropy structure of pahoehoe lava, and, in sedimentary rocks, ripple marks and rill marks (**60, 64**).

Scratches are always made by abrasion. Some secondary grooves are the product of scouring and others are made by weathering. Scratches on the floor and side of a groove, about parallel to its trend, may be accepted as proof of its origin by

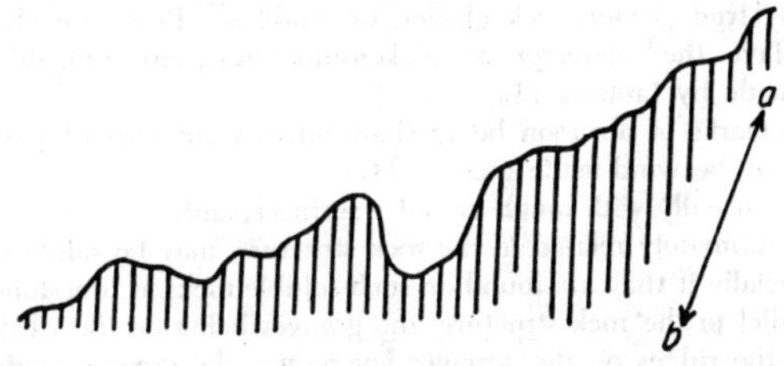

FIG. 4. Profile section of a rock surface worn by wave erosion. Note the definite relation between the joints, inclined in the general direction *ab*, and the outline of the rock surface.

scour. Scratches and abrasion grooves may be produced by ice, wind, landslides, mudflows and rock glaciers, by faulting, and by human means. Other secondary grooves may be made by solution and by differential weathering. All abrasion furrows indicate by their trend the general direction in which the agent moved, but whether the motion was in one way, along the line, or in the other, must be demonstrated by other criteria.

Below is a table to assist in the identification of scratches and grooves. The letters in parentheses refer to paragraphs in the succeeding context.

KEY FOR THE IDENTIFICATION OF SCRATCHES AND GROOVES

A. Scratches (always implying abrasion),
   1. If notably parallel,
      a. May be striae on slickensides (**H**) if they are on a rock surface that can be traced into the bedrock and if displacement is visible where this surface passes into the bedrock.

b. May be landslide scratches (**D**) if they are on a bare rock surface which is on a steep hill slope and is just above a mass of landslide débris, or if they are on a rock surface which is locally covered by landslide débris.

2. If showing some deviation in trend and if
   a. Present on a rock surface which is locally covered by till or other unsorted rock débris, may be glacial striae (**A**), or scratches made by mud flow or rock glaciers (**E**).
   b. Present on a rock surface which is locally covered by wind-blown sand, may be furrows made by wind scour (**C**).

B. Grooves with smoothed or polished surfaces and with evidences of abrasion,
1. The marks of abrasion being in the form of definite scratches which
   a. Have the characters of glacial striae, are probably grooves made by true glacier, rock glacier, or mudflow (**B, E**; see also **J**).
   b. Have the character of slickenside striae, are probably grooves made by faulting (**I**).
2. The marks of abrasion being short furrows and subordinate grooves, may be wind-made grooves (**C**).

C. Grooves, usually with rough granular surfaces, and
1. Not intimately related to the rock structure, may be solution grooves, especially if they are found on such soluble rocks as limestone (**F**).
2. Parallel to the rock structure, the grooves being on the weaker layers and the ridges on the stronger layers, may be grooves of differential weathering (**G**).

39A. *Glacial scratches or striae* (sing., stria) are found on rock surfaces that have been smoothed by ice scour in regions of past or present local or continental glaciation (Fig. 5, G). They may be present on horizontal, inclined, or vertical surfaces. On valley walls the striae are commonly inclined about parallel to the grade of the valley floor. Scratches with the same trend are said to belong to one set. When more than one distinct set marks an outcrop, the different sets are generally the effects of the symmetrical retreat of a single ice lobe (Fig. 6). They are not likely to belong to different ice advances, because the earlier marks would almost surely have been destroyed.

39B. *Glacial grooves* are in many respects similar to striae with which they are associated. They range in size from deep scratches to glacial valleys (**291, G**). They may be straight or sinuous, and they may be continuous for many feet. In cross section their profiles not infrequently show an angle or shoulder on each side, which divides the concavity of the groove from the

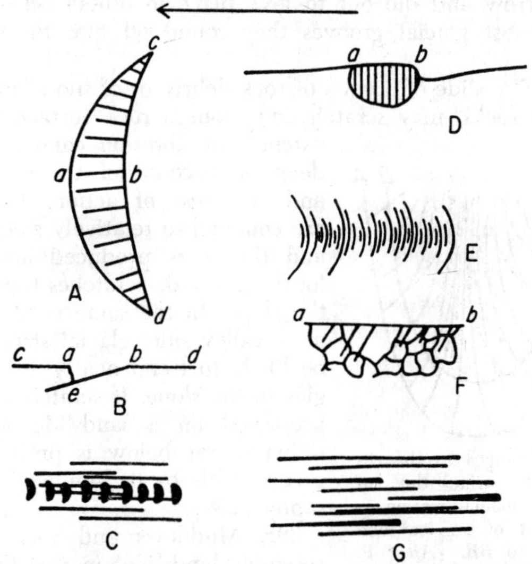

FIG. 5. Features produced on rock surfaces by glacial abrasion. The arrow points in the direction of ice motion. A, plan of a crescentic gouge. B, section of crescentic gouge, taken through *a* and *b* in Fig. A. *cabd* is the glaciated rock surface. A crack was formed along *be,* and then a chip broke off along *ae*. C, chatter marks associated with glacial striae. D, section of a pebble which has protected the rock matrix in its lee, *a,* and has caused the ice to gouge out this matrix on the thrust side, *b*. The depression at *b* may occur as a groove on three sides of the pebble, trailing out in the direction of ice motion. E, crescentic fractures in plan. F, microscopic section of quartzite showing six crescentic features extending downward from the glaciated surface, *ab*, of the rock (enlarged 14 diameters). G, glacial striae. Such striae sometimes begin abruptly and taper out in the direction of ice motion.

convexity or broader concavity of the adjoining rock surface (Fig. 7).

39C. *Wind-made furrows* are not common because their origin necessarily depends upon a very constant direction of wind motion. They have been described as occurring in the crater of Mt. Pelée, where heavy dust-laden steam clouds rolled over the ground down the slopes of the crater and scoured out furrows on the old lava.[9] Grooves of wind origin are short, and they

[9] Bibliog., Hovey, E. O., 1909.

soon narrow and die out to give place to others beside them. Unlike most glacial grooves they round off into the adjacent ridges.

39D. The slide of a mass of rock débris, or of snow laden with soil and rocks, may scratch and scour a rock surface to some extent, but abrasion cannot be very deep on account of the suddenness and shortness of action. Landslides are confined to relatively steep slopes and the scars produced are purely local. Landslide scratches trend down the slope. In the same position, high on a valley side, glacial striae would be likely to trend nearly at right angles to the slope. If scratches are still preserved on a landslide scar, the fallen débris below is probably still recognizable by its hummocky topography (298).

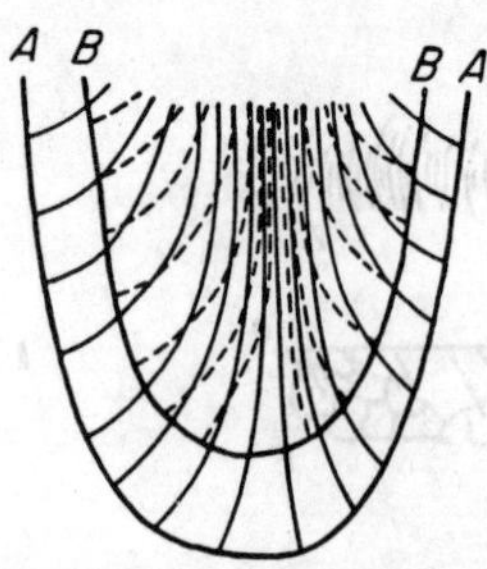

FIG. 6. Changes in the direction of striae due to change of glacial motion in the retreat of an ice lobe from *AA* to *BB*. (*After T. C. Chamberlin.*)

39E. Mudflows and rock glaciers resemble landslides in that they consist of rock detritus, but their motion is slower and may be continuous for many years. By the constant rubbing of the moving mass, bedrock may be scored in great U-shaped grooves sometimes many feet in depth and width. These grooves are broadly sinuous and are marked by smaller parallel furrows and scratches. They are exceedingly like glacial

FIG. 7. Profile section of a grooved glaciated rock surface, drawn transverse to the direction of ice motion.

grooves and their discrimination may be difficult. Careful search should be made for the materials—mud flow, rock glacier débris, or true moraine—which did the work.

39F. *Solution grooves* are more or less parallel furrows that sometimes develop on inclined and vertical surfaces of soluble and fairly homogeneous rocks like limestone and marble. They always trend down the slope, for they are made through slow corrosion by water as it trickles down over the surface. These furrows can be distinguished from abrasion grooves because they are often very uneven along their course, they are not scratched or striated, and the confluences between them are generally narrow and sharp.

39G. In rocks having a parallel structure, for instance, strata and schists, adjacent layers may differ in their susceptibility to decomposition or to disintegration. The layers which are easily affected will be eroded away more rapidly than the others, so that the rock will become ribbed and furrowed (Fig. 8). Since

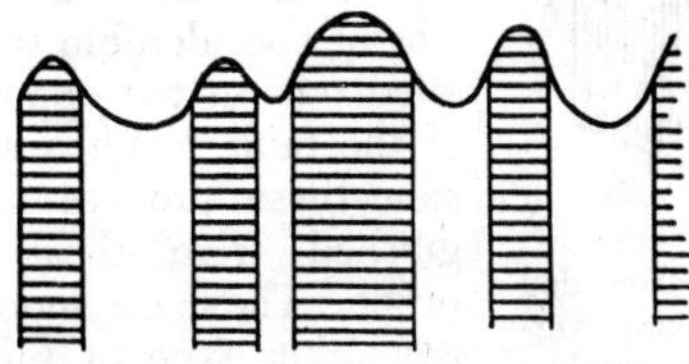

FIG. 8. Section of a ribbed rock surface. The ribs (horizontally ruled) are of calcareous shale which is here more resistant to erosion than the intervening layers of limestone.

layers which are highly liable to decomposition may be very resistant to disintegration, it follows that the rib-makers in a given rock in a dry, cool climate may be the furrow-makers in a climate that is moist and warm. Grooves of this class coincide with the outcropping edges of the layers. Like the solution grooves in homogeneous rocks, they are uneven along their length and they lack scratches. Their width is dependent upon the thickness of the layers.

39H. Slickensides, with the scratches and grooves produced by faulting (**207**), are sometimes exposed on the earth's surface when one of the fault blocks has been removed by erosion. The fault surface on which they occur may have any position, and on this surface the striae may lie in any direction. No rule can be laid down for their attitude. Striae and grooves on a given slickensided surface may be straight or they may curve, but they are always notably parallel. They may be interrupted at irregular intervals by steplike breaks (Fig. 9), with the drop always on the same side when well preserved.

In regions of glaciation, fault striae may be confused with glacial striae. If followed along their course, they will usually be found to pass into the rock where the eroded fault block has not yet been entirely removed. Glacial striae, if of Pleistocene or later age, are purely superficial on the bedrock. A possibility which must not be overlooked is that of an ancient glaciated surface which has been long concealed under solid rock and has been recently uncovered in part (**12**).

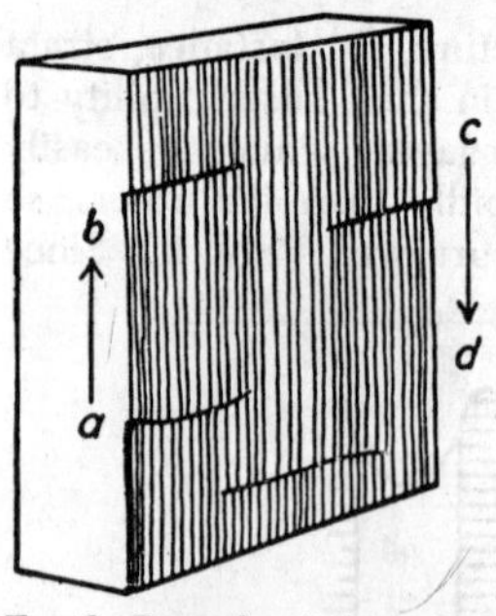

FIG. 9. Part of a slickensided fault surface, showing vertical striae. The steplike breaks across the slickensided surface here indicate that the block in the figure moved up (*ab*) with reference to the block which has been removed (*cd*). If the relative motion had been in the opposite direction, these steplike breaks would have been rubbed off.

39I. By the powerful grinding action of faulting, parallel grooves and ribs of considerable size may be chiselled out on the opposing rock faces of the fault.[10] When exposed by erosion these grooves must be distinguished from those of superficial origin. They are more regular than any other type of furrow. They are themselves lined with scratches, all parallel. In cross section their profiles usually display no shoulders. They trend nearly straight or in broad curves, and are not markedly serpentine. They are not limited to valley floors nor to any other topographic form. Along their length they may rise and sink, but this they do *as a group*. Individual variations are slight. Exposed fault grooves of large size are seldom seen, and where they do occur they are restricted to outcrops whose surfaces happen to coincide with the fault surface.

39J. Along cart paths and highways, scratches and ruts worn in low protruding rocks by the wheels of passing vehicles are sometimes mistaken for marks of glaciation. If there is doubt, comparison should be made with ledges beyond the reach of vehicles, where the real striae will be discovered if present.

[10] Bibliog., Gregory, H. E., 1914.

40. Pits and hollows. Pits and hollows of primary origin include large and small depressions on the surfaces of lava flows, and certain fossil impressions, such as footprints, made on muds and sands while these materials were still unconsolidated. Care should be taken not to confuse with fossil impressions any of the indentations described below.

Secondary pits and hollows in rocks may be the result of abrasion or of weathering. The more common varieties are classified below.

KEY FOR THE IDENTIFICATION OF PITS AND HOLLOWS ON ROCK SURFACES

A. Depressions definitely related to grains, pebbles, fossils, inclusions, or other bodies contained in the rock, are probably due to differential erosion. If these depressions
  1. Have rounded edges and smooth surfaces, and are present on smooth rock surfaces, they may be abrasion pits produced, for the most part, by wind or water (**A**).
  2. Have sharp edges and usually rough surfaces, and are present on rocks with rough surfaces, they may be weather pits due to the solution and removal of grains, pebbles, etc. (**F, I**).

B. Depressions not definitely related to grains, pebbles, etc.,
  1. If present on abraded rock surfaces, may be chatter marks, crescentic gouges (**B, C**), pits associated with hard obstructions (Fig. 5, D), potholes (**D**), or cupholes (**E**).
  2. If present on corroded rock surfaces, of limestone, gypsum, rock salt, etc., may be solution pits (**G**).
  3. When present on weathered or abraded rock surfaces, may be pits due to honeycomb weathering (**H**) or pits formed by organisms (**I, J**).

40A. Finely pitted surfaces are characteristic of wind erosion on granular rocks that are composed of minerals of different hardness. When dust or sand is blown against such a rock, the soft grains are worn away faster than the hard ones. At the same time all the edges and corners of the projecting hard grains are rounded. Thus, the surface of the rock becomes smooth to the touch, although closely indented with small rounded pits the dimensions of which depend upon the size of the eroded grains.

40B. Chatter marks and crescentic gouges[11] are indentations produced by glacial abrasion. *Chatter marks* are small dents that are found in rows of two or more, sometimes accompanying and running parallel to glacial scratches and grooves. They are pro-

[11] Bibliog., Chamberlin, T. C., 1888; and Gilbert, G. K., 1906.

duced by a rhythmic vibratory motion due to friction between the bedrock and rock fragments held in the overriding ice. In their origin they resemble the rows of dots made by drawing on a blackboard with a piece of chalk held nearly perpendicular to the board. Chatter marks are often distinctly convex on one side, and the convexity is turned in the direction from which the ice moved (Fig. 5, C).

40C. *Crescentic gouges* (Fig. 5, A, B), occasionally met with on the "upstream" or stoss slope of glaciated rocky knobs, measure from a few inches to 5 or 6 ft. from horn to horn and lie with their length perpendicular to the adjacent striae. Like chatter marks they are found in sets of two to half a dozen or more. Their convex edges usually point in the direction in which the ice moved.[12]

40D. Of much larger size than the depressions already noted are *potholes.* A pothole is formed by the constant swirl of an eddy which carries pebbles or sand round and round in one spot. Gradually a hole is bored downward into the rock. The sand and pebbles that served as the tools may often be found at the bottom of the depression. Whether the vortex be one in a current of wind or water or ice, the action is the same, although the rate of abrasion may vary. Potholes are most commonly of fluviatile origin. Occasionally they may be observed along rocky coasts and in glaciated valleys where the topographic configuration localized eddies; but many of the depressions of this nature in glacial valleys are made by water plunging through holes in the ice. These are called "*moulins*" or "mills." Here the concentration of action is due, not necessarily to a constant vortex, but to the maintenance of an opening in stationary ice for a time sufficiently long. Since true potholes open upward, the analogous excavations cut by wind rarely come under the definition, for wind eddies may work in any direction. Yet the process by which the holes are carved is identical.

40E. On a small scale abrasion, combined with solution, may wear cup-shaped hollows, called cupholes, on the surfaces of rocks like limestone (Fig. 10, A). In a certain sense they are miniature potholes.

40F. Decomposition and solution play an important rôle in modifying rock surfaces. Their action is generally differential. Soluble substances may be leached out from rocks which as a

[12] However, see Bibliog., MacClintock, Paul, 1953, where the occasional reverse orientation of these gouges is explained.

whole do not readily decompose and cavities may then remain, which indicate by their shape the nature of the material removed. Thus, from rocks that contain cubical holes, pyrite may have been carried away. Sometimes fossils are dissolved out and their impressions are left as small cavities on the surface of the rock. Similarly, limestone pebbles in conglomerate may be dissolved out from a shaly or sandy matrix. In moist climates basic segregations (**130**) are apt to decompose more rapidly than the granitic rocks in which they are contained. The hollows formed by their weathering have granular surfaces. In cases of this kind

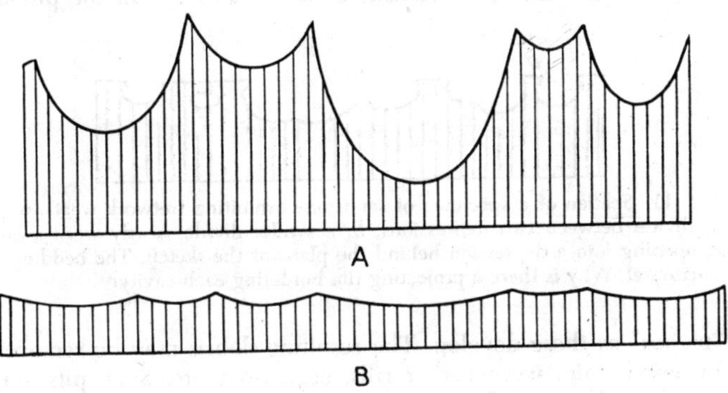

Fig 10. Profile section through the surface of a limestone exposure, showing two varieties of solution pit. (About ⅔ natural size.)

there are usually some depressions which still have a little of the original substance left in them. These should be sought in order to explain their formation.

40G. A very characteristic feature of corrosion surfaces on soluble rocks is the presence of abundant saucer-shaped pits, and this does not of necessity indicate any differential tendency in the chemical wear. Limestones and marbles may be very uniform and yet display this effect, generally on surfaces of low inclination. Where the slope is greater the pits may coalesce and become grooves (**39, F**). Between the hollows are sharp-edged divides (Fig. 10, B). If the divides are rounded, the corroding water probably carried some silt which did a little abrasion.

40H. On fine granular rocks such as sandy shale and sandstone, decomposition sometimes produces what is known as *fretwork* or *honeycomb weathering* (Fig. 11). At different spots on the exposure small pits arise through the decomposition of mineral grains. As these cavities grow deeper and larger and as they become more numerous, they unite at the surface while they are still separate below. In the less resistant laminae enlargement takes place more quickly than in those more resistant.

Fretwork weathering is characteristic of the surfaces of granular rocks, such as tuffs, granitoid rocks, sandstones, and conglomerates, where these are exposed in arid climates. Under these conditions, occasional action of hydration and solution, probably occurring for the most part immediately following infrequent showers, is concentrated more and more in the pits or

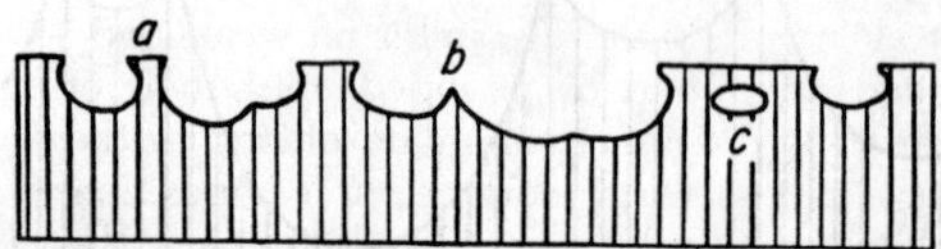

FIG. 11. Section of a specimen of sandstone exhibiting fretwork weathering. *a,* divide between two depressions; *b,* a similar divide, nearly worn away; *c,* opening into a depression behind the plane of the sketch. The bedding is horizontal. Why is there a projecting rim bordering each cavity?

"niches" as these develop. The resulting débris may be removed by wind, rain, wet-weather rills, organisms, etc. Such pits may grow to the size of caverns several yards in all three dimensions.[13]

40I. Corrosion of rock surfaces is not restricted to subaerial outcrops. It has been recorded as occurring below water level in lakes. Or, again, it may go on beneath the soil where moisture rich in products derived from vegetable decay may etch a pitted or corrugated surface. Subsequently the soil may be removed by natural or artificial means and so expose the rock.

Corrosion pits are generally a fraction of an inch to a few inches across. Their interiors are often roughened by projecting insoluble grains.

40J. Certain molluscs dissolve out cavities in which they dwell. The holes grow larger with the growth of the animal. Their organic origin may be indicated by the presence of the animals themselves, or of the shells, in some of the chambers.

[13] Bibliog., Blackwelder, E., 1929.

Chapter 3

ROCK PARTICLES AND FRAGMENTS

General Nature

41. Shape and surface markings. Rocks may be broken into fragments either by forces acting within the lithosphere or by processes at the earth's surface. Sometimes the fragments, as mere products of shattering, suffer no wear, and sometimes they are rubbed or ground or pounded until their original shape is modified. According to their mode of origin, they have distinctive characters of form, surface, or composition. For example, many glaciated pebbles are striated, just as is the glaciated bedrock. They served as the tools by which the ice scratched the rock, and the tools themselves suffered abrasion in the process. It follows that if we examine the constituents of a fragmental deposit or of a consolidated fragmental rock, we may be able to discover how that material was made, for very often the deposit or rock originated under the control of the same agents which were concerned in fashioning the individual constituents. In studying solid rocks there is need to discriminate between destructional fragments of the kind just mentioned and certain other bodies which are of quite a different nature (**47, C; 57**).

42. Dimensions of particles and fragments.[1] The distinction between gravel, sand, silt, etc., has arbitrary limits. According to a scale proposed by Wentworth,[2] and widely used, we have the classification shown in Table 1. In the present book, particles larger than coarse sand grains are discussed under the term of *rock fragments.* Ordinarily we think of pebbles, cobbles, and bowlders as fragments which have been more or less rounded through erosional processes.

Clastics of the intermediate groups may be passed through sieves or screens to grade their constituent particles. Sieves have

[1] Refer to Appendix 4.

[2] Bibliog., Wentworth, C. K., 1922. Also Krumbein, W. C., and L. L. Sloss, 1958, p. 70.

been standardized. There are two commonly used sets. One is known as the Tyler screen series, and the other is the series of the U.S. Bureau of Standards.[3] The differences between the two are slight, but the latter is perhaps more desirable because its mesh sizes (sieve openings) correspond with grades in the Wentworth classification. Table 2 shows the Wentworth grades and the

TABLE 1. GRADES OF CLASTIC SEDIMENTS

Range of dimensions, mm.	*Individual fragments, particles, etc.*	*Unconsolidated aggregate*	*Consolidated rock*
256 or more	Bowlder	Bowlder gravel	Bowlder conglomerate
64–256	Cobble	Cobble gravel	Cobble conglomerate
4– 64	Pebble	Pebble gravel	Pebble conglomerate
2– 4	Granule	Granule gravel	Granule conglomerate
1– 2	Very coarse sand grain	Very coarse sand	Very coarse sandstone
½– 1	Coarse sand grain	Coarse sand	Coarse sandstone
¼– ½	Medium sand grain	Medium sand	Medium sandstone
⅛– ¼	Fine sand grain	Fine sand	Fine sandstone
1/16– ⅛	Very fine sand grain	Very fine sand	Very fine sandstone
1/256–1/16	Silt particle	Silt	Siltstone
1/256 or less	Clay particle	Clay	Claystone

nearest corresponding sieve openings of both Tyler and U.S. Bureau of Standards systems. (Many intermediate and extreme screen sizes are omitted here.)[4]

CHARACTERS OF ROCK PARTICLES

43. Composition. Residual sands formed by disintegration are composed, for the most part, of the minerals present in the parent rock, for they have been subjected neither to attrition nor to decomposition on a large scale. On the other hand, sands that have been transported for a long time consist of minerals that are relatively resistant either chemically or physically or both.

[3] See Bibliog., Lange, N. A., 1946.

[4] For an ingenious method of measuring sand grains, see Bibliog., Huitt, Jim L., 1958.

TABLE 2. WENTWORTH GRADES AND SCREEN OPENINGS

Grain classification	Limiting dimensions, mm.	Tyler screen scale			U.S. Bureau of Standards screen scale			
		Sieve opening nearest to largest particle	*Number of meshes per in.*	*Number of meshes per cm.*	*Sieve opening nearest to largest particle*	*Number of meshes per in.*	*Number of meshes per cm.*	*Sieve number*
Granules	2–4	3.96	5	1.97	4.00	4.98	2.0	5
Very coarse sand	1–2	1.98	9	3.54	2.00	9.21	3.5	10
Coarse sand	½–1	0.991	16	6.50	1.00	17.15	7.0	18
Medium sand	¼–½	0.495	32	12.60	0.50	32.15	13.0	35
Fine sand	⅛–¼	0.246	60	23.62	0.25	61.93	24.0	60
Very fine sand	1/16–⅛	0.124	115	45.28	0.125	120.48	47.0	120
Silt	Less than 1/16	0.061	250	98.43	0.062	238.10	93.0	230

(Why?) Quartz is the most common ingredient of such sands, and in regions where micaceous rocks abound, muscovite and bleached biotite may be in considerable quantity. Garnet, magnetite, zircon, and rutile are also counted among the more indestructible minerals, but the last two are seldom abundant. If transportation has been comparatively short and rapid, the sand may contain mineral particles which would have been quite broken up under longer handling.

The composition of sand suggests not only the amount of transportation, but also the climate in the region where the erosion was in progress. A deposit which is rich in decomposable mineral grains is indicative of a very dry climate, and one that is strikingly lacking in such minerals points to decomposition as having been a very efficient erosional process. A high percentage of quartz indicates that the sand is a product of slow erosion in a warm, moist climate, where the more decomposable minerals had ample time to decay and pass away in solution. Feldspar is a decomposable mineral, yet it is not at all uncommon in sands of continental origin, even in moist climates. It is fairly resistant to chemical destruction, although less so than quartz. Consequently, its presence is not to be accepted as unquestionable proof of an arid climate. On the contrary, hornblende, augite, and particularly biotite, all iron-bearing silicates which are extremely liable to decay, are good evidence for aridity, or of erosion by ice.

The nature of the parent rock is likewise indicated by the composition of the derived sand. In this respect sands that have been subjected to little transportation are most valuable. Garnet and magnetite often come from gneisses and schists; quartz and feldspar from gneisses, granites, etc.; and micas from schists and certain igneous rocks.

The significance of clastic mica in muds and mudstones may well be mentioned here. Such mica is typical of continental sediments (**119**). When found in pelites that seem to be of marine origin, it usually means that they were accumulated near the shore.

44. Shape.[5] Most mineral particles owe their form partly to their manner of breaking and partly to the kind of erosion which has affected them. The grains may be angular, faceted, sub-

[5] Bibliog., Sherzer, W. H., 1910. Also Krumbein, W. C., and L. L. Sloss, 1958, pp. 78 *et seq.*

angular, rounded, or pitted. They may be nearly equidimensional, *i.e.,* with their three rectangular axes about equal—which is called "high sphericity"—or they may be oblong, rodlike, or tabular, all of which are included under the term "low sphericity." Their shape is seldom, in itself, a decisive criterion for the origin of the deposit in which they are found, but it is of considerable assistance. One must be careful not to draw conclusions from too brief an examination. Few fragmental deposits consist of grains derived in only one way. Wind-worn particles may be intermingled with those handled by water, and so on. It is the prevailing character of the majority of the particles that must be ascertained.

The key which is given below includes the more common varieties of broken or worn rock particles.

Key for the Identification of Rock Particles

A. Grains sharply angular,
   1. Consisting of volcanic glass or other volcanic material, are probably volcanic sands (**45, B**).
   2. Consisting of the mineral constituents of rocks especially susceptible to disintegration (usually rocks of relatively coarse texture), are probably disintegration sands (**45, A**).
   3. Present in a layer of limited thickness and consisting of fragments of the rocks on both sides of the layer, may be breccia particles (**45, D**).

B. Grains with one or more worn or broken facets which are marked off from the surrounding surface by sharp edges,
   1. Generally associated with glaciated pebbles, in till, etc., are probably glacial faceted sand grains (**45, C**).
   2. Associated with rounded eolian sands, are probably broken or chipped wind-blown grains.

C. Subangular grains, with edges and corners somewhat rounded may be aqueoglacial sands (**46**) or sands of the next class (D), not fully rounded:

D. Rounded grains which, if broken, show.
   1. Concentric structure on the fracture surface are probably constructional sands (**47, C**).
   2. No concentric structures on the fracture surface, and are
      a. Above 0.75 mm. in diameter, may be eolian, marine, and fluviatile sands (**47, A**).
      b. Below 0.75 mm. in diameter, are probably eolian sands (**47, A**).

45. Angular particles. **A.** Residual disintegration sands have sharp edges and corners (Fig. 12, A) because they have been detached from the bedrock along their contact surfaces with other grains and have suffered no corrosion and no rolling by wind or water. If they break up still further, minerals without cleavage, like quartz, crumble into highly irregular fragments, the micas separate into thin flakes, and most other minerals with cleavages fall into small irregular blocks faced by the cleavage planes.

45B. Volcanic sands (Fig. 12, B) are angular because they are largely the product of explosive shattering. They consist of chips and slivers of rock glass with here and there phenocrysts, broken or entire, and occasional pellets of glass rounded in the air by mutual attrition or by twirling, if thrown up as liquid drops.

Fig. 12. Characteristic grains from disintegration sand (A), volcanic sand (B), glacial sand (C), aqueoglacial sand (D), eolian sand (E), river sand (F), and oölitic sand (G).

45C. Ice-worn sand grains (Fig. 12, C) have faces which have been ground by glacial abrasion.

45D. Solid rocks are sometimes found to have been crushed by movements with the earth (**243**). The finer particles, so made, are angular or subangular.

45E. On the whole, angularity of grain signifies disruption in place or disruption followed by brief and rapid transportation. The glaciated particles noted in **C**, above, are an exception.

46. Subangular particles. If subjected to corrosion or to attrition for a sufficiently long time, angular grains may become subangular. Their edges become blunted. Aqueoglacial sands (Fig. 12, D), are commonly of this nature, for whatever angularity they may have acquired through fracture or through glacial abrasion has been modified by subsequent wear in running water. The larger grains may still show traces of the facets planed off by glacial scour.

47. Rounded particles. A. Long handling by wind or running water produces rounded grains. This shape is typical of eolian sands (Fig. 12, E). In river and beach sands, too, the grains are usually pretty well rounded (Fig. 12, F). Particles having a diameter less than a certain quantity are apt to escape rounding because they are held in suspension as long as they are swept by a current. The size below which the grains remain angular is about 0.75 mm. in running water and about one-fifth this amount in wind. The difference is due to the greater buoyancy of water.[6] Under special conditions marine sands may continue angular or subangular for a long while, even though they are larger than the size just noted. After the fall of the tide, they may be kept moist by capillary action between the grains. The moisture serves not only as a cushion to prevent the rubbing of the particles on one another, but also as a check to their transport and handling by wind. However, wind along low open shores soon rounds the dry grains in the upper layer of the beach, and consequently wind-worn grains are often scattered through beach deposits. Typical eolian sands occur only in desert regions. They may contain some particles which were broken or chipped by impact. As a general rule, sands that are well rounded and average considerably less than 0.75 mm. in diameter are probably of eolian origin.

47B. The student will probably have very little occasion to distinguish corroded sand grains from those mechanically rounded, since most sands are of mechanical origin. A difference may be mentioned here. Chemical agents tend to excavate small pits on the surface of a grain and the luster of the pits is like that of the whole grain. If there are indentations on abraded particles, these are the remains of the original uneven fracture, or of subsequent hard blows, and they are present merely because the particle has not been worn down enough to erase them. Rolling and repeated slight impact cooperate to fashion an evenly rounded surface, convex on all circumferences. The multitude of minute scars resulting from this sort of abrasion somewhat dull the luster of the particle, so that, in this case, the luster of remaining indentations is different from that of the grain as a whole. These features need a hand lens for their examination.

47C. Rounded sands of constructional origin (Fig. 12, G) compose oölites,[7] pisolites, and some greensands. Cross sections of these grains show them to have a concentric structure. Fur-

[6] Bibliog., Grabau, A. W., 1913, pp. 61, 226; and Ziegler, V., 1911, p. 654.

[7] Each "o" is pronounced separately as a long ō, as in "hope"; *not* together, as a diphthong, as in "mōōn."

ther description of their characters may be found in textbooks on petrology.

Characters of Larger Rock Fragments, Pebbles, Etc.

48. Identification. In Art. 22, pebbles and other detached rock bodies are listed principally according to their characters when seen in cross section. The following key is based almost wholly upon such features as roughness, smoothness, scratches, dents, etc., which may be observed on the surfaces of the pebbles or bodies. Reference is also made to form.

Key for the Identification of Rock Fragments[8]

A. Angular fragments, bounded by fracture surfaces, may result from various processes of weathering or of brecciation. References are given in the context (**49**).

B. Faceted pebbles which have
  1. The facets smoothed or polished, and sometimes pitted, may be wind-worn (**53**).
  2. The facets scratched or grooved, may belong to classes noted under C below.

C. Scratched and grooved pebbles, if
  1. Of various shapes (round, faceted, blunted, etc.), and with the scratches running in various directions, may be glacial pebbles (**50**).
  2. Of various shapes, and with one or more facets, each facet being local, usually separated from the adjacent surface by sharp edges, and marked by parallel scratches (running in but one direction), are probably slickensided fragments or pebbles (**50**).
  3. Elongate (sometimes spindle-shaped) or flat and sometimes bent, with the scratches or grooves running parallel to the length of the pebble, may be compressed (sheared) pebbles (**56**), especially if they are more or less coated with mica.

D. Pitted or dented pebbles or fragments, if they have
  1. The indentations definitely related to mineral grains, may be wind-worn pebbles (**53**).
  2. The indentations not related to the mineral constituents,
     a. These indentations usually being isolated and saucer-shaped, and generally
       (1) Unaccompanied by fractures, may be pebbles of a soluble rock, like limestone, the indentations having been formed by solution (**51**).
       (2) Accompanied by radiating fractures, may be pebbles of any sort of rock with compression dents (**51**).

[8] The reader's attention is called to Art. **57**.

b. These indentations usually being in groups converging at the blunted end of the pebble, are probably glaciated pebbles (**50**).

E. Pebbles or bowlders, ridged and furrowed on their upper surfaces and with a limey deposit of caliche on their lower surfaces, may be solution-morel pebbles (or bowlders), occurring in arid regions (**52**).

F. Subangular pebbles usually fragments which have not yet been fully rounded (see also B) (**54**).

G. Rounded pebbles and bowlders, if with

1. Smooth surfaces, may be river or beach pebbles.
2. Rough surfaces, may be pebbles or bowlders of disintegration (**55**).

49. Angular fragments. At the earth's surface, angular rock fragments may result from exfoliation, plucking, sapping, frost

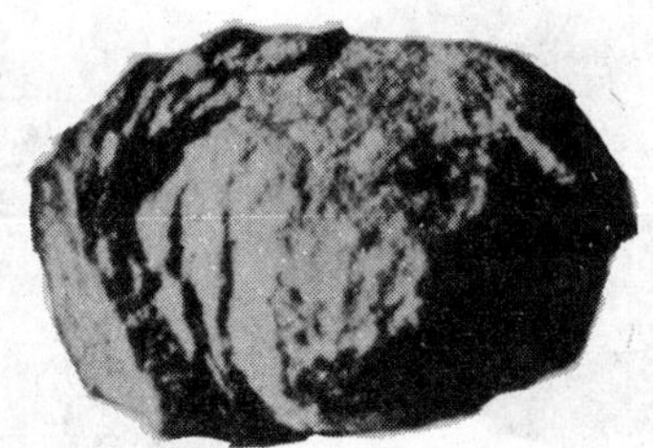

Fig. 13. Formation of a bowlder of exfoliation. Part of the original surface of the rock may be seen at the extreme left. The rough edges are the scars of flakes or spalls which have split off. Two such spalls (near the upper part of the figure) are nearly detached.

action, disruption by landslide and lightning, and by volcanic explosion. When massive rocks weather by exfoliation, relatively thin, curved, edged pieces split off. These are called *spalls* (Fig. 13). Fragments separated from the bedrock by plucking, sapping, or any of the other processes of disintegration, are bounded by surfaces of weakness (**35**). They are the negatives, as it were, of the outcrop surfaces produced in the same manner (**38**). Such fragments are generally found at the bases of cliffs where they have accumulated as slide rock in a heap or sheet called *talus*.

Landslide detritus is angular if the materials were solid bedrock before the slip. Both landslide débris and talus consist of fragments of all sizes and in both some of the fragments may have bruises or random scratches made in the downfall. The difference between the two kinds of deposit is mainly topographic (**301**).

Shattering of rocks by lightning has been recorded, but is very rarely seen or recognized In mountainous districts where the work of lightning would be most effective, frost and temperature changes are by far the most active forces of rock destruction.

Other kinds of angular fragments are described elsewhere, as follows: blocks made by volcanic outburst (**130, 243**); intraformational fragments (**107**); various kinds of breccia (**243**).

FIG. 14. A glacially striated pebble found by J. B. Woodworth in Pleistocene till in Gaspé, Quebec. Note the diversity in direction of the scratches.

FIG. 15. Striated pebble with splintered or snubbed end. (*Coll., J. B. Woodworth.*)

50. Scratched, faceted pebbles. Scratched, faceted pebbles are nearly always the result of glacial abrasion. They have been planed off by rubbing against bedrock while held in moving ice. Such pebbles may shift their position in the ice from time to time and thus receive several facets or "soles." Each facet is marked by striae which run in various directions (Figs. 14, 15). In this respect they differ from detached pieces of the striated bedrock, which are more apt to have a large majority of the scratches on only one face and, on this face, trending in one direction (Fig. 16). Sometimes a pebble which was held in one position for too short a time to become faceted may be round and yet bear striae.

Occasionally care may be necessary to discriminate between slickensided fragments and glaciated pebbles, especially in deformed rocks having relatively few pebbles in an abundant fine-grained matrix. Where surfaces of internal rock slipping have grazed a pebble, the slickensides probably continue across the pebble into the matrix. The fault striae, like the striae on detached fragments of a glaciated rock pavement, lie parallel to one another.[9] In fault breccias the fragments may be slickensided (**207**).

FIG. 16. Detached fragment of the striated rock floor over which glacial ice moved. Note the parallel arrangement of the striae. The figure shows chatter marks in the deepest scratch. (*Coll., J. B. Woodworth.*)

51. Pebbles with scars or indentations. A. Pebbles with concave fracture scars are as typical of ice abrasion as are striated pebbles. They are angular or subangular and may or may not have glacial scratches. The scars are thought to have been made by splintering or wedging of small chips from the pebble while it was pressed with great force by the ice against bedrock, or was jammed between two blocks of rock (Fig. 15). These scars should not be mistaken for the concave indentations next described.

51B. Circular or oval concave hollows may be produced, both by solution and by simple pressure unassisted by chemical processes, on the surfaces of the pebbles in a conglomerate. A solu-

[9] For further criteria see Bibliog., Woodworth, J. B., 1912 (*a*), p. 457: and Wentworth, Chester K., 1928.

tion hollow is formed where, in the compression of the rock, a small pebble is squeezed against a larger pebble. At their mutual contact the larger one is dissolved away and the smaller one is pressed into the hollow. Solution indentations are confined for the most part to pebbles of soluble rocks like limestone (Fig. 17).

51C. Concave hollows made by compression without solution are rare. They need special conditions for their origin. The paste of the conglomerate must be relatively weak and compressible, yet it must be strong enough to prevent complete fracturing of the pebbles when the rock is subjected to stress. As in the previous case, the small pebbles indent the larger ones. If the

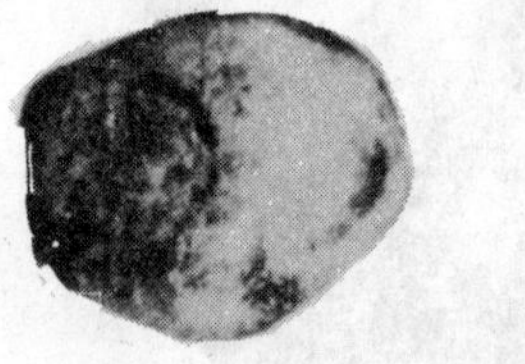

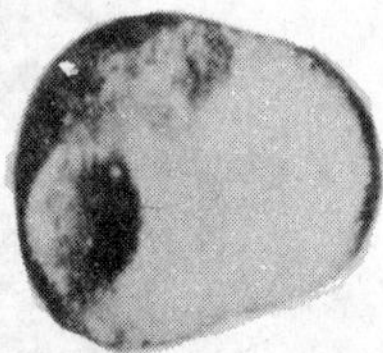

Fig. 17. Limestone pebbles indented by solution while they were under compression in a conglomerate. The pits mark the spots where adjacent pebbles were in contact.

pressure exceeds a certain quantity, variable under different conditions, the impressed pebbles crack.

Both types of indentation (**B** and **C**) interrupt the continuity of the original surface of the pebble, and in both the depth of the hollow is not more than a fraction of the diameter of the smaller pebble.

52. Irregularly grooved pebbles. A peculiar result of the effects of solution on impure limestone pebbles and bowlders in semiarid regions has been described by Scott.[10] Through corrosion by occasional rain water, the upper surface of a limestone pebble may develop furrows with intervening ridges, and these furrows may grow in depth and irregularity until the whole upper exposed surface of the pebble is a complex system of anastomosing ridges and furrows, which resembles the pattern of the morel mushroom. Hence these are called "solution-morel

[10] Bibliog., Scott, Harold W., 1947.

pebbles." The lime which is dissolved away from the upper surface of the pebble is carried down and deposited as a shell of caliche (see footnote, page 23) on the under side of the pebble, and this shell grows in proportion as the original limestone of the pebble is dissolved away. Pebbles of this nature may be found on alluvial gravel deposits in semiarid regions.

53. Polished, faceted pebbles. Polished, faceted pebbles are made by wind action. They are called *glyptoliths* (γλυπτός, carved; λίθος, stone) or *ventifacts* (*ventus*, wind; *facere*, make). A pebble too large to be transported is worn by the impact of

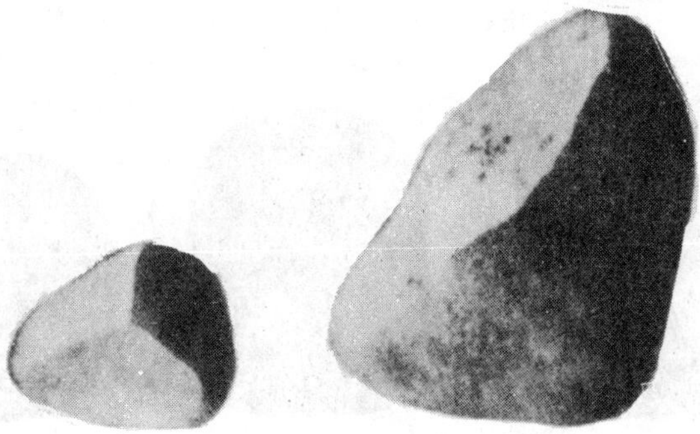

Fig. 18. Wind-worn pebbles. That on the right is an einkanter; that on the left is a dreikanter. (See footnote, p. 239.)

blown sand and dust. The side toward the prevailing wind direction is planed off and more or less polished, and if the pebble is granular, its surface is pitted. (Why?) Often there are two or three directions from which the wind blows most of the time, so that the exposed surface of the pebble acquires two or three facets which meet in rather sharp, smoothed edges; or, several faces may be worn because the pebble falls into a new position whenever the sand has been blown out from beneath it. If there is one such edge between two distinct faces, the pebble is called an *einkanter* (one-edge); if there are three edges and three faces, it is called a *dreikanter* (three-edge); and so on (Fig. 18).

54. Subangular pebbles. Subangular pebbles and bowlders are those which have had their edges and corners somewhat rounded, but which have not yet lost all traces of their original angular character. Glacial faceted pebbles, modified by running water, are typical of eskers and kames (**298, C, D**) and of other aqueoglacial deposits. Talus blocks may lose their angularity through the influence of weathering. Landslide fragments and the fragments in fault breccias sometimes have their edges blunted by rubbing during the movement.

55. Rounded pebbles and bowlders. Rounded pebbles and bowlders are shaped by rolling or by concentric weathering. River pebbles, rolled downstream, and beach pebbles, rolled up and down the beach, are indistinguishable. Both types pass through subangular stages and finally become well rounded with

Fig. 19. Three building bricks in successive stages of rounding by wave erosion.

smooth surfaces, free from scratches. Soft and hard grains are planed off alike, although here and there some brittle grains may have been chipped out by hard knocks. The ultimate form depends upon the original nature of the rock fragments. Cubical blocks become spherical, while flat slabs are worn to thin, oval pebbles (Fig. 19).

Concentric, or spheroidal, weathering is a passive process by which rounded bowlders of disintegration are formed. The agents include repeated freezing and thawing of water in the cracks and interstices of the rock and such chemical agents as carbonation, oxidation, and hydration of certain of the mineral constituents, resulting in localized expansion because the new minerals occupy more volume than the old. These agents work inward from the corners, edges, and surfaces of joint blocks. The

Fig. 20. Development of bowlders of disintegration. The bowlder in the center of the figure is still in place. It has been formed from a joint block by the gradual removal of the surrounding rock. Other joint blocks appear in less advanced stages of disintegration. (Owens Valley, Calif.) (*Drawn from a photograph by J. H. Blake.*)

Fig. 21. A pebble of quartzite elongated by compression in dynamic metamorphism. Length about 6 in.

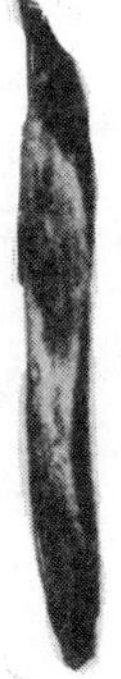

Fig. 22. A pebble of quartzite elongated, edged, and fluted by severe compression in dynamic metamorphism. Length about 9 in.

corners wear away faster than the edges, and the edges faster than the surfaces, so that a rounded internal core at length remains (Figs. 13, 20). From this the grains come off singly or in shells or spalls. Bowlders of disintegration differ from bowlders of attrition in being much weathered on the outside, and in having rough, granular surfaces (cf. 37).

56. Elongated and flattened pebbles. In metamorphic rocks pebbles and other rock fragments may have their original shapes entirely altered. Even equidimensional pebbles may be compressed in such a way that they become long, spindle-shaped rods, or they may be flattened into thin sheets. By rubbing against adjacent pebbles, during the shearing of the rock (**250**), they may be slickensided, fluted, and ribbed (Figs. 21, 22).

57. Pebble-like bodies. Sometimes rocks contain pebble-like bodies which are really not pebbles at all. In plutonic rocks rounded or oval masses may be segregations or inclusions (**130, 158**). They differ in composition from the matrix which surrounds them. Other pebble-like or bowlder-like forms include concretions (**77**), some kinds of fossils, volcanic bombs (**130**), and lava "pillows" (**130**).

Chapter 4

ORIGINAL SURFACE FEATURES OF SEDIMENTS

Classification

58. Identification of minor irregularities of surface. During the process of construction of sedimentary deposits, there are sometimes produced certain minor irregularities of surface. These may be of considerable value in determining the origin of consolidated strata in which they may be re-exposed either in cross section or, if the rock surface happens to coincide with the original bedding surface, in their old superficial aspect. These features may be grouped according to their general appearance, as follows:

Key for the Identification of Minor Surface Features of Unconsolidated Sediments

A. Ridges, or ridgelike forms, associated or not associated with depressions, if
   1. V-shaped in plan, measuring several feet from one to another, and if found near the upper borders of beaches, may be beach cusps (**59**).
   2. Parallel or subparallel ridges, generally between 2 and 6 or 8 in. apart, may be ripple marks (**60**).
   3. Very low ridges, somewhat irregular in form, generally less than ⅛ in. high, tending along beaches, may be wave marks (**62**).

B. Channel-like or groovelike forms, if
   1. Long grooves, single or in groups, on mud flats or on playa clay flats, may be *stone tracks* (**63**).
   2. Small channels, branching or not, trending down the slope of the beach or other deposit, may be rill marks (**64**).
   3. Cracks in mud or clay, occurring in a ramifying system, are probably sun cracks (**65**).
   4. Short, shallow, gashlike openings in clay or mud, may be ice-crystal marks (**68**).
   5. Resembling footprints, may be fossil trails (**69**).

C. Shallow depressions, if present
   1. As scattered circular, or nearly circular, saucer-shaped hollows, may be rain prints (**66**), spray imprints (**66**), hail prints (**66**), or bubble impressions (**67**).
   2. In series, may be fossil footprints (**69**).

Description and Explanation

59. Beach cusps. Along lake and sea beaches, particularly the latter, triangular ridges or cusps are sometimes found at regular intervals of 10 to 40 ft. or more (Fig. 23). "When most typically developed the beach cusp has the form of an isosceles triangle with its base parallel to the beach, but at its upper edge, and its apex near the water."[1] According to Johnson, beach cusps are formed through "selective erosion by the swash" which constructs "shallow troughs of approximately uniform breadth," beginning with "initial, irregular depressions in the beach."[2] Their ultimate size and spacing are proportional to the size of the waves.

60. Ripple marks. Ripple marks,[3] confined for the most part to coarse and fine sands, are alternating ridges and troughs,

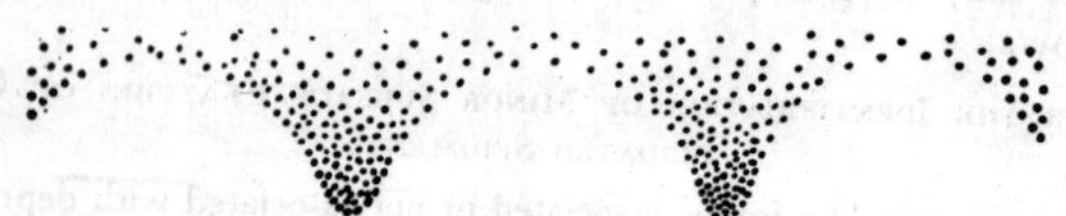

Fig. 23. Plan of beach cusps. The cusps point down the beach.

which are formed either (1) by the oscillatory motion of water waves or (2) by currents of wind or of water. Current-built ripple marks are sometimes called *current marks,* and wave-made ripples are *oscillation ripples.*

Ripple marks may be considered in plan, in profile, and in section (see **110**). In *plan* the ridges and troughs are usually subparallel, anastomosing at intervals, but sometimes two or more sets of ripple marks may cross one another and so complicate their pattern. Wave-made ripples are more regular in pattern than are current ripples. Evans points out that, where obstructions, such as pebbles, protrude through loose sand which is being rippled, wave-made ripples will extend up to the obstruction whereas current ripples will terminate a short distance from

[1] Bibliog., Grabau, A. W., 1913, p. 706.

[2] Bibliog., Johnson, D. W., 1910, p. 620. Also, Evans, O. F., 1938, 1945; and Kuenen, Ph. H., 1948.

[3] Bibliog., Bucher, W. H., 1919; and Twenhofel, W. H., 1926, pp. 451 *et seq.;* Twenhofel, W. H., 1939, pp. 518 *et seq.;* also Shrock, Robert R., 1948.

it against a groove scoured round the obstruction by the current.[4]

In *profile,* wave ripples (oscillation ripples) are usually symmetrical[5] (Fig. 24), and current ripples are always asymmetrical.

In defining the dimensions of ripple marks, it has been customary to describe them as if they were waves. Thus, in Figs. 24 and 25, the distance from crest to crest (*ab*) is called the wave length; the vertical distance (*cd*) from the crest to the bottom of the trough is called the *amplitude;* and the wave length divided by the amplitude (*ab*/*cd*) is the *ripple index.* A more consistent terminology would be to name *ab* the *width* of

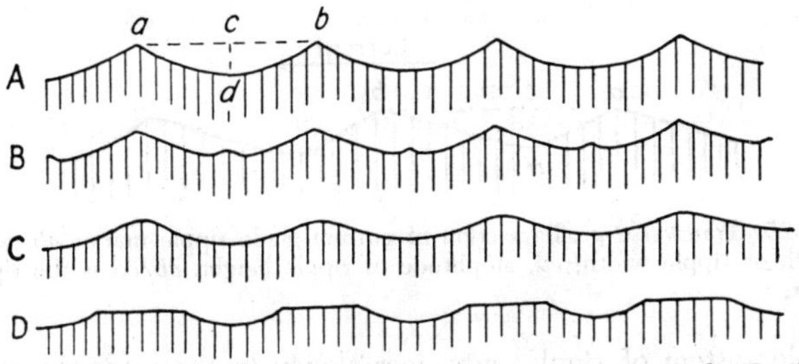

FIG. 24. Transverse profile sections of wave-made ripple marks. In A, *ab* is the wave length, or ripple width, and *cd* is the amplitude, or ripple height. *ab*/*cd* is the ripple index.

the ripple mark, *cd* its *height,* and, again, *ab*/*cd* the ripple index.

Wave-made ripple marks are common on the shallow bottoms of lakes and seas, where there is not much current action. While in process of formation they are practically stationary, their crests are sharp, and the intervening troughs are rounded (Fig. 24, A). Sometimes there are low "second-order" ridges in the troughs, one such second-order ridge lying along the bottom of each trough (Fig. 24, B). By slight changes in the strength of the

[4] Bibliog., Evans, O. F., 1949.

[5] Evans has shown that wave (oscillation) ripples may be asymmetrical where they travel on the bottom of shallow water, due to an alternation, during the passing of each wave, of a shorter more intense movement and a longer less intense movement in the water disturbed by the wave. See Bibliog., Evans, O. F., 1941.

waves or by a decrease in the resulting agitation of the water, the crests may be rounded off (Fig. 24, C). The rounding may proceed to such an extent, and the sand which has been removed from the crests may so far fill the troughs, that the system of ripples becomes a series of alternating relatively broad flattened ridges and narrow intervening depressions (Fig. 24, D).

In the case of *current ripple marks,* the shorter slope of each ridge, as seen in profile section (Fig. 25, *ad*), is always inclined in the direction in which the current is moving. Troughs and crests are both rounded. The sand particles are swept up the long (*stoss*) slope and are dumped over the crest down the short (*lee*) slope. On account of this migration of particles, the

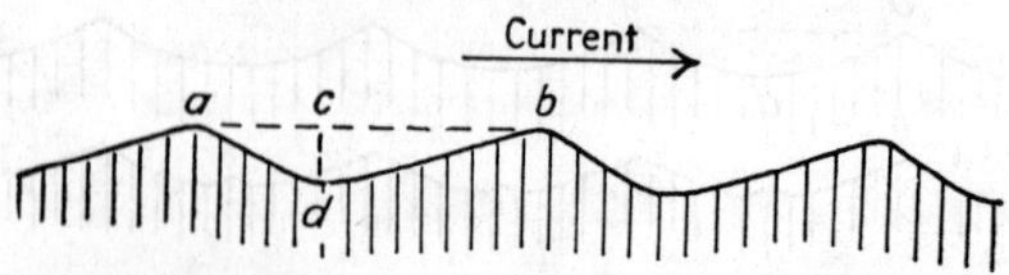

Fig. 25. Transverse profile section of current-made ripple marks. *ab,* wave length or ripple width; *cd,* amplitude or ripple height. *ab/cd* is the ripple index.

whole system of ripples advances slowly in the same direction as the current.

Current ripple marks, if made by water, may be on beaches, on lake bottoms and sea floors where there are currents, and locally in rivers; and if made by wind they may occur on the more exposed parts of sand beaches and especially on sand dunes along shores and in arid regions. Ripple marks may be made by wind on slopes inclined as steeply as sand will stand (267), and their trend is often up and down such a slope; but current ripples formed by water are seldom observed in unconsolidated sand on surfaces that slope more than 5° or 6°. Water-made current marks are much more likely to be preserved in consolidated sands (sandstones) than are those made by wind. The ripple index of water-made current ripple marks is commonly smaller than it is in wind-made ripple marks, *i.e.,* the latter have greater width in proportion to their height than do the former. In both wave-made ripples and current-made ripples, the size varies tremendously, although within a given set or system, made under similar conditions, there is not much range in size. Most commonly, in both classes of ripple marks, the breadth (wave length) is between 0.5 and 50 cm., the height (amplitude) is between 0.1 and 5 cm., and the ripple index is between 4 and 10.[6]

It is interesting to note the manner in which the sand grains come to rest in these ripple forms. In wave-made ripples, the heavier (usually larger) grains settle in the troughs and the finer grains lodge on the crests. In current-made ripple marks of aqueous origin, the coarser sand grains, rolling up and over the crest, come to rest in the troughs, and mica plates, if present, tend to accumulate in the troughs and on the lee slopes (**110**). In wind-made (eolian) ripple marks, the coarser material is likely to be on the ridges and the finer grains accumulate in the troughs.

61. Slump marks. Dry sand, which is blown up the windward side of a dune, accumulates at the crest or just over the crest until the angle of repose (**267**) is exceeded. Then there is a miniature avalanche, and the sand slides down the lee slope in a thin sheet, coming to rest with an irregular edge, often lobate downward. The individual lobes may be tonguelike. The small avalanches occur here and there on the lee side, and the result is a series of "irregular lines, roughly parallel to the direction of slope and marking the borders of the sand mass that has slumped downward." To these lines, McKee applied the name *slump marks.*[7]

62. Wave marks. Wave marks (also called *swash marks*) are very low, narrow, wavy ridges to be seen on sand beaches. They are seldom over 1/16 in. high and 1/8 in. wide, but may sometimes be several inches wide. Each is made at the upper edge of the swash of water that runs up the beach after the breaking of a wave. As the tide goes down, every swash more or less destroys the earlier wave marks and builds one of its own, so that it is common to find wave marks cutting into those next higher on the beach (Fig. 26). This relation may possibly be of some use in showing in which direction the sea lay when sediments, now consolidated, were deposited. Evans has suggested that greater width of these minute ridges may be correlated with lower slope of the beach.[8] Whenever the swash is diagonal to the trend of the beach, the water sweeping up and around and down again may produce a fanlike distribution of sand grains down-beach from each swash mark

[6] Bibliog., Twenhofel, W. H., 1950, pp. 570 *et seq.*
[7] Bibliog., McKee, Edwin D., 1945.
[8] Bibliog., Evans, O. F., 1938.

63. Stone tracks. Shallow grooves may be produced in very shallow water where fragments of rock, rafted by seaweed (on tidal mud flats) or by ice floes (in playa lakes) scrape the bottom muds or clays as they are moved along. Observations have shown that the former case, when it does occur, is usually caused by offshore winds. Not infrequently the pebble, bowlder, or rock fragment that scoured the groove may be found at the

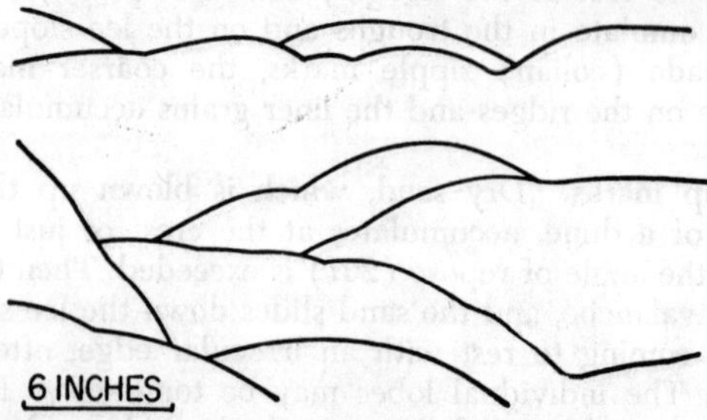

FIG. 26. Plan of wave marks on a sea beach. The land is above, and the sea below, the figure, as drawn.

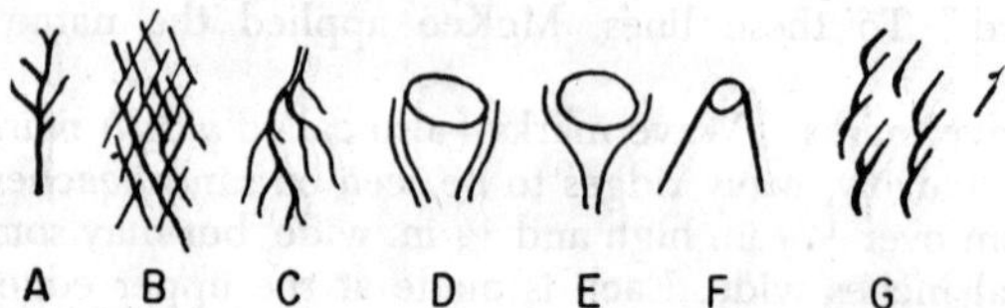

FIG. 27. Types of rill marks. In each case except G the water flowed in a direction from top to bottom of the diagram. In G the current moved with the arrow.

end where the action ceased. Association of this phenomenon with playas indicates that freezing temperatures may occur.[9]

64. Rill marks. The word "rill mark" has been applied to four kinds of structure. (1) After the swash of a wave up the beach, the returning water may scour little channels in the sand, which unite in trunk channels, and these again join with others, like a miniature river system. In this case each set of rill channels branches *up* the beach (Fig. 27, A). These little channels may unite in a reticulated pattern (Fig. 27, B). (2) Small streams that debouch on sandy or clayey flats sometimes divide and may

[9] See Bibliog., Stanley, Geo. M., 1956; also, Salisbury, C. L., 1956.

branch many times before the water finally runs off or passes into the ground. The channels or rill marks of this type branch *down* the slope (Fig. 27, C). They resemble the much larger channels made by the distributaries on deltas. (3) Water flowing down a sandy beach scours a small channel on each side of such an obstruction as a half-buried pebble or shell (Fig. 27, D–F). The two channels may unite in a short gully just below the obstruction (E). On the upstream side a low ridge may be built. (4) The fourth type of rill mark may be found where the sweep of waves or ebbing tidal currents, usually along the lower parts of beaches and under shallow water, has so scoured the sand that it is pitted with many asymmetrical depressions, roughly aligned in parallel position (see Fig. 27, G). These depressions are curved, with the deepest part against the apex of the curve. The current moved approximately in the direction of the longer arm of the curve, away from the apex.

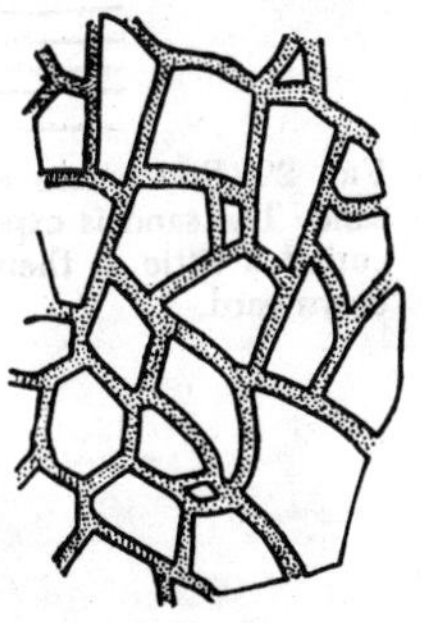

FIG. 28. Sun-cracked clay as seen in plan. The shrinkage of the clay has exposed an underlying bed of sand (stippled) in the cracks. (Cf. Fig. 29.)

65. Sun cracks. When dried under the sun's rays for a sufficiently long time, mud and clay shrink and crack in a network of fissures which inclose polygonal areas (Fig. 28). These fissures are called *sun cracks, mud cracks,* or *desiccation fissures.*[10] In cross section they may be wedge-shaped, thinning out downward, or they may have parallel walls (Fig. 29). They may be as much as several inches wide at the top and 10 ft. deep,[11] but they are generally much smaller. Their best development is found in localities where long exposure and a dry, warm climate are possible conditions. Sun cracks are therefore most characteristic of playas and the flood plains of large rivers in semiarid and arid regions. They may also be found on exposed, low, shelving shores of lakes in seasons of low water, and, more

[10] We prefer the term *sun cracks* to *mud cracks* because (1) in most instances desiccation is through exposure to heat of the sun, and (2) other materials (*e.g.*, some limestones) may be similarly cracked. "Mud-cracked limestone" is a little incongruous.

[11] Bibliog., Grabau, A. W., 1913, p. 709

rarely, on tidal mud flats. Locally they may be seen in the bed of any drying mud puddle. Near the edge of the evaporating pool the recently formed cracks are more widely exposed than they are farther from the water where continued drying has

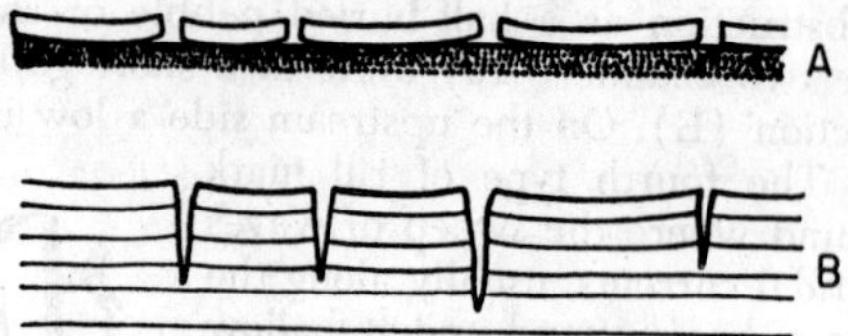

FIG. 29. Sun cracks in section. A, sun-cracked clay layer above a bed of sand. The sand is exposed in the cracks. (Cf. Fig. 28.) The clay chips have curled a little at their edges. B, sun-cracked clay, the cracks tapering out downward.

FIG. 30. Rain prints in clay. (About ⅔ natural size.)

developed more closely spaced cracks by repeated splitting of the mud. Sun cracks are essentially continental in origin and always indicate that the water in which the mud or clay accumulated was relatively shallow[12] (**101**).

66. Rain prints and hail prints. Clays, muds, and fine sands may preserve the impressions of rain drops. Each imprint is a shallow circular hollow with a very slight encircling ridge which was raised by the impact of the drop (Fig. 30). If there was no wind during the shower, the rim is of approximately equal height all around each impression; but if the rain fell obliquely,

[12] Bibliog., Barrell, J., 1906, p. 524.

the part of the rim on the lee side of the hollow is higher (Fig. 31). Rain prints are especially characteristic of continental mud deposits. Spray imprints, from the splash of breakers, may be formed on beaches. Hail prints are much like rain prints and, when small, may not be distinguishable, but hail stones may be up to several inches in diameter, and consequently their impressions may be correspondingly large.

67. Bubble impressions. Impressions made by bubbles of gas or air rising to the surface of mud flats, marsh deposits, beaches following the retreat of waves, and the muddy or fine sandy bottoms of water bodies, may very closely resemble rain imprints. Bubble impressions are circular depressions of small size which, unlike rain imprints, are more likely to be without marginal rims than with such rims.

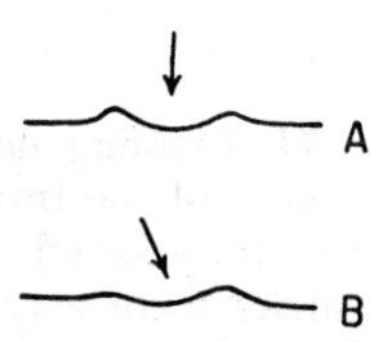

FIG. 31. Profile sections across rain prints formed during a shower (A) when there was no wind and (B) when the wind was blowing from left to right.

68. Ice-crystal marks. Frost as well as rain may leave its vestiges. When moisture in mud or clay freezes, it forms bladed and branching crystals of ice, casts of which remain after the crystals have melted and the water has passed away. Under the conditions for the preservation of sun cracks, rain prints, etc., ice-crystal marks may become lithified.

69. Animal tracks. Sometimes terrestrial animals leave records of their existence in footprints and trails in fine-grained sediments, particularly in clays of playas and river flood plains. If these impressions are left on marine sand or mud at low tide, they are generally, though not always, washed away by the next incoming tide. Depressions of various kinds, particularly those due to differential weathering of inclusions, segregations, pebbles, or other such bodies, are not infrequently mistaken for footprints (see Art. **12** for the discrimination between superficial and structural features).

70. Patterned ground. In polar, subpolar, and alpine regions, where frost action and soil movements (solifluction) are common, peculiar patterns are sometimes developed in the distribution of sediments and vegetation. These patterns may be comprised of circles or rings, nets, polygons, steps, or stripes. A full discussion of them and their classification may be found in the Bibliography, Washburn, A. L., 1956.

Chapter 5

ORIGINAL STRUCTURES AND STRUCTURAL RELATIONS OF SEDIMENTARY ROCKS

Stratification

71. Bedding in mechanical deposits. Mechanical deposits consist of the fragments of pre-existing rocks. If such fragments are transported prior to their accumulation, the agent that carries them may have the power of separating the lighter ones from those which are heavier. This process is called *sorting*. It is characteristic of handling by wind and by running water. As long as the transporting current is weak, it moves only light particles and these are somewhere spread out as a fine-grained layer. If the current becomes stronger, it may bear heavier fragments and may distribute them as a coarser layer above the earlier, finer materials. Thus, by variations in the efficiency of the transporting agent, a deposit may come to have a layered structure, known as *bedding* or *stratification* (Fig. 32) The *beds* or *strata* (sing., *stratum*), as the layers are called,[1] may differ from one another either: (1) in texture, that is, in the size of their constituent particles or fragments;[2] or (2) in composition, since variation in weight may be due to differences in specific gravity, a property closely related to chemical composition; or (3) in both texture and composition. Evidently, then, bedding in a deposit is a proof of changing conditions during accumulation. Where individual beds show a gradation from coarse below to fine above, the bedding is said to be graded (see Art. **99**).

72. Bedding in chemical and organic deposits. In chemical and organic deposits, likewise, bedding indicates that the condi-

[1] Very thin beds are usually termed *laminae* (sing., *lamina*).

[2] We may still further analyze texture for, with grains of a given composition, stratification may be produced by the arrangement of grains which vary, from layer to layer, in their size, in their shape, or in their orientation (see **110**).

tions of accumulation were not uniform. In superficial chemical deposits (salt, gypsum, sodium carbonate, bog iron ore, etc.), bedding may be produced, during sedimentation, by changes in the chemical substance precipitated or by variations in the quantity of contained chemical or mechanical impurities. These changes may owe their origin to oscillations in weather or climate.

73. Absence of bedding in sedimentary deposits. Provided we accept the statement that bedding is a result of changing

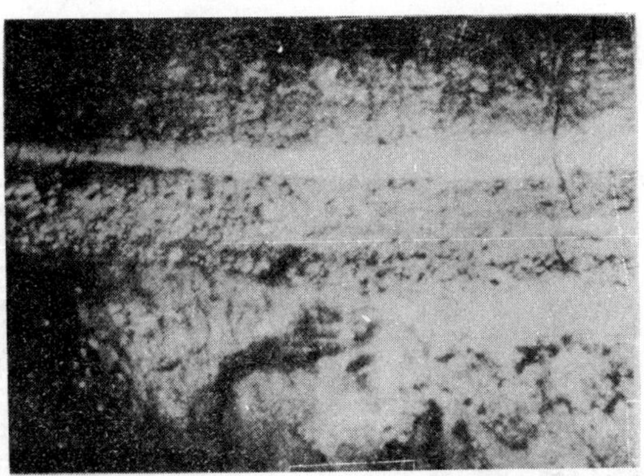

FIG. 32. Bedding consisting of layers of sand and gravel. The thick sand bed in the lower half of the figure was somewhat eroded by the stream that deposited the overlying layer of gravel. Length about 20 ft.

conditions, then absence of bedding, or perfectly uniform character, is what might be expected in deposits accumulated under very uniform conditions. However, there are other explanations for this feature. The several important causes for such absence of bedding in a sedimentary deposit may be summarized as follows: (1) the rate of accumulation may have been too rapid for sorting; (2) the transporting agent, by its nature, may have lacked the power of sorting; (3) the method of accumulation may have been unadapted to sorting; (4) the materials supplied may have been too uniform in character; (5) slumping of the materials after their deposition may have destroyed an original bedded structure; (6) chemical changes within the deposit, during or/and after its accumulation, may have prevented or modified any indication of bedding.

In the sudden fall and quick heaping up of landslide débris, there is no chance for sorting. Talus is practically free from bedding, although there may be a tendency for the larger blocks to roll to the base of the slope. The slow accumulation of materials by overriding ice (drumlins, etc.), the gradual lowering of englacial and superglacial débris in the melting of a stagnant glacier, and the falling of rock particles and fragments of all

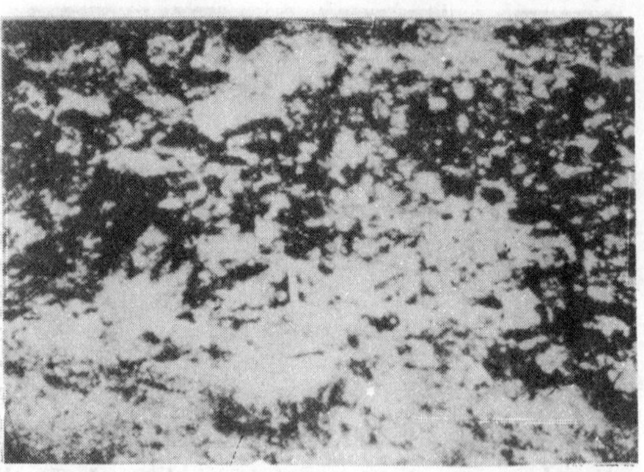

Fig. 33. Section in till. Note entire absence of bedding. The hammer handle is about 15 in. long. (*Photograph by R. W. Sayles.*)

sizes from ice walls or from the ice front—these are all processes which are not accompanied by sorting, provided water has no share in the deposition. Such deposits, of glacial origin, are called *till* (Fig. 33). Till may be defined as glacial material which shows no bedding, or, at best, bedding of very obscure and irregular character. Even in water-laid materials sedimentation may be too rapid for sorting. Thus, alluvial cone gravels (281, A) at the base of a steep mountain range may have very rude bedding and they may even closely resemble till, so poorly defined are the strata. Likewise, the gravels of eskers and kames (298, C, D) are rarely well stratified, because their formation is rapid, débris of all sizes falls out from the supporting ice walls, and the beds, such as they are, are obscured or destroyed by slumping after the supporting ice is removed by melting. Absence of bedding in coarse deposits of water-worn materials is sometimes called *pell-mell structure.*

In fine sediments absence of stratification indicates very uniform conditions of deposition, that is to say, there was probably very little action of waves or of currents to modify the process. This massive structure may be found sometimes in dust deposits (loess), in quiet water deposits, and in chemical and organic deposits.

74. Interstratification of materials of diverse origin. If one carries to an extreme the idea of changing conditions as related to stratification, one can easily understand how mechanical and chemical deposits, chemical and organic deposits, and other rock materials which are formed at the earth's surface, may be interstratified. Good examples of this phenomenon are: (1) the interstratification of salt and gypsum with layers of mud and sand in the basins of salt lakes which have suffered considerable variations in depth and salinity; (2) the interstratification of peat with clay or sand; (3) the interstratification of bedded with unbedded deposits, such as aqueoglacial sands and gravels with till (93); and (4) the interstratification of lava flows or pyroclastic débris with materials derived by ordinary processes of erosion (Fig. 34).

75. Lateral variations in sedimentary deposits of contemporary or of nearly contemporary origin. In an area where deposition is in progress, the sedimentary materials which are accumulating are seldom uniform in character throughout this area. For example, while sand may be deposited along a shore, just seaward of the sand mud may be accumulating. On an alluvial slope, flanking a mountain range, gravel may accumulate near the foot of the range, and this may grade outward, away from the mountains, into sand and still farther into fine clay, sometimes with salts precipitated from saline lakes. These materials will be essentially contemporaneous, and, when covered by later sediments, they will reveal a lateral gradation in character, *i.e.,* a gradation *along* the bedding. It is important to remember, in geology, that such changes in character (lithological, chemical, physical, organic, etc.) may be observed in individual strata, or formations, if traced far enough along the bedding.

76. Pseudostratification. Occasionally till deposits which have been overriden by ice (drumlins, etc.) exhibit a structure concentric with their surfaces and somewhat resembling stratification. This is not true bedding for it is not due to sorting. It is caused in part by the plastering of layer on layer by the ice and in part by shearing of the till by the great pressure of the ice.

The student should guard against confusing foliation in metamorphosed rocks (247) and sheet jointing in some eruptive rocks (236) with stratification. Both of these structures are of secondary origin (see also Art. 110).

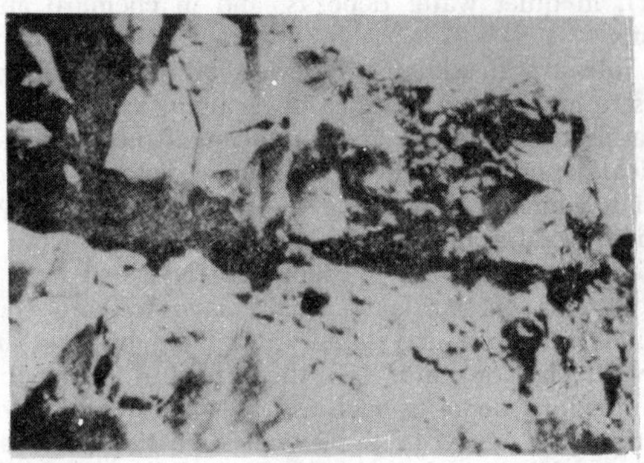

Fig. 34. Section of a basalt flow resting on alluvial cone gravels, as seen on the wall of a small canyon. The contact runs from left to right near the middle of the figure. The lava is vesicular near its upper surface and less so near its lower surface, and is compact in its middle portion. It is partly covered by later river-laid gravels, not shown. Note the rude hexagonal columnar jointing. (Owens Valley, Calif.)

Consolidation

77. Consolidation of mechanical sediments. Mud, sand, and gravel are unconsolidated mechanical sediments. Under certain conditions these may become mudstone, sandstone, and conglomerate, respectively. In like manner all fragmentals have their consolidated equivalents. Peat may become coal; till may become tillite. There are several ways in which consolidation may be brought about, and, while it is generally effected at considerable depths within the lithosphere, it may occur at the earth's surface. For instance, the baking of clay under the sun's hot rays is a surface phenomenon, but this kind of consolidation is only partial and the dried clay would hardly be called a rock in the popular sense of the word. Another example is that of the coquina, or shell rock, of Florida. This is a sandstone composed of shell and coral fragments which have been heaped together by wind and water. The process of solidification is thought to be going on at present. Rain water, descending through the deposit, dissolves lime carbonate from the particles and redeposits it a little lower down as a binder between the grains. Occasionally the same kind of thing may be seen in the case of ordinary sands or gravels where the fragments contain abundant iron-bearing minerals. The descending waters decompose these minerals and redeposit the iron, in the form of limonite (iron rust), as a cement. Superficial consolidation is generally accomplished by one of these two methods, namely, by drying or by the introduction of a cement.

At greater depths consolidation by cementation is a very common process, for the chemical activity of interstitial water increases with increment of temperature, and temperature increases with depth.[3] The weight of the overlying burden assists, too, for pressure is an aid to consolidation. In the formation of coal, compression may predominate as the cause of consolidation. In clay rocks the crystallization of original colloidal matter may cause cementation. Without going further into details, we may conclude that the most important difference between consolidated and unconsolidated mechanical sediments lies in the presence of a cement in the former and its absence in the latter. Like all rules, however, this one has its exceptions.

The cement may have been brought in from without or, more often, it has been derived within the deposit. The four most common binding substances are hematite (Fe_2O_3), limonite ($2Fe_2O_3 \cdot 3H_2O$), calcite ($CaCO_3$), and silica (SiO_2). Hematite is red. It is the chief binder in many red sandstones. Limonite is yellow, buff, or brown, and is the cement in brown sandstones. Calcite, colorless or white, may be detected by testing with dilute HCl. Silica, best recognized by means of a polarizing

[3] See footnote 7, p. 72.

microscope, is very hard and is often the cement in extremely hard sedimentary rocks, such as quartzite.

Occasionally evidences are found of cementation which has been concentrated about such objects as fossil shells, leaves, etc., in a sedimentary accumulation. Each fossil thus becomes surrounded by a jacket of cemented sediments, a jacket which thickens as long as cementation continues. If the unconsolidated sedimentary matrix be removed, these coated bodies, or *concretions*, are found to be of various shapes. Some are spherical, some ovoid, some disc-shaped, and some are very irregular if two or more have become attached in their growth. Fossils are not always found in the hearts of concretions. If chemical deposition once begins at any point, the minute portion already crystallized may stimulate further deposition about itself. The matrix is not always unconsolidated; it is merely less firmly consolidated than the concretions. Concretions may originate, also, by the localized deposition of substances which make room for themselves by actually forcing aside the surrounding rock.

By differential weathering concretions may be loosened from their matrix and accumulated as a residual gravel. They should not be mistaken for true pebbles.

78. Consolidation of chemical sediments. Chemical sediments do not undergo the same type of lithification as do fragmental sediments. Many chemical deposits are precipitated in the crystalline condition, and the resulting crystalline aggregate, if pure, is nearly as hard as the mineral composing it. Abundant impurities may weaken the adhesive properties of such a rock. In other cases the chemical sediment accumulates in a colloidal state and subsequently hardens by a gradual loss of moisture, or, sometimes, by ultimate crystallization. Bog iron ore is a rock probably consolidated from a colloidal condition by loss of water.

79. Consolidation of organic sediments. With respect to their consolidation, deposits resulting directly or indirectly from organic processes may be regarded as chemical or mechanical. Some of these sediments, like the unbroken central portions of coral reefs, are precipitated in solid form by processes which are as truly chemical as they are organic. Others, such as certain kinds of coal and the coral sand rock above described, are accumulations of plant débris or of the fragments of animal skeletons, and these, therefore, are mechanical. Their consolidation is accomplished by one or more of the methods described in Art. 77.

80. Porosity and permeability of sediments. All sedimentary materials contain small open spaces which are referred to as *pores* or *voids*. These pores are particularly conspicuous in coarse fragmental deposits and in some dolomitic limestones.[4] The *porosity* of a rock is the percentage volume of the total pore space in a given volume of the rock. This is usually deter-

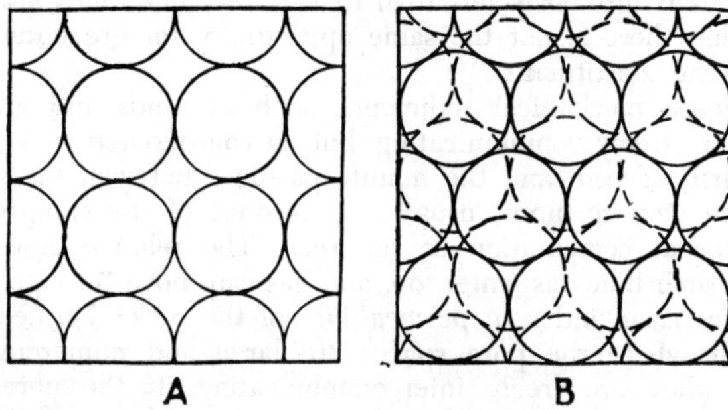

FIG. 35. A, open arrangement of spherical grains. The centers of the grains in each overlying layer would be directly over the centers of the grains below. The porosity is 47.64 per cent. B, close arrangement of spherical grains. In each layer the centers of the grains are above the centers of the open spaces in the next underlying layer, as indicated by the dashed circles. The porosity is 25.95 per cent.

mined by measuring the quantity of water that a sample of the rock will contain. Thus, if 1 cu. ft. of sandstone, when saturated, holds ¼ cu. ft. of water, its porosity is ¼, or 25 per cent.

Theoretically, on the assumption that all the grains of a mass of sand are spherical, are of uniform size, and are touching one another, the maximum porosity possible is 47.64 per cent and the minimum is 25.95 per cent (Fig. 35). Under these conditions, the size of the grains has no effect on the total pore space, provided the grains are arranged in the same way. In other words, the porosity of a gravel composed of essentially spherical pebbles 2 in. in diameter is practically the same as the porosity

[4] Alteration of calcite to dolomite involves a contraction of 12.3 per cent.

of a very fine silt composed of minute spherical particles, although the *size* of the pores, of course, is very different in the two cases.

Variations in the shape of the grains cause only slight differences in the porosity of the rock.

On the other hand, great variation in porosity results from an intermixture of particles of different sizes, for the smaller grains partly fill the pores between the larger grains. For this reason, since sands and gravels are nearly always composed of large and small particles intermingled, the porosity of these materials is ordinarily less than that of very fine muds and silts in which there is not the same opportunity for great range of size in the constituents.

In loose mechanical sediments, such as sands and gravels, pores are freely communicating, but, in consolidated rocks, they are partly closed, and the minute passages between the grains may be very tortuous, usually on account of the compression and partial cementation of the rock. The relative ease with which such fluids as water, oil, and gas can move through these passages is an index of *permeability* of the rock.[5] Permeability is high where the pore spaces are large and numerous *and* where they are freely intercommunicating. If the pores are large, but are not intercommunicating, the rock may have low permeability in spite of the fact that its porosity is high. A rock with pore spaces of given size, abundance, and continuity is more permeable by fluids of low than of high viscosity. Permeability is sometimes called *tightness*. An oil-bearing rock is *tight* if it yields its oil with difficulty, and it is *open* if it yields its oil freely.

The finer the rock and, therefore, the smaller the pores, the more do friction and other forces serve to retard the movement of fluids through rock materials and to reduce or check the yield of fluids from rock materials. Thus, although a clay may perhaps contain more water than a gravel, both being saturated, the gravel will yield its water very much more readily and more

[5] Permeability is expressed in *millidarcies* (sing., *millidarcy*). Rock permeabilities vary from a few hundredths of a millidarcy to several thousand millidarcies. Understanding of the significance of values of permeability is best obtained through observation of the behavior of fluids passed through core samples which are measured for their permeability. A millidarcy is 1/1000 of a *darcy*, which is the unit of measurement of permeability.

abundantly than the clay, other conditions being equal. The gravel is the more permeable.

81. Compression of sediments. During long-continued sedimentation in a region, the strata already laid down are covered by an increasingly thick and heavy overburden which tends to compress them by its weight. The compression, although produced by a force acting downward, is undoubtedly transmitted in all directions, so that the sedimentary material becomes more compact not only across, but also along, the bedding.

As proof of this compression in sediments, we may mention the bending of laminae about inclosed pebbles or other resistant bodies (Fig. 36), the flattening of fossils, and, possibly, the presence of cleavage in some shale formations which have not been folded or otherwise deformed.

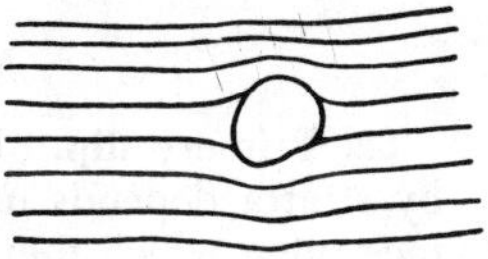

Fig. 36. Section of laminated slate, showing how the laminae have been bent against the pebble in the compression of the rock. The presence of an isolated pebble in deep-water sediments like this suggests that it was rafted out and dropped. When this happens, the mud layers immediately below the pebble may be bent. Consequently, arching of the layers above the pebble is the better indication of compaction.

The reduction in volume (compaction), consequent upon the compression, may be accomplished by: (1) partial squeezing out of interstitial water or other fluids; (2) closer crowding of the constituent particles; (3) bending and granulation of particles; (4) rearrangement of grains by crystal gliding; and, (5) chemical readjustment, as seen in the recrystallization of schists and gneisses (**244**). The first two methods, just listed, are especially effective in unconsolidated deposits and are more or less associated with the lithification of many rocks. The last three methods are more characteristic of changes within rocks already solid, such changes as occur in the metamorphism of rocks (Chap. 9).

Sedimentary materials may vary greatly in their compressibility. Sandstones, limestone, metamorphic and igneous rocks, are practically incompressible. Most of the compaction occurring in sandstones and limestones takes place before cementation has progressed far. Mud, clay, shale, and similar materials undergo considerable reduction in volume, which may be over 40 per cent of the original volume. Athy states that there is, in pure shales, definite relation between density (degree of compaction) and depth (pressure) of burial. His studies reveal in such rocks a compaction of roughly 25 per cent at 1,000 ft., 35 per cent at 2,000 ft., 40 per cent at 3,000 ft., and 45 per cent at 5,000 ft.[6] (180, ¶ 2). We may add here that the fluids that are present underground in the pores of rocks, such as gas, oil, and even water, are compressed to a degree dependent on depth and several other factors.[7]

Modes of Occurrence

82. Primary dip. During accumulation the attitude assumed by stratra depends upon the attitude of the constructional surface upon which they are being deposited. Alluvial cone gravels are laid down in rude beds approximately parallel to the surface of the cone (281). Sand blown over the crest of a dune falls on the steep lee slope where it is built up layer on layer. If a hole be dug in a beach, the strata will often be seen to dip seaward

[6] Bibliog., Teas, L. P., 1923; Hedberg, Hollis D., 1926; Athy, L. F., 1929 (*a*); and Nevin, C. M., and R. E. Sherrill, 1929.

[7] Experimental data indicate that pure water, if subjected to increasing pressures up to 500 atm. (7,350 lb. per sq. in.) at temperatures from 32° up to at least as high as 176°F., is compressible by roughly 2.1 per cent of its volume at atmospheric pressure and at the designated temperature. At atmospheric pressure, pure water expands about 2.87 per cent of its volume at 32°F. in being heated from 32° to 176°F.; and, at 500 atm., it expands 3.11 per cent of its volume at 32° in being heated from 32° to 176°F. Water containing salt (NaCl) or other impurities in solution is less compressible than pure water, and the degree of its compressibility decreases with increase in its content of solute. Similarly, saline waters, when heated, are subject to less expansion than pure water under like conditions.

These are statements of interest to geologists in view of the facts (1) that there is a general increase of temperature with depth (Art. **470**), which, though extremely variable, averages roughly 1°F. for every 50 to 60 ft. of depth in regions of thick sedimentary prisms; (2) that underground waters reveal an increase in content of NaCl and, to a less extent, of other solutes, with depth, the rate being variable but amounting to an average of at least 16,000 to 18,000 parts of solute per million parts of water (by weight) for each 1,000 ft. of depth in regions underlain by thick sedimentary prisms, like the Gulf Coastal Plain; and (3) that hydrostatic pressure in the lithosphere increases downward at a rate varying from 0.46 lb. per sq. in. per foot of depth for pure water to 0.502 lb. per sq. in. per foot of depth for water containing 250,000 parts per million of solids in solution.

References to statistical data may be found in the *Jour. Am. Chem. Soc.*, vol. LIII, p. 3783, 1931; and in International Critical Tables, vol. III, p. 40, McGraw-Hill Book Company, Inc., 1928.

parallel to the surface of the beach. Scores of other examples might be cited. The vertical angle between such an inclined layer and the horizontal may be called the *primary dip* or *original dip* of the layer. It is also referred to as a *constructional* or *depositional gradient,*[8] particularly as applied to the larger formations such as alluvial plain deposits, deltas, coastal plain formations, etc.[9]

Primary dip, in fragmental deposits, being mainly dependent upon constructional slopes, can never have angles greater than the maximum angle of repose for unconsolidated materials (**267**). Its values will range for the most part between 30° or 35° and 0°.

Probably a majority of strata of one kind or another are built with a primary dip; but the deeper offshore water deposits of oceans and lakes, the slowly settling dust accumulations of eolian origin, interbedded chemical and mechanical deposits of saline lakes, and a few other types of sediment, may be spread out with nearly or quite horizontal attitude.

83. Conformity and its significance. When sediments are being laid down, deposition may be continuous in a given area for long periods of time, and yet, because of variations in the strength of the transporting agent or in the nature of the depositing agent, the strata may differ, as we have seen, in texture and composition (**71**). Such beds, formed one above another, in uninterrupted sequence, are usually parallel to one another. Any stratum in the series is *conformable* with the beds above and below it. This relation between the beds is called *conformity*.

While conformity is often the result of uninterrupted deposition, it is not always so. Sedimentation may entirely cease for a few hours or days or even for several months or years, and, provided the part of the deposit already laid down suffers no kind of erosion or deformation, renewed sedimentation will be in conformity with the older beds. Within the formation evidence of a lapse of time of this sort would rarely be discernible. The essential fact to remember is, that *in a conformable series, there*

[8] "Initial dip," a term which probably should be synonymous with "original dip," was unfortunately applied by Bailey Willis to "original dip *plus* a certain secondary angle added by settling or tilting of the strata" (**180**).

[9] The primary dip of the basal layers of a sedimentary deposit may sometimes be determined, or at least partly controlled, by the slope of the destructional surface on which the deposit begins to accumulate.

has been no interval of erosion to interrupt the accumulation of the strata.

84. Relations between unconsolidated transported deposits and bedrock; regional unconformity; regional disconformity. The upper surface of the bedrock beneath any transported deposit is a sharply defined boundary between the rock and the deposit. It is usually an old destructional surface which is now protected to a large extent from further erosion by its cover of sediments. Such a buried surface of erosion is called a *surface of*

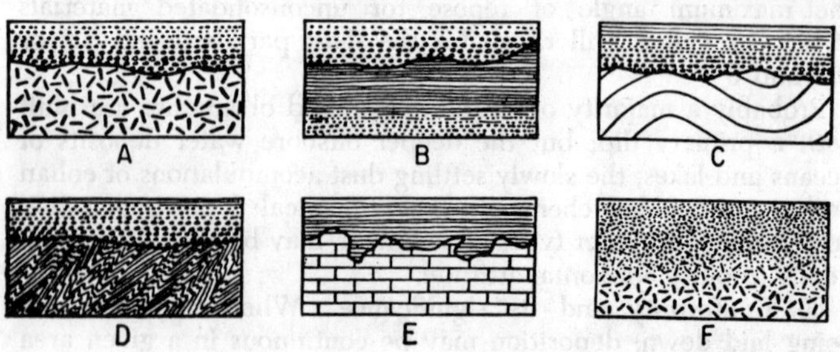

FIG. 37. Types of unconformity. A, unconformity between granite (below) and sediments (above); B, disconformity; C, D, nonconformity or angular unconformity; in D the underlying rocks are schists; E, unconformity between limestone and the residual product of its decomposition; F, blended unconformity between granite and the residual product of its disintegration.

unconformity. Furthermore, it is termed *regional unconformity* because the surface is of wide extent.

Four types of regional unconformity are possible. In each the rock upon which the surface was worn was consolidated at the time of its erosion.[10] This rock, in any given locality, may be: (1) a plutonic rock, such as granite or diorite (Fig. 37, A); (2) a sedimentary formation that has undergone consolidation but no folding (Fig. 37, B); (3) a folded series of consolidated sediment (Fig. 37, C); or (4) a body of regionally metamorphosed rocks (Fig. 37, D). Granite and other plutonic rocks are usually injected into some older *country rock* at considerable depth, and

[10] Regional unconformity between two unconsolidated sedimentary formations is possible, although uncommon. The best example is that of the superposition of the deposits laid down by continental ice sheets in two distinct glacial epochs (122).

at the time of intrusion the country rock forms a thick roof over the magma (**130**). Extensive consolidation of sediments rarely occurs except after deep burial. Finally, folding on a large scale and regional metamorphism are processes which are limited to depths of several hundreds or thousands of feet below the earth's surface. As each of these four types of rock requires a thick cover for the origin of its existing characters, this cover in each case must have been removed down to the level of the present surface of unconformity. Erosion of so much material, most of which was probably hard rock, takes a long time. *Regional unconformity, therefore, represents a long period of erosion.*

Two special cases of regional unconformity are mentioned above as existing between stratified formations. (1) Stratified rock which is essentially horizontal, never having suffered deformation, may be eroded and overlain by sediments with their bedding parallel to the strata beneath them. This relation is called *parallel unconformity* or *disconformity* (Fig. 37, B).[11] (2) On the other hand, if the older formation was tilted or folded before its erosion, there will be an angle between the strata of the two series. This relation is *angular unconformity* or *nonconformity* (Fig. 37, C). The angle may vary from place to place. The younger series will truncate the edges of the older series.

In the deposit above a regional unconformity are often found pebbles, fragments, or grains of the underlying bedrock. These have usually been transported some distance and they must not be regarded as having been derived necessarily from that part of the bedrock which is just below them. By the nature of the particles and fragments much can be learned of the depositing agent (Chap. 3). If the unconsolidated sediments can be removed, the exposed surface of the bedrock may exhibit features which will indicate the agent of erosion (see Chap. 2). Very often by such means deposition of the younger formation and erosion of the older rock will be found to have been performed by the same agent, the erosion antedating the sedimentation.

As examples of partially developed regional unconformity between transported unconsolidated deposits and bedrock the

[11] Although the older series was neither tilted nor folded before deposition of the younger series, there might still be observed some discordance in dips between the two if either or both series contained strata laid down with a primary dip (see **82**).

following may be cited: (1) river gravels on a rock floor formerly channelled out by the river; (2) eolian sands resting on wind-carved rock surfaces of desert regions; (3) glacial wash and till on glaciated bedrock; (4) beach gravels and sands upon a wave-cut bench (277).

85. Relations between unconsolidated residual deposits and bedrock; regional unconformity. In regions where *decomposition* prevails the residual deposits sometimes consist of substances which were contained in the bedrock and which cannot be removed in solution. Terra rossa, a red clay derived from limestone, is an example. An accumulation of this sort gradually thickens as a layer that covers and conceals the remaining bedrock (Fig. 37, E). The contact surface, or surface of unconformity, between the two is generally pretty sharp and, if artificially exposed, may exhibit superficial features of corrosive origin, for it is chiefly on this buried surface that the rock has been and still is undergoing chemical erosion.[12]

More commonly, where chemical weathering predominates, the regolith (soil mantle) derived from the underlying bedrock is found to be zoned from above downward in such a way that in the upper zone (A) soluble materials and colloids have been leached by downward percolating waters; in the middle zone (B) there has been precipitation of materials carried down from (A), with consequent enrichment of iron and aluminum in more humid regions or of calcium and magnesium carbonates in more arid climates; and in the lower zone (C) the material has been little altered and grades down into the original parent rock. These three zones are together referred to as the *soil profile.*[13]

Residual gravels and sands originating through *disintegration* grade downward into the rock from which they were derived (Fig. 37, F). If they are later overlain by other sediments and so become the basal portion of a deposit of some thickness, the relations between this sedimentary formation and the underlying bedrock are certainly those of regional unconformity; yet, in this

[12] *Laterite,* consisting of oxides of iron and aluminum plus other substances in smaller amount, is a residual soil, also usually reddish, produced through weathering of various kinds of rock (granites, basalts, shales, etc.) in tropical regions.

[13] See Bibliog., Shrock, R. R., 1948; and also Krumbein, W. C., and L. L. Sloss, 1958.

case, there is no distinct *surface* of separation; there is no surface of unconformity. This might be called *blended unconformity.*[14] As described in the preceding paragraph, zone C bears this same relation to the unaltered rock below.

86. Regional unconformity in bedrock. When sediments become consolidated, all the relations of unconformity are preserved. There are then two rock formations separated by the surface of unconformity. At least four distinct events are represented: (1) the origin of the older, subjacent formation; (2) the erosion of this body of rock down to the level of the surface of unconformity; (3) the origin of the younger, overlying formation; (4) sufficient erosion of this later series to bring evidence for the unconformity within the zone of observation. The old formation, as stated in the preceding articles, may consist of igneous or sedimentary rocks, metamorphosed or not, but the new formation can consist only of rocks which originate on the earth's surface (sedimentary or effusive). If the lower part of this younger formation consists of conglomerate or sandstone made of fragments of the older formation, it is called a *basal conglomerate* or *basal sandstone.* With a large percentage of feldspar it is a *basal arkose.*

For the methods of studying regional unconformity, see Art. 123.

87. Overlap; transgression and regression of sediments. The relations of regional unconformity show that a sedimentary formation is generally initiated by the accumulation of materials on an old erosion surface. It is hardly conceivable that the basal sediments of such a formation could have been laid down simultaneously throughout their extent. We must believe that deposition commenced in one or more restricted, but favorable spots and that the sediments, as they grew thicker and thicker, spread laterally and encroached upon the domain of erosion. In so doing, they *overlapped* the edges of the strata already formed.

Two kinds of *overlap* are recognized: the transgressive and the regressive. Each may be marine or nonmarine. *Transgressive overlap* may best be illustrated by the case in which the sea is advancing, or *transgressing,* upon a low shelving land mass (Fig. 38, A). At the shore line sand and pebbles accumulate. Their composition and texture depend upon the nature of the rocks

[14] Shrock calls this condition a *zone of unconformity.* (See Bibliog., Shrock, R. R., 1948, p. 49.)

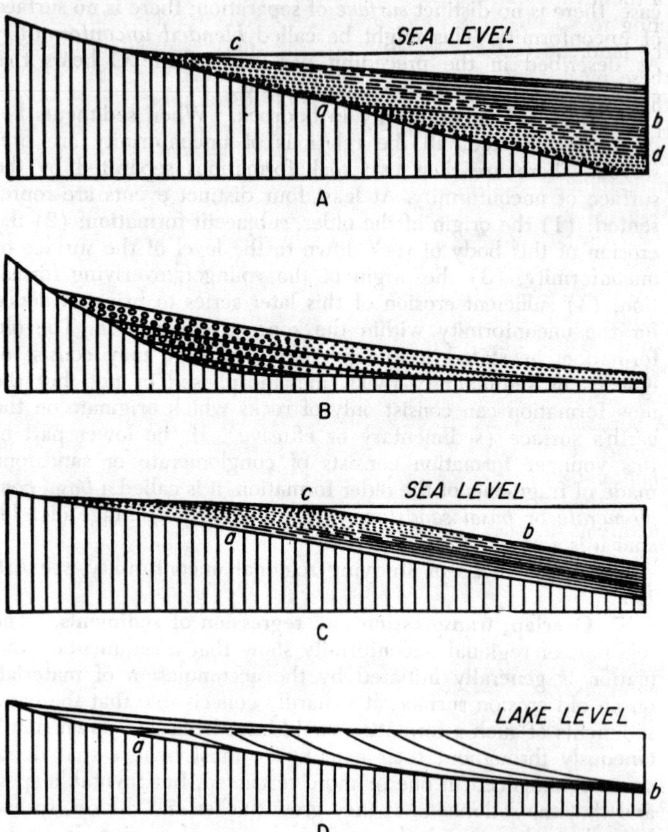

FIG. 38. A, marine transgressive overlap; lines parallel to the sea floor are called *time lines* (*ab*), for they run through materials deposited contemporaneously; lines essentially parallel to the gravel, sand, and mud deposits are called *formation lines* (*cd*). These "lines" are the intersections of surfaces with the plane of the diagram. In a three-dimensional sense, then, we have *time surfaces* and *formation surfaces*. B, transgressive overlap resulting from the upbuilding of an alluvial cone. C, marine regressive overlap; *ab*, formation line; *cb*, time line. D, lake regressive overlap; the lake floor muds (black) are gradually covered by coarser sediments. (Cf. Fig. 50.) Transgressive overlap is shown to the left of *a* in D.

of the invaded land area and upon the kind and degree of weathering to which these rocks may have been exposed. Away from the land, beyond the beach sands, are muds, and again beyond these muds there may be organic oozes on the sea floor. These three phases, the sandy, the muddy, and the limy, extend along the coast in roughly parallel belts. This mode of distribution has many exceptions and irregularities, and, indeed, sometimes it may actually be reversed,[15] but in a broad way it generally holds true so that we may use it for illustration.

As the sea encroaches on the land, the relative positions of these three types of deposit remain more or less constant and the beach sands and pebbles are laid down upon the old erosion surface; but the mud comes to overlie the sand deposited at an earlier date, and the ooze overlies an older portion of the mud body. The mud has lapped over the sand, and the ooze, similarly, has lapped over the mud. This is *marine transgressive overlap*. A vertical columnar section through the formation displays *finer clastics over coarser clastics*, or *deep-water sediments over shallow-water sediments* (Fig. 39, A).

Another type of transgressive overlap is that resulting from piedmont deposition by rivers. In the growth of an alluvial cone, the sediments are carried farther and farther out on to the plain, so that they overlap the lower edges of the older strata. Here the overlap is away from the source of supply, whereas in the marine type it is toward the source. To a less extent there is also a headward overlap at the upper margin of the cone where the materials are heaped up against the flank of the range (Fig. 38, B).

[15] Both the action of currents and the topographic configuration of the sea floor may be responsible for irregular and different local distributions of offshore clastics. In several regions, sand has been reported on submarine ridges, and mud and silt have been reported in the adjacent depressions.

Investigations of the offshore continental shelves have proved that there may be extensive areas of nondeposition on the sea floor, and also that the seaward decrease in grain size does not always hold. Shepard writes, "The discovery that sediments on the shelves lack outward-decreasing grain size should cause some hesitation in the use of variation in sediment texture in looking for shorelines in ancient sediments. Since there is some reason for believing that most old marine sediments now found on the continents were deposited in more or less protected basins and long arms of the sea rather than on the open shelf, the generalization [just stated] relative to texture variation may not be very significant." (Bibliog., Shepard, Francis P., 1948.)

Marine regressive overlap (Fig. 38, C) is produced where the sea recedes (regresses) from the land, *i.e.*, when sea level falls. By this process the beach zone migrates out over earlier offshore muds, and at their seaward ends these mud beds overlap the older oozes. In a vertical columnar section, *coarser clastics overlie finer clastics, or shallow-water sediments overlie deep-water sediments* (Fig. 39, B). Actual lowering of sea level is not necessary for the origin of marine regressive overlap, for a similar regressive section may be produced if the sea level is stationary and there is a sufficient supply of sediments, or even if sea level is rising, provided the rate of supply exceeds the rate of subsidence of the land.

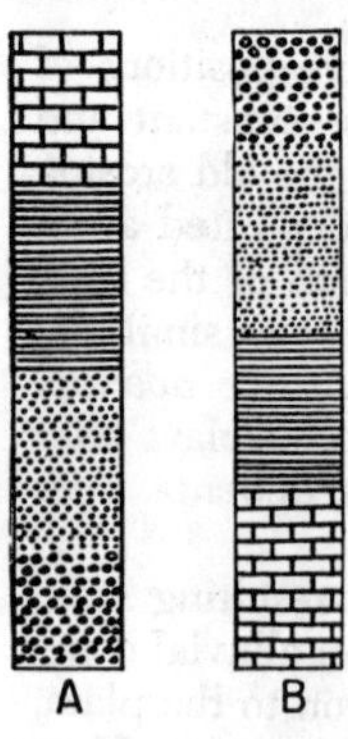

Fig. 39. Ideal sections to illustrate the sequence of deposits laid down (A) in a transgressing sea, and (B) in a regressing sea.

Lake regressive overlap is very much like marine regressive overlap. Feeding streams constantly tend to fill a lake, so that the shore sands and pebbles are forced to encroach upon the lake-floor muds. A vertical section through a choked lake exhibits *coarser sediments over finer sediments.* This is often called the *normal lake succession* (Fig. 38, D).

Different types of overlap may be combined in the same stratigraphic section. Thus, the sea may have advanced on the land and then receded, so that regressive overlap relations (*offlap*), are found above those of transgression (*onlap*), and this alternation may be repeated several times (Fig. 40). Again, marine overlap may be replaced by nonmarine overlap, or vice versa. The complications are too numerous for consideration in this volume.[16]

The term *overlap* is not restricted to major lithologic formations, but may be applied to the thinner beds within such formations where there are variations in texture or in composition and where these individual beds were laid down under similar conditions of transgression or regression, as the case may be.

There has been much discussion on the exact significance of this term *overlap.* As described above, in transgressive overlap (also called *onlap*) there are two connotations, namely, (1)

[16] For further information, see Bibliog., Grabau, A. W., 1913, Chap. 18.

overlapping of the wedge ends of older layers by younger layers *within* a conformable series *at the surface of unconformity* upon which this series rests (**123**), and (2) overlapping of older lithologic formations by younger lithologic formations *within* a conformable series of strata. In regressive overlap (also called *offlap*), only this second relationship is implied. There is the further implication, in this use of "overlap," that the process of overlapping was progressive, layer by layer, within the conformable series.

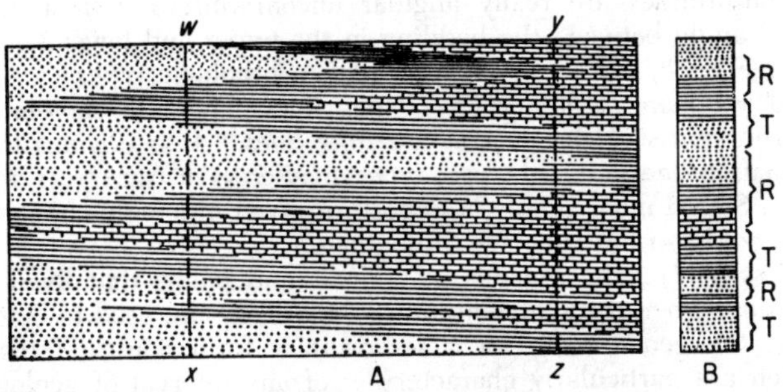

FIG. 40. A, diagrammatic cross section of deposits laid down during successive transgressions and regressions of the sea. Land to the left; sea to the right; sand, stippled; shale, ruled; limestone, brick pattern. At *wx* shallow-water sediments (shale and sandstone) predominate; at *yz* deep-water sediments predominate. B, columnar section taken at *wx* in A. Note that the changes in the character of the sediments in a columnar section like this are indicative of alternate transgressive (T) and regressive (R) conditions.

None of these connotations applies to the case of tilted strata which have been bevelled by erosion and then overlain by a truncating basal member of a younger series (Fig. 77C, *ad*). In this type of nonconformity (**84**), younger beds within the tilted older series do not successively *overlap* older beds in this same series, nor is there any implied or necessary process of *serial* blanketing of the older formation by the overlying younger formation. The latter merely covers the former, and the apparent overlap is not true overlap which, as we have said before, implies imbrication *within* the formation which exhibits overlap.[17]

[17] Melton suggested that this feature of the regular truncation of strata below unconformities (*ad*, Fig. 77C) be called "strike-overlap" (Bibliog.,

Referring to regional disconformity (84), the fact is that probably never in nature is there exact mathematical parallelism between the strata above and below such a disconformity. This may not be obvious in local exposures, or even when carried for some distance from outcrop to outcrop, but it becomes evident when regional studies demonstrate the gradual appearance of new strata in the section either just above or just below the surface of disconformity. This means that these strata occur in a very thin flat wedge, and it indicates that actually most regional disconformities are really angular unconformities with a very small angle between the bedding in the upper and lower series.

In Fig. 38, A and C, lines parallel to lithologic types (sands, mud, etc.) are *formation lines,*[18] and lines parallel to contemporaneous parts of the deposit are *time lines.*[18] It is obvious that formation lines, *i.e.*, lithologic types, may cross or transgress time lines. Stated more simply, a deposit of given lithologic character may not be of the same age throughout.

Fossils—*i.e.*, the remains of animals and plants that lived at the time when the sediments were deposited—are used to determine the geologic age of a sedimentary formation, and those which are particularly characteristic of any interval of geologic time are referred to as *index fossils.* At the time when they lived, these animals and plants flourished under special conditions of environment (temperature, clearness of water, salinity of water), conditions that, in considerable measure, were related to the kind of sediments in which the remains were finally entombed. Therefore, it is important to remember that fossil species, like lithologic types, may and often do transgress time lines in the greater sedimentary formations. Thus, animal or plant species associated with muddy waters might live in such waters throughout a long geologic period, moving inland during transgression and then seaward during subsequent regression. Their remains, preserved as fossils in the settling mud, would be geologically

---

Melton, Frank C., 1947), and Lovely referred to it as "overstep" (Bibliog., Lovely, H. R., 1948). We urge that only terms that denote unconformity (or nonconformity) and truncation of beds be employed here, and that the word overlap, in any form or combination, be restricted to those phenomena of sedimentation which the term appropriately describes (see also Bibliog., Lahee, F. H., 1949).

[18] In Fig. 38, A, the vertical cross sections of *formation surfaces* and *time surfaces.*

much older early in the transgression than late in the regression. Care has to be taken not to rely too implicitly on an index fossil or even on a group of index fossils, as proof that the containing strata in two localities are of exactly the same age.

88. Lithologic facies. We speak of the rock character, or lithologic character, of a stratum or of a formation as a *lithologic facies.* For example, within a certain area a certain formation may consist of limestone. As one passes into an adjoining area, this same formation may grade into a shale, and beyond this area, the shale may grade into a sandstone (see Fig. 40). We say, then, that the lithologic facies of this formation is limestone in the first area, shale in the second area, and sandstone in the third area. Similarly, within a given formation or group of formations, the fossil assemblage may change from one area to another, so that here we have different *biologic facies.* The study of lithologic facies and biologic facies of different formations is very important in helping to show the original relative positions of lands and seas, of mountains and plains, and so on, at the time when the sediments were deposited. These studies are properly embraced within the scope of the word "stratigraphy" (see **125, 505**).

89. Contemporaneous sedimentation. Because the particular lithologic and biologic facies of a sedimentary formation may not be, and probably are not, contemporaneous throughout their extent (as above explained), the question arises, How can contemporaneous deposition be determined? Is there any method by which we can determine that strata in one area were laid down approximately *at the same time* as those in another area, perhaps far distant? There are three kinds of finely divided material which help in the solution of this problem. These are volcanic dust or ash, pollen, and spores.

Volcanic dust, if violently erupted, may be blown over large portions of the earth and may then settle on land and in water. If this dust (bentonite, when decomposed; see Art. **132**) has characteristics that can be recognized, microscopically or chemically, in the sedimentary strata, it may serve as a key to contemporaneous deposition. Better, however, are the spores and pollen which are blown far and wide from many kinds of plants, and which are found to have characteristic shapes and markings that can be easily identified and classified through microscopic examination (see Fig. 41). These wind-blown substances are not

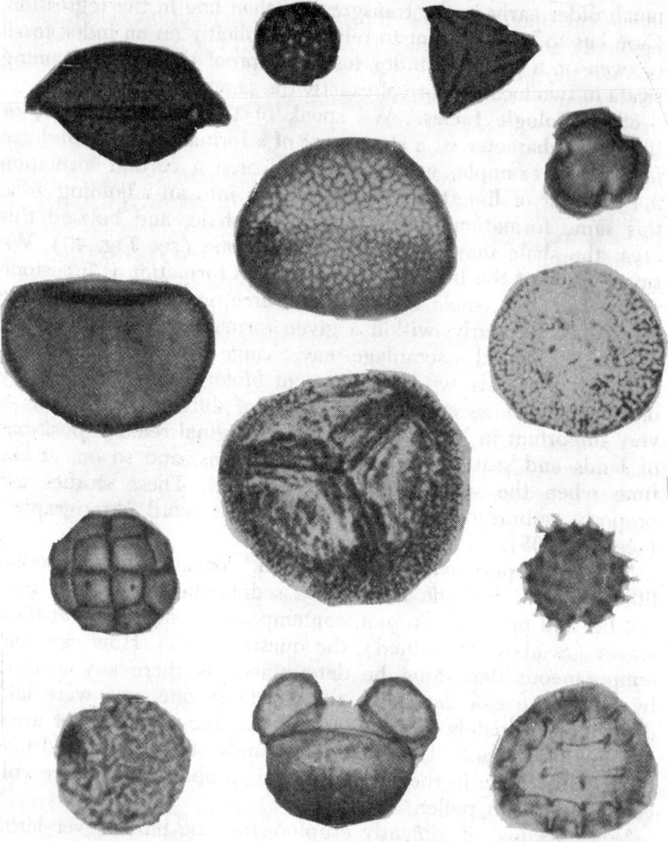

FIG. 41. Micropnotographs of pollen and spores selected to illustrate the wide variety of form and surface markings of these bodies. (Very much enlarged.) (*Kindly presented to the author for use in this book by Dr. John F. Grayson, with permission of Dr. Charles Ivan Alexander of Socony Mobil Field Research Laboratory.*)

dependent upon localized transport and deposition. They settle regionally and thus greatly facilitate the time correlation of the sediments in which they occur.[19]

90. Transgression and regression of bioherms. Many of the organisms that build a bioherm (see Arts. **104** and **299**) are closely limited, for their successful development, to a vertical range roughly corresponding with the range between low tide and high tide.[20] Their principal growth is near low tide. Consequently, if sea level remains constant, a bioherm can grow only laterally and, since the main supply of food is available from the open sea, lateral growth will be seaward; but in this direction as time goes on, increasing depth of water will more and more retard forward building of the reef mass. On the other hand, change of sea level may have some very important consequences on the development of such a bioherm. Too rapid a rise of sea level would drown the reef organisms. Too rapid a fall of sea level would kill them by exposing them to the air and removing their source of food. But if sea level were to rise gradually, not too fast to prevent the organisms from continuing their development, the reef might advance landward, or—perhaps more likely—a succession of bioherms might originate and grow each farther landward than the last, as the sea progressively advanced on the land, so that eventually these *transgressing* bioherms might occupy a rather wide belt. If, then, sea level should begin to fall, but not too rapidly, new reefs might develop successively seaward, and eventually there would be a *regressive* bioherm, or series of bioherms. These conditions are illustrated in Fig. 42. Note that although essentially the same type of organic assemblage may be responsible for the origin of all the bioherms represented in cross section here, from *a* to *b*, and *b* to *c*, the geologic age of *c* may be much younger than that of *a*. In other words, as explained above, the fossils have transgressed the time lines.

There are several important points which may be mentioned here. First, observe that bioherms may rest either on a basement

[19] The study of pores and pollen is called *palynology,* a term first proposed by Hyde and Williams. It was derived from the Greek word παλύνω, to *strew* or *sprinkle,* and this is evidently related to the Greek word πάλη. which means *fine dust* or *flour* (equivalent to the Latin *pollen,* also meaning *fine flour*). (See Bibliog., Hyde, H. A., 1944; and Cain, Stanley A., 1948.)

[20] Some reef-building organisms apparently flourish at considerable depths—possibly several scores or even hundreds of feet—below low-tide level.

unconformably beneath the stratigraphic series within which they occur, or on strata *within* this same series. Second, in a series like that shown in this figure (42), regressive reefs may be found in a vertical section above transgressive reefs; and of course the reverse is also true (Fig. 40). Third, the bioherms are pictured here in cross section as if, for example, *c* were almost directly over *a*; but actually, in nature, with many changing factors involved, *c*, although relatively of the same age and at the same distance from the old shore line as illustrated, might be far removed from *a*, either below or above the plane of the section as drawn through *a*. A fourth point refers to the nature of the

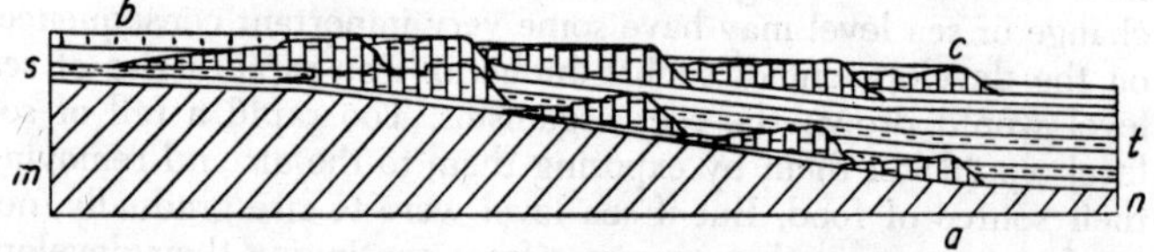

Fig. 42. Cross section of a marine series of beds, *st*, unconformably overlying a basement, *mn*. In the series *st* are several bioherms which were formed during transgression of the sea (from *a* to *b*) and then during regression of the sea (from *b* to *c*). (*After T. A. Link.*)

lagoonal and marine strata associated with these bioherms. Outside of the fringing talus deposits, these strata are often described as limy muds, but there is a question as to when, or how often, in these sequences, we may expect red beds and evaporites (perhaps lagoonal facies associated with regressing reefs), and also cherty limestones thought to represent silica gels brought in from an adjacent low-lying land area. Finally there is the problem as to what extent bioherm development was initiated on shallow submarine shelves or terraces or platforms.

91. Clastic dikes. The normal method of sedimentary accumulation is such that, in the terms of stratigraphy, any portion of a deposit must be younger than the materials which underlie it and older than the materials which overlie it (**100**). The age of a stratum is gradational from oldest at the bottom to youngest at the top. However, there are instances known of *clastic dikes*, that is, of layers of clastic material which intersect other rocks and which, unlike true beds, are of approximately the same age at opposite points in their sides. It is easy to imagine how sand, perhaps, might drift into and finally fill a fissure in bedrock at the surface of the ground or under water (Fig. 43). This mode of origin has been proposed for these dikes in some cases. Another suggestion offered is that detritus has slowly been let down *pari passu* with the opening of spaces by gradual leaching and removal of the original materials in solution (cf. Fig. 37, E). Generally the dike material seems to have come up from below in an unconsolidated condition (as loose sand, mud, etc.), probably mixed with water or other fluids. Upturned strata in the

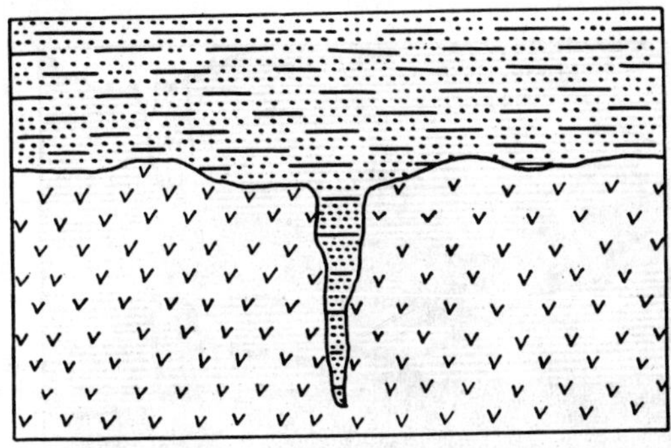

FIG. 43. Clastic dike formed by the filling of a fissure from above.

wall rock, upward thinning and termination of the dikes, evidence of flow structure parallel to the walls, inclusions of the wall rock in the dikes, the great size and continuity of some of the dikes,[21] and the similarity of the dike materials with underlying sediments—all these facts point to fairly rapid injection from a source below (Fig. 44). There are good reasons for believing that the injection was performed under considerable pressure (hydrostatic pressure, or pressure from gas, from the weight of the superjacent rocks, or from combinations of these forces).

Clastic dikes have been recorded as consisting of asphalt, clay, shale, gravel, conglomerate, bituminized and unbituminized

[21] Clastic dikes have been found ranging in thickness from mere films up to several hundred yards and in length from a few inches to over nine miles. See Bibliog., Newsom, J. F., 1903. For evidences of filling from above, see Bibliog., Vintanage, P. W., 1954.

sand, hard sandstones, and limestone, and as intersecting granite, sandstone, sand, shale, clay, limestone, and especially coal. The best condition for the origin of these dikes is the presence of unconsolidated sedimentary material overlain by a hardened, cracked stratum. They may have been caused by earthquake shocks and earth stresses which tend to fracture rocks and redistribute mobile substances.

92. Clastic pipes. Clastic "intrusions," instead of being sheetlike, may have one long and two short dimensions, like a rod.

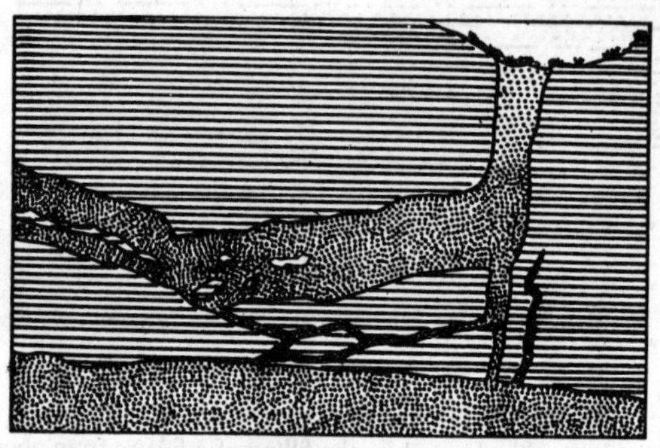

FIG. 44. Dikes of bituminous sandstone (stippled) in Miocene shale (lined). Section about 50 ft. high. (*Taken from folio* 163, *U.S. Geol. Survey*)

When they have this shape they are termed *pipes*. They are the fillings of irregular tubes and usually have approximately a vertical position. From the fact that the surrounding rock is nearly always limestone and from the structural relations of these pipes, they are believed to have originated either: (1) by the filling of sinks (**290**); or (2) by the slow settling of débris into a depression which, contemporaneously, was being made in the bedrock by solution. According to both explanations the materials enter from above.

Mutual Relations of Beds or Laminae

93. Local unconformity; contemporaneous erosion. Sometimes deposition is interrupted by a period of erosion. The beds already laid down may be somewhat dissected. After a relatively short time the accumulation of sediments may begin again and the eroded surface will be covered up by the later beds. In a deposit built in this manner the upper younger strata are *unconformable* with the lower older strata, and the buried surface of erosion is a *surface of unconformity;* but this structure differs in several respects from regional unconformity (84, 85). In the first place the area of erosion is often of small dimensions compared with the whole formation so that this may be called *local unconformity.*[22] Second, the erosion is accomplished during a short cessation in the upbuilding of the deposits, and is therefore spoken of as *contemporaneous* erosion. And third, the sediments below the surface of unconformity were not lithified at the time of this erosion (see footnote, page 74).

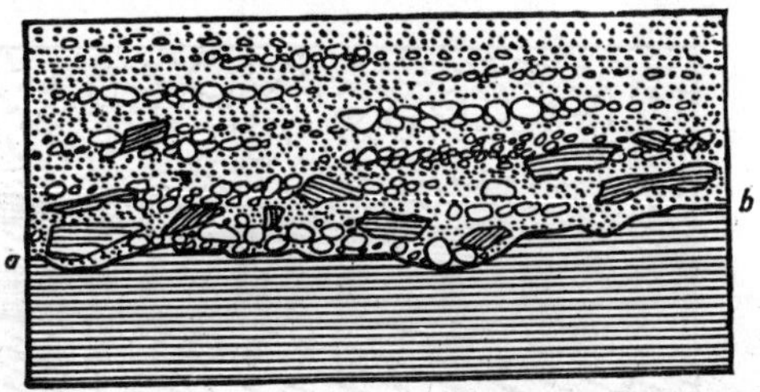

FIG. 45. Section of a surface of local unconformity, *ab,* between an older clay, now lithified to slate, and a younger sandy gravel, now conglomerate. The fragments of slate in the conglomerate are intraformational pebbles. They originated as such when broken away from the original clay bed.

The most common type of local unconformity is the result of stream action. At time of flood a river may cut into and sweep away part of the mud and sand deposited while its current was less impetuous. By its increase in velocity this stream is enabled to carry coarser sand and gravel. As soon as the speed begins to slacken again, deposition commences. The heavier fragments are dropped first and, while the flood subsides, finer and finer particles are deposited until normal conditions prevail.

A vertical cross section through beds separated by a local unconformity usually shows a finer stratum overlain by a coarser stratum and the two divided by an irregular line (of unconformity) which cuts across the bedding of the lower stratum (Fig. 45). The major stratification above the line of unconformity is parallel to that below.

[22] More precisely, it might be called *local disconformity.*

Contemporaneous erosion may be caused also by the shifting of aggrading streams on flood plains, deltas, and alluvial cones; in marine deposits by changes in the strength or direction of marine currents; in lake deposits by similar changes in currents; and in eolian deposits by variations in the wind. In all these cases the unconformity is local.

There is a somewhat similar relation between older and younger sediments which may be associated with glaciation. In front of an ice sheet or a mountain glacier aqueoglacial deposits accumulate. Beneath the ice till may be deposited. While the ice front is advancing the water-laid sands and gravels may be overridden, more or less eroded, and subsequently overlain by till

FIG. 46. Section of a surface unconformity, *ab*, between older cross-bedded sand and younger till.

(Fig. 46). The pebbles in such till are many of them waterworn, having been dislodged from the underlying wash, and those which are striated are characterized by very numerous and very fine scratches produced by rubbing against sand rather than bed-rock. On the other hand, in the retreat of the ice front, water derived from melting may flow over and erode somewhat earlier till and lay down aqueoglacial muds, sands, and gravels upon this till (Fig. 47). The latter relation is more common than the former because in most cases advancing ice completely destroys the wash over which it passes. The chief differences between local unconformity and the unconformity produced in each of these cases is that these are surfaces of such broad extent that they can hardly be termed *local*, and they are the result of a change in the agent itself. Nevertheless, they are examples of contemporaneous erosion, as the term has been defined (cf. 84, 122).

94. Sun cracks. Sun-cracked loam and silty clay disintegrate so quickly when moistened that there is little or no opportunity for the preservation of the cracks. Purer clays, if exposed long enough to dry thoroughly, may hold together until the

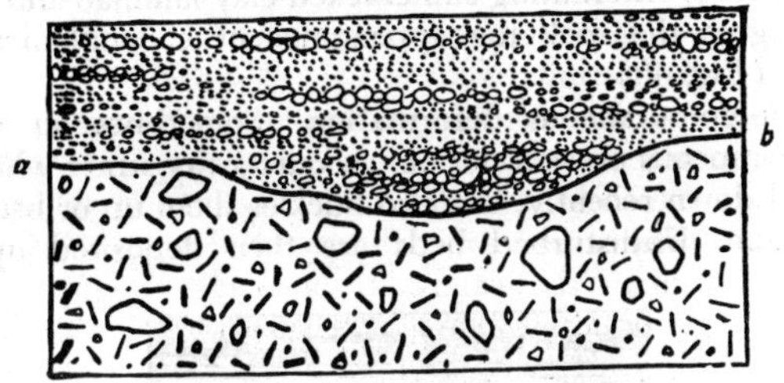

FIG. 47. Section of a surface of unconformity, *ab*, between older till and younger gravel.

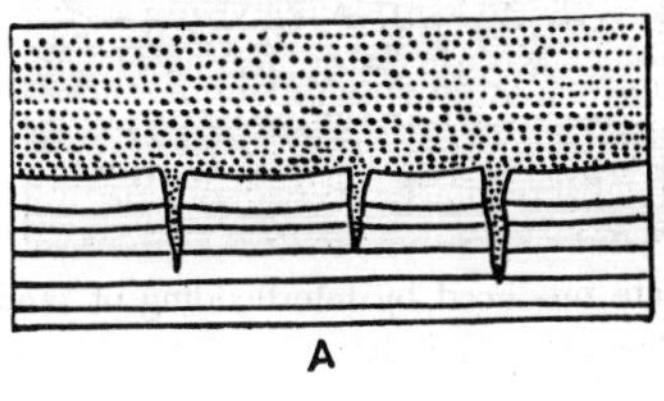

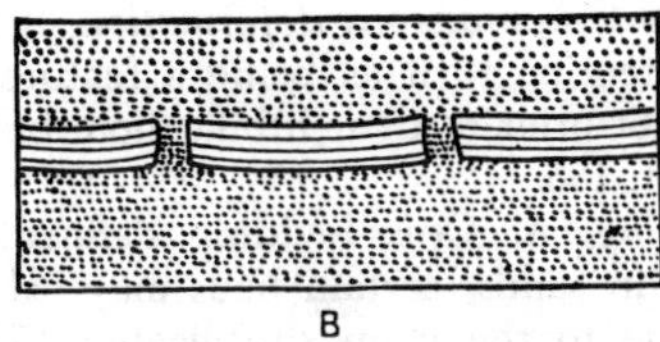

FIG. 48. Sections of sun-cracked clay which has been buried by sand. In B a thin clay layer rested on sand. (Cf. Fig. 29.)

cracks are filled with sand by an invading sheet of water. Sun cracks may be filled also with windblown dust or sand. In any case a cross section would show a fine mud or clay deposit overlain (usually) by a somewhat coarser stratum from which small projections, wedge-shaped or rectangular (**65**), would extend downward a few inches (Fig. 48). The contact between the two deposits would be sharp and would represent a time interval during which sedimentation ceased. In this interval erosion might or might not occur. It would not be unnatural to find contemporaneous erosion exhibited somewhere along the line of contact (107). Alternating sun-cracked clay laminae and laminae of sand give the rock the appearance of a conglomerate (or breccia) (Fig. 49).

95. Contemporaneous deformation. Sometimes an agent of contemporaneous erosion not only scours away strata which have been laid down recently, but also buckles them up or breaks and faults them. Undisturbed beds are then deposited upon the

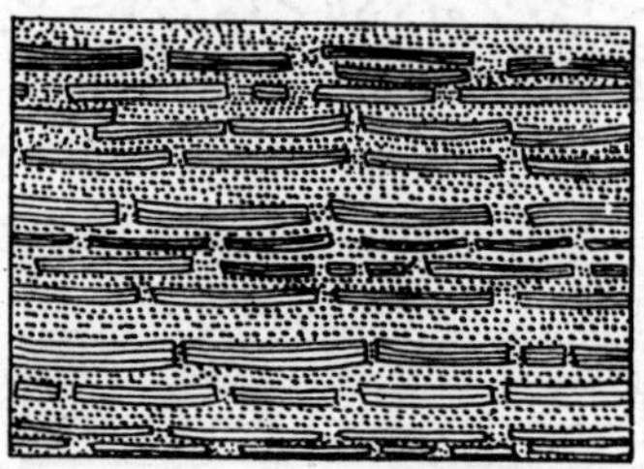

Fig. 49. Conglomerate produced by interbedding of sand laminae and sun-cracked clay laminae.

truncated edges of the dislocated layers. This structure, which may be called *contemporaneous deformation*, is mentioned here merely to call attention to it as being a feature which may be developed in strata prior to their lithification, but its description is reserved for Art. 188.

96. Cross-bedding. A. Cross-bedding defined. In some deposits, especially in sands, certain beds may exhibit an original lamination oblique to the main stratification. This structure is called *false bedding* or *cross-bedding*, or *cross-lamination*. It is generally caused by current action, either of wind or of water, and in some instances is produced by wave action. It is found in deltas, torrential deposits, sand bars in rivers, marine current deposits, sand reefs, and eolian deposits. It is produced only in granular sediments.[23] Ripple-mark, of both wave and current

[23] When occurring in limestones, cross-bedding is evidence that these limestones were laid down as granular materials, although at present such limestones may be dense and recrystallized.

origin, is a special case of cross-bedding. The principal kinds of cross-bedding are described in the succeeding paragraphs.

96B. Delta structure. In a delta that has been built under ideal conditions in a standing body of water there are three

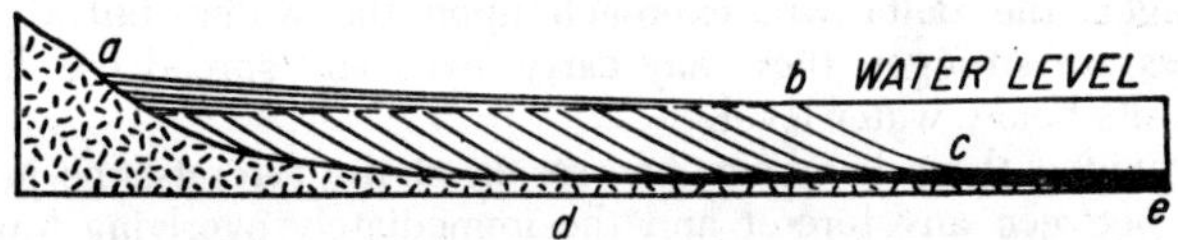

FIG. 50. Delta structure. *ab*, topsets; *bc*, foresets; *de*, bottomsets or prodelta clays. Note relation of water level to the angle between the foresets and the topsets.

series of beds, namely, topset, foreset, and bottomset beds (Fig. 50). The *topsets* have a primary dip equal to the angle of slope of the subaerial surface of the delta upon which they were laid down by an aggrading stream. The *foresets* consist of materials dumped over the front of the delta into the lake and hence their primary dip is the angle of repose of the materials under water (20° to 35°). The younger foresets of large deltas have lower primary dips than the older ones.[24] The *bottomsets* are nearly horizontal for they are formed of fine muds or silts that float out and gradually come to rest on the floor of the lake. They are often termed *prodelta clays.*

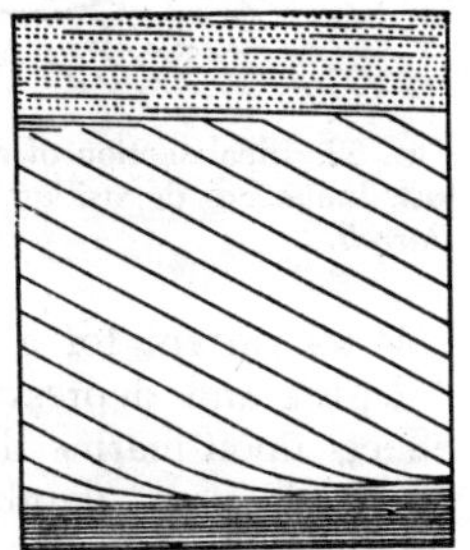

FIG. 51. Detailed vertical section through the deposits of a delta. *a*, topsets; *b*, foresets; *c*, bottomsets or prodelta clays.

The foreset group meets the topsets in an angle or in an abrupt curve and it merges with the bottomsets in a broader curve, concave upward (Fig. 51). Variations in load, course, or velocity may cause the aggrading stream temporarily to degrade its channel and so produce local unconformity between the topsets and the foresets; but erosion of this kind can never occur between the foresets and bottomsets. (How might contemporaneous erosion occur between the foresets and bottomsets?)

[24] Bibliog., Grabau, A. W., 1913, p. 702.

The upper ends of the foresets of deltas formed in large bodies of water are often broadly eroded if the action of tides or waves is strong. Whether or not a subaqueous plain of denudation can be maintained on the growing delta depends upon the comparative efficiency of river and waves. If the river is the stronger, the delta will encroach upon the water; but if the waves are stronger, they may carry away and spread the delta deposits below water level.

Provided there has been no erosion of the foresets, the junction between any foreset and the immediately overlying topset bed is a little below the water level at the time that foreset bed was deposited (Fig. 50). This is because the stream can main-

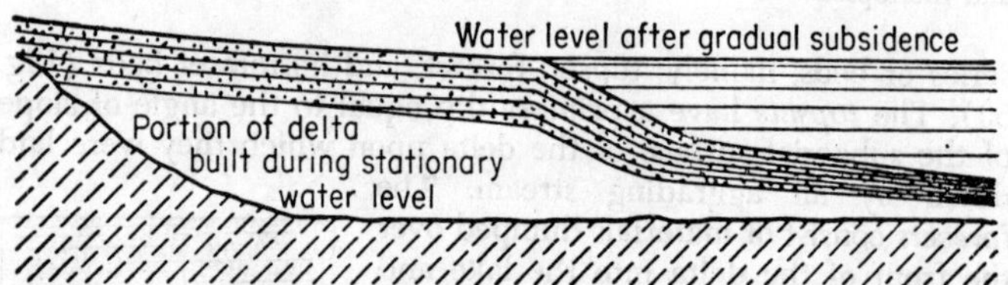

FIG. 52. Ideal section of a delta built out into quiet water while subsidence just balanced deposition. The shore line remained stationary. (*After J. Barrell.*)

tain its current for a short distance out from shore. (Explain.)

Uplift and depression of the sea floor may have significant effects upon marine deltas. Slow subsidence (normal condition) results in great depth and volume of topsets (Fig. 52), while small uplifts favor great volumes of foresets and tend to shift seaward the zone of terrestrial sedimentation.[25]

96C. Compound foreset bedding in deltas. The so-called normal delta structure is represented in radial vertical sections as in Fig. 50. If a vertical section were cut concentric with the front edge of a delta, *i.e.*, parallel to the strike of the foresets, no cross-bedding would be seen. All other vertical sections would expose foresets with an inclination less than their true dip. In the construction of a lobate delta (**281**), adjacent lobes interfere in such a way as to cause the building of foresets dipping now in one direction and now in another.[26] By changes in the

[25] Bibliog., Barrell, J., 1912, pp. 400, 401.
[26] Bibliog., Smith, A. L., 1909, p. 437.

stream, such as decrease in load, increase in volume of water, or shift in course, or by fluctuation of the lake or marine water level, foresets recently deposited may have their upper ends truncated and may then be overlain by new beds of similar nature dipping in the same or in a different direction. *Compound foreset bedding* produced in one or another of these ways is abundantly exemplified in glacial sand plains[27] (Fig. 53).

FIG. 53. Compound foreset bedding. Note that each set of laminae is truncated by the next overlying set. Section about 4 ft. long.

Of much less common occurrence is a type of cross-bedding where the successive sets of foreset beds have been deposited on those below without intervening erosion. This condition (Fig. 54) may occur locally within a series where truncation of lower sets by upper sets is the prevailing relationship.

Foreset bedding, although changing in direction and in observable angle of dip in a series of sets, may be so disposed that successive sets have essentially parallel top and bottom surfaces (Fig. 55); in other words, the cross-laminated sets are "tabular."

96D. Torrential cross-bedding. In torrential deposits, fine, horizontally laminated strata may alternate with uniformly cross-bedded strata composed of coarser material. The cross laminae meet the horizontal beds at an acute angle, both above and be-

[27] A special variety, called backset bedding, was described by W. M. Davis (see Bibliog., Davis, W. M., 1890).

FIG. 54. Foresets deposited on underlying sets with no erosion of the latter.

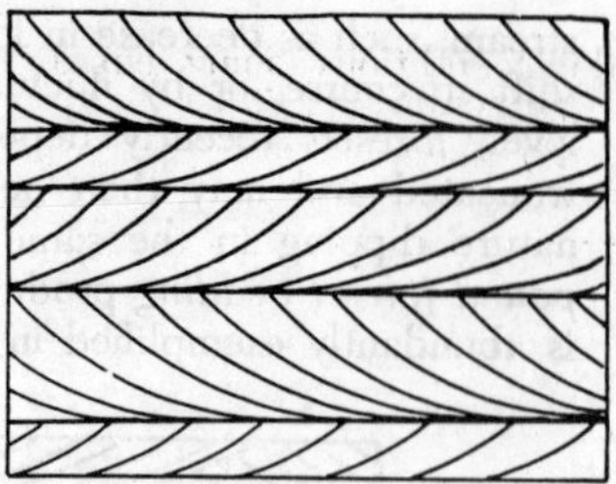

FIG. 55. Tabular sets of foreset laminae.

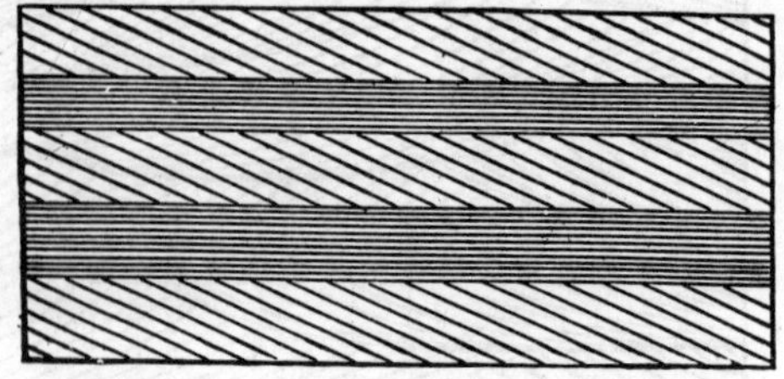

FIG. 56. Torrential cross-bedding.

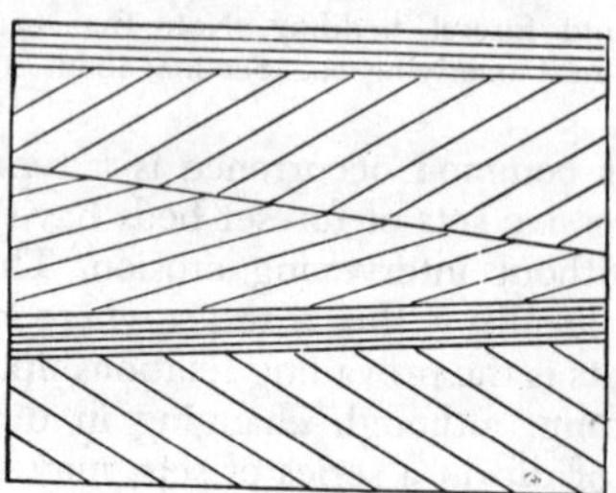

FIG. 57. A variety of torrential cross-bedding. (Cf. Fig. 56.)

low (Figs. 56, 57). The larger (or heavier) grains may be concentrated at the lower ends of the inclined laminae, having rolled down the slope as each lamina was deposited. This type of bedding is believed to originate under desert conditions of concentrated rainfall, abundant wind action, and playa lake deposition. The cross-bedded layers are built forward by temporary streams where they debouch upon the playa lake, and the horizontal layers are materials which settle from suspension from the playa lake waters after the feeding stream has withered away.

96E. Other types of foreset bedding in water-laid deposits. Sand lenses, such as those to be described in Art. 97, frequently exhibit a uniform cross-bedding of the foreset variety. In the building of a river sand bar, the materials are carried over the bar and are dumped on its front or downstream slope. Filling of hollows and deserted channels may proceed as in the construction of a normal delta, the sand being laid down in successive foreset beds. These may be seen in sections of the deposit.

Spits are built by the action of longshore currents. Sand is dumped over the growing end of the spit and there it slides down and assumes the angle of repose. The resulting bedding is therefore of the foreset type.

Under certain circumstances minor foreset bedding is produced by currents on the floors of lakes and seas, but it is not characteristic of deposits there accumulated. Yet it has been found even in marine limestones.[28] Cross-bedding of this origin is rarely seen in unconsolidated sediments.

96F. Wave-built cross-bedding. Lake beaches and marine beaches are built largely by the work of waves. Sand or gravel is thrown up layer upon layer and the beach thus grows toward the water. Since the slope and profile of a beach depend chiefly upon the strength of the waves, and since the stratification and surface of a growing beach are parallel, it follows that variations in wave efficiency may produce slight variations in the structure of the deposit . . . "The beach strata are considerably inclined" and "each layer or group of layers is apt to be intersected by other layers lying at different angles."[29]

This beach structure is not of the same origin as foreset bedding. The angles of inclination of the laminae are less than the ordinary angles of repose. Also, the angles between adjacent groups of laminae are usually only a very few degrees. Wave-built cross-bedding is not often visible in unconsolidated materials. It occurs chiefly on the outer parts of sand reefs. In gravel it is obscure and the arrangement of pebbles may suggest pell-mell structure. In sections of lake beaches it is to be distinguished

[28] See footnote 23, p. 92.
[29] Bibliog., Shaler, N. S., 1895, p. 165.

from the steeper, less regular structure produced by the shove of ice.[30] The portions of sand reefs above the reach of the waves are of eolian origin and the inner margins are built by the dropping of wind-blown sand into the neighboring lagoon (**305**).

96G. Eolian cross-bedding. Cross-bedding of wind construction is marked by its extreme irregularity (Fig. 58). This is due to the variability of direction of winds and the frequent alternation of scouring and deposition. The cross-laminae of a growing sand dune are of two sets: (1) the foresets which are built on the lee slope and dip at the angle of repose of dry sand

FIG. 58. Eolian cross-bedding.

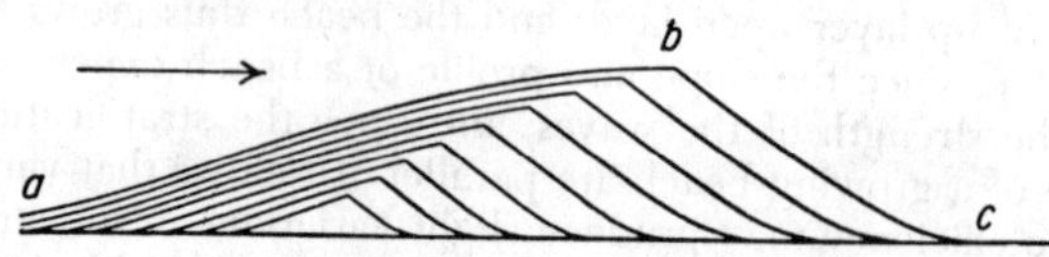

FIG. 59. Section of a dune, showing topset or backset bedding, *ab*, and foreset bedding, *bc*. The crest, *b*, has advanced a little in the direction of the wind (see arrow), but the dune as a whole has not migrated.

(about 30°); and (2) the topsets (or backsets) which are formed on the windward surface of the dune and have an average dip of 5° or 10° against the wind. (How does this differ from the topsets of deltas? What happens to the wind-blown materials corresponding to the bottomsets of deltas?) The topsets are rarely permanent and may be very thin or absent if the dune is migrating rapidly (Figs. 59, 60). The dip of the fore-

[30] See Bibliog., Fenneman, N. M., 1902, p. 31.

sets decreases down the slope so that these layers curve with their concave sides uppermost. As the dune moves forward, a part of the lower portion of the foresets may be left behind and upon these truncated foresets a new dune may advance from the same or a new direction. By a repetition of this process, the sand deposit comes to have a highly complex structure. The sets of cross laminae may be wedge-shaped, with the laminae of dif-

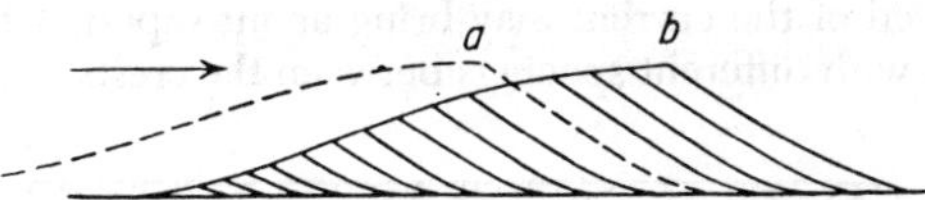

FIG. 60. Cross section of a dune, showing foreset bedding. The dune has migrated from *a* to *b* by the blowing of sand from the windward side (see arrow) to the lee side. Contrast this figure and Fig. 59 with reference to the quantity of sand supplied.

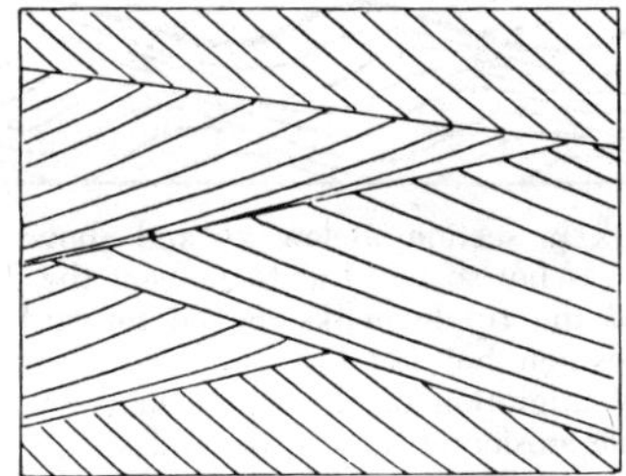

FIG. 61. Wedge-shaped sets of foreset laminae which dip in various directions.

ferent sets dipping in many different directions, as in Fig. 61. Care should be taken to discriminate eolian cross-bedding from compound delta structure and from wave-built cross-bedding.

96H. Ripple-mark.[31] The ripple marks seen in sections of deposits are more commonly of the current-formed species. Since each one of these ripple marks is a miniature dune, we may speak of the laminae which dip against the current as topsets (Fig. 25, *bc*) and those that dip with the current as foresets (Fig. 25, *ab*).

[31] "Ripple mark," in this book, is written unhyphenated to signify a single ridge of that name. The plural is "ripple marks." The hyphenated term, "ripple-mark," is used here for the structure which is seen in a cross section of a group of ripple marks.

Topsets are laid down provided deposition is sufficiently rapid during the process of ripple-making (Fig. 62); but if the strength of the current increases beyond a certain limit, which is variable according to several factors, migration of the ripple system is too rapid, and erosion instead of deposition will occur on the back slope of each ripple (Fig. 62). Change in direction of current may cause the superposition of rippled laminae in which the foresets are inclined in different directions. Variations in the speed of the current may bring about superposition of sets of ripples with different spacings between the crests.

FIG. 62. Ripple-mark in section. Below *ab* and above *ef* the migration of the ripple systems was not so rapid as to prevent the deposition of topsets. Between *ab* and *cd* the ripple marks moved forward just fast enough to prevent topset deposition but not fast enough for erosion of the foresets. Between *cd* and *ef* migration of the ripple marks was so rapid that the foresets suffered some erosion of their upper ends.

96I. Comparison of types of cross-bedding. Perusal of the foregoing descriptions of cross-bedding indicates that most of the varieties may be grouped under three classes, according to the arrangement of the cross-laminated sets, or units, as follows: (1) tabular (Figs. 51, 55, 56); (2) lenticular (Figs. 53, 54, 58); and (3) wedge-shaped (Fig. 61). Figure 57 is a combination of (1) and (3).

Clearly it is not always possible to tell at a glance whether a cross-bedded deposit is of wind or water origin. In most cases its accumulation must have been associated with current action, but sometimes the structure is the work of waves. The foreset type of cross-bedding is the commonest. In deltas it is usually of relatively large dimensions and is associated with topset and bottomset bedding. Torrential stratification is very regular and consists of alternate horizontal and cross-laminated beds. Compound delta structure (foreset and backset) much resembles eolian cross-bedding, but it is more regular, the sand is not windworn, and there are often gravel layers interbedded. The form of the unconsolidated deposit as a whole is that of a delta or a sand plain and not of a dune. In beach structure the laminae are inclined to one another at very low angles and there is not so much irregularity as in dunes and in compound foreset bedding. Ripple-mark is on a smaller scale. Sand reefs are not very permanent. They are ultimately thrown on shore and then become eolian deposits. Beach structure is really true bedding with

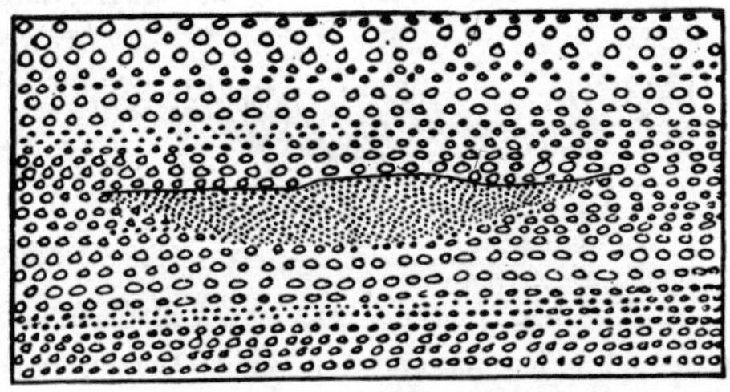

Fig. 63. Section of a lens of cross-bedded sand in gravel. The sand was deposited by a current flowing from left to right. The upper surface of the sand is a surface of local unconformity.

a rather steep primary dip. Bars may be more or less preserved. If they shift they may show some local unconformity. They are truly cross-bedded. Wind cross-beds are usually on a larger scale than water-made ones. The bedding of sand bars may perhaps resemble that of sand dunes. For the discrimination of eolian and aqueous deposits, it is worth while remembering the characteristic distribution of the coarser and finer sand grains on ripple marks (**60, 110**).[32]

97. Lenses. Gravel deposits sometimes contain isolated, roughly lenticular beds of sand, which thin out and terminate laterally (Fig. 63). These *lenses* may be the fillings of original hollows or channels in the gravels or they may be buried sand bars. They may exhibit a uniform cross-bedding of the foreset

[32] See Bibliog., McKee, Edwin D., 1957, for comparison of cross-bedding in beach and dune environments.

variety. There is often local unconformity between the lens and the overlying gravel. (Why?)

The opposite relation may be seen, in which sand contains gravel lenses, but in this case the local unconformity, if present, is between the lens and the underlying sand (Fig. 64). The gravel occupies a channel scoured out and then filled by a current of water. Other like associations may be found, *e.g.*, sand lenses in clay. It should be understood that in order that a channel filling may be of lenticular shape in cross section, the section must be more or less across the trend of the channel.

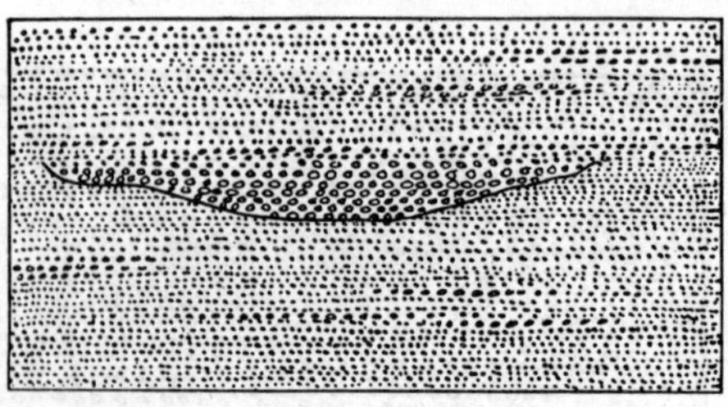

Fig. 64. Section of a lens of gravel in sand. The lower surface of the gravel is a surface of local unconformity.

Very long sand lenses (*e.g.*, a few hundred feet wide, a few score of feet thick, and several thousand feet to several miles long) are called *shoestring sands,* when they are found buried in mud deposits or in shale formations. They may be the fillings of old stream channels, or they may be old buried offshore bars (**305**). In the former case, the cross section of the sand deposit will have its greatest width at the top and will have a base convex downward; in the latter case, the cross section will be widest at the base and will have a relatively flat base and a top convex upward.[33]

98. Uniform lamination. Very fine and even lamination, free from cross-bedding and ripple-mark is often a sign of deposition under quiet conditions, yet under conditions which permitted sorting. This kind of bedding is especially characteristic of some muds and clays which settle gradually to the bottom of quiet water bodies after having been carried thither by surface currents or by wind.

[33] See Bibliog., Bass, N. W., 1934.

99. Transverse textural variation within single beds and laminae; graded bedding. It is not uncommon to find that individual beds which have been transported by wind or by water currents, notably by turbidity currents (Art. **3**),[34] grade from coarser below to finer above, and that there is a rather sharp transition between the fine part of any bed and the coarse lower portion of the next overlying bed. This is because the velocity (or volume) and therefore the carrying strength of a current generally increase much more rapidly than they decrease. The increase may be so sudden as to cause some local erosion (**93**). This kind of bedding is known as *graded bedding.*

Graded bedding is reported to be common in the stratification of graywacke,[35] a rock which may have been deposited from turbidity currents in relatively deep marine waters.

Fig. 65. A section of fine laminated sandstone, illustrating the gradation in texture in individual laminae.

The same kinds of variation, from coarse below to fine above, may be seen in thin uniform laminae of quiet water deposition and likewise in volcanic ash and tuff formations. With reference to laminae deposited in water, whether wind or water current was the transporting agent, after each accession of dust, mud, or silt, the larger grains dropped down before the smaller ones. The next time the water became turbid, large grains settled upon the finest particles of the layer last deposited (Fig. 65). This is characteristic of fine sediments (silts and clays) transported from melting snow and ice deposited in quiet water. The laminae are then called *varves* (*see* Art. **117**), and the material (whether unconsolidated or consolidated) is said to be *varved.* Each varve may represent a time interval of varying length, or each may represent a year, as in the case of the fine sediments brought down from melting snow and ice of glaciers through the seasonal changes of summer thawing and winter freezing.

100. Stratigraphic sequence. Since strata are accumulated by a process of upbuilding of layer on layer, any bed in a series of strata is younger than those below it and older than those

[34] See Bibliog., Kuenen, P. H., and C. I. Migliorini, 1950.

[35] Graywacke is described as a dark gray clastic rock composed of a fine-grained matrix containing angular quartz grains, with some feldspar and mica, and fragments of slate, chert, and other rock materials.

above it, provided always that such a series has not been upturned or overturned in severe crustal deformation (185). This is known as the *principle of superposition,* and the original succession of the beds from older below to younger above is referred to as *stratigraphic succession* or *stratigraphic sequence.* Although in most cases it remains *normal* after consolidation of the sediments, it may become *reversed* by overturning (185).

101. Stratigraphic interval defined. The distance, measured perpendicular to the bedding, between the corresponding parts of any two strata in a sedimentary formation is called the *stratigraphic interval,* or simply the *interval,* between these two beds. In Fig. 66, *ab* and *cd* are the stratigraphic intervals between the

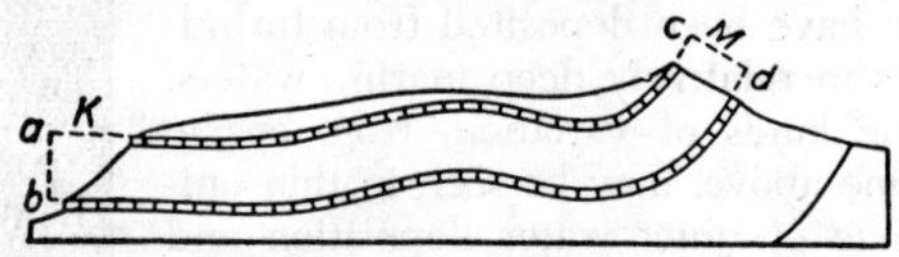

Fig. 66. Cross section to illustrate stratigraphic interval.

top surfaces of the limestone beds at two localities, *K* and *M,* where the strata are horizontal and inclined, respectively.

102. Variations in stratigraphic interval. The interval between any two beds in a sedimentary formation is seldom constant for any great distance. In other words, the strata thicken or thin in various directions. Ordinarily, on a large scale, shallow-water beds (sandstones) are likely to thin, and deep-water beds are likely to thicken, away from the shore line. Furthermore, an extensive formation, such as may have accumulated in a large lake or sea, after transportation from a land area, is likely to become thinner as a whole toward the region of deep water.

103. Pinching or lensing of strata. We have already described, in Art. 97, a minor variety of lens. A somewhat similar condition may occur on a larger scale. If a stratum continues to thin out in a certain direction, as suggested in Art. 102, it may finally "pinch out" or "lens out" altogether. The beds above and below it will then become contiguous (Fig. 67). Such a stratum is called a *tongue.* This condition is not uncommon, especially in the individual sandstone beds of formations consisting chiefly of shale and sandstone strata. It is sometimes the explanation of the absence, in one locality, of a stratum which is present in another locality in the same region. It may be very important in its effect upon the movements and distribution of water, oil, or gas, within the beds. Thus, the up-dip pinching of an oil-bearing sandstone may cause the accumulation of the oil near the termination of the bed, on homoclinal dip (**174**) or on the flank of a fold (Fig. 68). This kind of lensing should not be confused with up-dip termination of strata, due either to

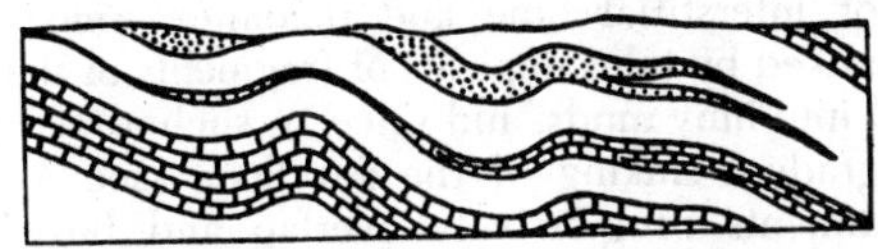

FIG. 67. Cross section illustrating the lensing or pinching of beds.

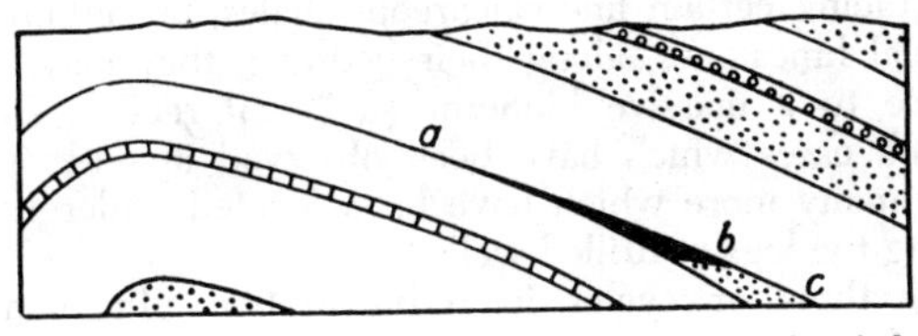

FIG. 68. Cross section of an anticline showing an example of the accumulation of oil and gas (black, *ab*) where a sandstone bed, *abc*, pinches out up the dip (at *a*). The lower portion, *bc*, contains water.

overlap (**87**) or to truncation by unconformity (**84** and Fig. 77, c).

104. Lateral variations in texture, porosity, and permeability. Not only do strata commonly vary in thickness from place to place, but also they are apt to vary in texture, porosity, and permeability, *laterally, along the bedding.* This feature has been described with reference to unconsolidated beds in Art. **75**. A sandstone layer, for instance, may gradually grow more and more fine-grained until, perhaps, it may blend into shale (we say, then, that the sandstone has "shaled up"); or the interstices between its grains may be filled by more and more original fine clayey material; or its pore spaces may contain an increasing amount of cement. Limestones, also, may vary considerably in porosity (**77–80**), and they may grade into shales. Informally, these variations in texture, porosity, and permeability, together with the pinching or lensing of beds (**103**), are frequently called *sand conditions.*

A rather special case of lithologic change that may be observed along the bedding is that of a buried calcareous reef, or bioherm. As explained in Art. **299**, a reef of this kind consists essentially of a structureless mass or core of limy skeletons of colonial organisms with intermingled similar fragmental material, and all with evidences of more or less solution and redeposition of interstitial lime and dolomite. Since these reef ridges are flanked by talus deposits of fragments of the reef, passing outward into limy muds, and since, as such a reef grows, perhaps with gradual sinking of the sea floor (see Art. **90**), the flanking sediments progressively overlap and bury the lower part of the reef core; consequently, when such a series has become part of a thick prism of stratified rocks, we may find that, in tracing certain fine calcareous shales, or certain marine or lagoonal limestones, along their bedding, they may abruptly give place to a massive bioherm (a "fossil reef"). There are many such cases which have been observed in outcrops (Fig. 69), and many more which have been located underground by correlating the logs of drilled wells.[36]

105. Rhythms or cycles in sedimentation. In many sedimentary formations, a more or less orderly repetition of a sequence of beds or laminae occurs, suggesting a cycle or repeated recurrence of certain conditions during deposition, such as might be related to weather, season, climate, sea level, etc. This is not quite the same thing as the transverse textural variations just described (Art. **99**), in which the repeated cycle was included within a single bed or lamina, and the cyclic repetition consisted of a repetition of this bed or lamina. As an example of a larger kind of cyclic deposition, we may observe, repeated again and again, upward through a thick sedimentary prism, a sequence which begins below with coarse sand and passes upward through shaley sand, then sandy shale, to shale, then fire clay (underclay), and finally coal at the top. Or a thick prism of sediments may be composed of several repeated sequences from marine limestone upward through cherty lime-

[36] Some of the ancient bioherms, because of their frequently high porosity, have become reservoirs for the accumulation of oil and gas where they have been inclosed within impermeable strata.

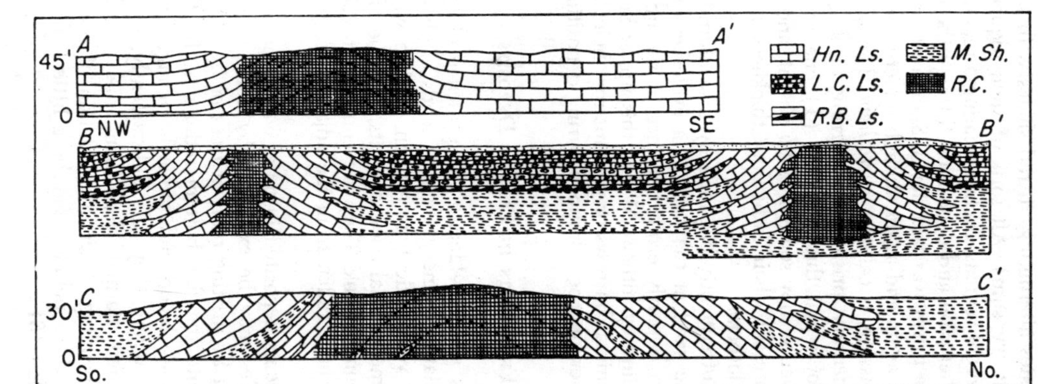

FIG. 69. Cross sections of local reefs (bioherms) in Indiana. *AA'*, reef in Huntington limestone near Georgetown. The core is about 400 ft. across. *BB'*, ideal section of two reefs, each about 2,000 ft. in diameter, with a core approximately 500 ft. across. Glacial drift is shown lying on top of the rock section. *CC'*, reef at Wabash, showing interfingering of shale and limestone on the flanks. This section is about 900 ft. long, the core being 250 ft. across. In the legend, *Hn.Ls.* means Huntington limestone; *L.C.Ls.* means Liston Creek limestone; *R.B.Ls.* means Red Bridge limestone; *M.Sh.* means Mississinewa shale; and *R.C.* means reef core. (*These diagrams have been copied with permission from Publication* 75 *of the Department of Conservation of Indiana. See Bibliog., Cumings, Edgar R., and Robert R. Shrock,* 1928.)

stone, gray and red shales alternating, to red shales with interbedded evaporites (salt, gypsum). All sorts of such sequences have been noted in different regions, each indicating a repetition of certain conditions of erosion and deposition through the time during which the whole prism was laid down. Such a sequence, which may be repeated again and again, though sometimes with part of the sequence missing, is called a *cyclothem*. The several cyclothems in a sedimentary prism, as occurring at a given locality, need not be of equal thickness, for (1) one or two of the beds in the sequence may sometimes be absent, and (2) even if all units are present, their individual thicknesses may vary in the different cyclothems.

Cyclothems are not infrequently bounded by disconformities. For instance, the coarse sand at the base of a cyclothem may have been deposited on a partly eroded surface at the uppermost bed in the preceding cyclothem. Where this upper bed is a shale, it may reveal animal burrows or perhaps root holes into which sand from the overlying bed dropped during deposition.[37]

Particles and Fragments in Clastic Deposits

106. Isolated pebbles and bowlders. The presence of large isolated bowlders in relatively fine gravels or sands of shallow water deposition is not very difficult to explain. Such bowlders are characteristic of some alluvial cone deposits, and they may be found in beach accumulations. They are common in eskers and kames where they have fallen from the adjacent ice walls, now long ago vanished.

In fine-grained sediments deposited in quiet water, the occurrence of isolated pebbles may be explained by flotation (Fig. 36). Pebbles floated out by drifting roots of trees or by ice may drop here and there into the fine bottom sediments. By their weight these pebbles may blend and somewhat compress the soft layers below them where they fall. Subsequently, if they are buried by continued normal deposition, the overlying laminae will show no bending. After consolidation of the material, the layers above these pebbles may be a little bent, but not so much as those below (81).

[37] For a more comprehensive discussion of cyclothems, see Bibliog., Krumbein, W. C., and L. L. Sloss, 1958.

The presence of scattered pebbles in muds or mudstones has been explained as a result of deposition by turbidity currents on sloping floors of lakes or seas (Arts. **4** and **63**).

107. Intraformational fragments. Under certain circumstances, when an unlithified surface deposit is exposed to erosion, it is sufficiently hard and compact to break into slivers or blocks instead of disintegrating into the grains of which it is composed. There are two main causes for such superficial hardening—sun-baking and freezing of interstitial water.

1. When muds, clays, or limy materials are dried by exposure to the atmosphere, sun cracks develop (**65, 94**). Under these circumstances polygonal fragments between the fissures may peel and become loosened from the underlying beds, and if deposition begins again they may be incorporated in the sediments immediately above the original sun-cracked surface. These fragments are said to be *intraformational*, and the strata containing them are *intraformational breccias or conglomerates.*[38] Usually they are angular and they may look as if they had been torn, but they are sometimes rounded by rolling. They are commonly seen in association with contemporaneous erosion (Fig. 45).

Sometimes in semiarid regions the dry, curled "clay shavings" are blown away and buried in sand. Then, in the following wet season, moisture, percolating through the sand, may soften the buried shavings and cause them to flatten out parallel to the bedding. In this form they are called *clay galls.* They are regarded as proof of the subaerial origin of the sand or sandstone in which they are found.

2. In cool climates water-soaked muds, sands, and gravels may become cemented by the freezing of their interstitial moisture and may then be disrupted by glacial erosion. If the broken blocks are deposited in till, they are preserved; but if they are handled by water they quickly fall to pieces. These blocks, also, are intraformational provided their erosion was of such a nature that it may properly be designated contemporaneous (**93**). They are angular, with shapes indicative of fracture (Fig. 70). In till deposits and occasionally in aqueoglacial wash, they are striking features, for when seen they are unconsolidated like the matrix that surrounds them. Similar ice-formed blocks have been observed in the lithified state (shale, slate, sandstone, etc.) in tillite (Appendix 4).

[38] Bibliog., Walcott, C. D., and J. E. Hyde.

Any intraformational fragments may be warped or bent either by the weight of the superincumbent beds or, as in the second example, by the force of the eroding ice.

108. Isolated masses of unconsolidated material in surface deposits. The ice-made intraformational blocks just described

Fig. 70. Section of till containing angular masses of unconsolidated sand and clay.

(107) are isolated masses of unconsolidated material as long as the matrix in which they lie remains unconsolidated. Short lenses of sand or gravel in till, contorted or not, are referred to as "nests" (Fig. 71). They are really *in situ*, having been deposited by water in association with the ice that formed the till. While they may closely resemble the intraformational blocks, they seldom have outlines which are suggestive of disruption.

Fig. 71. Section of till containing a deformed lens of gravel.

Till and wash deposits, and indeed any surface deposits of sufficient age, may contain entirely disintegrated pebbles and bowlders of such rocks as granite, schist, and gneiss. Their sharp outline, their rounded or subangular form, and sometimes the indications of surface markings of erosive origin, prove that these bowlders were fresh and hard when deposited and that they have disintegrated since they were buried. Their composition and usually their shape are sufficient to distinguish them from the incorporated blocks of sand, clay, or gravel.

109. Arrangement of pebbles. In bedded deposits pebbles which are not essentially spherical assume a definite position which varies according to several factors. On beaches composed of a great quantity of thin platy pebbles and beaten by a heavy surf, the pebbles often stand nearly vertically, wedged closely together, thus presenting the least resistance possible to the force of the waves (Fig. 72, A). When such pebbles are relatively few, they lie flat on the beach. Pebbles of greater thickness, but still thinner than wide or long, usually lie more or less flat on the beach (Fig. 72, B). In river beds where the pebbles lie closely packed, and are comparatively flat, they imbricate or overlap downstream, dipping upstream at a moderate angle, and thus offering least resistance to the current (Fig. 72, C). If the pebbles are few they lie flat on the bed of the stream. In alluvial cones, aqueoglacial deposits, and wind deposits, the pebbles and bowlders are ordinarily so few that they lie flat on the surface. Summarizing, in gravel accumulations where the pebbles are comparatively thin and are abundant they lie so as to present the least resistance to the force of waves or current; where they are associated with a large amount of sand or other fine débris they lie flat. A conglomerate having its pebbles arranged transverse to the main bedding (as A and C in Fig. 72) is called an "edgewise conglomerate." In unstratified deposits, the fragments are irregularly disposed. We may speak of a definite tendency toward parallel arrangement of pebbles or sand grains (**110**) or fossils (**111**) in a sedimentary rock as *preferred orientation* (see also Art. **131**).[39]

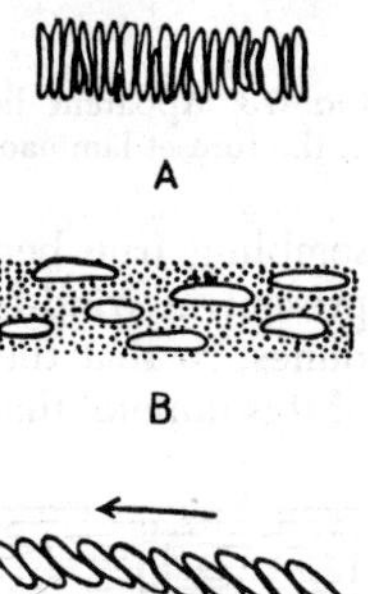

FIG. 72. Diagram to illustrate the arrangement of pebbles. The arrow in C points with the current.

110. Arrangement of sand grains. The position of sand grains which are not equidimensional is of some geologic importance. Most of the common minerals occurring in sand, namely, quartz, garnet, magnetite, etc., are such as wear with nearly equal dimensions; but mica (muscovite and, less commonly, biotite) splits along its perfect cleavage into very thin flakes. In sediments which accumulate in very quiet water, mica plates settle flat with the bedding. They are relatively light and may therefore be separated by sorting so that some laminae may have more

[39] See Bibliog., Knopf, Eleanora B., and Earl Ingerson, 1938, p. 202.

mica and some less. J. B. Woodworth[40] has called attention to the fact that the flakes may settle on the front (or lee) slopes of ripple marks, and that, as a sand deposit is built up, the position of the mica in the laminae may give rise to a structure re-

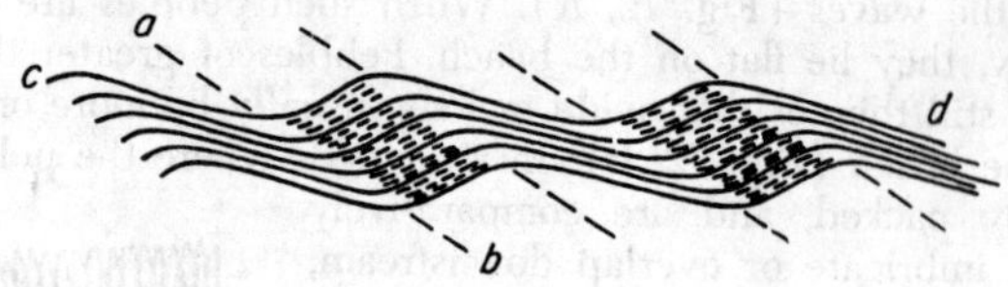

FIG. 73. Apparent bedding, *ab*, caused by the abundance of mica flakes in the foreset laminae of the ripple marks. *cd* is the true bedding.

sembling true bedding (Fig. 73). In the same manner mica, if present in wind-blown sand, accumulates on the front slopes of dunes, so that the forest beds contain a much larger proportion of this mineral than do the topset beds.

On this subject Dapples and Rominger[41] write: "A preferred elongation parallel to the current direction exists in fluvial and eolian environments; long dimension orientation in gravity sands is apparently random." However, in fluvial, eolian, and gravity environments the larger ends of the grains tend to lie toward the source (upcurrent).

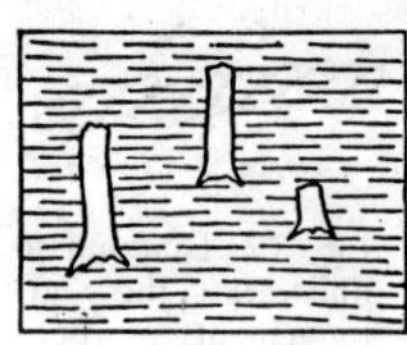

FIG. 74. Section through strata containing the trunks of ancient trees. The roots are embedded in the original soils. This fact and the position of the trunks in the bedding show that they were still standing when buried.

111. Position of fossils. The position of a fossil in a stratum depends upon the original mode of existence of the organism and on the method by which it was interred. Plant remains are sometimes exhumed in the attitude in which the plants lived. Ancient trees of the coal period have been found, their roots still buried in the lithified soil and their trunks projecting up through successive layers of the sediments which buried them (Fig. 74). Coal beds sometimes consist of vegetable remains *in situ*. Certain kinds of animal

[40] Bibliog., Woodworth, J. B., 1901.

[41] Dapples, E. C., and J. F. Rominger, 1945, p. 261. Also, Bibliog., Curray, Jos. R., 1956.

fossils (corals, etc.), also, may occur attached to their ancient rock supports. In such cases it is easy to see that the stratum containing the fossil must be younger than the stratum which served as the foothold for the organism while it lived.

Free-living, unattached organisms fall flat, and their remains are therefore found spread out parallel with the bedding. With possible exceptions, this is true for broad leaves, for thin, flat shells and tests, for skeletons of fishes, etc.

The valves of clam shells and other similiar concavo-convex shells, while sinking through water, settle with the concave side up and the convex side down (Fig. 75, *a*). If there is any motion

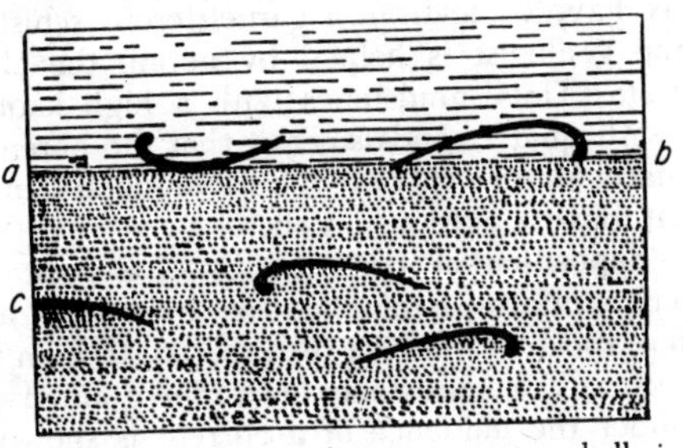

Fig. 75. Section showing position of concavo-convex shells in accumulating sand

in the water, they are soon overturned so that their convex surfaces are now uppermost (Fig. 75, *b*). In this attitude they offer least resistance to currents, and in this attitude they are apt to be buried (Fig. 75, *c*). It is quite common to find shell beds, or clastics containing such shells, with a majority of the valves lying convex side uppermost.

Field Interpretation of Sedimentary Materials

112. Nature of the parent rock. To determine the original character of the rock from which a sedimentary deposit was derived is a task which varies widely in its possibilities. If the sediment is easily recognized as residual and rests upon its parent rock, there is no difficulty. Even if there are no outcrops of the earlier formation, perhaps because it is quite buried or because it has been entirely eroded away, the problem is still easy provided the sediment is a product of disintegration which suffered little transportation, for its constituent particles are then merely the disarranged grains of the older rock. And in the case of a conglomerate or other psephite, the pebbles tell the story.

From sedimentary materials which were laid down after they underwent long transportation and sorting, or considerable decomposition, the facts are harder to ascertain. There is more chance for mistake. For instance, a highly micaceous sandstone may have been formed from a micaceous igneous rock or from a schist or a gneiss. A sandstone containing a large proportion of garnet may have come from a garnetiferous schist or gneiss. Sometimes the geologist is helped by noting the character of associated strata. Thus, mudstones with a high kaolin content interbedded with quartz sands suggest that the parent rock was granite or quartz diorite. (Why?) Further details must be left for the student to work out for himself.

113. Quiet deposition or current. Quiet deposition is indicated by very uniform lamination or by entire absence of bedding in fine rocks of uniform texture (98, 99). In both cases the rock is usually a mudstone or a fine-grained sandstone. Deposition under the influence of a current is shown by cross-bedding, local unconformity, current ripple marks, wave marks, rill marks, lenses, etc. Wind-laid sandstones and river-laid clastics nearly always bear evidence of current action. Lake and marine deposits may belong to either class.

114. Depth of water for lake and marine sediments. Since current action in lakes and seas grows less efficient away from shore, the coarser materials accumulate for the most part in shallow water. In a way, then, texture is indicative of depth of water. Likewise, the evidences for current action, just cited, appertain principally to shallow-water deposits. It should be remembered, however, that these structures are sometimes made far from land by deep-water currents; also, that far from land on submerged rises in the sea floor there may be sediments (sands) which are coarser than on the surrounding slopes and depressions (muds, silts). Density currents (Art. 3) may carry sands, sometimes relatively coarse sands, far out from shore.

Marine limestone has been said to form only in deep water, but we know now that the most important essentials for its origin are not depth so much as freedom from turbidity. While probably many limestones have been built up at depths greater than the average depth for the deposition of muds, still, some limestones may perfectly well have accumulated in relatively shallow water, provided the land waste was removed by long-shore currents.

115. Direction of current. Supposing that a rock does contain current-formed structures, we may desire to know in which direction the wind or water was moving, as the case may be. This is shown by cross-bedding, current ripple-mark, wave marks, rill marks, and to some extent by the attitude of included fossils. Seaweeds and other aquatic plants, which are attached at the base, may be trailed out with the current. If they are buried and fossilized in this position, they indicate the direction in which the water flowed. Direction of current may be shown by position of the valves of fossil shells where a majority settled on the bottom and were buried with the beak, or hinge, side of the shell pointing against the current. Also, direction of current may be indicated by the direction of imbrication of flat pebbles in a conglomerate (**109**).

116. Strength of current. Strong currents can handle heavier materials than weak currents. Also density currents (Art. **3**) can transport heavier materials than clear-water currents of the same speed. Provided a rock shows evidence of current deposition, its texture is roughly a measure of the efficiency of the agent. In this connection, one should not compare eolian and aqueous clastics. It is unsafe to deduce too definite rules referring to relations between size of grain and strength of current.

117. Climate. One of the most interesting kinds of information that the geologist is obliged to seek is the nature of the climate at the time of deposition of a given rock formation. Sometimes it is the climate in the area of deposition and sometimes it is the climate in the region where the sediments originated, but whence they were transported before their accumulation. Absence of fossils in marine or lake mudstones may mean that the water was unfavorable to life because of an excessive turbidity, or because of salinity, or because of too low a temperature. Coal is of two kinds, one being formed *in situ*, the fossil roots still passing down into the old soil from which the vegetation absorbed part of its nourishment (**111**), and the other formed from vegetable débris which was washed together and buried. Coal of the first type accumulated in marshes. It indicates, therefore, a climate which was moist and either warm or cool.

Mudstones containing a large percentage of kaolinite show that the land area whence they came was undergoing decomposition in a relatively warm, humid climate. Quartz sands and quartz-pebble conglomerates may be looked for as the coarser clastics associated with such mudstones. On the other hand, mudstones which have a high percentage of soluble mineral components, are evidence against thorough decomposition and therefore against a warm, moist climate. They are generally derived by severe glacial abrasion or by wind scour, so that in the former case they indicate a cool climate and in the latter case an arid or semiarid climate.[42]

The varves in clays and silts of aqueoglacial origin (99) vary in thickness according as the summer (period of melting) was relatively long or short. A succession of thin varves would thus point to a succession of cool years, and a succession of thick varves would indicate a succession of warmer years, with short, milder winters and long summers.

A semiarid climate is suggested in many cases by sun cracks, footprints, clay galls, etc., features which are best preserved where there are long spells of drought interrupted occasionally by showers, or once a year by a rainy season. Desert conditions are indicated by thick eolian sandstones together with playa-lake and sheetflood deposits and intercalated beds of salt, gypsum, nitrates, etc. Crystals of salt or their casts (Fig. 76) are considered evidence for aridity during sedimentation. Red color used to be regarded as proof of a desert climate, but it is also known to be characteristic of some widespread decomposition products in warm and temperate humid climates (32, 85). Rounded quartz sands of which the grains are coated with red iron oxide may be regarded as of desert origin. Arkose and highly feldspathic sandstone may signify a relatively dry climate, either warm or cold. Glacial deposits betoken a cool or cold climate with an excess of precipitation in the form of snow.

118. Physiographic conditions at time of deposition. Sedimentary rocks may give us information on the physiography of the ancient regions where they originated. It has been pointed out in the preceding article how they indicate desert conditions.

[42] For further discussion of the clay minerals, see Bibliog., Krumbein, W. C., and L. L. Sloss, 1958, pp. 150–153.

One may even go so far as to suggest that the arid region may have been flanked by a mountain range on the side from which the prevailing winds blew, and that this range caught the bulk of the rainfall on its windward slope. By the regional study of lithologic facies changes, much can be learned of the former relations of lands and seas (88).

Peat and coal, when *in situ*, mean that the area of deposition was flat and poorly drained. It was generally near sea level and

FIG. 76. Casts of salt crystals in argillite. (About ⅓ natural size.). (*After R. A. Daly.*)

was subject to occasional marine inundation. Hence the not uncommon interbedding of coal and marine clastics.

Products of long and thorough decomposition, such as decomposition clays, not only point to moist, temperate, or warm climate, but also to the fact that the lands where they originated were probably of low relief. They are suggestive of peneplanation. Likewise, the chert in some limestones may have originated from silica gels brought into a shallow sea from a low-lying land area. On the other hand, thick fluviatile gravels and sands generally belong to piedmont alluvial cone deposits and, therefore, indicate the proximity of mountainous country.

119. Characters of marine, littoral, and continental deposits. Sediments, consolidated or unconsolidated, are divided into three great classes, known as marine, littoral, and continental deposits. The littoral (*littus*, the seashore) zone lies between the average of the monthly highest flood tides and lowest ebb tides. All deposits within this zone are *littoral.* Deposits beyond the seaward margin of the littoral belt are *marine,* and those beyond its landward margin are *continental,* no matter whether the land mass is a true continent or only an island. The student may find it of advantage to have summarized the chief characters of these deposits, in order that their recognition may be facilitated. For the most part the discriminative features must be sought, not in small individual outcrops, but in large structural sections obtained through the correlation of many outcrops (see Appendix 6).

Marine deposits lack such structures as mud cracks, rain prints, etc., because they are never exposed to the atmosphere, but they may have ripple marks, and, occasionally, local unconformity. Wave-made ripple marks originate usually at depths of less than 100 fathoms. Marine deposits may attain enormous thickness, but their lithologic variation is less than in continental formations. Their bedding is comparatively uniform. Sand, silt, mud, and ooze, and their consolidated derivatives are the common members of the class. Clastic mica is a rare constituent. Exceptionally, pebbles and bowlders may be floated by ice and dropped into the finer sediments. Associated conglomerates are probably littoral.

Littoral deposits are not abundant because, being accumulated in a narrow belt, they are never very thick, and because they are especially liable to destruction. They have little variation. They consist chiefly of sand or sandstone with some conglomerate or mudstone associated. Conglomerate beds are seldom more than 100 ft. thick and are generally much less. Being situated between the marine and continental areas, littoral sediments share some of the characters of each of the other two classes. In common with continental deposits, they may contain rill marks, ripple marks, sun cracks, rain prints, imprints and fossils of land organisms, and clastic mica; and, in common with marine deposits, they may have brackish and salt water fossils. Sun cracks, rain prints, footprints, and other phenomena, preserved in mud by virtue of its property of hardening when sun-dried, are less apt to be found in littoral than in continental sediments, because they are destroyed by the advancing tide before they are hard enough for preservation. Wave marks, perhaps, are more characteristic of littoral sands than any other feature, yet even these are sometimes made on lake shores.

Continental deposits constitute the most varied group on account of the many diverse methods in which accumulation may be brought about. Changes from beds laid by one agent to beds laid by another agent are not uncommon. Eolian and glacial sediments are particularly characteristic, although they are not entirely limited to the continental class. The presence of numerous land or fresh-water fossils is a valuable criterion, but their absence is of negative value. Clastic mica in a fragmental rock is usually indicative of continental sedimentation. As regards the different rock types, conglomerates may attain great thickness, sometimes many hundred feet. Finer clastics may bear evidence of ripple-mark, cross-bedding, and local unconformity. Pelites may be variegated in color. They may contain sun cracks, rain prints, footprints of land animals, etc. Indeed sun cracks, formed as they are chiefly on the flats of river flood plains, low lake shores, and playas, are among the most reliable criteria for continental deposition. Coal beds *in situ* are of even greater significance. Limestones are apt to be continental if, like muds, they have been sun-cracked. Such limestones are rare and of restricted distribution. They may contain brackish-water fossils, but not marine ones.

Marine and lake sediments are typically well stratified, the beds being of pretty uniform texture and thickness. Fluviatile and glaciofluviatile deposits are stratified, but poorly so; their strata vary greatly in thickness; there is much textural variation; and such features as cross-bedding and local unconformity are characteristic. Eolian dust shows little or no bedding, whereas wind-blown sand is remarkable for its varied cross-lamination and excellent sorting. Deposits laid by ice, or resulting from volcanic outbursts, creepage, landslide, or weathering *in situ,* are generally heterogeneous and unstratified.

The principal and most permanent types of continental deposition are the accumulations of large deltas, piedmont slopes, interior basins in pluvial climates, and deserts. The significant characters of these classes of deposit are as follows:

1. *Large deltas.* Fluviatile muds or pelites, with mud cracks, etc. (see Appendix 6); associated soil beds and swamp deposits;

seaward gradation of the continental sediments into littoral and marine materials; intercalated wedges of marine strata, laid when the sea flooded the low delta flats, sometimes penetrating considerable distances landward between the continental beds.

2. *Piedmont slope deposits.* Fluviatile sands and gravels with characters such as are listed in Appendix 6.

3. *Interior basins in pluvial climates.* The deposits may be largely continental or marine according to (*a*) the depth of the basin, (*b*) the vigor of peripheral stream erosion, (*c*) the breadth and height of surrounding lands, (*d*) the proximity of the sea, and (*e*) the rate of subsidence of the basin floor, assuming subsidence to be in progress; if continental, the sediments may be fluviatile or lacustrine.

4. *Deserts.* Lag gravels, eolian sands, disintegration sands and gravels, and interbedded playa muds with associated saline precipitates are the common deposits; the sediments are partly eolian, partly fluviatile, and partly lacustrine; fossils are rare.[43]

120. Age relations of sedimentary materials. The age of a sedimentary deposit or rock, as indeed of any other geologic form or structure, may be regarded from three points of view: (1) If the deposit (or rock) is correlated with its immediate surroundings, it will be found to be younger than some geologic features and older than others. Stated in these terms of comparison, its age is called *relative*. The relative age of any bed within a given formation is obtained by determining the stratigraphic sequence (**110**). (2) Geologists have agreed upon a *time scale*, that is, a definite succession of formations for the whole world, and the divisions in this scale have received names (Appendix 1). In this time scale the major divisions of geologic time are called eras, periods, and epochs, and the corresponding bodies of rock are called sequences,[44] systems, and series. The former are referred to as *time units* and the latter as *time-rock units*. Throughout the whole succession of stratigraphic formations that constitute much of the upper part of the lithosphere, the assemblages of fossils reveal in general an increasing variety, an increasing complexity, and a higher state of organic development, progressively upward, from the older to the younger formations. This is known as the *principle of faunal succession*.

[43] For further information on this subject refer to Bibliog., Barrell, J., 1906; and *Idem.*, 1925.

[44] Seldom used in this sense.

Each division of the scale is characterized by a certain suite of fossils, which, though showing a good deal of variation in its species and even in its genera, is still sufficiently distinctive to be of use in settling the place of a fossiliferous deposit in the succession. The age of a body of sediments when referred to this time scale is its *geologic age*. (See last paragraph in Art. **87**.) If fossils are absent or scarce in the deposit, its geologic age can be obtained only by correlating it with other bodies of which the geologic age is already known. The geologic ages of all structures and of all rocks other than sediments must be found in this indirect way. (3) The *actual age* of a deposit, expressed in years or centuries, can seldom be ascertained. Even attempts to compute approximate values are likely to be far off.

Of these three methods of stating the age of sediments, the first and second are commonly followed. The second is the more definite of the two and is the more difficult to establish because fossil species must be identified. The third method, being rarely essayed, will receive no further comment in this book, except to state here that considerable study has been devoted to varves (**117**) as an index of the duration of interglacial and postglacial ages; and of other intervals of geologic time during which varved clays are deposited. Also extensive investigations of radioactive substances have been in progress with the purpose of measuring the length of geologic time.

Within a given sedimentary series, we may often say that beds of essentially the same age are at the same *horizon*. "Horizon" is defined as "any given definite position or interval in the stratigraphic column or the scheme of stratigraphic classification."[45]

121. Relative age of clastic dikes and pipes. Clastic dikes and pipes are clearly younger than their inclosing rock (country rock). If they have originated by filling from above, they are probably associated with some overlying stratum which bears unconformable relations with the country rock, wherefore they may be very much younger than this country rock; but if they were injected from below, the difference between their age and the age of the country rock may be relatively slight.

122. Discrimination between separate glacial epochs.[46] In regions of Pleistocene and later glaciation evidences have been

[45] Bibliog., Fay, A. H., 1920.

[46] For a more detailed discussion of this subject, see Bibliog., Salisbury, R. D., 1893. The writer has drawn freely from this source.

found which prove that the ice advanced more than once, that the periods between successive advances were often of considerable length, and that during these interglacial epochs the ice front retreated long distances. Some of the more important criteria for discriminating between the deposits of successive ice advances are briefly outlined below.

1. If beds of terrestrial origin, containing either plant or animal remains, are found between deposits of glacial drift, and if the organic remains are of species known to have existed in a temperate or warm climate, the evidence is strongly in favor of a long period between the laying down of the lower drift sheet and that of the upper. The mere presence of fossils is not always sufficient evidence, because sometimes life, especially plant life, flourishes near or even upon the ice. But this is more particularly true of local mountain glaciers and piedmont glaciers than of the larger ice sheets.

2. If between two sheets of drift there are found local beds of bog iron ore, or marine or lacustrine strata containing the remains of plants or animals that lived in temperate or warm water, a long interglacial period is indicated.

3. A weathered glacial deposit overlain by fresh drift with a sharp boundary between the two is another criterion for two separate glacial epochs. A red or reddish color in the weathered drift points to a warm, moist climate (32). The thickness of the zone of this decay roughly indicates the length of time of exposure to atmospheric influence.[47]

4. When bowlders of certain varieties of rock exhibit a distinctly greater degree of weathering in a given moraine or sheet of drift as compared with the degree of weathering in bowlders of *the same rocks* in an adjacent moraine or in an overlying drift sheet, respectively, the presumption is that the deposits were separated by an interglacial epoch of some duration. In both (3) and (4) care must be taken not to confuse superglacial materials of the older glaciation, which decayed while on the surface of the ice, with that part of the drift which may have weathered after its deposition.

[47] In cases of this kind we may have a "soil profile" or "weathering profile" in which, for example, in till an upper oxidized and leached zone may grade downward into an oxidized, but unleached zone, and this in turn, still lower, into the unaltered glacial material. (See Art. **85**; also Bibliog., Kay, G. F., 1931, pp. 456–458).

5. During the retreat of a glacier, streams from the ice are usually aggrading (why?); but after the ice front has retreated many miles, aggradation may cease and both aqueoglacial and till deposits may suffer erosion. Upon a readvance of the ice, channels cut into the older drift and even into bedrock beneath this drift may be filled up with a new glacial accumulation. Buried valleys of this origin are much larger than the gullies cut by contemporaneous erosion.

6. If, after the disappearance of the ice, a later drift sheet does not entirely cover an earlier one, the topography of the exposed part of the older deposit will show a more advanced stage of dissection than that of the younger. This is as true of the moraines of valley glaciers as it is of the deposits laid by continental ice sheets.

Other criteria, either of less value or more difficult of interpretation, are discussed by Salisbury in the article cited.

With reference to all the criteria mentioned above, the farther north the evidence is found in the case of continental glaciation (in the northern hemisphere), or the higher the altitude at which it is found in the case of mountain glaciation, the more reliable will be the deduction for two distinct glacial epochs. To base judgment on any one of these criteria alone is unsafe. Two or more should be sought in the field before drawing final conclusions. On the other hand, if these lines of evidence are wanting, their absence must not be regarded as absolute proof against two glacial epochs.

123. Conditions of unconformity. The field geologist must first of all be able to recognize a regional unconformity, and then he must be able to interpret its meaning. The criteria most useful in determining a regional unconformity are: (1) discordances of bedding at a line of contact; (2) evidence of a former weathered or eroded condition of one formation at its contact with another; (3) presence of a basal conglomerate or of a basal arkose at the line of contact; (4) faults in one body of rocks truncated by the beds of another formation (Fig. 77, A); (5) dikes or other igneous intrusive bodies in one rock formation truncated by the other (Fig. 77, A); (6) abundance of intrusive bodies (dikes, sills, etc.) of a particular kind in one group of rocks and an entire absence of the same in an adjacent formation; (7) a distinctly greater amount of folding or of metamorphism in one formation than in an adjacent formation; (8) discordances of

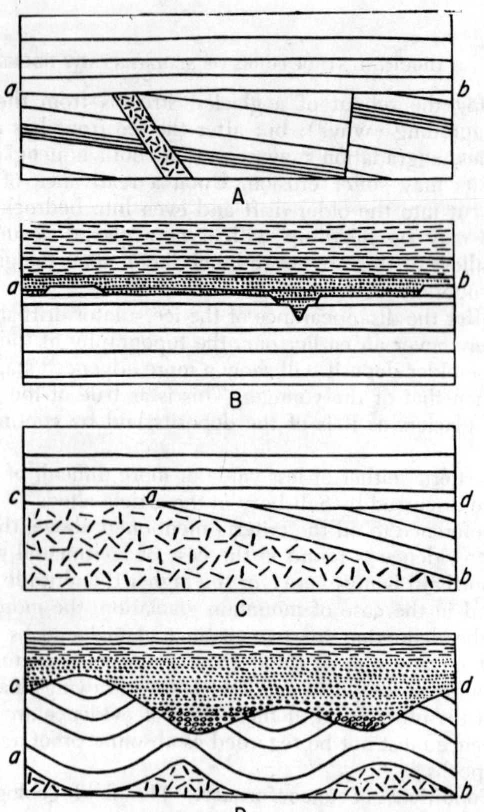

Fig. 77. Relations of unconformity. In A, the straightness of the line of unconformity (*ab*), together with the fact that this line bevels across various kinds of rocks and structures, suggests that it is the section of a buried peneplain. Clearly the dike and the fault are older than the beds above *ab*. In B, *ab* is a line of disconformity. It is the section of a buried land surface that was characterized by mesas and canyons. A basal sandstone is the lower bed in the younger formation. In C, two lines of unconformity are shown, *ab* and *cd*. How do we know that *ab* is older than *cd*? What two geologic events occurred in the interval between the deposition of the two sets of strata? In D, *ab* and *cd* are lines of unconformity. *ab* is older than *cd*. *ab* is sinuous because it has been folded together with the beds immediately overlying it. *cd* is sinuous because the land surface of which it is a section was a valley-and-hill topography. What features in the diagram prove the two foregoing statements? A basal conglomerate lies in the valleys above *cd*.

areal distribution of rocks or of structures as seen after plotting a geologic map of the region.[48]

Unfortunately there are many chances for error in the recognition of these criteria. (1) Discordances of bedding may be due to contemporaneous erosion, to cross-bedding on a large scale, or to faulting (**335**). Contemporaneous erosion might be confused with disconformity, and cross-bedding with angular unconformity. Nevertheless, both of these structures are usually local and they are not accompanied by the other criteria for regional unconformity. (2) The second criterion mentioned above is difficult to observe. (3) Autoclastic rocks (*e.g.*, fault breccias, crush conglomerates, etc.) may be mistaken for basal conglomerates. Van Hise has pointed out the following differences:[49] (*a*) Autoclastic rocks have derived all their material from the adjacent rocks, often both above and below, whereas in basal conglomerates there are apt to be at least a few fragments from foreign sources and all the materials are derived from the lower formation only. (*b*) In autoclastic rocks the fragments are usually less rounded than in basal conglomerates, but this statement is not intended to imply that the breccia fragments may not be somewhat worn—indeed, sometimes notably rounded—by rock movements, nor that the conglomerate pebbles are always well rounded. (*c*) The interstices of the autoclastic are often filled with vein material, while in the basal conglomerates the filling is finer detritus. Finally, (*d*) autoclastic zones may be seen to pass here and there into the unshattered rock, whereas basal conglomerates grade into other finer sediments. Criteria listed under (4) and (8) above should be clear and unmistakable before they are accepted as satisfactory. (6), (7), and (8) might result from extensive faulting instead of unconformity (**335**). In dealing with this problem, do not be contented to base conclusions on one fact. Search for many lines of evidence and, if all point the same way, then the inference is likely to be correct.

As for the interpretation of regional unconformities, the geologist should seek answers to the following questions: (1) What was the agent of the first erosion (**86**) and what was the nature of this erosion? (2) What was the rate of the first erosion? (3)

[48] See Bibliog., Van Hise, C. R., 1896, pp. 724–734, for a discussion of these criteria. Also, Bibliog., Shrock, Robert R., 1948, pp. 46–50.

[49] See Bibliog., Van Hise, C. R., 1896, pp. 680, 681, for a discussion of these criteria.

What was the nature of the old erosion surface? (4) What was the rate of deposition of the basal beds of the younger formation? (5) What was the source of these basal beds? (6) How long a period of time elapsed while the erosion represented by the unconformity was in progress? (See "time value," Art. **124.**) (7) What is the range of strata missing at the unconformity (see "hiatus," Art. **124**), as stated in the terminology of the geologic time scale? (Appendix 1.) (8) What thickness of rocks was removed in the first erosion? (9) What events are represented in the section? These questions can be answered only by studying the nature of the surface of unconformity and the characters and mutual relations of the two formations.

Since surfaces of unconformity are surfaces of past erosion, they should bear just such traces of erosion as would be sought on bedrock outcrops of the present day (see Chap. 2). The trouble is that the evidences are usually concealed beneath the overlying formation, although sometimes, it is true, recent erosion has exposed portions of the old surface. Ordinarily the surface must be studied in cross section, merely as a line. The greater the length of the exposed part of this line, the safer will be inferences based upon its examination; but even if it is not continuously exposed, the separate scattered outcrops may be levelled up and correlated so that a fair idea of its character may be obtained.

As explained in Art. **85**, a surface (or line) of unconformity does not necessarily accompany unconformable relations. A sharp dividing line between two formations which are unconformable with one another may be due: (1) to strong abrasion in the first period of erosion; or (2) to regional decomposition. A blended transition from the older formation to the younger one, with no sharp line of demarcation, points to deep weathering in the first period of erosion. Here the basal sediments are disintegration products of the underlying rock. Thus, the distinctness of the line of unconformity helps somewhat toward an understanding of the kind and rate of erosion.

Provided the line of unconformity is distinct, its form may indicate the nature of the old erosion surface. If the line is straight or gently undulating for a long distance, the surface was probably a destructional plain, or, less likely, a bench (**277**, **282**). Greater irregularity of the line points to a more uneven topography. Several possibilities are depicted in Fig. 77.

For interpreting the past, the basal portion of the upper series is of more value to the geologist than the actual line of unconformity. It should be studied with reference to its composition, texture, and structure, and as regards the shapes and surface features of its constituent fragments, if it is of mechanical origin. Information as to the climate at the time of deposition and as to the agent and rate of this deposition may be obtained in the manner described in Art. **117**. Conglomerate and arkose frequently appear as the lowermost stratum of the upper series. Arkose generally means short and rapid transportation and deposition which have been quickly inaugurated after a period of slow, long-enduring disintegration. A basal conglomerate, always containing abundant pebbles of rocks in the upper part of the lower formation, is significant of encroaching deposition and of effective abrasion during transportation from the source of supply. Sometimes rocks other than conglomerate and arkose are basal. Above an ice-scoured surface, tillite is to be expected; but if a glacial rock basin (**289**) were occupied for a time by a lake, finely stratified shale, originally lake clay, might rest on the grooved and striated surface. Limestone on an old erosion surface means: (1) that the initiation of the limestone-forming conditions was so quiet that no mechanical sediments were made; or (2) that such sediments were carried away to be laid down elsewhere as fast as they were formed. Basal sediments, then, need not be deposited by the same agents that eroded the subjacent surface of unconformity. There is no better aid to the interpretation of former conditions than a broad knowledge of present conditions.

Wrong impressions are sometimes formed regarding the source of the basal materials and the direction of their transport. For instance, if a basal conglomerate composed of granite pebbles were observed overlying, let us say, a quartzite, and half a mile away the granite of the pebbles were found as bedrock below the surface of unconformity, one might assume that the pebbles were derived and carried from the locality of the granite to the site of the conglomerate. It is to be remembered, however, that these features are seen only in a single plane, intersecting the unconformity in a line. The pebbles may have been shaped from this granite, but the granite mass may be of very great extent and the pebbles may have been borne, perhaps many miles, from another part of the same plutonic body, not necessarily exposed in the geologic section. Provided the rock was a transported deposit, there is no necessary relation between the trend of the section and the direction in which the materials were carried. Their true source can only be approximated, and even then only after an extensive investigation.

124. Time value and hiatus. From the standpoint of stratigraphy it is desirable to know what interval of geologic time was consumed in the erosion represented by the unconformity and how many geologic formations are missing at the unconformity. The former is called the *time value* of the unconformity and the latter is the *hiatus*. Hiatus can easily be determined if it is possible to ascertain the geologic age of the old and the young formations at the surface of unconformity (**120**). Time value need not be equivalent to hiatus, for there is no reason for assuming that erosion was continuous throughout the period of time represented by the unconformity. Thus, if the two formations are Upper Cambrian and Triassic (see Appendix 1), the Ordovician, Silurian, Devonian, Mississippian, and Pennsylvanian, but not the Permian, may have been deposited and then eroded before Triassic deposition commenced, or perhaps only the Ordovician was laid down and was worn away during the remaining time from Silurian to Triassic. In the first case the time value is represented by erosion during the interval from the end of the Pennsylvanian to the initiation of the Triassic; whereas, in the second case, the time value is represented by the interval between the end of the Ordovician and the beginning of the Triassic; yet, in both instances, the hiatus is the same. Time value is a difficult factor to determine.[50]

125. Stratigraphy and stratigraphic geology defined. *Stratigraphy* is briefly defined as "the arrangement of strata." *Stratigraphic geology*, or stratigraphy in the larger sense, is a broad science which deals with stratigraphic succession (**100**), faunal succession (**120**), relations of sedimentary deposits to unconformities, and so on—in fact, with a great deal of the subject matter of Chaps. 1–5 of this book. It includes the study of successive changes in the distribution of land and sea as interpreted from the character and fossil contents of sedimentary rocks (**88**).

126. Paleogeography defined. Just as geography refers to the description of presently existing lands and seas and other

[50] For further information on this subject, see Bibliog., Blackwelder, E., 1909; also Krumbein, W. C., and L. L. Sloss, 1958.

surface features of the earth, and the distribution of plant and animal life in relation to these earth features, so *paleogeography*[51] refers to the study and description of similar relationships at or during any past geologic time.

127. Paleogeology defined. Geology is a very comprehensive term. We may think of it as a science that includes the study of rock relationships on the surface of the earth (*field geology, areal geology,* Art. 9), and the study of rock relationships from the surface downward. We may consider that, at the time when a regional unconformity was in process of development, the areal

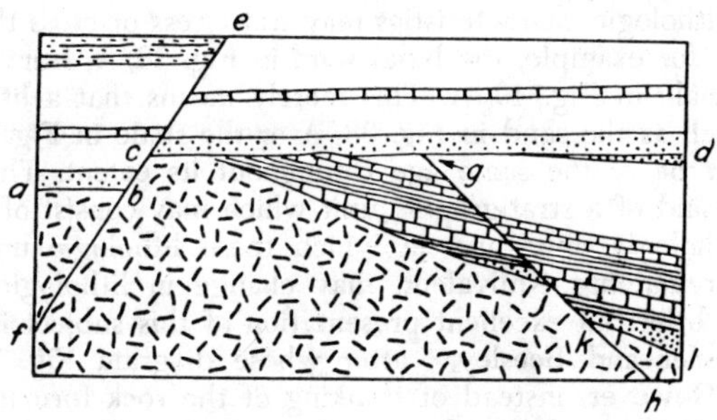

FIG. 78. Vertical cross section illustrating two periods of deposition, two periods of erosion, and two periods of faulting, all of which are geologic events younger than the origin of the igneous basement (below *abcijkl*).

geology *at that time* would have been the rock relationships at the surface of the earth and below that surface, "that surface" *now* being what we recognize as a regional unconformity. The study of these relationships as of the time of such an ancient surface of erosion (unconformity) is called *paleogeology.* Obviously such a study must be made of the rocks immediately beneath the basal formation of the upper series (86), and it must concern these rocks only as they were related before deposition of the younger series (86). Thus, a paleogeologic study of the conditions at and below unconformity *ijkl* in Fig. 78 would not take into account fault *gh* since this fault cuts, and was therefore subsequent to deposition of, the sediments resting on *ijkl.* Similarly, in the same Fig. 78, a paleogeologic study of

[51] This word was apparently first used by Robert Etheridge in 1881. See Bibliog., Schuchert, Charles, 1910, p. 431.

conditions at and below unconformity *abcd* would not take into account fault *ef*, but would include fault *gh* and all other geological conditions shown here below *abcd*. The paleogeology of any geologic time must, by definition, be correlated with a surface of unconformity of that time.

128. Time relations of stratigraphic units. Some of the most difficult problems of stratigraphy concern the time relations of stratigraphic units and of unconformities. There are three of these problems to which we wish again to call attention in closing the present chapter.

In Art. 87 we pointed out how a sedimentary deposit with certain lithologic characteristics may transgress or cross the time lines, as, for example, the basal sand in Fig. 38, A, from *d* to *c*, or the shale in Fig. 40, A. This merely means that a lithologic unit (such as the sand in Fig. 38, A or the shale in Fig. 40, A) need not be of the same age throughout its extent. The same may be said of a stratigraphic unit which may consist of one or more lithologic units and in which these lithologic units, although remaining equivalent, may change in lithologic facies (88). A brief but excellent presentation of this subject is given by Wheeler and Beesley,[52] after whose diagram Fig. 79 was copied. However, instead of thinking of the rock formations as crossing the time lines, these authors think rather of time as crossing the rock formations, and so they call this phenomenon *temporal transgression*.

We have also explained, again in Art. 87, how fossil assemblages, more or less closely related to lithologic facies, may transgress time lines (in space diagrams like Fig. 79, *time surfaces*).

A third concept of great importance relates to the fact that, since sedimentation must always imply concomitant erosion, and vice versa, every unconformity must correspond in some manner, somewhere, with a body of sediments. This means, of course, that a regional unconformity which, let us assume, separates Ordovician from Silurian in one area (A) must be represented by sedimentary deposits somewhere else (B, C, etc.), deposits which obviously cannot be contemporaneous with any of the strata in area (A).

129. Tectonic correlation of sediments. In recent years (late forties and fifties) a great deal of attention has been given to the

[52] Bibliog., Wheeler, Harry E., and E. Maurice Beesley, 1948.

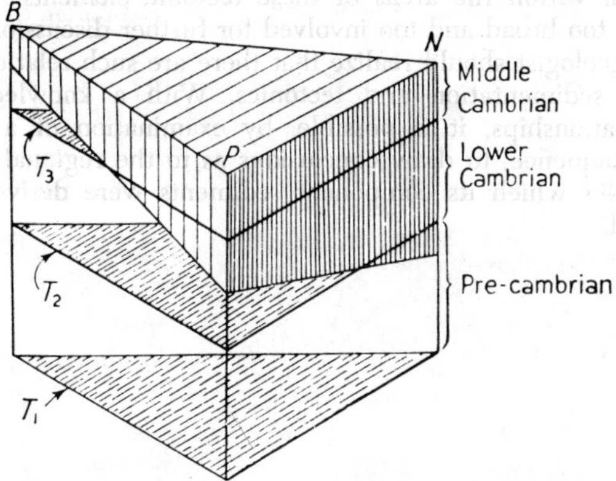

FIG. 79. Trigonal block diagram of a stratigraphic group (Bright Angel group) to illustrate differences in the time values of the group from one locality to another. *B*, *P*, and *N* are roughly between 150 and 200 miles apart. At *B* this group is 391 ft. thick and its base is well up in the Middle Cambrian. At *P* the same group of strata is 1,450 ft. thick and its base is near the middle of the Lower Cambrian. At *N* the group is 2,190 ft. thick and its base is well down in the Pre-Cambrian. Therefore, the geologic age of the basal part of the Bright Angel group is Pre-Cambrian at *N* and becomes younger (middle Lower Cambrian) at *P*, and still younger (Middle Cambrian) at *B*. These time values are indicated diagrammatically by the planes T_2 and T_3 which are, respectively, the boundary between Pre-Cambrian and Lower Cambrian, and the boundary between Lower Cambrian and Middle Cambrian. T_1 is an unidentified time horizon within the Pre-Cambrian drawn merely to add perspective to the diagram. Although, in this figure, we may regard the Bright Angel group as of essentially the same lithology at *B*, *P*, and *N*, it is evident that a group of strata which reveal variable time-space relationships might also vary in its lithology from locality to locality, which would introduce further complications in problems of correlation.

correlation of sedimentary associations with the major tectonic[53] elements of the earth's crust, such as the broad central parts of the continental masses, called *cratons;* the positive and negative areas[54] on the cratons; the shelf areas of the cratons; and the linear geosynclines bordering the cratons. Investigation has shown that certain types of sediment are characteristic of

[53] "Tectonic" refers to the broader structural features of the earth's crust.

[54] *Swells* and *basins*, respectively.

deposition within the areas of these tectonic elements. This is a subject too broad and too involved for further discussion here, but the geologist should realize that there are such relationships between sedimentation and tectonics. With a knowledge of these relationships, it is possible, by examination of a stratigraphic sequence, to draw conclusions as to the regional conditions under which its component sediments were derived and deposited.

Chapter 6

FIELD RELATIONS OF IGNEOUS ROCKS

Terminology and Classification

130. General definitions. While comparatively few people have actually witnessed a volcano in action, yet most of us know that a common phenomenon of volcanic eruption is the outpouring of lava; and we know further that this lava eventually cools and hardens into solid rock. Such lava, in all cases, has come up from within the lithosphere, and there are reasons for thinking that it may have come up a long way, perhaps many miles. Geology teaches us that molten rock does not always rise far enough to reach the earth's surface. Checked in its ascent, it may consolidate between walls of older, cooler rocks. Any rock which thus forms by consolidation from a molten condition is called an *igneous* rock (*ignis,* fire). Those rocks which become solid after ejection upon the earth's surface, either on land or below water, are *extrusive,* and those which harden from molten material injected below the earth's surface are *intrusive.* Molten rock is usually called *magma*[1] when it is well below the earth's surface, and *lava* when it is just below or upon the earth's surface; but "lava" may also be applied to the *consolidated* extrusive rock. "Lava" is not correctly used except with reference to volcanic extrusion.

All igneous rocks, or certainly a large majority of them, are *eruptive* in the sense that each has probably been derived from a magma that had moved or "broken out" from the place where it originated as *magma*, but the word does not necessarily imply "breaking out" at the earth's surface, *i.e.*, it is not synonymous with "extrusive."

Country rock is a purely relative term used for the older rock into which magma has been intruded. It has no significance as to the composition or structure of this older rock. Blocks of coun-

[1] Magma need not be wholly liquid, for it may contain solid phases, such as suspended crystals, but never in quantity or bulk sufficient to prevent mobility of the mass.

try rock entirely surrounded by igneous material in such a way as to indicate that they were immersed in the magma and were then frozen into it, are *inclusions* or *xenoliths*. "Inclusion" must not be confused with "intrusion." The original bounding surfaces of an igneous body, both before and after consolidation, are its *contacts*. Although this term is also applied to unconformities,

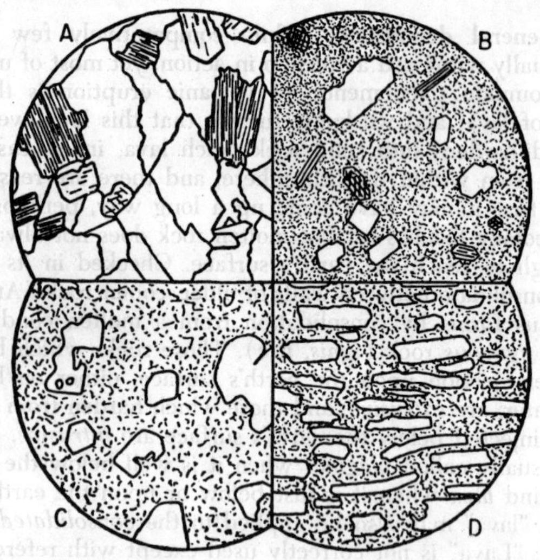

FIG. 80. Textures of igneous rocks. A, even-granular texture; B,C,D, porphyritic texture. In B the phenocrysts are sharply angular with definite crystal boundaries. In C the phenocrysts have rounded corners and embayments of the groundmass, both features being due to resorption. The parallel arrangement of the phenocrysts in D indicates the direction of flow of the original magma.

faults, etc. (17), in the present chapter it will be strictly limited to the walls of igneous bodies. A lava flow has a lower contact that separates it from the bedrock and mantle rock of the old land surface over which it spread, and an upper contact which may subsequently become the basal surface of younger sediments or of flows superposed upon it without intervening denudation. The contacts of an intrusive rock are the surfaces at which it touches its country rock.

Terms which refer to the grain of igneous rocks, *i.e.*, to its size or to its presence or absence, come under the head of *texture.* Some igneous rocks are distinctly *granular* others, so fine that no individual grains are visible, are said to be *dense;* and some are *glassy* or *amorphous.* The granular varieties are *even-granular* (Fig. 80, A) if the grains are of approximately uniform size, and *porphyritic* (Fig. 80, B and D) if one (or possibly two) of the minerals is conspicuously larger than the others so that the rock looks spotted. Such a rock is a *porphyry.*[2] The conspicuous grains in it are *phenocrysts* and the finer matrix in which they are scattered is the *groundmass.* The groundmass may be granular, dense, or glassy. If the variation in size of the grains of an igneous rock is so irregular that no distinction can be drawn between phenocrysts and a groundmass, and many of the grains are exceptionally large, or if all the grains are very large, the texture is *pegmatitic* and the rock is *pegmatite.* In some pegmatites crystals have been found measuring several feet in length.

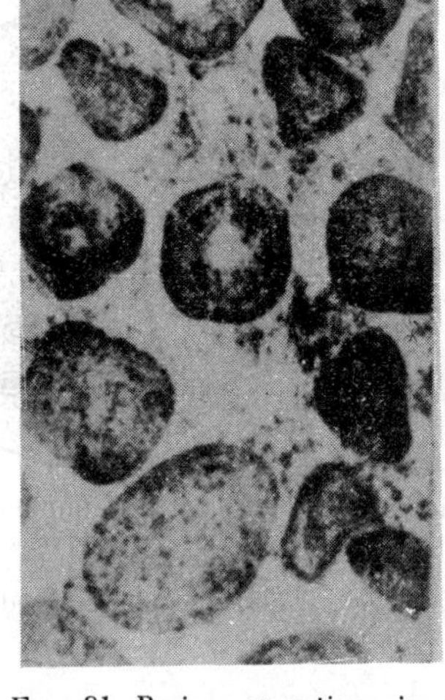

FIG. 81. Basic segregations in a granitic rock.

Features depending upon the arrangement of the constituents within a rock are *lithologic structures.* In the crystallization of molten rock certain minerals sometimes grow in groups, or *segregations,* or *clots* in the magma (Fig. 81). When these segregations are exposed they may appear as roundish spots and patches, commonly darker than the enclosing rock, and often with concentric structure; or they may appear as elongate streaks without any concentric structure. Layers and elongate "bundles"

[2] A spotted appearance due merely to differences of color is not porphyritic texture.

of the minerals composing the body of the rock, but in different proportions, and arranged so as to give it a streaky or platy appearance, are called *schliers* (*schlieren*). Lavas, when fresh, may be full of small pores or *vesicles*. They are then said to be *vesicular*. While the lava was still liquid, these pores were bubbles that contained gas or water vapor. If the vesicles are subsequently filled with minerals that are deposited from solution in water or gas, the fillings are called *amygdales*[3] and the structure is called *amygdaloidal* (Fig. 82). *Pillow structure* is

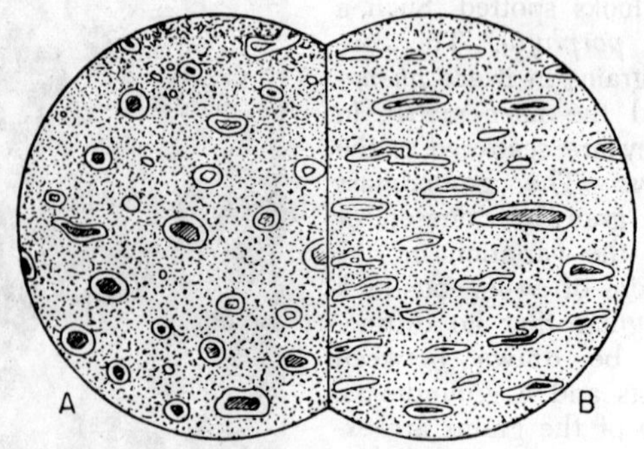

FIG. 82. Amygdaloidal structure in lava. Quartz (white) was deposited on the walls of the original vesicles, and subsequently epidote (lined) filled the remaining open spaces. The vesicles in which the amygdales of B were deposited were flattened and drawn out by the flowing of the lava. (Natural size.)

formed in mobile lavas under special conditions of viscosity, temperature, and pressure. It makes the surface of a lava flow hummocky. In cross section it is seen to consist of roundish bunches or "pillows" of the lava, piled irregularly upon one another (Fig. 83), with the spaces between the pillows filled with volcanic ash, clastic sediments, limestone, vein deposits, or other minerals.[4]

131. Flow structure. All igneous rocks must be regarded as having flowed into place. Those parts of the magma (or lava) that were adjacent to the original contacts cooled sooner and

[3] Amygdule, the diminutive, meaning "little amygdale," is commonly used.

[4] For an excellent paper on this subject, see Bibliog., Lewis, J. V., 1914.

therefore reached stages of relatively high viscosity and, finally, of consolidation, before parts farther inside the igneous body. Where crystallization occurred, some minerals crystallized out of the molten mass before others. These crystals, if elongate or platy in form, had a tendency to turn into parallel position as they were carried along, their long axes being brought into align-

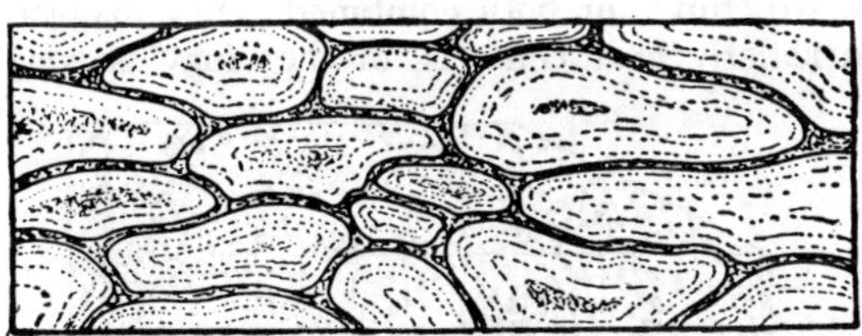

Fig. 83. Pillow structure in lava. The concentric rows of dots represent layers of vesicles. Observe that the lower sides of the "pillows" are shaped against the upper surfaces of the underlying "pillows." (1/25 natural size.)

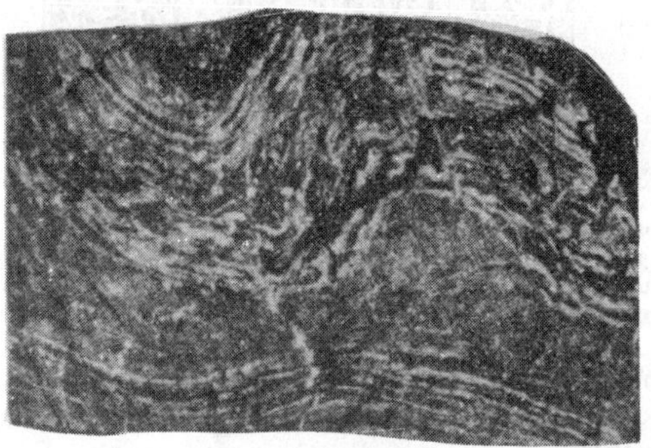

Fig. 84. Flow structure in lava. (1/3 natural size.)

ment with the direction of flow. Similarly, groups of crystals (schliers, segregations), elongate or platy foreign inclusions (xenoliths), and layers differing somewhat in composition or texture (Fig. 84), may have become orientated parallel to the direction of maximum flow. In lavas, gas bubbles may be pulled out or flattened (Fig. 82, B). All these parallel features in igneous rocks, due to the effects of flow, are called *primary flow structures.* They are *primary* because they developed during the time of origin of the inclosing rock.

Two definite kinds of flow structure are recognized. One is *linear*, and the other is *platy*. In the former we speak of *flow lines;* in the latter, of *flow layers*. If such flow structure is definitely linear, it falls under the head of "lineation"—here "primary lineation" (15). Figures 85 and 86 illustrate these features. An igneous rock may possess either one or the other of these lithologic structures, or both combined. They may be very distinct, particularly near contacts, or they may be very obscure;

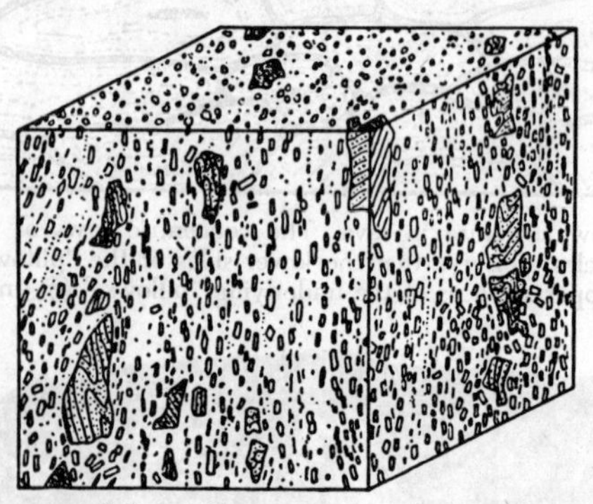

FIG. 85. Linear parallelism. Phenocrysts, mineral streaks, and xenoliths, arranged along roughly parallel lines, here vertical. In horizontal, and nearly horizontal, sections (top of block), the rock appears to be structureless. (*Figures 85 and 86 have been reproduced from Robert Balk's "Structural Behavior of Igneous Rocks," with kind permission of the author and the Geological Society of America.*)

but even in the massive granitic rocks, as has been pointed out by Balk,[5] careful search may reveal a faint tendency toward flow structure.

Where, during the origin of a rock, there have been forces that induced the constituent grains or crystals to assume a more or less parallel position, we say that these grains or crystals have *preferred orientation*. In the case of an igneous rock, the forces causing preferred orientation were related to flowage, and resistance to flowage, of the magma (or lava). It is important to note that preferred orientation may be exhibited not only by the shape of elongate or flattish grains (dimensional orientation)

[5] Bibliog., Balk, Robert, 1937. This is a full presentation of the subject of flow structures and fracture structures in igneous rocks.

but also by the arrangement of crystal axes (crystallographic orientation), as observed under the petrographic microscope.[6]

132. Pyroclastic rocks. Another group of rocks should be mentioned here, because, although they are like normal clastic

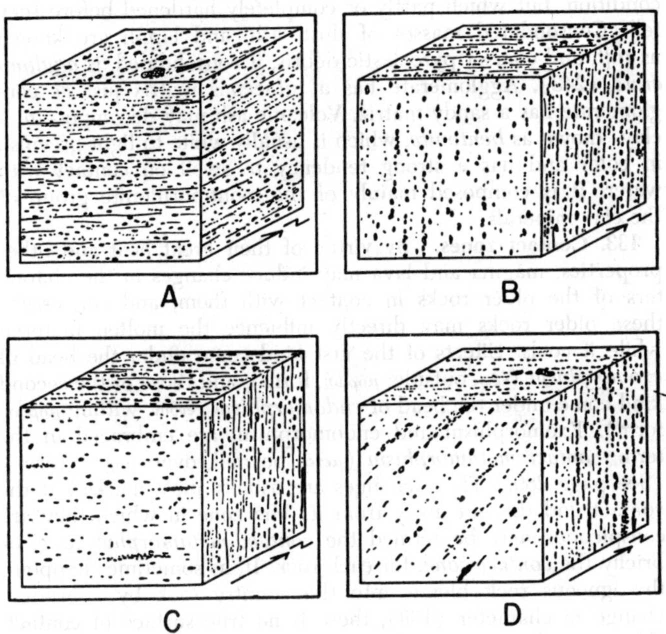

FIG. 86. Platy parallelism. Here, in contrast to Fig. 85, the phenocrysts, mineral streaks, and xenoliths are arranged in parallel layers, but parallel flow lines are also present in the layers. In A, the flow layers are horizontal, and the flow lines trend NE.-SW. In B, both the flow layers and the flow lines are vertical. In C, the flow lines are horizontal, and the flow layers are vertical. In D, the flow layers are vertical, but the flow lines are inclined at an angle of 45°. (*See caption for Fig. 85 for source.*)

rocks in their manner of consolidation (by pressure, cementation, etc.), they are igneous in their ultimate origin. These are the so-called *pyroclastics* ("fire-broken"). When unconsolidated, they consist of volcanic dust, volcanic ash, lapilli, bombs, and

[6] See Bibliog., Knopf, E. B., and E. Ingerson, 1938.

broken pieces, large and small, of older rocks that were shattered by the force of eruption. These materials are also called *ejectamenta.* Dust, ash, lapilli, and bombs are generally particles or lumps of lava which were thrown up into the air in a molten condition, but which partly or completely hardened before they fell. Consolidated masses of dust, ash, and lapilli are known as *tuff,* and coarser pyroclastic débris, if consolidated, is *agglomerate* (**243**). Agglomerate has a tufaceous matrix just as conglomerate has a sandy matrix. Volcanic ash may decompose to a clay, known as *bentonite,* which is usually white to light greenish in color and has a strong tendency to swell on contact with water. It is composed mainly of the montmorillonite group of the clay minerals.

133. Contact zones. By virtue of their great heat and other properties, magma and lava may induce changes in the characters of the older rocks in contact with them, and conversely, these older rocks may directly influence the molten material while it cools. Effects of the first kind come under the head of *exomorphism* (ἔξω, outside; μορφή, form), and those of the second kind come under the head of *endomorphism* (ἔνδον, within; μορφή, form). Exomorphism and endomorphism are embraced in the term, *contact metamorphism* (μετά, beyond, over; μορφ , form). (See page 289.) These changes are usually most marked at the contact and die out away from it. The zone in which they are conspicuous may be termed the *contact metamorphic zone,* or briefly the *contact zone,* for each rock. If, as sometimes happens, the igneous rock blends into the country rock by a gradual change in character (**139**), there is no true surface of contact; there is, rather, a *mutual contact zone.* Except for purposes of discrimination, this may still be called a contact (**140–153**).

134. Classification of eruptive bodies. Geologists speak of the *mode of occurrence* of an igneous rock, meaning by that the general form and size of the eruptive body and its relations to adjacent rocks. Extensive investigations the world over have shown that intrusive masses, all of which are included under the name *plutons,* are of two main varieties. Many were erupted *between* rock walls so that, at the time of their emplacement, they had older rock above and below them, and those which were vertical had side walls that corresponded to such upper and lower contacts; that is, the chambers occupied by these bodies seem to have had relatively small openings by which the magma gained admission. On the other hand, there are certain intrusive forms (batholiths, stocks, bosses) which, as far as observations demonstrate, enlarge downward and have no bottom contacts. No one has ever discovered a base for such bodies; only their upper or roof contacts and their side walls have been found. Accordingly, Daly[7] has proposed a division of intrusive forms into *injected*, those of the first type, and *subjacent*, those which enlarge downward and have no demonstrable basal contact. Plutons which were intruded into sedimentary country rocks are *concordant* if the magma was injected along the bedding planes, and *discordant* (or *transgressive*) if the magma was intruded across the bedding planes.

Concordant plutons include sills, laccoliths, lopoliths, and phacoliths. A *sill* is a layer of igneous material which has been in-

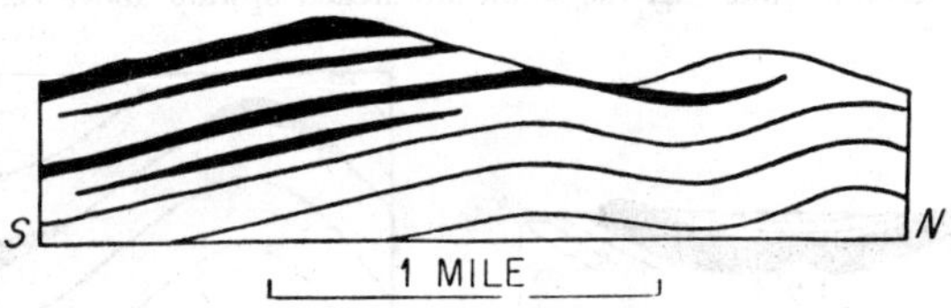

Fig. 87. Sills of porphyry (black) in the Carboniferous formation of the Tenmile District, Colo. (*Tenmile District Special Folio, No.* 48, *U.S. Geol. Survey*, 1898.)

jected between and along the beds of a sedimentary series (Figs. 87, 91, 92). It is relatively thin as compared with its lateral extent. Theoretically it tapers out at the edges, but this feature is seldom visible in a given sill. An *interformational sheet* is identical with a sill except that it has been intruded along a surface of unconformity. It is always essentially parallel to the younger, overlying formation. A *laccolith* is like a sill except that the ratio between its thickness and its width is much greater than in the sill. Its roof is distinctly arched (Fig. 88). When a laccolith has been intruded along an unconformity, it is said to be *interformational* (Fig. 88).

A *lopolith* is a concordant pluton which characteristically has a depressed, basin-like upper contact above which strata in the country rock are similarly depressed (see Fig. 89). Lopoliths,

[7] Bibliog., Daly, R. A., 1914, Chap. V.

like laccoliths, may be *interformational.* A lopolith may closely resemble a sill intruded between strata in a synclinal basin, but the ratio of thickness to lateral extent is commonly greater in the lopolith. The suggested distinction that the settling of the strata into which the lopolith was intruded was caused by removal (upwards) of magma from the deep-seated magma chamber is difficult to prove but is not impossible in the case of large sills under similar basin-like associations.

FIG. 88. Section showing three laccoliths. The feeder of *a* is not in the section. The magma followed a fault in rising to *b*. *c* is an interformational laccolith. Note that the strata are arched upward above each of the laccoliths.

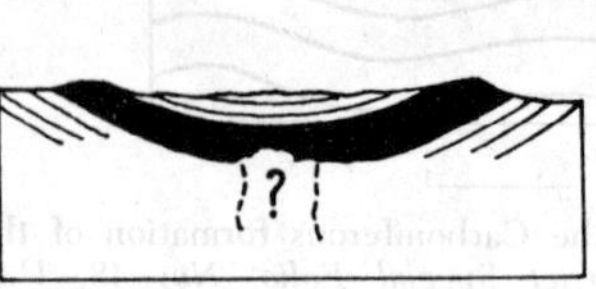

FIG. 89. Vertical section of a lopolith.

FIG. 90. Vertical section of two phacoliths, one anticlinal and the other synclinal.

A *phacolith* is an igneous body, lens-shaped in cross section, intruded between folded beds either on the crest of an anticline or in the trough of a syncline (Art. 174; Fig. 90).

Any of the plutons just described, although they are always concordant in their major relations, may break across the bedding locally (Fig. 91).

Discordant plutons include dikes, necks, chonoliths, batholiths, stocks, and bosses. The term *dike* is used in this book for any sheet of igneous material not concordant with bedding (Fig. 92). Its contacts need not be exactly parallel, *i.e.*, a dike may thin out or it may alternately pinch and swell along its length (162). An *apophysis* is a dike which extends out from a larger magmatic body and obviously tapers to a point (as seen in section) (Figs. 91, 95). A *neck* is a roughly cylindrical intrusive mass with one long and two short dimensions. Its axis is usually vertical or steeply inclined (Fig. 92). A *chonolith* is an injection irregular in that its characters are not those of a true dike, sill, sheet, laccolith, or neck, but, unlike the subjacent bodies, it has a floor (Figs. 93, 94).

FIG. 91. Section of a sill from which short apophyses extend into the country rock both above and below.

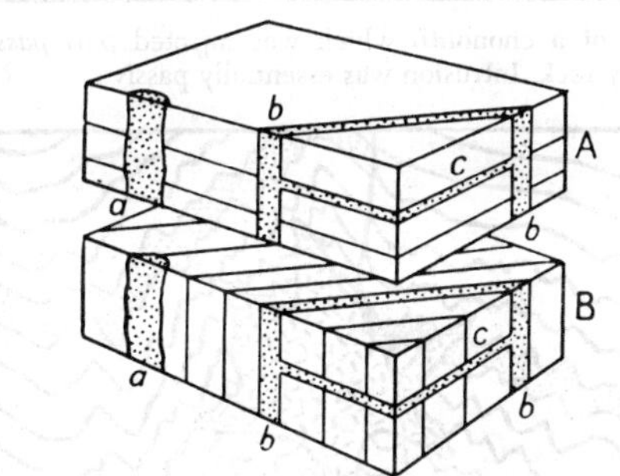

FIG. 92. Intrusive bodies in stratified rocks. *a* is a neck in both A and B. *b* is a dike in A and a sill in B. *c* is a sill in A and a dike in B.

A *batholith* is a large, irregular intrusive mass of igneous material which shows no evidence of having a base (Fig. 95). It is discordant in its relations to invaded strata. While its roof is roughly dome-shaped, there are often downward projections of the superjacent country rock which are called *roof pendants* (Fig. 95, *p*). Upward projections of the batholith are known as *cupolas* (Fig. 95, *c*). The side walls of batholiths appear to be steeply and outwardly inclined. A *stock* is a small batholith. A *boss* is a stock with a nearly circular ground plan. Stocks and bosses are sometimes cupolas of concealed batholiths.

Two special kinds of dike may be mentioned here, cone sheets and ring dikes, both of them the fillings of concentrically developed fractures in the roof rocks above boss-like masses of igneous rock. *Cone sheets* are steeply *inward*-dipping dikes in

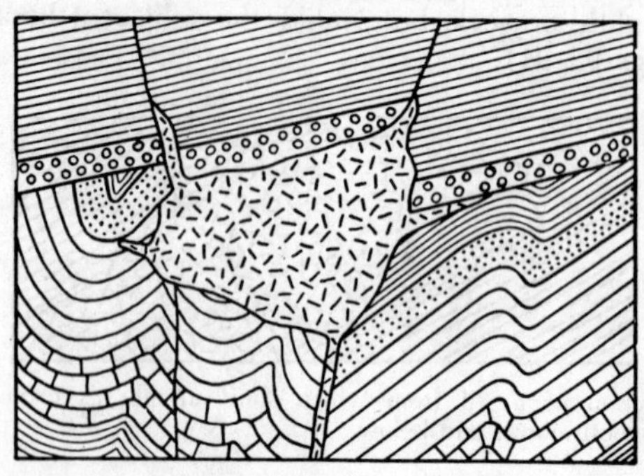

FIG. 93. Section of a chonolith which was injected *pari passu* with faulting of the country rock. Intrusion was essentially passive.

FIG. 94. Section of a chonolith which was intruded along a fault and which, in its injection, squeezed and contorted the country rock by the hydrostatic pressure of the magma.

concentric sets which by their arrangement indicate an inverted cone, or a group of concentric inverted cones, with the imaginary vertex some thousands of feet, possibly two or three miles, below the surface of the ground. These dikes are therefore arcuate in plan. In length, as seen in plan, they are seldom more than a short segment of the entire circle in which they lie. *Ring dikes* (Figs. 96 and 97) are essentially vertical dikes, arcuate in ground plan, partially encircling or sometimes wholly encircling a central area. This central area is the exposed transverse surface of a roughly cylindrical body of the country rock which, after or during the formation of the fractures into which the ring dikes came, settled downward into the magma. Depressed plug-like masses of country rock which originate through subsidence in this way are called *cauldrons.*[8]

As regards extrusion, it has been suggested that, perhaps sometimes in the past, magma may have reached the earth's surface

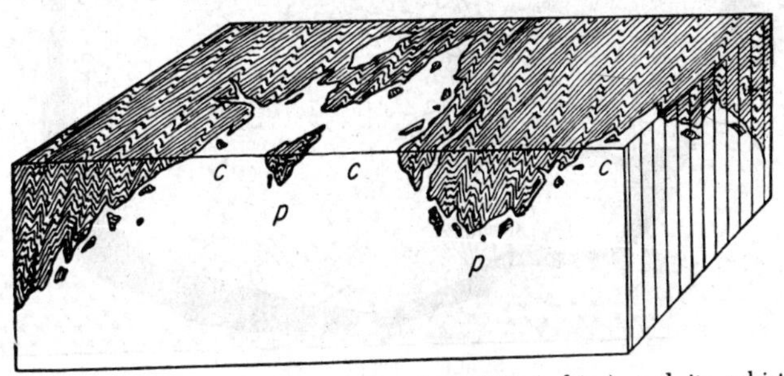

Fig. 95. Block diagram of part of a batholith (white) and its schistose country rock. *c*, cupolas; *p*, roof pendants. Several inclusions of the country rock have been frozen in near the contact.

by the foundering of part of the roof of a batholith (Fig. 98). This Daly called *extrusion by de-roofing.*[9] The two commonest methods, however, are by outflow from fissures and from tubular openings or pipes. These are known as *fissure eruptions* and *central eruptions*, respectively. When extrusion has ceased and the lava has become clogged in the conduit, the fissure type of filling is a dike or a sill, according to its relations, and the pipe filling is a *volcanic neck*. A *flow* is a sheet of lava. A *volcanic cone* is a conical, often symmetrical hill of volcanic material, either entirely ash or cinders, entirely lava, or partly lava and partly pyroclastic débris (Fig. 99). In any case it is apt to be intersected by dikes of lava.

[8] For further discussion and references on this subject see Bibliog., Billings, Marland, P., 1958, pp. 311–317.

[9] Bibliog., Daly, R. A., 1914, p. 121.

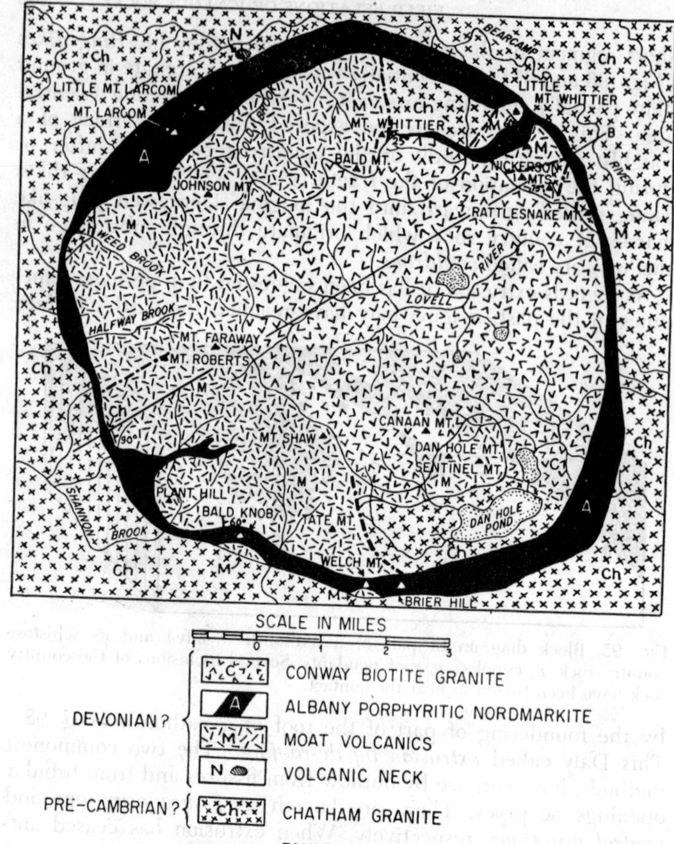

FIG. 96. Areal geology of the Ossipee Mountains in New Hampshire. The black circular area is a ring dike. (*Copied, with permission of Prof. Louise Kingsley and the American Journal of Science, from her article entitled "Caldron-Subsidence of the Ossipee Mountains," published in the Am. Jour. of Sci., vol. 22, 5th series,* pp. 139–168, 1931.)

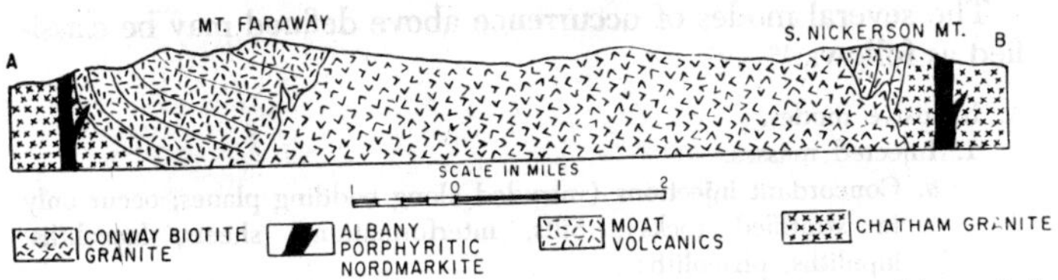

Fig. 97 Vertical section, along line *A-B* in Fig. 96. (*Like Fig. 96, copied from Professor Kingsley's article with her permission and that of the American Journal of Science.*)

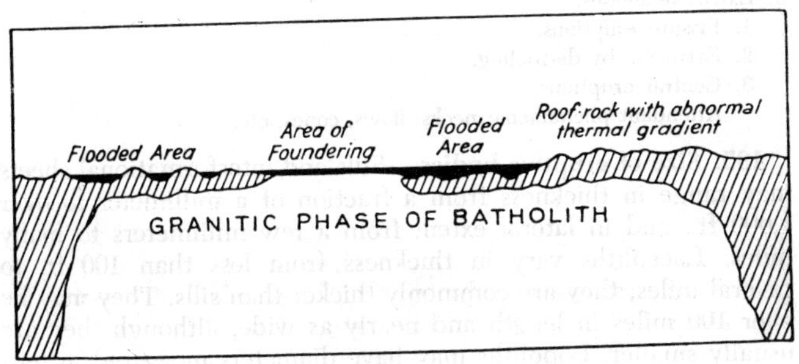

Fig. 98. Ideal section illustrating the hypothesis that the rhyolite and the thermal phenomena of the Yellowstone Park are directly related to the foundering of part of the roof of a late-Tertiary batholith. (*After R. A. Daly.*)

Fig. 99. Ideal section of a volcanic cone that has been built up on older rock (vertical ruling). The cone consists of pyroclastic material intersected by dikes of lava (black) which branch from the central neck. Along the course of each dike the lava rose until it broke out on the side of the cone, down which it flowed. The dike on the left is older than that on the right. (Why?) Bedding in the fragmental material has the characteristic angle of repose.

The several modes of occurrence above defined may be classified as follows:[10]

A. Intrusive modes.
   1. Injected masses.
      a. Concordant injections (intruded along bedding planes; occur only in stratified rocks). Sills, interformational sheets, laccoliths, lopoliths, phacoliths.
      b. Discordant injections (intruded across the bedding planes if in stratified rocks). Dikes, apophyses, cone sheets, necks, chonoliths.
   2. Subjacent masses.
      a. Batholiths, stocks, bosses.
B. Extrusive modes.
   1. Fissure eruptions.
   2. Extrusion by de-roofing.
   3. Central eruptions.
      Attendant phenomena; necks, flows, cones, etc.

135. Size of eruptive bodies. Sills and interformational sheets may range in thickness from a fraction of a millimeter to over 1,000 ft., and in lateral extent from a few millimeters to many miles. Laccoliths vary in thickness from less than 100 ft. to several miles; they are commonly thicker than sills. They may be over 100 miles in length and nearly as wide, although they are usually smaller. Lopoliths may have diameters measured in tens of miles, or more, and thicknesses up to thousands of feet. Dikes may be from less than 1 mm. to over a mile in thickness, and they may be traced a few millimeters or as much as 25, 50, or even 100 miles. The diameter of the ground plan arc of ring dikes ranges from several hundred feet to several miles. Cone sheets, usually only a few feet thick, outcrop in arcs that have diameters of several miles. Chonoliths have dimensions similar to those of laccoliths. With regard to area of outcrop, stocks and bosses are arbitrarily taken as less, and batholiths as more, than 40 square miles. A batholith may be exposed over thousands of square miles. Individual flows are generally several feet thick and they may be over 100 ft. thick. If successive flows have been poured out one upon another, the total thickness may amount to many hundreds of feet. Volcanic necks may be from 10 ft. to a mile in diameter, but are seldom as much as 1,000 ft.

[10] After Daly, with some omissions and modifications. Other less common types are described by Daly; A. W. Grabau, "A Comprehensive Geology"; and other authors of geological treatises.

NATURE AND CONSOLIDATION OF MOLTEN ROCK

136. Nature of molten rock. Magma may be regarded as a hot solution of certain volatile and nonvolatile substances. The nonvolatile ones include silica (SiO_2) and the oxides of Al, Fe, Mg, Ca, Na, and K, which, separate or in combination, compose the principal constituents of igneous rocks. There is a wide variation in the proportions of these ingredients in different magmas, and correspondingly igneous rocks vary much in chemical composition (Appendix 3). The volatile substances ("mineralizers"), such as water vapor, CO_2, HCl, etc., probably enter only in small part into the composition of the minerals. Most of them escape either into the wall rocks (**147**), or, in the case of lava, into the atmosphere. The explosiveness of some kinds of volcanic eruption is occasioned chiefly by the escape of gases and vapors under diminished pressure.

137. Consolidation of molten rock. By the process of eruption magma is brought up into regions of lower pressure and lower temperature. For subjacent eruption the change in both conditions is probably not large, but for injected and extruded bodies it may be very great. Reduction of pressure may have a number of effects of which, perhaps, the most important are the expansion of the magma itself, the expansion of its gases, and the increased chemical activity of these gases, which is an important cause of the high temperatures of lavas and probably magmas also.[11]

Reduction in temperature induces cooling which may be very gradual or rapid. When magma is cooling a temperature will at length be reached at which some of the nonvolatile constituents will begin to separate from the hot solution as crystals. Now, crystallization always implies that the molecules of which the crystals are being formed must have enough freedom in the liquid to move and orient themselves, and this freedom depends upon the fluidity or mobility of the magma. If the cooling is very slow, so that the magma does not soon become viscous, relatively few crystals will originate and these will grow by the addition of molecules until the mass has become a coarse crystalline rock. But if cooling is very rapid the magma may become so sticky that the molecules are unable to move about and combine. The

[11] See writings of Thomas A. Jaggar, Arthur L. Day, *et al.*

liquid becomes stiffer and harder, without crystallization, until it is a glass. If cooling is a little less sudden, yet not so slow as in the first example, there may be some opportunity for the molecules to move before the liquid becomes too viscous. Crystals may then originate at a great many points so near together that they will soon interfere and the resulting rock will be fine-grained. Evidently, then, *rate of cooling* is an important factor influencing the texture of an igneous rock.

The volatile constituents, or mineralizers, may be conceived of as lubricating the magma, as making it less viscous. By virtue of this property, not only do they increase the mobility of the molten material as a whole, but also they facilitate molecular movements within it, *i.e.*, they assist crystallization. In fact, the crystallization of some minerals, such as quartz, orthoclase, and albite (soda plagioclase), seems to be difficult or impossible without the aid of these volatile substances. Since ease of molecular migration in a cooling solution is conducive to the formation of relatively few, large crystals, an abundance of gases and vapors in a magma may function in the same way as a slow rate of cooling. Pegmatitic texture, which is thought to be due to the agency of an excess of mineralizers and particularly of water vapor, is often characteristic of the last portion of a magma to crystallize, because the volatile substances, being for the most part excluded from the composition of the minerals which they help to crystallize, are left in increasing proportion in the residual liquid.

There is still another factor which influences the fluidity of a magma, namely, the proportion of the nonvolatile components. Those magmas (*basic*) which have a relatively high content of lime, iron, and magnesium, and are low in silica, are thinner and more mobile than those (*acidic*) which are high in silica and the alkalies. Basic lavas flow quite freely and sometimes for long distances when they are poured out on the earth's surface, and the magmatic gases are readily given off from them; but acidic lavas are so viscous that the gases escape with much difficulty and generally with explosive violence. It might seem, therefore, that the basic, mobile magmas would consolidate with coarser texture than the acidic kinds, and undoubtedly this is sometimes true; but rate of cooling and volatile content are so much more effective, at least as far as visible results are concerned, that the degree of control by nonvolatile composition is usually indeterminate. Thus, an acidic intrusive may be of coarser grain than a basic igneous rock into which it was injected.

In brief, the viscosity and crystallization of magmas and the texture of igneous rocks are controlled by various factors of which temperature change and content of volatile substances are generally the most important. The beginner is advised to disregard pressure change and nonvolatile composition since the parts played by these are more difficult to gauge. Furthermore, he is warned not to make comparisons between the textures of different classes of rock and to draw conclusions accordingly. Because a granite happens to be coarse and a diorite is finer, the granite magma did not necessarily cool more slowly or have a larger proportion of volatile constituents than the diorite magma; but if the granite shows variations of texture within its own mass, these may be ascribed in most cases to the control of one or the other, or possibly both, of the factors named; and the same may be said of variations within the diorite.

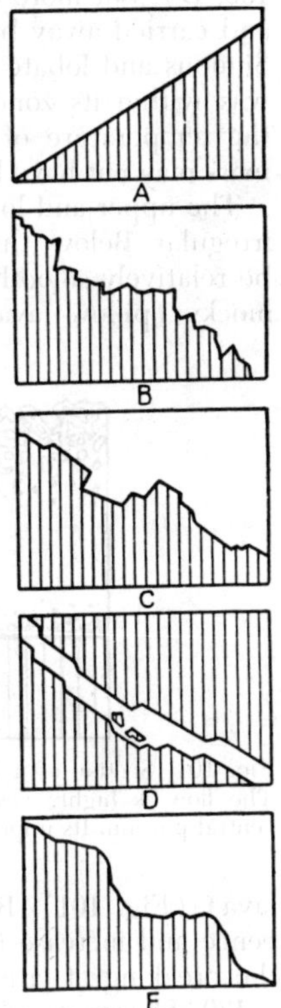

FIG. 100. Types of igneous contacts, as seen in cross section. The intrusive rock is blank and the country rock is lined. The contact is straight in A, jagged in B, blocky in C, blocky and matched in D, and sinuous in E.

CONTACTS

138. Shape of contacts. Intrusive contacts may be straight, jagged, blocky, sinuous, or lobate. These are shown in Fig. 100. Straight, jagged, and blocky contacts point to the invasion of fissures by the magma. They signify that the country rock was in its zone of fracture (173), and that probably it was relatively cool as compared with the molten material. In the case of thin injected bodies, such as dikes and sills, the two edges are some-

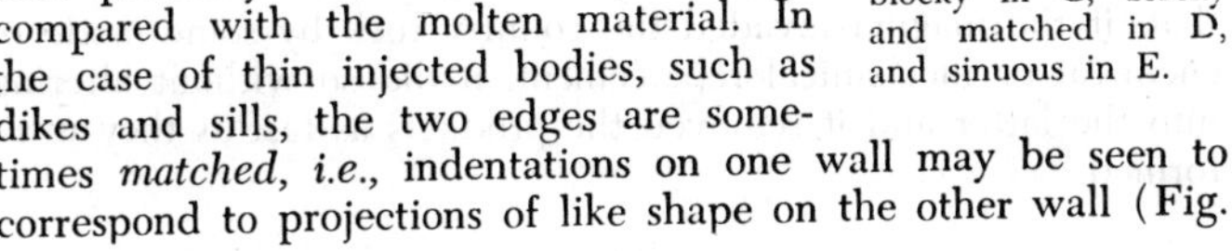

times *matched*, *i.e.*, indentations on one wall may be seen to correspond to projections of like shape on the other wall (Fig.

100, D); but more commonly small blocks have been broken off and carried away by the magma so that the walls do not match. Sinuous and lobate contacts often indicate that the country rock was within its zone of flowage (**173**). The difference between the temperature of the country rock and that of the intrusive mass may not have been very great.

The upper and lower surfaces of a lava flow are generally very irregular. Below, the sheet is often cavernous, and above, it may be relatively smooth and ribbed (ropy lava, pahoehoe), or hummocky (pillow lava), or exceedingly rough and jagged (block

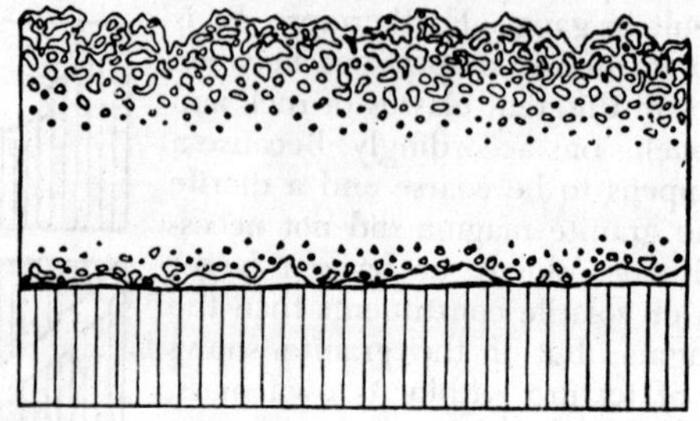

Fig. 101. Section of a lava flow resting on older material (vertical ruling). The flow is highly vesicular above, less so below, and is compact in its central portion. Its upper surface is scoriaceous. (Cf. Fig. 34.)

lava) (Fig. 101). Block lava owes its roughness to the coalescence and increase in size of vesicles at its upper surface and to the breaking of crusts which formed before its flow had ceased.

139. Sharpness of contacts. Some contacts are very definite, so sharp, in fact, that one can put the point of a pencil on the exact line (Fig. 102). In other instances there appears to be more or less blending between the country rock and the intrusive (Fig. 103). Sharp contacts may mean either: (1) that intrusion was rapid and the magma was soon chilled against the country rock; or (2) that there was not a strong tendency for the magma gradually to alter or dissolve the country rock (**147**); or (3) that, if the magma invaded the country rock by some mode of chemical or mechanical replacement, it did so without filtering into the latter and it removed the products as fast as they were formed.

Blended contacts suggest: (1) that the magma may have worked its way into the country rock and there crystallized in thin stringers or in isolated grains between the constituents of the older rock; or (2) that the magma had the property of gradually breaking down and altering the composition of the country

Fig. 102. Section of a sharp igneous contact between two igneous rocks. The rock on the left is the younger. This is determined by the fact that its texture becomes finer toward the contact, showing that its magma was chilled against the rock on the right, and that here, therefore, its crystallization was impeded. This is an example of a chilled contact zone.

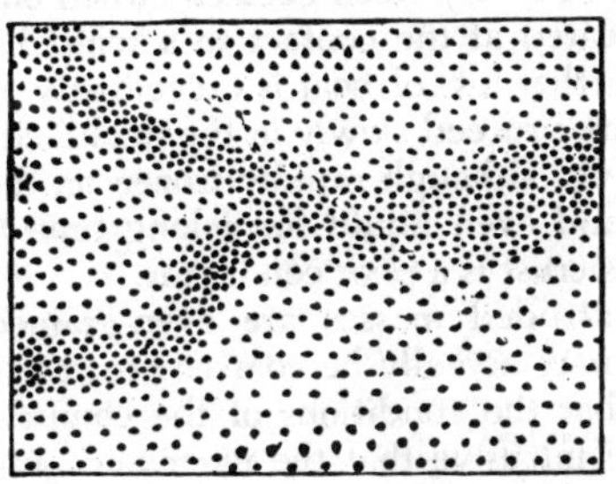

Fig. 103. Section of a branching dike and its country rock. The contacts are blended; that is, there is nowhere a sharp division line between the two rocks.

rock. Each of these alternatives points to long-continued magmatic conditions; there could have been no sudden chilling. In other words, the country rock must have been relatively warm. Here also may be mentioned the gradational contact between an original rock body and its granitized derivative in a pseudo-igneous pluton (Art. 255).

Contact Zone in the Eruptive Rock

140. Principal phenomena of the contact zone. The contact zone in an eruptive rock (endomorphic zone) may exhibit the following characters which are more or less dependent upon the influence of the country rock, or, in the case of lavas, of the atmosphere: (1) textural variation; (2) vesicular and amygdaloidal structures; (3) flow structure; (4) fracture structure (**234**); (5) chemical and mineralogical divergence from the normal or average composition of the eruptive as a whole; (6) schliers and segregations; and (7) inclusions (**154–161**).

141. Marginal texture. Many igneous bodies are of coarser grain centrally than they are near their surfaces. This is explained by the fact that the molten rock after its eruption was chilled by its cooler surroundings, so that its crystallization was hindered (**137**). For the same reason lavas may be glassy above and more or less crystalline inside. These fine-grained marginal zones are spoken of as *chilled contacts* (Fig. 102).

It is worth while noting in this place that rock is a poor conductor of heat. Hence, in large intrusive bodies the chilled contact zone may not be very thick because, when once the country rock has been heated at the contact to a temperature near that of the magma, further loss of heat is exceedingly gradual, so that crystallization may proceed slowly in the unchilled portion of the magma. Lava flows, although rapidly frozen on the surface, may remain red hot and even liquid for a long time beneath a thin crust because this crust is a poor conductor.

Occasionally intruded masses are even-grained up to their contacts or they may actually be coarser near the margins. Even grain indicates that the conditions of the country rock were so near those of the intrusive that the inner and outer parts of the latter were affected almost alike. For example, the country rock may have been so warm, either because of its depth or because the magma flowed by it for a long time, that it did not chill the magma. A coarser marginal phase may often be attributed to the local activity, near the contacts, of volatile constituents derived either from the magma itself or from the country rock.

142. Vesicular and amygdaloidal structures. Vesicular structure is characteristic of extrusive sheets, but it may sometimes be found in rocks which were injected under little pressure. The pores may be marginal or central or they may pervade the mass.

In sheets of lava (Fig. 101) they are commonly near the upper surface toward which they may become more and more numerous until the rock is scoriaceous or pumiceous. Vesicles near the lower contact of a flow in many cases originated on the upper surface or at the front of the moving lava and were then rolled under (**243**).

Since amygdales are merely the fillings of vesicles, their forms and relations are the same as those of vesicles.

143. Discrimination between vesicular structure and weather pits. Little cavities left by the removal of the grains of a soluble mineral (**40**) may give to a rock the appearance of a vesicular lava. To discriminate between these weather pits and vesicles, break off a piece of the rock. A short distance in from the surface of the outcrop the weather pits will be seen to have the angular shape of the crystals which were leached out, and, farther in, the original crystals may still be present. Vesicles, on the other hand, will be rounded and empty.

An exception to this statement is the case in which vesicles have been filled with amygdales and the amygdales have been dissolved out by weathering near the outcrop surface. The broken fracture of the rock may show the remaining amygdales. It will then be necessary to apply the rules for distinguishing between amygdales and crystals (**144**).

144. Discrimination between amygdaloidal and porphyritic structures. Well-developed amygdales and phenocrysts should be easily distinguished, for amygdales are typically rounded mineral aggregates with concentric structure and phenocrysts are generally single grains with crystal edges and angles (cf. Figs. 80, B, and 82). Sometimes, it is true phenocrysts have had their corners and edges rounded by resorption (magmatic solution) (Fig. 80, C), so that some of them look more like amygdales, but the other criteria just mentioned should be sufficient for their discrimination.

145. Flow structure. Flow structure has been briefly described in Art. **135.** When it bears a definite relationship to the contacts of an eruptive body, as in the dike in Fig. 104, it may be regarded as one variety of endomorphic effects. On a larger scale, Fig. 105 illustrates flow structure in a stock or batholith.

146. Fracture systems. In many eruptive bodies, both intrusive and extrusive, there are fractures that may be more or less regularly disposed and that may bear certain relations to the form of the body, or, in other words, to its contacts with the country rock. Since flow structure, also, is often related to these contacts, it follows that there may be a recognizable—often a very important—connection between the flow structure and the fracture systems within a given igneous body. More will be said on this subject in Art. 235, in the chapter on fractures and fracture structures.

147. Marginal variations in composition. Many eruptive bodies have a gradual change in composition toward their contacts in a way to suggest that the variation must owe its origin to some outside control. We can imagine two general methods by which a magma might be so affected, namely, either by solu-

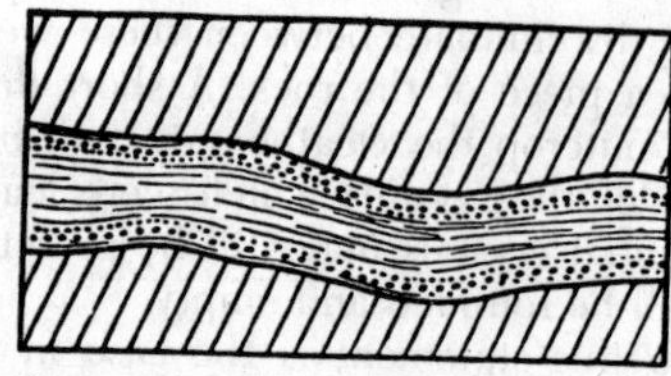

FIG. 104. Section of part of a dike and its country rock, showing the relation between the contacts and the flow structure of the dike.

tion and incorporation of some of the country rock, or by some internal process whereby certain mineral components might become separated from others and then segregated near the contacts or away from the contacts, as the case might be. The first and direct mode is *marginal assimilation;* the second, indirect way comes under the head of *differentiation.* Conceivably both might go on simultaneously. The products of assimilation are called *syntectics,* and those of differentiation are *differentiates.* Both processes, requiring high fluidity for their successful operation, might be expected to yield their most marked results in those intrusive bodies that consolidate least rapidly. Accordingly, we find that the best-developed contact zones of chemical or mineralogical variation are in the larger intrusive masses.

There has been much controversy about the relative efficiency of marginal assimilation and differentiation, and the problem is not yet solved[12] (see Art. 155). Without entering into the discus-

[12] N. L. Bowen (see Bibliog.) has published papers in which he discusses methods of differentiation: (1) by the gravitative settling of crystals as they are formed in the magma; and (2) by compression, due to the forces of rock deformation, which may squeeze some of the remaining magma from between the crystals of the partly consolidated igneous rock.

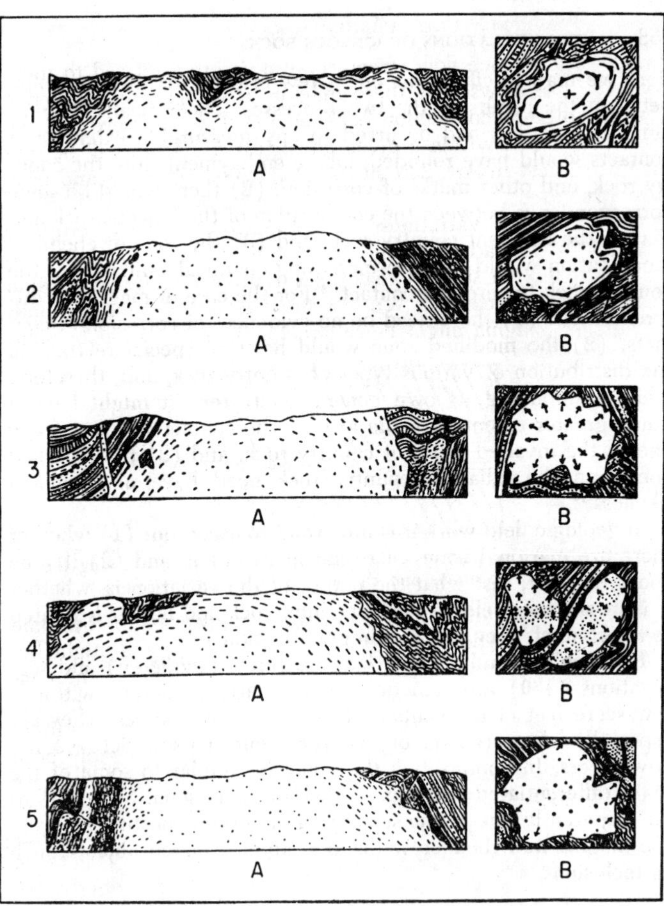

FIG. 105. Flow structure in a stock or batholith. In each of the five diagrams, A is a vertical cross section, and B is a horizontal plan. Diagram 1 shows a dome of flow layers; 2, arch of flow layers, with massive center; 3, dome of flow lines (not yet observed in the field); 4, arch of flow lines; 5, incomplete arch of flow lines. In 1 and 2, lines with black triangles indicate strike and dip of flow layers. A cross denotes horizontal flow structure. Arrows show plunge of flow lines. Double-barbed arrow denotes horizontal flow lines. In 4, B, the axis of the flow lines (stippled belt) coincides with the axis of the mass if on the right side of A and disregards it if on the left of A. (*After Balk. See caption for Fig.* 85 *for source.*)

sion, we may briefly point out a few criteria for distinguishing between the results of the two processes. Theoretically, if marginal assimilation had occurred to any measurable extent: (1) contacts would have rounded, lobate embayments into the country rock, and other marks of corrosion; (2) there would be some correspondence between the composition of the igneous rock and that of the adjacent country rock; and (3) the zone of chemical modification would have an increasing chemical similarity to the country rock toward the contact.[13] For the case of magmatic differentiation: (1) there need be no evidences of corrosion at contacts; (2) the modified zone would have no special relation to the distribution of various types of country rock, and, therefore, while maintaining its own general characters, it might have a much greater extent than the area of the contact surface of any one of the invaded types of country rock; and (3) the modified zone and the adjacent country rock need have no chemical likeness.[14]

In geologic field work it is important to ascertain: (1) whether there are marginal zones of chemical variation; and (2) if such zones do exist, just what the nature of the variation is, whether it is in any way related to the country rock and how it is related to the contact. (See Art. **255** on granitization.)

148. Schliers and segregations. Schliers (*schlieren*) and segregations (**130**) are sometimes particularly numerous within a few score feet of the contact of large intrusive bodies. They are especially characteristic of the subjacent masses. Schliers are flow layers. In composition they may be similar to some of the main differentiated portions of the frozen magma. Segregations are apparently due to the separation of certain constituents from the magma and their crystallization about isolated objects, such as inclusions.

Contact Zone in the Country Rock

149. Contact metamorphism. Physical and chemical changes induced in rock material by the influence of magma or of lava may be accomplished by heating, by the infiltration of volatile

[13] Observe that criteria 2 and 3 might equally well apply to pseudo-igneous plutons (Art. **255**).

[14] For further details see Bibliog., Barrell, J., 1907; Daly, R. A., 1914, Chaps. XI and XII.

and nonvolatile constituents of the magma, or, occasionally, by the pressure of intrusion. By chemical processes, discoloration, baking, and alteration in composition may be effected. Physical changes include tension jointing (**234**) and peripheral cleavage. The contact metamorphic zone (exomorphic zone) in which these features may be observed varies in thickness from a fraction of an inch to many hundred yards. It is usually thin adjacent to small intrusives and beneath flows. Its thickness and the extent of the alteration are roughly proportional to the size and temperature of the intrusive body, the duration of flow of the magma between the walls of a conduit, and the structure and composition of the country rock. For example, the roof above a

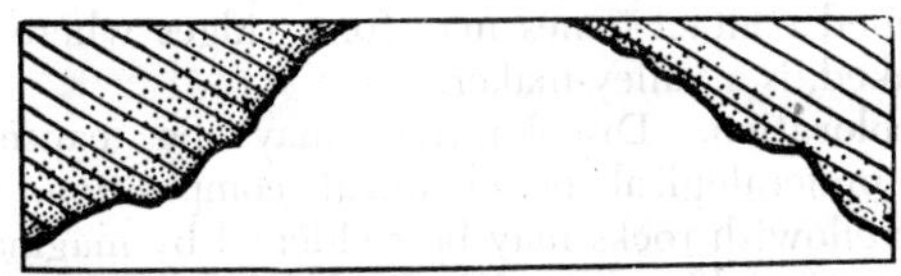

FIG. 106. Section of an igneous contact between an intrusive rock (blank) and its stratified country rock (lined). The latter has been metamorphosed (stippling) in a wider zone on the left where the bedding is transverse to the contact.

batholith may be altered a long distance, sometimes a mile or more, from the main contact, because batholiths are large and they lose their heat slowly. Likewise the contact zone about a volcanic neck may be disproportionately thick if the outflow of lava continued for a long time. Conduction of heat and infiltration of escaped magmatic substances are more easy along, than across, parallel structures, and therefore the thickest portion of the altered zone in rocks having cleavage, bedding, etc., is apt to be where these structures are perpendicular to the contact (Fig. 106). Finally, when magma is intruded into a rock having a composition very different from its own, the metamorphism is likely to be more intense and of greater extent than when the compositions of intrusive and country rock are similar. That is why a sedimentary country rock may be more severely altered than one that is igneous.

The physical and chemical features named above are described in Arts. **150–153**.

150. Baking. *Baking* refers to the hardening or toughening of rock material through the influence of magma or lava. Sometimes loose clays and sands are cemented just below a lava flow. Shale may become a very hard, flintlike rock, called hornstone, and quartz sandstone may become quartzite. Baking seems to be a process of cementation rather than compression. It may be due partly to the rearrangement and crystallization of substances already in the country rock, and partly to the infiltration and crystallization of some of the magmatic silica, etc. At exposed contacts in thinly and evenly banded shales, the banding may become obscure or fade away in the baked zone. Similarly, the cleavage of slates may gradually pass over into the irregular fracture of hornstone. Being comparatively resistant to erosion, these hardened contact zones may form ridges where the same rock, not baked, is a valley-maker.

151. Discoloration. Discoloration may be caused by a change in mineralogical or chemical composition. Greenish, grayish, or yellowish rocks may be reddened by magma through the dehydration of limonite ($2Fe_2O_3 \cdot 3H_2O$), or the decarbonation and oxidation of ferrous carbonate ($FeCO_3$), and the formation of hematite (Fe_2O_3).

152. Mineralogical and chemical alterations. Alterations more striking than baking or discoloration are common in the contact zones of invaded rocks. The changes are brought about largely through the agency of water vapor and gases, most of which have filtered in from the magma, but some of which may have been in the country rock prior to intrusion. Many of these changes come under the head of *pneumatolysis*. Even silica and other nonvolatile substances are believed to escape in solution from the magma, assisting in chemical reactions, cementing the rock particles, and forming veins in the open spaces (**257**). New minerals are formed by the crystallization of substances derived from the magma, by the breaking down and recrystallization of the original minerals, and by the combining of new and old constituents. Quartz, mica, garnet, andalusite, staurolite, vesuvianite, and tourmaline, are a few of the common species that may be developed in this way. Clay rocks sometimes become spotted in the early stages of metamorphism, the spots or "knots" often being small aggregates of carbonaceous matter or of newly formed minerals. Ordinarily the variety of the new minerals is greater if the original rock was impure, for then there are just so many more substances from which different combinations may be made. As a rule the effects of heat and of the infiltration of the magmatic juices proper are found to have been distinctly antecedent to the effects produced through the invasion of the volatile constituents (pneumatolysis).

It is important to note, with reference to contact zones showing chemical or mineralogical alteration, that greater changes are produced at high than at low temperatures and that, at different temperatures, the same chemical constituents may

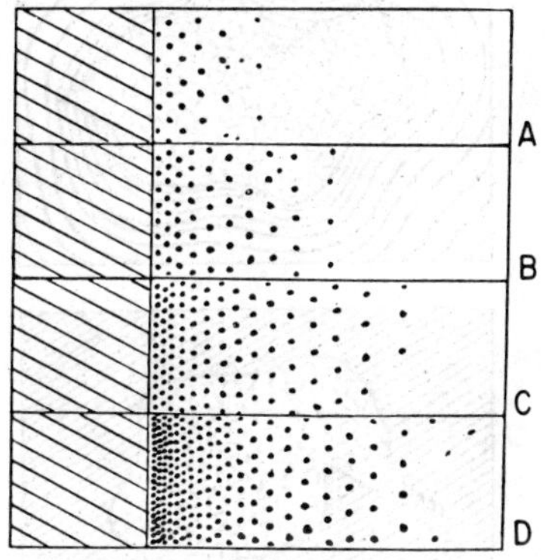

Fig. 107. Degrees of contact metamorphism. The intrusive rock is diagonally ruled. A, B, C, and D represent successive stages of increasing contact metamorphism (stippling) in the country rock. The more intense metamorphism is indicated by the closer stippling.

unite in different associations to make different minerals. From this it follows: (1) that the country rock near the contact will pass through successive stages of increasing metamorphism as long as it is being heated and otherwise affected by the magmatic agents; (2) that ultimately a given type of country rock will be most altered near the contact and less and less so away from it; and (3) that, other things being equal, the higher degrees of metamorphism existing close to the contact in broad altered zones will be wanting in narrow zones and that consequently a given degree of alteration may be expected nearer the igneous body in the narrower zones (Fig. 107).

Careful field mapping may reveal an aureole of metamorphosed rocks surrounding an igneous intrusive body, with roughly concentric belts of rock with increasing degrees of metamorphism (*metamorphic zones* or *facies*) inward toward the igneous mass. In some cases, where the intrusive body has not been exposed, but lies a relatively short distance below the land surface, the central area of such an aureole will have the highest metamorphism, suggesting proximity of the igneous body

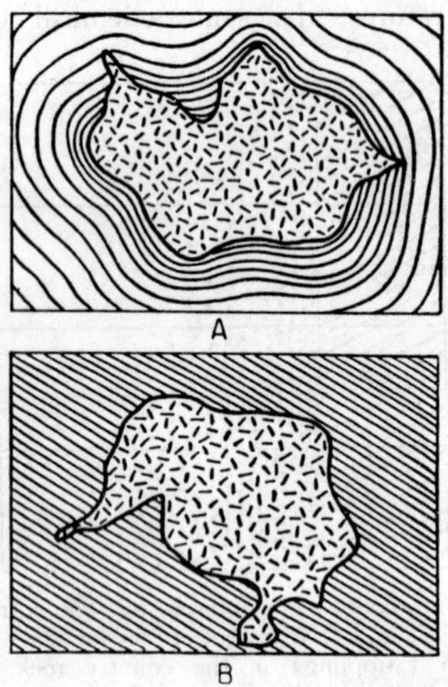

Fig. 108. Maps showing relations of cleavage to intrusive contacts. The dash pattern represents the intrusive rock. In A the cleavage is essentially peripheral, probably because it was produced by the hydrostatic pressure of the magma. In B the cleavage was formed prior to the intrusion of the magma.

beneath. (See Art. **251** for a description of metamorphic zones in regional dynamic metamorphism.)

153. Cleavage. As a result of eruption, cleavage (fissility) is not common. It is generally a product of dynamic metamorphism (see Art. **242**), with no relation to intrusion, a fact which is demonstrated in numberless exposures where the cleavage is *cut across* by the intrusive bodies (Fig. 108). Where it is a consequence of the force of intrusion, it dies out away from the contact and its attitude is directly related to the igneous mass. It is then roughly parallel to the contact and cases of intersection of this peripheral cleavage by the contact are local and insignificant.

Inclusions

154. Cognate and foreign inclusions. Inclusions have been defined as blocks of rock which were detached from the walls of a magma chamber and were eventually frozen into the resulting igneous rock. It is necessary to point out that not all inclusions are of the rock originally invaded by a magma. While a large body of molten material is undergoing differentiation, its

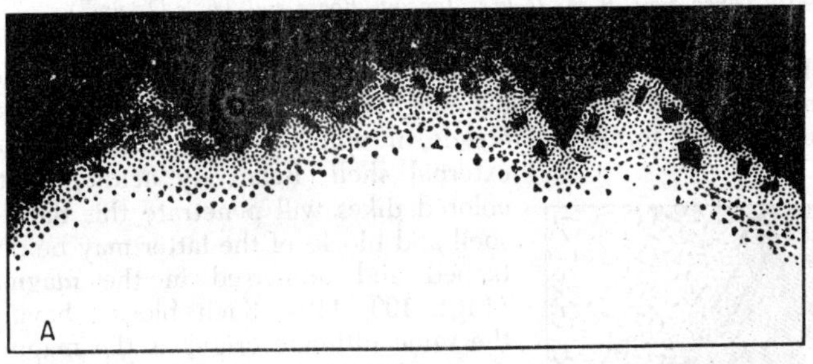

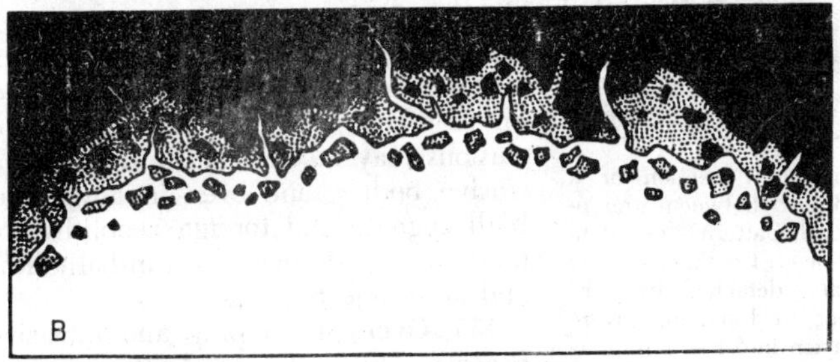

FIG. 109. Section of part of a batholith (blank and stippled) and its country rock (black) in successive stages of consolidation of the former. In A the stippling represents the portion which, having already crystallized, formed an outer envelope surrounding the still molten interior (blank). By further movements the magma was injected into this envelope (B). Black inclusions are foreign; stippled inclusions are cognate.

marginal parts are crystallizing, so that at length a stage is reached in which the body consists of an outer hardened shell covering a still molten residuum of different composition. Very

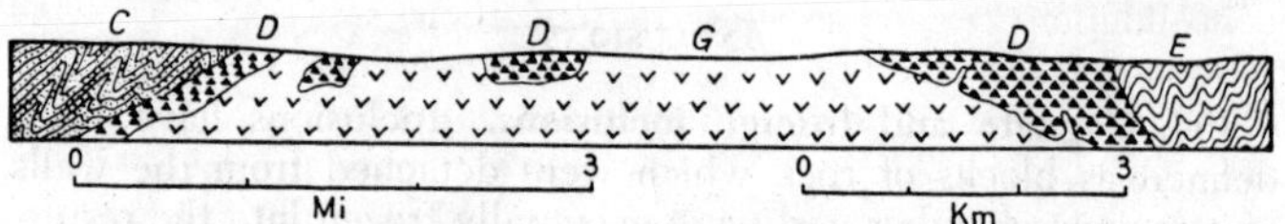

FIG. 110. Section of part of a batholith and its country rock, *C* and *E*. The batholith consists of granite, *G*, with a basic border phase of diorite and gabbro, *D*. The diorite and gabbro appear to be older chilled phases of the batholith in which the granite later differentiated and into which the granite was intruded. (*Penobscot Bay Folio, No.* 149, *U.S. Geol. Survey*, 1907. *Taken from R. A. Daly's "Igneous Rocks and Their Origin."*)

often the outer, earlier differentiates are more basic than the inner ones. If the residual magma for any cause is again disturbed and forced to intrude, it will have to invade its own external shell. Relatively acidic, light-colored dikes will penetrate this darker shell and blocks of the latter may be detached and immersed in the magma (Figs. 109, 110). Such blocks, having the same ultimate origin as the magma surrounding them, are called *cognate inclusions*. Inclusions of the country rock proper may be spoken of as *foreign*. Cognate inclusions are sometimes carried up in dikes, sills, etc., and foreign inclusions may be seen in all kinds of intrusive bodies, and even in flows; but both cognate and foreign xenoliths are most extensively developed in batholiths and large injected masses.

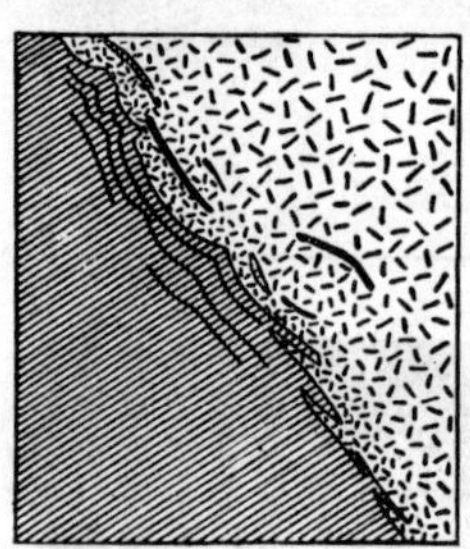

FIG. 111. Section of a contact between granite (dash pattern) and slate (lined). Fragments of the slate, detached by contact exfoliation, were frozen into the granite as inclusions. (*After T. N. Dale.*)

155. Overhead stoping and intrusive breccias. With reference to the large intrusive bodies, the passive rifting of blocks from the walls of the chamber Daly terms *overhead stoping*. He ascribes it to a sort of exfoliation consequent upon the heating and expansion of the wall rock (Fig. 111), assisted by the invasion of dikes (Fig. 112) and sometimes by the movement of the magma. In general the detached blocks sink as the magma remains sufficiently fluid. As the viscosity increases this settling is impeded and finally checked, so that the inclusions which are rifted off just prior to consolidation cannot move far from their sources. The consequence is that the big intrusive bodies may have an outer shell of *intrusive breccia,* in which inclusions, both cognate and foreign, are very abundant (Fig. 109), and this may pass into an adjacent surrounding cover of country rock ramified by numerous apophyses. If differentiation occurred and the magma was injected at intervals into its hardened portions, the contact zone of intrusive breccia might be very complicated in its nature.

Fig. 112. Section showing details of a contact between schist and an intruded igneous rock (dash pattern). The separation of inclusions is here due principally to the invasion of dikes. Observe the relation between the shapes of the inclusions and their schistosity. In which direction do the dikes appear to have penetrated with greatest facility?

156. Characters of inclusions. Seen in cross section on the surfaces of outcrops, inclusions appear as more or less irregular patches which may be sharply angular, subangular, well-rounded, lobate with embayments, or shredded (Figs. 113, 114). They may vary in size from a fraction of an inch to enormous blocks measuring several hundred feet in their visible dimensions. Their contacts may be clearly defined or blended for the same reasons that were mentioned in Art. **139.** Where sharp contacts and angular forms are common, marginal assimilation has probably played an insignificant part. Sometimes there is a complete and uniform transition from the surrounding igneous rock to the central, unaltered portion of the xenolith, as if the latter had been in process of absorption when freezing stopped further encroachment by the magma. Foreign inclusions may, of course, exhibit the same features, original or metamorphic, as the country rock. In them bedding, cleavage, etc., may still be preserved or, on the other hand, they may be baked, discolored, or mineralized. Their contact zones are concentrically arranged, the more extreme changes being in the outer parts. Since small inclusions are apt to be more thoroughly altered than large ones, original structures should be looked for in the latter.

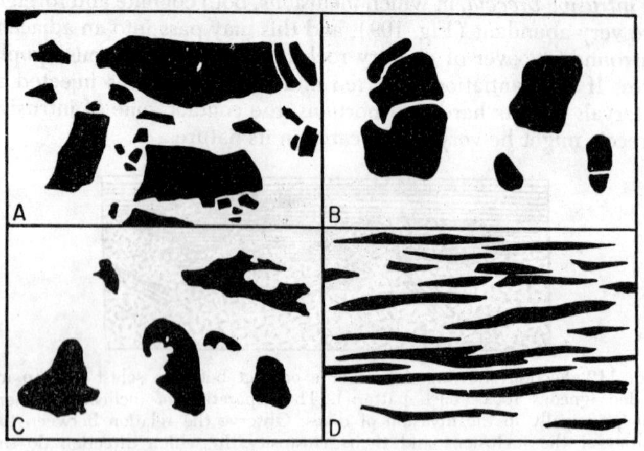

FIG. 113. Shapes and distribution of inclusions (black) in an inclosing igneous matrix (white). A, angular inclusions. Some of the fragments may be seen to have fitted together. B, inclusions with rounded corners, suggestive of magmatic solution. The small inclusion at the extreme right was evidently broken so late that the corners of the fracture suffered no rounding. C, scalloped inclusions, the embayments of the eruptive rock being places where the magma dissolved its way into the inclusions. D, sliverlike inclusions in parallel position. The form is the result of an original well-defined parallel structure in the country rock. The orientation may be indicative of the direction of flow of the magma.

157. Source of inclusions. When inclusions in an eruptive are situated near country rock of the same kind, as seen on an outcrop surface (Fig. 115), their source is fairly obvious, although probably they were not carried directly across from the part of the contact (*b* in Fig. 115) at present exposed. They may have come up from some point on the wall, *bc,* that is now within the rock mass, or they may have come down from a portion of the wall, *ab,* which has been eroded away, or they

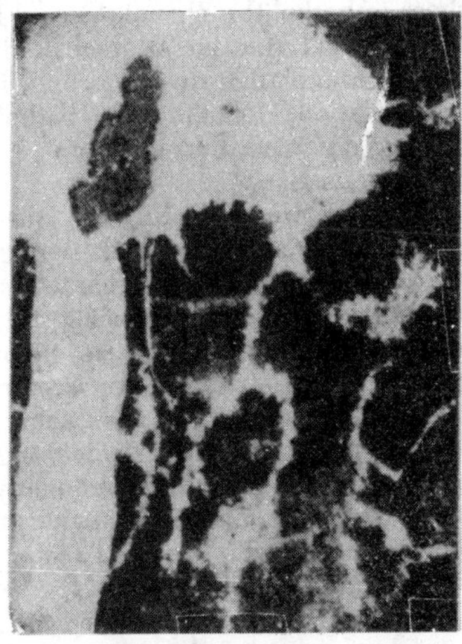

Fig. 114. A rock surface showing basic cognate inclusions in a more acidic matrix. Most of the contacts are irregular, suggesting that the magma was able to dissolve its way into the country rock; but the nearly straight matched contacts of the broad light dike on the left are clearly the result of fracture. They are of somewhat later origin than the irregular contacts. (Cf. Fig. 113, B.) (About ⅛ natural size.)

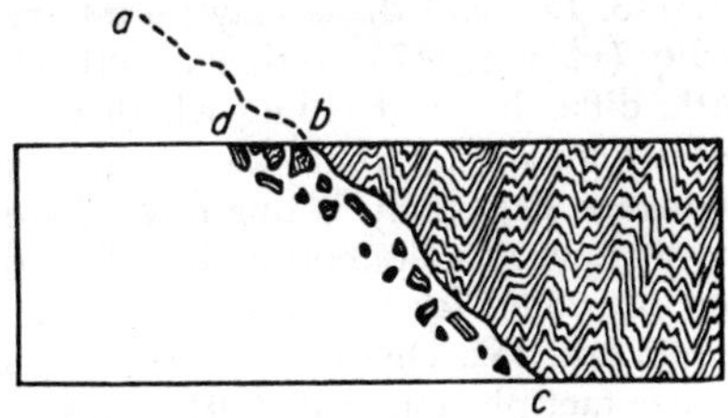

Fig. 115. Vertical section of a contact to illustrate the source of inclusions.

may have moved along the trend of the contact line. For the geologist they are of particular interest when no country rock remains in the vicinity or when the wall rock that does outcrop is of an entirely different nature. Under these circumstances it is likely, but not absolutely certain, that inclusions in dikes have risen and that those in batholiths, chonoliths, and laccoliths have sunk; in other words, that the parent rock in the first case is below the land surface and that, in the second, it has been removed through denudation. Xenoliths in a batholith which has been broadly uncovered may thus give one a notion of the character of the eroded roof.

158. Discrimination between inclusions and segregations. The distinction between inclusions and segregations is not always easy or possible. The following characters are generally typical of segregations: (1) relatively small size, often only a few inches across; (2) rather uniform size on outcrops a few square yards or rods in area; (3) oval or circular cross section; (4) concentric arrangement of the constituent minerals; (5) one or more minerals in common with the inclosing igneous rock. On the contrary, inclusions are more frequently of irregular shape and variable size. As pointed out in the preceding paragraph, the larger ones often retain original features. Hence, the true nature of small xenoliths that look like segregations may be determined by comparing their composition and structure with the composition and structure of the outer zones of the larger blocks whose derivation is certain. As for cognate inclusions, there is every gradation between them and segregations, for both are more or less directly related to differentiation.

159. Discrimination between inclusions and dikes. Inclusions, or xenoliths, may be long and narrow, as seen on rock exposures (Fig. 113, D), and dikes may be interrupted in their exposed continuity (cf. Fig. 117), so that sometimes the geologist may have a little difficulty in deciding whether he is observing xenoliths or very irregular, apparently discontinuous, dikes where the matrix is igneous. Especially is this true where this igneous rock has been somewhat metamorphosed. The discrimination must depend on searching for features such as are described in Arts. **140, 141, 149,** and **152.** Dikes should reveal some evidences of endomorphic contact phenomena (**140**), and xenoliths should, if possible, be correlated with the country rock into which the igneous matrix was injected.

160. Discrimination between large inclusions and roof pendants. In effecting the uncovering of a batholith, denudation isolates the roof pendants, if there were any such (Fig. 116). On a map they look like islands of country rock encircled by the intrusive rock, exactly the same relations, in fact, as are exhibited by xenoliths in ground plan. Outcrops of country rock in an area which is certainly inclosed by the eruptive rock may belong, then, either to a large inclusion or to a truncated roof pendant. There are some geologists who assert that it is impossible to tell the difference between the two. However, if several of these isolated exposures of country rock are found, and in all of them structures like bedding, cleavage, etc., have a parallel or otherwise orderly arrangement of strikes, they are probably roof pendants. In the case of xenoliths, even when they are very near one another, such structures are apt to have diverse directions

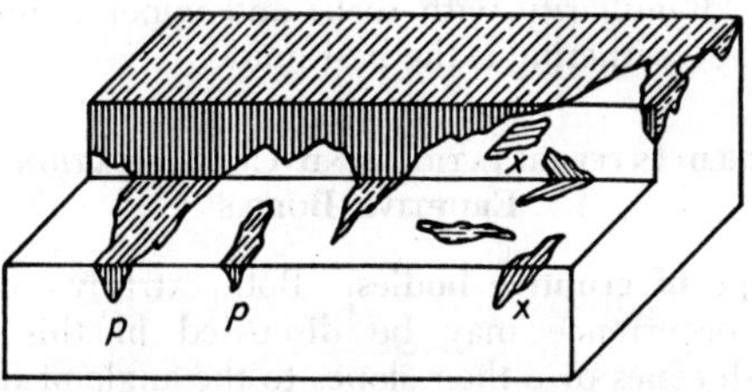

FIG. 116. Block diagram of a batholith (white) and its country rock (lined) in successive stages of erosion. At the lower level (front of block) one of the roof pendants, *p*, has been isolated and so looks like a xenolith. Compare the orientation of roof pendants, *p*, and xenoliths, *x*.

and no apparent relations, for blocks of country rock that have been detached from the walls of a magma chamber are free to change their positions.

161. Discrimination between inclusions and erosion patches. Small patches of rock left on a contact that has been laid bare by erosion are sometimes mistaken for true inclusions. These are described in Art. **170**.

Another erosion phenomenon which beginners too often confuse with inclusions is an effect of unequal weathering of igneous rocks. Exfoliation, it will be remembered, is a process by which the outer surface of an outcrop spalls or peels off in thin plates. If these spalls come off unequally, first in one place and then in another, the rock acquires a patchy look, for each slab that peels off leaves a scar that has a color somewhat different from the older surrounding surface. It is these scars that are sometimes taken for inclusions. They are especially common in glaciated regions which have been abandoned by the ice long enough for exfoliation to start on the smooth and polished surfaces. They may be distinguished by these characters: (1) often there are all gradations between the color of the latest scar and that of the original surface, for the spalls come off at different times, and with age the scars fade and so grow more and more like the old surface; (2) search may reveal some chips that have nearly come off and others which have separated so recently that they still lie loose on their own scars; (3) if it is possible to break the rock at the edge of a scar, the fresh fracture will be of uniform color both under the scar and under the old surrounding surface. Familiarity with rocks and minerals under various conditions of weathering is the best guide.

Field Interpretation and Classification of Eruptive Bodies

162. Shape of eruptive bodies. Both extrusive and intrusive modes of occurrence may be discussed in this connection. Volcanic ash cones owe their slopes to the angle of repose of the pyroclastic débris of which they are composed (**267**). It may reach 40°. The form of a mass of lava depends in part upon the topography and in part upon the viscosity of the molten rock. Mobile flows spread far and are relatively thin as contrasted with those which are viscous. A cone built of lava poured from a central vent may have an inclination of less than 10°. From this extreme there are all gradations to the type of ejection known as a "spine," a column of lava so rigid that it does not flow at all.

As regards intrusive bodies, their shapes are governed: (1) by the viscosity of the magma, (2) by the structure of the country rock, (3) by the weight of the overburden, and (4) by the manner of intrusion. Thinness, coupled with relatively great extent in other two dimensions (*e.g.*, many dikes, sills, etc.), implies rapid injection and a highly mobile magma, especially if the country rock appears to have been cool (**138, 139**) when it was invaded. A sticky magma would move sluggishly, and slow intrusion would soon be brought to a stop by chilling. Where the country rock was nearly as warm as the magma, thin sheets do not necessarily prove rapid injection. That the country rock was warm and plastic enough to be deformed by the force of intrusion is suggested by the pinch-and-swell form of many pegmatite dikes in schists (Fig. 117),[15] by the local bending of the schist folia against such pegmatite dikes (Fig. 118), and by other phenomena.

The effect of greater viscosity on concordant injection is exemplified in the typical laccolith (Fig. 88), the domical roof of

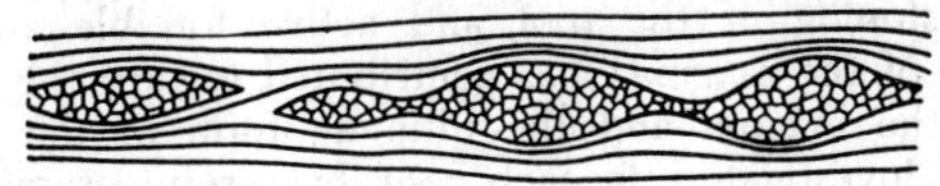

FIG. 117. Pinch-and-swell form of a pegmatite dike in schist.

which indicates that the magma, being too sticky to slip in rapidly and far between the beds, heaved them up and arched them by the force of its hydrostatic pressure. Many observed laccoliths are not quite typical, for minor irregularities in the roof and the presence of some inclusions in the igneous rock prove that the act of intrusion was not wholly a process of lifting and wedging, but was assisted by the disruption of blocks from the walls of the chamber. In batholiths this disruptive process (overhead stoping) seems to have predominated as is indicated by the marked irregularity of the contact as a whole, frequently by the abundance of xenoliths, and by the usual total lack of correspondence between the attitude of the contact and the attitude of bedding in the roof rock. However, although the shape of the contacts of a batholith must unquestionably be ascribed in part to the separation of inclusions, this does not preclude the possibility that the roof was uplifted. With wider and more intensive study of these large intrusive masses, evidence is increasing to the effect that upward pressure and upward expansion of the core of magma played a significant role in their emplacement. Such evidence includes doming and

FIG. 118. Section of a pegmatite dike cutting the foliation of a schistose rock.

[15] This structure may be explained as the result of severing of a once continuous layer (see p. 293).

arching of flow structure in the intrusive body; systems of tension fractures so disposed that they indicate upward movement of the magma after the outer shell has already consolidated; zones of marginal upthrusts, in steep-walled intrusives, showing the effects of upward and outward expansion of the liquid core; gneissic marginal shells, due to intense mechanical forces of intrusion, etc.[16] The degree to which each of these processes (passive stoping of the roof and active forcible ascent and expansion of the magma) has contributed toward the emplacement of the magma and the ultimate form of the batholith should be investigated, in each case, by careful examination of all available field criteria.

163. General summary with reference to the interpretation of contact phenomena. For ease of reference we may classify here the principal facts presented in the foregoing paragraphs. *Place of intrusion* within the lithosphere, *i.e.*, whether in the zone of fracture or in the zone of flowage, is indicated by shape of contact, sharpness of contact, marginal textures, tension jointing, and shape of the intrusive body. *Manner of eruption* is indicated by shape and sharpness of contacts, presence of inclusions, characters of inclusions, attitude of flow structure, and shape of the eruptive body. Evidences for *kind and amount of assimilation* may be found in shape and sharpness of contacts, marginal variations in the composition of the intrusive rock, shape of intrusive body, and characters of inclusions. Evidences for *differentiation* appear in schliers, segregations, and cognate inclusions, and in marginal variations in composition of the intrusive body. *Rate of injection, rate of flow,* and *viscosity of magma and lava* are indicated by the shape of the eruptive masses. *Conditions of the country rock at the time of intrusion* are suggested by shape and sharpness of contacts, marginal textures of the intrusive, characters of inclusions, kind and degree of contact metamorphism, and shape of the intrusive body.

164. Field recognition of eruptive bodies. The recognition of modes of occurrence of igneous rocks in the field depends upon a thorough understanding of the definitions given in Art. **134.** It is well also to have a notion of the sizes which are characteristic of eruptive bodies (**135**). Bear in mind that sills are essentially parallel to the bedding of their country rocks; that

[16] See Bibliog., Balk, Robert, 1937, pp. 122–129.

chonoliths, laccoliths, and lopoliths, as distinguished from batholiths, have basal contacts; and that the difference between a sill and a laccolith is principally one of the relations between thickness and lateral extent. There can be no such thing as a sill in a country rock which is not stratiform. For chonoliths, laccoliths, lopoliths, and batholiths, extensive field correlation is necessary because of the great size of these bodies.

Probably the most troublesome problem is the distinction between a sill and a flow which has been buried under later strata, now consolidated. (1) A flow is often vesicular or scoriaceous in its upper portion and may have pores and brecciated structure near its base. On the contrary, a sill is usually free from visible pores; but there are sometimes numerous short apophyses extending into the superjacent strata, and these, when viewed in cross section, may make the upper surface of the sill look as if it were a scoriaceous lava. If longer apophyses can be found, they are among the safest criteria for intrusion. (2) The cavities and depressions of a buried lava flow are generally filled with sediments that have their bedding lamination parallel to the main stratification above. If a sill has many short roof apophyses, the intervening downward projections of the country rock are apt to show more or less contortion. (3) A flow may rest upon beds of volcanic ash or other volcanic débris; yet it is not to be forgotten that sills, too, may be injected into pyroclastic materials. (4) Flows are not uncommonly overlain by sediments that contain angular blocks or water-worn pebbles of the lava. Eroded fragments of a sill cannot be present in the superjacent beds which were invaded by the sill. These overlying beds may seem to contain pieces of the sill rock if the magma was injected upward as a network of ramifying pipes (Fig. 119). Careful study of this case would show that the seeming fragments of sill rock have chilled margins and that the inclosing rock has a metamorphic aureole round each "fragment." (5) Inclusions of the superjacent beds may be found in sills, but never in flows. (6) The effects of contact metamorphism may be present in the roof strata of a sill, but not in the beds above a flow, provided there is no other outside influence by which such alteration might have been induced.

165. Field study of structures of igneous rocks. The two most significant kinds of structure in igneous rocks are flow structure (**131**) and fracture structure (**234**). Flow structure antedates fracture structure in time of origin, since the former develops while the rock is molten and the latter, after it has become hard enough to break or shear. For this reason it is best to begin the study of an igneous body by examining and mapping any flow structure that may be discovered in it; then the fracture systems should be mapped; and these should be studied and described in relation to the observed flow structure. Both features are usually best developed near the contacts. Both should be carefully examined on several surfaces of the rock as nearly as possible at right angles to one another. In recording notes and in mapping, discrimination should be made between

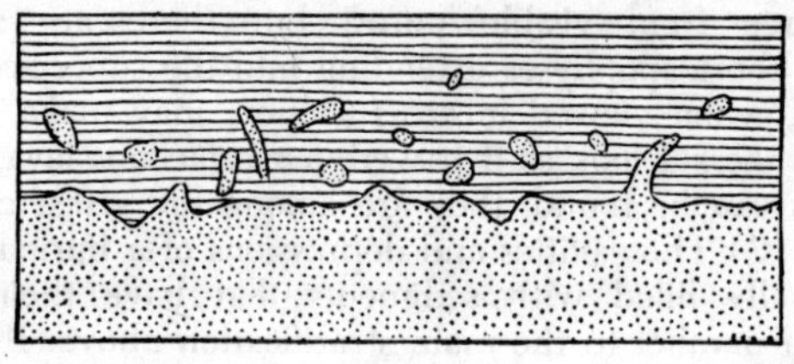

FIG. 119. Section of the upper contact between a sill (stippled) and its country rock of slate (lined), showing short roof apophyses which are pipelike in form. The roundish patches of the sill rock in the slate are sections of these "pipes." Section about 3 ft. long.

linear and platy flow structure; also between the different classes of fractures (234). Detailed investigation of these phenomena in the field is important because they are of great assistance in ascertaining the history and mode of occurrence of the igneous rock bodies with which they are associated.

ERUPTIVE BODIES IN RELATION TO THEIR TIME OF ORIGIN

166. Relative age. The age of an igneous rock is dated from the time when it was intruded, or extruded, and was brought into fixed relations with the adjacent older rocks. Thus, every intrusive body is younger than its country rock and every lava flow is younger than the underlying rocks and, if buried, older than the superjacent materials. In field work an important duty of the geologist is to determine the relative ages of the igneous rocks. This may be done in several ways. If, for instance, there are two kinds of dikes, outcrops should be searched until a place is found where one of these dikes cuts across the other (Fig. 120, A). Sometimes two or three periods of injection by the same type of rock may be demonstrated. Branching dikes must not be confused with intersecting dikes (Fig. 120, B). Where but one contact between two igneous rocks is exposed, the younger rock is apt to be progressively finer toward the contact (**141**). Even if the boundary line is concealed, the relations may occasionally be ascertained by discovering inclusions of one rock in the other, for inclusions are always older than the inclosing matrix.

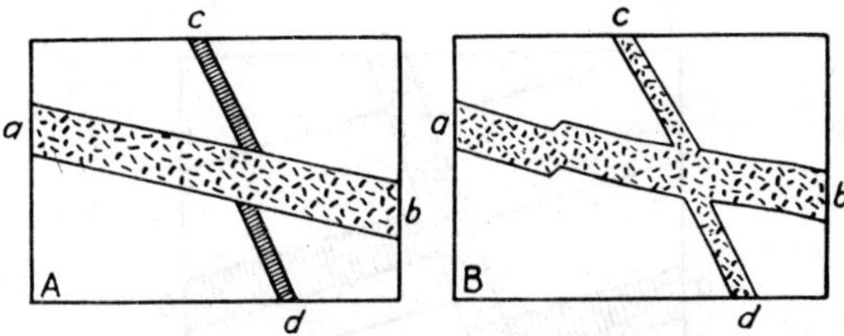

FIG. 120. A, intersecting dikes, *ab* being younger than *cd*. B, branching dikes, *ab* and *cd* being of the same age. How is the apparent displacement in A to be explained?

As regards batholiths and other large intrusive masses, there is probably a long time interval between the consolidation of the outer portions and the freezing of the final residuum. Consequently, in point of crystallization, not only are cognate xenoliths distinctly older than the surrounding rock, but also certain cognate inclusions may be older or younger than others in the same body. Within a given intrusive mass cognate inclusions are younger than foreign inclusions.

The age of an igneous body with reference to joints, faults, folds, and other structures, should likewise be noted. Straight and blocky contacts, particularly if they correspond to existing joints in the country rock, imply a fracture system antedating intrusion. Tension joints, due to contact effects (**234**), are clearly subsequent to the eruptive body that led to their origin.

A fault which intersects and displaces an igneous mass is younger than the latter (Fig. 121). A fault that is essentially coincident with a contact may be older or younger than the intrusive. Thus, a region may be dislocated and then invaded by magma along the faults (Fig. 121); or slipping may take place along the contact surface of an eruptive body. In the former case the contact and the fault would be one and the same surface, except perhaps where apophyses had branched into the fault blocks; whereas, if dislocation followed intrusion, places could surely be found where the fault and the contact were not coincident, and any apophyses would be intersected by the fault. On the earth's surface, lava flows and ash cones are sometimes aligned in such a way as to suggest that the magma ascended along a fault. The case may be proved by finding

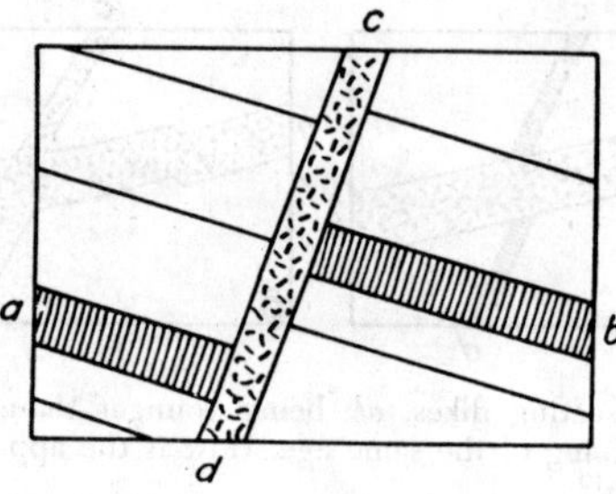

Fig. 121. Section of a dike, *cd*, which has entered a fault. The fault intersects a series of strata containing a sill, *ab*.

topographic evidences of displacement along the general trend of the volcanic vents (Chap. 8).

There are many reasons for believing that intrusion of large magmatic bodies and deformation of their country rocks are more or less synchronous. By definition, the updoming of the roof of a laccolith is accomplished by the invading magma. Batholithic intrusion seems often to have closely followed, or even accompanied, large scale deformation. These phenomena are regarded as parallel effects of the same cause.

167. Geologic age. Since igneous rocks do not hold fossils their geologic ages must be fixed by correlating them with sedimentary rocks whose age is known. Flows and pyroclastics are of the same geologic age as the sedimentary rocks with which they are interstratified. For intrusives, the following example may suffice to illustrate the method of correlation. In Fig. 122, *b* is intrusive into *a* and pebbles of *a* and *b* are found in *c*. Fossils show that *a* is Cambro-Ordovician and *c* is Devonian. Hence the age of *b* is between Ordovician and Devonian.

Eruptive Bodies in Relation to the Land Surface

168. Significance of the exposure of intrusive rocks. The presence of intrusive rocks upon the earth's surface is evidence of the work accomplished by erosion. Sometimes a thick covering has been removed and sometimes a thin one, for magma, in its eruption, reaches various levels within the lithosphere. Most striking is the case of batholiths. In these bodies the magma

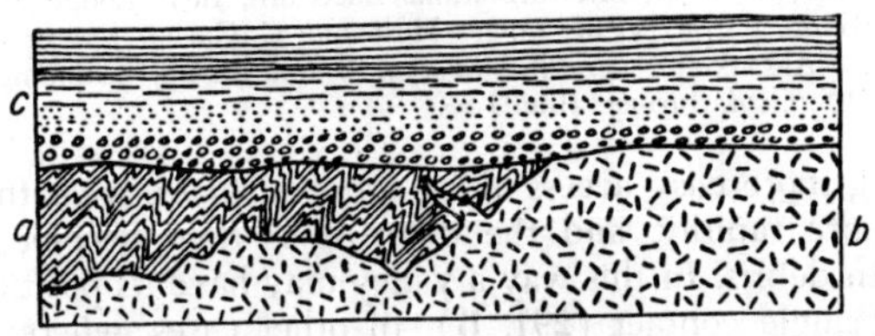

Fig. 122. Section of part of a batholith, *b*, and its country rock, *a*, both of which were eroded and overlain by later strata, *c*.

probably does not rise to within several hundred or even several thousand feet of the surface except, perhaps, in rare instances (**134**), so that where subjacent masses are exposed, a thick cover of country rock has, little by little, been worn away and the débris has been laid down elsewhere in some area of deposition.

169. Topographic expression of igneous bodies. Exposed intrusive bodies are so often more resistant than the inclosing country rocks that usually they have a more pronounced relief. The higher central parts of many mountain ranges consist of batholithic rocks. Unroofed laccoliths may form groups of hills that rise above the surrounding country (Fig. 123). The smaller injected bodies, such as necks, dikes, and sills, are generally more resistant or less resistant than the country rock, and, correspondingly, they may have positive or negative topographic relief (**265**) (Fig. 124). Horizontal or gently inclined sills and flows are sometimes the protective layers surmounting mesas and cuestas (**300**).

170. Relations of contacts to erosion.[17] The student who has arrived at the stage at which he undertakes his own geologic surveying will be disappointed to find how often important contacts—usually those he most wishes to map—are quite hidden beneath the soil. The reason is obvious. The agents of erosion,

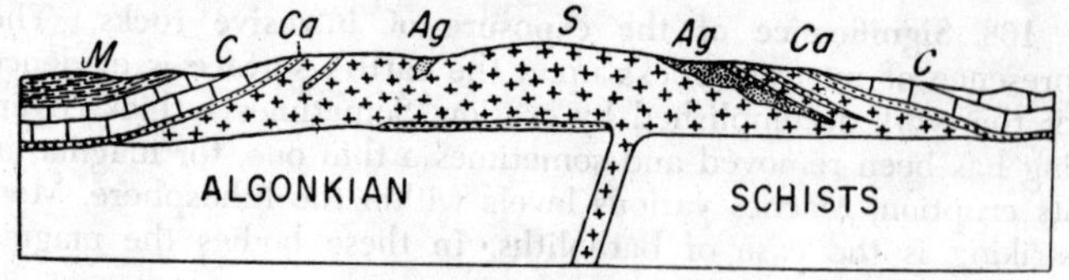

Fig. 123. Section of an interformational laccolith, Bear Lodge Mountains, Wyo. S, syenite porphyry; *M*, Lower Mesozoic; *C*, Carboniferous; *Ca*, Cambrian; *Ag*, "Algonkian?" granite. Section 6 miles long. (*Sundance Folio, No.* 127, *U.S. Geol. Survey*, 1905.)

obtaining more easy access along these surfaces, wear the rocks down more rapidly, and the depressions then become floored over with débris. In this way a valley may have its position fixed along a single contact (**291, B**). In other cases, where a weak rock lies between resistant materials, the former may be worn away, and the valley (or gully) will have its walls situated somewhere near the contacts (Fig. 124, A).

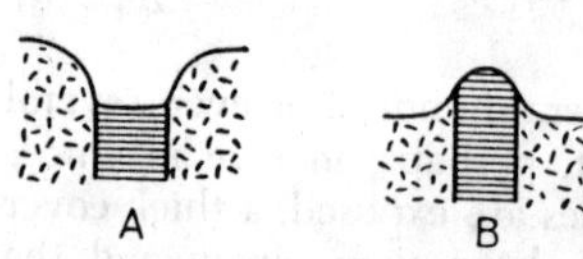

Fig. 124. Topographic relations of a dike and its country rock, as seen in vertical section. A, dike less resistant than country rock. B, dike more resistant than country rock.

If the rock on one side of a contact is much less resistant to erosion than that on the other side, the weaker rock, whether intrusive or country rock, may be worn away to such an extent that the outcrop surface practically coincides with the contact. At a certain stage in the erosion, when this coincidence has been all but accomplished, the more resistant rock will be exposed only in small areas where a thin remaining cover of the weaker material has been perforated (Fig. 125, A). A little later the weak rock will be removed except for a few scattered patches (Figs. 125, B; 126). The perforated spots in the earlier stage

[17] See also Art. 347.

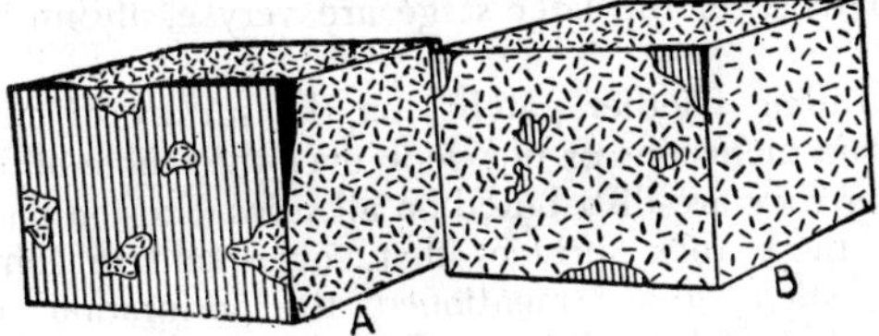

FIG. 125. The diagram shows an uneven contact between an igneous rock (dash pattern) and its country rock (lined on front face; black on top and side faces). The front face of each block is assumed to be a surface produced by erosion. In A the remaining layer of the country rock has been perforated, and in B, a somewhat later stage, only a few patches of the country rock are left.

FIG. 126. Patches of a trap dike (dark gray) still attached to its country rock. Here the dike was the weaker rock. (Cf. Fig. 125.) The largest patch is about 15 in. long.

and the patches in the later stage are very easily mistaken for inclusions.

To determine whether patches on the surface of an igneous rock are true inclusions or not, look over the whole outcrop and see whether they are distributed on all sides. Erosion patches are limited to those rock surfaces that correspond to contacts. In the earlier stage, above mentioned, the perforation spots can often be enlarged by splitting off some of the layer of weaker rock, and in the later stage the patches themselves can be broken off with a hammer. This weaker rock may be found in place in greater amount just beneath the soil at the foot of the outcrop or along the strike of the contact surface on other ledges in the vicinity.

On a much larger scale, the exposure of intrusive bodies presents some interesting problems. Consider, for instance, a batholith with an irregular roof. At first all the bedrock in the region is the normal country rock (Fig. 127, A). As denudation proceeds, the land surface at length reaches what we may call stage 2. In this stage, although the bedrock is still entirely the roof rock of the batholith, there are a few closed areas in which evidences of contact metamorphism may be recognized. These are the places where cupolas will soon be uncovered (Fig. 127, B). In the third stage several cupolas (stocks) are exposed, each being rimmed by a collar of the metamorphosed country rock (Fig. 127, C, *a*). There may be closed tracts of metamorphosed country rock which cap the shorter cupolas. The outcrop areas of the cupolas grow larger and coalesce, as erosion goes on, so that, in the fourth stage, the bedrock of the region consists principally of the intrusive, with here and there isolated tracts of country rock which are, in reality, truncated roof pendants (Fig. 127, D). In the fifth and last stage the land surface is entirely on the batholithic igneous rock (Fig. 127, E).

Possibly there are some regions where the roof contact of a batholith or of a flat-lying intrusive mass (sill, laccolith, etc.) has become the land surface over several square miles. The weaker superjacent country rock has been stripped off except for a few scattered remnants, and the resistant eruptive rock has been only locally incised by streams (Fig. 128). The evidences for this broad scale coincidence of erosion surface and contact include: (1) extensive distribution of like contact phenomena on the outcrops of the eruptive; (2) marked decrease in the

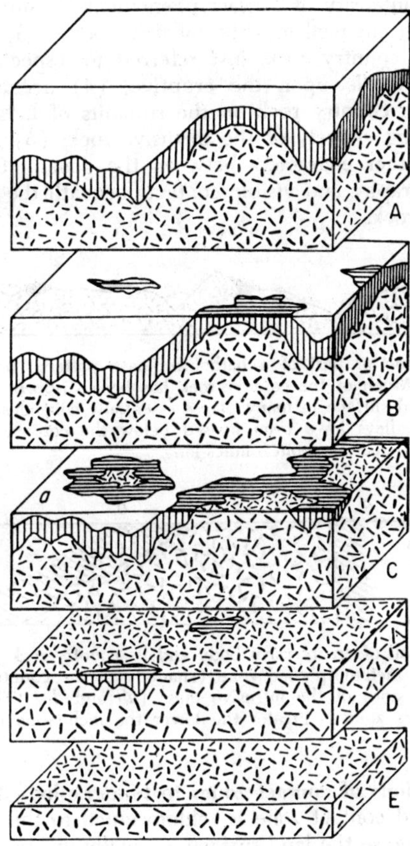

FIG. 127. Successive stages in the exposure of a batholith through erosion. Batholith, dash pattern; country rock, blank where unmetamorphosed, ruled where metamorphosed. *a* is a stock (cupola) surrounded by the metamorphosed country rock.

variety and intensity of contact phenomena downward in those valleys which cut well into the intrusive body; (3) the isolated remnants of country rock, just referred to, especially if these are clearly sessile upon the eruptive; (4) accumulations of débris of the country rock on the summits of hills and ridges now consisting entirely of the intrusive rock; (5) similarity in shape and other characters between the general configuration of the topography and visible contacts beneath the remnants of the country rock.

FIG. 128. Section of part of a batholith (dash pattern) and its country rock (black). Much of the country rock has been stripped off by erosion, so that the land surface in many places essentially coincides with the roof contact. The valleys have been incised below the contact well into the batholithic mass. Section about 8 miles long.

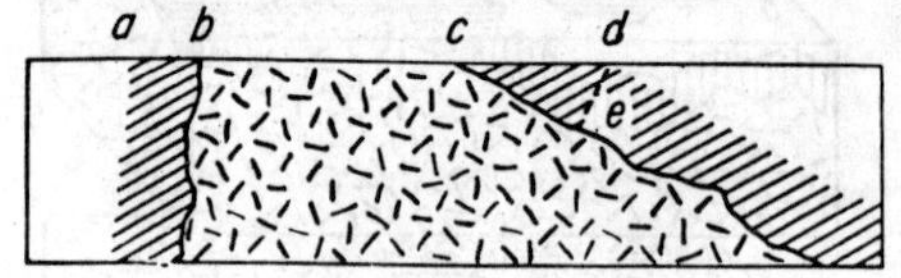

FIG. 129. Section of an intrusive body and its country rock. The thickness of the contact metamorphosed zone (shaded) of the country rock is the same on both sides of the intrusive mass (*ab* and *de*). The breadth of exposure of this zone is greater the lower the inclination of the contact (*ab* and *cd*).

171. Relations of contact zones to topography. The breadth of an exposed contact zone is seldom equal to the thickness of the zone, because the land surface is usually inclined to contacts at an angle less than 90° (Fig. 129). Instances of this kind should not be confused with cases like that illustrated in Fig. 106. Figure 130 shows two explanations for an observed increase in the degree of contact metamorphism without apparent cause.

172. Effects of topography on the shapes of outcropping dikes, sills, and contacts. The influence of topography upon the form of outcrop surfaces and layers is most conveniently treated with reference to stratified rocks. Consequently the subject is reserved for Art. **193**. The student has only to remember that, when dikes and sills are of comparatively uniform thickness,

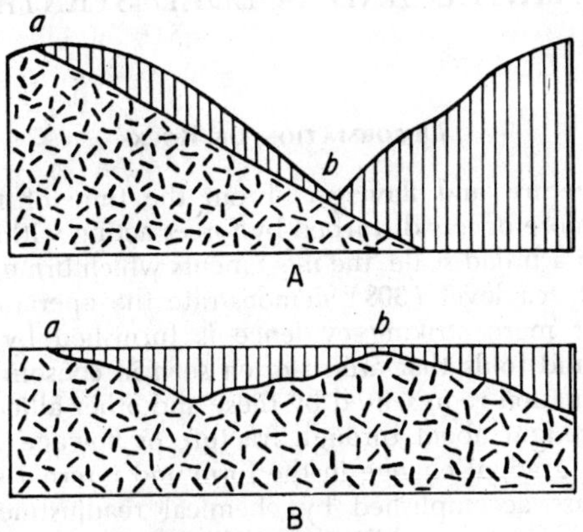

Fig. 130. Vertical sections showing relations of the land surface to the degree of contact metamorphism. Intrusive rock, dash pattern; country rock, ruled. In each case, A and B, the degree of contact metamorphism grows less in going from *a* toward *b*, and then increases again, reaching a maximum at *b*. The explanation is obvious.

their exposed edges are related to the land surface in exactly the same manner as are the exposed edges of strata, and that the same comparison may be made concerning regular igneous contacts and surfaces of conformity in sediments.

Chapter 7

TILTED AND FOLDED STRATA

Deformation of Rocks

173. Fracture and flowage. From the time of their origin rocks are more or less disturbed by forces acting within the lithosphere. On a broad scale, the movements which bring about slow changes of sea level (**308**) demonstrate the operation of these forces; but more striking evidence is furnished by the joints, cleavage, and folds that are so often seen in consolidated rocks. The deformation represented by these and other allied structures may be brought about through fracture or flowage. By flowage is meant a gradual change in the form and internal structure of a rock mass accomplished by chemical readjustment and by microscopic fracture while the rock remains essentially rigid. There is no igneous fusion during the process. The rock does not become molten. Under very great pressure and temperature, such as exist deep below the earth's surface, all rocks yield to stress by flowage rather than by fracture. High temperature and pressure, the presence of moisture, and the nature of the rock itself, are factors influencing this flowage. Nearer the surface rocks are more apt to break; but some rocks may flow even at depths of only a few hundred feet. For any rock subjected to differential pressure we have, then, a *zone of flowage* below and an enveloping shell or *zone of fracture* above. The maximum depth of the zone of fracture for rocks least capable of flowage is placed at about 11 miles.[1] Below that depth all rocks flow if deformed. However, when we speak in terms of all rocks, the outer 11-mile shell of the lithosphere becomes almost entirely a *zone of combined flowage and fracture,* because different rocks vary so much in their susceptibility to flowage when under stress.

Structures produced in the zone of fracture are joints, faults, brecciation, autoclastic structures, fracture cleavage, etc. (Chap.

[1] Bibliog., Adams, F. D., 1912.

8). In the zone of flowage originate flow cleavage, schistosity, gneissic structure, etc. (Chap. 9). Folds (flexures) may result from either fracture or flowage, and very often they are the product of both processes combined. They are not to be thought of as having been bent in the usual meaning of this word.[2]

Terminology and Classification

174. Principal kinds of folds or flexures. As seen in cross section, the principal forms of tilted and folded strata are as follows:

A *syncline* is a downfold opening upward (Fig. 131, A, D).

An *anticline* is an upfold opening downward (Fig. 131, B, E).

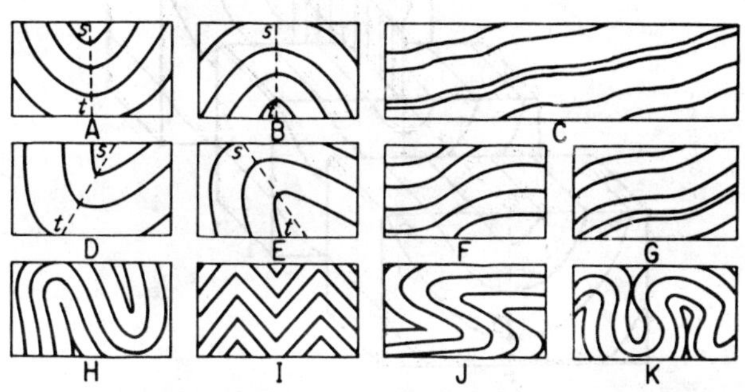

Fig. 131. Cross sections of types of folds. A, symmetrical syncline; B, symmetrical anticline; C, homocline; D, asymmetrical syncline; E, asymmetrical anticline; F, monocline; G. structural terrace; H, isoclinal anticline and syncline; I, chevron folds; J, recumbent folds; K, fan folds. In A, B, D, and E, *st* is the position of the axial surface.

A *homocline* is a group of strata which have a fairly regular amount of dip in the same general direction (Fig. 131, C).

A *monocline* is a steplike bend in otherwise horizontal or gently dipping beds. It consists of a change in the *amount* of dip from gentle to relatively steeper and back again to gentle (Fig. 131, F), but the direction of dip remains essentially unchanged.

A *structural terrace* is a steplike or shelflike flattening of the dip in more steeply inclined strata (Fig. 131, G). In a certain sense it is the reverse of a monocline.

[2] See Bibliog., Kelley, Vincent C., 1955.

The term *monoclinal dip* (also called homocline) refers merely to a dip in the same general direction. A homocline may be diversified by several monoclines and structural terraces.

175. Terms of general application. Folds are bodies of three dimensions, that is, they have height, breadth, and length, a fact which is too easily forgotten because they are usually represented in plane cross sections. Figures 132 and 133 show the directions of the three dimensions of the folds of which only the height and

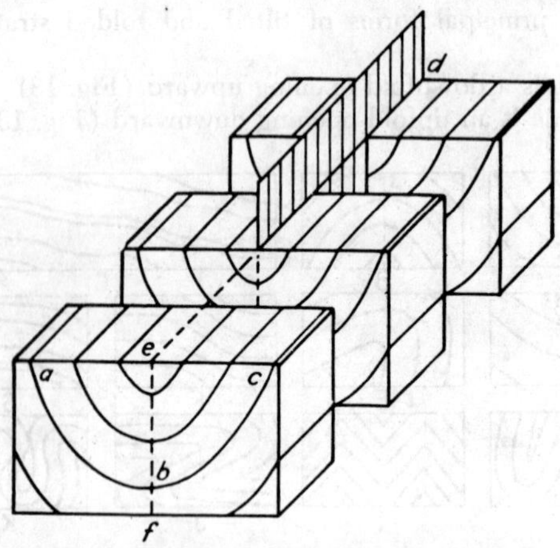

Fig. 132. Symmetrical syncline shown in three blocks. *ab* and *cb*, limbs; *de*, axis; *def*, axial surface. Note broadening of syncline with depth.

breadth are indicated in A and B, Fig. 131. In each of these diagrams (132 and 133), the fold is symmetrically divided into two essentially equal parts by a vertical surface (*def*), called the *axial surface*.[3] The line where this surface intersects any particular bed or horizon in the folded group of strata is called the *axis* of the fold in that bed or horizon (*e.g., ed*). The two parts of the fold, one on each side of the axial surface, are its *flanks* or *limbs* (*ab* and *cd*, Figs. 132, 133).

In Figs. 131, A and B, 132, and 133, the anticline and syncline are drawn with their axial surfaces vertical. If the axial surface

[3] Often called *axial plane,* though probably never a *plane,* since this surface is warped through the irregularities of folding.

of a fold is inclined, as in Fig. 131, D, E, the beds in the two limbs may have very dissimilar dips. It has been customary to describe the former type of fold as *symmetrical* and the latter as *asymmetrical,* referring to the mutual relations of the dips in the two limbs rather than to the geometrical relations of the limbs to the axial surface.[4]

In an asymmetrical fold, the axis does not coincide with the highest part, or crest, of an anticline, nor with the lowest part,

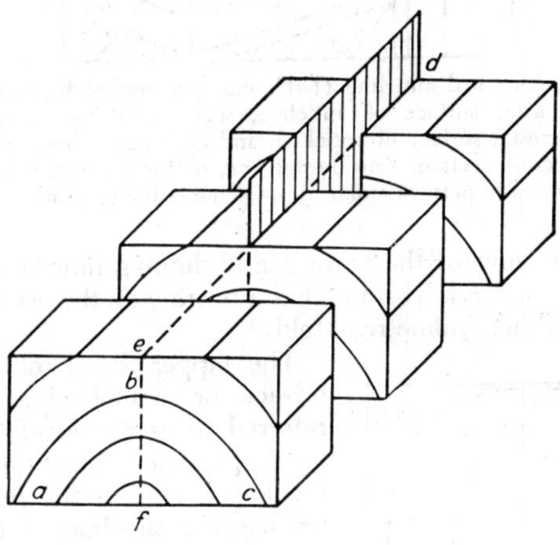

FIG. 133. Symmetrical anticline shown in three blocks. *ab* and *bc,* limbs; *de,* axis; *def,* axial surface. Note narrowing of anticline with depth, a feature of considerable importance in petroleum geology.

or trough, of a syncline (Fig. 134). This is a very important point to remember. In such folds, the line where any given bedding surface meets a horizontal plane may be called the *crest line,* in an anticline, or the *trough line,* in a syncline. The surface that includes the crest lines in successively deeper beds in an anticline

[4] There is a decided practical advantage in the first definition of symmetry, herein used and commonly understood, because, for the second definition, the whole underground form of the fold must be known, and this is rarely possible. Furthermore, if the whole form *is* known, terms other than symmetry and asymmetry may be applied to better advantage. Symmetry refers to the *dips* of the beds, and *dips* are measured from the horizontal.

is the *crestal surface* of that fold; and the corresponding surface in a syncline may be termed a *trough surface* (Figs. 134, 135).

Note that the axis of an asymmetrical fold migrates, in successively lower beds, toward the more steeply dipping limb in

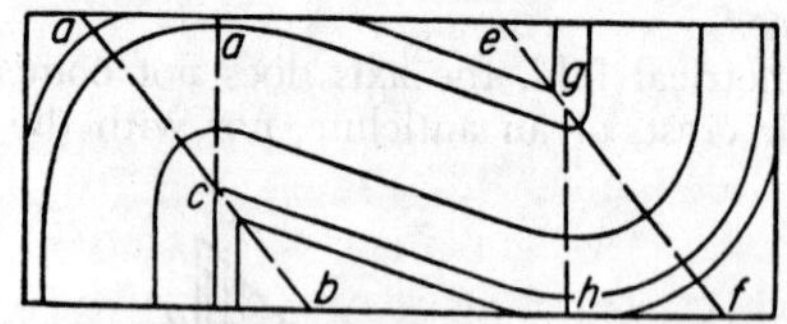

FIG. 134. Asymmetrical anticline (left) and syncline (right), seen in cross section; *acb*, axial surface of anticline, seen in section; *egf*, same for syncline; *dc*, crestal surface of anticline; and *gh*, trough surface of syncline, both seen in cross section. Any crestal *line*, or trough *line*, would be perpendicular, or nearly perpendicular to the plane of the diagram.

synclines and toward the more gently dipping limb in anticlines (Fig. 131, D and E). This fact has a bearing on the accumulation of oil and gas in asymmetrical folds.[5]

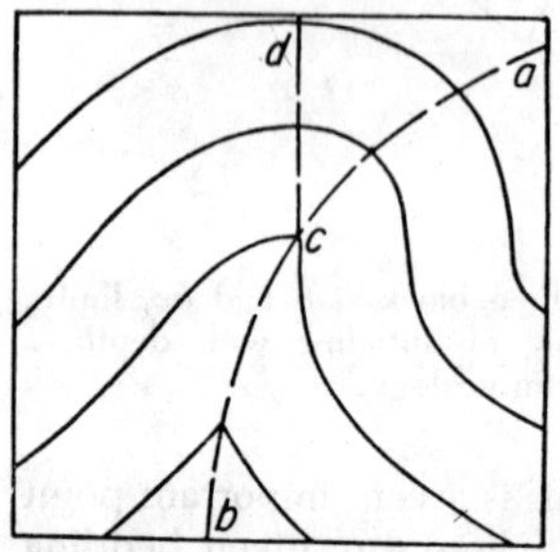

FIG. 135. Cross section of an anticline with a warped axial surface (*acb*); *dc* is the cross section of the crestal surface.

The upper bend of either a terrace or a monocline may be referred to as the *head*, or *upper break*, or *upper change of dip*, and the lower bend is the *foot* of the terrace or monocline, or the *lower break*, or the *lower change of dip*.

176. Varities of folds. Anticlines and synclines may be simple, composite, or complex. A fold is *simple* when its curve is simple; *composite* when it consists of smaller anticlines and synclines; and *complex* when its axis is folded, *i.e.*, when the fold is cross-folded. Simple folds are drawn in Fig. 131.

A composite anticline is called an *anticlinorium* and a composite syncline, a *synclinorium* (plurals, anticlinoria, synclinoria) (Fig. 138). Whenever a set of small folds is superposed upon a

[5] Bibliog., Hewett, D. F., and C. T. Lupton, 1917, p. 34.

group of larger folds, the former are called *minor* and the latter *major*. All major folds are composite. If the axial planes of the minor folds converge downward in an anticlinorium or upward in a synclinorium, the major fold is called *normal* (Fig. 136, A and B); if the opposite is true, the anticlinorium and the synclinorium are *abnormal* (Fig. 136, C and D).[6]

In many regions of the earth extensive areas have become the sites of accumulation of thick bodies of stratified rock materials (both sedimentary and volcanic) which were deposited, layer on layer, through long periods of time, with almost *pari passu* settling of the floor of deposition as the thickness, and therefore

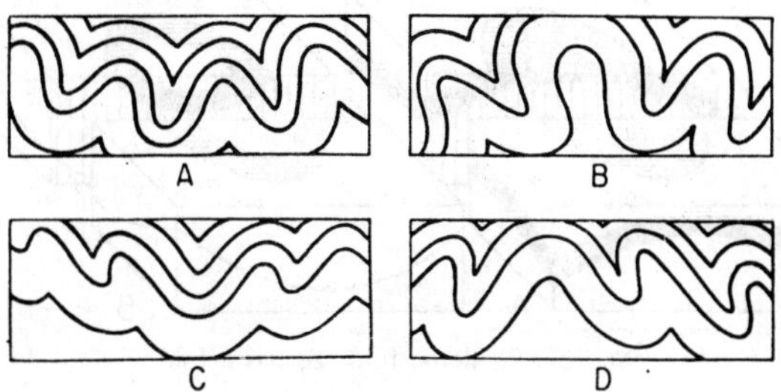

Fig. 136. Synclinoria (A and C) and anticlinoria (B and D).

the load, of the rock prism increased. The down-warped surface, basin-like or trough-like in its larger aspects, is called a *geosyncline*. As stated by Kay, "a geosyncline is a surface of regional extent subsiding deeply during accumulation of succeeding surficial rocks."[7] The term therefore not only specifies the downwarped floor, but also connotes the thick filling of surficial stratified rocks. The area of a geosyncline may be in thousands of square miles, and the thickness of the sedimentary prism within it may be in tens of thousands of feet. The geosyncline and its contained stratified rocks, after a long period of accumulation and concomitant subsidence, may eventually be compressed into a great folded massif. In this way the folds of the Appalachian Mountains resulted through lateral compression of

[6] Bibliog., Van Hise, C. R., 1896, pp. 608–612.
[7] See Bibliog., Kay, Marshall, 1951, p. 107.

the moderately warped sediments of the Appalachian geosyncline.

A *geanticline* is a great up-arched, or uplifted, massif, often associated with an adjoining geosyncline, and then serving as the source of eroded detritus carried into the geosynclinal area. Examples of geosynclines are the Michigan Basin, the Anadarko Basin of Oklahoma, the Appalachian geosyncline, and the geosyncline which parallels the Gulf of Mexico coast of Texas and Louisiana. Examples of geanticlines are the Nemaha uplift of Kansas, the Central Mineral Region of Texas, and the Sabine uplift of northen Louisiana.[8]

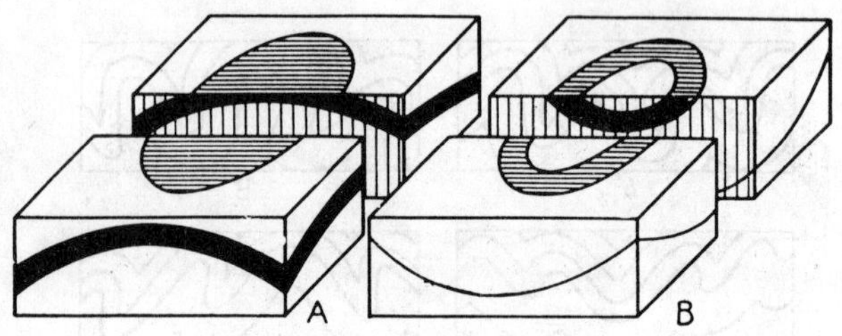

FIG. 137. A, dome fold; B, basin fold.

Where stratified rocks have an average inclination in some general direction over a wide extent of territory, this inclination is called a *regional dip*. It differs from a homocline in that it may be variously modified by changes in the amount and direction of dip, and even in *reversals* of dip, as long as the average is maintained. These reversals and less conspicuous variations are referred to as *local dips*. They are also called *abnormal* to distinguish them from the regional or *normal* dip. A regional dip is generally the limb of a geosyncline or of a geanticline.

Types of complex folds are the *dome fold* or *dome*, and the *basin fold* or *structural basin*.[9] A dome is anticlinal in two vertical sections at right angles to one another, and a basin fold is similarly synclinal (Figs. 137, 525). If the folding is much closer, *i.e.*, if the compression has been much more intense in one direction than at right angles to this direction, the folds are much longer

[8] For a full and excellent discussion of geosynclines and geanticlines, see Bibliog., Krumbein, W. C., and L. L. Sloss, 1958, pp. 320–349.

[9] See Art. 284 for the *topographic* basin.

in comparison with their width. The elongated basin fold may then be called a *canoe fold*, and the dome may be called an *inverted canoe fold*, or a *ridge fold* (Fig. 138). Domes and inverted canoe folds are referred to as *anticlinal closures*, and structural basins and canoe folds, as *synclinal closures*, on account of the fact that, when they are represented by structure contours (**497**), these contours are closed (Fig. 525).

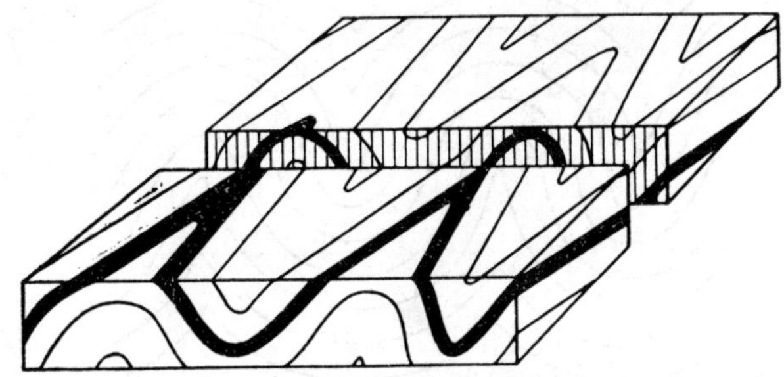

FIG. 138. Anticlinal and synclinal canoe folds, represented in part. The axes of the folds are inclined downward (plunge) toward the background.

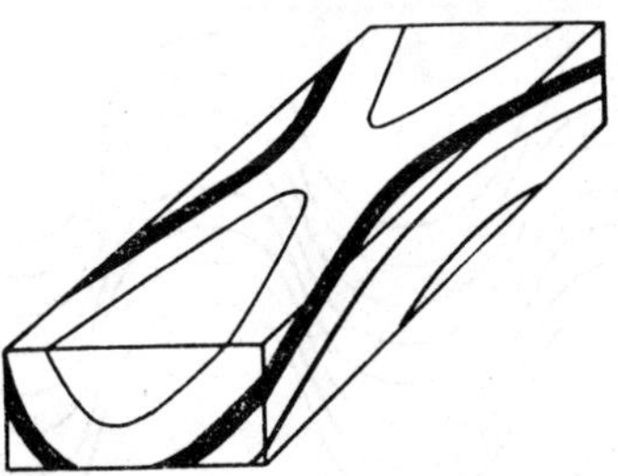

FIG. 139. A complex fold which is synclinal in one section and anticlinal in the perpendicular section.

Sometimes a fold which is anticlinal in one section may be synclinal in the perpendicular section (Fig. 139). Such a fold is termed a *saddle*. It may be an upfold along the axis of a syncline, or a downfold along the axis of an anticline.

A local anticlinal warping on the limb of a major fold or on any monoclinal dip is an *anticlinal bowing*, or *nose*, in reference to the fact that contours showing this type of structure bend or bow out toward the direction of the dip (Fig. 525). The corresponding synclinal structure, in which the contours bend in the up-dip direction, is a *synclinal bowing* (Fig. 525). Anticlinal and synclinal bowings pitch or plunge in the direction of the general dip.

Folding may be parallel or similar. In *parallel folds* (also called *concentric folds*) each bed is of approximately uniform

Fig. 140. Parallel folding.

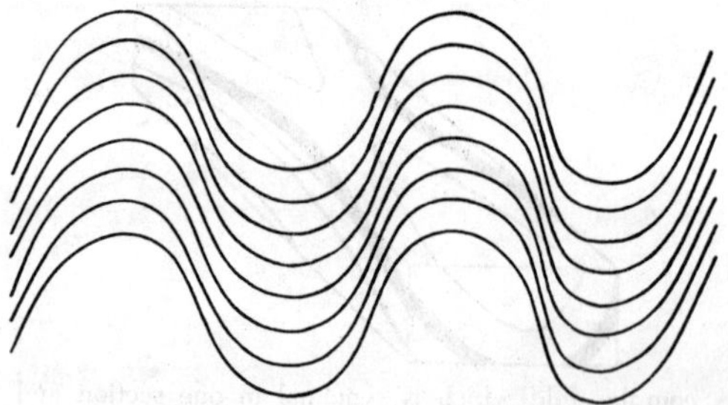

Fig. 141. Similar folding.

thickness throughout its course in both anticlines and synclines (Fig. 140). The effect of this relation is that the bedding surfaces are not of the same shape. Both upward and downward folds die out.[10] On the other hand, in *similar folds* the bedding surfaces are of similar shape and the beds vary in thickness (Fig. 141).

[10] The student is here reminded of another way in which an anticlinal fold may die out with depth. See Art. **504**, where the effects of convergence are described.

Their limbs are thinned and their axial regions are thickened. Such folds may be persistent upward and downward through a thickness of rock which is very great as compared with the amplitude of the contortions of any one bed.

Deformation in parallel folding is accomplished by adjustment between the beds, and in similar folding, by adjustment within the beds. In both cases the movement is differential. In parallel folding this movement is such that a given bed slides upward against the next underlying bed toward anticlinal axes (Fig. 142). Adjustment within beds is effected principally by rock flowage. It requires more energy than the shearing of strata one upon another. Hence we find that similar folds are characteristic of the zone of flowage, whereas parallel folds are characteristic of the zone of fracture (173). Similar folding is common in metamorphic rocks having flow cleavage (Fig. 143). The field classification of folds may be aided by the facts enumerated in Arts. **521** and **522**.

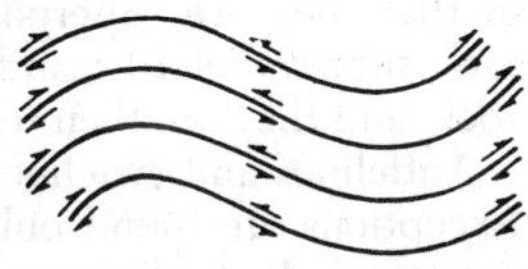

FIG. 142. Diagram illustrating the differential movement between adjacent beds in parallel folding.

FIG. 143. Sketch of contorted laminae in a specimen of mica schist. Length of figure about 1 ft.

A *diapir fold* is an anticline in which mobile material, such as salt, has been forced to break through overlying (younger) relatively brittle strata in the fold.

177. Size of folds. Folds range in breadth from very minute contortions, seen only by the aid of a microscope, to great arches and troughs many miles from axis to axis. Diminutive folds, naturally limited to fine-grained rocks, are always subordinate in that they are superposed upon larger folds. They may form low, subparallel ribs and furrows on the cleavage surface of a rock, and they are then termed *crenulations.*

Anticlines and synclines are usually lower than they are wide. Exceptions are found only where the strata have been intensely deformed. In folds large enough to map, the dips of the limbs vary from only a few feet per mile to 90°. They may be overturned (182, 185).

178. Competent or controlling beds. The unequal susceptibility of different rocks to deformation by flowage seems to indicate that if a sufficient force were applied laterally (parallel to the beds) to a formation consisting of layers of varying resistance, the individual beds would be affected in different ways; and, as a matter of fact, this is actually the case. In a series of this kind a strong stratum, if arched up, may tend to support the overlying beds and thus lessen the vertical pressure on the rocks below it. "Willis' experiments on the mechanics of Appalachian structure[11] showed that the thicker, more competent wax layers rise in simple outline under given conditions of pressure and load until they are unable to lift the load farther. Then they crumple and, in crumpling, thicken, enabling them to lift the load higher. Thus composite folds are really indications of incompetence. Simple folds are more characteristic of the zone of fracture; the bed is able to lift itself without interior adjustment, and without crumpling; it is competent."[12] As Leith and others have pointed out, this term, "competence," is one of relative value only. One rock may be competent with respect to a second and incompetent with respect to a third.

When a series of strata is subjected to lateral pressure, there is at first a tendency for the formation of parallel folds. This, as we have seen, means slipping between the beds. If the strata are of different degrees of resistance and the conditions are such that the stronger layers are in their zone of fracture while the weak beds are in their zone of flowage, the readjustment by slipping may be concentrated in the weaker, incompetent layers.

[11] Bibliog., Willis, B., 1892, pp. 241–253.
[12] Bibliog., Leith, C. K., 1913, pp. 111, 112.

The series will then be folded after the parallel pattern, being controlled as a whole by the competent strata; but the incompetent beds will bear evidence of flowage either in flow cleavage or in minor folds of the similar type. Minor folds of this origin are primarily the result of the differential movement or "drag" between the competent strata, and they have therefore received the name of *drag folds* (**184**). Since, in the differential movement between strata, a given bed slips over the subjacent layer in a direction toward the nearest anticlinal axis, the drag folds are

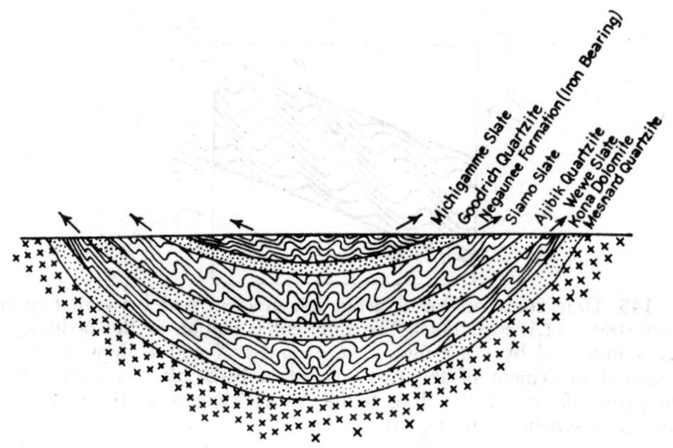

FIG. 144. Diagrammatic section showing differential movement between competent beds on the limbs of a fold with the development of minor drag folds between them. (*After C. K. Leith.*)

overturned in this direction and their axial planes generally converge downward in the major synclines and upward in the major anticlines (Fig. 144). The axial planes of the drag folds are inclined with the direction of differential movement (Fig. 145).

179. Strike, dip, plunge, and pitch. The definitions in Art. **14** hold for folded strata. In Fig. 146, A, the strike is east-west and the dip is 45° S. In Fig. 146, B, the strike is north-south and the dip is W. on the east side of the block and E. on the west side. The axis of the syncline shown in this diagram is horizontal, but in Fig. 146, C, the axis is inclined northward, and a vertical section through *a*, *b*, and *c* shows the angle of this inclination in its relation to the horizontal (Fig. 146, D). This angle is a special case of dip and is known as the *plunge* of the fold. Here, then, we have a syncline plunging 10° N. It is obvious from the diagrams that the strikes of the limbs of such a fold, the axis of which lies in a north-south vertical plane, are not parallel as in Fig. 146, B. In a syncline they diverge, and in an anticline they converge, in the direction of the plunge.

Beckwith[13] suggests that where a fold (anticline or syncline) is asymmetrical and where, therefore, its axial plane is inclined (see Fig. 134), *pitch* be used for the angle, *measured in the axial plane,* between a horizontal plane and the fold axis, and *plunge* be used for the angle, *measured in a vertical plane,* between a horizontal plane and the fold axis.

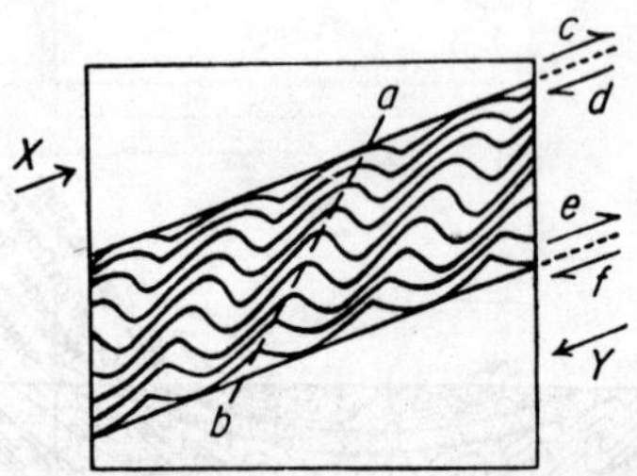

Fig. 145. Drag folds produced in an incompetent bed between two competent strata. (Cf. Fig. 144.) The differential motion at the bedding contacts is indicated by the arrows *c, d, e,* and *f*. *X* and *Y* show the relative differential movement of the two competent beds. *ab* is a section of the axial plane of one of the drag folds. An anticline is to the right of the figure and a syncline is to the left.

In its recommendations for adoption by the U.S. Geological Survey and by the geological profession, the Map Symbol Committee (see page 648) proposes the term *rake*, instead of *pitch*, for the angle of inclination of the axis in the axial plane, because pitch has been so often applied both to this angle and to the angle which we have here defined as *plunge*. (Cf. pitch, plunge, and rake, in connection with faulting, as explained in Art. 200.)

Causes and Conditions of Folding

180. Causes of tilting and folding. Although a detailed discussion of the causes of deformation of rocks is not within the

[13] Bibliog., Beckwith, R. H., 1947, p. 83.

province of this book, a few words of explanation may not be amiss. There are probably at least seven causes of tilting and folding of strata. These are: (1) settling due to weighting; (2) differential compaction; (3) tangential compression; (4) fault-

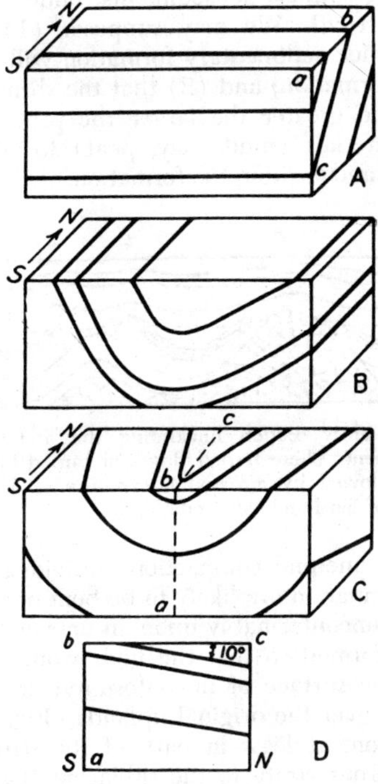

FIG. 146. Diagrams of dip, strike, and plunge.

ing; (5) igneous intrusion; (6) invasion of salt; (7) secondary changes including chemical alteration and unequal weathering.

1. In regions of long-continued deposition there seems to have been a gradual widespread settling of the floor in which the sediments have been accumulating, almost *pari passu* with the sedimentation. This settling, called *isostatic settling*, results in the bending of the strata, already deposited, downward toward the

area of maximum subsidence. The inclination of the beds, after such bending, has been termed "initial dip" by Bailey Willis.[14] In a thick series of sediments, it is greater in the lower beds, which have undergone more settling, than in the beds higher in the formation.

2. The compressibility of sediments under load has been mentioned in Art. **81.** We may suppose: (1) that the total shrinkage of a thick sedimentary formation will be greater than that of a thin formation; and (2) that the shrinkage of a given formation will be greater the larger the proportion of highly compressible materials (mud, clay, peat) to slightly compressible materials (sand) within the formation.

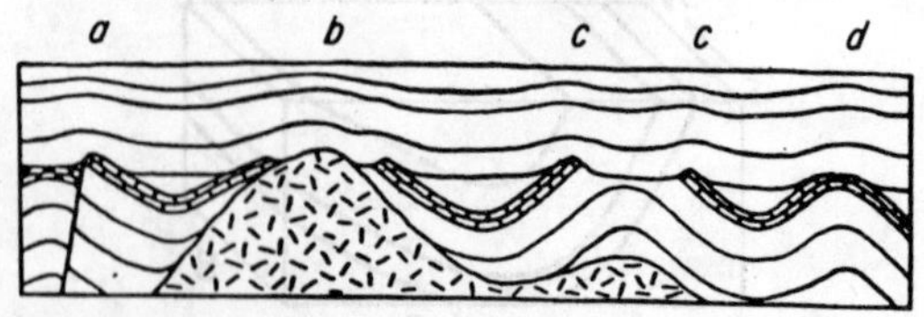

Fig. 147. Vertical cross section illustrating the arching of strata over ridges in the basement. These buried ridges or buried hills may have been due to faulting followed by erosion, *a;* exposure of a plutonic body, *b;* differential erosion of hard and soft strata, *c, d.*

As a result of unequal compaction, individual layers in such a sedimentary formation are likely to be bent or warped. A series of strata resting unconformably upon an uneven basement might thus become deformed so that the beds would sag toward the depressions in the surface of unconformity; or, in other words, they would arch over the original uplands (Fig. 147). This may be the explanation, at least in part, of the structural relations of the Carboniferous strata to the subjacent "Granite Ridge" in central Kansas.[15]

Another illustration of unequal compaction, but on a smaller scale, is that of marine shales and limestones which have been bent or warped downward over resistant calcareous reefs (bioherms) (**299**). This arching of the younger strata may be observ-

[14] See footnote 8, p. 73.

[15] This subject has been discussed at length by Sidney Powers, particularly in papers on buried hills. See Bibliog., Powers, Sidney, 1922; *Idem.*, 1926.

able over a thick reef through many hundreds of feet of the overlying sediments. Sand or sandstone lenses within a formation may induce bending of overlying, and even of underlying, more compressible strata. In cases of this kind we describe the arching of the overlying strata as *draping* of these beds over the incompressible body (granite knob or hill, bioherm, sand lens, etc.).

Assuming that the average distribution of sediments along a coast is such that sands predominate near shore, muds farther out, and limy oozes beyond the muds (87), in the progress of a transgression of the sea, the mud phase migrates over the basal

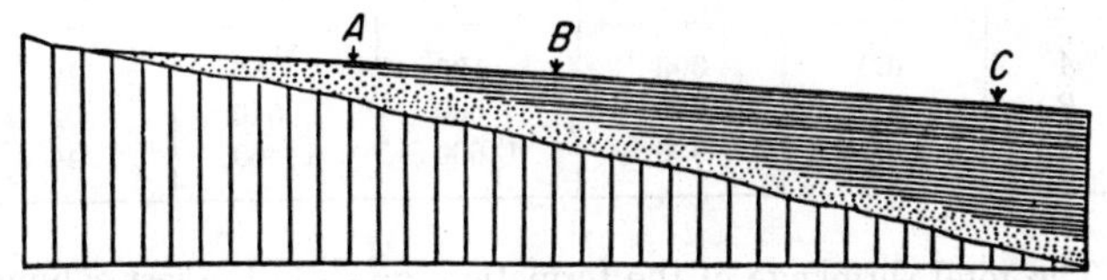

FIG. 148. Vertical section through littoral marine sediments laid down during a transgression of the sea from right to left. (Vertical scale exaggerated.)

sand phase. Between the principal sand body and the principal mud body there will be a transitional zone of considerable thickness in which layers of sand and mud will alternate, the mud increasing in amount upward and the sand increasing downward in the series. At any given time during the transgression, the proportion of mud to sand, as measured vertically from top to bottom of the growing sedimentary formation, will be greater seaward. Let us imagine a hypothetical case, illustrated in Fig. 148. The total thickness of mud and of sand, before compression, at points *A*, *B*, and *C*, is given as follows:

TABLE 3

Station	*Thickness of formation, ft.*	*Total sand thickness*		*Total mud thickness*	
		Ft.	*Per cent*	*Ft.*	*Per cent*
A	500	400	80	100	20
B	1,000	400	40	600	60
C	2,000	400	20	1,600	80

Considering only the strata represented in the figure, let us suppose that the sand will suffer 1 per cent vertical shrinkage and the mud 15 per cent vertical shrinkage, of its original thickness, after further transgression of the sea and the deposition of a heavy overburden of younger sediments. The figures will then be as follows:

TABLE 4

Station	*Original thickness of sand, ft.*	*Compressed thickness of sand, ft.*	*Original thickness of shale, ft.*	*Compressed thickness of shale, ft.*	*Total shrinkage of formation, ft.*
A	400	396	100	85	19
B	400	396	600	510	94
C	400	396	1,600	1,360	244

The total shrinkage of the formation, given in the last column, represents the quantity by which the original surface of the deposit, and, therefore, the beds which were at the surface, are lowered through the effects of the compression, using the foregoing hypothetical values (81).

From *A* to *B* a secondary dip of 75 ft. is produced, and from *B* to *C*, a secondary dip of 150 ft.

Although these figures are hypothetical, they suggest that the original inclination of the beds in extensive growing deposits may be increased not only by settling of the foundation (see 1, above), but also by the unequal compression of the strata, involving an increasingly great reduction in their thickness away from the source of supply.

3. Probably the folding ordinarily observed in strongly deformed strata is an effect of lateral or tangential compression within the lithosphere. *i.e.*, of compression by forces acting in approximately horizontal directions. Briefly, this compression is thought to be a consequence of strains and stresses induced by the earth's gradual shrinkage. Geologists believe that these stresses slowly increase until finally they somewhere overcome the resistance of the lithosphere to deformation. Then yielding occurs by breaking or by folding. In the earth's history this yielding seems often to have occurred in regions of heavy sedimentation where, already, there may have been some weakening

by bending due to isostatic settling (¶ 1) and differential settling (¶ 2).

The conception has been generally held that the compressive forces have operated essentially perpendicular to the axes of the resulting folds (Fig. 149). That such may not be the case was pointed out by Warren J. Mead,[16] who shows that overlapping, plunging folds, occurring in groups and with roughly parallel alignment of their axes—a condition frequently found in de-

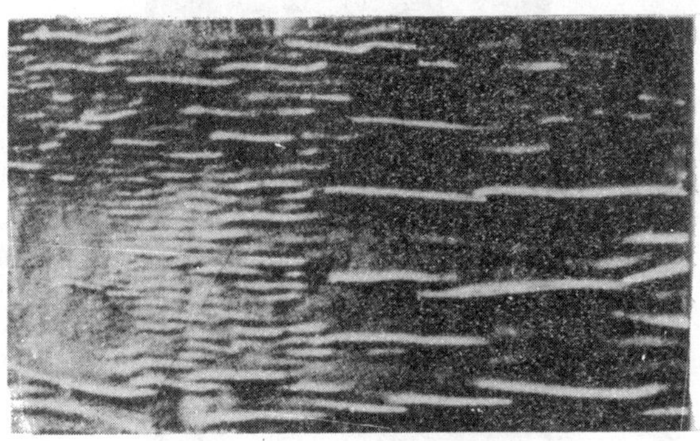

FIG. 149. Plaster of Paris positive of folds produced by compression or shortening. The force was applied perpendicularly to the length of the folds. (*After Warren J. Mead.*)

formed strata—may be produced by shearing stresses (Fig. 150). Mead writes, "It seems probable that the movements between great earth masses are in the nature of shears rather than simple straight-line compression. In other words, *the application of a compressive force directly toward the point of maximum resistance would be less probable than the development of a couple which would cause what has been called a rotational stress*" . . . He thinks that "most of the faults or folds" in deformed strata "are the result of the riding or dragging of the upper layers by" shearing movements in "the underlying materials."[17]

[16] See Bibliog., Mead, Warren J., 1920.
[17] *Idem.*, p. 521.

4. Flexing produced by faulting may be local, as in the case of drag dips (**199, 210**); or it may become rather extensive, where folds are associated with flat overthrusts, with zones of overlapping faults in the origin of which torsional forces operated, and, finally, in slump faults on the flanks of settling geosynclines (Art. **204**).

FIG. 150. Vertical view of reproduction, in plaster of Paris, of folds produced by shearing deformation. The direction of movement is indicated by arrows and the amount of deformation is shown by the shape of the block. (*After Warren J. Mead.*)

5. Deformation associated with, and produced by, the intrusion of magma is referred to in Art. **134.**

6. In some parts of the world, notably in Roumania, northeastern Germany, Holland, the Gulf Coastal region of Mississippi, Louisiana and Texas, and the Isthmus of Tehuantepec, there are dome-shaped uplifts of stratified rocks associated with

central plugs of salt. These structures are known as *salt domes* (Fig. 151). The salt core generally stands vertical or nearly vertical and has a roughly circular or oval horizontal section, measuring from 1,000 ft. to 2 miles or so in diameter. It extends downward several thousand feet. In North America wells have penetrated salt more than 3,000 ft. without going out of it, and there are reasons for believing that the plugs in Europe extend

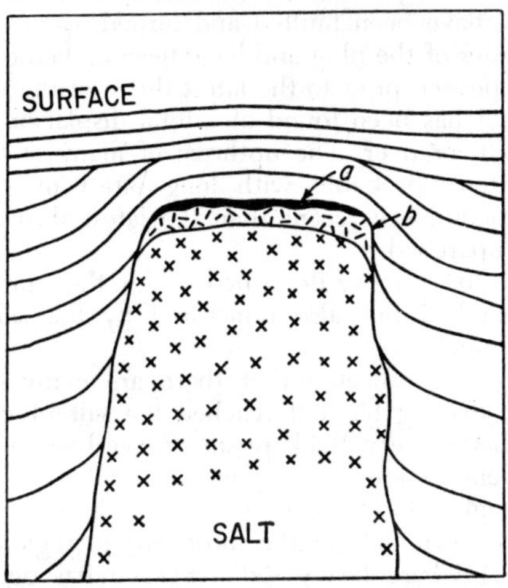

FIG. 151. Ideal vertical cross section of a salt dome showing salt, cap rock consisting of upper layer, *a*, chiefly of calcite (limestone), and lower layer, *b*, consisting of gypsum and anhydrite. An older series was intruded and uparched, then eroded, and finally covered by younger beds. Subsequently renewed uplift domed the younger strata.

downward 15,000 and even 20,000 ft. The sides of the plug dip at angles of 30° to 90°. The salt mass itself is composed of salt crystals which are sometimes columnar, having their long axes essentially in a vertical position. It may be marked by streaks closely resembling the flowage lines in gneisses, and these streaks may be parallel to the sides of the plug or they may be severely contorted, like the structure shown in Fig. 143.

A majority of the Gulf Coast domes are crowned with a so-called "cap rock" varying in thickness up to 1,000 ft. or more, and consisting essentially of crystalline anhydrite. Associated with the anhydrite may be gypsum, probably an alteration product of the anhydrite, and also limestone or dolomitic limestone, and in some cases sulphur. The uppermost part of a plug may flare out beyond the average position of its flank so that it has an overhang, which may consist of cap rock only or of salt covered by cap rock.

Adjacent to the salt, the surrounding sedimentary strata, generally ranging in age from Cretaceous to Recent in the Gulf Coast domes, have been faulted and turned up at sharp angles against the sides of the plug and have been arched over it where they were deposited prior to the latest thrust of the salt. In some instances proof has been found of a total displacement amounting to 5,000 ft. or over. The upthrust of many of these domes was intermittent, probably with long intervening periods of quiescence. Beds more recent than the latest thrust of the salt core are not uparched.

Domes like those above described, where the strata have been not only uparched but also punctured by the salt plug, are *piercement domes.*

Geophysics has indicated that there are many *deep domes* below which drilling has not reached the salt plug, which apparently arched a very thick prism of overlying beds without intruding them. These are sometimes called *nonpiercement domes,* although actually they may pierce the very deep strata.

Salt domes are found for the most part in regional synclines (geosynclines) where heavy sedimentation has occurred. Furthermore, they are distributed roughly along lines which parallel the major structural trends of the region.

Although many theories have been proposed to explain the origin of these salt domes, the view most commonly supported in America until the early 1920's was that the salt was deposited from ascending waters. However, serious objections to this theory have been presented.[18] In Europe, where the domes are often laid bare to considerable depths by erosion, and where, consequently, a more certain idea of their structure and origin is obtainable, geologists came to believe that the salt was thrust upward into the sediments like a punch, principally by mechanical means, assisted by the ordinary processes of granulation and recrystallization supposed to accompany the development of schistosity in metamorphic rocks (**244**). The source of the salt

[18] Bibliog., Rogers, G. Sherburne, 1918, p. 460; also DeGolyer, E., *et al.*, 1926.

is thought to have been in deep-lying salt beds (Lower Miocene in Roumania; Permian in Germany and Holland; probably Jurassic in Mississippi, Louisiana, and Texas), from which it was squeezed upward at points of minimum resistance.

In view of the many features common to our Gulf Coast domes and those of Europe, particularly the unmistakable indications of great mechanical upward force, we may conclude that the origin is similar in each case and that the salt of the Gulf Coast domes has been derived from sedimentary salt deeply buried in bedded deposits. The chief force involved was probably downward pressure of this great load of overlying strata, a force that caused the salt locally to move upward in a semiplastic condition along lines and at points of weakness. Many of the known domes are surrounded by "rim synclines," which were produced by settling of the strata into the space formerly occupied by the salt in its original bedded position deep in the sedimentary prism.[19]

7. In regions underlain by stratified formations which include some soluble members, these members may be gradually dissolved and carried away by subsurface waters. This may cause the overlying strata to sag toward the area of maximum removal by such solution (**344**).

Interpretation of Tilted and Folded Strata

181. Discrimination between primary and secondary dip. The inclination of layers, when not over 30° or 40°, may be original (**82, 267**). Sometimes it is hard to discriminate between primary dip and the secondary kind of dip induced by deformation. Ordinarily, laminae which have a primary dip as high as 25° or 30° are cross-beds (**96**) in the main stratification, and, therefore, they are of limited length. When the geologist is doubtful whether he is dealing with primary or secondary dip, he should examine other outcrops in the vicinity, and particularly large outcrops, since on these the major structure may be apparent. Cross-lamination is to be expected in eolian, fluviatile, and littoral sandstones.

Primary dips of lower angle are distinguished with less facility. In general, where cross-bedding is absent, the main stratification of coarse fragmental materials (sand or gravel) may be ex-

[19] For further discussion of salt-dome characteristics, see Bibliog., Balk, Robert, 1949.

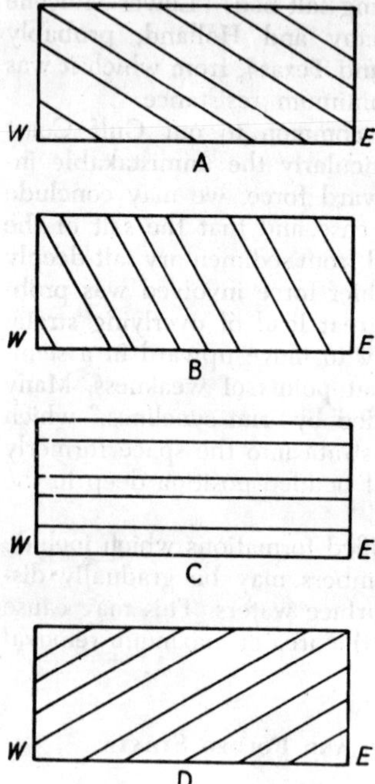

FIG. 152. Sections of strata illustrating the relations of primary dip to deformation. A, cross-bedding in its original position, with a primary dip of 30°E. B, the same cross-bedding after it has been tilted eastword through an angle of 30°; it now has a dip of 60°E. C, the same cross-bedding as that in A after it has been tilted 30° westward; it is now horizontal, in spite of the fact that the strata have been tilted. D, the same cross-bedding as that in A after it has been tilted 60° westward; it now has a dip of 30°W.

pected to have an original inclination of 2° to 5° or even 8°. This remark applies to piedmont alluvial deposits, topset beds of small deltas and sand plains, beach deposits, etc. If the rocks of a region belong unquestionably to these types, and if they have dips of these low angles, their inclination is not sufficient reason for assuming that they have been tilted since their accumulation. On the other hand, strata laid down with approximately horizontal attitude, now inclined at a low angle, have probably suffered slight deformation.

To understand how to solve this problem, one must have a knowledge of the manner in which different kinds of sedimentary material are deposited and one must correlate dips and strikes in many outcrops, sometimes over wide areas. Note that a single outcrop with a low dip, or a small group of exposures with low dips, may be situated in the axial region of a broad fold.

182. Amount of tilting. Provided beds were accumulated in a horizontal position, their dip is a measure of the angle through which they have been tilted, in any given locality; but if they were laid down with a primary inclination, the amount of their rotation is not correctly expressed by their present dip. Figure 152 illustrates three cases (B–D) where the axis of tilting was coincident with the original strike of the strata when deposited.

If a series of strata has been tilted to a position such, for example, that the beds dip 50° due north, we may say that they *face* north. If they have been upturned until they are vertical, they still *face* north. Finally we may say that they *face* to the north after they have been tilted past the vertical, let us say to such a degree that they dip 60° south, overturned. The word *face* is convenient to indicate the direction from older to younger beds in a vertical or overturned series of strata (see **185**).

183. Direction of forces. While it is impossible here to enter into a discussion of the dynamics of folding, a word or two may be said concerning the direction in which forces are supposed to have acted in the formation of folds. A monocline is often the product of a vertical or nearly vertical displacement consequent upon crustal tension; or it may be an effect of local adjustment in the vertical bodily uplift (or depression) of huge blocks of the lithosphere. In some cases basin folds may be made by downsagging of the area deformed, and dome folds may be due to local upthrust or to peripheral settling. In this connection it is well to bear in mind the possible origin of folds through differential compaction (**180**, ¶ 2). The forces in these instances have acted vertically.

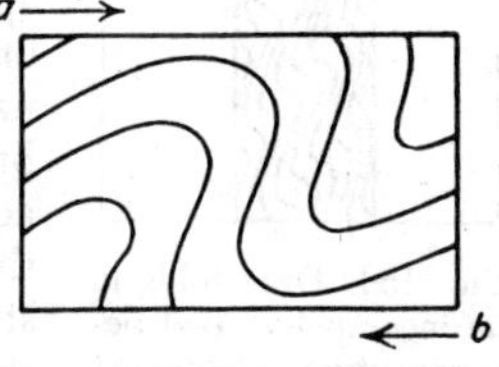

FIG. 153. Section of an asymmetrical fold which was formed by forces acting probably in the general direction of the arrows.

We have already mentioned the two hypotheses for the origin of typical diastrophic folds (**180**, ¶ 3). According to one the compressive force acted normal to the fold axes and according to the other this force was a component of a shear which operated oblique to the fold axes.

An asymmetrical fold suggests an overthrust force acting from the direction toward which the axial plane dips, *i.e.*, from the side of the less steeply inclined limb (Fig. 153). This force may have been a differential pressure applied through the mass of the folded zone or it may have been a drag consequent upon the overriding of a more rigid superjacent body of strata (Fig. 145); for there is no reason for assuming that the drag folds must necessarily be small because they are subordinate in a composite fold. The asymmetrical form of a fold might also be attained by an underthrust from the direction of the steeper limb (Fig. 153), a possibility which should be considered in reference to Mead's hypothesis of subjacent shearing (180, ¶ 3). The condition of asymmetry depends upon a multiplicity of factors, such as initial surface features of the folded tract, original inclination of the strata, relations of force and resistance, and the like.

184. Significance of minor folds in relation to major folds. Reference is made here only to folds produced by earth stresses. In contorted schists and gneisses, rocks which have undergone severe dynamic metamorphism, the folding is very irregular and all the layers have shared about equally in the deformation. The plications approach the similar type, although not uncommonly one fold may be seen to narrow and die out while beside it another broadens correspondingly. These are actually corrugations on larger folds and the larger ones may be superposed upon still larger ones, and so on. Originating in the same period and under the influence of the same forces, these sets of folds are apt to possess like characters. The difference lies principally in their dimensions. Naturally we should expect to find that the minor folds plunge if the major fold plunges, and probably in the same general direction. Careful study of these small folds[20] may, therefore, suggest the nature of the larger structure of a region and serve to guide the geologist in the methods to be adopted in his field investigation (346).

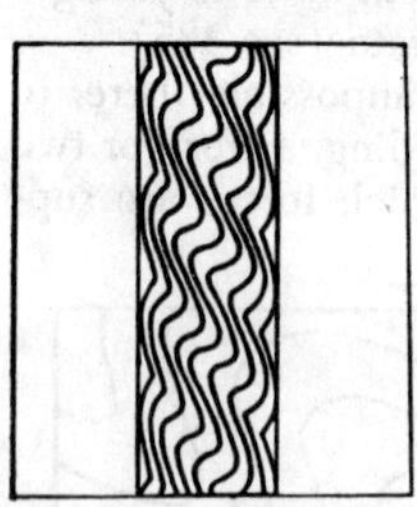

FIG. 154. Drag folds in an incompetent bed between two competent beds. According to the rule, the competent layer on the left moved up with respect to that on the right. Consequently, these beds must be in the limb between an anticline on the right and a syncline on the left, and the beds on the left must be stratigraphically above those on the right.

Drag folds produced in the manner described in Art. 178 may help to unravel the major structure. Since their axial planes are inclined with the direction of differential movement, they suggest the position of the major folds (Fig. 154). In a vertical or steeply dipping series this method also shows which is the top and which the bottom of the beds, for the younger and upper layers are toward the synclinal axes. (See also 248 and 249 on use of cleavage in interpreting folds.)

[20] For a detailed discussion of small en echelon folds, see Bibliog., Campbell, J. D., 1958.

185. Top and bottom of steeply inclined, vertical, and overturned beds. It is customary to assume that any layer in a series of strata is older than the overlying beds and younger than the underlying beds (**100**). When strata are vertical, their relative age cannot be determined by superposition. When they are steeply inclined this method of reasoning is unsafe, too, for they may have been turned beyond the vertical and thus be overturned. Indeed, in very severe folding, beds may be turned quite upside down (Fig. 131, J), but rocks thus affected would presumably show signs of considerable induration or early metamorphism. In the investigation of steeply dipping beds and

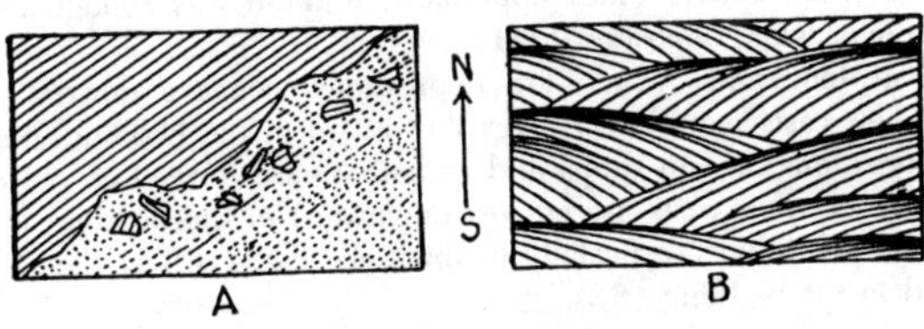

FIG. 155. Sections of steeply dipping strata as seen on a horizontal or nearly horizontal surface. The younger (upper) beds in both A and B are toward the south. Explain this fact.

indurated strata of lower inclination, the geologist must therefore seek criteria other than superposition to determine the direction of face (Art. **182**), *i.e.*, to demonstrate the true relative order of stratification (**100**).

The criteria for top and bottom of beds, and therefore for stratigraphic sequence, have been exhaustively described by Shrock.[21] Recognition of these criteria and a knowledge of how to interpret them are very important for any geologist who intends to map and study stratified rocks, especially those which have been strongly folded. The more important of these criteria are:

1. Regional unconformities with evidences of truncation and erosion of the lower rock formations and the presence of fragments of these in basal beds of the overlying formation (**86**).

2. Local unconformities with evidences similar to those under (1), but on a small scale (**93**; also Fig. 155, A).

[21] See Bibliog., Shrock, Robert R., 1948.

3. Gradational texture from coarse below to fine above in individual beds or laminae, with abrupt transition from fine below to coarse above at the junction between each two such beds or laminae (**99**).

4. Rhythms, or rhythmical repetitions, of a certain sequence of several strata, where the top and bottom of this sequence have already been ascertained in a stratigraphic series lying essentially in normal position (**105**).

5. Faunal successions already recognized in the stratigraphic sequence where still in normal position.

6. Presence of attached fossil forms of animal or plant life where still essentially *in situ* (*e.g.*, tree trunks, corals, etc.) (**111**).

7. Burrows made by worms or other animals in mud, subsequently filled by sand deposited above the mud (**105**).

8. Attitude of concavo-convex fossil shells, of which a majority are buried with their convex sides uppermost, if there was enough current to turn them over when deposited (**111**).

9. Fossil footprints, which are depressions, concave downward when formed. Their casts would be convex downward in the bedding (**69**).

10. Impressions of rain drops and of hail stones, formed as indentations. Like footprints, their casts are convex downward in the bedding (**66**).

11. Sun-crack fillings, especially in thick clay beds, where they terminate downward in the bedding (**65**).

12. Wave-made ripple marks, especially where the original crests were preserved, and where low second-order ridges were developed in the troughs (**60**).

13. Certain types of cross-bedding, especially those where each set of cross-laminae, concave upward, is truncated by higher (younger) sets (**96, C**). [Care should be taken not to confuse this type (Fig. 53) with that shown in Fig. 54.]

14. Relative position of drag folds in a folded sequence of strata (**184**).

15. Relative position of cleavage in a folded sequence of strata (**249**).

Folds in Relation to Their Time of Origin

186. Age of folds. In a folded series of strata the deposition of the beds antedated their deformation. The folds are younger than the strata. Generally, joints and faults in such a formation are younger than, or contemporaneous with, the folding. They should not be regarded as older than the latter unless there is definite proof of the fact.

The geologic age of folding is determined by correlation with strata of which the geologic age is known. In the district sectioned in Fig. 122, the folding was post-Ordovician and pre-Devonian, for the strata (*a*) are deformed, whereas the overlying series (*c*) is not so. Both folding and erosion, as well as the intrusion of *b*, must have occurred between the two periods of sedimentation.

187. Two or more periods of folding. To demonstrate that rocks have been subjected to two or more periods of folding is difficult if the evidences are sought in a conformable series of beds. Both complex folding and the superposition of small plications upon larger folds are phenomena commonly of contemporaneous origin. Cross-folding, so-called—*i.e.*, the deformation of fold axes—is not a criterion for a second period of folding (Figs. 149, 150). Moreover, variations in the intensity of folding, parallel or normal to the main axis, are perfectly characteristic of crustal blocks deformed in one diastrophic period.

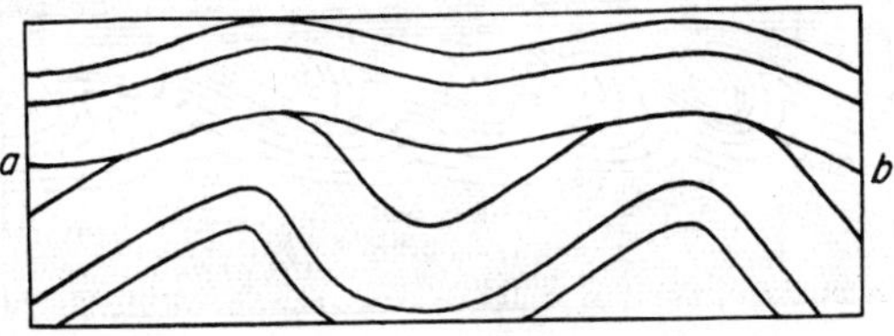

FIG. 156. Section of a surface of unconformity between two series of folded strata. The strata below the unconformity (*ab*) have been through two periods of deformation.

The only safe criterion for two distinct epochs of folding is found in undoubted cases of angular unconformity in which the younger beds have been folded (Fig. 156). Here the older strata must have suffered from deformation twice, once to account for the angle between the two series, and again, when the overlying beds were folded. The determination of successive periods of folding requires widespread geologic investigation and careful correlation of the observed facts.

188. Folds that originate in unconsolidated sediments. There are several ways in which folds may be produced in beds prior to consolidation. Some such plications fall under the head of contemporaneous deformation (**95**); others do not. Like cross-bedding and other primary structures, they may be preserved during the lithification of the strata in which they are formed, so that their occurrence is not limited to unconsolidated materials. In any case they are of peculiar interest in denoting certain conditions under which the sediments were deposited. Ten varieties are described below and an attempt is made to point out criteria which may be of service in their interpretation.

1. A block of ice floating in a lake or in the sea may scrape over the bottom and rumple up the muds and fine sands which are in process of accumulation (Fig. 157). Folds and faults thus produced are examples of contemporaneous deformation. When formed, they are confined to a relatively thin upper zone and they die out downward. Upward the folds are sharply truncated by the surface of erosion made by the berg, and they are overturned in the direction of its motion. Since deposition of the

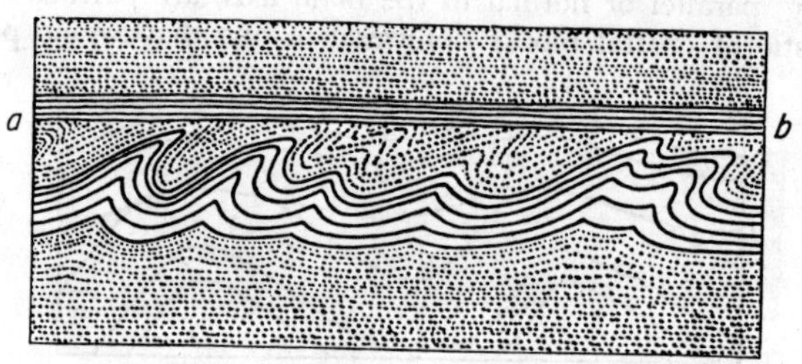

Fig. 157. Section of contorted fine sand and laminated clay overlain by like sediments which are not deformed. *ab*, line of local unconformity. The shape of the folds indicates that the deforming agent moved from left to right. What is the significance of the fact that the folds die out downward? Length of section about 2 ft.

mud or sand continues after the passage of the ice, the erosion surface is soon buried and so becomes a local unconformity.

A series of beds exhibiting this kind of contortion is usually characterized by fine texture, by thin, uniform lamination, and by general regularity except in the crumpled zones of the type just described. These zones may be few or many, according to the size and number of the bergs which made them. They are not apt to be of great extent in the plane of the main bedding. In formations that exhibit these features, search should be made for isolated bowlders (**106**) and other evidences of the association of ice in the work of deposition.

2. In the forward motion of glacier ice on land the ice may not only erode, but also dislocate, aqueoglacial sediments which have been laid down in front of the advancing ice margin. A

thickness of several feet of strata may be affected; the sediments are not limited to uniformly laminated fine sands and clays; and till often rests upon the eroded surface that truncates the deformed beds (Fig. 158). Many examples have been cited, in the literature, of glacial clays, esker and kame gravels, and other bedded deposits, which have thus been scoured and deformed. Overriden clay beds sometimes reveal grooves and scratches on the surface of unconformity, if this has been exposed. Overturned folds and reverse faults show by their attitude the direction from which the ice thrust came. This structure may also be classified as contemporaneous deformation.

3. A structure very similar to 2 is that of outwash beds which were spread out before a *retreating* glacier and were subsequently overriden and deformed by a new advance of the ice.

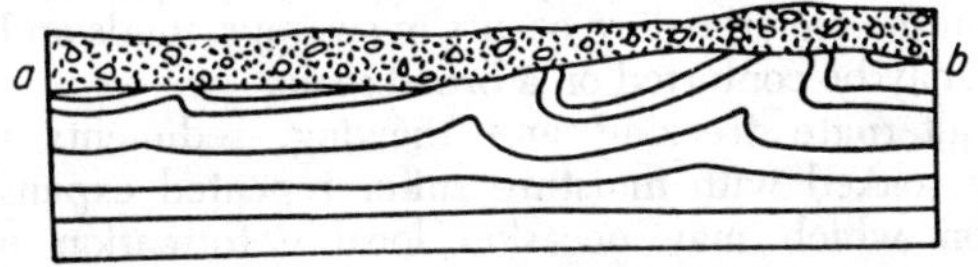

FIG. 158. Till overlying folded aqueoglacial strata. *ab* is a line of unconformity. The folding and the erosion, *ab*, were performed by ice moving from left to right. Length of section about 200 ft.

The time elapsed between the deposition of the strata and their erosion may have been scores, hundreds, or even thousands of years, so that this can hardly be called an example of contemporaneous deformation. The discrimination between the folding and erosion effected by ice moving over its own frontal outwash and the folding and erosion performed by ice moving over the retreatal deposits of an antecedent advance requires careful search for the criteria listed in Art. **122.**

4. During the winter season in northern climates, the expansion of the ice covering of ponds and lakes is relieved by crowding of the ice up the beach. This process, for which evidences may be seen in the bowlder piles of "walled lakes," may be accompanied by slight erosion and by deformation that may be called contemporaneous, provided the disturbed sediments constitute the beach. In most cases the ice probably rubs up over the beach materials, but it may carry along some sand and gravel which have been frozen into it, or it may push up a ridge

in front of it. The overridden layers are apt to be crumpled and dragged forward, so that small folds are overturned landward. They may be truncated above by an erosion surface (local unconformity); downward they grade into the uncontorted beds. At most this folded zone can be but a few feet in thickness, and between winters it is likely to be reworked and spread out by wave action. Normally only a narrow strip of sediments along the beach can be handled in this way; but if water level rises or falls during a succession of years, the effects may be distributed over a much wider belt. Stationary water level would result in excessive disturbance of the same materials; falling water level would result in the exposure of the contorted beds to erosion by rainwash, etc.; and rising water level would bring the deformed zone of each winter beneath the water surface where it might be preserved by subsequent lacustrine deposition.

5. When the ice crowding occurs in swamps, muds and organic materials may be contorted on a broad scale.

6. By alternate freezing and thawing, sediments that are ordinarily soaked with moisture suffer repeated expansion and contraction which may occasion local deformation in them. Properly speaking this would not be *contemporaneous* unless the time interval between the deposition of the sediments and their deformation were comparatively short.

Contemporaneous deformation originating on lake shores, in marshes, and in water-soaked sediments, is not necessarily associated with a capping surface of unconformity produced by the slight shove of the ice. It is much more probable that the folds will die out both downward and upward. They will grade upward into a zone in which any original bedding was destroyed by the upheaval and settling of the loose grains and pebbles.

7. Mud flow is a possible cause of folding in unconsolidated beds. The coefficient of friction is so low in moist clays and muds, especially under water, that slipping may be induced even on slopes of only 2° or 3°. The "flow" may be distributed in the form of contortion through the thickness of one or more beds. As might be expected, the folds are overturned toward the direction of motion. Sometimes this distributed crumpling develops into an actual sliding of the overlying mud or clay along a surface that truncates the tops of the little folds and lies approximately parallel to the bedding. The resulting structure, though closely resembling the contemporaneous deformation due to grounding ice

blocks, is likely to be of wider extent in the plane of stratification. Isolated bowlders and other evidences for the former presence of ice might serve as a means of discrimination were it not for the fact that there is nothing to prevent mud flow in bodies of water in which icebergs are floating.

8. Valley strata of various kinds, generally fluviatile, may be torn up, folded, and eroded by the sudden deployment of an avalanche. A vertical section would show the heterogeneous avalanche material resting unconformably upon the distorted beds.

9. Removal of mineral matter in solution from a rock which is undergoing decomposition may lead to irregular settling and contortion of overlying strata. Increase of volume induced by decomposition may crowd and fold rocks near the surface. Plications formed in these ways are not overturned in any particular direction.

10. Monoclinal folds, and sometimes more involved folding, may be produced in unconsolidated beds as an effect of faulting in the subjacent rocks.

In neither 9 nor 10 is local unconformity genetically associated with the deformation, and in neither instance is this deformation contemporaneous, as the term has been defined.

189. Discrimination between folds originating before and after consolidation. In folded shales, clay slates, and sandstones, and occasionally in other clastics some difficulty may be experienced in deciding whether minor folds were produced through superficial agencies or through earth stresses, in other words, whether they are to be interpreted as evidences for conditions of sedimentation or for conditions of diastrophic deformation. Unfortunately, there seems to be no constant and striking character peculiar to either class of deformation. Yet certain features may be noted, which are suggestive of one origin or of the other.

In the first place, superficial folds, having an origin unrelated to stresses and strains within the earth's crust, have no direct structural relation to the major deformation in the neighborhood. Herein they differ from minor diastrophic folds, but the fact is not always easy to ascertain. Second, superficial folds are often much more disorderly and involved than diastrophic plications, because there is less opportunity for readjustment under the pressure and confinement of relatively great depths. Again, superficial folds are usually localized in beds which are overlain and underlain by uncontorted strata. Very often the crests of the anticlines are bevelled off by a surface of contemporaneous erosion (iceberg, glacial ice, shore ice, landslide) or by a shear plane (mud flow, etc.), and more rarely the troughs of the synclines at the base of the folded zone are truncated by a shear plane; whereas small diastrophic folds commonly die out gradually upward and downward into the less deformed strata. However, there are exceptions in which, both upward and downward stratigraphically, superficial folds pass into uncontorted beds, and, on the other hand, diastrophic plications may be found in layers that are truncated above and below where there has been shearing of the undeformed beds over the crumpled zone, and of the crumpled zone over the subjacent undeformed beds. Truncation, then, is not a safe criterion.

The discrimination of these two kinds of folds is not a question that is likely to arise in the case of metamorphic rocks, flat-lying lithified sediments, or unconsolidated strata. In schists and gneisses any original plications that may once have existed have probably been masked beyond recognition. Minor contortion in metamorphic rocks is generally diastrophic and is usually of the similar pattern (Fig. 143). Highly crumpled layers or zones in flat-lying, unmetamorphosed strata, otherwise unfolded or only broadly warped, are pretty surely of primary origin. One important exception to this statement must be made: faults in the lithosphere may cause slips and accompanying local crumpling in the superjacent mantle rock.

Folds in Relation to the Land Surface

190. Topographic expression of folds. Provided folds are large enough and provided they are in strata of different degrees of resistance to erosion, they may exercise a marked control upon the form and distribution of hills and valleys. The harder beds stand up as ridges, and the weaker ones underlie longitudinal valleys (see Figs. 432 and 433). After long erosion the ridges may be carved into ranges of hills with intervening transverse valleys. If the axes of the folds are parallel to the general surface of the ground, the ridges and longitudinal valleys will have a parallel trend; but if the axes plunge, the ridges will zigzag back and forth, always pointing up the plunge in synclines and down the plunge in anticlines (cf. Fig. 138). In denuded dome folds and basin folds, the ridges and valleys are closed concentric curves (cf. Fig. 137).[22] In gently dipping beds that have been truncated by erosion, no matter what the shape of the fold may be, the hard layers stand out as cuestas, and in steeply inclined beds these hard layers form hogbacks (**300**).

191. Breadth of outcrop defined. The breadth of outcrop of an exposed bed may be defined as the distance between the stratigraphic top and bottom edges of the bed measured on the surface of the ground perpendicular to the strike (Fig. 159, *ab*, *cd*).

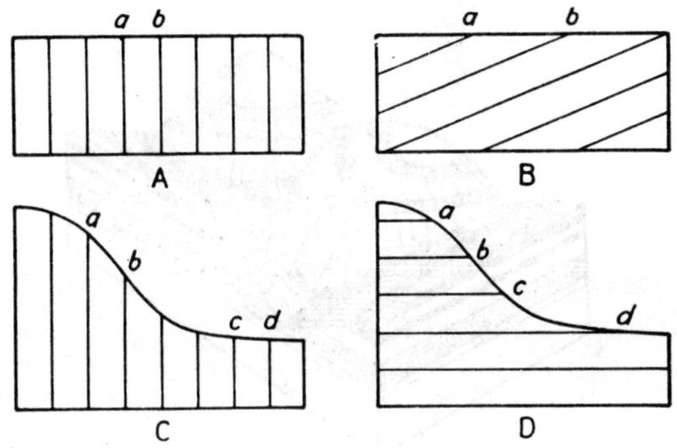

Fig. 159. Sections illustrating variations in breadth of outcrop (*ab* and *cd*) of strata. The thickness of the beds in all four diagrams is the same.

192. Effects of topography on breadth of outcrop. Figure 159, A–D, will explain more clearly than words how the breadth of outcrop of a stratum may be modified by topographic variations. The essential points to notice are: (1) that breadth of outcrop is least when the surface of the ground is perpendicular to the beds; and (2) that the more obliquely the surface bevels across the beds, the greater is the breadth of outcrop for a

[22] Salt domes (**180**) are seldom strongly marked on the earth's surface. Even where the deeper strata invaded by the salt may have been displaced many hundreds of feet, the surface expression of the dome may be only a low hill (Fig. 450). Sometimes the ground may be level, or again there may be a depression with or without a lake, probably due to partial solution of the salt plug at its top. The presence of an underlying salt dome may be manifested at the surface by springs of salt water or sulphur water, or by seepages of marsh gas or sulphur gas.

stratum of given thickness. (What would be the dip of a bed whose thickness is half its breadth of outcrop on a horizontal surface?)

193. Effects of topography on the distribution of outcrops. When strata are exposed on an uneven land surface, the trend of their outcropping edges varies according to their attitude. The edge of a horizontal bed bends out round the spurs and in up the valleys (Fig. 160). If it is followed upstream on one side of the valley, it is found to approach and finally cross the stream and then turn back on the other side. Isolated hills in the region

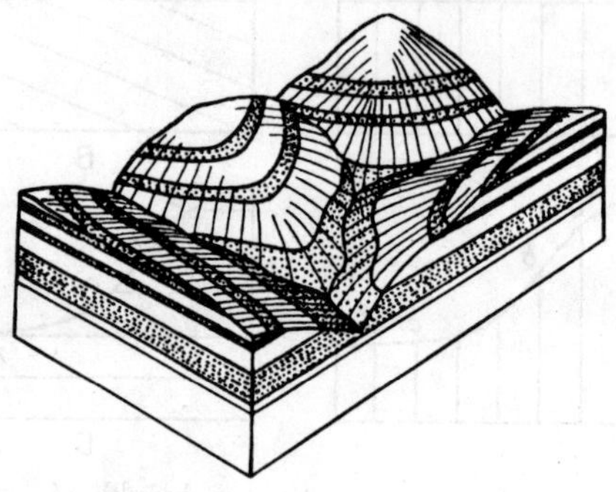

FIG. 160. Effects of topography on the outcropping edges of horizontal strata.

may be mesa-like, with the same beds exposed all round (**300**). Vertical strata outcrop in regular bands which trend straight across hills and valleys with no relation to the topography (Fig. 161). If beds are inclined, they outcrop in parallel zigzag belts with elbow-like bends which are situated in the valleys and on the spurs (Figs. 162, 163). In the valleys these bends point down the inclination of the strata, as measured in the general direction of the valley, unless the angle of this inclination is less than the gradient of the stream.[23] In the latter case, which is very rare, the bends point up the inclination. (What will be the effect if inclination of beds and valley gradient are equal?)

[23] If the strata strike perpendicular to the trend of the valley, this "inclination" is approximately the true dip; otherwise it is a component of the dip, taken along the valley trend.

It is to be observed that the foregoing rules, although referring to strata which are theoretically of uniform thickness, are equally applicable to either the top or bottom surface of any given bed, and to any relatively even surface of unconformity. The distance between the outcrop lines of any two parallel bedding sur-

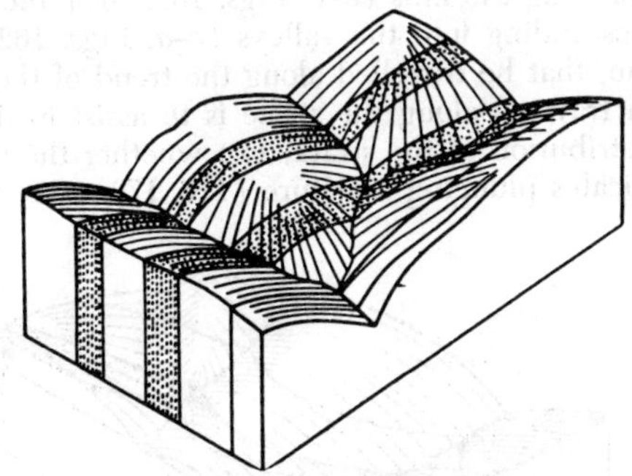

FIG. 161. Effects of topography on the outcropping edges of vertical strata.

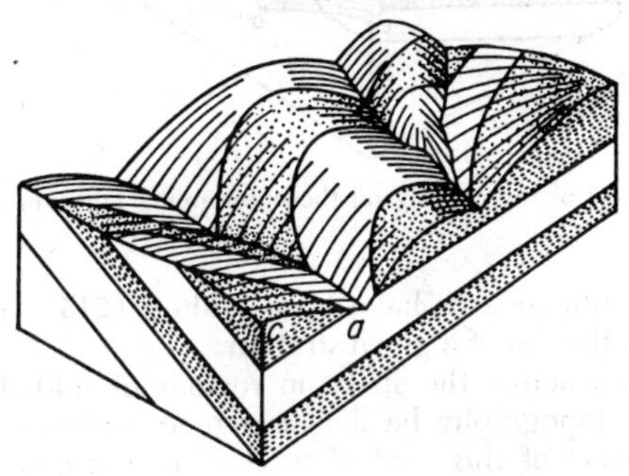

FIG. 162. Effects of topography on the outcropping edges of strata dipping downstream.

faces, *i.e.*, the breadth of outcrop, varies according to the slope of the ground as described in the preceding article.

194. Traverses across and along the strike. Unless the underground structure of a district on sedimentary rocks is exceptionally complex and irregular, a brief study of two or three outcrops should suffice to show in which direction one should walk in order to follow along, or to cross, the strike. In a flat country eroded upon folded strata, and in a hilly country where the strata are vertical, the geologist would keep on the same bed were he to travel parallel to the strike; but if the topography were rugged and the beds dipped less than 90°, he would come on to younger strata in climbing the hills (*a–c*, Figs. 162, 163) and on to older strata in descending into the valleys (*c–a*, Figs. 162, 163), provided, again, that he travelled along the trend of the strike. The object of a traverse along the strike is to assist in determining: (1) the distribution of the strata; (2) whether the strike curves and so indicates plunging structure (**176, 179**); (3) whether the

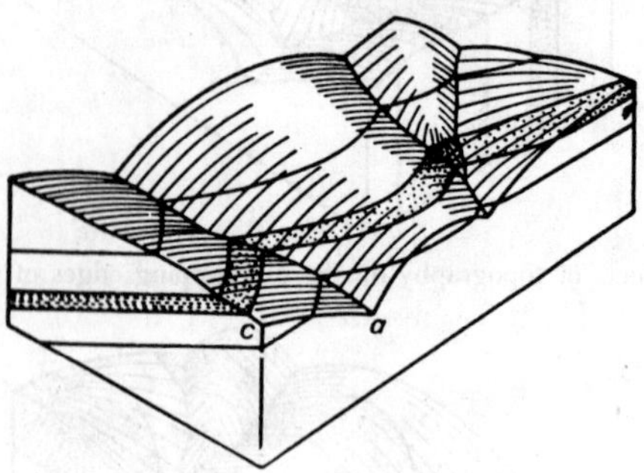

FIG. 163. Effects of topography on the outcropping edges of strata dipping upstream.

strata are continuous or have been faulted (**215**); and (4) the constancy of the dip of a given stratum.

In traverses across the strike in regions of folded sediments, whether the topography be flat or rugged, successive strata are met. The object of this kind of traverse is to ascertain: (1) the breadth of outcrop; (2) the nature of the folding; (3) the position of anticlines and synclines; and (4) variations in the dip.

195. Sequence of strata in a cross-strike traverse. As may be noted in Fig. 164, in synclines relatively younger strata, *a*, lie between the older, subjacent beds, *b*, and in anticlines older strata, *c*, lie between younger superjacent strata, *b*. In all cases except where the surface of the ground is parallel to the beds or where it slopes in the same direction as, and more steeply than, the dip of a series of inclined beds, or where the beds are vertical or overturned, successively younger strata are traversed in walking across the strike in the direction of the dip.

196. Correlation of outcrops. An outcropping stratum which is conspicuously and continuously exposed, or is exposed with only slight breaks in its continuity, can be traced on the ground without difficulty. This is called "walking a bed" (**333, 340**). When beds are exposed only in isolated outcrops, or in far-separated ledges, these exposures must be carefully studied and correlated with one another to determine their proper relationship. Correlation may be necessary from outcrop to outcrop along the general trend of the edges of the strata, either along the strike, or along the direction of dip, or in some direction oblique to strike and dip. This statement may be understood if the reader will imagine that the sandstone layers in Figs. 160–163 are exposed only in detached outcrops. Rocks may have to be correlated across a fold, as indicated in Fig. 165, where the sandstone outcrops, at *a*, *b*, and *c*, are found to belong to the same stratum.

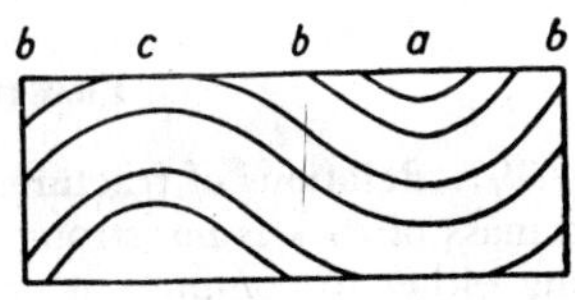

FIG. 164. Section illustrating the position of strata in eroded folds. *a*, youngest bed in section; *b*, beds of intermediate age; *c*, oldest exposed bed.

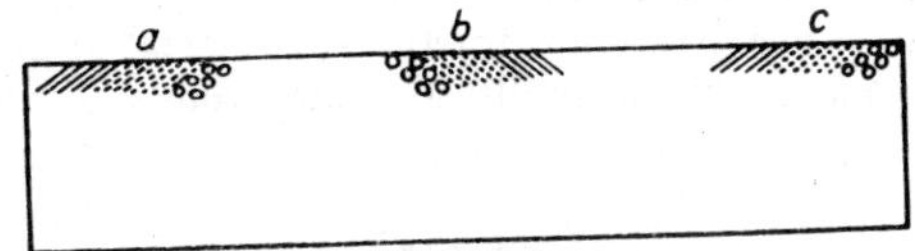

FIG. 165. Section to illustrate the methods of correlation of strata observed in different outcrops, *a*, *b*, *c*.

In cases of the two kinds just mentioned, the correlation of outcrops, being over areas of comparatively small extent, may be called *local correlation*. Where the relationship of rocks is studied over or across extensive areas, as in the entire Gulf Coastal Plain, or across the Rocky Mountains, the correlation may be termed *regional* (**345**).

Chapter 8

FRACTURES AND FRACTURE STRUCTURES

Fractures in Rocks

197. Relations of fractures to zones of the lithosphere. When a mass of rock is not strong enough to resist forces that are tending either to compress it or to stretch it, the rock suffers deformation. The change of form is brought about by flowage in the deeper parts of the lithosphere and by fracture in the upper parts. As pointed out in the foregoing chapter, the zone of fracture for any particular rock seldom coincides with that for another, because rocks differ in their capacity to "flow" under stress. However, since every rock which has been naturally exposed through erosion is within its zone of fracture, outcrops on the earth's surface are invariably and conspicuously traversed by cracks. A large majority of these fissures belong to the class called joints. Other types of rock fracture are faults, fracture cleavage, and breccia structure. Besides these there are certain kinds of fracture which are principally the effects of surface agencies. Such are crescentic fractures of glacial origin, exfoliation cracks along which spalls separate from a disintegrating rock, etc.

Faults

Terminology and Classification[1]

198. General nature of faults. A *fault* may be defined as a fracture along which there has been slipping of the contiguous masses against one another. Points formerly in contact have been dislocated or displaced along the fracture. Solid rocks or unconsolidated sands, gravel, etc., may be dislocated in this way. Faulting may result from compression, tension, or torsion. Some

[1] The author has drawn freely from Bibliog., Reid, H. F., *et al.*, 1913. In a few cases he has slightly modified the definitions as given therein, but the fact is noted.

faults in loose or weakly consolidated clays, sands, and gravels are produced by the removal of a support (**221**).

In many cases, especially near the earth's surface, the process of dislocation is probably intermittent, although the stresses may be applied continuously and uniformly. This is because the rock does not break until its resistance is overcome. Then it gives way suddenly, and the relief is followed by another period of quiet during which the stresses again accumulate until they occasion another movement, generally on the old fractures. Thus faulting may be accomplished, a little at a time, until the tension or the compression, as the case may be, ceases to be operative.

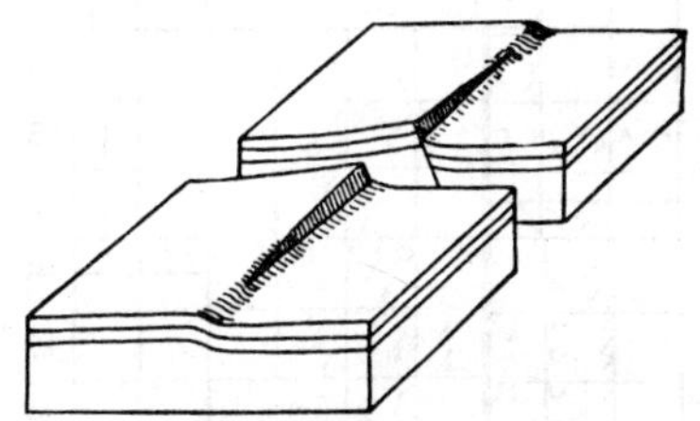

Fig. 166. A fault dying out and passing into a monoclinal fold at its two ends.

When the release is abrupt, the lithosphere is jarred and we say that there has been an earthquake.[2] Other things being equal, the greater a single movement is, the more violent is the shock and the farther do the perceptible earthquake vibrations travel from their place of origin. The displacement responsible for an earthquake is seldom more than a few inches, although occasionally it amounts to several feet; yet the sum of all the slipping that has occurred along a fault may be many hundreds or even thousands of feet.

If traced far enough a fault is found normally to die out at its two ends (Fig. 166). Consequently its displacement is apt to be at a maximum near the middle of its length, diminishing toward its extremities. Measured displacements vary from microscopic to many miles, and in length faults range also from microscopic to hundreds of miles.

[2] Not all earthquakes are so caused. Some are due to volcanic disturbances.

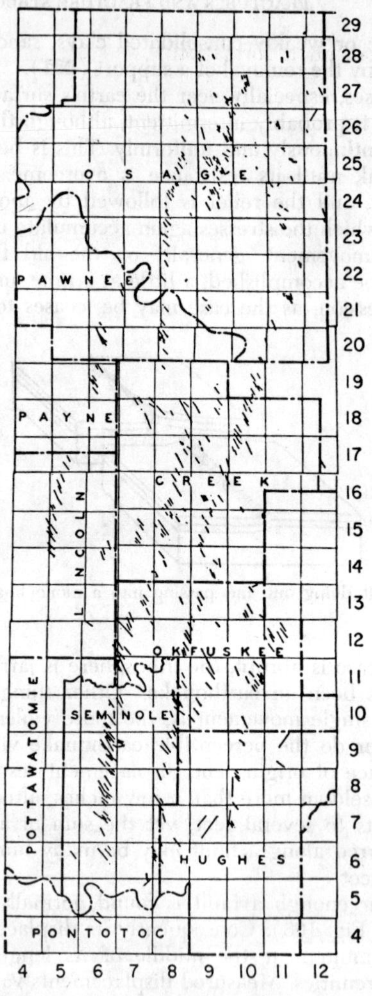

FIG. 167. Map showing distribution of the faults in certain counties in Oklahoma. The numbers on the right are townships north, and those in the lower margin are ranges east. (See Appendix 7.) (*Traced from the State Geologic Map.*)

In some districts there is a tendency for faults to occur in groups, or zones, within which the individual fractures not only possess many features in common, but also bear definite relations to one another. Thus, in Osage, Creek, Okfuskee, and adjoining counties in Oklahoma (Fig. 167), and likewise in eastern Texas (Fig. 168), there are fault zones in which the separate faults are arranged in overlapping order. Faults (or other features) which overlap in this manner are said to be *en echelon*. These zones usually trend about parallel to the regional strike of the strata. There can be no question that a majority of the faults in such groups or zones are effects of a common cause, which may be local settling over a deeply buried ridge; or, horizontal movement along steeply dipping faults in the basement; or, perhaps more commonly, regional twisting or torsion during uneven uplift or uneven subsidence involved in broad movements of the earth's crust. In the latter case, the twisting was probably such that there was relative tension more or less at right angles to the individual faults, and relative compression roughly parallel to them.[3]

199. Terms of general application. The characters of a fault are generally

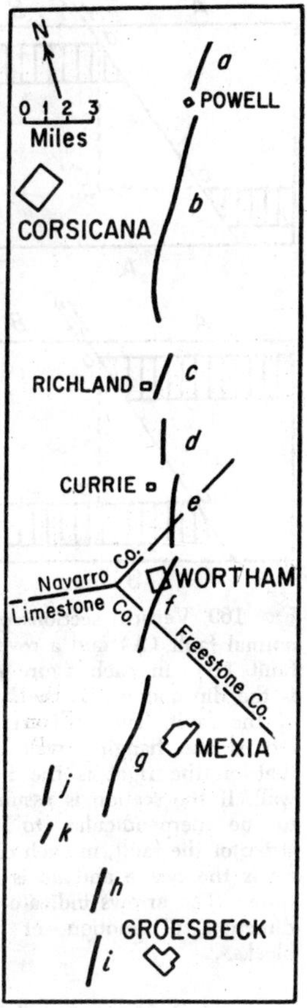

[3] For a discussion of this subject, see Bibliog.: Fath, A. E., 1920; Foley, Lyndon L., 1926; Link, Theo. A., 1929; Lahee, F. H., 1929, p. 357; and Sherrill, R. E., 1929.

FIG. 168. Sketch map showing distribution of major faults, *a* to *i*, in the Mexia fault zone, Texas. Faults *j* and *k* are in the Tehuacana fault zone. These faults are designated by the following names: *a*, Bazette; *b*, Powell; *c*, Richland; *d*, North Currie; *e*, South Currie; *f*, Wortham; *g*, Mexia; *h*, North Groesbeck; *i*, South Groesbeck.

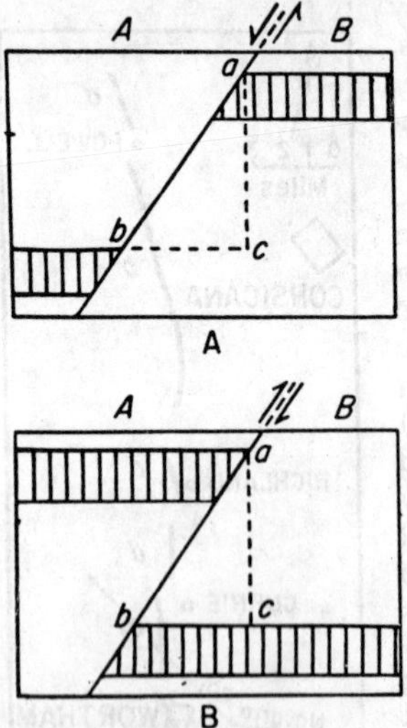

FIG. 169. Vertical sections of a normal fault (A) and a reverse fault (B). In each figure *abc* is the dip and *bac* is the hade of the fault. The wall on the left is the hanging wall and that on the right is the footwall. If the section is assumed to be perpendicular to the strike of the fault, in each case, *bc* is the heave and *ac* is the throw. The arrows indicate the direction of motion of the blocks.

different in different places. An illustration of this statement is the varying amount of displacement shown in the fault in Fig. 166. Consequently most of the terms in use refer only to part of the fault to which they are applied and not necessarily to the fracture as a whole. This must be kept in mind in connection with the definitions given below.

The contiguous surfaces of the two bodies of rock that have been displaced, in faulting, are called the *walls* of the fault. The upper walls of an inclined or horizontal fault is the *hanging wall*, and the lower one is the *footwall* (Fig. 169). When referring to these surfaces in contact with one another, or to either one, separately, we may speak of the fault surface or the *surface of faulting*.[4]

Although ordinarily fault walls are irregular in their minor details (**207, 39, H**), when looked at from a large point of view, they may be relatively flat or undulating. Their minor irregularities sometimes give rise to open spaces in which vein minerals may subsequently be deposited. The fracture is not always clean-cut and definite, for there may be more or less crushing of the wall rocks during the act of slipping. Finely pulverized rock flour of this origin is *gouge*. Coarser material, consisting of frag-

[4] The reader is reminded that the accompanying illustrations are diagrammatic. In the field fault zones may be found instead of the fault surfaces herein figured, and they may have much less regularity in direction and shape. Unfortunately, fault *plane* has often been used for fault *surface*, although, in nature, no fault surface is a plane.

ments of various sizes, usually associated with a more finely crushed matrix, is *fault breccia* (Fig. 170, C). The layer of gouge or breccia is termed the *fault zone* or the *shear zone.*[5] If such a shear zone is present, the walls are separated by the width of the zone. These fault zones may have vein minerals deposited between the fragments (243). The displaced masses on either side of a fault may be called *fault blocks.* A *horse* (Fig. 170, A) is a large fragment of rock broken from one block and caught between the walls of the fault. Sometimes bedding, or some other parallel structure in the fault blocks, has been turned up or dragged against the fault walls during the differential movement. Minor folding of this kind is called *drag* (Fig. 170, B). It is frequently well exemplified in faulted unconsolidated beds. It may

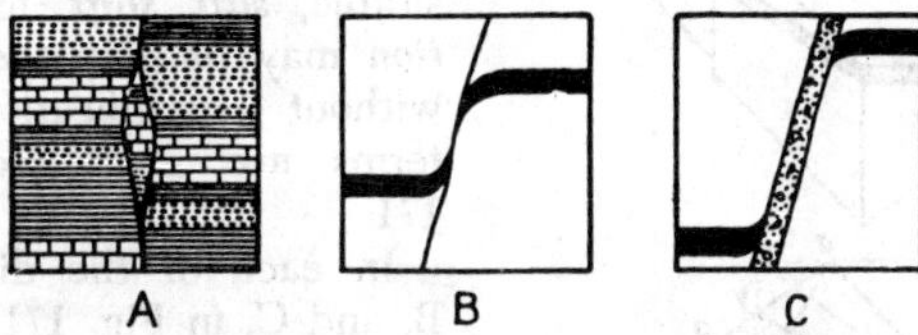

FIG. 170. Sections of faults showing, in A, a "horse"; in B, drag produced by bending; and in C, drag produced by brecciation.

produce sharp changes of dip and strike (*drag dips* and *drag strikes*) in the vicinity of a fault. The term is also applied by miners to the stringing out of fragments of a disrupted dike, ore body, etc., along the fault (Fig. 170, C). In the actual slipping the blocks may scratch, groove, or polish one another. The polished surfaces are said to be *slickensided,* and these surfaces, or *slickensides,* may be marked by parallel fault scratches or striae. Some geologists apply the name *slickensides* to both the polish and the scratches together.

Fault line, fault trace, and *fault outcrop* are used synonymously for the intersection of a fault with the surface of the ground.

The words *attitude, strike,* and *dip* are used for faults in the same way as for strata (14), and they may be applied to a sharp fracture or to a shear zone (Fig. 169). The *hade* of a fault, or of a shear zone, is the complement of the dip, *i.e.,* it is the vertical

[5] Not to be confused with the groups of related faults called *fault zones* (p. 225).

angle between the plane of the fault and a vertical plane containing the strike of the fault (Fig. 169, *cab*). In the interest of uniformity, when referring to the attitude of a fault, *dip* is to be preferred to *hade*. In other words, it is better to measure the inclination of a fault downward from the horizontal.

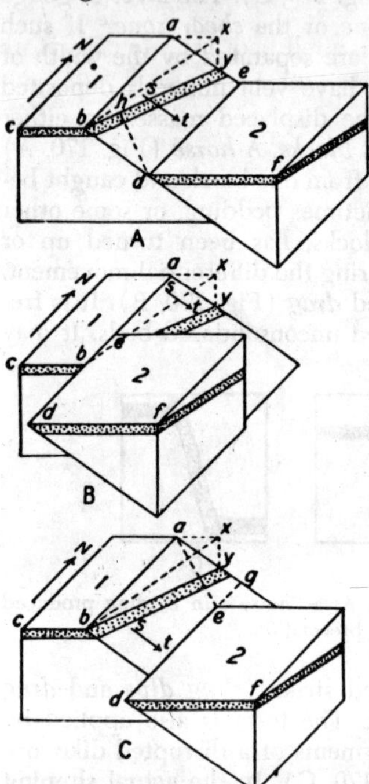

Fig. 171. Displacements of a fault. The upper and lower surfaces of each of the blocks are horizontal. In each diagram, a layer (bed, dike, vein, etc.), dipping toward the north, has been broken by a fault which strikes north-south and dips east. (See text for further explanation.)

200. Kinds of displacement. *Displacement* and *dislocation* are words used only with a general meaning in this book. When more accuracy is desirable, *slip, shift,* and *separation* may be employed with or without qualification. These terms are illustrated in Fig. 171.

In each of the diagrams A, B, and C, in Fig. 171, the strike of the fault is *ab* and the dip of the fault is *st*. In A, block 2 slipped down the dip of the fault from *a* to *e*; in B, the movement of block 2 was horizontal, along the fault strike, from *a* to *e*; and in C, the movement was diagonal, from *a* to *e*. In each of these cases, *ae* is the *slip*, or *net slip*, that is, "the relative displacement of formerly adjacent points on opposite sides of the fault, measured in the fault surface."[6] In Fig. 171, C, where triangle *age* is in the fault surface, *eg* (parallel to *ab*) is called the *strike slip*, and *ag* is called the *dip slip* (parallel to the dip of the fault). In Fig. 171, A, there is no strike slip. In Fig. 171, B, there is no dip slip. In Fig. 171, A, *hd* is the perpendicular distance be-

[6] The quotations in this article are taken from Bibliog., Reid, H. F., 1913.

tween corresponding parts (here top surface) of the dislocated bed (or other layer), measured in the fault surface. This is the *perpendicular slip* (*hd*).

In A and B the trace of the faulted bed, *by*, is clearly visible. The angle *aby* between this trace and a horizontal plane, meas-

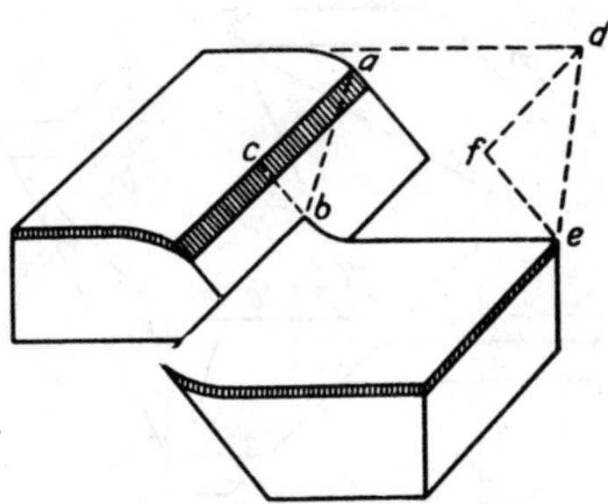

FIG. 172. Slip and shift of a fault. The curvature of the beds is drag. *ab*, slip; *bc*, dip slip; *ac*, strike slip; *de*, shift; *fe*, dip shift; *df*, strike shift. The words "dip" and "strike" are used for the components of slip and shift which are parallel to the dip and strike, respectively, of the fault. (*After H. F. Reid, with modification.*)

ured in the "plane" of the fault is the *pitch*, or *rake*, of this trace, and the vertical angle *xby* between this trace and a horizontal plane is the *plunge* of the trace.[7] (Cf. pitch, plunge, and rake in folds, as defined in Art. **179.**)

If there is drag or other distortion along the fault, the slip is not equal to the displacement that affects points situated outside the immediate zone of dislocation. This is illustrated in Fig. 172, where *ab* is the slip and *de* is the displacement of the point, *e*, in moving from its former position, *d*. This distance, *de*, is called the *shift*. It is distinctly greater here than the slip. Figure 173 shows another example of shift.

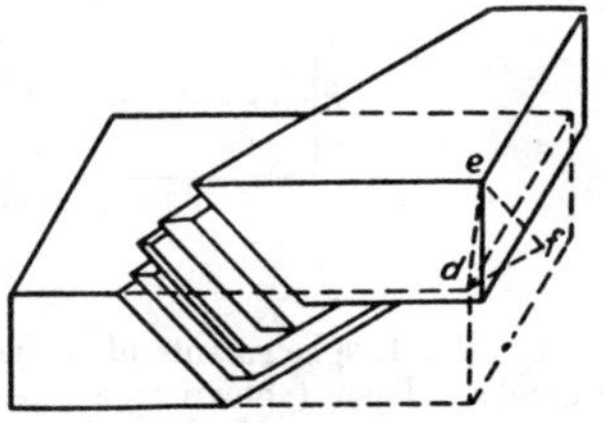

FIG. 173. Shift produced by a multiple fault. *de*, shift; *ef*, dip shift; *df*, strike shift. (*After W. Lindgren.*)

"The shift is of greater importance in the larger problems of geology than the slip." "The *separation* of a bed (Figs. 174–176), vein, or of any

[7] Bibliog., Beckwith, R. H., 1947, p. 82.

recognizable surface, is the distance between the *corresponding surface* of the two parts of the disrupted bed, etc., measured in any indicated direction. The distance must be measured between the *corresponding surfaces* on the two sides of the fault—for instance, between the upper surfaces of the two parts of the disrupted bed or between their lower surfaces

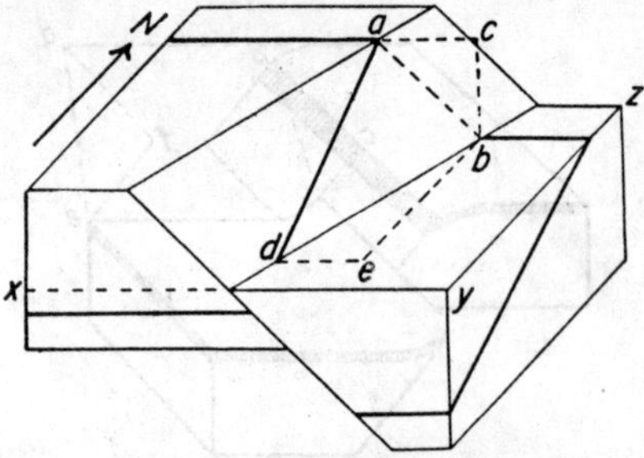

FIG. 174. Displacements of a diagonal fault which dips southeastward and breaks a layer (shown as a heavy line) that dips south. *ad* is the trace of this layer on the fault surface; *ab*, slip; *bc*, vertical separation; *ac* = *de*, horizontal separation along strike of bedding (*gap*); *be*, offset.

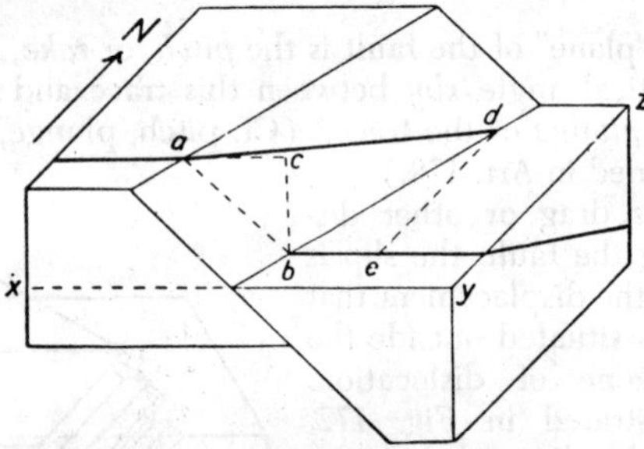

FIG. 175. Displacements of a diagonal fault which dips southeastward and breaks a layer (shown as a heavy line) that dips north. *ad* is the trace of this layer on the fault surface; *ab*, slip; *bc*, vertical separation; *ac* = *be*, horizontal separation along strike of bedding (*overlap*); *de*, offset.

—but not between the upper surface of one part and the lower surface of the other. Moreover, the surfaces considered must be parallel with the general extension of the bed, vein, etc., such as the upper or lower surface of a bed or the walls of a dike.

"The *vertical separation* is the separation measured along a vertical line (Figs. 174, 175).

"The *horizontal separation* is the separation measured in any indicated horizontal direction.

"The *normal horizontal separation* of a bed or other surface is its horizontal separation measured at right angles to the strike of the bed, etc. It is frequently determined from the outcrops of the bed at the surface of the ground; it is then usually called the *offset* of the bed."

If A and B, in Fig. 176, represent the ground plans of oblique faults on a level surface, *be*, and not *bd*, would be the offset of the bed. *bd* would be the horizontal separation along the fault

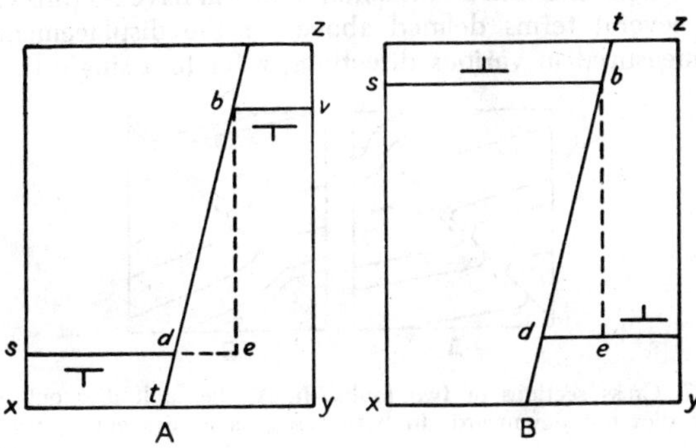

FIG. 176. Offset, gap, and overlap. A is a plan of the structures which would be seen in the plane *xyz* of Fig. 174; B has a like relation to Fig. 175. *be*, offset; *de*, gap in A, and overlap in B. Observe the symbols for dip and strike of the bedding.

strike. *de*, in the same figures, would be called the *gap* and *overlap* of the bed, respectively; they are measured parallel with the strike of the bed.

"The *perpendicular separation* is the distance between the planes of the two parts of a dislocated bed or other surface measured at right angles to these planes."

"The measures which will be most commonly made are the offset at the surface, and the vertical and horizontal separations in shafts and drifts, respectively" . . . .

"It is extremely important clearly to distinguish between the slip and shift and the separation. The first two refer to the actual relative displacement of the two sides of the fault, the last to the relative displacement of the surfaces of the two branches of a dislocated bed, etc.

"Movements of one side or of both sides of the fault parallel with the plane of a bed would not alter the separation of the bed, but would materially alter the slip and shift."

By *throw* is meant "the vertical distance between corresponding lines in the two *fracture surfaces* of a disrupted stratum, etc., measured in a vertical plane at right angles to the fault strike. The *heave* is the horizontal distance between corresponding lines in the two *fracture surfaces* of a disrupted stratum, etc., measured at right angles to the fault strike" (Fig. 169). A vertical fault can have no heave and a horizontal fault can have no throw.[8]

The several terms defined above for the displacement of a fault, measured in various directions, refer to a single line, or a

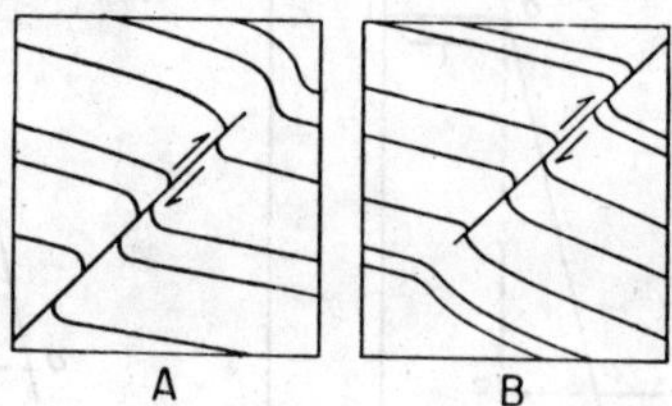

FIG. 177. Cross sections of two faults. In A, the fault dies out upward; in B, it dies out downward. In both cases, as it dies out, it passes into a flexure.

single surface, disrupted and separated in the movement. Because faults may die out upward, downward, or laterally, and because the broken strata or other rock materials may vary in rigidity, there may be considerable variation in the amount of displacement on the same fault, measured between points formerly in contact, at successively higher or lower levels in the disrupted mass (Fig. 177).

201. Classification of faults. Faults are classified according to: (1) the nature of their displacement; (2) their distribution; and (3) their relations to disrupted bedding or other parallel structures.

[8] Straley has discussed the confusion which apparently exists in the use of these terms, "throw" and "heave," by different geologists. It remains our opinion that these words should be applied with the meanings herein quoted, and not with any necessary connotation of fault movement. The terms previously given for fault movement should be adequate. (See Bibliog., Straley, H. W., III, 1934.)

1. In any rock formations, stratified or otherwise, a *dip-slip fault* is a fault that has its net slip essentially along the line of the fault dip (Fig. 178, A). A *strike-slip fault* has its net slip along the fault strike[9] (Fig. 178, B); and an *oblique-slip fault* has its net slip anywhere between the dip line and strike of the fault (Figs. 171, C, and 172).

A *normal fault* is one in which the hanging wall (199) has apparently slipped down with respect to the footwall (Fig. 169, A); and a *reverse* (not "reversed") *fault* is one in which the hanging wall has apparently moved up with respect to the footwall

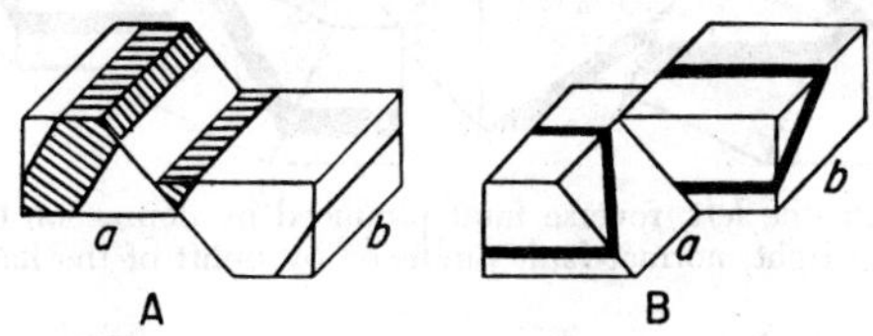

FIG. 178. A, a dip-slip strike fault. The slip is along the dip of the fault, and the fault strikes parallel to the strike of the bedding. B, a strike-slip dip fault. The slip is along the strike of the fault, and the fault strikes at right angles to the strike of the bedding.

(Fig. 169, B). We say "apparently" because a normal fault may be produced

1. If the footwall remains stationary and the hanging wall moves down.
2. If the hanging wall remains stationary and the footwall moves up.
3. If both walls move down, but the hanging wall moves farther than the footwall; and
4. If both walls move up, but the footwall moves farther than the hanging wall.

Four similar conditions may be associated with reverse faulting (merely exchange the words "footwall" and "hanging wall" in the above four clauses).

Sometimes the displacement characteristic of a normal fault may result from relative uplift of the hanging wall, and the dis-

[9] Although "rift" is used for a tension fault, the displacement of which is due to gravitational subsidence, the term has also been applied to strike-slip faults and to valleys caused by such faults (see Art. 285). Also, *wrench fault* has been applied to a strike-slip fault that dips steeply, particularly if it cuts across the regional structure. (See Bibliog., Moody, J. D., and M. J. Hill, 1956.)

placement characteristic of a reverse fault may result from relative depression of the hanging wall (Fig. 179). It is not always true, then, that there is extension of territory by normal faulting, as if tensile stresses had operated, nor that there is contraction of area in reverse faulting, as if due to compression. "Normal" and "reverse" should "be used purely for purposes of local description and not for the purpose of indicating extension or contraction, tension or compression, vertical or horizontal forces."[10]

Fig. 179. On the left, reverse fault produced by depression of the hanging wall; on the right, normal fault produced by uplift of the hanging wall.

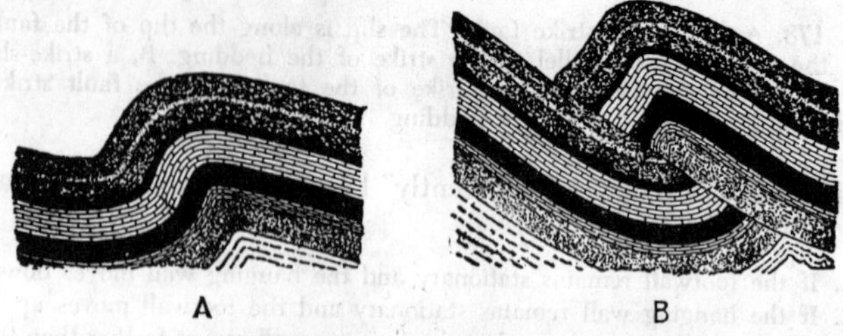

Fig. 180. Sections illustrating the origin of a break thrust. The position of the overthrust fault shown in B was determined by the fracture represented in the massive limestone bed in A. Observe that in this kind of faulting, and also in the varieties shown in Figs. 181 and 182, older rocks come to lie above younger rocks. (*After B. Willis.*)

Sometimes a steeply dipping fault may change its attitude along its course from dipping in one direction, through vertical, to dipping in the opposite direction, its downthrown block always being the same. This results in its changing along its course from normal to reverse.

A fault due to gravitative settling, resulting from tension, is

[10] Bibliog., Reid, H. F., *et al.*, 1913, p. 178.

called a *rift*.[11] *Thrust* may be reserved for faults that are demonstrably due to compression. Three varieties of thrust are noted by Willis: (*a*) *break thrusts,* when the fault follows a previously formed tension fracture (Fig. 180); (*b*) *shear* or *stretch* thrusts, when the break follows the sheared and stretched underlimb of

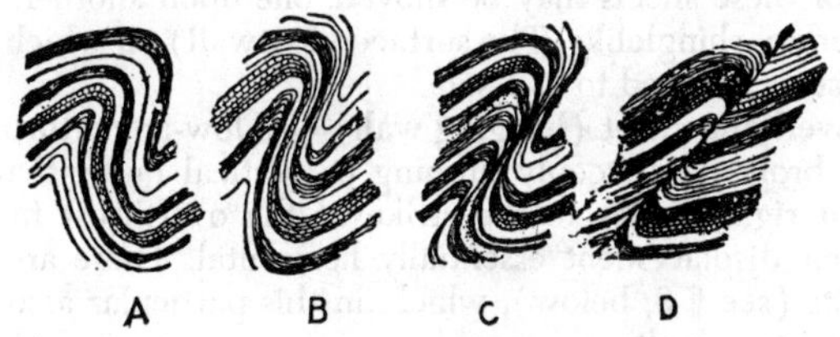

FIG. 181. Development of a stretch thrust from an overturned fold. (*After B. Willis.*)

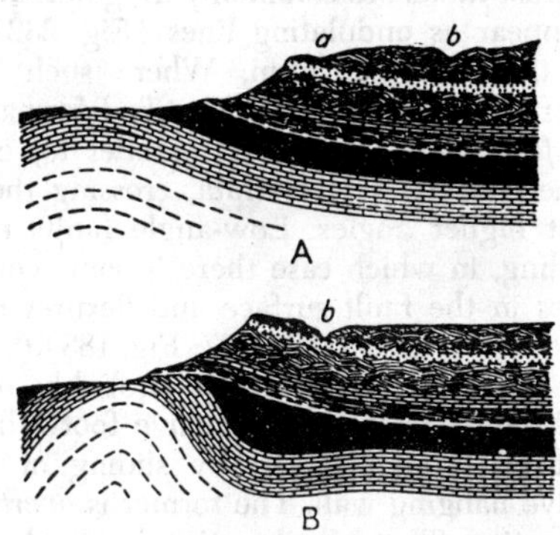

FIG. 182. Sections illustrating the origin of an erosion thrust. The position of the overthrust shown in B was determined by the land surface condition represented in A, where a weak rock (dark shading) outcrops at the base of a scarp. The force acted from right to left. Erosion is supposed to have continued during the faulting. (*After B. Willis.*)

an overturned fold (Fig. 181); and (*c*) *erosion thrusts,* when the competent layer carrying the thrust is weakened by erosion at or near the crest of the anticline (Fig. 182).[12] A thrust having a relatively high angle of dip is a *ramp*. An *overthrust* is any thrust fault having a low dip (large hade) (Figs. 180–182).

[11] See footnote 9, p. 233.

[12] Bibliog., Willis, B., 1892, pp. 222–223; Leith, C. K., 1913, pp. 46–48.

Overthrusts are very common in regions of intense folding. Their displacements may amount to several miles.[13] They have been traced as single faults for as far as 200 miles, or even more. The overlying block, or *sheet,* is termed a *nappe* (pl., *nappes*) or *decke* (pl., *decken*). Because of successive overthrusting several of these sheets may be shoved, one upon another, so that they overlap, shinglelike. The surface (footwall) on which a fault sheet rests is referred to as a *sole.*

The overlying sheet (hanging wall) of a low-angle thrust fault may be broken by steeply dipping or vertical faults that strike nearly at right angles to the strike of the overthrust fault and have their displacement essentially horizontal. These are strike-slip faults (see ¶ 3, below), which, in this particular association, are called *tear faults.*

Low-angle thrust faults are commonly irregular, and their cross sections may appear as undulating lines (Fig. 232) even when they preserve their original form. Where such a fault cuts obliquely upward across a series of stratified formations, it may be a *bedding fault* (*i.e.,* essentially parallel to, or along, the bedding) in the *less* competent strata, crossing the *more* competent strata at higher angles. Low-angle faults may undergo warping or folding, in which case there is some correspondence between flexures in the fault surface and flexures in the folded strata above and below (see *a,* Fig. 227; Fig. 183).[14]

Most of the low-angle thrust faults probably resulted from sliding of the hanging wall *over* a passive footwall; but similar relations might be brought about by sliding of the footwall *beneath* a passive hanging wall. The former is *overthrusting;* the latter, *underthrusting.* That overthrusting has probably occurred in most cases is suggested by these facts:[15] (1) the relative direction of movement of the hanging wall is usually in the direction of convexity of the trends of associated arcuate folds, and the axes of such folds curve outward, away from the deforming force; (2) there would be less resistance to the lifting and sliding of an *overthrust* mass than to the downward and forward driving of an *underthrust* mass; (3) the rocks of the overlying sheet being

[13] See Bibliog., Bevan, A., 1929, p. 447; also Willis, Bailey, 1923.

[14] For a detailed discussion of complicated thrust faulting, see Bibliog., Hume, G. S., 1957.

[15] Bibliog., Nevin, C. N., 1936, pp. 130–133.

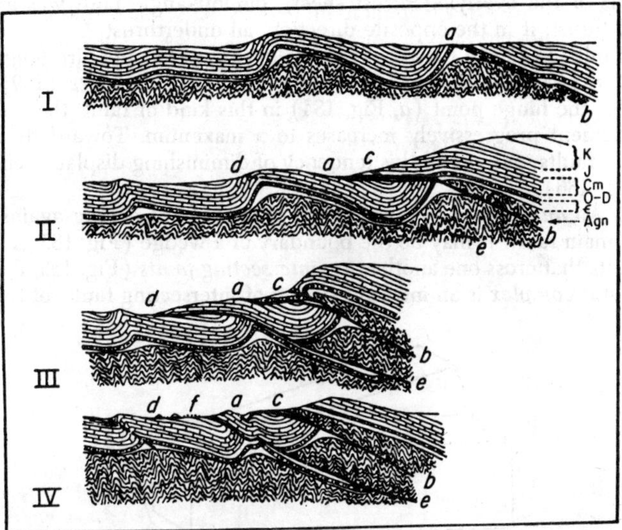

FIG. 183. Cross section showing successive stages (I to IV) of thrusting in the eastern part of the Canyon Mountain area, Montana. In each stage the dashed line indicates the position of development of the next thrust. Stage I shows the hypothetical condition before thrusting, with two anticlines truncated by erosion. A shear, propagated from the pre-Cambrian (Agn) through the Middle Cambrian shales to the surface at the crest of the northern anticline, gives rise to stage II. A second shear (*de*) cuts through the Madison limestone (Cm) where that formation has been weakened by flexure and erosion (at *d*); and a branch shear from *ab* reaches the surface at *c*. On this the formations above the fault surface are overturned (stage III). In stage IV, further compression has folded the thrust planes, and erosion has produced the present topography. The section in stage IV is about 8 miles long. (*After D. C. Skeels, with some modifications. See Bibliog. Reproduced through the courtesy of the author, the Journal of Geology, and the University of Chicago Press.*)

older and more rigid, would be better able to stand the strain of overthrusting than the younger rocks of the footwall could stand underthrusting. According to Lovering,[16] if the active wall of a tear fault moved in the same direction as the relative move-

[16] Bibliog., Lovering, T. S., 1932.

ment of the overlying thrust sheet, this low-angle fault was an overthrust; if in the opposite direction, an underthrust.[17]

Faults on which the blocks rotate during dislocation are *hinge faults, pivotal faults, scissors faults,* or *rotational faults* (189). From the hinge point (*a*, Fig. 184) in this kind of fault, the displacement progressively increases to a maximum. Toward their ends, faults may reveal this tendency of diminishing displacement (Fig. 166).

2. An *auxiliary* or *branch fault* is a minor fault ending against the main fault. It may be the boundary of a wedge (Fig. 185, A). Faults that cross one another are *intersecting faults* (Fig. 185, B). A *fault complex* is an intricate system of intersecting faults of the

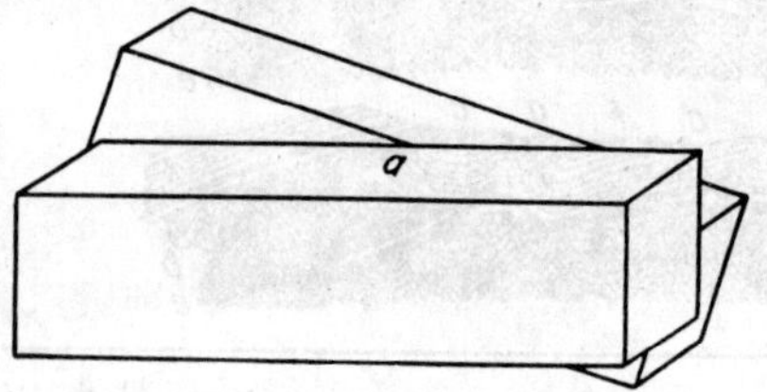

Fig. 184. Rotational fault.

same age or of different ages. When several parallel faults are close together and the intervening fault slabs or slices are not distorted, the group may be termed a *multiple fault*. A multiple fault in which the downthrow is on the same side of each component fault, is a *distributive fault*. A multiple fault, consisting of thrust faults, is called *imbricate structure*. It may divide the

[17] Stuart K. Clark has grouped most varieties of faults into six categories, of which five are shears (involving failure under stress) and one is a simple type of tension fault. His six classes are: (1) normal diagonal shears (including most normal faults); (2) reverse diagonal shears (including most thrust faults); (3) horizontal (or nearly horizontal) faults (bedding-plane shears); (4) tension faults (of shallow origin, dying out downward); (5) lateral shears (including strike-slip faults, tear faults); and (6) vertical shears (apparently a theoretical group). For further discussion and examples, see Bibliog., Clark, Stuart K., 1943.

In his analysis of faulting in Britain, Anderson groups all faults, according to their relations to the stresses involved in their origin, into (1) normal faults, (2) transcurrent faults (equivalent to strike-slip faults), and (3) reverse faults. (See Bibliog., Anderson, E. M., 1942.)

major blocks in regional overthrusting into minor slices (Fig. 186).

3. In strata, a *strike fault* (Fig. 178, A) has its strike parallel to the strike of the beds; a *dip fault* (Fig. 178, B) strikes at right angles to the strike of the beds; a *diagonal fault* is one in which the strike is oblique to the strike of the beds (Figs. 174–176); a

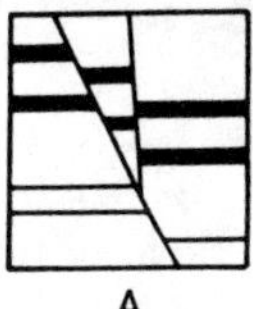

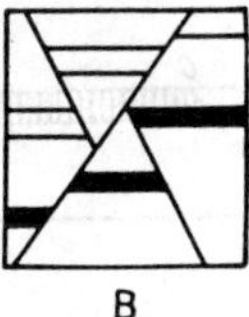

FIG. 185. A, branching fault; B, intersecting faults. Which fault is the older one in B?

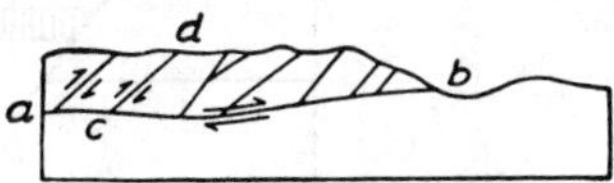

FIG. 186. Imbricate structure in the overhanging block (*adbc*) of a thrust fault (*ab*).

bedding fault is parallel to the stratification (Fig. 187); a *longitudinal fault* strikes parallel to the general structure (fold axes, schistosity, etc.) of a region; and a *transverse fault* strikes across such structure.

202. Terms for fault blocks. A wedge-shaped block between two faults is a *fault wedge* (Figs. 185, A; 188, 189). Wedges are sometimes indicative of considerable lateral motion (Fig. 190). An upthrown block between two downthrown blocks is a *horst*[18] (Fig. 191, A). A downthrown block between two upthrown blocks is a *graben* or *fault trough* (Fig. 191, B). In both definitions the movement of the blocks is relative. Thus, in the graben, the middle block may have gone down, or the walls on both sides may have gone up, or all three may have settled with respect to their original position, but the middle one more than

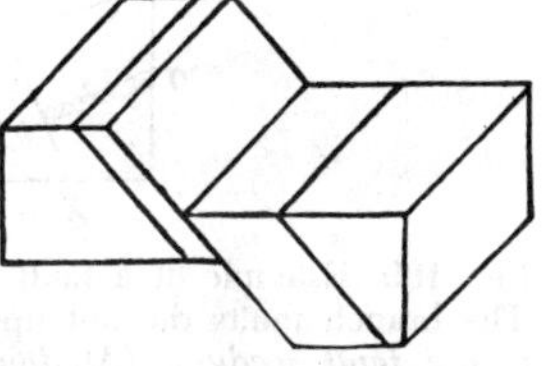

FIG. 187. A bedding fault.

[18] Some authors anglicize such words as "horst" and "graben" by adding "s" for the plural, instead of using the native plural (Horste, Gräben). Some say "horsts," but retain graben (without the umlaut) for the plural. We believe that as far as possible these words should be treated consistently. Therefore, in the absence of any rule, in this book, for the plurals, we say horsts, grabens, klippes, fensters, dreikanters, einkanters, etc.

the other two. Similar reasoning may be applied to a horst. In the diagrams (Fig. 191, A and B) tension faults, or rifts bound the middle block. Conceivably these faults might dip in the direction opposite to that shown, and they would then be thrust faults, or ramps. A graben might thus be defined as a *rift trough*, or a *ramp trough*, according to the nature of its bounding faults. Again, corresponding nomenclature might be applied to horsts.

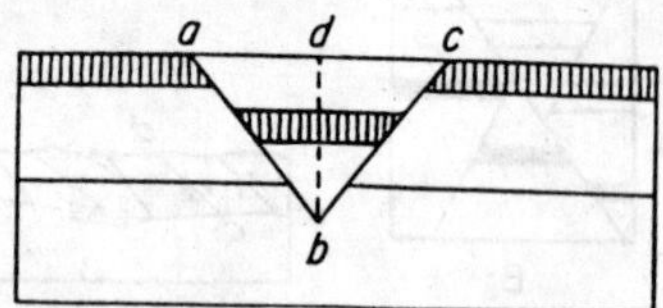

FIG. 188. Section of a fault wedge, *abcd*.

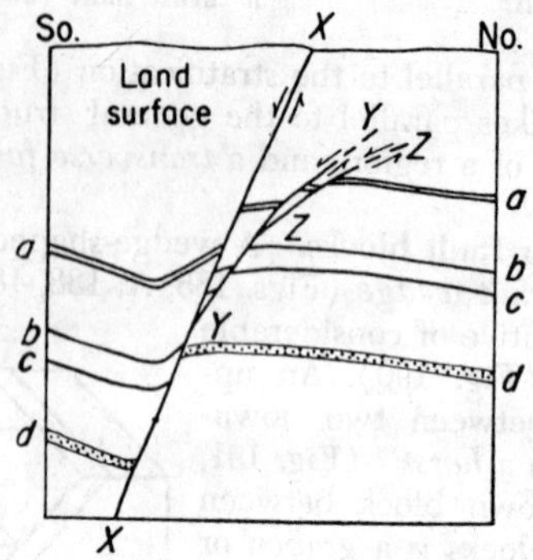

FIG. 189. Example of a fault (*x*) with two associated branch faults (*y,z*). The branch faults die out upward. Between *x* and *y*, and between *y* and *z, are fault wedges. (Modified from section of Fitts Oil Field structure in Pontotoc County, Okla. See Bibliog., Clark, Stuart K.,* 1943.)

Grabens may occur on or near the crest of broad arches; also, on the crests of domes associated with deep salt intrusion (¶ 6, Art. **180**), as indicated in Fig. 192. These relations suggest some expansion and settling of the rock masses following the compression, or uplift, that produced the arch. Faults like those in Fig. 168, with downthrow on the side up the regional dip of the strata, may be the down-dip walls of *strike grabens,* which are

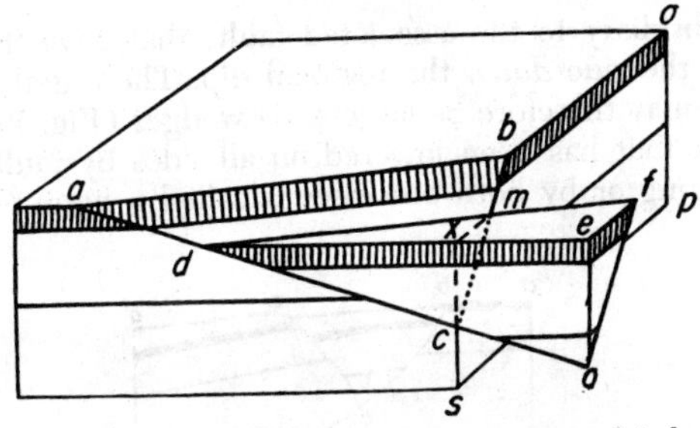

FIG. 190. Block diagram showing a possible explanation for the dislocation of such a wedge as that drawn in Fig. 188. *efg* corresponds to *dcb* in Fig. 188. *d* has slipped from *a*, and *f* from *b*.

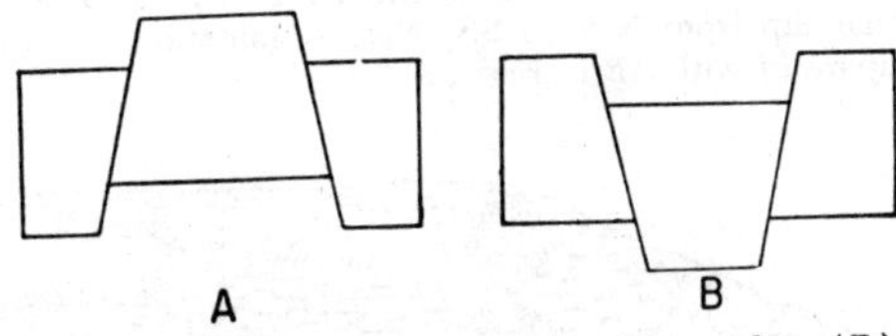

FIG. 191. Sections of a horst (A) and a graben (B).

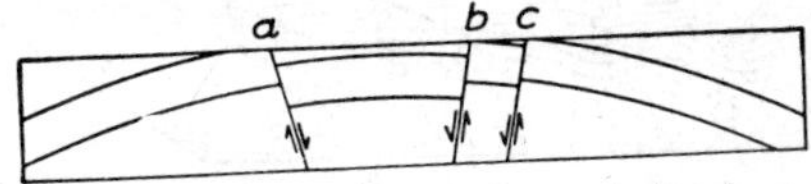

FIG. 192. Cross section of a deep salt dome (salt plug not reached by deep drilling) where the crest has broken and dropped to form a compound graben, between *a* and *c*.

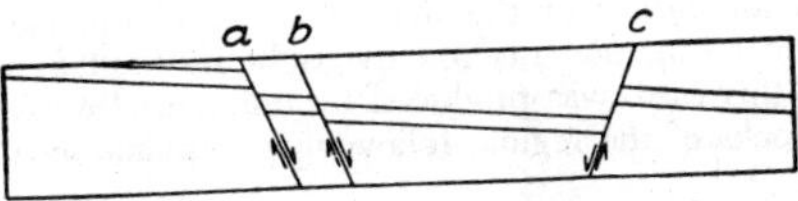

FIG. 193. Cross section of a graben (*ac*) that trends essentially parallel to the regional strike (perpendicular to the plane of the page).

bounded 2 or 3 miles up dip by tension faults (rifts) that have their downthrow on the down-dip[19] side (Fig. 193). In such cases deep drilling indicates that the Mexia-type faults (downthrow on the side *up* the regional dip of the strata) are essentially second-

[19] These references to dip are to the regional dip of the faulted strata.

ary or subsidiary to the associated faults that have their downthrow on the side *down* the regional dip. These grabens (as in Fig. 193) may therefore be large-scale wedges (Fig. 194).

A block that has been lowered on all sides by faulting or by downwarping or by both processes is called a *basin* (Fig. 195).

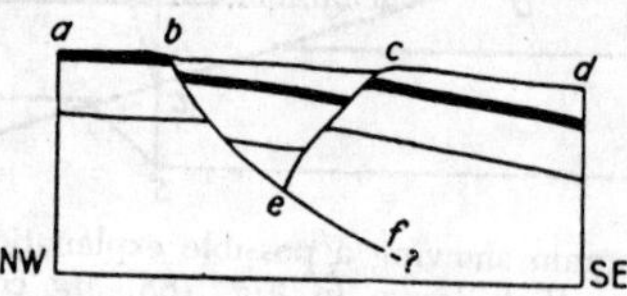

FIG. 194. Diagram to illustrate apparent relation of faults of the Balcones (*bf*) and Mexia (*ce*) types. *abcd* is the land surface. The faulted beds have a regional dip from NW to SE. Note termination of fault *ce* against fault *bf*. Compare *bf* with *AB* in Fig. 197.

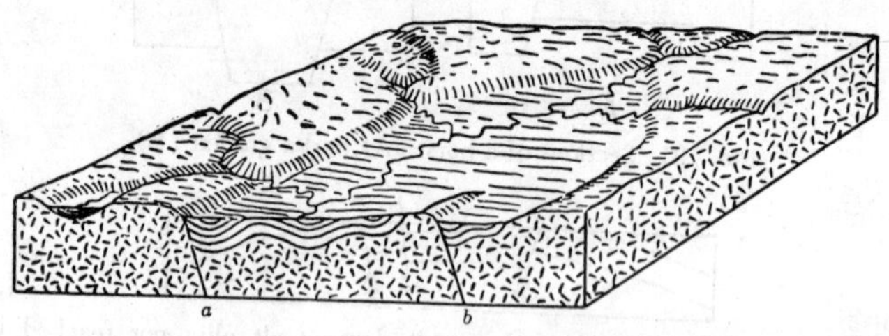

FIG. 195. Block diagram of a structural basin. The dash pattern represents a hard crystalline rock formation upon which a series of strata (lined) rests unconformably. The strata occupy the basin. The little basin on the extreme left is an *outlier* of the main basin, and the mass of crystalline rocks within the basin, bounded on the right by fault *b*, is an *inlier*. The topography, in this case, was produced by differential erosion acting on the hard and soft rocks of the region, following peneplanation (Art. 282).

These terms (*horst, graben, basin*) are structural in their significance, and they are used irrespective of the topographic form of the block (224).

When a fault is approximately parallel to the strike of the strata, the block on the side of the fault toward which the dip of the beds is measured may be termed the *down-dip block,* and the other one is the *up-dip block* (Fig. 178, A). Note that the word, dip, in these two terms refers to the inclination of the beds.

On the down-dip side of any given stratum, the strike of a diagonal fault makes an acute angle with the strike of the beds (angle *sdt*, Fig. 176, A) on one side of the fault, and an obtuse angle with the strike of the beds on the other side (angle *dbv*, Fig. 176, A). The block containing the acute angle on the down-dip side of an outcropping bed may be called the *acute-angle block*, and the other, the *obtuse-angle block* (see also Fig. 176, B).

203. Omission and repetition of beds defined. Erosion after strike-faulting of stratified rocks may bring about the entire elimination of some beds (Fig. 196, A), or, on the other hand, it may cause repetition of some beds, with the same sequence, on

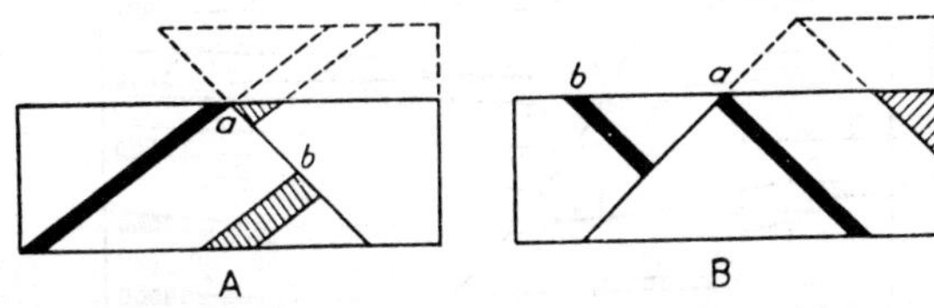

Fig. 196. Sections showing omission (A) and repetition (B) of strata. In A, the beds between *a* and *b* are entirely concealed beneath the surface of the ground. In B, beds between *a* and *b* are exposed twice in the same succession on the surface of the ground.

opposite sides of the fault (Fig. 196, B). The first is spoken of as *omission of beds* and the second as *repetition of beds*, respectively.

204. Variations in dip and displacement of faults. When faults are exposed in cross section over a distance of many hundreds of feet or when their underground form can be ascertained by numerous deep well logs or by seismographic methods, they are often found to change in dip with increasing depth. Thrust faults may steepen with depth (Fig. 183). On the contrary, normal faults—especially strike faults with downthrow on the side down the regional dip of the strata—may reveal a decreasing angle of dip with increasing depth (Fig. 197).

205. Relations of faults to folds. Flexing or folding of strata may be associated with faulting. Figure 166 shows a tension fault passing into a flexure at each end. A fault of this kind may also pass into a flexure either upward or downward. Similarly, a thrust fault may pass into a fold either laterally or upward or downward (Fig. 177). In these cases, bending of the strata no doubt occurred first, and then, with further application of the stress, fracturing followed where this stress was most effective (Fig. 183).

Drag (Fig. 170, B) is another variety of flexing associated with faulting. It is generally very local, but it may assume larger proportions, as represented in Fig. 198.

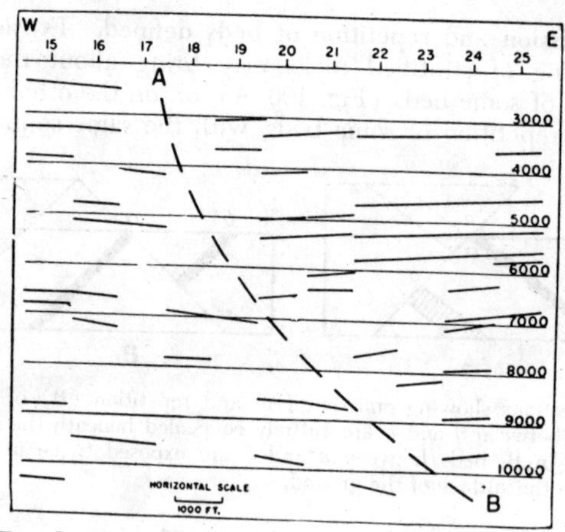

FIG. 197. Dip data secured by reflection seismographic work (see p. 804) in an area in south Texas. Note the zone of poor records, indicated by the dashed line, *AB*, which is interpreted as a fault, the dip of which decreases with depth. Note also that the strata dip toward the fault on both sides. Its displacement, though not revealed by these data, is down on the east side. (Cf. Fig. 199.)

A very interesting relation between folding and faulting is depicted in Fig. 199, where, for some distance out from the fault, the strata dip in toward it. This condition has been recognized by seismograph (Fig. 197) and then by drilling, in association with many strike faults of the Gulf Coastal Plain. It has also been observed exposed in mountain districts of considerable topographic relief. Comparison of Figs. 197, 199, and 297 suggests that the tilt of the beds toward the fault (from *a* to *b* and *c* to *d*, in Fig. 199), on the downthrown side, may be genetically associated with this kind of fault that so closely resembles the landslide slip. The thickening of the strata from *a* and *c*, toward *b* and

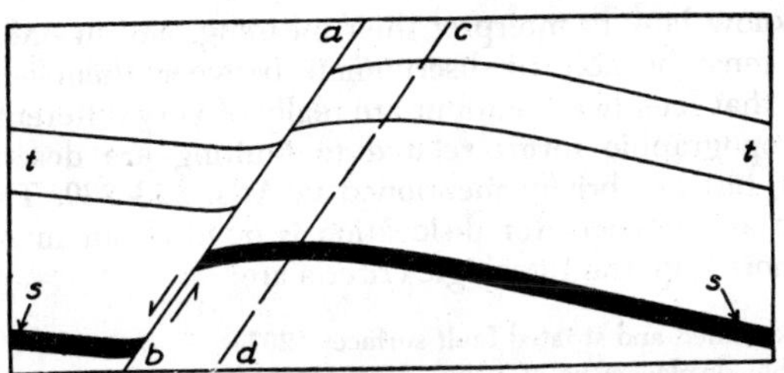

FIG. 198. Cross section of a normal fault (*ab*) with upthrow on the regional down-dip side. (The regional dip here is toward the right.) Some flexing, on a relatively large scale, seems to be genetically related to the fault, since the crestal surface (in section, *cd*) of the anticline in the upthrown block is parallel to the fault.

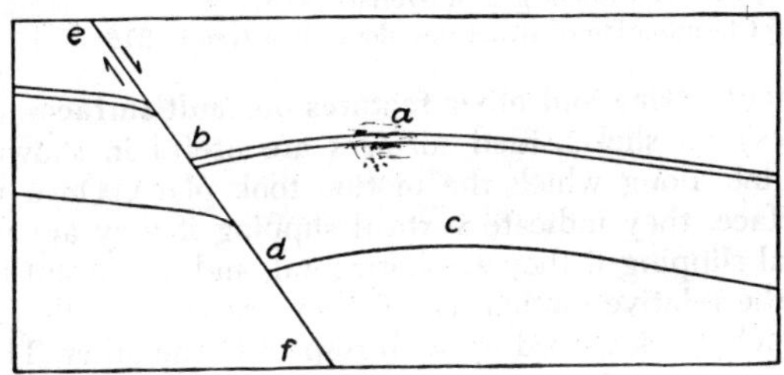

FIG. 199. Faulting of the normal type (*ef*), where there is dip of the strata *into* the fault on both sides of the break. (Cf. Fig. 197.)

d (Fig. 199), may mean that sliding on the fault was progressive during sedimentation.

EVIDENCES FOR FAULTING

206. Principal evidences of faulting. That faulting has occurred in any locality may be indicated in various ways. Sometimes slickensides or other marks of slipping may be observed on a fault surface exposed by natural or artificial means. More often the evidence is found in the relations of the rock structures on the two sides of the fault when the latter is viewed in horizontal, inclined, or vertical cross section. Or, again, the criteria may be topographic in character. These features, whether geologic or topographic, the field geologist should learn to recognize. He should know how to interpret their meaning, and in order to do this, he must be able to discriminate between them and other features that look like them but are really of very different origin.

The topographic forms related to faulting are described in Chap. 9, but are briefly mentioned in Arts. **223–230.** Their significance as evidences for dislocation is pointed out in Art. **230.**

The more important geologic criteria are:

1. Slickensided and striated fault surfaces (**207**).
2. Visible displacement of veins, dikes, strata, etc., on opposite sides of an exposed fault line (**208**).
3. Zones of breccia (**209, 243**).
4. Drag (**210**).
5. Repetition of strata (**211, 212, 214**).
6. Omission of strata (**211, 213, 214**).
7. Offset, with or without gap or overlap (**215**).
8. Abrupt termination of structures along their trend (**216**).

207. Fault striae and other features on fault surfaces. Striae (scratches) on slickensided surfaces are useful in showing the general line along which the motion took place. On a vertical fault surface, they indicate vertical slipping if they are vertical, horizontal slipping if they are horizontal, and so on; but they do not tell the relative motion, *i.e.*, if they are vertical, they do not show which block moved up with respect to the other. This relative displacement is sometimes indicated by steplike jogs that trend across the slickensides (**39, H**). The student should be careful not to place too much importance on these little irregularities. One or two are not sufficient evidence, but if they are numerous and all face in one direction, then they are fairly conclusive. Polish is of no value as a criterion for displacement.

Fault striae on outcrop surfaces may look like glacial striae. For the most part, the former, on any given surface, are parallel, whereas glacial striae generally—not always—vary in direction within 10° or 15° of arc. On steeply inclined surfaces, fault scratches are apt to run up and down, whereas glacial striae are likely to trend in a nearly horizontal direction. When the scratched surface can be traced to a place where it passes into the rock,[20] it is usually a fault surface; but exception must be made for the rare case in which ancient (pre-Pleistocene) glaciated surfaces

[20] Not merely under superficial deposits, such as till, alluvium, etc.

are found to have been re-exposed by the partial removal of the overlying younger rock. When the scratched surface is glaciated, any overlying material, consolidated or not, is apt to be of glacial or of aqueoglacial deposition. For other kinds of scratches, grooves, and polish, which may be mistaken for fault striae, the reader is referred to Art. **39.**

Fault striae are not invariably accurate indices of the direction or distance of slipping. Successive movements on the same fault may have different directions, and the grinding and polishing of the last dislocation may have destroyed all traces of earlier fault striae. Thus, the total distance travelled by a point from its first position may be greater than the striae would lead one to believe, and the present direction between two points which were formerly in contact may be different from the course along which they acquired their ultimate positions. In making measurements on a given fault the geologist should ascertain, if possible, whether the striae are reliable data for obtaining the direction and amount of slip.

208. Visible displacement of veins, dikes, strata, etc. There can be no better evidence for faulting than the case in which the two ends of a dislocated bed, dike, vein, or other structure, are visible where they abut against the fault, also exposed in section (Fig. 169). The geologist will discover few instances in which this kind of evidence is questionable; but he will also find that it is a phenomenon which is seldom seen except on a small scale (**215**).

209. Fault breccia zones. This subject is reserved for Art. **243.**

210. Drag. Drag is not observed unless in the immediate vicinity of a fault. It need not be exposed on both sides of the fracture in order to ascertain the direction of displacement, for, normally, if the slipping had a vertical component, the faulted structures are turned up in the downthrown block and down in the upthrown block (Figs. 170, B; 172). However, due to complex conditions of the forces acting and of the consequent displacement, or because of two successive periods of slipping, one up and the other down, on the same fracture, or because monoclinal folding has been followed by faulting with the relative directions of displacement reversed, instances of faults have been observed where the drag turned up in the upthrown block and down in the downthrown block, except perhaps within a very few feet or a few inches of the actual surface of slipping.[21]

211. Repetition, omission, and offset. The terms repetition, omission, and offset, when used in connection with faulting, generally refer to stratified rocks, but they may be applied to any sequence of faulted rocks or to any faulted geologic surface where they can be recognized. As criteria for faulting they are usually less evident than the first four above noted (**207–210**) because they more often occur on a large scale. Considerable field exploration may be necessary to find proof of repetition, or of omission, or of offset, on the surface of the ground, and careful study of well logs may be needed to discover repetition or omission in a vertical sense (see **214**).

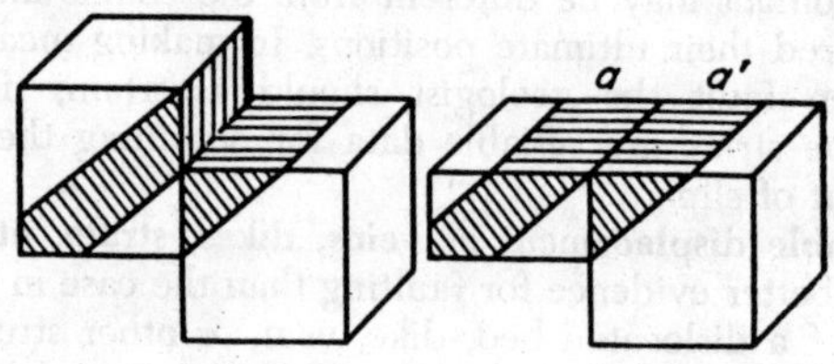

FIG. 200. Repetition of strata caused by erosion (right diagram) succeeding dislocation by a vertical dip-slip strike fault (left diagram). (Cf. Fig. 205.)

In the following explanations of the different ways in which these criteria for faulting may be produced, we have adopted a purely geometric method. In each illustration (Figs. 200–208 and 210–220) the diagram on the left shows the theoretical relative positions of the two fault blocks and the attitude of the displaced strata (one black between two white; or, in some cases, one cross-hatched between two white), after faulting and before erosion; and the diagram on the right shows the relations of the fault and the faulted strata as seen on the surface of the ground (top of block) after the upthrown block has been eroded down to the level of the downthrown block. The surface of the ground is assumed here to be horizontal. In nature, of course, it would be more or less uneven because of topographic variations.

212. Repetition of strata. Figures 200–203 illustrate four ways in which repetition of beds may be produced. The repeated bed

[21] See, for example, Bibliog., Brucks, Ernest W., 1929, vol. I., p. 266.

(or succession of beds) is cross-hatched in Fig. 200; it is the series above the black layer in Figs. 201 and 203; and it is the white layer just below (to the left of) the black layer in Fig. 202. Note that repetition may result from vertical faulting, normal

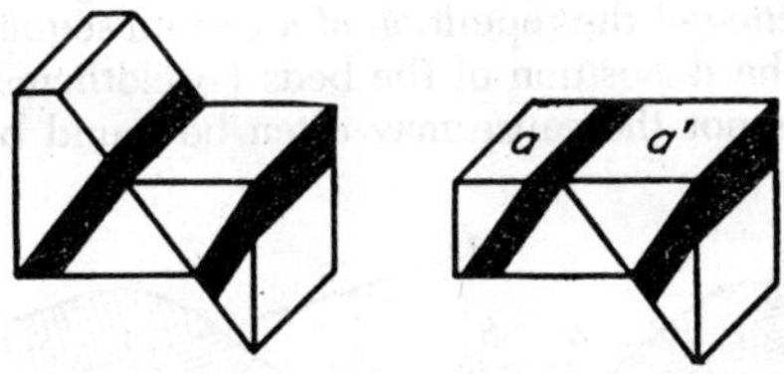

FIG. 201. Repetition of strata caused by erosion (right block) succeeding dislocation by a dip-slip strike fault that dips in the opposite direction from the dip of the broken strata. (Cf. Fig. 206.)

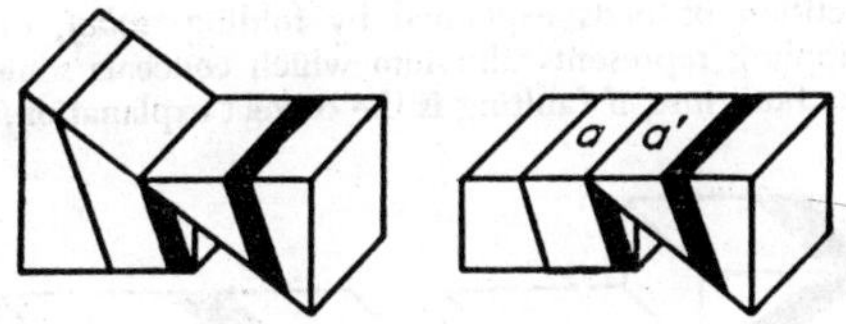

FIG. 202. Repetition of strata caused by erosion (right block) succeeding dislocation by a dip-slip strike fault that dips in the same direction as the broken strata. (Cf. Figs. 203, 207.)

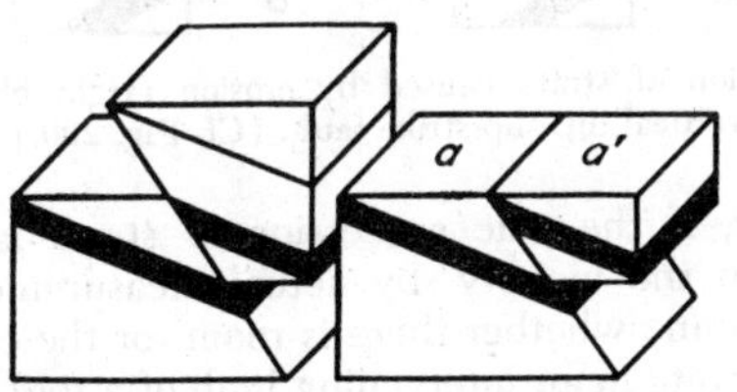

FIG. 203. Repetition of strata caused by erosion (right block) succeeding dislocation by a dip-slip strike fault that dips in the same direction as the broken strata. (Cf. Figs. 202, 208.)

faulting, or reverse faulting. All four of the examples shown are strike faults, where repetition is at a maximum. In diagonal faulting, especially where the angle between the strike of the fault and the strike of the beds is oblique, there is a certain amount of repetition. Furthermore, repetition may be associated with rotational faulting, as suggested in Fig. 224 (cf. with Fig. 202).

Repetition of beds (**203**) is a very satisfactory indication of faulting, but it is not conclusive evidence. It may be due to folding where an intervening limb is concealed (Fig. 204), or it may be a consequence of the repetition of a certain sequence of conditions during the deposition of the beds (cyclothems, **105**). Proof that folding is not the cause may often be found by wider field

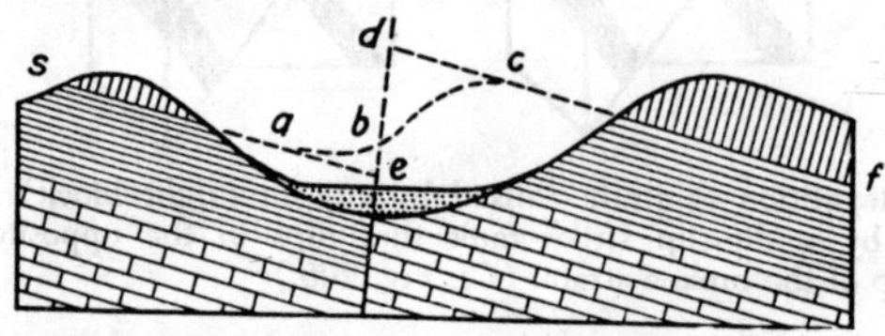

Fig. 204. Repetition of beds explained by folding, *sabcf*, or by faulting, *saedcf*. The stippling represents alluvium which conceals some of the beds and likewise the fault line, if faulting is the correct explanation.

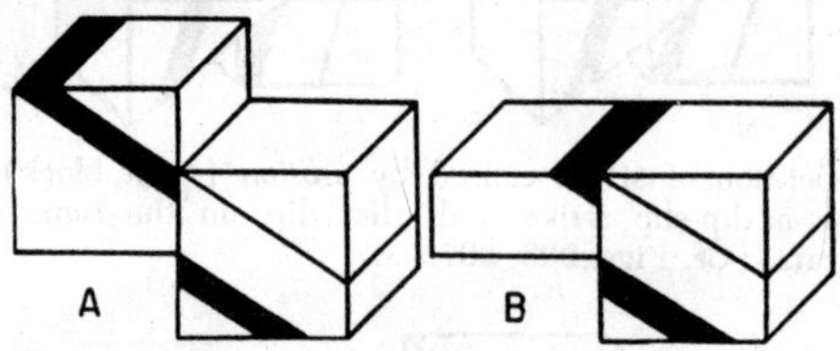

Fig. 205. Omission of strata caused by erosion (right block) succeeding dislocation by a vertical dip-slip strike fault. (Cf. Fig. 200.)

correlation, or, if the true succession of strata is known from observations in the vicinity, by actual measurement across the strike to determine whether there is room for the concealment of the repeated strata in an intervening limb of a fold. To be certain that the repetition is not that of a cyclothem, related solely to sedimentation, the geologist must pay careful attention to the nature of the stratigraphy and the evidences of deformation in the region.

213. Omission of strata. Figures 205–208 illustrate four methods by which omission of beds (**203**) may be caused. In Fig. 205 the omitted stratum is that immediately above the black layer. In Figs. 206, 207, and 208 the omitted bed is that which is cross-hatched. As with the phenomenon of repetition, omission may be caused by vertical faulting, normal faulting, or reverse faulting; and again it is at a maximum in strike faulting. Like-

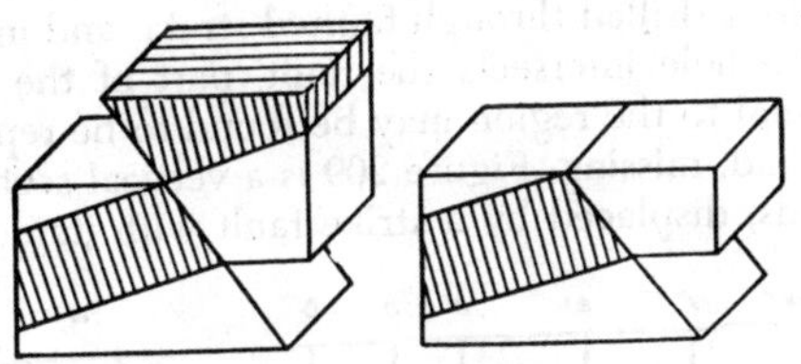

FIG. 206. Omission of strata caused by erosion (right block) succeeding dislocation by a dip-slip strike fault that dips in the opposite direction from the dip of the broken strata. (Cf. Fig. 200.)

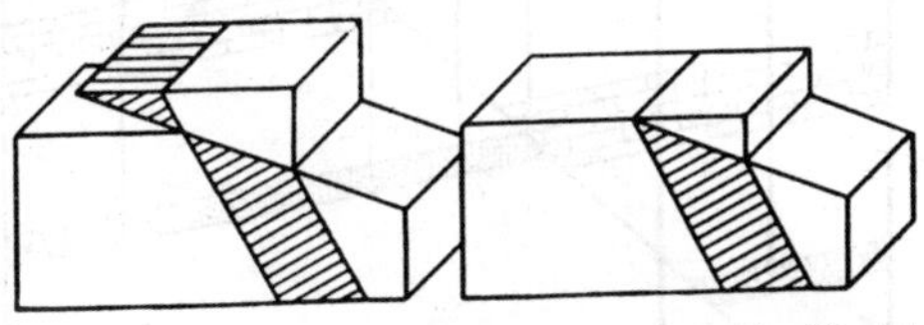

FIG. 207. Omission of strata caused by erosion (right block) succeeding dislocation by a dip-slip strike fault that dips in the same direction as, but less steeply than, the broken strata. (Cf. Figs. 202, 208.)

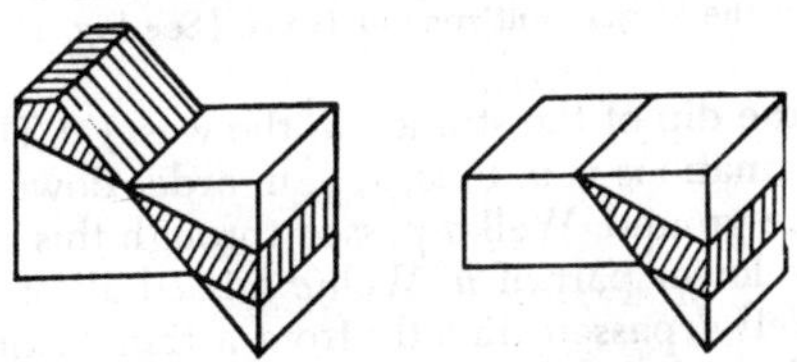

FIG. 208. Omission of strata caused by erosion (right block) succeeding dislocation by a dip-slip strike fault that dips in the same direction as the broken strata. (Cf. Figs. 203, 207.)

wise, it is a condition associated with diagonal faulting, but to a less and less degree as the angle between the strike of the fault and the strike of the beds increases in value. As in the case of repetition, omission too may result from rotational faulting.

The ability to recognize omission of beds in the field demands thorough acquaintance with the stratigraphic sequence (**125**) in the region; for obviously, unless one knows what strata to expect, one cannot tell whether or not some beds are missing.

214. Omission and repetition of beds observed in drill holes. When a hole is drilled through faulted strata, and in such a position that the hole intersects the fault, part of the stratigraphic section normal to the region may be found to be repeated, or, on the other hand, missing. Figure 209 is a vertical section of gently inclined beds, displaced by a strike fault with its downthrow on

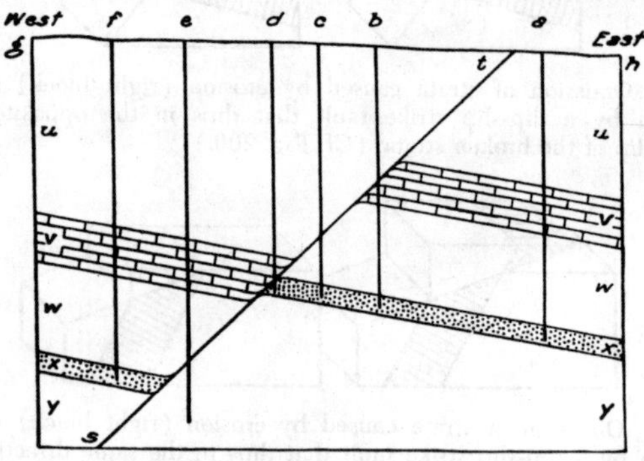

FIG. 209. Vertical section of strata broken by a normal fault which dips in the direction opposite to the dip of the strata. This is the kind of fault characteristic of the Mexia fault zone in Texas. (See Fig. 168.)

the side up the dip of the strata (on the west).[22] The normal succession of formations is *u*, *v*, *w*, *x*, *y*, in order downward from the surface of the ground. Well *a* passed through this sequence. Well *b* missed the lower part of *u*. Well *c* missed all of *v* and parts of *u* and *w*. Well *d* passed directly from a thin section of *v* into *x*, missing *w* altogether. Well *e* missed *x* and part of *w*. Well *b* had the normal sequence as deep as it was drilled, but at a much lower level than the same formations were encountered in well *a*.

In the study of vertical sections by means of well logs (498) an understanding of these relations is essential, for the discovery of a fault may be made on just this sort of evidence, even where there are no indications on the surface of the ground.

[22] See Bibliog., Lahee, F. H., 1929.

By carefully analyzing the relations in Figs. 201–208, the student will note that either repetition or omission of beds may be observed in a *vertical hole which intersects* either a normal fault or a reverse fault. Whether the fault is associated with repetition or omission of beds depends on the particular relations of direction and amount of dip of both the fault and the strata. Note that a strike fault (or a diagonal fault which has a relatively small angle of divergence from the strike of the beds) will produce repetition in a vertical direction, as demonstrated by drilling, if it produces repetition in a horizontal or nearly horizontal direction, as seen on the land surface. Likewise, if omission of beds is observed in a vertical sense, omission will also occur with the same fault in a horizontal sense. In more simple language, where there is repetition horizontally, there is repetition vertically, and where there is omission horizontally, there is omission vertically.

215. Offset, with or without gap or overlap. A dip fault or a diagonal fault, intersecting beds or other regular structures across their strike, is usually indicated by some type of offset. For example, a bed which has been dislocated in this way may be traced on the surface of the ground, generally in a series of separate outcrops, to a point beyond which it terminates and some other rock takes its place; but somewhere, to the right or left, the same bed will be discovered, probably trending in the original direction. The relations are essentially like those described in Art. **208**, but here the fault intersection (fault line) is concealed, so that merely its approximate position can be determined.

For the correct interpretation of offset the faulted bed, dike, vein, igneous contact, or other structure must have characters sufficiently distinctive for unquestionable recognition. On the assumptions: (1) that inclined stratified rocks have been dislocated; (2) that the bedding has the same strike and dip on both sides of the fault; and (3) that the land surface is essentially horizontal, the conditions of offset may be grouped according to whether the fault is (*a*) a dip fault or (*b*) a diagonal fault. Figures 210–214 are examples under *a*. In each of the five cases pictured, the offset is the same as the horizontal separation along the strike of the fault. In Figs. 215–218, which illustrate cases under *b*, the offset is not the horizontal separation along the strike of the fault, but is the shorter distance, measured perpendicularly between the two corresponding parts of the disrupted bed, in a horizontal plane (refer to Figs. 174, 175). In cases under *b* the horizontal separation is the hypotenuse of a right triangle of which one leg is the offset. In all cases of diagonal

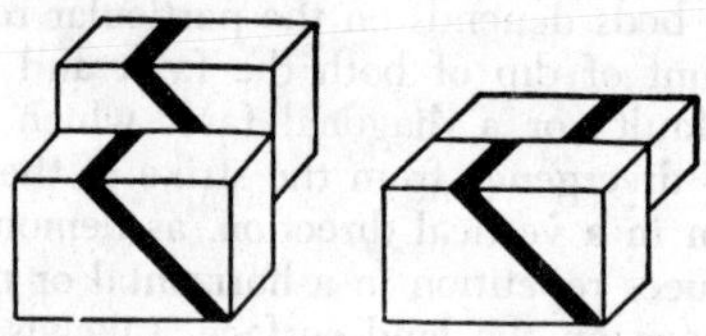

FIG. 210. Offset produced by a vertical dip-slip dip fault. Left, without erosion; right, after erosion.

faulting (group *b*), either the ends of the offset traces of the disrupted bed may *overlap* (Figs. 215, 216), or they may *appear* to have been drawn apart (*gap*) (Figs. 217, 218) (see Figs. 174, 175). In dip faults there is neither overlap nor gap.

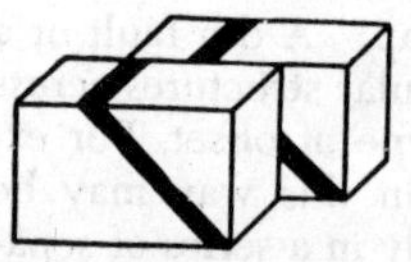

FIG. 211. Offset produced by a vertical strike-slip dip fault.

In the examples shown in Figs. 210–218, the dip of the strata is the same, or essentially the same, in direction and amount in both fault blocks. Offset may be produced by rotational dip faulting in which event the dip of the strata will be different in the two blocks (Figs. 219, 220). Similarly, rotational diagonal faults may reveal either overlap or gap, according to the relations between the attitudes of the strata and the fault.

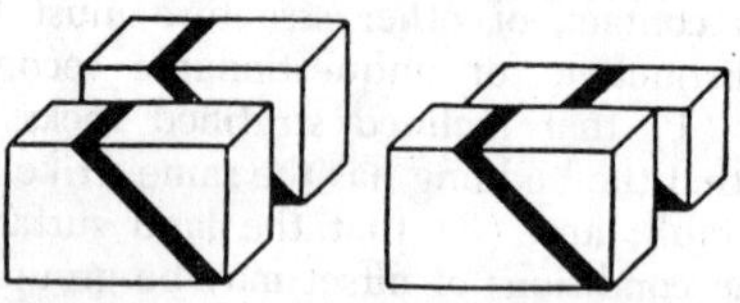

FIG. 212. Offset produced by a vertical oblique-slip dip fault. Left, without erosion; right, after erosion.

216. Abrupt termination of structures along their trend.[23] In dip faulting and diagonal faulting, where strata, dikes, veins, or other structural features have been disrupted, the two parts of

[23] The word "trend" here implies outcrop on the land surface.

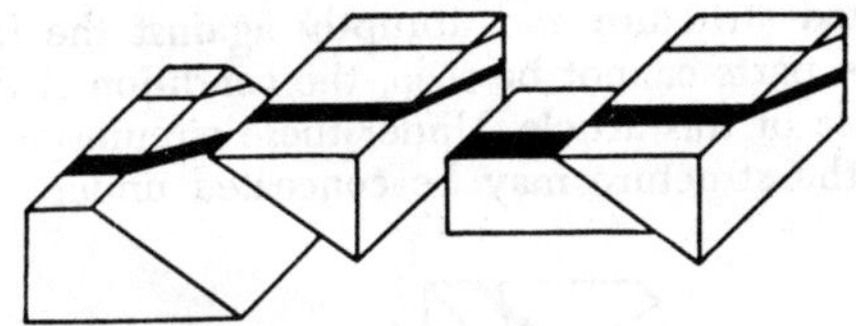

FIG. 213. Offset toward the direction of dip of the beds in the downthrown block of a normal oblique-slip dip fault. Left, without erosion; right, after erosion.

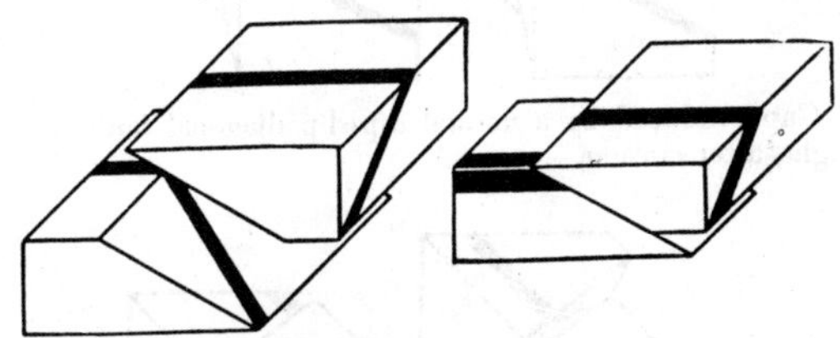

FIG. 214. Offset toward the direction of dip of the beds in the downthrown block of a reverse oblique-slip dip fault. Left, without erosion; right, after erosion.

FIG. 215. Overlap caused by a normal dip-slip diagonal fault. Left, without erosion; right, after erosion.

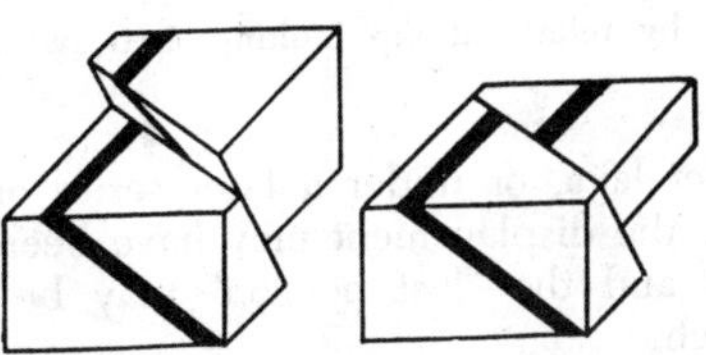

FIG. 216. Overlap caused by a reverse dip-slip diagonal fault. Left, without erosion; right, after erosion.

the dislocated structure end abruptly against the fault line. If one of these parts cannot be seen, the condition is that referred to in the title of this article. Under these circumstances, the lost portion of the structure may be concealed under water, under

FIG. 217. Gap produced by a normal dip-slip diagonal fault. Left, without erosion; right, after erosion.

FIG. 218. Gap produced by a reverse dip-slip diagonal fault. Left, without erosion; right, after erosion.

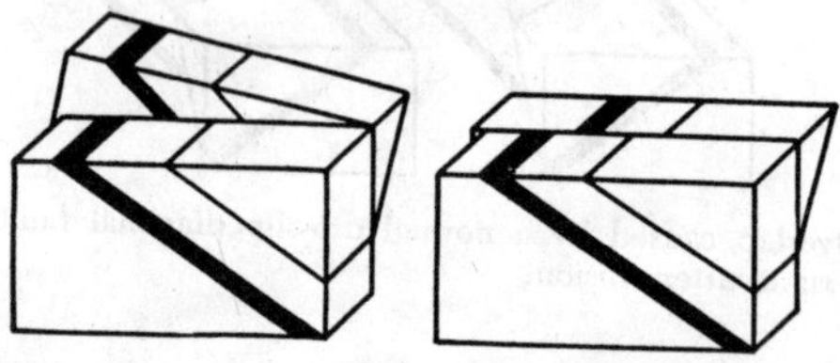

FIG. 219. Offset by rotational dip faulting. Left, without erosion; right, after erosion.

alluvium, under lava, or under a later series of stratified rocks (Fig. 221); or the displacement may have been greater than at first imagined and the "lost portion" may be found by more extended search.

Rotational faulting may bring about some special relations which are mentioned here. Thus, in Fig. 222, a rotational fault cuts horizontal beds. The back block has been tilted, with the result that eroded outcrops of the beds in this block abut against the fault. In Fig. 223, A, the beds in both blocks dip in the same general direction, and in 223, B, the same statement may be

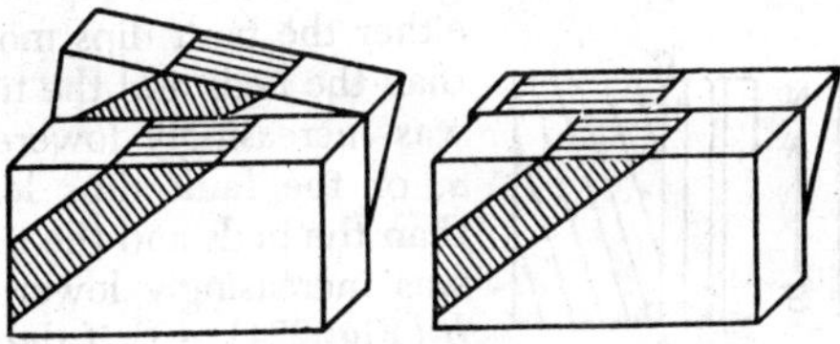

FIG. 220. Offset by rotational dip faulting. Left, without erosion; right, after erosion.

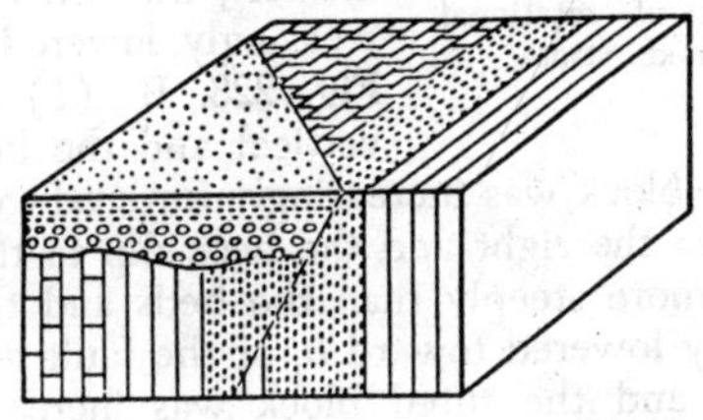

FIG. 221. Abrupt termination of strata (right) against a fault. The same strata on the left of the fault, are concealed beneath the body of horizontal sediments. These younger horizontal sediments have been eroded from the right fault block.

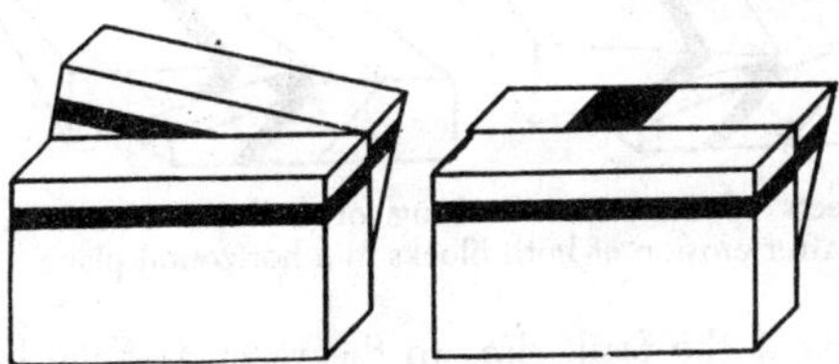

FIG. 222. Effects of rotational faulting of horizontal strata. Left, without erosion; right, after erosion.

made. In both A and B the beds strike parallel to the fault on the left of each diagram, but, on the right side, they strike into the fault, to the west of north in A and to the east of north in B. In a case of this kind the strata which abut against the fault are usually in the tilted or rotated block (on the right in both A and B). Several interpretations of these conditions are possible, as follows: In Fig. 223, A: (1) if the fault is vertical and the beds dip to the right, the tilted block was increasingly lowered toward *a*; (2) if the fault dips to the right and the beds dip to the right, either the fault dips more steeply than the beds and the tilted block was increasingly lowered toward *a*, or the fault dips less steeply than the beds and the tilted block was increasingly lowered toward *b* (Fig. 224); (3) if the fault dips to the right and the beds dip to the left, the tilted block was increasingly lowered toward *b*. In Fig. 223, B: (1) if the fault is vertical and the beds dip to the right, the tilted block was increasingly lowered toward *b*; (2) if the fault dips to the right and the beds dip to the right, either the fault dips more steeply than the beds and the tilted block was increasingly lowered toward *b*, or the fault dips less steeply than the beds and the tilted block was increasingly lowered

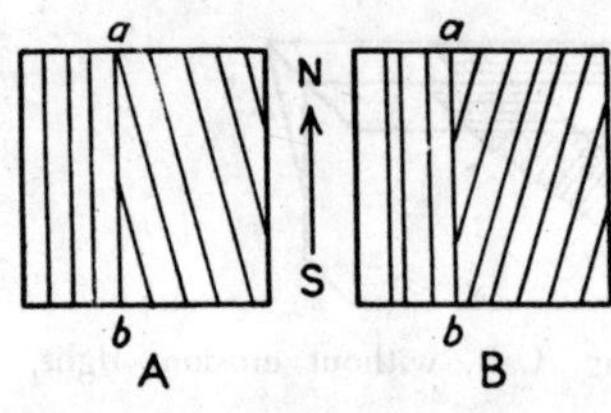

FIG. 223. Effects of rotational faulting of inclined strata, as seen in plan.

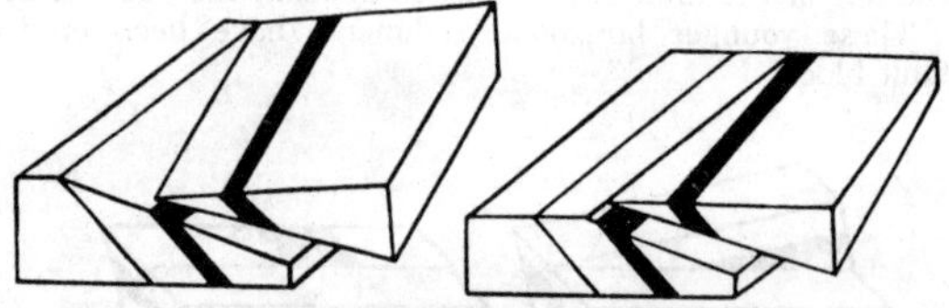

FIG. 224. Effects of rotational faulting of inclined strata. Left, without erosion; right, after erosion of both blocks to a horizontal plane.

toward *a*; (3) if the fault dips to the right and the beds dip to the left, the tilted block was increasingly lowered toward *a*.

On the assumption, above made, that the land surface is horizontal, the relations shown in Fig. 225 may be caused by rotation in both blocks; but in nature the same thing is more apt to be due to the fact that the ground slopes.

The abrupt termination of structures along their trend is not necessarily a result of faulting. The same phenomenon is common in association with igneous contacts and lines of unconformity. Furthermore, one should not overlook the fact that since beds, dikes, veins, fractures, and the like, may come to an end in their original form, within short distances, apparent truncation is not always real (Fig. 226). The natural termination may be con-

Fig. 225.

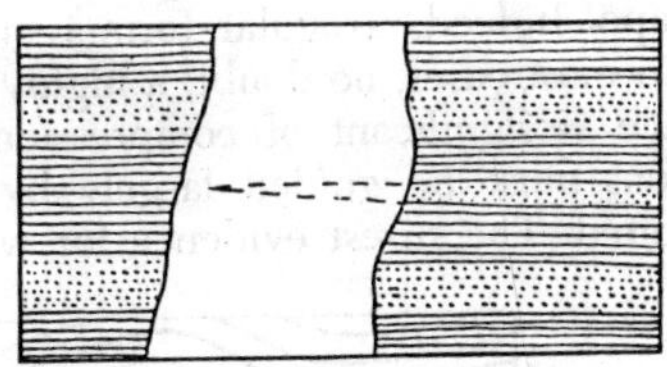

Fig. 226.

Fig. 225. Effects of rotational faulting, as seen in plan.
Fig. 226. Sketch map of a body of inclined strata partly covered by alluvium (white). The middle sandstone bed (stippled) on the right thins out beneath the alluvium and thus looks as if it had been dislocated by a fault, also concealed beneath the alluvium; but the fact that the other beds match across the alluvium cover proves that the suggestion of a fault is incorrect.

cealed and so lead one to infer the presence of a covered fault where no fault exists.

Faults in Relation to Their Time of Origin

217. Relative age of faults. A fault is younger than the rocks which it intersects. A fault which is clearly dislocated by an intersecting fault is older than the latter (Fig. 185, B). Yet there are many cases of intersecting faults which are essentially contemporaneous, although some are slightly dislocated by others. Such faults generally occur in definite sets which, like intersecting joint sets (**238**), have been formed during one and the same period of deformation. In a given region tension faults are generally younger than compression faults.

218. Warped and folded faults. Faults have been recorded as folded or warped; that is to say faulting is supposed to have been accompanied or followed by folding or warping. Overthrusts are particularly liable to bending, because, like most folds, they are products of compression, and they may be followed as well as preceded by folding (Fig. 183). Tension faults are less apt to be warped unless the rocks which they intersect are buried and subjected to folding in a later geologic period. Note, however, that the fact that a fault has an undulose shape and looks as if it had been flat and had been bent is no proof of subsequent deformation. A great many faults originate with such a shape. Indeed, irregular form is more typical than is flatness. Yet in most cases, no doubt, a highly undulose shape of the fault surface is significant of compression after faulting. One's conclusions must be guided largely by the degree of irregularity exhibited. The surest evidence for warping or folding of a fault

FIG. 227. Section of a fault, *a*, which is intersected by a surface of unconformity, *bc*. Since the surface of unconformity and the beds above it have been folded, the irregularity of the subjacent fault is probably also a consequence of deformation. The little patch of stippling (to represent sandstone) in the upper middle part of the diagram was displaced along fault *a* from the crest of the anticline just to the left of *a*.

includes all the following features in association (Fig. 227): (1) the fault has an undulating form; (2) it cuts a rock formation which has clearly been folded; (3) it terminates upward at a surface of unconformity which separates the dislocated formation from an overlying series of strata; (4) this younger series is likewise folded. In the absence of obscurity of one or more of these structural relations, the conclusion that the undulose fault has been bent after its origin becomes less reliable and it is often safer to believe that the shape is primary.

219. Geologic age of faults. The geologic age of faults is ascertained from their relation to the adjoining rocks. An example is shown in Fig. 77. On many of the major faults, displacement has been recurrent, sometimes through long periods of geologic time, so that they have to be dated as to both their first and last movements.

220. Post-Pleistocene faults in bedrock. In countries which were glaciated in the Pleistocene, signs of postglacial dislocation are sometimes found in low scraps or edges, of a fraction of an inch to a few inches in height, which interrupt the continuity of striated and glacially smoothed rock surfaces (Fig. 228). Although the throw of these faults may be small individually, the total displacement of several on a single ledge, all with the downthrow on the same side, may amount to a number of feet. Demonstration of the origin of these faults subsequent to the erosive work performed by the ice lies in the facts: (1) that the displaced scratches and grooves on the two sides of the fault clearly match as to their direction, shape, and size; and (2) that the edge of the upthrown block at the fault is sharp, not bevelled off as it would be had the dislocation antedated glaciation.[24]

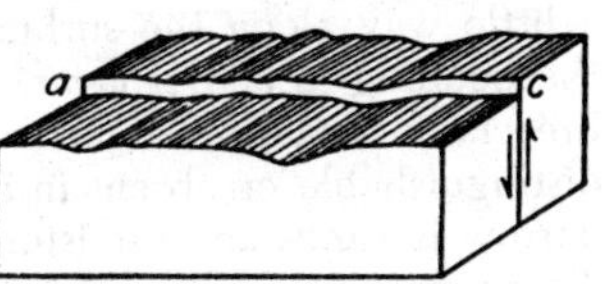

Fig. 228. A small postglacial fault, *ac*, which interrupts the continuity of a glacial rock surface. The edge made by the fault is about ¼ in. high.

221. Faults that originate in unconsolidated sediments. Faults may be formed in unconsolidated sediments in all the ways described for folds (188). They are usually reverse faults when the deformation was produced by an overriding mass, and, like the overturned plications, they indicate by their attitude the direction in which the agent moved. If due to settling the faults are commonly normal. Settling may be induced by faulting in the underlying rock (cf. 188, ¶ 10), by decomposition of the underlying rock and removal of the products in solution (cf. 188, ¶ 9), by mechanical washing out of the finer grains from a bed of sand or gravel, or by the removal of a support, such as ice. It is possible that many of the small faults in aqueoglacial sands are to be explained by one or both of the last two processes.

222. Discrimination between faults originating in sediments before and after consolidation. After faulted sediments have become consolidated, it may be difficult to decide whether the observed displacements were formed before or after lithification.

[24] Bibliog., Matthew, G. F., 1894.

1. If such faults are thrusts, they are probably associated with crumpling, and the criteria outlined in Art. **189** for the discrimination of contemporaneous folds may be applied.

2. Gravity faults, occasioned by settling of purely superficial origin and therefore limited to sediments which were unconsolidated at the time of the displacements, are seldom more than a few inches or a few feet in length when measured across the bedding. They are spaced typically at short intervals, their trends and mutual relations are irregular, and they are lacking in definite relations to the axes of diastrophic deformation in the rocks of the region. A fault of this kind is often slightly blurred because some of the grains of the unconsolidated deposit slipped or rolled a little way along the surface of displacement and so obscured the bedding in a thin layer. Such a layer corresponds to a fault breccia in fractured solid rocks. Usually, not always, it is indistinguishable or absent in muds or clays and their derivatives, narrow in sands and sandstones, and broader in coarse materials. These gravity faults commonly terminate upward where the original surface of the deposit was at the time of dislocation (Fig. 229, A).

3. Faults, either single or multiple, which were produced in unconsolidated sediments by displacement in the subjacent rock, intersect a regional unconformity (Fig. 229, B). In the younger formation, which was unconsolidated at the time of their origin, they exhibit many features like those mentioned for the second group, but necessarily they are definitely related to the faults in the rocks below the unconformity. In the underlying formation they are apt to have clean-cut edges, true breccia zones, and other characters such as develop in the dislocation of consolidated rocks. Sometimes the grains of the younger formation are found to have slipped down into the fault crack in the older formation.

Topographic Expression of Faults

223. Classification of topographic forms related to faulting. The topographic expression of faults may be original or subsequent. Original are all those land forms produced by faulting and not so modified by erosion that their primary characters are not still recognizable. These include fault scarps (**269**), faceted spurs due to faulting (**275**), fault valleys, faults gaps, and rifts (**285**), kernbuts and kerncols (**275**), and horsts, grabens, and structural basins bounded by fault scarps (**202**). All topographic forms which have been derived through the extensive erosion and consequent extensive modification of original topographic features due to faulting are subsequent. Such are fault-line scarps (**274, F**), fault-line gaps (**291, E**), and horsts, grabens, and basins, bounded by fault-line scarps (**224**). Here also may be mentioned alignment of solution-made sink-holes (Art **290**).

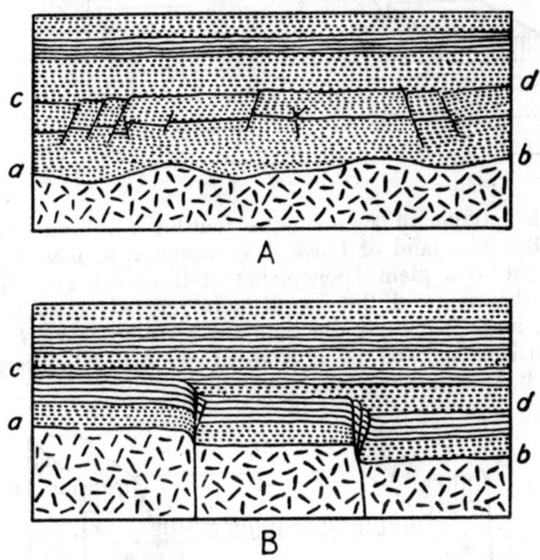

Fig. 229. Sections to illustrate the difference between faults which were limited to superficial sediments (A) and those which, although appearing in the superficial sediments, had their origin in the underlying bedrock (B). *ab,* line of unconformity between ancient rock foundation (dash pattern) and sediments which were unconsolidated at the time when they were dislocated. *cd,* original land surface at time of faulting. In both cases this surface was later buried under younger sediments.

224. Topographic expression of horsts, grabens, and basins. Horsts, grabens, and basins are included in the list just given because, if they are comparatively small, or if their characters are very pronounced, they are recognizable as topographic forms; but ordinarily they are so large and their surfaces are so varied in relief that their study can be accomplished only by extensive field investigations. Consequently, although the scarps, valleys, and other land forms are described in Chap. 11, horsts, grabens, and basins will receive consideration here.

A horst has been defined as a relatively elevated block of the lithosphere between two downtown blocks; that is, in its original surface form, a horst is a ridge (Fig. 230, A), or, if erosion has modified the block, it has a hilly or mountainous expression,

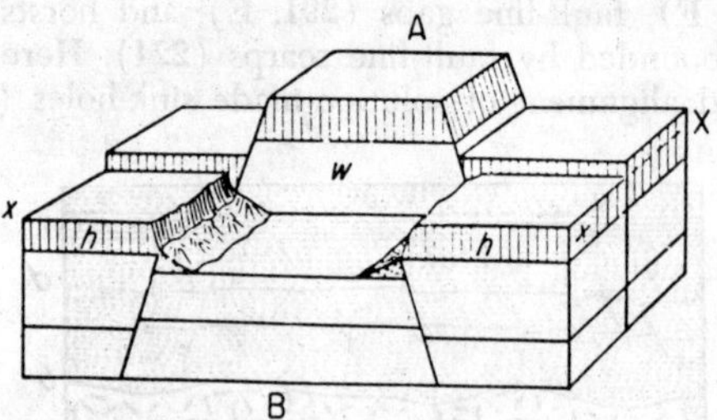

Fig. 230. Block diagram of a horst after faulting (A) and after considerable erosion (B). The land of block A is supposed to have been reduced by erosion almost to a plain (peneplain) at the level, *xxx*. Then, after a general uplift, the rivers of the region were revived. They cut away the weak rocks, *w*, much more rapidly than the resistant rocks, *h*, so that the lowlands of block A became the uplands of block B. The scarps in A are fault scarps; in B, fault-line scarps.

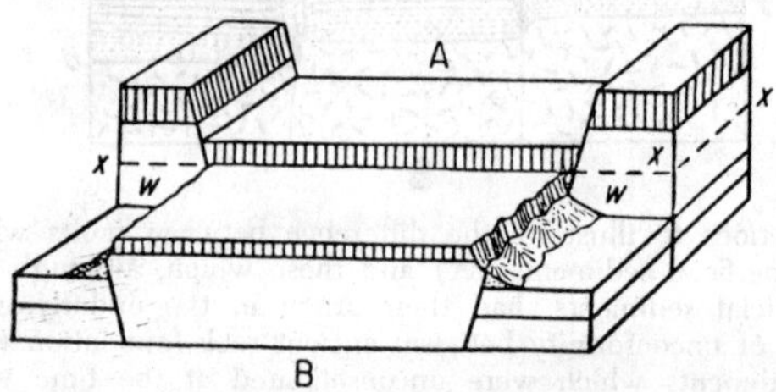

Fig. 231. Block diagram of a graben after faulting (A) and after considerable erosion (B). The land of A was reduced to a plain at the level, *xxx*. After uplift and rejuvenation of the rivers, the weaker rocks, *w*, were eroded away more rapidly than the hard rocks (lined), so that the lowlands of A became the uplands of block B. The scarps in A are fault scarps; in B, fault-line scarps.

provided the block is a large one. In the same way, the original topographic form of a graben is a lowland which may or may not have an even floor (Fig. 231, A).

If such a valley is bounded by tension faults (rifts), it is a *rift valley;* if by thrust faults (ramps), it a *ramp valley* (202). If a region in which there is a graben or a horst is exposed to denudation for a long period, hard and soft rocks may be so distributed in the fault blocks that the relief may become reversed. The horst may become a lowland and the graben may become an upland (see B in Figs. 230, 231). Likewise, theoretically, the relief of a geologic basin may be reversed.

The student should observe that even if a basin or a graben is still a lowland, and if the horst is still an upland, this seemingly primary form may be of subsequent development. In other words

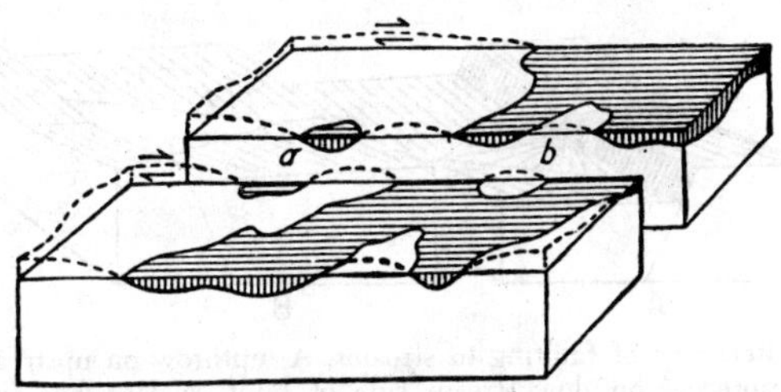

FIG. 232. Relations of an overthrust fault to the land surface. The figure is drawn as if a single block had been cut and the pieces had been separated a short distance. The land surface (top of the blocks) is represented as flat. Erosion has removed a large part of the older overthrust block (shaded), thus exposing the underlying younger rocks (white). (Cf. Fig. 180.) The base of the shaded formation is the fault, drawn as a full line where still present, and as a dashed line where eroded. The arrows indicate the relative motion of the blocks in the faulting. *a*, a fault outlier; *b*, a fault inlier. Quite commonly in nature fault outliers are hills, and inliers are basins, topographically.

the scarps which bound the basin, graben, or horst, may be fault-line scarps (**271, F**) which front in the same direction as the original fault scarps.

225. Effects of topography on the trend of fault lines. Major faults are more apt to trend along valleys or along the bases of scarps, but where a fault runs across hills and valleys the form of its outcrops is regulated by the topography in just the same way as is that of an exposed stratum (**193**). The rules governing the outcrops of vertical, inclined, and horizontal faults are identical with those for strata with like attitudes; and the exceptions are the same. The trace of an overthrust may be highly complex and irregular (Fig. 232).

226. Inliers and outliers produced by erosion of faults. Like low-dipping strata, the outcrop lines of overthrusts are very involved and sinuous in lands of marked relief. Cases are known in which the overlying (overthrust) block (decke, or nappe) has been locally perforated by erosion so that the lower block has become uncovered (Fig. 232, *b*). An isolated exposure like this has been termed a *fenster* (German, window).[25] With reference to the main mass of the overriden block, a fenster may be called a *fault inlier.* In analogous fashion, a remnant of the upper, overthrust block, separated by erosion from the main area of this

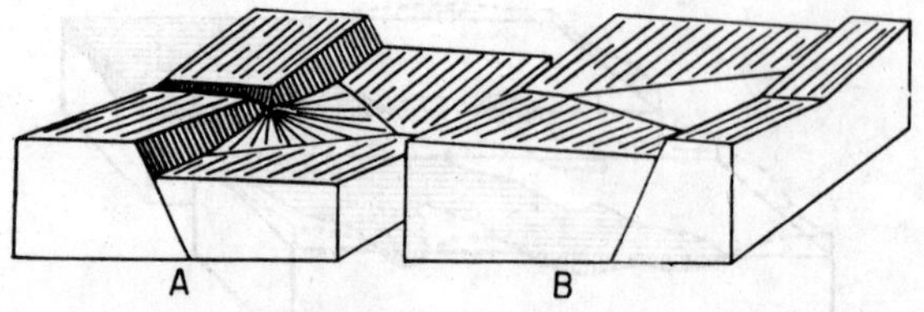

FIG. 233. Relations of faulting to streams. A, upthrow on upstream side of fault; B, upthrow on downstream side of fault. A lake has formed upstream from the fault in B.

block and surrounded by the worn surface of the lower block, is termed a *klippe* (pl., *klippen*),[26] or *fault outlier* (Fig. 232, *a*) (cf. Fig. 195).

227. Effects of faulting on streams. A and B in Fig. 233 show two cases in which dislocation has occurred across the channel of a stream. If downthrow is on the downstream side of the fault, the stream will incise its course in the upthrown block and will build a small alluvial fan in front of the scarp (Fig. 233, A). This process will continue until the river's channel is reduced to a uniform grade. Following relative upthrow of the downstream block (Fig. 233, B), the fault scarp serves as a dam above which a lake may be impounded. The lake will rise until it spills over at the old channel. The outlet will then be degraded until the lake is drained and any sediments which may have been spread over its floor will be incised.

228. Displacement relative to sea level. When we say that one fault block has moved up or down with respect to another,

[25] See footnote 18, p. 239.
[26] See footnote 18, p. 239.

we do not imply anything as to the actual change of position computed from sea level. Fault striae and measured relative displacements do not solve this problem. Both fault blocks may be lowered, but if one sinks more than the other, the latter appears to have been raised. For ancient faults it is practically impossible to determine the true change of position. Recent earth movements can be studied by levelling. A comparison between old and new triangulation records may establish results as to uplift or downthrow with respect to sea level. This is really the only satisfactory method, although certain physiographic features, when observed not too far from the coast, may be significant. For instance, where there is evidence that a late young topography, adjacent to the coast, has had its valleys suddenly aggraded from the shore line inland to a fault scarp which shows downthrow toward the sea, the seaward block has probably been depressed with respect to sea level. In this, as in other problems, the correlation of geologic and physiographic phenomena is of great importance.

229. Original inclination of a fault scarp. The average inclination of a fault scarp may be less than the dip of the fault (or faults) either because the displacement is a distributive fault or because the scarp has been lowered by erosion. Professor Wm. M. Davis suggested a physiographic method of determining in a rough way how steep a dissected scarp may have been before it was modified by erosion.[27] If the fault had been very steep, as in Fig. 283, a talus would probably have accumulated at the base of the scarp between the notches, and this rock waste would have been conspicuous in front of each triangular facet for a long time during the erosion of the fault block. The absence of a talus with these relations would therefore indicate that the scarp was originally of comparatively low inclination, perhaps not much over 30° or 35° (**267**). However, we might assume that, for a steep fault, slipping might have been intermittent through a period sufficiently long to permit erosion to keep the scarp reduced to a low angle and to remove the waste.

230. Topographic forms as evidences of faulting. None of the land forms listed in Art. **223** can be accepted as *prima facie* evidence for faulting. Perhaps the most significant are rifts, kerncols, and kernbuts, and certainly: (1) scarps which interrupt the continuity of slope on constructional surfaces (**269**); (2)

[27] Bibliog., Davis, W. M., 1909, p. 754.

local abnormal changes in stream courses associated with transverse scarps or rift valleys in the banks on either side (**227**); and springs in linear arrangement. But rift valleys, kernbuts, and kerncols are not always easy to recognize; scarps, faceted spurs, gaps, and valleys may originate in other ways than by dislocation; and springs may be arranged in linear fashion where a water-bearing stratum comes to the surface in a long narrow belt. Faceted spurs may be made by glacial scour or by marine erosion (**272**); valleys may be eroded upon belts of weak rock, or along lines of igneous contact and of unconformity (**291, B**); erosion scarps often look very much like fault scarps (**269**), and raised beaches, river terraces, etc., may resemble low fault scarps in unconsolidated gravels or in other loose deposits (**273–278**). A common fallacy is to ascribe joint-faced erosion scarps to faulting. Such scarps are especially numerous in glaciated lands and they may be very striking in their regularity and in their extent. They are often the plucked sides of roches moutonnées. As in the case of many of the geologic structures mentioned in the preceding pages, these topographic forms suggest the possibility of faulting, but they do not prove it. Before they can be attributed to faulting, the geologist must demonstrate that there is no other reason for their being. In other words, he must be able to discriminate between them and other similar features of the land surface. For the comparison between like topographic forms, the reader is referred to Chap. 11.

Joints

Terminology and Classification

231. Definitions. Well-defined cracks in a rock divide it into blocks. If, along such a crack, there has been no slipping of one block on another, or if one block has slipped only a very little against the other, the crack is termed a *joint*. Slight displacement may sometimes be seen when, for instance, a pebble in conglomerate has been split by a joint and the pieces have subsequently been cemented together in their altered position by vein material. The blocks between adjacent joints, or blocks bounded by joints, are called *joint blocks*. Their breadth depends upon the *spacing* of the joints. The opposing surfaces of two blocks at a joint are the *walls* or *surfaces* of this joint. Short or long, straight or curving, regularly or irregularly distributed, joints display great variety of character. They may be arranged in definite *sets,* all those belonging to one set having the same general direction. Often the fractures of one set are better developed than those of the other set or sets in a locality, and we then call the former the *master joints* or *major joints.* The strike and dip of a joint may be taken on the outcropping edge of the crack, or if one block has been removed, upon the joint wall that still remains *in situ.*

232. Classification. Theoretically, joints may be classified according to whether they have been formed by compression, tension, or torsion. Since torsion is a special case involving both tension and compression, it will not be included here. Due to compression are: (1) irregular cracks induced by the expansion of rocks consequent upon chemical alteration; (2) diagonal joints in igneous rocks; and (3) probably a majority of the regular joint systems in stratified rocks. Tension joints include: (1) irregular cracks formed in the shrinkage accompanying certain kinds of rock alteration; (2) hexagonal columnar structure and associated fractures due to cooling; (3) cross joints in igneous rocks; (4) small local cracks, opened in folding, in the upper parts of some anticlines and less often in the lower parts of synclines; (5) gash joints transverse to cleavage in sheared rocks; (6) fractures clearly associated with tension faulting; (7) cracks due to the drying of muds, clays, and argillaceous limestones.

To say whether the origin of this or that joint or set of joints is to be ascribed to tension or to compression is not always possible. The criteria are too indefinite and the problem is often too complex for solution. Typical tension fractures bear on their surfaces evidences of pulling apart, of disruption. From their walls project the grains or pebbles or other physical constituents of the broken rock, and each projection on one joint surface is matched by a hollow from which it was torn on the other surface. Thus, tension cracks characteristically have rough, granular walls. On the other hand, joints arising from compression are really shear surfaces along which there has been a small differential gliding of the blocks. Such fractures cut across pebbles and large grains indiscriminately, so that the joint walls are apt to be comparatively smooth. Mathematical flatness and smoothness are prevented by the imperfect elasticity of rocks and by other interfering factors. More significant than these surface features in determining the nature of the causal force are the larger relations to folds or to adjacent igneous bodies. These will be mentioned below in dęscribing the more important types of joints.

Description of Joints

233. Primary fracture systems in igneous rocks. In igneous rock bodies several kinds of primary fracture are recognized. These are primary in the sense that they originate through forces acting during what may be called the emplacement period of the eruption. These classes of fracture include the columnar and transverse jointing observed in many flows and some thin intrusive sheets (Art. **234**); and th the following six kinds of fracture, usually rather definitely related to flow structure in the larger eruptive bodies: (1) cross joints, (2) marginal fissures, (3) longitudinal joints, (4) diagonal joints, (5) flat-lying primary joints, and (6) flat-lying normal faults (Art. **235**).

234. Columnar and transverse jointing related to igneous eruption. In the consolidation of magma which has been erupted in the zone of fracture, or in the consolidation of lava, there is often an accompanying diminution of volume. A tensile stress is set up thereby in the cooling igneous body and the strain at length may become so great that the rock may crack. Since cooling and consequent increase of tensile stress begin at the contacts of the eruptive body and proceed inward, the cracks likewise open first at the outside and then grow inward. If the igneous mass is chilled uniformly over a flat contact surface, according to a well-known physical law the fissures develop in three plane directions, each at 120° to the other two, and all at right angles to the contact surface at which they started. The blocks beween the fissures are hexagonal columns (Fig. 234). At the same time transverse joints form parallel to the contact and therefore perpendicular to the lengths of the columns.

This kind of tension jointing is best exemplified in some sills, dikes, and lava flows, and it is sometimes found in laccoliths and necks, but it is by no means a constant feature in these eruptive bodies, for conditions are rarely suitable for its origin. There is usually a great deal of variation in the shape and perfection of the columns. They may curve, especially if the contact surfaces are not parallel. In cross section they are irregularly hexagonal and some may be found which are pentagonal or even quadrilateral. The transverse joints may be flat or curving and one such fracture may intersect one or several columns.

More commonly the tension cracks in eruptive bodies are so irregular that any tendency toward hexagonal columnar structure is hardly discernible. Yet, even in such cases, a master set of joints may be observed essentially parallel to the contact, while the associated fractures lie in various plane directions at right angles to it.

The joint structures resulting from cooling tension in an eruptive rock may also originate, though less frequently and with less regularity, in the adjoining country rock; for the latter, as first heated, later cools and contracts. The same relations as

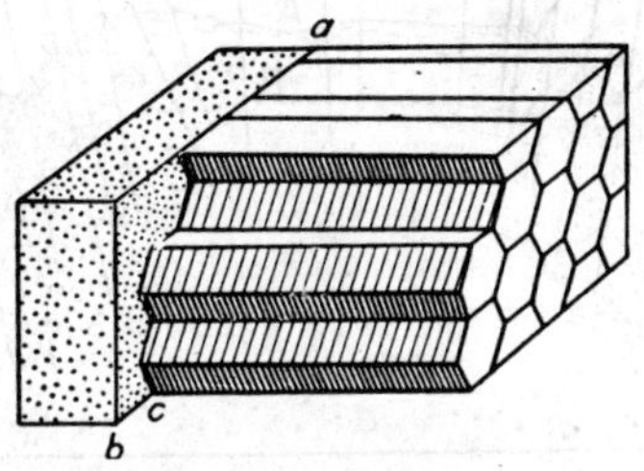

FIG. 234. Ideal diagram of hexagonal columnar joints in an intrusive rock (lined and blank) in their relation to the contact, *abc*. Country rock stippled.

those above described exist here between joint directions and contact attitude.

All these tension fractures characteristically have granular, rough surfaces. Both types, columnar and transverse, whether in the eruptive or in the country rock, are best developed and have the closest spacing nearest the contact. Away from it their regularity decreases, their spacing increases, and they may actually fade away and disappear.

235. Primary fracture systems related to flow structure in igneous rocks.[28] *Cross joints* are roughly at right angles to flow lines (**131**). They are of tension origin. Flow structure must be present for their designation. Where they pass down into the more massive part of the igneous body, where flow lines may be wanting or indistinguishable, they are called *tension joints;* but, to be so classified, their relationship to the true cross joints must

[28] In writing the following, we have freely used Robert Balk's "Structural Behavior of Igneous Rocks." See Bibliog.

be established. If the flow lines form an arch or dome in the igneous mass (Fig. 105), the cross joints will be arranged in a fan (Fig. 235). This fan of cross joints may extend into the country rock, which suggests that the wall rocks as well as the intrusive suffered some stretching or elongation in a direction normal to these joints (Fig. 235).

The steep border regions of some large intrusions are accompanied by systems of aplite and pegmatite dikes, quartz veins,

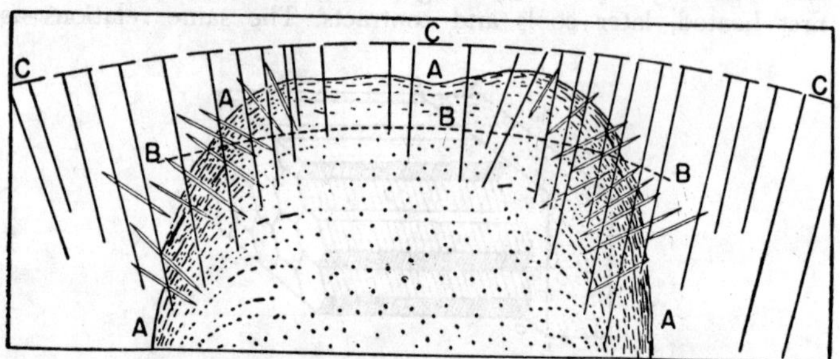

FIG. 235. Ideal superposition of flow-structure types and fracture systems in a massif, or plutonic body of moderate size. The oldest structure is a dome of flow layers (*AAA*); next younger are marginal fissures, with or without upthrusts, frequently accompanied by dikes (double lines). The position of an arch of flow lines is indicated by line *BBB*. Cross joints may be arranged perpendicular to this arch or may be referable to a still larger (imaginary) arch (*CCC*), which indicates harmonious arching of a considerable portion of the wall rocks. (*Figures* 235, 236, *and* 237 *taken from Robert Balk, Bibliog.,* 1937, *p.* 103. *Permission to copy them given by Professor Balk and by the Geological Society of America.*)

and fissures, which dip into the igneous body at angles between 20° and 45°. These belong to the class of *marginal fissures*, probably caused by local stretching involved in the upthrust of the eruptive mass (Fig. 236).

Quoting Balk,[29]

"In border zones where flow structures are vertical, these fractures have distinct dip angles, whereas true cross joints would lie horizontal. . . . In nature . . . steeply dipping flow layers and flow lines represent the earliest stage; marginal fissures dip gently into the intrusive because they were formed a little later—*i.e.*, the magma had stiffened somewhat during their

[29] Bibliog., Balk, Robert, 1937, p. 101.

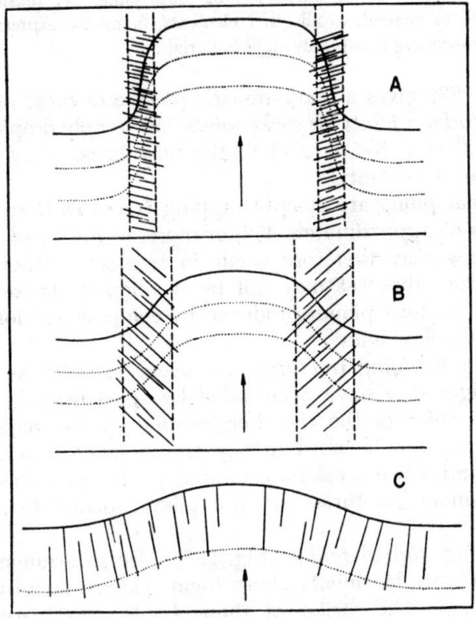

FIG. 236. Diagram to illustrate bending of weak and strong material and attendant development of marginal fractures or joint fans. In A, a weak substance protrudes in the direction of the arrow, between stationary walls to the left and right. The zones of intense lengthening (between the dashed lines) are relatively narrow, as shown by the curvature of the three lines. Under suitable conditions, tension joints open within these zones, approximately normal to the lines of local elongation. In nature the marginal fissures near intrusive contacts are due to a similar lengthening of the magma. In B, the material is stronger than in A. The zone of bending is wider, the elongation per unit area less intense. Fractures within the border zones are more widely spaced, and the dip is steeper. In C, a strong substance is bent. Distinct zones of bending disappear, and a continuous symmetric arch results. The fractures are arranged in a broad fan. The fans of tension joints in massifs are believed to form under similar conditions; hence, they are steeper than marginal fissures and reach from one end of the massif to the other. (*After Robert Balk, Bibliog.*, 1937, *p.* 102. *See caption for Fig.* 235.)

period of origin. . . . A broad fan of cross joints (or tension joints) is superposed, in general, to all other elements, being the expression of slight bending or arching in a highly rigid material."

Figure 235 gives a diagrammatic picture of these relations.

Longitudinal joints, or *strike joints,* are steeply dipping fracture surfaces that strike parallel to the flow lines. They are not so smooth as cross joints.

Diagonal joints are steeply dipping fractures that tend to lie at angles of approximately 45°, or more, to the trend of the flow lines. They may therefore occur in two sets, although locally one or the other set may not be developed. These joints are regarded as shear planes produced by compression normal to the trend of the flow lines.

Primary flat-lying fractures may occur in sheetlike intrusions. Their origin may have been aided by approximately horizontal floors or roofs (of the chamber invaded by the magma) or by low-dipping flow layers; but they are not limited to associations of this kind. Care must be exercised in discriminating between these primary fractures and the joints opened by exfoliation (**236**).

Flat-lying normal faults (Fig. 237) "are so arranged that the sum of all displacements along them widens an intrusive horizontally. . . . The strike of these faults may vary, but the azimuth of the slickensides on them is parallel to that of the flow lines."[30]

236. Sheet jointing in massive rocks. *Sheet structure, sheet jointing,* or *sheeting* may be seen to good advantage in granite and other massive, homogeneous rocks. The joints are broadly undulating and are roughly parallel to the surface of the ground. They divide the rock into flat sheets, or into lenticular slabs that lie so that the thick part of one rests upon the thin ends of two underlying lenses (Fig. 238). The vertical spacing of the blocks, *i.e.,* the thickness of the slabs, increases downward. The fracturing is believed to be due to relief of pressure, and consequent vertical expansion, through removal of the overlying rock by erosion.[31]

When sheet jointing is present in massive sedimentary rocks considerable care is sometimes necessary to distinguish between

[30] Bibliog., Balk, Robert, 1937, p. 107.
[31] Bibliog., Dale, T. N., 1907, pp. 30–38.

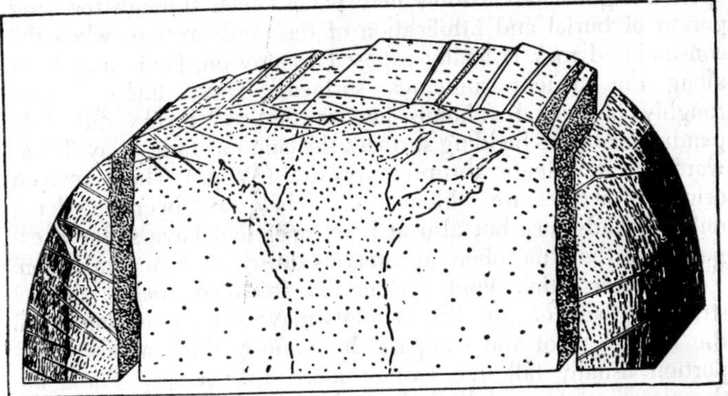

FIG. 237. Association of flat-lying normal faults with marginal fissures and thrusts. Along steep contacts (left and right), marginal fissures prevail. They lengthen the massif upward and outward. The flat-lying normal faults (center) distend the intrusive horizontally and seem to develop especially near subhorizontal contacts. In some instances, the expansion along these fracture systems seems to be caused by continuous intrusion of magma into the core of a massif. (*After Robert Balk, Bibliog.,* **1937,** ***p.* 107.** ***See caption for Fig.*** 235.)

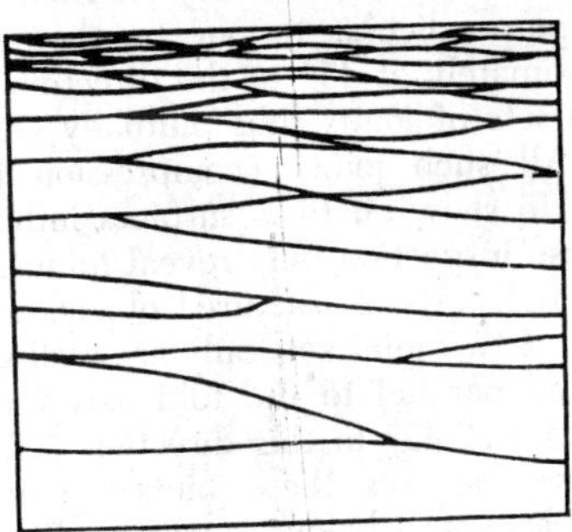

FIG. 238. Vertical section of sheeted granite. The joints or sheets inclose roughly lenticular slabs of the rock between them.

it and stratification. Even granites and other igneous rocks that are well sheeted may look very much like strata from a distance.

237. Columnar and transverse jointing not related to igneous eruption. Sun cracks are an example of original or contemporaneous hexagonal columnar jointing (**65**). The tendency to open along the old fissures may persist even through the long period of burial and lithification of the mud, so that, when the consolidated rock is finally exposed by erosion, joints may form along the ancient sun-crack surfaces. These inclose short, roughly hexagonal columns just as the sun cracks did. Perpendicular to the bedding surfaces the columns fade away downward but terminate abruptly upward. (Why?) These revived original fractures are seldom found. They have been noted not only in mudstones but also in limestones that have suffered exposure to the atmosphere at intervals during their accumulation.

238. Intersecting joint systems in stratified rocks. In the stratified rocks of any district joints may be seen striking in all the directions of the compass, but among these a large proportion usually fall into two or more distinct sets. These are the major joints, and it is these that the following description concerns. The minor fractures are merely the outcome of the complex conditions of force and resistance that must obtain in a strained series of variable beds. Probably the majority of joints in stratified rocks are the result of compression or of torsion, seldom of simple tension.

1. Compression along a single axis may produce two, four, or more joint sets, and there is a tendency for fractures in intersecting sets to be perpendicular to one another and for all the sets to be approximately at 45° to the direction of compression (Fig. 239). Two sets of joints thus mutually related are called *conjugate sets.* All such joints (compression joints or shear joints) are likely to show on their surfaces indications of slight shearing, and close inspection may reveal minute displacements between the severed parts of fractured objects in the rock. In a region of folding, if two joint sets only are well developed, both may strike roughly parallel to the fold axis (*strike joints*), or at an average angle of 45° to this direction (cf. A and B, Fig. 239). If parallel to the axes, these joints dip so that they converge above anticlines and below synclines (Figs. 240; 241, A). If the joints strike oblique to the fold axis (Fig. 239, B), they will have a nearly vertical dip. The first condition, A, is best developed where vertical relief is comparatively easy upward and the second condition, B, where relief under the compression is more easy in a roughly horizontal direction. It is possible also for joint systems to result from compression acting along the fold axes in the condition of strain for the formation of complex

folds (**176**). If, through this *minimum* compression, fractures arise striking perpendicular to these lines of force, their average strike will be nearly in the plane of the dip of the main folds. They will be *dip joints.* Their dips will approach 45°.

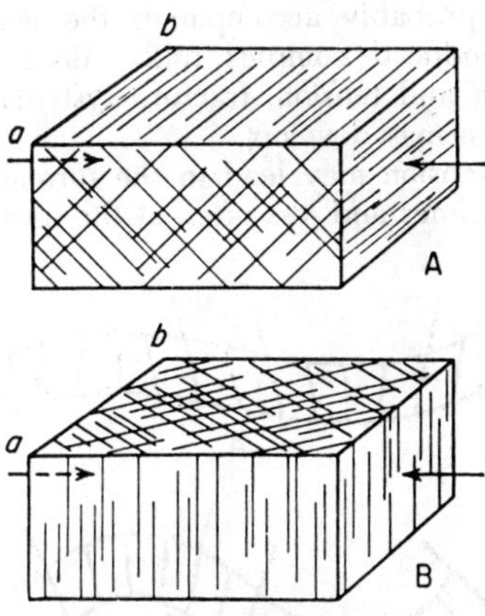

FIG. 239. Compression joints, in conjugate sets, made by forces acting in the direction of the arrows. *ab* would be the approximate strike of beds folded by these forces. In A both sets of fractures are strike joints; in B both sets are diagonal joints. All four sets might well be produced in a single rock mass. They are shown separately here merely for comparison.

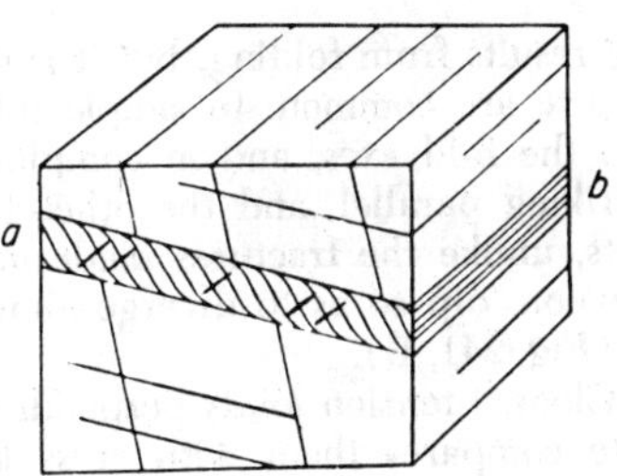

FIG. 240. Block diagram of a thin, weak bed (*ab*) between two thick, strong beds. The fractures in the strong beds are strike joints formed by compression. Those which are parallel to the bedding are bedding joints. In the weak bed the curved fractures are fracture cleavage, and the five short cracks are gash joints formed by tension. (*After E. Steidtmann, with modification.*)

For the significance[32] of certain kinds of compression joints in folded strata, refer to Art. 248.

2. Torsion, like compression, may give rise to two, four, or more sets of joints that bear similar relations to one another and that tend to make an angle of 45° with the axis of twisting. Torsional stress probably accompanies the warping and compression that produced complex folds. Since torsion involves both compression and tension, fracture systems related to both conditions of stress may develop.

3. Sometimes tension may lead to the formation of cracks at the crests of anticlines and less often at the troughs of synclines,

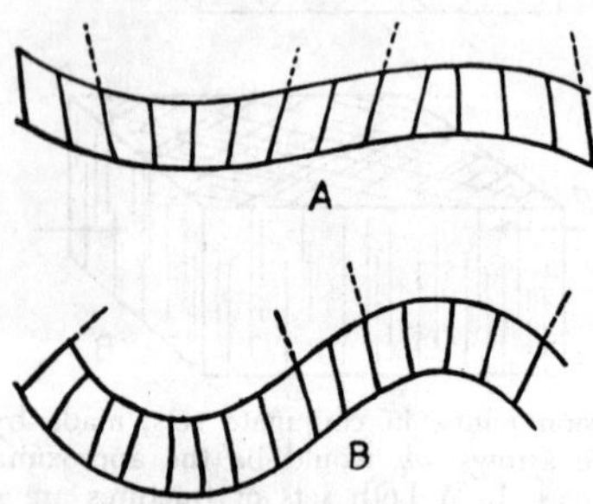

Fig. 241. Sections of folded strata intersected by strike joints. In A the fractures are compression joints, and in B they are tension joints.

where stretching results from folding; but it is doubtful whether joints of this nature are common. In simple folds tension joints strike parallel to the fold axes, and in complex folds there are two sets, one striking parallel, and the other transverse, to the axes. These joints, unlike the fractures made in analogous positions by compression, dip so as to diverge above anticlines and below synclines (Fig. 241, B).

According to Cloos,[33] tension joints perpendicular to fold axes are common. He compares them with cross joints in igneous rocks, since, in both cases, they are essentially normal to the direction of greatest elongation (fold axes; linear flow structure).

Gash joints are short, local tension fractures (Fig. 240).

[32] See also Bibliog., Bucher, Walter H., 1920–1921.
[33] Bibliog., Cloos, Ernest, 1946, p. 74.

The geologist may take for granted that lithified, flat-lying strata have nearly always suffered broad-scale warping, although in small areas no dip may be apparent. These "horizontal" beds are commonly intersected by two main vertical joint sets approximately perpendicular to one another. Extended field work in some regions has demonstrated not only the existence of broad undulations in such strata, but also the fact that the two master fracture sets strike respectively perpendicular and parallel to the axes of the low folds and dip so as to converge above anticlines and below synclines. For these particular areas, then, the joints would seem to be of compressional origin. In distinctly folded rocks conspicuous joint sets are more numerous and more closely spaced, and their study is correspondingly more difficult.

No individual joints, not even the master ones, are continuous for long distances.[34] When a fracture ends it is usually replaced, on one or the other side, often with a few inches or a few feet of overlap, by other joints having the same trend. In strata of variable resistance joints in one bed often end abruptly against an adjacent bed or they may turn and pass through the latter bed in a different direction.[35]

Interpretation of Joints

239. Interpretation of joints. Careful field investigation of joints may assist in the interpretation of local and regional geologic structures. Take, for example, hexagonal columnar jointing (234). We know that the columns are apt to develop perpendicular to the igneous contact at which their growth commences. Therefore, if a rock has vertical columnar jointing, the contact is probably horizontal, and if the columns are horizontal the contact is vertical. If such columns are present, they are apt to be vertical or steeply inclined in recent lava flows, perpendicular to the adjacent strata in sills and laccoliths, and in dikes that cut stratified rocks that are parallel or inclined to the bedding.

In proportion as the columnar structure is less perfect, the transverse joints become more conspicuous. They may be of

[34] However, Billings refers to joints that may be traced continuously for hundreds, or even thousands, of feet. (Bibliog., Billings, Marland P., 1958, p. 107.)

[35] For important papers on joints see Bibliog., Mead, Warren J., 1920; and Bucher, Walter H., 1920–1921.

use because of their approximate parallelism with the contact. Following is an actual example: A certain outcrop of trap was intersected by what appeared to be a very complex system of joints. Upon close examination one fracture set seemed to be better developed than the rest. It had a definite trend and the cracks belonging to it were, many of them, continuous for several yards. They had a strike between N. 10° W. and N. 10° E. and a dip of about 50° eastward. There were several other less prominent joint sets more or less perpendicular to the master set. Knowing that trap occurred in this region generally in straight-edged dikes and assuming that the fissures were of the tension class, the geologist inferred that the master set corresponded to the transverse variety of joints, that the contact might have approximately the same attitude, and that, therefore, search should be made on the eastern and western edges of the outcrop. By removing the sod here and there this conclusion was proved to be correct. The country rock was found, the igneous rock was shown to be a dike, and the attitude of the dike was obtained. The value of this method lies, not in its infallibility, for it is by no means certain, but in its suggestiveness where contacts are hidden.

In field studies of the larger eruptive bodies, the geologist should investigate and map both flow structures and fracture systems in order to ascertain their mutual relations. From such data he should be able to learn a great deal concerning the form of the igneous body, the nature and attitude of its contacts, and the mechanics of its emplacement (Art. **485**).

In regions of folded strata, whether the folds are broad and low or are close and indicative of strong deformation, the master joint systems usually exhibit a marked degree of regularity over an area much more extensive than the individual folds. Consequently, if carefully mapped and properly interpreted, they may reveal valuable information as to the history and larger structural features of the regional geology.

Joints in Relation to Their Time of Origin

240. Age of Joints. From what has been stated above certain important conclusions may be drawn: (1) Joints having different attitudes may be of the same age, whether they are intersecting or not. (2) If, in homogeneous rocks, the joints of one set, *A*, are relatively short and always terminate against the fractures of another set, *B*, *A* may be younger than *B*. (3) If joints in a given bed terminate abruptly against an overlying bed, they are not necessarily older than the latter; rather they are almost surely younger. (4) Conjugate sets of joints in folded strata striking at approximately 45° to the direction of maximum compression are essentially contemporaneous with the folding. (5) Joints due to the cooling of an intrusive rock are younger than the adjacent country rock (**234**). (6) Joints due to the cooling of a lava flow are younger than the underlying rock. (7) Joints that are due either to drying or to cooling are essentially contemporaneous with the origin of the material in which they occur. (8) In the larger igneous bodies, cross joints, marginal fissures, diagonal joints, and other fracture systems belong to the later stages of intrusion when the magma had already become too viscous to flow but while it was still under the stresses involved in its emplacement. To these statements may be added the following: (9) Joints may be synchronous with cleavage (*q.v.*). (10) Compression joints may be contemporeaneous with compression faults (*q.v.*), and tension joints may be contemporaneous with tension faults (*q.v.*).

The geologic age of joints may sometimes be ascertained by their relations to dikes. For instance, in a certain region where late Carboniferous strata were folded before the Triassic period commenced (see Appendix 1), the beds were abundantly cut by several prominent sets of fractures. Parallel with these fractures and showing every sign of having been intruded into some of them, are numerous dikes of Triassic age. Obviously the joints are pre-Triassic and post-Carboniferous, and they must, therefore, have been contemporeaneous with the folding, or a little later.

Joints were no doubt developed near the earth's surface in the past just as they are today, and we might, therefore, expect to find signs of old fracture systems at surfaces of regional unconformity. However, it would require a shrewd geologist to prove that existing cracks in the underlying formation (below the unconformity) are old fissures reopened and are not joints of the same series as those in the overlying younger formation. More satisfactory evidence is necessary. This may be found where the old joints were filled, previous to the first erosion period, by vein material or by dikes, or later, at the close of the erosion period, by sediments belonging to the overlying formation.[36] By their shape and relations to the surface of unconformity, these joint fillings may indicate something of the original character and arrangement of the fractures in which they were formed (Fig. 242).

Joints in Relation to the Land Surface

241. Relations of joints to erosion and topography. Joints are the commonest kind of fractures in rocks. In promoting erosion they are of the utmost importance, for they serve as channels for waters that cause decomposition, they facilitate the wedge action of ice in disintegration and in glacial quarrying, and they invite concentrated attack by abrasive agents. Many

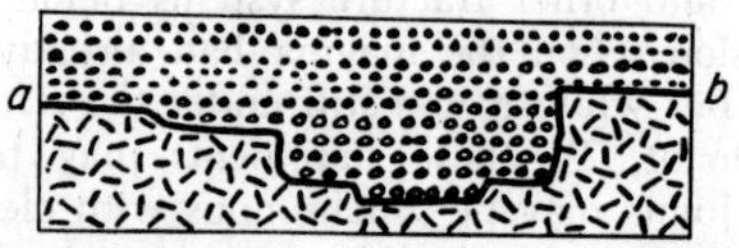

Fig. 242. A line of unconformity, *ab*, which indicates by its form that the older formation (dash pattern) had vertical and horizontal joint sets prior to the deposition of the overlying sediments.

erosional processes are accomplished by the removal of joint blocks. The surface configurations of ledges, cliffs, and mountain summits are generally conditioned by joints. Indeed, it has been demonstrated that the pattern of drainage and topography in a region often reveals a marked dependence upon the existing fracture systems. Thus, the elbow turns in many young streams are not infrequently due to a shift of the current from one joint set to another. The student should be on the lookout for this kind of topographic control, not only in the field, but also by comparing joint directions as plotted on a contour map with the pattern of rivers, lakes, and divides.[37]

Fracture Cleavage

242. Definition and origin. *Rock cleavage* has been defined by Leith as a "structure by virtue of which the rock has the

[36] It must be clear that the old fissures were not opened along faults.
[37] Bibliog., Hobbs, W. H., 1905.

capacity to part along certain parallel surfaces more easily than along others."[38] He goes so far as to include within the definition such primary parallel structures as bedding, flow structure in igneous rocks, etc. Ordinarily, however, in speaking of rocks, geologists apply the term "cleavage" to secondary structures only. This is the sense in which it is used in the present book.

Cleavage in rocks—also called *fissility*—may be induced by fracture or by flowage. The discussion of flow cleavage is re-

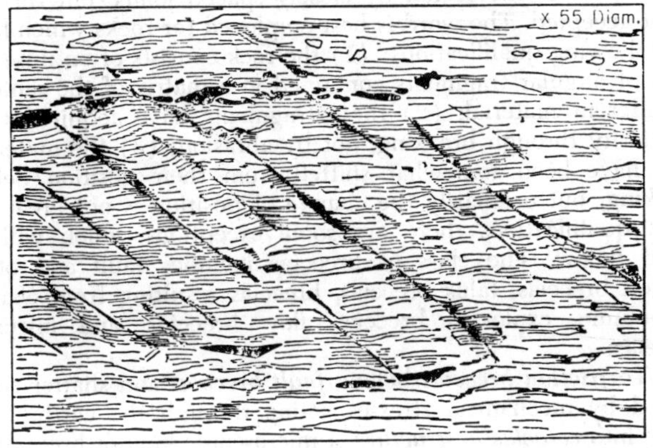

FIG. 243. Microscopic section of fracture cleavage (diagonal) crossing flow cleavage (horizontal). (*After T. N. Dale.*)

served for Chap. 9. *Fracture cleavage* may be regarded as a special case of jointing or of faulting in which the displacements are minute and the "blocks" are thin sheets. Not infrequently it occurs in two or more intersecting sets that divide the rock into small polygonal blocks. In thin sections, for microscopic examination, fracture cleavage is seen to consist of true fissures (Fig. 243). Sometimes the microscope reveals columnar or platy minerals distributed in the planes of the fracture, with their long dimensions parallel to it, so that they give the appearance of flow cleavage (*q.v.*). They may have acquired this arrangement by growth after the origin of the fracture cleavage

[38] Bibliog., Leith, C. K., 1905, p. 11.

or by rotation of the parallel mineral grains of flow cleavage into parallelism with a subsequent fracture cleavage.

For further details on fracture cleavage refer to Chap. 9.

Breccias and Autoclastic Structures

243. Definition and classification. The term *breccia* (pron., bretchia, not breck-chia) is derived from a root which means to break. As far as its origin is concerned, it might be applied to a rock which is intersected by closely spaced joints, but this use is not accepted. The word is best employed for rocks which have the following qualifications: (1) the rock consists of an unsorted mass of angular fragments contained in a matrix of the same or of different material; (2) these fragments have acquired their angularity through breaking, not by abrasion; (3) the materials may have been somewhat shifted from their position before breaking, but ordinarily the change of position is not great. To these qualifications there are some exceptions which will be noted below. The class of breccias includes fault and other friction breccias, talus breccias, breccias resulting from change of volume, explosion breccias, flow breccias, and intrusive breccias.

1. To *friction breccias* belong *fault breccias* and shatter zones caused by mechanical stresses acting through the earth. They grade into *cataclastic structure*, a microscopic kind of brecciation present in many gneisses and schists. Both compressional (thrust) and tensional (gravitational) faulting may cause irregular fracturing by the grinding of the blocks against one another, and sometimes the fragments may show evidences of rubbing (Art. **50**). By excessive attrition due to shearing such fragments may become more or less rounded. The matrix of a friction breccia generally consists of the same substance as the larger fragments, but in a more finely pulverized condition. Friction breccias such as those just described are called *autoclastic* ("self-broken") rocks. In general, as contrasted with normal clastics, they are apt: (*a*) to consist of homogeneous material like that of the adjacent rocks; (*b*) to contain a large proportion of vein cementing substance; and (*c*), when in strata, to trend across the bedding; but none of these criteria is decisive.

Under friction breccias may be put certain fracture structures of superficial origin. Breccia structures may result from overriding ice. The disrupted material may have been solid rock or unconsolidated gravel, sand, or mud, temporarily cemented by interstitial ice (Art **107**). Evidences of associated glacial deposits and signs of ice abrasion should be sought. Landslide débris and breccia structures caused by other kinds of gravity slipping of essentially superficial origin may also be listed here.

2. Since talus débris is the product of a disruptive process it is properly classified as a breccia; but it differs from friction breccias in that the fragments accumulate many feet or even several hundreds of feet from their source. Coarse-grained rocks may suffer rounding by disintegration so that the talus fragments may lose their angularity. Criteria for consolidated talus are: (*a*) the materials show different degrees of weathering; (*b*) the matrix is of the same materials as the larger blocks; (*c*) the deposit is often associated with other sediments as a basal accumulation above a regional unconformity; (*d*) the deposit is banked up against a cliff (usually buried if the talus is consolidated rock). The materials of talus are homogeneous or heterogeneous, depending upon the nature of the cliff rock from which they were derived.

3. Rocks may be broken as well as folded (9 in **188**) by change of volume effected by decomposition. Breccia structure of this origin does not in itself cause removal of the fragments. If they remain essentially in place, they constitute a mass which grades down into the subjacent unshattered rock of the same kind. Being for the most part only slightly dislodged, they can often be seen to have once fitted together. There are no signs of faulting. Interstitial material between the fragments is in relatively small amount and is apt to be foreign.

4. Tuff and agglomerate are varieties of breccia, the fragments having been broken and thrown up by volcanic explosion. The larger blocks in agglomerate may be of lava or of the country rock which was pierced by the conduit, and the matrix may consist of tuff, with or without finely comminuted country rock (Fig. 244, A). Vein cementing substances are common. The best criterion for pyroclastics, aside from their lithologic characters, is their interstratification with recognized lavas.

5. *Flow breccias* (Fig. 244, B) are formed by hardening and breaking of the crust of a lava sheet while still flowing. The fragments and the matrix are of the same material, the matrix having frozen about the fragments from a molten condition. Various lava structures are usually present both in the fragments and in the matrix.

6. The process of intrusion may be accompanied by brecciation of the country rock, or brecciation by some other method may be followed by invasion of the shattered zone by magma, and in either event the injected magma will congeal as a matrix round the fragments of the country rock. Plutonic differentiates may harden and then be broken by movements of the residual

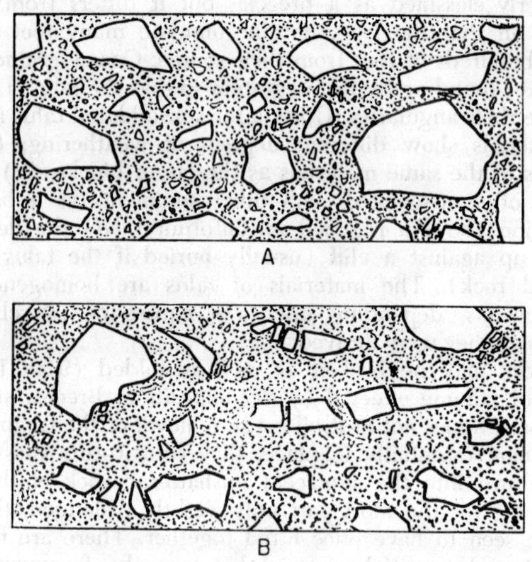

FIG. 244. Breccia structures. A, agglomerate; B, flow breccia. In B many of the fragments seem to have fitted together and to have been separated by only a little distance. This is because they were broken essentially *in situ*. The fragments in A were thrown by volcanic explosion some distance from the place of their shattering.

magma which subsequently freezes about the inclusions. Again, by magmatic stoping, blocks split from the roof of a magmatic chamber (batholith, etc.) may be preserved as angular masses in the marginal parts of plutonic bodies. All these are ordinarily classed as *intrusive breccias* (plutonic breccias, shatter breccias, neck breccias, etc.) (refer to Arts. **154–157**). The only rocks with which they are likely to be confused are flow breccias. Their recognition depends upon the determination of the matrix rock as unquestionably intrusive in its relations.

Chapter 9

METAMORPHIC ROCKS

Metamorphism in General

244. General conditions and effects of metamorphism. It has been pointed out in Art. 173 that the lithosphere is divisible into a lower zone of flowage and an upper zone of fracture. All through the lithosphere water is present, but it is in relatively small amount in the lower zone. In the upper zone it occupies fractures and other open spaces. From the zone of flowage upward to a level near the earth's surface, called *ground-water level* or the *water table,* the rocks are saturated with moisture. Above the water table is a thin shell which has a variable water content and in which the principal movement of the water is downward. This outer shell of the zone of fracture is known as the *belt of weathering,* for processes of weathering are here predominant. Since the water table may fluctuate, rising in wet weather and falling in dry seasons, and since, locally, it may even reach above the earth's surface, as seen in ponds and rivers, the belt of weathering has a thickness which varies from zero to several hundred feet. The saturated rocks between the water table and the zone of flowage are in the *belt of cementation,* so called because many substances dissolved in the belt of weathering are carried down and deposited in this underlying region, thus cementing grains together and filling open spaces. It is here that most vein deposits originate (Chap. 10).

All rocks are more or less subject to alteration if the conditions under which they were formed are changed. Such alteration is called *metamorphism.* It may be induced chemically or mechanically. *Gases* and *liquids, heat, static pressure* (simple downward pressure), *differential pressure,* and *duration of time* are the important factors concerned in both chemical and mechanical changes. On account of the different conditions existing at various depths within the lithosphere, different chemical processes assume chief importance in the zones and belts referred to above. In the zone of fracture, oxidation, hydration, and carbonation prevail, the first being particularly characteristic of the belt of weathering and the other two, of the belt of cementation. Complex silicates break down and simpler, less dense minerals form. These processes are therefore said to be katamorphic (κατά down μορφή, form) and the zone is called the *zone of katamorphism.* In contrast to this, reactions in the zone of flowage may involve deoxidation, dehydration, and decarbonation. Here silicates are built up, and the great pressure leads to the formation of denser minerals and a compact crystalline structure. This is known as the *zone of anamorphism* (ἀνά, up; μορφή, form).[1] According to definition, any kind of alteration that any rock has undergone, whether katamorphic or anamorphic, comes under the head of *metamorphism,* but there are many geologists who prefer to restrict the meaning of this term so that it does not include weathering. It will be used in this restricted sense in the present book.

In the processes of metamorphism, the original mineral grains (1) may be crushed, rearranged, and recrystallized, but without change in the bulk composition[2] of the rock, or (2) new chemical elements may be brought in from the outside, with the formation of new minerals, *i.e.*, with a change in the bulk *composition* of the rock, but usually with no significant change in the bulk volume of this rock. This latter kind of metamorphism is known as *metasomatism.* It includes granitization (see Art. **255**).

Four important processes leading to change of the conditions under which rocks originate are erosion, sedimentation, eruption, and mountain building.

1. Through erosion rocks that were once at great depths are brought into regions of lower temperatures and pressures than those which prevail farther down in the lithosphere.

2. Sedimentation works in the opposite direction. Materials accumulated on the earth's surface, volcanic products, and high-level intrusive bodies (after their crystallization) suffer a gradual

[1] The reader is referred to Bibliog., Grout, Frank F., 1932, for a general discussion of the subject. Much later treatises on metamorphism are Turner's "Evolution of the Metamorphic Rocks" (Bibliog., Turner, F. J., 1948), and Hans Ramberg's "Origin of Metamorphic and Metasomatic Rocks," published in 1952 (see Bibliog.).

[2] Composition of the rock as a whole.

increase in temperature and pressure as they become more and more deeply buried, and ultimately they may enter the influence of anamorphic conditions. The weight of the overlying rocks is to be regarded as a simple downward static pressure which induces little or no rock flowage. Hence the new minerals that develop are apt to be those with equidimensional forms (*e.g.*, garnet) or, if they are bladed or tabular (hornblende, staurolite, ottrelite, biotite, etc.), they grow in all sorts of positions (Fig. 245). This is *static metamorphism* (cf. 4, below).

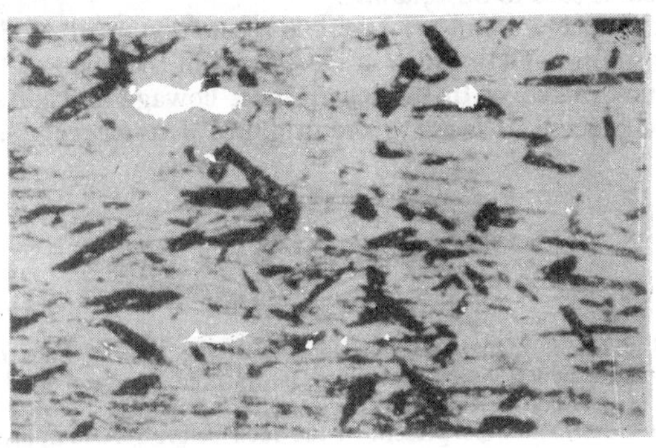

FIG. 245. Metacrysts (porphyroblasts)[3] of hornblende in gneissic rock. The metacrysts were formed after the development of the parallel gneissic structure. (About ⅓ natural size.)

The increasing weight of accumulating sediments may sometimes so far compress the strata, vertically, that there is some differential lateral slipping and the consequent growth of mica plates parallel to this slight motion (cf. 4, below) (see Arts. **81, 180** ¶ 2).

3. Through intrusion of magma or overflow of lava the adjacent materials may be heated, invaded by gases and liquids, and otherwise affected. Of the several agents concerned, pressure is usually of least importance. For the most part the alterations are chemical and mineralogical and they are often of the anamorphic type, even within the zone of katamorphism. They come under the head of *contact metamorphism* or *thermal metamorphism* (**149–153**).

[3] See footnote 6, p. 294.

4. The forces which give rise to folds and compressional faults in the processes of mountain building are very effective agents of metamorphism. At any given point in a rock subjected to differential pressure, the forces may be regarded as resolvable into three components at right angles to one another. These may all be unequal (three-dimensional stress), or two may be equal and the third greater or less than the others (two-dimensional or plane stress). A rock under this kind of unequal compression may be deformed by fracture or flowage. The metamorphism is said to be *dynamic.*

Rock cleavage (fissility) (242) is a common result of dynamic metamorphism. That which is developed in the zone of fracture is *fracture cleavage.* In the lower zone, flowage is itself a metamorphic process. It leads to the origin of *flow cleavage,* a structure consequent upon the parallel orientation of platy and columnar minerals and of minute lenticular aggregates of grains (Figs. 246, 247). This parallel arrangement of the mineral constituents is called *foliation,* and rocks having this internal structure are *foliates.* Locally, along surfaces of slipping, a parallel arrangement of minerals may be produced in the zone of fracture. Flow cleavage is called *slaty cleavage* when it is so perfect that the rock splits into thin plates of uniform thickness, and it is called *schistosity* when the rock splits easily, but not always very regularly. Rocks exhibiting these features are called slates and schists, respectively. Micas are the commonest of the thin, flat minerals that give rise to flow cleavage. They often cause a distinct sheen on the broad surfaces of the cleavage fragments. Many schists have the mica flakes distributed in wavy lines (seen in cross section) which alternately meet and separate, and so inclose lenticular areas in which the constituents other than

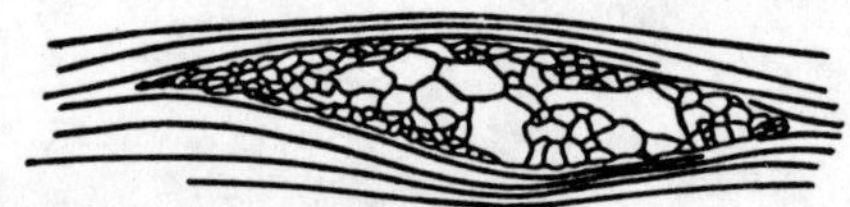

Fig. 246. Lens of quartz granules in schist. The curving lines represent layers of mica, which wrap around the quartz. The lens originated through crushing of a large quartz grain. The mica was formed by recrystallization of substances which were present in the rock before metamorphism. (Enlarged 15 diameters.)

the mica predominate. These lenses range from less than an inch to many feet in length. A *gneiss* is a metamorphic rock in which a banded distribution of its constituents is more conspicuous than a parallel orientation of the individual grains. Many gneisses contain feldspar, quartz, and mica, so that they

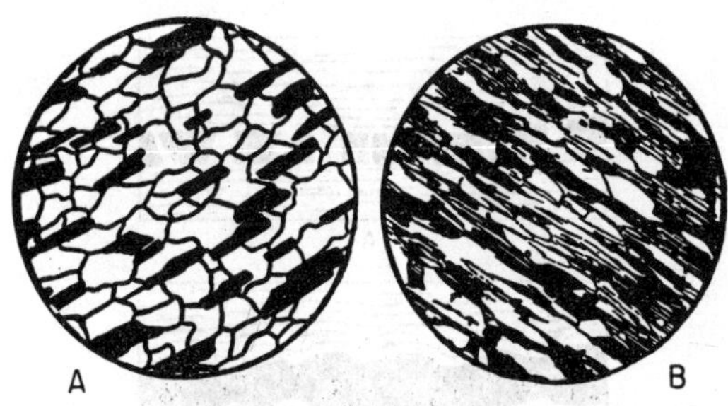

FIG. 247. Microscopic sections of cleavage structure developed through rock flowage. In A the biotite (black) is arranged with its laths all parallel and the quartz grains (white) have a slight tendency to be elongate parallel to the mica. In B there are three different minerals, all of which are oriented in parallel position. Which rock would probably have the better cleavage? (*B is after Blackwelder and Barrows.*)

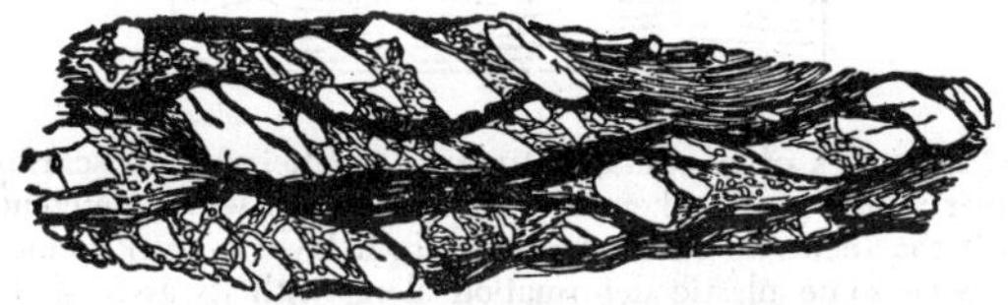

FIG. 248. Microscopic section of "sliced" feldspars (white) in mica schist. (*After C. K. Leith.*)

look like granitic rocks, especially if their banding is not pronounced (**253**). In gneisses, foliation is not so well developed as in schists.

Flow cleavage is produced, *i.e.*, rock flowage is accomplished, by granulation, recrystallization, and rotation, thus: (1) Brittle minerals are crushed and the aggregates of minute fragments are flattened in planes at right angles to the maximum stress (Figs. 246, 248). This is *cataclastic structure.* (2) From the old constituents new minerals are built and these are apt to be species with tabular or columnar shapes (Figs. 247, 248). If tabular, they grow with their flatness normal to the maximum stress, and if columnar, they grow in various directions, in planes normal to the maximum stress (*plane schistosity*), or, if the mean and maximum forces are approximately equal (plane stress), such

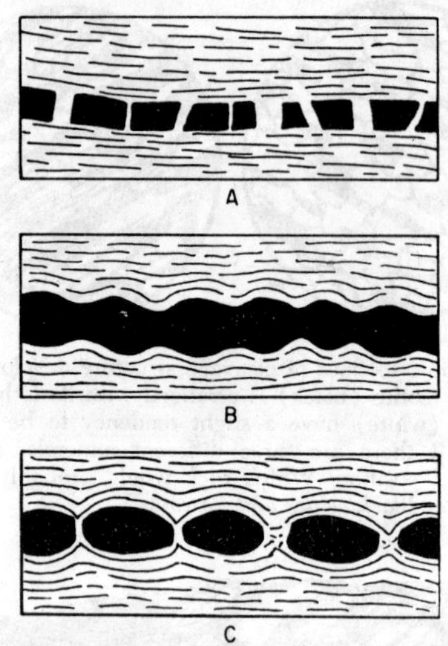

FIG. 249. Examples of boudinage structure in gneissic and schistose rocks. A, the layer which was broken into angular blocks was competent as compared with the inclosing sheared matrix. B, a layer of rock (black) which has undergone some plastic deformation along with its associated schistose matrix, but not enough to pinch off the narrowed "necks." C, the boudin layer, by plastic flowage has been squeezed into a series of separate bodies (boudins).

crystals may develop with their lengths parallel and in line with the minimum stress (*linear schistosity, parallel linear structure*) (Figs. 250, 251). Minerals like quartz and calcite may or may not display elongation of grains, but, even when the grains are roughly equidimensional, they may reveal orientation of their crystal axes, if examined under a polarizing microscope.[4] (3)

[4] Crystals of the various minerals that compose rocks have definite properties in fixed directions, or related to fixed directions, within them, and

Old or new constituents may be rotated into approximate parallelism.

Rocks which have been subjected to compressive forces may differ in their response to these forces. The less resistant materials may be compressed in the direction of the compression, with plastic flowage and relative elongation transverse to this direction. On the other hand, associated layers of more brittle rock (hard strata, dikes, etc.) may resist plastic flowage and instead may break or may be pinched off into a series of detached

FIG. 250. Side view of a specimen of gneiss having parallel linear structure. (Cf. Fig. 251.)

fragments. These are called *boudins* (French for sausage), and the structure is called *boudinage* or *pinch-and-swell structure* (Fig. 117). It is very commonly seen in highly metamorphosed bodies of rock of both igneous and sedimentary derivation (Fig. 249).[5]

After flowage has ceased, and static conditions have been resumed, heat, moisture, etc., may still continue to operate and so produce minerals without parallel arrangement. These will

---

these directions, called *crystallographic axes,* can be studied by examining thin slices of the minerals with a special type of microscope. Properties thus definitely related to these crystal axes are referred to as *vectorial properties.*

[5] See Bibliog., Ramberg, Hans, 1955.

lie scattered in various positions through the schist or slate, that is to say, the features of static metamorphism will be superposed upon those of dynamic metamorphism. Often these later crystals are large and conspicuous. Being of origin *subsequent* to that of their inclosing matrix, they are termed *pseudophenocrysts* or *metacrysts*,[6] and the structure is *pseudoporphyritic* (Fig. 245).

Quartzite and marble are not infrequently seen interbedded with schists, yet as a general rule neither displays much evidence of flow cleavage. Both may originate under either static or dynamic conditions, through pressure or through contact metamorphism. In quartzite that was formed under dynamic conditions, the quartz grains are usually a little longer than wide, and they are oriented in parallel position, but the elongation is not enough to be recognized by the eye. The massive character of marble is probably to be accounted for by the ease of recrystallization of calcite. Under static conditions following the cessation of differential pressure, the calcite readily recrystallizes without linear arrangement of its grains. If impurities are sufficiently abundant in these rocks, minerals such as the micas, amphiboles, etc., may be developed with distinctly parallel orientation in dynamic metamorphism, but without orientation in static metamorphism.

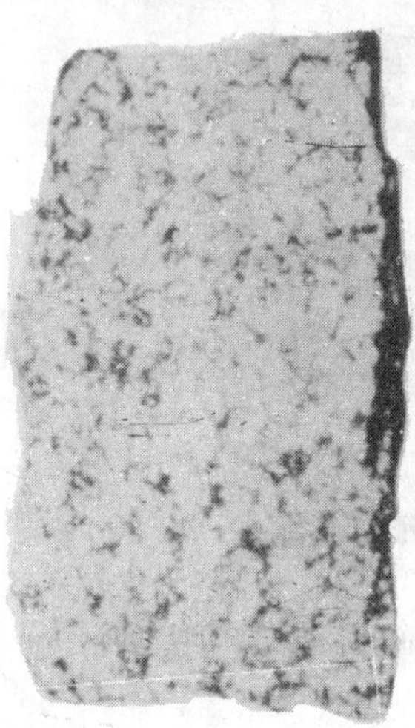

FIG. 251. End view of a specimen of gneiss having parallel linear structure. (Cf. Fig. 250, another view of the same specimen.)

In the foregoing paragraphs, we have referred to "parallel orientation" of mineral constituents of rocks having foliated structure. A better term would be "subparallel orientation," for

[6] They are also called *porphyroblasts*, but this term has been applied by some petrologists to sheared or otherwise modified phenocrysts in metamorphosed porphyritic igneous rocks.

actual parallelism is rare, except in very small sections. The important feature is the tendency toward parallelism, or the approximation to parallelism, which is well expressed by the term "preferred orientation," which, as defined by Knopf and Ingerson,[7] describes the spatial relations of the individual grains and also implies that these relations were effected through movement within the rock at the time of its origin.

Preferred orientation is applied to *any* rock in which the constituents acquired orientation as a consequence of forces acting during the origin of the rock. Thus, the term includes orientation of the phenocrysts in certain igneous rocks; orientation of clastic flakes or mica in sedimentary rocks; orientation of micas, hornblende crystals, quartz grains, etc., in metamorphic rocks; etc. (see Arts. **109, 131**).

Schistosity, gneissic structure, foliation, slaty cleavage, etc.—all these phenomena, which are conspicuous as the result of preferred orientation of one or more constituents of a rock, come under the head of *lineation* (see Art. **15**). Where the lineation in metamorphic rocks is carefully mapped, very significant trends may become evident, and these may be genetically related to the stresses which have acted in the region (see Fig. 252).

As suggested in previous statements, preferred orientation includes dimensional orientation, *i.e.*, orientation of grain shape, and also crystallographic orientation (orientation by crystal vectorial properties), as in the constituents of many quartzites, gneisses, marbles, etc. *Rock fabric* is a term used to include not only the pattern and granularity exhibited by the shape of the constituents but also the pattern made by the orientation of the internal crystal structure of the individual grains.

The study of rock fabric, as thus defined, is *petrofabrics,* which is beyond the scope of this book. However, we do want to emphasize this fact, that, just as minor folds and cleavage may be of great assistance in interpreting the nature of major folding, so also the microscopic examination of rock fabric may serve to unravel problems in structural geology. This the student should keep in mind in case he wants further evidence that may bear on his field studies and conclusions.

In the words of Knopf and Ingerson,[8]

[7] See Bibliog., Knopf, Eleanora Bliss, and Earl Ingerson, 1938, p. 7.
[8] Bibliog., *Idem.*, p. 27.

"The purpose of the final microscopic analysis of the internal grain structure of the rock is to block out an accurate ground plan by which to check and, if necessary, to modify the interpretation of megascopic structure as determined from field evidence. This kind of analysis may wipe out many futile speculations as to whether such and such joints are tension joints or

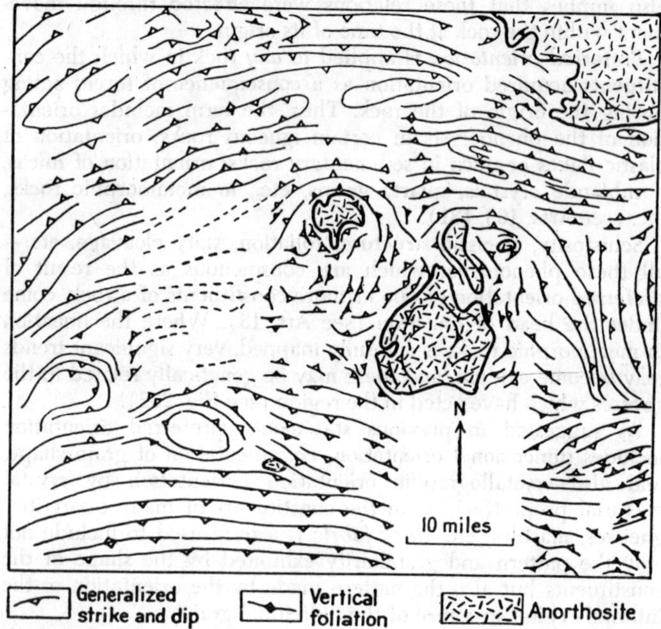

Fig. 252. Generalized trends of foliation in metamorphosed plutonic rocks of Pre-Cambrian age in the Adirondacks. The foliation here, although in part related to plastic flow of the solid rock in metamorphism, may be genetically related to original directions of flow of the liquid magma at the time of its intrusion. (*Bibliog., Turner, F. J.,* 1948, *p.* 314. *The map is after A. F. Buddington.*)

shear joints, whether a given schistosity has developed at 45° or 90° to the direction of applied force, whether a given structure is the result of tangential shearing stress or of compression. An intimate and exact knowledge of rock fabric and of the movements that formed the fabric has already been acquired by the use of this tool and has thrown new light upon the processes of sedimentation, ore deposition, rock deformation, and metamorphism."

Several kinds of metamorphism have already been mentioned. Such are static, dynamic, and contact metamorphism, anamorphism, and katamorphism. *Regional metamorphism* is a term often used in contrast with contact metamorphism, because the latter is generally rather local; but this distinction is unfortunate for alterations caused by intrusion are sometimes very extensive in their distribution. It would be less confusing further to qualify the word "regional" by "static," "dynamic," or "contact," when the discrimination is necessary.

Study of Rock Cleavage

245. Relations of flow cleavage and fracture cleavage. Fracture cleavage may originate in rocks which have not been below their zone of fracture, or it may be developed in rocks which have already been folded and had a flow cleavage induced upon them in the zone of flowage and which have later been subjected to further compression in the zone of fracture. In the latter case the fracture cleavage is nearly always preceded by minute folding (crenulation) of the older flow cleavage. These relations are represented in Fig. 253. In rocks which have had fracture cleavage induced upon them and then flow cleavage, the earlier cleavage is destroyed.

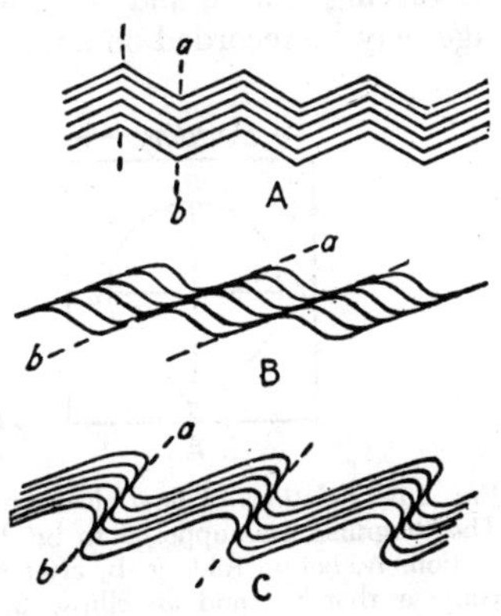

Fig. 253. Three ways in which fracture cleavage, *ab*, may develop by deformation of a pre-existing flow cleavage.

246. Discrimination between flow cleavage and fracture cleavage. When fracture cleavage occurs in several sets, the planes of parting are equally good in different directions, whereas if flow cleavage is found in intersecting planes, one set is usually much smoother and better developed than the other.[9]

247. Discrimination between bedding and cleavage. One of the mistakes which many of the old-time geologists made and which students are very apt to make at first, is to confuse cleav-

[9] For further distinctions between the two varieties of cleavage the reader is referred to Bibliog., Leith, C. K., 1905, p. 125.

age with bedding. The error is most natural, for on weathered rock surfaces both structures may look much alike. But cleavage, in its superficial expression, often appears as parallel fractures, whereas bedding consists of parallel layers of different textures and often different colors. The parallel layers of foliation (flow cleavage, schistosity) are due to parallelism of constituents, especially mica, rather than to parallelism of adjacent layers of varying texture and composition. The strike and dip of cleavage may be recorded on a map, but on such a map there must be

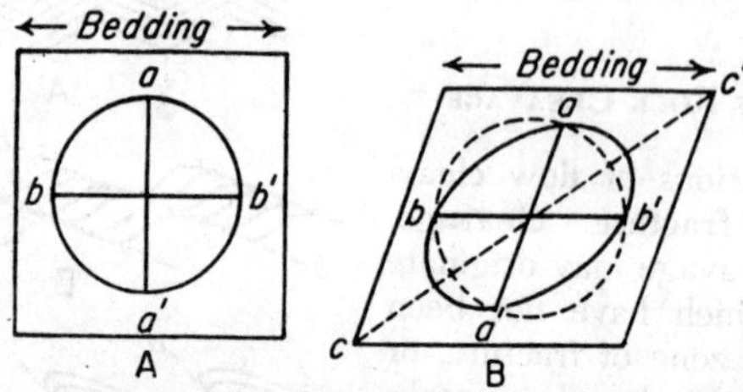

FIG. 254. Relations of flow cleavage and compression joints to deformation. The diagrams are supposed to be drawn on the edge of a bed, as seen in section. A, before folding. B, after folding. The square and circle of A become a rhombus and an ellipse in B. In its proper position in the fold, *aa′* in B should be vertical. The bedding and the line *bb′* would then be inclined toward the left. B has been placed in its present position to emphasize the relations between it and A. The lines *aa′* and *bb′* in B indicate the positions of compression joints and fracture cleavage which may be produced in the deformation. *cc′*, the direction of greatest elongation of the rock, is the position for flow cleavage. (Cf. Fig. 255.)

clear indication which symbols are for cleavage and which for stratification.

248. Relations of cleavage and bedding in folds. It has been stated (**176**) that in parallel folding adjustment is accomplished by the shearing of contiguous strata on one another. Each bed on the limb of a fold slips on the next underlying bed *toward the nearest anticlinal axis*. This differential movement has a tendency to produce cleavage planes or joints either parallel to the stratification or at an acute angle to it (Figs. 254, 255). In the latter case the cleavage planes "lean toward the direction of motion." They dip so as to converge upward in anticlines, like the axial planes of drag folds (**178, 184**). When beds differ in their competency, cleavage may be developed in this way in the weaker layers only (Fig. 255). It may change a little in direction where it approaches the contacts between beds of different resistance (Fig. 240), and its average attitude in one stratum may vary several degrees from its average attitude in an adjacent stratum.

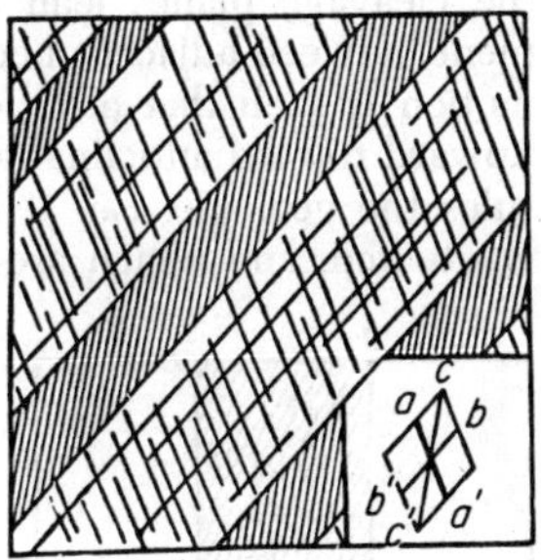

Fig. 255. Section of alternating competent and incompetent strata in the limb of a fold. The beds dip to the left. The weak layers have flow cleavage, parallel to *cc'*: the strong layers are intersected by two sets of compression joints, parallel to *aa'* and *bb'*. (Cf. Figs. 240, 254.)

In similar folds, with which flow cleavage is usually associated, since both are produced in the zone of flowage, this cleavage may be extensively developed with a uniform dip regardless of its position in the folds. It is approximately parallel to their axial planes (Fig. 256). Hence, while it is nearly or quite perpendicular to the bedding in the axial parts of the folds, it may be essentially parallel to the bedding on the limbs. As a matter of fact these are the relations which exist on a much smaller scale between minor drag folds and cleavage when both structures occur together (cf. Figs. 154, 257). It would seem, then, that the major folding and its associated monoclinal cleavage might be concomitant effects of a powerful control, such as the overriding of a great rock mass in the process of overthrusting just as the drag folds are a smaller product of differential shearing between separate beds.

Fig. 256. Relations of flow cleavage to folds.

249. Uses of cleavage in geologic interpretations.[10] The relations between bedding and cleavage as described in the last section are useful as criteria in the interpretation of geologic structure. An outcrop in which cleavage is perpendicular to the bedding is probably near the axial region of a fold, and one where cleavage is inclined to the bedding

[10] See Bibliog., Leith, C. K., 1913, p. 129, the source for many of the following statements.

at an acute angle is probably in the limb of a fold. Of great importance in this connection are the two rules which have been stated before with reference to parallel folding, namely: (1) the cleavage planes lean in the direction of differential movement between adjacent beds (Fig. 255); and (2) this differential motion is such that any bed slips over the next underlying bed upward toward anticlinal axes (178). By the application of these rules the geologist can tell on which limb of a fold an outcrop is situated, and which are the upper and lower beds in cleaved vertical strata. Thus, in Fig. 257, at the contact *a–b* the cleavage cracks in bed 2 lean toward *a* and so indicate that 1 moved over in this direction. Similarly, 3 slipped along 2 toward *c*. This section, then, must be a part of a limb between an anticline on the right and a syncline on the left. Successively younger beds are crossed up to the axial region of the syncline in passing from right to left across the outcrops (cf. 185). "Cleavage in a slate area may strike east and west and dip south at an angle of 45°. The inference is that here are similar composite folds with east-west trend and axial planes dipping to south; further, that the structure was developed by the relatively northward movement of some overlying competent rocks which have been removed; finally this inferred major control suggests a major anticline to the north."[11]

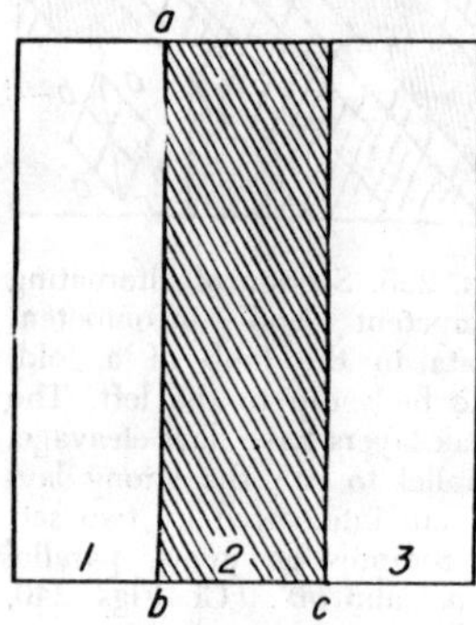

FIG. 257. Section of vertical strata. 1 and 3 are competent beds; 2 is an incompetent bed with cleavage.

250. Distortion of original structures, fossils, pebbles, etc. Of the two kinds of metamorphism, static and dynamic, the former is least apt to blur and destroy original structures in a rock. Pebbles, fossils, and such lithologic features as ripple-mark and cross-bedding are little, if at all, altered in shape, except in so far as they are flattened by compression of the rock as a whole (Fig. 258). Indeed, the lithologic structures may be made more conspicuous by the growth of new minerals in layers or lines such

[11] Bibliog., Leith, C. K., 1913, p. 132.

as to emphasize contrasts. Dynamic metamorphism, and especially rock flowage, has a marked distorting effect. In similar folding, beds are thinned on the limbs and thickened in the axial regions (Art. **176**). Sometimes, as previously explained (p. 293), strata may be irregularly thinned and thickened so that they "pinch and swell," as seen in cross section. Pinching may go so far that a bed which was once continuous now consists of a series of detached lenses.

Obviously distortion which can have these results must seriously modify the forms of original minor structures. The laminae

FIG. 258. Section of the trunk of an ancient tree (Sigillaria), flattened by simple compression. (About ⅓ natural size.)

FIG. 259. Section of deformed curved cross-bedding in vertical strata. By the rule stated in Art. **185**, in which direction would one go to find younger strata?

in cross-bedding may be folded (Fig. 259) or their curvature may be flattened (Fig. 260).[12] In proportion as they suffer deformation, their usefulness in determining stratigraphic sequence lessens (**185**); and the same is true of ripple-mark. Pebbles may be squeezed into spindle-shaped rods (linear schistosity) (Figs. 21, 22) or they may be flattened into thin sheets (plane schistosity), the deformation in both cases being accomplished by rock flowage. Fossils also may be distorted (Figs. 261, 262), and

[12] Schists sometimes have a wavy streaking of their constituents in thin lines that may be mistaken for cross-bedding.

unfortunately only a little shearing is enough to deprive them of their value so far as this depends upon the recognition of species.

In the deformation of any lithologic feature, all stages may exist between very slight change and very great change (**251**), and in rocks that have been intensely metamorphosed such original features may have been obliterated. Thus, curious though it may seem, the distinction between sheared quartz veins and sheared quartzite pebbles may be almost impossible in cases of

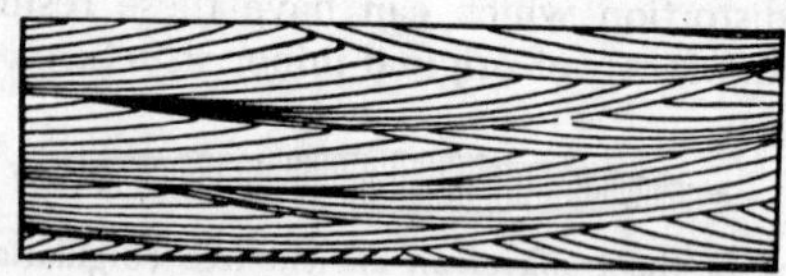

FIG. 260. Section of curved cross-bedding which has been somewhat flattened by compression.

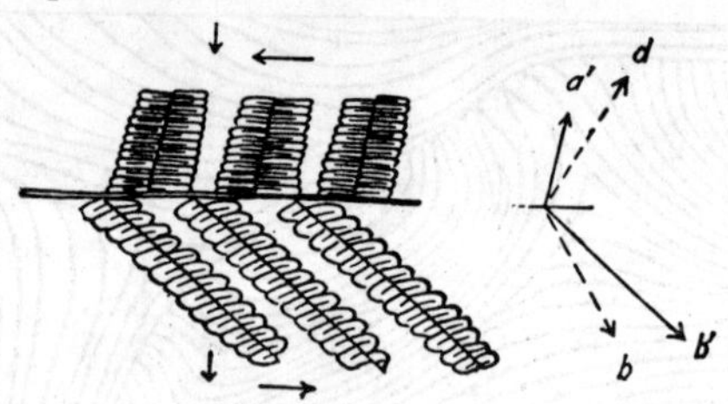

FIG. 261. Part of a fossil frond deformed by shearing. The midribs of the leaflets once had the positions *a* and *b*. By the shearing the leaflets above have been shortened and rotated toward the left, *a′*, and the leaflets below have been lengthened and rotated toward the right, *b′*. (About ½ natural size.)

extreme metamorphism. Lithologic structures in igneous rocks may likewise be deformed, but here one must be careful not to confuse phenomena due to magmatic flow with those which are of truly metamorphic nature (**253**). If possible it is good policy for the beginner to postpone studying highly metamorphosed rocks in the field until he has first become familiar with the primary characters of sediments and igneous rocks.

DEGREES OF METAMORPHISM AND ORIGIN OF METAMORPHIC ROCKS

251. Degrees of dynamic metamorphism in clastic sedimentary rocks. Like contact metamorphism, dynamic metamorphism exhibits various degrees of intensity (**152**). To be sure there is great complexity in the latter type of alteration on account of many factors, such as the composition and texture of the rock, yet certain stages can be recognized. (1) The first indications of metamorphism, as seen in hand specimens, are a poor secondary cleavage and a faint gloss on the cleavage surfaces, both due to the presence of a little white mica (sericite or paragonite) in fine laths that have roughly parallel orientation. (2) When shearing has been somewhat more intense, the white mica

FIG. 262. Deformed impression of the shell of a Spirifer. (About natural size.)

laths have more perfect parallelism and there are more of them, so that the rock cleavage is better and the sheen on the fracture surfaces is more conspicuous. Sometimes other secondary minerals, like biotite and ilmenite, are found, although these may have originated under static conditions after the cessation of rock flowage (page 294). Fossils are somewhat distorted. Pebbles are slightly, if at all, deformed, but they have thin coats of mica. (3) In what may be called the third stage, secondary cleavage is good and is often consequent upon the parallelism, not only of the white mica, but also of ilmenite, biotite, etc.; that is, all these cleavage minerals grew during rock flowage. Fossils are much distorted. Pebbles, too, are distorted and are thickly coated by white mica. (4) Maximum metamorphism is represented in the fourth stage. Original structures and fossils are largely obliterated and pebbles have been very much deformed. All the minerals in the rock are secondary.[13]

To quote from Billings,[14]

> "During the last few decades the principle of metamorphic zoning or metamorphic facies has become well established. The zones or facies are based on the mineralogy of those rocks most sensitive to progressive changes during metamorphism; argillaceous sediments and basaltic rocks are especially susceptible to change . . . Barrow[15] fifty years ago . . . recognized that in going from an area of unmetamorphosed sedimentary rocks into progressively more highly metamorphosed rocks new minerals appear in orderly succession. Thus, in a series of argillaceous rocks subjected to regional metamorphism, the first index mineral to appear is chlorite, followed successively by biotite, garnet (almandite), staurolite, and sillimanite. A line can be drawn on the map indicating where biotite first appears. This line is the biotite *isograd;* the less metamorphosed argillaceous rocks on one side of this line lack biotite, whereas the more metamorphosed rocks on the other side contain biotite. An isograd can be drawn for each new mineral. Actually the isograds are surfaces, and the lines we draw or the map are the intersections of these surfaces with the surface of the earth."[16]

We may speak of the successive zones of increasing metamorphism as the chlorite zone, the biotite zone (chlorite and biotite), the garnet zone (chlorite, biotite, and garnet), and so on. As emphasized by Billings in the article just cited, these metamorphic zones, or facies, apply only to argillaceous rocks and not to other classes of sedimentary rock.

Here we may mention the alterations of carbonaceous materials, such as coal and petroleum, which may be associated with sediments. These substances react under compression much more readily than do shales, and they may react under both static and dynamic forces. Peaty or coaly materials consist essentially of fixed carbon, volatile hydrocarbons, other volatile substances, such as water, sulphur, etc., and nonvolatile impurities classed as "ash." With increasing compression, probably assisted by moderate heat, the volatile components gradually pass off, thus

[13] These stages were observed and described by the author many years ago. (See Bibliog., Lahee, Frederic H., 1913.)

[14] Bibliog., Billings, Marland P., 1950, p. 436.

[15] Bibliog., Barrow, George, 1893; and *Ibid.*, 1912.

[16] Quoted with the kind permission of Dr. Billings and the Geological Society of America.

resulting in an increasing proportion of fixed carbon to remaining volatile hydrocarbons. In any coal, the ratio of the fixed carbon to the fixed carbon plus the volatile hydrocarbons, expressed in percentage, is known as the *fixed carbon ratio* of that coal. The proportions of these ingredients are determined in the laboratory by proximate analyses.

This process of metamorphism is undoubtedly in part dependent upon the abundance and openness of avenues by which the volatile constituents can escape.

In general, within a given coal-bearing formation, the fixed carbon ratio is found to increase downward from the earth's surface, to be somewhat greater on anticlines than on adjacent synclines, and to be relatively high near faults.[17] In two unconformable coal-bearing formations, the fixed carbon ratio is higher in the older formation.

Apparently there is a more or less definite relation between the characters of petroleum in its native state and the degree of metamorphism to which its containing rock formation has been subjected.[18] The greater the metamorphism, and, therefore, the higher the fixed carbon ratio of any coal which may be present in the formation, the lighter is the associated petroleum, *i.e.*, the greater is its gravity expressed in degrees Baumé. This rule, however, may have many exceptions, for the reason that petroleum compounds are usually fluid and are capable of extensive underground migration. The consequence is that heavy *residual* petroleum substances may occur in a rather highly metamorphosed formation, and vice versa, an abnormally light migratory petroleum compound may be found in a series of beds containing coal having a low fixed carbon ratio.

We wish to point out again that these changes in coal and petroleum, if recognizable, are commonly found as indices of metamorphism in sedimentary rocks which have not suffered enough alteration to exhibit even the lowest degree of metamorphism in the associated shales. Sericite does not appear in the latter until the fixed carbon ratio of the coals is very high.

252. Field study of metamorphic rocks. The study of metamorphic rocks in the field involves a number of major problems, such as these: (1) Was the original rock, now metamorphosed,

[17] See Bibliog., Fuller, M. L., 1920.

[18] This relation was first described by David White. See Bibliog., White, David, 1915.

igneous or sedimentary? (2) What was its original classification (*a*) as an igneous rock, or (*b*) as a sedimentary rock? (3) To what kind of metamorphism was this original rock subjected, *i.e.*, what were the agents of metamorphism? (4) What is the regional distribution of the metamorphosed rocks? (5) Do these rocks exhibit any indication of metamorphic zones? (6) What was the geologic age of the metamorphosed rocks? These and other questions may be answerable partly through local examination of rock samples or of rock outcrops, and partly through regional mapping and correlation.

Locally the geologist may look for original structures that are surely identifiable, such as contacts in the case of igneous rocks and pebbles, fossils, cross-bedding, etc., in sedimentary rocks (Art. **250**). Faults and unconformities must not be mistaken for igneous contacts (Art. **335**). Original textures, such as porphyritic texture, may be preserved, but this should not be confused with pseudoporphyritic texture (p. 294). Intercalation of beds of limestone or quartzite is good evidence for sediments, but sometimes calcite and quartz veins may be misinterpreted for beds. Graphite may be sparsely distributed through an igneous rock or it may occur in veins. However, if it is uniformly disseminated in distinctly argillaceous or quartzose layers, or if it forms beds intercalated between such layers, it and its associated rocks are probably of sedimentary origin. Great preponderance of quartz is characteristic of some sediments. Confusion may arise in the case of sheared quartz veins and highly quartzose pegmatite dikes. For other criteria, which are mostly microscopical and chemical, the reader is referred to Trueman and to Leith.[19]

As we have expalined in Art. **251**, clayey or argillaceous sediments are particularly susceptible to mineralogic changes which can be identified through a series of stages (metamorphic zones or facies) that represent increasing metamorphism. Associated sandstones may be altered to quartzites and associated limestones to marbles, so that a metamorphic rock complex consisting of layers of quartzite, marble, and chlorite schist (or biotite schist, or garnet schist, etc.) must have been derived from a sedimentary sequence of intercalated beds of sandstone, limestone, and shale. Recognition of this relationship may require regional study. Also, tracing of a schistose or slaty rock through its several metamorphic zones to its least altered, or unaltered, phase will require

[19] Bibliog., Trueman, J. D., 1912; Leith, C. K., 1913.

regional coverage. Increasing intensity of the observed metamorphism may be related to greater intensity of folding and faulting where the strata underwent dynamic metamorphism or to closer proximity to an intruded igneous body where the strata were invaded by magma (contact metamorphism). The geologic age of metamorphosed sediments can best be determined either (1) by finding in some of the associated strata remains of index fossils that have not been deformed beyond recognition or (2) by tracing the altered formations to regions of least metamorphism where their age has been satisfactorily determined.

253. Discrimination between primary and secondary gneisses. Primary gneisses are igneous rocks which possess a foliation produced before crystallization was complete. Secondary gneisses are those which acquired their structure through true rock flowage and not through the viscous flow of a stiff magma. Certain characters of primary gneisses, useful as criteria for distinguishing between the two classes of rock, are noted in the following quotation from Trueman:[20]

"Field evidence: Banding in apophyses from the gneiss parallel to the walls and at an angle to the schistosity of the inclosing rock; dikes of pegmatite belonging to the same magmatic series as the gneiss and either parallel to the gneissic structure and foliated with it or cutting the gneissic structure and undisturbed; lack of sharp contact between the acidic and more basic portions of the gneiss, indicating high temperature during the solidifications of the different bands; presence of inclusions of foreign rocks, which are but slightly deformed, in a matrix of well-banded gneiss; presence of distinct bands of widely different composition, none of which may show evidence of shearing; flowlike curves of the banding, some of which may close in a circle.

"Mineralogical evidence: Presence of minerals formed characteristically only from igneous melts and arranged in a manner impossible of formation from solid rocks by metamorphism, *e.g.*, nepheline and olivine; textures due to crystallization from an igneous melt."

254. Original depth of metamorphic rocks. A rock which has characteristics due to rock flowage must have once been within its zone of flowage. A comparatively weak rock, like shale, may have undergone anamorphic changes at a moderate depth; but if all the rocks in a formation, even the more resistant types, have flow cleavage or other features unquestionably of anamorphic origin (not contact metamorphism), probably these

[20] Bibliog., Trueman, J. D., 1912, p. 231.

rocks were altered in the zone of flowage, that is, below the region where both fracture and flowage are possible. On the assumption that the upper part of the zone of flowage is several miles below the earth's surface (173), this would mean that these rocks have been exposed through the erosion of a cover of that thickness.

255. The granite problem. In our discussion of plutons (Chap. 6), we referred almost wholly to only one method of derivation of the rock material, namely, through cooling and consolidation of magma. The composing rocks, so derived, are truly igneous. But extensive research has indicated that some batholiths, formerly thought to have been of magmatic origin, have apparently developed through metasomatic replacement of minerals in a sedimentary sequence, or in a metamorphosed body of rock, by minerals common to granite, so that the derived rock resembles granite consolidated from magma. This process is therefore called *granitization*. The rocks originating in this way may be referred to as *pseudo-igneous*. The word *pluton* is used both for the true igneous bodies and also for those which may be pseudo-igneous. It is a convenient "basket term."

In the field, the geologist should endeavor to determine whether observed bodies of granite, or of granite gneiss, were formed from magma or by metasomatic replacement. Evidences for differentiating between these sources are: (1) Contacts between magmatic derivatives and their country rocks are likely to be sharper, *i.e.*, less gradational, than those bordering replacement granites. (2) Regional investigation may reveal a gradual passage of structural features (foliation, etc.) of the country rock into a replacement granite. (3) Fragments of the country rock in the granite may be sharp and angular if they were inclosed in magma, but they may be rounded and scalloped if they were in process of replacement. Sure proof of one or the other of these two modes of origin of granitic rocks is very difficult to determine. This is the reason for the long-continued arguments on this so-called "granite problem."[21]

[21] For a comprehensive discussion of this topic, see Bibliog., Gilluly, James, *et al.*, 1948.

Chapter 10

MINERAL DEPOSITS

Mineral Deposits in General

256. Terminology and classification. A mineral deposit is a natural concentration of one or more mineral species. The concentration may be brought about by sedimentary, igneous, or metamorphic processes. Such deposits are *primary* if they still preserve their original characters and relations to adjoining rocks, and they are *secondary* if they have suffered partial or complete chemical or mechanical alteration since their origin. In the formation of a secondary deposit the materials often change their position. With reference to the time of their origin as compared with that of the inclosing rock (country rock), primary bodies are either *contemporaneous* (*syngenetic*) or *subsequent* (*epigenetic*). The contemporaneous varieties are further divided into those which are *igneous* and those which are *sedimentary*. Subsequent mineral deposits include *open-space deposits* and *replacement deposits*. Secondary deposits, produced by various processes of erosion, may be concentrated by chemical or mechanical means.

It is not the author's purpose to enter into detail concerning mineral deposits. All classes are abundantly represented by ores, *i.e.*, by deposits which are of economic importance, and therefore, if the student wishes full information on the subject he should consult books devoted to economic geology.[1] We are here interested particularly in structural and field relations. With respect to the different types noted above, all discussion of contemporaneous primary mineral deposits and of secondary mineral deposits will be omitted from this chapter. Igneous

[1] See Spurr, J. E., "Geology Applied to Mining," McGraw-Hill Book Company, Inc., 1926; also Gunther, C. G., and R. C. Fleming, "The Examination of Prospects," McGraw-Hill Book Company, Inc., 1932. See Arts. **457–459.**

primary deposits, resulting from processes of magmatic differentiation and segregation, answer to statements made in Chap. 6; sedimentary primary deposits are merely beds which, in general, have structural and field relations like those described for stratified rocks in Chap. 5; and many of the facts outlined in Chap. 5 and 9 are applicable to secondary mineral deposits. The only types left for description here are open-space and replacement deposits.

Study of Subsequent Mineral Deposits

257. Origin of subsequent deposits. Underground waters whether they have descended into the lithosphere from the earth's surface or have been given off by intruded magmas, contain a variable proportion of mineral substances in solution. In their circulation these waters may come under certain influences which induce the deposition of some of the solutes. Precipitation may be caused by cooling, by the mingling of different solutions, by chemical reactions between a solution and the rock through which it is passing, and in other ways. The same is true of gaseous solutions which probably emanate from magmas in considerable quantities (**152**). In the zone of fracture the precipitated minerals may incrust the walls of open spaces and line them with layer upon layer until the openings are partly or wholly filled. Thus originate open space deposits (Fig. 263). Under certain circumstances mineral-bearing solutions may attack a rock, removing its constituents in solution and precipitating new ones by a process of substitution or *replacement,* generally without change in the bulk volume of the rock (Art. **244**). This is known as *metasomatism.* Such *replacement deposits* may be formed either in the zone of fracture or in the zone of flowage. Metasomatism is often associated with intrusion as one of the important phases of contact metamorphism (Fig. 264).

Although any rock may be altered by replacement if the conditions are favorable, some kinds are much more susceptible than others. Limestone is one of the types that are metasomatized with comparative readiness (Fig. 264). Fossils are often preserved because their constituents have been replaced by more stable compounds. Not uncommonly the wall rocks of open space fillings are more or less metasomatized in the vicinity of these deposits (Fig. 263).

258. Forms of subsequent mineral deposits. Subsequent mineral bodies with tabular or sheetlike form and genetically associated with fractures are called *veins* (Fig. 263). They may originate by the filling of a fissure (joint, fault, cleavage plane, etc.) or by more or less replacement of its wall rocks, or by a combination of both processes. Simple open space fillings of any variety naturally have the shape of their inclosing chamber

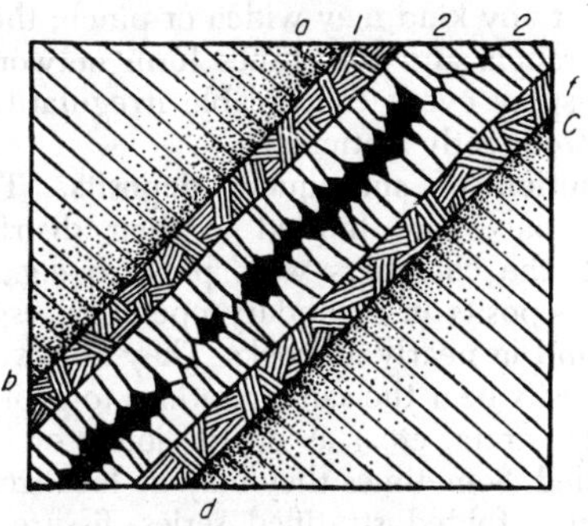

Fig. 263. Section of an open space vein. The mineral numbered 1 was deposited before that numbered 2. The black represents spaces still unfilled. *ab* is the hanging wall and *cd* is the footwall. The stippled part of the country rock adjacent to the vein has been metasomatized.

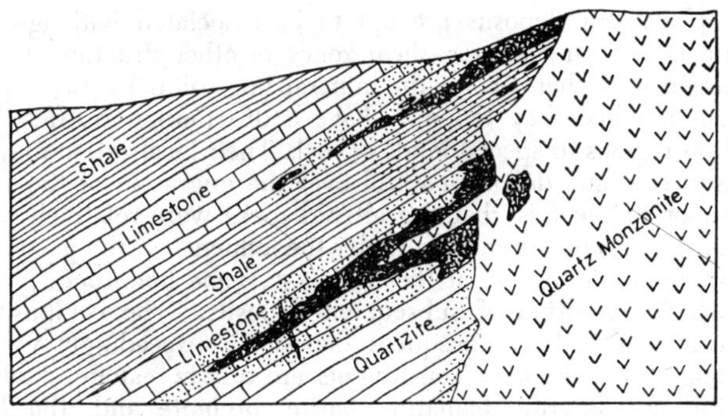

Fig. 264. Vertical section of a contact metamorphic deposit. Ore, heavy stippling; altered country rock beyond ore, light stippling. The alteration was induced by the intrusion of the quartz monzonite. The ore is almost entirely limited to the limestone. (*After W. Lindgren.*)

or fissures. Examples are amygdales (page 136); geodes, which are subspherical incrustations in cavities an inch to a foot, more or less, in diameter; *vugs*, similar to geodes but more irregular in shape; and gash veins, occupying gash joints (Fig. 240) and some other kinds of tension fractures. Stalactites and stalagmites are peculiar types belonging to the group of open-space deposits. Replacement bodies are usually very irregular in shape. This is true even of replacement veins, although in the main they are tabular. Veins of any kind may widen or pinch; they may turn in their course, branch, and sometimes form networks; indeed, as a class they display every conceivable irregularity. In schistose rocks they are frequently lenticular.

259. Distribution of subsequent deposits. The fillings of primary open spaces are limited in their distribution to the rocks in which the chambers were present; *e.g.*, amygdales in certain lavas. Deposits in secondary openings, especially fissure fillings, are found in nearly all rocks. They are exceedingly common. Such deposits bear the same relations to geologic structures (folds, contacts, strata, etc.) as do the joints or faults in which they were formed. Sometimes they may be localized in particular rocks. Thus, in a folded stratified series, fissure veins may be found only in the harder, more brittle members which suffered prominent fracturing (178), whereas the less competent beds, which were deformed by flowage, are barren or have only thin, poorly defined veinlets.

Replacement deposits are apt to be associated with igneous contacts or with fractures, shear zones, or other structures which functioned as channels for the mineralizing solutions. Like open-space deposits, they too may have a distribution restricted in certain regions to special kinds of rock. Their localization may be caused by some definite control over the migration of the solutions, or to the fact that the altered rocks were relatively very susceptible to metasomatism under the influence of the particular solutions in circulation at the time; *e.g.*, some limestones.

260. Composition of subsequent deposits. The composition of veins and other subsequent deposits is exceedingly varied. Among the commonest constituents are quartz, calcite, epidote, pyrite, chalcopyrite, hematite, barite, prehnite and, the like. Ore-bearing veins generally consist of one or more minerals which have a commercial value associated with other substances, known as *gangue minerals*, which have no value. Within the gangue the ore minerals may be disseminated as fine particles, or distributed in threads, or segregated in masses, or otherwise arranged. Although ore minerals are sometimes native, as gold, copper, platinum, and mercury, they are usually sulphides, oxides, carbonates, sulphates, chlorides, or other compounds.

261. Size of vein deposits. In thickness veins may range from a fraction of an inch to many yards, and in length they may range from a fraction of an inch to several miles. Many have been followed downward to depths of 3,000 or 4,000 ft.

262. General field relations of veins. The attitude of a vein is referred to in the same terms as that of a fault, a dike, or a bed. Strike, dip, and hade are used with the same significance as defined in Art. **199.** A majority of veins have dips steeper than 50°. When a vein is inclined the wall above it is the *hanging wall* and that below is the *footwall* (Fig. 263).

The geologic age of a mineral deposit is determined by correlation with fossiliferous strata or with other rocks whose age has been established.

With reference to their relations to the land surface, veins may be more resistant or less resistant to the influences of weathering than their wall rocks. If stronger, they project as ridges. When small and numerous, they give to an outcrop a ribbed surface or a honeycombed appearance according as they are in parallel or intersecting sets. If they are less resistant than their country rock, they weather down below the general level and become covered with their own residual débris (gossan, etc.).

The trends of outcropping veins conform to the rules which have been set forth in Art. **193** for strata.

263. Discrimination between open-space deposits and replacement deposits. No infallible rule can be laid down for ready discrimination between open-space and replacement deposits. There is generally some alteration in the walls of open-space deposits and, on the other hand, replacement bodies may be situated along fissures which conducted the mineralizing solutions. Every gradation exists between the two classes. Nevertheless there are certain features which are especially characteristic of one group or the other, and these, when properly interpreted, may be of considerable assistance as distinguishing marks. (1) Usually, not always, replacement deposits have rather indistinct or blended contacts and open-space deposits have sharply defined boundaries. (2) Open-space bodies ordinarily have a banded or crustiform structure parallel to the walls of the original chamber, this being due to the deposition, one upon another, of successive layers of varying mineral composition. Banding, if present in replacement deposits, is rarely symmetrical. (3) Replacement veins are apt to be less regular in shape than fissure veins. The latter often exhibit matched walls. (4) Blocks, or "horses," of the wall rock, completely detached and with their original structures unchanged in position, have been isolated by replacement of the intervening rock (Fig. 265). If detached fragments of the wall rock are found in an open-space deposit, they usually touch

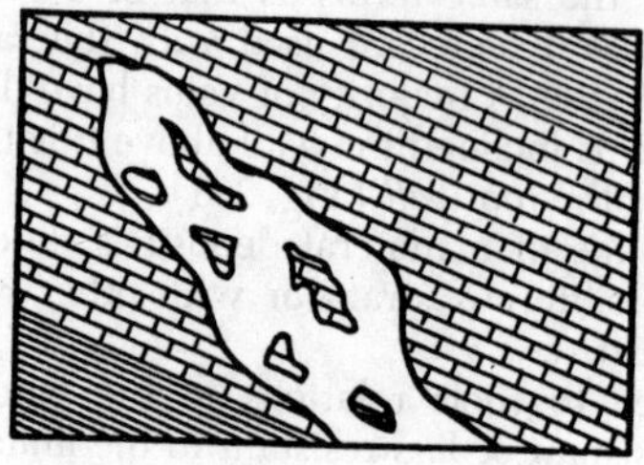

Fig. 265. Section of a replacement mineral deposit (white) containing isolated blocks of the country rock in their original position.

one another and they have altered their position as shown by the various orientations of their structures.

264. Discrimination between veins and dikes. In their field occurrence dikes and veins are very much alike. Typically they are sheetlike and their irregularities of shape are of similar nature, so that they cannot be distinguished by their form and structural relations. As for their manner of origin, there is a complete gradation between them. Vein materials are deposited from solutions. Dikes are formed by the consolidation, usually the crystallization, of magma in which is present a variable quantity of gases and vapors. The greater the proportion of these mineralizers, the more mobile is the magma and the more nearly does it resemble a hot solution from which certain types of vein are precipitated. Pegmatite dikes (or veins) are on the border line in the classification. Pegmatite apophyses from granitoid bodies often verge into true quartz veins at their outer extremities.

From these facts it is evident that a satisfactory code of rules for the discrimination of dikes and veins cannot be made. There are too many exceptions. However, texture, lithologic structure, and mineral composition are often helpful guides. Dikes are usually compact without visible open spaces, and not uncommonly they have porphyritic texture. Chilled margins are typical of many. On the contrary, veins are apt to have open spaces into which numerous crystal ends project (drusy cavities), and they may have a banded distribution of their mineral constituents parallel to the walls. Perhaps the most important criteria are mineral composition and especially the relative proportions of the different species. There are certain minerals which, while sometimes found in dikes, are of much more frequent occurrence in veins; and vice versa. For example, characteristic of veins are calcite, epidote, and the other minerals cited in Art. **260**, and species more typical of dike rocks are feldspar, hornblende, augite, biotite, and muscovite. Yet, even in this case, great care must be exercised not to confuse calcite, epidote, and the like, in veins, with the same minerals occurring as secondary constituents of dike rocks.

Chapter 11

TOPOGRAPHIC FORMS

Topographic Forms in General

265. Topographic forms and their recognition. Hills, valleys, plains, beaches, cliffs, and the like, are classified as *topographic forms.*[1] Although most of them are products of the erosional and depositional agents which are working at the earth's surface, some have been made through the operation of subterranean forces. To the latter category belong volcanoes, lava flows, fault scarps, etc.

Of the topographic forms resulting from erosion and from deposition, those which project upward (hills, etc.) are *positive,* and those which have the nature of depressions are *negative.* Those which are direct effects of wearing down are *destructional,* and those which have been built by processes of accumulation are *constructional.* Destructional topographic forms are immediately dependent upon the relative resistance of the materials eroded. Underlying structure is of secondary account, although it naturally governs the shape and distribution of the topographic elements. Constructional forms are nearly always situated in regions lower than the sources of the materials.[2] This, of course, is because the products of erosion are generally carried downward.

The ability to recognize topographic forms is not only indispensable for the geologist, but it is also a valuable acquisition for persons engaged in many other pursuits. One should be able to tell the difference between valleys made by ice and those made by rivers; between hills of eolian, glacial, or volcanic origin; between plains built by rivers and plains due to the work of

[1] Most topographic forms may also be called *land forms,* for, even though now partly or wholly submerged, they may have originated on land. Some, such as calcareous reefs, develop between low-tide level and high-tide level or even below low-tide level (see **Art. 299**).

[2] Obviously, volcanic cones are an exception.

waves; and so on. The criteria are included for the most part among the following characters of topographic forms: (1) surface features; (2) general shape, including ground plan and profiles in significant directions; (3) position with reference to topographic surroundings; (4) internal structure; and (5), for constructional deposits, the characters of constituent grains or fragments.

266. Geomorphology defined. The science that treats of the surface features of the earth—their form, nature, origin, development, and interrelationships—is known as *geomorphology*. Much of the subject matter of Chaps. 11 and 12 belongs under geomorphology.[3]

SLOPES

267. Significance of the inclination of land surfaces. Topography may be said to consist of sloping surfaces. Even plains have some undulations, and those which are essentially flat often

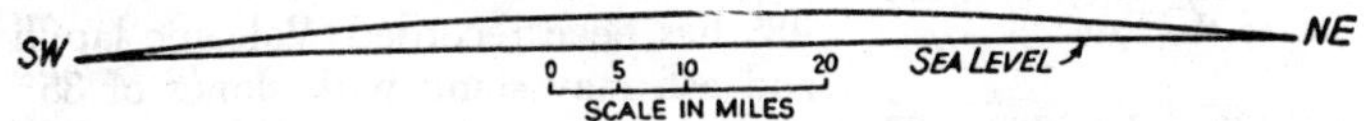

FIG. 266. Profile section of Mauna Loa, a lava cone. (*After C. E. Dutton.*)

have an inclination one way or another. The slope of any such surface is a feature which deserves an explanation, for it is related to the mode of development of the topographic form with which it is associated.

Land surfaces may be on consolidated or on unconsolidated rocks. The average inclination of the surface of a lava sheet, or a lava cone, is indicative of the original viscosity of the liquid rock. Very mobile lavas spread far and have a slope which may be as low as 3° (Fig. 266). Surfaces eroded on bedrock often owe their inclination to a balance between the rates of passive weathering and of active corrasion. Their case will be taken up in more detail below. Any destructional surface which approximately coincides with the stratification of dipping beds is called a *dip slope*. It is due to natural stripping of an overlying weak stratum from an underlying resistant layer (**300, C**).

[3] For an excellent reference on this science, see Bibliog., Thornbury, Wm. D., 1954.

Surfaces on unconsolidated sediments may be either destructional or constructional. In the case of stratified deposits, a surface coincident with the bedding is probably constructional, and one intersecting the bedding is probably destructional. The most important angle of slope in unconsolidated deposits is that known as the *angle of repose* or *angle of rest.* If sand or gravel has been held up by a support, and this support be removed, the sediments will slump down of their own weight and will continue to slide until friction between the particles prevents further slipping. The vertical angle between a horizontal plane and the surface in which sliding ceased is the angle of repose for these materials (Fig. 267). The maximum angle of repose for coarse gravels consisting of angular fragments is about 35°. Even 42° has been recorded. Volcanic lapilli and ash may stand with slopes of 35° to 40° (Fig. 268). The angle of repose for rounded gravels is lower. For mixed sand and gravel and for sand alone, 28° to 30° is common. Damp sand can stand more steeply than dry, and angular sand more steeply than well-rounded sand. The angle of repose for sand is somewhat higher under water, provided there is no current, for a current can easily reduce the slope to a much lower inclination. Clay, loess, and similar materials, which are capable of a sort of semiconsolidation, may stand in vertical

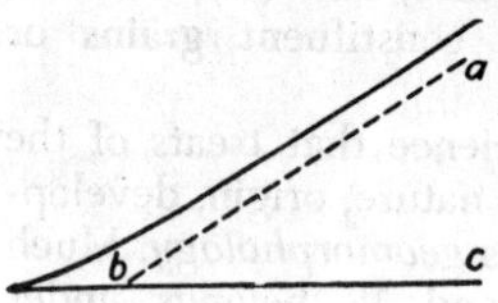

FIG. 267. Profile section of a slope on loose gravel. *abc,* angle of repose. The larger bowlders may accumulate at the foot of the slope, although the reverse may be true where these large fragments disintegrate on the upper part of the slope instead of rolling to the base.[4]

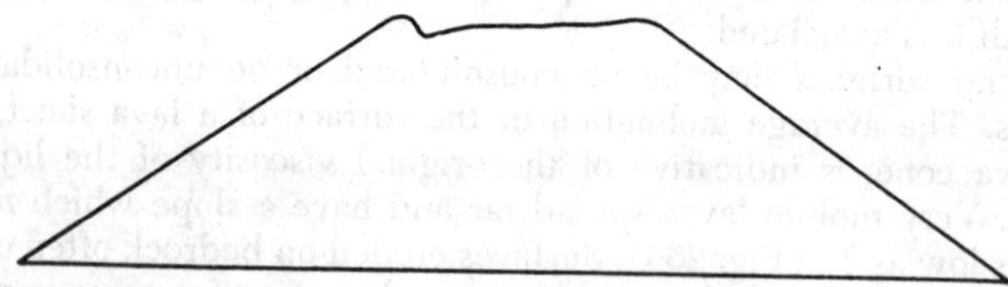

FIG. 268. Profile of a volcanic cinder cone. The breadth at the base is a few hundred feet. (*After J. S. Diller.*)

[4] Bibliog., Behre, Charles H., Jr., "Talus Behavior above Timber on the Rocky Mountains," *Jour. Geol.,* vol. 41, p. 624, 1933.

cliffs (Fig. 269), but, when well soaked with water, mud and clay may slide on slopes of only 2° or 3°. In fact, the relative quantity of water between the particles of any kind of mantle rock has a very significant bearing on the angle above which the material will begin to slide. This is important in considering mass movement (3). On many hill slopes, often of moderate inclination, there is a constant tendency for downhill creep, a process that is usually intermittent, being facilitated by moisture and

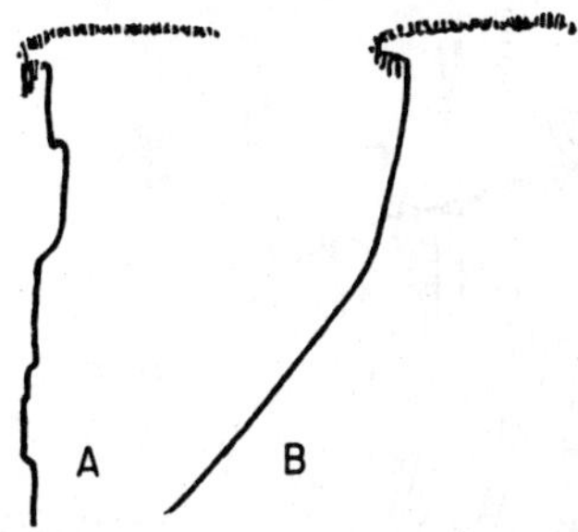

FIG. 269. A, profile of a bluff in loess; B, profile of a bluff in till. The upper steep slope in B is due to rain erosion; the lower more gentle slope is due to a balance between deposition by rainwash and landslips, on the one hand, and erosion by rain, on the other hand.

frost. Figure 270 illustrates several evidences for creep (see also 394).

CLIFFS

268. Cliffs in general. To vertical or very steep faces of rock and partially consolidated sediments are given such names as cliffs, scarps, escarpments, precipices, bluffs, etc. The word cliff will be used here in a general sense. The more common varieties will be classified as follows:[5]

KEY FOR THE IDENTIFICATION OF CLIFFS

If a cliff

A. Bears scratches and grooves which
   1. Trend principally along the cliff, either horizontal or with a low inclination, the cliff was probably made by glacial abrasion (271, D).

[5] Faceted spurs (272) are not included.

2. Trend up and down the slope, being vertical or steeply inclined, the cliff may be a fault scarp (**269**) or a landslide scar (**271, G**).

B. Bears no scratches or grooves, but is rough on account of the separation of grains or joint blocks (**38**), and

1. Evidence is found of dislocation (faulting) of bedrock structures,

   a. And of topographic forms, along the cliff, the latter is probably a fault scarp, somewhat weathered (**269**).

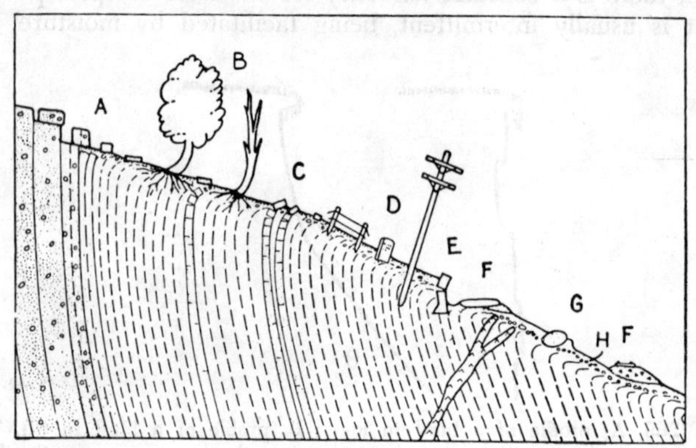

FIG. 270. Common evidences of creep. A, moved joint blocks; B, trees with curved trunks concave upslope; C, downslope bending and drag of bedded rock, weathered veins, etc., also present beneath soil elsewhere on the slope; D, displaced posts, poles, and monuments; E, broken or displaced retaining walls and foundations; F, roads and railroads moved out of alignment; G, turf rolls downslope from creeping bowlders; H, stone line at approximate base of creeping soil. A and C represent *rock creep;* all other features shown are due to *soil creep.* Rather similar effects may be produced by some types of landslides. (*Reproduced from Sharpe's "Landslides and Related Phenomena" by permission of Columbia University Press. See Bibliog., Sharpe, C.F. Stewart,* 1938, *p.* 23.)

   b. But not of topographic forms, along the cliff, the latter is probably a fault-line cliff (**271, F**).

2. No evidence of dislocation is found along the cliff, the latter

   a. Being situated along an existing shore line or, if not so situated, being associated with a wave-cut bench at its base (**277**), this cliff is a wave-cut cliff (**271, A**).

   b. Not being associated with a shore line or with a wave-cut bench, and if

      (1) The cliff truncates a particular stratum or layer in a series of eroded horizontal or inclined layers, this cliff is an erosion scarp produced largely by weathering (**38**).

(2) The cliff is the front edge of a recent lava flow, this cliff may be original (**270**).

(3) The cliff is the inclosing rim of a crater or of a caldera, and intersects rocks of volcanic origin, this cliff may be a consequence of volcanic explosion, or of the infall of blocks from the sides, accompanied or not accompanied by fusion at the base, or by these processes in cooperation (**287**).

(4) The cliff is not related to any particular kind of rock, but

(*a*) Forms the wall of a river valley (or channel), this cliff is probably due to weathering assisted by basal undermining accomplished by the river (**271, B**).

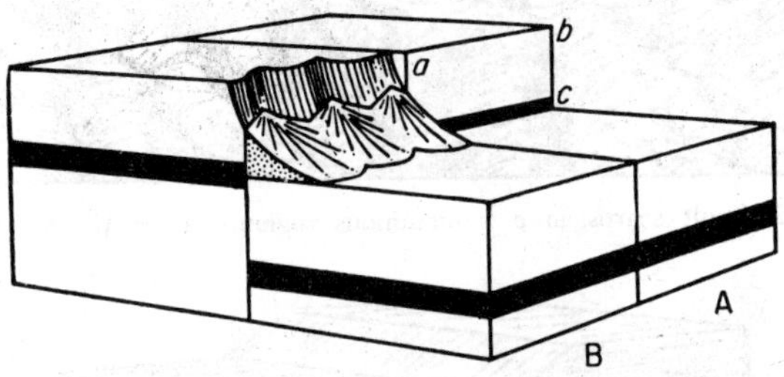

Fig. 271. Fault scarp interrupting a level land surface. A, hypothetical condition before erosion; B, aspect after moderate erosion. Talus cones have accumulated at the base of the fault cliff.

(*b*) Forms the wall of a glacial valley or of a cirque, the cliff may be the result of glacial scour, somewhat weathered, or of glacial sapping (**271, D and E**).

(*c*) Forms the lee side of a roche moutonnée, the cliff is probably a result of glacial plucking (**271, E**).

269. Fault cliffs. Fault scarps are cliffs of varying height and length, formed by faulting. The scarp always fronts upon the lower land of the downthrown block. Most fault scarps, especially the high ones, are the result of recurrent dislocation along the same surface of fracture or along close, parallel fractures. The shape of the original scarp depends upon the topography of the land mass that was broken. If the ground was level, the cliff is pretty regular in height (Fig. 271), but if a rugged surface was intersected by a fault transverse to the trend of the ridges and valleys, the scarp crest zigzags up and down (Fig. 272). In some cases the scarp may be the actual fault surface, but generally all marks of slipping are destroyed by weathering soon after their exposure. Fault scarps in sands, gravels, and the like, are seldom steeper than the angle of repose, because such materials are prone to slump (Fig. 273).

When on alluvial cones and other deposits with definite constructional slopes, fault scarps may be distinguished from aban-

FIG. 272. Fault scarps in a mountainous region. (*After W. M. Davis.*)

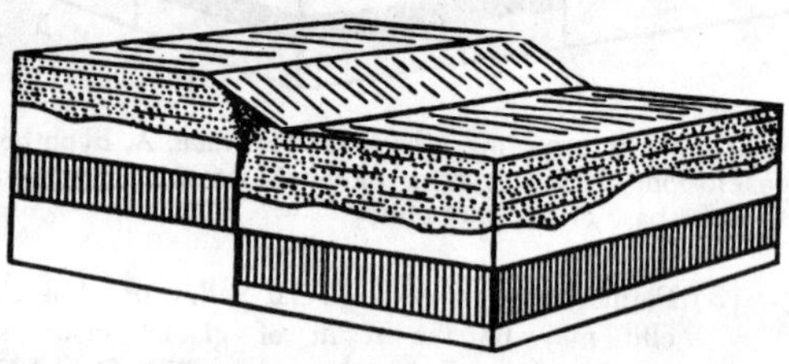

FIG. 273. Fault scarp in gravel, produced by a displacement in the underlying bedrock. The slope of the scarp is the angle of repose of the gravel.

doned shore-line cliffs (**308**) by their lack of relation to the contours. Shore-line features follow the contours (Fig. 274).

270. Volcanic cliffs. The front edges of lava flows are often abrupt and may be fairly straight for many hundred feet, so that they resemble fault scarps. Indeed, it is sometimes a difficult matter to determine whether or not such a steep face in lava is a product of faulting. Evidence for the continuation of a line of displacement must be sought beyond the edge of the lava flow. The inner rims of explosion craters might also be mentioned here. They are steep slopes on which are usually exposed the truncated ends of the outward dipping ash deposits and interbedded flows which constitute the volcanic cone. They are distinguished with some difficulty from the bounding walls of volcanic sinks (285).

271. Destructional cliffs. Erosion cliffs include sea cliffs, river cliffs and bluffs, cuesta scarps, ice-scoured rock walls, ice-quarried cliffs, fault-line cliffs, and landslide scars. Some are made by weathering, some by abrasion, and some by both. Ordinarily one may assume that a cliff exists either because it is still

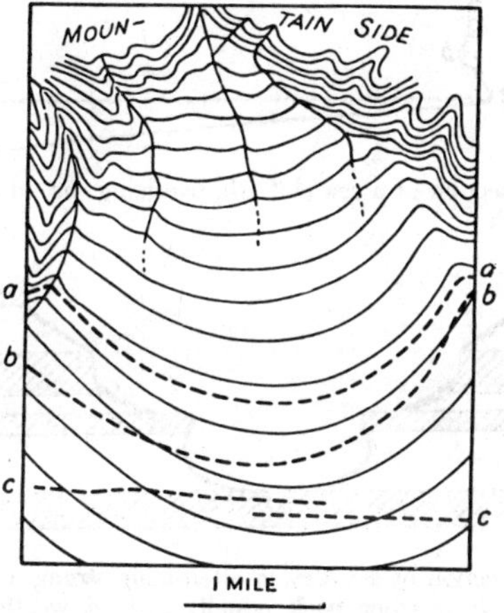

FIG. 274. Contour map of an alluvial cone at the base of a mountain range. The dashed lines indicate the relations between the contours and the hypothetical positions of an abandoned shore line, *aa,* a tilted, abandoned shore line, *bb,* and an interrupted fault scarp, *cc.*

in process of formation or because it was made so recently that the forces of erosion have not yet had time to erase it.

271A. Sea cliffs are maintained by cutting at the base. In hard rock the *locus of attack,* or place where the waves do their principal work, is seen in an undercut, or notch, at about high-tide level (Fig. 275). From time to time joint blocks are dislodged from the overhanging rock by frost or by other agents of disintegration. Where weak dikes or strata offer less resistance to the onslaught of the waves than do the adjacent rocks, fissures and cliffs may be cut landward. This is a case of differential erosion. In materials like till, which are apt to slip if undermined, the cliff may be steep, but rarely has the compound nature of undercut and overhang (Fig. 269, B). Gravels and sand slump to their angle of repose just as fast as they are attacked below.

271B. River cliffs are cut by the lateral swinging of the stream. In respect to basal undercutting, dislodgment of blocks from the cliff face, and relation of materials to slope and form, they

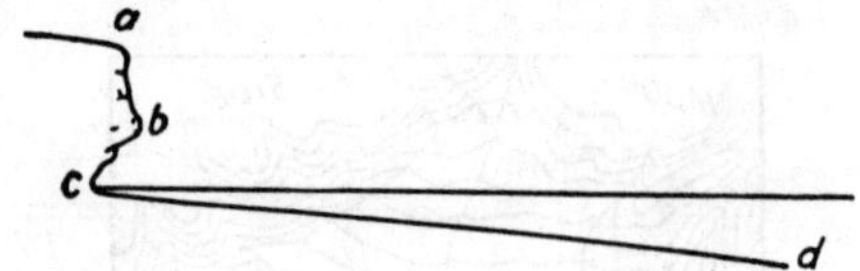

Fig. 275. Profile section of a sea cliff. *ab*, overhang; *bc*, undercut, or notch; *cd*, wave-cut bench.

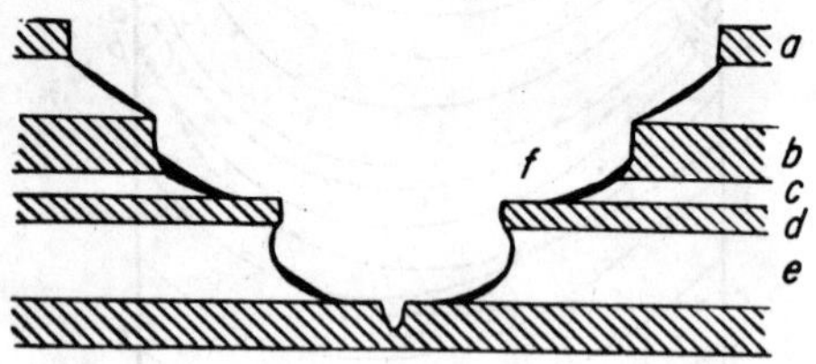

Fig. 276. Profile section of a valley in alternating strong and weak horizontal strata; *a* and *b* weather back equally fast; *d* weathers more slowly than *b* and, therefore, a rock bench is developed at *f*; *c* is so thin that the talus (black) overlaps the base of *b* (cf. *e*).

correspond to sea cliffs. Wherever streams are rapidly incising their channels in horizontal strata of varying resistance to erosion, the valley walls usually consist of alternating vertical cliffs on the more resistant rocks, and talus slopes with the angle of repose on the weaker strata (Fig. 276). This type of valley wall may be seen in the Colorado Canyon.

271C. Cliffs like those just mentioned may form the sides of mesas and buttes (Fig. 277). Each hard layer serves as a protective cover for the underlying softer rock. To some extent erosion may undermine the weak stratum beyond the edge of the strong, but if undermining goes too far, masses of the overlying rock fall off. Thus, while the cliff or escarpment is gradually worn back, its steepness is maintained as long as the hard stratum, or cliff-maker, stands well above the level attained by the streams of the region when they reach grade (**303**). If the layers have a low inclination (say up to 20° or 25°), the escarpment is called a *cuesta face* or a *cuesta scarp,* and the cliffmaking rock is spoken of as a *cuesta-maker* (Fig. 346).

271D. The ice of mountain glaciers scours deep the valleys through which it moves and, in so doing, greatly steepens the valley walls. This is called *oversteepening* (Fig. 278). Such over-

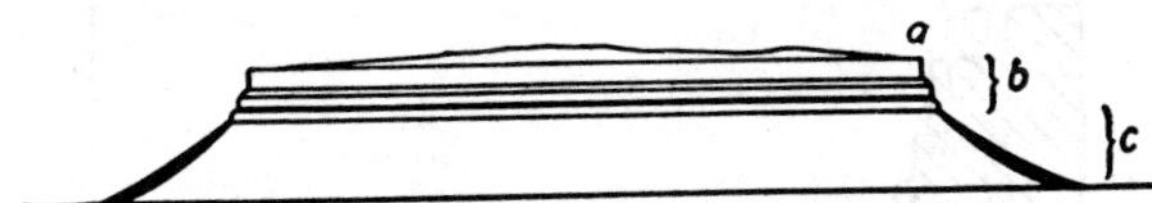

FIG. 277. Profile section of a mesa. *a,* remains of a weak stratum, nearly worn away; *b,* alternating strong and thin weak beds; *c,* weak stratum with its edges covered by talus (black).

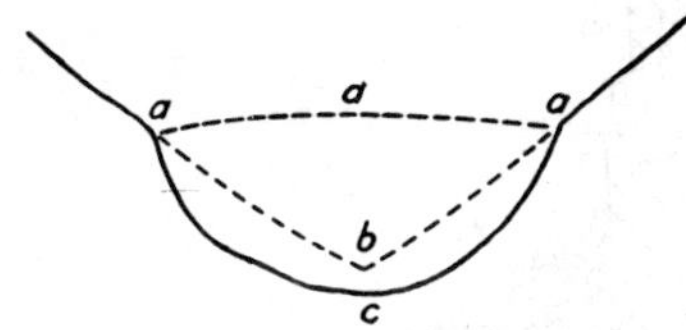

FIG. 278. Transverse profile section of a glaciated valley (*aca*). *aba,* valley before glaciation; *ada,* original surface of ice. Note the shoulders at *a.*

steepened, ice-scoured rock walls are polished and striated unless postglacial weathering has effaced the marks of glaciation. In the latter event the origin by ice abrasion may be demonstrated by other signs of glacial erosion in the vicinity, or by associated glacial deposits.

271E. Ice-quarried cliffs (Fig. 279) are quite different from the preceding type. At the head of a mountain glacier, where abrasion is little or nil, alternate thawing and freezing operate exactly as does the frost action of disintegration, but on a larger scale, and blocks are riven off along the joints. These blocks of rock settle into the ice (Fig. 280) and are slowly carried away by the glacier. If long continued, this process of *sapping* or *quarrying* may develop cliffs up to many hundreds of feet in height, but they are not exposed, except to a certain extent within the bergschrund, until after the glacier has dwindled away and disappeared. They form the walls of cirques (**291, H**).

Smaller cliffs of somewhat similar origin may be seen on roches moutonnées, and on hills of like nature, where moving ice detached or *plucked* joint blocks from the lee sides of the rock

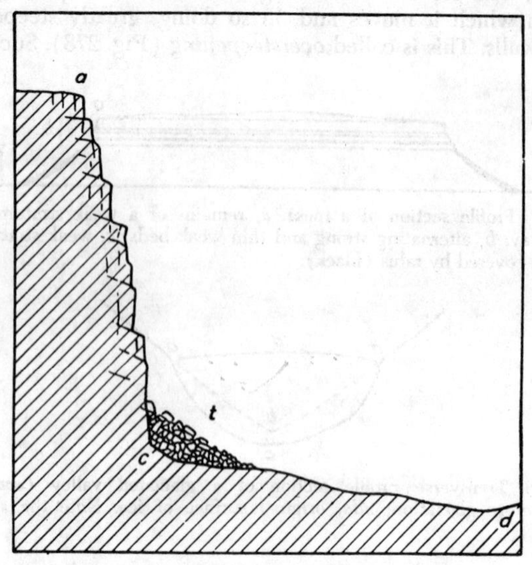

Fɪɢ. 279. Profile section of the ice-sapped cliff, *ac*, and the ice-scoured floor, *cd*, at the head of a glacial cirque. *t*, talus (of postglacial origin).

masses over which it rode (**300**). Sapping or quarrying is accomplished entirely by the passive process of wedging, whereas plucking, although more or less assisted by wedging, is largely dependent upon the overriding of a moving body.

271F. Fault-line scarps are erosion scarps developed along lines of faulting. They are not direct effects of displacement. They are phenomena belonging to a second cycle of erosion (**307**). The original fault scrap was eroded to low relief, the land was then uplifted and a second cycle was inaugurated, in which weaker rocks on one side of the fault were worn away more rapidly than more resistant rocks on the other side. Thus, a scarp was developed along the line of faulting. Two conditions are possible: the lower land toward which the fault-line scarp faces may be (1) on the block which was the downthrown side of the fault (Fig. 281, C) or (2) on that which was the upthrown side (Fig. 281, B). In other words, a fault-line scarp may face the

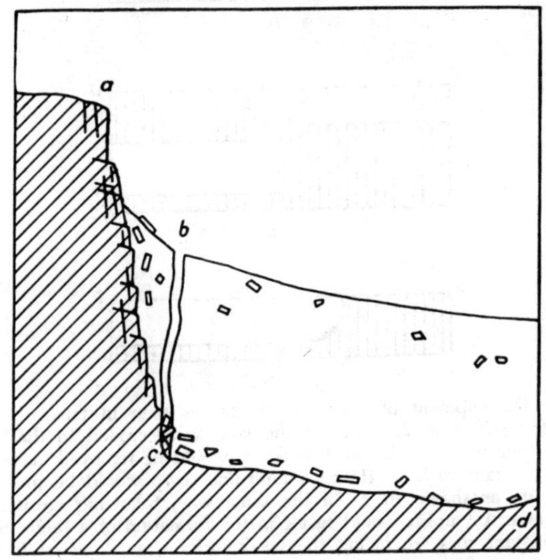

FIG. 280. Same as Fig. 279, with the ice restored to its original position, *ac*, rock wall from which alternate thawing and freezing of water loosen blocks that settle into the ice. At *b* is a deep crevice, known as the *bergschrund*, which is commonly observed at the head of a glacier and which may facilitate the entrance of water. *cd* is the scoured rock floor over which the ice moves.

same way as the original fault scarp or in the opposite direction. Figure 282 represents a fault-line scarp formed in the first cycle of erosion.

271G. Landslide scars are the bare surfaces left by the fall of masses of rock or of unconsolidated materials. The greatest dimension of a landslide scar is generally up and down the slope (**288, F**).

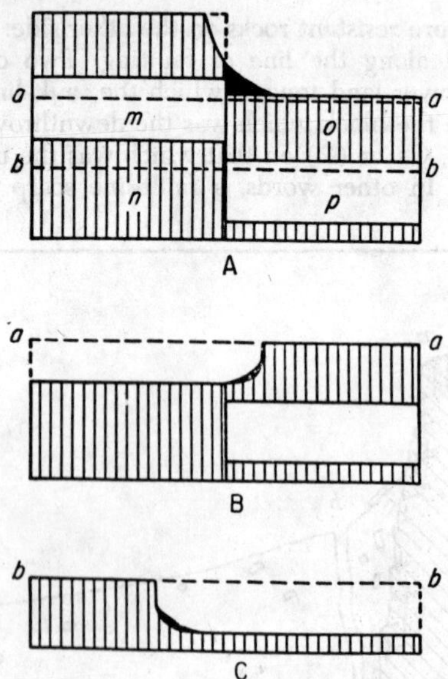

FIG. 281. Development of fault-line scarps, as seen in cross section. A, fault scarp. (Cf. Fig. 271, B.) If the land were eroded to the level *aa* and were then uplifted, the weak rock, *m*, would be removed more rapidly than the resistant rock, *o*. Hence a fault-line scarp would be produced in *o*, facing *m*, as shown in B. In the same way, following erosion to the level *bb* (see A), uplift would result in the formation of a fault-line scarp in the resistant rock, *n*, facing the weak rock, *p*, as depicted in C. The black is talus.

FIG. 282. Section of a fault scarp and a fault-line scarp. Strong beds, ruled; weak beds, blank; talus, black. *a* has been worn back faster than *c* because the weak rocks are exposed in *a*. Before the faulting, the strong rock stratum at *a* and *c* was continuous.

Here, also, might be mentioned the scars left by mudflows, although these scars are likely to be broad in area, with relatively low bounding edges and on lower slopes than the sites of landslide scars. At the down-slope side or end of a mudflow scar will be found the mudflow débris.

272. Faceted spurs. Let us consider the topographic development of a fault scarp in a land mass that was essentially level before its displacement. Take

"the ideal case of a faulted block of homogeneous structure whose faulting has progressed at a slow and relatively uniform rate, so that the sides of the ravines that are eroded in it shall be weathered back to graded slopes

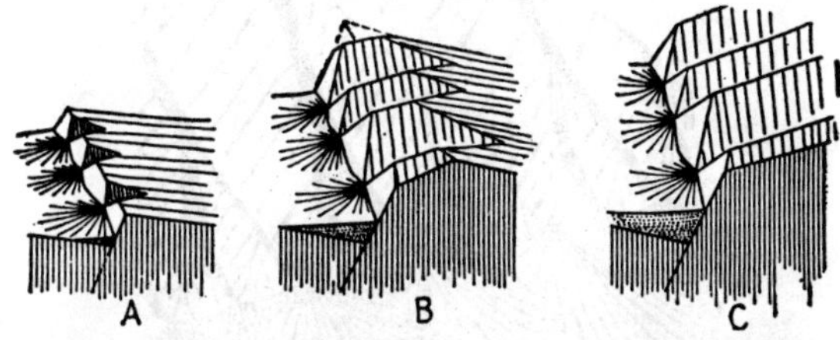

FIG. 283. Dissection of a fault scarp. A, displacement moderate; g, ges short; part of the original front edge of the uplifted block remains. B, the same region after more displacement and erosion; none of the front edge of the uplifted block is left; the fault scarp still persists in a series of triangular facets. C, spurs and deep ravines in the uplifted block after further displacement and erosion. The upper surface of the block is not shown in C. Actually, the spur facets would have suffered some erosion in B, and more in C, and the slopes of these facets would tend, therefore, to decrease (see Fig. 284). (*After W. M. Davis.*)

about as fast as the fault block is raised. . . . In an early stage (Fig. 283, A) the low fault scarp is notched by ravines whose location and length are determined by the site of pre-faulting inequalities in the upper surface of the block. Adjacent ravines have not yet widened sufficiently to consume the edge at the top of the block between them. In a later stage (Fig. 283, B) the block is raised higher, the ravines are worn deeper and farther back, some of them being larger than others. Nothing of the upper front edge of the block now remains, for the flaring walls of the ravines now meet in a sharp ridge crest that rises backward from the vertex of a *triangular facet on the block front*[6] toward the top of the block. In the third stage (Fig. 283, C) the block is raised still higher, and the

[6] The italics in the quotation are not original.

ravines have become still longer and deeper; at this stage the mountain crest might become serrate, and its back slope would be well dissected. The long, sharp-crested ridges between the larger front ravines are still terminated by triangular facets, very systematic in form and position, with their bases aligned along the mountain front. The spur sides and the facets themselves will have suffered some carving, as is shown in Fig. 284, where some of the terminal facets are enlarged. The moderate dissection of the large facet by small ravines results in the development of several little basal facets along the fault line, where they form the truncating terminals of several little spurs. These basal facets are of

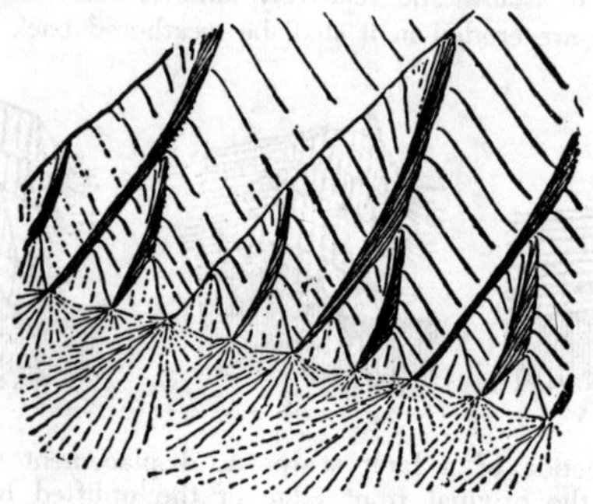

FIG. 284. Dissected terminal facets of main spurs. (Drawn on a larger scale than Fig. 283.) (*After W. M. Davis.*)

importance in this stage of dissection, for they have suffered the least change of any part of the mountain front.

"We are thus led to conclude that the features of special significance as the necessary result of long-continued faulting, persistent into the recent period, are, first, the sharp-cut, narrow-floored valleys which have already been considered; and secondly, the large and small terminal facets of the spurs, whose bases show a notable alignment along the mountain front.

"If faulting be supposed to cease after the stage of Fig. 283 is reached, the valleys will widen without much deepening at their mouths, the spurs will be narrowed, and the truncating terminal facets will in time be so far consumed that the spurs will become pointed."[7]

Faceted spurs may be made also by glacial erosion, or by wave erosion upon a submerged ridge-and-valley topography along a lake shore or a sea coast. If the ice should retreat or if the lake

[7] Bibliog., Davis, W. M., 1909, pp. 745–747.

waters or the sea should withdraw, these triangular spur terminations might be mistaken for fault facets. Wave-cut triangular facets, however, would rise from the inner margins of triangular wave-cut benches (**277**) (Fig. 285), and the valleys would show evidences of aggradation succeeded by rejuvenation, caused, respectively, by the advance and later by the retreat

FIG. 285. Triangular facets due to wave erosion. *ABCD*, initial shore line at time of submergence; *DKF*, cliff facet cut back in spur *DEF; FGH*, spur platform fronting its cliff facet, *FLH*, after withdrawal of the water. (*After W. M. Davis.*)

FIG. 286. Triangular facets due to glaciation. The lowland in the foreground is part of a broad trunk glacial valley. (*Drawn from a photograph, after F. H. Moffit.*)

of the waters. Triangular facets made by ice are sometimes found terminating the ridges between adjacent tributary glacial valleys where they enter the trunk glacial trough (Fig. 286). In this case marks of ice scour (**36, 39, 40**) are generally present on the walls and floors of the valleys and on the facets, and more or less glacial débris is distributed in the neighborhood.

A more complex type of faceted spur is developed by a series of transverse, essentially parallel step faults. On such divides downdropped strips of the old upland surface may be preserved at different levels (**275**).

BEACHES[8]

273. Classification and general characters. All constructional shore-line deposits, built principally by the work of waves and longshore currents, and consisting of sand or of pebbles and bowlders, are herein classed as *beaches*. Under this head may be listed barrier beaches, bay-head or pocket beaches, spits, baymouth bars, tiebars, and cuspate forelands.

FIG. 287. Barrier beach and lagoon (Great South Bay), south of Long Island, N.Y. The overlap of Fire Island Beach south of Oak Island Beach indicates transportation of sand in the direction of the arrow. Shaded, dry land; stippled, sand beach; unshaded land area, marsh. (Islip quadrangle, N.Y.)

Along a coast where the mainland is very low (coast of elevation), the waves break some little distance offshore. They churn up the bottom sand and build up a *sand reef* or *barrier beach* (*offshore bar*) (Fig. 287), between which and the main shore there is a strip of quiet water called a *lagoon*. Reefs of this kind are well represented along the Atlantic coast from Long Island southward. Along steeper coasts, where the shore line is comparatively straight, a beach often lies at the foot of the sea cliff, forming a thin cover over the wave-cut bench.

[8] For a discussion of beaches, see Bibliog., Johnson, J. W., 1956.

Beach construction on irregular coasts is varied. At the heads of the bays there is a tendency for the accumulation of débris worn from the neighboring headlands. These deposits are *bay-head beaches* (Fig. 288). Sometimes currents sweeping by headlands or islands distribute the rock fragments and sand in *spits* which tail off into deep water (Fig. 289). Spits may be hooked, or recurved (Fig. 290). If a spit or a barrier beach finally closes in the entrance to a bay, it is termed a *bay-mouth bar* (Figs. 291, 292). If it is carried out so far as to join an island with another island, or with the mainland, it is a *tiebar* (Fig. 293). A *cuspate foreland* is a triangular point of land, often inclosing a small triangular lagoon, built out from a shore line by currents (Fig. 294).

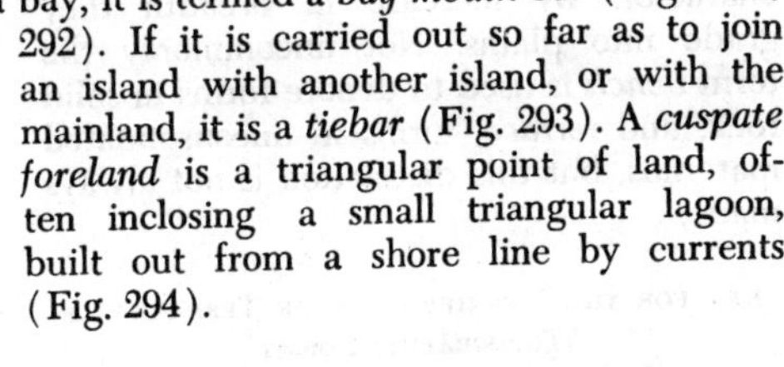

Fig. 288. Bay-head beach (stippled) consisting of wave-washed sediments. The land is to the left. The arrows show the direction of transportation. Sea cliffs are represented by short hachures.

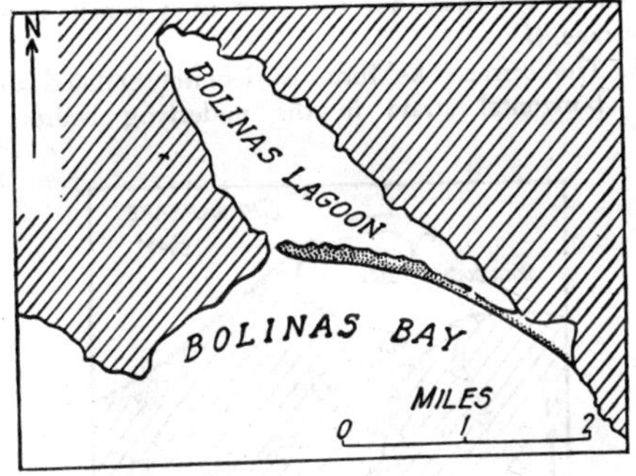

Fig. 289. Spit (stippled) at the head of Bolinas Bay, Calif. (Tamalpais sheet, Calif.) In which direction were the materials of the spit transported?

In general beaches are coarser at the top than they are near the water. Sea beaches often consist of pebbles above high-tide level, grading downward into sand, and, below low-tide level, into mud. On very low, shelving shores, mud flats are exposed at low tide. Coarse pebble beaches are usually situated near cliffs from which the materials are supplied. A sand beach may have its surface diversified by ripple marks, rill marks, wave marks, and other features which have been described in Chap. 4.

Benches and Terraces

274. Definitions and identification. Benches and terraces are relatively flat, horizontal or gently inclined surfaces, sometimes long and narrow, which are bounded by a steeper ascending slope on one side and by a steeper descending slope on the opposite side. Both forms, when typically developed, are steplike in character. By increase in breadth they grade into plains. Not uncommonly the term *bench* is used to denote forms in solid rock, and *terrace*, forms in unconsolidated materials, but this distinction is not always made.

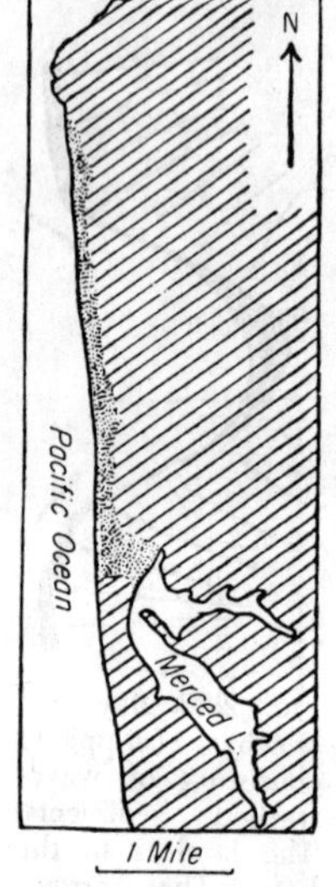

Fig. 291. Merced Lake, Calif., a bay closed by the forward growth of a spit. (San Mateo and San Francisco sheets, Calif.)

Key for the Identification of Terrace-like Topographic Forms

The land surface has the form of a bench or a terrace. If

A. The terrace-like form is definitely related to horizontal strata in the underlyng bedrock being situated between two abrupt slopes or cliffs whch truncate relatively hard strata, it is probably a bench or a step produced by differential erosion (**277**).

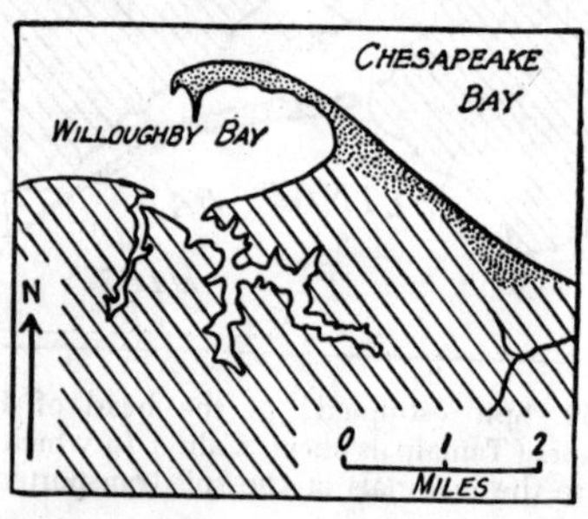

Fig. 290. Willoughby Spit, Va. (Norfolk quadrangle, Va.–N.C.)

B. The terrace-like form is not definitely related to horizontal strata in the underlying bedrock, and

1. Is situated along an existing shore line, beachlike, usually just above high water level, it may be a wave-built terrace or an ice-pushed terrace (**276**).

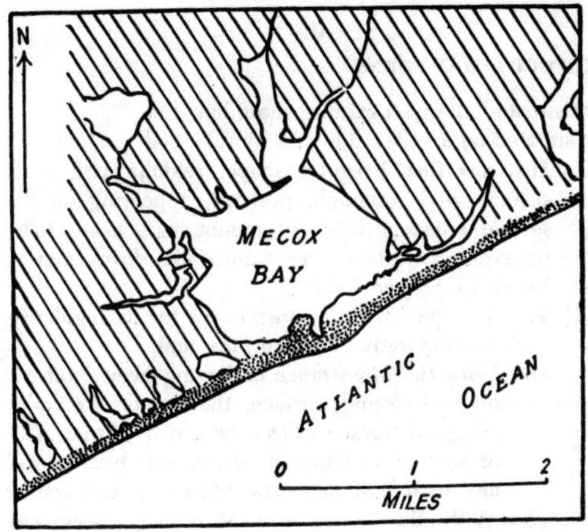

FIG. 292. Mecox Bay, L.I., a bay closed by the landward advance of a barrier beach. (Sag Harbor quadrangle, N.Y.)

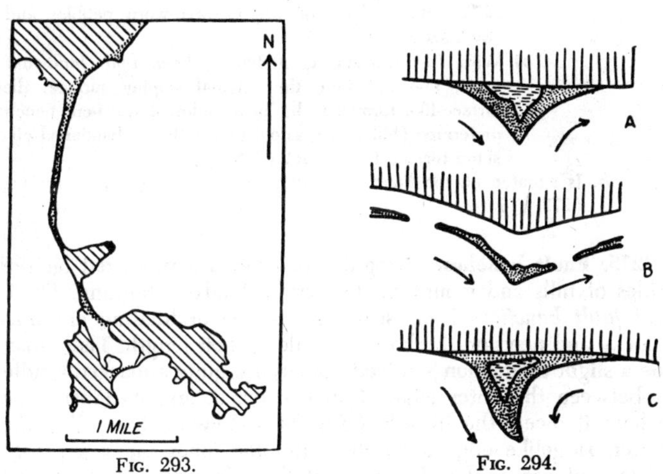

FIG. 293.

FIG. 294.

FIG. 293. Lynn Beach (the long narrow stippled area) connecting Nahant (shaded areas on the south) with the mainland (NW. shaded area). Lynn Beach is a tiebar (*tombolo*). Nahant once consisted of two islands, now themselves united by a tiebar. (Boston Bay sheet, Mass.)

FIG. 294. Three varieties of cuspate foreland (stippled). The mainland is shaded. In A and C the forelands inclose lagoons. The arrows indicate current directions.

2. Is not situated along an existing shore line, but
   a. Is situated on a valley side or a hillside, and
      (1) Has a rather irregular shape, seldom with a flat or level surface, and although, perhaps, appearing on the flanks of several adjacent hills (or mountains), never follows up the intervening valleys, the terrace-like form may be a fault bench or terrace (**275**).
      (2) Has a shape which is conspicuous for its regularity, generally with a comparatively flat surface, and
         (*a*) With the appearance of having been *built out upon* the original sloping surface, the terrace-like form may be a marginal terrace (**276**), or a river terrace (**278**), or one of several varieties of abandoned beach (**273, 308**), in any case bounded downhill by a relatively steep slope.
         (*b*) With the appearance of having been *cut into* the original sloping surface, the terrace-like form may be a wave-cut bench (**277**) or a wave-cut terrace (**278**), in either case bounded uphill by a steep wave-cut cliff (**271**) at the base of which wave-worn pebbles and bowlders may be present.
         (*c*) With the appearance of having been *both built out upon, and cut into,* the original sloping surface, the terrace-like form may be an abandoned wave-cut bench or terrace (cut in) in association with an abandoned offshore terrace (built out) (**308**).
   b. Is situated on the floor of a valley, it is probably a river terrace (**277, 278**).

275. Fault benches. Irregular benches are produced on the sides of hills and mountains by certain kinds of faulting. These are *fault benches.* Their surfaces may be undulating or hummocky and need not be horizontal along their length. There may be a slight depression—indeed, sometimes quite a marked saddle—between the outer edge of such a bench and its inner edge where it meets the hillside (Fig. 295). Lawson has called the outer, ridgelike edge a *kernbut,* and the inner sag a *kerncol.*[9] Two explanations for the origin of these features are illustrated in Fig. 296. Such benches are not to be confused with similar forms of landslide origin and, therefore, purely superficial (Fig. 297). Benches like that in Fig. 297 may be produced on a smaller scale, either singly or in steplike groups, by slumping.

[9] Bibliog., Lawson, A. C., 1902–1904, pp. 331 *et seq.*

276. Constructional terraces. Constructional terraces include offshore terraces (also called wave-built terraces), marginal deposits and abandoned beaches. An *offshore terrace* (Fig. 298) is a deposit of sand which is built out into deep water by the combined action of waves and currents. It trends parallel to the shore. The materials are dumped over its outer edge. Its upper surface is a continuation of the shore bench or wave-cut bench with which it is associated. Shore terraces are not exposed except by sufficient subsidence of the water level.

Wave-built terrace is a term sometimes given to the upper coarser portion of a beach where the waves have thrown the pebbles up in low ridges parallel to the shore line and a few feet above mean high water level. An *ice-pushed terrace* is made along some lake shores by the thrust of ice up the beach. Similar features have been observed on the shores of fiords and inlets of the sea in northern latitudes.

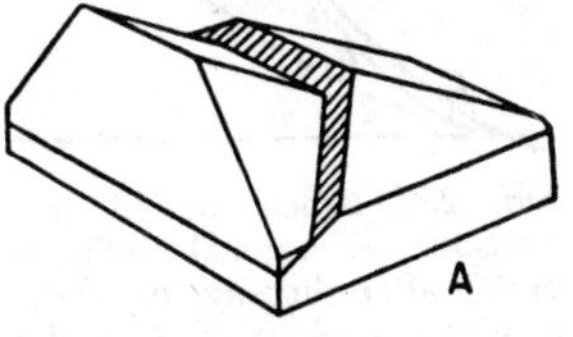

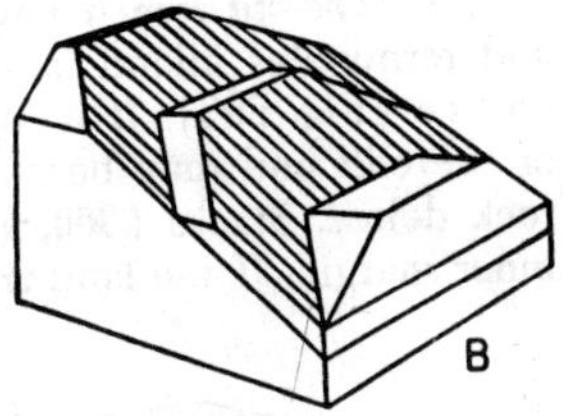

FIG. 296. Two explanations for the origin of kernbuts and kerncols. In A the mountain flank consists principally of pre-faulting land surface, and the uphill side of the kernbut is the fault surface (lined). In B the mountain flank is chiefly fault surface (lined), and the uphill side of the kernbut is the pre-faulting land surface.

FIG. 295. Map of a hillside ridge made by faulting. (*After the California State Earthquake Investigation Commission.*)

During the later Pleistocene, when the ice was fast melting away, gravels and sands were sometimes deposited between withering ice tongues and the adjacent valley walls. After the complete disappearance of the ice, these deposits were left as terraces on the hillsides. While, for several reasons, they are not common, the chance of their existence should not be forgotten when studying terraces in regions of past glaciation.

Beaches and other associated shore-line deposits which have been abandoned by the water body at whose margin they were formed, may constitute terraces which may be difficult to distinguish from river terraces. They are discussed in a separate section (**308**).

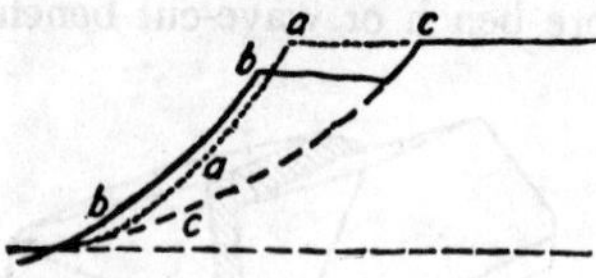

Fig. 297. Bench caused by a landslide. *aa*, original profile; *bb*, profile after slipping; *cc*, surface of slipping. (*After M. L. Fuller.*)

277. Destructional benches and terraces. Wave-cut benches, canyon benches, plateau steps, and river terraces may be described in this category.

The *wave-cut bench* (*marine bench*) usually has a rock floor and terminates inland in a marine cliff and seaward in a shore terrace (Fig. 298). It is made by the gradual landward erosion of the cliff and may be more or less covered by a thin layer of rock débris. Stacks (**300, F**) may rise above the bench near its inner margin. If the land rises or the sea level falls, such a bench

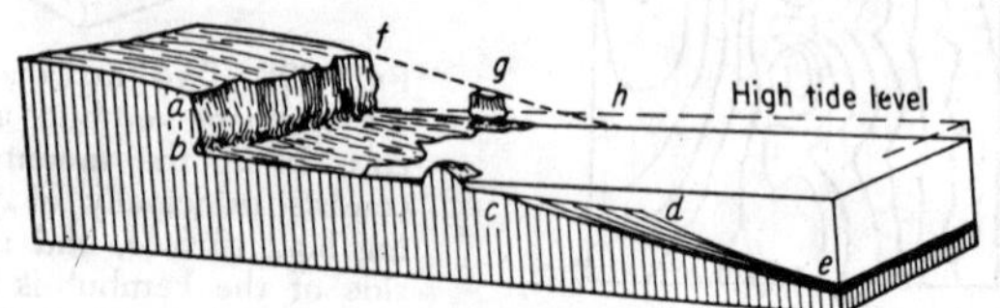

Fig. 298. Shore-line features. *ab*, sea cliff; *bc*, wave-cut bench; *cde*, wave-built terrace; *fgh*, outline of land surface before wave erosion; the same surface lies beneath the terrace; *g*, a stack.

becomes *abandoned* (**308**). Its associated terrace will be quickly destroyed, wholly or in part, and a new sea cliff and sea bench may be cut into the rocks. The abandoned bench will then be bounded both landward and seaward by sea cliffs (Fig. 299). It may be incised by streams that traverse it to the new shore line.

Marine erosion of *unconsolidated* rock materials may produce a similar wave-cut bench, but the *sea cliff*, at the head of the bench, or fringing residuals corresponding to "stacks," may be less pronounced than in solid rock and may lack the undercut or notch at the base. Forms analogous to those just described may be developed by the action of waves along lake shores; and successive stands of lake level, during a long period of shallowing of the lake waters, may result in several such groups of abandoned shore-line features on the slopes forming the lake basin.

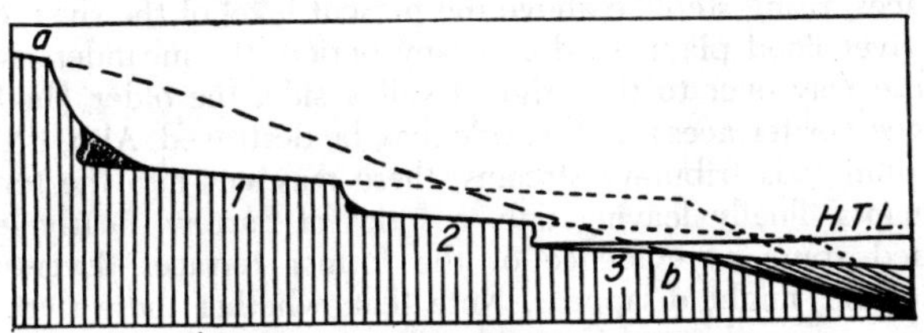

FIG. 299. Profile section of abandoned (probably elevated) wave-cut cliffs and benches. Stippled, talus; *ab*, outline of land before erosion; *H.T.L.*, high-tide level. The oldest bench is 1, the next is 2, and the youngest is 3.

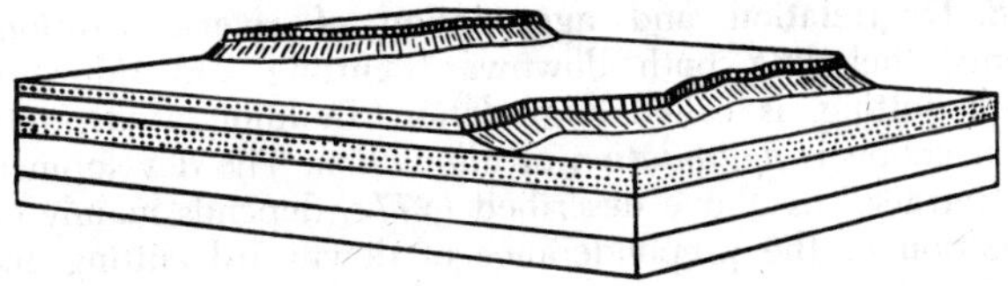

FIG. 300. Steps, or "stufe," made by erosion of alternating strong (stippled) and weak (blank) horizontal strata.

In regions of horizontal strata the walls of deep valleys may be steplike. The cliffs between the *treads* or bench levels are in hard strata. In each case the upper surface of the hard layer roughly coincides with the tread above the cliff (Fig. 276). These are *canyon benches.*

Where erosion has greatly broadened benches like those just described, they are called *steps* (German, *stufe*) (Fig. 300). They are characteristic of the high plateaus of western America. Exact counterparts of these steps, as far as their origin is concerned, are the cuesta in low-dipping strata and the hogback in steeply dipping strata (**300, C**).

If the *downward* cutting by a river becomes retarded for one reason or another, *lateral* cutting may become predominant, and, by virtue of the swinging and migration of the meanders of the river, a long narrow plain may be formed, beveling across rocks and structures below (**282**). Provided the stream now undergoes *rejuvenation*, which means a return of the preponderance of downward over lateral cutting, it will erode below the level of this plain, parts of which will be left as *river terraces;* and, if this process is repeated, there may be several sets or pairs of such terraces, rising steplike above the present level of the river, or of the river flood plain. If, during any period, the meanders swing all the way over to the original valley side, the older (higher) terrace (or terraces) on this side may be destroyed. Also, if there are numerous tributary streams, these may cut into the terrace remnants, finally leaving only a series of narrow, nearly level-topped spurs as evidence of the former terraces. Eventually these, too, might disappear. Note that, whether these river terraces are carved out of consolidated or unconsolidated rock materials, this fact may not at once be apparent because there is nearly always a thin layer of river alluvium (mud, sand, or gravel) covering the destructional surface of the terrace.

278. Degradation and aggradation of rivers. Erosion by streams, including both downward cutting and sidewise, or lateral, cutting, is called *degradation*. Building of deposits by stream action is *aggradation* or *alluviation*. The development of river terraces, as above described (**277**), depends mainly on an alternation of the preponderance of downward cutting and of lateral cutting; but terraces may likewise be formed through alternation of degradational and aggradational processes. There are several reasons why degradation may succeed aggradation. (1) In its normal development a river constructs an alluvial plain in its lower course. The surface of this plain is above the level to which the stream can cut in a later stage. Subsequently, therefore, the river incises its channel in the alluvial deposits and, by meandering, may broaden its flood plain (**281, A**) until only remnants of the old, higher plain are left. These remnants appear as terraces on either side or on both sides of the flood plain. They are usually not very conspicuous features. (2) Much more striking are the terraces formed by the downcutting of a stream into thick alluvial deposits which it laid down during a period when it carried an excessive load. Many of the rivers of northern regions were thus overloaded by abundant débris derived from melting ice in the waning stages of glaciation. With the disappearance of the ice, the supply decreased so much that aggradation gave place to degradation. Terraces made in this way may be preserved for long periods of time when the river, in swinging from side to side, encounters projections of the bedrock below the alluvium. The rock outcrops are generally situated near the terrace cusps (Fig. 301). (3) If the volume of a stream is augmented while the load remains unchanged, the stream will incise

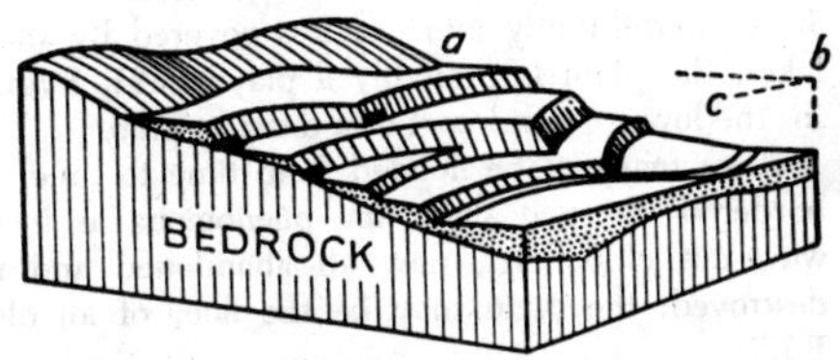

FIG. 301. River terraces. Black spots at the terrace cusps represent bedrock exposures. *abc*, former level of terrace gravels.

its channel. (4) By uplift of the land, rivers may be rejuvenated and so forced to cut into their old alluvial deposits.

PLAINS

279. Terminology and identification. Topographic forms which are comparatively flat and of low inclination and which are not better classified under the head of benches or terraces are placed here under *plains*. They vary in area from a few acres to many square miles. While their continuity may be interrupted by isolated hills or by occasional valleys, flatness is their predominating quality.[10]

[10] The word "plain" is often reserved for low-level expanses, usually constructional, whereas "plateau" is applied to extensive, flat, or nearly flat areas which are at relatively high levels, dropping off abruptly on one or more sides to much lower topography. Plateaus may be either destructional or constructional, and they may be incised by deep canyons.

Key for the Identification of Plains

The land surface is a flat, or nearly flat,[11] plain which may be horizontal or gently inclined. If

A. The materials beneath the plain are till, the plain is a till plain (**281, D**).

B. The materials beneath the plain have a stratiform structure with which the plain is essentially parallel, and these materials consist principally of

1. Superposed lava sheets, often with intercalated beds of volcanic ash, etc., the plain is of volcanic origin (**280**).
2. Stratified muds, sands, or gravels, and if

a. The plain constitutes the floor of a basin which

(1) It is intermittently more or less covered by shallow alkaline lakes, the plain is probably a playa (**281, F**) and is situated in the lower central part of a desert region.

(2) May or may not be flooded from time to time, and which is bordered by such shore-line phenomena as beaches, deltas, wave-cut cliffs, etc., now all abandoned and more or less destroyed, the plain may be the floor of an old lake (**281, E**).[12]

b. The plain borders a range of hills or mountains away from which it slopes downward with an inclination of 5° to 8° at its upper margin, this angle decreasing inversely as the distance from the range, the plain may be a piedmont alluvial cone or a piedmont alluvial plain (**281, A**).

c. The plain constitutes the floor of a valley along which a stream flows, the plain may be a valley train (**281, C**) or a flood plain (**281, A**).

d. The plain borders upon a lake, down to which it has a gentle inclination, and

(1) Is local, being situated at the mouth of a stream which empties into the lake, the plain is probably the exposed upper surface of a delta (**281, B**).

(2) Is continuous round a large fraction or the whole of the periphery of the lake, and is underlain by mud or clay, the plain may be an exposed portion of the lake bottom at time of low water.

[11] Such a flat plain need not be continuous. It may be incised by valleys or broken by faults, or perhaps diversified by an occasional volcanic cone, sessile upon its surface; but provided its original character is still recognizable, its remaining visible portions may be classified as if it had not been modified since its origin.

[12] Such features may be found in valleys which were once basins produced by some temporary natural barrier (**308**).

e. The plain borders upon the sea, down to which it has a gentle inclination, and

(1) Is local, being

(*a*) Situated at the mouth of a stream and not being inundated except, perhaps, in rare instances and then only at its outer margin, the plain is probably the exposed surface of a delta (**281, B**).

(*b*) Part of the floor of a bay, and being inundated at high tide, the plain is probably an estuarine flat (**281, E**).

(2) Is continuous for many miles along the coast and is not inundated at high tide, the plain may be a coastal plain (**281, E**).[13]

f. The plain, having a gentle southward inclination, is bordered on the north by an irregular hummock-and-hollow topography of glacial origin (refer to the key in **295**), it may be a frontal apron or a sand plain (**281, C**).

C. The materials beneath the plain are rocks of various kinds and often with diverse structure, and these rocks and structures are truncated by the plain, the latter may be a plain of marine denudation, a graded river flood plain, a peneplain, or a plain of arid denudation (pediment) (**282**). Note, however, that in many cases, such destructional plains are thinly veneered with gravel or other loose sediments that conceal the typical erosional features and thus make them look like constructional plains.

280. Volcanic plains. Volcanic plains are the surfaces of broad sheets of lava or of volcanic ejectamenta. They may be many square miles in area. They are usually diversified by other volcanic forms.

281. Constructional plains. River flood plains, alluvial cones, piedmont alluvial plains, delta plains, glacial frontal aprons, outwash plains, valley trains, kame terraces, till plains, lake-floor plains, estuarine flats, coastal plains, and playas are all constructional in their mode of origin. Swamps might also be listed here, but they are treated in Art. **283**. All have been built up in one way or another.

281A. Plains of several kinds are constructed by rivers. When a stream has its volume diminished (as by evaporation in deserts) or has its efficiency lowered by a decrease in its velocity, it may become overburdened with detritus so that it will have to deposit part of its load. *Aggraded flood plains,* characteristic of mature

[13] A coastal plain may consist of isolated portions at the heads of the bays on an irregular coast which has suffered only a small emergence.

rivers (**303**), are alluvial flats which are often covered by water at times of flood. When the waters subside a new layer of sediment is deposited on the plain. On piedmont slopes streams are forced to deposit where they pass out from their steeply graded mountain valleys on to broad lowlands. Each stream builds an *alluvial fan* or *cone*, a gently sloping deposit (Fig. 302), which focuses at the point where the stream leaves the mountains. Ordinarily the channel is not so deep but that the stream can break out at times of high water and take a new route on a lower part of the cone. When deposition has gone too far in one place there is a shift in the water course to a new position, so that the cone is formed symmetrically, banked up against the mountain

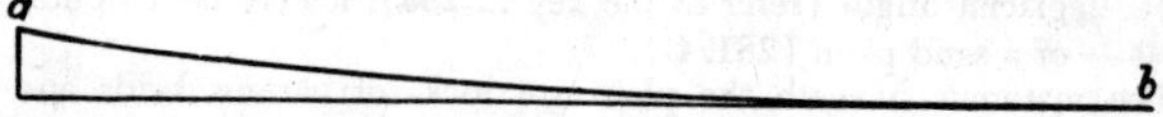

FIG. 302. Radial profile section of an alluvial cone. The distance from *a* to *b* is about 8 miles.

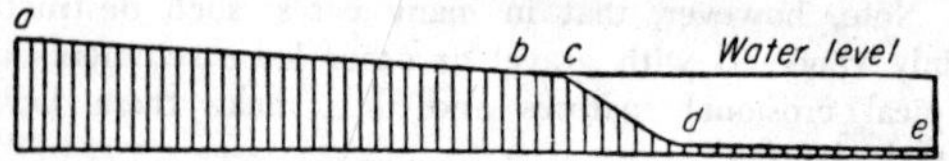

FIG. 303. Radial profile section of a delta, *abc,* top surface, of which *ab* is exposed and *bc* is submerged; *cd,* front slope; *de,* prodelta clays and muds.

side. In arid regions these fans are built intermittently largely by torrential outbursts and by mudflows. If these cones coalesce, they make a piedmont alluvial plain, or, in arid regions, a *bajada* (pronounced *bahada*), which spreads like an apron along the front of the range. A bajada is characterized by a succession of groups of radiating dry channels, each group focusing at the head of its fan. The radial profile is concave upward (Fig. 302). "Parallel to the mountain range the convexities of the component fans impart to the bajada an undulating surface."[14]

281B. A delta is a familiar type of river deposit. It is made where a stream loses carrying power by passing into a body of water with little or no current. Topographically it consists of three parts (Fig. 303): (1) a broad, gently sloping upper surface most of which is above the level of the quiet water body;

[14] Bibliog., Blackwater, Eliot, 1931, p. 136.

(2) the steeper front slope which is submerged and has the angle of repose of materials under water; and (3) the submerged muds and silts (*prodelta clays*) which extend out in a gently undulating sheet from the foot of the front slope. Deltas are described here because the exposed portion, (1) above, is conspicuous as a plain. On this surface the river may split into distributaries which reach the front at different points on the periphery (Fig. 304, A). The plan of a delta depends on several factors among which the presence or absence of longshore currents and variations in the load transported by the river are important. Were it not for these disturbing factors the delta would be semicircular in outline. Longshore currents sweep away much of the material dumped by the stream, and so truncate the delta (Fig. 304, B). When the load of the river is diminished, the several distributaries may temporarily degrade their channels, bear the resulting sediments to the front, and drop them there as small deltas. This makes the main delta lobate.[15] Highly irregular delta fronts show that river construction dominates over wave erosion. Delta structure has been described in Art. 96.

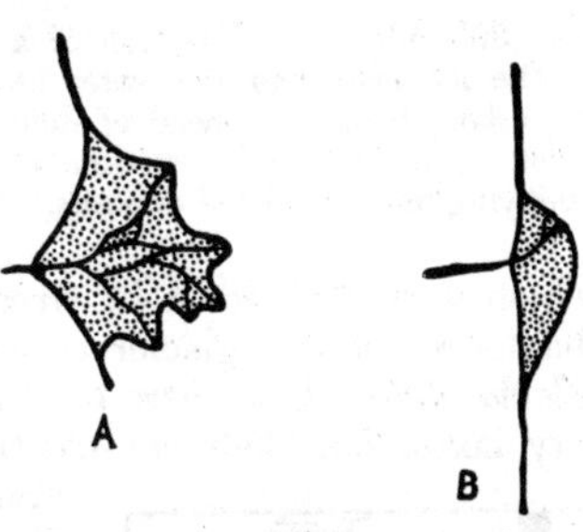

Fig. 304. A, lobate delta with distributaries. B, a delta which has had its form modified by a current flowing in a direction up the page, as the figure is drawn. In each case the mainland is on the left and the water body on the right of the shore line.

281C. The construction of outwash plains was an important accomplishment of aqueoglacial waters just outside the margin of the continental ice sheet. Frontal aprons, valley trains, and glacial delta plains were so formed. *Frontal aprons* correspond to alluvial plains. They consist of sands and gravels which were spread out in front of the ice. Their length is parallel to the ice margin and they often head against frontal moraines. The largest ones were made south of the main terminal moraine. Probably those portions of the loess plains of central United States which were water-laid constitute parts of very large outwash plains. *Valley trains* are nothing more than restricted frontal aprons.

[15] Bibliog., Smith, A. L., 1909.

They are valley floor deposits of sand and gravel laid down by heavily overloaded streams that flowed from the melting ice. Some of them are many miles long. Many have since been terraced. *Kame terraces* are terrace-like deposits of gravel and sand

FIG. 305. Ideal radial section of a glacial delta plain showing its relation to the ice mass and the water level. Both ice and lake were temporary. *ab*, esker channel; *b*, head of delta plain; *d*, front of delta plain at water level; *o*, backset beds; *st*, line of unconformity between rock floor and overlying unconsolidated deposits. (*After W. M. Davis.*)

which were laid down by streams between the valley walls and the flanks of the glacier or ice-lobe that occupied the valley. *Glacial delta plains* were built by aqueoglacial streams in temporary lakes. For their construction the ice front must have been stationary (298, E). Subsequently they were exposed by the natural draining of these lakes. There are a great many of them in New England, New York, etc. They consist of the three parts mentioned above for modern deltas. The prodelta clays are now often covered by marsh. At their northern edge, these delta plains usually terminate in ice-contact slopes where formerly the deposits rested against or upon the ice (Fig. 305). Often an esker north of a delta plain marks the course of the original stream (Fig. 306). Any of these outwash plains, consisting chiefly of sands and gravel, and deposited by water in proximity to glacial ice, may be called *sand plains*. Some sand plains are *pitted* by kettle holes (288) and some show the old stream channels, or *creases*.

FIG. 306. Map of the Barrington delta plain, R.I. Stippled, esker and delta plain; vertical ruling, brick clays, largely marsh land; horizontal ruling, water. (Scale, approximately 1 in. to 1 mile.) (*After J. B. Woodworth.*)

281D. Till plains are produced by more or less uniform deposition of till, usually in lands of low relief. The ice must retreat at a fairly constant rate, for otherwise the débris is apt to be heaped up in morainal ridges. The till of these plains is no doubt partly subglacial, partly englacial, and partly superglacial. In sections the deposit is seen to have no stratification (**73**).

281E. While silts and muds are in process of accumulation on the floor of a lake there is a tendency to fill depressions and thus to make the bottom more even. The same thing may be said of sea floors. If the lake is drained or evaporated away, the exposed floor will be a *lake-floor plain*. In section the underlying deposits will be seen to be very fine and evenly stratified (**98**). They may carry fresh water fossils. If the floor of a bay is laid bare at low tide we speak of it as a *mud flat* or an *estuarine flat*. If the land should suffer relative uplift with respect to sea level, a larger area of sea floor would be exposed as a *coastal plain*. Where there is gradual exposure of sea-floor deposits, inflowing rivers are likely to be aggraded, and so it happens that extensively uplifted coastal plains consist, not solely of littoral and marine sediments, but of littoral and marine strata interbedded with fluvial or river-laid deposits (**87; 96, F; 98**).

281F. *Playas* are level plains underlain by clays, locally alternating with salt and gypsum, deposited in broad shallow ephemeral lakes in basins in desert regions. Deposition is intermittent. It is accomplished by inflowing mud-laden streams after local cloudbursts. Drought of many months duration may succeed a short period of accumulation, and in this dry season the muds may crack and peel under the sun's rays and undergo a considerable amount of eolian erosion. While dry, playas are often whitened by a crust of soluble salts. (Where did these salts come from and why are they found here?) Some playas, marking the loci of discharge of groundwater by evaporation, are soft and wet most of the time.

Plains are sometimes diversified by great numbers of scattered shallow depressions (p. 363), or similarly by hundreds or thousands of low mounds,[16] in each case having an origin which is still uncertain.

282. Destructional plains. The plain of marine denudation, the graded river flood plain, the peneplain, and the plain of arid denudation (pediment), are the principal members of this group. The *plain of marine denudation* is merely an enlarged marine bench (**277**), a level area cut by the waves. Its distinguish-

[16] See Bibliog., Knechtel, Maxwell M., 1952.

ing characters are as follows: (1) a sea cliff surrounds any residual stacks or other elevations that rise above the plain; (2) there is a scanty covering of wave-worn pebbles and beach sand; (3) the surface bevels across rock structures. The sand and gravel, being poor supporters of plant growth, are not likely to be densely covered by vegetation even in old uplifted plains.

A *graded river flood plain,* or "river grade plain"[17] is really a destructional plain, beveling across structures in the bedrock that is concealed by a veneer of river deposits. Such a plain is commonly narrow, its width being determined by the breadth of the meander belt (see footnote 4, page 394), for the plantation is accomplished largely by side cutting as the stream meanders. The graded river flood plain may easily be mistaken for the aggraded flood plain (**281, A**), which, however, has a much thicker underlying deposit of alluvial material than in the former.

A peneplain[18] (*pene,* almost) is a nearly flat or broadly undulating land surface produced by normal subaerial erosion, that is, by erosion which is accomplished chiefly by the work of rivers assisted by weathering. A stream-made topography passes through a series of stages of development, known as youth, maturity, and old age (**303**). The valleys, at first narrow, become broad; the hill slopes grow gentler; the relief as a whole becomes less and less rugged; and finally the rivers with their branches, aided by weathering, reduce the land to an almost level plain. This is the peneplain. It is the ultimate stage of the erosion cycle. A true peneplain has the following characters: (1) the relief is very low, but there may be a few scattered residual hills (monadnocks) which have not yet been cut down to the level of the surrounding country; (2) the streams meander at grade (**303**) in broad, shallow valleys; (3) thick residual soils carpet the interstream areas, for slopes are so low that weathering is more rapid than removal of the débris; (4) the surface of the plain bevels across the underlying rocks without regard to variations in their hardness and structure (Fig. 307, A). Pene-

[17] Bibliog., Blackwelder, Eliot, 1931, p. 134 .

[18] We have retained the original spelling, *peneplain,* instead of the revised spelling, *peneplane,* which is found in some recent textbooks, because William Morris Davis, who first used the term, intended to convey the idea, not that the land had been worn down almost flat or almost level but that it had been almost, rather than completely, worn down. His emphasis was on degree of completion of the process rather than on approach to a geometrical plane.

plains on nearly horizontal strata are difficult to determine as such, but the geologist usually finds that, by travelling across the plain in certain directions he traverses different strata or formations which successively come to the surface (Fig 307, C). A peneplain is first completed near the sea coast and its development progresses inland, for rivers generally reduce the land to late stages of erosion in their lower courses long before they have lost even their youthful appearance up in the hill country.

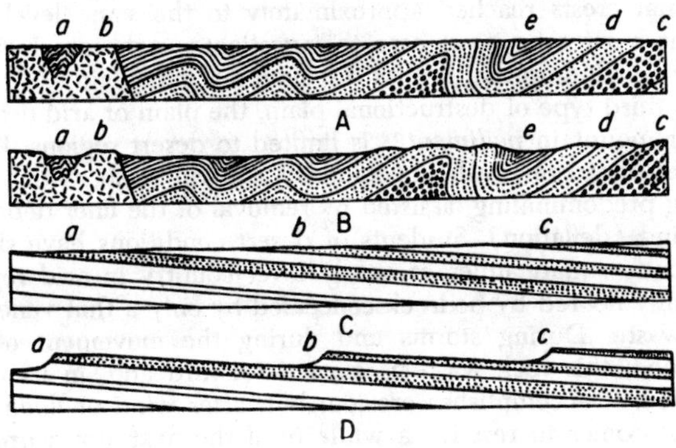

Fig. 307. A, the section of a peneplain upon rocks of varying hardness and with complicated structure. B, the same region after moderate uplift, revival of erosion, and removal of the weaker rocks to a level below that of the old peneplain which is now preserved in the hill tops. *a*, schists, intruded by *b*; *c*, basal conglomerate laid down unconformably on *b* and overlain by sandstone, *d*, and shale, *e*. C, a peneplain bevelling inclined strata. D, the same region after uplift and erosion. Here the harder rocks, *a*, *b*, and *c*, form cuestas.

A peneplaned surface of great extent is rare because erosion becomes excessively slow in advanced maturity and old age. Relative depression of the sea level, tilting, crustal warping, and other changes may interrupt the cycle of erosion before it has reached its normal conclusion.

If a peneplaned land mass is uplifted with respect to sea level, a new cycle is inaugurated. Beginning at the shore line and cutting headward, the rivers will incise their channels as young valleys below the upland surface. They will have a new base level (**303**) toward which they will work. As time goes on, the upland area, the old peneplain, will be diminished until, in the mature topography of the new cycle, it is represented perhaps merely by the crests of the hills. Yet it will still be called a peneplain—*a dissected peneplain.* It will be recognized by the fact that a majority of the hills rise to about the same level (Fig. 307, B, D). In the distance it will be indicated, though not demonstrated, by the "even sky line." We say "not demonstrated," for an even sky line in a hilly topography may be due to the dissection of some other kind of plain, or it may be the result of differential erosion on strata which have been folded so that the anticlinal crests reached approximately to the same level. The student must take great care to investigate each case by itself before concluding that he has discovered a peneplain.

The third type of destructional plain, the plain of arid denudation or mountain *pediment,*[19] is limited to desert regions. It is a product of stream wash, sheetfloods[20] and rill wash, with lateral cutting predominating, assisted by removal of the finer débris by the wind (deflation). Students of desert conditions have shown that many square miles of nearly level country in arid regions are really floored by bedrock concealed by only a thin veneer of rock waste. During storms and during the movement of the sheetflood, this rock waste is carried forward and, in its transportation, it accomplishes erosion; but, after wind or flood subsides, it comes to rest for a while until the next storm urges it forward again. In this manner a plain may be worn on the bevelled edges of rock strata so that the relations resemble those of true peneplanation. Residual hills and ranges ("island mounts") of relatively resistant rock may rise as monadnocks above the plain of arid denudation (**289, A**).[21]

Because of its veneer of rock waste, the pediment may be confused with the bajada (**281, A**), especially since the bajada may grade downward into a pediment. However, in contrast with the undulating profile of the bajada, parallel to the mountain front,

[19] Bibliog., Keyes, C. R., 1908.

[20] A sheetflood is a broad, shallow sheet of running water, which rises rapidly, generally following a cloudburst, and soon subsides again and disappears. Temporary streams of this kind are characteristic of some semi-arid regions. When heavily loaded with mud and other rock débris, the sheetflood becomes a mudflow which may be a powerful agent of transportation of huge bowlders (Bibliog., Blackwelder, Eliot, 1928).

[21] For a detailed comparison between erosion features in arid and humid climates, see Bibliog., Davis, W. M., 1930. On the origin of pediments, see discussion on p. 288 *et seq.*, in Bibliog., Thornbury, Wm. D., 1954.

and its series of groups of radiating drainage channels, the pediment is a nearly flat plain, slightly concave upward, with a nearly level profile parallel to the mountain front, and its drainage consists of braided stream courses.

Broad, closed desert basins flanked by mountains, which are fringed by bajadas and pediments, passing centrally into flat playas, are referred to as *bolsons* (Spanish for *purse*) (Fig. 308).

SWAMPS

283. Definition and classification. A large proportion of the land surface receives its moisture in the form of rain, snow, hail, dew, or frost, but there are some places which are watered by

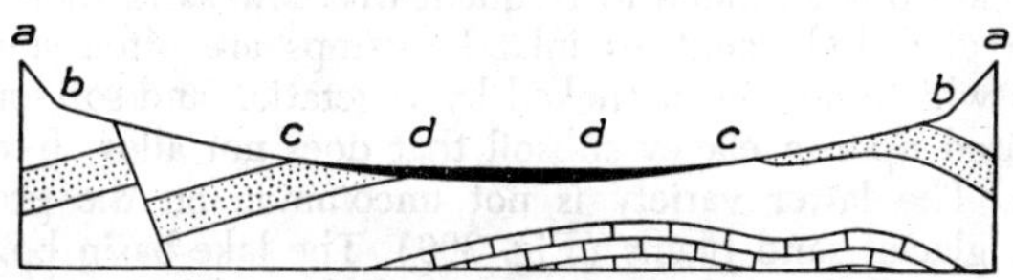

FIG. 308. Ideal cross section of a bolson. *ab*, exposed mountain flanks in process of erosion; *bc*, pediment, meeting *ab* with abrupt change of slope; *bc* is thinly veneered with rock waste, which is shifted intermittently toward lower part of basin *cddc*, where it may accumulate. The floor of the basin, under alluvium (black), may be irregular instead of smooth, as shown. In special cases, a bajada of coalescing fans may be built out from the mountains, covering the lower part of *ab* and the upper part of *bc*.

springs, and there are others which are periodically or occasionally flooded. Whatever may be the source of supply, the water ordinarily passes away within a very short time. Some of it runs off over the ground in thin sheets or in little rills; some of it sinks into the soil and into fissures in the bedrock, and so becomes groundwater; part of the underground water combines with part of the *run-off* to form streams; and, last, a considerable quantity of moisture is evaporated. These modes of removal may be referred to as drainage (including run-off and streams), percolation, and evaporation. Thorough drainage may be prevented by the levelness of the land; percolation may be impeded by a relatively impervious soil, subsoil, or underlying bedrock, or by a thick mat of plant roots and plant remains; and evaporation may be checked by a dense foliage. If, in any region, these processes are incompetent to carry away all the water that is supplied, the ground may become swampy and perhaps stay so for an indefinite time. A *swamp* may be defined as a land area where the soil contains an excess of moisture.

A majority of swamps are nearly or quite level, yet the soil on mountain sides and hillsides is sometimes soggy either because of the constant downslope percolation of moisture from melting snow fields above or because of a local subsurface discharge of underground water. These may be termed *hillside swamps. Coastal plain swamps,* like the Everglades, owe their existence primarily to their flatness and consequent poor drainage. Although they are situated on uplifted portions of the sea floor, they are usually fresh, most of the original salinity having long ago disappeared. *Delta-plain swamps* and *river flood-plain swamps* are due as much to frequent overflow as to their levelness. In glaciated countries inland swamps are often the sites of lakes which have been choked by vegetation and soil, or they are located upon a clayey subsoil that does not allow free percolation. The latter variety is not uncommon on the prodelta clays of glacial sand plains (Fig. 306). The lake-basin bogs are sometimes called *muskegs.* Portions of the tundra in northern climates are kept saturated by melting snow. Small boggy places may be found even in deserts. For instance, the ground is moist and there is generally some vegetation in the vicinity of springs, and at points where intermittent streams sink into the ground, or where they come near the surface in their subterranean course. A swampy belt may be situated in soil that conceals a bedrock fault, if the fault serves as a conduit for ascending underground waters. Along sea coasts several kinds of salt marsh are recognized. Some are caused by the filling of lagoons with mud, sand, and plant remains (**305**); others are due to the slow uplift of the sea floor; and others, on the contrary, are indicative of subsidence. The evidence for the origin of this last type rests on these facts: (1) the marsh deposit is relatively thick and consists of mud mixed with the relics of plants (mostly grasses) which can exist only if they are moistened by salt water for a short period each day; (2) this marsh deposit rests upon a floor which was once undoubtedly under subaerial conditions; and, (3) the present upper surface of the marsh is just within reach of the high tide.

In many cases the origin of a swamp is suggested by its topographic surroundings, but whenever possible corroborative proofs should be looked for in the structure of the marsh deposit itself. This can be done with an instrument for cutting test holes.

VALLEYS AND BASINS

284. Terminology and identification. The word *basin*[22] is here used for topographic depressions which are rimmed round on all sides. They may be deep or shallow, large or small, and they may or may not contain water. *Valleys* are topographic depressions that are open, although in some cases their floors may be diversified by small basins. They may or may not be occupied by streams.

In attempting to draw up a table for the recognition of valleys and basins, it has been thought best to treat them separately, as follows:

KEY FOR THE IDENTIFICATION OF TOPOGRAPHIC BASINS

The land has the form of a basin, being rimmed on all sides. If

A. The basin, after careful investigation, is found to be due to the direct effects of faulting (**224**) or of tilting or warping of the underlying rocks, it is a tectonic or diastrophic basin (**285, 286**).

B. The basin is due to the damming of a valley by a barrier of lava, morainic débris, ice, mudflow, or landslide débris, or if it is situated near the sea coast and is separated from the ocean merely by a sand or gravel beach, it is a barrier basin (**288**).

C. The basin is not the consequence of diastrophism nor of the construction of a barrier across a valley. It

1. Is entirely rimmed by bedrock,[23]
   a. Being generally shallow and
      (1) Veneered by a thin deposit of transported (wind-blown) dust or sand, it may be a wind-scoured basin (**289**).
      (2) Covered by a deposit of residual material, it may be a basin due to some localized process of weathering (**289**).
   b. Being comparatively deep, but generally not so deep as it is wide or long, and if it
      (1) Has steep inward facing walls which are rough and irregular and have no scratches or grooves, or, if exhibiting such marks of abrasion, have them trending up and down, the basin may be a volcanic crater (**287**), and a caldera (**287**), and the surrounding rock is probably lava.[24]

[22] Note that *basin* is also used in a structural sense (p. 190).

[23] Sometimes this fact is obscure because the bedrock is more or less covered by surface débris.

[24] The lava may have intercalated beds of volcanic ash, etc.

(2) Has walls which are steep in some places and of gentler declivity in others, showing marks of abrasion which trend, for the most part, along the walls and parallel to the length of the basin, the latter is probably an ice-scoured basin (**289**).

c. Having a depth generally equal to, or greater than, its horizontal dimensions, and if it

(1) Has smooth, often polished, rock walls which may bear irregular circumferential grooves, the basin may be a large pothole (**40**).

(2) Has walls which are rough, or, if somewhat smooth, have vertical channels due to solution (**39**), and is in limestone, the basin may be the upper end of a sink hole (**290**).

2. Is entirely rimmed by unconsolidated materials, and

a. Is situated at the crest of a conical hill which consists of volcanic ash, etc., the basin is probably a volcanic crater.

b. Is situated in an irregular hummocky land area which is

(1) Underlain by glacial till, the basin is probably a kettle hole in a moraine (**288**).

(2) Underlain by rather poorly stratified gravel and coarse sand with subangular pebbles predominating, the basin is probably a kettle hole associated with kames and eskers (**288**).

(3) Underlain by fine, cross-bedded, wind-blown sand, the basin is probably a "blow-out" (**289**), or less probably a constructional depression, between sand dunes (**288**).

c. Is situated on a nearly flat plain, which is

(1) Underlain by well-bedded, often cross-bedded sands, not infrequently overlain by gravel, the basin is probably a kettle hole in a glacial delta plain or a frontal apron (**288**).

(2) Underlain by gravel, sand, or mud, the basin being crescentic in form and associated with a meandering stream, the basin is probably a deserted meander (**288**).

(3) Underlain by essentially flat-lying sands and clays which contain permafrost, it may be a cave-in basin or a thaw basin (**289**).[25]

Key for the Identification of Valleys

The land surface has the form of a valley. If

A. The valley has rock walls,[26] and

[25] See also references to oriented lakes (**291**) of Alaska and the Carolinas. These are so restricted in their regional distribution that they are omitted from this "key."

[26] This fact is not always clear at once, for the bedrock may be more or less concealed by surface débris.

1. Its floor bears evidence of glacial abrasion, with more or less glacial deposition, and its cross section is U-shaped, the valley is probably of glacial origin (**291, G, H**).
2. Its floor bears no evidence of glacial erosion or deposition, and it is
   a. Definitely elated to, or controlled by, the underlying rock structure, in this respect, that
      (1) The valley crosses or intersects a ridge across its trend,
         (*a*) The ridge being a cuesta, the valley is a transverse valley and is probably "consequent" in the sense that its stream originally flowed down the constructional surface of the dipping beds.
         (*b*) The ridge being a hogback or a similar exposed edge of a steeply dipping stratum or other layer, the valley may be some variety of gap (**285, 291, E**).
      (2) The valley trends along the course of one or more of a series of parallel rock layers, it is a longitudinal valley and may be
         (*a*) Due to corrosion, particularly if the underlying rock is not markedly soluble, or
         (*b*) Due to solution, if the underlying rock is soluble, *e.g.*, limestone (**291, D**).
      (3) The valley is situated above a fault (single or multiple), this valley may be a rift (**285**) or a fault-line valley (**291, B**).
      (4) The valley is bounded on one side by a fault scarp or a fault-line scarp, this may be a fault valley (**285**), or a fault-line valley (**291, B**), respectively.
      (5) The valley is bounded on both sides by fault scarps or by fault-line scarps, this valley may be situated upon a graben, or upon a horst of which the relief has been reversed by erosion (**224**).
   b. Not definitely related to, or controlled by, the underlying rock structure, it is probably a river valley in a region of complex geologic structure or in a region of horizontal strata.

B. The valley lies between a rock wall on one side and a wall of unconsolidated materials on the other side, this valley is probably a result of construction, and the unconsolidated materials may belong to a moraine (**288, E**), an esker (**298, C**), etc.

C. The valley has walls of unconsolidated materials, and
1. Lies between two typical constructional deposits (two moraines, two eskers, an esker and a drumlin, etc.), the valley is of constructional origin (**288**).
2. Interrupts the continuity of an otherwise essentially flat surface, the valley may be a stream channel
   a. Associated with the upbuilding of the deposit (channels on alluvial cones, deltas, etc., and creases; refer to **288**).
   b. Of purely destructional origin (**291, F**), (rainwash gullies, etc.).

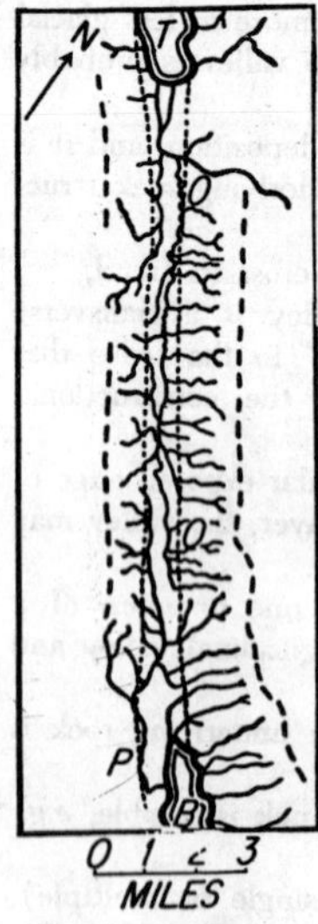

FIG. 309. Drainage map of the Bolinas-Tomales Valley, Calif. Heavy broken lines, crests of bounding ridges; light broken lines, limits of rift topography; *T*, Tomales Bay; *O*, Olema Creek; *P*, Pine Gulch Creek; *B*, Bolinas Lagoon. (*After the California State Earthquake Investigation Commission.*)

285. Fault valleys and basins. In faulting the blocks may be tilted in such a way that a depression lies at the base of the fault scarp (Fig. 283), or a block may slip down between two opposing fault scarps (Fig. 231, A), or a block may be left between two other blocks that have been uplifted. Sometimes long, relatively narrow depressions or *rifts* are formed along lines of multiple fracture (Figs. 309, 310). The San Andreas rift[27] in California, along which differential horizontal movement occurred in the earthquake of 1906, is "a trough coinciding in general trend with the Coast Ranges, but crossing various mountain ridges obliquely, or even following their crests. In detail it comprises many small ridges and hollows, approximately parallel but otherwise irregularly disposed, and evidently caused by splintery dislocation. Streams zigzag more or less about the ridges and the hollows contain many small ponds and marshes."[28] This rift is traceable for several hundred miles. On this subject, refer also to Art. 224.

Another possible phase of fault valley is the *fault gap*, a depression between the offset ends of a ridge developed on a resistant rock layer that has been displaced by a transverse fault (Fig. 311). *Fault-line gaps* are more common than fault gaps (291, E).

In volcanic regions roughly circular or oval depressions, called *volcanic sinks*, may be formed by the broad-scale downfaulting of the land surrounding an old vent. The settling may be caused by subterranean removal of lava which had served as a support. These sinks are bounded by steep fault

[27] In this usage the word *rift* seems to include both the depression due to faulting and the fault or faults, but it does not imply the kind of displacement. See p. 233.

[28] Bibliog., Gilbert, G. K., 1909, p. 48.

scarps upon which fault striae or other evidences may sometimes be found, indicating the direction of the slipping (**39, 207**). The floor of a volcanic sink is of much larger area than the cross section of any associated vent.

286. Basins caused by tilting and warping. Some basins, usually of large size, have resulted from tilting or warping of a topography that may be flat or irregular. In this manner, through diastrophic agencies, sags may be produced in a previously even land surface, or low ridges may be uparched across original drainage courses.

287. Volcanic basins. By volcanic outbursts craters are formed, either as holes in more or less level ground (pit craters),

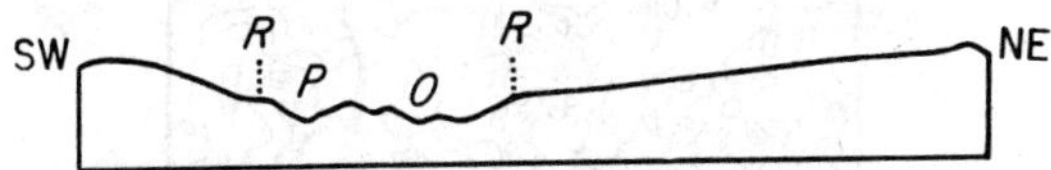

FIG. 310. Profile section of Bolinas-Tomales Valley. *RR*, limits of rift; *P*, valley of Pine Gulch Creek, running S.E.; *O*, valley of Olema Creek, running NW. (Vertical and horizontal scales are equal.) (*After the California State Earthquake Investigation Commission.*)

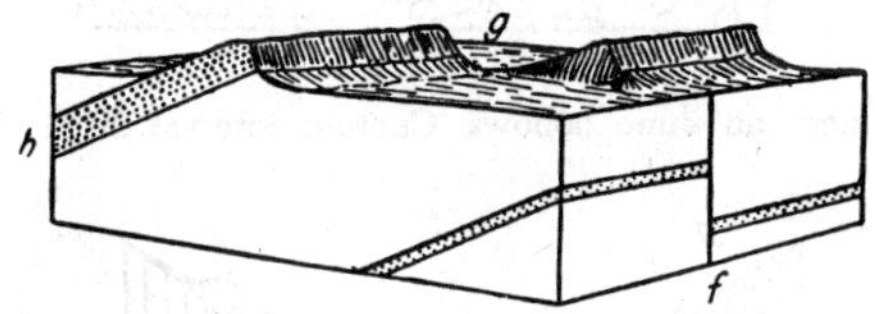

FIG. 311. Diagram of a fault gap, g, caused here by horizontal movement on a vertical fault, *f*, with consequent displacement of the ridge of hard rock, *h*.

or as cup-shaped depressions on the summits of volcanic peaks. The floor of such a crater is of the same size as the cross section of the vent through which the explosions occurred. Explosion-made depressions of considerably larger size than the accompanying associated volcanic vents are called *calderas* (sing., caldera) (cf. volcanic sink, Art. **285**). Lakes may gather in the craters of extinct volcanoes.

288. Constructional valleys and basins. When deposition by wind, water, ice, or vulcanism is irregular, or when natural barriers are thrown up across valleys, constructional valleys and basins may result. Basins, some constructional and some destructional, are typical elements in the topography of dune areas (Fig. 312). Valleys may be formed between parallel morainal ridges of mountain glaciers, or between the lateral moraines (298, E) and the adjacent valley walls (Fig. 313).

FIG. 312. Dunes and dune hollows. Contour interval 20 ft. (Lakin sheet, Kans.)

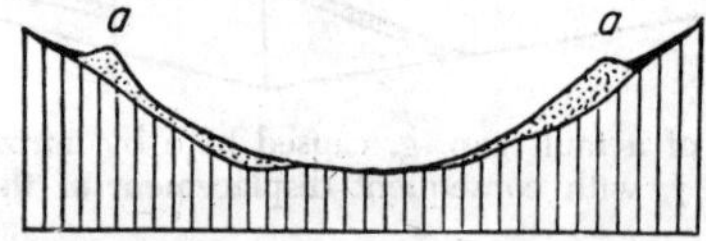

FIG. 313. Section of a glaciated valley with lateral moraines (stippled). Talus (black) has partly filled the small valleys between the moraines and the bedrock (vertical lining).

They may be formed also between parallel ridges deposited by a continental ice sheet. Terminal moraines especially are characterized by numerous hollows of all sizes and shapes (Figs. 314, 315). At the ragged edge of the melted ice sheet, outwash sands and gravels [kames, eskers, sand plains, etc. (298)] may be spread round and even over detached ice blocks, which, by subsequent melting, leave depressions (kettle holes, ice-block

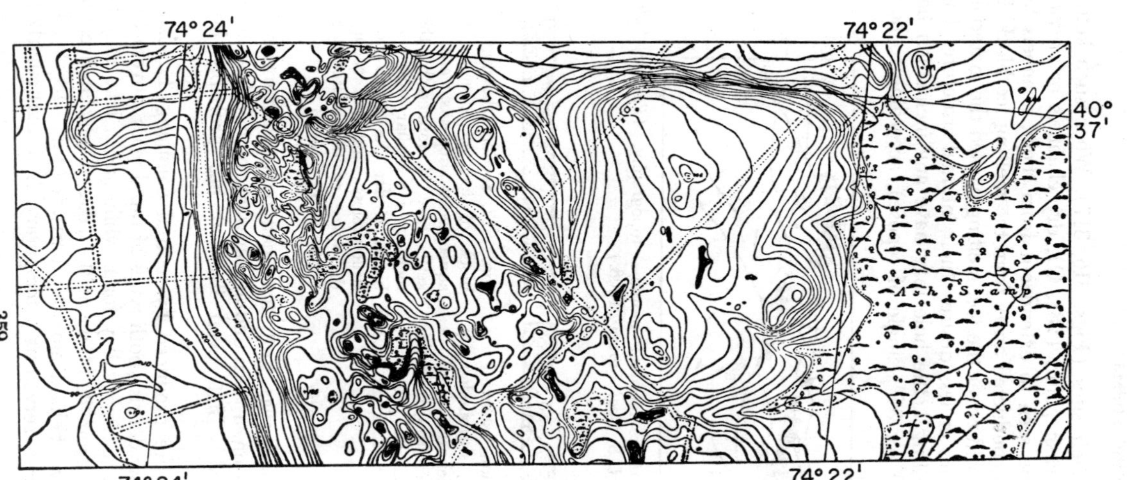

Fig. 314. Moraine and outwash-plain topography in Union Co., N.J. The two fine straight lines running up and down in the figure are meridians, that to the left being 74°24′, and that to the right being 74°22′. The similar line near the upper part of the left two-thirds of the figure is parallel 40°37′. The eastern half of the map shows ground-moraine topography. The rough belt of country just east of meridian 74°24′ is a terminal moraine. The land sloping westward from the terminal moraine is an outwash plain. Ponds are represented by horizontal ruling. Contour interval 5 ft. Length of mapped area 3.4 miles. (*After R. D. Salisbury and W. W. Atwood.*)

holes) to mark their sites (Figs. 316, 317). When such kettle holes are in outwash plains (281, C), dry channels or *creases* may sometimes be seen to extend out from them, channels by which water was conducted away from the melting ice block. If the wash deposit did cover the ice, melting caused the materials to sag and so more or less destroy their internal structure. The sides of the resulting kettle hole may have any inclination between 0° and 30° or 35° (angle of repose), according to how

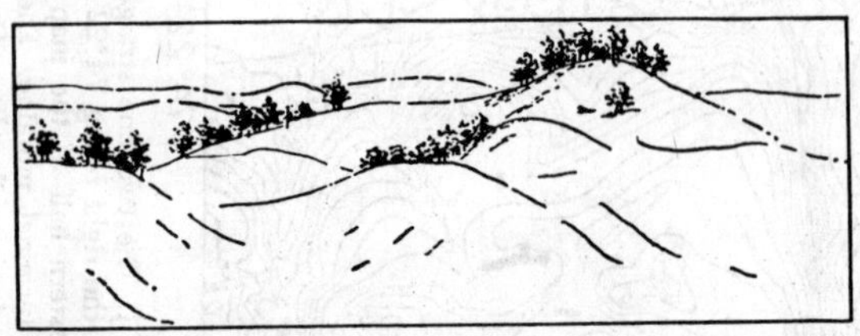

FIG. 315. Characteristic terminal moraine topography. (*Passaic Folio, N.J.–N.Y., No.* 157, *U.S. Geol. Survey*, 1908.)

FIG. 316. Section showing a mass of ice, *a*, surrounded by aqueoglacial deposits, and a kettle hole, *b*, resulting from the melting of a similar projecting ice block. (*After M. L. Fuller.*)

FIG. 317. Section showing a block of ice, *a*, covered by aqueoglacial deposits, and a kettle hole, *d*, formed by the melting of a similar buried ice block. Under the kettle hole structureless sands, *c*, occupy the space of the melted ice. (*After M. L. Fuller.*)

much sagging there was, and there can be no accompanying drainage creases on a surrounding outwash plain. If a kettle hole has a notably flat, even floor, it has probably been alluviated.

Barrier basins are produced by natural damming. Landslide débris, or mudflow débris (both types of rapid mass movement), may choke up a narrow valley for a while and a lake may be formed upstream from it. Many of the lakes in glaciated countries lie in hollows behind morainic barriers (Fig. 318, A). Ice itself has sometimes served as a temporary dam, particularly in the valleys of northward-flowing streams. Two bends of a meandering stream sometimes meet, and the stream, breaking through the narrow neck, adopts the shorter course. The deserted meander, at length silted up at its cut-off ends, becomes an ox-bow lake (Fig. 319). When a side stream brings down more detritus than the main stream can handle, the latter may be ponded upstream from the confluence; and, vice versa, if a river carries an excess of load, it may aggrade its bed and impound the lower reaches of its branches just above its confluence with them. (Under what topographic conditions might these events occur?) Another type of barrier basin may be made by a sheet of lava which blocks a main valley, or, by moving down a main valley, dams up the side valleys. Barrier basins include lagoons (**305**) and bays which have been closed in by bay-mouth bars (**273**).

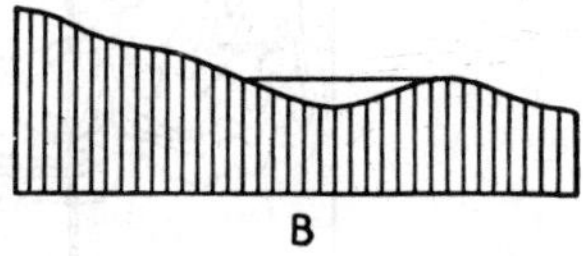

FIG. 318. Section to illustrate the nature of glacial lake basins. A, lake retained by moraine dam; B, lake held in rock basin.

289. Destructional basins. Basins of destructional origin are comparatively rare. Some are made by ice, some by wind, and some by unequal weathering. In glaciated districts these rock basins are not infrequently occupied by lakes which may be very deep (Fig. 318, B). The process by which they are gouged out by the ice is often called *overdeepening*. On their rocky rims are unmistakable signs of their glacial origin, in striae, grooves, and numerous knobs or roches moutonnées (**300, E**). *Wind-scoured basins, i.e.,* basins maintained or developed by deflation of the finer rock waste, are shallow, but they may cover large areas, sometimes many square miles in extent. They are characteristic of deserts. At irregular intervals their lower central parts may become the sites of broad, shallow sheets of water called *playa lakes,* which quickly gather and almost as quickly evaporate, leaving mud flats, or *playas,* to mark their sites (**281, F**). Destructional hollows carved out by wind in dune areas are called *blow-outs*. Their sides are often steep and intersect the bedding of the adjacent dunes. Shallow basins are sometimes produced by unequal weathering (chiefly decomposition) in uniform rocks or by differential weathering in rocks of varying resistance where the surface of the ground is too level for thorough drainage. Moisture, collecting in the hollows, maintains a luxuriant vegetation and, with the help of soil acids, brings about the decay of the underlying rock. Such basins may

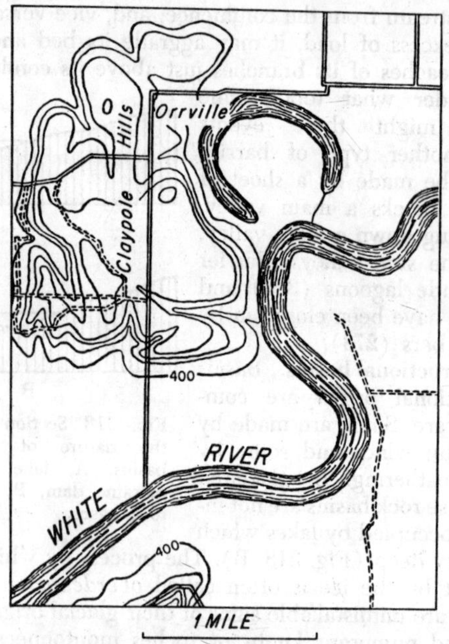

Fig. 319. An oxbow lake in the site of a deserted meander of the White River, Ind. Contour interval 20 ft. (Princeton sheet, Ind.–Ill.)

broaden more rapidly than they can deepen, for decomposition is greatly retarded by increase of depth.

Under the heading of destructional basins, we may call attention to certain kinds of lakes and lake basins which have been described as occurring on low-lying constructional plains, but of which the origin is not yet fully known. We are listing them here because, from what is known of them, they appear to result from local destructional causes rather than from constructional causes, although possibly both may have had a part in their origin. We are including the "cave-in lakes"[29] and "thaw lakes"[30] of Alaska, the "oriented lakes" of Alaska,[31] the oriented "bays" of the Carolinas,[32] and the "frost-thaw basins" of New Jersey.[33]

The first three classes of these lakes (and their basins) occur where the moisture in the soil is permanently frozen (permafrost), except for local surficial thawing during the summer. The cave-in lakes and thaw lakes are explained as largely dependent on this temporary thawing with its attendant phenomena (see references cited). The oriented lakes of Alaska and the oriented "bays" of the coastal plain in South Carolina and adjoining parts of North Carolina and Georgia are mutually similar in a great many respects,[34] although present climatic conditions in the two areas are very different.

All of the types of lake and lake basin mentioned in the last two paragraphs are regionally so restricted in their occurrence that we shall not go further with their description here. Full descriptions may be found in the references cited.

290. Destructional sinks. The word *sink* is applied to vertical holes in the ground, which lead downward into subterranean passages and chambers that have been formed by the solution of a soluble rock. It should not be confused with the volcanic sink (**285**), which is of diastrophic origin. Sinks are generally limited to countries where limestone underlies the soil and the climate is humid (Fig. 320). They are of two kinds: some are produced by the caving in of the roofs of subterranean chambers, and others are channels which were opened up along joints and which have been enlarged through solution by descending surface waters. The cave-in type of sink reveals signs of fracture on the edges of the hole, generally increases in diameter downward from the surface, and contains shattered débris of the roof rock on the cave floor beneath the opening (Fig. 321, A). On the other hand, solution sinks often flare, funnel-like, at the surface,

[29] Bibliog., Wallace, Robert E., 1948.

[30] Bibliog., Hopkins, David M., 1949.

[31] Bibliog., Black, Robert F., and William L. Barksdale, 1949.

[32] Bibilog., Johnson, Douglas, 1942.

[33] Bibliog., Wolfe, Peter E., 1953; and Rasmussen, W. C., 1953.

[34] See Bibliog., Black, Robert F., and William L. Barksdale, 1949, p. 116.

and the edges and walls of the hole bear marks of corrosion, not of fracture (Fig. 321, B) (Chap. 2).

By gradual lateral solution of the upper layer, or layers, a sink may expand into a broad, shallow, nearly circular depression. A land surface that consists of many sinks, with irregular divides

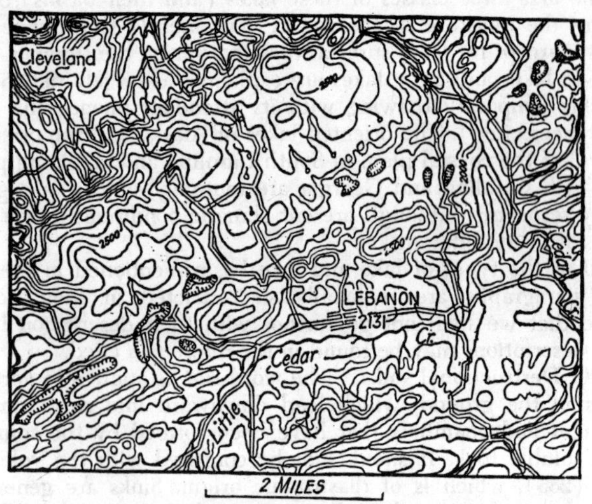

Fig. 320. Sink holes in limestone. The depressions, producing karst topography, are situated on the NE.-SW. diagonal of the map. Contour interval 100 ft. (Bristol quadrangle, Va.)

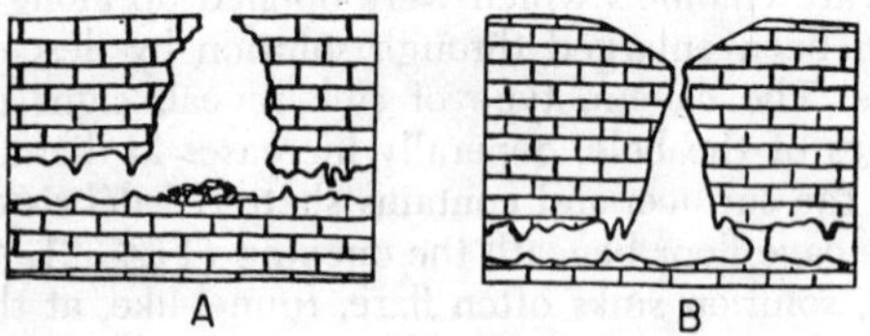

Fig. 321. Sections of sink holes. In A the roof has fallen in; in B the upper opening has been made entirely by solution.

between them, is called a *karst topography* (see Fig. 320). Favorable conditions for the development of karst topography are (1) jointed, fairly thinly bedded limestone, (2) sufficient rainfall, and (3) occurrence of the limestone well above the streams in the area.

In regions where limestone strata, near the surface of the ground, are horizontal or low-dipping, numerous sink-holes, arranged in a row, may indicate the position and trend of faulting.

291. Destructional valleys. A. In general. Valleys carved by erosion differ very greatly in respect to size, shape, and pattern. In size they grade down into grooves (*q.v.*). Their shape may be considered in terms of their profile sections, their longitudinal sections, and their plan. These characters depend upon a number

FIG. 322. Section of a valley due largely to the disintegration of the weaker rocks which are principally sandstones and shales. Here granite, *a*, and the massive Bighorn limestone, *cd*, form the uplands. The section is roughly 1,500 ft. long. (*Cloud Peak–Fort McKinney Folio, Wyoming, No.* 142, *U.S. Geol. Survey,* 1906.)

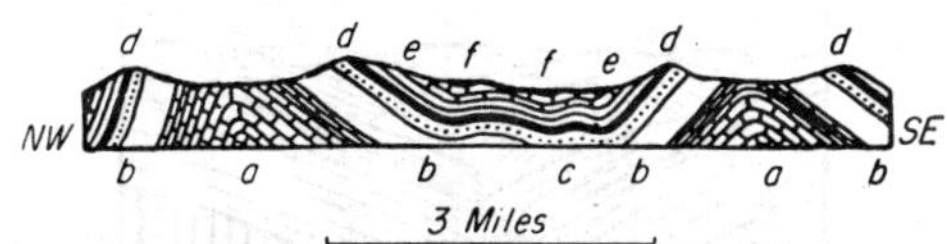

FIG. 323. Section across the Appalachian Mountains in Virginia. The principal valleys are situated on limestone. The ridges are on sandstone and quartzite. *a*, Shenandoah limestone; *b*, Martinsburg shale; *c*, Juniata formation; *d*, Tuscarora quartzite; *e*, Lewistown limestone; *f*, Monterey sandstone. (*Monterey Folio, Va.–W.Va., No.* 61, *U.S. Geol. Survey,* 1899.)

of factors, the most important of which are the agent of erosion, the nature of the material or rock eroded, and the stage of erosion (**302**).

291B. Valleys of differential erosion; contact valleys. Where rocks differ in their resistance to erosion, the weaker ones become the sites of valleys and lowlands, while the stronger ones remain as uplands. It may be that the difference in resistance is merely mechanical, the weaker ones perhaps being softer or more closely jointed, or the weaker rock may be more soluble or otherwise more easily decomposable than the hill-maker (**Figs. 322, 323**). Valleys are often opened up along the outcropping edges of such surfaces of weakness as igneous contacts, upturned unconformities, conformable bedding contacts, and faults (Fig. 324) (see **190, 224**). These may be called *contact erosion valleys,* and those on fault lines are further defined as *fault-line valleys.* The fault-line gap is a special variety of fault-line valley.

291C. V-shaped valleys. Gully, gorge, ravine, and canyon, are all general names applied to destructional valleys with comparatively steep sides. Those which are stream-made are characterized by two important features: they are V-shaped in cross section, and their plan is more or less sinuous or zigzag, so that a person standing near the stream and looking along the valley cannot see far because of overlapping upland spurs (Fig. 325). The breadth or angle of the V is largely dependent upon the stage of erosion (**302**). In young valleys it is narrow and relatively deep. In valleys which are said to be in early maturity it is broader, and it opens wider and wider and becomes more and more shallow as maturity advances to old age.

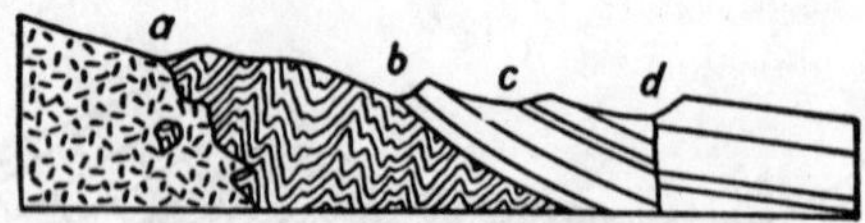

FIG. 324. Geologic section illustrating valleys situated upon contacts as follows: *a,* intrusive contact; *b,* unconformity; *c,* conformable bedding contact; *d,* fault. Note that the contact localizes the valley but often because resistant and weak rocks are there in juxtaposition.

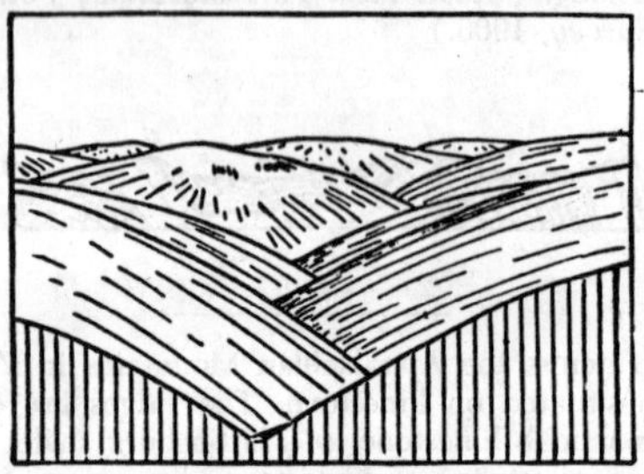

FIG. 325. A river valley showing overlapping spurs. The line at the top of the vertical ruling is a profile line, the ruling being a section of the ground.

291D. Solution valleys. The V-shaped types of valley just described are due to corrasion. In moist climates soluble rocks, like limestone, may wear chemically with greater facility than they wear mechanically. The resulting *solution valleys* are often broadly U-shaped in cross section, and their trend parallels the outcrop of the soluble rock. There is the possibility that these valleys may be confused at first glance with those of glacial origin; but, in general, solution valleys are seen only south of the limits of continental glaciation. Within the glaciated area examples may be found of valleys started by solution, but subsequently deepened by ice abrasion.

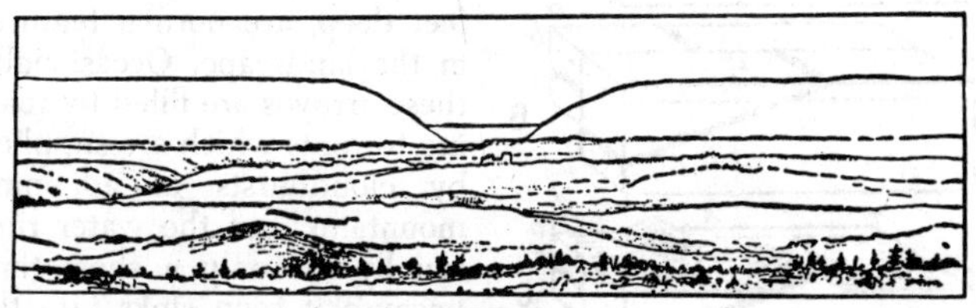

FIG. 326. The Delaware Water Gap, from Jenny Jump Mountain. The high ridge in the background, interrupted by the gap, is the Kittatinny Mountains. Its top marks the level of an ancient uplifted peneplain. (*After W. M. Davis.*)

291E. Destructional gaps. A short valley which opens across a ridge and connects lowlands on opposite sides of the ridge is termed a *gap*. The fault gap has already been described and figured (**285**).

Under certain conditions a river may be forced to incise its course as a narrow gorge in a hard rock ridge while it opens out a broad lowland in the less resistant rocks on each side. This gorge is called a *water gap* as long as the stream flows through it (Fig. 326); but if, for any reason, the water is diverted, the original water gap becomes a *wind gap*. A gap, whether or not containing a stream, is called a *fault-line gap* provided it is due primarily to erosion and is located along the line of outcrop of a dip fault or a diagonal fault that intersects the ridge-making rock layer (Fig. 327).

291F. Valleys and channels without streams. Two cases have already been noted of channels which have been abandoned by the streams that made them. These are the wind gap (**E**) and the glacial crease (288). Further comment on them is unnecessary; but there are several other types of channel, gorge, or valley, which are temporarily or permanently without streams.

By differential weathering steeply inclined dikes and strata may be eroded so much faster than the rocks on each side that clefts and even considerable valleys may be produced. Often there is no stream in these depressions. The rock waste is removed by rainwash or, in dry countries, by the wind.

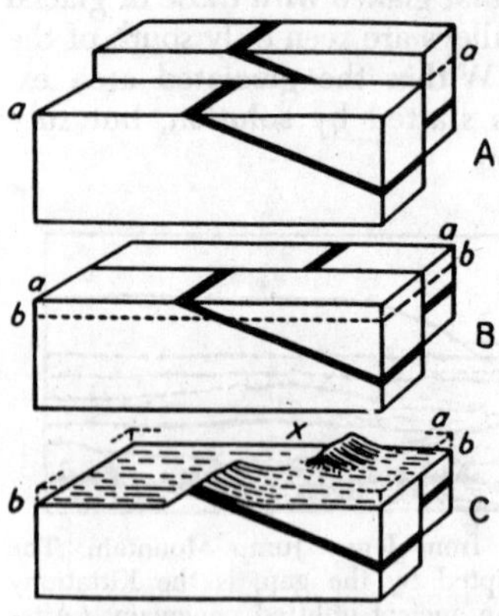

FIG. 327. Origin of a fault-line gap. A, a region after faulting and before erosion; B, the same region after erosion to a plain at the level *aa*; C, the same region after revival of erosion and removal of the weak rocks to the level *bb*. The fault-line gap is at *x* in C. Hard rocks are black.

In deserts dry channels or *arroyos*, some of them many feet deep, are normal features in the landscape. Occasionally these arroyos are filled by roaring torrents which are supplied by cloudbursts in adjoining mountains, but the water runs usually for only a short time because it soon sinks into the ground or is evaporated. The typical arroyo has a flat floor and almost, if not quite, vertical walls, for the effects of the excessive erosion performed by the torrents are scarcely modified in the intervals between successive floods.

Alluvial fans in dry regions are built intermittently. The streams pass into the loose sand or gravel far up on the deposit and abandon their lower channels except at times of heavy rainfall in the mountains. Shallow depressions are common on alluvial plains where the streams, in their meandering, have deserted their former courses.

Above the level of saline lakes, in relatively low places in the rims about their basins, abandoned outlets may exist by which the lake waters once drained out. More common, however, are the abandoned channels in lands which have been under the influence of continental glaciation, channels which served for a while as main drainage lines for the glacial waters (Fig. 328).

They were made where the lower, older valleys were blocked by ice or moraine and the water was forced to follow new routes. They often start at the level of abandoned shore lines, showing that they were the outlets of temporary lakes. Some of these gorges were subsequently buried under later drift, but those that were not so filled display many of the normal characters of destructional stream courses, except that they are often out of harmony with the present drainage systems.

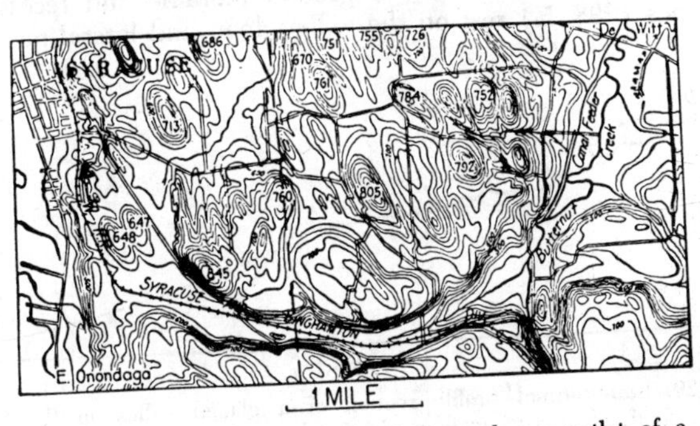

FIG. 328. An abandoned stream channel, formerly an outlet of a glacial lake. The Syracuse and Binghamton Division of the railroad follows the channel. Contour interval 20 ft. (Syracuse sheet, N.Y.)

291G. Glaciated valleys. Glaciated valleys have been scoured either by mountain glaciers or by ice sheets. In both cases it is probable that many of the valleys were formerly made by streams and were then modified by ice. The glaciated valleys of mountain districts are characterized by several or all of the following features: (1) the transverse profile is U-shaped, not V-shaped as in a majority of stream valleys; (2) the valley is straight or broadly curving, without overlapping spurs;[35] (3) its rock walls are steep (oversteepened stream-valley walls) and are more or less polished, striated, and grooved by ice abrasion; (4)

[35] An occasional exception to this is the so-called "bastion," a projecting shoulder from the wall of the glaciated valley, occurring, when present, just down-valley from the confluence with a branch valley. Bastions seem to have been formed where a high-level tributary glacier prevented or hindered lateral erosion by the trunk glacier just below the point of confluence. (See Bibliog., Ives, Ronald L., 1946.)

the ice-scoured walls sometimes terminate upward in an obtuse angle or *shoulder* above which the mountain slope is less steep; (5) the valley's longitudinal profile is broadly steplike, the *treads* being of gentle grade and sometimes holding lakes in rock-rimmed or moraine-dammed basins, and the *risers* being steep, ice-plucked cliffs, sometimes well nigh impassable (Fig. 329); (6) the rock floor of the valley bears evidence of powerful ice abrasion in polish, striae, grooves, etc., and is often irregular with roches moutonnées; (7) ground moraine and recessional moraines (**298, E**) rest on the valley floor, and lateral moraines

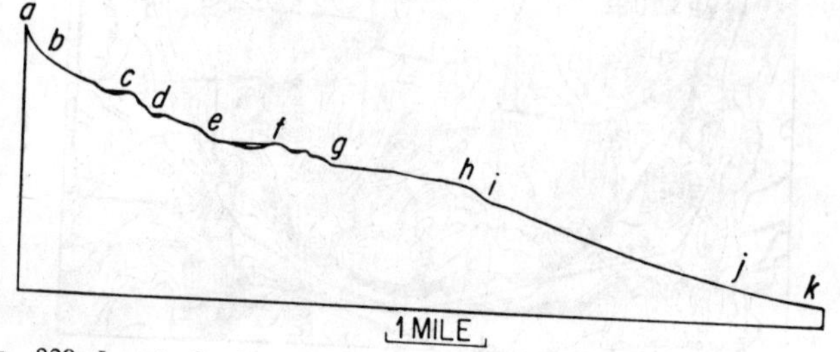

FIG. 329. Longitudinal profile section of a glacial valley in the Sierra Nevada, Caif. *ab*, cirque wall; *c, d, ef*, lakes; *gh*, tread; *hi*, riser; *jk*, head of alluvial cone at foot of mountains. (The vertical scale is twice the horizontal scale.)

are plastered up against the valley sides; (8) tributary valleys usually enter at levels considerably above the main valley floor (**292**).

Valleys overrun by ice sheets do not possess so many distinguishing marks of their origin. Their profile is U-shaped if they happened to trend about parallel to the ice motion, but those which lay athwart this direction often suffered plucking (and therefore steepening) on the side toward the source of the ice and abrasion (hence reduction of slope) on the other side (Fig. 330). Although an ice sheet tends to straighten original valleys parallel to its advance, although it polishes, striates, and grooves their floors and walls, and here and there scours out rock basins or forms roches moutonnées, it does not have a special propensity to oversteepen these walls, or to produce *shoulders*, or to erode *giant steps*. There are no true lateral moraines. In fact, the distribution of morainic material shows regional rather than local control. Outwash sediments very often cover the bedrock floors of these valleys, sometimes to considerable depths.

Glaciated valleys may lose their distinctive marks so that there may be some trouble in distinguishing them from solution valleys on the one hand, and from certain mature stream valleys on the other hand. For instance, weathering may remove striae and other tokens of glacial abrasion, and, in mountain valleys, talus accumulations may obscure the U-profile or conceal morainic deposits. As with solution valleys, so too with U-shaped mature stream valleys, they are not found in areas which have suffered continental glaciation because there has not been time enough for their development since the ice retired. All such original valleys in the glaciated area were modified by the ice.

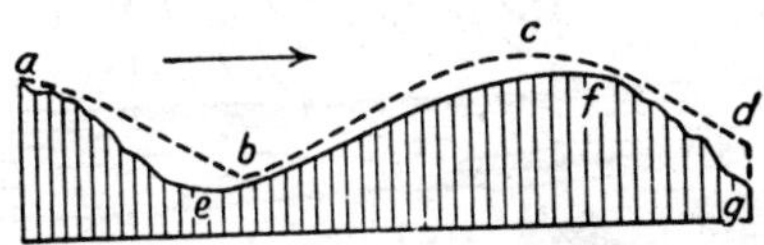

FIG. 330. Transverse profile of a valley overrun by an ice sheet in the direction of the arrow. *abcd*, profile of valley before ice erosion.

291H. Cirques and drift hollows. At its head the valley made by a mountain glacier normally opens out into a broad half-amphitheater bounded by steep precipices on all sides except at the junction with the valley. This is a *cirque*. Its floor resembles the floor of the associated valley in bearing evidences of very powerful ice abrasion, but its walls, unlike those of the valley, are generally free from marks of scour. They are cliffs made by sapping (**271**). They are bounded by joint faces.

The earliest phase of the cirque is to be seen in the small drift hollow on a hillside. During the day the snow melts. At night the water freezes in the interstices of the underlying rock and wedges off a few small chips. The next day these chips are washed away down the slope. Thus, as the process (called *nivation*) is repeated from day to day, the snowdrift comes to rest in a hollow of its own making. When the drift hollow (*nivation hollow*) grows larger it becomes a small cirque and the deeper snow changes to névé.

Landslide scars (**271, G**) may partially resemble glacial cirques, especially where well developed by repeated slides from the same place on the mountain side and also where the bedrock is relatively soft and therefore not likely to preserve for long the marks of glacial abrasion.

HANGING VALLEYS

292. Definition and classification. A *hanging valley* may be defined as a valley whose floor "is not in even adjustment with the bottom of the lower depression with which it unites."[36] Be-

FIG. 331. View of a glacial hanging valley on the south side of Nunatak Fiord, Alaska. (*From a photograph, after R. S. Tarr and B. S. Butler.*)

tween it and this lower depression—valley or basin as the case may be—there is a steep, generally precipitous slope over which the stream of the hanging valley plunges. (1) A majority of hanging valleys owe their origin to glaciation (Fig. 331). This is because a trunk glacier cuts its bed to a lower level than do its tributary glaciers, and when the ice disappears the tributary valleys are left hanging above the main valley. In like manner cirques may be hanging. However, there are methods other than ice erosion, by which valleys may be made to hang. (2) If waves wear back a coast line more rapidly than the inflowing rivers can cut down their channels, the latter become hanging with respect to sea level (Fig. 332). (3) A river may erode faster than its side streams so that their valleys are made to hang with respect to the main valley. (4) Finally, if a fault crosses a valley, the part of the valley in the upthrown block may be hanging

[36] Bibliog., Russell, I. C., 1905, p. 76.

above the lowland of the downthrown block, provided the displacement was more rapid than the stream erosion. From the foregoing it is clear that any kind of a valley may become hanging under the proper conditions.

Caves and Natural Bridges

293. Caves. Caverns in lava, which result from the very irregular way in which viscous lava moves, may be classed as volcanic. Most caves are destructional. Among these, the largest are formed by solution of limestone where the water table (**244**) is low and the products of solution are carried away in underground streams. The Mammoth Caves of Kentucky and the Carlsbad Cavern of New Mexico are well known examples.

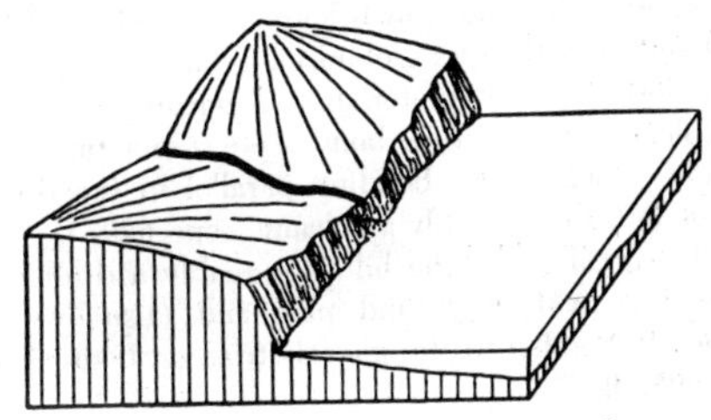

Fig. 332. A hanging valley resulting from rapid wave erosion.

In regions of horizontal strata weathering may locally gnaw back the weak rock underlying a cliff-maker and thus produce broad, shallow caves. Of somewhat similar nature are undercut caves formed at the base of an abrasion cliff, where winds, stream currents, or waves, deliver their most efficient attack. Such caves are especially liable to occur in weak rocks or along joints or faults that invite concentrated erosion.

294. Natural bridges. Natural bridges may be found in irregular lava sheets. The majority, like caves, are destructional products of denudation, and as such they are merely a later stage of cave erosion. They are remnants of cave roofs of which the main portion has fallen in or has been eroded away. Consequently, they may result from solution or from abrasion. Some are cut by wind and some by water. In regions of flat-lying strata, the undercut soft rock on opposite sides of a divide may at last be removed, leaving the hard capping layer to span the opening.

Hills, Ridges, and Other Positive Topographic Forms

295. Terminology and identification. According to the definition previously given (**265**), positive topographic forms include hills, ridges, pinnacles, and any other relief forms which project upward and are surrounded on all sides by lower land.[37] Following is a key to aid in their identification:

Key for the Identification of Positive Land Forms

If the land surface has the form of

A. An isolated knoll or hill, not much longer than wide, and, in general,
  1. With its height less than its ground plan dimensions, and
    a. The underlying rock materials are unconsolidated, consisting of
      (1) Volcanic ash, scoriae, bombs, etc. (sometimes associated with flows), with their bedding parallel to the slopes of the hill, the latter is probably a volcanic cone (**297**).
      (2) Glacial till (**73**), the hill is probably a drumlin, if it is more or less oval in ground plan and (usually) has its length nearly parallel to the glacial striae on bedrock in the vicinity (**298, B**).
    b. The underlying rock materials are consolidated, and consist of
      (1) A particular rock association composed of
        (*a*) Lava in flows (sometimes interbedded with volcanic ash, etc.), the flows being parallel to the surface of the hill, the latter is probably a volcanic cone (**298**).
        (*b*) Flat-lying strata, the hill is
          (a_1) A mesa if its top is flat (**300, B**).
          (b_1) A butte if its top is peaked (**300, B**).
        (*c*) Igneous rock which has the shape of a neck, cutting across the rocks of the surrounding region, the hill is probably a volcanic butte (**300, B**).
        (*d*) Limy skeletal material of organic origin, the form may be a table reef (page 386).
      (2) Not necessarily a particular rock association, and if
        (*a*) The rock knob or hill is more or less well rounded and
          (a_1) Has glacial scratches and grooves on its surface, the knob or hill is probably a roche moutonnée (**300, E**).
          (b_1) Has no glacial scratches or grooves, but shows evidence of the separation of spalls or slabs from

[37] Islands are not treated here as a separate class.

its surface and is more or less surrounded at its foot by talus of these spalls, the hill is probably an exfoliation dome (**300, D**).

(*b*) The knob is usually rugged, and is surrounded by a wave-cut cliff and bench, it is probably a stack (**300, F**).

2. With its height often several times greater than its ground plan dimensions, the elevation may be a stack (**300, F**), a rain pillar (**300, G**) or any sharp, pinnacle-line remnant of erosion (**300, H**).

B. A definite ridge, usually many times longer than wide, and either continuous or broken by transverse valleys, and if

1. The underlying rock materials are unconsolidated, consisting of
   a. Loose bowlders with no, or little, intervening finer débris, the ridge may be a bowlder belt (**298, E**), or a winter talus ridge (**298, G**), or a wave-built terrace (**276**).
   b. Glacial till, the hill is probably a moraine of one kind or another (**298, E**).
   c. Rather poorly stratified sand and gravel, many of the pebbles and bowlders being subangular, the ridge may be an esker (**298, C**) especially if it is associated with kames and kettle holes (**298, D**).
2. The underlying rock materials are consolidated,
   a. Consisting of inclined strata which dip nearly parallel to the land surface on one side of the ridge, but are truncated by the other side of the ridge, the latter may be a cuesta or a hogback (**300, C**).
   b. Consisting of the calcareous skeletons of colonial growths of corals, bryozoans, etc., and occurring at or near low-tide level as a shoreline feature, the ridge is some type of calcareous reef (**298, A**).

C. A group of hummocks and hollows, generally with a relief of 150 ft. or less and the underlying materials, which are unconsolidated, are

1. Fine, cross-bedded sands, the hummocks may be dunes (**298, A**).
2. Coarse sand and gravel, rudely stratified, the hummocks may be kames and the hollows kettle holes (**298, D**).
3. Unstratified, heterogeneous débris, the deposit as a whole may be of glacial till, or it may have been produced by landslide, earth flow, mudflow, or rock glacier (**298, B, E, F**).

D. A range of hills or mountains, with intervening valleys, the hills are the interstream divides left in the process of erosion of the valleys which have been incised into a broad upfaulted or uparched land mass.

296. Fault mountains. *Block mountains* are ridges due to faulting. Ordinarily one slope is gentle (back slope) and the other is steep, the latter being a fault scarp (**269**). Since the uplift of a block mountain is generally slow and erosive agents are constantly working, the ridge is seldom seen as an unbroken unit. It is usually dissected by valleys, and, when very old, it becomes a low range of hills (Fig. 283). The same remark applies to the horst (**224**).

297. Volcanic cones. A volcanic peak consists principally of volcanic materials—lava, or ash and other fragmentals, or lava and fragmentals interbedded. Typically it is conical in form, often quite symmetrical, and if sufficiently recent, it may have a crater at its summit. Its slopes may vary between 2° or 3° and 40° (**267**). Denudation may eventually destroy the crater and reduce the original elevation of the peak (Fig. 333).

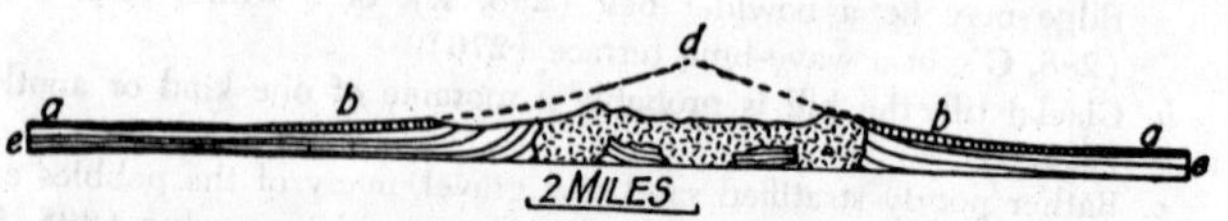

FIG. 333. Geologic section of Marysville Buttes, a group of hills resulting from the denudation of a volcanic cone. *a*, alluvium resting on volcanic tuffs, *b*; *e*, Tertiary sedimentary rocks; *bdb*, hypothetical original profile of volcano. (*Marysville Folio, Calif., No.* 17, *U.S. Geol. Survey*, 1895.)

298. Constructional hills and ridges. Constructional hills and ridges built of materials derived through erosion include dunes, drumlins, kames, eskers, several types of moraine, landslide hummocks, and winter talus ridges.

298A. In arid regions, along the shores of seas and lakes and along or near the courses of streams that vary greatly in volume, *dunes* may be constructed if there is an abundant supply of sand and if winds are prevailingly strong and from certain definite directions (onshore in case of seas and lakes). Sand dunes vary greatly in shape, probably depending upon the relations between wind strength, wind direction, and available supply of sand. In Fig. 334 are shown several types of dune in horizontal plan. Some are crescentic (Fig. 334, A) with the horns opening *with* the wind (called *barchans*). Others are roughly crescentic or parabolic, but with the convex curve of the dune facing *with* the wind (Fig. 334 B). Others are almost sprawling, with finger-like lobes extending to leeward, and with irregular windward edges (Fig. 334, C). Some are ridgelike, elongate across the course of the wind, and these may have finger-like lobes to leeward (Fig. 334, D). And, finally, some are long, subparallel, and elongate *with* the prevailing wind direction (Fig. 334, E).

Sand dunes are usually in groups. Their heights are commonly between a few and 200 or 300 ft., though they may be considerably higher. The windward slope is gentle and the lee slope is steeper, with an angle of from 25° to 35° (Fig. 335). Sand is blown up the gentle slope and is dropped over the crest, whence it slides down the lee slope.

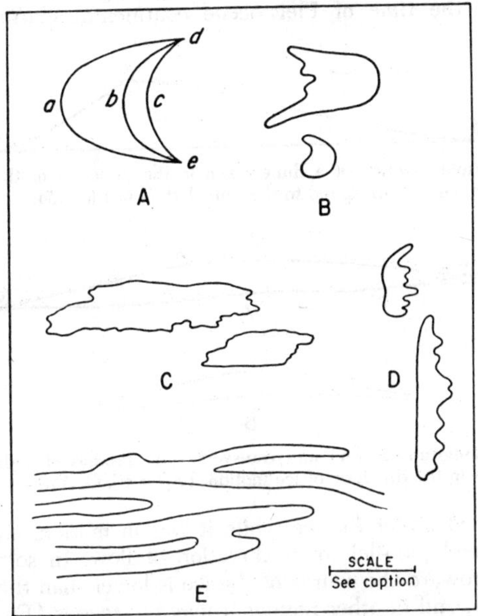

Fig. 334. Sand dunes, in plan. The graphic scale represents 500 ft. for A, B, and D, and 4,000 ft. for C and E. For all five types of dune, as here represented, the prevailing wind blows from left to right.

In areas where clays are broadly exposed (tidal flats, playas, etc.) and where, after occasional moistening, they then undergo a period of desiccation, their upper layers may crack and curl, and strong winds may sweep away chips and pellets of the clay (Art. **107**), piling these up in dunes where further progress is impeded. This may be within the clay-belt area, or at or near its lee margin. During the next rain, the particles soften and coalesce, and, in the ensuing dry spell, the clay hardens and so tends to build up compact mounds, or *clay dunes*.[38]

Sand dunes and clay dunes may be grassed over and covered with vegetation to such an extent that their identity is very obscure. Examinations should then be made for their internal structure (**96, G**).

298B. *Drumlins*[39] are hills consisting of glacial bowlder clay (till). At the time of Pleistocene continental glaciation, they

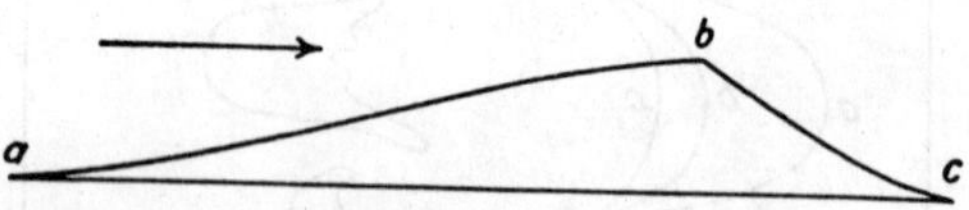

FIG. 335. Profile section of a dune taken in the direction of the wind (see arrow). *a, b,* and *c* correspond to the same letters in Fig. 334.

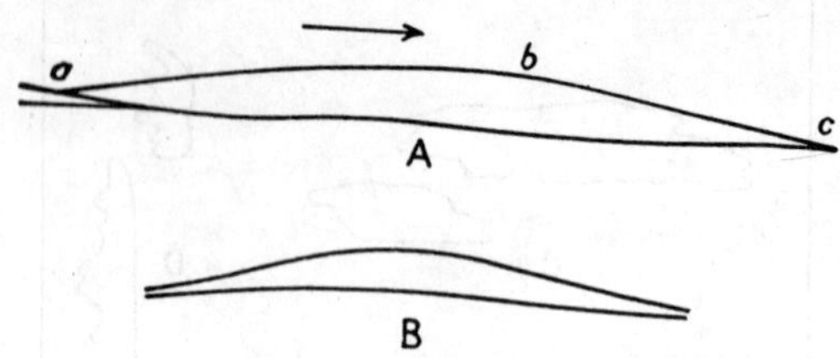

FIG. 336. Longitudinal (A) and transverse (B) profiles of a drumlin. The arrow points in the direction of ice motion. (*After W. C. Alden.*)

were formed under the ice while it was in motion, and so they have a trend parallel to its direction of flow. In some regions the slope toward the source of the ice is lower than the lee slope (Fig. 336), and in other regions it may be steeper (Fig. 337). In plan, drumlins are typically oval, although irregularities in shape are not uncommon (Fig. 337). Few have a relief of more than 200 ft. While some were evidently built round projecting rock ledges, many have no such rocky cores. In cross sections isolated strata may occasionally be seen in the till, and these may be contorted (**108**). At the time of their formation drumlins are thought to have been between 5 and 30 miles north of the ice front. As for their distribution, they are numerous in many

[38] See Bibliog., Coffey, G. N., 1909; Price, W. Armstrong, 1936, p. 226; also Huffman, George G., and W. Armstrong Price, 1949.

[39] Bibliog., Alden, W. C., 1905.

states within 100 miles or so north of the southern limits of Pleistocene glaciation (Fig. 338).

298C. *Eskers* are relatively long, narrow, winding ridges of mixed sand and gravel. In longitudinal profile their crests are seen to be sinuous (Fig. 339, A). They range in height from 10

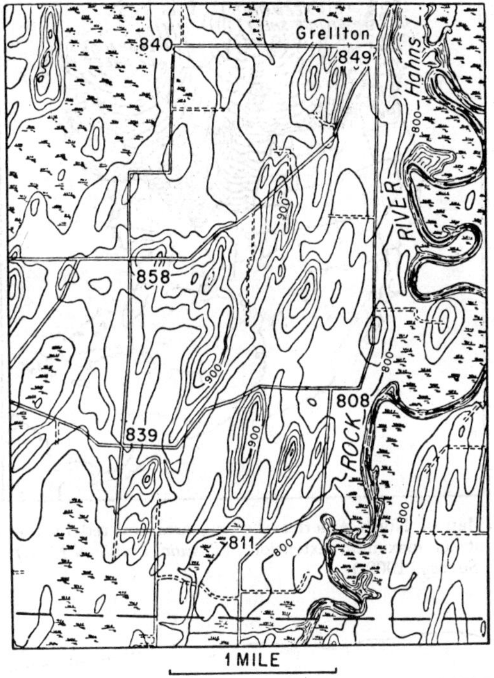

Fig. 337. Drumlins in Wisconsin. The ice moved a little west of south. Contour interval 20 ft. (Waterloo sheet, Wis.)

or 15 ft., to 100 ft. or even more. They may cross valleys or bend round hills, seldom more than 200 ft. above the valley floor. Usually they terminate in outwash plains (**281, C**). Cuttings in them show that they consist of somewhat waterworn, rudely stratified materials. The pebbles range up to 18 in. or 2 ft. in diameter and are typically subangular, although sometimes

FIG. 338. Map of North America showing area covered by the Pleistocene ice sheet at its maximum extension. (*Passaic Folio, N.J.–N.Y., No.* 157, *U.S. Geol. Survey,* 1908.)

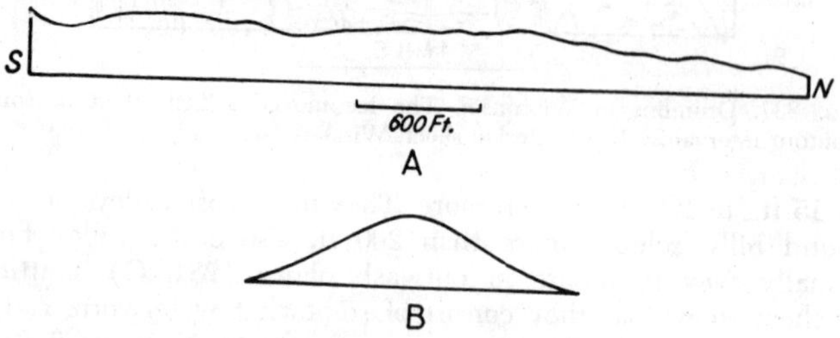

FIG. 339. Longitudinal (A) and transverse (B) profile sections of an esker. (B is drawn on a somewhat larger scale than A.)

pretty well rounded. These esker ridges were laid as stream bed deposits in channels in the ice during the retreat of the glacial sheet. Their shape, their structure, and their relations to outwash plains, prove that the ice was stagnant when they were formed. After the supporting ice walls melted away, the deposits slumped down to the angle of repose for gravel (**267**). It is on account of their rapid accumulation and their later settling that their stratification is generally so poor.

298D. *Kames* are similar to eskers in composition, structure, and origin, but in shape they differ. Instead of being long, narrow ridges, they are more or less oval or irregular knolls and hummocks. They were deposited in irregular openings in the ice. Eskers and kames are associated with kettle holes.

Fig. 340. Lateral and ground moraines deposited in two successive advances of a valley glacier.

298E. Ridges and irregular deposits laid down by ice are spoken of as *moraines*. Some are associated with valley glaciers and others with ice sheets. Lateral, medial, terminal, and recessional moraines are made by valley glaciers. *Lateral moraines* are built of débris, part of which falls upon the ice as talus from the mountain sides, and part of which, having been carried for some distance within the ice, is returned to the surface by shearing or by surface melting (ablation). When the glacier shrinks by excessive melting, it leaves these lateral moraines as embankments on either side of the valley. They consist of till or of great agglomerations of bowlders (**73**). They may rise above the valley floor to heights of over 1,000 ft. Frequently there is a descent of a few score feet from the crest of the moraine to the original valley side. A readvance of the glacier front, if of great extent, may destroy the moraines of the earlier advance; but if the advancing ice tongue is not so large as the first glacier, lateral moraines of the second may be constructed, terrace-like, against the inner sides of the older moraines (Fig. 340). On account of the tendency of glacier termini to oscillate up and down their valleys, this superposition of lateral moraines is not uncommon, and care must be taken to discriminate between the minor variations of one ice epoch and the much more significant effects of distinct glacial epochs. The two sets of moraines shown in Fig. 341 might belong to two ice oscillations during one glacial age

Fig. 341. Sketch map showing the distribution of moraines deposited in two successive advances of a group of valley glaciers. (*After W. W. Atwood.*)

were it not for the fact that criteria other than relative position proved them to represent two glacial ages widely separated by an interglacial interval (**122**).

When two ice streams coalesce, the inner lateral moraines of the two unite to form a *medial moraine* downstream from the point of junction. Medial moraines are very rarely left on the floor of the valley after the disappearance of the ice. They are not so well marked as lateral moraines and they are more apt to be modified or destroyed by subsequent erosion.

At the front of the ice, as at its sides, a great deal of detritus is deposited. Some of this débris accumulates in a *marginal* or *terminal moraine,* and the rest becomes aqueoglacial material in so far as it is handled by water derived from the melting of the ice. Terminal moraines, composed of till or of bowlder heaps, are curved with the convex side pointing down the valley. In the recession of the glacier a distinct marginal moraine may be formed every time the front pauses in its migration. These are often termed *recessional moraines* (Fig. 342). Many such may be built in a single valley. Terminal moraines often unite with the contemporaneous lateral moraines. Where glaciers deployed upon broad piedmont slopes, terminal and lateral moraines may be finely developed.

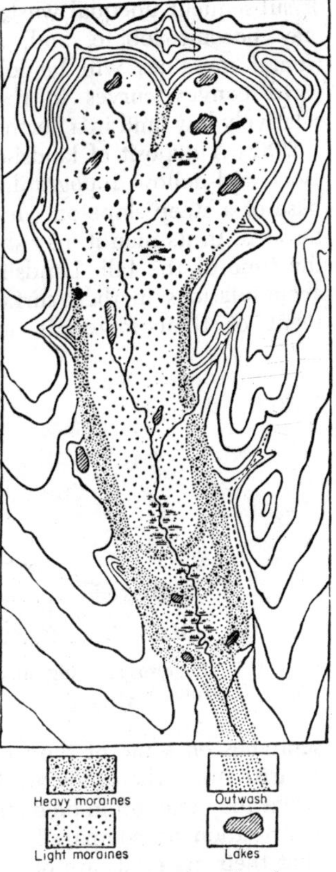

FIG. 342. Diagrammatic sketch map of a glaciated valley, showing lateral and recessional moraines, several blocked tributary streams, and the head of a valley train. (*After W. W. Atwood.*)

Terminal and recessional moraines are also formed by ice sheets, both piedmont and continental. In origin they are similar to the deposits of the same name made by mountain glaciers, but in form they may be more hummocky, and they are of much greater size. They may consist of till or of loose bowlders (bowlder belts). Either because an ice sheet, advancing over an uneven topography, may migrate farther in the valleys than on the uplands, or because of subsequent unequal wastage of the ice, the front of the sheet may become lobate, and, as a consequence, its marginal or frontal moraines will be lobate. In North America the southward convex curves in the terminal moraine often indicate relatively low land in a northerly direction.

298F. A deposit of landslide débris has a very irregular, hummock-and-hollow topography, and is generally situated at the base of a steep slope on which the original scar of the slide may be seen. In its plan it may show evidence of having spread out at the time of the fall. Landslide deposits may resemble morainal accumulations in their surface features, in the chaotic arrangement of their materials, and in the occasional presence of

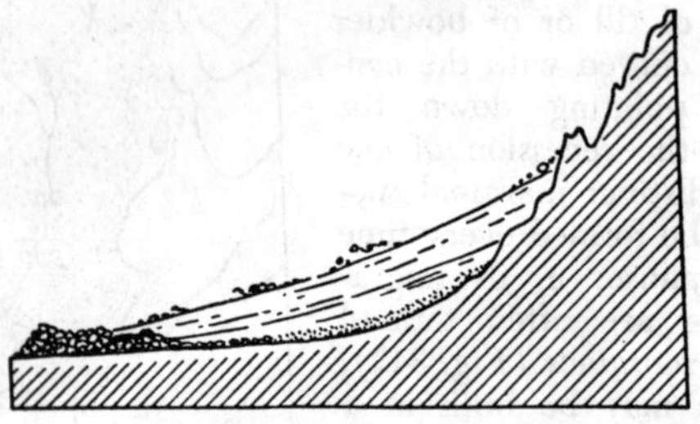

Fig. 343. Diagram showing mode of formation of a winter talus ridge. (*After E. Howe.*)

scratches on some of the rock fragments, but confusion is likely to arise only when they are in valleys that look glaciated. In this event they may often be distinguished by their local and irregular distribution as compared with most moraines, and by the fact that their materials are of the same rock as that on the mountain side *above* them. In unglaciated valleys no other suggestions of ice action will be found. In valleys that were formerly glaciated, the landslide materials have probably slumped down over any morainal débris that happened to be in the way. Other constructional forms, which may have either a hummock-and-hollow topography or an irregular ridgelike shape, are the deposits of earth flows and mudflows and rock glaciers (**4; 271, G**).

298G. In mountain regions, snow banks lead to the formation of *winter talus ridges* (Fig. 343). Rock fragments slide down the snow surface and accumulate at the foot of the drift. In summer, after the snow has melted away, a curving ridge of rock fragments remains, convex away from the source of the slide. If the snow banks of successive winters are smaller, a series of concentric talus ridges may result. Since these ridges are formed in front of any true talus that may have accumulated at the foot of the rocky slope during the summer season, they are also called *pro-talus ramparts.*

299. Bioherms or calcareous reefs. Some shore lines are characterized by the presence of calcareous reefs (limestone reefs, coral reefs, algal reefs). These reefs, technically known as bioherms,[40] may be properly included among positive constructional topographic forms. Except for their uppermost parts, they are submerged, and even these uppermost parts may be exposed to the air only when the tide is low, and not always then.

Most commonly a calcareous reef (bioherm) is a ridge built up of the limy skeletons of colonial growths of corals, bryozoans, algae, sponges, crinoids, etc., animals and plants which flourish in shallow seas under special conditions of temperature, salinity, clearness of water, etc. At the top of the reef, especially along its seaward margin, are the living organisms and, as these die, their skeletons become part of the limy core of the ridge. Through partial solution and redeposition of the limy materials, and also through the action of boring organisms, the original organic structures of the mass may be largely destroyed, and there may be more or less alteration to dolomite. As a result, the core of the reef may become essentially structureless—a solid, practically incompressible rock, but still containing abundant pore spaces. Except in early stages of their development, these bioherms are much longer than they are wide or thick, and their length is roughly parallel to the shore along which they are built. They may vary greatly in size, ranging up to several hundred feet in thickness, several miles in width, and several hundred miles in length. They may be separated from the mainland by a lagoon,

[40] The word *bioherm* was first applied to calcareous or limy reefs ("coral reefs") by Cumings and Shrock. In their detailed report on Niagaran coral reefs, we read "The authors have for some time used the term 'bioherm,' from the Greek root *bio-*, having the meaning *organic*, and ἕρμα, the word for a reef." (Bibliog., Cumings, Edgar R., and Robert R. Shrock, 1928, p. 599.) If a calcareous deposit, consisting of the same organic remains as those which constitute a bioherm, is not ridge-shaped, but is spread out blanket-like, similar to any other normal stratum, it is designated a *biostrome.*

in which case they are called *barrier reefs;* or they may be much closer to the mainland, just offshore, without an associated lagoon, and then they are called *fringing reefs.* A more or less circular reef inclosing a lagoon is an *atoll.*[41]

The outer or seaward side of a bioherm is steep, sometimes locally even vertical or overhanging, especially where the organisms are actively growing seaward. Flanking this reef core is a submarine talus of broken fragments of the reef materials dipping off steeply and grading outward, at considerable depth, into marine muds. On the landward side of the bioherm, there may be a fringe of reef detritus, but in the case of atolls and barrier

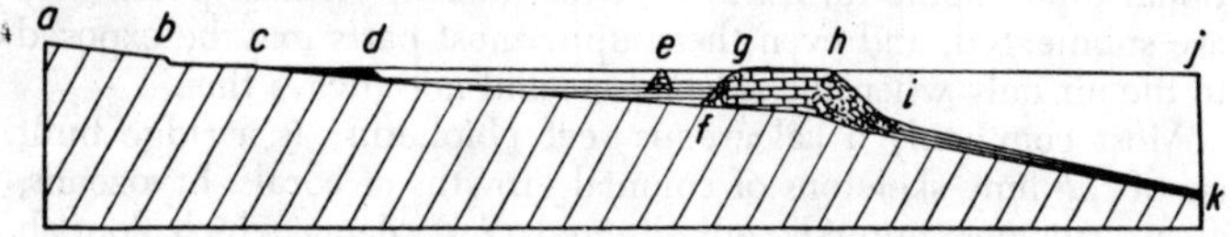

FIG. 344. Ideal section of barrier reef (bioherm) and lagoon. The reef is imagined to have started growth on a terracelike change of slope on the sea floor. Growth of the reef has been upward and somewhat seaward. *ab,* land surface on exposed old land mass (cross-hatched below *abck*); *bc,* sea bench, largely exposed at low tide; *b,* sea cliff; *cd,* clastic deposits carried into lagoon (*cg*) from land; *df,* limy clay deposits on lagoon floor; *e,* pinnacle, based on lower lagoon clays; *gh,* barrier reef; *fg, hi,* talus from wave erosion of reef; *fg,* back-reef; *hi,* fore-reef; *hjk,* ocean, on floor of which (*ik*) are limy muds which grade basinward (seaward) from outer fore-reef talus; *dghj,* approximate low-tide level.

reefs this grades into even-bedded fine calcareous muds of the lagoon. These relations are illustrated in Fig. 344.

300. Destructional hills and ridges. Destructional hills and ridges are outstanding topographic forms which owe their existence to the deeper erosion of the land that surrounds them. That

[41] A fourth type, referred to as important by Shepard (see Bibliog., Shepard, Francis P., 1948, p. 252), is the *pinnacle* or *coral pinnacle,* which is usually of small size, is built in the same way and of the same materials as in the other types, and may occur in large numbers rising from the floor of the lagoon and reaching upward close to the surface of the lagoon water. Closely related is the *table reef* which, like the pinnacle, is a column of reef material, completely surrounded by water. Its top surface may be from less than a mile to 5 or 6 miles in diameter, yet it may rise from depths of as much as 2 miles (see Bibliog., Ladd, Harry S., 1950, p. 204). A table reef may spread out radially like a mushroom, where the outward growth of the building organisms predominates over erosion by the onslaught of waves.

they have not been worn to a lower level is often due to the superior resistance of the materials of which they are composed, but it may be merely because they are interstream areas or *divides* which have not yet had enough time for their complete erosion. This class of elevations may be regarded as including sharp pinnacles, small rocky knobs only a few hundred square feet in area, and larger peaks and ridges. The following forms will receive consideration: monadnocks, mesas, buttes, cuestas, hogbacks, exfoliation domes, roches moutonnées, stacks, and rain pillars. Mention is made of nunataks, baraboos, and steptoes.

300A. By long continued erosion a land surface may be reduced to an almost level plain (**282, 303**), but there may still be a few hills, which, having as yet escaped final destruction, rise

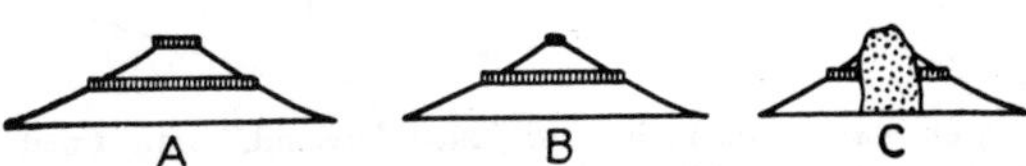

FIG. 345. Sections of buttes. A and B, buttes consisting of horizontal strata. B has been more eroded than A. C, volcanic neck. A thin talus cover lies on the edges of the weaker strata in each of the diagrams.

conspicuously above the plain. These are *monadnocks*. The term connotes nothing in regard to form or structure; it means merely a residual of an old topography standing above a plain of subaerial erosion.

A similar residual type in arid regions is the *island mountain*, or *island mount* (German, Inselberg)[42] (**306**)

300B. A *mesa* is a flat-topped *table mountain* consisting of horizontal or nearly horizontal beds and bounded on all sides by steep erosion scarps (**38, 271**). Mesas sometimes occur as outliers of plateau steps (**277**). When erosion has reduced a mesa so far that there is practically nothing left of the original flat upper surface, the hill is called a *butte* (Fig. 345). Steep-sided hills consisting of relatively hard igneous rock are likewise termed *buttes* (Fig. 345, C). Many mesas and buttes are monadnocks.

300C. If strata of varying hardness are tilted at a low angle, say between 10° and 20°, erosion will develop ridges or *cuestas* on the resistance rock layers. From the crest line of a cuesta there is a steep descent in one direction and a gentle descent in the

[42] A term proposed by W. Bornhardt. See Bibliog., Davis, W. M., 1912, p. 366; and *Idem.*, 1930, p. 6.

opposite direction (Fig. 346). The steep slope is the cuesta face, an erosion escarpment, and the gentle one is the *back slope* of the cuesta. The latter is nearly a dip slope. In beds inclined at angles higher than 20° the slopes of an erosion ridge developed on a hard rock layer have angles of inclination which are more nearly equal. The side corresponding to the cuesta face (across the stratum) becomes less steep and the back slope, about parallel with the beds, becomes steeper. A ridge of this type is a *hogback*

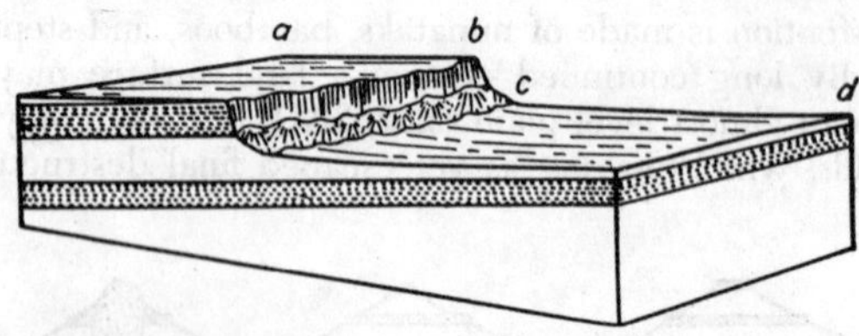

Fig. 346. A cuesta. *ab*, back slope or "outer lowland," approximately a dip slope; *bc*, escarpment with its base covered by talus; *cd*, "inner lowland." Hard strata are stippled.

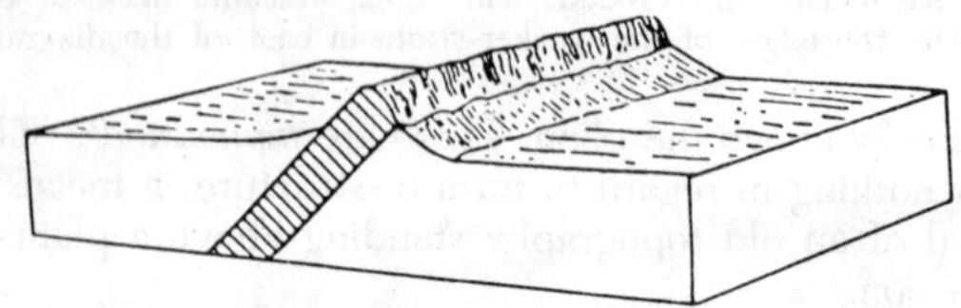

Fig. 347. A hogback, due to the slower erosion of a resistant stratum (lined).

(Fig. 347). Evidently, then, there are all gradations between the plateau step in horizontal strata (Fig. 300), through the cuesta, to the hogback in beds with a relatively steep dip.

300D. Rounded knobs or *domes* are sometimes produced in the erosion of granitic rocks, conglomerates, etc., by exfoliation (**37**). They may range from a few feet to several hundred feet in height. At the base of a hill of this origin the talus consists largely of great spalls of which some may be seen on the hillside in all stages of separation from the parent rock.

300E. In glaciated regions many of the rounded rocky knobs and hills were so made by ice abrasion. Glacial striae, polish, and grooves, on their surfaces bear witness to this fact, but on high hills and rarely in other places, postglacial disintegration may have destroyed these evidences. These rounded rock knobs and hills are called *roches moutonnées* (sing, roche moutonnée). They have a more gentle slope on the side from which the ice thrust came and a steeper, ice-plucked slope on the other side (Fig. 348).

300F. Along rocky coasts there are sometimes outstanding projections of rock, *stacks* or *chimneys*, which have been separated from the sea cliff by the concentrated attack of the waves round and behind them. They are still bedrock in the sense that they are in place. They rise from the wave-cut bench (**277**) from which they will ultimately be razed (Fig. 298).

300G. Relatively soft, fine-grained strata, containing scattered pebbles, or perhaps concretions, may be cut into by the

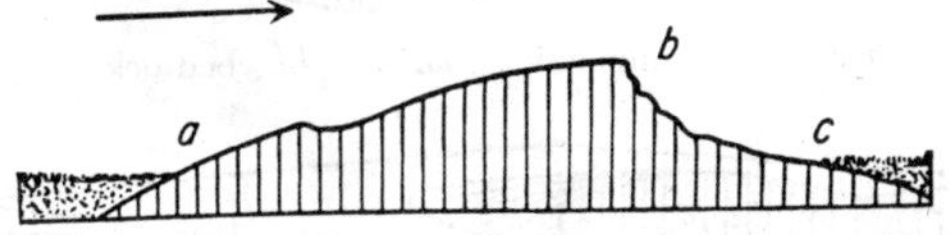

Fig. 348. Profile section of a roche moutonnée, showing thrust side, *ab*, and lee side, *bc*. Arrow indicates ice motion.

force of falling rain. About any one of these pebbles the matrix may be worn away until the pebble at length rests as a cap on the top of a pillar of the less resistant material. Such *rain pillars* may reach heights of several feet.

300H. Pillars (*hoodoos*) may be developed by the erosion of horizontal strata of varying hardness in regions where most of the rainfall is concentrated during a short period of the year. Below hard layers of the soft materials may be so far worn away that columns of the latter remain capped by remnants of the overlying resistant rock. The height of the pillar depends in part upon the thickness of the weaker stratum.

300I. Ancient calcareous reefs (bioherms) buried within a series of strata may later—possibly millions of years later—be re-exposed through erosion. If, after such re-exposure, they form ridges or hills, due to their relative resistance to the erosive processes, they are called *klintar* (sing., klint).

300J. Three or four other forms may be mentioned here, although they have no particular relation to destructional or constructional origin. These include the nunatak, the steptoe, and the baraboo. A *nunatak* is an island of bedrock in a glacial field, a hill projecting through, and entirely surrounded by, the ice (Fig. 349). A *steptoe* is a similar island of bedrock in a lava flow. The lava spread out around the hill and froze about it (Fig. 350). Finally, a *baraboo* is a monadnock which has been buried by a series of strata and subsequently re-exposed by the partial erosion of these younger strata.

A hill or mountain of older rock, entirely surrounded, but not covered, by any kind of later sedimentary deposit, has been

FIG. 349. A nunatak, *c*. *aa*, ice; *bb*, bedrock.

FIG. 350. A steptoe, *c*. *aa*, lava; *bb*, bedrock and soil which were overflowed by the lava.

referred to as a *lost mountain* or an *island hill*,[43] a term which to some extent conflicts with the more restricted definition of *island mountain* or *inselberg* (**300, A**). Robert T. Hill states[44] that the term *huerfano* (Spanish for orphan; pronounced ware-fa-no, with the accent on the first syllable) is frequently applied to mountains of this character in southwestern United States and Mexico. These terms—steptoe, baraboo, island hill, island mountain, inselberg, and *huerfano*—are not in general use, but since they do occasionally appear in the literature and since they do refer to special cases, they have been included in the present chapter.

[43] E. W. Shaw, on p. 489 in "Preliminary Statement Concerning a New System of Quaternary Lakes in the Mississippi Basin," *Jour. Geol.*, vol. 19, 1911.

[44] In a conversation with the writer.

Chapter 12

TOPOGRAPHIC EXPRESSION

Topographic Expression in General

301. Mutual relationship of topographic forms. The study of topography cannot stop at the description and interpretation of land forms as mere isolated phenomena. Not only must we be able to recognize these individual elements, but also we must be able to interpret their meaning as they appear in their mutual relations (**266**). The various relief features of a region as a whole are the product of some common cause or interacting causes. Their shape and distribution are dependent partly upon the underlying rock materials and geologic structure, partly upon the number and kind of geologic agents which have been engaged in their formation, and partly upon the length of time during which they have been under the control of these agents. Using the term *topographic expression* with reference to the general appearance of a land area,[1] we may say, then, that topographic expression is conditioned by four important factors, namely, rock materials, geologic structure, erosion process, and stage of topographic development. In the succeeding pages topographic expression in its relation to these four factors will receive some consideration, though by no means in an exhaustive way. Topographic development will be treated first; then the association of unlike types or facies of topography, which were produced in successive cycles, and, last, valley pattern, which depends chiefly upon underground structure. In studying a land surface from this broad standpoint, the geologist should never lose sight of the fact that the topographic elements must always be examined individually before they can be explained in their ensemble.

[1] We may speak, likewise, of the topographic expression of a particular kind of rock or type of structure.

Cycles of Topographic Development

302. Definition. No land forms are strictly permanent. Wind, water, and ice are constantly engaged in modifying the configuration of the ground. In the change successive stages of development are recognized, and these are called youth, maturity, and old age. The sequence, from the beginning of youth to late old age, is known as a *geomorphic* or *physiographic cycle*. As a matter of fact, old age is seldom attained, for the process of erosion becomes increasingly slow as the cycle advances and various accidents and interruptions interfere with the work (**307**). Since each agent of erosion operates in its own peculiar way, there are several different kinds of geomorphic cycle. There are the *normal* or river cycle, the cycle of mountain glaciation, the cycle of marine erosion, and the cycle of arid erosion.

303. Cycle of river erosion. No river can cut its channel more than a few feet below sea level because its speed is quickly reduced as soon as it empties into the sea. A few hundred feet inland the stream cannot cut even as low as sea level, for there must be some slope to enable it to flow. Carrying out this line of reasoning, we find that there must be a slope for the course of every river, below which further erosion is no longer possible. When any stream has cut down to this critical slope it is said to be *at grade*, or at *base level*.[2] Probably grade has never been attained by any river, for as time goes on a stream must have a constantly diminishing load, and a diminishing load will enable it to cut nearer and nearer to sea level, so that its grade will be a constantly vanishing quantity; but for purposes of general description grade may be regarded as something having a fairly definite value.[3]

[2] Unfortunately "level," which properly implies horizontality, has here come to mean a gently sloping surface which is not, and cannot be, strictly level.

[3] "A graded stream," says J. Hoover Mackin, "is one in which, over a period of years, slope is delicately adjusted to provide, with available discharge and with prevailing channel characteristics, just the velocity required for the transportation of the load supplied from the drainage basin. The graded stream is a system in equilibrium; its diagnostic characteristic is that any change in any of the controlling factors will cause a displacement of the equilibrium in a direction that will tend to absorb the effect of the change." (Bibliog., Mackin, J. Hoover, 1948, p. 471.) For a comprehensive discussion of "base level" and "grade," see Bibliog., Thornbury, Wm. D., 1954, pp. 105–110.

Streams that have not yet reached grade are apt to have waterfalls where they cross hard rocks, and lakes where they flow through basins. They are then said to be young and their valleys are in an early stage of erosion. In this condition they are actively cutting downward and headward. For a time a lake may reduce the inflowing streams to temporary grade (Fig. 351), but at last the lake will be drained and the streams will renew erosion

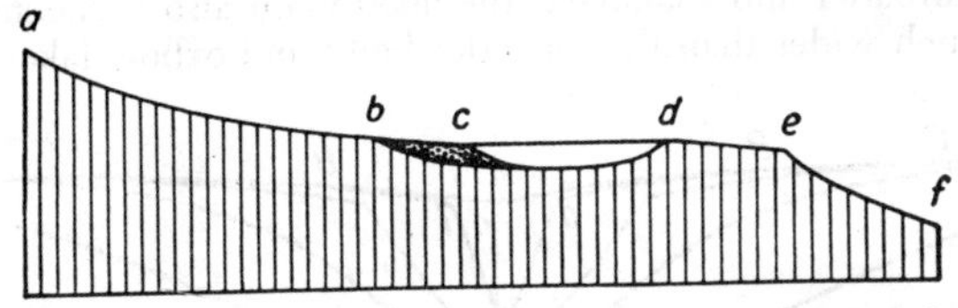

Fig. 351. A temporary grade (*ab*) determined by the lake *cd*; *bc*, delta; *de*, portion of original slope of stream channel; *ef*, upper part of stream profile which is being cut downward to a grade controlled by conditions downstream from *f* (possibly another lake or a hard rock layer). As soon as *e* reaches *d*, by headward cutting, the draining of the lake, *cd*, will begin.

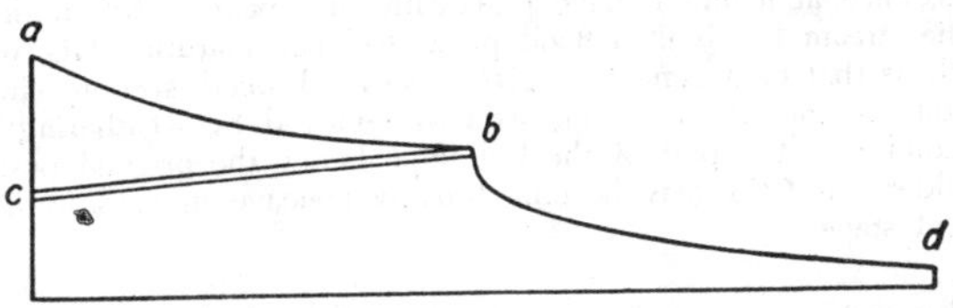

Fig. 352. Profile of a stream channel, showing how a hard rock layer, *cb*, retards the erosion of the channel upstream from *b*. *b* is a local base level.

toward a new grade. In like manner, a resistant rock may bring the stream above it to a temporary grade (Fig. 352).

While the stream in its youth is eroding its channel, weathering, soil creep, earth flow, and landslides cooperate to lower the valley walls. At first the walls are comparatively steep and the V-section is narrow (Fig. 353). As grade is approached vertical erosion becomes slower, and with the slackening of this process, weathering and mass movement relatively gain in speed, so that the V broadens, *i.e.*, its angle becomes more obtuse. When at grade the river is said to be mature. If all the streams in a region are at grade, the topography is mature. The valleys are broad, there is no sharp dividing line between hills and valleys, and there are no waterfalls and lakes.

From the inception of maturity, lateral erosion becomes more effective than downward cutting. The river builds a flood plain on which it meanders. On the outer curve of each bend the current erodes and on the inner curve it deposits. The beginning of maturity marks the end of the distinct V-section of the valley (Fig. 353, E). During maturity the hills are lowered, the valley grows broader and shallower, the flood plain also broadens until it is much wider than the meander belt,[4] and oxbow lakes result

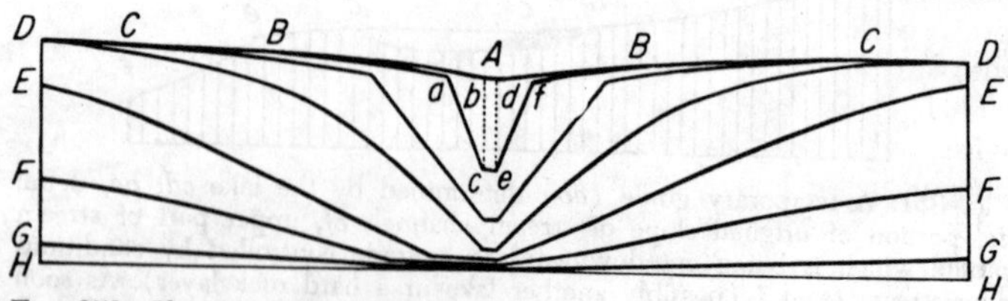

FIG. 353. Changes in the profile section of a valley from youth to old age. *A*, initial stage. *BB*, youth. *CC*, late youth. *DD*, early maturity; here the shoulders, once at *a* and *f*, have practically disappeared. *EE*, middle maturity; the stream has built a flood plain. *FF*, late maturity. *GG*, old age; the profile is that of a peneplain. *HH*, base level. *bced*, section which was cut by the stream; *abc* and *def*, sections removed by weathering. Under certain conditions the part of the hill slope below the original position of the shoulder (in *CC*) may become broadly concave upward in *DD* and subsequent stages.

from the coalescence of meanders (**288**). Without any sudden change river and valley pass into old age and so complete the normal cycle of erosion. When the uplands have all been reduced to low swells and all the streams meander on broad flood plains, the topography as a whole is old (**282**).

Summarizing with reference to the cycle of erosion of streams and valleys: youth is marked by relatively steep valley sides, occasional waterfalls and lakes, and a V-shaped transverse section of the valley; maturity is characterized by a meandering stream, absence of lakes and waterfalls, a flood plain which is not much wider than the meander belt, and a rolling hill-and-valley topography; and old age is characterized by broad,

[4] The part of a flood plain between two lines tangent to the outer bends of all the meanders is called the *meander belt*

shallow valleys, broad flood plains, much wider than the meander belts, and the presence of numerous oxbow lakes.

The foregoing description applies more especially to the cycle in regions which have a normal rainfall and a fair covering of vegetation. Where the rainfall is deficient and the vegetation scant, the topographic history approaches that of the arid cycle (**306**). Furthermore, the differences in the relative resistance of the rocks to erosion may distinctly modify the topographic forms at any particular stage in the cycle. For instance, in areas underlain by approximately horizontal strata, the hard layers may preserve steep cliffs at their outcropping edges from youth even into late old age of the district (cf. **300, B**).

304. Cycle of mountain glacier erosion. As with rivers, so with mountain glaciers, it is possible to recognize a progressive change in the topography according to the amount of erosion to which the region has been subjected. Imagine an upland on which glaciers are beginning to make themselves manifest. The first work of erosion will consist of the carving of drift hollows and then of small cirques. As the process goes on, the cirques will grow larger and will lead out to glacial valleys. That portion of the old upland which has not yet been touched by ice abrasion will constantly diminish in area, for, by headward sapping, cirques on the opposite sides of a divide will approach one another. Thus the upland will become *scalloped* (Fig. 354, A). To a less degree the divides between adjacent valleys that open in the same direction will grow narrower as the valleys are scoured deeper and wider. If glacial erosion continues long enough, adjacent cirques may meet in sharp-edged ridges, and the old upland will then remain only in isolated areas (Fig. 354, B). At a still later stage the last remnants of the upland will disappear and all the divides will be knife-edge ridges rising at junction points into abrupt peaks (Fig. 354, C).

305. Cycle of marine erosion. There are two phases of the cycle of marine erosion, that for coasts which have been relatively elevated with respect to sea level (coasts of emergence), and that for coasts which have been relatively depressed (coasts of submergence). The elevated coast may at first be characterized landward by a coastal plain which slopes gently to the water's edge and then continues with the same inclination beneath the water. The shore line is relatively straight and monotonous. Since the water is shallow, the waves are forced to

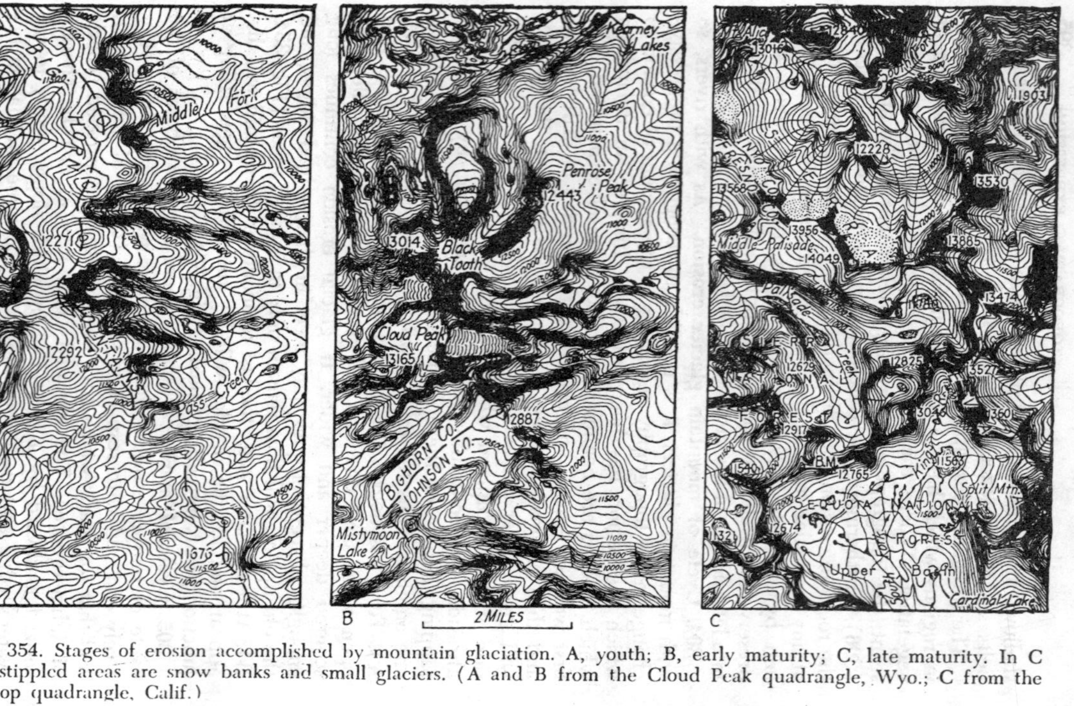

FIG. 354. Stages of erosion accomplished by mountain glaciation. A, youth; B, early maturity; C, late maturity. In C the stippled areas are snow banks and small glaciers. (A and B from the Cloud Peak quadrangle, Wyo.; C from the Bishop quadrangle, Calif.)

break some little distance offshore, and where they break they churn up the bottom sediments and pile them up seaward as an offshore bar (Fig. 355, I and II) (273). Between the bar and the mainland is a lagoon of clear salt water. The shore is now in a young stage. Meanwhile the waves cut deeper and they begin to cut into the seaward side of the bar; winds blow the dry sands of the bar over into the lagoon; and streams carry mud and sand into the lagoon from the land side. Thus, two important changes

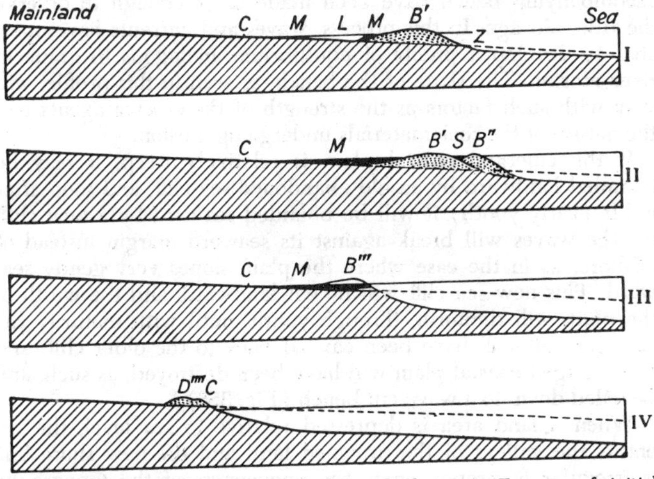

Fig. 355. Development of a shore line of elevation. Z, zone of initial wave attack; *B'*, *B"*, *B'''*, offshore bar; *C*, original shore line; *D''''*, dunes; *L*, lagoon; *M*, marsh. (*After W. M. Davis.*)

are in progress: the bar is migrating landward and the lagoon is filling up. Gradually plants take root in the shallowing lagoon which eventually becomes a marsh. Over this marsh the bar travels, usually as a body of sand dunes, and at length the edge of the marsh is exposed on the sea side of the bar, that is, on the beach (Fig. 355, III). It is recognizable as a dark band of peat, and very often lumps or *bowlders* of peat, more or less rounded by the waves, may be seen on the beach. Finally, there comes a time when the bar has crossed the entire width of the marsh and has advanced on to what was the land side of the lagoon while the latter existed. The shore line is now mature (Fig. 355, IV). It is still nearly straight, but it has a low cliff or *nip* where the waves are cutting into the original coastal plain. The fact is that the waves, by this complicated process, have so far deepened the water that they now break against the shore instead of far out as formerly. They have moved their locus of attack to the land. Henceforth, during maturity, they may cut inland, but the process will slacken and the land will probably suffer elevation or depression and so start a new cycle before the cliff and its accompanying bench have been made large enough to deserve the title, old age. In this process, waves and currents have operated to develop a profile of equilibrium analogous to grade in river erosion. The slope of the bench, as seen in this profile, will vary with such factors as the strength of the erosive agents and the nature of the rock materials undergoing erosion.

If the emerged coastal plain is relatively steep, it may be bounded landward by an old abandoned sea cliff, and soon after uplift (early youth) it will be bounded seaward by a new cliff, for the waves will break against its seaward margin instead of offshore, as in the case where the plain slopes very gently seaward. This new sea cliff will be cut landward, and the width of the plain will diminish, through youth, until with maturity the younger cliff will have been carried back to the older cliff, and the emerged coastal plain will have been destroyed, as such, and bevelled down to a wave-cut bench (Fig. 356).[5]

When a land area is depressed relative to sea level, the sea enters the valleys of the drowned land and the new shore line is irregular in proportion to the unevenness of the topography at the time of submergence. The headlands and islands are more strongly attacked by the waves, and the débris, distributed by currents, finds lodgment here and there in bays or on the lee sides of promontories and islands. This is the youthful condition of the depressed coast. Spits, tombolos, bayhead beaches, baymouth bars, etc. (**273**), are abundantly represented. In the lapse of time the islands are demolished, the headlands are cut far back, and the bays are well filled with sediments, partly marine and partly dropped by inflowing rivers, so that the shore line becomes nearly straight (Fig. 357). This is maturity. Old age is approached, as in the case of the elevated coast, by long continued landward erosion of the coast by the waves.

[5] See Bibliog., Putnam, William C., 1937.

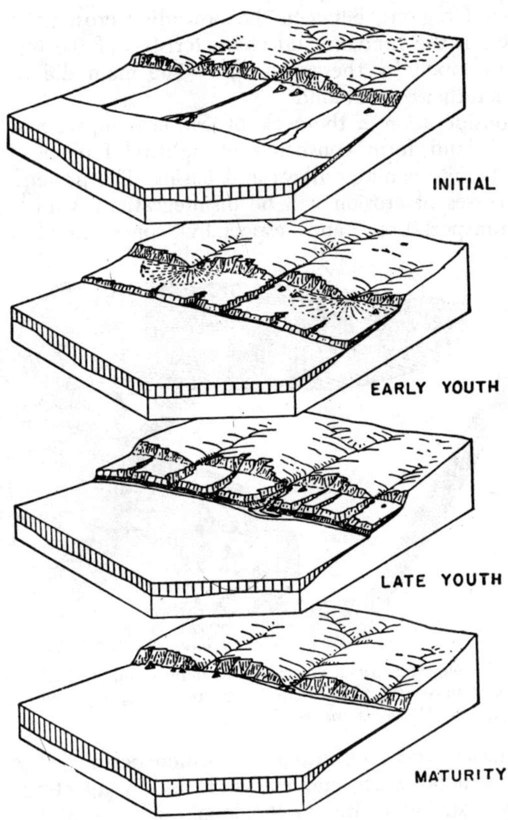

FIG. 356. Development of an emerged, relatively steep coastal plain, where the land mass is bordered by deep water close to shore. (*After Putnam, with permission of the Journal of Geology and the University of Chicago Press. See Bibliog., Putnam, W. C.*, 1937, *p.* 848.)

Lake shores may undergo the same types of erosion as sea shores, but the existence of a lake is generally too short for the complete development of its shore.

306. Cycle of arid erosion. As has been pointed out by W. M. Davis,[6] there is no radical difference, in arid regions as compared

[6] Bibliog., Davis, W. M., 1930.

with humid regions, between the prevailing erosional processes nor between the fundamental characteristics of the topographic forms developed by these processes. The main differences are in degree rather than in kind.

For consideration of the cycle of arid erosion, we may assume an initial land form consisting of uplifted fault-block mountains, with intervening valleys and basins. The principal agents and processes of erosion will be disintegration; wind scour and wind transportation; and especially concentrated abrasion,

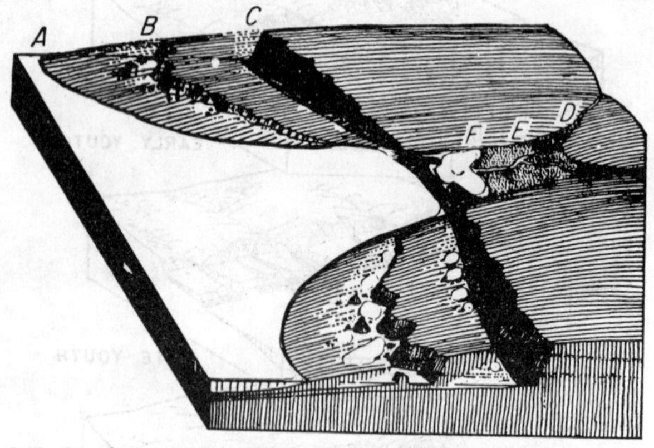

FIG. 357. Development of a shore line of depression. *A*, initial shore line; *B*, shore line in youth; *C*, same in maturity; *D, E, F*, deposits made by rivers. (*After W. M. Davis and W. H. Snyder.*)

transportation and intermittent deposition performed by stream wash, sheetflood wash, and rill wash, locally affecting areas irregularly distributed, but in the long run more or less equally affecting all parts of the region. Landslides, mudflow, and soil creep also play an important role in lowering slopes and in furnishing waste for transportation. Because of the absence, or paucity of vegetation, detritus is coarser, in relation to the time or period of development in this cycle, than it is in the case of erosion under a humid climate.

During the earliest stages in the cycle of arid erosion, stream valleys and branch valleys develop; the uplands are vigorously dissected; and the products of erosion are carried out on to the valley or basin floors. Streams tend to cut down to a grade which will have a slope depending on distance of transport, amount and size of material carried, etc., and the same may be said of sheetfloods and rill wash. By these methods of erosion of running water, assisted by the important process of deflation, a rock-floored plain is carved out of the front of the mountain mass, an apron-like plain, sloping basinward. This is known as a *pediment*. One of the striking features of arid physiography is the pediment, thinly and discontinuously veneered with sand and stony waste, and usually cut out of the same rock materials as the adjacent mountains themselves. This plain, the pediment, is the homologue of the peneplain in humid climates. In the lower central parts of the basins, where sedimentation prevails, are shallow lakes, playas, and salinas (see Fig. 308).

Under the conditions just described, the region may be said to be in youth. As erosion progresses, the pediment flanking each mountain mass is extended, encroaching more and more upon the uplands, and adjacent pediments may at length coalesce as a *pediplain*.

"Maturity will be reached when the drainage of all the arid region becomes integrated with respect to a single aggraded basin base-level, so that the slopes lead from all parts of the surface to a single area for the deposition of the waste . . . . There will appear . . . large rock-floored plains sloping toward large waste-floored plains; the plains will be interrupted only where parts of the initial highlands and masses of unusually resistant rocks here and there, survive as isolated residual mountains [Inselberge, or island mountains] . . . . In so far as the plains are rock-floored they will truncate the rocks without regard to their structure"[7] (**282, 300, A**).

With further extension of the pediplain, an old-age stage may be conceived at which all island mountains will have disappeared and only a monotonous undulating plain remains.

Topographic Expression Developed in Two Successive Cycles

307. Topographic unconformity defined. *Topographic unconformity* is a term applied to land surfaces which consist of two parts that are out of adjustment with one another. This condition is brought about by an interruption in the ordinary course of an erosion cycle. For instance, rivers and agents of weathering may have produced a late mature topography which is then uplifted and subjected to mountain glaciation. If the invading glaciers disappear before they carry their erosion beyond youth,

[7] Bibliog., Davis, W. M., 1909, pp. 303, 304.

the area will show two kinds of topography: (1) the mature upland incised by (2) the new glacial valleys, and these two topographic phases will be out of harmony with one another, that is, they will be topographically unconformable. Their relation will be that of *topographic unconformity* due to an *interruption* in the normal cycle (Fig. 358). The same mature upland, incised by streams with young valleys of a new cycle, would be another case of such unconformity (profile B, Fig. 353). Abandoned shore lines (308) are a third illustration of topographic unconformity.

308. Abandoned shore lines. Shore-line features—beaches, bars, reefs, benches, and the like—originate for the most part

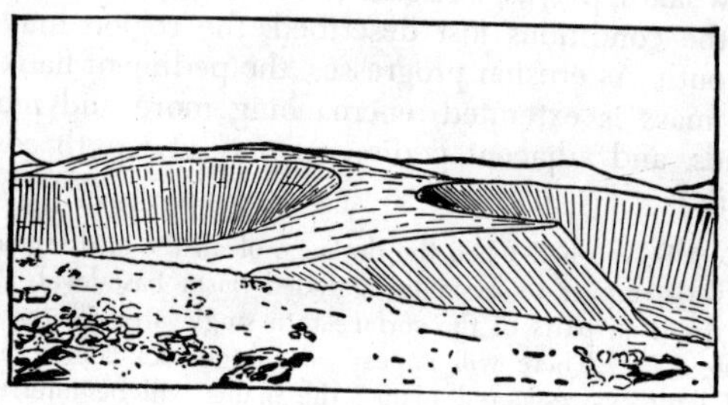

FIG. 358. Topographic unconformity. A gently rolling preglacial land surface has been invaded by ice which has produced a series of steep-sided cirques. The land is in an early mature stage of glacial erosion. (*After W. W. Atwood.*)

at or near the level of the lake or sea where they are formed. If the water level rises a few feet, relative to the land, they will be submerged; but if it suffers relative lowering, they will be left stranded, as it were, some distance above the new shore line. They are then said to be *abandoned*. Such shore lines are too often called *elevated* before substantial evidence has been brought forward to prove that the land rose, rather than that water level was lowered. *Abandoned* is a better epithet for it implies nothing as to the manner in which the change in relative water level was effected. A shore line may be abandoned, in the case of the sea, either by actual uplift of the land or by actual depression of the sea, and, in the case of lakes, either by differential tilting of the land such that at one end the lake floor is more or less exposed, or by lowering of the lake as a whole through draining or evaporation (Fig. 359). Whatever the real cause may be, the

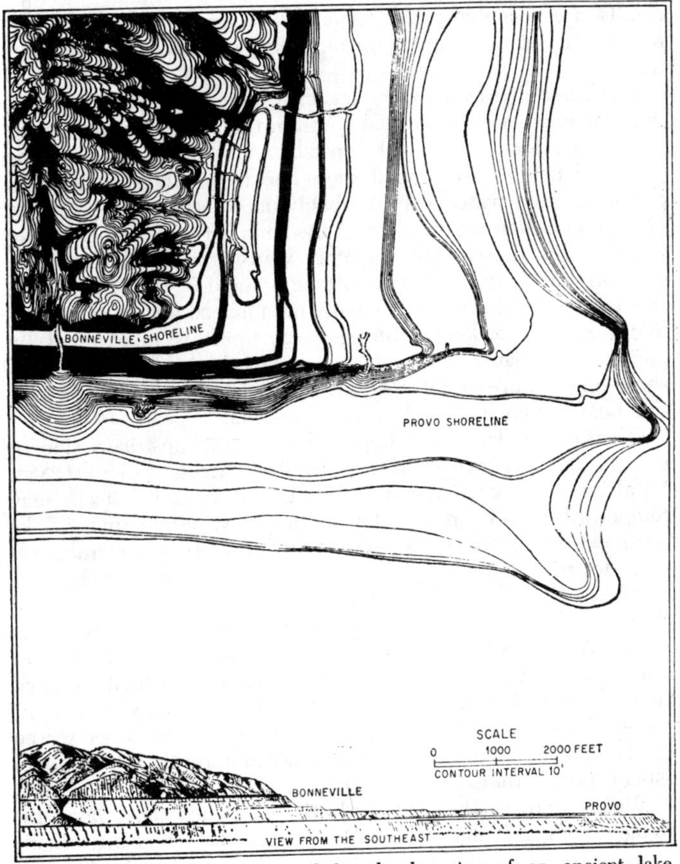

FIG. 359. Shore terraces exposed by the lowering of an ancient lake. Near Dove Creek, Utah. Map above, view below. (*After G. K. Gilbert; drawn by G. Thompson.*)

results are essentially the same. These abandoned shore-line features are in topographic unconformity with the adjoining land forms.

If relative depression of water level sets in after a long period of constancy, and continues at a uniform rate until it is succeeded by another long interval of constant water level, there will be only one belt of abandoned shore-line forms, those of the first period of fixed water level. Probably no other evidence of wave or current action will be seen in the zone between this old shore line and the present one. In other words, for the development of shore-line features there must be a stand of the water level, and the longer this stand, the more pronounced will be the shore-line forms. If a long-enduring great uplift is interrupted by pauses, each pause will be represented by a belt of abandoned shore-line features (Fig. 299). Naturally, the older, higher ones will bear evidence of most subaerial erosion.

Occasionally lakes are impounded on the upstream side of natural barriers which have been built across valleys (**288**). Landslide débris, morainal material, and even ice itself, may temporarily block up a valley in this way. While such a lake is in existence, various shore-line features, both constructional and destructional, may be formed. Beaches may be built; a small *nip* (bench and cliff) may be cut in original unconsolidated deposits of the valley side; and inflowing streams may construct deltas. After the barrier has been cut through, or, in the case of ice, has melted away, the lake will be drained, and small beaches, deltas, wave-cut benches, etc., may be seen on the slopes of the valley through which, perhaps, a stream now flows. If ice served as the dam, the shore-line phenomena end abruptly at the former site of the ice front.

With regard to the field study of abandoned shore lines, the geologist should note that their original characters are usually more or less concealed by vegetation and by erosion. Their recognition depends, first, upon a knowledge of the typical features of shore-line phenomena in their natural position, and likewise upon the ability to distinguish between them and topographic forms of similar appearance (**274**). River terraces are especially apt to be mistaken for abandoned lake beaches. However, river terraces are not associated with abandoned deltas which extend out from their outer margins (Fig. 359), and riverlaid gravels are usually mingled with more sand and fine clastic material than are beach gravels. The latter are relatively *clean*. Also, beach materials grade from pebbles and bowlders at the inner margin to finer pebbles and sand toward the outer margin (87), whereas river terrace gravels exhibit no such regular gradation.

Topographic Expression in Its Relation to Rock Materials and Geologic Structure

309. Valley pattern. Valley pattern,[8] or what commonly amounts to the same thing, drainage pattern, depends on the

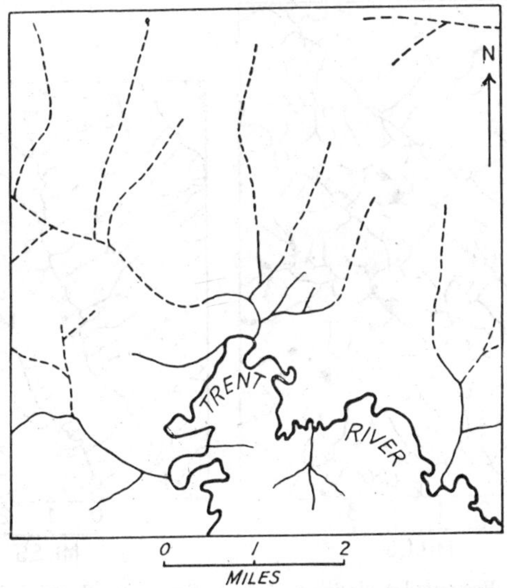

Fig. 360. Insequent drainage pattern. (Trent River quadrangle, N.C.)

distribution of bedrock, the attitude of stratiform rocks, the arrangement of surfaces of weakness, such as joints and faults, and on a number of other structural features. Consequently it may be used to assist in the interpretation of geologic structure as well as in the study of land forms.

Young streams, flowing on a nearly level plain or upon irregular superficial deposits of indefinite form and structure, are likely to wander here and there in following the irregularities of the ground. This type of drainage is called *insequent* (Fig. 360).

[8] See Bibliog., Zernitz, Emilie R., 1932.

A rectangular, or trellis-like pattern may result from the control of a rectangular joint or fault system (Fig. 361), or from the influence of tilted or folded, alternating resistant and weak strata (Fig. 362). By the updoming of a relatively flat area, a radial drainage may be induced (Fig. 363). If the radial streams intersect concentric belts of hard and weak rocks, this pattern may be taken as substantial evidence for there having once been such an updoming. The dendritic (treelike) arrangement of rivers and

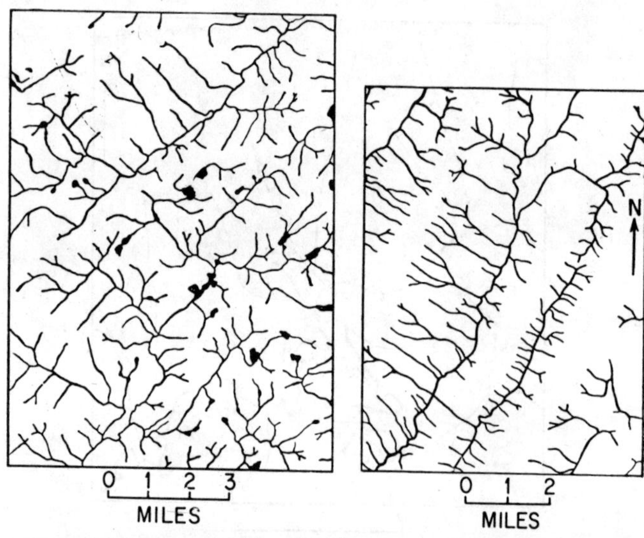

Fig. 361. Rectangular drainage pattern controlled by joint and fault systems. (Elizabethtown sheet, N.Y.)

Fig. 362. Rectangular drainage pattern controlled by folded strata. (Monterey sheet, Va.–W.Va.)

their branches is most common, and is characteristic of regions where structural controls are not exaggerated (Fig. 364).

In many parts of the country, where soils are mostly residual and where the underlying rocks are gently folded strata, hills and divides may roughly correspond with domes and anticlines, and valleys, with basins or synclines. Under these circumstances it is often a question whether the beds have sagged, as erosion proceeded, and thus have produced what might be termed *false structures* (344), or whether the inclinations of the beds are true structural dips which controlled the direction and pattern of the drainage. Where folded structure does govern the drain-

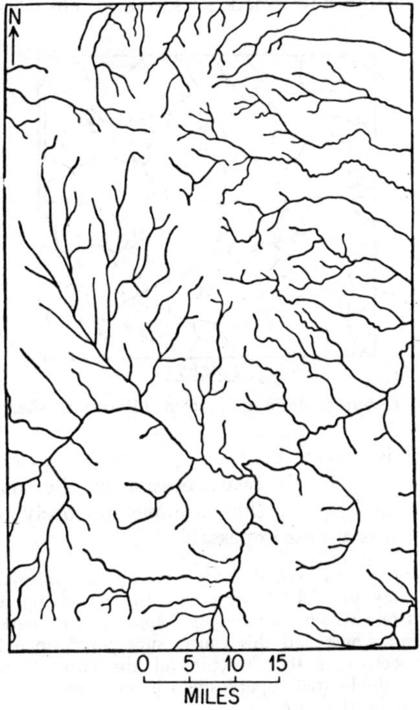

FIG. 363. Radial drainage pattern of the Black Hills of Wyoming and South Dakota. The range is situated principally in the upper half of the map. (*After N. H. Darton.*)

age, the control is effected principally by the harder layers which resist erosion and tend to hold up the land surface. The smaller streams are likely to exhibit the closer relation to the dip, for the master streams not only may cut downward irrespective of the structure, but also may swing sideways out of the area of any possible original control. This statement may apply whether the main drainage is consequent or superposed.[9]

310. Badland topography. Badlands are a special case of young topography in which gullies are numerous and are separated by divides having steep to vertical walls. *Badland topography* is typically developed in semiarid climates where the

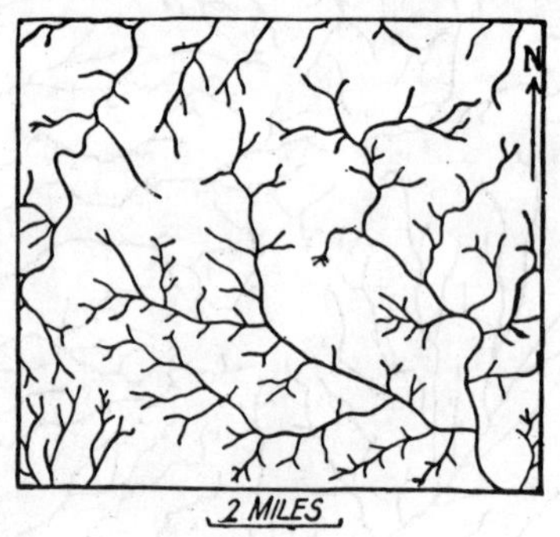

Fig. 364. Dendritic drainage pattern. (Wartburg sheet, Tenn.)

rock material is clayey, containing scattered clastic grains and fragments, and where headward erosion by the smaller streams is active. The land surface thus becomes so closely and so deeply dissected that it is almost impassable.[10]

[9] A *consequent stream* is one having its course controlled by, and its direction essentially parallel to, the dip of the underlying strata. A *superposed stream* is one which acquired its course on a formation now mostly eroded away and which had this course superposed upon the underlying formation irrespective of the structure of the latter formation. Melton (Bibliog., 1959) thinks that superposition is much more common than has been assumed to be the case.

[10] See Bibliog., Carman, Max F., Jr., 1958.

Chapter 13

TOPOGRAPHIC MAPS AND PROFILE SECTIONS

Features Shown on Topographic Maps

311. Classification of features. A *topographic map* is one that shows the size, shape, and distribution of features of the earth's surface. On the topographic maps published by the U.S. Geological Survey[1] these features are classified in three groups: (1) *relief*, including hills, valleys, plains, cliffs, and the like; (2) *drainage* or *water*, including seas, lakes, ponds, streams, canals, swamps, etc.; and (3) *culture*, including many of the works of man, such as towns, cities, roads, railroads, boundaries, and names. Relief is printed in brown, drainage in blue, and culture in black. In addition to these, on some maps, forests are indicated by a green tint. The significance of the conventional signs employed[2] is often given in a key either on the back of the map or in the right margin. Such a key is called a *legend*. In it the various signs are arranged in a column with those for relief above, those for drainage next, and those for culture at the lower part of the table. Each symbol or line is inclosed in a small rectangle, and all the rectangles are of equal size. If the student has to prepare a topographic map of any kind, he will do well to make the legend for it according to the scheme just outlined. In any case the map must have a legend.

312. Contours. Relief may be represented on topographic maps by contour lines, by tinting, by hachures, or by shading. In some cases a combination of two or more of these methods is adopted. We shall concern ourselves only with contour maps, since these alone can be used for making satisfactory measurements of height, slope, and distance.

A *contour* is a line drawn through points having the same altitude. The shore line at mean sea level is called the contour of

[1] Lists of these maps for each state may be obtained from the Director, U.S. Geological Survey, Washington, D.C.

[2] Bibliog., Salisbury, R. D., and W. W. Atwood, 1908.

zero elevation, mean sea level being taken as the datum plane from which other contours are measured. A contour representing an elevation of 20 ft. is the line of intersection of the land surface with a horizontal plane 20 ft. vertically above mean sea level. If the sea were to rise 20 ft., the new shore line would coincide with this contour. In the same way, if the sea were to rise 40 ft., the new shore line would coincide with the 40-ft.

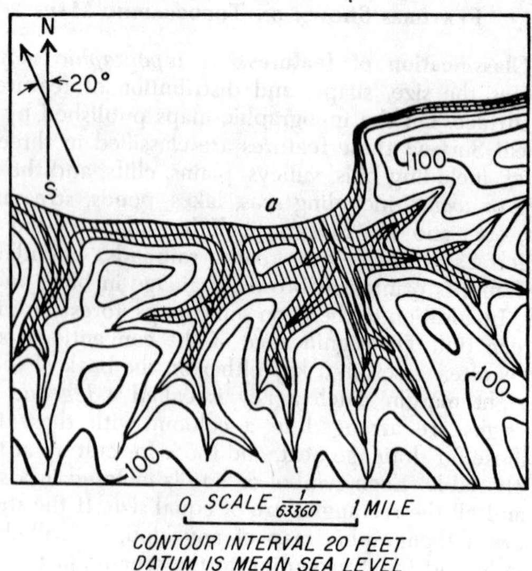

FIG. 365. Contour map of a land area bordering a shore line. If sea level were to rise 40 ft., the shaded portion of the present land would be submerged and the new shore line would be the present 40-ft. contour. The hill south of *a* would become an island.

contour (Fig. 365); and so on. When the contours thus indicate differences of level of 20 ft., the vertical distance of 20 ft. is termed the *contour interval.* Other contour intervals, such as 1, 5, 10, 50, 100, 200, and 250 ft. are sometimes chosen instead of 20 ft., but ordinarily only one contour interval is used on a given map.

Certain contours are printed more heavily than others. When the contour interval is 20 ft., the 100-ft. contours are heavy (Fig.

365). A broad contour line of this kind may be called an *index contour*, for it is labelled here and there along its length by a small number which denotes its elevation above mean sea level.

If sea level were to rise, the water would extend up the valleys and so form bays, while the hills and ridges would become headlands. Some hills, having been entirely cut off from the mainland, might become islands. In the present connection the significance of these facts is that: (1) contours bend or "loop" upstream in valleys; and (2) the upper contours on hills are relatively short, closed curves. Hollows without outlets are also indicated by closed contours, but they are distinguished from hill contours by having short hachures on the inner (downslope) side of the line (Fig. 312).

For portrayal of a given type of topography, a contour interval should be chosen sufficiently small to reveal the details of that topography. For example, in deep canyon country, where the relief is many hundreds of feet within distances of only a few miles, an interval of 250 ft. may be adequate. On the other hand, on a nearly flat constructional plain, such as a coastal plain adjacent to the sea, or a broad delta flat, where the relief between local swells and depressions may be only 5 or 10 ft., a contour interval as small as only 1 or 2 ft. may be advisable, for otherwise significant surface details may be completely overlooked.

313. Scale. The scale of a topographic map is usually noted in the lower margin. It may be expressed in several ways. For instance, it may be denoted by such a statement as, "one inch = one mile," or it may be represented graphically by a measured straight line as in Figs. 365 and 366. Again, the scale may be expressed as a ratio or a fraction, the latter being known as the *representative fraction* (R. F.). Thus, if the scale is 1:125,000, or 1/125,000, this means that the distance between any two points on the map is 1/125,000 of the actual distance between the originals of the two points on the earth's surface; or, to put it in another way, a map 6 in. long on a scale of 1:125,000 shows an area 6 × 125,000 in. = 11.8 miles long.

Most of the maps of the U.S. Geological Survey are constructed on one or another of these scales: 1:24,000; 1:31,680; 1:62,500; 1:63,360; 1:125,000; or 1:250,000. A scale of 1:24,000 is a scale of 1 in. equals 2,000 ft. On maps with a scale of 1:31,680, 1 in. equals ½ mile, and where the scale is 1:63,360, 1 in. equals 1 mile. Maps with scales of 1:62,500, 1:125,000, or

1:250,000 are 15-min. maps, 30-min. maps, and degree maps, respectively.[3] On the scale of 1:62,500, 1 in. on the map represents a distance a little less than 1 mile; on the scale of 1:125,000, 1 in. represents a little less than 2 miles; and on the scale of 1:250,000, 1 in. represents somewhat less than 4 miles.

314. Direction. Compass directions are sufficiently indicated on many maps by meridians and parallels of latitude. On large-scale maps, however, a full arrow is commonly drawn, properly oriented, pointing to true north, and a half arrow, intersecting the full arrow in its center, for magnetic north (Fig. 365). The angle between these two arrows should be marked, and also the

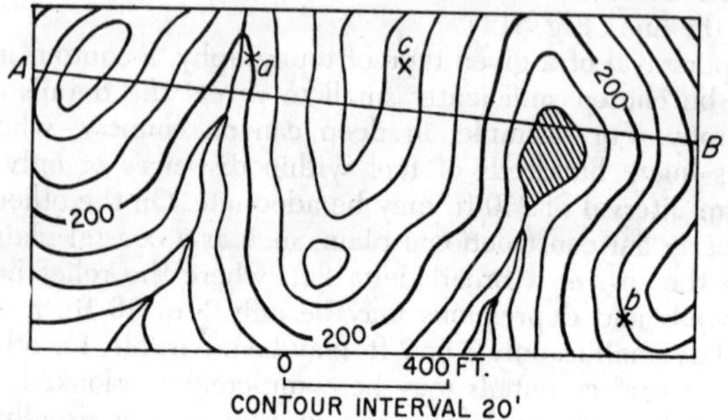

Fig. 366. Contour map of a land area of moderate relief. Diagonal ruling, lake; *AB*, line of section.

date when the observations were made, for the magnetic variation changes from year to year (**356**).

315. Requisite data on a completed contour map. The more important features of contour maps have been described above. A contour map is not complete unless it has a name, is accompanied by a legend, and has designated upon it the scale, the contour interval, the datum plane from which the contours were measured, and compass directions.

316. Air photographic maps. The subject of air photographs and their use as maps is reserved mainly for Chap. 17. Such photographs, taken from a considerable height, looking vertically downward, are essentially topographic maps. They display in

[3] For example, a 15-min. map covers a rectangular area 15 minutes of latitude by 15 minutes of longitude.

remarkable detail the form and distribution of features of the earth's surface. When properly prepared, they can be accurately contoured (**456,** Sec. 4), and they can be used for measuring distances and slope angles, but these operations require the use of certain precise instruments in the hands of trained specialists.

Profile Sections

317. Nature of profile sections. A *profile section* is a diagram showing the shape of the surface of the land as it would appear in vertical cross section. A profile section consists of four lines which completely inclose a space (Fig. 367). They are the profile line, the base line, and the two end lines. The profile line, which is the top line in the diagram, represents the intersection of a vertical plane with the land surface. The base line is drawn horizontal and is chosen at a convenient distance below the lowest

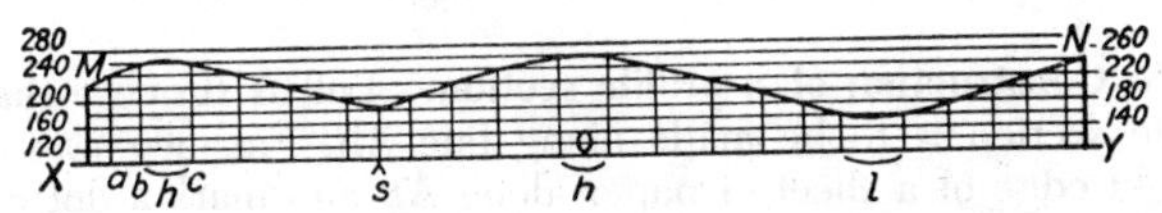

Fig. 367. Profile section along line *AB* in Fig. 366. (Drawn to natural scale.)

point of the profile line. The end lines are perpendicular to the base line.

The position of a profile section should always be indicated by a line, called a *line of section*, on an accompanying map (*AB*, Fig. 366), for a section has no practical value unless its location is known. The line of section is really the top line of the profile section as seen in plan.

Every profile section has a horizontal scale, measured in units on the base line, and a vertical scale which is measured in units of elevation perpendicularly above the base line. If these two scales are the same, the section is said to be *drawn to natural scale*. Sometimes the vertical scale is *exaggerated, i.e.*, it is made two or more times as great as the horizontal scale (Figs. 367, 368). Exaggeration is useful for profile sections of lands of very slight relief merely to emphasize the positions of hills and valleys. Ordinarily natural scale should be employed. Unless accurate measurements are to be made, the vertical scale may be 1 in.

to 5,000 ft. if the horizontal scale is approximately or actually an inch to a mile (1:62,500 or 1:63,360). This is so near to natural scale that it is satisfactory for most purposes, and it has the advantage that the contour interval is commensurable with the vertical scale.

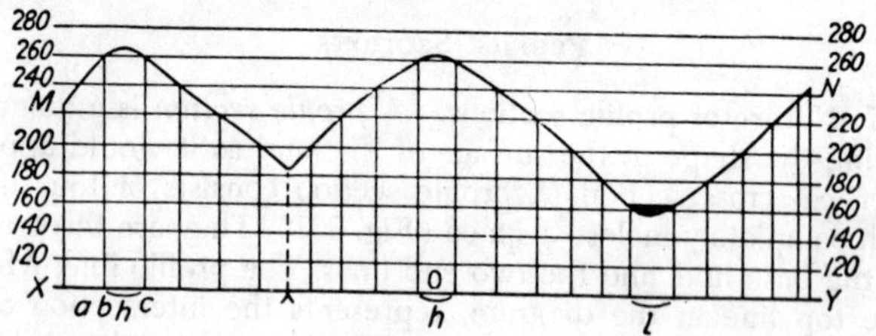

FIG. 368. Profile section along line *AB* in Fig. 366. Similar to Fig. 367 except that the vertical scale is three times as great as the horizontal scale. Therefore, in Fig. 368 the vertical scale is exaggerated three times.

318. Construction of a profile section. Let us suppose that a profile section is to be made along line *AB*, Fig. 366. Lay the straight-edge of a sheet of paper along *AB* and mark a dot on it at each point where a contour is crossed by *AB* and a small caret at each point where a stream is crossed by *AB*. Connect the dots for the upper contour on each hill by a curved line (*h*, Fig. 367), to show where the hills are situated. In the same way connect dots representing the two margins of a lake (*l*, Fig. 367). It is well also to label some of the index contours by their elevation numbers. Upon a piece of profile paper ruled with coordinates to $\frac{1}{20}$ in., draw $XY = AB$ for the base line of the section. Transfer the points, carets, etc., to *XY*, marking them lightly with a lead pencil. The first three of these points are lettered *a, b,* and *c,* the summit contour is *h,* and the stream is at *s* (Fig. 367). Since $XY = AB$, obviously the horizontal scale of the section is equal to that of the map. If we let $\frac{1}{20}$ in. = 20 ft. for the vertical scale, this section will be drawn to natural scale.

The lowest point crossed by *AB* happens to be at the lake where the elevation is somewhat less than 180 ft. Therefore, 100 ft. above sea level would be a convenient elevation for the base line. Sea level itself may be chosen if preferred. The first contour cut by *AB* is the 240-ft. line, represented by *a* on *XY*. Make a dot vertically above *a* on the coordinate for 240 ft. Vertically above *b*, the position of the 260-ft. contour, mark a dot on the 260-ft. coordinate. Similarly, mark a dot on the proper coordinate above each point on *XY*. Connect these points by a curved line, *MN*, which is the profile line of the section. Note that the hilltops are a little higher than 260 ft., but not so high as 280 ft.; that the stream channel is lower than 200 ft., but not so low as 180 ft.; and that the lake surface is below 180 ft., but above 160 ft.

319. Enlargement of profile sections. Profile sections may be enlarged by multiplying both the vertical and horizontal scales by the same factor. This may be done in two ways. Suppose that the section of Fig. 367 is to be enlarged twice. Draw a base line double the length of *AB* (Fig. 366) upon a piece of

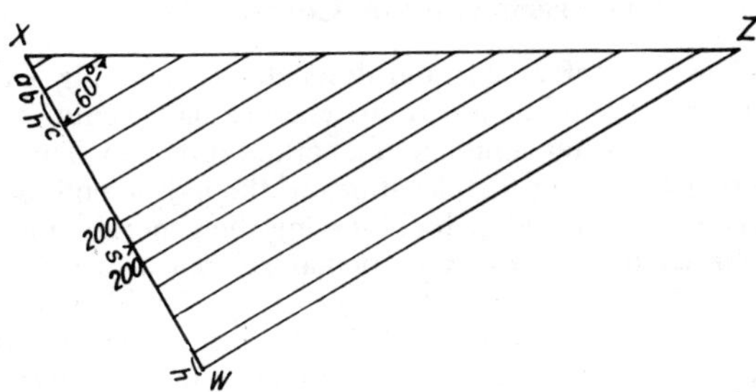

FIG. 369. Diagram illustrating a method of enlarging a profile section. $XZ = 2XW$. $XW = XY/2$ in Fig. 367.

profile paper. As described in the preceding article, mark on the edge of a sheet of paper the positions of the contours and streams intersected by *AB*. Lay this paper against the base line so that the point, *A*, will coincide with the left end of the line. Then transfer the contour positions in such a way that the space between each two adjacent points will be doubled, that is, the spaces, beginning at the left, will be equal to 2*Xa*, 2*ab*, 2*bc*, and so on, in order (cf. Fig. 359). Having set off all these points, continue as in Art. **318**, but with a vertical scale of $\frac{1}{20}$ in. = 10 ft. instead of $\frac{1}{20}$ in. = 20 ft.

The second method is illustrated in Fig. 369. For convenience only half the length, *XO*, of the section in Fig. 367 is here enlarged. Lay off the base line $XZ = 2XO = 2AB/2$, as in the first method. From *X* draw $XW = AB/2$, making an angle of 60°

with *XZ*. Mark on *XW* the contour and stream positions, as explained in Art. **318**, from *X* to *W*. Draw *ZW*, and from each of the points on *XW* draw a line to *XZ* parallel to *ZW*. These lines will intercept distances on *XZ* just double the distances which they intercept on *XW*.

Enlargement may be accomplished more readily as follows: Let *XW*, Fig. 369, represent the line of section on the map. Place the paper, on which the enlarged section is to be plotted, so that the base line, *XZ*, of this section (drawn as many times longer than *XW* as the desired enlargement) is at an angle to *XW*, as shown. Draw *WZ*, and, parallel to it, draw lines through other points to be transferred from *XW* to *XZ*.

Interpretation of Contour Maps

320. Direction of ascent and descent. In studying a contour map one may want to ascertain whether one would go up or down hill in crossing contours in a certain direction. This may be done either by noting the elevations of the index contours which are successively crossed or by observing the general arrangement of all the contours without particular reference to those which are numbered. The latter method is often preferable where index contours are not crossed or where the map is so obscured by various features that finding and tracing the index contours is difficult. This second method is simple enough if it is remembered: (1) that the contours bend upstream in valleys (Figs. 365, 366); and (2) that the ground must rise away from stream courses. In crossing a valley the last contour met before reaching the stream is the first one to be passed on the other side of this stream. Similarly, the highest contour on a divide between two streams must be crossed twice without meeting any intervening higher or lower contour. Ordinarily divides are characterized by knobs or hills which are shown by closed contours. The innermost of such closed contours is the highest. The divide summit is a little higher, but less than a contour interval higher, than this uppermost contour. Obviously the position of the divide summit between two adjacent valleys must be determined in order to avoid the mistake of estimating too great an ascent in passing up from the valley floor.

321. Elevation of a given point. Suppose that one wants to know the elevation of a certain point on the map. The point may be: (1) on an index contour; (2) on a light contour; or (3) between contours. In the first case (*a*, Fig. 366) the elevation of the point may be found by following the index contour along to the nearest number which gives its height above mean sea level. The second case is illustrated by *b* in Fig. 366. To obtain the elevation of this point, first determine the elevation of the nearest index contour, here 200 ft., and whether the point is uphill or downhill from this index contour. In the figure, *b* is on the second contour uphill (see stream) from the 200-ft. line. Since the contour interval is 20 ft., *b* is 2 $\times$ 20 ft. above 200 ft.: *i.e.*, its elevation is 240 ft. above sea level. The third case is left for the student to explain. In Fig. 366, *c* may be taken as the point.

322. Spacing of contours. Figure 370 illustrates the relations of contour spacing to the steepness and form of a sloping surface.

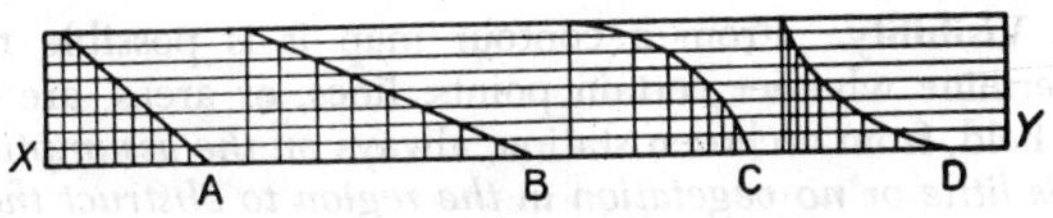

FIG. 370. Ideal profile sections of slopes.

A, *B*, *C*, and *D* are profile sections of slopes. *A* is steep; *B* is relatively gentle; *C* is convex upward; and *D* is concave upward. *XY* is the base line for all four. The vertical lines are drawn from the intersections of the profile lines with the elevation coordinates. The spaces between the verticals are equal to the distances between the contours on a map representing these slopes. This diagram shows that, with a given contour interval: (1) contours are more closely spaced on steep slopes than on gentle slopes; (2) contours are more closely spaced at the base of a surface which is convex upward, and near the top of a surface which is concave upward. When several contours run together into a single line, this line indicates a cliff, or, if the scale of the map is small, a very steep slope.

323. Distance between two points. In Fig. 371, *abc* is the profile of a hill. On a contour map the distance from *a* to *c* over the hill would be shown by the length of the straight horizontal line *de*. *abc* may be called the original of its projection, *de*. Stated in general, any line that crosses contours on a map represents a distance shorter than the actual distance along the original of that line on the earth's surface. An approximation to the real distance between two given points may be obtained by constructing a natural scale profile section between them and measuring the profile line; but this method cannot be quite accurate because contour maps can be approximately correct only at the contours. Within the limits of two adjacent contours the ground may slope uniformly or it may be irregular.

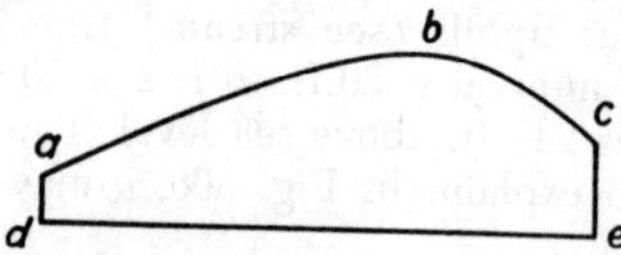

FIG. 371. Profile section of a hill to show relations between base line and profile line.

324. Visibility. From a contour map it is possible roughly to determine whether certain points, lines, or areas, are visible, in the field, from a chosen station, always *on the assumption that there is little or no vegetation in the region to obstruct the view.* In the first place we state the rules that: (1) on a convex land surface where the contours are spaced more closely at the bottom of the hill than near the top (322), points are not intervisible; and (2) on a flat surface, or on a concave surface (322), points are intervisible, in both cases (1) and (2) *in directions across the contours.*

To find out whether a distant point, *C* is hidden or not, from the observer's position, *A*, by an intermediate high point, *B*, draw a horizontal line on a chosen scale to represent the distance between A and *C*, and measure off the distance *AB* on this scale on the horizontal line. Let the lowest of the three points lie in the horizontal line. Choose a convenient vertical scale and plot the proper positions of the other two higher stations, on this scale, above the horizontal line. Draw a straight line from *A* through *B* toward *C*. If *C* lies above this line (the line of sight), *C* is visible from *A*. If it lies below the line of sight, it is not visible from *A*.

In ascertaining what areas may be visible from a given station, A, skeleton profiles of the type just described may be constructed from A across all adjacent critical points, such as hilltops and low points on gaps between hills, and the points at which these

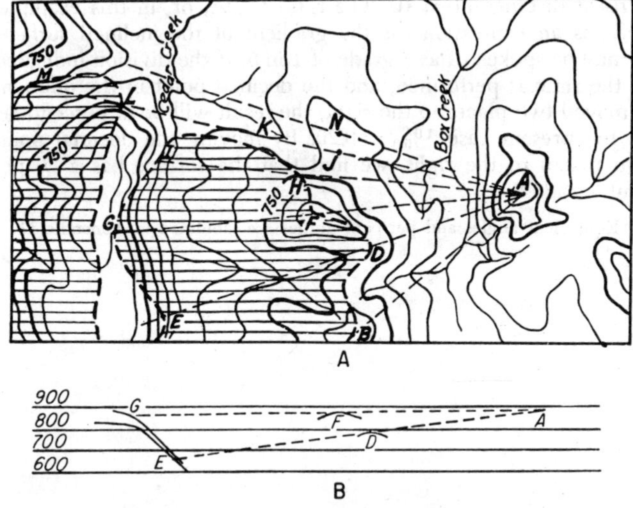

FIG. 372. A, topographic contour map. Contour interval 50 ft. The observer standing at A and looking westward (toward the left) can see the area not shaded west of Box Creek, provided the land is not forested. The shaded areas are determined by constructing skeleton profiles on lines *AB*, *AE*, *AG*, *AM*, and *AN*, as illustrated by the two profiles in the lower cross section, B.

lines of sight meet the more distant topography may then be connected by a flowing line (Fig. 372).

325. Inclination of a slope. The inclination, grade, or gradient, of a sloping surface or of a sloping line may be expressed

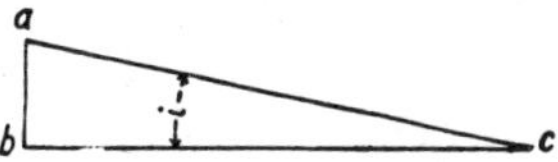

FIG. 373. Diagram showing the methods of measuring a slope.

as a ratio, as a percentage, or as an angle measured in degrees from the horizontal. Let Fig. 373 be a profile section of a sloping surface, *ac*, and suppose that $ab = 10$, and $bc = 50$, no matter in what units. i is the angle of inclination of the surface. In travelling the horizontal distance $cb = 50$, one would ascend a vertical distance $ab = 10$. The ratio ab/bc, or, in this example, $^{10}/_{50}$, is an expression for the gradient of the inclined surface. It may be spoken of as a grade of 1 in 5. If the division indicated in the ratio is performed, and the decimal point in the quotient is moved two places to the right, the result will be in percentage. In the present case $^{10}/_{50} = 0.20$. By moving the decimal point two places to the right, we find that the surface has a 20 per cent grade.[4]

[4] Equivalent angles and per cent grades are tabulated in Appendix 11.

Chapter 14

GEOLOGIC SURVEYING

PART I. GENERAL OBSERVATIONS

Nature of Geologic Surveying

326. Definition and aim. *Geologic surveying,* a term practically synonymous with geologic field work or field mapping, is the systematic examination of any region for geologic information. Its purpose may be economic or purely scientific. If economic, the investigation may be somewhat limited in its scope, the object being merely to study the phenomena which bear directly on some particular problem; but it is becoming more and more evident that the broader the range of any field examination, the more accurate and otherwise satisfactory the results are likely to be, for the interrelations of geology are numerous and intricate; and it is further true that the broader and more varied has been the training of a geologist, the more efficient he is in analyzing any kind of restricted geologic problem, be this theoretical or practical.

327. Uses of geologic surveying. Geologic surveying is fundamental to all geologic knowledge. Its uses are, therefore, numberless. It assists the engineer in determining the location and cost of tunnels, bridges, aqueducts, reservoirs, dams, and many other structures. It facilitates the work of the prospector. It shows the farmer what kind of soil he may expect to find in one place or another. It provides valuable information in reference to mining, quarrying, and the production of oil and gas. One of its principal advantages is that it locates for the manufacturer the most accessible sources of his raw materials and so enables him to obtain them at a relatively low cost. Finally, it yields to the scientist facts by which he interprets the structure and history of the earth.

328. Diversity of surveys. There are many conditions which egulate the nature of geologic surveys. Work is apt to be difficult in swampy regions, on heavily forested land, and in places where the soil cover is thick and extensive. Marked relief and high altitude increase the physical labor of exploration, and certain climates seriously handicap the geologist. Accessibility to towns and railroads is a significant factor. If the field area is far removed from civilization, a large supply of provisions has to be transported across country and travel is difficult. Where topographic maps have already been published, geologic work can be done more easily and more quickly than where such maps are poor or wanting. If air photographs (Chap. 17) are available, or if it is practical to make them in advance of field work, for an area to be surveyed, procedures may be different in many respects from the course of an investigation where such photographs are not available. Again, there are such factors as the time at the disposal of the geologist, the scale on which the geologic mapping is to be done, and, finally, the nature of the problem itself. The consequence is that geologic surveys are very diverse in respect to their needed equipment, their thoroughness, and their manner of execution.

329. Scope of geologic field work. Geologic field work usually involves: (1) the study and interpretation of rocks, topographic forms, etc.; (2) the determination of the location of points or outcrops where observations are made; and (3) the plotting of these points or outcrops, and of other geologic data, on a map. The interpretation of rock structures and topographic forms we have already discussed at some length in the foregoing pages of this book, but there remain a few facts of general significance to be mentioned in the present chapter. The nature and use of instruments for geologic surveying will be discussed in Chaps. 15 and 16. Air photographs and air photography are described in Chap. 17.

Study of Outcrops

330. Most likely places for exposures. The best places in which to look for exposures of bedrock are precipices, hilltops, steep hillsides, stream beds, and coasts, along railroads and roads, and in artificial excavations. Cuts in unconsolidated materials may be sought along the banks of streams, along coasts, roads, and railroads, and in artificial excavations.

331. Examination of outcrops. The beginner is often at a loss as to the best manner of attacking a rock exposure. The writer has always advised his students to start by quickly walking round and over an outcrop which they have just found, before attempting to take any notes. In this way they soon gain a general idea of the rocks and structures which are exposed, and they are better able to decide what parts of the rock should be examined in more detail. Unless this plan is followed much time may be wasted. For instance, one may spend several minutes trying to determine the attitude of a sedimentary rock where its bedding is obscure, whereas further search on the same outcrop may reveal a place at which the bedding is distinct and easily studied. This method of rapid reconnaissance followed by detailed examination is recommended, on a larger scale, for the geologic investigation of extensive areas (**350**).

332. Discrimination between bowlders and outcrops. Care should always be taken not to mistake large, half-buried bowlders, such as are common in glaciated districts, for outcrops of true bedrock. A safe rule to follow is, never accept as bedrock anything that is small enough to be a bowlder, but this is unsatisfactory because there are many places in which large exposures are very scarce and where the small ones are exceedingly useful. It is better to spend some time in studying the questionable rock and correlating it with its surroundings. Bedding, joint systems, cleavage, schistosity, etc., are apt to have similar, though not necessarily exactly the same, character and arrangement in adjoining outcrops of bedrock, whereas in scattered bowlders such structures are usually very variable, especially in trend.

333. Tracing outcrops. The mapping of veins, dikes, and stratified rocks is best accomplished if these rocks are continuously exposed so that they may be easily followed. However, continuous exposure for long distances is rare. It may be observed sometimes where there is great dissimilarity in the resistance of the rocks to erosion, the stronger ones then constituting scarps (Fig. 346) or ridges (Fig. 347), and the weaker ones the adjacent soil-covered slopes or lowlands. The thicker the alternating hard and soft members of a series of sediments are, the more pronounced the ridges on the harder layers are likely to be. If the resistant beds are relatively thin, or if the difference in resistance of the several members of a series is not marked, there is more chance that the harder rocks will be locally covered with soil.

Where the edge of a bed, dike, or vein, is more extensively

covered than it is exposed, the following or *walking* of the outcrop may be very difficult. Under these circumstances the approximate position of the concealed rock may often be indicated by a particular variety of soil, or by a characteristic type of vegetation, or by the topography. As an example of the last, hard beds in a nearly horizontal sedimentary formation may be indicated on the hillsides by topographic benches which are continuous with occasional outcrops of the bench-forming rock. Mapping of distinct belts characterized by certain species of vegetation not only may assist in charting the distribution of rock bodies but also may roughly reveal the direction and amount of dip of sedimentary formations. Another aid in tracing concealed rocks is the occurrence, in some districts, of moist ground or a line of springs along the contact of a lower less pervious rock and an upper more pervious rock (see also Art. **335**).

Characteristic soils may indicate the position of rocks which are mostly covered. Thus, *gossan* (**262**) may assist in mapping veins, and *coal bloom*[1] similarly may aid in the tracing of coal beds.

The *walking* of beds is often an essential procedure in the mapping of low-dipping strata (**436,** ¶ 4; **440**).

334. Importance of contacts. Contacts (**17**) are of the utmost importance in the construction of geologic maps, sections, and diagrams, as well as in the interpretation of underground structure and geologic history. This cannot be too strongly impressed. It is, therefore, obligatory upon the geologist: (1) to find the position of contacts in the field, and (2) to map them with as much accuracy as circumstances will allow. These *circumstances* are factors such as the time available and the degree to which a boundary line may be concealed under superficial débris.

335. Discrimination between igneous contacts, unconformities, and faults. Sometimes the relations between two adjoining rock bodies are so obscure that difficulty is experienced in deciding whether their mutual contact is an *igneous contact*, an *unconformity*, or a *fault*. Two specific instances should be noted, in which one of the three possibilities may be discounted: (1) if

[1] *Coal bloom* is soil darkened by the content of coal débris. The "bloom," on a slope which intersects a coal bed, appears most pronounced just below the position of the coal and fades away in the soil down the slope (see also **336**).

both bodies are sedimentary, their contact cannot be igneous; and, (2) if both bodies are intrusive, they cannot meet in a surface of unconformity. In all other cases, including that of an intrusive mass against an extrusive rock, the mutual surface may be any one of the three types of contact. The problem must be approached with a clear understanding of what features are to be looked for in association with faults, unconformities, and igneous contacts, and then the region must be diligently searched for whatever evidence it has to reveal. Several phenomena that may be misinterpreted are mentioned below.

1. The trend of the boundary line cannot be accepted as a safe criterion. Igneous contacts, faults, and unconformities, may all outcrop in lines that are straight, undulating, or very irregular, although, generally speaking, igneous contact lines, particularly of subjacent bodies, are more commonly irregular, and fault lines and lines of unconformity are more often broadly undulating.

2. Apophyses of an intrusive may extend into the country rock, but sometimes they are conspicuous for their absence. In any event one should look for them. In the case of unconformities, the younger rock may have filled fissures or chasms in the old land surface. Such a filling, if of sedimentary materials, can hardly be misinterpreted; but one of lava might be mistaken for an apophysis, especially if the flow were overlain by lithified strata (**164**). As for faults, there can be no finger-like projections of the rock of one block into the other unless the displacement occurred close to a pre-existing igneous contact or unconformity (**166**).

3. Angular or subangular fragments of country rock may be contained in an eruptive body near the contact. Likewise angular, subangular, or rounded fragments of the rocks below an unconformity may constitute the lower layers of the overlying formation. However, an intrusive breccia has an igneous matrix, whereas the matrix of a basal conglomerate is sedimentary. For the special case of sills, see Art. **164**. Contrasted with intrusive breccias and basal conglomerates, fault breccia zones are relatively narrow and they are composed of pieces of the rocks from both walls (**243**).

4. An intruded country rock may reveal evidences of more or less contact metamorphism, both by heat and by pneumatolysis, and these effects are usually proportional in their intensity and

kind to their distance from the contact (149–152). Also, the eruptive may exhibit textural and other variations which are dependent in character upon the distance from the contact (141). Such conditions are not to be expected in association with unconformities. Faults sometimes serve as conduits for volatile substances rising from underlying magmatic bodies, and these gases and vapors may considerably alter the wall rocks on both sides, so that effects in some degree resembling those of contact metamorphism may be produced.

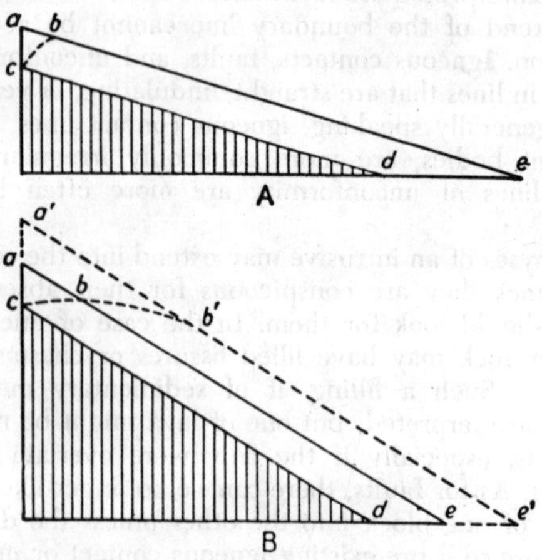

FIG. 374. Ideal profile sections to illustrate the downhill migration of rock waste in the soil. Shaded, bedrock; blank, soil. Rock fragments reach the surface of the soil (*c* to *b*) a shorter distance downhill where the slope is moderate (*ab* in A) than where the slope is steep (*ab* in B); and, on a given slope, they reach the surface a shorter distance downhill where the soil is thin (*ab* in B) than where it is thick (*a′b′* in B). (Cf. Fig. 270.)

336. Location of contacts buried under a soil mantle. A contact hidden under surface débris may be located by observing the distribution of rock chips and fragments in the soil derived from the underlying bedrock. Precision depends upon: (1) the inclination of the ground; (2) the thickness of the soil cover; (3) climatic conditions; (4) the trend of the contact line; and (5) the regularity of the contact. The steeper the slope of the ground and the thicker the mantle rock, the farther the loose materials may slide from their source before they work up to the surface where they may be seen (Figs. 270, 374). If the inclination is less than 25°, sliding is usually not great enough to occasion serious error in fixing the location of the contact. Climate has various effects. Of these as important a one as any is the action of frost in facilitating soil creep. When a straight contact line runs directly up a slope, its location may be accurately determined by the soil method. If it is either oblique to the slope or parallel to the contours, allowance must be made for factors (1) and (2), above noted. Its actual position is higher than is indicated in the mantle rock. Bends and angles of an irregular contact line are exaggerated by the distribution of rock fragments in the soil. This method proves useful in locating any kind of concealed contact, provided the rocks on either side are unlike one another (see also **333**).

337. Sinuous contacts in low-dipping beds. In regions where the strata have low dips, and the topographic relief is low, pronounced swings in a contact may indicate anticlinal structure if an older formation is partly included between or within a younger formation, and synclinal structure if the reverse is true (Fig. 375). The swings must not be confused with the normal downdip bending or looping of the contacts (and outcrop belts) in valleys (**193**).

338. Location of eruptive contacts. The line at which an igneous rock touches its country rock on the surface of an outcrop may be hard to distinguish, even though exposed, either because the two rocks are of like color and texture, or because surface staining due to weathering has impaired an original contrast in hue. There is only one thing to do in this case, and that is to scrutinize the rock surface very carefully. Form the habit of examining one rock inch by inch in a direction toward the other, and then you are not likely to miss the dividing line, provided it is visible. Error is most apt to be made where, by local scaling or exfoliation, relatively fresh surfaces of rock are laid bare next to older surfaces that look different because they have been exposed for a much longer time. Do not let some crack or the edge of a conspicuous stain mislead you into calling this the contact, and, on the other hand, do not be too prone to conclude that a contact is blended and that for this reason no *line* is present (**139**).

Whether or not the boundaries of an igneous body are concealed, they may often be located and traced by the phenomena of contact zones. Thus, if an igneous rock displays a regular diminution in the size of its grains in a definite direction, its contact is likely to be found in this direction. In Art. 239 is explained the value of flow structures and fracture systems for this purpose. Great abundance of inclusions in an igneous rock may signify proximity to the contact, especially to the roof of a large

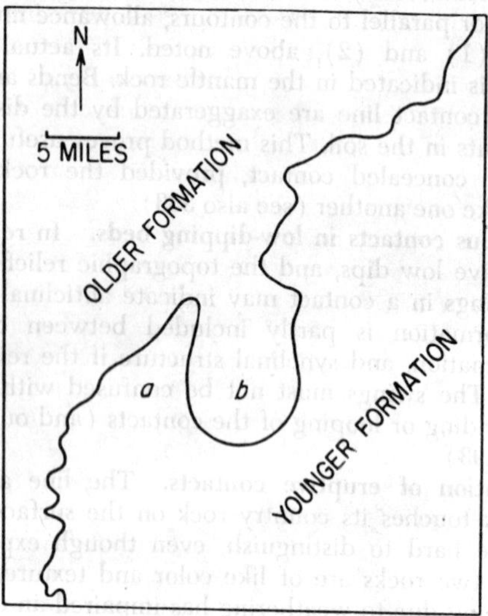

FIG. 375. Map of a contact between two conformable formations. The dip is about 50 ft. to the mile southeastward. At *a*, a shallow synclinal depression is suggested, and at *b*, an anticlinal uplift. Why is this so?

intrusive body (batholith, etc.). When once the geologist has made out the characteristic variations of the contact zones in a given region, he may use this knowledge in seeking the same contact where exposures are poor or infrequent. By the degree of baking, discoloration, or mineralization observed on outcrops of the country rock, he may be able to tell roughly how far he is from the eruptive body (171).

339. Obscure bedding. There is hardly need to say that sedimentary rocks should always be examined for their bedding, for if this cannot be found, the attitude of the strata and other important facts cannot be determined. Stratification may be difficult to see on a rock exposure either because the materials were accumulated under very uniform conditions (**73**), or because the rock was metamorphosed (**245, 246**), or because of surface discoloration. Although, occasionally, sediments are devoid of bedding, perfect uniformity is of rare occurrence. The rock which at first sight appears to be structureless is almost sure to reveal some degree of lamination upon careful scrutiny. When studying an outcrop which is seemingly of even texture, look for sandy streaks in conglomerates, for pebbly or fine sandy streaks in sandstones, for very fine sand laminae in mudstones, and for impure streaks in limestones and chemical deposits.

340. Determination of strike and dip of strata. Wherever strata are exposed, the attitude of their bedding should be found (**339**). In general, we may say that dips of two or three degrees and less are more conveniently recorded in feet of vertical descent per mile of distance than in degrees (Appendices 12–15). Such dips are difficult to read by clinometer. They are determined by finding the elevation, above sea level or above some assumed datum, of scattered points on some chosen *key horizon,* such as the top or bottom of a particular bed. In the field an effort is made to trace or *walk out* the key bed (**333**). Sometimes it may disappear, either because it has been eroded away, or because it dips below the surface. If it has been removed by erosion, elevations may be determined on some other bed, stratigraphically lower, and to these elevations may be added the stratigraphic interval between this bed and the key horizon in order to obtain elevations in the latter. If the key bed dips below the surface of the ground, its position may be ascertained from the records of borings deep enough to reach it (Art. **499**), or the stratigraphic interval between it and some higher bed, which *can* be mapped, may be subtracted from elevations on this higher bed to obtain elevations on the key horizon.

Ordinarily, where dips are very low, as above described, field mapping is accomplished principally by either the barometric method (**407–424**) or the plane-table method (**425–439; 440**), and the geologic structure is represented by a contour map (**497**). Air photographic maps are also used for this kind of work (Art. **456**).

If dips are greater than two or three degrees, they are usually read by clinometer (358). The actual process of taking strike and dip would be simple enough if it were not for the fact that bedding surfaces are more or less irregular and rarely conform with the surfaces of outcrops. To avoid error the compass should never be placed against the rock. Always stand off a few feet and endeavor to gain a correct notion of the strike and dip by a single observation for a length of several feet of outcrop rather than for only a few inches. Where dipping beds are exposed on a horizontal rock surface, the trend of their edges is their strike; but if they are exposed on an inclined rock surface, as they are 99 times out of a 100, the geologist must appeal to his geometric

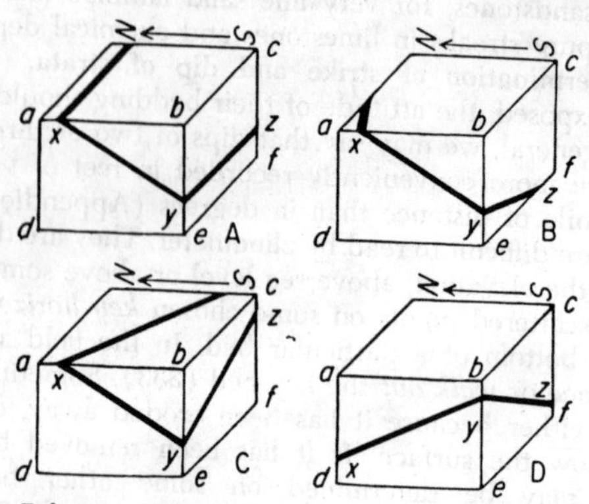

Fig. 376. Relations of dip and strike of bedding to outcrop surfaces.

imagination. The same statement holds for dip, since outcrop surfaces exactly perpendicular to strike are rare. Four possible cases are illustrated in Fig. 376. For convenience the structure is shown in diagrams of rectangular blocks, but it must be remembered that these are unavoidably much more regular than natural outcrops. A, B, and C, in Fig. 376, represent three instances in which the dip might be taken as 30° S. and the strike as E.–W. if only the face *abed* were seen; but an examination of another surface, *bcfe*, proves that Fig. 376, A, alone answers to this suggestion. In Fig. 376, B, the eastward inclination of the strata on face *bcfe* indicates that the real dip (steepest inclination) is southeastward and the real strike is northeastward; and in Fig. 376, C, the westward inclination of the beds as seen on face *bcfe* shows that the real dip must be southwestward and the real strike northwestward. Figure 376, D, is another case which may arise. It will be noted in all these examples that observation on at least two outcrop surfaces, not parallel to one another, and preferably as nearly perpendicular to one another as possible, is requisite in order to arrive at a correct inference as to strike and dip. The chief aim is to ascertain the position of the plane of stratification. Points *x*, *y*, and *z*, in each diagram, determine this plane. This follows from Plane Geometry. If, on a curved or highly irregular outcrop surface, pebbles be placed at three points, not in the same straight line, on the outcropping edge of a given layer, these pebbles may help to visualize the plane of the bedding.

On a small scale this illustrates the principle involved in dip determinations made by geometric analysis of elevations found by careful methods of field surveying on three separate outcrops of the same bed. For example, suppose that a given stratum is exposed at *A*, *B*, and *C*, these being at the apices of a triangle and being so spaced that *A*, is 500 ft. from *B*, and *C* is 400 ft. from both *A* and *B*. The elevations on top of the same bed at *A*, *B*, and *C*, are determined to be 200, 210, and 230 ft., respectively, above sea level. By the solution of triangles, the true dip may be obtained. It will lie in a direction from *C* toward a point between *A* and *B*, and nearer to *A*. This method of finding dip is more accurate than the measurement of local dips by clinometer, where dips are very low. It eliminates the minor variations, common in folded beds, and especially it reduces the errors which may result from local settling (**534**, **342–344**). We cannot too strongly warn the field geologist to guard against mistaking original dip (**82**), cross-bedding (**342**), and the results of soil creep and other mass movements (**3**, **344**), for dips caused by actual secondary deformation of deep-seated origin.

341. Degree of accuracy in taking strike and dip of strata. The accuracy with which dip and strike should be read depends upon the nature of the problem in hand and upon the character of the folding. In regions where dips are low, averaging, let us say, 5° or 6°, fold axes are apt to be irregular in trend. The strata are warped and strikes vary notably. In such cases dips should be read with an error of less than 1°, and strikes should be taken with care. On the other hand, where high dips point to intense deformation, an error of two or three degrees in dip or strike is unimportant, for the actual variations in the beds themselves amount to this or even more within short distances. In this case pains should be taken to obtain correct averages, rather than to make absolutely accurate local readings.

342. Cross-bedding. Several types of cross-bedding have been described in Art. **96.** In studying outcrops of strata with the purpose of determining the dip, great care must be exercised lest cross-bedding be mistaken for true bedding. This confusion is less apt to occur in steeply dipping strata than in gently dipping strata, and the relative error in the resulting structural interpretation is generally less in the former than in the latter.

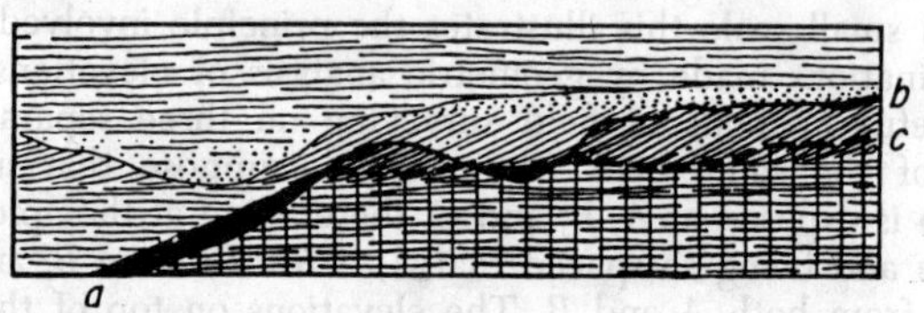

Fig. 377. Vertical section of a series of irregularly bedded, nearly horizontal sandstones and shales. The portion (lightly drawn) above *ab* has been eroded away. The black represents soil. If only the rocks between *ab* and the dashed line *c* were exposed, the cross-bedding might be mistaken for true bedding.

One should remember that the transverse laminae in a cross-bedded stratum may be several, or even many, feet long, so that sometimes an outcrop may expose nothing but these cross laminae (Fig. 377). In regions of low-dipping beds, the wisest course is to ascertain the structure, not by attempting to read strikes and dips at obscure or unreliable outcrops, but by determining the elevations at well distributed points on some chosen bed (key horizon) and then drawing structure contours in reference to these established points (**340, 497**). This method of representing structure by contours also eliminates, to a considerable degree, errors which may be occasioned by such causes as are described in Arts. **343** and **344.**

343. Bevelling of outcrops. In the erosion of some kinds of rock, especially of rather soft sandstones, the upper portion of the outcrop may be bevelled off so that the exact position of the upper surface of the bed is rather hard to determine (Fig.

378). This is a source of error which must be considered particularly in districts where sandstones are the only satisfactory beds to use in mapping and where mapping is done by contouring a key horizon (497).

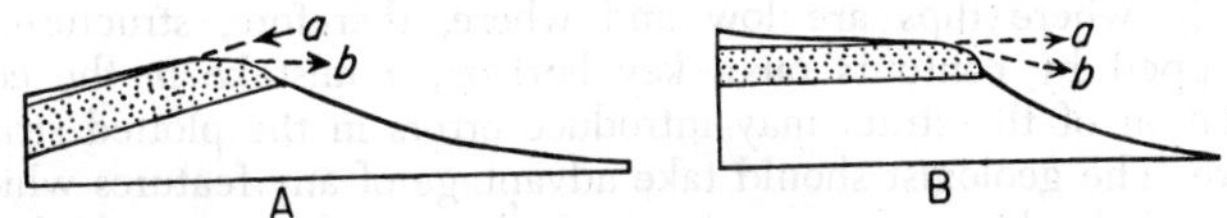

Fig. 378. Vertical sections of thick sandstone beds (stippled), which have been bevelled at their outcrops by erosion. The true attitude of the bed in each figure is shown by *a*; a possible erroneous idea of the dip, due to the bevelling, is indicated by *b*. The black is soil.

344. Settling of beds. Superficial dips, which have no relation to the true structural dips of a region, are very common effects of uneven sagging and settling of sedimentary rocks. This settling is usually manifested in the exposed harder rocks (Fig. 379). It may be caused by the gradual washing away of an

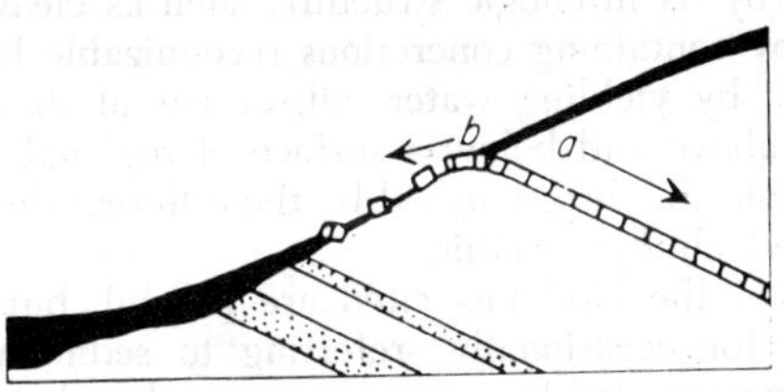

Fig. 379. Cross section of strata dipping toward the right, *a*. Observations at the outcrop of the limestone bed might lead one to suppose that the dip is to the left, *b*, where sagging of the outcrop has been caused by erosion. The black is soil. (See also Fig. 270.)

underlying clay or silt, or by the removal of an underlying soluble material such as salt or limestone. On hillsides, a sagging of the beds toward the valley is often seen in regions of moderate folding. Every precaution should be taken lest these false dips be misinterpreted for true dips. Where the object is to obtain elevations on a key horizon (340), possible errors, which may be occasioned by settling, may be reduced by eliminating the more doubtful outcrops, or by estimating and allowing for the probable amount of settling.

345. Field correlation. In order to obtain satisfactory results in field work, correct correlation of the outcropping rocks is essential. The reader can easily understand that very serious errors may be caused by mistaking one rock for another which may *look* like the first, but actually may be quite different. Especially where dips are low and where, therefore, structure is mapped by contours on a key horizon, a mistake in the correlation of the strata may introduce errors in the plotted structure. The geologist should take advantage of any features which may help him to recognize and distinguish one rock from another.

Rocks are correlated principally by reference to: (1) their lithologic character; (2) their topographic expression (footnote 1, page 391); (3) the nature of the vegetation which grows upon their derived soils; (4) their stratigraphic sequence; and (5) their fossil contents.

1. In the first place, a rock is recognized by its classification as igneous, sedimentary, or metamorphic. It may further be marked by a conspicuous color; by its chemical composition; by its texture; by its lithologic structure, such as cleavage, lamination, etc.; by containing concretions recognizable by their form; or, perhaps, by yielding water, oil, or gas at its outcrop. The formations above and below a surface of regional unconformity may sometimes be distinguished by the different degree of metamorphism which they exhibit.

Features of the kind just cited are helpful, but not final, in correlation, for occasionally—referring to sedimentary rocks—two strata may so closely resemble one another that the geologist may *jump* the beds in crossing an area where there are no outcrops, that is, he may map one bed thinking he is mapping the other. On the other hand, the characteristics of a rock may so far change, laterally along the bedding (**104**), that two separate outcrops of one and the same bed may perhaps be entirely unlike, even though they are not far apart.

2. Topographic expression may be of great assistance in correlation, since, if a rock keeps its general nature, it will usually affect the topography in the same way wherever it is exposed to erosion. Thus, a hard limestone is likely to crop out in distinct ledges, or, at least, it will probably cause a bench or a ridge, whereas a weaker rock is likely to make valleys.

3. The vegetation is apt to be different according as the soil

may be derived from an underlying shale, limestone, sandstone, or other rock. The particular flora characteristic of a certain rock must be learned for each new locality, but, once known, it may be serviceable in problems of correlation.

In the last two cases (¶¶ 2, 3), the geologist must watch for possible variations in the nature of the rock, for lithologic variations are bound to be more or less definitely reflected by changes in the topographic expression and the type of vegetation.

4. Strata may be correlated in reference to their stratigraphic sequence. In Fig. 165, the similar order of like beds—conglomerate, sandstone, and shale, from below upward—suggests that these three beds are the same at the three outcrops. If, at the three localities, the conglomerate were found to rest unconformably upon an older rock formation, this relation would still further establish the correlation of the three beds.

5. Some fossil species, or fossil genera, are found through a considerable stratigraphic range, whereas others are much more limited in their distribution across the bedding. A species which is characteristic of a definite geologic horizon, and occurs only in beds at the horizon, is called an *index fossil.* Such a fossil species may be of great value in the correlation not only of different exposed parts of the bed in which it is found, but also of overlying and underlying strata which may be referred to this bed. Sometimes not one fossil, but a group of fossils, is characteristic of a stratum or series. By way of example, in Fig. 165, the outcrops of sandstone might be recognized as belonging to the same bed because of containing the same fossil species or group of fossil species at *a, b,* and *c.*

Like the other criteria for correlation, fossils are not always dependable. Judgment must be exercised in their use. The same stratum, which may be rich in organic remains in some places, may have few or none in other places. Not uncommonly several beds in a formation hold the same fossil species. This causes no trouble in the correlation of the formation, but it may lead to mistakes in the identification of a particular bed which has been chosen as a key horizon for mapping.

Another source of error, applying rather to regional than to local correlation, is lateral change in fossil floras and faunas. This important feature is too often overlooked. One has only to compare the conditions and types of modern life, as they vary from place to place, to appreciate the fact that lateral variations are to be expected in fossils within a given bed or formation of the same geologic age. On account of some original barrier, very different fossil groups may be found in beds of the same age at localities not far distant from one another.

Again, with the transgression or regression of sedimentary deposits (87), floras and faunas may have been forced to migrate along with their shifting environment. The result is that we may have a transgression of a fossil flora or fauna diagonally across a formation or group of formations, much as a basal sandstone may diagonally cross successively higher and younger formations. For this reason we may sometimes find the same fossils in beds of different age at more or less widely separated localities.[2]

346. Attitude of contorted strata. A word of caution may be given in reference to taking the dip and strike of contorted

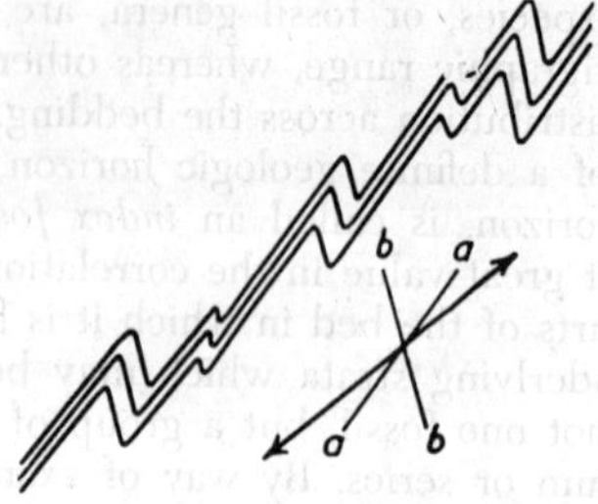

FIG. 380. Section of two layers in a contorted schist. The section is drawn looking north.

strata. Figure 380 is a local vertical section of two layers in a series deformed by minor similar folding. The small folds are from 1 to 5 ft. from crest to trough and the dips of their limbs are approximately 48° W., *aa*, or 82° E., *bb*. Yet the general inclination of the strata is neither 48° W. nor 82° E. It is indicated by the double-headed arrow and is about 33° W. Evidently dips which are measured on the limbs of minor folds cannot be used for the major structure. The same is true, but to a less degree, of strikes. In dealing with highly crumpled sediments the geologist must be careful to discriminate between principal and subordinate folds, and he must not record angles for the minor

[2] For a more lengthy discussion of this subject, the reader is referred to Bibliog., Grabau, A. W., 1913, Chap. XXXII.

folding, which he intends to use in sections and maps of the major structure.

347. Attitude of eruptive contacts. The position of an igneous body with reference to horizontality and to structure in the adjacent rocks can be ascertained by studying the attitudes of its contacts. The dip and strike of flows and of uniform dikes and sills may be obtained by clinometer and compass just as in the case of strata (**340**). It is important to remember, however, that even the straightest intrusive sheets, as seen in cross section (vertical, horizontal, or inclined), not uncommonly have jogs or elbow-bends, the effect of which, if the bends are all on the

Fig. 381. Apparent offset in two outcrops of a dike of which the strike, where observed, is parallel to the front edge of the block. V-pattern, dike rock in section; stippling, alluvium.

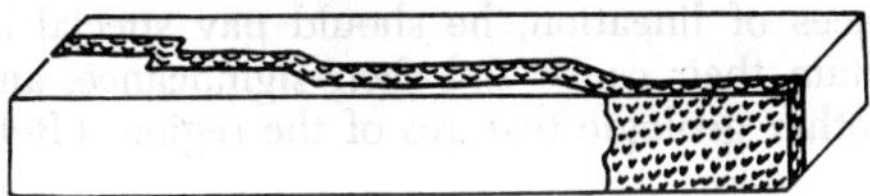

Fig. 382. Explanation of the apparent offset shown in Fig. 381, the soil having been removed and the top of the block being represented as a horizontal plane.

same side, is like that of transverse faults with the offset always in the same direction. One part of the sheet may be far out of line with another part (Figs. 381, 382).

In obtaining the trend or the inclination of very irregular contacts, like those which are typical of many batholiths, chonoliths, etc., the degree of precision necessary must be determined by the geologist. Just how much he may generalize the line depends largely upon the scale of the map on which he is plotting. For instance, he may disregard local turns and angles 150 or 200 ft. deep if his map is on a scale of 1 mile to an inch. Nevertheless, observe that this statement does not signify that the details of such a contact are not to be studied. Not only should they be carefully examined, but also their shape and other characters should be illustrated by large scale plans and sketches made in the field.

After a contact has been located for a considerable distance and its line of outcrop plotted on a topographic map, its general attitude may often be made out from an inspection of this map, as explained in Art. **520**.

Attention is here called to Art. **165**, where mention is made of the value of field studies of flow structure and of fracture systems in and adjoining intrusive igneous bodies.

348. Lineation. Lineation has been defined and described in Art. **15**, and it has been mentioned in several other places in this book. It is a term of such broad application that no one method can be recommended for its study. The important points to remember are: (1) that the field geologist should always be on the watch for parallelism of geologic features, whether he is examining an outcrop, or is mapping in reconnaissance or in detail (**391**), or is studying an air photograph or an air mosaic (**451**); (2) that he should likewise be on the watch for single linear features, or for two or more such features widely spaced, or perhaps in intersecting sets; and (3) that if he detects any such evidences of lineation, he should pay special attention to them, ascertain their cause and their significance, and correlate them with other geologic features of the region. (Refer again to **15**.)

Field Observations

349. General data to be observed and recorded. Many of those who are engaged in geologic work, particularly in the earlier years of their training, find that a table of the facts which should be looked for in the field is often very helpful. Excellent schedules may be found in Hayes' "Handbook."[3] They refer to the description and interpretation of land forms, to petrology, geologic structure, glaciers, and glacial deposits, ores, building stones, and other materials of economic worth. For general purposes, however, the following outline may be found useful. If desired, it can be expanded or shortened or otherwise rearranged to suit the particular needs of special districts or special problems. Also, the various items listed in it may be tabulated, with spaces for recording the observed facts.

[3] Bibliog., Hayes, C. W., 1909.

Schedule for Field Observations

Topography. Note: Relief (flat, low, hilly, mountainous; also rough estimate of vertical distance between valley floors and hilltops); shapes and arrangement of uplands and lowlands; lineation, if any; relations of topographic forms to rock distribution; destructional and constructional origin; evidences for agents and processes of erosion and for stage of development in erosion cycles; effects upon human activities.

Rocks. 1. *For any outcrop,* note: Color, luster, grain, and irregularities of surface; shape, size, and arrangement; distribution with relation to topographic forms; evidences, nature, and attitude of any observed lineation.

2. *For any rock,* note: Texture; mineral composition; kind and degree of weathering; color and nature of weathered surface; color of fresh fracture; relations to other rocks as regards structure and age (contact relations, stratigraphic sequence, unconformity, etc.).

(*a*) *If an igneous rock,* note further: Mode of occurrence; dimensions of igneous bodies; attitude (for dikes, sills, etc.); fracture systems; lithologic structures (flow structure, schliers, primary gneissic structure, segregations, etc.); contact relations; contact metamorphism; and inclusions (kind, shape, size, arrangement, and source).

(*b*) *If a sedimentary rock,* note further: Whether detrital (clastic, fragmental), chemical, or organic; mode of occurrence (bed, lens, clastic pipe, clastic dike); dimensions (thickness, lateral extent, etc.); attitude; direction of face in regions of intense folding (**182**); breadth of outcrop; degree of consolidation (unconsolidated, loose, compacted only by adhesive properties of some constituents, consolidated by virtue of a cement); composition, shape, size, and arrangement of constituents in detrital (fragmental) rocks, (larger fragments, matrix, cement); lithologic structures (cross-bedding, ripple-marks, sun cracks, local unconformity, contemporaneous deformation, etc.); inclusions (concretions, nodules, geodes); kinds, attitude, distribution, and abundance of fossils; stratigraphic sequence.

(*c*) *If a metamorphic rock,* note further: Kind and degree of metamorphism; evidences of metamorphic zoning; any preserved original structures (see igneous and sedimentary rocks, above); secondary lithologic structures (slaty cleavage, plane schistosity, linear schistosity, gneissic structure, etc.); attitude of structure; relations of original structures to secondary structures; classification of original rock before metamorphism.

(*d*) *If a vein,* note further: Its shape, size, attitude, and relations to the wall rock and to the topography; species, arrangement, and relative amount of mineral constituents.

Structures. 1. *For uncomformities,* note: Kind, extent, and nature of surface; relations of the two unconformable formations; kind and source of basal sediments of the younger formation; age relations.

2. *For folds,* note: Shape; dimensions; classification; major or minor; parallel or similar; with horizontal or plunging axis; relations to topography; relations to rocks; relations of minor to major folds; age relations.

3. *For faults,* note: Extent, attitude, shape, classification as far as can be observed; slickensides, gouge, brecciation, drag, etc.; exposed rocks on each side of fault line; amount and direction of visible displacement; relations to other structures (bedding, folds, joints, etc.); relations to topography; age relations.

4. *For joints,* note: Extent, attitude, shape, spacing, regularity, classification; rocks affected; relations to other structures; relation to topography; age relations.

The foregoing outline will probably not fit all cases, for geologic relations are almost infinite in their variety. The best rule is, search for anything and everything of geologic interest and record all you see. Do not overlook surficial deposits merely because they are unconsolidated. All earth features are but parts of a whole, and you can never tell when seemingly trivial things are going to furnish decisive evidence for the solution of important problems.

General Suggestions

350. Beginning a field problem. A few words may be added here in reference to beginning field problems. Some facts concerning the equipment and management of large parties and professional surveys may be found in Hayes' "Handbook."[4] Elementary studies, let us say undergraduate field work, should be approached without any previous knowledge of the locality. In this way the student can be trained to observe on his own initiative. More advanced work, of postgraduate grade, and all professional work, should be preceded by reference to the available geologic literature on the region. It is important to learn all that is possible of the results of earlier investigations before going into the field. The geologist should know where to look for the writings of others. For this purpose the "Bibliography of North American Geology," published by the U.S. Geological Survey, is of inestimable service.[5] Other valuable lists of books and

[4] Bibliog., Hayes, C. W., 1909.

[5] This bibliography comprises the following publications of the U.S. Geological Survey: *Bulletins* 746 and 747 (1785–1918); *Bulletin* 823 (1919–1928); *Bulletin* 937 (1929–1939); *Bulletin* 1049 (1940–1949);

shorter papers are usually given as bibliographies accompanying such publications.

In the search for information on an area to be examined in the field, one should give consideration to the following points:

1. The name, character and geologic age of each of the formations exposed.
2. The names and geologic ages of formations which may underlie the exposed formations.
3. The structural and genetic relationships of these formations.
4. The average or approximate thicknesses of sedimentary formations.
5. The normal or average regional dip of such formations.
6. The amount and direction of any thinning or thickening which may have been recognized in sedimentary formations.
7. The topographic and physiographic conditions in the region, and the relations between these conditions and the various formations.

Passing over the details of equipment, preparation of the notebook, choice of hotel or camping site, etc., we are brought face to face with the actual field work. What is the best thing to do first? To plunge right in at the outset and make a careful traverse is a rather blind proceeding. It has to be done sometimes, but only when time is very short or when the work is to be restricted to a definite route. Ordinarily several hours or days, depending upon the magnitude of the problem, should be spent in going over the area rapidly, for by such a reconnaissance one can learn enough about the frequency of exposures and about the nature of the rocks and probable underground structure to enable one to plan a systematic mode of carrying out and completing the entire investigation. Several days may be saved in this way. After the preliminary reconnaissance the geologist may continue with the more detailed surveying according to one or another of the methods outlined in Chaps. 16 and 17.

351. Collecting and trimming specimens. In these days of sedulous laboratory study comparatively little can be learned of the true nature of rocks in the field. Hence the necessity of collecting specimens. Judgment must be exercised in doing this. Do not bring in chips from the surface of a weathered exposure.

---

and *Bulletins* 985 (1950), 1025 (1951), 1035 (1952–1953), 1054 (1954), and 1065 (1955). See also the "Annotated Bibliography of Economic Geology," published by the Economic Geology Publishing Company, since 1929.

Get as fresh a fragment as possible, for the classification of a rock cannot always be made from the products of its decomposition. Representative samples, typical of the rock, should be selected. If time is pressing, irregular fragments may be collected. Otherwise the specimens should be trimmed to a flat rectangular shape, either 4 by 5 by 1 in. or 3 by 4 by 1 in. They are then called *hand specimens*. The width and length should be measured with considerable exactitude, but the thickness may be somewhat variable.

Fig. 383. Hammer head, *b*, and rock specimen, *a*, in proper position for trimming.

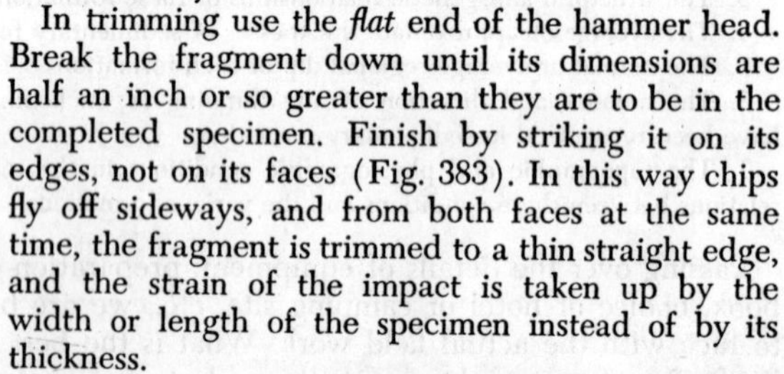

In trimming use the *flat* end of the hammer head. Break the fragment down until its dimensions are half an inch or so greater than they are to be in the completed specimen. Finish by striking it on its edges, not on its faces (Fig. 383). In this way chips fly off sideways, and from both faces at the same time, the fragment is trimmed to a thin straight edge, and the strain of the impact is taken up by the width or length of the specimen instead of by its thickness.

If a rock is to be thoroughly studied it must be examined by the petrographic microscope and must be chemically analyzed. For the microscope thin sections have to be cut. Therefore, in order to avoid sawing into the hand specimens, a geologist usually takes, in addition to these, a small chip of every rock that he thinks will need to be sectioned. Of any rock that he considers deserving of chemical analysis he collects several pounds; but chemical analysis is seldom undertaken, unless with some special object, on account of the expense.

Hand specimens and chips *must* be wrapped in paper bags to prevent their scratching and bruising one another. A badly bruised specimen is almost worthless. A label bearing the name, number, and locality of each specimen should be wrapped up with it. Always mark *on* the specimen its original orientation within the rock body. This is important for petrofabrics analysis.

Under the head of collecting specimens, we may mention the cuttings and cores which are secured from holes drilled for oil, gas, water, or for other purposes. These are discussed in more detail under Subsurface Geologic Surveying, especially in Arts.

461, 464. Whether such well samples are cuttings, or samples of mud, or cores, they should be carefully wrapped and correctly labelled at the well, so that there will be no mistake as to the depth from which they came. These samples may be briefly examined before they are wrapped, but their principal study is in the laboratory.

352. Taking photographs. In many respects photographs are the most valuable means of geologic illustration. Miniature cameras, especially the better grades, are excellent for recording many features that might be overlooked, or might be slighted, in the field notes. Original photographs can be enlarged and used to illustrate finished reports. For distant photography, the best results can be obtained only by employing special films and ray filters. Stereoscopic and panoramic views are very much worth while. Kodachrome may be used to record the colors of rocks, soils, and vegetation.

Do not take a picture merely because it shows something within your area of investigation. Choose only such views as have a definite bearing on the subject in hand. It is best to photograph very irregular rock surfaces on a dull day, for the shadows made by projecting edges and corners on sunny days appear on the print as black patches. Not infrequently contact lines and other rock structures are exposed on granular, pitted, ribbed, or scratched surfaces. If one's aim is to bring out the grain, ribs, etc., take the picture on a bright day when the sun is rather low so that these minor irregularities will cast shadows; but if the structures are to be emphasized, the photograph should be made on a cloudy day.

In spite of the fact that the subject of the picture should be of geologic interest, the view should be taken in such a way as to secure an artistic balance. Experience has demonstrated that the balance is best attained in the following manner: Imagine that the field of the picture is divided by two vertical lines and two horizontal lines into nine equal spaces (Fig. 384). These lines, and particularly the intersections of these lines, are the strong parts of a picture. One should aim, therefore, to place the camera in a position such that: (1) the prominent upright lines or objects (trees, edges of cliffs, etc.) in the view will fall along the vertical division lines (*aa*, *bb*, Fig. 384); (2) the prominent horizontal lines or objects (horizon line, etc.) will come on the horizontal division lines (*cc*, *dd*, Fig. 384); and (3) the principal centers of interest or the conspicuous centers of light or of shadow will be at the intersections of the division lines. It is not necessary that there should be features in the picture coinciding with all the division lines and their intersections, but merely that those important objects which are present should be arranged as above described.

353. How much shall be undertaken in the field? This is a question which deserves consideration. An inexperienced geologist is often tempted to do little more than tramp over the ground and record what he sees at the moment, leaving the rest to be done in the office after the field season closes. This is very poor policy. When this man, two or three weeks or months later, sits down to prepare his geologic maps and reason out the geologic structure, he will soon discover that he cannot remember

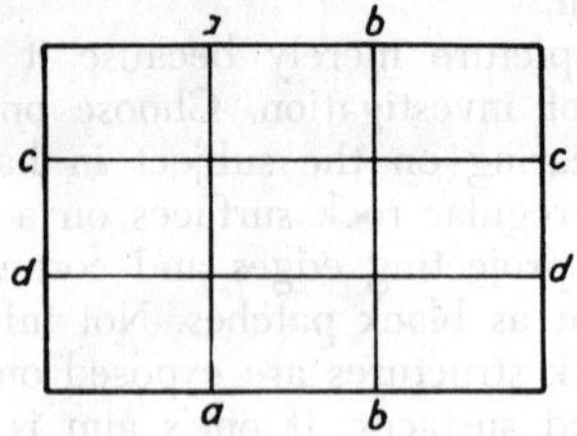

FIG. 384. Strong lines and points in a picture.

just where he saw this thing or just how that one looked. Indeed, either he may have to go back to the district next field season or he may have to write a report that is lacking in certain details, some of which, perhaps, are very important.

The moral of this is that you should accomplish in the field all that is possible. Make your geologic maps and sections, and draw your sketches, plans, and block diagrams. They do not have to be finished for publication. They may be done—in fact, they should be done in the field—in pencil, black or colored. You will find that this preliminary drawing will be of the greatest assistance in showing you what you have omitted and what you should reexamine, if possible, before you leave the region. Write a summary of your notes every night, or at least at the end of every week. This will stimulate new ideas and reveal deficiencies or errors of interpretation which may need attention before the completion of the work.

354. Degree of accuracy in field work. Brief mention has been made of the question of degree of accuracy to be sought in field work (**328, 341, 347**). This is an important matter for consideration in advance of, and during, most kinds of field exploration. It also applies to the preparation of the final maps. Rules worth remembering are: (1) for any map no greater degree of precision is desirable or necessary than is commensurate with the scale of the map; and (2) for any map no set of data need be charted in the field by a method more precise than the methods applied in charting the other sets of data for this map.

Possibly these statements are obscure. To be specific, where low-dipping formations are to be contoured (**312**) with a contour interval of, let us say, 50 ft., application of a field method of mapping elevations to a final limiting error of 1 or 2 ft. would be waste of time. An error of as much as 10 ft. would not be serious. And, similarly, for such a map, too great exactitude in horizontal location of points used for contouring would not be warranted. The whole endeavor should be to see that vertical and horizontal controls, the location of geologic features, and the scale of the final maps and sections are all reasonably related to one another in degree of precision or, to express it in another way, in permissible limit of error.

These remarks are made here so that they may be kept in mind in reading the chapters that follow (Arts. **388, 390, 391, 422, 423, 424, 434, 440, 552**).

Chapter 15

GEOLOGIC SURVEYING

PART II. INSTRUMENTS AND OTHER EQUIPMENT USED IN GEOLOGIC FIELD MAPPING

355. The compass and clinometer. The compass, with its clinometer attachment, is indispensable for geologic field work. The Gurley and Brunton compasses are the types most commonly employed.

The *Gurley compass* is provided with a square metal base, a pendulum (swinging) clinometer, folding open sights, and a rectangular spirit level. The edges of the base are bevelled, two being graduated in inches, and two in degrees of arc for use as a protractor. With the sights turned up, this instrument may serve as a short open sight alidade (**372**). The pendulum clinometer is excellent for reading dips, but is not always satisfactory for determining slopes.

The *Brunton compass,* or *Brunton pocket transit,* is oomprised of an ordinary compass, folding open sights, a mirror, and a rectangular spirit level clinometer. It cannot be employed as a protractor and it is unsatisfactory as an open sight alidade. The clinometer, which is operated by a short arm on the back of the compass box, serves better for taking slope angles than for taking dips.

356. Use of the compass. Direction and strike (**14**) are measured by means of the compass. Concerning the use of this instrument, there are certain rules and facts with which the beginner must familiarize himself at the outset.

1. Degrees for direction and strike are read on the *outer* circular dial.

2. In taking direction or strike, hold the compass so that its face is horizontal and its "length," *i.e.,* the line between the letters, "N" and "S," on the dial, lies in the direction of the strike (Fig. 385, A, arrow).

3. When the needle is at rest it points in a constant direction for any given locality. Hence readings should be made from one or the other end of the needle, and not from the letters "N," "E," "S," or "W," printed on the dial. Thus, in Fig. 385, A, the compass length, or line between the letters "N" and "S," lies in the NW. and SE. quadrants and thus indicates a NW.–SE. direction. This is suggested by the position of the needle between "N" and "W," and between "S" and "E."

4. Strikes and directions are to be recorded exactly as one reads the compass. If the instrument is in the position shown in Fig. 385, A, and one is looking in the direction of the arrow, the

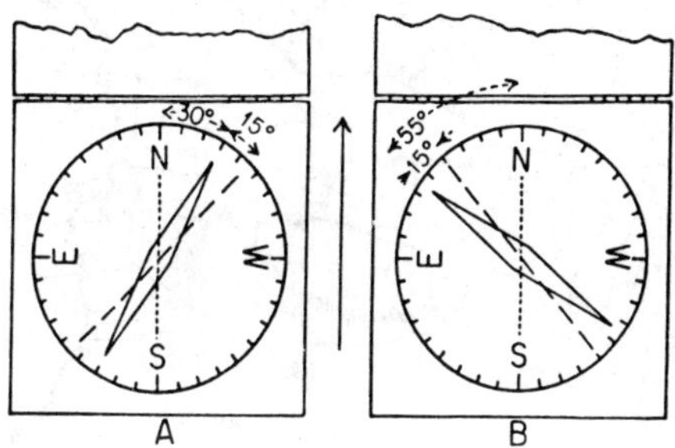

FIG. 385. Diagrams to illustrate the use of the compass. Dotted line, "length of compass"; dashed line, true north-south line.[1]

north end of the needle, being the nearest end to this line of sight, should be noted first. Next should appear the angle or number of degrees between the needle and the required direction, and finally is written the direction in which this angle was measured *from the needle end.* If the angle is 30° in this case, the strike is N. 30° W.

5. All readings are made from north and south, or sometimes from north only, but never from east or west. Thus, the strike mentioned in the last paragraph would not be recorded W. 60° N. A direction 30° east of south may be written S. 30° E. or N. 150° E., but not E. 60° S.

[1] Note that the letters "E" and "W" are reversed so that the needle will lie between the letters which designate the quadrant in which the bearing is taken.

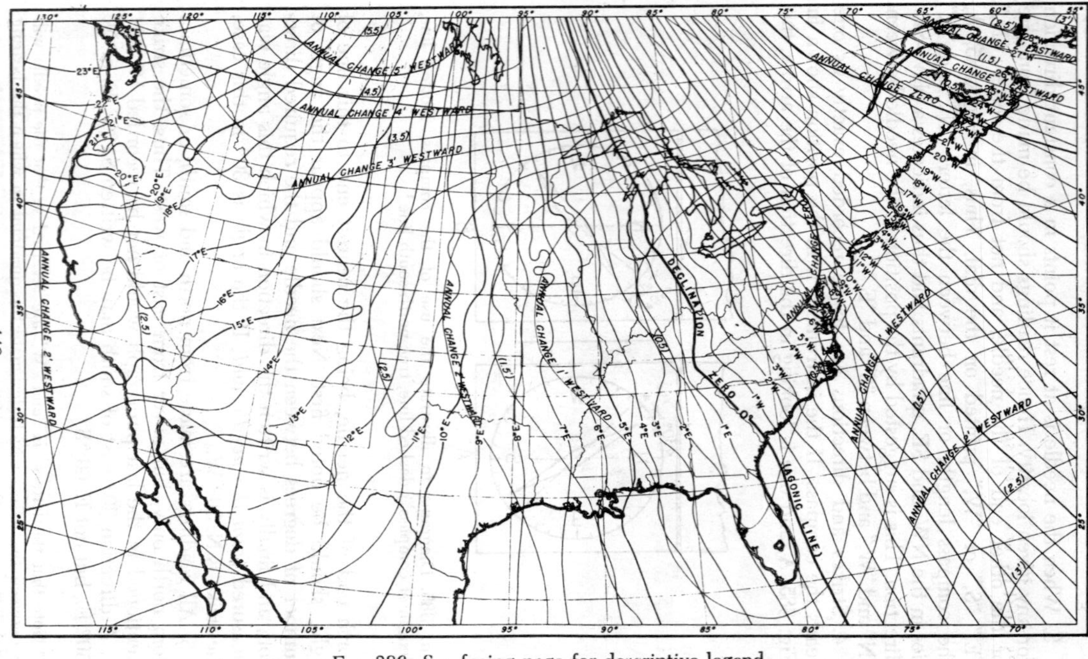

FIG. 386. See facing page for descriptive legend.

6. A bearing made as just described is spoken of as *magnetic*. There is nearly always a correction which has to be made for this compass reading because the needle seldom points to the *true north*. The compass north (*magnetic north*) may lie a variable number of degrees to the east or west of the true north. East of the zero isogonic line (agonic line) (Fig. 386) magnetic north is west of true north (west declination), and west of this line magnetic north is east of true north (east declination). Suppose, in Fig. 385, A, that true north is 15° to the east of magnetic north (and, therefore, that true east is 15° south of magnetic east, etc.); the true bearing is then 30° + 15° to the west of true north, or N. 45° W., instead of N. 30° W. Similarly a magnetic bearing of S. 30° E. would become a true bearing of S. 45° E. If the compass reads N. 55° E., as in Fig. 385, B, obviously one must subtract the correction of 15° and the true bearing is then N. 40° E. Likewise, S. 55° W. would be corrected to S. 40° W. All cases are covered in the following rules: If true north is to the east of magnetic north, to all magnetic bearings in the NW. and SE. quadrants add the correction, and from all magnetic bearings in the NE. and SW. quadrants subtract the correction. If true north is to the west of magnetic north, add the correction to NE. and SW. readings and subtract it from NW. and SE. readings. Additions and subtractions are algebraic. (How would you correct a magnetic bearing of N.–S.? of E.–W.?)

Since the magnetic variation is not the same for different localities and since it changes gradually from year to year in any given locality, one must ascertain the proper correction for any place in which geologic field work is to be performed (Fig. 386).

7. Be scrupulously careful not to have your hammer or any other steel near the compass while making observations. Magnetic ore, steel nails, electric wires, etc., seriously affect the needle.

Fig. 386. Isogonic chart for the United States. The lines of equal magnetic declination (isogonic lines) are given for every degree. They apply to Jan. 1, 1955. East of the isogonic line marked "zero" (agonic line) the north end of the compass needle points west of true north. West of this line, it points east of true north. The north end of the compass needle is moving eastward for places in the extreme NE part of the area, and westward elsewhere over the chart, at an annual rate indicated by the lines of equal annual change (isoporic lines). (*After the U.S. Coast and Geodetic Survey.*)

8. In reading directions, the sights of the Gurley and Brunton compasses increase the accuracy of the results. The Gurley, however, must be placed on a horizontal support, such as a plane table, whereas a Brunton can be held in the hand. This is a distinct advantage of the latter instrument, where a plane table is not desired. To read the direction to a distant object, hold the Brunton compass level, with the mirror nearest you and the open sight away from you. The sight should stand vertical and the mirror should be tilted at such an angle that the sight and the distant object can both be seen reflected in it. With the reflected object and the slot in the sight both bisected by the cross-hair in the mirror, read the compass angle and so determine the required direction (4–6, above.)

357. Setting the compass. In both the Brunton and Gurley compasses the dial can be so adjusted that, for a given locality, true instead of magnetic bearings may be read directly. In Fig. 387 the dashed line represents the direction of true north, here

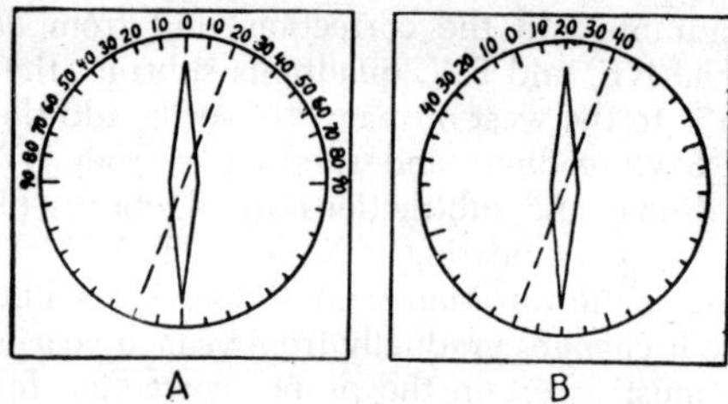

FIG. 387. Diagrams illustrating the method of setting the compass dial for true readings. Dashed line, true north-south line.

assumed to be 20° to the east of magnetic north (the north end of the needle). As shown in Fig. 387, A, the magnetic reading is due north and south, and the corrected reading is N. 20° W., for the "0" on the dial is 20° to the west of true north. If the dial is turned in the compass box 20° to the west (counterclockwise), and the needle and box are in the same relative position as in Fig. 387, A, the bearing when read directly will be N. 20° W. (Fig. 387, B), *i.e.*, the "0" on the dial will now be 20° to the west of the needle. Hence, the rule for setting the compass is this: rotate the dial through an angle equal to the magnetic declination (the angle between magnetic and true north), *west-*

ward (counter-clockwise) if true north is to the *east* of magnetic north, and *eastward* (clockwise) if true north is to the *west* of magnetic north. Do not overlook the fact that magnetic declination is usually different in different regions.

358. Use of the clinometer. The clinometer is used for measuring vertical angles of slope and dip. The compass box must be held with its plane vertical. If the clinometer is of the pendulum type, the angle will be indicated on the inner, nearly semicircular scale, where the swinging pointer comes to rest. If the clinometer is of the friction type, as in the Brunton, the angle will be read on the inner semicircular scale opposite the zero of the vernier, after this has been properly set as described below.

1. In taking the dip, hold the compass vertically with its length parallel to the outcropping edge of the stratum and its face in a plane *perpendicular to the strike*. "Care must be taken to have the eye as nearly as possible in the extension of the plane whose inclination is being measured, and to sight on a horizontal line,"[2] *the strike line.* If the compass is a Brunton, while holding it with its plane vertical and perpendicular to the strike, and with its long edge apparently coinciding with the bedding, turn the clinometer arm until the bubble in the longer level is centered. Then read the angle of dip on the inner dial.

2. In recording dip, the vertical angle from the horizontal and the direction of inclination must be noted. Dip is always measured *downward.* If the strike is E.–W., then the dip may be either northward or southward. If the strike is N. 50° E., the dip may be northwestward or southeastward. It is necessary to give only the quadrant in which the dip lies, for the exact direction can be determined from the strike, since the *direction* of the dip is always perpendicular to the strike. A record of a strike of N. 25° W. and a dip of 45° (downward) toward the NE. is written, N. 25° W.; 45° NE. Observe that the 45° NE. does not mean N. 45° E.; it signifies a vertical angle of 45° in a general northeasterly direction.

A shorter way of recording attitude is to show only the amount and *exact* direction of dip. Thus, in the example just cited, instead of writing "N. 25° W.; 45° NE.," we could write "45° N. 65° E." Strike, always being at right angles to the direction of dip, would then have to be N. 25° W.

A Brunton compass may be employed in other ways. To find

[2] Bibliog., Hayes, C. W., 1909, p. 24.

the angle of a slope, while looking up or down the slope, hold the Brunton with its plane vertical and parallel to the direction in which you are making the observation, and with the mirror farthest from you. Open the sight at right angles to the plane of the compass and have the mirror about three-quarters closed. Look simultaneously through the open sight and the peephole near the base of the mirror at a point, up or down the slope, which is as high above the ground as your eye, and bring the point, the center line of the open sight, and the cross-hair of the mirror into alignment. Then, without changing position, turn the clinometer arm until the bubble in the longer level is centered, *as seen in the mirror*. The angle of slope will be indicated at the

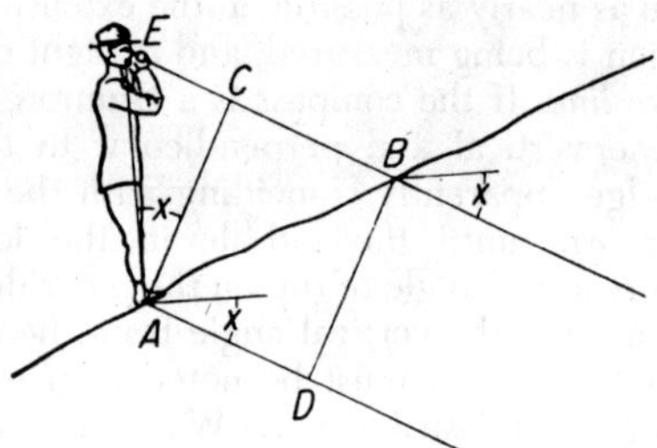

FIG. 388. Determination of thickness of inclined beds. (*After D. F. Hewett.*)

point on the inner dial of the compass opposite the zero of the clinometer vernier scale.

Sometimes the Brunton may be used to verify a supposed slight dip or slope. In this case, set the vernier scale with its zero against the zero of the inner dial, and sight at the questionable dip or slope across the top edge of the compass as above described. The supposed dip is proved to exist if the bubble does not move to the center.

The Brunton may be of service in measuring the thickness of inclined beds. In Fig. 388,

"the geologist stands at *A*, the base of the section to be measured. The clinometer level of the Brunton compass is turned to equal the angle of dip of the beds. When, therefore, the observer looks through the sights, he observes a spot on the ground that is the distance $AC = BD$ stratigraphically higher than the point A at which he stands. Now $BD = AC = AE \cdot$ cosine of the angle of dip $= AE \cdot \cos x$, and AE is constant for each observer. If, therefore, he prepares a table such as that given below, in which $AE = 5.25$ ft. he can readily determine the proper unit for each degree of dip."[3]

From A he will go to B and repeat this procedure, and so on to the top of the section. The sum of the distances, equivalent to $AC = BD$, will be the required thickness. (See also Art. **361.**)

TABLE 5. Thickness Values for Stepping with Inclined Sight[1]

Dip = *x*	$AC = AE \times \cos x$	*Dip* = *x*	$AC = AE \times \cos x$
0	5.25	22	4.86
2	5.24	23	4.83
4	5.24	24	4.79
6	5.23	25	4.75
8	5.20	26	4.72
9	5.18	27	4.67
10	5.16	28	4.63
11	5.15	29	4.59
12	5.13	30	4.54
13	5.11	32	4.45
14	5.09	34	4.35
15	5.07	36	4.25
16	5.04	38	4.14
17	5.02	40	4.02
18	4.99	42	3.90
19	4.96	44	3.77
20	4.93	46	3.64
21	4.90	48	3.51

[1] After Hewett, D. F., 1920.

359. The Locke level. The Locke level consists of a straight metal tube or barrel about 5 in. long and ¾ in. in diameter, which the observer holds horizontal as he looks through it. Attached near one end is a small spirit level, to be held uppermost when the instrument is in use. Under the level tube, inside the barrel, is a mirror which covers one-half the field of vision, up and down. It (the mirror) is inclined at such an angle that the

[3] See Bibliog., Hewett, D. F., 1920, pp. 383, 384.

observer can sight through the barrel at a distant object, and, at the same time, see the bubble reflected in it. When the bubble is bisected by the horizontal cross-hair, a distant object which appears to be opposite the middle of the cross-hair is at the same level as the observer's eye, provided the instrument is in adjustment. The geologist should know the height of his eyes above the ground.

The Locke level may be employed as indicated in Fig. 389. *ag* is a hill slope. Standing at *a*, and being careful to hold the level so that the bubble is centered, the observer looks through the tube at some point, *b*, at the same elevation as the instrument; *i.e.*, *a′b* is horizontal. He then proceeds to *b*, noting the distance *ab*, and repeats the process at *b*, looking toward *c*. The

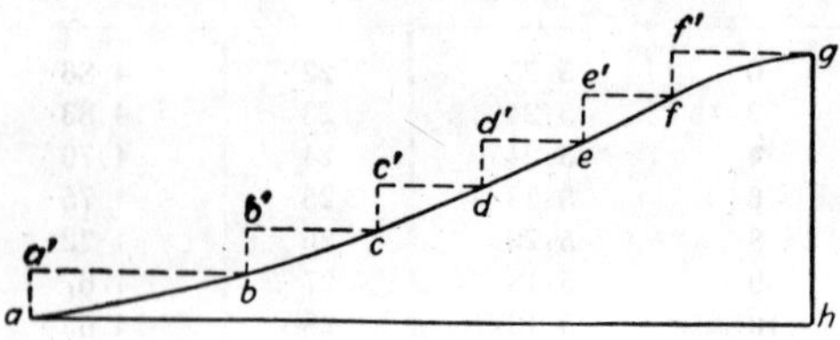

FIG. 389. Profile section of a slope, illustrating the method of finding difference of elevations by hand level.

height of the instrument, *aa′* is known. Hence the elevation of g above *a* is, in this case, 6*aa′*.

360. The Abney level. The Abney level (or pocket altimeter) has a vertical graduated arc, a square sighting tube, and a pivoted clinometer with attached spirit level. With the clinometer set at 0° it can be employed just like a Locke level. The Abney level can also be used as a clinometer to measure slope angles. In Fig. 390, *abcd* is a slope with a change at *b* and another at *c*. The observer stands at *a* with the instrument at *a′*, and, sighting through the tube at *b′*, at the elevation $bb' = aa'$ above the ground, he simultaneously rotates the spirit level until the bubble is centered. The angle of the slope, $\angle b'a'f$, may then be read directly from the graduated arc. The height of *b′* above *b* is generally estimated from *a* by eye. It may be obtained with greater precision if an assistant at *b* holds a rod known as a *grade rod,* having the proper length, *aa′*, indicated upon it. At *b* the observer sights at *c′* and reads the slope angle, $\angle c'b'g$. Notice that these readings are always made at changes of slope. At *c* he would sight forward to a position on another change of slope, and so on. The Abney level can also be used like the Brunton

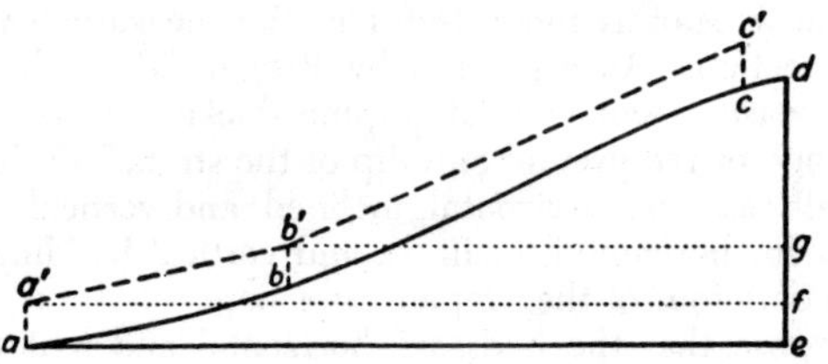

FIG. 390. Profile section of a slope, illustrating the method of finding slope angles by clinometer.

compass (page 452) for measuring the thickness of a stratigraphic section. This is explained in Art. **361.** The principle involved is illustrated in Fig. 391.

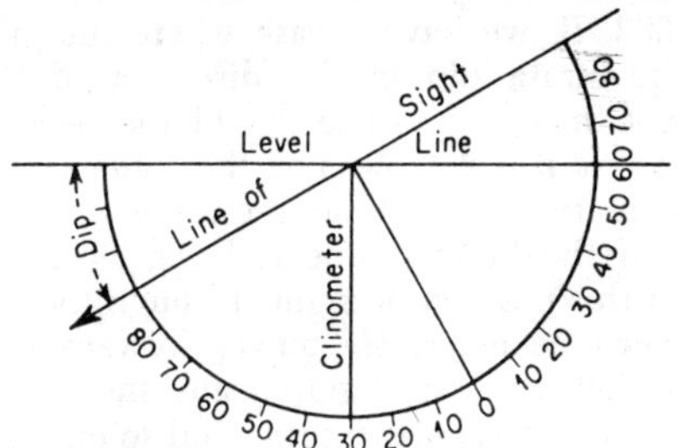

FIG. 391. Principle of the Abney level when used to measure the thickness of a stratigraphic section. With the bubble in the level tube centered, the sighting tube is rotated through an angle, here 30°, equal to the dip of the strata. Since the clinometer is firmly attached to the level tube, it will always be vertical, and will indicate the degrees of dip measured from 0° on the scale.

361. The Jacob staff.[4] A Jacob staff (or Jacob's staff) is a straight rod, usually 5 ft. in length, rubber-tipped or iron-shod at its lower end and having, at its upper end, a rack or ball-and-socket joint to which a Brunton compass or an Abney level can

[4] See Bibliog., Broggi, J. A., 1946; and Robinson, G. D., 1959.

be firmly attached with the length of the open compass or the sight-line tube of the Abney level perpendicular to the rod. The rod serves as a support while the observer is sighting with the compass or level.

The Jacob staff is most useful in the measurement of stratigraphic sections. As explained by Broggi, "the field conditions for the measurement of stratigraphic thicknesses vary according to the slope of the ground and dip of the strata." He lists and describes all cases for horizontal, inclined, and vertical ground surface and for horizontal, inclined, and vertical bedding. We shall mention only four of the simpler cases here.

1. Suppose that the beds are horizontal and that the ground slopes upward from the observer (Fig. 392, A). Since there is no dip, he sets the clinometer arm at zero on the graduated arc.[5] At *a*, holding the rod vertical (*i.e.*, the level horizontal), he sights through the tube at a point *b*. He then moves to *b* and sights at *c*. He carefully records the number of such "steps" (rod lengths) to the top of the measured section. The total thickness will be this number multiplied by the rod length.[6]

2. In Fig. 392, B, we have a case where the ground is horizontal and the strata dip in the direction of the observer's traverse (*a* to *b* to *c*, etc.). The dip of the beds is first determined. In this case it is 20°. Zero on the clinometer arm is set at 20° on the graduated arc. Holding the rod at *a*, the observer tilts it forward until the bubble tube is level, as indicated by the bubble, and in this position he sights through the hollow tube at a point *b*, which he notes. He moves forward to *b* which, as shown in Fig. 392, B, is stratigraphically the length of the rod (5 ft.) above *a*. He repeats at *b* for *c*, and so on, again recording the number of rod lengths from the bottom (*a*) to the top of the section measured. This number times 5 ft. is the thickness of the section.

3. In Fig. 392, C, where the dip of the beds is 30°, the clinometer arm is set at 30° and the observer proceeds, just as in case 2, setting up first at *a* and sighting through the tube at *b* while the rod is tilted at such an angle that the bubble tube is level; then setting up at *b* and repeating to *c*; and so on.

[5] For convenience we shall hereafter refer to the Abney level in its attached position on the rod.

[6] The rod length (here 5 ft.) is the distance from the lower end of the rod up to the central axis of the sighting tube.

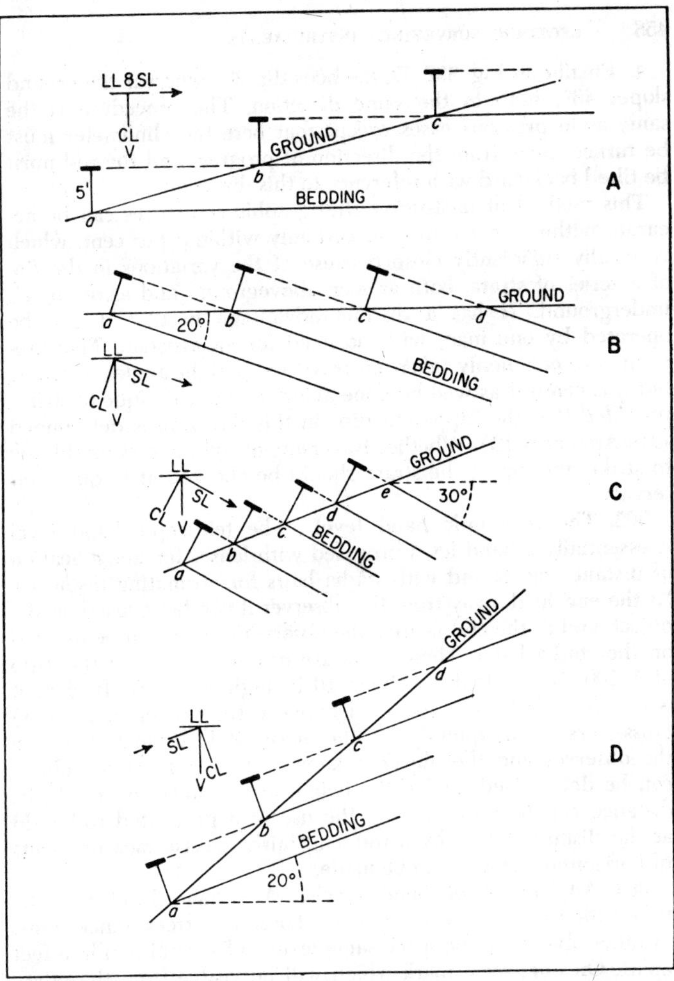

Fig. 392. Sketches to illustrate four different conditions of ground slope and dip of the bedding where measurements are made of the thickness of a stratigraphic section by use of a Jacob staff. At the left of each diagram is a small insert showing the positions of the level line (*LL*); the sight line (*SL*), always parallel to the dip of the beds; the clinometer (*CL*); and the vertical line (*V*). The four cases, A to D, inclusive, are explained in the text.

4. Finally, in Fig. 392, D, the beds dip 20° whereas the ground slopes 40°, both in the same direction. The procedure is the same as in previous cases except that here the clinometer must be turned away from the direction of progress and the rod must be tilted backward with reference to this direction.

This method of measuring stratigraphic sequences can be accurate within 3 per cent, and certainly within 5 per cent, which is usually sufficiently close because of the variations in the dip of a series of strata, both as seen aboveground and as occurring underground. It has a distinct advantage in that it can be operated by one man, with no need for an assistant. Measurements are commonly taken on traverses at right angles to strike, but this can just as well be done along traverses oblique to strike, *provided* that the "apparent dip" in this direction is determined (see Appendix 13). Whether traversing at right angles or oblique to strike, the dip of the strata should be checked at frequent intervals.

362. The telescopic hand level. The telescopic hand level is essentially a hand level provided with lenses for magnification of distant objects and with stadia hairs for estimating distances. At the end held away from the observer it can be focused on the object, and at the end nearest the observer's eye it can be focused on the stadia hairs. These hairs are usually spaced on the ratio of 1:100, *i.e.*, so that an object 10 ft. high and 1,000 ft. distant will appear to be just included between the two outer (stadia) cross-hairs. Consequently, if the horizontal distance between the observer and the object is known, the height of the object can be determined; and if the height of the object is known, its distance can be obtained. By the use of a graduated rod, held at the distant station by a rodman, fairly precise measurements of horizontal distance can be made.

363. Adjustment of hand levels. Any hand level may be tested for its accuracy as follows: choose two trees, fence posts, or other objects at about the same level and several hundred feet apart. On one, set a mark which will be visible from the other. Hold the level at this mark and carefully sight at the other tree (or fence post, etc.), noting a point which is cut by the cross-hair while the latter bisects the image of the bubble. Go to the second tree and, with the level against the observed point, sight back at the mark on the first tree. If, now, the bubble is not bisected by the cross-hair, the level is out of adjustment. To correct, turn the screws at the end of the level tube until the apparent error in the position of the bubble is halved. Go back to the first tree and repeat, if necessary.

364. Comparison of hand levels. The Abney level is seldom used as a level in ordinary geologic field work, but, as part of the Jacob staff, it is valuable for measuring stratigraphic sections (see Art. **361**). Of the Locke and telescopic (stadia) levels, the latter is more accurate than the former for short sights, provided, of course, that the instruments are in perfect adjustment. In the case of either instrument, the relative error is similar for short or for long sights, but the absolute error is greater for long sights.

365. The aneroid barometer. An aneroid barometer is a case containing a metal vacuum chamber which responds to differences in atmospheric pressure. By a mechanism within the case, changes of pressure are communicated, very much magnified, from the vacuum chamber to an index needle which rotates over a circular dial. In view of the fact that atmospheric pressure diminishes with increasing altitude above sea level, the dial is provided with an outer scale in feet of elevation and an inner scale in inches of mercury. The smallest subdivisions of the former scale are usually 10 or 20 ft. Smaller values may be estimated.

Some instruments have the scales fixed, with the zero of the scale in feet opposite 31 on the inch scale, whereas others are constructed so that the outer scale is movable against the inner. If the geologist has an aneroid of the latter kind, he should be careful to *keep the zero mark in feet against* 31 *in.* Otherwise he may introduce considerable errors into his readings for the reason that the divisions of the altitude scale are not of uniform size, but are progressively smaller from zero to the upper registry of the instrument. Under normal atmospheric pressure, 31 in. represents an elevation of 890 ft. below sea level. The zero point of the altitude scale was chosen arbitrarily as equivalent to 31 in. on the pressure scale so that the needle would seldom, by rises of atmospheric pressure (**413**), go as low as zero. If atmospheric pressure should rise to more than 31 in. a negative elevation would be indicated on the scale in feet.

Aneroids are made in sizes varying from about 2 to 6 in. in diameter. They register up to 2,000, 3,000, 5,000, 6,000, 10,000 ft., etc. One registering to 5,000 or 6,000 ft. is generally most satisfactory in regions where elevations above sea level are not over 4,000 ft. Under no circumstances should a barometer be used at altitudes near the limits of its registry. Hence, the geologist who expects to undertake barometric work should ascertain the probable range of elevations in the district to be investigated.

For all geologic work the barometer must be reliable. Few aneroids are good enough. Before an instrument is selected for purchase, it should be carefully tested. This may be done in several ways as follows:

"1. Gently tap the glass case with the fingers. The needle should jar slightly, not too freely, and should return to the same point at which it stood before being disturbed. If it stops now at one place and now at another, after successive tappings, while it is held always in the same position, it is unreliable.

"2. Read the instrument, carry it to an upper floor in a building, or 30 or 40 ft. up a hill; read it; return to the starting point and read again. Two or three minutes after arriving here the needle should record the same elevation as at first, provided the ascent and descent were made within 5 or 6 minutes. Go up to the upper station once more, wait a minute or two, and read. Any considerable differences in the elevations recorded at the same station, especially if these differences are unrelated, usually indicate a poor barometer. The pause after reaching the station is to allow for a possible lag.

"3 Take out the new barometer on a day's traverse and compare its readings with those of another barometer known to be reliable. In doing this observe that both barometers may not show the same elevations, estimated from zero, nor equal amounts of rise and fall, but both should rise together and fall together, and *after the readings have been corrected* (**413, 416**), the elevations obtained by both instruments should be approximately the same for the station."[7]

Since an aneroid is always a delicate instrument, it should be handled with care. It should be carried where it will not be severely jolted and where it is subject to as little variation in temperature as possible (**413**). In reading the instrument, hold it horizontally in the open palm of your hand. Do not grasp it.

366. The Paulin altimeter. A special type of aneroid barometer, called a Paulin altimeter, has been devised to overcome, as far as possible, some of the instrumental defects[8] of the ordi-

[7] Bibliog., Lahee, F. H., 1920, p. 151.

[8] Such as frictional resistance in the operation of the mechanical parts, elastic hysteresis, and lag.

nary aneroid. We cannot go into the details of construction here. Suffice it to say that, while "the ordinary aneroid may be likened to a spring balance where the reading of weight depends upon the proportional elongation of the spring," the Paulin altimeter "is comparable to the type of scale used in laboratories or for other accurate weighing where known weights are placed on one pan and the object to be weighed is placed on the other, the true weight then being determined by adding to or subtracting from the known weights until the 'tendency pointer' is at zero on the scale."[9] Except for some differences in the method of reading the elevations, the Paulin altimeter is handled like an aneroid barometer. Corrections for temperature, weather conditions, and diurnal range must be made in using either instrument (**413–423**).

367. The barograph. A barograph may be described as a self-recording aneroid barometer. The movements of the vacuum chamber, caused by variations in atmospheric pressure, are communicated to an arm which carries a pen. This pen, which is constantly filled with ink, rests on a piece of specially prepared ruled paper wrapped round a drum which revolves by clockwork. The motions of the pen are thus recorded on this paper. At the end of each day the record is removed and a new piece of paper is substituted. Barographs are made in different sizes. A small one is almost useless for geologic purposes (**415**, ¶ 8), because the divisions on the ruled paper are too small for careful reading of pressure variations. A large instrument, if any, is the only kind that should be used, but this has the disadvantages of bulk and weight.

368. The watch. An ordinary watch is absolutely essential in some types of field work (**408**). It ought to be of workmanship sufficiently good to insure its proper running, with ordinary care, while the geologist is in places where no repairs can be made. A wrist watch is most convenient.

369. The plane table. A plane table is a drawing board mounted on a tripod in such a way that the board can be turned horizontally, when the table is set up, without moving the tripod. Geologists ordinarily prefer boards 15 by 15 in., 18 by 18 in., or 18 by 24 in. The small size is convenient for some kinds of reconnaissance work (**438**). The 18- by 24-in. board is the best size

[9] Bibliog., Hill, Raymond A., 1929. See also Bibliog., Hodgson, Robert A., 1957, on the use of the Paulin altimeter.

for mapping unsectionized country and for mapping a single township, on the scale of 2,000 ft. = 1 in., in sectionized country (Appendix 7), since, in the latter case, there is room for the title, legend, etc. (**484**). The 18- by 18-in. size is useful in sectionized country where several townships must be mapped and the maps must later be fitted together.

The paper for the map may be attached to the board by thumb screws or thumb tacks.

The plane table may be used oriented or unoriented. When *unoriented,* the table is set up at a given locality without reference to directions. It serves merely as a page in the notebook, but is a more convenient support for the map. Lines between stations are plotted by protractor with respect to north-south and east-west coordinates ruled on the map sheet. An *oriented* plane table is set up at every station in exactly the same position relative to true or astronomic bearings (**356**), and lines between stations are plotted by sight alidade (**372**) or telescopic alidade (**373**). Some plane tables have a compass needle for orienting, sunk in the board at one edge. More often, however, the board is not provided with such a needle, for the Gurley compass (**355**) or the alidade may serve the same purpose if this instrument is properly placed on the map.

370. Paper for the plane table. On account of the fact that paper consists of fibers, it generally expands and contracts unequally in different directions. To overcome this tendency, plane table paper is mounted on cloth, or two or three thicknesses of paper are mounted together with the fibers in the different sheets in different relative positions. The most satisfactory type is made of two sheets of paper with a sheet of cloth between them (double mounted egg shell paper). This may be used first on one side and then on the other. The surface should be slightly rough, hard enough to take a 7-H or 8-H pencil line, and slightly tinted to lessen the glare of the sunlight. The sheets should be cut to the dimensions of the plane table. Often several sheets are carried attached to the board at the same time. When a map sheet is finished, it is placed under a clean one. Celluloid sheets may be used in regions where wet weather is continuous for many weeks, but otherwise the cloth-mounted paper is to be preferred. On rainy days office work can be done instead of mapping in the field.

371. Stadia and levelling rods. In plane-table mapping a stadia rod is used in connection with the telescopic alidade. This is a collapsible jointed wooden rod, 12 to 15 ft. long when open, and 3 or 4 in. wide, graduated in feet and tenths of feet. It should be painted in contrasting colors, preferably with white background and a black saw-tooth design to mark feet and fractions of a foot. Such a design can be read at great distances. The rod is carried by a "rodman." When set up for a reading, it should be vertical and the graduated side should be held facing directly toward the "instrument man" who, at some distant point, is looking at it through the telescope of his alidade.

Sometimes mapping is done by means of a telescopic hand level and a level rod. This rod may be from 5 to 15 ft. long. It may be provided with a sliding disc or *target* which can be set at a chosen elevation above the ground.

372. The open-sight alidade. An open-sight alidade consists of a flat rectangular metal base with one edge bevelled and graduated, about 10 in. long, provided with an open folding sight at each end. It is used in conjunction with the plane table. In practice the sights are turned up at right angles to the base. They should be at least 4 or 5 in. long, for observations up or down slopes. The observer, having set up the plane table at a station (428), places the fiducial (bevelled) edge of the alidade against the point that represents this station on the map, and rotates the alidade about this point until he brings some distant object, which he has selected as the next station, into line with the cross-hair of one sight and the slit of the other sight. He then draws a line on the map along the fiducial edge from the point for his present location toward the distant object. The use of the alidade is further described in Chap. 16.

373. The telescopic alidade. The telescopic alidade most commonly used in geologic field work is of the Gale type. It has a flat metal base, 11 in. long and 2¾ in. wide, with one edge bevelled and graduated to fiftieths of an inch. Upon this base are two short vertical pillars on which a small telescope is so mounted that it may be rotated in a vertical plane parallel to the bevelled edge of the base. The line of sight of the telescope is always in this vertical plane when the instrument is properly adjusted. On the right side of the base is a tangent screw for raising and lowering the telescope. On the left side of the base is a magnetic needle. This should be kept locked when not in use. With the alidade resting flat on the plane table, the latter can be levelled by means of a round spirit level, or bullseye level, on the alidade base. A detachable striding level, which is employed in levelling the telescope, is supported by two wyes, each resting on a metal collar, one on one side and the other on the other side of the sleeve in which the telescope is set. A graduated arc, firmly attached to the telescope, shows, by reference to a vernier, the angle through which the telescope is rotated.

At the objective end of the telescope are a vertical and a horizontal diametric cross-hair and two horizontal stadia hairs, these being carefully fastened in proper relative position on a reticle, or cross-hair ring. The two stadia hairs are at equal distances above and below the horizontal cross-hair. They are spaced, as in the telescopic hand level, so that they will exactly include a distance of 1 ft. on an object 100 ft. away, or 2 ft. on an object 200 ft. away, and so on, when this object is viewed through the telescope. The vertical distance thus covered between the stadia hairs is called an *interval* or a *step*, and half this distance, between either stadia hair and the horizontal cross-hair, is a *half interval* or a *half step*. The reticle, as a whole, is movable by four capstan screws. For purposes of adjustment it is very necessary to understand how these screws control the movement of the cross-hair ring. Before tightening one screw, the opposite one should be loosened, for otherwise the ring cannot move and the screw threads may be damaged. By loosening the lower screw and tightening the upper screw the whole ring may be drawn upward, or by reversing the process, it may be turned downward. By working the side screws in a similar manner, the ring may be turned to one side or the other. All this can be done without turning the ring, while the vertical hair remains vertical, and the horizontal hair remains horizontal.[10]

A telescopic alidade may be equipped with a Beaman stadia arc for simplifying the reading of differences of elevation, and with a gradienter screw and Stebinger drum for measuring distances and determining vertical angles. The Beaman arc is at-

[10] After Mather, following J. C. Tracy. Bibliog., Mather, Kirtley F., 1919, p. 101. This is a very excellent treatment of the subject. With the kind permission of Professor Mather and also of the Scientific Laboratories of Denison University, we have quoted extensively from this article.

tached to the horizontal axis of the telescope. The drum, which is attached to the tangent screw, is so graduated that if it is rotated through one complete revolution, the telescope will be raised (or lowered) through one interval, as above defined (see Art. 437, 4, 5).

374. Care of the alidade. Like all instruments of precision the alidade must be handled with extreme care. It should never be placed on the ground or on a rock pile. If for any reason it must be removed from the plane table, return it to its leather case and close the case tightly. Its base must be kept free from dirt. When in constant daily use, all screws and moving parts should be carefully wiped clean with a soft rag dampened in light oil. The springs which play against the bearing studs on the opposite sides from the vernier and tangent screws should be removed from their housings, wiped clean, stretched a little, and replaced. At all times the instrument should be protected against jars and shocks which might cause changes in adjustment of cross-hairs, level bubbles, or other delicate parts.

"If the Stebinger drum is used in determining the elevations, the tangent screw must be treated with special care. Experience indicates that very trivial and unobtrusive things may change the relation of the screw to the arc sufficiently to make a Stebinger table no longer applicable and necessitate the construction of a new one. If possible, the gradienter screw should be entirely withdrawn every week or two and wiped absolutely clean with the oily cloth. The bearing plate stud against which the point of the micrometer screw pushes must be kept securely tightened. Should it become loose very erratic readings will result. The surface of this plate will gradually wear at the point where the micrometer screw bears against it until a distinct socket is made. Ultimately this becomes so pronounced that not only does it throw out the relation of the straight line push of the screw to the circular movement of the arc, but the point of the screw will not hit exactly the same spot on successive readings, and as a result three or four readings from the same station to the same object will fail to check. When that happens, the bearing plate should be surfaced with a file and a new gradienter table constructed. (See Art. 437, 5.)

"The compass needle should always be raised from its pivot and clamped immediately after it has been used . . . . Place the alidade as nearly as possible in the magnetic meridian before releasing the needle, and thus avoid the blow to the needle resulting from sudden contact with the compass box. The danger of destroying the polarity of the needle is another reason for guarding against reckless treatment of the alidade as a whole. When working in the rain, the compass box is the most vulnerable part of the instrument. Unless the glass cover is securely sealed all around, moisture will penetrate the box and put the needle out of commission by causing it to adhere to the inside of the glass. If this occurs, the box must be opened, the needle removed, and all parts thoroughly dried before proceeding with the work."[11]

375. Adjustment of the alidade.

"The most important adjustments of the miniature or explorer's alidade, which require attention in the field, are those for collimation and of the striding level. All other adjustments are reasonably permanent as made in the factory. It is, however, well for the instrument man to be able to detect, and if possible correct, faulty workmanship or damage for mistreatment or accident.

"The line of sight through the telescope is determined by the intersection of the cross-hairs, whatever their position in the tube, and the nodal point in the objective lens. This line is correctly collimated when it coincides with the optical axis of the objective. That is, the intersection of the cross-hairs should remain stationary in the field of vision when the telescope is rotated on its horizontal axis. The telescope is mounted between 180-degree stops in the axis-sleeve for this purpose.

"Sight some distant fixed object of small size and center the cross-hair exactly upon it. The telescope need not be horizontal. Rotate the tube carefully half way round and twist the prismatic eye-piece back into position. Note whether the cross-hairs are still centered upon the object. If not, correct half the discrepancy by means of the diaphragm adjusting studs, which may or may not be concealed beneath a ferrule which forms a guard against accident or tampering . . . . Move the vertical hair to left or right by turning both lateral studs in the same direction, first slightly loosening the one, then tightening the other. If the alidade is of the erecting type with field reversed from right to left, as is commonly the case, loosen the screw *away from which* the *vertical* hair must apparently be moved, and tighten the opposite screw. Move the horizontal hair up or down by turning top and bottom studs in the same direction, first slightly loosening the one and then tightening the other. If the eye-piece is of the erecting type, loosen the screw *towards which* the *horizontal* cross-hairs must apparently be moved and tighten the opposite screw. Having corrected half the discrepancy in this way, shift the alidade until the cross-hairs are again centered upon the distant object, and rotate the telescope as before. The line of sight should now remain fixed upon the distant point; if it does not do so, correct half the apparent error as before. Repeat until the hairs are properly centered.

"The test for collimation should be frequently made. No important triangulations should be begun until one is certain that the cross-hairs are

[11] Bibliog., Mather, Kirtley, F., 1919, pp. 141, 142.

properly located. Should the instrument be subjected to any unusual jar, it must be collimated before it is again used. In the normal routine of field work the position of the cross-hairs should be examined at least once each week."[12]

Probably the most important adjustment of the alidade to be made in the field is that of the striding level. The bubble of the striding level is sensitive to changes in temperature, shocks, etc., and must be watched carefully in order to do accurate work. It should be checked at least three or four times daily, and especially before starting work in the morning and in the middle of the day. If the temperature change is great, or if many stations are visited, the bubble should be checked more frequently.

For making such adjustments a screw will be noted at one end of the bubble carriage. By means of a spring a slight turn of the screw raises or lowers one end of the carriage. To make correct adjustment, bring the bubble to level by means of the vertical tangent screw. Reverse the bubble carriage and if the bubble does not return to the central position, adjust for one-half of the error by means of the adjustment screw. To be in perfect adjustment, the bubble should remain in the center when the bubble carriage is reversed. A number of trials may be necessary to obtain the correct adjustment. While a slight error of adjustment does not make an appreciable difference in short shots, it increases largely the percentage of error in long shots.

376. Stadia reduction tables. If, in plane-table work, the observer's station is higher or lower than the observed station, the solution of a right triangle is involved. The inclined distance along the line of sight is the hypotenuse, the horizontal projection of this inclined distance is one leg, and the vertical difference of elevation of the two stations is the other leg. The inclined distance (hypotenuse) and the vertical angle between the line of sight and its horizontal projection (horizontal leg) are read by the instrument man. By reference to a stadia reduction table, or conversion table (Appendix 18), he finds the length of the vertical leg of a right triangle similar to the one above described, but with its hypotenuse 100 ft. long. This factor he multiplies by the number of hundreds in the inclined distance between the two stations in order to determine their difference in altitude (**434**).

[12] Bibliog., Mather, Kirtley, F., 1919, pp., 137–139.

377. Stadia slide rule. A stadia slide rule is a mechanical device which may be substituted for stadia reduction tables. The stationary part of the rule is graduated above for horizontal and below for vertical distances. The movable scale is marked in angular degrees. When the horizontal distance to a given station, *A*, is known, and the angle of inclination of the line of sight to this station is also known, the vertical difference in elevation between the observer's station and *A* can be found by setting "0" (marked on the side of the movable scale nearest to the fixed scale for horizontal distances) opposite the value of the given horizontal distance. The required vertical distance, on the other fixed scale, will be against the observed angle. It is important to remember that, if the horizontal distance is greater than the vertical distance, one fixed scale is used for horizontal distances, and if the vertical distance is greater than the horizontal distance, the other fixed scale is used for horizontal distances.

378. Scale for plotting. A *plotting scale*, or a scale for plotting, is a straight-edge graduated in intervals representing feet, yards, meters, or paces, on whatever scale is adopted for the mapping. Such a scale is best graduated in inches and tenths of inches when plane-table mapping is done on a scale of 1 in. = 1,000 ft., or 1 in. = 2,000 ft.

379. The protractor. A 4- or 5-in. protractor is often very useful for laying off angles in any kind of mapping. Probably it is employed most frequently in plotting compass traverses (**399**), dip-and-strike symbols, and locations taken by intersection on known points.

380. The steel tape. The steel tape is of especial importance in measuring base lines for triangulation nets (**436,** ¶ 2). It is also serviceable in measuring stratigraphic sections, in determining pace lengths, and in measuring other short distances where considerable accuracy is required. For geologic mapping there is practically never any necessity for correcting taped distances for tension, temperature, sag, or standardization of the tape.

381. The odometer. When an automobile is used in geologic mapping, the car must have an odometer registering the distance travelled in miles and tenths of miles. This instrument constitutes part of the mechanism in a speedometer, as usually provided. By keeping watch of the trip gauge, the geologist can estimate distances to less than 0.05 mile, which is close enough for most reconnaissance work (**391**).

382. The tally register or pace counter. A tally register is an instrument, about the size of an ordinary watch, used for keeping count of paces. In traversing on foot, the geologist holds it in his hand and presses the small knob at every second or every fourth step. With a little practice, this becomes so much a habit that it requires hardly any thought. If one is traversing moderately hilly country, perhaps with a fairly open growth of vegetation, the average length of two steps will be very nearly 5 ft.; that is, one can allow about 1,000 double paces to the mile, a convenient quantity for approximate measurements of distance. If the land is less rolling, or more open, the geologist will probably go a mile in less than 1,000 double paces.

383. The camera. A camera is almost an essential part of a geologist's field equipment. There is considerable divergence of opinion as to which is the most satisfactory kind to use. Some prefer one of vest-pocket size, whereas others choose a larger type. Much depends upon conditions of climate and travel in any particular field investigation, for sometimes the pack must be reduced to the lowest possible weight and dimensions. Ordinarily the writer prefers a Leica, or other miniature camera, because of its size and the large number of pictures that can be carried. In any case the lens should have good definition. In moist climates, and particularly in tropical regions, films should always be carried in watertight tins, and they should be developed as soon as possible after exposure (352).

384. Base maps. For most kinds of geologic field work, some sort of a preliminary map of the region is of great advantage. This may be a simple property plat; a road or railroad map; a township plat (Appendix 7); a county or state map; a plotted triangulation net (436) or other control system; a sketch map of the drainage; or, better than any of these, a good topographic contour map, or an air photograph or photographic mosaic (454). Such a map, which has been previously prepared and on which the geologist can plot his data in the field, is termed a *base map* or a *working map*. Sometimes the base map must be enlarged or reduced to bring it to the scale adopted for the field work.

385. Additional equipment. In addition to the instruments which may be used, the geologist will need various other articles. A few words will be said concerning notebooks in the next chapter which treats of the methods of field surveying. If the work necessitates the collection of rock specimens, the geologist should provide himself with a geologic hammer, a collecting bag, small paper bags or newspapers in which the specimens can be separately wrapped, and paper labels (**351**). The style of hammer depends partly on the preference of the individual and partly on the nature of the work and the character of the rocks. Hard crystalline rocks require a heavier hammer than fissile shales. The fossil collector generally chooses a hammer with a peen shaped for splitting.

For plane-table mapping, a 7-H or 8-H pencil is best. A 4-H to 6-H pencil is better for recording information in the notebook. Colored pencils are convenient for marking, on a working map, the distribution of the different formations encountered. The boundaries of the formations are first outlined and then the areas between are filled in with the colors.

A hand lens is always useful, and is almost indispensable for work in regions of igneous or metamorphic rocks.

For automobile work, in rough country, the geologist will do well to prepare himself for trouble. He will be wise if he carries two spare casings, three or four spare inner tubes, an extra tin of gasoline (3, 4, or 5 gal.), a tin of lubricating oil, a spade, mud chains, 30 or 40 ft. of stout rope, an axe, some baling wire, extra spark plugs and valve caps, and so on, besides all the usual equipment that belongs with a car.

Chapter 16

GEOLOGIC SURVEYING

PART III. INSTRUMENTAL METHODS IN FIELD MAPPING

General Considerations

386. Procedures in geologic mapping. As stated in Art. 329, geologic mapping requires the following three procedures: (1) the examination of the rocks; (2) the determination of the location of outcrops or points where observations are made; and (3) the plotting of the field data on a map. All three of these procedures are important, but the extent to which each is carried and the manner in which each is executed depend on the nature of the country, the kind of rocks, the rate at which the mapping must be done, the character of the results desired, and many other factors. Geologists should be impressed with the necessity of carefully locating outcrops and stations, not only in reference to natural objects and to one another, but also—and particularly—in relation to established survey corners, land lines, and other such features. The significance of this remark is often brought out in those phases of geologic surveying which have an economic purpose. If air photographs of an area to be surveyed are available, they may be of great assistance in this matter of locating outcrops, stations, and other points of interest (see Art. 456).

387. Traverse defined. In studying an area a geologist proceeds along the route which he thinks will show him most in the time at his disposal. His course, known as a *traverse,* is a line, or a system of lines, connecting outcrops or stations where observations are taken. Obviously several traverses have to be made when an area is to be investigated. Traverses are often designated by the instrument which figures most largely in their making. Thus, there are compass traverses, plane-table traverses, transit traverses, barometer traverses, etc.

388. Quantities measured. The accurate location of points involves measurements of horizontal distance, vertical distance or difference of elevation, and horizontal direction. Distances are determined by direct measurement, as in pacing, taping, chaining, etc., by reference to the stadia interval (**373**), or by triangulation (**436**). *Horizontal* distances can seldom be measured in actual practice. They can be obtained by right angle calculations when inclined distances or slope distances have been determined, but, except in accurate mapping, the allowable limit of error in geologic work rarely demands the reduction of the measured inclined distances to their horizontal equivalents. Such reduction is necessary only when the ratio of the length of the inclined distance between two stations to the difference of elevation of the two stations is relatively large. The limiting ratio, which will decide whether or not a given inclined distance should be corrected to its horizontal equivalent, varies according to the degree of refinement wanted in the results (**391**). Ordinarily no such correction is necessary for slopes of

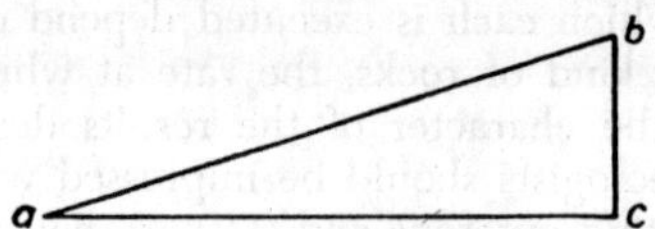

FIG. 393. Section of a slope to illustrate slope distance, *ab*, horizontal or map distance, *ac*, and difference of elevation, *bc*.

less than 5°. If, in Fig. 393, *ab* is a rather steeply inclined slope distance, *bc* the elevation of the point *b* above *a, ac* the horizontal or map equivalent of *ab*, and $\angle bac$ the slope angle, then *ac* may be obtained by the equation, $ac = ab \cdot \cos \angle bac$, or by the equation, $ac = \sqrt{ab^2 - bc^2}$, according to whether the slope angle, $\angle bac$, or the difference of elevation, *bc*, has been determined.

Differences of elevation are found by stepping (**359, 437**), by vertical angle computations (**360, 437**), and by barometric readings (**387,** *et seq.*).

Directions, always regarded as horizontal in mapping, are determined by compass or by triangulation (**436**).

In addition to these quantities, geologic work often requires the measurement of dips of strata, faults, veins, etc. Dips are found by clinometer (**358**) unless they are very low, in which case they may be determined by obtaining elevations of points on a given key horizon (340).

389. Correction of pace lengths. Pacing is a common method of measuring distances on the ground. If a certain distance is paced from one known point, by way of several unknown stations, to a second known point, and an error in the distance is found at the second known point, this error may be divided proportionally among the several parts of the traverse, from station to station. If long distances are to be paced, without control stations for checking, the geologist should measure his pace lengths in the different types of country traversed. His paces will be longer in smooth open country than in rough topography, or on

TABLE 6. REDUCING PACES ON SLOPES TO THEIR EQUIVALENTS IN TERMS OF HORIZONTAL PACES

Angle of slope	0°	5°	10°	15°	20°	25°	30°
Gradient of slope	....	1/11.4	1/5.7	1/3.7	1/2.7	1/2.1	1/1.7
Factor for paces going uphill	1.000	0.907	0.799	0.717	0.625	0.542	0.413
Factor for paces going downhill	1.000	0.959	0.929	0.905	0.860	0.753	0.591

land overgrown with tall weeds or grass, or thickly overgrown with shrubbery or trees. They will be longer on level ground than up or down a relatively steep slope. If desired the foregoing table may be used for finding the value, in terms of horizontal paces, of any number of paces on a slope of 30° or less.[1] Multiply the number of paces recorded on the slope by the factor in the table for that slope, thus: if a distance on a slope of 20°, going uphill, is 300 paces, the actual distance on the slope is equal to $0.625 \times 300 = 187.5$ horizontal paces. If the horizontal pace is

[1] Before using this table each individual should test it for his own paces measured on different slopes. He will do well to make a similar table for himself. As a matter of fact, however, many geologists standardize their paces by walking several miles uphill and downhill over the kind of country to be mapped and computing an average pace length for the whole distance. This average pace is then adopted for all measurements of distance without reference to slope.

equal to 2.5 ft., the distance *on the slope* is 2.5 × 187.5 ft. = 468.75 ft. After making this correction for the slope value of the paces, the slope distance obtained, here 468.75 ft., must be reduced to the horizontal by one of the equations given in Art. 388. In using the table for slope factors, interpolate for slope angles not multiples of 5.

Where the traversing is done on horseback, the length of the horse's pace must be determined under different conditions, just as in the case of a man's pace, and these values may be used as units of measurement of distance.

390. Controls for mapping. Geologic mapping, like all kinds of mapping, is done by determining and plotting the locations of certain chosen points or stations and then sketching in the details with reference to these points. Gannett has well defined a map as "a sketch, corrected by locations." These selected points may be said to *control* the map. Their horizontal directions and distances from one another are termed the *horizontal control,* and their elevations the *vertical control,* of the map. Occasionally, in regions which have not yet been surveyed, the geologist has to establish the entire system of control points for his map; but generally he finds that a control of the district to be investigated has already been plotted, perhaps by the U.S. Geological Survey, or the Coast and Geodetic Survey, or by a survey conducted by state or township, by a railroad or mining company, or by some other interest.[2] Yet, even in this case, because the fixed control points are too far apart or because, as is usual, they have been chosen with little regard for geologic structure, he will have to locate a secondary group of stations whose horizontal and vertical positions will be determined in relation to the original or primary control points. The control system for any geologic work should be laid out more accurately, *i.e.,* with a smaller allowable limit of error, than is demanded for the geologic mapping itself.

391. Detail and reconnaissance mapping. The degree of accuracy with which field mapping may be done, is open to wide variation. In some kinds of work every outcrop and every geologic contact must be located with precision, whereas, in other cases, only a sketch is required of the position and size of

[2] The control points may be triangulation stations, U.S. Geological Survey bench marks, township corner posts or quarter posts, claim corner posts. etc.

the larger structures and rock formations. In general, the more precise methods are included under the term, *detail mapping*, and the less precise methods are *reconnaissance mapping*. In the former progress is slower and, therefore, more time is needed for covering a given area. The mapping is performed with as small an error as is consistent with the limits of error of the geologic structure (**442**). On the other hand, in reconnaissance work, speed is often of paramount importance, and a large limit of error may be permissible. For the field work for each problem, instruments are chosen and field methods are pursued, which will be best adapted to the needs of the particular case in hand.

Reconnaissance surveying, if properly done, is far more difficult than detail work. It requires wide experience, thorough training, quick judgment, constant observation of soils, vegetation, outcrops, and topography, and the ability to remember the impressions obtained during the part of the work already completed. The geologist must be able mentally to picture in three dimensions structures and formations which he can actually see, usually poorly exposed, in but two dimensions. In geologic training one should become proficient in detail mapping before attempting reconnaissance mapping. A good reconnaissance man is always on the alert. We know of one instance where such a man, accustomed to driving an automobile in his field work, noticed that his rear wheels became clogged with mud in a manner not characteristic of the wet mud of the locality. From this he was led to make a search which revealed a small area of exposure of an older formation uplifted by salt doming (**180, 6**). Hundreds of geologists would have passed by this incident without notice. Again, a good reconnaissance man, even if he must drive over the same route many times, will always be trying to account for the geology and physiography which he is traversing. The best reconnaissance man is one who records all he sees, not all he thinks he should see, and clearly enough so that his notes can be used when later ideas evolve.

392. Note-taking in general. Geologic notes should always be full and accurate. Do not rely on your memory. Write down all your observations and impressions. Be careful to distinguish between facts and theories. If you are not quite sure of a statement, punctuate it with a question mark in parentheses. Notes may be abbreviated to save time; but if scientific knowledge is to be increased by the investigation, abridgment of the field notes should not be of such a character as to impair their lucidity for any geologist who may subsequently read them. Symbols and unintelligible abbreviations should be listed with their meanings near the front of the notebook. Following are a few common abbreviations which may well be learned and put into practice. Others will suggest themselves as occasion demands.

ABBREVIATIONS OF GEOLOGIC TERMS FOR FIELD NOTES

about, ca.
basalt, b.
bedding, stratification, bd.
conglomerate, cg.
diorite, di.
from, fr.
granite, gr, γ.
joint, or jointing, jt.
limestone, ls.
metamorphosed, met.
outcrop, otc.
rocks, rx.
sandstone, ss.
shale, sh.
slate, sl.
specimen, sp.
trap, tr.

Strike and dip of bedding may be recorded in short form by always writing them in the same order: N30E40NW, meaning strike, N. 30° E., and dip, 40° NW.; or, as stated in Art. **358**, using the same example, both dip amount and dip direction may be recorded thus: 40° N. 60° W.

It is good policy to write on only every other page so that plenty of space will be left blank for future additions and corrections. Illustrate all significant geologic structures and other features by sketches and diagrams. These are the briefest and most satisfactory means of recording information (Chap. 19).

On the last pages of the field notebook the rock specimens and photographs should be separately catalogued (**351, 352**). For each specimen give its number, locality, field name, date of collection, and the page on which it is described, and leave spaces for additional remarks and for the numbers of thin sections if these are to be made. For each photograph give its number, locality, name, the direction in which it was taken, and also remarks on time of day, light value, length of exposure, diaphragm, and focus (**352, 383**).

393. Four principal methods of field mapping. Although the methods of geologic field mapping are innumerable and diverse, depending upon such factors as the nature of the country, the mode of travel, the degree of precision demanded in the work, and the individual preferences and notions of the geologist himself, yet most of these are simply variations of the following four principal methods: (1) the compass-and-clinometer method, (2) the hand-level method, (3) the barometer method, and (4) the plane-table method. These will be described below. To these might be added (5) the methods of air (aerial) mapping (Chap. 17), and (6) the methods of mapping by the application of electronics (Art. **552**).

The Compass-and-Clinometer Method

394. Definition. In the *compass-and-clinometer method,* frequently used in reconnaissance mapping, the clinometer is employed for taking dips and the compass for determining strikes and directions (**355–357**). Distances are often paced, on foot or on horseback, or are measured by odometer (**381**), and differences of elevation are commonly obtained by barometric readings, properly corrected (**413**). Where the topographic relief is comparatively low and the dips of strata are high, no attempt is made to ascertain the relative altitudes of stations or outcrops, for under such circumstances the resulting error is practically negligible. On the other hand, if dips average only 5° or 10° and the relief is considerable, the elevations of outcrops should not be disregarded (**193**).

395. Equipment. For the compass-and-clinometer method of mapping, the Brunton compass with its clinometer attachment is most convenient. Besides this instrument one needs a tally register, a notebook, a working map if such is available, a protractor, pencils, hand lens, probably a hammer, a camera, and an aneroid barometer if elevations are to be determined. A Locke level may be of service. *The compass should be set for magnetic declination* (**357**).

Notebooks of various shapes and sizes are used according to the preference of the geologist. A convenient kind is 5 by 7½ in., opening at the shorter edge, and having its pages ruled with coordinate lines ⅕ in. apart. This easily fits in one's pocket.

396. Preparation of the notebook. Before you begin field work, the notebook should be made ready. Write your name and address on the inside of the front cover. On the first blank page, facing the front cover, record the name of the region where the investigation is to be made, and the year and date of beginning the work. The magnetic variation of the compass needle (**356, 357**) in the region is noted on the first ruled page. On page 3 you will start your notes unless you can secure a good topographic map of your area for a working map.

If you have a line base map,[3] its scale, contour interval, and name are to be recorded on the first ruled page, as well as the magnetic variation. Cut this map into rectangles of equal size and somewhat smaller than a page of the notebook, so that, if mounted, there will be at least ¼-in. margin on the ruled page on all sides. Topographic sheets of the U.S. Geological Survey may be cut into nine rectangles, each bounded by parallels and

FIG. 394. Method of numbering the divisions of a working map.

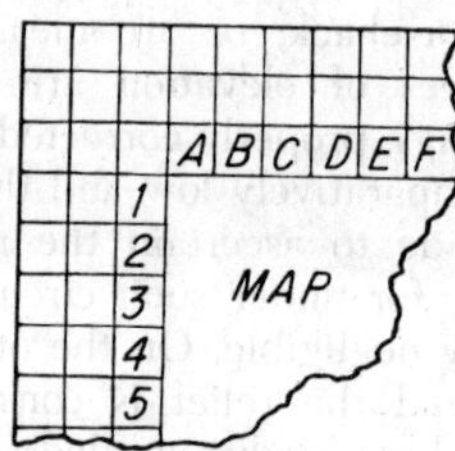

FIG. 395. Method of mounting a working map.

meridians.[4] These rectangles may be mounted on a piece of linen or they may be pasted in the notebook. If mounted on linen, the sections should be separated a little to facilitate folding. When so mounted, all parts of the map are together and the whole can be folded and kept in a pocket in the notebook. If they are to be pasted separately in the book, number them as shown in Fig. 394. Glue rectangle 1 on page 3, making its upper and left edges flush with horizontal and vertical coordinates, respectively (looking at the open book with its length up and down). On page 5 mount rectangle 2 in a position exactly analogous to that

[3] As distinguished from an air photograph (see Art. **456**).

[4] These are called rectangles although actually the corner angles are not quite 90° on account of the northward convergence of the meridians.

of rectangle 1, but leave an inch or so near the upper margin of this map free. The lower edge of rectangle 1 can then be bent down to touch the upper edge of rectangle 2, if you wish to see the relations of contours, roads, etc., near this common margin. The other portions of the working map may be mounted like rectangle 2 in proper order on pages 7, 9, 11, 13, etc. Above each rectangle write its number. If you intend to adopt the *coordinate system* in taking your notes (398), letter the coordinate spaces (not the lines) above each rectangle, and number the spaces on the left of each rectangle, beginning at the top left corner (Fig. 395). In just the same manner letter and number the corresponding spaces on the even-numbered pages facing the maps. If the *point system* (398) is followed, the coordinate spaces need not be numbered or lettered. All the preliminary writing should be done in waterproof India ink, not in pencil nor in an ink that will wash off.

It is hardly necessary to say that the exact manner in which each geologist will keep his notes will depend on his own personal taste. The writer believes, however, that the student should be taught several accepted methods so that he may be able better to choose his own course in later work.

397. Compass traverses. When a good base map of a region to be surveyed cannot be procured, and the mapping is done by the compass-and-clinometer method, the geologist generally follows a course across country from point to point, finding the directions of the different parts of his route by compass. His course is a *compass traverse*. Even if a base map is available, traversing by compass may be necessary because the scale of the map is too small or because it has some comparatively large areas so lacking in geographic features that stations cannot be readily located by reference to it. Sometimes, also, short compass traverses are run from stations in a triangulation net or a stadia traverse (**436**).

Let us now briefly consider the manner of conducting a compass traverse. The first thing to do is to find, in the field, some point which has been definitely established by previous surveying. It may be a triangulation station, a land survey post, a geographic boundary monument, a claim post, etc. If a topographic map is provided, it may be the intersection of two roads, the confluence of two streams, etc., as shown on this map. Call this point Station 1.

Having located Station 1, find the bearing to any conspicuous object, preferably an outcrop, in the general direction in which the traverse is to be run, and pace to this object. Call it Station 2. If it is of geologic interest, record your observations. Proceed in the same way to Stations 3, 4, and so on. In this work it is always a good plan to check the course by sighting back to the last station, or by sighting from two or more of the stations to some recognizable point on one side or the other of the traverse (Resection, page 532). For areal surveying traverses should be run as near one another as time will permit and near enough for the geologist to feel reasonably sure that he has seen most of the district. They should be connected at intervals by cross traverses.

Before setting out on a compass traverse, you should ascertain the approximate average length of your stride. This is best done by counting the number of paces in walking half a mile or some other known distance across country of the type you are to investigate, and then dividing this distance in feet by the number of paces. Two circumstances must be allowed for: (1) the length of a pace in going uphill or downhill is not the same as in travelling on level ground; and (2) the map value or horizontal projection of any interval on a slope is less than the actual distance (**323, 389**).

If elevations are to be determined, the aneroid barometer should be read at each station. For methods of correcting such readings, see Art. **415.**

A compass traverse should be tied with a known point at its end as at its beginning. This point may be some new locality not yet visited on this particular route, or it may be Station 1. In the latter case the traverse is said to be *closed.* If the end does not tie up precisely, the gap distance should be measured and this error is subsequently to be divided up proportionally along the whole traverse when the final map is made (**400**). For closer checking the traverse may be tied in at other stations in the route or at previously established points.

398. Notes for a compass traverse. With regard to recording the data of a compass traverse in the notebook, the student would do well to begin conforming to a prescribed system. Then, if he prefers, he is at liberty to change his method later. Following is an illustration of a convenient form for field notes:

July 17, 1950

Up a tributary of ______________ River, starting at Sta. 46.

From 46, N 10E–60 × N 60 E–35, banks low, evidently of drift × N75E–55 to Sta. 47, a 40′ terraced bank of solid well-stratified highly plastic blue clay, showing thin laminae of fine brown sand ½″–1″ apart. Strata nearly horizontal. If not well-sorted Pleistocene, are Tertiary ×

From 47, E-260 (at 160 are otcs[5] of massive ss and sh in S. bank, N 40 E 40 SE (g). At 200 sh seems N 35 E 35 SE) × S70E–80, no rx. Bank slowly rising × N75E–100 to Sta. 48, large blocks of massive ss in stream, ca in place, seems N 10 W 20 NE (o) ×

From 48, N80E–240 (at 60 are large otcs of fine and coarse sandy tuffs and agglomerates (Sp. 268)..............................etc.

Observe that each compass bearing for the traverse is followed by a dash and the distance (in paces) of the line along which this bearing was taken; that a large cross (×) indicates a change in direction of the traverse; that notes for stops along a given part of the traverse, between changes in its direction, are put in parentheses; that the number for a hand specimen is given, also in parentheses, after the name of the rock from which it was collected; that strike and dip are recorded thus, N. 40 E. 40 SE.; and, that each such record for attitude is immediately followed by parentheses containing a letter to show how well the bedding was exposed and, therefore, how reliable the readings are for dip and strike. In the sample notes above, "g" means *good* or *bedding well exposed*, and "o" means *bedding obscure*.

Some geologists prefer to *plot* the traverse while *en route* (**399**), carrying it from page to page of the notebook, and recording all the notes in their proper places beside it. This plot, rough though it be, has the advantage of revealing errors which might be made in a *written* record of directions and distances.

Provided a base map can be secured for a working map, the geologist must first know: (1) how to locate, on the map, outcrops and other points of interest seen in the field; (2) how to record certain data on the map; and (3) the best methods of note-taking. He must be able to understand and interpret contour maps (Chap. 13), since these, if well made, are most satisfactory for working maps.

Whether the working map is mounted in the notebook or separately, every outcrop or station at which observations are

[5] See Art. 392.

made is indicated on it by a dot or a small cross at the correct place. Where strata are exposed, the dip, strike, and rock type may be recorded by the symbols given in Art. **478.** The different rocks seen, igneous, sedimentary, or metamorphic, may be colored in on the map as far on each side of the traverse as can safely be done without fear of serious error. In this case the distinction must be drawn between alluvium and the several varieties of bedrock. Where the alluvium is so thin and outcrops are so numerous that there can be little chance of misnaming the covered bedrock, the map is colored for rock rather than alluvium.

If the working map is on a large scale, all possible information is entered on it rather than in the notebook in order to simplify the task of recording. If the scale of the map is small, little more than the locations of the outcrops or stations can be indicated, and the other data must be written in the notebook.

There are two commonly accepted methods of note-taking, the coordinate system and the point system. For the *coordinate system* the working map is cut into rectangles which are pasted in the notebook, and the pages bearing the maps and those opposite the maps are lettered and numbered as explained in Art. **396.** The dots or crosses, by which outcrops and stations are located on a given map, fall on the coordinate lines or in the intervening spaces. Suppose that the station is in the vertical space *B* and in the horizontal space, 5. It is then called *B*:5. If it is on the vertical line between *A* and *B* and is still in 5, its position is denoted by *A–B*:5. Similarly, *B*:5–6 indicates a station in *B* and on the line between spaces 5 and 6; and *A–B*:5–6 refers to the intersection of the two lines. If two or three stations are in the same square, they may be called, *e.g.*, *B*:5 W, *B*:5 SE, etc., where the final letters signify compass directions

The notes are started on the first odd-numbered page after the last map rectangle. In the middle of the page at the top write the date. Just below this, at the extreme left of the page, note the number of the map rectangle on which the traverse starts. On the next line, set in a little from the left margin, record the location of the first station or outcrop, *e.g.*, *B*:5. Then continue with the notes concerning *B*:5. Follow the same method for each outcrop. If the traverse runs on to a new rectangle, write the number of this new map in the same way as you did that of the first. Head each day's traverse with the date in the middle of the page. Below is an example:

SAMPLE OF GEOLOGIC NOTES
June 5, 1950

Map 4.

G:26. Small exposure of sandstone. Bedding well shown: N20°W, 30°E.

K:30. Conglomerate with rounded pebbles of quartzite and granite, quartzite predominating. Average, 3 in. in diam. Largest 5 or 6 in. No bedding seen.

Map 5.

H:2. Sandstone like that seen at 4, G:26. Bedding not seen.

The lettered and numbered page opposite each map is to serve as an index to the notes relating to the stations located on that map. For instance, if an outcrop in *C*:25 is described on page 41, 41 should be written in square *C*:25 on the page facing the map.

For the *point system*[6] the map, either with its original scale or photographically enlarged, may be mounted in any way, but preferably on linen. It can then be folded so that any rectangle is face out and can be held thus in the notebook with rubber bands. The stations at which observations are recorded are shown on this map by small crosses. The crosses in any rectangle (or other division of the map) are numbered consecutively from first to last.

The note-taking is essentially like that in the coordinate system except that the remarks on each locality are headed by its station number. When the book is filled a page index (*point index*) to the notes may be made in which each group of station numbers is listed in consecutive order, *e.g.*,

Rectangle III

Stations	Pages
1	21–22
2–5	22–23

etc.

[6] A more detailed account is given by C. H. Clapp on pp. 177–181 in "Economic Geology," vol. 8. This is one contribution in Bibliog., Irving, J. D., *et al.*

With regard to the advantages and disadvantages of the two systems . . . "locations can be fixed more quickly and more accurately on the map and can be referred to more quickly by this method than by the system of coordinates more commonly used. It is unlike the coordinate system in that the localities at which notes were made cannot be relocated if the map accompanying the notes is lost."[7]

It is a good habit, at night or on rainy days, to copy in full the abbreviated notes recorded during the day. A separate book should be kept for this purpose. Here, too, lists of specimens and of photographs are to be rewritten. Indices arranged according to maps and station numbers, dates, and subjects, may be prepared, so that facts can easily be found when one starts in with the office work.

399. Plotting compass traverses. Compass traverses should be plotted as soon as possible, preferably in the field. This is

TABLE 7. RECTANGULAR VALUES FOR PLOTTING COMPASS TRAVERSES

Angle, in degrees measured from coordinate line	*Distance, in number of squares, on short coordinate (leg)*	*Distance, in number of squares, on long coordinate (leg)*
5	¼	3.0
10	½	3.0
15	½	2.0
20	1	3.0
25	1	2.5
30	1	2.0
35	1	1.5
40	1	1.25
45	1	1.0

done on a piece of paper, or on one or more pages of the notebook, a certain direction having been chosen as north and a certain distance having been selected as the unit of scale. A very convenient method is to rule the paper with coordinate lines spaced according to the adopted scale. Beginning at Station 1, the different parts of the traverse, from station to station, are drawn in with protractor and plotting scale.

In plotting directions on coordinate ruled paper, the course

[7] Bibliog., Irving, J. D., *et al.*, vol. 8, p. 181 (C. H. Clapp).

from any station to the next can be approximately laid out as the hypotenuse of a right triangle by measuring distances, equal to the two legs, along the E.–W. and N.–S. coordinates. Thus, suppose that Station *B* is N. 30° E. from Station A. Measure a unit distance of 1 *eastward* from A to *x*, and from *x* measure two units due *north* to *y*. Draw *Ay*, which will trend N. 30° E. On *Ay*, produced if necessary, mark off the distance *AB* on the adopted scale, thus obtaining the location of *B*. Paying due heed to compass directions, the values[8] shown in Table 7 may be used for rough plotting in this manner.

400. Correction of plotted compass traverses. If the last station of a plotted compass traverse does not tie up accurately,

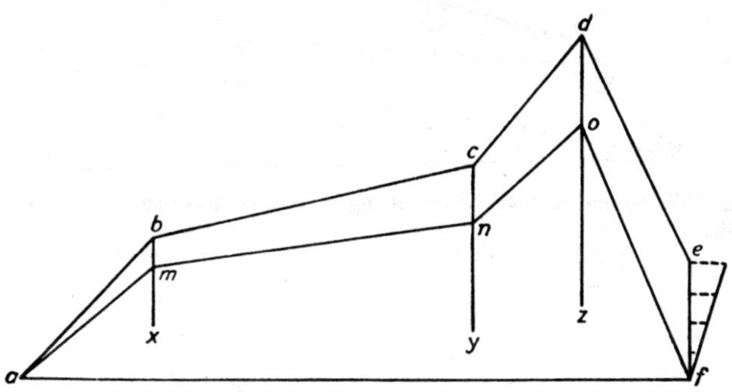

FIG. 396. First method of correcting a compass traverse. (Cf. Figs. 397, 398.)

that is to say, if it is a little out of place, the whole traverse must be corrected. This may be accomplished as follows: let *abcde*, Fig. 396, represent a traverse of which the last station, *e*, should fall at *f*. Draw a line from *e* to *f* and, parallel to *ef*, rule lines from the other stations (*bx*, *cy*, and *dz*). Divide *ef* into as many equal parts as there are stations in the entire traverse, less one. Here there are five stations. Therefore *ef* is divided into four equal parts. On *bx* mark a point, *m*, ¼*ef* from *b;* on *cy* mark a point, *n*, 2/4*ef* from *c*; and on *dz* mark a point, *o*, ¾*ef* from *d*. Draw *amnof*, which is the corrected traverse.

[8] After M. L. Fuller. Bibliog., Fuller, M. L., 1919, p. 414. This paper is an excellent description of practical methods in rapid surveying by compass, clinometer, and aneroid barometer.

A more exact method is illustrated by Fig. 397. Here *abcde*, again, is the traverse as plotted from the notes, and *f* is the point at which *e* should fall. Determine what percentage of *af* is represented by *ae*. Here *ae* is 101 per cent of *af*, *i.e.*, *ae* is 1 per cent too long. Therefore the length of each part of the traverse (*ab*,

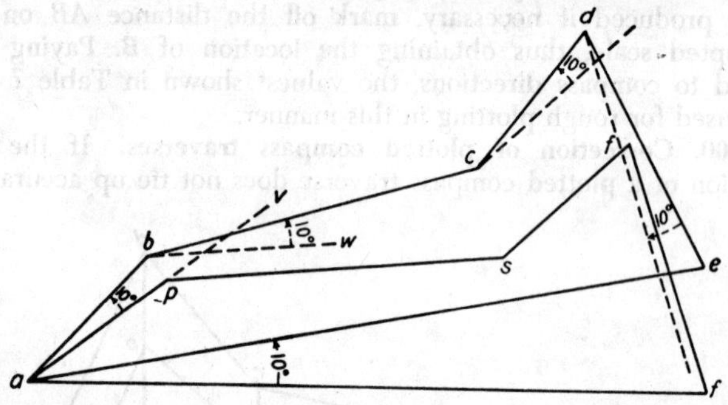

FIG. 397. Second method of correcting a compass traverse. (Cf. Figs. 396, 398.)

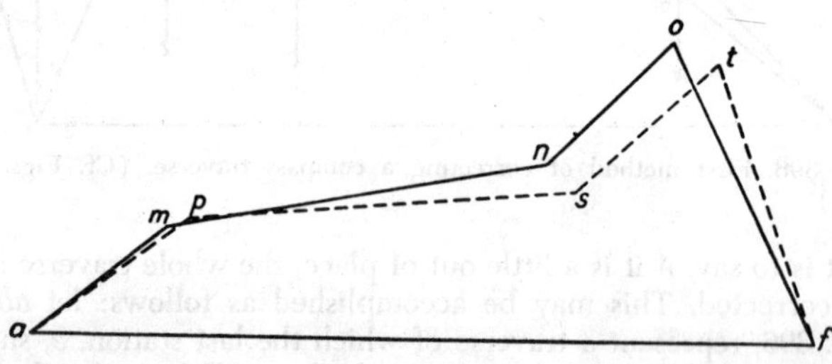

FIG. 398. Corrected traverses of Figs. 396 and 397 shown together for comparison.

bc, etc.) must be reduced by 1 per cent of its present length. The angle between *ae* and *af* is 10°, and *af* is to the south of *ae*. Hence the direction of each part of the traverse (*ab*, *bc*, etc.) must be shifted southward 10°. The procedure is as follows: draw *av* making an angle of 10° with *ab* at *a*. From *a* measure off *ap* = 99 per cent of *ab*. From *b* draw *bw* making an angle of 10° with *bc*. From *p* draw a line parallel to *bw*, and on this line measure off $ps = 99$ per cent of bc. Proceed in the same way with cd and de.

The first method is not accurate because it takes no account of angles, yet it is usually satisfactory for compass traverses. It requires less time than the second method. The difference in the results obtained by both operations is shown in Fig. 398.

THE HAND-LEVEL METHOD

401. Definition. The hand-level method may be used in regions where stratified rocks have dips too low for satisfactory measurement by clinometer. The hand level is employed for taking differences of elevation on any given stratum. The dip of this stratum can then be indicated as a fall of so many feet per mile between certain designated points. Distances may be obtained by pacing, odometer, etc., or by stadia if a telescopic stadia hand level is used. Directions are found by compass.

402. Equipment. The equipment necessary for the hand-level method includes a Locke level or a telescopic hand level, a Brunton compass, a tally register or other instrument for recording or measuring distances, a notebook, a base map if one can be obtained, pencils, etc.

403. Determination of strike. To find the approximate strike of an inclined bed, stand on the top[9] of the bed at some point from which the same bed is visible at a distance either across a dip slope or across a valley. Sight through the hand level at the distant outcrop of the bed where this is about at the same level as the observer. Holding the instrument horizontal, swing it back and forth until the top of the bed in the distant outcrop is on a level with the middle cross-hair. The direction in which the instrument is pointed will then be the approximate strike. Determine this direction by compass.

404. Determination of dip. To find the dip of an inclined bed, stand on the top of the bed[9] and select a distant outcrop of the same bed as the station to be observed. Choose some object, the height of which can be easily judged, near the distant outcrop. Taking this height as a unit of vertical measurement, a

[9] The *top* of the bed is here mentioned, but any recognizable horizon within the bed, or its bottom surface, can be used, provided the same horizon is sighted at the distant exposure.

step, see how many times it will be included in the vertical distance between a horizontal line from the observer's eye toward the distant outcrop and a point which is the height of the observer's eye above the top of the bed in the distant outcrop. The approximate inclination of the bed between the two points will be the height of the *step* times the number of *steps* recorded. This is usually expressed in feet per mile.

Unless the strike of the inclined bed is known and the measurement of the dip is made at right angles to the strike, the observed inclination, obtained as described above, will not be the true dip. It will be a component of the dip, measured in a certain direction not perpendicular to the strike. If the geologist finds several dip components in as many different directions, he can make an estimate of the approximate value of the true dip and its direction (**534**).

405. Hand-level traverses. For the most part the hand level is used only for short branch traverses, or for side shots from traverses mapped by other methods. Sometimes, however, extensive areal mapping can be done by this instrument. Directions and distances will then be run and corrected as in the compass and clinometer method. Elevations, obtained by stepping or levelling, may be checked by planning the traverses to meet or intersect at certain stations, and the errors in elevation, discovered by failure to tie in at these stations, can be divided proportionally, in each case, among the several stations of the traverse since the last similar station where correction was made.

406. Note-taking. Since the hand-level method is seldom applied in extensive mapping, there is no special system of note-taking devised for it. Notes may be kept much as in the compass and clinometer method. If a base map is supplied, all the written information and also arrows for dips or dip components can easily be recorded on this map.

The Barometer Method

407. Definition. The barometer method of field surveying[10] involves the measurement of relative elevations by an aneroid

[10] For earlier descriptions of the use of the aneroid barometer in this connection, see Bibliog., Gilbert, G. K., 1882; Bibliog., Campbell, M. R., 1896. M. R. Campbell described this method as he applied it in investigations for coal.

barometer (Art. **365**) or by a Paulin altimeter (**366**).[11] The method is employed principally in regions of stratified rocks where dips are so low that they are most satisfactorily determined by obtaining elevations on a chosen key bed (**340**), rather than by using a clinometer. Although, in the name of this method, emphasis is placed on the importance of the barometer and on the measurement of vertical distances, the geologist should realize that directions and horizontal, or essentially horizontal, distances between stations must also be measured. Directions may be found by compass or by triangulation, and distances by pacing, odometer, etc., or by triangulation. If a good base map is provided (Art. **408**), the locations of stations may often be estimated by reference to recognizable landmarks, and plotted by eye.

408. Equipment. In addition to the aneroid barometer, or the altimeter, the geologist will need a compass, a watch, a coordinate-ruled notebook, a hand level, and a base map upon which to mark the positions and elevations of stations along his traverse. He will find a tally register serviceable for pacing and an odometer indispensable in automobile work. In some cases he may use a small plane table and open sight alidade (**372**). The compass should be corrected for the local declination (**357**). When two or more men work together in the same area, their watches should be set together. The notebook is most serviceable when ruled in fifths or tenths of inches. Any fairly accurate county, state, or property plat will generally do for a base map. Air photographs may be particularly useful (Art. **456**). There is no special need to have a base map that shows topographic features, although it is well to have streams indicated. If the geologist cannot procure a satisfactory map of some sort, he should make or have made a simple outline map showing a few prominent landmarks in their correct relative positions, so that he can *tie* his traverses to these. When the land is sectionized he can often sketch his own base map along with his geologic

[11] Because this method was originally performed with an aneroid barometer, it is referred to as the *barometer method,* but it might better be called the *altimeter method.* Actually the process of determining the absolute elevation of a point above mean sea level, or the relative differences in elevation between two points, is known as *altimetry* when these values are calculated from barometric or altimetric measurements of atmospheric pressure.

work. The degree of precision demanded in the work will determine the kind of base map necessary.

409. Horizontal control for mapping by barometer. Before considering in detail the use of the aneroid barometer, we may well give some attention to the subject of the horizontal control. By horizontal control is meant the system of measured horizontal distances and directions between the stations included in the mapping. These stations may be classified under two heads: (1) certain relatively few points, known as control stations, which are located with considerable accuracy; and (2) those stations which are less precisely located and which have their positions established in reference to the stations of the first class. As a matter of fact, the *control stations* govern the positions of all the other stations not only in respect to their horizontal distances and directions, but also in respect to their relative elevations. The student should bear in mind the distinction between these terms *horizontal control* and *control stations.*

There are many variations in the methods adopted in establishing the horizontal control for barometric work. If a satisfactory base map is provided, the horizontal locations of stations are often simply estimated by reference to recognizable charted landmarks and are accordingly plotted by eye on the map. The degree of accuracy of this method depends on the number and distribution of such recognizable points, and also on the class of workmanship of the map. In any event the limit of error is likely to be large.

Ordinarily the geologist will find it necessary to prepare some kind of a horizontal control along with his barometric work. This he may do by running a system of compass traverses in which distances are measured by pacing, by horse paces, by the revolutions of a wheel, by odometer, etc. (397), or he may use a small plane table and an open sight alidade or a Gurley compass. In sectionized country where roads lie on nearly every section line, directions of road traverses are along north-south or east-west lines and are easily mapped. In such country travel is generally accomplished by automobile. Only occasional branch traverses, on foot or in the automobile, must be run by compass and measured by pacing or odometer, as the case may be. For the running of irregular compass traverses and their correction see Arts. **397–400.**

The use of the small plane table and open sight alidade, rather than a compass, is chiefly a matter of individual preference.

With the plane table, the features may be mapped as a route traverse with branch sights where necessary or as a triangulation network (Art. **436**).

410. System of recording stations.[12] The writer has found it most convenient, for note-taking, to designate days by letters and stations by numbers. Thus, in a given area, the first day will be *A*, the second *B*, and so on until the investigation is finished. The next area will be commenced *A*, again. If more than 26 days are spent in one district, the 27th day will be *AA* or 2*A*, the 28th *BB* or 2*B*, and so on. The stations on the first day will be *A*1, *A*2, *A*3, etc.; on the second day, *B*1, *B*2, etc. These symbols are plotted on the base map and are recorded in the notebook, as will be explained presently. Some geologists use consecutive numbers for an entire field season or for an entire district or problem, even when more than a single season is consumed in the work.

411. Graphic method of note-taking. According to the method devised by M. R. Campbell, the notes may be recorded in the form of a profile section. Figure 399 illustrates one. To explain this let us assume that the geologist is at Station *A*1. He has a sufficiently clear idea of the area to know that Station *A*1, his starting point is rather low and that most of the stations which he will visit will be above the level of Station *A*1. The barometric elevation at this station he finds is 2,460 ft. Consequently, holding the notebook with its length right and left, he chooses a horizontal line rather low on the page, in order to leave room above for higher points, and he labels the left end of this line, "2,400." Letting 1 in. = 100 ft., the other horizontal lines are labelled accordingly, upward and downward from the first line (Fig. 399).

Suppose that he arrives at Station *A*1 at 8 A.M. On the intersection of the 2,460 line and a vertical line at the left of the page, he marks a small cross or a dot to represent *A*1. Let the direction from *A*1 to the next station be due north. Along this same vertical line he writes, "*A*1, 8.00 A.M., No.," and any other necessary information. If, as we may suppose, *A*1 is on the top of a bed of limestone, this is plotted by the usual symbol.

He now proceeds 110 double paces to Station *A*2, a point here

[12] This article and much of the following description of the barometer method have been taken from *Economic Geology,* vol. 25, pp. 150–169. Bibliog., Lahee, F. H., 1920. For a very good explanation of procedures followed with the altimeter. see Bibliog., Hodgson, Robert A., 1957.

assumed to be on a 10-ft. bed of sandstone, at an elevation which he reads as 2,500 ft. He arrives at A2 at 8.10 A.M. Letting the horizontal scale of the section be 1 in. = 100 double paces (equals approximately 1/10 mile), he plots A2 according to the adopted scales. As before, he writes on the vertical line through the point for A2, "A2, 8.10 A.M., N10E.," the direction being from A2 to A3. To save time that might be lost later in measuring distances in the notebook, he records the number of paces from A1 to A2. He represents the sandstone bed by the convention for that rock (478).

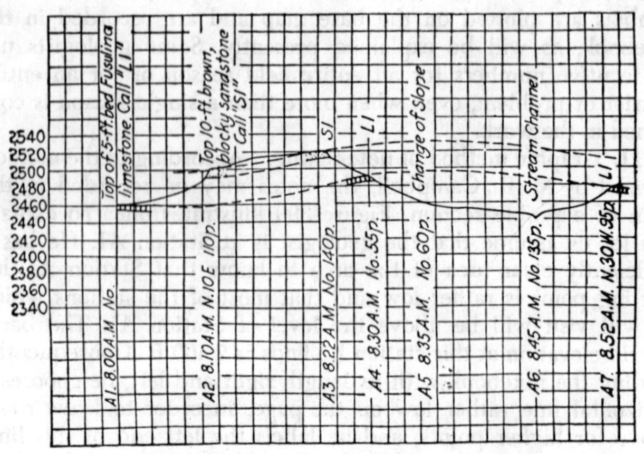

FIG. 399. Profile section of features observed on a traverse.

In this manner he continues from station to station, recording whatever information seems to be of importance and sketching the topographic profile along his traverse.

Every effort should be made to settle the correlation of the strata during the course of the field work, and the correlations should be suggested in the section by dashed lines, as in Fig. 399. The profile section is carried from page to page, care being taken to keep the elevation coordinates as nearly as possible in the same relative positions on the sheet. The section should terminate on each page at a station and should begin on the succeeding page at the same station at about the same level on the page, so that the pages may be matched for comparison.

412. Tabulation method of note-taking. In many cases much time may be saved by keeping the notes in tabulated form. This may be done especially when speed is required, when travel is done by automobile, and when a structure contour map, and not a geologic section, is the principal graphic result to be attained. The following plan of tabulation has been found to be serviceable. The facts indicated in Fig. 399 are recorded in this table.

TABLE 8. TABULATED NOTES

Station	*Time*	*Barometer*	*Corrected barometer*	*Direction from last station*	*Distance from last station (paces)*	*Remarks*
	A.M.					
*A*1	8.00	2,460	....	No.	...	Top of 5 ft. bed yellowish ls. Abundant Fusulina. Call "L1."
*A*2	8.10	2,500	....	N10E	110	Top 10 ft. brown blocky ss. Call "S1."
*A*3	8.22	2,520	....	No.	140	S1.
*A*4	8.30	2,490	....	No.	55	L1.
*A*5	8.35	2,460	....	No.	60	Change of slope.
*A*6	8.45	2,440	....	No.	135	Stream channel. No outcrops.
*A*7	8.52	2,475		N30W	95	L1.

If an automobile is used, the trip distance is recorded in the sixth column. The fourth column is left blank to be filled in subsequently with the corrected barometric readings (413 *et seq.*). As in the graphic method of taking notes, the positions of the stations are to be marked on the base map.

413. Necessity for the correction of barometric readings. An aneroid barometer is in principle a sensitive air pressure gauge. If properly made, it is "compensated for temperature," *i.e.*, it will read correctly any pressure irrespective of the temperature of the instrument. In this it has an advantage over the mercurial barometer which requires correction due to the unequal expansion or contraction of the mercury and the containing glass under varying temperatures.

The aneroid barometer and the Paulin altimeter are used for registering differences of elevation. If the temperature of the air were constant, a scale for altitude could be made to correspond to a scale for pressure; but since air density varies with changes in temperature, these instruments can be made to read altitude correctly only at one temperature. This is known as the *temperature of calibration* of the instrument. Generally speaking, aneroids and Paulin altimeters are calibrated to register correct altitudes at 50°F. If the air is warmer than 50°, the elevation indicated on the barometer will be too high, because the air, being lighter, will have a pressure corresponding to a higher altitude

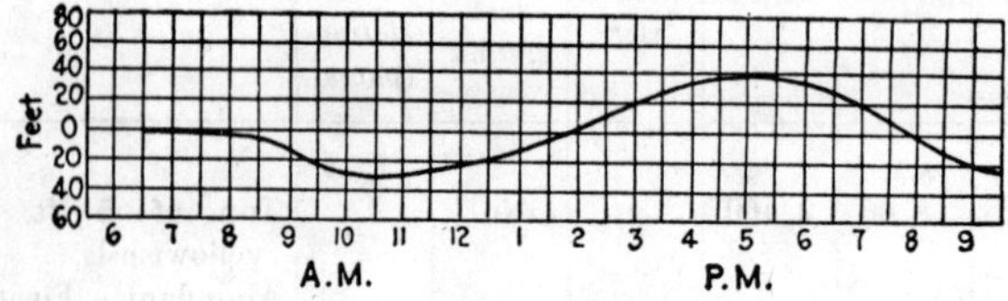

FIG. 400. Type curve illustrating diurnal variations in atmospheric pressure from 6.30 A.M. until 9:30 P.M. on a day when conditions were exceptionally steady. (Cf. Fig. 402.)

at 50°. On the other hand if the air temperature is below 50°F., and, therefore, abnormally heavy, the aneroid will record an elevation too low. Obviously, therefore, barometric readings must be corrected for these errors due to the effect of temperatures above or below the temperature of calibration of the instrument.

Another very important source of error in the use of the barometer lies in the fact that atmospheric pressure is subject to almost continuous and often violent changes. Thus, if an aneroid is left undisturbed in the same place for 24 hours, the needle will gradually alter its position. Under ordinary conditions, it will swing slowly downward[13] from dawn until 9 or 10 o'clock, after which it will remain nearly steady for an hour or two; then it will rise, at first slowly and later, by 1 or 2 P.M., more rapidly

[13] *Downward* and *upward* are here used in reference to the scale in feet, for elevations. When the needle points to successively lower elevations, it naturally indicates higher pressure in inches of mercury.

until between 4 and 6 P.M., when it will again change and begin to fall. These movements are illustrated in Fig. 400. There is some variation, both from day to day and from season to season, in the time of the changes from rise to fall, and from fall to rise.

The regular curve of diurnal barometric variation is more or less modified by local fluctuations in atmospheric pressure such

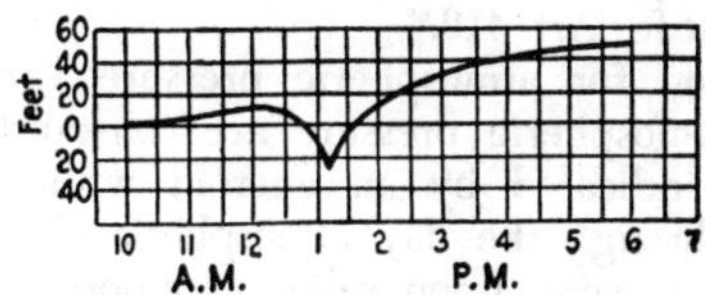

FIG. 401. Curve of atmospheric pressure variation during a thunderstorm, plotted from observations made at frequent intervals at a single station.

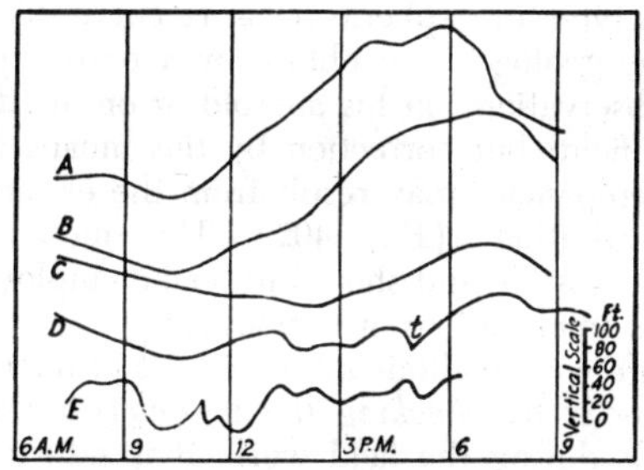

FIG. 402. Examples of atmospheric pressure curves, as indicated by barometric readings, on different days. *A* to *D* are by the same barometer. *E* was plotted from the record of a poor barometer. *A* and *B* show abnormally large increases of pressure during the afternoon. *C* is abnormally flat. *D* is characterized by several rises and falls due to unsteady weather conditions. A thunderstorm occurred during the drop at *t*. The great diversity of these curves shows how great may be the errors due to correcting barometric readings by the use of a type or average curve.

as may be caused by gusty winds, "twisters" or "baby tornadoes," irregular air currents due to the effects of strong topographic relief, and especially by storms (Figs. 401, 402).

Just as in the case of errors due to atmospheric temperature barometric readings must be adjusted for this second class of errors caused by atmospheric pressure changes, if such readings are to be correct. Although corrections for temperature should properly be made before those for pressure variation, we shall describe the latter first, partly because the temperature factor may often be omitted from consideration (**422**), whereas correction for pressure change must always be made; and partly in order to avoid confusing the reader in explaining this subject of correcting for pressure variations. The matter of temperature corrections is left for Art. **419**.

414. Correction for atmospheric pressure variations. Since variations in atmospheric pressure are constantly in progress, the elevations indicated by an aneroid while traversing are incorrect. All through the day atmospheric changes are being superposed, as it were, upon relief variations, and before the recorded barometric readings can be regarded as truly representing differences in topographic relief, the atmospheric variations must be eliminated. To a certain extent this may be done by reference to a type atmospheric pressure curve, like that in Fig. 400, which the geologist can obtain by a barograph (**367**; **415**, ¶ 8), or by observations on his aneroid or on another while not in use in the field; but correction by this means is very rough and large discrepancies may result from the effects of the local atmospheric variations (Fig. 402). This method should be avoided when possible and should never be employed unless the allowable error in elevations of stations is large.

The only safe way to eliminate the effects of fluctuating atmospheric pressure is by *checking the barometric readings* at frequent intervals during the field work. It is safe to say that the proficiency of the geologist in the barometer method of mapping and the accuracy of his results depend almost wholly upon his skill in checking and correcting the barometric readings. The more important methods of checking are described below.

415. Methods of checking barometric readings. 1. *Checking on an established control.* If there are points, such as U.S. Geological Survey bench marks, U.S. Geodetic Survey monuments, railroad stations, etc. of which the true elevations have already been established, in the region to be geologically surveyed, these points may serve as a control for correcting the barometric readings. The traverses should be planned so as to include such stations. In sectionized country bench marks are usually to be found at the section corners or the township corners.

To illustrate this method, let us suppose that Fig. 403 is the plot of a traverse. The crosses are stations of which the true elevations have been determined. If the true elevations of 1 and 6 are 700 and 630 ft. above sea level, respectively, and the barometric elevations at these same stations were recorded as 775 and 750 ft., respectively, the barometer was reading 75 ft. too high at Station 1 and 120 ft. too high at Station 6; that is, while the geologist went from 1 to 6, the atmospheric pressure curve rose 120 − 75 ft. = 45 ft.

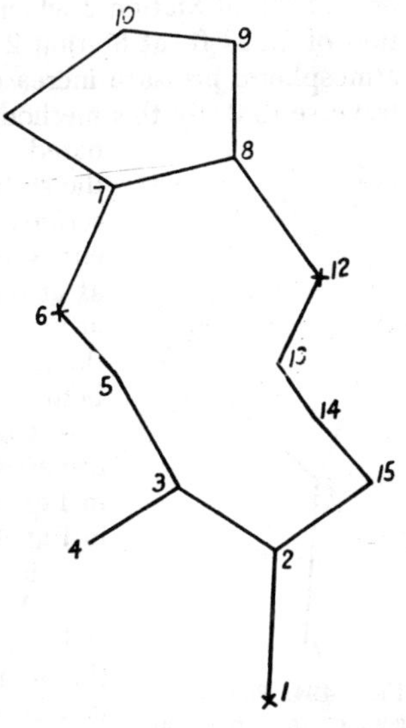

Fig. 403. Plot of a traverse. The correction curve for the barometric elevations on this traverse is shown in Fig. 406.

Checking by reference to established control stations is the best method of ascertaining the variations of the barometer provided the elevations of these stations are reliable, but ordinarily such control points are too infrequent, and, accordingly, other methods of checking must be employed.

2. *Checking by two or more readings at a station.* When several minutes are spent at one station, perhaps in studying the fossils or rocks, or in automobile delays, the aneroid should be read shortly after arrival and just before leaving. It is better to wait two or three minutes after arriving to allow for lag of the instrument. Otherwise, the first reading might perhaps be made immediately after a considerable ascent or descent from the preceding station, whereas the second reading would be made after the aneroid had been kept at rest for some time. With some instruments the results obtained under these unlike conditions would not be exactly comparable.

A distinct rise or fall in the barometer during a stop of 30 minutes or more is probably atmospheric and should be recorded, as at Station 7 in Figs. 403 and 406. Usually changes observed during shorter stops should be given little weight.

3. *Checking by branch traverses.* Figure 404 shows a map of a traverse. The geologist's course, in the order of stations visited, was 1, 2, 3, 2, 4, 5, 4, 6. At 2 and 4, each, he obtained two readings which served to indicate whether the atmospheric pressure curve was steady, rising, or falling, while he visited 3 and 5, respectively. For example, if his instrument showed an elevation of 1,140 ft. at Station 2 when he first arrived there, and an elevation of 1,150 ft. at Station 2 after his return from Station 3, the atmospheric pressure increased 10 ft. while he made the branch traverse to 3. By this method, the effects of lag are largely eliminated by reading always upon arrival at the station; but it has the disadvantage that serious discrepancies may appear at the end stations of adjoining branch traverses, as at 3 and 5. When such branch traverses are near, the geologist should connect them, going, for instance, from 5 to 3, before he returns to 4.

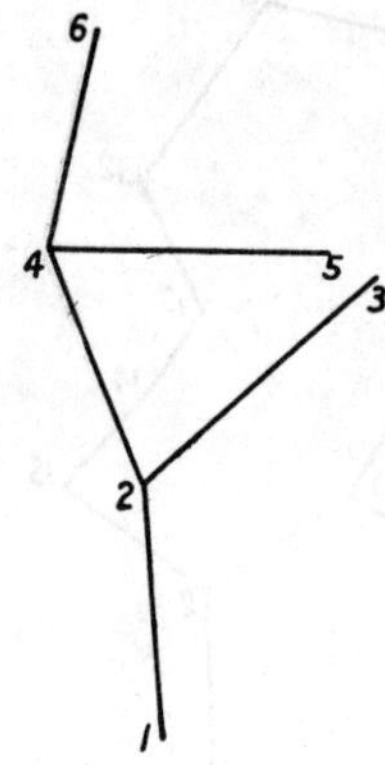

FIG. 404. Plot of a course to illustrate checking by branch traverses.

4. *Checking by closed and intersecting traverses.* A closed traverse is illustrated in Fig. 405, A, and an intersecting traverse in Fig. 405, B. The progress of the geologist was in the sequence of the station numbers. When he returned to 1 from 6, Fig. 405, A, his aneroid reading showed what the total change in atmospheric pressure had been since he departed from 1 toward 2. In the method of Fig. 405, B, a check was obtained on the atmospheric curve at 2 and at 1.

The reader should observe that there is nothing in these methods of checking to indicate just how the atmospheric pressure varied in the intervals between checks. Thus, it might have risen 10 ft., or it might have dropped 10 ft. and risen 20 ft., and the result, as far as could be detected by the checking, would have been the same in either case. The error would be in the elevations at the intermediate stations. The closed and intersecting traverses have the advantage of distributing such errors among all the stations in the closure, so that the error at any one station is relatively small. Obviously the shorter the time allowed to elapse between checking, the less opportunity will there be for large errors (**441**).

5. *Checking by return traverse.* If the geologist returns on the same day along the same route, he may read his barometer a second time at several, not necessarily all, of the stations of his traverse. The double record at each of these check stations will indicate the amount of atmospheric pressure change between the visits to their particular station. This is like a combination of the second and third methods of checking. It is useful especially in automobile work in rough country where roads are few

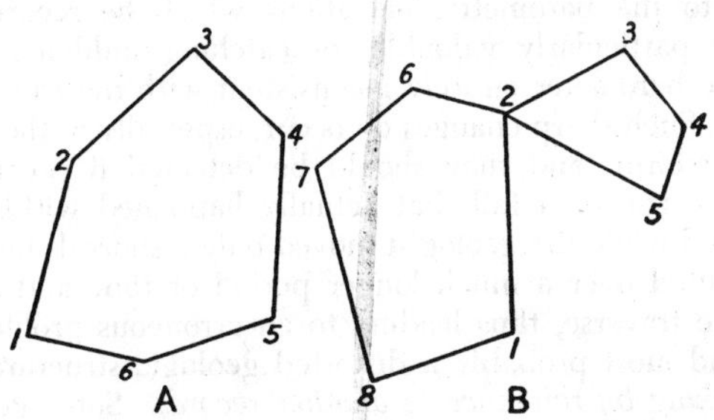

Fig. 405. Plots to illustrate checking by closed and intersecting traverses.

and are more or less parallel, perhaps following steep-sided divides or narrow canyons. It will suffice for a single day's work, or it may be repeated on successive days, but before the mapping in such a region is completed, these parallel or radiating traverses must somewhere be connected and tied in on one another by occasional cross-country traverses, even if these have to be made on foot.

6. *Checking by hand level.* Both sight and telescopic hand levels may be used to considerable advantage in checking barometric readings at stations of approximately the same altitude. The geologist may level from one point to another visible point from which he has come or to which he is going, and if the two stations differ in elevation, he may estimate this difference. Assuming, for example, that the hand level shows Station 1 to be 10 ft. higher than Station 2 and the barometer indicates that Station 1 is 20 ft. higher than Station 2, then the atmospheric

pressure has risen 10 ft. in the time elapsed while going from Station 1 to Station 2. Whenever a check is made by hand level, the fact should be recorded in the notebook. Care should be taken to see that the hand level is in perfect adjustment.

7. *Checking by eye.* The constant comparison, by eye, of the observed barometric readings with the true slopes and elevations of the ground traversed is fairly difficult, for it requires experience and judgment. It means that the geologist must have an idea not only of the topography, but also of the structure, which he is crossing, and it means that he must give constant attention to the barometric elevations which he records. This method is particularly valuable for catching sudden rises and falls of the barometer entirely inconsistent with the true relative elevations. Such sharp changes do occur, especially in the vicinity of thunderstorms and they should be detected if possible, for otherwise a rise or a fall that actually happened within a few minutes and while the geologist moved only a short distance may be distributed over a much longer period of time and a larger part of the traverse, thus leading to an erroneous profile of the ground and most probably a distorted geologic structure.

8. *Checking by reference to another record.* Some geologists take a barograph into the field with them and place it somewhere near the center of the area to be surveyed during the day. Or an assistant at camp, or at some chosen spot in the field, may note and record the readings of a second stationary aneroid every 15 minutes or half hour during the day. The record made automatically by the barograph, or the curve plotted by the assistant from the record of his aneroid, can then be used to correct the readings of the field man's barometer. Besides the fact that a barograph or a second aneroid is an unnecessary burden, this method of checking and correcting is generally unsatisfactory because the stationary instruments may fail to record sharp local atmospheric pressure changes that may affect the field aneroid, and, on the other hand, they may register changes which escape the field aneroid. In other words, atmospheric pressure variations, even though pronounced, may sometimes affect areas of relatively small extent.

416. Plotting the correction curve. The following is a brief explanation of the plotting of the atmospheric pressure curve, or, as we have called it here, the *correction curve.*[14] Let Fig. 403

[14] This curve, as it is derived from observations by the aneroid barometer, is to a large extent indicative of actual variations in the pressure of the

TABLE 9. BAROMETRIC READINGS RECORDED ON A TRAVERSE

A Station	*B* Time	*C* Barometer	*D* Corrected barometric readings	*E* Elevations previously established
	A.M.			
1	6.00	625	700	700
1	7.30	620	700	700
2	8.00	575	660	
3	8.20	580	665	
4	8.50	685	780	
3	9.15	565	665	
5	9.30	535	640	
6	9.40	525	630	630
7	10.00	540	650	
8	10.25	505	615	
9	10.45	520	630	
10	11.10	550	660	
11	11.45	595	700	
	P.M.			
7	12.15	550	650	
7	1.00	560	650	
8	1.15	535	625	
12	2.00	560	635	635
13	2.20	570	640	
14	2.35	590	655	
15	3.00	620	680	
2	3.30	605	660	
1	3.50	650	700	700
1	5.30	655	700	700
1	7.05	640	700	700

represent a traverse in which several methods of checking have been employed, yielding the results listed in Table 9.

Camp is at Station 1 which happens to have its elevation already established as 700 ft. above sea level. It is therefore a

atmosphere; but it no doubt includes, also, certain indeterminable irregular fluctuations consequent upon the individual peculiarities of the barometer. These fluctuations, as well as the atmospheric pressure variations, are for the most part eliminated by the application of the correction curve. The reader should remember that, in this explanation, we are still disregarding errors which may have been occasioned in the records as a result of atmospheric temperature (**413, 419**).

control station. Stations 6 and 12 are also control stations (column E, Table 9). At 6 A.M. the barometric reading was 625 ft., or 75 ft. too low, at Station 1. For plotting the curve, take a piece of coordinate-ruled paper and, holding it with its length right and left, label every other vertical line for the hours, beginning at 6 A.M. (Fig. 406). Every space, right and left, will correspond to 30 minutes, and smaller intervals of time can be interpolated. Label a horizontal line near the middle of the page "0"; label the next line, both above and below the "0" coordinate, "20," the next "40," and so on, as far as seems necessary. The horizontal coordinates below the zero coordinate represent quantities, in feet, to be added to the barometric readings to

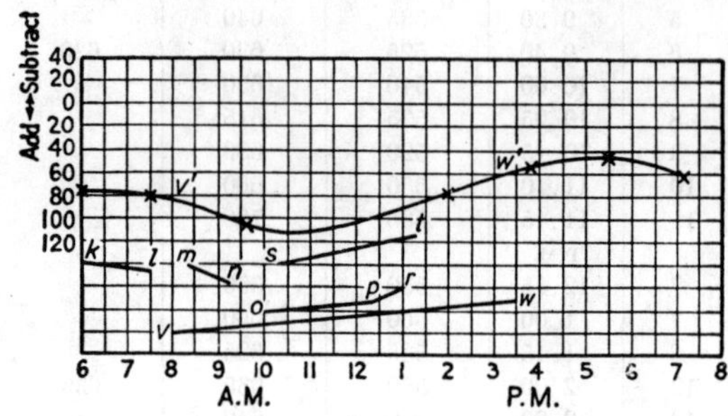

FIG. 406. Correction curve (curve of atmospheric pressure variation) for barometric elevations recorded on the traverse plotted in Fig. 403. The diagram illustrates the lower part of a page in the notebook.

obtain corrected elevations, and those above the zero coordinate represent quantities to be subtracted from the barometric readings to obtain corrected elevations. Since the first reading, at 6 A.M., was 75 ft. too low, 75 ft. must be added for correction. Mark a cross (for an established control station) at a point on the 6 A.M. vertical line one-fourth of a space up from the 80 ft. horizontal line. At 7.30 A.M., the barometer read 80 ft. too low. Mark the intersection of the 7.30 vertical line and the 80 ft. horizontal line.

Between the two visits to Station 3, at 8.20 and 9.15 A.M., the barometer fell 15 ft. Somewhere well below the probable position of the curve to be drawn through the points just plotted, mark a point (*m*, Fig. 406) on a horizontal line at 8.20 and another point (*n*, Fig. 406) three-fourth space (= 15 ft.) below *m* on the 9.15 line. Draw a straight line between *m* and *n*. *mn* may be called a *guide line*. It is not necessarily parallel to the ultimate correction curve (cf. *st* and *vw*, two other guide lines), but merely indicates to the eye that points in the curve corresponding to the ends of the guide line are related to one another exactly as they are in the guide line. This will become clearer presently.

At Station 6, at 9.40 A.M., the barometric reading was 105 ft. too low. Mark a cross (again for an established elevation) where the 105 coordinate intersects at 9.40 coordinate.

At Station 7 readings were made at 10.00 A.M., and at 12.15 and 1.00 P.M. 12.15 to 1.00 was the lunch period. Again, below the region of the curve, construct another guide line, *opr*, *o* being at the intersection of any horizontal line and the 10.00 A.M. vertical, *p* being 10 ft. above *o* and on the 12.15 coordinate, and *r* being 10 ft. above *p* and on the 1.00 P.M. coordinate. The 10-ft. intervals correspond to the rise of the barometer from 540 at 10.00 A.M. to 550 at 12.15 P.M., and from 550 at 12.15 P.M. to 560 at 1.00 P.M.

A guide line is plotted for Station 8, visited twice, and for Station 2, visited twice. Also crosses are plotted at 2.00 P.M. and 75 ft. for Station 12 (columns *C* and *E*, Table 9), and at 3.50 P.M. and 50 ft., at 5.30 P.M. and 45 ft., and at 7.05 P.M. and 60 ft., these last three being readings at Station 1.

The correction curve is drawn through the plotted crosses, which indicate the actual corrections to be made, and in such a way that points in this curve are the same distances apart, vertically and horizontally, as the end points of the several guide lines, vertically below. For example, *v′* is in the curve at 8.00 A.M. and *w′* is in the curve at 3.30 P.M., 30 ft. higher than *v′*. These are exactly the relations of the end points of the guide line, *vw*, but, to repeat what was stated above, the curve between *v′* and *w′* is not by any means necessarily parallel to the guide line, *vw*.

The curve is drawn smoothly except for storm depressions (Fig. 401) and the effects of sudden jars. It is not drawn as a series of connected straight lines.

Observe that two or more readings may be taken at the same station before starting in the morning and after returning in the afternoon. These additional observations are seldom made by geologists, but the writer has found them to be of considerable value in showing the slope and general tendency of the curve. Note also that the curve is drawn through the crosses, that is, through the points which indicate the corrections to be applied at stations whose elevations have been previously established. The guide lines are obtained by checking. In this traverse (Fig. 403) checking was accomplished by reference to control stations at 1, 6, and 12; by closure at 2, 7, and 8; by branch traverse at 3; and by two readings with intervening wait at 7.

417. Application of the correction curve. By means of the correction curve, constructed after the manner above described, any barometric readings made during the day may be corrected. If notes were kept by the graphic profile method, the corrected elevations may be written against the proper points in the profile section. If the notes were tabulated, the corrected elevations are to be written in a column for the purpose (see Tables 8 and 9).

For illustration of the way in which corrections are made, let us take Station 14 (see Table 8). The barometric elevation for 14 was observed to be 590 ft. at 2.35 P.M. A point at 2.35 P.M. in the curve, Fig. 406, is just below the horizontal line that would represent "add 65 ft." Approximately 65 ft., then, should be added to the recorded reading, 590, thus giving the true elevation of Station 14 as 655 ft.

Where stratigraphic intervals must be added to or subtracted from the elevations of certain strata in order to obtain elevations on a chosen key horizon (**101, 102, 340**), this may be done at the same time as the correction of the barometric readings, and the *corrected elevation of the key horizon* may then be entered in the notebook, in the manner suggested above, ready to be copied on to the map.

418. Comparison of different correction curves for the same route on different days. The beginner sometimes finds it difficult to understand how dissimilar correction curves can give essentially the same results for the corrected elevations of the same stations visited on different days. We have, therefore, added Table 10 in which are listed the data obtained in repeating the traverse shown in Fig. 403 on a second day. Figure 407 represents the correction curve based on these data.

All barometric readings, on this second traverse, were lower than on the preceding day (Fig. 406), so that quantities of over

TABLE 10. BAROMETRIC READINGS RECORDED ON A TRAVERSE

A Station	*B* Time	*C* Barometer	*D* Corrected barometric readings	*E* Elevations previously established
	A.M.			
1	7.00	580	700	700
1	7.18	570	700	700
2	8.00	520	660	
3	8.30	525	665	
4	9.00	645	780	
3	9.15	530	665	
5	9.40	500	640	
6	10.00	480	630	630
7	10.30	485	650	
8	10.50	435	615	
9	11.15	440	630	
10	11.50	460	660	
	P.M.			
11	12.15	495	700	
11	12.45	490	700	
1	1.30	500	700	
7	1.55	460	650	
8	2.10	435	615	
12	3.00	475	635	635
13	3.30	485	640	
14	3.45	505	655	
15	4.10	530	680	
2	4.45	500	660	
1	5.05	535	700	700
1	5.30	545	700	700
1	7.00	570	700	700
1	9.00	555	700	700

100 ft. had to be added for correction. By careful study of this figure, and comparison with Fig. 407, the reader will observe that the elevations obtained from either curve are practically identical for each station. There is opportunity for a variation of perhaps 5 ft.—hardly 10 ft.—in elevations adjusted from the part of the curve (Fig. 407) between 3.15 and 4.15 P.M. Also, a 5-ft drop or a 5-ft. rise of the curve at 10.30 A.M. (Station 7), either of which would be possible, might cause a difference

of 5 or 10 ft. in the corrected elevations of Stations 8 and 11, visited between the two records at Station 7. Note, however, that variations of this degree would only very slightly alter the *relative* elevations of adjacent stations; and the errors which might affect stations rather far removed from one another would usually be less than the probable limit of error of the stratigraphy (442).

419. Correction for atmospheric temperature. As stated in Art. 413, aneroid barometers are calibrated to record elevations correctly only at a specified temperature. The difference between the elevations (pressures) read at two consecutive stations will be too small if the temperatures at the stations are above the

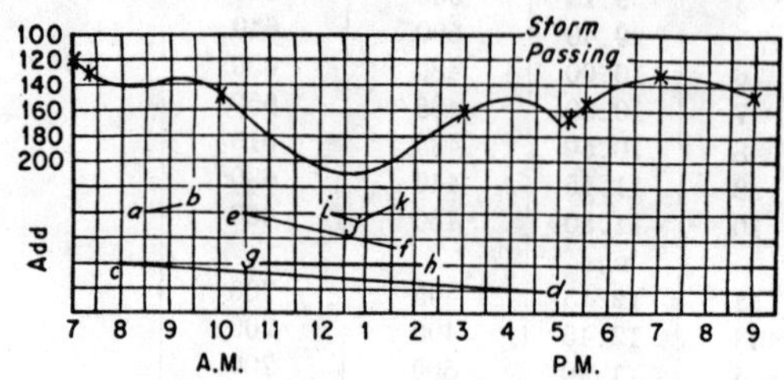

FIG. 407. Correction curve based on data recorded in going over the traverse illustrated in Fig. 403 on a stormy day. (Cf. Fig. 406.)

calibration temperature (here assumed to be 50°F.), and vice versa. "These differences . . . amount to approximately $\frac{2}{10}$ of 1 per cent" (of the difference of elevation at the stations) "for each degree of temperature above or below 50°F. If air were a true gas its density at any temperature would be inversely proportional to the absolute temperature . . . and a 1° change would cause a pressure variation of 0.1961 per cent. Actually, the rate of change, due to the fact that air is not a true gas, is 0.2039 per cent for each degree above or below 50°F."[15]

For example, if the temperature at Station *A* were 60°F. and at Station *B* were 70°F., the average temperature would be 65°, or 15° above the temperature for which the instrument is calibrated. Let us suppose that the recorded elevation at *A* is 200 ft. lower than at *B*. Using $\frac{2}{10}$ of 1 per cent for each degree (15°), the correction would be $0.2 \times 15 = +3$ per cent. The

[15] Bibliog., Hill, Raymond A., 1929, p. 3.

true difference of elevation would be, not 200 ft. as read, but 200 ft. + 3 per cent of 200 ft., *i.e.*, 200 + 6 = 206 ft.

Generally it is simpler to use the sum of the temperatures at each two successive stations, and to multiply by 1/10 of 1 per cent. If the sum is greater than 100°, the percentage factor is positive; if less than 100°, it is negative. Thus, in the example above cited, the temperatures, 60° and 70° are added, making 130°, from which is subtracted 100°, leaving 30°. Multiply this result by 1/10 of 1 per cent and multiply the result of the difference of elevations, here 200 ft.

$$0.1\ (30) = +3 \text{ per cent}$$
$$3 \text{ per cent of } 200 = +6$$

The corrected difference of elevation is 200 + 6 = 206 ft.

If the temperatures had been 30° and 50°, and the recorded difference of elevations 160 ft., the procedure would be:

$$30° + 50° = 80°$$
$$80° - 100° = -20°$$
$$0.1\ (-20) = -2 \text{ per cent}$$
$$-2 \text{ per cent of } 160 = -3.2$$

This means that the quantity 3.2 ft. is to be subtracted from 160 ft., making the difference of elevations actually 157.8 ft.

In order to facilitate the correction of barometric (aneroid or Paulin altimeter) readings for the temperature factor, we have prepared the chart shown in Fig. 408. On the left are shown feet of difference of elevation between successive stations. For differences greater than 100 ft., use tens and multiply the final result by 10 or 100, as the case may be. Thus, if the difference in elevations is 320 ft., make the calculations for 32 ft. and multiply the final result by 10. Similarly, if the difference is 1,100 ft., calculate for 11 and multiply the final correction by 100. The radiating lines in the diagram represent the number of degrees by which the sum of the temperatures at the two stations exceeds 100° or is less than 100°.[16] On the base line are marked feet to be added to, or subtracted from, the difference of elevations in order to obtain the corrected relative elevation for the last of the

[16] This explanation is for the case where the aneroid or altimeter is calibrated for 50°. If the instrument is calibrated for 60°, the radiating lines represent the number of degrees by which the sum of the temperatures at the two stations exceeds, or is less than, 120°

two stations visited. For example, let the difference of elevations at *A* and *B* equal 75 ft., *A* being the lower of the two, and suppose that the temperatures at *A* and *B* when the readings were made, were 65° and 75°, respectively.

$$65° + 75° = 140°$$
$$140° - 100° = +40°$$

Find the point of intersection (*a*, in the figure) of the radial line marked 40° and the horizontal line for 75 ft.; then, from this point of intersection, follow the vertical line down to the base line where the correction is indicated. In the present case this

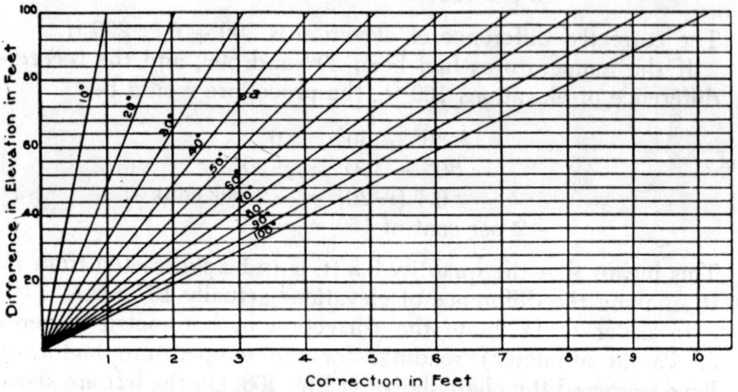

FIG. 408. Graph for making temperature corrections in barometric readings.

correction is +3.05 ft., or simply 3 ft. The true difference in elevations between *A* and *B* is therefore 75 + 3 = 78 ft.

If the difference of elevations, as read on the aneroid, had been 750 ft., the calculations would have been made on the quantity 75, and the final result would have been 10 × 78 = 780 ft.

If the temperatures at *A* and *B* had been 35° and 50°, and the difference in recorded elevations 75 ft., as before, we should have:

$$35° + 50° = 85°$$
$$85° - 100° = -15°$$

The vertical through the point of intersection of the horizontal for 75 ft. and the diagonal line for 15° indicate a correction of 1.15 which will be minus, *i.e.*, subtracted from the recorded elevation at *B*, since the sum of the temperatures at *A* and *B* was *less than* 100°.

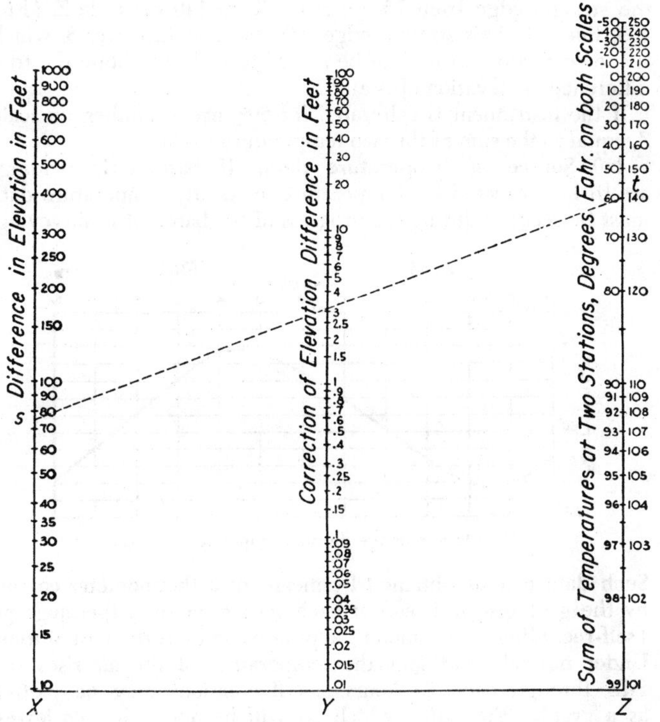

FIG. 409. Alignment chart for temperature corrections in barometric readings.

Figure 409 represents another method of correcting aneroid readings for differences in temperature at the observing stations. The difference of observed elevations at the two stations, recorded in feet, is shown on scale *X*; the sum of the temperatures at the two stations is given on *Z*; and the correction (to be added if the sum of temperatures is over 100° and subtracted if the sum is less than 100°, as given on Z) is shown on scale Y. Take the example already mentioned, where two stations, A and B, differed in elevation by 75 ft. and the sum of the temperatures recorded at the two stations was 140°. Lay the straight-edge from 75, on scale X, to 140 on scale Z (Fig. 409, line *st*). This straight-edge will cut Y at just over 3, which is the correction, in feet, to be *added* to 75 ft. to obtain the true difference in elevation of A and B.

If the instrument is calibrated for 60°, use a number, on scale Z, equal to the sum of the two temperatures —20°.

420. Source of temperature data. If barometric readings are to be corrected for temperature, evidently temperature data must be secured during the progress of the barometric surveying.

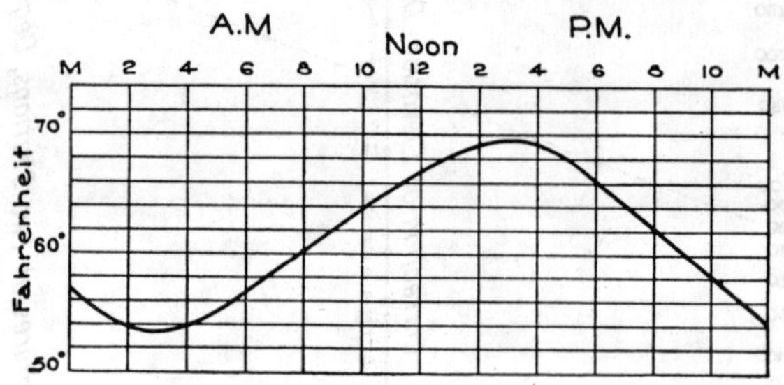

FIG. 410. Average diurnal temperature curve.

Such data can be obtained by means of a thermometer carried by the geologist and read at each station, or by a thermograph (self-recording thermometer) kept at camp or at the base station. Under normal conditions the temperature of the air rises and falls through each 24 hours. Its fluctuations may be plotted as a graph (Fig. 410), which, as will be noted, has its lowest point near dawn and its peak between 2 and 4 in the afternoon. Only in the event of abrupt weather changes is the normal form of this graph radically modified. Where the topography is not very rugged and the relief is not more than a few hundred feet, the method of obtaining temperature variations by a stationary thermograph is satisfactory.

421. Method of correcting for both temperature and pressure variations. In Arts. 415–418, we described the methods of correction for pressure variations. These methods were discussed first in order not to confuse the student; but he is reminded that in practice he must correct for temperature *before* he corrects for pressure. To illustrate this procedure, we have used, in Table 11, the data of Table 9 (page 501). In column *A* (Table 11) are the station numbers; in *B*, the time; in *C*, the elevations read on the aneroid; in *D*, the temperature readings; in *E*, the drop (—) or rise (+) in elevation from one station to the next (cf. *C*); in *F*, the sum of the temperatures at each two stations; in *G*, the percentage adjustment in temperature equals (the sum of the temperatures —100)/10; in *H*, the actual correction (factor in *G* times factor in *E*); in I, the number of feet to be added to, or subtracted from, the recorded elevation (*C*) to give the altitude reading *corrected for temperature;* and in *J*, this reading (*C*) corrected for temperature.

At this point a few words of explanation may be given. Take Stations 7 and 8 as an example. The aneroid readings at 10 and 10.25 A.M. were 540 and 505 ft., respectively; that is, a drop of 35 ft. from Station 7 to Station 8. The temperatures were 77° and 79°, which, when added together, equals 156°, or 56° more than 100°. The percentage adjustment is therefore 5.6 (column *G*). Multiply 35 by 5.6 to obtain the actual adjustment, 1.96, which is here negative because Station 8 was lower than Station 7. The last correction in column *I* was —2, obtained from the data for Stations 6 and 7. The present correction, —1.96, is essentially —2, which is to be algebraically added to the —2 for Station 7, making —4 as the correction at Station 8. That is, 4 is to be subtracted from the elevation 505 ft. recorded at 8 (column *C*). In this manner each *actual correction* figure is to be added algebraically to the last total correction figure in column *I* to find the next total correction figure, which is then added to, or subtracted from, the recorded elevation (column *C*) to obtain the corrected reading (column *J*).

In column *J*, then, are the elevation values to be used in constructing the correction curve for *pressure* variations as explained in Arts. **415–417.** Figure 411 is based on the data in column *J*, Table 11. In column *K* are listed the elevations as corrected by the use of this graph. By reference to column *E*, in Table 9, the reader will note that the altitudes of Stations 1, 6, and 12 had already been established.

The field notebook may be ruled in columns for recording these data (columns *A* to *K*, in Table 11), and spaces may be

TABLE 11. Correction of Barometric Readings for Temperature and Pressure

Station no.	*Time*	*Barometer reading*	*Temperature*	*Elevation change*	*Sum of temperatures*	$\frac{E-100}{10}$	$\frac{G \times E}{100}$	*Feet corrected for temperature*[1]	*Elevation corrected for temperature*[1] $(C + (I))$	*Elevation corrected for pressure*	*Cf. K and D in Table 9*
A	*B*	*C*	*D*	*E*	*F*	*G*	*H*	*I*	*J*	*K*	*L*
	A.M.										
1	6.00	625	65					0	625	700	0
				− 5	132	+3.2	−0.16				
1	7.30	620	67					0	620	700	0
				− 45	135	3.5	−1.58				
2	8.00	575	68					−2	573	658	− 2
				+ 5	138	3.8	+1.9				
3	8.20	580	70					0	580	670	+ 5
				+105	142	4.2	+4.41				
4	8.50	685	72					+4	689	784	+ 4
				−120	145	4.5	−5.40				
3	9.15	565	73					−1	564	669	+ 4
				− 30	148	4.8	−1.44				
5	9.30	535	75					−2	533	643	+ 3
				− 10	150	5.0	−0.5				
6	9.40	525	75					−3	522	630	0
				+ 15	152	5.2	+0.78				
7	10.00	540	77					−2	538	658	+ 8
				− 35	156	5.6	−1.96				
8	10.25	505	79					−4	501	626	+11
				+ 15	159	5.9	+0.885				
9	10.45	520	80					−3	517	642	+12
				+ 30	163	6.3	+1.89				
10	11.10	550	83					−1	549	669	+ 9
				+ 45	168	6.8	+3.06				
11	11.45	595	85					+2	597	712	+12
	P.M.										
				− 45	173	7.3	−3.28				
7	12.15	550	88					−1	551	661	+11
				+ 10	179	7.9	+0.79				
7	1.00	560	91					0	560	655	+ 5
				− 25	183	8.3	−2.075				
8	1.15	535	92					−2	533	623	+ 2
				+ 25	186	8.6	+2.15				
12	2.00	560	94					0	560	635	0
				+ 10	189	8.9	+0.89				
13	2.20	570	95					+1	571	641	+ 1
				+ 20	190	9.0	+1.8				
14	2.35	590	95					+3	593	658	+ 3
				+ 30	190	9.0	+2.7				
15	3.00	620	95					+6	626	681	+ 1
				− 15	189	8.9	−1.335				
2	3.30	605	94					+5	610	655	+ 5
				+ 45	188	8.8	+3.96				
1	3.50	650	94					+9	659	700	0
				+ 5	186	8.6	+0.43				
1	5.30	655	92					+9	664	700	0
				− 15	181	8.1	−1.215				
1	7.05	640	89					+8	648	700	0

[1] This correction, at each station, consists of the algebraic sum of the last recorded item in column *I* plus the next correction in column *H*, given in full numbers.

added before column *A* for tabulating information descriptive of the station and for recording the distance from each station to the next.[17]

422. To what extent is correction of barometric readings for temperature fluctuations desirable? In column *L*, Table 11, are the amounts in feet, by which the adjusted elevations of this traverse, as corrected for both temperature and pressure, differ from the adjusted elevations when correction has been made for pressure only (*D*, Table 9). Observe that the greatest difference is 12 ft., at Stations 9 and 11; also that the greatest difference in relative values, *i.e.*, from station to station, is only 7 ft. (between Stations 2 and 3, at 8.00 and 8.20 A.M.). In view of

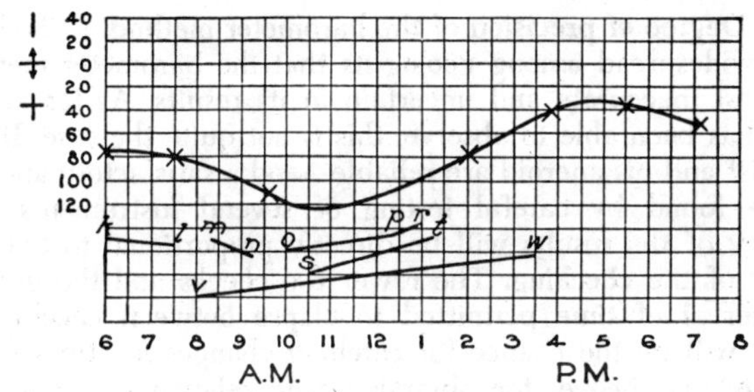

FIG. 411. Correction curve based on same data as those used in Fig. 406, but here first corrected for temperature.

the facts: (1) that, in plotting these correction curves and in applying them, there is easily room for an error of 5 ft. or even 7 or 8 ft.; and (2) that a contour map based on the corrected altitudes of Table 11 would not materially differ from a contour map based on the corrected altitudes of Table 9, one may conclude that temperature corrections are not always necessary. To lay down a rule as to when they should be made, and when not, is practically impossible. One must remember that the greater the difference is between 100°F. and the sum of the temperatures at two consecutive stations, the greater will be the resulting correction. If barometric surveying is being done in very cold weather or very warm weather, the aneroid or altimeter

[17] The American Paulin system has published a useful notebook for recording data under these several headings.

readings should be adjusted for temperature. In general, we would say that, if, in Fig. 408, the point of intersection of the diagonal and horizontal lines falls to the left of the vertical line for a correction of 5 ft., and the difference in elevations is 100 ft. or less, correction for temperature is unnecessary. If the difference in elevation of consecutive stations is more than 100 ft., the geologist will have to use his own judgment as to whether disregard of the temperature factor will introduce too large an error into his results, always bearing in mind the amount of permissible error is governed by the rate of travel (424), the area to be covered within a specified time, the regularity of the geology, the contour interval to be adopted for the map, and so on.

423. Degree of precision of the barometer method. The feeling is widespread among geologists that the barometer method is at best inaccurate and uncertain in its results. As far as the writer has been able to observe, this is not quite the case. If the geologist and his aneroid are reliable—and a satisfactory aneroid *can* be found by careful testing of several instruments—the accuracy of the results will be directly proportional to the frequency of the checking. The fewer the checks and the greater the interval of time permitted to elapse between checks, the smaller will be the chance for catching changes in atmospheric pressure and, hence, for obtaining true relative elevations by reference to the correction curve. On the other hand, there is a practical limit to the number of checks which should be made. Too many checks merely add to the work of correction without yielding a corresponding or necessary increase in the accuracy of the results.

For detail mapping, check stations should not be over a mile or two apart, and not over an hour should elapse between checks. When, on the other hand, the object is to prepare a small scale map of an extensive area and to show only the larger structures, travel is usually much more rapid, minor details are omitted, check stations are selected at 5, 10, 15, or even 20 miles apart, depending on the rate of progress possible, and the barometric elevations are checked at intervals of from 1 to 3 hours.

The reader will perceive that the barometer method is highly elastic. It can be made slow and fairly precise, or rapid and less accurate. In other words, it may be adapted to both detail and reconnaissance geologic mapping. Under ordinary circumstances, whether progress is slow or rapid, the average relative error may be made less than 1 vertical in 1,000 horizontal, which is usually less than the variations in thickness of mappable groups of strata.

424. Rate of mapping. Detail mapping, involving sufficiently careful field work to enable the geologist to prepare a reasonably accurate contour map of the geologic structure on the scale of ½ to 2 miles to the inch with a contour interval of 10 to 20 ft., may be done by the barometer method at rates varying from 2 to 50 square miles per day. Two to four square miles should be mapped in a day where foot traversing is necessary. From 10 to 50 square miles may be mapped by automobile. More than 25 square miles as a day's work is exceptional.

In more rapid reconnaissance, for a map, let us say, on a scale of 2 to 10 miles to an inch and with a contour interval of 25 to 100 ft., as much as 100 square miles, or even more, can sometimes be surveyed by automobile in a day.

For both detail and reconnaissance work the size of the area examined in a day depends upon the number, condition, and distribution of roads, the abundance of outcrops and ease of correlation of strata, and whether or not the geologist has a helper to drive the car.

The Plane-table Method

425. Definition. In the plane-table method of geologic mapping, directions, horizontal distances, and vertical distances are all determined by plane table and alidade, and the map is plotted in the field.[18]

426. Equipment. The equipment used in this method includes a plane table of convenient size, a telescopic alidade, usually of the Gale pattern, a stadia rod, plotting scale, several sheets of plane-table paper, two notebooks, a stadia slide rule or stadia tables, pencils, eraser, thumb tacks, etc. An *instrument man* carries the plane table, alidade, one notebook, and other articles needed for making the map; and a *rodman*, who is usually the geologist, carries the rod, the other notebook, etc. He may also carry a Brunton compass and an aneroid barometer for occasional side traverses.

[18] An excellent text on plane-table mapping is given in Bibliog., Low, Julian W., 1952.

The instrument man's notebook is commonly ruled by vertical lines, the columns being labelled for the various data to be assembled. In these columns are recorded the station number; the level reading or reading of the vernier when the telescope is level; the vertical angle of the line of sight, and a notation whether this angle is positive or negative;[19] the distance to the next station; the difference of elevation between the instrument station and the rod station; the height of the instrument, or "H.I.";[20] the elevation of the distant station; and other data. Sample pages from an instrument man's field notebook are shown in Figs. 412 and 413. In every such book there should be a table giving values for vertical heights up to at least 9° or 10°, and also horizontal corrections for distances (Appendix 18). A natural tangent table for minutes and for degrees up to 20 may be found useful (see Appendix 19).

427. Preparation of the map paper. In preparation for the field work, several sheets of paper of the proper kind are generally fastened, one on top of another, on the plane-table board. This is the easiest way of carrying them. These sheets should be ruled in coordinate squares, parallel to the edges of the board, on the scale to be used in the mapping. One set of lines is assumed to run north and south, and the other set, east and west. Somewhere near the middle of the sheet, through the point of intersection of an east-west coordinate and a north-south coordinate, a line should be ruled in the direction of the magnetic north in the district to be surveyed. Methods of determining the magnetic declination are described below (429).

[19] A positive vertical angle is one between a horizontal line of sight and the inclined line of sight when the objective of the telescope is raised to observe a higher station; a negative vertical angle is included between the horizontal line of sight and the inclined line of sight when the objective is lowered to observe a lower station.

[20] The height of the instrument (H.I.) is the vertical distance from sea level to the horizontal axis of the telescope when the instrument is set up on the plane table for use. The instrument man sets up the plane table at approximately a constant elevation above the ground, making no record of this quantity unless, for some reason, the table must be set up exceptionally high or low. Since, in some cases, especially where mapping is on a large scale, the height of the instrument (here also called "H.I.") is taken as the vertical distance of the center of the instrument above the ground just below it, the instrument man should always indicate, for a plane-table survey, which definition of "H.I." he uses.

						REMARKS
1	2	3	4	5	6	
7	8	9	10	11	12	
13	14	15	16	17	18	
19	20	21	22	23	24	

FIG. 412. Page from an instrument man's field notebook. (See Fig. 413.)

DATE ______ 193__ GEO. ______ INSTR. ______ PAGE ______ GEO. COL.

PLANE TABLE SHEET NO. ______ MAP AREA NO. ______

	NO. STA. INSTR.	NO. STA. ROD.	LEVEL	ANGLE: LEVEL	ANGLE: + OR −	ANGLE: DIFF.	DIST.	DIFF. ELEV.	H. I.	ELEV.	DIFF. TO DATUM	DATUM	GEO. COL.	
1														
2														
3														
4														
5														
6														
7														
8														
9														
10														
11														
12														
13														
14														
15														
16														
17														
18														
19														
20														
21														
22														
23														
24														

FIG. 413. Page from an instrument man's field notebook. When the notebook is open this page is to the right of the page shown in Fig. 412.

428. Centering and levelling the plane table. When the plane table is to be set up for use at a station, it must be centered, levelled, and oriented. Orienting is explained in Art. **430.** To center the table, bring the point for a station on the map over the corresponding point on the ground. In geologic work this may be done by eye without introducing serious errors.

For levelling, set up the plane table and roughly level it by eye. Place the alidade near the middle of the board. Then, by slightly tilting the board this way and that, center the bubble in the circular spirit level of the alidade. When this bubble is centered, clamp the angular motion of the board.

429. Determination of declination. Ordinarily the magnetic declination (**356**) in a given region can be found by reference to published records or to an isogonic chart (Fig. 386); but sometimes the geologist must determine the declination for himself. Below are outlined three methods of doing this.

1. If there are any previously established control stations in the district, such as U.S. Geological Survey bench marks, etc., two of these, which are intervisible, may be chosen for the following operation. They should have been carefully plotted on the map sheet. Set up the plane table at one of these stations, levelling it as described in Art. **428.** Clamp the angular motion. Move the alidade on the board until its bevelled edge coincides with the line between the plotted points for the two established stations. Rotate the board in a horizontal plane until the other station, in the distance, is in the line of sight of the alidade. Fasten the horizontal motion of the board and release the compass needle. Rotate the alidade about the point of intersection of an east-west coordinate and a north-south coordinate until the needle points to magnetic north. Draw a line along the fiducial (bevelled) edge of the alidade. This will be the declination line, making an angle with the north-south coordinates equal to the magnetic declination.

2. Where the country has been sectionized and roads are laid out accurately along the section lines, the declination may be found by reference to these roads. Select a point on the road from which you can see the road for 2 or 3 miles preferably across a valley. Set up the plane table at this point and level it. The alidade should be placed with its bevelled edge against a north-south coordinate. Center the vertical cross-hair on a point in the road 2 or 3 miles away, endeavoring to choose this point

in the same relative position across the road as the site of the plane table. After releasing the compass needle of the alidade, rotate the alidade about the intersection point of an east-west and a north-south coordinate near the middle of the board, until the needle swings freely and points to magnetic north. East of the zero isogonic line (agonic line) (Fig. 386), the alidade will be turned counter-clockwise in this procedure, and west of the zero isogonic line it will be turned clockwise. Draw a line along the fiducial edge of the alidade. This line will lie in the direction of magnetic north and south, and will make an angle with the north-south coordinates approximately equal to the magnetic declination for the district.

3. With a suitable book on astronomy, or with the aid of a person who knows the stars, first learn to recognize the constellations, Cassiopeia, Ursa Minor (the "Little Bear"), and Ursa Major (the "Great Bear"), and the stars called Delta Cassiopeia, Mizar, Polaris (the "Pole Star"), and the "Pointers" in Ursa Major. Ascertain at what time of night an imaginary line connecting Delta Cassiopeia, Polaris, and Mizar (Fig. 414), will appear to be vertical. Either Delta or Mizar may be below Polaris. Fifteen minutes or so before this time go out and carefully level the plane table. Set the alidade with its bevelled edge exactly parallel to a north-south coordinate on the map sheet, but support the objective end on a rectangular block of wood of which the right-and-left edges are perpendicular to the length of the alidade. This is to enable the observer to raise the objective end of the telescope enough to see the higher star. Turn the board horizontally until, by raising and lowering the objective end of the telescope, Polaris is brought into the line of sight. Raise and lower the telescope alternately until the time when both Polaris and the "Guide Star" (Delta or Mizar) may be brought successively into the line of sight. When this is possible, the north-south coordinates on the map are lying due north and south. Now lock the table, releasing the compass needle of the alidade, and turn the alidade, resting flat on the board, about a coordinate intersection until the needle points to magnetic north. Draw the declination line along the fiducial edge of the alidade.[21]

[21] Other methods, "suitable tor work of medium accuracy under conditions where time is at a premium, or where visibility conditions permit only one or two 'sights' a week," are outlined by Ronald L. Ives (Bibliog., 1948).

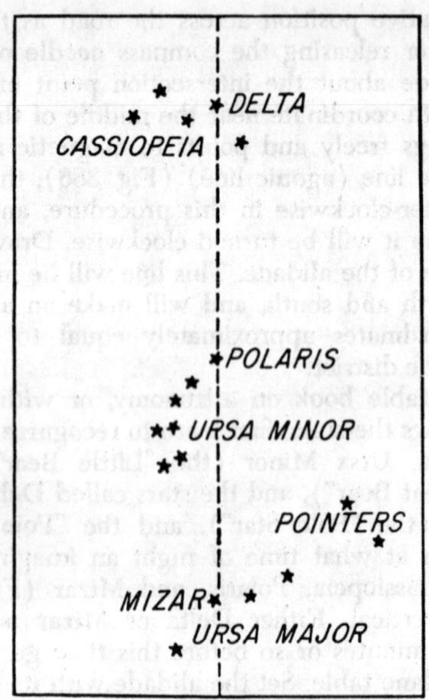

Fig. 414. Stars and constellations near the Pole Star.

430. Orienting the plane table. In most plane-table mapping the board is set up, at any station, so that its edges bear exactly the same relations to compass directions as at all other stations. The process of setting up in this way is called *orienting*. Following are three methods of orienting the board:

1. Set up the plane table. Place the alidade on the board with its fiducial edge coinciding with the declination line (427), and with its objective end toward the north. Turn the board horizontally until the released compass needle points north. This is *orientation by compass.*

2. To *orient by backsight,* set up the table at a given station, *B,* and see that the north edge of the board is toward the north. Place the alidade so that its fiducial edge coincides with the line drawn from the station previously visited, *A,* to the station now occupied *B.* Rotate the board until Station *A* is brought into the line of sight of the alidade. The board is now oriented.

3. Still another method of orientation makes use of the Baldwin Solar Chart. The angle between the apparent position of the sun and true north is graphically determined by means of this chart which is so constructed that when turned until the proper pivot point on an arrow and the *sun time point* on a latitude arc are on a line parallel to the shadow cast by a plumb line upon a level table the arrow points true north. A copy of this chart and full directions for its use may be found in "Topographic Instructions of the U.S. Geological Survey," pages 219–225.[22]

431. Lining in a station.

"After the table has been properly oriented at a station, the location of which has been plotted on the map, the bearing of any visible object may be drawn directly. The alidade is moved until the straight-edge touches the side of the needle-hole or pencil dot representing the occupied station and the vertical cross-hair in the telescope bisects the distant object, the bearing of which is desired; a line drawn along the straight-edge will then represent the compass-bearing plotted to position on the map under construction.

"The best method to pursue in lining in a distant station is to grasp the ends of the alidade base with either hand; shift the instrument until the line of sight through the telescope falls upon the desired objective and the fiducial edge rests within an inch or two of the dot locating the occupied station; then move the alidade diagonally forward and to the right, keeping the vertical cross-hair on the distant object, until the ruler edge touches the proper point. If the alidade is equipped with a parallel-edge ruler, it is only necessary to place the instrument somewhere near and to the left of the plotted point in such a position that the vertical cross-hair cuts the distant station; then push the parallel straight-edge outward until it touches the proper point. Some surveyors make it a practice to stick a needle vertically into the plane table at the point representing the occupied station, and to pivot the alidade on the needle when lining in a station. This practice is not recommended. Although it is an easy way for the novice to increase his speed, it involves inaccuracies of considerable import. If the needle is inserted far enough to hold its upright position, it makes a hole several times as large as necessary; the point becomes a space which on the customary scales represents an area on the ground, 30 to 60 ft. in diameter.

"Lines representing bearings should be drawn with the chiseled edge of a 9-H pencil, being careful always to hold the pencil at the same angle, and to see that the contact of rule and paper is perfect. By placing the ruler-edge in a position tangential to the tiny circle formed by a needle-hole or dot, the line when drawn should exactly cut the center of the 'point.' If the

[22] Bibliog., Birdseye, C. H., 1928. (Quoted from Mather, Kirtley F., 1919, p. 109. See Bibliog.)

distant station is subsequently to be occupied and orientation there is to be by backsight, the foresight line should be the full length of the alidade base; if not, the foresight line may be short, covering only the estimated position of the point. It is better not to draw lines through the dot or needle-hole representing the occupied station; break the line for a fraction of an inch."[23]

432. Determination of horizontal distances. Let *A* and *B* represent two intervisible stations at the same elevation above sea level. *A* is occupied by the instrument man, and *B*, by the rodman. The distance *AB* is to be determined. Set up the plane table at *A*. Line in *B* and *A* as explained in Art. 431. Looking through the telescope, set the lower stadia hair on a foot mark on the rod held at *B*, and count the number of feet on the rod

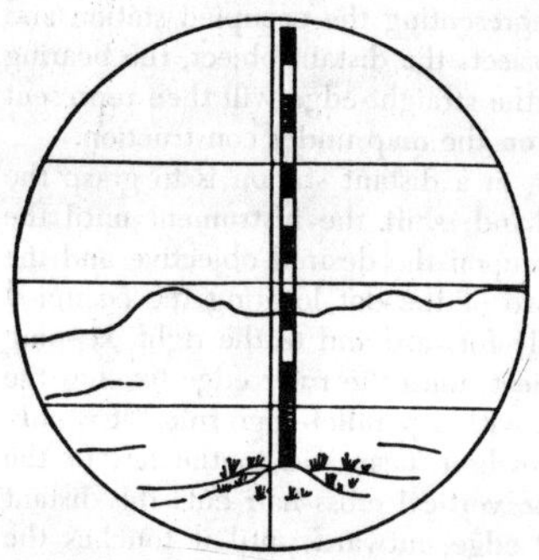

FIG. 415. Stadia rod in field of view at a distance of 720 ft. (*After Kirtley F. Mather; reproduced with permission of Scientific Laboratories of Denison University.*)

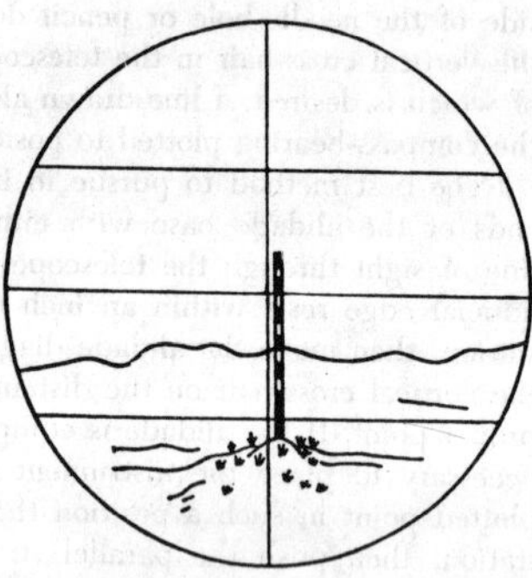

FIG. 416. Stadia rod in the field of view at a distance of 1,740 ft. (*After Kirtley F. Mather; reproduced with permission of Scientific Laboratories of Denison University.*)

intercepted between the two stadia hairs. Multiply this intercept by 100 to obtain the distance from *A* to *B* (373). If *B* is so far away that the rod does not extend across the space between the two stadia hairs, read the intercept on the rod between the lower stadia hair and the horizontal cross (diametric) hair, and multiply this intercept by 100 × 2 to obtain the distance *AB* (Figs. 415, 416).

[23] Bibliog., Mather, Kirtley F., 1919, pp. 110, 111.

433. Long sights.[24]

"Occasionally, it is necessary to measure distances greater than 200 times the rod length with an alidade equipped only with three stadia hairs. Several different methods of procedure are available; the choice of the one to use depends upon the equipment of the instrument, the geographic environment, and the custom of the individual surveyors. Some of the methods are in effect schemes to provide a longer rod. Others depend upon trigonometric principles. The method numbered 5 is probably best suited to the more common conditions met in geologic mapping.

"1. Rotate the telescope 90° in its sleeve so that the stadia hairs are vertical instead of horizontal. Signal rodman to mark his station with a flag or to select a certain sapling or post for his station. Place one hair on the station and signal rodman to move at right angles to the line of sight until the rod, held vertically, is in line with the other stadia hair. The rodman will then measure the distance horizontally on the ground from his second position to his first, using the rod as a measuring stick, and report the result of the instrument man. Distances of 4,000 to 7,000 ft. may be determined with a fair degree of accuracy by this method. It may be used to advantage only when the two men are able to communicate freely by signals such as the two-arm semaphore code.

"2. Rotate the telescope as before. Signal rodman to hold rod horizontally and to be prepared to move laterally so that the base of the rod will occupy the point now occupied by its top. Intersect base of the rod with one stadia hair. Signal rodman to move over in the desired direction a sufficient number of rod-lengths so that the other stadia hair will finally intersect the rod. Read intersection; add the number of feet indicated by the length of the rod multiplied by the number of moves; multiply by 100 or 200 depending upon which hairs were used.

"3. If instrument is equipped with a Stebinger gradienter drum attached to the fine adjustment screw, proceed as follows: place bottom hair on lowest visible primary division of the rod; read and record Stebinger. Turn Stebinger drum until middle hair rests on the top of the rod; read and record Stebinger. Take the difference of the two Stebinger readings; turn an equal number of divisions in the direction which brings the middle hair down onto the rod; observe the number of feet between the top of the rod and the intersection of the middle hair. Add this to the length of the rod which was above the bottom hair at the first reading; the sum multiplied by 200 is the horizontal distance. For example:[25] 12 ft. of the rod are entirely visible and the middle hair is well above the rod when the bottom hair rests 12 ft. below its top. In that position the Stebinger drum reads 24. Turn

[24] See Art. 435.

[25] This, and the following examples apply only to those instruments in which a clockwise rotation of the Stebinger drum depresses the objective end of the telescope.

down until middle hair touches the top of the rod; Stebinger reading is now 60. The difference between the two readings is 36. Turn down 36 divisions more, to 96. The middle hair now intersects the rod 3.4 ft. below its top. The horizontal distance is $200 \times (12 + 3.4)$ or 3,080 ft.

"4. If instrument is equipped as in 3 and there is at hand a table previously prepared for this particular instrument, showing Stebinger factors,[26] *i.e.*, the differences in elevation at the unit distance of 100 ft. corresponding to the vertical swing of the telescope denoted in divisions of the Stebinger drum, proceed as follows: place one hair on the top of the rod; read and record Stebinger. Turn down until that hair cuts the lowest visible primary division of the rod; read and record Stebinger. Take the difference of the two readings. Repeat for each of the other two hairs. The three results should check. Select from the table the Stebinger factor corresponding to that number of divisions. Note the number of feet passed over on the rod; multiply it by 100 and divide by the factor. The result is the horizontal distance. For example: 13 ft. of the rod are visible. With the middle hair resting on the top of the rod, the Stebinger reading is 62. When the middle hair is turned down to the primary division 13 ft. lower, the reading is 106. Difference of the two readings is 44; corresponding factor is 0.4111; horizontal distance is $1{,}300 \div 0.4111 = 3{,}160$ ft.

"This method is frequently employed by ingenious surveyors to good advantage in determining distances without the use of the stadia rod. Any two points, one above the other, at known distances apart suffice; two flags at a measured interval, the crown plate and girths (commonly 8 ft. apart) of a standard derrick, the eaves and lower copings of a church tower, are listed merely as suggestions. If the location of such a target is plotted, the surveyor may *shoot himself in,* with a fair degree of accuracy, at any point from which it is visible.

"5. If alidade is equipped as in 3, an alternative method which may be used is as follows: place middle cross-hair on top of rod; read and record Stebinger, denoting the record as *A*. Turn down until middle hair intersects the lowest visible primary division; read and record Stebinger (record *B*). Turn down until top hair rests on top of rod; read and record Stebinger (record *C*). Compute distance by the formula

$$D = 200r\,\frac{C - A}{B - A},$$

in which *D* represents the distance, *r* the length of the rod above lowest visible primary division, and *A*, *B*, and *C*, respectively, the three readings of the Stebinger drum. For example: a 13-ft. rod is entirely visible. The middle hair on top of rod gives a Stebinger reading of 31; middle hair on bottom of rod gives a reading of 54; top hair on top of rod gives a reading of 78.

[26] The preparation of such a table and the mathematical principles on which it is based are discussed on pp. 544–545.

$$\text{Distance} = 200 \times 13 \times \frac{78 - 31}{54 - 31} = 5{,}300 \text{ ft.}$$

"The formula may be more easily recalled if one has grasped the principle upon which it is based. The Stebinger difference, $C - A$, is theoretically a constant, the measure of the angle between the rays converging from the top and middle cross-hairs to the focus of the telescope. If the rod at the distant point were of sufficient length, the intercept subtended by this angle could be read and, multiplied by 200, would give the distance to the rod. That is, if i be taken to mean the length in feet of that hypothetical intercept,

$$i = D \div 200.$$

But

$$i:r::C - A:B - A,$$

for the Stebinger difference $C - A$ is the measure of the angle defined by the chord i and $B - A$ is the measure of the angle defined by the length of the rod at the same distance. Therefore,

$$(D \div 200):r::C - A:B - A$$

or

$$D = 200r\frac{C - A}{B - A}.$$ [27]

434. Inclined sights.

"This discussion of the measurement of distances with the stadia (**432, 433**) has been based on the assumption that the rod is always held perpendicular to the line of sight and that the desired distance is to be measured along that line. As a matter of fact, most of the sights in stadia work are taken not on a level, but on a slope or inclination, as suggested in [Fig. **417** (**376**)]. Consequently if the rod is held vertically, the stadia intercept is somewhat more than it would be when held perpendicular to the line of sight, and an element of error is introduced. This error amounts to 1 per cent of the distance for a gradient of 8°, 2 per cent for 11°, and 3 per cent for 14°. It may obviously be corrected by tilting the rod so that it is perpendicular to the central visual ray from the telescope. This may be accomplished by attaching a short pointer to the rod at right angles to its face and aiming this pointer at the instrument when the sight is taken. It is, however, difficult to hold the rod steadily in this position and this corrects only one of the two discrepancies. It is, therefore, customary to hold the rod vertical no matter what the angle of slope may be and make the correction in the tables for distance and elevation.[28] The second discrepancy is due to the fact that the distance to be plotted is the horizontal distance from telescope to rod, not the inclined distance. So far as plotting is concerned, this

[27] Bibliog., Mather, Kirtley F., 1919, pp. 114–117.

[28] See footnote 1, p. 863.

discrepancy, and, therefore, the angle of inclination, must be fairly large before it need be taken into account; how large depends upon the scale of the map, but for most work it may be neglected for all angles of less than 3°. [See Art. 388.] With an angle of 5½° this discrepancy amounts to about 1 per cent, which for a distance of 1,000 ft. is little more than the diameter of a needle hole on a scale of 1:321,250.[29]

"The stadia tables ordinarily used include the correction for horizontal distance of inclined sights. In practice, such tables (Appendix 18) should be consulted before plotting distances determined by sights which depart more than 3° from the horizontal. Reference to the accompanying diagram

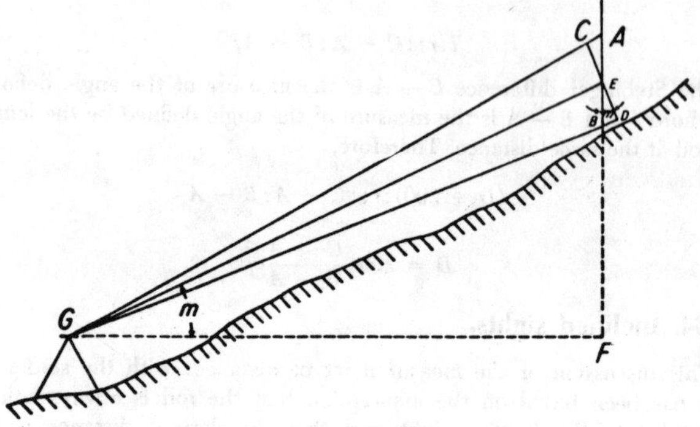

Fɪɢ. 417. Diagram illustrating the stadia principle applied to inclined sights. (*After Kirtley F. Mather; reproduced with permission of Scientific Laboratories of Denison University.*)

(Fig. 417) will make clear the mathematical formula upon which the correction tables are based. In the diagram, *AB* represents the intercept on the rod held vertically, *CD* the intercept on the rod held perpendicular to the line of sight from *G*, *GE*, the distance from table to rod in the line of sight, and *GF* the horizontal distance from set-up to station. The angle of inclination of sight and the equal angle between the two positions of the rod are indicated by *m*. For all practical purposes, ∡ *ACE* and *EDB* may be assumed to be 90°. By trigonometry,

$$CD = AB \cos m$$

and

$$GF = GE \cos m.$$

But

$$GE = 100CD = 100AB \cos m;$$

[29] See Bibliog., Threet, Richard L., 1953.

therefore, by substitution,

$$GF = 100AB \cos^2 m,$$

by means of which the horizontal distance may be computed from the rod intercept and the angle of inclination."

For the vertical distance EF (Fig. 417), we have the following:

$$EF = GE \sin m$$

and

$$GE = 100AB \cos m,$$

as stated above. By substitution,

$$EF = 100AB \cos m \sin m.$$

From trigonometry,

$$\sin 2m = 2(\sin m \cos m).$$

Therefore, again by substitution,

$$EF = 100AB \cdot \tfrac{1}{2} \sin 2m.$$

"The correction to be applied to the observed distance on inclined sights may be determined without reference to tables or formulae by means of the Beaman stadia arc, an attachment for the mechanical solution of the stadia problem. . . . The arc carries two scales, a multiple scale and a reduction scale, having coincident zero points marked 50 and 0, respectively. The reduction scale is, of the two, the more distant from the adjustable index and gives percentages of correction that may be used to reduce observed stadia distances to horizontal. The adjustable index should be set opposite the zero of the reduction scale when the telescope is level. To get the necessary correction, simply read the same scale with the line of sight cutting the distant station. Reading to the nearest per cent is usually sufficient. For example: the reduction scale reads 3 with an observed rod intercept of 16.2; then 3 per cent of 1,620 = 48.6; 1,620 − 48.6 = 1,571.4 = corrected horizontal distance."[30] (See Art. 437.)

435. Correction for curvature and refraction.[31] No matter what method of determining vertical distances is used, a correction for curvature and refraction must be applied to all 'shots' of a mile or more in length. The level datum to which all elevations are referred is a surface having the curvature of the earth; the line of sight through the telescope in a level position is tangential to this curved surface; therefore, distant objects appear to

[30] Bibliog., Mather, Kirtley F., 1919, pp. 117–119.
[31] See Appendix 20.

be lower than they really are. In the greatly exaggerated Fig. 418, for example, point *B* appears to be at the same level as the instrument, whereas it is really at a height *CB* above the level line. The result of curvature can be determined with reasonable accuracy. It varies directly as the square of the distance and

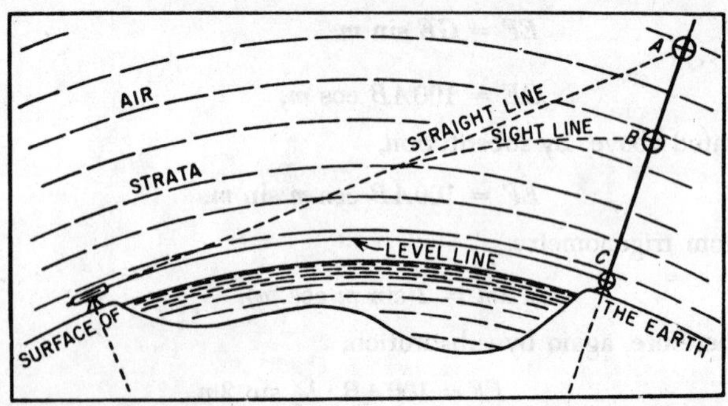

Fig. 418. Diagram, greatly exaggerated, to illustrate influence of curvature and refraction upon observations for determining differences in elevation between two points. (*After Kirtley F. Mather; reproduced with permission of Scientific Laboratories of Denison University.*)

may be computed by the formula: curvature $= 0.667 \times D^2$, where *D* is the distance in miles.[32]

"Refraction, on the other hand, has the opposite effect. When light rays pass obliquely from one air stratum to another of different density they are bent or refracted from their original position. In Fig. 418, the light from the target at *B*, passing into air strata of increasing density as it travels to the alidade at the left, is bent downward and enters the telescope as though it had come by a straight line from *A*. Thus, the effect of normal atmospheric refraction is to make distant objects appear higher than they really are. It, therefore, tends to decrease the curvature correction, as shown in the figure. The amount of refraction depends upon the density of the air and is, therefore, quite variable. It is much greater near the ground than 3 ft. above it, and generally greater at midday than early in the morning or late in the afternoon.[33] The empirical valuation ordinarily placed upon the

[32] Bibliog., Mather Kirtley F., 1919, pp. 117–119, with some changes.

[33] Obviously, the refraction to which reference is here made is not that of the direct rays of light from sun or stars. The refraction for which correction must be made in determining sun azimuth is least between 9 A.M. and 3 P.M.

effects of refraction gives the combined formula: curvature plus refraction $= 0.57135 \times D^2$.

"A table showing corrections based on this formula may be found in the ordinary stadia tables. The correction amounts to only 0.1 ft. for distances of 2,200 ft., 0.2 ft. for 3,125 ft. and 0.5 ft. for 4,940 but increases rapidly to more than 5 ft. at 3 miles and 20 ft. at 6 miles. It may safely be disregarded for the great majority of rod 'shots,' which will of course be less than 3,000 feet long."[34]

The correction is always a positive quantity for foresight readings (intersection) and a negative quantity for backsight readings (resection). It should be added algebraically after the proper sign has been placed in front of the vertical distance as instrumentally determined, an angle of elevation giving a plus sign and an angle of depression giving a minus sign. Occasionally, for nearly level sights, the correction to be applied for curvature and refraction will be greater than the observed difference in elevation, but no confusion will arise if the rule stated in the first sentence of this paragraph be rigidly observed.[35]

436. Methods of determining location. There are four methods of locating points for map construction by the plane table, all of them embraced in the term *triangulation*. They are radiation, intersection, resection, and progression or traversing. Intersection and resection are the two principal modes of triangulation.

1. The *method of radiation* is illustrated by Fig. 419. *a*, *b*, *c*, and *d* are stations to be located. Set up the plane table above any point, *s*, from which the stations are visible. If an open-sight alidade is used these stations must also be accessible from *s*. Orient if necessary. Let *s′* be the position of this point on the map. *s* is vertically below *s′*. Place the fiducial edge of the alidade against *s′*, sight at the rod held at *a*, and draw a line from *s′* toward *a*. Measure *sa* (**432**). Lay off *s′a′* on the scale adopted for the map. In like manner plot *s′b′*, *s′c′*, and *s′d′*. In each case find the elevation of the distant point and record it on the map (**437**).

2. The *method of intersection* is illustrated in Fig. 420, where *a*, *b*, *c*, *d*, *e*, and *f*, are points to be plotted. Set up the plane table at a given station, *a*. Let *a′* on the map represent *a* on the ground.

[34] Bibliog., Mather, Kirtley F., 1919, pp. 135–137. The original text has been somewhat modified.

[35] This paragraph has been modified from Kirtley Mather's article. Appendix 20 is a table for curvature refraction corrections.

Sight with the alidade at *b*, *c*, *d*, *e*, and *f*, and draw lines from *a′* toward these points. From *a* measure the distance to one of the stations, *c*, and lay off *a′c′* on the scale adopted for the map. Set up at *c* by backsight on *a* (430). From *c* sight at *b*, *d*, *e*, and *f*,

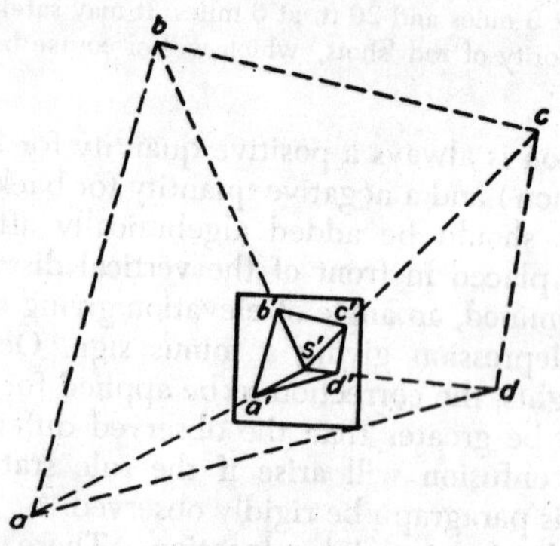

FIG. 419. Mapping by the method of radiation. The square represents the plane-table board.

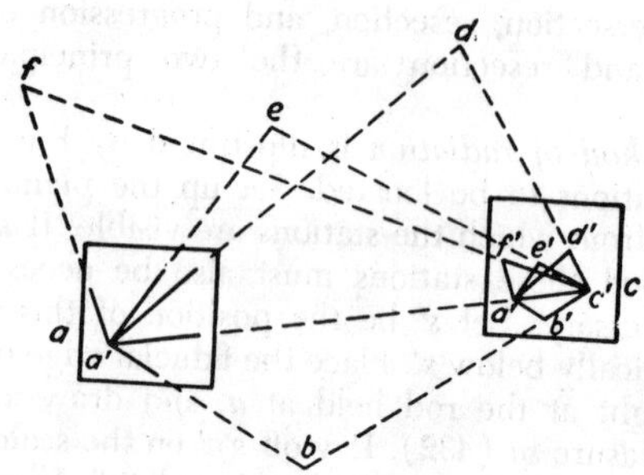

FIG. 420. Mapping by the method of intersection. The squares represent different positions of the plane table.

and draw lines toward these points from *c′*. The intersection of the two lines of sight from *a′* and *c′* to each point will determine the position of this point on the map. The angle made by these two lines at each point (*e.g.*, *a′e′c′*) should not be less than 30° or more than 150°. Whenever possible it should approximate

90°. Elevations of the distant stations may be determined as described in Art. 437.

To check the work, the observer should always sight from a third station at all points previously located by two-line intersections (Fig. 421). If the line from the third station does not pass through the intersection point for any other station, there has been an error in the plotting and the mapper may have to go back and repeat until his error has been discovered and corrected. The elevation of any station can be checked by reading the vertical angle to this station from a second and a third station and computing the elevation in each case.

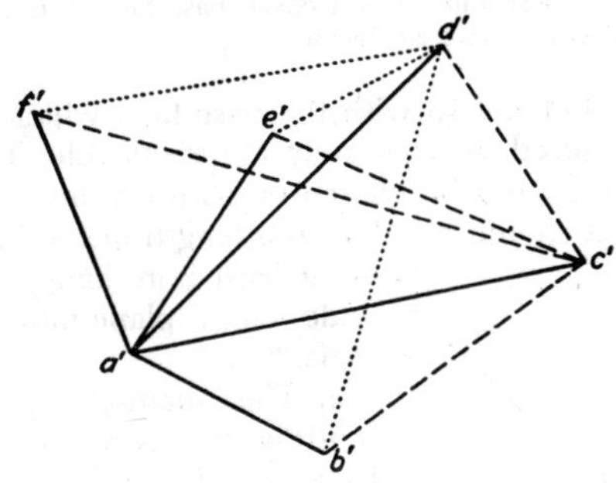

Fig. 421. Enlargement of the plot shown in Fig. 420. All points are fixed by the intersection of at least three lines. Full lines were sighted from *a*, dashed lines from *c*, and dotted lines from *d*; *a*, *c*, and *d*, being the stations represented by *a'*, *c'*, and *d'*.

By advancing from station to station, always locating points by intersection in the manner just described, any number of stations may be plotted. The lines joining stations will form a network of triangles, a *triangulation net*. The process of developing this net is called *expansion*. Expansion may be accomplished by building up a series of triangles, quadrilaterals, or polygons (Fig. 422).

The method of intersection requires the actual measurement of the length of but one line, termed the base line (*ac* in Fig. 420). In most cases, however, the system should be tied to a check base line at the other end of the net (Fig. 422, D). The accuracy of the whole net is proportional to the degree of precision with which the base line is measured. Errors in triangulation tend to

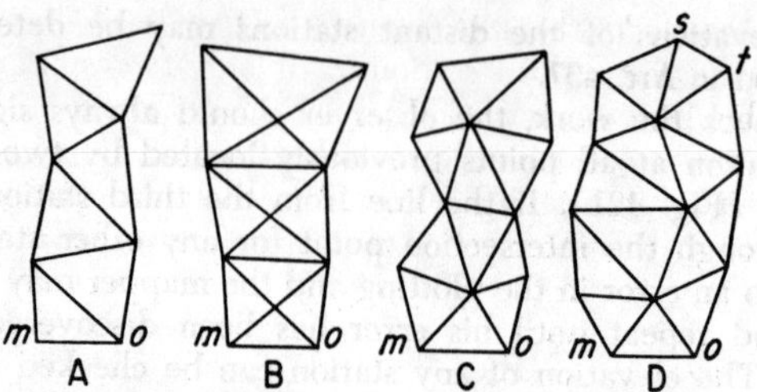

FIG. 422. Triangulation nets consisting of a series of triangles (A), quadrilaterals (B), polygons (C), and intersecting polygons (D). In each figure *mo* is the base line. *st* is a check base line. A is the least accurate method. B and D are most satisfactory.

balance out, but not so with the base line, which should, therefore, be measured as accurately as practicable. The position of the base line should be chosen on as open and as level ground as possible. It should be of such a length in the field that it will be at least 2 in. long when plotted to scale on a plane-table map of any scale.[36]

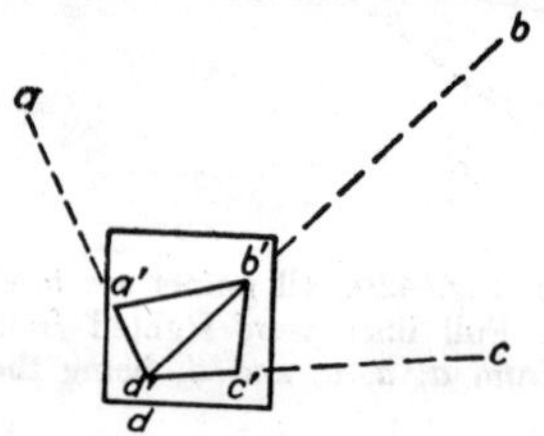

FIG. 423. Mapping by the method of resection. The square represents the plane table.

3. The *method of resection,* or "cutting in," is virtually intersection backward. Let *a, b,* and *c,* in Fig. 423, be three stations previously determined, and let *a′, b′,* and *c′* represent these stations on the map. The observer is at *d* and wishes to ascertain his location with respect to *a, b,* and *c,* which are visible from *d.* These stations should be selected so that the rays (lines) drawn from them intersect at angles as wide as possible. Do not select stations from which the rays are nearly parallel. Set up the plane table at *d* and orient it by compass. Lay the fiducial edge of the alidade at *a′* and turn it until *a* is in the line of sight. Draw a line from *a′* away from *a.* Place the alidade against *b′*, turn it until *b* is in the line of sight, and draw a line from *b′* away from *b.*

[36] This does not mean that the line on the map should not be drawn 6 or 8 in. long when its *direction* is plotted, in order to facilitate laying the alidade along it.

This line intersects the line from a' at d'. Check by repeating this operation for a third station, c. If only two stations, a and b, are visible from c, no satisfactory check of this kind is possible.

If the line from c' intersects $a'd'$ and $b'd'$ at d', d' is the correct location of the point (Fig. 423). If it does not, the three lines (rays) will form a *triangle of error*, which may lie inside

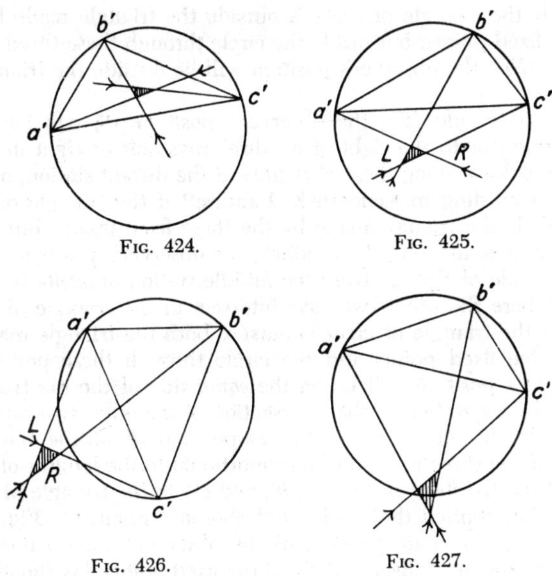

FIG. 424.

FIG. 425.

FIG. 426.

FIG. 427.

FIGS. 424 to 427. Different aspects of the three-point problem. a', b', and c' are the mapped positions of the stations a, b, and c, on the ground. The small shaded triangle is the "triangle of error," in each case. The arrowheads point along the lines of sight (rays) toward the stations a, b, and c, respectively.

(Fig. 424) or outside (Figs. 425–427) the triangle made by the three fixed points (a', b', and c') on the map, and inside (Figs. 424, 425) or outside (Fig. 426) a circle which passes through these three fixed points. If the *triangle of error* falls on, or nearly on, this circle (Fig. 427), substitute another station for one of the three fixed points, and repeat the operation of resection from this new station. Having obtained a triangle of error which corresponds with one of the conditions illustrated in Figs. 424, 425, or 426 (not 427), the correct position of the observer can be found through a series of approximations by application of the following rules:

1. If the triangle of error is *inside* the triangle made by the three fixed points (Fig. 424), the observer's position, *d′*, is *inside* the triangle of error; and vice versa.

2. If the triangle of error is outside the triangle made by the three fixed points, but inside the circle through these three points (Fig. 425), the observer's position will be outside the triangle of error.

3. Under rule (2), the observer's position, *d′*, will be either to the left or to the right of all three rays, left or right meaning when looking along these rays *toward* the distant station, in each case. According to Kenneth K. Landes,[37] if the triangle of error is outside the triangle made by the three fixed points, but inside the circle connecting these points, the observer's position will be on the side of the ray from the middle station *opposite* from the side where the other two rays intersect in the triangle of error; and if the triangle of error is outside both the triangle made by the three fixed points and the circle through these points, the observer's position will be on the *same* side of the ray from the most distant station as the intersection of the other two rays.

4. The distance of the observer's position, *d′*, on the map from each of the three rays will be proportional to the lengths of these rays from the fixed points (*a′*, *b′*, and *c′*) to the triangle of error.

Having applied these rules and chosen a point, *d′* (Fig. 423), for the approximate position of the observer, draw a line from *d′* to *b′*, the most distant of the three fixed points, lay the alidade against *d′b′*, and turn the *board* until the sights are in line with *b*. Check by sighting along *d′a′* at *a* and along *d′c′* at *c*. If there is still a triangle of error, it should be much smaller than the one first obtained. The procedure may be repeated to secure greater accuracy, but usually this is not necessary.

Another solution of this *three-point problem*, as it is called, may be accomplished by describing circles on the map as follows: After the triangle of error has been drawn, a circle through *a′*, *b′*, and the vertex of the triangle of error corresponding to the lines drawn from *a* and *b*, will pass through the observer's posi-

[37] See Bibliog., Landes, Kenneth K., 1947.

tion on the map. Similarly another circle, through b', c', and the vertex formed by the lines drawn from b and c, will pass through the observer's position. Therefore, these two circles will intersect at the observer's position, d'. Generally this method is found to be more laborious and to require more time than the method of approximation, first outlined above.

The solution of the *three-point problem* may be performed graphically as follows: If a triangle of error is obtained by drawing lines from the three fixed points, as described above, rotate the table a little and, in just the same way, draw three more lines from the same three points, making another like triangle of error. If this second triangle of error is larger than the first, rotate the table in the opposite direction, and try again. It will be found that the triangle will reach a minimum size and then, with continued rotation of the table in the same direction, will become larger again and *inverted*. In seeking the correct position of the occupied station, refer to a triangle of error in normal position and another in inverted position. Draw straight lines connecting the corresponding apices of these two triangles. The corresponding apices in the two triangles are those from which sight lines were drawn from the same distant station. The three lines connecting these apices will intersect in a point which will be the observer's correct position on the map.[38] Lay the alidade against this point and the most distant fixed point, rotate the table until the station represented by this fixed point on the map is in the line of sight of the alidade, and then check by sighting at the other two stations.

A third useful, but less accurate, solution is accomplished by means of tracing paper. Fasten the tracing paper to the board, orient the table by compass, let a point near the center of the paper be the observer's position, lay the alidade against this point, and sight successively at three distant stations already determined, each time drawing a line from the station of the set-up. Unfasten the tracing paper and shift it on the board until the three lines fall over the plotted points for the three distant stations. Prick through the observer's position. Test the correctness of the location in the way described for the preceding methods.

[38] These lines do not meet mathematically in a point, but, on the scale of ordinary plane-table work, they will so nearly meet at a point that for all practical purposes they may be considered to do so.

From the vertical angles measured from *d* to *a*, *b*, and *c*, of which the elevations are already known, the elevation of *d* can be calculated (437).

4. The *method of progression*, commonly termed *stadia traversing* when a telescopic alidade and rod are used, is illustrated by Fig. 428. *a*, *b*, *c*, and *d* are points to be plotted. Let *a′* on the paper represent *a* on the ground. Set up the plane table at *a* and orient it by compass or, preferably, by backsight or resection from some fixed points. Place the fiducial edge of the alidade against *a′* and sight at *b*. Draw a line from *a′* toward *b*. Determine and lay off the distance, *ab*, on the scale adopted for the

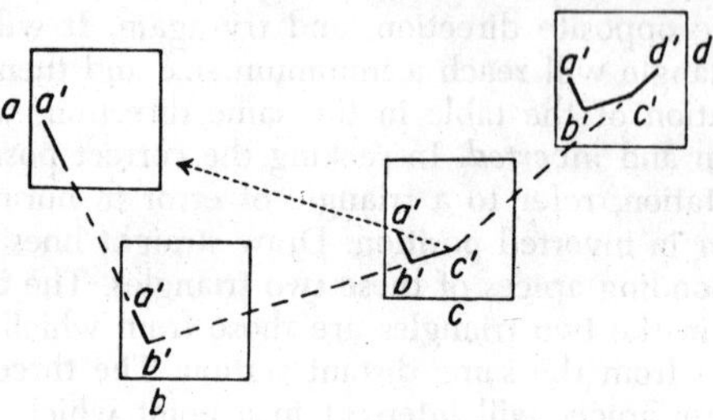

Fig. 428. Mapping by the method of progression or traversing. The dotted line is a check sight line made by the observer at *c* looking toward *a*. The squares represent different positions of the plane table.

map, along the line just drawn. This will locate *b′*. Set up at *b* and orient by backsight on *a*. Place the fiducial edge of the alidade at *b′* and sight toward *c*. Draw a line from *b′* toward *c*. Determine *bc* and lay off *b′c′*. Set up at *c*, orient by backsight on *b*, and continue as before. When possible sight back from a given station, such as *c* (Fig. 428), to an earlier station, such as *a*, and note whether the direction from *c* to *a* coincides with the line *c′a′*. This will serve as a check on the work. In passing, always tie the traverse to fixed points, previously located, and if there is an error of closure, correct that part of the traverse which has not yet been corrected, as explained in Art. **400.** At its end, too, the traverse should be tied to a fixed point, and any error of closure should be corrected.

Features on one or the other side of the course are plotted in by eye estimate, by perpendicular offset with measured distance (*s* and *t* in Fig. 429), by radiation (*w*, *x*, *y*, in Fig. 429), or by intersection from two or more of the stations of the traverse (*m* in Fig. 429). Such intersection often helps as a check on the traverse.

In common practice, when mapping outcropping strata, the instrument man occupies one station, *A*, and reads the rod held by the rodman at *B*. This is a foresight reading. He then proceeds to Station *C*, after having been signalled to do so by the rodman, and again reads the rod held at *B*. This is a backsight reading. Then the rodman goes to *D* and the instrument man reads the rod held at *D*; and so on. Thus, instrument man and

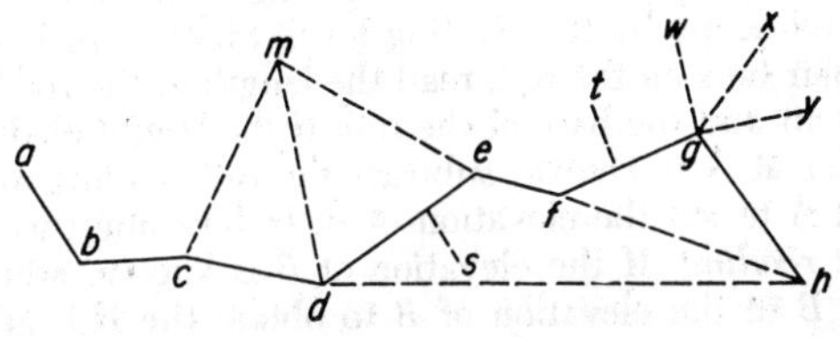

FIG. 429. A plotted traverse, showing side points located by intersection, *m*, perpendicular offset, *s*, *t*, and radiation, *w*, *x*, *y*. *hf* and *hd* are check sight lines from *h*.

rodman alternate along the main traverse. The rod stations (*B*, *D*, etc.), on which foresight and backsight readings are made, are *turning-points* (cf. page 538).

The rodman, who is the geologist, selects his own route which is governed by the nature of the geologic evidence sought. In regions of moderately dipping strata, he endeavors to walk the beds (333, 340). He holds the rod at points which he chooses with a view to the subsequent mapping of the structure. Most of these points lie on one or the other side of the main traverse. They are called *intermediate stations*, and the sights (lines) made by the instrument man toward them are popularly termed *side shots*. The reader will understand that relatively few rod stations are turning-points. Only when the rodman signals the instrument man to proceed to a new station does he (the rodman) establish his location as a turning-point. Notice, further, that the choice of route therefore rests with the rodman (geologist).

437. Determination of elevations. When plane-table mapping is undertaken with a small plane table and an open sight alidade, the differences in elevation of the various stations may be overlooked, or they may be determined by barometer (**407**, *et seq.*). On the other hand, if a telescopic (stadia) alidade is used, an effort is generally made to obtain the altitudes of the stations with some degree of accuracy. In the latter case, the difference in elevation between two stations may be found by direct level reading, stepping, vertical angle, Beaman stadia arc, and Stebinger drum.

1. Suppose that *A* and *B* are two intervisible stations of nearly the same altitude. Set up and orient the table at *A* and place the alidade in proper position for sighting at the rod held at *B*. Level the telescope by the striding level. Sight at *B*. If the middle cross-hair falls on the rod, read the length of the rod between this cross-hair and the base of the rod. If the height of the intsrument (H.I.) at *A* is known, subtract the rod reading at *B* from the H.I. at *A* to get the elevation of *B*. In levelling this is called a *foresight reading*. If the elevation at *B* is known, add the rod reading at *B* to the elevation of *B* to obtain the H.I. at *A*. This is a *backsight reading*. A station upon which a backsight is taken to establish the H.I. is a *turning-point* (cf. page 537). The student should remember that an error made at a turning-point will affect every succeeding reading.

2. In *stepping*, proceed as follows: level and orient the board at Station *A*, place the alidade in proper position, sight at the rod held at *B*, and draw the alignment, *ab*. Determine the distance, *AB* (**432**). Let us assume that *B* is higher than *A*. Level the telescope by the striding level. Looking through the telescope, choose some recognizable object, such as a rock, bush, etc., which is crossed by the horizontal cross-hair. Revolve the telescope on its horizontal axis until the lower stadia hair is on this object. This is a *half step*, or a *half interval*. Note a new object crossed by the upper stadia hair. Revolve the telescope till the lower stadia hair is on this object. Repeat, recording the number of *steps* until the upper stadia hair falls on the rod at *B*. Read the rod and wave the rodman to proceed. The elevation at *B* is the total number of *steps* times the vertical stadia interval for the distance, *AB*, minus the rod reading. If *E* is the elevation at Station *B*, H.I. is the height of the instrument above sea level at Station *A*; *N* is the number of steps, including the last one

which brought the upper stadia hair on to the rod; S is the vertical stadia interval (373) for the distance AB; and R is the reading of the rod where crossed by the upper stadia hair; then

$$E = (\text{H.I.}) + (N \times S) - R.$$

If B is lower than A, the process consists of *stepping down*, and the formula becomes,

$$E = (\text{H.I.}) - (N \times S) + R.$$

"The *step* method when used by an experienced instrument man is very fast and fairly accurate. It is not, however, sufficiently accurate for important work, as there is wide margin of error involved in the placing of one hair in the position previously occupied by another. Moreover, there is no

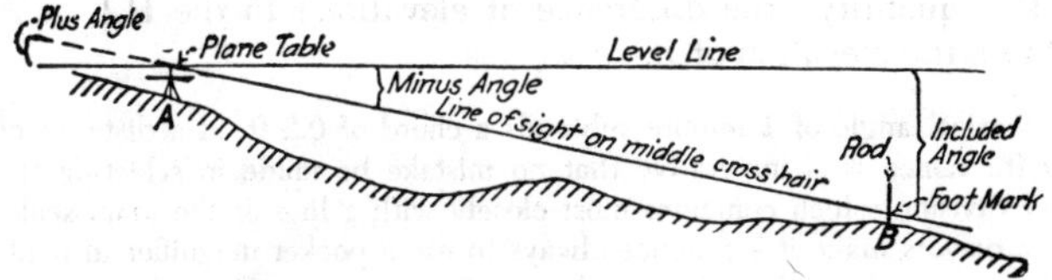

FIG. 430. Illustration of a method of determining vertical angles.

simple way of correcting the error resulting from the inclination of sight to the rod when the intercept is read. The *step* method should never be used when more than six steps are necessary, nor to determine the elevation of a turning-point or set-up. It is well fitted to serve as a check upon the more accurate methods next described, when there is need for especial care to guard against error."[39]

3. The elevation of Station B can be found by measurement of the vertical angle between the horizontal line of sight at Station A and the inclined direct line of sight from A to B (Fig. 430). After setting up the plane table and placing the alidade with its fiducial edge parallel to AB, raise or lower the telescope, with its clamp loosened, until the middle cross-hair rests near the foot mark of the rod. Tighten the clamp and by the tangent screw accurately place the middle hair on the foot mark. Record this foot mark in the notebook and wave the rodman off the station. On the vertical arc read the angle of inclination of the telescope

[39] Bibliog., Mather, Kirtley F., 1919, pp. 123–124.

to the nearest minute and record this under "Angle." Level the telescope, read the vernier again, and record the reading under "Level." Angles upward from the horizontal are positive, and those downward from the horizontal are negative. Algebraically subtract the plus or minus angle (as the case may be) from the level reading to obtain the included vertical angle (Fig. 430). The difference of elevation corresponding to the included angle for a horizontal distance of 100 ft. can be found by using a stadia conversion table or a stadia slide rule. Multiply this quantity by the number of hundreds of feet in the distance, *AB*, to get the difference in elevation between these stations. If the base of the rod was not used, the computed difference of elevation must be corrected accordingly. The corrected quantity is to be recorded under "Difference of Elevation," and is to be marked minus if *B* is lower than *A*, and plus if *B* is higher than *A*. Algebraically add this quantity (the difference of elevation) to the H.I. at *A* to obtain the elevation of *B*.

"A vertical angle of 1 minute subtends a chord of 0.3 ft. at a distance of 1,000 ft.; hence it is imperative that no mistake be made in selecting the vernier division which coincides most closely with a line of the main scale. Most surveyors make it a practice always to use a pocket magnifier in reading the vernier. It is also easier to detect offsets of the main scale and vernier division lines if one looks obliquely along the lines at an angle of 30° or 40° with the face of the scale than it is when observing the vernier face from a direction perpendicular to it . . . .

"The procedure of the instrument man should be planned explicitly to minimize the length of time the rodman is kept at a station. Just as much of instrument work as possible should be done after the rodman has been 'waved on.' With this in mind, the instrument man signals the rodman as soon as the cross-hair is set on the selected mark on the rod; after the rodman has departed he reads and records the vernier, levels the telescope, reads and records the new position of the vernier, wherever it happens to be, and determines the vertical angle by subtraction. He is then under no pressure of haste in reading the vertical arc and in centering the level bubble. To increased speed of geologic work is added thereby greater accuracy in instrumental observations . . . ."[40]

When directions and distances between stations are carefully plotted on the map, in methods of triangulation, the difference in elevation between any two stations, *A* and *B*, can be obtained by multiplying the scaled map (horizontal) distance between

[40] Bibliog., Mather, Kirtley F., 1919, pp. 127–128.

them by the tangent of the vertical angle of the inclined sight between them (see Appendix 19).

"4. *Beaman Stadia Arc.* The reading of vertical angles may be avoided by the use of the Beaman stadia arc . . . . This is a specially graduated vertical arc which may be attached to the vertical limb of a transit or telescopic alidade. It carries two scales, of which the one nearer the adjustable index is known as the multiple scale because it indicates multiples for obtaining difference in elevation. The zero point of this scale is marked 50 and its divisions are so spaced as to be proportional to one-half the sine of twice the angle through which the telescope moves.

"To determine differences in elevation read the distance subtended on rod and express in feet (for example, 8.7 = 870 ft.). Clamp telescope and level. Set index exactly at 50, by means of the tangent screw back of arc, and do not touch this tangent screw again.

"Then, by means of the customary clamp and tangent movement, raise or lower telescope until there is brought exactly opposite the index such a graduation on the multiple scale as will throw the middle stadia wire somewhere on the rod, it does not matter where. The arc reading, minus 50, multiplied by the observed stadia distance gives the difference in elevation between the instrument and a known point on the rod—that is, the height on rod indicated by middle wire. Settings of both index and arc should be made carefully under reading glass.

"Example: suppose observed stadia distance is 6.3 (630) ft. and that telescope is so inclined that multiple scale reads 58, at which exact setting the middle wire on rod reads 7.2 (7.2 ft. above base of rod) then multiple is 58 − 50 = +8, and computation for a foresight would be

$$\begin{array}{r l} 6.3 & \\ 8 & \\ \hline +50.4 & \\ -7.2 & \\ \hline +43.2 & \text{ft. base of rod above H.I.} \end{array}$$

"If middle wire were set on H.I. or top or other fixed point on rod and the arc were read by estimation (for example, 54.2) to obtain a multiple, the result would be approximate only; therefore, this method is not to be used with this attachment.

"If the half-wire interval is read and this reading is then doubled to get the stadia distance, it occasionally happens that no even multiple arc setting which will throw middle wire on rod can be found. In this case make arc setting that will throw the lower wire anywhere on rod; the middle wire will then be somewhat above the top of the rod. Then take multiple as read on arc, but compute position of middle wire above base of rod by adding one-half the expressed stadia distance (in feet subtended) to the reading of the lower wire.

"Example: if the half wires subtend 7.2 on rod, the distance would be $7.2 \times 2 = 14.4$ (1,440 ft.). If the lower wire cuts the rod 8.7 ft. above its base, the computed middle wire reading would be $8.7 + 7.2 = 15.9$ ft. above base rod. Then compute as before.[41]

"The advantages of the stadia arc are readily apparent. The use of stadia tables, slide rules, or diagrams is entirely obviated, nor is there any vernier to be read. The accuracy of the result is identical with that obtained from formula or table computations; in fact, differences in elevation may be read more closely than is possible where vertical angles are determined only to the nearest minute. Moreover, the simplicity of the process eliminates many of the chances of error which are incidental to the use of other methods and gives final results in minimum time. The use of the arc is, however, limited to sights which involve the reading of the stadia rod, and for most 'shots' it holds the rodman on the station longer than is necessary with certain other methods.

"5. *Stebinger Gradienter Drum.* The accuracy of a sensitive bubble vial in the striding level is greater than that implied by the reading of the vertical angle only to even minutes. The fine adjustment tangent screw is so threaded[42] that a complete revolution deflects the telescope about 34 minutes, so that if the unit of measurement be 1/500 a revolution of that screw, the accuracy of reading vertical angles is greatly increased. This is especially important in determining the difference in elevation of a station 2 to 8 miles distant as is frequently done in triangulation work. The Stebinger gradienter drum surrounding the tangent screw is graduated into 100 divisions, so broadly spaced that the drum may be read accurately by estimation to 0.2 division, and so quickly legible that there is marked saving of time and increased safeguard against error in observation when it is used in preference to the vertical arc. It is in reality simply another method of reading the vertical angle, denoting the angle by an arbitrary unit instead of by degrees and minutes. The value of that unit in length of chord at known distances may be expressed in tables similar to those provided for computation from vertical arc readings.

"In most instruments a clock-wise rotation of the Stebinger drum depresses the objective end of the telescope by pressing against a little stud fixed to the inside surface of the right-hand standard. A counter-clock-wise rotation permits a spiral spring to expand against the opposite side of the stud and thus to raise the objective end of the telescope. Experience indicates that it is unsafe to trust the spring to act with uniform regularity and

[41] "Topographic Instructions of the U.S. Geological Survey," Washington, Government Printing Office, 1918, pp. 131, 132.

[42] "The intention of the makers commonly is to calculate the pitch of the screw and the length of the clamp arm so that one complete revolution of the screw head moves the line of sight 1 ft. vertically at a horizontal distance of 100 ft., but this ratio may not be safely depended upon except as a broad approximation."

TABLE 12. ANGULAR VALUES OF BEAMAN INTERVALS[1]

Number of interval	*Angle*		*Difference in minutes*	*Number of interval*	*Angle*		*Difference in minutes*
	°	′			°	′	
0	0	00.00					
			34.38				36.16
1	0	34.38		16	9	19.89	
			34.39				36.42
2	1	08.77		17	9	56.31	
			34.42				36.70
3	1	43.19		18	10	33.01	
			34.47				37.00
4	2	17.66		19	11	10.01	
			34.52				37.32
5	2	52.18		20	11	47.33	
			34.59				37.71
6	3	26.76		21	12	25.04	
			34.68				38.08
7	4	01.44		22	13	03.12	
			34.77				38.49
8	4	36.21		23	13	41.61	
			34.88				38.95
9	5	11.09		24	14	20.56	
			35.02				39.44
10	5	46.11		25	15	00.00	
			35.16				39.97
11	6	21.27		26	15	39.97	
			35.33				40.54
12	6	56.60		27	16	20.51	
			35.50				41.16
13	7	32.10		28	17	01.67	
			35.71				41.85
14	8	07.81		29	17	43.52	
			35.92				42.58
15	8	43.73		30	18	26.10	

[1] Reproduced by permission from "Metro Manual," Bausch and Lomb Optical Co., Rochester, N.Y., 1915, p. 114.

smoothness. It is, therefore, necessary in using the Stebinger method always to read vertical distances in one direction—usually downward[43]—the direction in which the telescope is moved by clock-wise rotation of the drum. If the station is higher than the telescope, the first reading is taken with the horizontal cross-hair cutting the target; the telescope is then turned down to the level position for the second reading. If the station is lower than the instrument, the telescope is leveled for the first reading of the Stebinger drum and then turned down till the cross-hair cuts the target for the second reading.

"The fine adjustment screw to which the Stebinger drum is attached is a tangent screw; *i.e.*, its motion is tangential to the arc described by the arm of the clamp of the telescopic axis. Therefore, a revolution of the screw, when it is near one of its limits of motion will elevate or depress the telescope through an arc slightly different from that resulting from an equal turn of the screw when it is midway between its limits. Therefore, it is necessary always to begin an angle reading with the tangent screw in approximately the same position as that from which the determination of the Stebinger factors was made. This position, generally about a quarter turn of the screw after it first 'takes hold,' should be indicated by a mark on the celluloid or steel index. After each reading the tangent screw should be withdrawn to that position, ready for the next reading.

"In practice, then, the first reading is made with the Stebinger drum somewhere near the predetermined starting point and with the cross-hair on the distant object, if it is higher than the instrument or with the telescope level if the sight is a *down shot*. The reading, a figure between 0 and 100, is recorded in the proper column of the notebook. The telescope is then turned down by means of the tangent screw to position for the second reading. As the Stebinger drum revolves the total number of revolutions should be counted. The count may be verified by the graduations on the index bar if present and is set down on the left of the two digits which indicate the Stebinger division beneath the index. For instance, after completing eight revolutions, the Stebinger drum is brought to rest at 67; the second reading is therefore recorded in the appropriate column at 867. With an alidade which *reads down*, as is the more common arrangement, the smaller of the two Stebinger readings will be in the 'Sight' column if the target is higher than the instrument, and in the 'Level' column if lower than the instrument. The difference of the two readings expresses the size of the vertical angle in terms of Stebinger divisions. From the Stebinger tables prepared for the individual instrument the corresponding 'Stebinger factor' is selected. This factor multiplied by the apparent distance gives the difference of elevation of target and plane table.

[43] In some instruments the screw is fixed to the telescope standard and the stud is attached to the arm of the clamp of the telescope axis; when so attached the direction of movement to be used in reading the gradienter is upward.

"The preparation of the Stebinger tables is essentially the determination of the value of Stebinger units in terms of circular measure. Withdraw the micrometer screw to the position from which determinations of vertical angles will be started. Set the drum on an even division and read the vertical arc; turn the drum through 100 divisions and read the arc again. Turn through 200, 300, etc., divisions, reading the arc at each hundred until the screw has reached the farther limit of its play. Usually 9 or 10 hundred divisions will suffice. Repeat the operation at least five times and take the average value in minutes for each hundred divisions. Determine the corresponding difference in elevation for each of these angles by interpolation of regular stadia tables or from a table of natural sines by the formula:

$$\text{Difference of elevation} = \tfrac{1}{2} \text{ sine of twice the angle.}$$

The first value thus determined divided by 100 is the difference in elevation corresponding to each Stebinger division between 0 and 100. The second value minus the first and divided by 100 is the difference in elevation corresponding to each Stebinger division between 100 and 200. The third minus the second and divided by 100 is the value for Stebinger divisions between 200 and 300, etc. Carry the quotients in each case to the fifth decimal. With an adding machine set at the difference in elevation for one division between 0 and 100, print 100 additions for the factors corresponding to the second 100 Stebinger divisions. Then with the machine set at the difference in elevation per division between 100 and 200, print 100 additions for the factors corresponding to the second 100 Stebinger divisions. Complete the table in this manner, changing the addition figure after each 100 additions. Number the divisions, strike out the extra decimals beyond the third for the first 50 divisions and beyond the second, thereafter, and typewrite into tabular form in parallel columns; the number of divisions in one column, the corresponding factors in another. Brief tables for correction because of curvature and refraction as well as for conversion of observed to horizontal distances should be added at the margin. The whole, if properly planned, will occupy a sheet about 5 × 7 in. in size when photographed to one-half reduction for field use.

"A slight modification[44] of the above method will give a still more accurate series of factors. Read the vertical arc at each 50th division of the Stebinger drum instead of each 100th; determine the corresponding difference in elevation for each Stebinger unit as before; with the factors thus obtained plot a curve using the numbers of divisions as the abscissas and the values as the ordinates. From this curve the point will be readily apparent at which the micrometer screw begins to work with reasonable uniformity; begin constructing the table to be used at that point. From the curve determine the points where the factors for two successive divisions differ by 0.00005 and compute the factors for the number of divisions

[44] Suggested by K. C. Heald.

represented by each of these points; interpolate between the values thus obtained to complete the table.

"The table of Stebinger factors should be checked every few weeks by comparing a half dozen Stebinger readings, made at haphazard intervals well distributed throughout the range of the micrometer screw, with the corresponding readings of the vertical arc. The Stebinger factor should be identical, on the average, with the vertical distance corresponding to the arc reading.

"In reading the Stebinger drum the observation should be made from directly above the celluloid or steel index so as to project the index line vertically downward to the drum. Ordinarily, a reading to the nearest Stebinger division is sufficiently close, but for low angles and long 'shots' it is better to estimate half divisions, and for the nearly horizontal 2–5 mile 'shots' of triangulation it is frequently worth while to estimate to tenths of a division. For these long sights, the distance of which is determined by scaling off the space on the map, there is a theoretical error in using tables based on the formula involving one-half the sine of twice the angle, but there is practically no discrepancy here for the difference between the sine of a small angle and one-half the sine of twice the angle is negligible."[45]

438. Application of the methods of location. The method of radiation is practicable for small areas, quarries, etc., and for side shots from the main traverse or triangulation net. It has the disadvantage of giving no check upon the accuracy of the work.

The method of intersection is the only one by which inaccessible points may be located and their positions checked. For general mapping it is usually too slow, since several readings have to be made on every station in the triangulation net. Consequently it is seldom used by the geologist except for the location of single stations. In some kinds of open country, and particularly in unsurveyed regions, a triangulation net may be prepared by engineers in advance of the geologic work.

Resection is of great value to the geologist who is provided with a base map and wants to locate himself by reference to visible stations previously established. In some kinds of open country and in unsurveyed regions, an engineering party may go out and prepare a triangulation net. The engineers build monuments or set flags at conspicuous triangulation points, and make an accurate map of the system of stations established by them. Provided with this map, the geologist can then go into the field and, whenever he wishes to locate an outcrop or other point of

[45] Bibliog., Mather, Kirtley F., 1919, pp., 128–135.

interest, he can do so by resection from three or four of the triangulation stations. They constitute his control system. A disadvantage of this method is that, unless he is accompanied by an assistant, the geologist is encumbered with plane table and alidade. With an assistant to carry the instruments, he can use an ordinary plane table and telescopic alidade, but, if alone, he will do well to reduce this equipment to a small plane table, a Gurley compass or other open sight alidade (**355, 372**), and an aneroid for elevations.

Stadia traversing is especially useful for route maps along roads, streams, or across country, and for general mapping of exposed stratified rocks. In comparison with triangulation it has the advantage: (1) that ordinarily each station has to be visited only once; and (2) that the course, being open to more modification than in triangulation, is more adaptable to the tracing of exposures.

439. Variations in plane-table parties. We have stated that plane-table mapping with telescopic alidade is performed by a rodman, who is commonly the geologist, and an instrument man. These two individuals constitute a plane-table party. To each such party a specific area may be assigned for mapping. Under certain circumstances larger parties may be used to advantage. There may be an instrument man, a geologist, and one or two rodmen. The geologist will then be the chief of party, and it will be his duty so to direct the work that all members of his party are kept busy while he, himself, has time, not only to supervise their work, but also to reconnoitre ahead of the mapping and lay plans for their advance. He may have to spend a day or two looking over the field before his party begins work.

Conclusion

440. Comparison of the methods of field mapping. The four methods of field surveying, described in the foregoing pages, differ in respect to the accuracy of the results which may be obtained by using them. Named in the order of increasing possible precision, they are, the hand-level method, the compass-and-clinometer method, the barometer method, and the plane-table method.

The hand-level method is of value chiefly in certain kinds of rough reconnaissance work, and more often for ascertaining local strikes and dips of gently inclined stratified rocks. It is very seldom employed in areal mapping.

The compass-and-clinometer method is satisfactory in the mapping of areas underlain by igneous and metamorphic rocks and sedimentary rocks which have dips of about 5° or more. It should not be chosen for work in regions of low-dipping strata. The degree of accuracy of the results depends primarily on the number and precision of location of the control stations to which the compass traverses are tied.

Both the barometer method and the plane-table method may be used in many types of mapping, but they probably have their greatest value in the mapping of moderately dipping stratified rocks. There can be no question that the plane-table method, when performed by competent men, is more precise than the barometer method. On the other hand, the latter has several advantages which make its practice more desirable under certain conditions. Among the advantages of the barometer method, we may mention the following:

1. It requires only one man, whereas the plane-table method requires at least two, namely, the instrument man and one or more rodmen.

2. It is very elastic in its possibilities of speed and degree of precision attainable, and these factors are to a considerable extent within the geologist's control. The plane-table method is more limited in this respect.

3. The equipment for the barometer method is much lighter and more easily portable than that for the plane-table method.

4. The barometer method is more satisfactory than the plane-table method in forested areas and regions of low relief, where the intervisibility of points is poor.

Some of the disadvantages of the barometer method are:

1. Satisfactory aneroid barometers are difficult to secure.

2. In general this method requires a more experienced and therefore a more highly salaried man than does the plane-table method.

3. Since, in the barometer method, it is customary to follow north-south or east-west lines, or roads, or property boundaries, or other definite directions, the traverses usually cross outcropping strata, making correlation very difficult where the beds are not easily recognized. Under these circumstances the plane-table

method is more satisfactory since the rodman may walk or trace the outcropping beds and so facilitate their correlation.

4. The barometer method necessitates the correction of the barometric readings before the map can be made, whereas, by the plane-table method, the mapping may be practically completed in the field and errors may thus be more readily detected.

441. Sources of error. Errors, which may affect the results in geologic mapping, may be classified as: (1) instrumental errors; (2) errors in procedure; (3) errors caused by geologic conditions; and (4) personal errors.

1. Instrumental errors are occasioned by imperfect adjustment or defective manufacture. To determine the efficiency and accuracy of his instruments, the geologist should at least know how to test them. He will often find it of advantage to be able to make minor adjustments. For complex adjustments he should send the instrument back to the maker.

2. Errors in technical procedure are due to carelessness, insufficient training, or lack of practical experience. These errors may come through misuse of the instruments and equipment or through misinterpretation of such geologic features as cross-bedding, settling, etc. (**342, 344**).

3. Errors caused by geologic conditions include certain variable quantities which are dependent on the number and size of outcrops, the amount and kind of weathering of exposures, changing stratigraphic intervals between beds, ease of correlation, etc. These errors are sometimes large and sometimes small. They are never entirely eliminated. The geologist, however, should always endeavor to estimate about how great such errors may be in his work.

4. Personal errors are those which are attributable to the habits and state of mind of the geologist himself. They come under the head of the *personal equation*. Each man should try to discover his own personal equation and reduce it as far as possible.

442. Limits of error. Every instrument, if carefully used, can yield results which are accurate within certain limits; but beyond these limits greater precision is practically impossible. In the same way, each method of field surveying has its limitations. Instruments and methods are usually chosen for field investigations with a view to: (1) the precision required; and (2) the precision attainable. If the work must be done rapidly and great accuracy is not demanded, field procedure and equipment are selected with rather large limits of error; in other words, with a rather large permissible error; and vice versa. In every case, however, the geologist should know the limits of error of his instruments and of the field method which he adopts.

Distances obtained by pacing may be correct to 3 per cent or less. The error may be reduced to 1 per cent if the paces are frequently standardized. In very rough country with heavy underbrush, the error will probably amount to more than 3 per cent. Taping, with ordinary precautions, is much more accurate, being correct to at least 1 in 3,000. On automobile traverses measured by odometer, readings may be in error as much as ⅒ mile for any distance, if the odometer is perfectly regulated. Usually such an instrument registers a little more or a little less than a mile for every map mile (horizontal mile) traversed, on account of imperfect adjustment, rough roads, strong topographic relief, use of oversize casings, etc. Errors of this kind the geologist must ascertain for his particular machine.

Triangulation performed with sight alidade and oriented plane table should be correct to 1 in 500, and with telescopic alidade and oriented plane table, to 1 in 1,000 or 1,200. In stadia traversing, with oriented plane table, telescopic alidade, and stadia rod, reasonable care will yield results correct within 1 in 200 for horizontal closure or better, and within 3 to 5 ft. of closure in elevation, provided the shots are not over 2,000 ft. in length and provided both foresight and backsight shots are of approximately equal length; for in this way, no matter how long the traverse may be, the errors are largely compensating. On the other hand, where shots are longer, and especially where foresights are considerably longer than backsights (or vice versa), the vertical error is likely to be larger. For smaller scales under like conditions, the limits of error are larger.

In barometric work, the permissible error in relative elevations ought not to be more than half a contour interval, as the map is finally constructed.

Something has already been said in reference to errors in determining dips (**341**).

It should be noted that the error in location of a point is equal to the error of the least precise method of measurement employed for the three quantities of direction, horizontal distance, and vertical distance. For instance, a compass traverse or a traverse with plane table and sight alidade is correct to only about 1 per cent if the distances are measured by careful pacing. In any mapping the error permissible for elevations should be similar to that allowed for the horizontal control. For this reason, on the basis of the limits of error cited above, reduction of slope distances to their horizontal equivalents is unnecessary on slopes of 1 in 7 (about 8°), or less, for work in which distances are paced; on slopes of 1 in 12 (a little under 5°), or less, for compass traverses in which distances are measured by tape; on slopes of 1 in 15 (about 3° 30′), or less, for triangulation with sight alidade; and on slopes of 1 in 25 (a little under 2°), or less, for ordinary triangulation with telescopic alidade.

For further remarks on the subject of degree of accuracy, and sources and limits of error, see Arts. **328, 341, 347, 388, 390, 391, 422, 423, 424, 434, 440, 441.**

443. Factors affecting choice of method. In view of the great variety of the problems which may require field mapping, we can do no more here than mention some of the factors which may influence the geologist in his selection of the field method. Such factors are:

1. The kind of rocks prevailing in the region.
2. The type of geologic structure.
3. The type and extent of vegetation.
4. The topographic relief, steepness of slopes, and altitude of the region.
5. The purpose of the investigation, *i.e.*, whether purely scientific or economic.
6. The scope of the result desired, *i.e.*, whether information is wanted on all related phases of a general geologic problem or information is sought only in reference to some one particular question.
7. The kind and scale of base map, if such is available.
8. The accuracy of the results required.
9. The number of men available.
10. The number and condition of the roads, and the methods of travel.
11. The source of food and other supplies.
12. The time available for the work.
13. The funds available for the work.
14. Whether or not the work is to be done in a foreign country.
15. The general climatic conditions.

444. Topographic contour sketching. Occasions not infrequently arise when the geologist finds it of advantage to sketch the topography by contours. To do this, a contour interval adapted to the relief of the land and to the scale of the map must first be selected. In general a smaller interval will be used for low relief and for large scale. Mean sea level is commonly taken as the datum plane. The position of the first contour drawn on the map will depend upon the altitude of Station 1 above sea level and upon the slope of the ground between Stations 1 and 2. As the mapping proceeds, the points where successive contours intersect the lines of sight are interpolated according to the differences of elevation between stations. The spacing of these points will naturally be close on steep slopes and wide on gentle slopes. Observations for relief should always be made at changes of slope. The contours themselves are sketched in by eye, the observer having due regard for the changes of slope, and for valleys, hills, and other topographic forms. Contour sketching is often done in connection with traversing. If the traverse runs across a slope, the geologist stops at any favorable locality, notes the distance from the last station, sights uphill or downhill perpendicular to the contours, and reads the slope angle in this direction. He plots the sight line on the map and marks off the points where the contours intersect this line at intervals which are determined by the slope angle. If the traverse runs up or down the slope, he can sight parallel to the contours and plot their directions adjacent to his course. When a few such lines with the contour intersections have been plotted, the contours themselves can be sketched.

445. Schedules for mapping. To summarize the procedure in certain types of geologic mapping, the following schedules have been prepared. In using them the reader must bear in mind that, since it is impossible to make such schedules applicable to the great variety of conditions which may arise, they may require modification and enlargement.

Schedule I. A Compass Traverse

Method. Directions by Brunton compass; distances paced; elevations by barometer; plotting with notebook or unoriented plane table.

Conditions. A control system established; a base map with a few control stations plotted; camp (or headquarters) near one of the control stations.

Procedure. *Preliminary.* (*a*) Rule base map with N.–S. and E.–W. coordinates. (*b*) Set the compass for true bearings. (*c*) Find the elevation of camp with reference to the adjacent control station, which may be called Station 1. (*d*) Record the reading of the barometer an hour or so before leaving camp. (*e*) Record the reading of the barometer just before leaving camp.

At Station 1. (*a*) Check barometer. (*b*) Mark a point on the map for Station 1, and record the elevation of Station 1. (*c*) Select a suitable point in the field for Station 2, or decide in which direction to walk from Station 1. (*d*) Find the bearing from 1 toward 2 and plot this bearing on the map. (*e*) Observe and plot the bearings of any other objects to be located from Station 1.

Between Stations 1 *and* 2. (*a*) Pace toward Station 2. (*b*) If necessary stop to make and plot offsets, or to record useful geologic information. (*c*) Always note and scale off the distance from Station 1 to the point of stopping. (*d*) Continue pacing toward 2.

At Station 2. (*a*) Make a note of the distance, 1–2. (*b*) Check bearing by backsight on 1. (*c*) Scale off distance, 1–2, on map. (*d*) Read barometer and record this reading. (*e*) Select a suitable point in the field for Station 3. (*f*) Find the bearing from 2–3; etc. (Continue as before. See (*d*) under Station 1.)

Whenever possible tie the traverse to another control station and make any necessary corrections for distance and direction. Keep a record of the barometric readings and correct them by a plotted correction curve after returning to camp (**413–417**).

Schedule II. Traverse with Oriented Plane Table

Method. Directions by sight alidade; horizontal distances by pacing; vertical distances indirectly by clinometer; contours by reference to differences of elevation; plotting with oriented plane table.

Conditions. A control system established; a base map with a few control points plotted; one of these control points is taken as Station 1; another control point, *X*, is visible from Station 1.

Procedure. *Preliminary.* (*a*) Rule base map with N.–S. and E.–W. coordinates. (*b*) Select a contour interval to be used in contouring the topography.

At Station 1. (*a*) Set up the plane table at Station 1 and orient it by the method of backsight on *X*. (*b*) Select a suitable point in the field for Station 2. (*c*) Sight at 3 and draw 1–2. (*d*) Determine the slope angle from 1–2 and record it. (*e*) Observe and plot the bearings of any other objects to be located from 1, or of slopes for contouring (444). (*f*) Fix the position of contours and sketch them in (444).

Between Stations 1 *and* 2. (*a*) Pace toward Station 2. (*b*) If necessary stop to make and plot offsets, or to record useful geologic information, or to take slope directions and slope angles for contouring. (*c*) Always note and scale off the distance from 1 to the point of stopping, correcting for pacing and slope. (*d*) Continue toward Station 2.

At Station 2. (*a*) Set up the plane table at 2. (*b*) Make a note of the distance, 1–2. (*c*) Correct this distance for paces on slope and reduce to horizontal equivalent (389). (*d*) Scale off the corrected distance, 1–2, on the map. (*e*) Orient the plane table by backsight on 1. (*f*) Select a suitable point in the field for Station 3. (Continue as before. See (*c*) under Station 1.)

Schedule III. A Stadia Traverse

Method. Directions, distances, and differences of elevation by telescopic alidade and stadia rod; plotting with oriented plane table.

Conditions. Control system of widely spaced stations established; base map available; elevation of Station 1 may be known or assumed; magnetic declination known.

Procedure. *Preliminary.* Rule the map sheet in coordinate squares on the scale adopted for the work. Rule the magnetic north-south line on the map. Select an established station on the ground and locate it on the map as the starting point. Call it Rod Station 1.

At Instrument Station 1. The instrument man goes to a point, designated Instr. Station 1, from which he can see Rod Station 1 and a wide stretch of surrounding country. Here he sets up, levels, and orients his board, and sights back at the rod held at Rod Station 1. He reads the distance and difference of elevation, determining his position and the height of the instrument (H.I.). When ready he waves down the rodman (geologist), who proceeds to Rod Station 2. The instrument man locates this point and determines its elevation, and then waves the rodman to Rod Station 3; and so on, until the rodman, having been to as many points as he wants located in the vicinity of Instr. Station 1, signals the instrument man to plot and record the last Rod Station as a turning-point, and then to proceed to Instr. Station 2.

At Rod Station 1. The geologist, as rodman, first goes to Rod Station 1, the elevation of which is known or assumed, and examines the rocks while the instrument man is on his way to Instr. Station 1. He then holds the rod for the instrument man to make the observations noted above.

At Rod Station 2. After the instrument man has waved the rodman down from Rod Station 1, the latter follows the outcrops, and holds the rod at any points—Rod Station 2, 3, 4, etc.—which he will need for making the map. If he is surveying an area in which stratified rocks outcrop, he takes elevations above or below his key horizon whenever practicable, thus determining and checking the exposed geologic section. When he has examined all the exposures surrounding Instr. Station 1, he signals the instrument man a *turn* (T), and holds his station until the instrument man has set up at Instr. Station 2 and has located this station (Instr. Station 2) by backsight on the turning-point. After this is done, the process is repeated as before.

SCHEDULE IV. TRIANGULATION

Method. Directions by telescopic alidade; base line measured by tape; other horizontal distances plotted by triangulation; vertical distances computed by stadia method; plotting with oriented plane table.

Conditions. The elevation of Station 1 is either known or assumed; no plotted control; no base map; magnetic declination not known.

Procedure. *Preliminary.* (*a*) Rule the paper for the map with N.–S. and E.–W. coordinates. (*b*) Choose a suitable position for the base line. (*c*) Call one end of the base line Station 1 and the other end Station 2.

At Station 1. (*a*) Mark a point on the map sheet for Station 1 and record its elevation. (*b*) Determine the magnetic declination (**429**). (*c*) Set the compass (to be used for any necessary radiation, traversing, strike-reading, etc.) for true bearings (**357**).

(*d*) With the table oriented, sight at the rod held at Station 2 and draw 1–2. (*e*) Note angle of declination from 1–2, and compute elevation of 2. (*f*) Sight at other stations to be located from 1 and draw lines from 1 toward them. (*g*) Compute elevations of these stations.

Between Stations 1 *and* 2. Measure base line by tape.[46]

At Station 2. (*a*) Scale off 1–2. (*b*) Carefully orient the table by backsight on 1 and check for inclination and elevation. (*c*) Sight at all stations located from 1, and at any additional stations; draw lines on the map from 2 toward these stations; note angles of inclination from 2 to each of them; and recalculate their elevations and check with their elevations as determined from Station 1. Call one of these stations 3.

Between Stations 2 *and* 3. Proceed to Station 3.

At Station 3. (*a*) Orient by backsight on 2 and check for elevation. (*b*) Check also by sighting at other stations located from 1 and 2. (*c*) Sight at any additional stations, draw lines toward them, note angles of inclination from 3 toward them, and compute their elevations.

Continue thus from station to station, each time using one of the plotted sides of a triangle as a base for the further expansions of the system.

The reader should understand that all sights are made from instrument stations at the rod held at the distant stations.

[46] It is often better to measure the basic line twice, once in each direction before locating stations from 1 and 2.

Chapter 17

GEOLOGIC SURVEYING

PART IV. AIR RECONNAISSANCE, AIR PHOTOGRAPHY, AND AIR MAPPING[1]

446. Air reconnaissance. Rapid examination of an area from the air may greatly facilitate the selection of localities to be explored on the ground, especially in countries where roads are few, where accessibility is difficult, and where geologic features can be reasonably well seen from the air. In this *air reconnaissance,* the airplane is controlled by an experienced pilot, and the surveying is done by a geologist who, as a passenger in the plane, is provided with a base map on which he sketches such features as he wishes to record. He makes his observations by eye. The base map has on it the main roads, railroads, towns, ponds, and stream courses in the country to be examined. Sometimes two, or even three, geologists fly together in the same plane and endeavor to sketch the same geologic features, each on his own base map, thus facilitating comparison and correction of the results at the end of the flight. Since the progress of the plane is rapid, this kind of sketching requires constant attention and

[1] The word "aerial" has come into wide use as applied to photographs of ground features taken from an aircraft. Becaus of the close similarity in sound between "aerial" and "areal," we are using the simpler, and just as appropriate, word "air" for "aerial" (and for "airplane" when used as synonymous with "aerial") when referring to photographs and photographing from the air. This, we believe, is entirely justified for the sake of simplicity, to avoid confusion with "areal," and by definition. In Webster's "New International Dictionary," 2d ed., 1947, we find that "air" and "aerial" are defined with exactly the same meanings, and without indicated preference for either, in this connection.

The writer here wishes to express his thanks for assistance generously and abundantly given to him in the preparation of this chapter in the fifth edition of "Field Geology" by Laurence Brundall, Leavitt Corning, Jr., Louis Desjardins, Vincent C. Kelley, and Sherman A. Wengerd, and by William A. Fischer and Laurence Brundall in the 6th edition.

uninterrupted observation of details. It is very exacting work and cannot be done well for more than a few hours at a time. Provided with a preliminary sketch map of this kind, the geologist can then pick out those places which he thinks merit special attention on the ground, and he can decide how to reach them. During the flight he can, of course, take any photographs that he thinks will assist him, but these are usually snapped with an ordinary camera held in the photographer's hand. Where conditions permit, helicopters may provide a better means for visual reconnaissance than do airplanes.

447. Air photography; air mapping; air photogrammetry. The science (and art) of precision photographing of the surface features of the earth from an aircraft is called *air* (*aerial, aero-, airplane*) *photography*. The photographs so taken are *air photographs*. The applications of air photography in the construction of maps may be called *air mapping*. The science of obtaining reliable measurements of horizontal distance, direction, and elevation by means of air photography is *air photogrammetry*.[2] Although a geologist need not himself be a photogrammetrist, he should know something of the scope of this science.

The uses of air photography are innumerable. Either the photographs themselves or maps made from them are valuable in their applications in civil engineering (town and city planning, highway construction, dam construction, railroad engineering, reservoir construction, harbor work, etc.), the mining industry, military engineering, land surveying, agriculture, forestry, flood control, archeology, and many branches of geology and geophysics. For discussion of the geological applications, see Art. **456.**

448. Air photographs classified. Air photographs may be taken with the camera pointing vertically downward, or they may be taken with the camera set obliquely, as the plane travels horizontally. The former are called *vertical photographs* or *verticals*, and the latter are *oblique photographs* or *obliques* (Fig. 431). If obliques are taken at a high enough angle to the vertical, they will include the distant horizon, but if they are pointed more directly downward, at a lower angle to the vertical, they will not show the horizon. These are, respectively, *high*

[2] For the convenience of those who may be mapping in different latitudes, Appendices 21 and 22 are provided, listing the variations in lengths of segments of meridians and parallels of latitude, in miles.

obliques (or *horizon obliques*) (Fig. 433, A) and *low obliques* (Fig. 432, A).

A *vertical photograph* has essentially uniform definition over its entire area; *i.e.*, objects are as clearly shown in one part as in another. The area covered is rectangular, usually square (Fig. 434). The scale of the photograph and the dimensions of the area covered by it depend upon the focal length of the camera and the height from which the picture was taken. The greater the height and the smaller the focal length, the greater the area

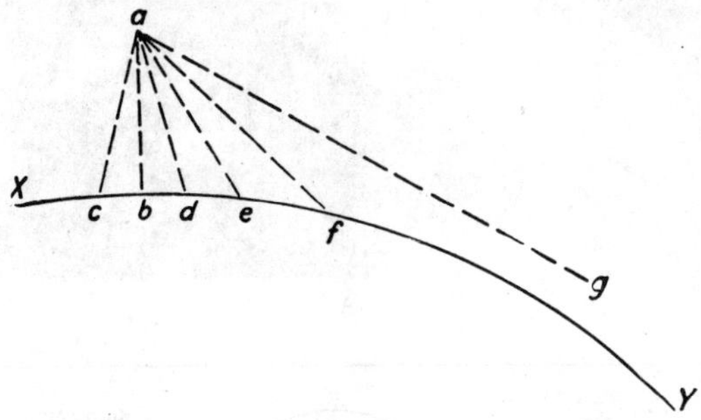

FIG. 431. Diagram to illustrate coverage of vertical and oblique air photographs. *XY*, earth's surface in section; *a*, position of camera in airplane; *b*, point on earth's surface vertically below *a*. A vertical photograph, with camera lens pointed vertically downward, would cover an area corresponding to *cd*. A low oblique might cover *be* or *df*. A high oblique would include the horizon and would therefore cover *eg*.

covered. The scale is usually stated as a representative fraction (R.F.) or as a ratio (see Art. 313). The R.F. equals the focal length (f) of the camera lens, divided by the height (H) of the camera, *i.e.*, f/H, all expressed in feet (or meters—*i.e.*, always in the same units). Thus with a 12-in. focal length in a camera flown at 20,000 ft. while photographing, the R.F., or scale, of the photograph is 1:20,000 or 1/20,000 (approximately 3 in. = 1 mile). Other focal lengths which will give approximately this same scale at other altitudes are:

A focal length of 5.25 in. at 8,750 ft.
A focal length of 6 in. at 10,000 ft.
A focal length of 8.25 in. at 13,750 ft.

A

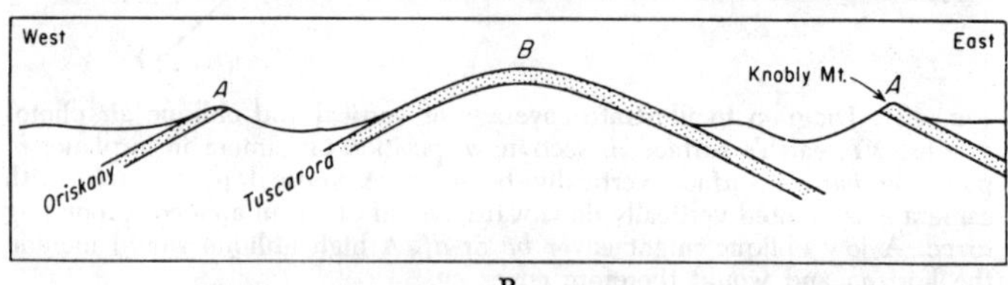

B

Fig. 432. A, low oblique air photograph of an area in West Virginia. B, sketch cross section to show geological structure. The Oriskany sandstone and Tuscarora quartzite are hard, resistant formations. Note that the hill (B in the section) is anticlinal. (*Figure 432, A, reproduced from Rich, with permission of the American Geographical Society of New York. See Bibliog., Rich, John L.,* 1939, *Fig.* 25.)

The last of these—8.25 in. focal length and flight at 13,750 ft.—is the combination usually recommended as most satisfactory for geological interpretation.

A *high oblique*, or *horizon oblique*, may be compared with the view one would have if looking toward the horizon from a high point on a mountain. It gives a good idea of perspective and it shows hills, valleys, and other land forms more nearly as we are accustomed to seeing such features. However, while

A

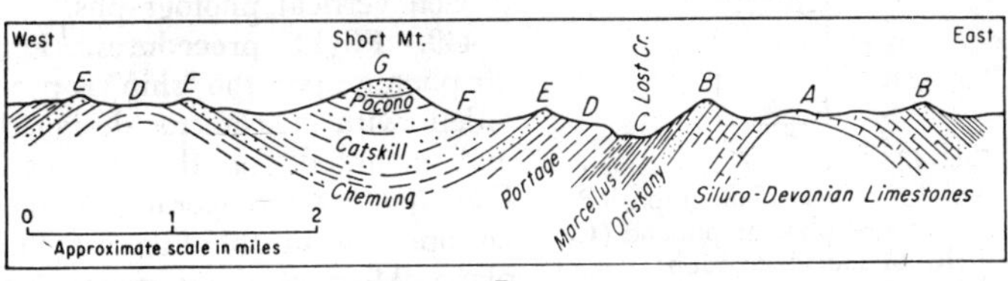

B

FIG. 433. A, high oblique air photograph of an area on the Virginia–West Virginia line. B, sketch cross section to show geological structure. (*A and B reproduced from Rich, with permission of the American Geographical Society of New York. See Bibliog., Rich, John L.,* 1939, *Figs.* 16 *and* 17.)

details may be clear in the foreground, a high oblique photograph loses in definition toward the background (cf. foreground and background in Fig. 433, A). Its coverage, on the other hand, is greater than that of a vertical taken from the same point, because, toward the horizon, it includes a rapidly increasing breadth of landscape, as measured in distance units at right angles to the line of sight. The ground area covered in an oblique photograph is trapezoidal in shape, with the narrow base in the foreground (Fig. 434).

Low obliques vary in the angle of the line of sight from near high obliques to near verticals. Accordingly, their coverage varies. It is less, other conditions being equal, the nearer they approach verticals. Also, they lose less in definition from foreground to background, the lower their angle from the vertical.

In any oblique photograph the scale is the same on any given line parallel to the horizon, but it decreases on these parallel lines from the foreground of the picture to the background. In all other directions the scale progressively decreases along the line from front to back. (Cf. discussion of scale in parallel perspective in block diagrams Art. 511, pages 717, 718.) In high obliques the rate of change of scale from foreground to background is greater than in low obliques, and obviously it is least in those low obliques which approach vertical photographs.

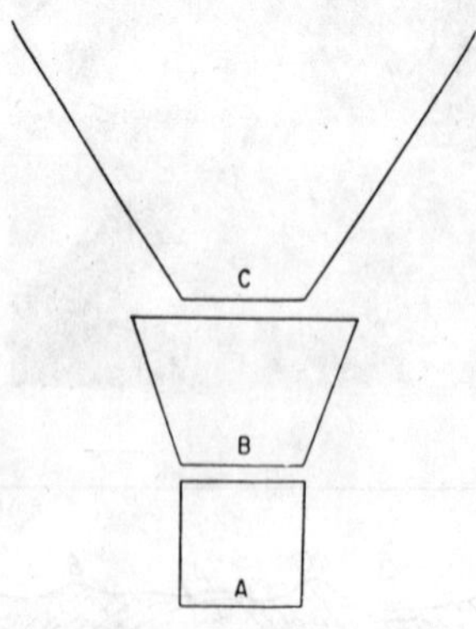

FIG. 434. Shape of area covered by (A) vertical photograph, (B) low oblique photograph, and (C) high oblique photograph.

449. Flight procedures. For air photography the "ship" is provided with a camera designed and mounted for the purpose. Usually it is set to operate through an opening in the floor of the plane. Most of the cameras for this work take pictures 9 by 9 in., or 7 by 9 in., or on roll films in lengths of 75 ft. or more. To bring out color differences and to reduce the effects of haze, color filters are used on the lens, and the films are panchromatic.

For regional coverage of an area by vertical photographs, the airplane is flown at a mean elevation along level parallel courses at a distance apart such that there will be an overlap of 30 per cent by the photographs of adjoining flights (Fig. 435). This is called *side lap.* If the flying is at a mean elevation of 13,750 ft. and the focal length is 8.25 in., this 30 per cent of side lap requires that the parallel flights be about two miles apart. The photographs are taken automatically at intervals such that, along a given course, they will overlap 60 per cent (Fig. 435). At 13,750 ft. this results in taking a picture every mile along the flight. Naturally, there are variations in shutter control and in ground area covered, depending on focal length of lens, mean altitude of flight, speed of plane, etc.

High obliques may be "shot" as single views, or in overlapping sequence for panoramic effects.

A procedure which involves both verticals and high obliques is called *trimetrogon air photography*. In this a combination of three cameras is mounted in the airplane, one adjusted to take vertical photographs, and the other two (one on each side of the vertical camera) adjusted to take horizon obliques (high obliques) simultaneously with the verticals, one to the right and

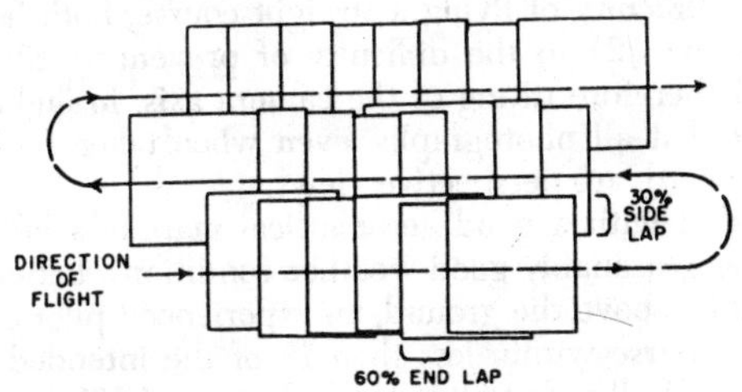

Fig. 435. Diagram showing ideal flight line and overlap spacing for air photography. (*Kindly furnished by Laurence Brundall.*)

the other to the left, of the flight line. On each side, the oblique photograph overlaps the central vertical photograph by a reasonable margin. Thus each triplet gives a complete view of the ground from the horizon on one side of the airplane to the horizon on the other side. This triplet of pictures is repeatedly shot as the plane travels, and at intervals such that there is adequate overlap of each triplet by the next. Because of the decrease in definition toward the horizon in high oblique photographs, satisfactory information cannot be obtained from the whole width of coverage of the trimetrogon triplet. Only the part of the obliques near the central vertical strip is usable, so that the practical coverage from side to side, across the line of flight, is about 35 miles. In other words, for complete coverage of an area to be surveyed by trimetrogon photography, flight lines may not have to be closer than 35 miles apart, and consequently air photography by this method is much more rapid than surveying by vertical photography; but trimetrogon is less accurate. Trimetrogon air photography is distinctly a reconnaissance method for covering large areas rapidly.

If a multilens camera is used, with four lenses oriented to produce four low obliques in azimuths perpendicular to one another, or with five lenses oriented to produce one central vertical surrounded by four low obliques, the result is a group of partly overlapping pictures which, after adjustment of the obliques to the vertical, can be assembled as a *composite*. Such a composite is in many respects similar to a vertical.

450. Errors, displacement, and distortion in air photographs. Air photography, even when conducted under the most favorable conditions, is subject to certain inaccuracies. These are due (1) to the difficulty of flying a straight course, both horizontally and vertically; (2) to the difficulty of preventing tilting of the plane, and therefore tilting of the camera axis, in flight; and (3) to the fact that all photographs, even when taken looking vertically downward, are perspective views.

If provided with a good aeronautical map as a guide, and if flying under reasonably good weather conditions, between 10,000 and 15,000 ft. above the ground, an experienced pilot can usually maintain a course within less than 1° of the intended direction, and changes of altitude will not greatly exceed 100 ft. over flat or moderately rolling country.[3] At lower levels air conditions become much more variable, and consequently steady flying becomes difficult or impossible. For this reason air photographic mapping is seldom attempted at altitudes of less than 7,500 ft. When there is a cross wind and the airplane is blown somewhat out of its intended course, the effect is called *drift*. Each picture, although *oriented* correctly as related to the planned course, is shifted a little to leeward with respect to the picture taken just before (see Fig. 436, A). Because of this drifting of the plane, adjacent lines of flight which are intended to be parallel may converge or diverge. If, on the other hand, the airplane is kept on its proper course by flying somewhat toward the wind, but without adjusting the camera to compensate for this "angling" of the airplane, the successive photographs will be at an angle to the flight direction (see Fig. 436, B). This is called *crab*.

Tilting of the plane, caused by variable winds and air currents, is almost impossible to prevent. This means that there may be

[3] See Bibliog., Davis, Foote, and Rayner, 1934, pp. 784–785.

some distortion (called *tilt*)[4] in the photographs. However, the statement is made[5] that, in photographs taken between 10,000 and 15,000 ft. above the ground, with careful flying under satisfactory conditions, 50 to 80 per cent of the pictures will be tilted less than 1°, and rarely will any be tilted over 3°. In contract flying, a tolerance of 3° is the maximum permitted.

The relations of tilt are comparable to those in a low oblique, which are diagrammed in Fig. 437. Here are shown the position of the lens, the negative, and the ground photographed. *PP'* is

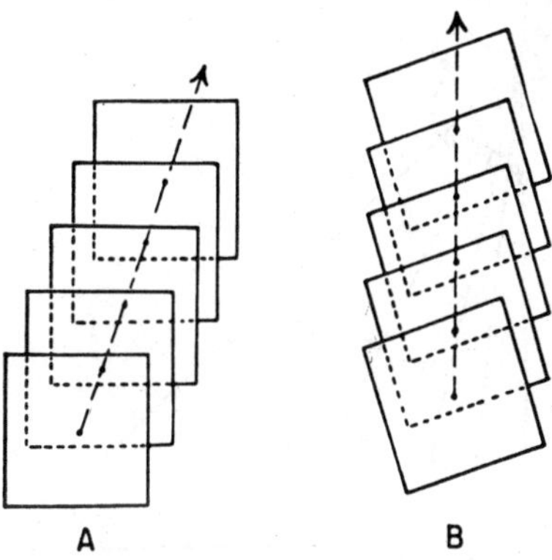

FIG. 436. Relative positions of air photographs in case of (A) drift and (B) crab. The arrow points along the flight line.

the position of the positive in front of the lens the same distance (focal length $= LC$) as the negative is behind the lens. The axis of the camera is *LT* which bisects the angle covered by the photograph (*SLS'*). *C* is the *center point* or *principal point* of the picture, where *LT* cuts it. *N* is the plumb point, or nadir point, vertically below the lens. The bisector (*LB*) of the angle

[4] Sometimes an effort is made to discriminate between tilt along the line of flight and tilt across (at right angles to) the line of flight, the former retaining the name *tilt* and the latter being called *tip*. In this book we use *tilt* for all azimuths.

[5] See Bibliog., Davis, Foote, and Rayner, 1934, p. 785. This book, "Surveying: Theory and Practice," was completely revised for the third edition by Davis and Foote, the chapter on Photographic Surveying being replaced by Photogrammetric Surveying by Capt. B. B. Talley.

(*NLT*) between *LN* and *LT* cuts the picture at *X*, which is called the *isocenter*. In a vertical photograph which has no tilt, *LN*, *LB*, and *LT* all coincide; but if there is tilt, there is a small angle between *LN* and *LT*, and the plumb point does not coincide with the principal point.

A photograph taken looking vertically downward includes only a single point that is *directly* beneath. This is the *plumb point*

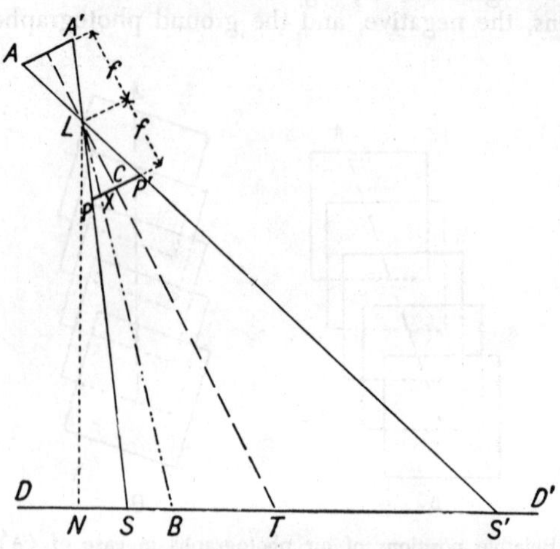

FIG. 437. Diagram drawn in the *principal plane* (the vertical plane which includes the optic axis of the camera lens and a plumb line dropped from the lens). The lens is at *L*; the ground is *DD'*; the photographed area lies between S and S'; *AA'* is the negative, and *PP'* is the positive, of the picture; the focal length is *f*. (For further explanation, see text.)

or ***nadir point***. All objects with vertical dimensions, not at the nadir point, are distorted by radial displacement, since they are actually viewed in perspective. In other words, an air photograph is a radial projection and not, like all drafted maps, an orthographic projection. We may explain this as follows: Imagine two points, one vertically above the other. For convenience we may assume that these two points are the top (*A*) and bottom (*B*) of a tall vertical pole (Fig. 438). If the camera is vertically above *A*, it is also vertically above *B*. If, however, the camera is off to one side of *A*, so that the rays of light from *A* and *B* enter the lens (*L*, in Fig. 438) along inclined paths *AL* and *BL*, respectively, the rays from *A* will reach the film in the camera farther from the center of the picture than the rays from *B*. Both the top and bottom of the pole will be *displaced,* and since points at equal intervals, measured up from *B* to *A*, will be increasingly displaced, there will be some *distortion* in the image of the pole.

If the points *A* and *B* are assumed to be at the top and bottom of a vertical cliff, the position of both the top and bottom of the cliff will be displaced and the image of the cliff face will have some distortion. Since, in photographing terrane with topographic relief, we are concerned mainly with points, like *A*, on the land surface and at varying elevations above, or below, an assumed level datum surface, we are concerned only with displacement. Where the land surface is not horizontal, all points not directly below the lens will be more or less displaced in the photograph, and this displacement, which is called *perspective displacement* or *topographic displacement*, increases radially in all directions from the plumb point. It will be greater in the case of wide-angle lenses with short focal length than in the case of narrow-angle lenses with long focal length. Therefore, we may say that the amount of radial topographic displacement will vary directly with the relief of the country and with the distance from the plumb point of the photograph, and inversely with the focal length of the camera lens and with the height at which the picture was taken. Photographing from a given height, lenses with short focal length exaggerate the vertical component of the terrane. Hills appear to be steeper, and also dips of inclined strata appear steeper, than they really are. Consequently, where slopes or dips are steep, lenses with longer focal length are used.

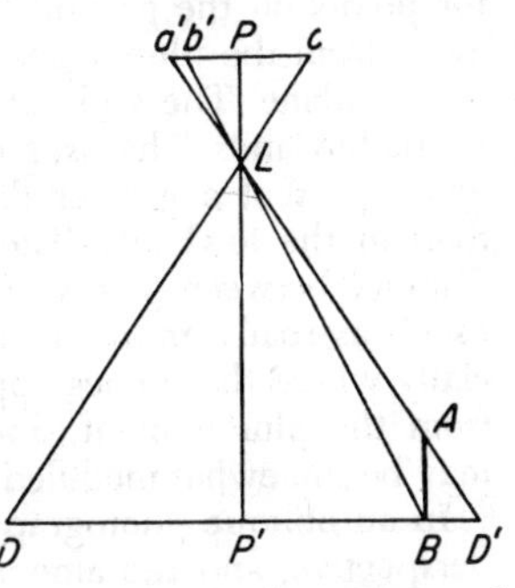

FIG. 438. Grossly exaggerated diagram to illustrate perspective distortion in a vertical photograph. *L*, position of lens; *a'c* is the negative; *P*, plumb point, vertically above *P'*; *DD'*, area covered in photograph; light rays from *A*, vertically above *B*, reach the negative at *a'*, farther from *P* than the rays at *b'* coming from *B*.

In areas of low relief or with low dips (up to 4°), short-focus lenses are preferred.

Since vertical photographs are taken from an airplane flying along a level course, the vertical distance from the lens to the ground will vary according to the topography. We may imagine a level surface or *datum plane* which is at a distance, equal to the *average* height of the airplane, below the level of the flight. Hill tops will be above this datum plane, and valley floors will be below it. Radial displacement will be toward the plumb point for points on the ground below the datum plane, and it will be away from the plumb points for points on the ground above the datum plane. The scale of the uplands will be greater than that of the lowlands. That is, a given unit of length on the photograph will represent a greater distance on the ground on the uplands than in the lowlands. There is distortion of both direction and distance between points.[6] Because of this distortion, straight lines (such as roads, railroads, fence lines) may seem to curve, especially where these lines approach perpendicularity with the radii from the plumb point, and the appearance of sloping surfaces may be somewhat modified.

In an oblique photograph there is always displacement due to perspective, and the amount of displacement increases from the foreground toward the background. Other conditions being equal, there is less displacement in a low oblique than in a high oblique. Where the land surface is relatively flat, the horizontal or near-horizontal shapes of ponds, shore-lines, river courses, meanders, etc., may be distorted in this way; but where there is considerable relief, similar slopes may be differently distorted according as they face toward the camera, away from it, or at an angle to it, and according to their distance from it. Thus, in Fig. 439, slopes *ab, bc, de,* and *ef* are all equal in area (section in the figure) and angle; but *ab* would be concealed, *bc* would be shorter in the picture than *ef*, though facing toward the lens, and *ed*, facing away from the lens, would be much shorter than *ef*.

It is well to remember, in using air photographs, that the area of least displacement in obliques is nearest the foreground and that the area of least displacement in verticals is the central part of the picture. This central part of a vertical photograph has been called the *effective coverage* by H. T. U. Smith, who says this

[6] See Bibliog., Smith, H. T. U., 1943, pp. 39, 40. Directions of straight lines through the plumb point are true.

term "is defined as the area nearer to the center of one particular photo than to the centers of any adjoining photos."[7]

451. Methods of using air photographs for study. Air photographs may be examined as single contact prints, individually, either as aids to finding local features in the field, or as "base maps" on which to enter geologic data in carrying on field surveying. These prints are seldom rectified, that is, corrected for tilt (see footnote 4, page 565). Or such photographs may be

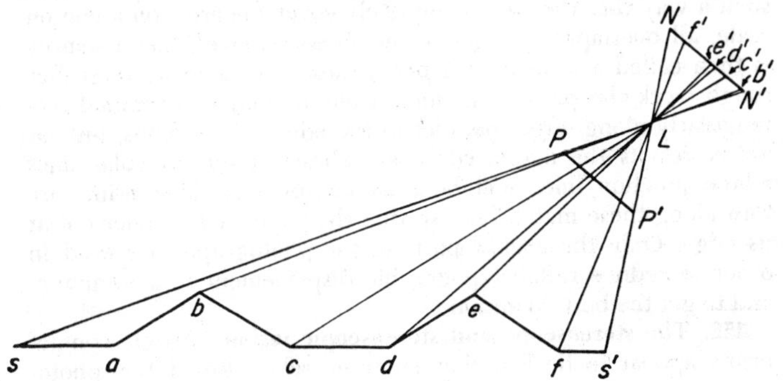

Fig. 439. Effects of displacement in an oblique photograph. Area covered by photograph, *ss'*; negative of oblique, *NN'*; positive, *PP'*; lens, *L*; *SabcdefS'* is profile section of ground, with slopes shown straight and slope angles sharp, for purposes of illustration.

used in overlapping pairs, or in groups of three or more. Discussion of the stereoscopic examination of paired photographs is reserved for Art. 452.

If a series of vertical photographs has been taken along a flight course, with the usual 60 per cent of overlap between adjacent pictures, the contact prints, or, more commonly, reductions of these prints to half scale, may be laid down, overlapping one another in just the same order and position in which they were taken, and they may be fastened thus to a stiff sheet of beaverboard, or masonite, or something similar. Each is attached by its front (in direction of flight) edge only, so that it may be turned up for examination of the picture below. As far as possible each

[7] Bibliog., Smith, H. T. U., 1943, p. 32.

photograph is matched with that below. This series of mounted photographs is called a *photo strip*. Either singly, or in proper combination with adjacent photo strips, mounted with 30 per cent of sidelap, such a group of pictures may be consecutively numbered to serve as a *photo index*. A disadvantage in a photo index lies in the commonly present abrupt discontinuities, from picture to picture, in scale, in tone, and in photographic image.

If the vertical photographs of a flight, or of a group of parallel adjacent flights, are matched and glued to a firm flat base in such a way that they will completely cover the area, on a chosen scale, all overlapping edges having been removed, the assembly is then called a *mosaic*, or a *photo mosaic*, or a *photo map*. For rough work the pictures in such a mosaic may be trimmed rectangularly along edges parallel to the edges of the films, but for better results the match edges are chosen along irregular lines where junction lines will be least conspicuous. The prints are torn along these match lines so that the paper will feather out at its edge. Only the central parts of the photographs are used in order to reduce radial topographic displacement to a minimum and to get the best definition.[8]

452. The stereoscope and stereoscopic vision. Single contact prints appear to be flat; they show no relief. But if two photographs are taken of the same object, from somewhat different viewpoints, and the two images are presented to the eyes in such a way that one appears to be superimposed on the other, the effect is three-dimensional; *i.e.*, features that actually have height, breadth, and thickness stand out in relief in the picture. This effect is called *stereoscopic*. The principle is essentially the same as vision by two eyes (binocular vision) that see an object in slightly different directions.

Stereoscopic observations of two partly overlapping photographs may be accomplished by viewing the two photographs placed in correct position side by side (1) by ordinary light, or (2) in complementary colors, or (3) in polarized light. In this book we are concerned only with the first two methods.

In air photography one of the main objects of requiring overlap between adjacent pictures, both along the flight line and between flight lines, is to permit stereoscopic examination because, from a three-dimensional image, much can be learned

[8] For a full description of the making of mosaics, see Bibliog., American Society of Photogrammetry, 1952, Chap. 10.

that could not be seen in a single contact print. Indeed, stereoscopic study of air photographs is exceedingly important in both photogeology and photogrammetry.

For stereoscopic examination, a pair of overlapping photographs is called a *stereo pair*. Three such pictures so arranged that the middle one is wholly overlapped, partly by the picture on one side of it and the remainder by the picture on the other side of it, are together called a *stereo triplet*. The area of overlap, viewed stereoscopically, is called the *spatial model, stereo model,* or simply the *model*. The model is the area within which the three-dimensional, or stereoscopic, effect is seen.

An instrument used for stereoscopic examination of pictures is a *stereoscope*. There are two kinds of stereoscope, the lens type and the mirror type. The lens type has two lenses, one for each eye, with some magnification, preferably not more than 2.5 times. The mirror type has four mirrors set at 45° to the plane of the photographs. There is no magnification unless the instrument is provided with auxiliary lenses. Advantages in the lens or refraction stereoscope are its compactness, portability, and magnification, but its field of vision is smaller than in the mirror stereoscope. The mirror stereoscope is made large enough to include all of two prints, 9 by 9 in. in size, within its field of vision. A small folding pocket stereoscope is almost an essential part of the equipment of a field geologist.[9]

453. Control and corrections of air photographs. For their more accurate uses, air photographs—singly, as composites, or as mosaics—must be carefully tied to a precisely surveyed ground control. Such a ground control is usually tied to established bench marks or to Coast and Geodetic Survey monuments, both as to horizontal location and as to elevation above sea level; but it may sometimes be tied to an assumed elevation. Adjustment to ground controls may include reference to horizontal controls only, or to both horizontal and vertical controls.[10]

[9] A very useful modification of the folding pocket stereoscope is a pair of spectacles prepared for stereoscopic observation.

For application of the stereoscope in geological work, see Bibliog., Hemphill, William R., 1958.

[10] Bench marks or other ground control stations may be recognized in the photographs if they are conspicuously marked by strips of cloth on the ground before the pictures are taken. Sometimes they are selected from a study of the photographs and are then surveyed on the ground.

Several sources of error and displacement in air photographs have been described in Art. **450.** For some purposes corrections must be made for these, particularly where measurements must be accurate within small limits of error. Under other circumstances, as in the case of air photographs for general illustrative purposes or for rapid reconnaissance, correction may be needed for only some of the sources of error or displacement, or perhaps corrections may not be needed at all.

When precision is necessary, flight specifications may call for certain definite limits of error in the process of air photography.

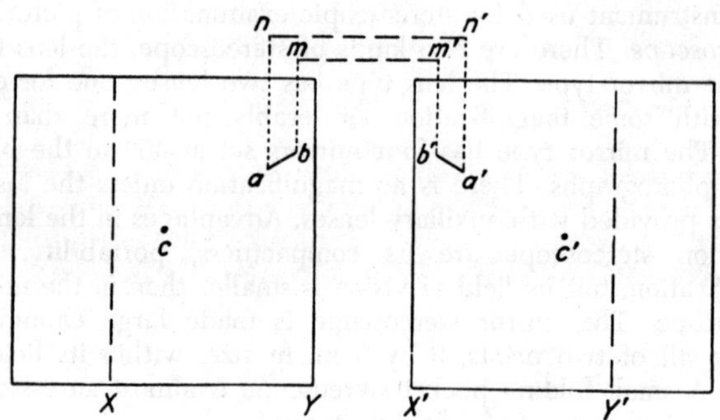

Fig. 440. Diagram to explain parallax. (See text.)

For instance, if the tolerance for tilt is limited to 3°, any photographs with more than 3° of tilt must be retaken. However, correction for tilt can be accomplished by a process of photographically projecting the negative, carefully oriented in the position in which it was taken, onto a horizontal sensitized sheet of paper. This is called *rectification.*[11] In the same manner an oblique photograph can be rectified, *i.e.*, converted to a vertical, a procedure followed in the case of the obliques of composite photographs (trimetrogon, etc.).

Radial displacement was mentioned in Art. **450.** In the "model," or area of overlap in a stereo pair, this effect produced *parallactic displacement* (stereoscopic parallax). Thus, in Fig. 440, *c* is the center of one photograph, and *c′* is the center of the

[11] Rectification is accomplished by use of a special camera called a *rectifier*, or *rectifying camera.*

adjoining photograph of a stereo pair, *xy* and *x′y′* being the areas of overlap (the model) within which a three-dimensional image may be seen by stereoscope. Let *a* be the base of a high chimney in the photograph to the left, and *a′* be the base of the same chimney in the right-hand photograph. In the former the top of the chimney, *b*, is radially displaced *ab* from its correct position vertically above *a*, and in the latter, this same point, here *b′*, is displaced *a′b′*, similarly. *ab* is along a radius from *c*, and *a′b′* is along a radius from *c′*. By placing both photographs in such a way that they are correctly oriented along the line of flight from *c* to *c′*, we have

$$nn' - mm' = \text{parallactic displacement (stereoscopic parallax)}.$$

For measurement of this difference it is obvious that the two pictures should not be placed in overlapping position.

Summarizing, air photographs may be controlled or not controlled, *i.e.*, tied to a ground control, or not so tied; and they may be rectified or not rectified, *i.e.*, corrected for scale, tilt, and perspective displacement, or not so corrected. For precise work they are both controlled and rectified.

454. Transfer of data from air photographs to planimetric maps. Correcting, rectifying, and adjusting to controls, in the application of air photographs, and the operations used in constructing planimetric or two-dimensional maps[12] and contour maps from partially or wholly controlled photographs and mosaics belong for the most part under the head of photogrammetry. For the benefit of the geologist we shall describe here only a few of the techniques employed, and these very briefly. It is important that the geologist should know enough of these techniques to be able to decide whether or not he should call in the service of a photogrammetrist.

One of the simplest photogrammetric instruments is the *sketch-master,* which is essentially a camera lucida in principle. It is not infrequently used by the geologist himself when he wishes to transfer details from an air photograph to a base map. It can be adjusted for scale, and correction for tilt is possible by lengthening or shortening one or more of the three legs of the frame of the instrument. These adjustments in the so-called "universal sketch-master" have sufficient range to permit transfer of

[12] Planimetric maps do not show topographic relief, either by contours or in any other way.

features from an oblique photograph into their correct position on the horizontal map sheet. Figure 441 illustrates the principle of the sketch-master, in this case where lines are to be transferred from a vertical photograph to a horizontal planimetric base map.

Adjustment to a system of controls and at the same time approximate correction of parallactic displacement may be accomplished in vertical photographs by one or another of several *radial-plot* or *radial-line* methods, which are based on the common surveying principles of intersection and resection in triangulation (436). A simple radial-plot procedure may be described

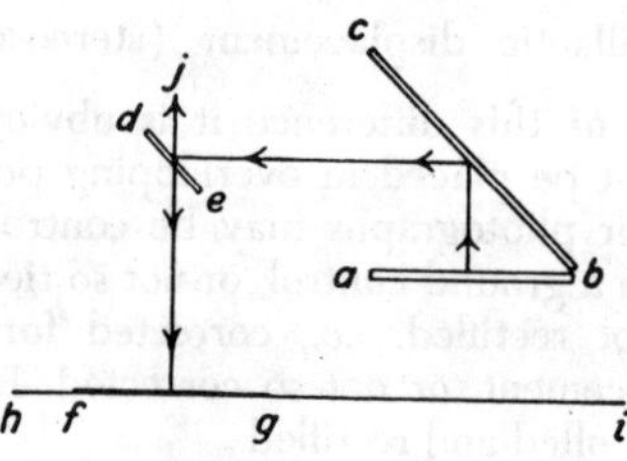

FIG. 441. Principle of the sketch-master. *ab*, air photograph on supporting frame; *bc*, opaque adjustable mirror; *de*, semitransparent adjustable mirror; *fg*, image of *ab* on table (*hi*) on which map sheet is fastened; *j*, points to position of observer's eye when viewing reflection of *ab* which seems to be projected on to *hi* at *fg*, thus enabling him to sketch features from the photograph directly onto the map.

as follows. Let us assume that we have a series of vertical photographs, taken with 60 per cent of overlap between adjacent pictures, along a horizontal flight line. Take the first two photographs and carefully mark on each its center (principal center)[13] and also the position of the principal center of the other picture of the pair. On each connect these two points by a fine straight line (the *principal point base*). On each picture also indicate the positions of *ground control points* and any other selected recognizable *picture control points* (such as stream junctions, road intersections, etc.) within the area of overlap. For precise matching of photo strips (see Art. 451), two easily recognizable ground points, called *wing points*, are adequate, one to the left and one

[13] Obtained by ruling lines from the "collimation points" on opposite sides of the photograph, points which are always indicated on the film.

to the right of the principal point, and far enough from it to be within the 30 per cent area of sidelap. Draw short (1 to 1½ in.) straight fine lines through the indicated control points on both pictures, these lines being drawn radially from the principal center points. Repeat this procedure for photographs 2 and 3; then for photographs 3 and 4; and so on.

Select a sufficiently large sheet of tracing cloth (or cellulose sheet) to serve as a base map on which to plot the features shown in the several photographs of the assemblage. Place the first photograph under this sheet, and orient it so that the flight will not run off the sheet when data from all pictures in the assemblage have been plotted. Carefully trace on to this sheet the points and radial lines drawn on photograph 1, also the principal point base line from center of 1 to transferred center of 2. Next place photograph 2 beneath the cellulose sheet, and adjust it so that its center and the transferred center point of photograph 1 will exactly coincide with these same points already plotted from photograph 1. Then trace all new control points from photograph 2 and also the radial lines from the principal center of 2 to all these control points. Proceed in this manner from photograph to photograph until all control points, radial lines, and sections of the principal point base line have been traced.[14] When the center points and wing points of all pictures have been properly marked on the overlay sheet, the area of each picture, except the edge pictures of each group, will include three principal centers and six wing points (Fig. 442).

Under ideal conditions it will be found that each control point will be indicated on the overlay sheet at the intersection of three rays, drawn, respectively, from three center points. However, due to a number of factors, the three rays may not mutually intersect, but may form a small triangle of error (cf. Art. **436,** 3) in which case the location of the point is to be regarded as essentially correct at the center of the triangle of error. If plotting is carried forward over several photographs without ground control points,

[14] If it seems best not to draw the radial lines directly on the photographs, a piece of tracing cloth, cut to the size of the print (9 by 9 in.), may be laid over each photograph from which the control points and principal center points can be pricked through, and the radial lines can be ruled in on this tracing cloth or templet (template). The several templets will then be treated just as we have described for the photographs in transferring points and lines to the main planimetric base (cellulose sheet).

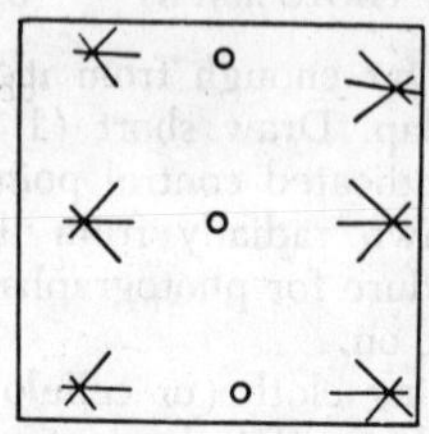

FIG. 442. The square represents the area, on the transparent overlay, immediately above a vertical photograph which is one of a series arranged in a photo strip. Call this photo VI. Then V will be the adjacent picture below (to the rear, in the direction of flight), and VII will be the adjacent picture above (forward, in the direction of flight). *A* is the principal center of photo V; *B*, of photo VI; and *C*, of photo VII. Wing points are numbered 1 to 6. Within this area (of photo VI), principal centers *A* and *B* and wing points 1 to 4 all lie within the 60 per cent overlap of photos V and VI; and principal centers *B* and *C* and wing points 3 to 6 all lie within the 60 per cent overlap of photos VI and VII. Wing points 2, 4, and 6 lie within the 30 per cent sidelap of the adjoining strip on the right, and wing points 1, 3, and 5 lie within the 30 per cent sidelap of the adjoining strip on the left.

there may be an accumulated error which, when finally checked at the next available ground control points, may have to be proportionally adjusted backward, much as in plane surveying. For further details concerning the radial-plot methods, see publications by P. G. McCurdy, H. T. U. Smith, and others.[15]

The radial-plot methods of constructing a planimetric map from air photographs are not too accurate. Most photogrammetrists, who are concerned with precision techniques, regard them as distinctly of reconnaissance value. Nevertheless for geologic base maps these radial-plot methods may often be adequate. Where the terrain photographed is fairly level, a radial plot with good control can be quite accurate.

Greater accuracy is obtained in using the so-called "multiplex," or other similar devices which belong in the class of precision instruments. We may describe the multiplex as an example. This instrument consists of two or more projectors mounted on a horizontal bar above a table in such a way that they can be adjusted exactly to duplicate, on a reduced scale, the altitude, tilt, and position of the camera at each of two or more stations along the line of flight. Each photograph to be viewed is reduced from its original size to a diapositive (like a lantern slide) only 64 mm. square, and the diapositives are inserted in their respective pro-

[15] Bibliog., McCurdy, P. G., 1940; Eardley, A. J., 1941; and American Society of Photogrammetry, 1952.

jectors. Alternate blue-green and red filters are placed on the projectors, and the operator wears glasses provided with one blue-green and one red lens. These glasses filter the projected images so that each eye sees an image of the same area taken from adjacent air stations. One eye sees the image blue-green and the other sees it red, and the effect of superposing these two complementary colors is stereoscopic. It is another method of producing a three-dimensional image.

Working in a darkened room, the operator sees an image of the topography on a small horizontal *tracing table* which can be moved in any direction on the plotting table. By raising or lowering the tracing table, a small bright dot, called a "floating dot," may be brought into such a position, on the stereoscopic image of the topography, that it will seem to be exactly "on the ground." This "floating dot" is set correctly on one elevation control point, and the projector is then tilted until it appears to be "on the ground" at the other control points. By setting the tracing table at a fixed elevation, on the vertical scale adopted, and keeping the floating dot always "on the ground," this dot can be made to travel along a contour as the tracing table is moved. Then, by raising the tracing table a contour interval, on the adopted scale, the next higher contour can be traced; and so on. Below the tracing table a pencil at the same time automatically traces the contour on a sheet of paper over which the tracing table is moved. By tying in to a known elevation control point, and by using a vernier for vertical scale, it is possible to use a selected contour interval and to refer the contours to sea level datum. Within the horizontal plane of each contour elevation, radial displacement is corrected. Thus this instrument may be employed to construct a topographic contour map controlled for horizontal and vertical position and corrected for tilt, radial distortion, and scale.

Other instruments often used in preference to the multiplex are the Kelsh and ER-55 plotters in which the models are sharper and more easily measurable.[16] For preliminary observations some geologists, before going into the field, compile maps of their assigned areas, using high-altitude (scale: 1/60,000) photographs in conjunction with these plotters.

An instrument developed by the U.S. Geological Survey, called

[16] For brief descriptions of these plotters, see Bibliog., Pillmore, C. L., 1957; also Ray, Richard G., 1956.

an orthophotoscope, converts perspective photographs to the equivalent of orthographic photographs, that is, it eliminates parallactic displacement, producing a corrected photograph in which the scale in all directions is uniform. This instrument is used in conjunction with the ER-55 plotter, or the Kelsh plotter, or the multiplex. The orthophotograph

"offers a combination of the wealth of detail supplied by photography . . . with the accuracy of measurement supplied by a map. . . . It can be made in a fraction of the time required for a map, thus eliminating months, or even years, of waiting for a reliable base on which to plot strikes, dips, fault lines, lithologic contacts and other features shown on geologic maps. . . . Whenever there is an advantage in being able to determine accurately on an aerial photograph the positions of points, the lengths or directions of lines, or the shapes or areas of given tracts, the orthophotograph offers a potential means of accomplishing the desired end."[17]

For further details on techniques and instruments, the reader is referred to texts on photogrammetry.[18]

455. Availability of air photographs. For geologic field work it is well to know where one may secure air photographs. The U.S. Geological Survey publishes two index maps, one showing "all areas known to have been photographed by or for federal, state, and commercial agencies," and the other showing "all areas for which aerial mosaics or photo-maps are known to have been compiled by or for federal, state, and commercial agencies." With each of these maps is furnished an explanatory circular. Those who would secure any air photographs or air mosaics for use in mapping should apply to the Map Information Office, Geological Survey, Department of the Interior, Washington, D.C., for these index maps and for whatever other information is desired concerning scales, sources of procurement, etc. The U.S. Geological Survey, through the cooperation of the Army Map Service, sells copies of high-altitude photographs on a scale of approximately 1/60,000. These together now cover nearly all the United States.

In Canada an index map of "Air Photographic Coverage" is available from the Map Distribution Office, Department of Mines

[17] Quoted from Bibliog., Bean, Russell K., and Morris W. Thompson, 1957, p. 178.

[18] Bibliog., Eardley, A. J., 1941; Smith, H. T. U., 1943; American Society of Photogrammetry, 1952; Ray, Richard G., 1956; and Pillmore, C. L., 1957.

and Resources, Ottawa, Canada. Information on the areas covered, as shown on this map, may be obtained from the National Air Photographic Library, Department of Mines and Resources, Ottawa.

456. Air photographs for geologic uses; photogeology. Air photographs are of inestimable value in many kinds of geologic, topographic, and physiographic work. They present a bird's-eye view of the land surface—the shape and distribution of land forms; the distribution and larger features of rocks and soils; the attitude of stratified rocks; the form, trend, and relations of folds; the positions and relations of faults; and the relations of roads, railroads, and other man-made elements to these natural phenomena—a wealth of detail that cannot be matched by the methods of ground surveying (Chap. 16); and these air photographs, with all their detail, can be made, corrected, and assembled into mosaics for study in less time than was required for mapping by the usual methods of surveying. Often they may reveal geologic features that can be entirely overlooked in field exploration. They have the advantage of easily reaching areas which are difficult or impossible of access on the ground, either because of the nature of the land surface (swamps, rugged mountains, escarpments) or because of trespass restrictions. Maps made from air photographs, with precise plotters and proper ground control, can be more accurate than maps made entirely by ground surveying.

The study of air photographs and of maps constructed from such photographs for geologic information is called *photogeology.* A geologist who specializes in this study is a *photogeologist.* Such a person must be well trained in the principles of geology. He must be an experienced field geologist who knows rocks, structures, and topographic forms and their significance, and who, also, can translate the surface expressions of these phenomena into their subsurface meanings. Also he should be fully cognizant of the ways in which he can be helped in his work by photogrammetry.

For an understanding of air photographs for geologic interpretation, the geologist must learn to recognize roads, railroads, houses, water, various kinds of vegetation, stream courses, slopes, etc., as these appear on the photographs. Most roads are either very irregular, or they may be in rectangular patterns. Except along well-graded highways, they usually have sharp, angular turns. On the other hand, railroad turns are always curved. Houses and other buildings may be conspicuous by their shadows. On some pictures shadows cast by trees, and especially by hills and escarpments in lands of high relief, may obscure some of the important, but less conspicuous geologic features. Also cloud shadows may be disconcerting. For these reasons the photographs should be taken in the middle of the day and in perfectly fine weather, and in making mosaics, adjoining photographs should not have strongly conflicting shadow angles. Shadows should be kept at a minimum. Air photographs in hilly or mountainous country should not be taken when shadows are long enough to reach across valleys to opposite slopes.

Lake waters, if calm, may look black or dark gray, but if ruffled by a breeze, they may look white, or light gray. Stream courses commonly branch headward, thus indicating the direction of the general slopes controlling them. Rough checks on elevation differences can often be made by reference to the streams if one remembers that mature and old streams have uniform gradients, but that young streams are characterized by abrupt and sometimes considerable changes in elevation along their channels.

Vegetation—woods, grass, brush, cultivated fields, etc.—has various appearances on air photographs. These differences, which may be accentuated by the use of filters, are seen as changes in tone value on black-and-white prints. They merit careful attention because vegetation is closely related to soil, and soil, if residual, is closely related to the underlying bedrock, so that study of the photographs for characteristics that depend on the kind and distribution of vegetation may assist in deciphering the geology. It is remarkable how distinctly some soil effects, due to geology, are shown on these air photographs made by camera and color screen, in spite of the fact that they would pass quite unnoticed on the ground. An instance of this was noted in California. A soil contact, invisible on the ground, was readily traceable on the air photograph even where it crossed a field of full-grown wheat. Figure 450 represents a circular area within which the soil contrasts and drainage pattern are largely a result of the uparching of strata by a salt plug. Color photographs are especially effective in emphasizing contrasts in vegetation, soil, and rock types.

In most cases the geologist will probably use verticals, but obliques may be of service. His object may be to cover a wide area in a reconnaissance manner,[19] or to examine a smaller area in detail. For reconnaissance, trimetrogon photography yields most rapid coverage. Photo indices and uncontrolled mosaics, in each case composed of verticals, are valuable for giving the geologist a general idea of the country. As far as possible air photographs should be examined stereoscopically; *i.e.*, photographs should be paired, or adjacent prints should be duplicated in part by overlap, and the geologist should be provided with a stereoscope.[20] The study of mosaics may be facilitated by stereoscopic examination of paired prints of the separate photographs that go to make up the mosaic. For very detailed results, in regions of inclined and folded strata, the geologic structure can be shown by structure contours photogrammetrically plotted either on the controlled mosaic itself or on a planimetric base map constructed from this mosaic (**454**).

Air photographs may be used in several ways by the geologist. Such a photograph may serve him (1) as a general guide for field work, (2) for direct interpretation of the geology, (3) as a base for field mapping, (4) for topographic contouring, (5) for structure contouring, or (6) for construction of stratigraphic sections. For these purposes he may employ contact prints singly or in groups, or he may work with mosaics.

1. If the geologist is provided with good air photographs of an area in which he is to undertake field work, not only can he gain a fair idea of the nature of the country that he must traverse, but also he can intelligently plan his program in relation to roads, topography, and geologic features. He can see whether roads are numerous or few and to what extent he may have to resort to horseback or to walking, rather than to automobile in examining the land. If pack train or foot traversing is necessary, he can route these to avoid such difficulties as marshes or precipices. Even for this simplest application of air photographs, he will find the use of a stereoscope very advantageous.

[19] The high-altitude photographs, available from the U.S. Geological Survey (see Art. **455**), may be used for preliminary reconnaissance.

[20] By practice one can acquire the ability to look at a stereo pair without a stereoscope and, by focusing the eyes on an unseen point far behind the photographs, cause the pair to appear to be superposed, with the resulting three-dimensional effect. Exercises for practising are described by H. T. U. Smith (see Bibliog.).

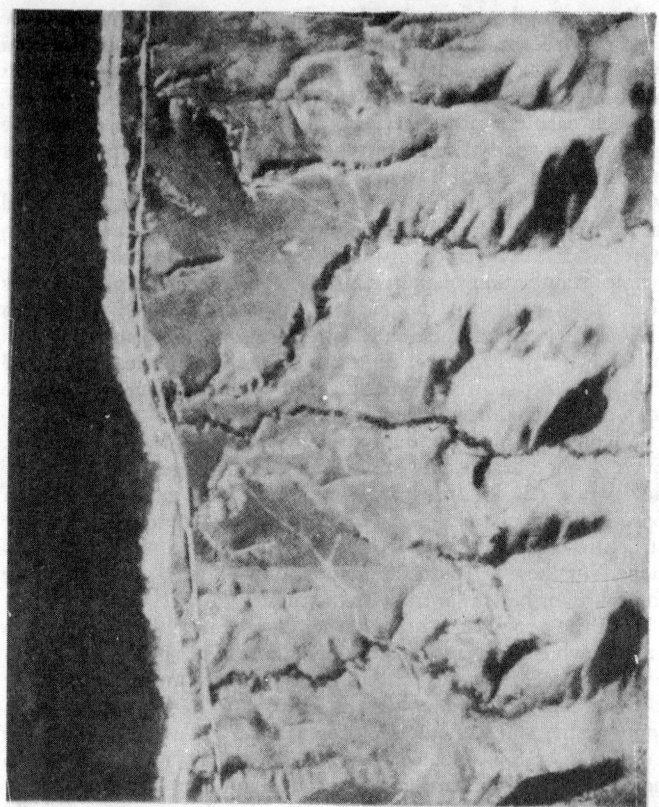

FIG. 443. California coast west of Santa Barbara. Monocline of Tertiary beds dipping toward ocean at angle of 45°. (Scale: width of picture equals 8,250 ft.) (*Published through the courtesy of the Continental Air Map Company of Los Angeles.*)

As a single illustration of the value of air photographs, consider a region where outcropping strata are nearly horizontal and are dissected by a drainage system that has produced a dendritic and intricate pattern of scarps on the hard layers. If either barometer or plane-table mapping is to be done, a great deal of time may be saved if the field men are furnished with air photographs or with a photomosaic of the area before beginning the field work. They can very easily trace and correlate the exposed beds shown in the photograph, picking points at which to record elevations on a selected key horizon at properly distributed stations in the field without the need of "walking" this bed through all its ramifications of outcrop.

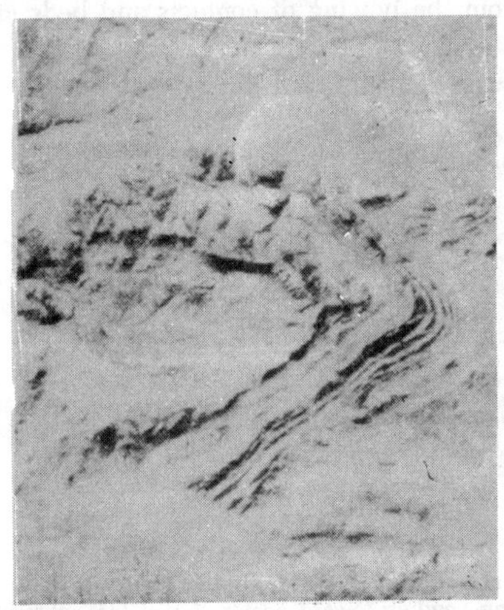

FIG. 444. An anticline in the Imperial Valley, Calif. Note small fold developed on NE. flank of large fold. Relief is due to hard and soft Tertiary strata. Desert conditions exist, with the ground almost bare of vegetation. (Scale: width of picture equals 3,000 ft.) (*Published through the courtesy of the Continental Air Map Company of Los Angeles.*)

In countries where rock exposures are few and difficult of access and therefore hard to find, but where there is not too much forest cover to hide them, air photographs may indicate the positions of these rare outcrops which may then be quickly visited and investigated in the field.

Where field reconnaissance is to be done, preliminary stereoscopic examination of paired overlapping air photographs, which cover the area in one or more flights, will permit the geologist to select features of special interest that may require inspection on the ground. Thus, suggestions of dip, especially of ***reverse dip***, in a region where the normal direction of dip is known, may lead to the discovery, in the field, of geologic structures that might be favorable to oil accumulation.

2. Air photographs may be used for direct interpretation of the geology, as illustrated in Figs. 443–450. If well-exposed strata are inclined more than 10° or 15°, the direction of their dip may be evident from the bowing of contacts and beds in the valleys

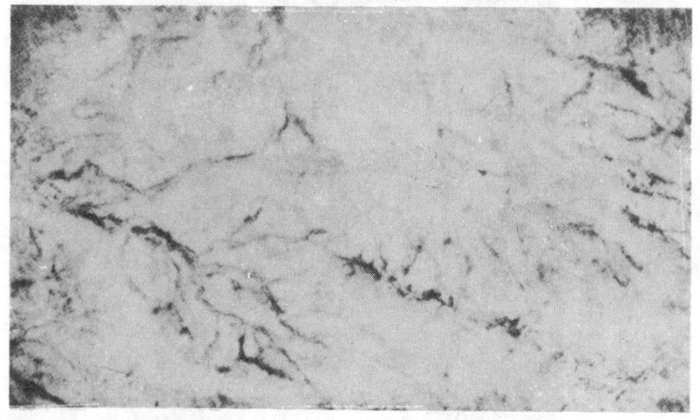

Fig. 445. A synclinal basin seen from the air. Note how some outcrop belts can be seen bending toward center of structure where they cross the valleys. View taken in northern Mexico. Conditions arid, with little soil. (Scale such that area shown covers 22 square miles.) (*Published through the courtesy of Fairchild Aerial Surveys, Inc.*)

(Figs. 443, 567; also Art. 193). An experienced photogeologist, if aided by stereoscope, can make fair estimates of the amount of dip of stratified rocks, provided the air photographs had very little tilt. "Dips observed under the stereoscope invariably appear steeper than their actual inclination. This is, of course, a help in extremely low-dip country but a source of confusion in areas where dips are steeper. However, dips ranging from 3 degrees to 20 degrees can usually be estimated with a reasonable degree of accuracy," after some practice with actual checking on the ground. "Dips in the range of 20 to 45 degrees should be estimated with an error of no greater than 5 degrees, whereas dips from 45 degrees to near vertical are difficult to estimate closer than within 10 degrees of their true value."[21] Some photogeologists admit that for dips over 40° or 45° they cannot safely make estimates from the stereo model. Dips as high as 75° may look vertical or even overturned. Since radial displacement increases toward the edges of the picture, estimates of dip should not be attempted too far from the central area.

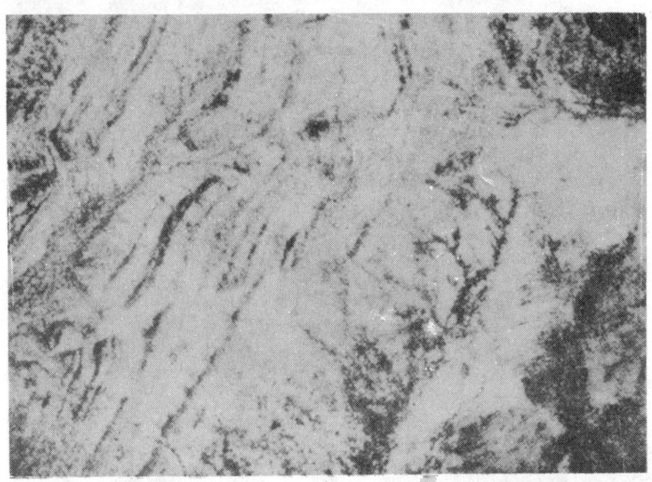

FIG. 446. Air photograph of a series of outcropping strata broken by two faults, which trend about N. 80° E. (Scale: width of picture about 6,000 ft.) (*Published through the courtesy of Edgar Tobin Aerial Surveys, San Antonio, Tex.*)

Both anticlinal and synclinal folds may be clearly shown on air photographs by the trend of the strata and their downdip bowing in the valleys (Figs. 444, 445).

Faults, which perhaps are inconspicuous on the ground, may be brought into prominence (Figs. 446, 447). Joint systems may show up very strikingly (Fig. 448).

On some air photographs either the geologic structure, or the particular class of rock, or the topography, may have a more or

[21] Bibliog., Brundall, Laurence, and A. R. Wasem, 1950, p. 54.

less distinct linear appearance. Whatever the cause may be, this effect is called *lineation* (see Art. **15**). It is illustrated especially well in Figs. 433, A, 446, and 448. It is a phenomenon which should by all means be investigated and explained by the photogeologist. Often it will prove to be of real significance in unravelling the geologic structure and history of a region.

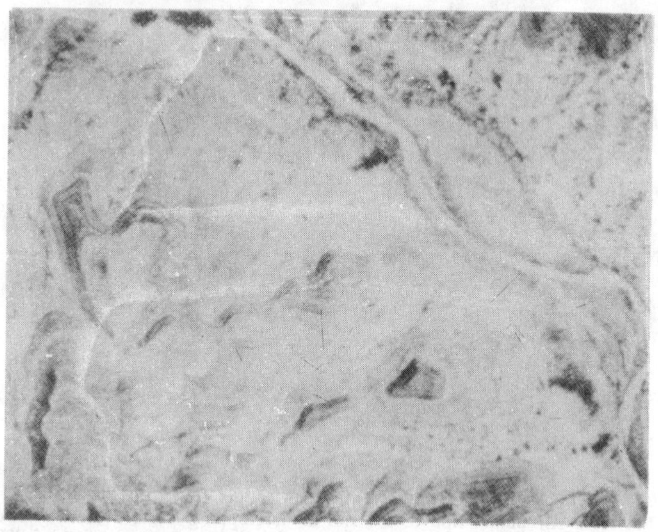

FIG. 447. Nearly horizontal strata cut by a group of parallel vertical faults of small displacement (striking NW.–SE.) and then eroded. These faults are scarcely visible to an observer on the ground. Note how closely erosion is controlled by the faults. The river is the Pecos River, the picture having been taken in northern Pecos County, Tex. (Scale: width of picture just over 2 miles.) (*Published through the courtesy of Fairchild Aerial Surveys, Inc.*)

In starting to work in unfamiliar regions the photogeologist can be greatly assisted by advance acquaintance with any peculiar or abnormal geologic conditions, either from the study of existing geologic maps or reports, or from reconnaissance field work. Such conditions might include glacial deposits, caliche, major unconformities, igneous features, wind deposits, alluvia-

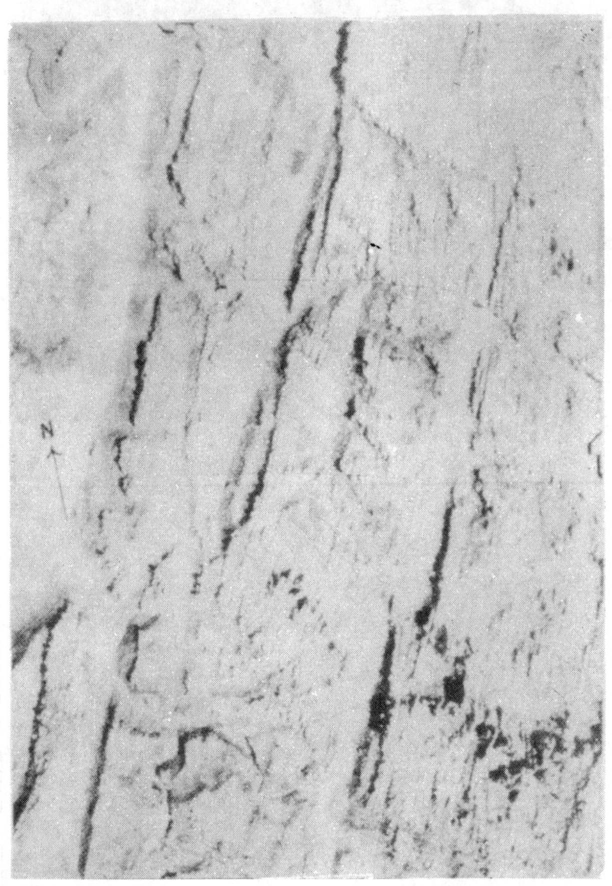

Fig. 448. Air photograph of an area in the Moab district of southeastern Utah. North is shown by the arrow. The prominent lineation, both N. 25° E. and N. 42° W., is due to two sets of jointing in the Cedar Mesa sandstone of Permian age. The three main valleys, trending N. 25° E., are narrow grabens, named, from left to right, the Cyclone Canyon, Devil's Lane, and Devil's Pocket grabens. The bedding is actually nearly horizontal here, as may be seen in the northwest corner of the picture, but at first sight the main jointing gives the impression of vertical bedding. (*This picture is reproduced with permission of Jack Ammann Photogrammetric Engineers, San Antonio, Tex.*)

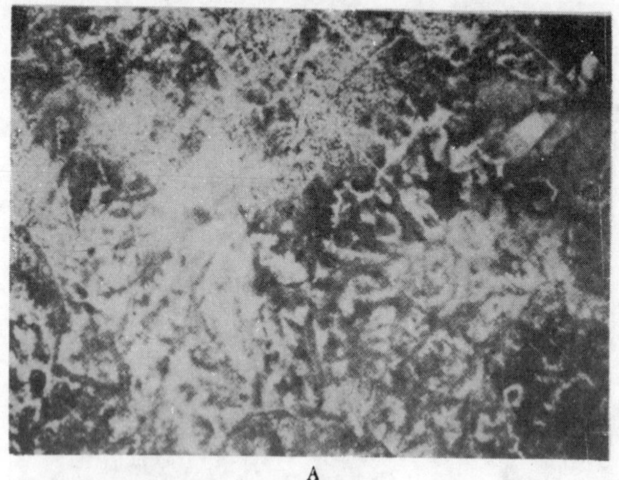

A

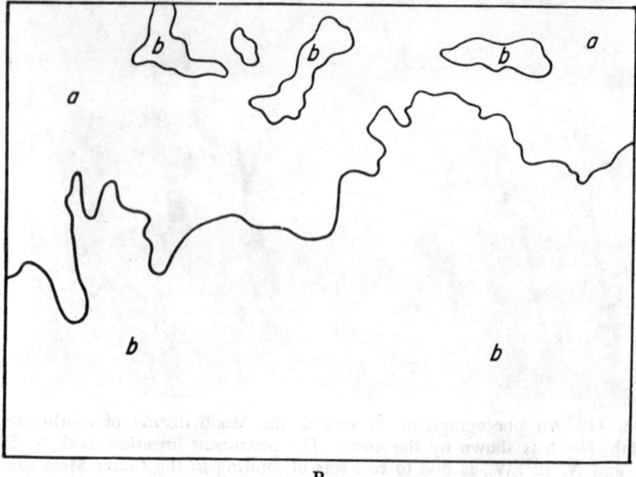

B

FIG. 449. A, air photograph and B, outline map of same area, showing two gently dipping formations, one (*a*) characterized by rather smooth topography and a growth of scattered live-oak trees, and the other (*b*) characterized by dendritic topography and a growth of mesquite trees. The contact can be very easily traced on the photograph, whereas in the field it would require a great deal of time. The contacts are shown on the outline map, B. (Scale: width of picture about 3.9 miles.) (*Published through the courtesy of Edgar Tobin Aerial Surveys.*)

tion, faulting, etc. It is not necessary to know the details of these; they will probably be supplied from his stereoscopic study; but fair warning that such abnormal features may occur often saves time and labor. He should be constantly on the watch lest

Fig. 450. Air photograph of the Barbers Hill salt dome, in Chambers County, Tex. No bedrock is exposed. The effect of the uparched formations is brought out by slight differences in the soil. A lighter central area, nearly circular in outline, may be discerned surrounded by soil of darker shade. The edge between these two areas is most distinct on the north and northeast. The picture shows cultivated fields, wooded areas, roads, drainage features, etc. (Scale: width of picture about 3.4 miles.) (*Published through the courtesy of Edgar Tobin Aerial Surveys.*)

he draw false conclusions. Landslides, mudflows, and outwash deposits and various kinds of mantle rock may be confusing in an interpretation aimed at subsurface structure. At this point we may emphasize the importance of geologic supervision of the making of mosaics for geologic uses. The match lines between photograph segments should never be *along* geologic features of any kind, if this is avoidable.

3. On the air photograph geologic features observed in the field can be sketched. The positions of outcrops, traces of scarps, and symbols for rocks can be plotted in their proper relations to topography and culture. Contacts, faults, and strike-and-dip symbols can be indicated. If desired two copies of each such photomap can be used, one for the field and the other for camp or field office. By following this plan, the office copy, onto which the field data are transferred each night, is kept clean and is available if the field copy happens to be damaged or lost. The office copy may be a mosaic, whereas separate contact prints are taken into the field, and in this case the geologic data are plotted only on every other print, for there is no need to duplicate these annotations in the whole area of overlap. Sometimes, instead of having two copies of each air photograph, a blueprint from the original film or a photostatic copy of the photograph, or an accurate planimetric map of the more important features of the photograph, may serve for field use, and the air photograph is then kept for the office. Or, again, annotations concerning the geology may be kept on the field copy of the photograph, and subsequently these may be transferred by means of a sketchmaster (Art. 454) to a planimetric base map. Such a base map may be available,[22] or it may have to be constructed by the geologist himself. When geologic annotations are not wanted permanently on the print used in the field, they may be entered on it with a soft 5-B pencil which will not injure the emulsion surface and which can easily be removed by a cloth dampened with benzene after the data have been transferred.[23]

The geologic annotations may be drawn directly on the face of the photograph itself, or on a transparent overlay. "The advantages of the overlay are that they keep the photos clean and untouched, and give in one step all the interpretational data in the form of a sketch map, usually showing also a selected amount of drainage and other geographic data, which is traced

[22] As for instance in regions of the United States where the Soil Conservation Service has made planimetric maps by photogrammetric techniques from government air photographs.

[23] Personal communication from Prof. Vincent C. Kelley, Albuquerque, N.M.

all at the same time."[24] The disadvantages are in some obscuring and loss of stereoscopic relief in the finer details. The better way is to make the annotations directly on the photograph, neatly, with fine lines and with removable colored pigment inks.

4. The drawing of topographic contours on an air photograph is possible by the use of an ordinary stereoscope, and considerable proficiency can be attained by a "stereo-topographer" in this work. Desjardins considers that the training acquired in mastering the art of free-hand topographic contouring is so important that no one can become a competent photogeologist without it.

If the geologist does not care to concern himself with topographic contouring, this can be carried out by the use of a precise plotter in the hands of a trained photogrammetrist (Art. 454). For further discussion on topographic contouring the reader may consult manuals on photogrammetry.

5. Provided with a photomap on which geologic boundaries of stratified rocks have been drawn and with another identical photomap on which topographic contours have been drawn, one can produce a structure contour map of the strata. The picture bearing the geology is then combined, under the stereoscope, with the one bearing the topography, and a single image showing geology and topographic contours is the result (Fig. 451, A, B, and C).[25]

In his more recent paper,[26] Desjardins explains at some length photogrammetric methods of structure contouring under conditions of low dip (under 2°), moderate dip (2° to 10°), and high dip (over 10°). The same subject is discussed by Nugent.[27]

Following is a brief outline of the procedure adopted where the country to be examined had not yet been mapped from the air. The area to be surveyed was characterized by rather extensive dissection of low-dipping strata of weak or moderate resistance to erosion, so that scarps were not too pronounced, but still were often traceable between actual exposures by low benches. This area was outlined for the photogrammetrist and the tolerances for tilt and scale were designated, the object being

[24] Bibliog., Desjardins, Louis, 1950, p. 2288. For further details on this subject, reference may be made to this article.

[25] Bibliog., Desjardins, Louis, and S. Grace Hower, 1938.

[26] Bibliog., Desjardins, Louis, 1950.

[27] Bibliog., Nugent, L. E., Jr., 1947.

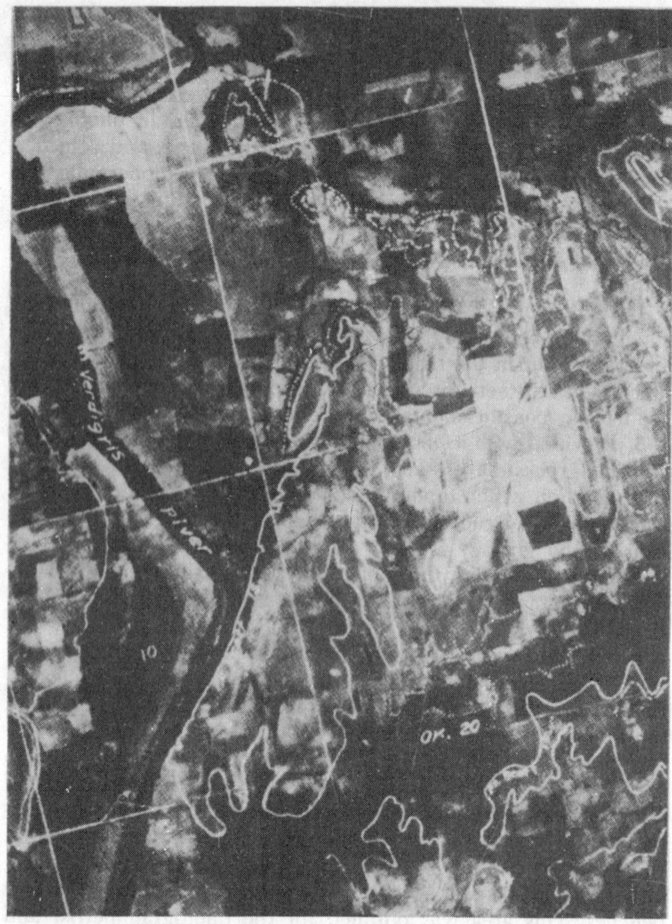

FIG. 451A. Air photo map of an area in Oklahoma, showing geologic contacts (top of Fort Scott limestone and top of Prue sandstone) which have been sketched in on the picture. (*Figures 451, A to C, are reproduced through the courtesy of the Aero Exploration Company, Tulsa, Okla.*)

Fig. 451B. Same view as in Fig. 451, A, but with topographic contours sketched in. Contour interval, 20 ft.

FIG. 451C. Same view as Figs. 451, A and B. By superposing the contours of Fig. 451, B, on the formation boundaries of Fig. 451, A, as described in the text, structure contours may be drawn on a selected key horizon. This has been done in Fig. 451, C, where the top of the Fort Scott limestone has been contoured, using a 10-ft. contour interval.

to secure sufficient accuracy for multiplex requirements. To keep within these specifications the area was photographed only under the most favorable weather conditions.

After the desired air photographs had been taken, each couple of adjoining (partly overlapping) pictures was examined by stereoscope by the geologist and on each, with a moderate amount of overlap, the several formation edges were carefully indicated, each by a different colored ink. This procedure was carried from picture to picture until all outcropping lithologic units were marked over the whole area.

Next the geologist selected certain points on these formation boundaries to serve as control points, pricking them through the photograph with a fine needle and ringing each such hole with a penciled circle, for recognition. He picked these points on the more pronounced ledges, evenly scattered and with 16 to 20 to a square mile.[28] These were given to the photogrammetrist who was directed to survey these points in the field, tying them to any available bench marks, as to both horizontal position and elevation. Before this was done, however, the geologist made a trip into the field to check his interpretation as made from the photographs.

After completing the survey of the control points on the ground, the elevations of these points were given to the geologists by the photogrammetrist. A key bed was chosen by the geologist and, with the elevations provided at the mapped control points, he was able to contour the structure of the key bed, subtracting or adding to other beds whatever interval might be needed to adjust for overburden or erosion, respectively. In this way, in approximately one-third of a year, he finished a structure map which would have taken a year and a quarter by the usual plane-table method, and, moreover, a map which was more complete and more accurate than could have been prepared by plane table.[29]

[28] Not more than four or five such control points should be necessary per stereo model under ordinary circumstances.

[29] A method, which may come to be of considerable importance in highly dissected terranes on nearly horizontal and very gently warped strata, is called *radar altimetry*. Flights of an airplane are made along parallel courses, 1 or 2 or 3 miles apart. At greater intervals—10 to 15 miles apart—cross traverses are flown at right angles to the first set. Along these courses an altimeter registers the height of the plane above sea level, or above some selected horizontal datum, and this altitude is automatically

6. Stratigraphic or columnar sections may be constructed from stereoscopic study of air photographs. Quoting from Desjardins:[30]

"The photo-derived columns, naturally, are not quite like those measured in the field, where every thin layer can be shown and complete lithological and fossil composition noted (outcrops permitting). They can, however, rival those from the field for accuracy of thickness determinations for larger units, and especially for accumulated thickness or total thickness where this is great. The photo method is free from a common source of field error, that of mismatching tie beds or misjudging covered intervals in piecing together partial sections made at different outcrops into a composite section. It also has an advantage over field methods of attaining greater accuracy where dips are steep, if the dip angle is used as a factor in computing the formational thickness. This is because the photo-measured dip has an accuracy within a degree, and it applies to a dip surface over a sufficient distance to rule out small local variations such as affect dips encountered on the outcrop. The proved accuracy of the photo-columnar thicknesses has greatly added to their general value and usefulness.

"Suitable scales for the columns have been found to range from 1:500 to 1:2000. They can be made, of course, to any scale desired, and it is an advantage to have them on the same scale as columnar sections made in other ways, such as from well samples, for the purposes of mutual comparison. The columns should be plotted on long paper strips of about 5 centimeters in width. They are extremely useful in laying side by side for comparison with each other.

"The stratified sequence to be portrayed by the columns is that which is appropriate for the source of the data, namely, the stereoscopic photo view of the topography. The now popular 'geomorphic' column, where hard layers overhang softer intervals, on one side of the graphic column,

---

recorded as a continuous line. At the same time the height of the airplane above the land surface, vertically below it, is indicated by radar and is automatically recorded as a continuous topographic profile. The elevation of the ground at any point on any course is the altitude of the airplane above sea level (or above datum) minus the height of the airplane above the land surface. The cross traverses permit correction of the altimeter readings (for diurnal variation, etc.) at every intersection of the flight lines. By carefully tying in this corrected elevation profile grid with the exposed stratigraphy, as shown on the photographic map, and if feasible with a few established bench marks, it is possible to plot enough points on the photographic map to permit contouring of a selected key bed. Approximately what the limit of error may be in this procedure is not yet known. To be of use, it must of course be considerably less than the structural relief of the folded or warped strata.

[30] Bibliog., Desjardins, Louis, 1950, pp. 2307–2308.

should be used (cf. Fig. 562). The greater the degree of topographic expression of a given layer the more prominently it should be drawn so as to protrude. Since in the majority of cases the photo annotation of bedding is made by drawing lines along the outcrop of the tops of the hard layers, these will be the positions in the column computed as to their respective stratigraphic intervals, and everything between will be sketched proportionally according to what is seen in the stereoscope. For each of these hard layer tops a bottom surface will also be drawn giving the layer a thickness estimated from the stereo inspection. At the protruding end these top and bottom lines are properly joined to give the bed a solid appearance. Conventional symbols may be called into play to express the lithology of this bed if it is known from field notes, or interpreted from the photos. Many hard beds cannot be so interpreted, and the photogeologist is under no obligation to indicate lithology in his column. The meagerness and incompleteness of his lithologic indications will be made up by the greater fullness of his topographic or geomorphic notes opposite the individual beds, such as 'ridge-maker,' 'intermittent bench,' etc. The outcrop of intervals between the prominent hard beds must be carefully studied, because it is not necessarily all shale. There may be evidence of poorly bedded massive rock of considerable thickness. The relative degree of hardness or softness can be shown by appropriately narrowing the graphic column even when lithology is not certain. With experience the photogeologist may recognize the lithology rather completely, but the emphasis here is that the column does not necessarily have to show it to be broken down into a very detailed sequence. Wherever the photo annotations indicate particular beds in particular colors, or accompanied by identifying numbers, letters, or symbols, these should all be indicated at the corresponding positions in the columns, so that columns and photos serve as indexes to each other."

As in the case of detailed structure contouring, precise photogrammetric techniques are best employed for measuring the thicknesses of stratigraphic units, separately or in combination, so that again we shall refer the student to texts on photogrammetry for further information.[31]

[31] Smith, H. T. U. (see Bibliog.), in Appendix B of his excellent book on "Aerial Photographs," gives both valuable information on sources for procuring air photographs and suggestions for their laboratory study.

In addition to the references cited in the preceding pages of this chapter, we call attention to publications, listed in the Bibliography, by Armand J. Eardley, Frank R. Melton, Sherman A. Wengerd, and Gonzalo Medina Vela. Doctor Vela's contribution, in Spanish, is a well-illustrated, clear presentation of many of the problems in air mapping.

Chapter 18

SUBSURFACE GEOLOGIC SURVEYING

457. Scope. Subsurface or underground geologic surveying includes two distinctly different classes of work. These are (1) mine surveying and (2) the study and correlation of data obtained from drilled holes. The first of these is largely independent of surface geologic surveying except within the regions where mines have been excavated. It is a broad subject and one that is fully treated in textbooks on mining geology.[1] Consequently, in the present volume we shall mention only a very few mining terms, with only brief mention of some special practices followed in mine surveying (see Art. **458**). On the other hand, with reference to the second class of subsurface work, in many regions field interpretations of the geology are greatly assisted by data from drilled holes. Indeed, the geologist may have to be responsible, through his recommendations, for the drilling of holes for this very purpose. Intelligent study of well data is therefore a proper function of the field geologist. The fund of knowledge which has been contributed to the science of geology as a result of the study of data from wells is immeasurable. This branch of subsurface geologic surveying is treated below in Arts. **461–476** and **498–508.**

Mine Surveying

458. Definitions. In referring to mines, the term *working place* includes all underground openings where excavating has been done or is in progress. A group of openings, or "workings," all at approximately the same elevation, is known as a *level.* In most mines levels are spaced at fairly regular intervals of depth. For instance, they may be 100 ft. apart, or 200 ft. apart, etc. A horizontal underground passage is called a *drift* if it follows a vein, or other similar geologic structure, or a *crosscut*

[1] See Bibliog., Forrester, James Donald, 1946; and McKinstry, Hugh Exton, 1948.

if it intersects such structure. A *shaft* is a vertical or steeply inclined opening extending downward from the surface to reach underground workings. It is usually rectangular in cross section. A *winze* is a similar downward excavation, but it starts from a point underground. A *raise* is a vertical or inclined underground opening driven upward from one level to reach a higher level. A *stope* is an underground opening, usually of relatively large size, from which ore has been, or is being, extracted. The *breast* or *face* of a tunnel (drift, crosscut, raise, winze) or stope is the end where the work of excavating is in progress or was last in progress. The *back* of an underground excavation is the top or roof of the opening.

459. Practices in mine surveying. For mine surveying it is often necessary to take special precautions against damage to the map by dripping water. The paper may be attached to an aluminum sheet with a hinged cover to which a blotter can be fastened. The pencils should be sharp and water-resistant. In operating mines every effort must be made to cooperate with the authorities and to avoid anything that will interfere with the miners. Always, too, the geologist should be alert for dangers that might be caused by bad ground, water flooding, caving, old or insecure timbering, blasting, etc.

If a geologic survey is to be made of a mine, the geologist will save time (1) by making a rapid reconnaissance trip through the working place in company with the superintendent or other officer who is familiar with the property, and (2) by securing from him, for use as a base map, a surveyed plan of the workings showing outlines of drifts and crosscuts, positions of survey stations, and elevations of the track (used for hauling the ore) at every station. If such a plan is not available, the geologist will have to make his own as he proceeds with the mapping of the geologic features.

Let us assume that the geologist must chart the mine workings as well as the geology. He will use a Brunton compass for directions and a tape for distances. Actual plotting is to be done underground, rather than from notes in the office. Paper 8½ by 11 in. is preferred by many. Where the plat is carried from one sheet to another, it is repeated in a strip an inch wide so that there will be this much overlap. The scale to be used will be large as compared with most surface mapping. It may be 10 ft. equals 1 in., or 50 ft., 100 ft., or perhaps 200 ft. equals 1 in., depending on the complexity of the geology and the degree of detail required.

In mine surveying all features are mapped at breast height. This applies both to the *ground lines* (intersections of the walls with the floor) of the openings (drifts, crosscuts, etc.,) and to the geologic features. When geologic structures intersected by the working place are vertical or steeply dipping, their plotted positions on the breast-high plane of the map will not be far from their positions on the floor or on the roof of the opening; but if they have low dips there may be a considerable difference between such positions. In this case they may be plotted on the level of the roof (or back), but this fact should be noted on the map. The walls should be carefully examined from top to bottom, and if significant geologic features cannot be shown satisfactorily on the map, they may be sketched and properly labelled in vertical sections. This should be done for low-dipping structures. If, as sometimes happens, a geologic structure is in such a position that, when projected to breast height, it will lie *outside* the mapped walls of the opening (the ground lines), it is nevertheless plotted in this correctly projected position with its dip properly indicated.

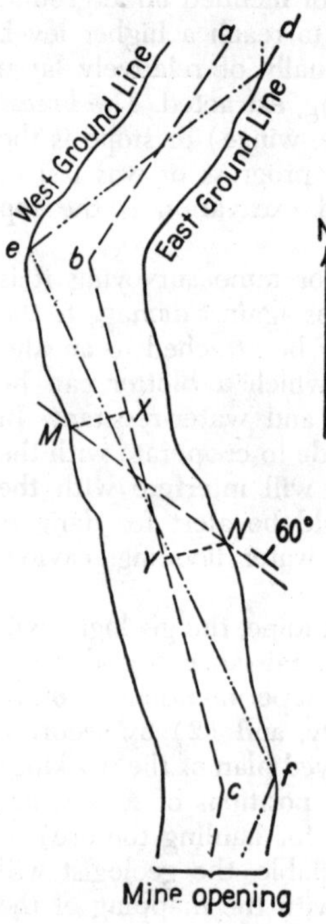

Fig. 452. Simple plot of a mine opening crossed diagonally by a fault (*MN*).

Figure 452 is a part of a mapped opening in a level. Two methods of plotting the traverse are shown. *abc* is a surveyed traverse essentially along the center line of the opening, with angles or turning points at *b* and *c*. *def* is a line surveyed from wall to wall, with turning points at *e* and *f*. *abe* is the commonest procedure. At each turning point a foresight reading is made to the next station, and also, as a check, a backsight reading may be made to the last station. A fault is intersected by the opening, as observed on both walls. Its breast-high position is at *N* on the east wall and at *M* on the west wall (Fig. 452). These points are related on the map by perpendiculars (*NY* and *MX*) to the traverse line. If these points are correctly plotted, the strike of the fault will be along *MN*. It can be checked by compass by standing at *M* and sighting at *N*, or vice versa. The dip of the fault, which should be measured from *M* looking toward *N*, or from *N* looking toward *M*, is recorded on the map as 60° northward. Irregularities of the wall should also be plotted, for they help in locating geologic features.

If the behavior of the compass indicates the proximity of magnetic disturbances at a point where the strike is read and if one has a surveyed base map, comparison can be made between the plotted azimuth of the traverse line at this same point and its direction as indicated here by the compass, and the discrepancy can then be applied as a correction to the observed strike. Local magnetic disturbances can usually be passed by foresight and backsight readings between turning points chosen on each side of the questionable area.

If an underground passage has a low slope rather than being horizontal, it can still be mapped in horizontal plan, but the amount of this slope must be noted. In plotting winzes and raises, the slope, length, and direction of the opening may be approximated by stretching a cord between corresponding points at its upper and lower ends, and measuring the inclination (allowing for sag), length, and azimuth of this cord. The inclined or vertical opening (raise, winze) can be plotted to scale in vertical section in which, also, may be shown details of the geologic structure projected to one wall. The cross-sectional dimension of the opening should be recorded.

For further details on mine surveying methods reference may be made to texts by Forrester, McKinstry, and others.

Study of Data from Drilled Holes

460. Purposes for drilling bore-holes. The purposes for which bore-holes—or, as we often say, wells—are drilled may be classified mainly under four heads: (1) to determine the stratigraphic or rock sequence penetrated by the hole; (2) to locate and evaluate, within the section penetrated, any substances (solid or liquid or gaseous) that may be of economic value; (3) if feasible to extract and bring to the surface any such economically valuable substances; and (4) to provide data for correlating, from hole to hole, the lithologic sequences penetrated in order to facilitate the plotting of underground stratigraphy and structure. The pages which follow will have particular reference to the first, second, and fourth of these purposes.

461. Methods of drilling. There are three principal methods of drilling bore-holes. These are cable drilling, rotary drilling, and diamond drilling. For the better understanding of logs, these three methods are described below, but only in the briefest way.

1. *Cable drilling* is also known as *cable-tool drilling*, the *percussion method*, or the *standard method* of drilling. The outfit consists essentially of a "string of tools," at the lower end of which is a heavy steel bit, suspended on a manila or wire cable which can be lowered or raised by controlling machinery near the mouth of the hole. In drilling, the tools are alternately lifted and dropped, the rock being cut by the repeated blows of the bit. Some water is always kept in the hole. Enough may drain in from the rocks penetrated, but if they are dry, water must be added from above. If there is too much water the impact of the bit, and therefore its effectiveness in cutting, is reduced because of buoyancy. If a water-bearing stratum yields too copious a flow, it must be "cased off" by sinking a "string" of pipe, or "casing" to a point below it. In the same way, relatively soft materials may have to be cased off to prevent their "caving."

The rock cuttings are removed in a bailer which is lowered at intervals sufficiently frequent to keep the bottom of the hole fairly clean of débris. These cuttings are dumped into a "slush pit," at the mouth of the well. They serve as specimens of the rocks drilled. Other indications of the rocks penetrated are found: (1) in mud or clay stuck to the bit; (2) in exceptional wear on the edge of the bit, caused by the drilling of sand, sandstone, or other hard, abrasive materials; (3) in the "kick," or vibration, of the cable, noticeable while drilling in hard rocks; and (4) in the observed rate at which the drilling proceeds, since hard rock is more slowly cut than soft rock.

2. *Rotary drilling*, as generally understood, is accomplished by the rotation of a perforated fishtail bit (or, in harder formations, a "rock bit") which is screwed firmly to the lower end of

a string of pipe, known as a "drill stem." The drill stem itself is rotated by a turn-table at the mouth of the hole. It is lengthened by the addition of new "joints" of pipe whenever the increasing depth of the hole demands. When the bit requires sharpening, it is raised to the surface by unscrewing the joints of the drill stem, usually in threes ("thribbles") or fours ("fourbles"), and these thribbles (or fourbles) must be screwed together again when the bit is lowered to resume drilling. During the drilling, a thin mud is kept constantly flowing downward inside the drill stem, out through the perforations in the bit, upward between the drill stem and the walls of the hole or the innermost casing, if casing has been set, and out at the mouth of the hole. This mud serves the double purpose of keeping the bit cool and supporting the walls of the uncased part of the hole by virtue of the hydrostatic pressure exerted by it (the mud fluid). By this means, in many cases, loose materials may be prevented from caving and water may be kept from entering the hole when water-bearing sands are penetrated. Where the driller expects to encounter natural gas under high pressure, he thickens the mud or adds certain heavy ingredients to it in order to hold the gas back in the sand; for otherwise the whole column of mud may be blown out, an event which may entail serious consequences. In deep holes part of the weight of the drill stem is held off the bit to prevent the hole from "going crooked," *i.e.*, deviating from a vertical course (Art. **475**). The amount of weight applied on the bit is shown by a recording weight indicator on the derrick floor.

In regions where experience in drilling one well, or perhaps several wells, has demonstrated that a considerable thickness of the formations to be penetrated is essentially dry, without danger of encountering water-bearing sands, air may be used instead of mud while drilling through these dry formations. This air is pumped down, under pressure, through the drill stem, out through the bit, and up to the surface outside the drill stem, just as in the case of the mud circulation. This so-called *air drilling* permits rapid penetration by the bit, but it does not prevent escape of gas from any possible gas-bearing sands cut in the drilling, and if sparked by friction in the drilling, it may, through its contained oxygen, ignite any such gas. To guard against this danger, gas itself (with no oxygen content) may be used in place of air. And to prevent accidents from fire at the well, equipment is used here to carry off any gas (either that discovered in the formations or that used for drilling in place of air) to some distance from the rig, where it may be safely ignited to dispose of it.

The mud, or the air or gas, returned from the bottom of the hole brings up with it cuttings of the materials drilled. They are not always easy to recognize, and furthermore, they do not appear at the surface until some minutes after they were cut. The determination of their source is assisted by the driller's observations on the behavior of the bit, indicating whether it is cutting soft or hard rock. When better samples of the rock are required, the driller uses a bit constructed to cut and retain a core of the formation penetrated. The *conventional* core bit, like the ordinary fishtail bit, is screwed to the lower end of the drill stem. Centrally, inside it, is a barrel into which the core passes as the bit cuts deeper. The drilling mud, meanwhile, passes down between this barrel and the outer metal shell of the bit; thence out at the lower end of the bit; and from there up outside the bit and drill stem. When the desired length of core has been cut (usually from 10 to 20 ft.), the core is raised to the surface for examination by the slow process of "breaking down the drill stem" in thribbles or fourbles.

For quicker results, it has become common practice to use what is termed a *wire-line core barrel.* In this tool the bit is so made that the core barrel is removable at will. During drilling, the barrel is held in place within the bit. After the core has been cut, a wire line is lowered, and the barrel is caught and raised by this line *through* the drill stem, which remains in the hole. This is a great saving of time, since it does away with the necessity of "breaking down" and "making up" the drill stem for each core, as in the case of the conventional type. (See remarks on side-hole sampling, Art. **463.**)

3. *Diamond drilling* is another process in which the cutting tool is rotated. The bit used in this method is a hollow cylinder of soft steel in the lower edge of which black diamonds are set so that they project a little way beyond the outer and inner edges of the cylinder.[2] The bit is screwed to a "core-shell" which is screwed to the lower end of a "core barrel," and the core barrel,

[2] For drilling in formations that are medium hard, a bit may be used in which, instead of diamonds, irregular pieces of specially hardened steel, such as *haystellite* and borium, have been set.

in turn, is screwed on to a string of hollow steel rods which reach to the top of the hole. In drilling, the string of rods and the tools attached thereto are rotated. The rods are clamped to a hydraulic feed which enables the driller to control the pressure applied to the bit. A stream of clear water or of thin mud is kept flowing down inside the rods and core barrel and up between the rods and the walls of the hole or the casing. This keeps the tools cool. The diamonds on the bit cut a way for the metal of the cylinder, and a core of rock is left inside the hollow bit, shell, and core barrel. As soon as the core extends to the top of the barrel, the rods must be pulled and the core removed. The pieces of the core, preserved in the order in which they were obtained, furnish an excellent record of the rocks penetrated by the hole. To check the positions at which the rock materials change in character, the rock cuttings washed up by the circulating water are examined and the action of the tools is watched.

462. Applications of drilling methods. Holes are drilled for water, or for gas or oil, or for exploratory purposes. If formations are generally soft, rotary drilling is employed. If formations are hard, rotary drilling with rock bit, or diamond drilling, or cable-tool drilling may be used. Where formations change from relatively soft to much harder at depth, or, as sometimes happens, from very hard near the surface to softer at depth, the hole may be drilled by a combination rig—partly rotary and partly percussion.

Diamond drilling of small-diameter holes to depths of a few hundred feet may serve in the mining industry to block out ores or to help decipher the subsurface geologic structure. In regions of stratified formations, shallow-hole explorations are more often done by simple rotary drilling, with or without coring. If cores are *not* taken, study of the stratigraphy and structure is then accomplished by using electrical logs (Art. **468**). The shot holes for seismographic work (see **566**) are sometimes utilized in this same way. If the shallowest available source of reliable stratigraphic information is deep—perhaps several thousand feet deep—and holes are drilled for the purpose of securing geologic information from these depths rather than primarily for oil or gas or water, they are called *stratigraphic tests,* or *slim holes* (the latter because they are drilled with smaller diameter than would be the practice if they were to be cased for production of fluids).

Shallow exploratory holes are usually drilled in groups of two or more, whereas, in the case of the deep stratigraphic tests, one such hole may be sufficient. This is because the shallow holes are drilled to secure scattered points on some underground key horizon, for subsurface correlation and structure mapping (**465**), whereas the deep tests are more commonly drilled to ascertain the vertical lithologic and other conditions in the deep stratigraphic sequence. In either case, locations for these holes are selected by the geologists. For the sake of economy they are distributed in the manner or in the order which he thinks will yield the data sought with the drilling of the smallest possible number of holes. Thus, where a dome is suspected, one test hole might be located on the supposed crest, and three or four others might be placed surrounding the first. Or, if faint indications of a fault are to be checked by coring, one or two rows of three or four holes in each should be laid out to cross the possible fault at right angles to its trend. Slim-hole drilling is useful in seeking the position and direction of stratigraphic pinch-outs (Art. **103**).

463. Reliability of samples. As far as the geologist is concerned, the type of record obtained in drilling is of great importance. The reader will perceive, from the foregoing article, that the samples secured in different methods of drilling are likely to vary considerably in their reliability. The rock core that is cut in diamond drilling, or by any improved type of core bit in ordinary rotary drilling, is by far the best index of the formations penetrated, although even this may not always be entirely accurate, since, in drilling through some kinds of rock, unless adequate provision is made, particles may be washed out of the core by the circulating water. Complete recovery of the entire length of the core that has been cut is rare.

The record obtained in cable drilling is fairly reliable if kept by a competent driller and properly interpreted by a geologist. It is subject to errors caused by: (1) too infrequent bailing; (2) loss or confusion of rock particles bailed up; (3) occasional caving of materials from points above the bottom of the hole; and (4) incorrect measurements of depths.

The least satisfactory record is that secured from the cuttings in rotary drilling, for the rocks are thoroughly ground up, the particles are mixed with mud, and considerable time may elapse between the drilling of a given rock and the appearance of its particles at the mouth of the well. Rock variations having a thickness of only a few feet are likely to escape notice. The driller pays more attention to the reaction of the bit than to the cuttings. He may call a hard sandstone layer a *lime shell,* simply because, in his experience, this sandstone has the same effect on the drilling as a limestone. The geologist must familiarize himself with the significance of the driller's terms.

Because of the many difficulties experienced in securing adequate subsurface information in cable-tool and rotary drilling, a great deal of time and thought has been devoted to inventing and perfecting the various types of core barrel. There are now in use coring devices for both cable-tool drilling and rotary drilling. Coring in cable-tool holes is done only when there is a very special reason for securing a sample of rock, since ordinarily the cuttings brought up by the bailer are sufficient. In drilling *wildcat wells* (that is wells far from known oil or gas production) by the rotary method, the hole is sometimes cored all the way down from a few feet below the surface, in order to avoid missing any possible oil or gas sands, and also in order to secure a complete record of the formations penetrated. When this is done, the hole may be cored by a relatively small bit, and then reamed to full diameter by a large bit, or the hole may be cored and simultaneously drilled to its full diameter. In the former case, coring and reaming are alternated, usually 50 to 100 ft. of depth at a time.

Most varieties of core barrel can cut the core from the bottom of the hole only, so that once the drilling has progressed beyond a given point or formation, there is no possibility of going back and taking a sample. To overcome this deficiency, several kinds of *side-hole sampler* have been devised. These take small-diameter cores from the walls of the hole, at selected points, after it has been drilled to a given depth (sometimes the total depth), but before it has been cased. These *side-hole cores* may be punched out or they may be cut by a rotary mechanism that operates at right angles to the axis of the hole.[3]

464. Oriented cores. Usually, in securing cores from a borehole, no attempt is made to ascertain how the core was oriented before it was cut out of the rock formation. On the assumption

[3] On the subject of sampling and coring, see Bibliog., Kraus, Edgar, 1924; Clark, Stuart K., and Jas. I. Daniels, 1928; and Officer, H. G., Glenn, C. Clark, and F. L. Aurin, 1926. In some respects these papers are out of date, but they are excellent presentations, each of the particular phase of the subject treated.

that the hole is vertical, if the bedding is horizontal (Fig. 453), there is no particular reason for wanting an *oriented core;* but if the strata are inclined as in Figs. 454 and 455, the determination of the *direction* of their dip may be very important. In Fig. 456 are shown an incorrect (A) and a correct (B) interpretation of an observed dip of 30° in each of four cores taken from different depths in a hole. To understand these dips correctly, their direction must be known. Actually, as indicated in B, a pronounced angular unconformity was crossed in this well. Figure 457 is a

Fig. 453

Fig. 454

Fig. 453. Core showing bedding perpendicular to axis of hole and therefore horizontal if hole were vertical. (*Figures 453–457 and Figs. 473–476 are reprinted from Bull. Am. Assoc. Petr. Geols. See Bibliog., Lahee, F. H., 1929, b.*)
Fig. 454. Core with moderate dip.

diagram of the record of a hole which, after passing through 3,500 ft. of nearly horizontal beds, unexpectedly entered a series of steeply dipping strata, which were penetrated for 400 ft. before the hole was abandoned. If an oriented core of this lower series could have been secured, the geologist would have known in what direction he must go to approach the axis of the deeply buried structure.

Several varieties of instrument have been devised for cutting cores and marking them at the time when they are cut, so that their true original orientation can be determined after they have been brought to the surface. By such means the true orientation of such cores as those diagramed in Figs. 456 and 457 can be ascertained.

An ingenious method has been developed for determining the original orientation of a core by observing its magnetic properties. As will be explained in Art. 557, the earth may be regarded as a large magnet. The system of its magnetic forces is known as its magnetic field. These forces vary in direction and intensity in different parts of the earth. Because some of the mineral constituents of common rocks have the property of acquiring and retaining a certain amount of polarity from the earth's magnetic field, cores of these rocks, having been examined by a special instrument of high sensitivity, are found to reveal polarity that they had while *in situ*. In this instrument a core under investigation is slowly rotated in a position such, with reference to two suspended magnets, that its magnetic north and south sides can be determined. For reliable results a core that is to be examined for its magnetic polarity must be carefully labeled at the well as to its top and bottom. Since the main object is to find out the direction and amount of true dip at the depth from which the core was secured, only cores with good lamination should be used, preferably shales or sandy shales. Shales with no observable bedding and sandstones with cross-bedding are of no value. The rough core, as received from the well, is accurately ground to the form of a perfect cylinder, and on it the strike and direction of dip of the lamination are marked—also its top—before it is tested for its polarity. Thus, after the examination has been completed, the original position of the core before it was cut in the hole can be correctly determined.[4]

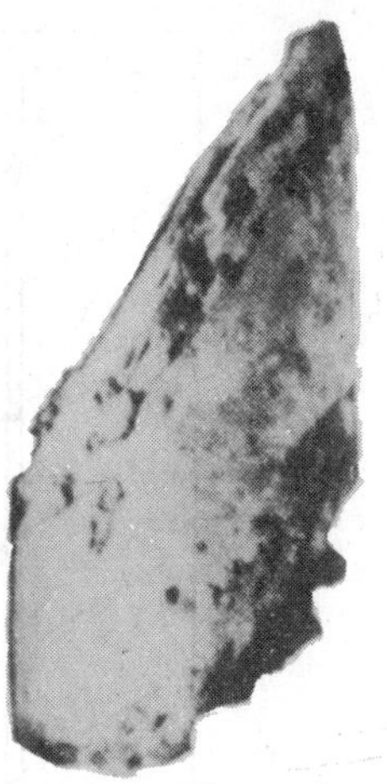

FIG. 455. Core with steep dip. This was taken in a fault zone. The dip is drag. The isolated crystals are of pyrite.

Three significant facts must be impressed upon the geologist, in considering the subject of taking oriented cores: (1) Assuming

[4] See Bibliog., Lynton, Edward, 1937, 1938.

that perfect cores can be secured, there will always be present the danger of misinterpreting cross-bedding for true bedding. This has been mentioned above. The only safeguard is to take plenty of cores for comparison and to place more reliance on laminated shales than on sandstones. (2) A dip, even if correctly measured in a core, may not correctly reflect the average or

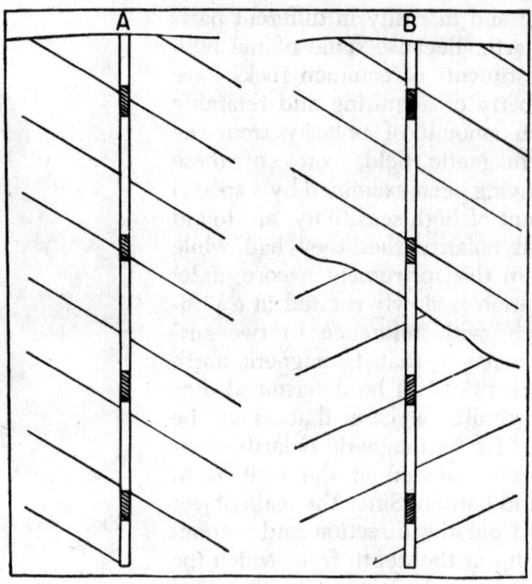

Fig. 456. Two interpretations based on four cores taken from a drilled well, as seen in vertical section.

general dip of the strata in the area where the hole was drilled. (3) If a bore-hole is not drilled vertical, the original orientation of the core in the inclined hole can be learned, but, before the true dip of the strata from which this core was cut can be determined, the angle and direction of inclination of the hole must be ascertained, and corrections must be made accordingly (**475**).[5]

Dipmeter surveying (Art. **473**) is a quicker and less expensive method for determining the attitude of beds penetrated by a

[5] For an interesting paper relating to this subject, see Bibliog., Mead, Warren, J., 1921.

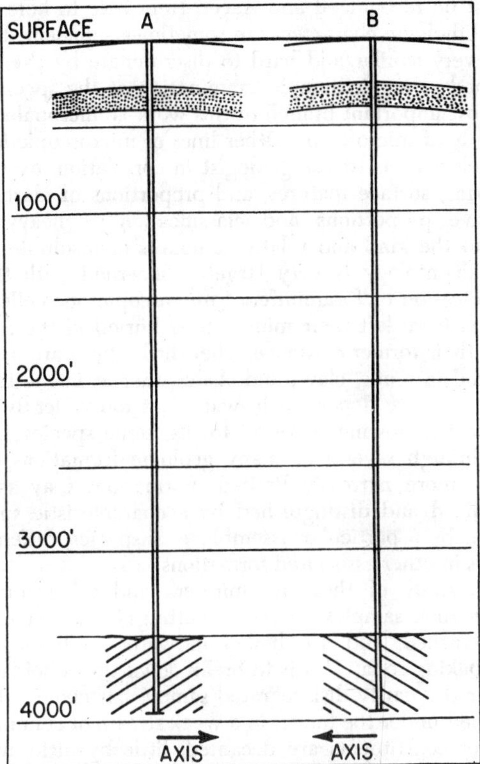

FIG. 457. Vertical section through strata penetrated by a hole which encountered steeply dipping beds at 3,500 ft. Without knowing orientation of cores from below 3,500 ft., the geologist could not tell in what direction to go to reach the axis of the deeply buried anticline.

hole and measured within the small circumference of the hole, but, like the use of oriented cores, it is subject to the three limitations just described.

465. Correlation of samples from bore-holes. In order that the records of bore-holes may be used for constructing subsurface maps and determining subsurface geologic structure, the strata penetrated by the drill must be correlated; *i.e.*, the formations must be recognized and traced from hole to hole. For this purpose, lithologic characters are sometimes sufficient; but if the beds are very similar and hard to discriminate by eye, recourse may be had to a microscopic examination of the specimens. By far the most important branch of this work is micropaleontology, or the study of microfossils. Other lines of microscopic investigations which may assist the geologist in correlation are the study of the forms, surface features, and proportions of clastic grains, the relative proportions and classification of heavy mineral grains, and the kind and relative amounts of insoluble residues.

Micropaleontology is very largely concerned with the study and classification of foraminifera,[6] microscopic one-celled organisms which have left their minute tests buried in the rocks as a record of their former existence. Their little shells are most likely to be found in muds, clays, and shales, that is, in the finer sediments which were deposited in water not too violently agitated nor too swiftly flowing. Like all fossils, some species are found ranging through several or many geologic formations, whereas others are more narrowly limited. Formations may sometimes be recognized and distinguished by a characteristic species, or more often by a particular assemblage of species, different from the species in other associated formations.

For the study of these foraminifera and other microscopic fossils, the rock samples (cores or cuttings) are first crumbled, but not crushed, and are boiled in water containing a little ordinary baking soda. This is to break down the colloidal matter. Next, after the partly disintegrated sample has cooled, it is carefully washed under the faucet in a weak stream of running water. The lighter constituents are decanted, little by little, until only a heavy residue remains. The rest of the water is then poured off and the residue is dried on the stove. In this residue will be found the shells of foraminifera, if any were present in the specimens. They can now be put on a slide and examined under the microscope.[7] The micropaleontologist must be warned always to be on his guard lest the samples be contaminated by material from higher up in the hole.

[6] Other microscopic fossils of value in this connection are diatoms, ostracods, conodonts, etc.

[7] For references on this subject see Bibliog., Cushman, Joseph A., 1924; Schuchert, Charles, 1924; Applin, Esther Richards, *et al.*, 1925; Galloway, J. J., 1926; Cushman, Joseph A., 1928; Milner, Henry B., 1929.

Where foraminifera are absent, correlation of the formations or strata may perhaps be possible through a careful study of their content of "heavy minerals," for in many localities investigation has proved that the proportions in which these mineral grains occur may differ markedly in different beds, yet hold fairly constant in one bed or formation over an area of considerable extent. These "heavy minerals" are clastic, sometimes altered in shape by secondary crystallization. Following is a list of the more common varieties, with their specific gravities. Quartz, muscovite, and biotite are noted for comparison.

Mineral	Specific gravity
Andalusite	3.16–3.20
Apatite	3.17–3.23
Biotite	2.7–3.1
Calcite	2.713
Cyanite	3.56–3.67
Epidote	3.3–3.51
Garnet	3.15–4.3
Ilmenite	4.5–5
Magnetite	5.17–5.18
Muscovite	2.76–3
Pyrite	4.5–5.1
Quartz	2.65
Rutile	4.18–4.25
Staurolite	3.65–3.75
Topaz	3.4–3.65
Zircon	4.68–4.7

In preparing samples for heavy mineral determinations, crush the rock in a mortar. If calcareous, treat with hydrochloric acid, decant, wash with distilled water, and dry. If the material is impure sand or sandy shale, boil with soda, decant, thus removing colloids, wash with distilled water and dry. If the sample contains oil, wash with benzol, chloroform, or alcohol, and dry. The dried cleaned material is then poured into bromoform having a specific gravity of 2.69 (test with a hydrometer), and contained in a funnel. The mineral grains of higher specific gravity will sink. They may be drawn off through the stem of the funnel into an evaporating dish. After the small quantity of bromoform which escapes has been decanted, the heavy residue is then washed with alcohol. To clean grains of iron coatings, heat residue with nitric acid or aqua regia, which will remove pyrite, marcasite, limonite, and other iron compounds. After drying, the grains may be mounted in balsam on a slide ready for study.

The comparison of sands by their heavy mineral content is tedious unless very striking differences are discovered. In general practice a rough count is made of the relative proportions of each such mineral in a type sample of the rock, and this assemblage is taken as the criterion for comparison.[8]

A great deal can sometimes be learned, in the way of correlation, by studying the shapes of the clastic sand grains, their surface features, such as pitting, gloss, etc., and other such features, which are largely dependent upon their mode of origin, for after all, sediments must have characteristics imposed upon them by virtue of the particular climatic and physiographic conditions under which they were transported and accumulated. To a considerable degree, a like statement applies also to microscopic fossils and "heavy minerals."

Another avenue of approach to the problem of subsurface correlation is by water analyses.[9] Within reasonable distances, the water from a given stratum may have roughly similar chemical properties, which may differ strikingly from those of the waters from overlying or underlying strata. Care must be exercised, however, in using this means of correlation, for: (1) water from the same sand may reveal very different mineral contents adjacent to faults, or other passages for fluid circulation *across* formations; and (2) from point to point the water in any given stratum is likely to show a progressive change in mineral content. Not infrequently, for example, water in a "sheet sand"[10] will contain a higher proportion of chlorides in the upper part of a closed anticlinal structure than lower on the flanks, for the reason that any circulation within the sand has probably been more active, and consequently the original connate nature of the water has been more modified by dilution, low on the flanks, nearer to the synclinal troughs or basins. Similarly, in a given sand which has a regional dip for many miles from its surface exposure, the water is apt to be freshened and modified updip toward the outcrop, where meteoric waters have ingress.

[8] For further information on this subject and on the study of insoluble residues, see Bibliog., Reed, R. D., 1924; Tickell, F. G., 1924; Ross, Clarence S., 1926; Reed, R. D., and J. P. Bailey, 1927; Milner, Henry B., 1929; McQueen, H. S., 1931.

[9] Bibliog., Ross, J. S., and E. A. Swedenborg, 1929.

[10] A sand entirely blanketing over a structure.

If samples of water cannot be obtained from bore-holes, cores of the water-bearing sands may be tested instead, and thereby a fair approximation to the composition of the water may be made. The rock specimen for analysis must be solid and as free as possible from contamination by drilling fluid, etc. It should be broken from inside the core. First, its porosity is roughly determined, thus:

1. Weigh sample, cool to 40°F. in a closed vessel to prevent condensation, dip in melted paraffin, cool to room temperature, and weigh again. The difference in weight times the specific volume of paraffin equals the volume of the paraffin.

2. Using a wide-mouthed specific gravity flask, weigh flask plus sample, then flask plus sample plus distilled water. Subtract the difference of these weights from the calibrated volume of the flask (indicated by a mark on the neck of the flask). Result is a volume of sample plus paraffin plus pore space. Subtract volume of paraffin to obtain volume of sample plus pore space.[11]

3. Peel off paraffin, crush sample, dry in oven at 212°F., cool in a desiccator, and weigh sample plus specific gravity flask. Add enough distilled water to cover sample, stir out all air bubbles, place top on flask, fill to mark on neck (for calibrated volume) and weigh again. Calculate volume of sample as in (2).[11]

4. Volume of sample plus pore space minus volume of sample equals volume of pore space.

5. Percentage porosity equals volume of pore space divided by volume of sample plus pore space.

6. Specific porosity (cubic centimeters of pore space per grain of sample) equals pore space divided by weight of original sample.

Having thus determined the approximate porosity, add to a large portion of the crushed and dried residue of the sample 250 cc. of distilled water. Run the analysis on the leachings and calculate the results in parts per million based on the volume of the pore space in the core specimen.

While this method is open to some criticism, it has met with considerable success. It has often been checked by comparing the analysis of the sample with the analysis of the water subsequently obtained from the same sand, and the results have been very satisfactory.

[11] Temperatures of water used in (2) and (3) should be observed so that corrections for volume may be made.

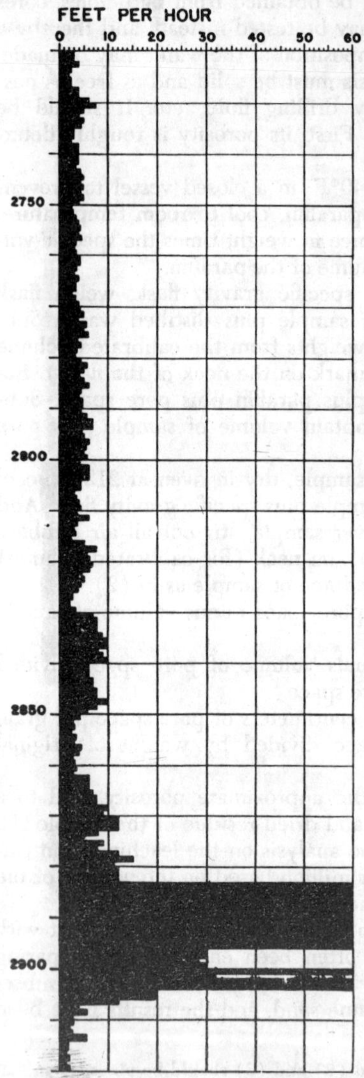

Most of the efforts at correlation so far referred to in this article concern the carrying of certain lithologic facies or sequences from well to well, and often this is the kind of correlation desired. But, as explained in Art. 89, broader problems of geology or of stratigraphy may require *time* correlations, which may cross lithologic facies, and in this case the microscopic examination of well cores and cuttings may yield valuable information from contained pollen or spores, or possibly from associated dust (bentonite) layers.

466. Drilling-rate charts. Of assistance in correctly correlating samples of strata penetrated in drilling is the driller's time chart or drilling-rate chart. Figure 458 illustrates such a chart. It records the rate at which drilling progressed through

Fig. 458. Drilling speed record. In this record, made of a well in west Texas, the rate of drilling, in feet of depth per hour, is recorded for every foot of hole drilled between certain limits (here between 2,720 and 2,920 ft.). The greatly increased rate beginning at 2,882 ft. indicates penetration of a highly porous, or soft, zone, which, in this case, carried oil. The base of this zone was between 2,904 and 2,907 ft.

formations between the depths of 2,720 and 2,920 ft. From 2,720 to 2,883 ft., drilling was relatively slow, because the formations were hard, but at 2,882 ft. there was an abrupt increase in the rate of drilling where a soft rock (here sandstone) was encountered. After passing through this zone, hard limestone was drilled at a very slow rate down to the total depth, 2,920 ft. It should be evident that this chart, when checked against the drill cuttings, may help the geologist to place the top and bottom contacts of strata that differ in their hardness. Similar records in adjoining wells facilitate subsurface correlations (Art. **499**).

467. Caliper logging. Bore-holes are never perfectly cylindrical openings from top to bottom. Hard rocks are likely to retain the diameter of the hole as it was drilled, but soft rocks, or loosely granular rocks, or materials which swell when wet, may break away to a variable extent, thus enlarging the opening by a process referred to as *caving.* To measure such variations in hole diameter, a special kind of caliper is employed, an instrument which has movable arms that press against the walls, usually in four directions, as it is hoisted from the bottom. These arms trace the configuration of the wall, and their movements are electrically transmitted to the surface where a record of the shape of the hole is automatically made as a curve called a *caliper log.* In general, limestone, dolomite, hard sandstone, and anhydrite stand up well in the hole; medium and soft sands tend to cave; and shale and salt are most susceptible to slumping with the consequent enlargement of the hole. Caliper logging is generally done in conjunction with micrologging, microlaterologging (Art. **468**), and dipmeter surveying (Art. **473**). Among other uses, caliper logs are of particular value in enabling an engineer to determine how much cement will be needed to fill the space behind the casing in certain selected parts of a hole. Also, for the geologist, they may assist in localizing the boundary surfaces of lithologic units.

468. Electrical surveying of bore-holes. The exact position from which samples come, in a drilled hole, may be more or less open to question. Cores can be more accurately located than cuttings, but often there is considerable loss of material, so that the precise depth to the top or bottom of any stratum represented by the well samples may be difficult to ascertain. Furthermore, the fluid content of cuttings and cores received at the surface is not likely to be the same as the original fluid content of the rock from which these samples came. To determine, even qualitatively, what this original fluid may have been, is frequently very desirable. For the purpose of learning more about the lithology and fluid content of rocks in the walls of a bore-hole, and in conjunction with this, for more accurately fixing the top and bottom contacts of rocks of varying character, a procedure known as *electrical surveying*,[12] or *electrical logging*, has been developed and improved to such an extent that it has become common practice in nearly all holes drilled for oil or for geologic information. In the following paragraphs electrical surveying and electrical logs are briefly described, and the uses of these logs, for the purposes just mentioned, are outlined. Their application in subsurface correlation is discussed in Art. **500**.

In electrical surveying two classes of electrical potential are measured. In the first, only currents come into play that are generated as a result of chemical and physical reactions set up between natural conditions in the rocks and certain conditions in the drilling mud in the bore-hole; whereas in the second, an electrical field is artificially imposed. Observed effects are automatically plotted as lines or "curves," called, respectively, *natural*, or *potential*, or *self-potential*, or *spontaneous potential* (*SP*) *curves*, in the first case, and *resistivity curves* in the second case (Fig. 459). The "natural curve" is also known as a *porosity curve*, or, better, a *permeability curve*. Measurements are made by lowering certain apparatus into the hole while the hole is full of drilling mud (**461**) and before it is cased, *i.e.*, while its rock walls are still exposed to the drilling fluid.

The *potential* (*natural*) *curve* represents the algebraic sum of three kinds of electrical potential resulting from pressure differences and chemical differences between the drilling fluid and the fluids in the rock formations.

1. A flow of electric energy may be caused by filtration of water out of the drilling mud (**461**) and into a porous medium (such as a sandstone penetrated by the hole) or from the porous medium into the hole. The former direction of filtration (and electrical current flow), regarded as of negative sign, is much more common, because ordinarily the mud column at any depth

[12] See Bibliog., Schlumberger, C. and M., and E. G. Leonardon, 1934; also, Bibliog., Houston Geological Society Study Group, 1939. Also Bibliog., Schlumberger Well Surveying Corporation, 1958, an excellent explanation of many kinds of logging.

in the hole is heavier (exerts more pressure) than the hydrostatic pressure at that depth. Water from the mud may be squeezed into the pores of the rock for a distance of several inches or even several feet back from the face of the hole. Occasionally the flow is in the opposite direction (positive) if strong artesian pressure or strong gas pressure forces fluid from the porous rock into the hole in spite of the resisting pressure of the mud column. These effects (negative and positive) are referred to as *electro-filtration.*

2. A second kind of electrical effect, called *half-cell electro-chemical potential,* is produced as a result of chemical conditions at the surface of a metal electrode. In a very thin layer small currents can rapidly change the chemical conditions and "polarize" the electrode. Since this action may obscure and perhaps conceal the effects of electro-filtration, precautions are taken to reduce the

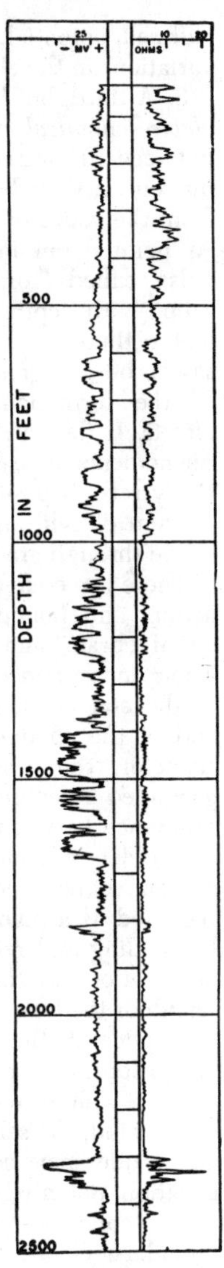

FIG. 459. Example of electrical log, showing two curves, one on each side of the central vertical column, the divisions of which mark hundreds of feet of depth in the hole surveyed. The curve on the left is called the "first curve," or "potential curve," or "permeability curve"; and that on the right is the "second curve," or "resistivity curve." A scale of millivolts (MV) is given for the first curve, and a scale of ohms for the second curve, both at the top of the log. Note (1) that permeability of sands is not well shown in the upper part of the log (say down to 1,000 ft.), where there is little difference in the composition of the drilling mud water and water in the formations; (2) that in this upper zone, where the formation waters are fresh or brackish, rather high resistivity is indicated (second curve); (3) that, with increasing depth, the positions of sands are clearly marked by indications of high permeability; and (4) that salt water present in these deeper sands shows little or no evidence of resistivity. However, near the bottom of the log is a sand that contains oil or gas, as evidenced by high resistivity. (Cf. Fig. 460.)

half-cell potential to a minimum, so that, as nearly as possible, variations in the electro-filtration potential alone will be recorded.

3. A third, but less important, electrical effect, called *boundary electro-chemical potential,* is produced by an exchange of ions between the water in the mud and the water in the porous formation, at their boundary or interface. An electric current flows from the water of lower salinity into the water of higher salinity. As pointed out in footnote 7 on page 72, underground waters (also called "formation" waters) become progressively more saline with depth. Since drilling mud is usually made with fresh water, there may be little or no electro-chemical action in upper sands, but, as greater depths are reached, the increasing salinity of the formation waters produces stronger electro-chemical effects. If the current flows from the mud into the formation the phenomenon is called negative. The reverse, which is comparatively rare, is positive. It may occur when a hole is drilled into a stratum of salt, and the mud, in its circulation, becomes highly saline through gradual solution of this salt.

These three effects—electro-filtration, half-cell electro-chemical action, and boundary electro-chemical action—are recorded as an algebraic sum in the self-potential or permeability curve. Their measurement is accomplished by lowering an electrode at the end of an insulated conductor into the hole. The upper end of the conductor is connected to one terminal of a potentiometer, the other terminal of which is connected with a grounded reference electrode near the mouth of the hole. The difference between the electrical potential of the ground (reference) electrode and the potential at any point in the hole (at the suspended electrode) is indicated by the potentiometer and is recorded as a point in the permeability curve, which is built up by reading and recording this quantity in a continuous series of observations as the suspended electrode is moved through the length of the hole.

In general, the three components of the self-potential curve are proportional to the permeability of the rock, although their absolute values may vary with the weight, viscosity, and salinity of the mud, the salinity of the formation fluid, etc. Their order of magnitude may be roughly expressed as follows: (*a*) electro-filtration potential, up to hundreds of millivolts; (*b*) half-cell electro-chemical potential, up to hundreds of millivolts; (*c*) boundary electro-chemical potential, up to tens of millivolts.

Provided variations in the half-cell electro-chemical effect are successfully reduced to a minimum, electro-filtration thus becomes the major component in the permeability curve.

Rock materials in the lithosphere differ in respect to their electrical conductivity or, conversely, their resistivity. Dense rocks, like granite, quartzite, gneiss, marble, gypsum, rock salt, anhydrite, and coal, have high electrical resistivity (Figs. 460, 461). In porous rocks the resistivity is determined by the nature and composition of the contained fluids. Fresh water has high resistivity; salt water has low resistivity; and, again, oil and gas have very high resistivity (Fig. 459). In shales and fine sediments the water held in the pores is usually relatively saline, even at shallow depths where interbedded sands may carry fresh or only brackish water. The sands that contain oil have more or less absorbed saline water on the surfaces of the mineral grains (*i.e.*, on the walls of the pores), and the effect of this water may sometimes mask or reduce the opposite effects of the oil, especially in fine sands. In view of these facts, wide variation may be expected in the resistivity characteristics of rock materials at different depths, in different stratigraphic and structural associations, and in different localities.

The characteristics of the potential curve depend largely on the *relative* electrical resistivities of the drilling mud, of the formation fluid (fluid in the pores of the rock), and of the rock itself. If the mud resistivity is about equal to that of the formation-fluid resistivity, the potential curve is featureless. If the mud resistivity is greater than the formation-fluid resistivity, the potential curve "throws" to the left, that is, toward the negative side; and vice versa (see Figs. 459–461).

As previously stated, the second class of electrical potential is measured by artificially producing an electrical field. The electrical resistivity of rocks penetrated by the hole is usually determined by sending an electric current through the ground, by battery or otherwise, and by measuring the variation in intensity of current, where only one electrode is used; or by measuring the difference in potential between two exploring electrodes where a system of four is used, one being on the surface of the ground and the other three being lowered into the hole; or by measuring certain electrical quantities by various other methods, all of which yield results that, from a practical viewpoint, are comparable. The electrical characteristics of the formations are auto-

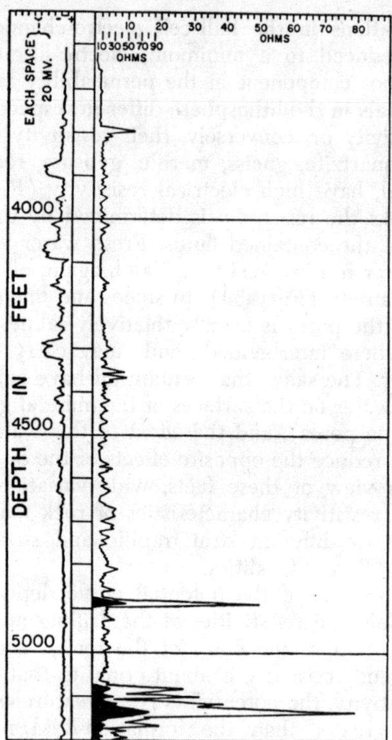

FIG. 460. Electrical log of the lower part of a hole drilled for oil. Here the beds showing very high resistance are of anhydrite, which, as indicated opposite in the first curve, is highly impermeable. (Contrast this with the oil sand near the bottom of the log in Fig. 459.) Because of the inconvenient width of a log where high resistivity is shown, as in this case, it is common practice to reduce the scale of ohms to one-fifth of the usual scale (see top of log) for the outer parts of the peaks in the curve, which are then shown shaded or, as in this diagram, solid black.

matically recorded in the form of the so-called *resistivity curve* (Figs. 459–461).

If the three suspended electrodes (in a system of four) are relatively close together, electrical effects that are measured will be the result of conditions in the immediate vicinity of the electrodes. The radius of investigation may reach only a few inches into the wall of the hole, a distance that may be less than the distance of infiltration of water from the drilling mud into a porous formation. In this case the measured electrical resistivity will not be that characteristic of the particular rock and due to its true fluid content. To obviate this difficulty, additional resistivity curves are sometimes run, with wider spacing of the suspended electrodes so that the radius of investigation of the electrical effect will be greater than the distance of infiltration of the drilling fluid. Such additional curves are commonly referred to

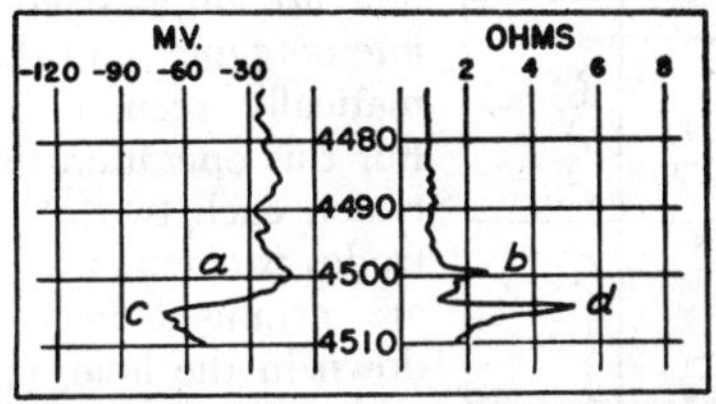

FIG. 461. Electrical log of a small part of a deep hole in south Texas. Lignite with low permeability (*a*) and relatively high resistivity (*b*), and oil sand with good permeability (*c*) and high resistivity (*d*) were penetrated in drilling this section.

as third and fourth curves (Fig. 462). The student should note that, because of the wider spacing of the electrodes for third and fourth curves, the measured resistivity is an average for a thicker zone of rock materials and is therefore less detailed than the second curve run with more closely spaced electrodes. In other words, the third and fourth curves may more surely indicate the nature of the fluids originally present in a porous stratum, but they may not so accurately determine the top and bottom and thickness of this stratum. These, however, can often be ascertained from the potential curve.

In practice, the readings for the potential (permeability) curve and for the resistivity curve (or curves) are made in the same run of the electrodes in the hole. By electrical controls it is possible to separate the measuring of these two kinds of curves although both are plotted on the same strip of paper.

The electrical logging described so far is referred to as *conventional.* It includes recording of the self-potenial (first) and resis-

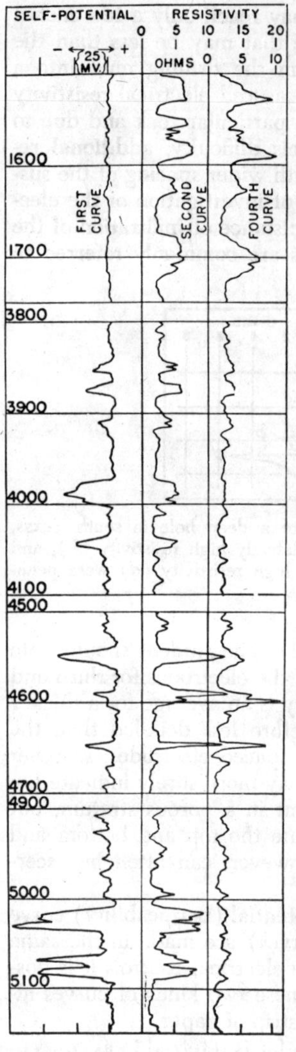

tivity (second, third, and fourth) curves as what may be called *macrologs.* Instead of increasing the distance between the three electrodes for greater penetration of the electric current, as for the third and fourth curves, the opposite procedure may be followed with the result that the penetration is much less, but details of the lithology immediately adjacent to the hole are emphasized. This is called *micrologging,* and the record automatically secured is a *microlog.* For this operation the distance between each two of the three electrodes is commonly 1 in. The three are arranged in a row, up and down in the hole, in an insulating pad which is pressed against the wall of the hole. Two records are made, one of the effects of a current which enters the hole from the lowest electrode *A,* passes through a small volume of the wall material, and goes out through the middle electrode *B;* and the other, of

Fig. 462. Electrical log showing first, second, and fourth curves (third curve omitted for sake of clarity). At shallow depths the second and fourth curves are similar (fresh water). With increasing depth, peaks in the second curve are not always duplicated in the fourth curve. Fresh water from the drilling mud may have penetrated a few inches into the wall, but not far enough to affect the fourth curve. A definite peak in both second and fourth curves may indicate an oil sand or a gas sand if the first curve shows a fair degree of permeability.

the effects of the same current which enters from A, but goes out through the upper electrode C, by a somewhat longer path than that through B. These currents reflect the resistivity effects of the mud, called the "mud cake" (from the drilling fluid), which is plastered against the wall of a rotary hole and which, in the more permeable beds, invades the rock formation some distance. Micrologging is essentially logging of the thickness of the mud cake, the thickness being greatest where permeability has facilitated maximum infiltration. Therefore, micrologging presents an index of the relative permeability of the individual beds in a sedimentary series, and also it serves clearly to mark the boundaries of these beds. It is of particular value in discriminating sandstone layers from shale layers (or sand layers from clay layers) in an alternating series of these materials, and it helps to indicate the positions of porous zones within a limestone or dolomite (see Figs 463–465). It can be used for quantitative determinations of porosity but not of permeability.

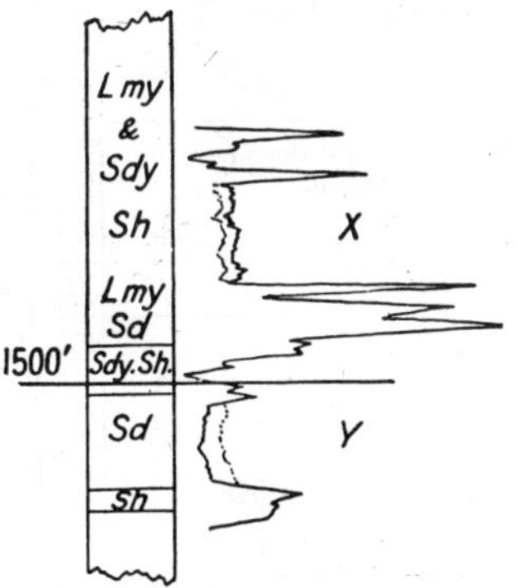

FIG. 463. Part of a microlog showing variations due to an alternation of more permeable (throw to left) and less permeable (throw to right) layers in a series of shales, sandy shales, sands, and limestones. The solid line is the curve for one exploring electrode (B), and the dotted line (obscured or lost at the strong kicks to the right and therefore here omitted) is the curve for the other exploring electrode (C). The amount and direction of separation of these curves may have significance. It is negative separation opposite X and positive separation opposite Y.

Summarizing then, we may say that electrical surveying of bore-holes provides us with a record of certain characteristics of the formations drilled. On one side of the conventional electrical log (macrolog), we have the first, or potential, curve reflecting permeability variations in the rocks; on the other side we have one or more (second, third, fourth, etc) resistivity curves that, by high figures may indicate dense, nonporous rocks or fresh water, sulphur water, oil, or gas in porous rocks, and, by low

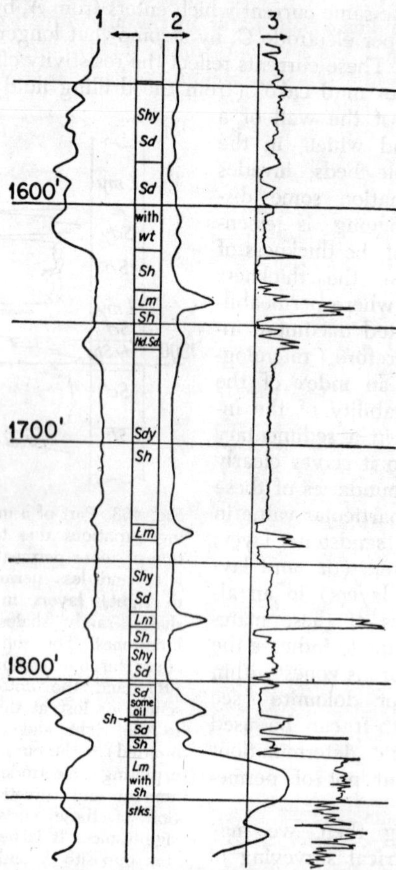

Fig. 464. Part of a conventional electric log with potential (1) and resistivity (2) curves, and, to the right for comparison, a microlog (3) through the same section of the hole. The lithologic facies are indicated in the column. Depth is shown on the left. Note high permeability and low resistivity (salt water) of sand near 1,600 ft. depth; low permeability and high resistivity of limestones near 1,645, 1,740, and 1,775 ft. and below 1,825 ft.; low permeability and low resistivity of shale (*e.g.*, between 1,660 and 1,730 ft.); high permeability and high resistivity of sand carrying oil just below 1,800 ft.

figures, may indicate salt water in porous formations, whether permeable (sand, etc.) or not (mud, shale). For more precise delimitation of the top and bottom contacts of thin strata, and for additional quantitative determinations of permeability in these beds, we can use the microlog. The student must always

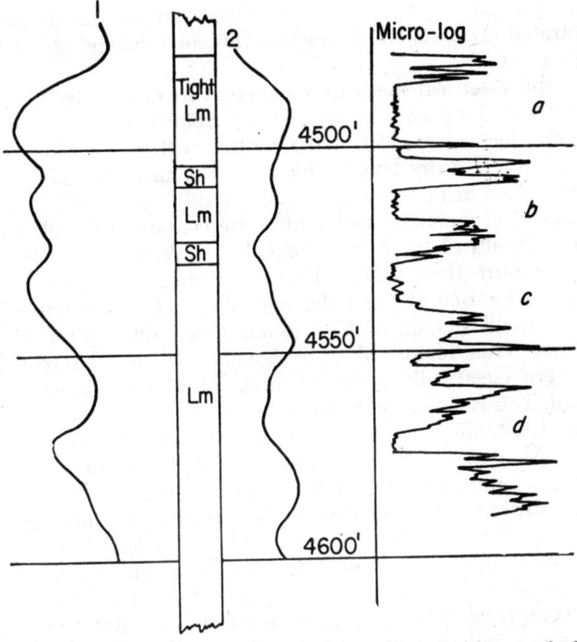

FIG. 465. Short portion of an electric log through limestone which has porous streaks. The potential (1) and resistivity (2) curves are of very little value here, but the microlog clearly demarks the porous zones (*a, b, c, d*) from the intervening impermeable zones.

remember that these electrical logs picture a resultant of many factors, so that rules cannot be too rigid as to the significance of individual peaks and depressions in the lines, nor as to the quantitative measure of these peaks and depressions on the horizontal scales employed (millivolts for self-potential curves; ohms for resistivity curves).

Conventional electrical logging and micrologging are used for the most part in holes drilled with mud that has a fresh-water base. When saline mud is used, or when fresh-water mud becomes saline in drilling through salt formations, electrical logging requires certain changes in the arrangement and number of electrodes and in the order of activation of these electrodes for satisfactory recording of the characteristics of the formations penetrated. These methods include "microlaterologging," "laterologging," etc.[13]

All the electrical methods mentioned so far involve the artificial sending of an electric current from a source of energy through electrodes which make contact with the mudded walls of the hole. In a dry hole (cable-tool hole, air-drilled hole) or in a rotary hole drilled with an oil-base mud (*i.e.*, a mud in which oil instead of water is used), adequate contact of the electrodes with the walls of the hole is difficult or impossible. In this case the rock formations surrounding the logging apparatus, as it is lowered or raised in the hole, are energized by induction, and (omitting all details of description here) differences in conductivity (the reciprocal of resistivity) in the different rock types are electrically recorded on a log at the surface of the ground. This is called induction logging.

469. Continuous velocity logging, or sonic logging. In the year 1951 a new method of logging called *continuous velocity logging*, or *sonic logging*, or *acoustical logging*, was in the process of experimentation. The method consists of automatically recording the variations in acoustical properties of the formations penetrated by the bore-hole. The instrument, when lowered in the hole, is kept parallel to the axis of the hole by centralizers. It is comprised either of a transmitter and one detector or of a transmitter and two detectors. In all cases these elements of the instrument are separated by acoustic insulators. The space between the detectors varies according to the nature of the results required. One foot has been regarded as most satisfactory, but a spacing of 3 ft. may be preferred. Sharp pulsations are produced in the transmitter at the rate of 1 to 10 per second, and these in part travel across the mud in the hole into the rock wall, through a short section of this rock wall, back across the drilling mud column, and into the detectors. The variations in acoustic

[13] Detailed explanations of these methods may be found in Bibliog., Schlumberger Well Surveying Corporation, 1958; and Welex, Inc., 1959.

velocity of the rock section, recorded at short time intervals as the instrument is lowered (or raised) at a uniform rate of 100 to 150 ft. per min., are transmitted electrically to the surface and are there automatically recorded as curves, similar in appearance to electric logs.

The sonic log records *transit time, i.e.*, the time required for sound to travel a distance of 1 ft. through the rock formation. The unit of measurement is the microsecond (or one millionth of a second) per foot. Transit times vary from 40 microsec. per ft. in hard formations to as high as 200 microsec. per ft. in recent beds or in ordinary drilling muds. These times correspond to velocities of 25,000 to 5,000 ft. per sec.[14] Table 13, which is taken

TABLE 13. SONIC VELOCITIES AND TRANSIT TIMES FOR VARIOUS MATERIALS

Material	*Sonic velocity, ft. per second*	*Transit time, microseconds per ft.*
Oil	4,300	232
Water	5,000–5,300	200–189
Neoprene	5,300	189
Shale	6,000–16,000	167–62.5
Rock salt	15,000	66.7
Sandstone	Up to 18,000	55.6
Anhydrite	20,000	50.0
Limestones (carbonates)	21,000–23,000	47.6–43.5
Dolomites	24,000	42

from the article by Tixier *et al.*, just cited, shows approximate sonic velocities and transit times for several types of rock material.

In the harder formations the sonic log reflects the amount of fluid in the rock, so that it bears a direct relation to the porosity. Sonic logs are often run in conjunction with self-potential electric logs, or with gamma-ray logs (see Art. **471**), to facilitate interpretations of the records. As may be seen in Fig. 536, sonic logs may be useful in stratigraphic correlation. In hard-rock country, with limestone, dolomite, and anhydrite sequences, the

[14] These statements are from Bibliog., Tixier, M. P., R. P. Alger, and C. A. Doh, 1959. See also Bibliog., Breck, H. R., S. W. Schellhorn, and R. B. Baum, 1957.

correlation with lithology is in many instances superior to that of electric logs. Not only are these sonic logs of value for purposes of stratigraphic correlation, but also, because of the detailed velocity information furnished by them, they may greatly assist the seismologist in his interpretations of the records obtained in conventional seismic exploration (see page 790).

470. Geothermal data in relation to geology; temperature logging. That the temperature of the lithosphere increases with depth is a well-known fact. The rate of increase with depth is called the *temperature gradient*. In different localities it has a wide range in values, but, in general, the average may be regarded as 1°F. increase for every 50 to 60 ft. of depth. Estimates are usually made from the mean annual soil temperature at the earth's surface, this value being added to depth in feet times the rate of temperature increase per foot. Tables giving data on temperature gradients have been prepared by Van Orstrand, who pioneered in this study.[15]

Measurement of subsurface temperature is usually made by a resistance thermometer in preference to the old type of fluid thermometer. The effectiveness of the resistance thermometer is based on the fact that the electrical resistance of a conductor varies as a function of its temperature. As the thermometer is lowered into a well, the temperature changes are continuously recorded at the surface. These observations, referred to as *temperature logging*, may be made along with electrical logging of the hole (Art. 468).

The causes of temperature increase with depth and the causes of variation in the gradient are problems still under investigation. Some causes for abnormally high (steep) gradient are (1) proximity to igneous intrusive bodies; (2) proximity to a granitic (or other crystalline) basement; and (3) ascending hot water or hot gases. Causes for an abnormally low gradient are (1) freely circulating cool waters and (2) expanding gas.

Subsurface temperatures are of interest to geologists in two ways: (1) They may be indicative of certain lithological and fluid conditions in the rocks penetrated by drilling; and (2) they may suggest certain structural conditions, especially when they have been recorded and correlated in numerous wells in a given district.

[15] Bibliog., Van Orstrand, C. E., 1926; 1934, pp. 1009–1021.

1. The release of some gas from a sand, in which it has been under considerable pressure, results in its expansion, and, since expansion is a cooling process, this may cause a distinct lowering of temperature, as measured in a drilled hole, opposite the gas-bearing stratum (Fig. 466). Similarly, an oil-bearing sand may be indicated by a drop in temperature opposite the sand, because of expansion of the gas released from the oil. Where, in drilling for petroleum, mud in a rotary hole is heavy enough to prevent escape of gas from the formation, there is no expansion and therefore no cooling effect. But if the mud is too light in weight gas may escape and perhaps cause a blow-out, in which case its source can be determined. Also, in cable-tool holes and in rotary holes drilled with air, gas sands can be located by the cooling effect of the expanding gas. Strata containing cool subsurface water—usually only at shallow depths—produce local cooling effects. On the other hand, strata carrying hot water may be shown on the graph by an abrupt temperature rise. Changes of temperature of this kind are most evident when there is opportunity for the fluid (gas, oil, or water) to pass into the hole. Even when a hole has been cased, the temperature effects may sometimes be detected through the casing, especially if extraction of these fluids from adjacent wells has brought about their movement, or has facilitated expansion of gas, through the body of the containing porous strata.

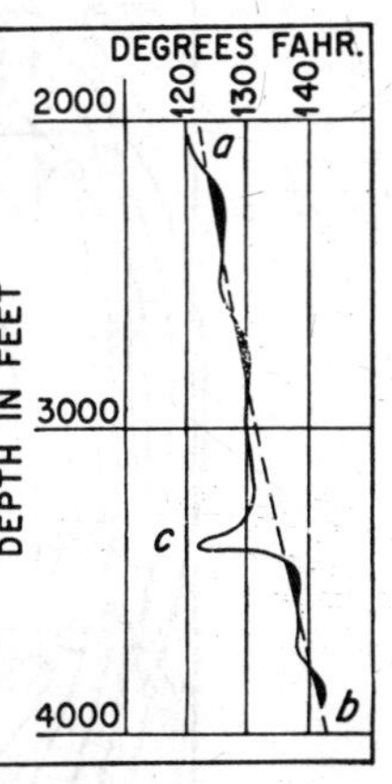

FIG. 466. Part of a temperature curve run in a hole drilled for oil. The average increase of temperature with depth is indicated by line *ab*. The sharp lowering of temperature at *c*, about 3,400 ft. below the ground surface, suggests a gas sand at this depth.

2. Of much more significance for geologists are the particular relations of subsurface temperatures to geologic structure. Investigations made in Wyoming and California by Van Orstrand,[16] beginning as far back as 1920, indicated that temperatures measured in a well on the crest of an anticline increase more rapidly with depth than the temperatures in wells drilled lower

[16] Bibliog., Van Orstrand, C. E., 1924; 1926; also, Thom, W. T., Jr., 1925.

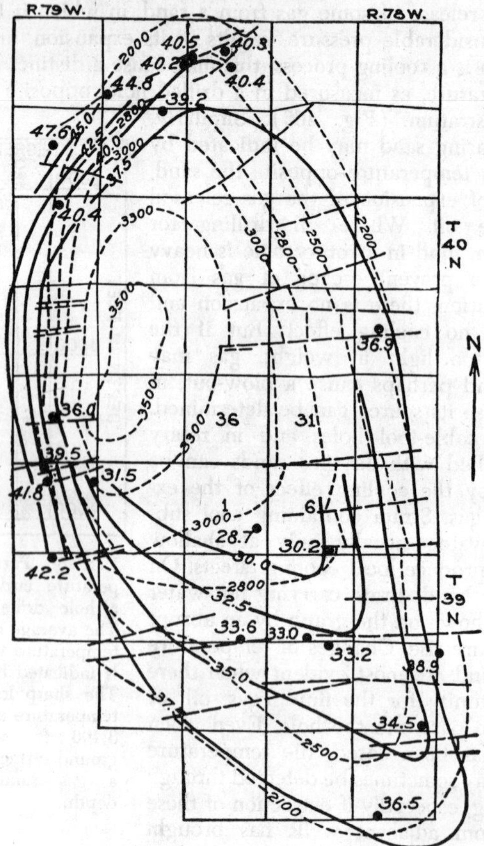

FIG. 467. Salt Creek Dome, Wyo. Dashed contours show elevation of top of Second Wall Creek sand above sea level; solid lines are of equal temperature gradient; dots and heavy figures show locations of wells and temperature gradients (showing ratio of increase in feet per 1°F.). (*Prepared by W. T. Thom, Jr., from data furnished by C. E. Van Orstrand. Reprinted with permission of Economic Geology.*)

on the flanks of the structure; in other words, that in any given horizontal plane across the structure, the temperature is higher at the crest of the fold than on the flanks (Fig. 467).

In Oklahoma, Kansas, Texas, and California, careful research under the auspices of the American Petroleum Institute revealed the interesting relations described below.[17] In all cases measurements were made in drilled wells.

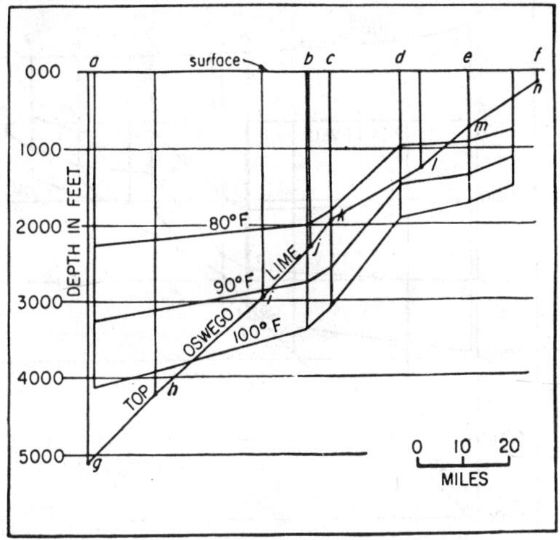

Fig. 468. Cross section showing depth to isothermal surfaces as determined in wells along a general line from Tulsa to Oklahoma City. (The profile on top of the Oswego lime was added by the present writer to show the general relations between the geothermal surfaces and the regional dip. The letters refer to locations of wells in the section.) (*After John A. McCutchin; reproduced with permission of the Am. Assoc. Petr. Geols.*)

In Oklahoma, a most striking condition brought out by these studies is the general westward dip of the isothermal (equal temperature) surfaces, in the direction of the regional dip of the strata, and the convergence of these surfaces eastward. "The 100° isothermal surface is only approximately 1,500 ft. deep near Tulsa, although this surface is more than 4,000 ft. deep

[17] Bibliog., Heald, K. C., 1930; McCutchin, John A., 1930.

near Oklahoma City,"[18] some 70 miles down the regional dip from Tulsa. In other words, the steeper gradient (more rapid rate of increase) and the higher temperatures at any given depth are found where the basement rock complex, on which the sediments rest, is at shallowest depth. In Fig. 468, copied from McCutchin, we have drawn a line roughly corresponding to the top of the Oswego lime, encountered in wells approximately along

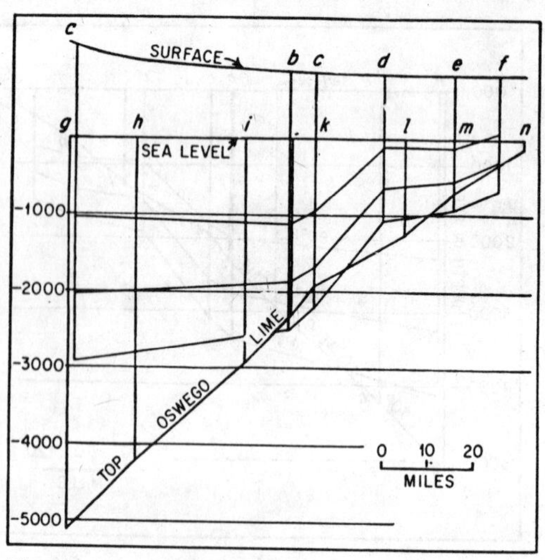

Fig. 469. This diagram shows the same data as those in Fig. 468, but we have referred both the geothermal measurements and the position of the Oswego lime to sea level. The letters merely designate the location of wells in the section (*Prepared by F. H. L.*)

the course of McCutchin's profile. In Fig. 469 the same facts are shown more nearly in their correct relations, for here account is taken of the westward rise of the land surface, from which McCutchin plotted his data referred to depth, and not to sea level. Although the dip of the strata and the dip of the isothermal surfaces are similar northeast of *i*, there is a distinct rise in the latter in the region of the Oklahoma City anticline (not shown in Fig. 469).

[18] Bibliog., McCutchin, John A., 1930, p. 541.

In Oklahoma and Kansas a definite relation between local structure and geothermal gradients was observed, though not in all instances. "The variations within individual fields (oil pools on structure) are ordinarily small but measurable and fairly uniform. The variations from area to area are large and seem to bear a relation to the regional dip of the formations."[19]

In Texas, the symmetrical, domelike structure of the Big Lake field in Reagan County was "clearly reflected by the temperature measurements,"[20] but only by the temperatures below a depth of 2,000 ft. On four salt domes examined, temperatures were highest on top of the dome, and less on the flanks.

In California "the results of this work . . . show conclusively that in fields of the Los Angeles Basin type the temperatures . . . reflect structure. Higher temperatures are found over the centers of domes or anticlines than near the edges of the folds."[21]

In general, a large proportion of the structures investigated showed "a well-defined variation with the highest temperature always at or near the crest of the anticline."[22] Although these relations are subject to considerable variation and may not always be evident, their study and correlation offer a useful method of seeking concealed geologic structures, through measurement of temperatures in comparatively shallow holes.

471. Use of radioactivity in logging bore-holes.[23] Rocks of various kinds are radioactive in different degrees. Their radioactivity may be due to minerals that were formed in their origin, as in igneous rocks, or to minerals transported and redeposited, as in sedimentary rocks. In the present connection the important fact is that apparently the radioactivity of a given stratum, or of a given rock type, may be remarkably constant and therefore characteristic over wide areas. Among sedimentary rocks, shales are commonly most highly radioactive, particularly black or dark-colored shales; whereas sandstones, limestones, and dolomites are less radioactive.

The measurement and recording of radioactivity variations in drilled holes is called *radioactivity logging*. Two classes of radio-

[19] Bibliog., McCutchin, John A., 1930, p. 554; also, Van Orstrand, C. E., 1934, p. 998.

[20] Bibliog., Heald, K. C., 1930, p. 107; also, Van Orstrand, C. E., 1934, p. 993.

[21] Bibliog., Heald, K. C., 1930, p. 109.

[22] Bibliog., Van Orstrand, C. E., 1934, p. 1004.

[23] Bibliog., Schlumberger Well Surveying Corporation, 1958.

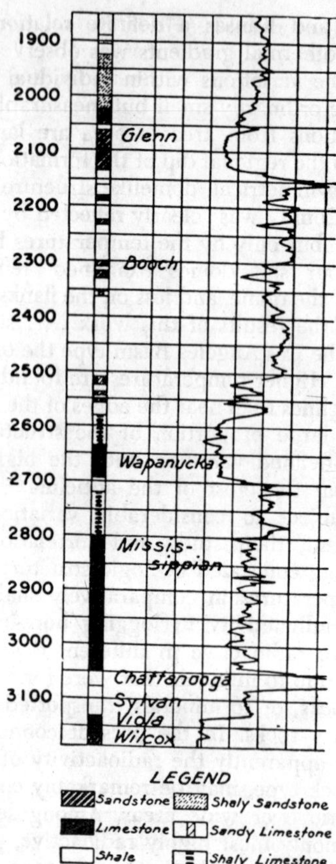

FIG. 470. Gamma-ray log of part of a hole in Oklahoma. To the left of the gamma-ray curve is a lithologic log for comparison. Note the high peak indicated in the gamma-ray curve for the Chattanooga shale. (*Reproduced with permission of Well Surveys, Inc., Tulsa, Okla.*)

activity are studied, namely, gamma rays and neutrons, and although each of these must be measured in a separate run of the instrument into the hole, both records are usually plotted on the same strip of paper as a *radioactivity log*. On this log the *gamma-ray curve* is on the left, and the *neutron curve* is on the right, of the center line. In both cases, increase in intensity is toward the right (see left side of Fig. 471).

The most essential part of the instrument which is used to survey radioactivity variations in a bore-hole is the ionization

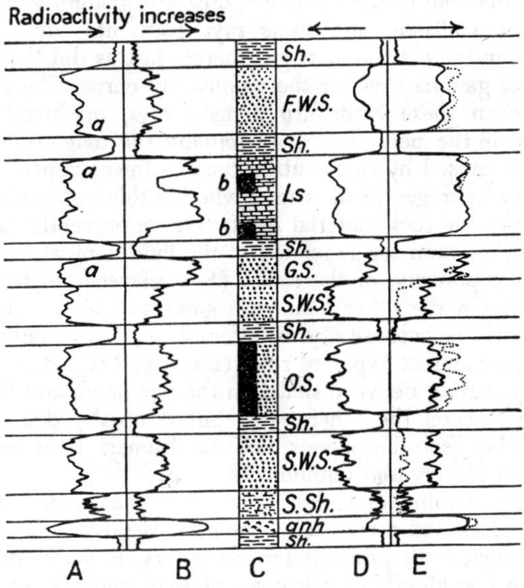

FIG. 471. Comparison of radioactivity logs (A,B) and electrical logs (D, E), and their correlation with rock conditions (lithologic log, C) encountered in a bore-hole. A, gamma-ray curve; B, neutron curve; D, natural potential curve; E, resistivity curves (full line, shallow penetration; dotted line, deep penetration). *Sh.*, shale; S.*Sh.*, sandy shale; *F.W.S.*, fresh-water sand; S.W.S., salt-water sand, G.S., gas sand; *O.S.*, oil sand; *anh.*, anhydrite; *b*, porous zones in limestone. Note that the positions of contacts between different lithologic units are taken midway of the sloping transition lines of the curve, as at *a*. The dotted resistivity curve is the "fourth curve" on a smaller scale, in ohms, than that for the "second curve," which is drawn solid. (*Reproduced with permission from "Tomorrow's Tools Today," Vol.* 13, *p.* 5, *published by Lane-Wells Company.*)

chamber. In this chamber is an inert gas under considerable pressure. Gamma rays, which penetrate from the rock formations into this chamber, cause the gas to conduct an electrical current which, after amplification and transmittal to the surface of the ground in the equipment, is there recorded as the gamma-ray curve (Fig. 470). For neutron logging, there is, below the ionization chamber, a "source chamber" within which is a "source of fast-moving neutrons." These neutrons,[24] by bombarding the strata in the wall of the bore-hole, create *secondary* gamma rays by atomic collision, and these rays pass into the ionization chamber and affect the inert gas therein just as did the *primary* or *natural* gamma rays for the gamma-ray curve. The curve resulting from these *secondary* gamma rays, produced by the neutrons, is the neutron curve. Actually the magnitude of the radiations caused by this neutron bombardment depends on the amount of hydrogen in the strata, whether this hydrogen is in oil or water or the rock material itself, and consequently to a large extent the neutron log is related to the fluid content, and therefore to the porosity, of the rocks. (See reference to porosity in Art. 469.) On the other hand, the gamma-ray log marks lithological changes because of the different degrees of radioactivity present in different types of rock (see Fig. 471). It is effective in discriminating between shale, on the one hand, and limestone or sandstone, on the other hand, but it usually does not distinguish between limestones and sandstones. It is especially useful in exploring for uranium ores.

The great value of radioactivity as a means of subsurface study rests on the fact that it can be measured in cased holes. Gamma rays, both primary and secondary as above described, penetrate considerable thicknesses of iron, and also of cement, so that, with proper equipment for measuring radioactivity, it is possible to determine the top and bottom contacts and correct thicknesses of strata that were not satisfactorily logged when the hole was drilled. Other methods of log determination and correlation must be applied only in open (uncased) holes.

472. Density logging.[25] A special application of radioactivity in recording lithologic variations in a bore-hole is *density logging*, or *densi-logging*, in which scattered gamma rays are utilized after these rays have passed through selected intervals of the rock formation. The density, or "bulk density," of any rock is the combination of the density of the rock material (grain

[24] Neutrons are certain constituents of atoms. The theory relating to their nature need not concern us here.

[25] See Bibliog., Baker, P. E., 1957; also Campbell, John L. P., and John C. Wilson, 1958.

material) and the fluid contained in the pores of the rock. In density logging, the bulk density is measured. Therefore, since the grain density can be separately determined, the porosity, *i.e.*, the pore space occupied by any fluids (such as water, oil, or gas), can be calculated. The instrument used in density logging contains a gamma-ray source and, above this, a detector. Because contact with the wall of the hole is essential for satisfactory results, a spring on one side of the instrument is used to press the latter into close contact with the opposite side of the hole. To provide data for correction of the density records, the hole is caliper-logged (Art. **467**) and the mud weight is noted at the time of logging. Since high-density material absorbs more gamma rays than material of lower density, changes in the bulk density of the rock material are measured by the detector and these are transmitted by the suspending cable to the surface of the ground, where they are recorded as a log. Not only can these logs be used to assist in subsurface stratigraphic correlations (Fig. 537) and in determinations of porosity and fluid content, but also they can furnish valuable data for interpretation of gravity surveys (Art. **556**).

473. Dipmeter surveys.[26] An electrical method is often employed, instead of oriented cores (Art. **464**), for measuring the amount and direction of dip of the strata penetrated by a drilled hole. This is accomplished by an instrument called a *dipmeter*, a long cylindrical assembly, with flexible spring guides at the upper and lower ends, and in the middle of its length, a triple electrode. These three electrodes are set 120° apart on a circle perpendicular to the length of the instrument (and the axis of the hole). In operating, the three electrodes are pressed by springs against the wall of the hole, and a continuous record is made by each as the instrument is raised in the hole. The point at which each electrode meets a given formation contact (as between sandstone and shale) is electrically indicated both as to depth and as to azimuth, for the dipmeter includes, as an integral part of its assembly, a photographic means (photoclinometer) of registering directions of the contact points of the electrodes. This photoclinometer also determines the inclination, or drift, of the hole from the vertical and the azimuth of this

[26] The following description refers chiefly to the apparatus serviced by Schlumberger Well Surveying Corporation, and is used with their kind permission.

drift. Whether the hole is vertical or inclined, the dip of a recognizable contact in the stratification can be determined either by descriptive geometry (see Fig. 472) or better by a machine which is provided for the purpose. Since the directions are here found by magnetic compass, the recorded directions will

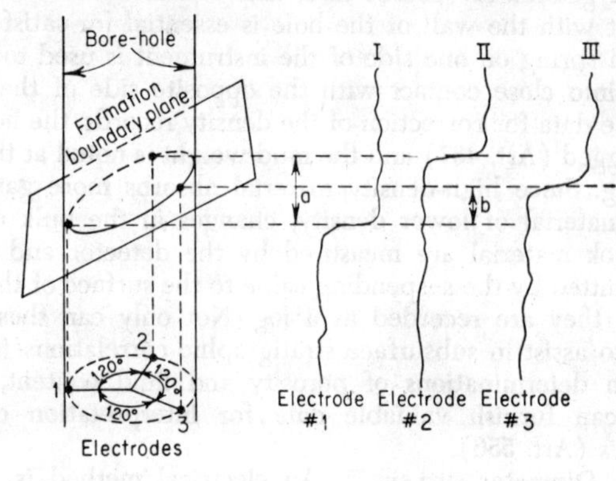

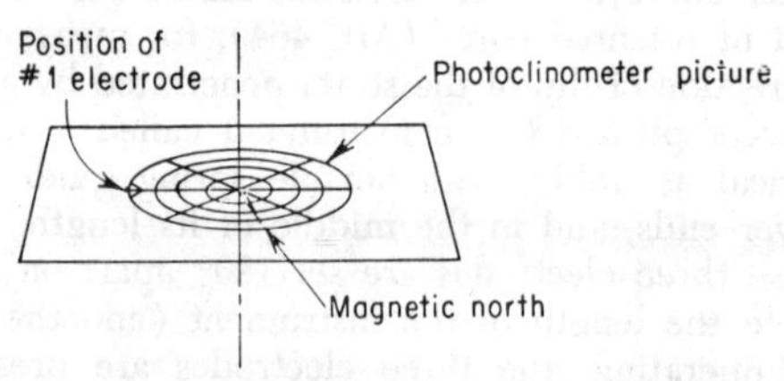

FIG. 472. Diagram to illustrate the relations of the three electrodes of the dipmeter to an inclined formational contact. If the dipmeter is raised in the hole, the electrodes, as pictured here, would record the position of the contact successively in the order, 1, 3, and 2. (*Copied, with permission of the Schlumberger Well Surveying Corporation, from their circular "Photoclinometer Directional Surveys and Dipmeter Surveys."*)

be magnetic, and these will have to be corrected to obtain true directions (see Art. **356**). Two of the three limitations, mentioned near the end of Art. **464** for oriented cores, apply equally well to dipmeter survey readings (see Art. **475**). These are (1) the risk of measuring cross-bedding instead of true bedding and (2) the possibility that local dip and strike measured in the hole do not exactly reflect the attitude of the strata in the adjacent area.

474. Applications of sampling and logging methods. In Art. **465**, following a discussion of rock samples and cores from drilled holes, we considered how these samples and cores could be used in the subsurface correlation of geologic formations. In our descriptions of the various logging methods (Arts. **468–473**), we referred mainly to their use in recording conditions in, or close to, the individual well. However, these logging methods are of great value to the geologist in defining formation contacts for local and regional correlation in the study of subsurface stratigraphy and structure. Both kinds of information, from rock samples and from logging methods, should be studied together, for their mutual relationships may often yield better results than either taken alone. For a brief outline of the applications of these logging methods in subsurface correlation, see Arts. **500** and **501.**[27]

475. The problem of crooked holes. Except under special conditions, when a hole is drilled into the ground for water, or oil, or gas, or simply for information as to subsurface geology, the intention is to drill it vertical. One can easily realize, however, that if too great pressure is put upon the bit by forcing it, or by not lifting some of the weight off the drill-stem in deep holes, the drill-stem is likely to bend or lean in the hole and crowd over to one side, with the result that the hole wanders off a plumb line. To illustrate, holes have been found to go off the vertical as much as 30° or more with no indication of this condition in the drilling. Several very curious instances are known where two wells, started on the surface several hundred feet apart, ran into one another at depth.[28] This, of course, would apply to diamond drilling and rotary drilling, but not to the cable-tool method, though even here *crooked holes*[29] have been drilled.

There are several important causes for this tendency of holes to deviate or drift, but we cannot discuss them now.[30] The main points to remember are, that while a great deal of careful study was given to this problem in 1927 to 1929 with the result that

[27] Explanations of the various kinds of logging are given in Bibliog Haun, J. D., and L. W. LeRoy, 1958.

[28] Bibliog., Lahee, F. H., 1929 (*b*).

[29] By *crooked hole,* a drilling term, we mean simply any hole wh deviates from its predetermined course—generally a hole that devi from the vertical.

[30] Bibliog., Dodge, John Franklin, 1930; also Lahee, F. H. *op. cit.*

better drilling methods have very greatly reduced the amount of deviation of holes and the number of holes which are still drilled off plumb, nevertheless: (1) in some regions and on some types of structure the drilling of vertical holes is difficult; (2) the increasing depths of drilling for petroleum[31] mean that holes that have only a small angular deviation may be far to one side of their intended position at the bottom; and (3) if a hole is not vertical, then obviously certain geologic inferences, based on the data recorded in the well, may be in error, and perhaps seriously so.[32] Resulting misinterpretations of geologic structure are illustrated and described in Art. **508.**

A phase of this problem in which the geologist is vitally interested is the correct interpretation of oriented cores (Art. **464**) and of dipmeter surveys (Art. **473**). On the assumption that cores can be secured in such a manner that their original orientation before they were cut, can be ascertained (Art. **464**), then it becomes necessary, in a hole which deviates from the vertical, to find out in what direction and how much the hole is off plumb; for otherwise estimates of the position of the cores from this hole are incorrect. Similarly, with a dipmeter survey, the dip estimated from the three electrode records on a given stratigraphic contact must be corrected for the inclination of the hole.

"The study of cores for their orientation and the determination of the direction of true dip is not easy. For instance: (1) in a vertical hole penetrating horizontal strata, the lamination is at right angles to the axis of the

[31] The deepest well in the world in July, 1930, was the Mascot No. 1, drilled, but not then completed, by the Standard Oil Co. of California, in the Midway field of California. It was 9,629 ft. deep on July 1. On Jan. 1, 1940, 427 holes had been drilled, in different parts of the world, to over 10,000 ft. The deepest hole drilled up to that time was completed in 1938 in California to a total depth of 15,004 ft. This was the Continental Oil Company's KCL A-2 in Kern County (see the *Oil Weekly*, vol. 96, Pt. 8, pp. 68–74, Jan. 29, 1940). At the end of 1950, the deepest hole in the world was the Pacific Creek well, drilled by the Superior Oil Company in Sec. 27, 27 North, 103 West, in Sublette County, southwest Wyoming. It was abandoned as a dry hole 20,521 ft. deep in June, 1949. In 1959, the deepest hole in the world was Phillips Petroleum Company's University 1-EE in Pecos County, Texas. It was plugged and abandoned at a total depth of 25,340 ft. after 2½ years of drilling.

[32] Contracts for drilling commonly require that the hole be kept within a stipulated small angle (3° or 5°) of deviation from its intended course. This angle is usually 2° for shallower holes, increasing to 3° or 4° for deeper holes.

core. If (2) the beds are horizontal and the hole is inclined, the angle between the axis of the core and the lamination is equal to the inclination of the hole (Fig. 474). If (3) the beds dip, let us say, 30° due south, and the hole is vertical, the lamination in the core makes an angle of 30° with the axis of the core. But, unless the angle of deviation of the hole is known in case (2) and unless the orientation of the core is known in case (3), we cannot interpret the dip in the core.

"Now if we suppose that (4) the beds dip 30° due south, as in case (3), and the hole is inclined 30° off the vertical in a due north direction, the core will show lamination perpendicular to its axis, as in case (1); or, (5) the hole may be inclined more than 30° from the vertical in a due north direction; or (6) less than 30° due north; or (7) at an angle of less than 30° from the vertical due south.

"These are all comparatively simple cases, for the hole is inclined in the plane of the dip of the strata. They are illustrated in Figs. 473–475. The real difficulty lies in the fact that extremely few crooked holes are inclined in the plane of the dip of the bedding, even in the short length of hole from which the core came. Thus, in Fig. 476, the core, represented by the graduated glass tube, slopes toward the left in the plane of the picture. The surface of the black liquid marks the horizontal line. The bedding (white line) dips toward the background, almost at right angles to the plane of the picture. It is evident from this picture that if the relations of the bedding (white line) to the horizontal plane and to compass directions were not known, nothing could be determined from the relations of the bedding to the core alone, and this is true even if the correct attitude of the hole were known.

"This topic is stressed to make it thoroughly evident that oriented cores ought to be secured from drilling wells, but in order to secure them the hole must be surveyed as to both its angle and its direction of deviation from the vertical."[33]

FIG. 473. Illustration of dip in a core supposed to have been taken from a vertical hole. The glass tube represents the hole, the surface of the dark liquid marks the horizontal plane, and the strip of tape represents the bedding in the core.

Where dipmeter surveys are made in holes that are inclined off the vertical, the time-consuming computations for correction of the recorded data may be avoided by the use of an instrument designed especially for making these computations.

[33] Bibliog., Lahee, F. H., 1929 (*b*), pp. 1135–1141.

Fig. 474. Similar to Fig. 473, but here the hole (and core) is inclined in such a way that the bedding, actually about horizontal, would be said to dip the amount of inclination of the hole if this latter figure were not known.

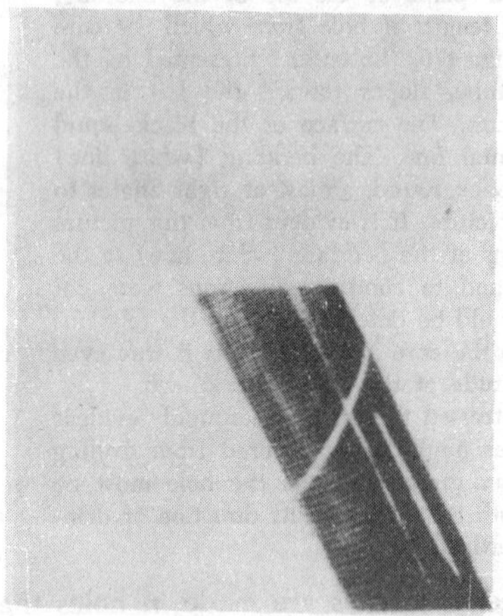

Fig. 475. Similar to Fig. 473, but dip is about 65° to left and hole is inclined about 30° off vertical toward right, giving impression of bedding dip of about 35°.

We cannot enter into a discussion of methods of measuring the deviation or drift of bore-holes. Many types of instrument have been made for determining the vertical angle of deviation only, and several devices have been used for measuring both the vertical angle and the direction of deviation.[34]

476. Directional drilling. In this place we may briefly mention what is called *directional drilling*, or *inclined drilling*, which means purposely drilling a hole off the vertical. This is not uncommon practice, where, for example, an inclined hole can be

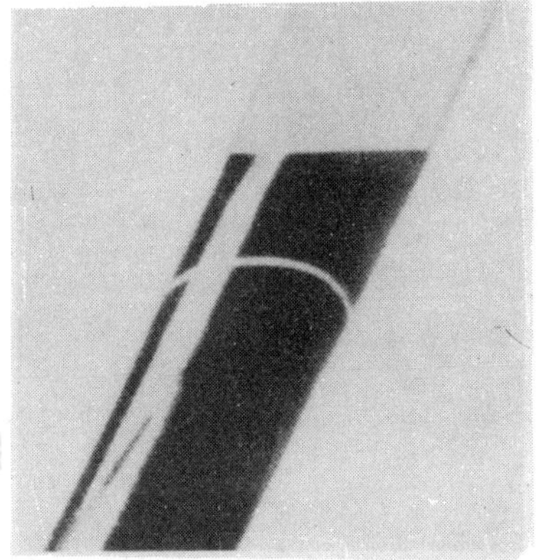

Fig. 476. Similar to Fig. 473, but here hole is inclined to left and bedding is inclined from front to back, in figure.

drilled onshore to reach a desired point offshore or where, by drilling several inclined holes from one derrick location (as in the case of offshore drilling), a great deal of money can be saved as contrasted with drilling these holes at locations directly above the points that they must reach at depth. Thus, in deep-water offshore drilling (as off the coasts of California, Louisiana, and Texas), four or five holes can all be drilled from the same platform. If these inclined, or directional, holes bend off their

[34] For various methods of surveying holes for verticality, see the different oil-trade journals; also, Bibliog., Lahee, F. H., 1929 (*b*), and Dodge, John Franklin, 1930; also sections contributed by J. B. Murdoch, Jr., in "Subsurface Geologic Methods." (Bibliog., LeRoy, L. W., 1950.)

intended course, they are brought back approximately into line again. The important thing is that a hole of this kind must be carefully surveyed at frequent intervals during its drilling, and, when completed, not only must it reach its predetermined destination, but its exact course must be charted. Obviously the proper correlation of formation tops and other geologic phenomena encountered in such a hole must involve corrections for the inclined course just as in the case of "crooked" holes drilled inadvertently off the vertical (**475**).

Chapter 19

MODES OF GEOLOGIC ILLUSTRATION

Geologic Maps

477. Definitions. Any map that shows the distribution of rocks and the form or distribution of geologic structures is a *geologic map.* An areal geologic map or formation map shows the distribution of formations. A structure contour map represents the form of geologic structure by contour lines (**497**). A special type of geologic map is an *outcrop map* which represents only the actual outcrops. In the preparation of a geologic map the geologic features are plotted on a land map, showing survey or ownership divisions, or on a topographic map, or on an air photographic map (**456**). In any case this map is referred to as a *base map.* The distribution of rocks is indicated on a geologic map by various patterns or colors; and linear features, such as fault lines, igneous contact lines, boundaries, etc., are shown by lines of different kinds and weights. If there are many formations to be represented, a literal abbreviation may be printed at intervals in each color area (see folios published by the U.S. Geological Survey). In the margin of a geologic map is a legend, that is, a key to the meaning of the colors, patterns and lines used on that particular map (**311, 483**).

478. Conventional patterns, lines, and symbols. The color or pattern to be employed on a geologic formation map depends largely upon the inclination of the investigator unless he is working for some organization which has already adopted a scheme. On the maps of the U.S. Geological Survey certain colors and patterns have a definite significance.

"Patterns composed of parallel straight lines are used to represent sedimentary formations deposited in the sea, in lakes, or in other bodies of standing water. Patterns of dots and circles represent alluvial, glacial, and eolian formations. Patterns of triangles and rhombs are used for igneous formations. Metamorphic rocks of unknown origin are represented by short dashes irregularly placed; if the rock is schist the dashes may be arranged in wavy lines parallel to the structure planes. Suitable combination patterns are used for metamorphic formations known to be of sedimentary or of igneous origin. The patterns of each class are printed in various colors. With the patterns of parallel lines, colors are used to indicate age, a particular color being assigned to each system."[1]

In Figs. 477–487 are sketched many of the symbols used on maps and sections by the U.S. Geological Survey.[2]

"In the use of line symbols for contacts, faults, and folds the solid line is used throughout to denote accurate locations, the dashed line for approximate or indefinite locations, and the dotted line for concealed locations (Figs. 477–478). . . .

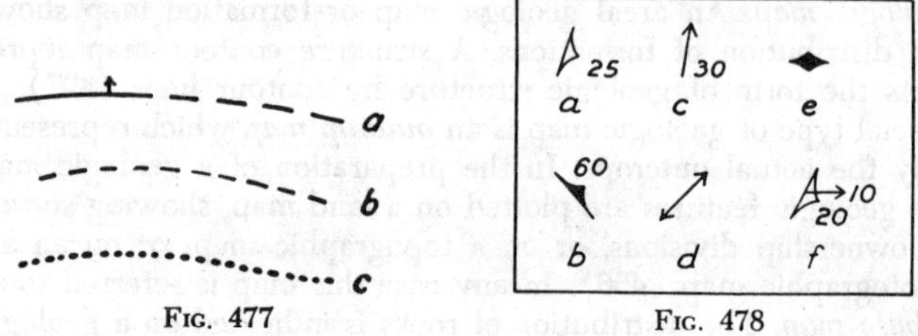

FIG. 477 FIG. 478

FIG. 477. Contacts (boundary lines between geologic formations). *a*, contact showing dip (dashed where approximately located); *b*, indefinite contact; *c*, concealed contact.

FIG. 478. Symbols used on maps of igneous rocks. *a*, flow layers, strike as plotted (N. 18° E.), dip 25° eastward; *b*, flow layers, strike N. 45° W., dip 60° NE. (dips below 30° shown as open triangles; over 30°, as solid triangles); *c*, flow lines, trend plotted, plunge 30° nearly north; *d*, horizontal flow lines, trend as plotted; *e*, vertical flow lines; *f*, combination of flow layers and flow lines. These symbols represent lineation in igneous rocks. If properly explained, they can also be used for other kinds of lineation.

"Different kinds of arrows are used to distinguish the various types of linear structures. The barbed arrow is used for flow lines, alinement of minerals and inclusions, etc., and it can also be used for other special types of lineations if such uses are indicated in the explanation of the map. The half-barbed arrow is used to denote direction of relative movement; the spear-point is used for slickensides, grooves, and striations; and the triangular arrow is used for axes of folds."[3]

[1] Geologic folios published by U.S. Geological Survey.

[2] Copied here with permission of the Director of the Survey.

[3] From "New List of Map Symbols," distributed by the U.S. Geological Survey.

Note that symbols that indicate directions of geologic features are to be carefully oriented in their correct positions on the map. Strike and dip of bedding are represented by a symbol like a broad, low T, which is so placed that the intersection of the two lines is at the point for the outcrop on the map. The upper line of the T (*a*, Fig. 479) marks the strike, and the stem of the T is drawn at right angles to the strike, pointing *down* the dip. Sometimes an arrowhead is drawn on this dip line to emphasize the

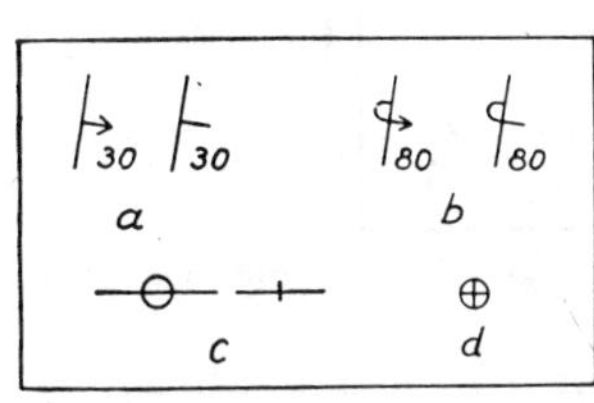

FIG. 479. Symbols for strata. *a*, strike plotted (N. 10° E.), dip 30°; *b*, strike plotted (N. 10° E.), dip overturned 80°. These symbols may be used with or without the arrowhead. In *b*, the strata have been turned through an angle of 100°, *i.e.*, up to 90° and then 10° beyond the vertical. *c*, strike east-west, dip vertical; *d*, beds horizontal.

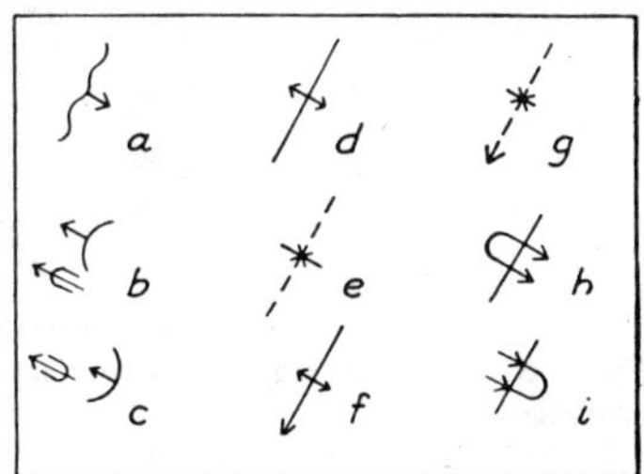

FIG. 480. Symbols for folded strata. *a*, general strike and dip of minutely folded beds; *b*, direction of plunge of minor anticline; *c*, same for minor syncline; *d*, axis of anticline; *e*, axis of syncline; *f*, plunge of axis of major anticline; *g*, same for major syncline; *h*, overturned anticline, showing trace of axial plane and direction of dip of limbs; *i*, same for overturned syncline.

direction of dip. The *angle* of dip is recorded beside the symbol. In Fig. 480 are symbols for folds. Figure 481 indicates anticlinal structure on the west and synclinal structure on the east. Figure 482 is more complicated. The folds are overturned, as shown in the section.

The type of rock, also, may be shown with the symbols for strike and dip (Fig. 483). A second line drawn parallel to the strike line, close to it and just the other side of it from the dip line, stands for shale or slate; a similar line with short cross lines between it and the strike line means limestone; a row of dots parallel to the strike line, in the same place as the shale line, is for sandstone; and a row of small circles signifies conglomerate.

Figures 484–487 represent symbols for faults, joints, cleavage, and schistosity. On both colored and black-and-white maps faults may be indicated by heavy black lines (*a*, Fig. 486) and boundaries between adjacent areas of different color or pattern by fine black lines. These fine boundary lines may stand for conformable contacts between adjacent strata, lines of unconformity, and

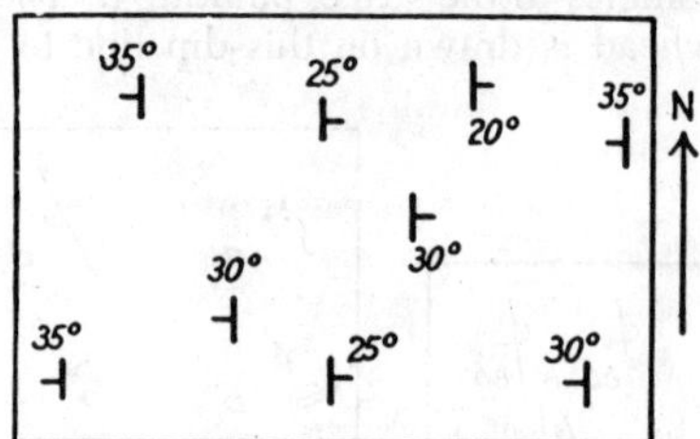

Fig. 481. Outline map of sedimentary rocks, showing dip and strike symbols.

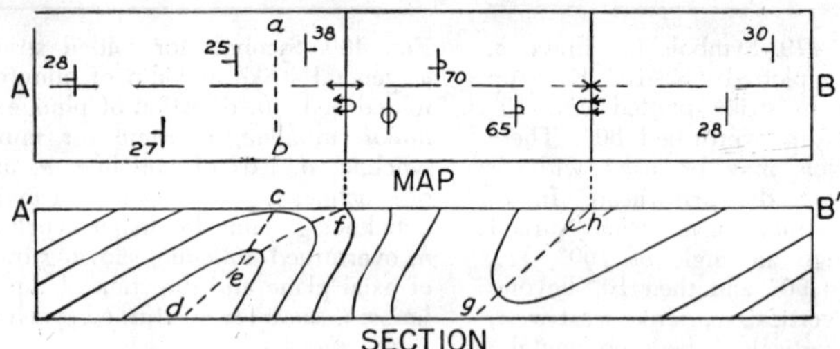

Fig. 482. Map and cross section of overturned anticline and syncline. *ab*, in map, is crestal line of anticline; *ce*, cross section of crestal surface of anticline; *def*, section of axial surface of anticline; and *gh*, section of axial surface of syncline. (See symbols in Fig. 480.)

igneous contacts. A fault line may be drawn full where its position is reasonably certain, dotted where it is partly buried or where its location, likewise, is reasonably certain, and dashed where its location is less sure (*a* to *d*, Fig. 486).[4]

[4] There are many symbols and patterns used for special purposes in geology, as for instance in mapping glacial deposits (see "Outlines in Glacial Geology," F. W. Thwaites), or in mining geology (see Bibliog., Forrester, J. D., 1946), and so on. See also Bibliog., LeRoy, L. W., and Harry M. Crain, 1949.

479. Position of boundaries between rock bodies. Areal mapping consists largely of plotting boundaries (Fig. 477). When these have been correctly placed, filling in the spaces with arbitrary colors or patterns is a simple matter. Before a line can be properly located on a map, its position must be determined in the field (**336, 338, 339**). Some maps represent only mantle rock with or without the actual outcrops of bedrock; others give the distribution of bedrock only, as if the overlying débris had been entirely removed; and still others, the most common variety, show both bedrock and mantle rock, but the latter is indicated merely where it is comparatively thick.

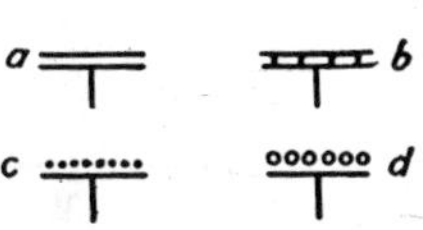

FIG. 483. Symbols for rock type combined with symbol for dip and strike. *a*, shale or slate; *b*, limestone; *c*, sandstone; *d*, conglomerate.

In field work a good deal of trouble may be experienced in locating boundaries for the second and third types of map. When bedrock only is to be shown (second type), the division lines

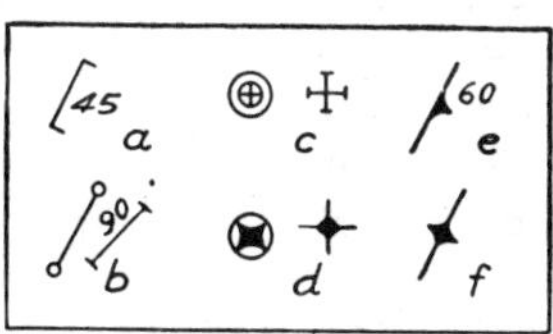

FIG. 484. Symbols used for cleavage and schistosity on maps. *a*, strike (long line) and dip (45° in direction of short lines) of cleavage of slate; *b*, strike of vertical cleavage of slate; *c*, horizontal cleavage of slate; *d*, horizontal schistosity or foliation; *e*, strike and dip of schistosity or foliation; *f*, strike of vertical schistosity or foliation.

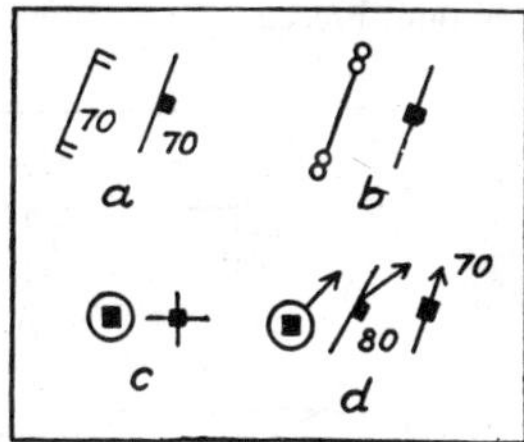

FIG. 485. Symbols used for joints on maps. *a*, strike and dip of joint; *b*, strike of vertical joint; *c*, horizontal joint; *d*, direction of linear elements (striations, grooves, or slickensides) on joint surfaces and amount of plunge of these linear elements on a vertical joint surface. Linear elements here shown in horizontal projection.

between rock bodies are often concealed. In this case their position may be suggested by the topography. To take examples from sedimentary rocks, a weak stratum may form a valley

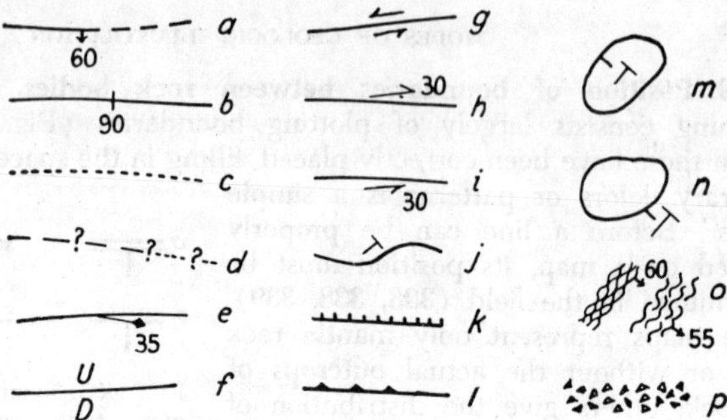

FIG. 486. Map symbols for faults. *a*, fault showing dip (barbs on dip arrow may be omitted); *b*, vertical fault; *c*, concealed fault; *d*, doubtful or probable fault, dotted where concealed; *e*, fault showing bearing and plunge of grooves, striations, or slickensides; *f*, high-angle fault (*U*, upthrown side, *D*, downthrown side); *g*, relative movement of fault blocks; *h*, normal fault, showing bearing and plunge of relative movement of downthrown block; *i*, same for reverse fault; *j*, thrust, or low-angle fault (*T*, upper overthrust plate); *k*, normal fault, hachures on downthrown side; *l*, thrust or reverse fault, sawteeth on side of upper plate; *m*, klippe, or outlier remnant of low-angle fault plate (*T*, overthrust side); *n*, window, fenster, or hole in overthrust plate (*T*, overthrust side); *o*, fault zone or shear zone, showing dip; *p*, fault breccia.

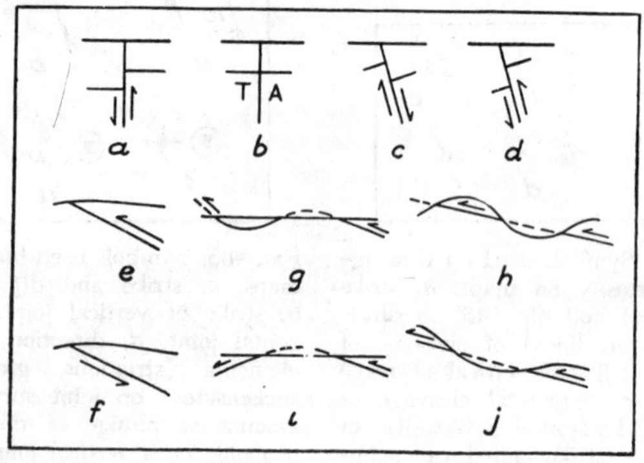

FIG. 487. Symbols for faults in sections. *a* to *d*, high-angle faults; *e* to *j*, low-angle faults. *a*, vertical fault, with principal component of movement vertical; *b*, vertical fault with horizontal movement, block *A*, moving *away* from the observer and block *T* moving toward the observer; *c*, normal fault; *d*, reverse fault; *e*, overthrust; *f*, underthrust; *g* and *h*, klippen, or fault outliers; *i* and *j*, fenster, windows, or fault inliers.

between two resistant beds; or a valley may be situated along the junction of two strata which are of nearly equal resistance to erosion (**291, B, D**). Frequently further investigations along the general trend of the line may reveal some substantial key to the relations. Provided the boundary between two outcrops with parallel strikes is neither visible nor can be closely located by the topography, it is usually drawn halfway between these

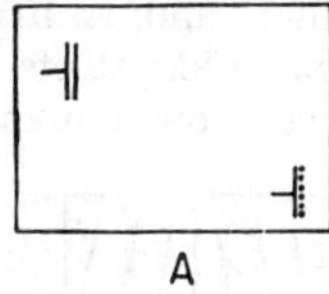

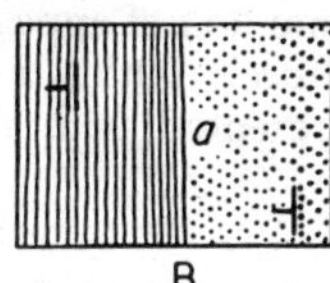

FIG. 488. Maps illustrating the method of locating a concealed bedding contact between outcrops of different strata. The boundary is drawn through *a*, halfway between the outcrops.

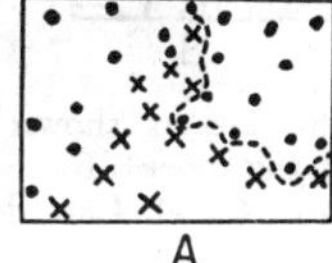

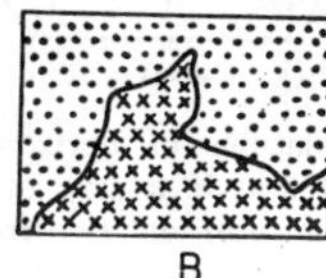

FIG. 489. Maps illustrating the method of locating a concealed irregular boundary. In A the dots and crosses represent outcrops of two kinds of rock. On the left no boundary is shown; on the right its approximate position is indicated. In B the boundary has been completed and the map filled in with symbols for both rocks.

outcrops and parallel to the strikes (Fig. 488). This is on the assumption that the beds in the two outcrops are mutually conformable. Care must always be taken to avoid errors that may be occasioned by unconformity or faulting. For rocks of two kinds, having no definite structure like bedding, the contact line may be put halfway between the nearest outcrops, but its trend must be determined by correlation with exposures over an extensive area (Fig. 489).

When the geologist prepares a map of the third type, he tries to mark out areas where outcrops are numerous and mantle rock is relatively thin and discontinuous from areas in which exposures are rare or absent and the surficial deposits are comparatively thick. Such a boundary is purely arbitrary and is seldom drawn in exactly the same way by different geologists.

480. Relations of topography to geologic mapping. A map is a projection of lines and areas upon a horizontal plane, lines and areas which, in reality, are usually distributed over an uneven land surface. A line which trends without deviation across hills and valleys is therefore straight on a map; its sinuosities in the vertical plane do not appear. On the other hand, an irregular line which is entirely within a horizontal plane has all its bends and angles represented with their true shape on a map. When a

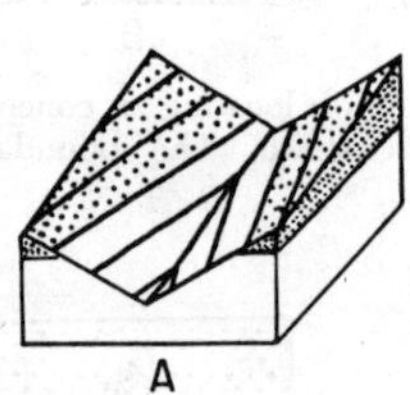

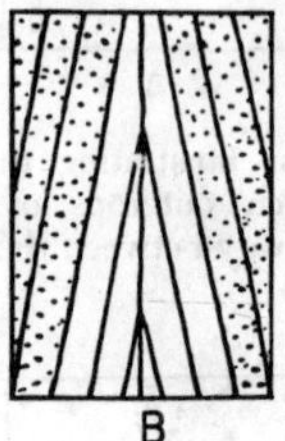

FIG. 490. Relations of horizontal bedding to contours shown in a block diagram (A) and in a map of the surface of the block (B). Stippled and blank portions represent two rock strata. Figures 491–494 are drawn in the same way.

crooked line lies in any plane other than one which is vertical or horizontal, its projection on a map has the same number of bends in the same relative positions, but the arcs of curves are broader and angles are more obtuse. It follows from this that the rules laid down in Arts. **172, 193, 225,** with reference to the effects of topography on the distribution of outcrops must be applied in map construction. These rules are repeated below, although in modified form. For the sake of simplicity the relations of a surface only are considered. The surface may be any kind of geologic contact, *i.e.,* the top or bottom of a stratum, the walls of a vein, an igneous contact, a surface of unconformity, or a fault. It is assumed to be flat or nearly so.

(1) If the given surface is horizontal its outcropping edge on a hill-and-valley topography will have all the characters of a contour; in its directions and curves it will closely correspond to the nearest contour lines on the map (Fig. 490) (2) If the

surface is vertical its outcropping edge will be a straight line on a map no matter how rugged the topography is (Fig. 491). (3) If the surface is inclined, its outcrop will be an irregular line with elbow-like bends. In valleys these bends will point upstream

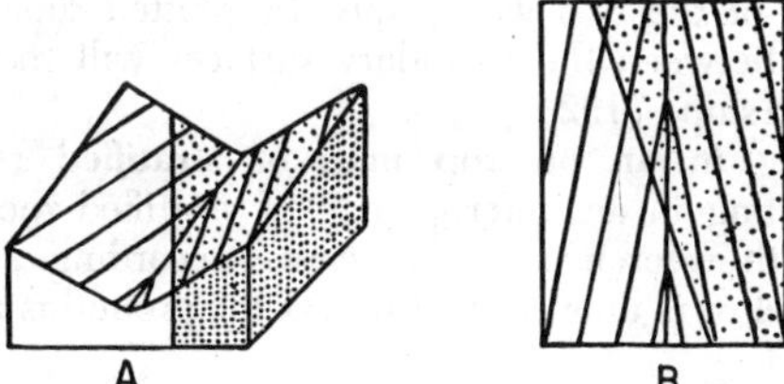

FIG. 491. Relations of vertical strata to contours. (See Fig. 490.)

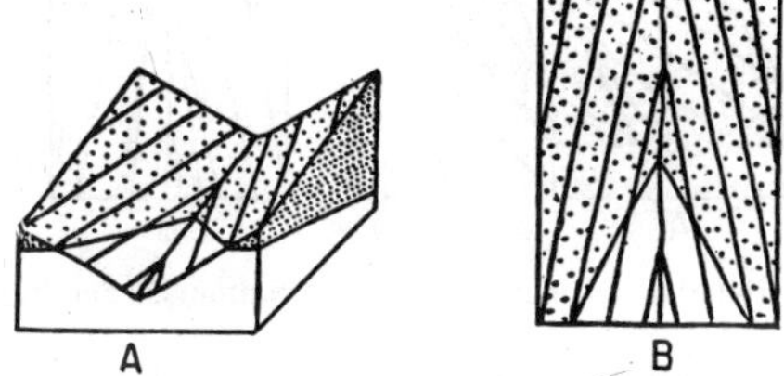

FIG. 492. Relations of inclined strata to contours. (See Fig. 490.)

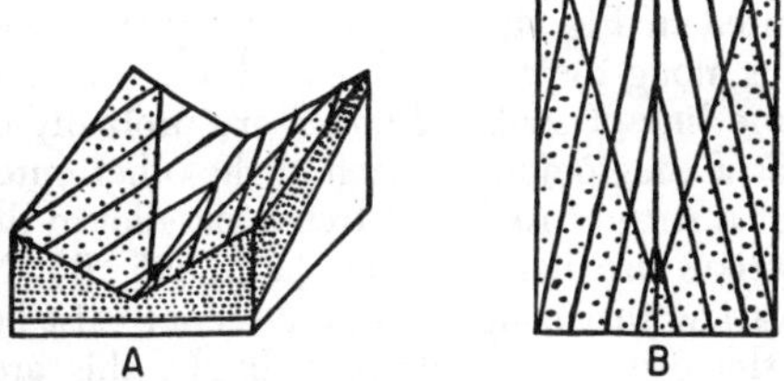

FIG. 493. Relations of inclined strata to contours. (See Fig. 490.)

if the dip is opposed to the slope of the valley bottom (Fig. 492), and they will point downstream if the dip is in the same direction as the slope of the valley bottom (Fig. 493), unless the dip is less than the slope. In this case, which is rare, the bends point upstream (Fig. 494). Note that the apex of the bend in valleys falls at the stream channel. The more uneven a surface is, the more irregular will be its line of outcrop. Dikes, sills, veins, and strata, when of approximately uniform thickness, may be treated as surfaces if they are thin. Otherwise the top and bottom, or each of the two walls, must be plotted separately, and the distance between the boundary surfaces will then vary according to the slope (**192**).

481. Filling in an outcrop map of stratified rocks. The method of filling in an outcrop map of stratified rocks may be described with reference to two cases, according as the land surface is level or is uneven. In Art. **481** the ground is assumed to

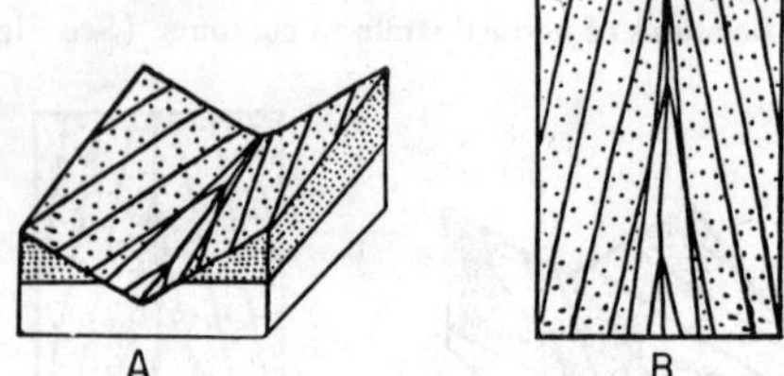

Fig. 494. Relations of inclined strata to contours. (See Fig. 490.)

be level. Article **482** deals with the problem of geologic map construction where the topography is uneven.

Let us suppose that the geology is to be plotted on the outcrop map represented in Fig. 495, A. Presumably the exposed strata are continuous along their strikes beneath the soil mantle. Being along the same line of strike, *d* and *e* are probably outcrops of the same bed of conglomerate. Each of the other outcrops is the visible part of a strip of rock that trends parallel to the *e–d* bed, for all the strikes are here parallel (Fig. 495, B). Now, there is nothing to show that conglomerate does not exist between the *c* strip and the *e–d* strip, and, accordingly, this area may be marked for conglomerate. Similarly, shale probably occupies the space between *g* and *h* along the strike. It will be observed that there are indications of six different belts of rock, as follows: shale on the west, including outcrop *a*; sandstone next east, including outcrop *b*; then conglomerate, including outcrops *c*, *d*, and *e*; then sandstone, *f*, followed eastward by shale, *g* and *h*,

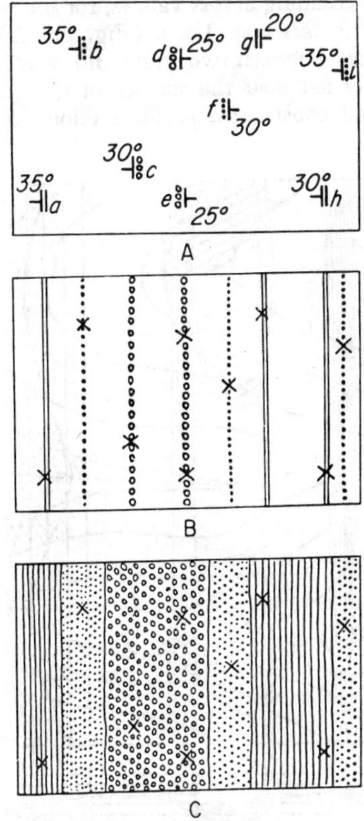

Fig. 495. Stages in the construction of a geologic map of folded strata which outcrop on a level land surface. The crosses in B and C are in the positions of the outcrops in A.

and finally sandstone, *i*, at the extreme east. By locating the boundaries between these belts, as directed in Art. **479,** the map is completed (Fig. 495, C).

482. Use of profile sections in geologic map construction. Few regions are flat as in the hypothetical case just described. If the topography is varied, the construction of the geologic map is more complicated. An example is chosen here in which strikes are regarded as trending across valleys, for the relations are better brought out in this way. Let *n* (Fig. 496, A) be an outcrop exposing a contact between two strata and imagine that this contact is essentially flat near the surface of the ground. Choose a vertical scale and construct a profile section through *n* perpen-

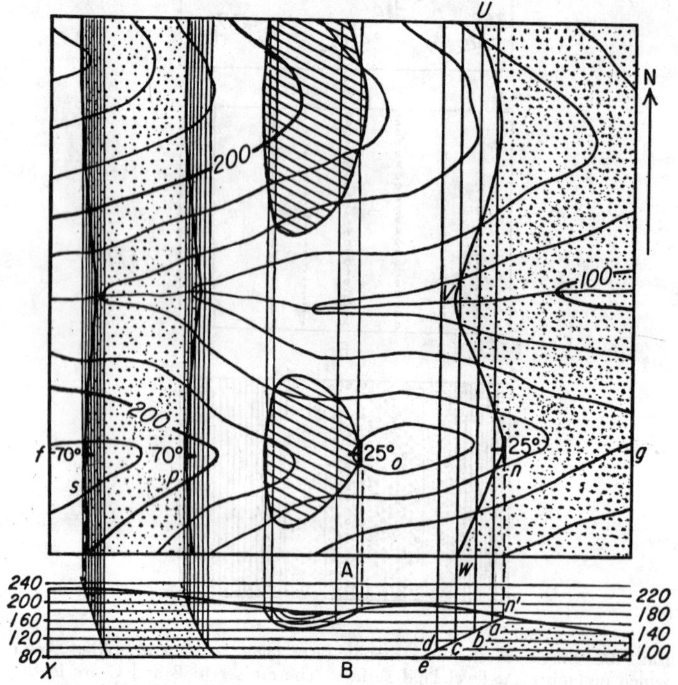

FIG. 496. Construction of a geologic map of folded strata which outcrop on an uneven land surface. Contour interval 20 ft.

dicular to the strike (Fig. 496, B) (**318**). The base line, *X–Y*, of this section may be drawn on the same sheet of paper as the map, but it must be drawn actually perpendicular to the strike. Project *n* upon the profile line of the section at *n′*. From *n′* draw a line, *n′–e*, westward and downward at an angle of 25° to the horizontal. *n′–e* is the intersection of the plane of the section with the bedding contact plane through *n*. It cuts the 160-ft. contour level in the section at *a*, the 140-ft. contour level at *b*, the 120-ft. contour level at *c*, and the 100-ft. contour level at *d*. From these four points draw lines perpendicular to *X–Y* upward and across the map. Wherever the line from *a* crosses the 160-ft. contour on the map, the bedding contact plane comes to the surface at this point; wherever the line from *b* crosses the 140-ft. contour line on the map, the contact plane meets the surface at the level of 140 ft.; and so on. Between these points of intersection on the map a curved line, *UVW*, is drawn, this line being the position of the continuous outcrop of the contact plane on the surface of the ground. The line from *d* does not meet the 100-ft. contour because the valley in the middle of the map is not deep enough to reach this contact.

Now let *fg*, Fig. 496, A, be a traverse across the strike of a series of strata. Suppose that, at outcrops *o*, *p*, and *s*, contacts between strata have been recorded and that *n* and *p* are at the same horizon. The structure, inferred to be synclinal, may be shown on a profile section along the traverse, as directed in Art. **491.** If one desires to make a geologic map of the rocks and structure represented in this section, each outcrop is to be separately treated as has been explained for *n*. Figure 496, A, shows the distribution of the contacts exposed in the five outcrops. Between them the different strata are indicated by cross-hatching and stippling. The boundary that runs through *o* is not continuous across the valley, for the stream has cut below this horizon, entirely removing a large part of the overlying bed (diagonally lined in Fig. 496, A).

In ordinary geologic mapping it is not customary to locate contacts with such mathematical precision unless great accuracy is particularly desirable. After one has gained some familiarity with the general effects of topography on the distribution of outcrops, one can sketch the boundaries between strata on a contour map with sufficient precision without the assistance of geometry, provided dips are known and the relief is observed, and provided, also, the different beds in the series have been located along several traverses.

483. Nature of the legend. The nature of the legend of a geologic map is illustrated in Fig. 497. The conventional signs and colors should be tabulated in a column of small rectangles of equal size. On the U.S. Geological Survey maps, the signs for rocks are above those for such features as faults, glacial striae, lines of section, etc. Igneous and sedimentary rocks, metamorphosed or not, are grouped separately, the sediments being above. For metamorphic rocks whose origin cannot be determined, the signs may be placed under the head "Unclassi-

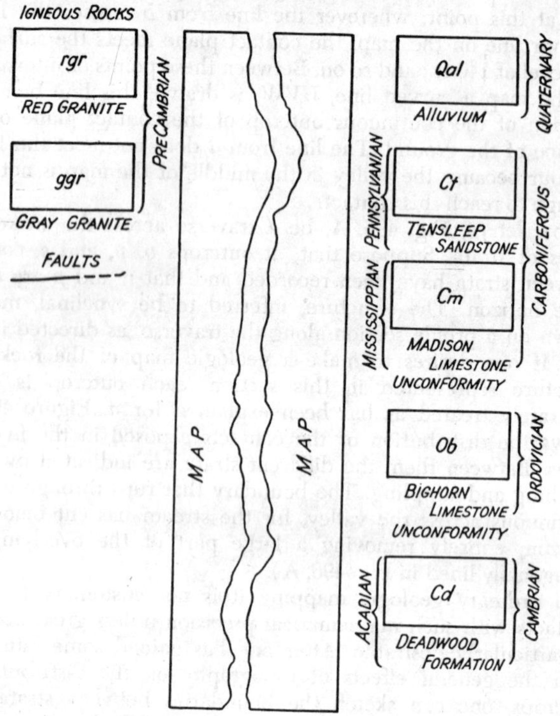

FIG. 497. Arrangement of the legend for a geologic map. The rectangles would be filled in with the colors or symbols employed on the map.

fied" below those for igneous rocks. In each group the formations are placed in the order of their relative age, youngest being at the top. Unconformities, when present, are often noted between the symbols for the unconformable formations. The geologic ages are printed beside the column. The legend is put in the right margin of the map and, if too long, it is continued in the left margin (Fig. 497). In this case the left portion really belongs below the part in the right margin.

484. Requisite data for a completed geologic map. A geologic map is incomplete unless it has a legend, a scale, compass bearings, both magnetic and true, and lines of section (**486**) if any geologic sections have been drawn to accompany this map. It must have a name, and the year in which it was made must appear somewhere upon it. If it was constructed on a contour base map, the contour interval and datum plane must also be recorded. If possible, it should have at least one parallel of latitude and one meridian correctly indicated on it. With regard to scale, compass bearings and contours, what was said in Arts. **312–314** is applicable here.

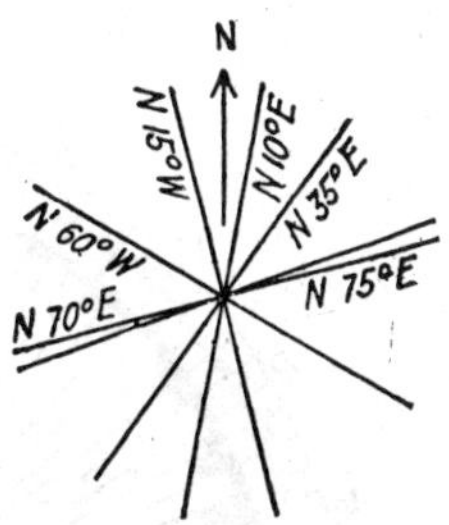

FIG. 498. Diagram showing the strikes of joints observed on an outcrop.

JOINT DIAGRAMS AND MAPS

485. Methods of representing the attitude of joints. The field geologist should not neglect to study the joints in his area of investigation. Not until their attitudes and relations to one another are known can deductions be made as to their origin. They are an important aid toward the elucidation of structural and genetic problems in many kinds of rock formations (**233–239,** see Fig. 485 for symbols for joints). For the larger fracture systems it is well to prepare special maps or diagrams to show the dips and strikes of the joint sets observed. For each station on a traverse the strikes may be plotted on a map as a radiating group of lines which intersect at the station (Fig. 498). Along each line the strike and also, if it is desired, the amount and direction of dip may be noted. If one wishes graphically to represent in a single diagram all the joint trends in a region, this may be done by plotting all the strikes about a single center; or the following method may be employed.[5] Tabulate all the joint strikes in groups of 3° each, beginning at the west and passing through north to east. In the first group will be all strikes between N. 90° W. (= E.–W.) and N. 88° W., inclusive; in the

[5] Bibliog., Shaler, N. S., 1889, pp. 583–588; and Sheldon, P., 1912.

next group of three, readings from N. 87° W. to N. 85° W., inclusive; and so on. Having tabulated the strikes in this way, construct a diagram like that in Fig. 499, in which: (1) the radii are drawn at intervals of 3°, beginning at the west, and thus intercepting segments corresponding to the joint groups; (2) the radial distance between the middle and inner circles is measured in any convenient unit and is made proportional to the greatest number of joints falling in any one of the groups; (3) the number of joints in each group is recorded between the middle and outer circles; (4) the number of joints in each group is graphically shown by blackening the corresponding segment inward from

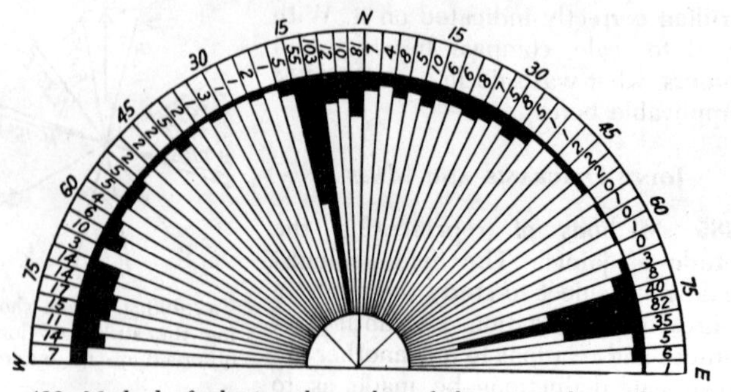

Fig. 499. Method of plotting the strikes of the joints observed in a given region. (*After P. Sheldon.*)

the middle circle a distance proportional to this number and measured in the chosen unit; and, (5) the compass directions are indicated just outside the outer curve.

Dips may be plotted in like manner; but for this the reader is referred to the reports above cited. Needless to say, the attitudes of veins and dikes may be illustrated by diagrams similar to that above described, if the veins and dikes are comparatively uniform in trend and thickness.

Geologic Sections

486. Definitions and general nature. If it were possible to make a deep vertical cut in the ground and then remove all the soil and rocks on one side of the cut, the other side might stand up as a flat vertical wall upon which rock structures and rock relationships could be seen in cross section. While incisions of this kind are impossible, except for very slight depths, the geologist can draw vertical sections of the underground structure as he thinks it exists from data obtained from outcrops, artificial excavations and bore-hole data (**498**). Such sections, whether actually seen or merely inferred, are called *geologic sections.* They depict geologic structure by means of certain conventional lines and patterns or colors, and, therefore, like geologic maps, they must have a legend.

The line of intersection of the land surface with the plane of a geologic section, as shown on a map, is called a *line of section,* exactly as in the case of profile sections (**317**).

For every geologic section one must first make a *base section* upon which the geologic features may be drawn. This may be a profile section, (Fig. 501), prepared as described in Art. **318**, or a simple rectangle (Fig. 504). The simple rectangular base consists of two horizontal lines connected by two vertical end lines. The lower horizontal line corresponds in every way to the base line of a profile section (**317**). The upper horizontal line is intended to represent the intersection of the plane of the section and a horizontal plane which may be taken at any convenient elevation. The advantage of the rectangular base section is that it eliminates the necessity of plotting the topography; but since it does not depict the actual nature of the land surface, it should not be used except where the scale is so small that the relief variations would be negligible in a profile section of the same district on the same scale (**492**).

487. Methods of indicating geologic structure. Within the closed space of a geologic section all lines for faults, contacts unconformities, etc., are drawn full, and between these lines, as on a geologic map, the rocks or formations are filled in by conventional colors or patterns (Fig. 500). It is a common practice further to indicate the geologic structure by extending the *lines,* now *dotted,* beyond the confines of the base section (Fig. 501); but observe that the colors (or patterns) for the rocks should be restricted to the area of the base section. Above the top line of the base section these dotted lines stand for the inferred structure of the rocks which have been removed by erosion. Below the bottom line such dotted lines represent the structure where it is uncertain on account of its great depth. Note that the general characters indicated by the full line for a particular contact should be simply represented by the dotted prolongation of the same line (cf. *ab* and *cd*, Fig. 501).

488. Position of sections across folded strata. The location of a geologic section depends upon the exact features which the geologist wishes to emphasize. Ordinarily it is drawn perpendicular to the strike of stratified rocks, so that it will show their true

Limestone Shale & Slate Sandstone Conglomerate

Schist Granite and other massive rocks

FIG. 500. Symbols used in geologic sections for different types of rock.

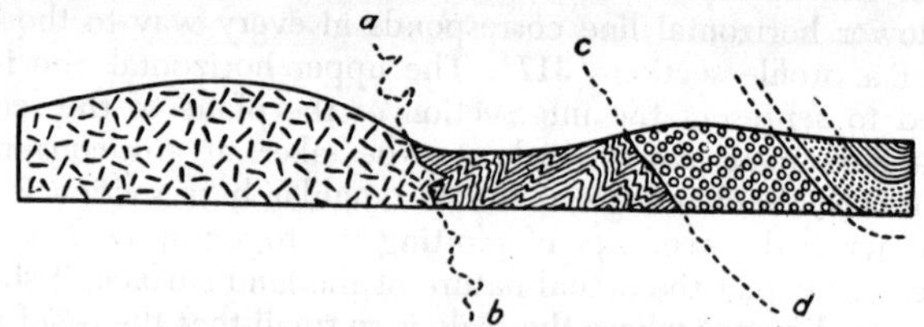

FIG. 501. Illustration of the nature of a geologic section.

dip. When plunge is to be figured, the section must be drawn parallel to the axis, and it is then called an *axial section*. In districts where the bedrock is abundantly exposed, locating a section is easy; but if outcrops are few and scattered, the rocks and structures which they reveal must be projected along the strike (Fig. 502, B, C). Frequently strikes vary 10° to 15° to one side or the other of their average direction. For a large-scale section, covering a short distance, it may be important to make allowance for these variations; but for a small-scale section they are insignificant if the outcrops are situated relatively near the line of section. Experience will soon teach the student how to deal with these cases. He must not confuse this indiscriminate and slight variation of strikes with a gradual or sudden, pronounced and regular change in direction. The latter phenomenon may be due to a fault, an unconformity, or some other important cause.

To illustrate the relations between the trend of a geologic section and the position of outcrops and structures, several examples are given below. In all, the land surface is assumed to be horizontal.

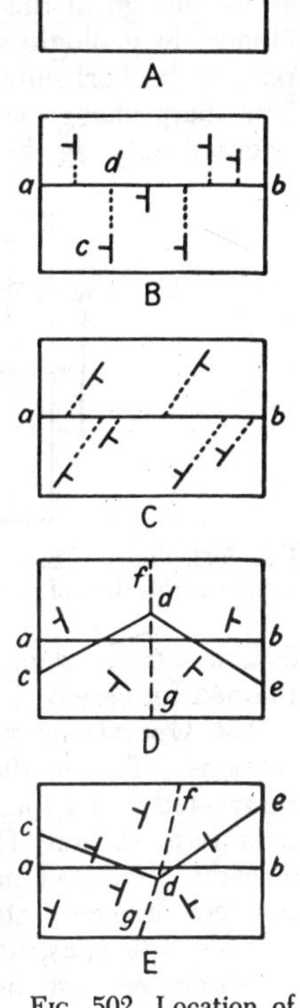

Fig. 502. Location of a geologic section across stratified rocks.

1. The bedrock is broadly exposed, or the outcrops are situated in a row trending perpendicular to the strike (Fig. 502, A). Draw the section along a line from *a* to *b*.

2. Outcrops are scattered. Strikes are all identical or very nearly so (Fig. 502, B). Project the rocks and dips of the several outcrops along their strikes to points on the line *ab*, which is perpendicular to the strike. Thus, the rock exposed at *c* and the dip of the beds at *c* would be represented in the section at *d*.

3. For some reason, not here stated, the section must be drawn at an acute angle to the strikes, along such a line as *ab* in Fig. 502, C. Project rocks and dips along the strikes of the outcrops to points on the line *ab*, just as in example 2. Since a section perpendicular to the strike shows beds with their maximum inclination or dip, and since, in a section parallel to the strike, the beds would appear to be horizontal, obviously a section located between the dip and strike directions must show the beds inclined at an angle more than 0° and less than their true dip. In other words, in cases like the present one, a correction must be made for the inclination of the beds as this would be seen in the section, and this correction will depend upon the actual dip and upon the angle between the strike and the line of section (Appendix 13).

4. When strikes vary regularly, as in D and E, Fig. 502, the line of section may be straight, *ab*, or it may be drawn with one

or more changes in its direction, *cde*, the object in this case being to keep it as nearly as possible perpendicular to the strikes. In Fig. 502, D, the curve in the strikes indicates a plunging fold. Let us assume that the axis of this fold lies along *fg*. The outward dip of the beds shows that the plunge is toward *g*, and, as far as the map reveals, there is every reason to believe that the strata plunge in this same direction at all points along the axis. Hence, in geologic sections on *ab* and *cde* the beds would appear to be horizontal where *ab* and *cde* cross the axis. (Why?) The sharp change in strikes in Fig. 502, E, suggests a fault or an unconformity, *fg*, between the two sets. In either D or E, Fig.

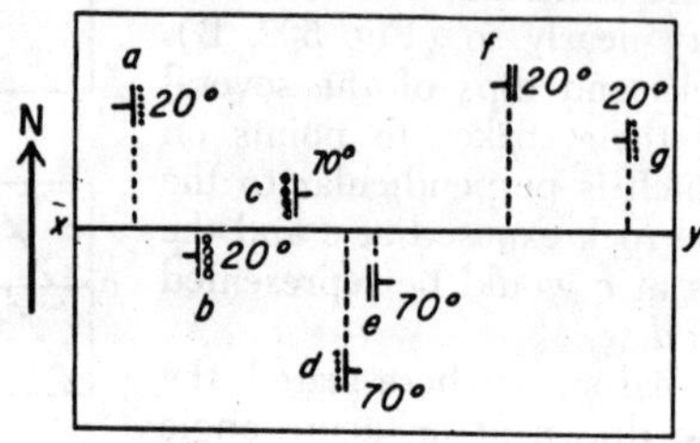

Fig. 503. Outcrop map of folded strata. A geologic section is to be made along *xy*, the "line of section." (See Fig. 504.)

502, a section along *ab* would need correction for dips as explained for case 3.

489. Operations necessary in the construction of geologic sections. The method of constructing geologic sections may be treated under four heads: (1) the transfer of data from a map to a base section; (2) the correlation, in the section, of rocks already correlated in the field; (3) the location of boundaries between adjacent strata or formations; and (4) filling in the section. The construction of a rectangular geologic section will be discussed first, and then that of a profile geologic section. In both cases we shall consider a region in which all the rocks are folded strata. Geologic sections may be enlarged as described in Art. 319.

490. Construction of a rectangular geologic section across folded strata. A. Transfer of data recorded on a map. Let Fig. 503 be a map of an area in which the relief is relatively low as compared with the length of the section to be drawn. *xy* is the line along which the section is to be made. Upon *xy* project the rocks and dips of the outcrops as directed in Ex. 2, Art. **488**, and transfer the points of intersection, *a–g*, to *xy* in Fig. 504, A. At point *a*, Fig. 504, A, lay off a row of dots inclined downward and westward and making an angle of 20° with the horizontal line *xy*. This denotes sandstone (**478**) dipping 20° W., and it stands

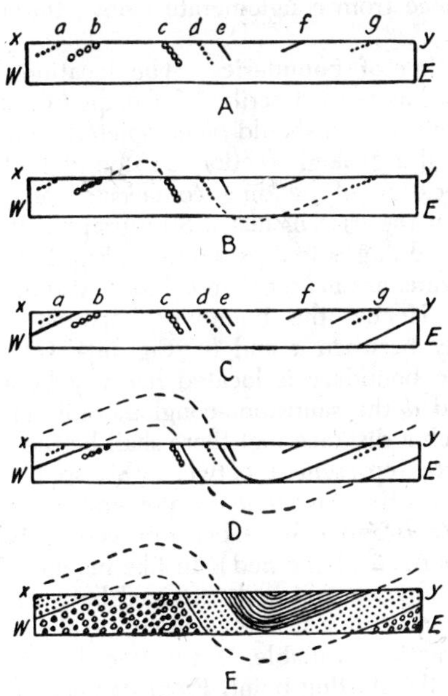

FIG. 504. Stages in the construction of a rectangular geologic section along line *xy* in Fig. 503.

for outcrop *a* in Fig. 503. Follow the same method for each of the other points, always observing the proper rock and dip to be used. Conglomerate is to be represented by a row of small circles parallel to the dip, and shale by a straight line parallel to the dip. Figure 504, A, is the result of this work. It is well not to make the symbols, *i.e.*, the rows of dots or circles, or the lines for shale, extend more than a very short distance down from the top of the figure, merely far enough to show the dip.

490B. Correlation of rocks. In Fig. 504, A, *d* and *g* may be connected in a syncline (Fig. 504, B), since they are parts of the same bed, a fact which we shall assume has been ascertained by one or more of the methods of field correlation mentioned in Arts. **196** and **345.** For the same reason, the outcrops of conglomerate at *b* and *c* may be drawn as if they had formerly been joined in an anticline. The structure, then, indicates a stratigraphic sequence from conglomerate below, through sandstone, to shale above.

490C. Location of boundaries. The location of boundaries between strata has been described for maps in Art. **479.** In general the map of a region should be completed before the sections are made; but if a geologic section is to be plotted directly from field notes, location of bedding contacts is determined in the same way as in the case of maps. Stratigraphically, *i.e.*, at right angles to the bedding, outcrops *a* and *b* (Fig. 504), of sandstone and conglomerate, are nearer than *c* and *d*, also of sandstone and conglomerate. Hence, the boundary between these rocks is placed halfway between *a* and *b* (Fig. 504, C). Similarly, the shale-sandstone boundary is located halfway between *d* and *e*. Between *c* and *d* the sandstone-conglomerate contact is placed east of *c* at such a distance that there shall be the same thickness of conglomerate represented between this spot and *c* as there is between *b* and the sandstone-conglomerate contact west of *b*. This is because *b* and *c* have been proved to be at the same stratigraphic horizon (same bed). In like manner the position of the shale-sandstone contact is determined between *f* and *g*.

When locating boundaries between strata, always use the most accurate information available. If a contact is exposed, this contact should be the starting point. From its position other boundaries may be fixed, provided the thickness of each bed is known. If no contact is exposed, determine the position of the boundary between the nearest outcrops of two adjacent strata, and then locate other contacts.

490D. Filling in the section. It is now possible to complete the section by extending the rock contacts and filling in the inclosed rectangular space with the proper symbols for conglomerate, sandstone, and shale. The boundaries are drawn, as full lines in the section and as dotted lines beyond the confines of the base section, parallel to the structure shown in the anticline between *b* and *c* and in the syncline between *d* and *g* (Fig. 504,

D). The last step is the filling in of the section proper (Fig. 504, E).

491. Construction of a profile geologic section across folded strata. Let Fig. 505, A, be an outcrop contour map of an area and suppose that a section is to be made through the line *xy* which marks a cross-strike traverse. A profile base section must be constructed (**318**). This is illustrated in Fig. 505, B, where

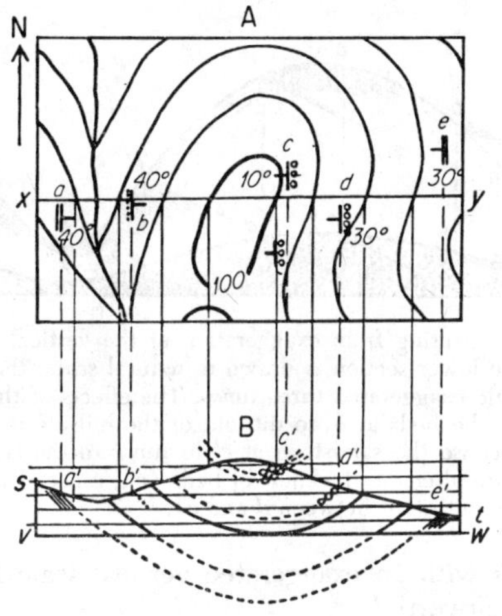

FIG. 505. Construction of a profile geologic section.

vw is the base line which corresponds to *xy* on the map. Here the points of intersection of the line of section (*xy*) with the contours may be transferred to *vw* most conveniently by dropping perpendiculars from these points of *vw*, it being understood that *vw* has been drawn equal in length to *xy* and, like *xy*, perpendicular to the strikes. Just as the intersections of the contours with *xy* are plotted on *vw*, so also the positions of the outcrops, *a–e*, projected along their strikes, are located on *vw*. The perpendiculars from the outcrops meet the profile line, *st*, at the proper sites of the outcrops *a′–e′*. At these points on *st* the dip and rock type are to be correctly indicated (**490**, **A**) and then the section is to be completed in the manner outlined in Art. **490, B–D.**

The vertical and horizontal scales of a geologic section should be the same.[6] Exaggeration of the vertical scale necessitates adjustment of all the dips, and this not only involves a great deal of labor but also gives a false notion of the structure. On the other hand, if the dips are plotted with their correct values in a section with its vertical scale exaggerated, several absurdities may result, as illustrated in Fig. 506. How to make a scale for

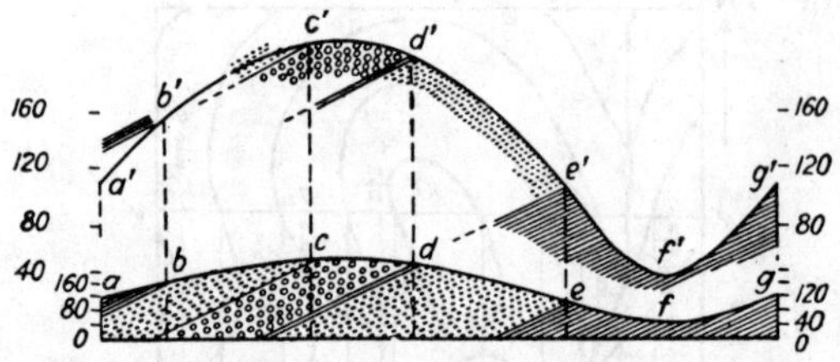

Fig. 506. Errors resulting from exaggeration of the vertical scale of a geologic section. The lower section is drawn to natural scale; the upper section has a vertical scale exaggerated three times. The effects of this exaggeration are (1) to cause the beds at b' to dip out of the hillside instead of into it, as at b; (2) to cause the sandstone at c' to run into the slate at b' (cf. b and c); and (3) to alter the thickness of beds (cf., especially, the sandstone between d' and e' with that between d and e).

use in sections with an exaggerated vertical scale has been described by Wentworth.[7]

492. Comparison of rectangular and profile sections. The student should observe that rectangular geologic sections are more or less incorrect except when the land surface is flat and horizontal. The profile section, drawn to natural scale, is the most accurate mode of showing geologic structure. Figure 507 contrasts the results obtained by projecting the same data upon both rectangular and profile sections. Upon a map (not shown) are two stations at each of which the dip is 30° E. The land slopes uniformly 17° W. (Fig. 507, A). The stations, as projected, are at a and b. From these points the dip is plotted. Measure-

[6] Five thousand feet to an inch, for the vertical scale, is satisfactory when the horizontal scale is 1 mile = 1 in.; and the same may be said of multiples of these scales.

[7] Bibliog., Wentworth, Chester K., 1930.

ments indicate that the thickness, *T*, between the beds *a* and *b* is considerably reduced in the rectangular section. It is correct in the profile section. If the beds were projected down their dip to the horizontal level represented by the top line of Fig. 507, B, they would have a breadth of outcrop, *cd* (Fig. 507, A), longer than *ab* in Fig. 507, B. *cd,* however, is the correct horizontal distance between the beds at the level, *cd*. Obviously, then, profile sections are always to be preferred to rectangular sections when actual geologic structure is to be depicted. Rectangular

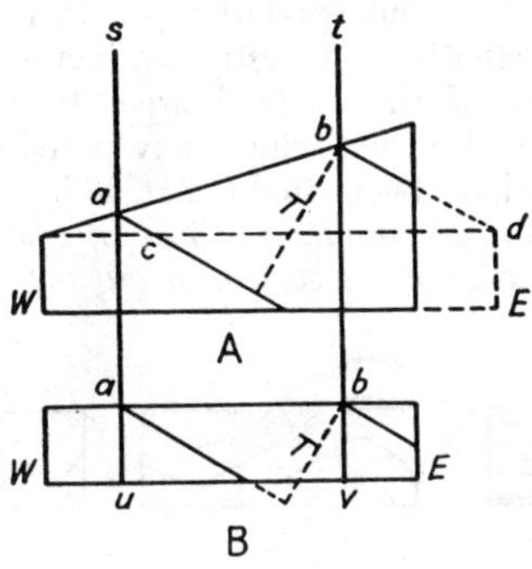

Fig. 507. Errors introduced by the use of a rectangular section. A, profile section, and B, rectangular section, of a bed whose breadth of outcrop is *ab*, as projected from the map along the lines *su* and *tv*.

sections are useful for diagrams of general application, such as many used in this book.

493. Interpretation of dips in the construction of geologic sections. In many cases after the dips and rock types of folded strata have been plotted, the final interpretation of the structure requires a good deal of thought. Several variations may be suggested by the data. In order to assist the student in completing his sections, a number of relations for dipping strata are noted below, together with their possible interpretations. In these examples it is assumed that field observations on rock type, strike, amount and direction of dip, etc., have been recorded. Simple symmetrical folds, asymmetrical and overturned folds, isoclinal folds, and parallel and similar folds, are considered. Strikes are regarded as parallel in all outcrops unless otherwise stated.

493A. Observations on homoclinal dips. 1. *On a single outcrop or on several adjacent exposures the dip is found to be of nearly constant value and in the same direction. There is no duplication of beds.* Let Fig. 508 be a section of the structure beneath the area examined. Beds with this dip may belong in a monocline (Fig. 509, A), or in the limb of an upright anticline or syncline (Fig. 509, B) or in the limb of an overturned fold (Fig. 509, C). To determine which interpretation is correct, the country must be more extensively investigated across the strike and beyond the limits of the original area. In Fig. 509, C, the strata are overturned, a fact which may perhaps be ascertained by such criteria as have been cited in Art. **185**.

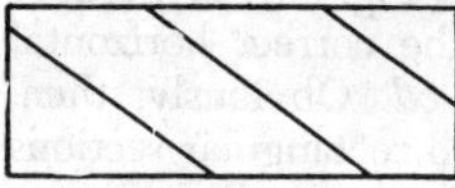

FIG. 508. Section of beds with homoclinal dip.

2. *The conditions are similar to those of case* 1, *but beds are repeated in inverse order as seen in a cross-strike traverse.* The

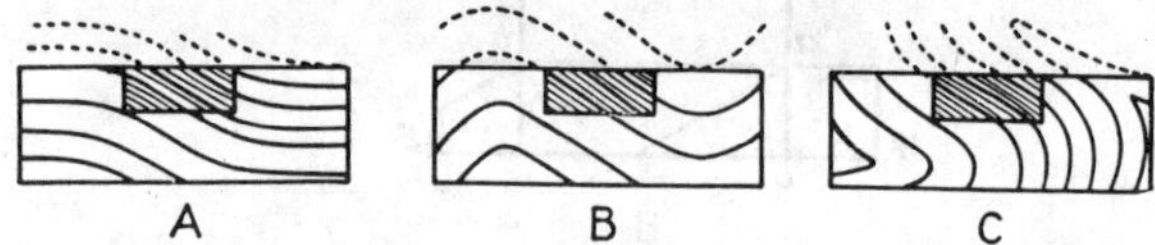

FIG. 509. Structures inferred from observations on homoclinal dip. The small closely ruled rectangle in each diagram corresponds to Fig. 508.

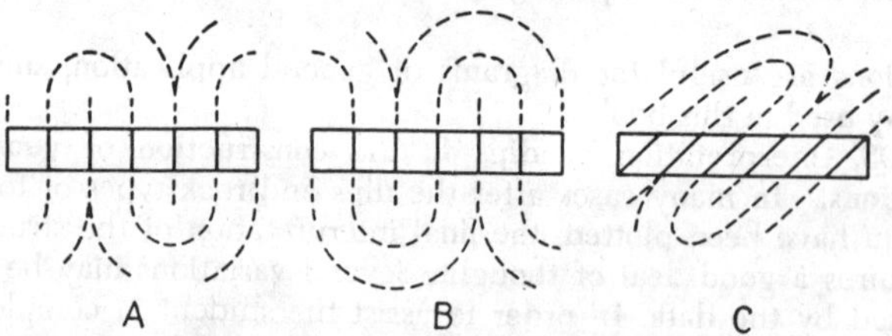

FIG. 510. Structures inferred from observations on beds which have homoclinal dip and which outcrop alternately in normal and reversed order.

strata have been duplicated once or several times by isoclinal folding (Fig. 510). Obviously, correct interpretation of this kind of structure requires search for the top and bottom of individual strata (**185**) and for stratigraphic sequence (**100**).

493B. Observations on dips of varying amount and direction. 1. *A bed, which is surely identifiable, is exposed in two localities where the strikes are alike and the dips, though equal, are in opposite directions.* There are two possibilities: if the dips converge downward, the outcropping stratum is probably continuous underground as a syncline (Fig. 511, A), and if the dips diverge downward, the bed once extended above the ground as an anticline from which erosion has removed the crest (Fig. 511, B). Both folds are symmetrical and the axis is midway between the outcrops. This rule for converging and diverging equal dips

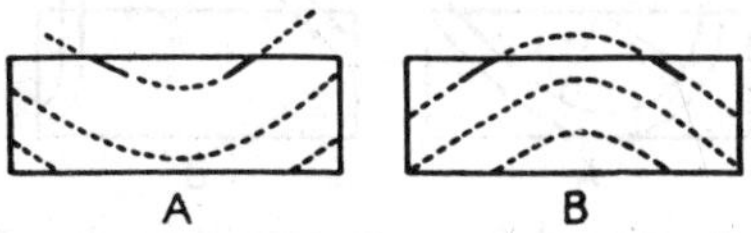

Fig. 511. Structures inferred from observations on dip. The short black lines indicate the dips as plotted at two outcrops.

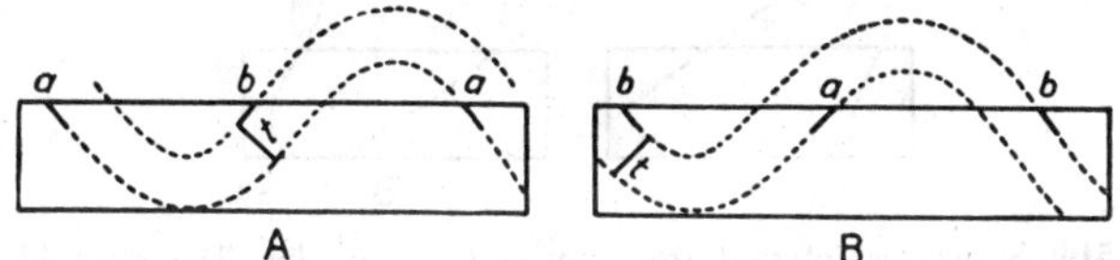

Fig. 512. Structures inferred from observations on dips recorded at outcrops labelled *a* and *b*.

is applicable to all folds except fanfolds. Observe that it is customary to draw the crests and troughs of folds *rounded* unless there is evidence to the contrary.

2. *In two localities two different strata are exposed, one, a, being older than the other, b. Dips are about equal in value and are in opposite directions.* As far as any observations reveal, the folding is symmetrical. The dips suggest a syncline on the left and an anticline on the right, in both A and B, Fig. 512. The axis is nearer the younger exposed bed, *b*, in synclines and nearer the older bed, *a*, in anticlines. In order most accurately to determine the position of the axis, the thickness, *t*, of the concealed beds stratigraphically between *a* and *b* should be computed (531).

3. *As in case* 1, *under* **493B**, *above, the same stratum outcrops in two localities, but here the dips are unequal and opposite and one of them is vertical.* The fold is asymmetrical, the axial surface being inclined, and the axis is nearer the steeper limb (Fig. 513). The axis should be placed so that the perpendicular distances, *t*, from it to the given bed in each of the two limbs are approximately equal, unless there is good evidence for actual inequality. As will be explained presently, not all instances of

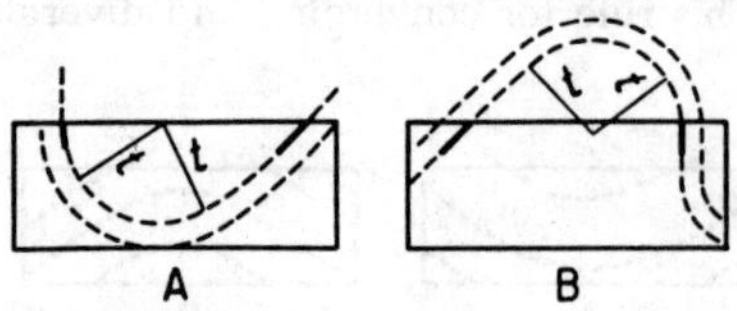

FIG. 513. Structures inferred from observations on dip. The short black lines indicate the dips as plotted at two outcrops.

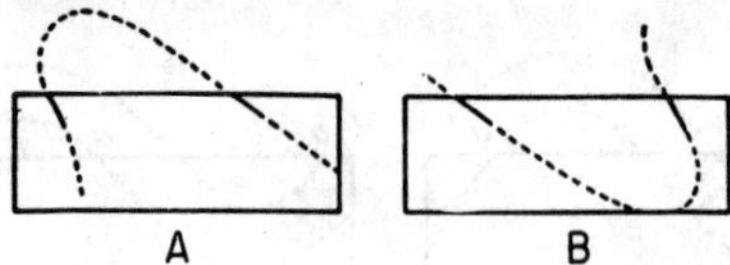

FIG. 514. Structures inferred from observations on dip. The short black lines indicate the dips as plotted at two outcrops.

unequal dips are to be attributed to asymmetrical folding (see **493C**, below).

4. *The same bed outcrops in two localities, and the dips are unequal and in the same direction.* Great care should be exercised in searching for criteria for overturning in the more steeply dipping rocks (**185**). If proof of overturning is forthcoming, the folds are overturned or recumbent according to the attitude of the axial surface, and the axis is nearer the steeper limb (Fig. 514); but if the steeper beds have not been turned beyond 90°, the structure must be that described in **493C**, 1.

5. *If available exposures are not of the same bed, but otherwise the conditions are such as were stated in* 3 *and* 4 *above,* the folding may be asymmetrical (see, however, **493C**). As in **493B**, 2, the thickness, *t*, of the concealed beds stratigraphically be-

tween *a* and *b* should be ascertained if possible (**531**). Study the diagrams carefully (Fig. 515).

6. *A succession of strata is exposed, all inclined in the same direction, but with some variation in the angle of dip.* This is a phenomenon of frequent occurrence, chiefly because beds are not likely to undergo exactly the same amount of tilting when subjected to the complex forces of deformation. In this case,

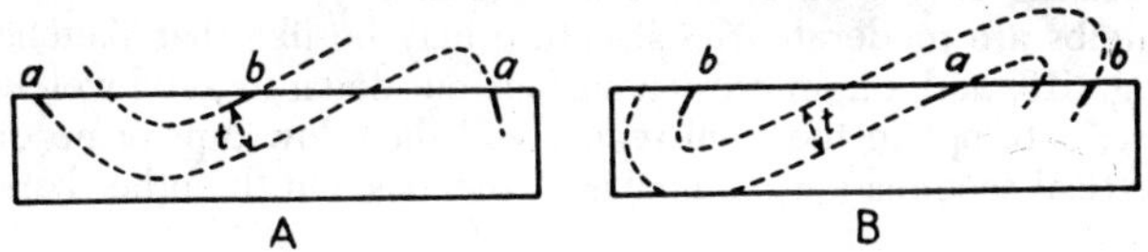

Fig. 515. Structures inferred from observations on dips recorded at the outcrops labelled *a* and *b*.

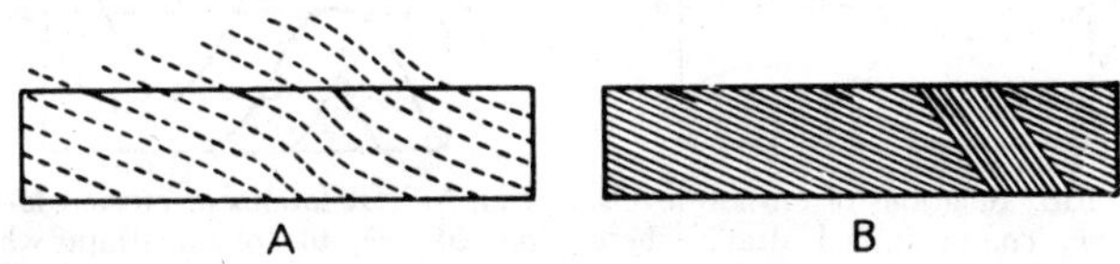

Fig. 516. Correct (A) and incorrect (B) interpretations of structures based upon observations on varying dips.

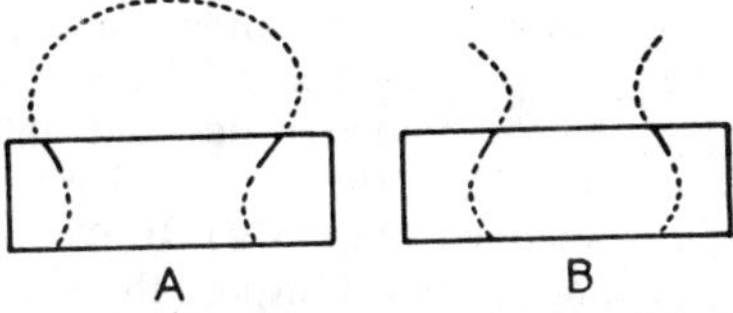

Fig. 517. Structures inferred from observations on dip. The short black lines indicate the dips as plotted at two outcrops.

unless there is conclusive evidence to the contrary, the beds should be drawn as in Fig. 516, A. A mistake too commonly made by beginners is illustrated in Fig. 516, B, where a curious anomalous structure is given for the interpretation of the dip relations.

7. *The same bed is exposed in two localities. Dips are opposite and equal or unequal. The strata are found to be overturned in both localities.* The structure is that of a fanfold (Fig. 517).

493C. Studies across axial regions. The student will notice that all the diagrams used for this article are of parallel folding. This is because the major folds in a set of deformed strata are apt to be more nearly parallel than similar, for similar folding is produced only under extreme compression (**176**). Figures 510 and 515 would perhaps be more natural if the folds in them were made on the similiar pattern. Let us assume, now, that we are dealing only with folds of the parallel type. If the dips on the limbs are moderate, the structure may be like that sketched in Fig. 518, and, on an erosion surface cut down to any level, *aa, bb, cc,* outcrops in the axial region will show low dips or no dip in vertical sections perpendicular to the axis. On the other hand,

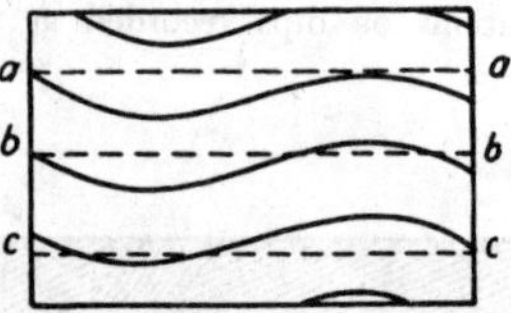

Fig. 518. Relations of erosion levels, *aa, bb, cc,* to folded strata where deformation has been moderate.

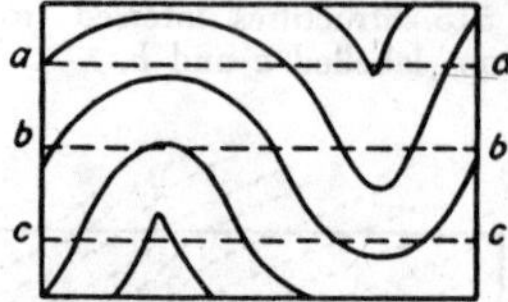

Fig. 519. Relations of erosion levels, *aa, bb, cc,* to folded strata where deformation has been greater than that shown in Fig. 518.

if the compression has been more intense and the dips on the limbs are relatively steep, synclines will be pinched, or *carinate,* in the upper part of the folded series and anticlines will be carinate in the lower part of the series, whether the axial surfaces are upright or inclined (Fig. 519). If agents of erosion cut down to a level, *aa,* outcrops will expose the lowest dips in anticlinal axial regions and the steepest dips in synclinal axial regions. If the land surface has reached a level, *bb,* the steepest dips will be on the limbs, and the lowest dips will be in both synclinal and anticlinal axial regions. And, if erosion has cut down to level *cc,* the steepest dips will be in the anticlinal axial regions and the lowest dips in the synclinal axial regions. In any of these cases the dips recorded on a cross-strike traverse may look like Fig. 520 when they are plotted, but as brought out by the dotted lines, this divergence of dip does not signify actual upward fanning of the strata. The stratification surfaces may still be parallel.

When the folds are even closer, the carinate crests of the anticlines may overlap the carinate troughs of the synclines (Fig. 521). Then, although erosion surfaces at *aa* and *cc* will be the same as in Fig. 519, at any erosion level in the middle belt, ***bb***, both anticlines and synclines will be pinched. With the extremely close compression of isoclinal folding there may be no overlap of the carinate axial parts of the folds (Fig. 510).

494. Sections across igneous bodies. If a dike is to be the principal feature in a section, the latter is drawn perpendicular to the strike of the dike. More commonly, dikes are incidental phenomena in a section of a sedimentary formation or of a larger igneous body, and in this event they may lie in various positions

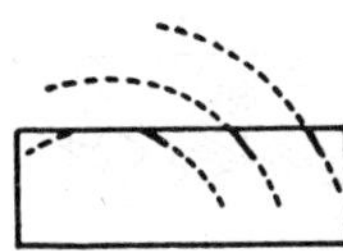

FIG. 520. Variations in dip (short black lines) due to position of outcrops in a fold.

FIG. 521. Relations of erosion levels, *aa, bb, cc,* to folded strata where deformation has been more intense than that shown in Fig. 519.

with respect to the trend of the section. Corrections for their inclinations, as represented in the sections, may then be necessary (Appendix 13). Sills are treated like strata. A section through a laccolith or a chonolith is made preferably in the plane of the dip of the basal contact. A section across a rock complex, such as is seen in the case of many of the larger intrusive bodies (batholiths, etc.) and their associated country rocks, may be oriented so that it will cut certain rocks, but generally without fixed relations to their boundaries.

As a rule one may safely infer that the nature of an igneous contact, as indeed, of any other geologic contacts, is similar in all directions, *i.e.,* that the features to be shown in its section are probably like those exposed in its horizontal, or nearly horizontal, outcrop. Hence, the details observed on rock exposures of contacts may often be drawn in the same general manner, whether on a map or in a vertical section (cf. the different sections shown in Figs. 92 and 95).

495. Vertical sections of faults. A section across a fault should be made as nearly as possible at right angles to the strike of the fault. For a dip-slip fault such a section gives the actual displacement; for all others, any displacement in the diagram is a rectangular component of the net slip. If the section is not perpendicular to the fault strike, the inclination of the fault must be corrected (Appendix 13).

In a geologic section a fault is represented by a heavy line, full within the base section and dotted (or dashed) above and below the base section (Fig. 522). On each side of the line, preferably just outside of the base section, a small arrow should

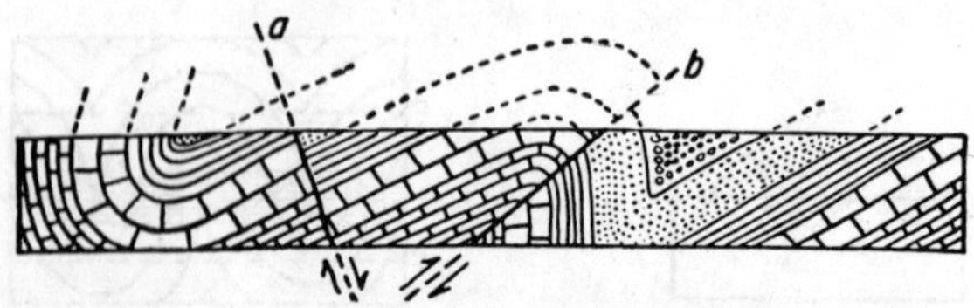

Fig. 522. Method of representing faults and faulted structures in a geologic section.

be drawn to show the *relative* direction of displacement of the blocks. The structures (bedding, igneous contacts, etc.) in the fault blocks, if indicated above the base section, should be drawn in dotted lines to the positions which they are imagined to have had against the dotted (or dashed) part of the fault line, *after faulting, but before erosion cut them down* to the present level of the land surface (Fig. 522) (cf. Arts. 198 and 515).

The construction of difficult fault problems may be simplified by sketching on scrap paper a section of the rocks before the displacement, cutting the paper along the line of the fault, and shifting the pieces along this cut until the rocks and structures are in their present relations.

496. Requisite data for a completed geologic section. No geologic section of existing structures is complete which is not accompanied by a legend, vertical and horizontal scales, and some indication of its direction. With reference to scales, see Art. 317. The direction of a section may be shown by labelling its ends with the proper points of the compass, or by stating that it is drawn looking in such and such a direction[8] or by labelling its ends by letters or by numbers which are also placed at the corresponding ends of its line of section on the map. A common error of beginners is to mark the top and bottom of a section by points of the compass, an impossible condition since all sections are vertical and all compass directions are horizontal.

Structure Contour Maps[9]

497. Nature of structure contour maps. Most geologic sections of stratified rocks are far from being accurate in the information which they convey of the thickness and depth of the individual layers. They are usually diagrammatic inferences based on such scattered facts as can be assembled from the observation of outcrops and from bore-hole and mine records. When such sources of information are especially abundant and reliable, the folds may be indicated by structure contour maps better than by geologic sections. A *structure contour map* (Fig. 523), like a topographic contour map, depicts the configuration of a surface by lines of equal elevation, generally referred to mean sea level as the datum plane. These lines are the intersections of the surface with a series of equally spaced horizontal planes, the vertical distance between any two adjacent planes being known as the contour interval. For a shallow structure contour map the surface chosen is that of the top or bottom of some bed which is easily recognized, is persistent over large areas, has not suffered much erosion, and is not too far below the land surface. The elevation of this *key horizon,* as it is called, above mean sea level is obtained in the field at as many points as possible, both at actual outcrops and from the records of drill holes, and the data are plotted at the several stations on a base map. Sometimes it is necessary to secure these elevations by adding to or subtracting from the elevations of outcrops of other known beds, but this method is liable to error on account of the possible variations in thickness of the intervening strata (**101, 102**). For a deep structure contour map, the key horizon is again the top or bottom of some recognizable bed, but the data used come from subsurface geology (**502–508**).

[8] Common practice is to draw east-west sections looking north (east end on right) and north-south sections looking west (north end on right).

[9] See also Art. **502** on Subsurface Maps.

FIG. 523. Structure contour map of the Amity, Brownsville, Waynesburg, and Masontown quadrangles, Pa. Axes of folds are indicated by dashed lines. The contours are lines of equal elevation of the base of the Pittsburgh coal bed above mean sea level. Contour interval 50 ft. (*After F. G. Clapp.*)

To illustrate the method of drawing a structure contour map, let Fig. 524 represent a chart of the stations examined and plotted in the field. At stations to the left of the dashed line, *ST*, elevations were determined on the chosen key horizon. At stations to the right of this line, *ST*, elevations were found on a bed 30 ft. above the key horizon, so that 30 ft. must be subtracted from each of these quantities to obtain elevations on the key

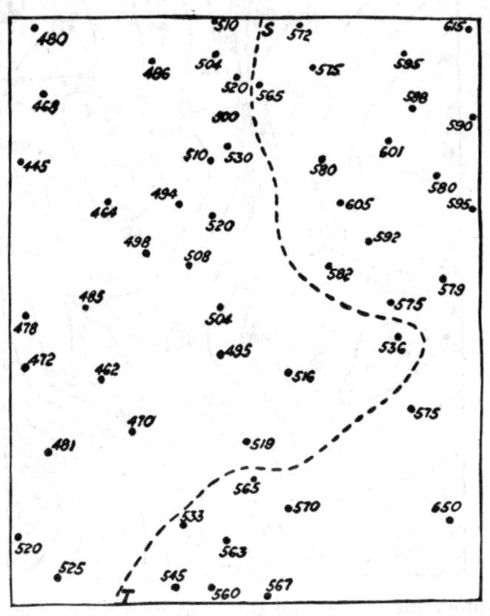

FIG. 524. Map of elevations determined at scattered stations on two outcropping beds. (See text.)

horizon. In Fig. 525 this subtraction has been done. On the assumption that a 10-ft. contour interval will be satisfactory, we may start by drawing a line through *a*, midway between *b* and *c*, through *d*, ⅓ way from *e* to *f*, ⅕ way from g to *h*, just south of *i*, and so on. This will be the 520-ft. contour line. In the same way the other contours may be drawn, either through stations having these elevations, or interpolated between stations of higher and lower elevations.

In Fig. 525 the 560- and 570-ft. contours are closed, representing a dome, *A′*; and the 470-ft. contour is closed to indicate a structural basin, *B′*. Note the closed basin contours are hachured.

As regards the accuracy of these maps, the steeper the dip of the strata and the less reliable and less numerous the available data, the greater is the chance for mistake in placing the structure contours. There are often places where generalization is a

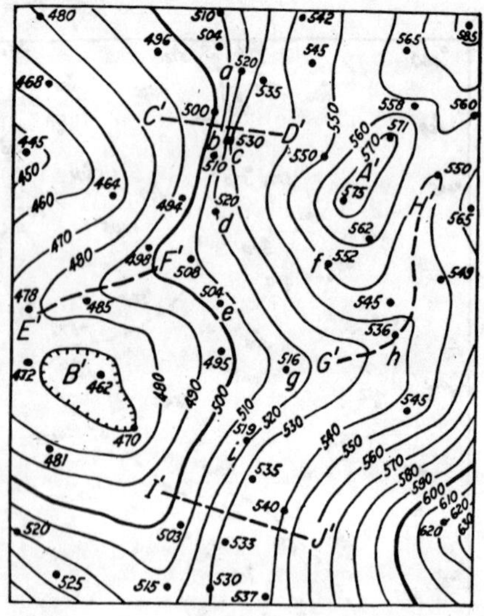

FIG. 525. Contour map drawn on the basis of the data shown in Fig. 524. The contours represent an anticlinal closure or dome at *A′*; a synclinal closure or structural basin at *B′*; an anticlinal nose with its axis along *E′F′*; a synclinal bowing or "chute"[10] with its axis along *G′H′*; a monoclinal flexure at *C′D′*; and a structural terrace at *I′J′*.

necessity, simply because the facts are too few. The more doubtful contours on a map should be dashed (Fig. 538). The contour interval is selected with a value such that it is not less than the *limit of error* for the district. "For example, if over a given area the elevation of" the key horizon "was determined to an accuracy of within 50 ft., it would be useless to attempt to draw contours

[10] Bibliog., Johnson, R. H., and L. G. Huntley, 1916, p. 65.

with a 25-ft. interval. Moreover, such a representation would be misleading to the reader, who would be led to believe that the elevation at any given point was accurate within 25 ft., which would not be the case."[11]

The intersection of a structure contour with a topographic contour of the same elevation marks a point on the outcrop of the key horizon. Where the land surface is higher than the key horizon, the approximate depth of the latter below the ground surface may be found by subtracting the elevation of the structure contour from that of the topographic contour at that place. When the land is lower than the key horizon, the latter has been eroded away and the structure contours indicate its probable former position. In this case they would better be dotted.

If one wants to ascertain the depth of some horizon other than that chosen for the *key*, one must first know the thickness of the beds between the two horizons. Thus, in Fig. 526, *dc* is the key horizon, parallel to the bedding, *c* is a point of which the depth, *fc*, below the surface of the ground, *gfh*, may be determined on the structure contour map, and *b* is a point vertically below *c* in a horizon, *eb*, with a thickness of intervening beds equal to *ab*. The required quantity, *cb*, can be obtained by solution of the right triangle *abc* in which *ab* and the angle *acb* are known.

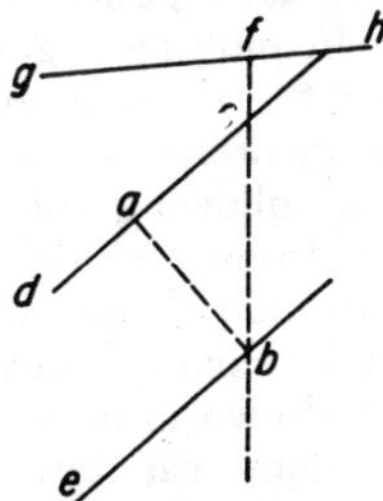

FIG. 526. Vertical section to illustrate the method of computing the depth of a horizon below the key horizon of a structure contour map.

WELL LOGS

498. Definition. When a deep hole is drilled into the ground, a record of the rocks penetrated is usually kept by the driller or by the field geologist. Such a record is called a *lithologic* or *formation log*.[12] It may be made up in written or typewritten

[11] Bibliog., Clapp, F. G., 1897, pp. 37, 38.

[12] As previously described, there are several other kinds of well logs which are often used in conjunction with lithologic logs in the study of subsurface geology (see Arts. **468–473**).

form, as shown below, or it may be plotted graphically to scale (Figs. 527, 528). In the laboratory a more detailed log is made of the same well, showing any data, discovered in the samples, pertaining to paleontology, lithology, etc.

Observe that every well log should have recorded on it the name of the locality or property where the well was drilled, the name of the organization which drilled the well, the elevation of the mouth of the well above sea level, the method of drilling, depths of casing seats, positions where the formation caved (see Art. 467), positions of water sands, oil or gas sands, etc.

In plotting a graphic log, various symbols or colors are used for the different rocks. Colors are better, since they stand out in greater contrast. For sedimentary rocks, the writer has found the following color scheme satisfactory: conglomerate, gravel, sandstone, or sand, yellow; shale, slate, clay, gumbo, and similar materials, blank; red shale, clay, or slate, red; limestone, chalk, and dolomite, blue; coal or peat, black. The sea level line should be drawn in its proper position across the log (Fig. 531).

Many varieties of printed log form are in use. In our experience the most convenient form is prepared as shown in Fig. 527. Here A is for sectionized country and B is for unsectionized country (Appendix 7). This outline is printed on heavy paper of good quality. The scale is 100 ft. = 1 in. The paper is about 2 in. wide. It should be long enough to plot a log of an average deep well. For an exceptionally deep hole, an extra strip may be glued at the bottom of a blank log form.

Example of a Well Log

State—Texas. County—Stephens. File number—6,836
Owner—XXXX Company. Farm—T.S. Hatch. Well number—2.
Location of Farm— Lot number XXX; Survey————.
Location of well—500 ft. from east line; 500 ft. from south line.
Casing record: set 18 in. . . . ; 15½ in., 615 ft.; 12½ in., 1,310 ft.; 10 in., 2,020 ft.; 8¼ in., 2,425 ft.; 6⅝ in., 3,075 ft.; 5³⁄₁₆ in., ...
Pulled 18 in. . . . ; 15½ in., 615 ft.; 12½ in., 1,310 ft.; 10 in., 2,020 ft.; 8¼ in.; 6⅝ in., ... ; 5³⁄₁₆ in., ...
Production: initial, 154 bbl.; settled, ... ; after shot, 750 bbl.; shot from 3,200–3,260 ft.; shot with 200 qts.
Total depth, 3,260 ft. Elevation, 1,245 ft.
Remarks: 2,425 ft. of 8¼ in. and 3,075 ft. of 6⅝ in. casing left in hole. Drilling began 8/27/40. Drilling completed 11/22/40.

TABLE 14. DRILLER'S LOG (*Continued from p. 684*)

Formation	*Top*	*Bottom*	*Remarks*
Clay	00	15	
Clay	15	30	
Blue mud	30	115	
Blue shale	115	210	
Brown lime	210	225	
Brown shale	225	345	
White lime	345	390	
Dark sand	390	410	Water
White lime	410	425	
Blue shale	425	460	
Broken lime	460	478	
Brown shale	478	595	
Lime	595	605	
Shale	605	630	
White lime	630	740	
Brown shale	740	765	
White lime	760	805	
Brown shale	805	1,005	
Lime	1,005	1,045	
Shale	1,045	1,060	
White lime	1,060	1,115	
Brown shale	1,115	1,125	
Gray lime	1,125	1,170	
White lime	1,170	1,195	
Black shale	1,195	1,223	
Gray sand	1,223	1,275	Water
Blue shale	1,275	1,310	
White lime	1,310	1,325	
Brown shale	1,325	1,500	
White lime	1,500	1,525	
Brown shale	1,525	1,700	
Gray lime	1,700	1,750	
White sand	1,750	1,755	Water
White lime	1,755	1,785	
Soft gray lime	1,785	1,790	
Brown shale	1,790	1,980	
Gray sand	1,980	1,990	Hole full of water
Dark shale	1,990	1,995	
Lime	1,995	2,000	
Gray sand	2,000	2,020	
Lime	2,020	2,035	
White shale	2,035	2,105	
Gray and white shale	2,105	2,315	
Gray lime	2,315	2,325	
White sand	2,325	2,330	Water. Gas show
Gray sand	2,330	2,425	
Blue shale	2,425	2,530	
Brown shale	2,530	2,600	
Blue shale	2,600	2,630	
Gray sand	2,630	2,645	Water
Brown shale	2,645	2,735	
Blue mud	2,735	2,752	
White sand	2,752	2,785	Water
Brown shale	2,785	2,900	
Blue shale	2,900	2,950	
White sand	2,950	2,960	Dry
Sandy shale	2,960	3,055	
Blue shale	3,055	3,075	
Hard lime	3,075	3,080	
Black slate	3,080	3,200	
Black lime	3,200	3,210	Steel line measure, 3,220 top black lime
Brown lime	3,210	3,245	
Gray lime	3,245	3,260	
		3,260	Total depth

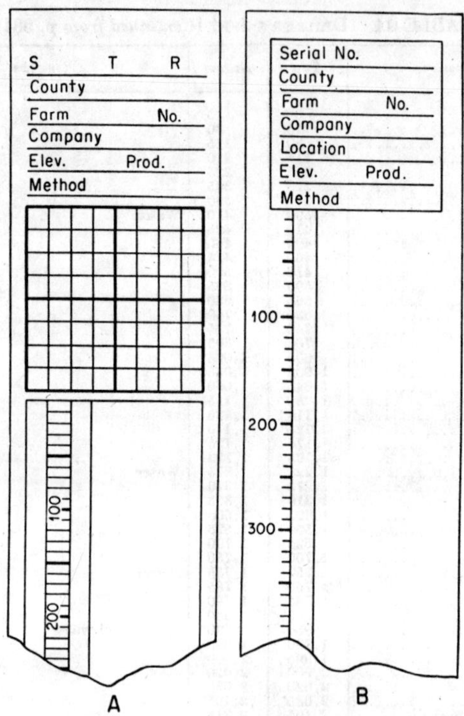

FIG. 527. Illustration of two types of log form used for plotting well records. That on the left (A) is used for sectionized country and that on the right (B) for regions which are not sectionized (Appendix 7). In these forms, "S" stands for section; "T" for township; "R" for range; "No." for well number; "Elev." for elevation of the mouth of the well above sea level; and "Prod." for initial production. The vertical scale is 1 in. = 100 ft. in the original form.

499. Correlation of lithologic logs. The correlation of lithologic logs involves the matching of plotted graphic records of two or more drilled holes, with a view to establishing the identity of the formations penetrated in these holes. The following two methods of correlation are frequently practiced.

1. Let *A* to *K*, Fig. 529, represent the locations of several wells of which the ground elevations are known. Plot the logs

graphically and then place them, side by side, as close together as possible, in such a way that their sea-level lines (**498**) are opposite (Fig. 530). Their order should not be selected at random, but should be chosen, according to the distribution of the wells in the field, with the object of placing together the logs of adjacent wells and of wells probably along the same line of strike. The sequence may often be one that a person might follow in going from well to well, provided no obstacles were in his way. Thus, here the order is *A*, *B*, *C*, etc., to *K*. Any scattered arrangement, such as *A*, *J*, *C*, *G*, *K*, etc., would be highly inadvisable.

Having placed the logs in this order, they may be shifted a little up or down until they match. If they do not exactly match—and they probably will not—they may be lined up on either the top or bottom of a definite bed (Fig. 531), or on the best average position for some bed or group of beds (Fig. 532). In the former case, the horizon on which the logs are correlated (matched), *ST* in Fig. 531, may be adopted as a key horizon for making a *subsurface map* (**502**). In the latter case, an arbitrary line may be drawn horizontally across the logs and used as the key horizon (*SS′*, Fig. 532). In matching the geologist will do well to remember that sharp and distinct changes in the hardness of rocks, either from hard to soft or vice versa, are more likely to be detected, and therefore correctly reported, by the driller than any other variations in materials.

2. In the second method of correlation the logs are arranged with their

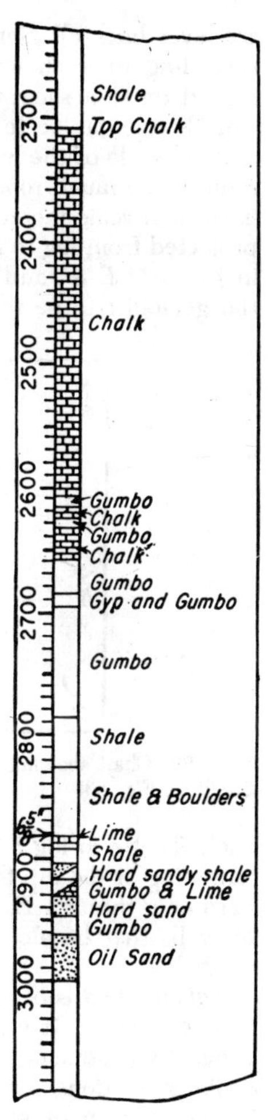

Fig. 528. Lower portion of a plotted well record showing method of recording data on the log form.

sea-level lines all along a horizontal line, and they are spaced according to a chosen horizontal scale. They may be thumbtacked on to a sheet of beaver board or on to a drafting table. The horizontal scale may be considerably smaller than the vertical scale of the logs, since too great a horizontal scale would require too much room. This method of arranging the logs on a horizontal scale facilitates their correlation in that strata may be projected from log to log along the inferred or known dips. Thus, in Fig. 533 *E*, *F*, and *G* are sufficiently close to one another for the geologist to be reasonably certain that bed *a* is the same in

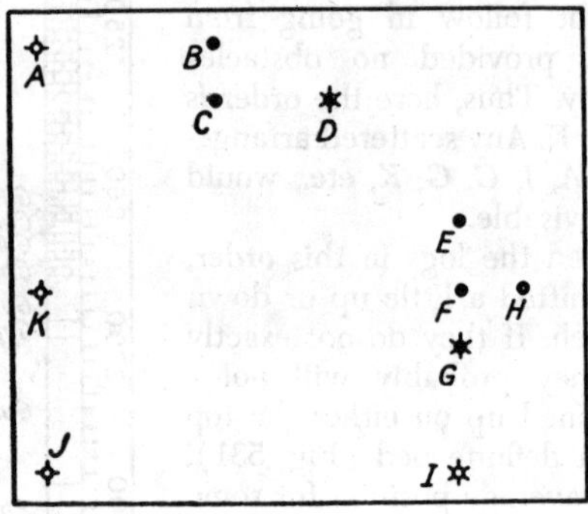

Fig. 529. Chart showing location of wells used in plotting structure illustrated in Fig. 538.

each. That *a* in log *I* is this same bed is indicated by the general flattening of the dip toward *I*, as shown by the line drawn on the base of *a* through *E*, *F*, and *G*. Observe that logs are used only of wells that lie along straight lines, or nearly straight lines, in the field.

This method is of value chiefly where the wells are fairly close to one another. It cannot safely be applied to widely scattered wells. In producing oil fields, it is often used in constructing geologic sections. For a subsurface structure contour map, the top or bottom of some easily recognized bed—frequently the pay sand in oil and gas wells—may be taken as the key horizon (503).

In difficult problems of correlation, both of the methods above described may have to be used, first one and then the other.

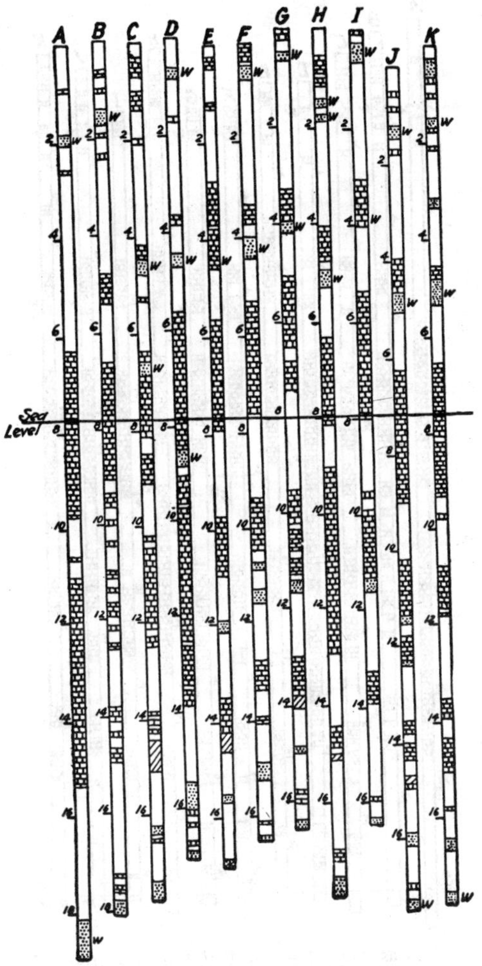

FIG. 530. Logs of the wells shown in Fig. 529 grouped in their proper vertical positions relative to sea level. Depths below the ground surface are shown for every 200 ft. *w* means "water-bearing."

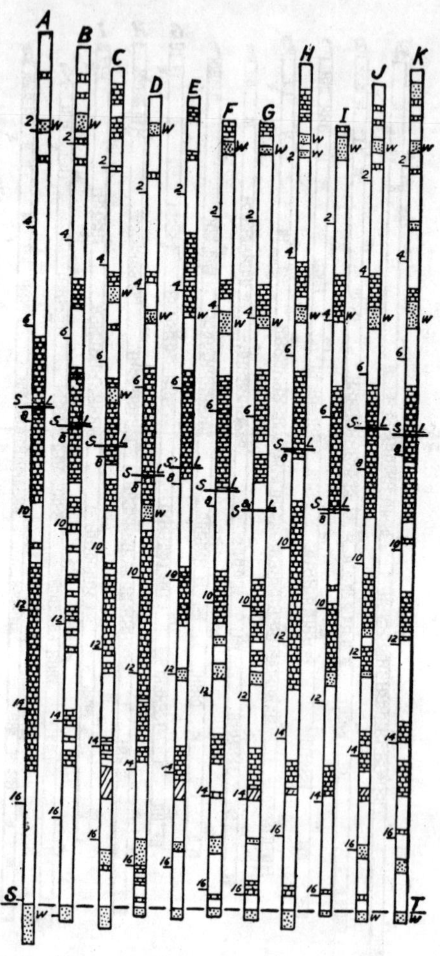

FIG. 531. Same logs as those shown in Fig. 530, here arranged so that they line up on the top, *ST*, of the oil sand at the bottom of each hole.

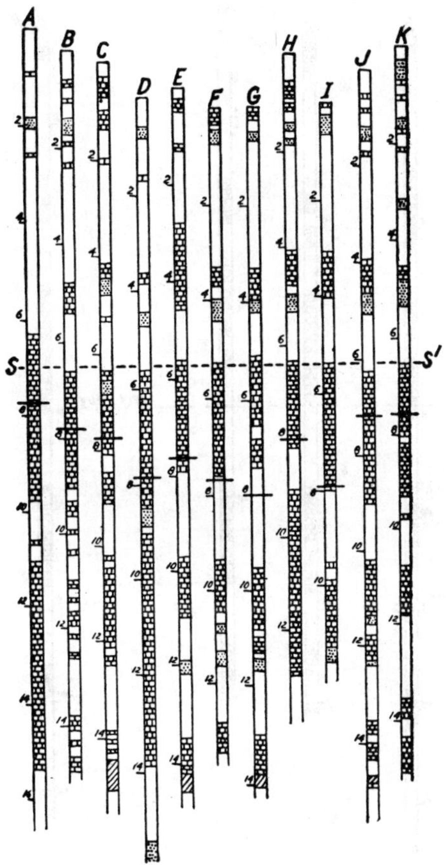

FIG. 532. Same logs as those shown in Fig. 530, here arranged so that they match most closely. Observe that this correlation was made before any of the holes, except *D*, had been drilled deep enough to reach the oil sand on which the correlation in Fig. 531 is based.

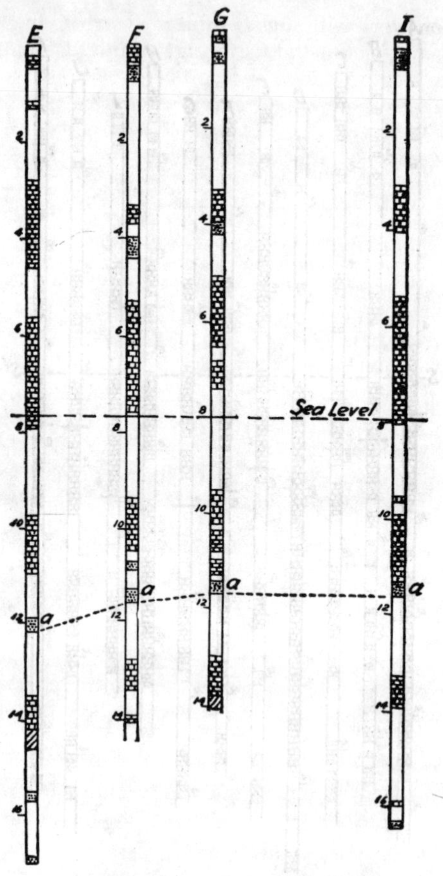

FIG. 533. Logs of *E*, *F*, *G*, and *I* (from Fig. 529), arranged on a chosen horizontal scale in their correct positions relative to sea level. Correlation is here made on the base of bed *a*. (Cf. contour map, Fig. 538, B.)

All correlation work with logs is subject to errors which should be understood and eliminated as far as possible. Certain important sources of error are these:

1. The elevations determined for the mouths of the wells may be more or less in error on account of inaccurate or careless instrumental work, or because they were found by individuals representing different companies and using different instrumental methods or different reference points.

2. Misunderstanding of driller's terms for rocks, and failure to appreciate the difference between cable-tool records and rotary records, may lead to misinterpretation of the logs.

3. Errors may be made in measuring, and therefore in recording, the depths of points in the hole. These may be caused by failure to make steel-line measurements, or by actual mistakes in measuring, or by the use of different steel lines for successive measurements. Great care is always necessary in these measurements of depth. The length of cable or drill stem extending down to any important point in the hole should be compared with the record obtained by the steel line to this point. Measurement of depth is often made as part of the operation of electrical logging (**468, 500**).

4. Mistakes often creep into the written logs in copying and recopying them.

The methods of correlating logs, as discussed above, apply more especially to drillers' logs or to logs in which there is some latitude for interpretation, because of the scarcity or uncertainty of scientific data. If accurate determination of one or more horizons is possible, there is no necessity for shifting the logs up and down to select an average position for correlation. If the stratigraphic interval between any two definite beds changes across the area, a subsurface map on each may be advisable (**504**).

500. Electrical logs for correlation. As we have explained in Art. **468**, electrical surveying of bore-holes has a decided advantage over former methods of logging, since it permits more accurate determination of the points where changes in lithology occur. Electrical logs more surely indicate the positions of the tops and bottoms of strata—points, in other words, that may be used in correlation. However, we want to make clear the fact that, even where these logs are employed as the main basis for correlation, this cannot be done to the complete exclusion of lithological and paleontological data from each hole; for we must have knowledge of what the rocks are and what fossils they contain before we can have a satisfactory understanding of the subsurface geology.

Figure 534 illustrates the use of electrical logs in correlation. These logs are arranged in the actual field relations of the wells that they represent and on a horizontal scale here equal to one-fifth the vertical scale. Only the lower part of each log is shown, beginning at a subsea depth of 3,500 ft. Depths from the surface of the ground, in each well, are indicated in the middle part of each log—40 meaning 4,000, 50 meaning 5,000 etc. The dashed lines (*a*, *b*, etc.) are correlation lines connecting, as nearly as possible, horizons that seem to be the same, from well to well. In making these correlations, the geologist first laid his electrical logs close together so that corresponding peaks and depressions in the potential and resistivity curves (**468**) could be more easily measured. (This is like the method of correlating lithologic logs, described under 1, Art. **499.**) The capital letters *D* and *H* mark the highest points at which certain fossils, usually regarded as determinative, were recorded from examination of samples. Matching of key horizons across the logs, when properly arranged to scale (as in Fig. 534), reveals the presence of a fault that cuts well 2 between *c* and *f*. This fault has its downthrow on the west. Its angle of dip is such that it does not cut holes 1 and 3 within the depths represented in the diagram.

Careful study of this section (Fig. 534) reveals these facts:

1. There are several distinct porous zones, here sand (strong negative anomaly in potential curve), and these, for the most part, contain salt water (low resistivity).

2. One sand contains oil (high resistivity), and the oil in this sand is banked up against the fault (cutting hole 2) that has its downthrow on the updip side of the regional eastward dip of the strata.

3. Between the sands are shales (low porosity) that, no doubt, contain saline water (low resistivity) in their fine pore spaces.

4. The heavy sand, indicated by the high porosity curve in hole 6 between depths of 3,900 and 4,250 ft., thins westward (holes 4, 3, 2, 1), and becomes less porous and more broken by shales eastward (holes 6 and 7).

5. The two sand zones *ac* and *de*, conspicuous in holes 3, 4, and 5, seem to merge into a less porous but thicker sandy zone eastward to hole 7; the shale break *cd* thins eastward.

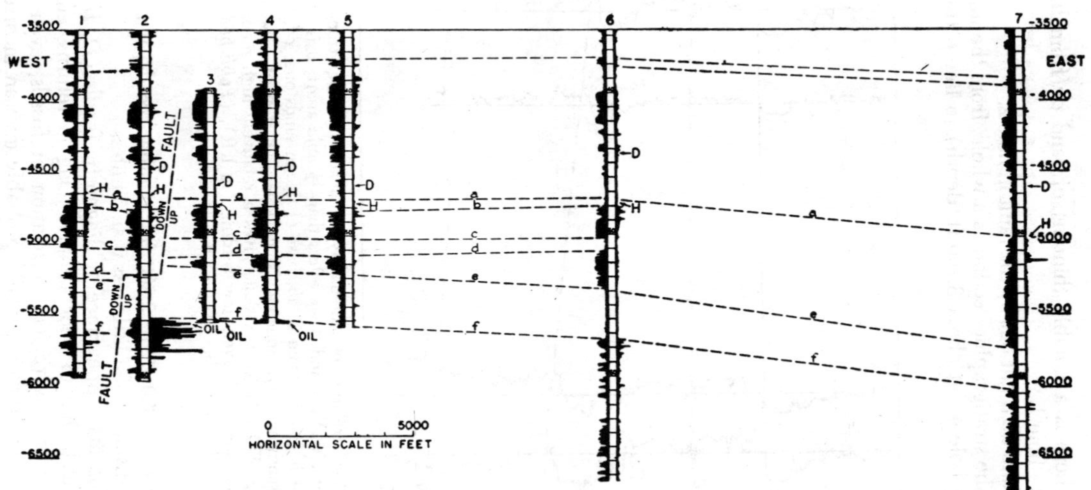

FIG. 534. Correlation of electric logs. These are logs of wells in south Texas. (See text.)

6. There is a notable thinning of sand *de* from hole 6 westward to hole 1.

7. Sand *de* is cut out by the fault in hole 2.

8. The stratigraphic section as a whole, from the upper dashed line in hole 4 (at about 3,760 ft. depth) to line *f*, thickens east-

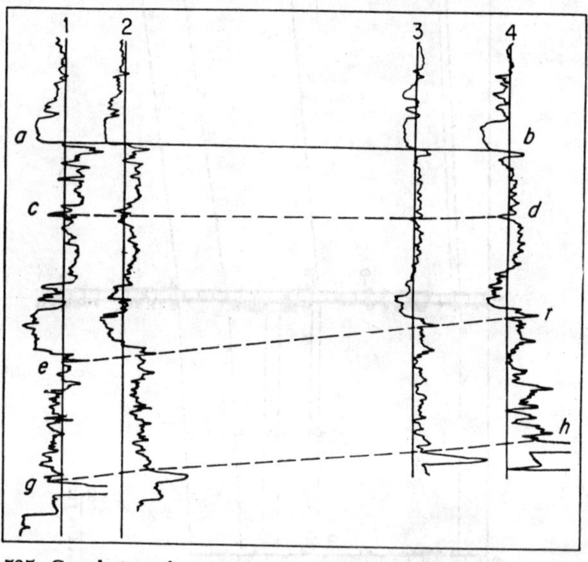

FIG. 535. Correlation of gamma-ray (radioactivity) logs from four wells in Oklahoma. Wells 1 and 2 were less than ½ mile apart; 3 is 3½ miles from 2; and 4 is ¾ mile from 3. *ab*, base of Glenn sandstone; *cd*, base of lower Booch sandstone; *ef*, unnamed shale layer; *gh*, top of Chattanooga shale (see Fig. 470). Note that shale gives a relatively high reading (to right) and sandstone a relatively low reading (to left). (*Published with permission of Well Surveys, Inc., Tulsa, Okla.*)

ward from 1,850 ft. to 2,200 ft.; in other words, it thickens 350 ft. in a distance of a little less than 5 miles.

9. The first appearance of diagnostic fossils (*D*, *H*) is rather theoretical, due to poor sampling, lag in returns, etc., so that, certainly in this region, correlation of fossils, even if assisted by study of lithology, would probably give an incorrect picture

of stratigrapnic and structural conditions. The electrical logs greatly assist in checking the geologic data.

501. Sonic logs, density logs, and radioactivity logs in correlation. Just as electrical logs (Art. **500**), so also sonic logs, density logs, and radioactivity logs can be of service in correlat-

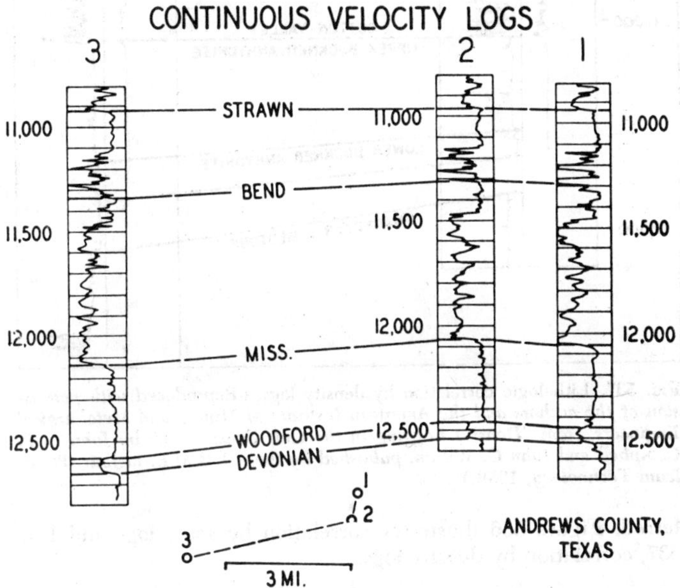

Fig. 536. Lithologic correlation by continuous velocity (sonic or acoustic) logs. (*Kindly furnished by G. H. Westby, and reproduced with permission of Breck, Schoellhorn, and Baum, and the American Association of Petroleum Geologists, from their article "Velocity Logging," published in Bull. Am. Assoc. Petr. Geols.*, 1957. *See Bibliog.*)

ing the formations penetrated in drilling. As we have stated, radioactivity logs can be secured from holes already cased and therefore not available for the usual methods of sampling and electrical logging. In Fig. 535 correlation by gamma-ray curves only is shown, but in practice the complete radioactivity log, with both its gamma-ray curve and its neutron curve, is pre-

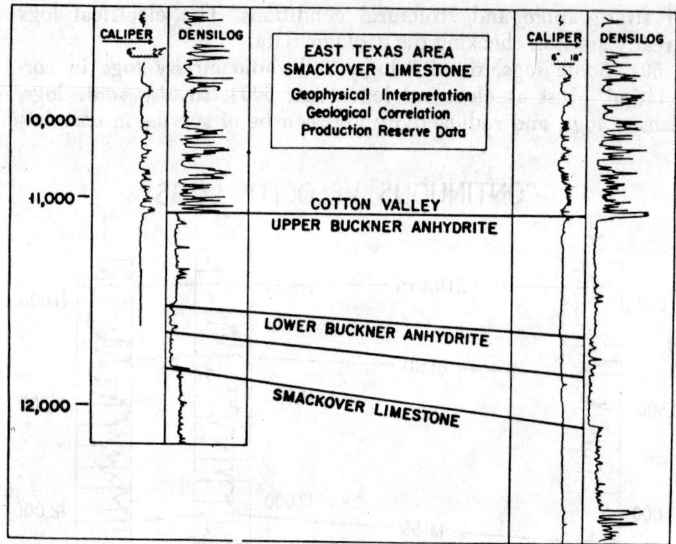

FIG. 537. Lithologic correlation by density logs. (*Reproduced with permission of the authors and the American Institute of Mining and Metallurgical Engineers, from "Density Logging in the Gulf Coast Area," by John L. P. Campbell and John C. Wilson, published by the A.I.M.M.E. in Jour. Petroleum Technology,* 1958.)

ferred. Figure 536 illustrates correlation by sonic logs and Fig. 537, correlation by density logs.

SUBSURFACE MAPS

502. Definition. The kind of structure contour map described in Art. 497 is constructed largely from data secured at or near the earth's surface. Outcropping strata furnish most of the evidence. A structure map contoured on some deep-lying key horizon, elevations on which have been obtained from well logs or mine records, is known as a *subsurface map*.

503. Construction. In Art. 499 we have briefly described methods of correlating well logs and selecting a key horizon for a subsurface map. Having chosen the key horizon, its elevation, in reference to sea level as datum, is to be found for each well by algebraically subtracting its depth from the elevation of the mouth of the well. Thus, if the key bed is at a depth of 800 ft. in a well which has a ground elevation of 1,000 ft., the elevation of the key horizon is 1,000 ft. − 800 ft. = 200 ft. If the key bed is found at a depth of 1,300 ft. in a well with a ground elevation of 1,000 ft., the elevation of the key horizon is 1,000 ft. − 1,300 ft. = −300 ft., or 300 ft. *below* sea level. The elevation of the key horizon is determined in this manner for all the wells in the area to be mapped, and these elevations are recorded on the map sheet in their proper places. A contour interval is chosen large enough to be somewhat greater than

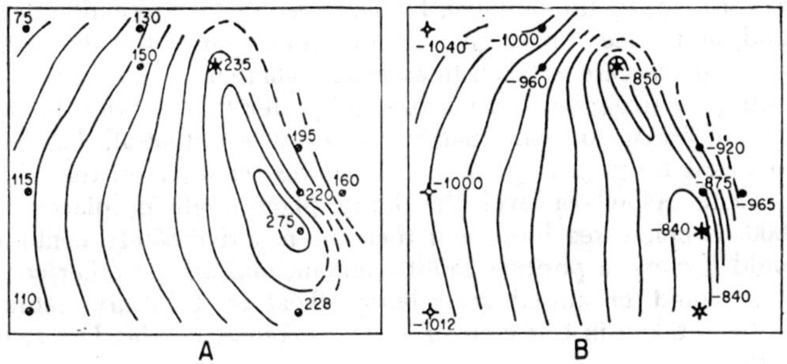

Fig. 538. Structure contour maps of the area shown in Fig. 529. A, preliminary interpretation based on correlation of Fig. 532. (Contours are above sea level. Key horizon is *SS′* of Fig. 532.) B, final interpretaton based on correlation of Fig. 531. (Contours are below sea level. Key horizon is *ST* in Fig. 531.)

the probable error involved in the correlation of the logs, and the contours are drawn as explained in Art. 497. The completed map should have a title, legend, scale, etc., just as in the case of an ordinary surface structure contour map.

In oil fields, where wells are being drilled in fairly close proximity to one another, it is often desirable to make one or more preliminary subsurface maps from data obtainable from the wells during the progress of the drilling. Naturally such maps are likely to be somewhat in error on account of the incompleteness of the well logs. To illustrate the difference between a preliminary map and a final map of a given area, we have prepared Fig. 538, in which A has been plotted on elevations determined by the correlation of Fig. 532 and B on the elevations derived from the correlation of Fig. 531. Note that the structure is essentially the same in both maps, although the form of the contours varies a little. Map A would certainly be of value for choosing locations for new wells before all the wells shown on this map had reached the oil pay.

When the contours of a subsurface map are above sea level they are *positive,* and when they are below sea level they are *negative.* A map with positive contours has the greater contour numbers on the higher parts of the structure, whereas a map consisting of negative contours has the greater contour numbers on the lower parts of the structure (Fig. 538). Since the latter type of map is a little difficult for some people to read and understand, and since it may give a false impression of the structure shown unless care is taken to ascertain whether the contours are positive or negative, some geologists prefer to raise the datum plane of a map to such a height above sea level that all the contours will be positive. Thus, if the lowest contour on the map is 850 ft. below sea level, the datum plane might be placed at 1,000 ft. below sea level, and then the negative 850-ft. contour would become a positive 150-ft. contour, and all the other contours would be raised accordingly. That an arbitrary datum has been taken in this manner must, of course, be clearly stated on the map.

In the writer's opinion this practice should be discouraged, for, although it simplifies the mere reading of the map, it greatly increases the time and labor incurred in making the calculations of depth, etc., based on the map. In the long run, the most practicable map is the one constructed on sea level as datum whether the contours are positive or negative.

In constructing Fig. 538, the contours were spaced essentially in mathematical relations to the elevation points recorded on the map. This is called *mechanical contouring.*[13] When there are numerous well-scattered elevation points, this method is fairly satisfactory, but if such points are few, the resulting contouring may be unreasonable, and even absurd, perhaps entirely out of accord with the known structural trends and forms of the region. Under these circumstances, the geologist must use his imagination, guided by his knowledge of the prevailing conditions. To illustrate these relations, Fig. 539, A to D have been drawn.

[13] Bibliog., Rettger, R. E., 1929.

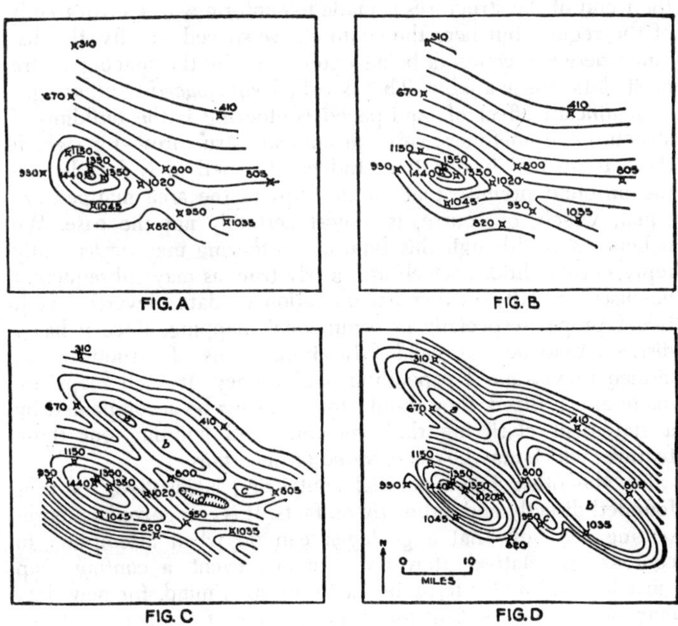

Fig. 539. Four interpretations of subsurface structure, all based on the same data obtained from the same wells. On each map the elevation of the key bed is given at the location of all wells. In A, the spacing is mathematically determined; in B, although proportionate spacing between wells controls the contouring for the most part, some latitude of interpretation has been employed in order to make the form of the structure look a little more reasonable. In C and D, equal spacing of contours has governed, the assumption being made that dips are everywhere essentially equal, which of course is unwarranted. Note that, in both C and D, certain anticlines (*a*, *b*, *c*) and synclines (*d*) appear, whereas they are entirely absent in A and B. Contouring such as that done in C and D is not justified and should be discouraged.

Figure 539, A, represents a mechanical contouring of the data plotted at 12 stations. Figure 539, B, shows another contour map, based on the same data, but with the contours drawn more nearly parallel, and in a form suggestive of the known type and alignment of other structures in the district. This is termed *parallel contouring*. Figure 539, C, and D, again, are based on the same data as Fig. 539, A and B, and also, as in Fig. 539, B, the trend of the structures is made to conform with known trends of the region; but here the contours are spaced equally, the distance between contours being determined by the spacing where most data are available. This is called *equispaced contouring.*[14] A significant effect of equispaced contouring is the building of structures—sometimes very prominent structures—for which there is no real justification. Indeed the method is founded on the unsound premise that all the dips in the area mapped are equal, which, of course, is almost certainly not the case. We believe that, although this type of contouring may occasionally represent conditions which are nearly true, as may subsequently be discovered by further accumulation of data, nevertheless it is not proper, especially in commercial mapping, since it has a distinct tendency to yield false impressions of structure and induce unwarranted expenditures of money. If such maps are made and utilized, they should by all means be accompanied by a statement clarifying their meaning and pointing out those features which may be exaggerated or uncertain.

On the other hand, parallel contouring is justified, for it is founded directly and indirectly on facts. It is recognized as representing the best that a geologist can do when attempting to contour on relatively few data. In any event, a contour map must be read and interpreted with an open mind, for new data may necessitate altering the minor details of the contour lines. Usually the major features will persist through various modifications, provided correlations have been correct.

504. Comparison of surface and subsurface maps; isopach maps. On account of variations in the thickness of beds and unconformity between formations, surface structure may often differ considerably from the structure in deeper beds below. These differences are well brought out on structure contour maps. Figure 540 illustrates two maps, one of surface beds and the other of the strata a few hundred feet below. The discordance here is due to thinning of the beds westward within a conformable series. In Fig. 541, the difference between the two maps is due to unconformable relations between two series of strata.

Certain rules may be formulated in reference to the effects of convergence on local structures. Anticlinal axes transverse to the direction of general convergence are shifted *toward* the direction of this convergence in successively lower beds. Thus,

[14] Bibliog., Rettger, R. E., 1929.

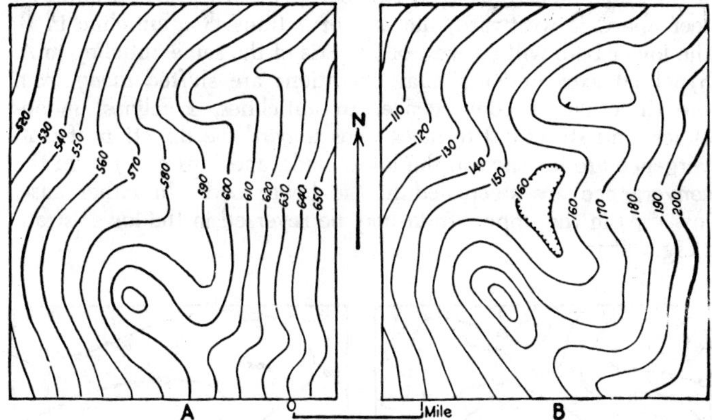

FIG. 540. Structure contour maps of an area in which there is westward convergence between the beds in a conformable series. A shows the surface structure. B shows the subsurface structure as mapped on a key bed directly below the area of A. The interval between the key beds of the two maps increases about 40 ft. from west to east across the area

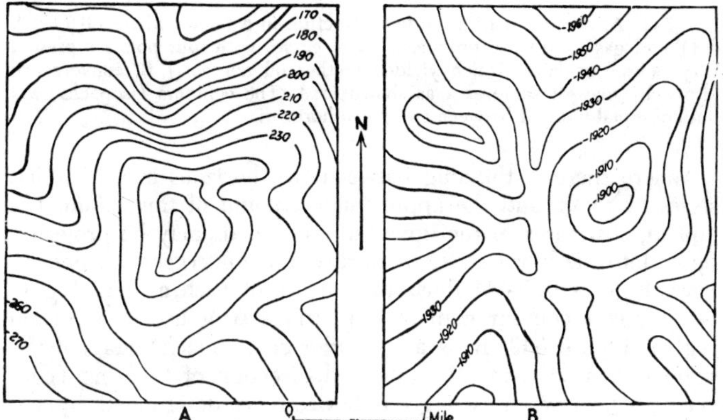

FIG. 541. Structure contour maps of an area in which there is convergence between two unconformable series of strata. A illustrates the structure of the exposed beds, and B shows the subsurface structure of the older formation which lies unconformably below the series mapped in A.

if the convergence between two beds, *A* and *B*, several hundred feet apart, is westward, the axis of a transverse anticline in *B*, the lower bed, will be west of the axis of the same anticline in *A*. Synclinal axes under similar conditions are shifted *away* from the direction of convergence. In anticlines, synclines, monoclines, and structural terraces, dips *toward* the direction of convergence are lessened in the lower beds, and dips *away* from the convergence are steepened in the lower beds. In either case, low dips in the upper strata may be reversed in the lower strata (Fig. 546).

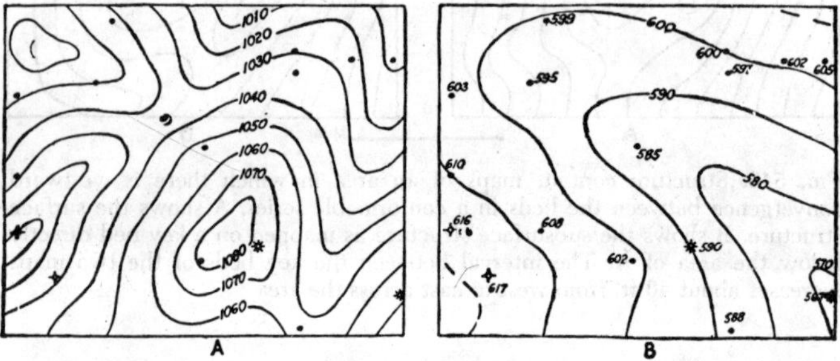

Fig. 542. A, contour map of surface structure in a region where oil (black dot) and gas (star) are produced. (The circles with four points represent "dry holes," or holes which yielded neither oil nor gas.) B, convergence (isopach) map of same area as shown in A. The contours (isopachs) are lines of equal interval between two given horizons.

Where there is thinning between two horizons in a stratified series of rocks, and the approximate amount of this thinning is known, structures in the upper series of beds may be projected down into the lower series by means of a *convergence* (*isopach*) *map.* Figures 542–544 illustrate the use of such a map. Figure 542, A, is a contour map of the surface structure in a certain region. Figure 542, B, is a convergence (isopach) map of the same region, showing the rate and direction of thinning (convergence) between two given horizons as determined by the records of wells or by measurement of exposed strata. By superposing the convergence map (drawn on tracing paper) upon the surface structure map (Fig. 543) elevations on the deep horizon may be marked at every point where a convergence contour (*isochore* meaning "equal interval," or *isopach,* meaning "equal thickness") crosses a surface structure contour. For instance, if the isopach showing an interval of 600 ft. between the two given horizons crosses the surface structure contour of 1,040 ft., the elevation of the deep horizon at the point of intersection of these two lines (*a,* Fig. 543) is 1,040 ft. − 600 ft. = 440 ft. After the elevations have been established in this manner on the deep horizon, contours are drawn in reference to these points (Fig. 544).[15]

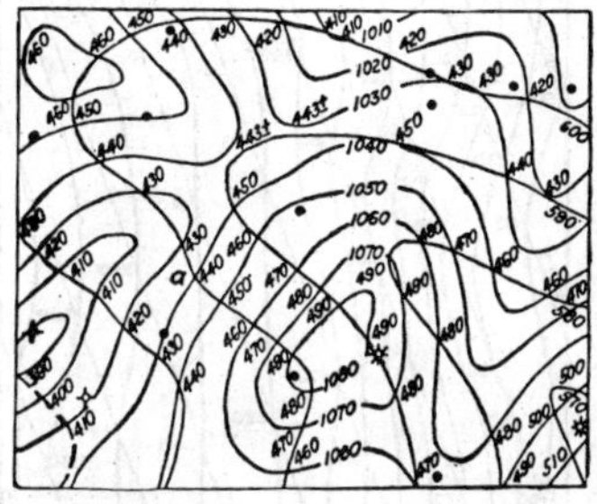

FIG. 543. This figure shows Fig. 542, B, superposed on Fig. 542, A. At every point where the contours of the two maps intersect, the difference between the elevations of the intersecting contours is calculated and recorded.

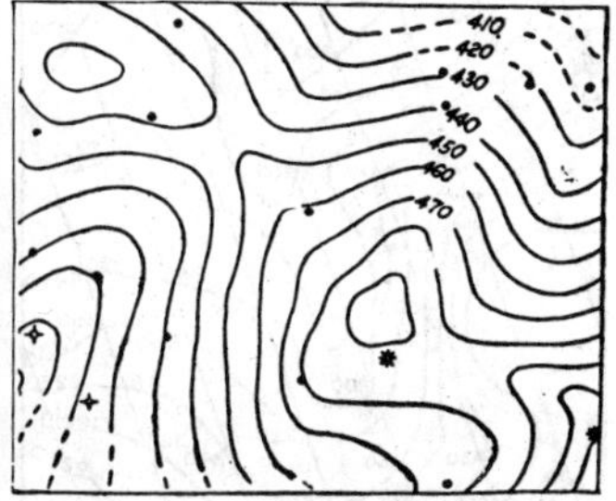

FIG. 544. Contour map of the deep horizon in the area mapped in Figs. 542 and 543. The contours here are drawn through the intersection points of the contours as established in Fig. 543.

The deep horizon maps in Figs. 540, B, 541, B, and 544 are decidedly similar to the shallow horizon maps of the same areas (540, A, 541, A, and 542, A, respectively); but it is important to note that such close similarity does not always occur. For example, compare Fig. 545, A and B, and Fig. 546, A and B. Also observe that, unless strata have low dips—let us say of 5° or less—errors may result from the fact that the distance between the top and bottom of a bed, as measured in a bore-hole, may not represent true thickness (Fig. 548).

[15] Two excellent papers referring to convergence have been published by Corbett and Levorsen. (Bibliog., Corbett, C. S., 1919; and Levorsen, A. I., 1927.)

505. Lithofacies maps and biofacies maps. In Art. 88 the meaning of lithologic facies and biologic facies was explained. To show the regional distribution of the different lithologic facies of a given formation, *lithofacies maps* are made. These may indi-

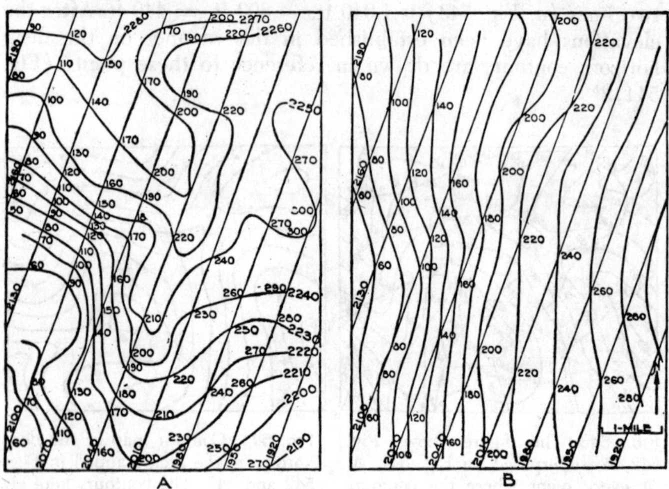

Fig. 545. A, surface contour map of an anticlinal nose. From data obtained in several wells in the district, it is known that the upper series, which has an average southeastward dip of 15 ft. per mile, lies unconformably on a lower series which dips nearly due westward 30 ft. per mile. From these dips, the convergence of these formations is estimated to be about 45 ft. per mile S. 70°E. Lines of equal average interval, showing this convergence, are drawn straight across A and B. At each intersection point of these lines with the contours in A the interval is calculated. The quantities obtained are transferred to B, in the same relative positions, and they are then contoured with the result shown in B. In other words, B represents a contour map of the deep-lying formation, unconformably below the beds contoured in A. Observe that nothing is left, in B, of the structure in A, except a slight terrace effect.

cate the facies in terms of rock types, as, for example, conglomerate, sandstone, shale, limestone, dolomite, etc.; or they may be prepared on the basis of varying proportions of clastic (sand, shale, etc.) and nonclastic (limestone, anhydrite, etc.)

constituents of the rocks, expressed in percentages. Thus, in Fig. 547 the symbols represent the percentages of each of these two classes of rock material as measured in local vertical sections of the entire thickness of the formation under consideration, here called "A." For correct interpretation such measurements of thickness should of course be perpendicular to the stratification. Bear in mind that these percentages do not reflect absolute

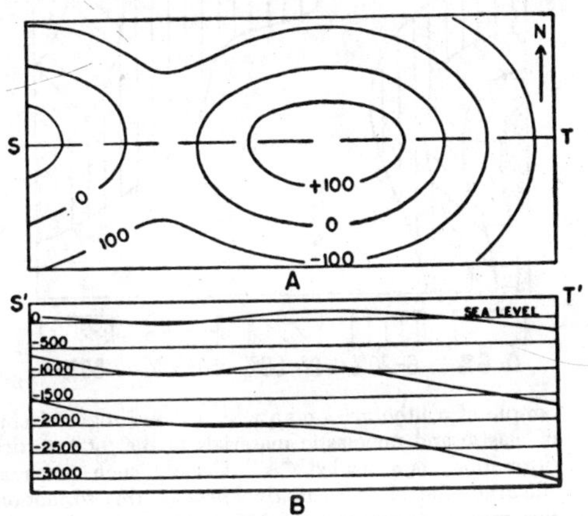

FIG. 546. Effect of convergence of beds on structure. The section (B) is drawn along *ST* as shown on the map (A). The key horizon contoured on the map is shown by the upper curved line in the section. This horizon has nearly 200 ft. of closure, but, because of westward convergence in the underlying strata, this closure becomes less with depth until it disappears, and instead there is a terrace (lower curved line in the section). Length of section about 3½ miles.

thicknesses. Similarly, biofacies maps may be constructed to show the distribution of percentage relations of one fossil to another, or of one distinctive group of fossils to another, within a selected stratigraphic sequence and within a defined area.

506. Isolith maps. Closely related to lithofacies maps are maps which portray the variations in aggregate thickness of a given lithologic facies as measured perpendicular to the bedding at selected points. For instance, let us suppose that there are five

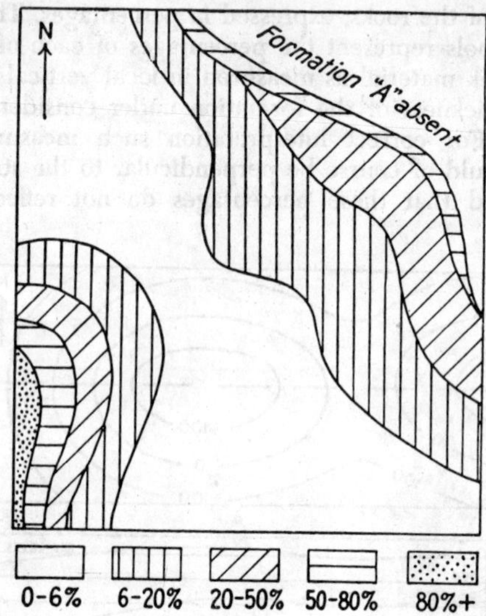

FIG. 547. Example of a lithofacies map which shows regional changes in the proportions of clastic and nonclastic materials in the total vertical thickness of a given formation, here called "A." Usually such maps also include isopachs to illustrate the changes in thickness of this formation. The area covered by this map is approximately 150,000 square miles. (State boundaries and locations of cities, etc., have been omitted.)

localities at which, through measurements in drilled holes, a certain formation varied in total thickness and in the thickness and distribution of its constituent lithologic members, as follows:

Locality 1...... Formation totals 500 ft. and contains 2 sandstone beds, each 50 ft. thick.

Locality 2...... Formation totals 500 ft. and contains 3 sandstone beds, one 40 ft., one 50 ft., and one 70 ft. thick.

Locality 3...... Formation totals 400 ft. and contains 5 sandstone beds, one 40 ft. thick and four each 20 ft. thick.

Locality 4...... Formation totals 350 ft. and contains 6 sandstone beds, respectively, 5 ft., 10 ft., [illegible] ft., 20 ft., 30 ft., and 40 ft. thick.

Locality 5...... Formation totals 200 ft. and contains 10 sandstone beds, each 10 ft. thick.

Thus, there would be 100 ft. of sand at Locality 1, 160 ft. at Locality 2, 130 ft. of sand at Locality 3, 120 ft. of sand at Locality 4, and 100 ft. of sand at Locality 5.

After these aggregate thicknesses have been plotted in their proper positions on the map, lines of equal aggregate thickness (*isoliths*) are drawn to produce the *isolith map*.

507. Paleogeographic maps; paleogeologic maps. A map which shows the distribution of the ancient lands and seas at the time when a given formation was deposited is a *paleogeographic map* (see Art. **126**). Such maps are very generalized since, as usually constructed, they portray a body of strata which were

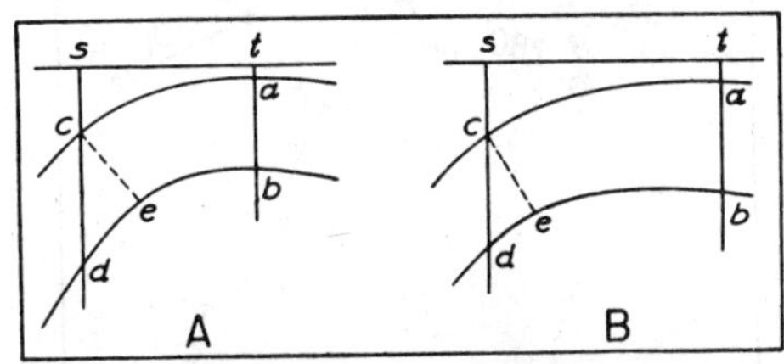

Fig. 548. Sections to illustrate errors in measuring the thickness of formations in holes (*s* and *t*) where dips are relatively steep. *ab* and *ce* are true thicknesses. *cd* is an incorrect thickness measured down from *c* to *d* in hole *s*. In A, *ce* actually equals *ab*, but *cd* is much greater than *ab*, giving the impression that the formation thickens from hole *t* to hole *s*. In B, there is actual thinning of the formation from *t* to *s*, but *cd*, being equal to *ab*, gives no clue to this thinning. (See **533**.)

laid down through a very long period of time, and we can be practically sure that during that time the shore lines may have undergone many and extensive migrations. Thus, a paleogeographic map of the Devonian system could approximate the positions of Devonian shore lines only in the broadest way.

A *paleogeologic map* is a map which shows the geology of a selected ancient land surface, now represented by an unconformity (see Art. **127**).

508. Effects of crookedness of bore-holes on subsurface mapping. The subject of crooked holes has been touched upon in Art. **475**. We wish now to point out some of the errors in interpretation of subsurface conditions which may be occasioned by the false assumption that holes, actually inclined, are vertical. Figure 549 illustrates a possible spacing of the points at which

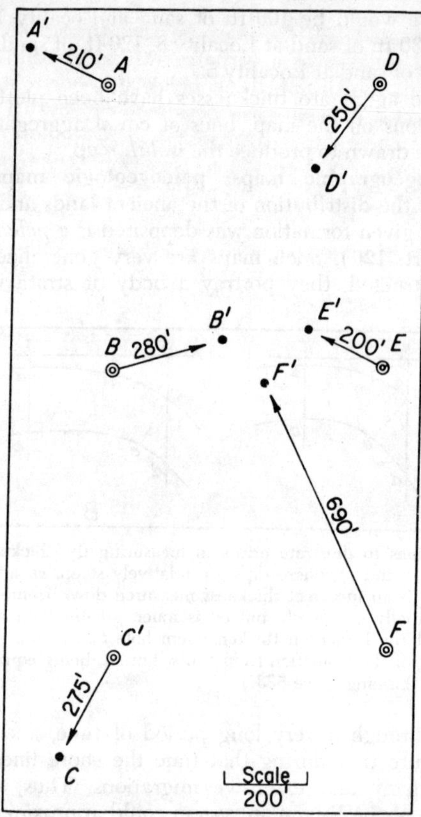

FIG. 549. Map of six well locations (*A* to *F*) on the surface of the ground (double circles). On the assumption that these holes were drilled off the vertical in the directions indicated by the arrows and to a horizontal distance shown beside the arrows, the bottoms of the holes would be at points *A'* to *F'*, respectively. (*Figures 549 to 553 are reprinted from the Bull. of the Am. Assoc. Petr. Geols. See Bibliog., Lahee, F. H., 1929.*)

six holes, located 660 ft. apart on the surface of the ground, encountered the top of a certain stratum, S. The arrows show the direction of drift of these holes, the horizontal migration being indicated in each case beside the arrow. If the facts of deviation of these holes were not known, and the holes were assumed to be vertical, the data (elevations, etc.) on S would be incorrectly recorded on a map at the points *A* to *F*, instead of at

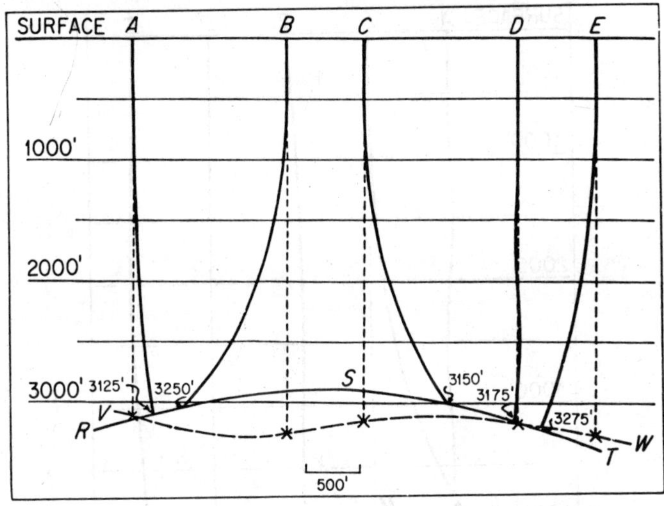

Fig. 550. Vertical section to illustrate misinterpretation of subsurface geologic data from crooked holes.

A′ to *F′* where they really belong. It is not difficult to imagine how misinterpretations of this kind may lead to errors in contouring subsurface geologic structure, in estimating per-acre yields of oil from a given property, in trying to solve problems of porosity and rate of flow of fluids between wells, and so on. Furthermore, in regard to contour maps, there is a vertical error as well as a horizontal error in the plotting of any data from a crooked hole. No doubt in a majority of wells, taking into consideration all regions where holes are drilled for oil, gas, or water, this vertical discrepancy is small; but it may be large without any suggestion in the drilling that the hole is going off plumb.

Figures 550–553 represent other anomalies and misinterpretations which may result from deviation of holes from the vertical. In Fig. 550, "five holes are shown in vertical section. From measurements in these holes, from the surface down to the key horizon, *RST*, the structure represented by line *VW* was inferred.

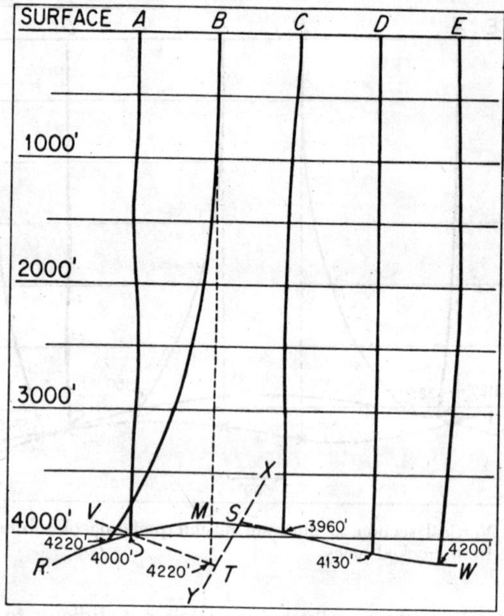

Fig. 551. Hypothetical vertical section showing how incorrect geological structure may be inferred from data from wells not drilled vertical.

Actually, however, the structure was that indicated by the full line, *RST*. The misinterpretation was due principally to the abnormal depth at which holes *B* and *C* reached the key horizon . . . ."

Figure 551 "is another example of false interpretation. Here the excessive depth of hole *B*, at the key horizon, *RMW*, led to the conclusion that a fault of approximately 400 ft. displacement lay between *B* and *C*, the strata on both sides of the fault having a dip toward *W*. Yet actually *RMW* is an unbroken anticline."

In Fig. 552, "*C*, between two wells, *B* and *D*, should have produced oil; and *G* should have been dry. As shown, however,

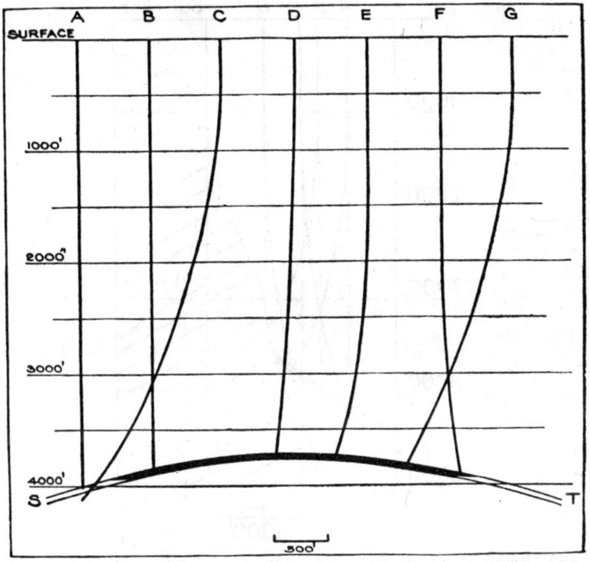

FIG. 552. Vertical section of an anticline carrying oil (black) on its crest. *A* to *G* represent wells drilled for the oil, but not all drilled vertical. (See text.)

C would have been a puzzle since it was dry and apparently missed the 'pay' altogether. *G* was a surprise in that it was a much better well than *F* . . . ."

Figure 553 "illustrates one side of a salt dome in cross section. If the four wells had been vertical, *A* would have been a deep edge well; *B* and *C* would have been good producers; and *D* would have gone into salt several hundred feet above the 'pay.' Due to the deviation of these holes, *C* was an edge well, *A* and

D were big producers, and *B*, between two oil wells, went into salt."[16]

These examples are sufficient. They emphasize the need for making daily checks on the verticality of holes that are in process of drilling, and the importance of surveying completed holes for their true position underground, when they are known to be

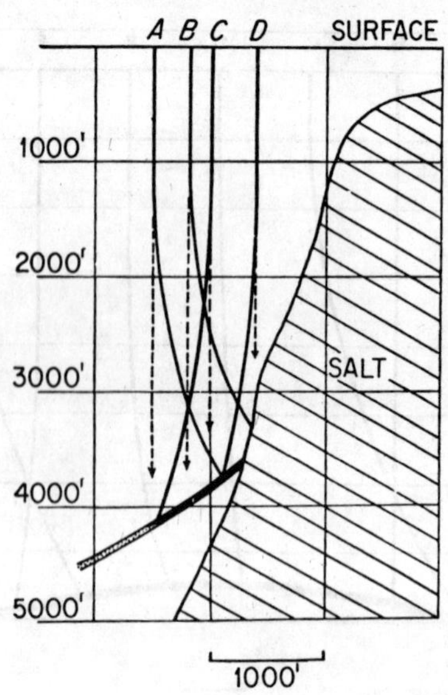

FIG. 553. Relations of crooked bore-holes to the salt plug of a salt dome.

more than a few degrees off the vertical. If their courses in three dimensions are determined, the geologic data which they reveal can be plotted in correct relations.

CONTOUR MAPS OTHER THAN STRUCTURE CONTOUR MAPS

509. Examples mentioned. Without entering into detail, we may say that the method of drawing lines or contours through mapped points of equal value is applied to many other features besides structure. For instance, contour maps have been made

[16] Bibliog., Lahee, F. H., 1929 (*b*), pp. 1129, 1133.

showing lines of equal magnetic anomaly (**560**), lines of equal chlorine content in water, lines of equal Baumé gravity of oil, lines of equal gasoline content in natural gas, and so on. With the explanation of ordinary structure maps clearly in mind, the student should be able to prepare any kind of contour map to solve his own problems.

Block Diagrams

510. Definitions. One of the most successful methods of geologic illustration, both for popular and for scientific demonstration, is the so-called *block diagram*. In brief this is a view of an imaginary rectangular block of the earth's crust. It is as if upon a rectangular block of wood, let us say, two geologic sections had been drawn on two adjoining sides and a map on the top face, and then the block itself had been sketched in a position such that these three faces were visible to the eye (Fig. 95). Frequently the top surface is drawn as if it were a model of the topography, with all the hills and valleys (Figs. 160, 195, 207, 347, etc.). There are, then, two varieties of block diagram. For easy reference the term, *map block*, will be used for the kind with a flat top, and the term, *relief block*, for the kind that shows the topography. The first brings out the relations of geologic structures in normal planes, and the second, the relations between geologic structure and topography. Relief blocks are best constructed in perspective, but map blocks may be made in isometric or cabinet projection or in perspective (**511**). Like geologic sections and maps, a block diagram represents the geology by different lines and patterns, less often by colors, and consequently it must have a legend.

511. Construction of block diagrams. Before the geology can be depicted on a block diagram, the outlines of the block itself must be drawn. This may be done in isometric projection, in cabinet projection, or in perspective. Figure 554, A, illustrates the isometric projection, and Fig. 554, B, the cabinet projection, of the same rectangular parallelopiped. In each case lines parallel in the block are drawn parallel, vertical lines are drawn vertical, and equal lines (those with the same letter in Fig. 554) are equal in the diagram. In Fig. 554, A, the angles marked x are each of them 120°, and measurements along any of the lines of the diagram are on the same scale. In Fig. 554, B, angle $x = 45°$

and angle $y = 90°$; measurements parallel to a and c are equal, but parallel to b the scale is one-half its value parallel to a and c; that is, if an inch or a foot or a mile is measured off as an inch along a and c, the same distance is represented by ½ in. parallel to b. A very useful variety of cabinet projection is one in which angle x (Fig. 554, B) is 30°, angle y is 90°, parallel edges of the block are drawn parallel, and measurements in directions parallel to all the edges are on the same scale. In both isometric and cabinet projections, then, measurements of length can easily be made in directions parallel to the edges of the block.[17]

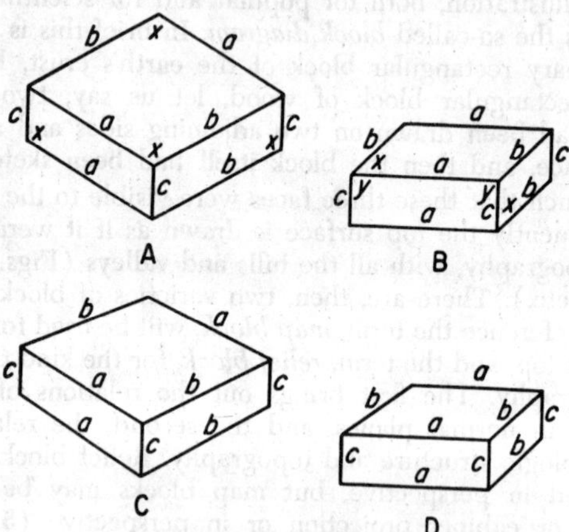

FIG. 554. A rectangular block drawn in isometric projection (A), cabinet projection (B), angular perspective (C), and parallel perspective (D).

On the other hand, in a perspective sketch of a rectangular parallelopiped, equal parallel lines are seldom equal or parallel in the figure. Vertical lines are drawn vertical, but horizontal parallel lines generally converge toward the background in such a way that, when produced, they will all meet in a single point, and the several points in which different sets of horizontal lines meet are all on the same straight line, the *horizon line* (*ab* in Figs. 555, 556). If all sets of horizontal lines in the object meet in the horizon line, the perspective is angular (Figs. 554, C, and

[17] Measurement of angles and distance in nonperspective blocks is explained by Ives (see Bibliog., Ives, Ronald L., 1939)

555), but if one set of horizontal lines in the object is drawn in the plane of the picture, the perspective is parallel (Figs. 554, D, and 556). Parallel perspective differs from cabinet projection in that the edges marked *b* in *D* and *B*, Fig. 554, are parallel in the latter, but converge to a point on the horizon line in the former. Parallel perspective involves a certain amount of distortion, as may be seen in Fig. 554, D, for if a rectangular block were looked at perpendicular to one of its faces its other sides would not be visible.

Measurements can be made on block diagrams in both parallel and angular perspective,[18] but with very much less facility than

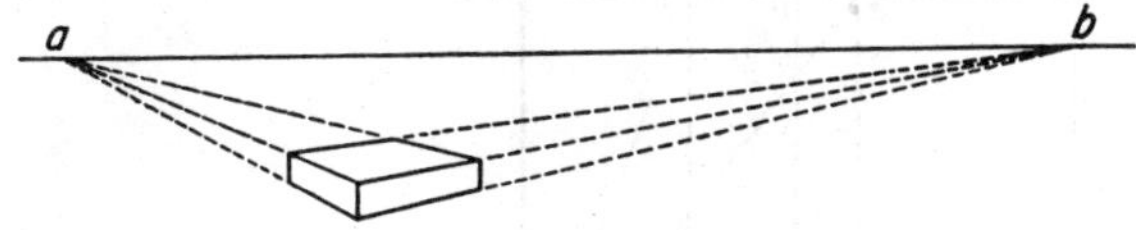

FIG. 555. Block drawn in angular perspective, showing its relation to the horizon line, *ab*.

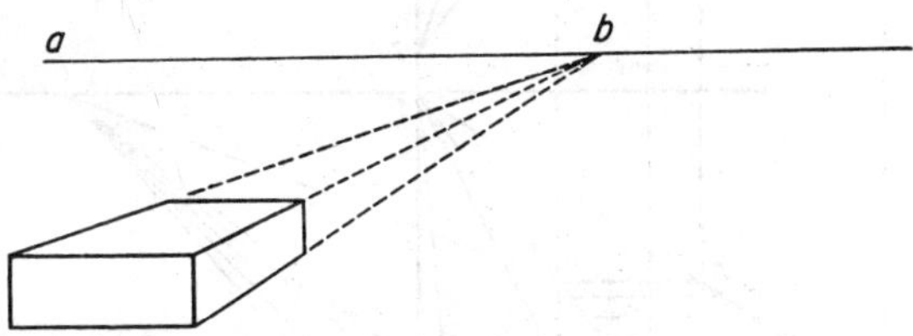

FIG. 556. Block drawn in parallel perspective, showing its relation to the horizon line, *ab*.

in cabinet and isometric projections. Let us consider an example of parallel perspective. Suppose that in Fig. 557, *ljkmnop* represents a rectangular block which is 3 ft. thick and 5 ft. square on its top. The construction of this part of the figure may be stated briefly as follows: *abcd* is the square top (or bottom) of the block as viewed from above, drawn to the scale of ⅙ in. = 1 ft. Choose a point, *g*, for the *view point*. Produce *dc* a certain distance to the right to *c′*. Draw *ag* and *bg*. *ag* intersects *dc′* at *e*, and *bg* intersects *dc′* at *f*. Next draw *hi* parallel to *dc′* and at a convenient distance below *dc′*. Drop perpendiculars to *hi* from *d* and *c*, meeting *hi* in *j* and *k*, respectively. Mark off

[18] See Bibliog., Secrist, Mark H., 1933.

lj and *mk*, each 3/6 in. long. Draw *lm*. Then *lmkj* represents the front face of the block constructed on the chosen scale. Through *g* draw a line, *c′v*, perpendicular to *dc′* and *hi*. On this line select a point, *s*, at a convenient distance above *hi*. From

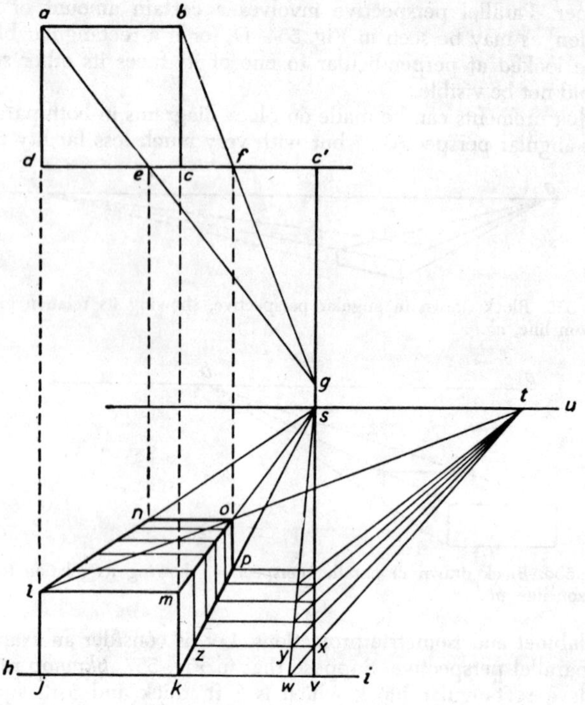

FIG. 557. Construction used for measurements on a block drawn in parallel perspective.

l, *m*, and *k*, draw lines to *s*. From *e* and *f* draw lines perpendicular to *hi*, intersecting *ls*, *ms*, and *ks*, at *n*, *o*, and *p*, respectively. Draw *no* and *op*. Then *noml* is the top, and *mopk* is the side, of the block, both seen in perspective.

Now, the reader will notice that although, in the block, $jk = lm = no$, and $lm = mo = kp$, and $lj = mk = op$, this is not true in the diagram. Evidently the same scale cannot be used for all edges. The front face is here made with both horizontal and vertical scales the same, *i.e.*, ⅙ in = 1 ft. Because of foreshortening, 1 ft. must be represented by less than ⅙ in. on edges *no* and *op*. To obtain the scale for these two edges, divide *no* into five equal parts and *op* into three equal parts. The divisions of *no* and *op* are equal.

As for edges *ln*, *mo*, and *kp*, each consists of five parts, and each part represents 1 ft. in the block, but in the figure these parts are necessarily smaller toward the background. They are obtained thus: referring to Fig. 557 again, draw through *s* a line, *su*, parallel to *hi*, and through *l* and *o* draw a line intersecting *su* at *t*. From *v*, on *hi*, mark off a distance, *vw*, equal to ⅙ in. (the unit of the scale) toward *k*, and draw *ws* and *wt*. *wt* intersects *sv* at *x*. From *x* draw a line parallel to *hi* and meeting *kp* in *z*. *kc* represents 1 ft. *xz* intersects *ws* at *y*. Draw *yt*. From the point of intersection of *yt* and *sv* draw a line parallel to *hi* until it meets *kp*. Proceed in this manner until *kp* has been divided into five unequal spaces, each representing a length of 1 ft. in the original block. The divisions of *mo* may be obtained by erecting perpendiculars to *hi* through the points fixed on *kp*, and the divisions of *ln* may be obtained by lines drawn parallel to *hi* from the points on *mo*.

For further discussion of scale in perspective blocks, both parallel and angular, the student may consult the article by Secrist, already cited.

With regard to the advantages and disadvantages of these methods of illustration, perspective drawing looks more natural than either kind of projection, but it greatly increases the difficulty of measuring distances. Therefore, cabinet or isometric projection should be employed when the block diagram is intended to facilitate computations (see figures in Chap. 21). Of the two, cabinet is preferable to isometric projections. For geologic illustration parallel perspective has a distinct advantage over angular perspective since it shows the structures in their true relations on at least one face, the front one.

Having completed the outline of the block, the next thing to do is to decide upon its orientation, or, rather, the orientation of the geology to be indicated upon it. A good rule to follow is, let the front of the block be perpendicular or parallel to some important structure. Thus, it is well to make the front face normal to the axis of a fold or normal to the strike of a fault, bed, or dike, on any of which measurements are to be computed.

When you have determined the orientation of the block, you are ready for the third stage. This consists of sketching in the geology and, on a relief block, the topography. The sides of vertical faces of the block are filled in first, and then the top surface. For any block in cabinet projection or in parallel perspective, complete the front face, which is parallel to the plane of the paper, exactly as you would a geologic section. If the finished diagram is to be a map block, this front face is treated as a rectangular base (**490**); if a relief block, it is treated as a profile base (**491**).

In any block diagram, for sides not parallel to the plane of the paper begin by making a preliminary true geologic section on a rectangular base or on a profile base according as the figure is to be a map block or a relief block, respectively. Do not complete this preliminary section; merely carry it far enough to get the locations of important points, and then transfer these points to their correct places on the side of the block diagram. In transferring, remember the rules for measurement in cabinet and isometric projection and in perspective. When the geologist has become proficient in making block diagrams, he seldom needs to construct these preliminary sections unless great accuracy is requisite. He is able to draw the geologic structure directly on the sides of the block in spite of the distortion of projection or perspective.

After the sides of the diagram are finished, the positions of structures and boundaries on its top surface may be obtained from points in the upper edges of the side faces. If it is a map block, this is fairly easy; but if it is a relief block, the topography is difficult to sketch properly. Indeed, good execution requires a true sense of proportions.

512. Requisite data for a completed block diagram. A block diagram should have a legend arranged in the same way as for geologic maps and sections. The directions of the block's upper edges must be indicated. This may be done either by lettering the front corners with the appropriate compass points, or, if an edge lies in a north-south position, by drawing an arrow, pointing north, parallel to this edge (Fig. 146). Isometric and cabinet projections should be accompanied by the adopted scales. For blocks in parallel perspective the scale for the front face should be indicated. A general idea of the horizontal scale in perspective may be given by labelling various known localities, such as lakes, towns, hills, etc., on the upper surface.

SKELETON DIAGRAMS

513. Definition and description. Skeleton diagrams are made to show the probable relations of geologic structures inside the

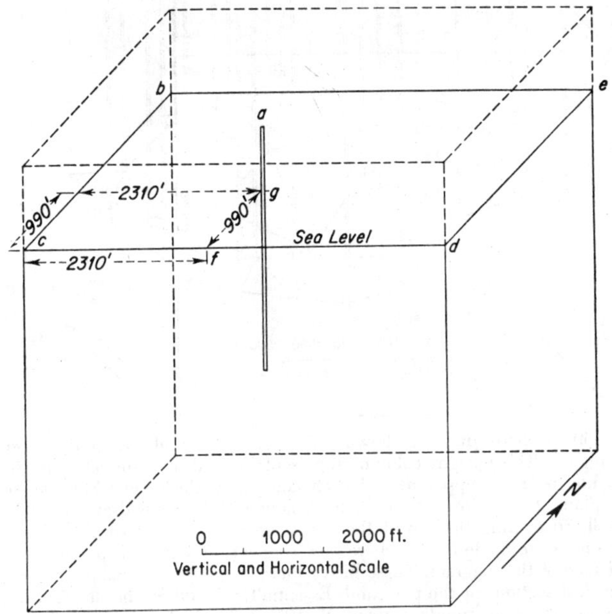

FIG. 558. Construction of a skeleton diagram. (See text.)

space of a block. They are essentially sketches of section models and peg models.[19] They are drawn to scale in their true field relations, on the principle of block diagram construction (**510–512**). In Fig. 558 each side of the block is supposed to represent a dis-

[19] Section models are constructed of parallel or intersecting sections, usually on glass, but sometimes made of wire. These sections are prepared and spaced to scale. Peg models are groups of wooden sticks made to represent well logs, and placed, according to scale, in an upright position on a horizontal wooden base.

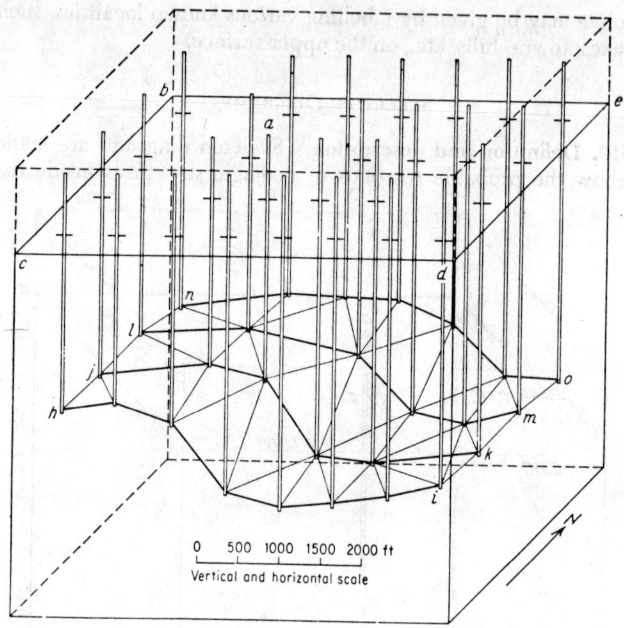

FIG. 559. Skeleton diagram showing structure on the oil pay sand in a certain region. The upright columns represent holes drilled for oil. The short cross line near the upper part of each hole marks the point where the sea-level plane, *bcde,* intersects the hole. A network of lines is drawn from well to well, connecting the top of the pay sand near the bottom of each well. These lines are made heavy where they connect rows of wells parallel to the front face of the diagram. These heavy lines, *hi, jk, lm, no,* may be regarded as vertical sections of the pay sand. Essentially, therefore, the diagram illustrates an anticline, trending about N. 10° or 20°E., with a steep east dip and a gentle west dip.

tance of 1 mile. The plane, *bcde,* is taken for sea level. The site of each well is plotted by reference to the three coordinates which correspond to the three edges of the block, thus: well *a* is 2,310 ft. east of edge *bc,* 990 ft. north of *cd,* and its elevation is 750 ft. above sea level. To find the site of this well, scale off $cf = 2{,}310$ ft. from *c* on *cd*; then scale off $fg = 990$ ft. northward (parallel to edge *bc*) from *f*; and then $ga = 750$ ft. vertically up from g. From *a* plot the log of this well downward and on the scale of the block. All other wells are similarly located and their logs plotted graphically. After this has been done, lines may be

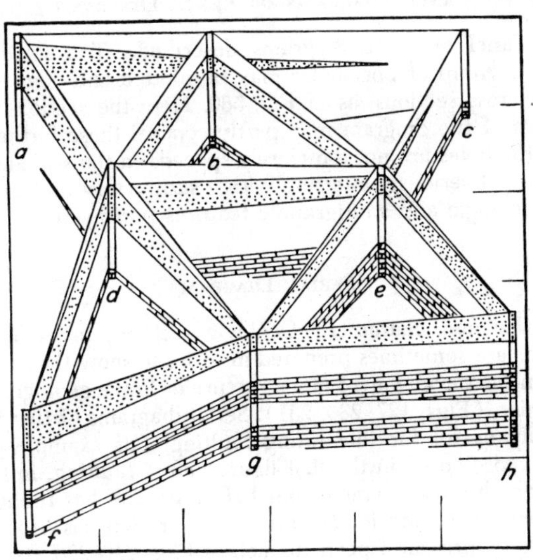

FIG. 560. Panel diagram. The upright columns (*a* to *h*) are well logs plotted to scale, with the base of each column at the well site as located on the map, here a township plat 6 miles on each side [see position of section lines along right (E.) and bottom (So.) boundaries of township]. The vertical scale of the logs is exaggerated. Sandstone is stippled, shale is blank, and limestone is in brick pattern. Note pinching out of sand toward northeast and thinning of limestone and corresponding thickening of shales toward southwest. In constructing a panel diagram the front sections must be completed first and then those successively farther and farther toward the rear. This diagram might have been constructed as a block diagram on either isometric or cabinet projection with the top of the block representing the mapped area 6 miles on a side. (See Arts. **510** and **511**.)

drawn connecting points at any given horizon as shown in the different logs.

Such blocks may be used for various purposes. For example, in oil fields, if the pay sands and water sands are plotted (Fig. 559), the depths at which these horizons are likely to be encountered in drilling other wells can be calculated, provided the locations and elevations of such new wells are known.

Panel Diagrams or Fence Diagrams

514. Panel or fence diagrams described. The stratigraphic data in a group of bore-holes may be plotted and connected by vertical cross sections, as in Fig. 560. Here the sections toward the front of the diagram may partly conceal those farther back, but, if the holes are not too closely spaced, on the scale adopted, this will not seriously interfere with a satisfactory understanding of the geologic and stratigraphic features portrayed.

Serial Diagram

515. Use and character. Geologic sections, maps, or block diagrams are sometimes prepared in series to show the successive stages in the development of a structure or in the geologic history of a region (Figs. 127, 230, 231). Serial diagrams of this sort are especially useful for illustrating faulting. For example, a rock mass is represented in the first figure before faulting; in the second, after the displacement, but before erosion has reduced the upthrown block; and in the third, after erosion has brought the region to its present aspect. In each of Figs. 210–220, the second and third stages are drawn, but the first is omitted. This method is, of course, quite unnatural since, under ordinary circumstances, denudation more nearly keeps pace with faulting (**198**).

Columnar Sections

516. Definition. A *columnar section*, or *geologic column* (Fig. 561), is made to show the sequence and original stratigraphic relations of the formations in a region. The height of each formation in the column represents the approximate relative thickness of this formation. The column cannot be drawn absolutely to scale since the formations vary in thickness from place to place. If the strata are inclined or folded, the thickness of each member must be computed (**531**). In this respect a columnar section differs from a well log, unless the well penetrates horizontal strata.

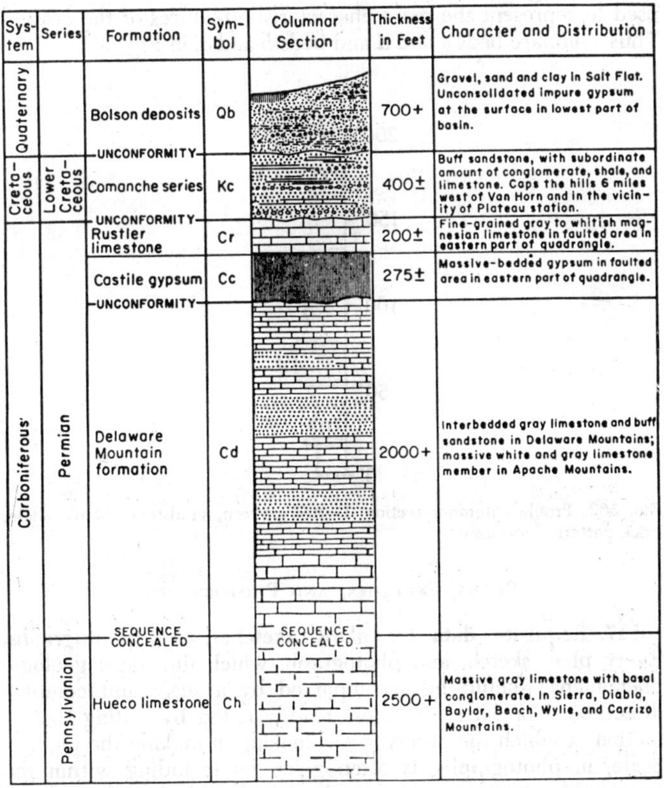

System	Series	Formation	Symbol	Columnar Section	Thickness in Feet	Character and Distribution
Quaternary		Bolson deposits	Qb		700+	Gravel, sand and clay in Salt Flat. Unconsolidated impure gypsum at the surface in lowest part of basin.
		UNCONFORMITY				
Cretaceous	Lower Cretaceous	Comanche series	Kc		400±	Buff sandstone, with subordinate amount of conglomerate, shale, and limestone. Caps the hills 6 miles west of Van Horn and in the vicinity of Plateau station.
		UNCONFORMITY				
Carboniferous	Permian	Rustler limestone	Cr		200±	Fine-grained gray to whitish magnesian limestone in faulted area in eastern part of quadrangle.
		Castile gypsum	Cc		275±	Massive-bedded gypsum in faulted area in eastern part of quadrangle.
		UNCONFORMITY				
		Delaware Mountain formation	Cd		2000+	Interbedded gray limestone and buff sandstone in Delaware Mountains; massive white and gray limestone member in Apache Mountains.
		SEQUENCE CONCEALED		SEQUENCE CONCEALED		
	Pennsylvanian	Hueco limestone	Ch		2500+	Massive gray limestone with basal conglomerate. In Sierra, Diablo, Baylor, Beach, Wylie, and Carrizo Mountains.

FIG. 561. Example of a columnar section. The rocks listed in the column are found in the region mapped for the folio. (*Van Horn Folio, No.* 194, *U.S. Geol. Survey,* 1914.)

Another variety of columnar section,[20] which may be called a *profile columnar section* or a *geomorphic columnar section,* is illustrated in Fig. 562, where the amount by which the several beds extend out to the right roughly indicates their relative resistance to erosion. Those beds which protrude farthest are the strong scarp makers, or ridge makers. The profile line may be

[20] First used in this form by Raymond C. Moore.

used to represent the more characteristic features of the erosion. Thus, compare beds *a* and *d* and beds *b* and *c*, in Fig. 562.

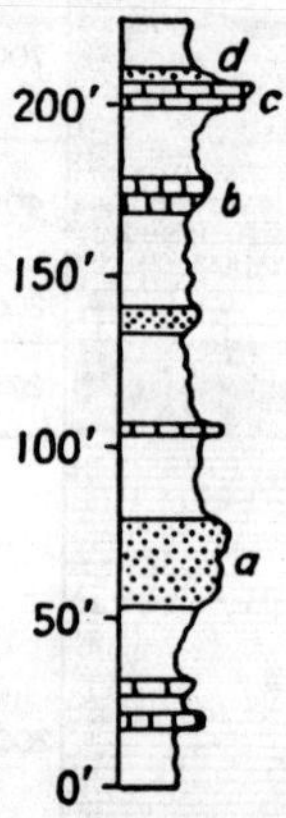

FIG. 562. Profile columnar section. Dotted pattern, sandstone; blank, shale; brick pattern, limestone.

PLANS, SKETCHES, AND PHOTOGRAPHS

517. Requisite data for plans, sketches, and photographs. Every plan, sketch, and photograph, which illustrates geologic phenomena, should be accompanied by a scale and compass directions. The latter are most readily noted by stating the direction in which the observer was looking in making the picture. Scale, in photographs, is often given by including within the view a ruler, hammer, or some other article of known dimensions. Plans and sketches may be treated like maps and sections. Locality should also be mentioned, and if any conventional signs are employed these are to be tabulated in a legend.

Chapter 20

INTERPRETATION OF GEOLOGIC MAPS

518. Significant features on geologic maps. From an examination of a geologic map a great deal may often be learned of the geologic structure, provided the topography is shown by contours. In general three things must be considered, namely, the contours, the outcrop areas marked with different colors or patterns to represent different rocks, and the boundary lines between these areas. Contours have been discussed in Chap. 13. Outcrop areas and boundary lines will be treated in the following paragraphs.

519. Outcrop areas. For the interpretation of a geologic map one should begin by ascertaining the meaning of the colors or patterns of the different outcrop areas. From the legend one should find out which colors or patterns are for igneous rocks, which for sedimentary rocks, and which for metamorphic rocks, and wherever the map shows that two rock bodies are in contact, their relative ages should be determined, also from the legend. For this purpose the geologic time scale must be known (Appendix 1). The forms of the outcrop areas, being consequent upon the trends of the inclosing lines, may be described under the head of boundaries.

520. Boundaries of outcrop areas. Geologic boundary lines on maps represent the exposed edges of contacts, such as surfaces between conformable strata, surfaces of unconformity, igneous contacts, and faults. Rules pertaining to the nature of these lines, as controlled by topography, have been stated in Arts. **193**, and **480.** In the present connection the rules may be reversed: (1) if the outcrop of a surface does not cross contours, the surface is horizontal (Fig. 490); (2) if this outcrop line is straight and has no fixed relation to the contours, the surface is vertical or dips steeply (Fig. 491); (3) if the outcrop line has a sinuous course and intersects the contours, the surface is moderately inclined. In the latter case the line has elbow-like bends which point down the dip in the valleys (Figs. 492, 493), unless the inclination of the given surface is in the same direction as, but is less than, the slope of the valley floor (Fig. 494). The longer and more acute the bends are, the lower is the dip of the inclined surface. These statements are based on the assumption that the given surface is essentially flat. If it is undulating or otherwise irregular its outcrop is likewise irregular, but with a little experience one can distinguish the disorderly bends and

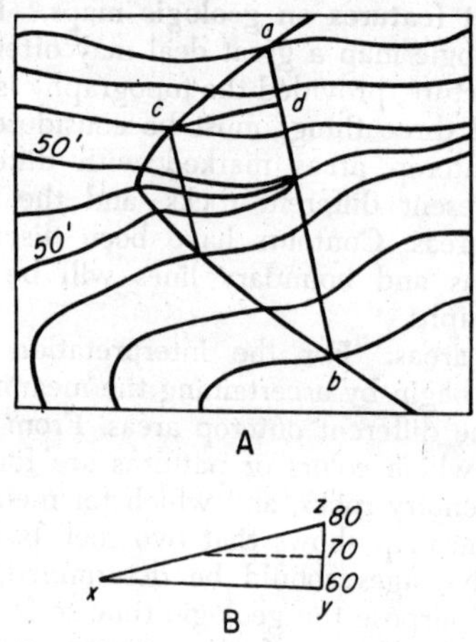

FIG. 563. Method of computing the strike and dip of an inclined layer by reference to its outcrop on a contour map.

angles of a line of this sort from the more uniform curves due to the topographic intersection of a flat surface.

The strike of an inclined flat surface may be obtained by drawing a straight line between two points of intersection of a given contour with the outcrop of the surface (*ab* in Fig. 563). The approximate dip of such a surface may be found thus: from the intersection, *c* (Fig. 563, A), of the outcrop of the surface with any contour except that containing points *a* and *b*, draw a line, *cd*, perpendicular to *ab*. In Fig. 563, A, the second contour below *a* is used. Lay off a horizontal line, *xy* (Fig. 563, B) equal to 2*cd*[1] and at the end for the higher contour (*y*, corresponding to *d* in Fig. 563, A) erect *yz* perpendicular to *xy*, making the length of *yz* four times[1] the contour interval. These lines, *xy* and

[1] For convenience, here, Fig. 563, B, is enlarged twice.

yz, must be drawn to natural scale. Complete the right triangle *xyz*. Angle *zxy* will then be the dip of the inclined surface, and this angle may be calculated since *xy* can be measured on the map and *zy* is known. It is hardly necessary to remark that accuracy in the result depends not only upon the flatness of the surface, but also upon the care with which the map was made.

521. Strike symbols. On outcrop maps of folded strata the general trend of the strikes may give one an idea of the structure. Three varieties of strike arrangement are noted below. If several possible interpretations are mentioned, the correct one

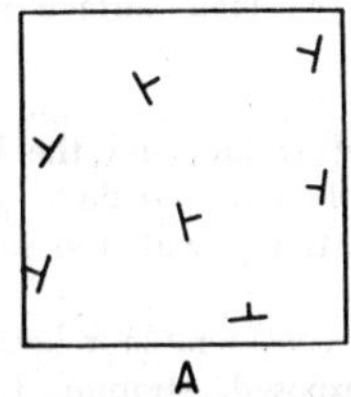

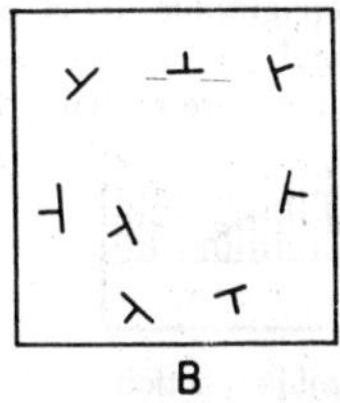

FIG. 564. Strike and dip symbols on outcrop maps, indicating plunging folds in A and a dome fold in B.

can be determined by a knowledge of the dip directions at the several outcrops.

1. Strikes are straight and parallel. The folding may be homoclinal, monoclinal, synclinal, or anticlinal. If anticlinal or synclinal, the fold axes are horizontal (Fig. 502, A, B, C).

2. Strikes converge alternately, first in one direction and then in the opposite direction, and at the angles of convergence they swing round sharply or broadly (Fig. 564, A). The structure consists of plunging anticlines and synclines.

3. Strikes run round in a complete curve which may be rudely circular or oval. The structure is a dome fold (Fig. 564, B) or a basin fold.

522. Conformable strata.[2] Unless the dip of a stratified series exactly coincides with the slope of the ground—an exceedingly rare condition—the beds are exposed in belts. The two edges of any belt on the map are the outcrops of the upper and lower surfaces of a stratum, and for each belt these lines, in their relations to the contours, conform with the rules given in Art.

[2] See also p. 683.

520. When the top and bottom surfaces of a given bed are approximately parallel, as they often are, the trend of the outcrop belt as a whole is naturally governed by these same rules. The breadth of the belt varies according to the dip of the stratum and the slope of the land (**192**). To facilitate the interpretation of geologic maps of conformable strata, the following key is given.

Key for the Interpretation of Maps of Conformable Strata

1. The color or pattern used on the map indicates that only one stratum outcrops over a broad area.
   a. The topographic relief is low and the land surface is essentially horizontal.
      The beds are probably horizontal.
   b. The relief is low and the land surface as a whole has a definite slope.
      The beds dip with the surface of the ground.
   c. There is considerable relief.
      The exposed stratum is essentially horizontal and is at least as thick as the measure of the relief (Fig. 565).

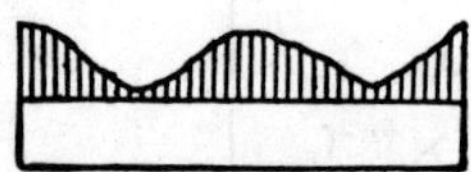

Fig. 565. Profile section showing the relation between the thickness of a stratum (lined) and the topographic relief.

2. Different strata outcrop in relatively straight, parallel belts.
   A. The beds are exposed in regular sequence across the strike.
      a. The land surface is a nearly flat, horizontal plain.
         The beds are inclined or vertical.
      b. The land surface is a nearly even plain which has a definite inclination.
         The beds are horizontal, inclined, or vertical. If they are inclined, their dip is not parallel to the slope of the ground.
      c. The relief is marked and may be rugged (Fig. 566). In case the topography consists of parallel ridges and valleys, the outcrop belts show no deviation in transverse valleys that may interrupt the continuity of the ridges.
         The strata are vertical.
      d. The relief is marked and the topography consists of parallel ridges and valleys. In transverse valleys the outcrop belts make sharp elbow-like bends.
         The beds are inclined (cf. Art. **520**).
   B. Across the strike the stratigraphic succession is alternately normal and then reversed. Thus, if the digits 1, 2, 3, and 4, stand for the beds in the sequence of their deposition, the order of exposure may be 1, 2, 3, 4, 4, 3, 2, 1, or it may be, 4, 3, 2, 1, 1, 2, 3, 4.

a. The relief may be low, or the topography may consist of parallel ridges and valleys which coincide pretty closely with the outcrop belts (Fig. 567).

The structure is anticlinal if older beds are flanked on both sides by younger beds, and it is synclinal if younger beds lie between older ones. Variations in the width of these belts may point: (1) to symmetrical folds in which opposite limbs are exposed on a uniform slope or on slopes of different inclinations; or (2) to asymmetrcial folds outcropping on a surface of low relief and of no or uniform inclination (**192**).

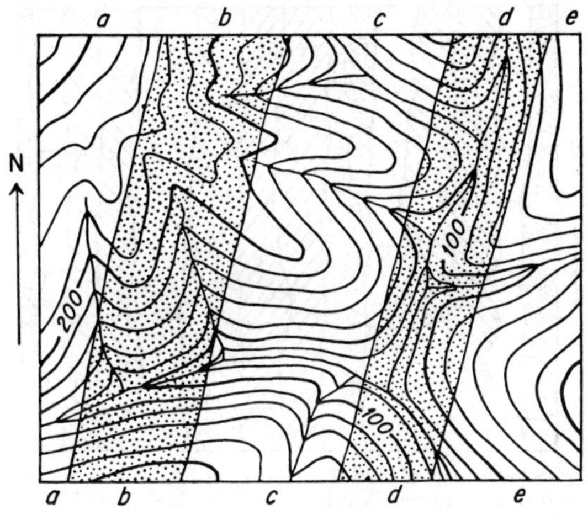

Fig. 566. Geologic map of vertical strata, *a, b, c, d, e.* Contour interval 20 ft.

3. Different strata appear in sinuous or zigzag belts.

a. The relief is considerable. The boundaries between strata are roughly parallel to the contours, following these up valleys and thus giving a treelike, branching, or *dendritic* pattern to the rock distribution on the map (Fig. 568). When traced up the valleys, the belts are seen to make elbow-like turns which point upstream. Followed down the valleys, the same belts bend round projecting spurs of the uplands, here pointing down the slope.

The beds are horizontal or very nearly so.

b. The topography is strongly rolling or rugged. The boundaries between adjacent strata cross the contours. The turns of the belts are situated on the valley floors and on the upland spurs. In the valleys the bends are convex toward younger beds, and on the spurs, toward older beds, but whether on spurs or in valleys, the convexity may point up the slope or down the slope.

The beds are inclined. The turns in the belts are convex down the dip in the valleys and up the dip on the spurs, provided always that the dip is greater than the inclination of the ground (cf. Fig. 567).

c. The relief may be low or considerable. In the latter case the hills are generally long ridges which trend parallel to the outcrop belts.

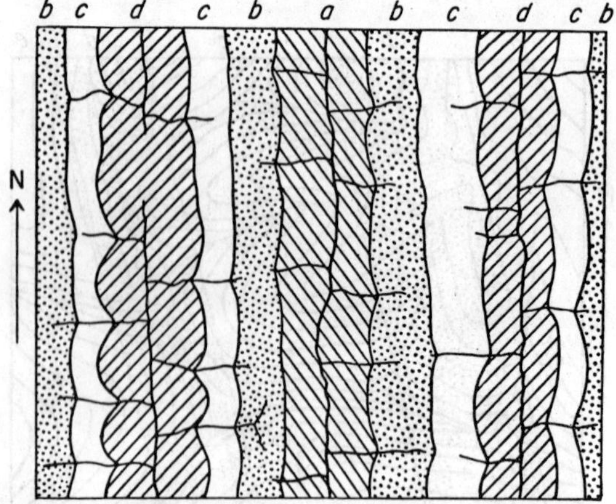

Fig. 567. Geologic map of folded strata, *a*, *b*, *c*, and *d*. *a* outcrops in an anticline and *d* in synclines. Which is the oldest bed shown? The youngest bed? Note how the contacts between strata bend in the direction of the dip in the valleys (see streams). Contours not shown.

The boundaries between adjacent strata are roughly parallel to the contours in the valleys which are parallel to the ridges (longitudinal valleys), but they cross the contours in the valleys that are transverse to the ridges (transverse valleys).

The strata are folded in plunging anticlines and synclines. Older beds outcrop between younger beds in anticlines; vice versa in synclines. In anticlines the beds are convex down the plunge; in synclines, up the plunge. At the sharp bends the ridges usually have a gentle slope in the direction of the plunge and a steep slope on the opposite side of the crest.

4. Different strata appear in roughly concentric closed belts.

a. The relief is considerable. The boundaries between strata are parallel to the contours. The closed belts appear only in isolated hills. Elsewhere on the map, in valleys and on spurs, the dendritic pattern prevails (Fig. 568).

The strata are nearly or quite horizontal (cf. 3, *a*).

b. The relief is low or considerable. If the latter, the uplands are concentric ridges parallel to the outcrop belts. The boundaries between adjacent strata are about parallel to the contours in longitudinal valleys, but they cross the contours in transverse valleys.

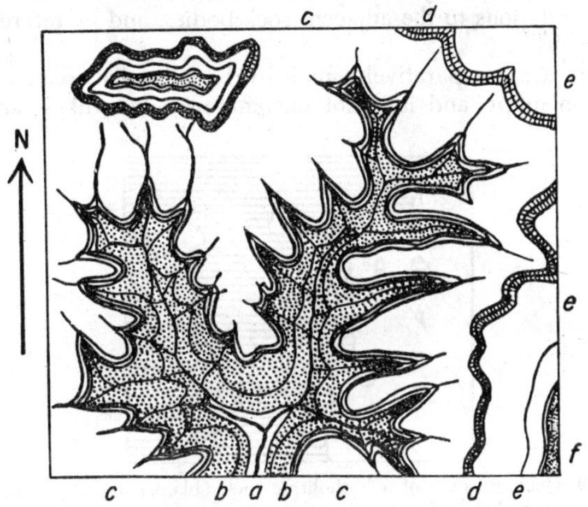

FIG. 568. Geologic map of horizontal strata, *a*, *b*, *c*, *d*, *e*, and *f*. Which is the oldest bed shown? Which the youngest? In the northwest corner of the map is a mesa. Contour interval 100 ft.

The structure is that of a basin fold if the strata are successively older outward in all directions from the center of the curving belts and if the boundary lines bend inward in the transverse valleys; and the structure is that of a dome fold if the strata are successively younger outward and if the boundary lines bend outward in the transverse valleys.

5. An outcrop belt, whether continuous or interrupted, becomes gradually narrower and finally disappears.

This signifies that the bed represented by this belt has thinned out to an edge. Do not confuse this phenomenon with the narrowing of a belt which passes on to the face of a steep slope or a cliff, nor with the abrupt termination of an outcrop belt at a fault, an igneous contact, or a line of unconformity.

523. Igneous rocks. Since sills and flows are like strata in their field relations, they also look like strata on geologic maps. They may be distinguished by their colors or patterns by referring to the legend. Most of the cases cited for stratified rocks in the preceding article are applicable to eruptive sheets. Dikes, too, have their outcrop belts controlled by the topography in the same manner as sills, flows, and strata. They usually dip pretty steeply. They are readily distinguished by their cross-cutting relations to the adjacent rock bodies, and by reference to the legend.

Necks are comparatively small oval or circular areas, as indicated on maps, and it is not uncommon to see dikes radiating

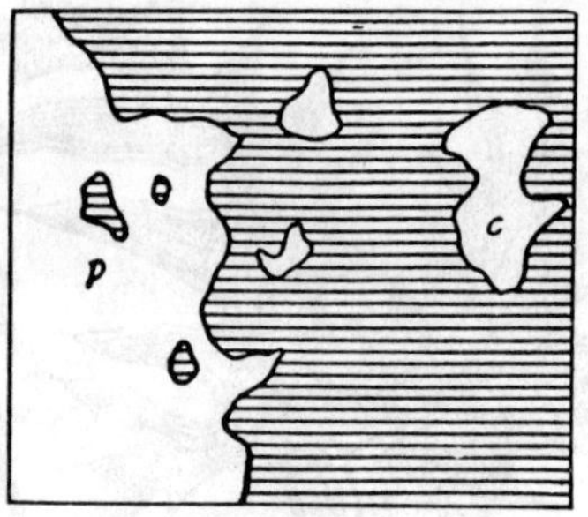

Fig. 569. Geologic map of a batholithic rock (blank) and its country rock (lined). *p*, roof pendant or large inclusion; *c*, cupola.

from them and also to find the remnants of flows somewhere in the neighborhood. Volcanic cones are recognized by the fact that they consist of pyroclastic débris or of lava (see legend) and, when fresh, they often have craters. Laccoliths appear as larger closed areas surrounded by sediments which have an outward dip if the intrusive body is essentially horizontal. If the laccolith is inclined, its outcrop may be lenticular. Exposures of batholiths are usually of still greater extent and of very irregular form. The edges of the map area of a batholith commonly truncate the outcrop belts of adjacent older sedimentary rocks. Isolated patches of these older rocks within the confines of the batholithic area are roof pendants or large inclusions (**160**), and isolated areas of the batholithic rock in the older sediments outside the main boundary are cupolas or pipes (Fig. 569) (**170**)

524. Unconformities. Unconformities are noted in their proper places in the legend. Of the types described in Arts. **84** and **85**, disconformity is the hardest to detect on geologic maps. Its presence is indicated in the legend by the fact that formations which should come between the disconformable strata are wanting. Angular unconformity between two groups of stratified rocks appears on a geologic map as a line, regular or irregular, against which abut the beds of one or both formations. Lines of unconformity of this sort may separate older bedrock from younger overlying surface deposits or lava sheets. Unconformity between an *intrusive* igneous rock and a body of any kind of igneous, sedimentary, or metamorphic rocks, may be mistaken for an intrusive contact. If the intrusive (A, Fig. 570) is older than the rocks on the other side of the doubtful line, this line (*no*, Fig. 570) is one of unconformity; but if the intrusive is younger, the line is an igneous contact. The relative ages can be obtained from the legend.

Fig. 570. Geologic map of a regular contact, *no*, between an intrusive rock, *A*, and a body of sedimentary rocks, *B*. If *A* is younger than *B*, *A* is intrusive into *B* and *no* is an igneous contact; but if *A* is older than *B*, *B* was laid down unconformably on *A* and *no* is a line of unconformity.

Unconformities and faults cannot be confused on a map because they are represented by lines of different weight (**478**).

525. Faults. Before one can interpret the relations of a fault which is shown on a geologic map, one must secure all possible information on the characters, structures, and relative ages of the rocks in the two contiguous fault blocks. These facts are to be sought by aid of the statements made in Arts. **520** and **522–524.** The next step is to ascertain the attitude of the fault. For this see Art. **520.** Ordinarily a fault with a low dip, and therefore a highly sinuous exposure where the relief is marked, is an overthrust (Fig. 571). In this case there may be associated isolated areas, each entirely inclosed within a fault line. Such an area is a *fault inlier* if the rocks within the closed fault line are younger than the rocks outside, and it is a *fault outlier* if the opposite condition holds (**226**) (Fig. 571).

Having determined the general attitude of a fault and the relations of the rocks on either side of it, we may proceed to classify it. If the fault is vertical, younger rocks are exposed at a given elevation near the fault line in the downthrow block. If the fault is inclined, younger rocks are exposed in the block toward which the fault dips in the case of a normal fault, and in the block away from which the fault dips in the case of a reverse fault. These statements refer to dip-slip and oblique-slip faults. Strike faults, dip faults, and diagonal faults which dislocate stratified rocks can be recognized at a glance.

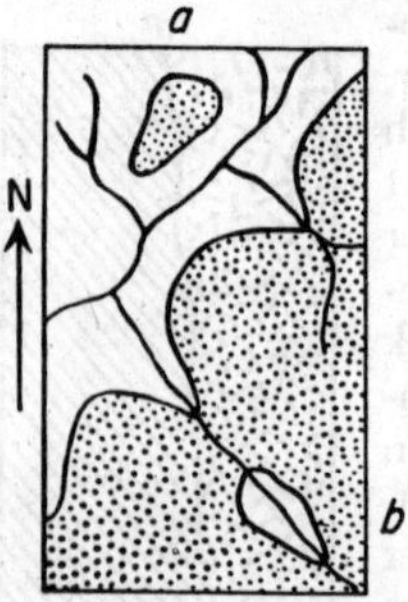

FIG. 571. Geologic map of a region where an overthrust fault is exposed. Older rocks, stippled; younger rocks, blank. All the boundaries between these two formations are fault lines. *a*, fault outlier; *b*, fault inlier. The main NE.-SW. fault line dips southeastward. How may this fact be ascertained from the map?

With regard to repetition, omission, and offset, the reader is referred to Arts. **203**, **212**, **213**, and **215**, where many of the rules laid down for the field interpretation of faults will be found to be applicable to the interpretation of mapped faults.

A word may be said of the appearance of faulted synclines and anticlines which have been truncated by erosion. The effect of dip faults and diagonal faults upon such folds is to increase the perpendicular distance between the outcropping edges of a stratum on opposite limbs of an open syncline (*s*, Fig. 572), and to decrease this distance in an open anticline (*a*, Fig. 572) always on the side of the downthrown block. From the map it is possible to tell which is the downthrown block if the nature of the folding is known, or, on the other hand, to ascertain the nature of the folding if the relative displacement is known.

526. Geologic history. In the interpretation of geologic maps, one should be able not only to decipher the structural conditions, but also to read the geologic history represented on them. Every geologic map shows certain features which, if properly understood, can be described in the chronological order in which they originated. The same may be said of geologic sections and block diagrams. Take Fig. 573 for example. Here the strata *f* and *g* dip gently southwestward, as shown by the bends of their contact lines at the streams. This series, *f* and *g*, is overlain un-

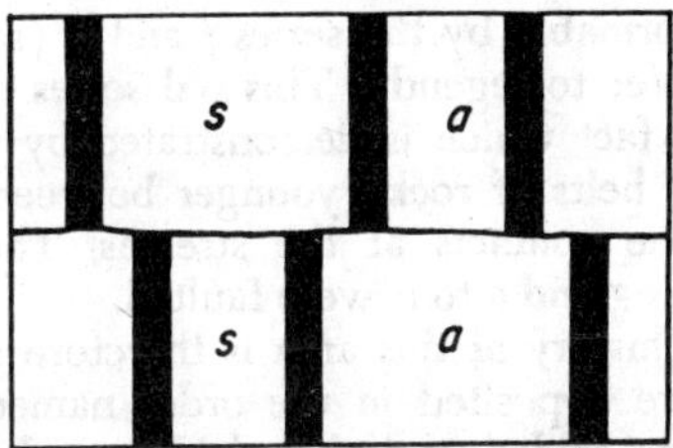

FIG. 572. Geologic map of folded beds dislocated by a transverse dip fault. *s*, syncline; *a*, anticline.

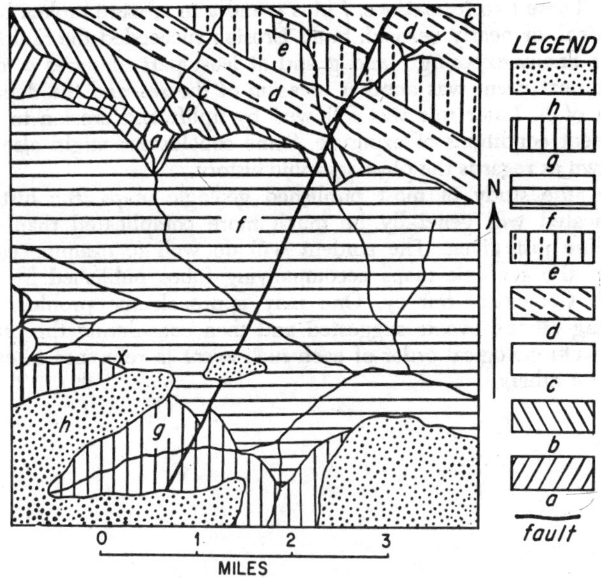

FIG. 573. Geologic map illustrating geologic history. In the legend, the formations are successively younger from below upward. (See text.)

conformably by *h*, for this stratum occurs only on the uplands, whereas *f* and *g* outcrop as low as the stream channels, and *h* apparently conceals *f* and *g* (see near *x*, Fig. 573). Furthermore, the legend indicates that *h* is younger than *f* and *g*. In the northern part of the map a folded series of strata is seen to be overlain unconformably by the series *f* and *g* (see north contact line of *f* and refer to legend). This old series *a* to *e*, is folded in a syncline, a fact which is demonstrated by the sequence of the outcropping belts of rock (younger between older) and by the bends of the contacts at the streams. The two stratified formations, *f* plus *g* and *a* to *e*, were faulted.

The geologic history of this area is therefore as follows: *a*, *b*, *c*, *d*, and *e* were deposited in the order named. Subsequently these strata were folded and then laid bare by erosion, these processes probably consuming a long period of time. Upon their truncated edges, beds *f* and *g* were laid down in a transgressing sea. These two formations, *f* plus *g* and *a* to *e*, were broken by a vertical, or nearly vertical, fault. Erosion succeeded the faulting, thus finally exposing *f* and *g* and at least part of series *a* to *e*. The next event was another invasion of the sea and the deposition of *h*. Later this was followed by uplift and erosion to the present conditions of exposure. Some conclusions might also be drawn as regards the physiographic history.

In the study of most published geologic maps, the history indicated will generally be much more complicated than the outline just given. The student will do well to examine carefully the geologic maps accompanying folios published by the U.S. Geological Survey. One may approach the problem by listing all the events suggested and then considering the probable chronological order of each such event in reference to each of the others.

Chapter 21

GEOLOGIC COMPUTATIONS

Computations in General

527. Measurements and computations previously discussed. Certain problems of measurement and construction have been discussed in the preceding chapters. The more important of these may be listed here for reference, as follows: distance, on the surface of the ground, between two points on a contour map (**323**); inclination of a slope (**325**); correction of a compass traverse (**399**); depth of a horizon below the "key horizon" on a structure contour map (**497**); dip and strike of an inclined surface as determined from the outcrop line of the surface on a contour map (**520**).

528. Application of computations explained in the present chapter. In geologic computations it is sometimes necessary to ascertain the direction and angle of inclination of the intersection of two planes which are not parallel, or the position of the point of intersection of a line and a plane. The intersecting planes may be two faults, a fault and the contact between two conformable beds, a bedding surface and the wall of a dike, etc. Accuracy in the results requires that such surfaces be as nearly plane as possible and that the lines be essentially straight. The methods of solving these two problems are outlined in Arts. **529** and **530**. Computations for thickness (**531**) are applicable to any inclined layers of uniform, or nearly uniform, thickness, such as strata, dikes, sills, veins, etc. Variations in thickness introduce errors into the results. Computations for the depth of a point in an inclined surface (**532**) may refer to the top or bottom surface of a bed, dike, sill, or vein, or to a fault or any comparatively flat surface. Measurements of slip and shift (**534**) pertain only to faults.

Solution of Particular Problems

529. Line of intersection of two planes, not parallel.

Given: The dips and strikes of two intersecting planes.

Required: The angle of inclination and the direction of inclination of the intersection of these planes.

Solution:[1] Since strikes and compass directions are horizontal, the construction for this problem is assumed to be in a horizontal plane. Draw *MN* and *OP* (Fig. 574), the intersections (strike

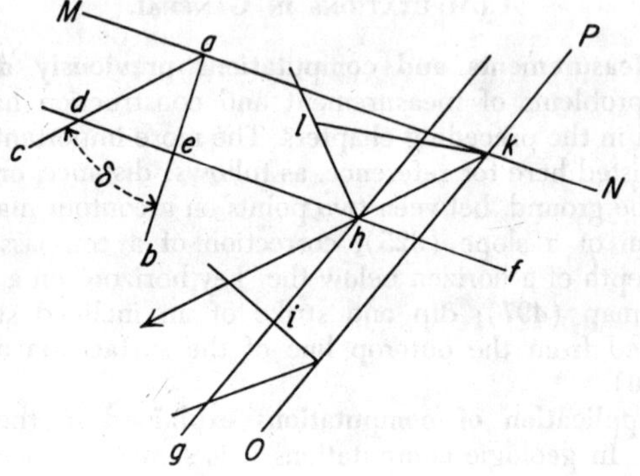

Fig. 574. Method of computing the angle and direction of inclination of the intersection of two planes. (*After H. F. Reid.*)

directions) of the given planes with any horizontal plane. *MN* and *OP* will be called *lines* where reference is made to the intersections, and *planes* when reference is made to the inclined planes passing through these intersections. From any point, *a*, on line *MN* erect a perpendicular, *ab*, in the direction of the dip of the plane *MN*. From *a*, also, draw a line, *ac*, making with *ab* an angle δ, equal to the dip of the plane *MN*. Through *e*, on *ab* at a convenient distance from line *MN* draw *df* through *ac* parallel to the line *MN*. The triangle *ead* may be regarded as a vertical triangle rotated about *ae* into a horizontal position. In its vertical position, *ad* would be in the plane *MN* and *de* would be vertical. *df* is the intersection of the plane *MN* and a

[1] This problem and the next are modifications of those presented by Dr. Reid. Bibliog., Reid, H. F., 1909, pp. 173–176.

horizontal plane which is at a depth, *de*, below the horizontal plane in which lines *MN* and *OP* are situated.

Use the same method of construction for *OP*, but draw the line *gh*, corresponding to *df*, parallel to line *OP*, and at such a distance from line *OP* that *gi* shall be equal to *de*. Then *df* and *gh* are, respectively, the intersections of planes *MN* and *OP* with a horizontal plane at a depth equal to *de* ($= gi$) below the plane of the figure; and *h*, the point of intersection of these lines, is also a point in the intersection of the given inclined planes. Therefore, a straight line through *h* and *k* will be the projection of the line of intersection of the inclined planes upon any horizontal plane. The direction of inclination of this line of intersection will be downward in the semicircle that contains the dip directions of the given planes. The amount of this inclination may be found thus: from *h* erect a line, *hl*, perpendicular to *hk* and equal to *de*. Draw *lk*. In right triangle *hlk*, $\angle lhk$ is the dip of the intersection of the inclined planes. $\angle lkh$ may be obtained from the equation, $\tan \angle lkh = lh/hk$, in which *lh* and *hk* are known.

Another method of solving this problem follows:[2]

"1. Construct the angle *ACB* (Fig. 575), the sides of which have the directions of the strikes of the given planes, and produce one of the sides, as *AC*, so as to obtain the angle *BCD*, supplementary to the angle *ACB*.

"2. On *CD* lay off *CE*, the graphic tangent of the angle of dip of the plane whose strike is *AC* (either using a tangent scale for this purpose or else obtaining the value of the tangent from trigonometric tables and setting off this value according to any scale suited to the problem and the degree of accuracy required. The latter method is, in general, preferable, especially with very high angles of dip which are beyond the limit of the fixed tangent scale).

"3. On *CB* lay off (by the same scale) *CF*, the graphic tangent of the angle of dip of the plane whose strike is *CB*.

"4. Draw *EF* and, through *C*, the parallel line *CH*. *CH* is the required direction of inclination of the line of intersection of the two given planes.

"5. Draw *CG* perpendicular to *EF*. The length of this line when determined in degrees by means of the tangent scale used for plotting *CE* and *CF*, will give the required angle of inclination of the line of intersection of the given planes. This angle, it may be noted, is an apparent dip angle common to the two planes.

"By a slight modification of the method just given, the cotangents of the angles of dip may be used instead of the tangents in solving this problem,

[2] After W. S. Tangier Smith, in personal communication.

although the solution is a little less simple when the cotangents are used. The cotangents are especially useful when the dip angles are large and a fixed tangent-cotangent scale is used.

"If the dips of the given planes do not exceed 10°, the numerical values of these angles may be used instead of the tangent values in solving this problem. This is of small importance, however, since intersecting planes,

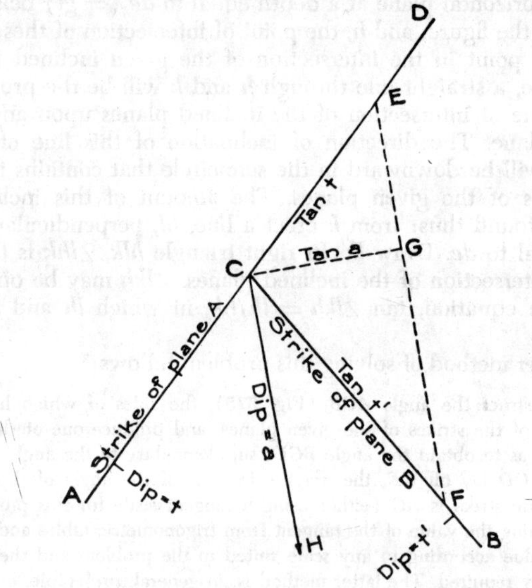

FIG. 575. Diagram for finding angle and direction of inclination of intersection of two planes not parallel.

both with low angles of dip, rarely occur. On the other hand, if the dips of the given planes and the angle of inclination of their line of intersection are between 80° and 90°, the numerical values of the complements of the angles of dip may be used in place of the cotangent values in the cotangent method of solving the problem. The error involved in using numerical values instead of tangent or cotangent values is small, not to exceed a few minutes."

530. Point of intersection between a line and a plane.

Given: The dip and strike of a plane and the angle and direction of inclination of a line not parallel to the plane.

Required: The point of intersection of the line and the plane.

Solution: Two cases are figured (Figs. 576, 577). The letters apply to both diagrams. *MN* is the trace of the given plane on a horizontal reference plane. *MN* will be used likewise to designate this plane. *ST* is the projection of the given line upon the reference plane. Through *a*, that point on *ST* in which the given line intersects the plane of reference, draw *OP* parallel to line *MN*. Let *OP* represent the trace of a plane containing the given

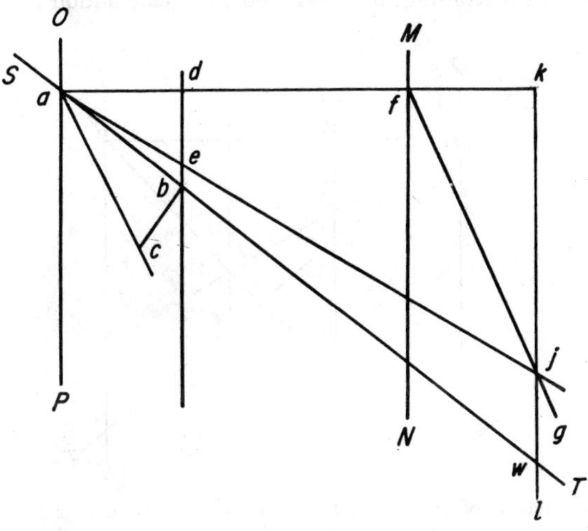

FIG. 576. Method of computing the point of intersection of a line and a plane when the line and the plane are inclined in the same direction, the plane more steeply than the line.

line of which *ST* is the horizontal projection. From *a* draw *ac* making an angle with *ST* equal to the inclination of the given line. From any point, *b*, on *ST* draw *bc* perpendicular to *ST*. *bc* is the depth of the given line below its horizontal projection, *ST*, at *b*. Draw *af* perpendicular to *OP* and *MN*, through *a*. Through *b* draw *bd* parallel to *OP*, intersecting *af* at *d*. From *d* lay off *de* = *bc*. Draw *ae*. Then ∠*dae* is the inclination of the plane *OP*.

From *f* draw *fg*, making an angle with *af* (produced in Fig. 577) equal to the dip of the plane *MN*. *fg* must be drawn on the side of line *MN toward the dip* of plane *MN*. In Fig. 576 the dip is on the right, and in Fig. 577 on the left, of *MN*. Produce *ae* until it meets *fg* at *j*. Through *j* draw *kl* parallel to line *MN*. Then *kl* is the projection, upon the horizontal reference plane, of the line of intersection of planes *OP* and *MN* at the depth, *kj*, below *k*. The intersection of *ST* and *kl*, at *w*, is the projection, on the reference plane, of the intersection of the given line and the given plane.

531. Thickness of a layer. When an estimate is made of the thickness of a stratum, dike, vein, etc., the calculation is usually

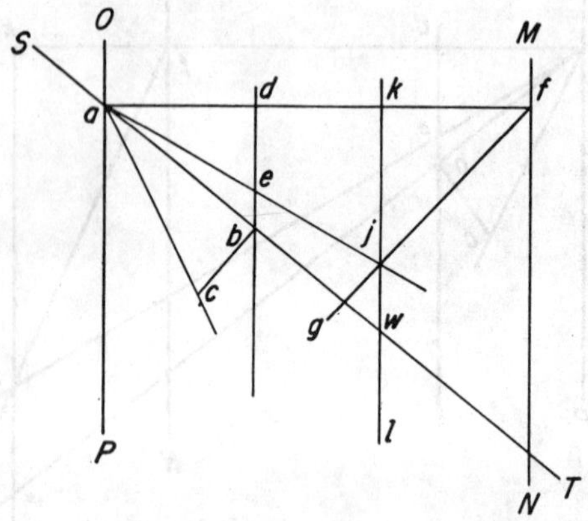

FIG. 577. Method of computing the point of intersection of a line and a plane when the plane and the line are inclined toward one another.

based upon a distance measured along a traverse perpendicular to the strike of the layer; that is to say, the breadth of outcrop must first be known. For folded beds, if the deformation is complex, the breadth of outcrop should be measured if possible along the axis of the fold rather than across the axis, for in this direction of least compression there is less likelihood of contortion and of other disturbing factors, and the results are less liable to error.

Thickness can be measured directly only when the surface of the ground or of an artificial excavation is perpendicular to the beds. In all other cases right angle computations must be made. Thus, in Fig. 578, *ab* is the breadth of outcrop and *bc* is the required thickness. Let the dip (here angle *bac*) be represented by δ. In triangle *abc*, $\sin \delta = bc/ab$, and, therefore, $bc = ab \cdot \sin \delta$.

Two other cases are illustrated in Figs. 579 and 580. In Fig. 579 the strata dip 20° E. (δ) and the surface of the ground slopes 10° W. Call the latter *i*. We want to find the thickness, *bc*. For the solution of right triangle *abc* we must determine the angle *bac*. $\angle dac = 20° = \delta$. $\angle bad = 10° = i$. Therefore,

$$\delta + i = 20° + 10° = 30°.$$

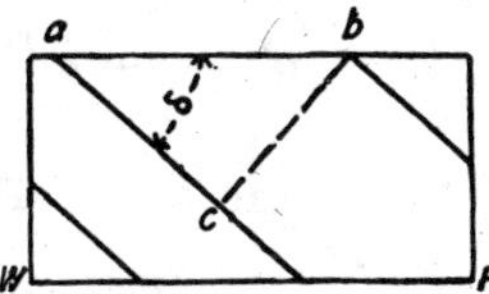

FIG. 578. Thickness of a dipping layer, the land surface being level.

Then, as in the first example, $bc = ab \cdot \sin(\delta + i)$. In Fig. 580 the beds dip 40° E. and the ground slopes 10° in the same direction. The thickness, *bc*, is required. $dab = i = 10°$, the inclination of the ground, and $\angle dac = \delta = 40°$, the dip. *bac* in right triangle $abc = \delta - i = 40° - 10° = 30°$. Therefore, $bc = ab \cdot \sin(\delta - i)$.

If the traverse along which local measurements of dip and strike have been recorded is oblique to the general strike, the

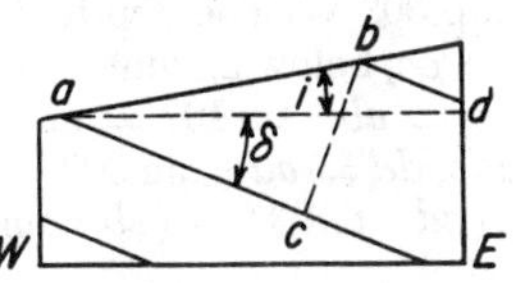

FIG. 579. Thickness of a dipping layer, the land surface sloping in a direction opposite to the dip of the layer.

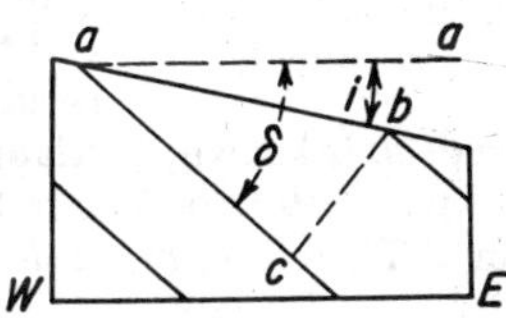

FIG. 580. Thickness of a dipping layer, the land surface sloping in the same direction as the dip.

dip data should be projected along strike to a line perpendicular to strike, as in Fig. 581. Across wide areas with variations in strike and in direction of traverse, several such adjustments by projection may be desirable, each for a strip of the terrain examined, and then the results can be added together for the total thickness of strata traversed.

532. Depth of a point in an inclined surface. Another problem that must be solved by right triangles concerns the depth, below the surface of the ground, of a point in an inclined surface. Again, the calculation is based upon the breadth of outcrop. The problem may be illustrated by three cases. In Fig. 582 the beds dip east at an angle of 25° ($\angle bac$). We wish to know the depth, bc, of the bedding surface outcropping at a below some point, b, on the ground surface. In right triangle abc, ab is known and

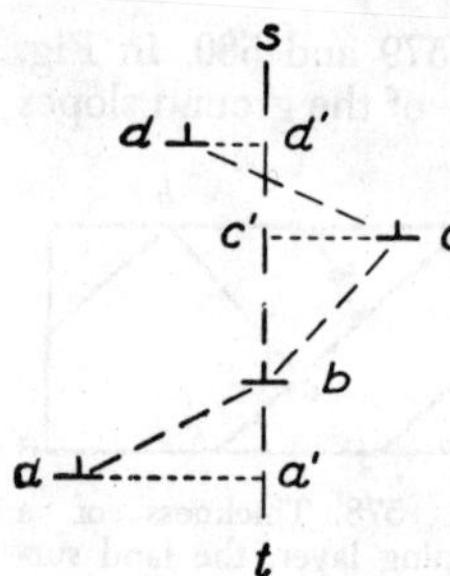

Fig. 581. Sketch map of traverse, $abcd$, oblique to strike of beds exposed at these four points. For a section perpendicular to the strike (st), the dips at a, c, and d are projected along the strike to st at points a', c', and d', respectively.

$$\tan \delta = \tan 25° = bc/ab.$$

Therefore, $bc = ab \cdot \tan 25°$.

In Fig. 583 the strata dip 25° E. and the ground slopes 15° W. ab is known. In triangle abd, $ab = ab \cdot \cos 15°$. Also,

$$bd = ab \cdot \sin 15°.$$

In triangle adc, $dc = ad \cdot \tan 25°$. Therefore,

$$bc = (ab \cdot \sin i) + (ad \cdot \tan \delta),$$

where i is the inclination of the ground and δ is the dip.

In Fig. 584 the ground slopes 10° W. and the beds dip 30° W. The depth of the bedding surface, ac, below a point, b, is required. ab is known. In triangle adb, $db = ab \cdot \sin 10° = ab \cdot \sin i$ and $pa = ab \cdot \cos 10°$. In triangle adc, $dc = ad \cdot \tan 30° = ad \cdot \tan \delta$. Therefore, $bc = dc - db = (ad \cdot \tan \delta) - (ab \cdot \sin i)$.

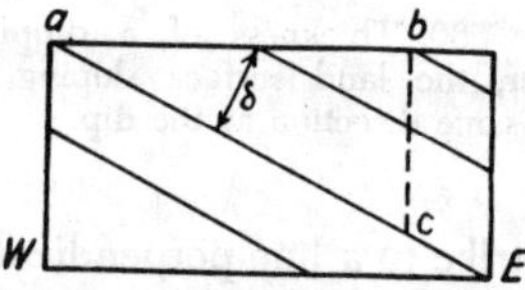

Fig. 582. Depth of an inclined surface, the land surface being level.

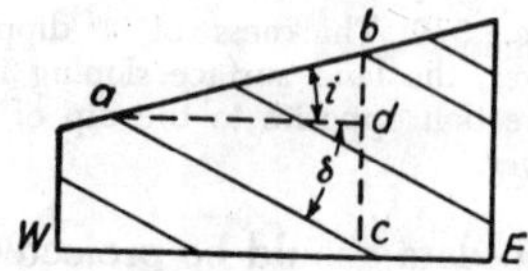

Fig. 583. Depth of an inclined surface where the ground slopes in the opposite direction.

In Appendix 16 will be found a table for computing depth and thickness.

Observe again (as in Art. 531) that if measurements in the

field are made along a traverse oblique to the strike the dip data should be projected along strike to a line (or vertical section) perpendicular to strike for the solutions as given in Figs. 582–584.

533. Errors in thickness and depth calculations. The calculations outlined in Arts. 531 and 532, if applied to considerable thicknesses of folded strata, may introduce significant errors. To illustrate, we may assume that a series of strata has been rather strongly folded on the parallel pattern (see Fig. 140 and accompanying text). In Fig. 520, which shows such a fold, incorrect estimates of thickness and depth may result from a failure to realize the changing relations of dip to breadth of outcrop across the fold. Figure 585 indicates, in a highly diagrammatic way, how calculations of thickness based on depth and dip, and calculations of depth based on thickness and dip, may be in error because of the change of dip with depth. General rules cannot be laid down for avoiding all such errors because there are so many variable factors involved, but it is important that the geologist be aware of

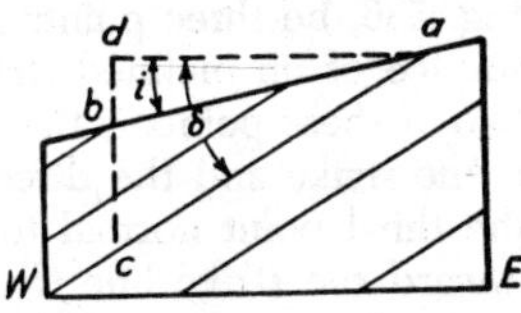

FIG. 584. Depth of an inclined surface where the land slopes in the same direction.

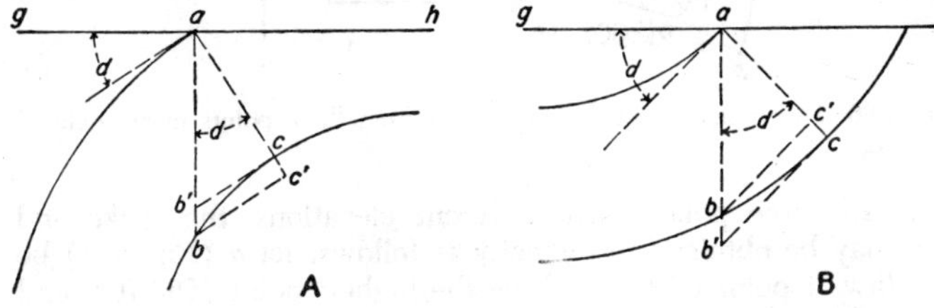

FIG. 585. Anticlinal (A) and synclinal (B) parallel folding. In both diagrams, *gh* is the ground surface, shown here as horizontal; *a* is a point below which calculations are to be made on the thickness (*ac*) of a series of the folded strata or on the depth of the base of this folded series (*b*) vertically below *a*. The dip of the strata measured at *a* is *d* (cf. Fig. 548). In both diagrams the calculation of *ac*, based on angle *d* and depth *ab*, will give *ac'*, with an error of *cc'*; and in both, the calculation of the *ab*, based on angle *d* and *ac* (the true thickness here), will give the depth as *ab'*, with an error of *bb'*

the possibility and reasons for such errors and that he guard against them in making his own estimates.[3]

534. Determination of strike and dip when the elevations of three points in an inclined surface are given. Let *a*, *b*, and *c*, Fig. 586, be three points at which the elevation of the flat upper surface of an inclined stratum is known. If the elevation at any two of these points is the same, the line between these two points is the strike and the direction of dip is along a line drawn from the third point normal to the strike line. The dip will be down toward the strike line if the third point is higher than the other two points, and it will be toward the third point if this point is lower than the other two points.

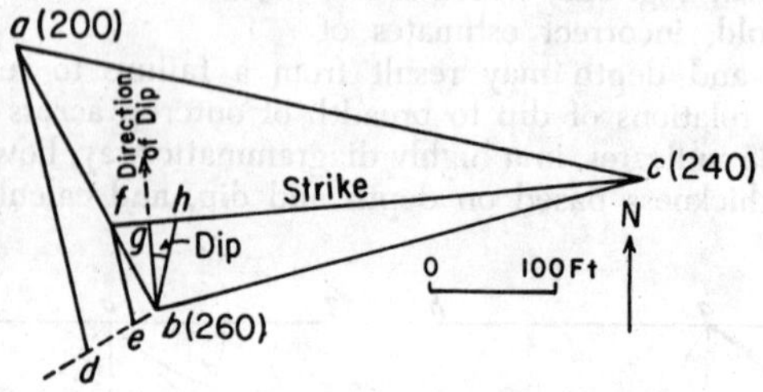

Fig. 586. Determination of dip and strike from three points in an inclined surface.

If all three points have different elevations, the strike and dip may be obtained graphically as follows: let *a* (Fig. 586) be the lowest point (200 ft.), *b* be the highest point (260 ft.), and *c* be of intermediate elevation (240 ft.). The directions are, from *a* to *b*, S. 30° E.; *b* to *c*, N. 75° E.; and *a* to *c*, S. 80° E. The distances between the stations are known. Having selected a convenient horizontal scale, plot these stations in their correct relative positions. Draw *ab*, the line connecting the lowest and highest points. At *b* erect a perpendicular to *ab*, and on it lay off *bd* = the difference in altitude between *a* and *b*, here

$$260 \text{ ft.} - 200 \text{ ft.} = 60 \text{ ft.}$$

This should be done on the same scale as the adopted horizontal scale. Lay off *de* = the difference of elevation between

[3] See papers by Mason L. Hill (Bibliog., 1942) and Luis G. Duran S. (Bibliog., 1948).

a and *c*, here 240 ft. − 200 ft. = 40 ft., on the adopted scale. Draw *da* and, parallel to it, draw *ef*. Draw *fc*, which will be the line of strike of the stratum. From *b* draw a line perpendicular to *fc*, meeting *fc* at *g*. *bg* is the direction of dip. From *g* lay off *gh*, equal to the difference in altitude of *b* and *c*, here

$$260 \text{ ft.} - 240 \text{ ft.} = 20 \text{ ft.}$$

Draw *bh*. Angle *gbh* is the angle of dip. The direction of strike and dip and the angle of dip can be determined by measurement, since the diagram is drawn to scale in reference to north-south and east-west coordinates. *db* need not be perpendicular to *ab* for the solution of this problem.

Dr. W. S. Tangier Smith[4] has outlined a simple method for determining the strike in this problem, as follows:

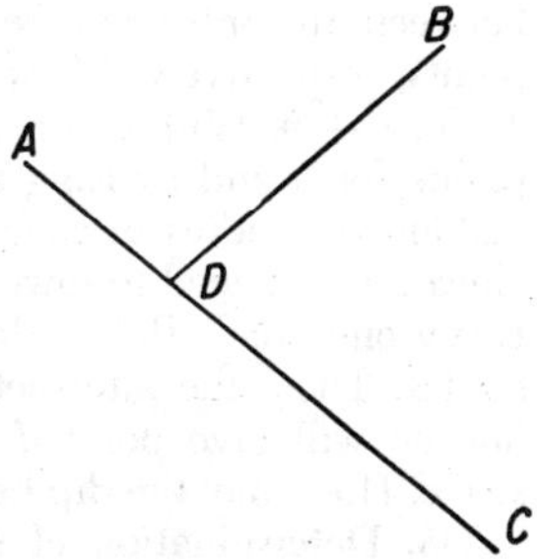

A B D C

Fig. 587. Diagram for determining strike of a plane in which three points, not in same straight line, are known.

"1. Having platted, on a map or a separate sheet, the three given points, *A*, *B*, and *C* (Fig. 587), *A* being the highest and *C* the lowest, measure, as accurately as possible, the distance between *A* and *C* on the plat. Let us suppose the measured distance to be 1.242 in.

"2. Determine the difference in elevation between *A* and *B*; also that between *A* and *C*. Express these two differences as a ratio in fractional form, and reduce this ratio to its simplest terms. If, for example, the difference in elevation between *A* and *B* is 70 ft., and that between *A* and *C* is 230 ft., the ratio of these differences, expressed fractionally ($^{70}/_{230}$) and reduced to simplest terms, is $^{7}/_{23}$.

"3. Multiply the measured distance between *A* and *C* by the fractional ratio obtained from the differences in elevation. The resulting distance, when laid off from *A*, along the line *AC* of the plat, will give the point *D*. Using the figures given above, the distance

$$AD = 1.242 \text{ in.} \times {}^{7}/_{23} = 0.378 \text{ in.}$$

"4. *D* is the plat of a point lying in the given plane and having the same elevation as the point whose plat is *B*. The line *BD* will, therefore, be the required strike of the plane."

[4] Personal communication.

The following graphic method of obtaining the attitude of an inclined bed from three given points on the bed has been suggested by W. S. Tangier Smith as a modification of Moon's method.[5] For illustration of this problem, assume that the three points, *a*, *b*, and *c*, (as in Fig. 586), are on the top surface of a certain stratum where this stratum is intersected by three drill holes. Let the elevations of *a*, *b*, and *c*, be 830, 860, and 900 ft., respectively, above sea level. Each of these elevations was obtained by subtracting the depth of the stratum below the mouth of the well from the elevation of the mouth of the well. The sites of the wells are plotted to scale. Take the differences of elevation between the intermediate point, *b*, and the highest and lowest points, respectively. These differences are here 30 ft., $b - a$, and 40 ft., $c - b$. With compasses describe circles round the location points for *a* and *c*, using any convenient scale for the radii, and making the radius in each case proportional to the differences of elevation, reduced to lowest terms (*i.e.*, 3 and 4 in this example). Draw one (or both) of the *interior* tangents common to the two circles. Then, the intersection of the tangent (or tangents) with line *ac* will give point *d*. Line *bd* will be the required line of strike. How may the dip be found in feet per mile?

535. Determination of strike and dip from two components. The geologist sometimes finds it necessary to determine true dip and strike from observations made on components of these quantities; in other words true dip and strike for various reasons may not be subject to direct measurement. Following are examples of graphic solutions of this problem.

1. Let us assume that the amount of inclination from the horizontal (*i.e.*, dip component) and the direction of this inclination are recorded, respectively, as 6° and N. 20° W., as measured on a certain horizon exposed on one side of an outcrop, and that the similar quantities are 8° and N. 60° E. on the same horizon on another face of the same outcrop. The same conditions might apply to a given stratum exposed at two widely separated outcrops, say on opposite sides of a valley, or of a ridge. To find the true dip and strike of the horizon (top or bottom of a bed, etc.), proceed thus:[6]

Lay off a long north-south line on a sheet of paper (Fig. 588, NS). At any convenient point, *a*, on this line, lay off with a pro-

[5] Bibliog., Moon, F. W., 1913.

[6] Somewhat modified, after Kitson. See Bibliog., Kitson, H. W., 1929.

tractor the lines *am* and *ap* with the bearings N. 20° W. and N. 60° E., respectively. At *a* draw perpendiculars to *am* and *ap* with the protractor, and on each lay off equal distances, *ad* and *ae*, any convenient length being used. From *d* lay off a line at an angle of 6° to *am* and intersecting *am* at *b*. From *e* lay off a line at an angle of 8° to *ap*, intersecting *ap* at *c*.

Draw *bc*, which is the line of strike of the inclined horizon. The strike of this horizon is the acute angle, N*ob* or *co*S, which may be measured with the protractor. Here it is S. 28° E.

Draw *af* perpendicular to *bc* from *a*. At *a* draw a line *ag*, perpendicular to *af*, and lay off *ag* equal to *ad*. Draw *fg*. Then angle *afg* is the true angle of dip of the inclined horizon. As measured by protractor, this angle is here 9° SW.

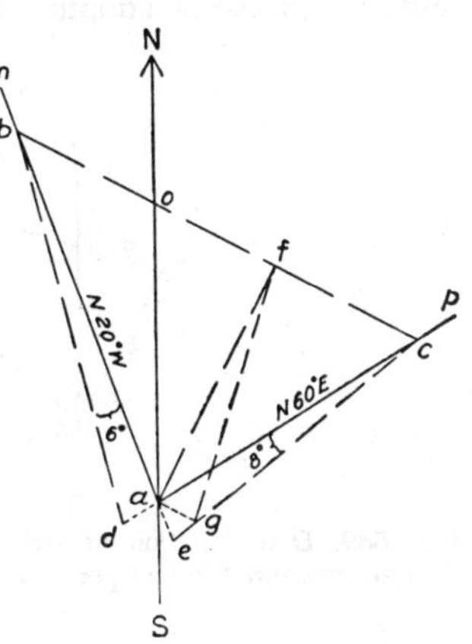

Fig. 588. Determination of strike and dip from two components where dips are measured in degrees.

Where the vertical angles of the components are small, a more accurate method is to lay off the natural cotangents of the vertical angles along lines *am* and *ap*, respectively, to a convenient scale, thus locating points *b* and *c* without drawing the perpendiculars *ad*, *ae*, and *ag* or platting the vertical angles. Then *bc* is drawn, and *af* is drawn perpendicular to *bc*. Thus, the natural cotangent of 6° is 9.5144; that of 8° is 7.1154. Therefore, scale off $ab = 9.5$ and $ac = 7.1$. With the same scale measure *af*, which is here 6.1, which is the natural cotangent of the true angle of dip, namely, just under 9°.[7]

If dips are so low that they are recorded, not in degrees, but in feet per mile or as 1 ft. in so many feet, a method described by Rich[8] may be used. Let us suppose that field observations indicate a dip component of 1 ft. in 50 ft. in the direction N. 30° W.

[7] This method is described by Kitson. See Bibliog., *op. cit.*

[8] Bibliog., Rich, John L., 1932. In a later note Rich credited this method to Prof. G. D. Harris (Am. Assoc. Petrol. Geols., *Bull.*, vol. 20, p. 1496, 1936).

and another dip component, on the same horizon, of 1 ft. in 125 ft. in the direction N. 50° E. (if the vertical difference in elevation is recorded as inches in so many feet, the ratio should be raised or lowered to the form 1 ft. in *x* ft.). The observations are then plotted. From a convenient point, *a* (Fig. 589), on a north-south line (NS), draw a line, *am*, bearing N. 30° W. and, using any convenient scale, lay off on it a distance *ab* equal to 50 units. Draw a line *ap* and on this measure *ac*, equal to 125 units on the scale adopted. Draw *bc*, which is the true strike.

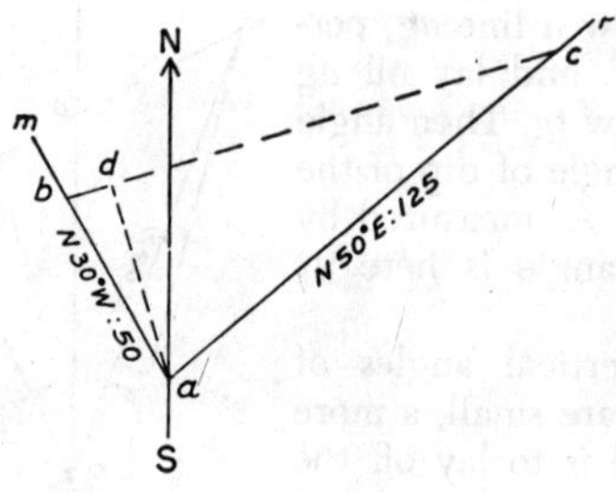

FIG. 589. Determination of strike and dip from two components where dips are measured in feet per mile.

Draw *ad* perpendicular to *bc* from *a*; *ad* is the direction of the true dip, the amount (angle) of which can be ascertained by scaling off the distance *ad*. This is 48. In other words, the true dip is 1 ft. in 48 ft. in a direction N. 17° W.

536. Slip and shift of faults. A visible displacement between corresponding points in the broken sides of a faulted dike, vein, or other recognizable structure, is almost never the true displacement (net slip) of the fault, for there is small chance that a surface of erosion or an artificial section will coincide with the direction of the net slip which, as we have seen, may lie in any position in the fault surface. Consequently, direct measurement of net slip is seldom possible. Likewise, estimates of shift, when based merely upon superficial evidence of dislocation, are apt to be incorrect. Yet in nearly all cases where fault measurements are to be made—and they must often be made—the net slip or the net shift is the quantity which must be obtained. This is done by the solution of right triangles, as will be explained below.

All fault computations depend upon facts observed and recorded in the field. When, for one reason or another, a geologist suspects the presence of a fault, he should search for the following: (1) the attitude of the faulted dike, bed, vein, igneous contact, etc.; (2) the measure of the visible displacement along an exposed portion of the fault; (3) the amount of gap, overlap repetition of strata, or omission of strata, if such relations exist (**212, 213, 215**); (4) the strike and dip of the fault; (5) the attitude of the fault with respect to the dislocated structures; (6) the direction of slipping of the blocks as indicated on the fault surface (**207**); (7) the direction of relative displacement of the blocks, *i.e.*, which one seems to have moved in a certain direction with respect to the other.

With reference to the first two factors, dislocated structures may change their attitude in the immediate vicinity of the fault (**210**), and consequently, if displacement is visible *at the fault* it may be related to slip and not to shift; but shift is the quantity most desired and the one which will probably be obtained when the displacement is not visible along an exposed fault. This last remark applies especially to gap, overlap, repetition, and omission.

Since a majority of large important faults are more or less concealed, their attitudes with respect both to a horizontal plane and to the structures which they intersect must often be found in the field by indirect observations. If a fault can be approximately located at several points in a hill-and-valley topography, its line of outcrop can be plotted on a contour map and its attitude can be determined from its trace (**520**).

The sixth factor, the direction of slipping, is best ascertained by fault striae and other features on the fault surface (**207**), but these cannot always be seen. The same information can be secured in another way if two intersecting structures are cut by the fault. For example, let the structures be a dike and a bed. The attitudes of dike, bed, and fault must have been recorded in the field. Construct a diagram as described in Art. **529**, and so determine the position of the line of intersection of any chosen surfaces in the dike and the bed. Then find the two points at which the separated portions of this line—one in each block—meet the plane of the fault (**530**). These points, formerly in contact, will show by their mutual relation the direction and amount of the slip (or shift).

This method is not practicable when the fault is parallel to the line of intersection of the dislocated structures. Furthermore, while it may give essentially correct results for slip or shift, as these have been defined, it is subject to misinterpretation as regards the true direction of slipping, just as are fault striae, if there was any change in this direction before the faulting ceased (**207**). It indicates merely the resultant of the combined movements.

We shall now suppose that enough data have been secured in the field to make possible the necessary computations. If the required quantities can be obtained by reference to but one right triangle, the figure should be drawn to scale; but if, as is usually the case, the problem demands the solution of two or more right triangles in different planes, these are best constructed in block diagrams made in cabinet or isometric projection (**511**). This is the most satisfactory method of visualizing the complex relations of faulted structures. This warning, however, must be heeded: in block diagrams *you cannot construct all angles and lines to scale on account of the unavoidable distortion due to projection.*

Below are outlined a few examples to illustrate the use of right triangles in solving fault problems. Although the first one might just as well be represented in a plane figure, it is shown in a block diagram so that it may be compared with the more involved cases that follow. In all these examples the surface of the ground (upper surface of the block) is regarded as horizontal and the fault surface is assumed to be flat.

1. *Given:* A vertical strike fault intersecting a series of beds which dip 40° due east. The displacement was vertical. A knowledge of the stratigraphic sequence in the region proves that a certain thickness of beds is missing.

Required: The net slip (or net shift).

Solution: Construct a block diagram in cabinet projection, having its front face in the plane of the dip of the beds (Fig. 590). Draw lines for the stratification and the fault. Field observations prove that the east block dropped with respect to the west block, for beds are missing on the east side of the fault trace. Draw a right triangle, *abc,* in which one leg, *bc,* meets the point *c,* which was formerly in contact with *a,* in the west block.

bc is the thickness of the missing beds and the hypotenuse, *ac*, is the required displacement. Since *bc* is known, and

$$\angle bac = \angle dac - \angle dab = 90° - 40° = 50°,$$

ac may be found by the equation, sin $\angle bac$ — sin 50° $= bc/ac$.

2. *Given:* The same conditions as those stated for Problem 1, with the exception that the direction of slipping is inclined southward (forward in the block) at an angle of 30° to the horizon.

Required: The net slip (or net shift).

Solution: Construct triangle *abc* (Fig. 591) as in Problem 1, and determine the length of *ac*. *ae* is the outcrop of the fault.

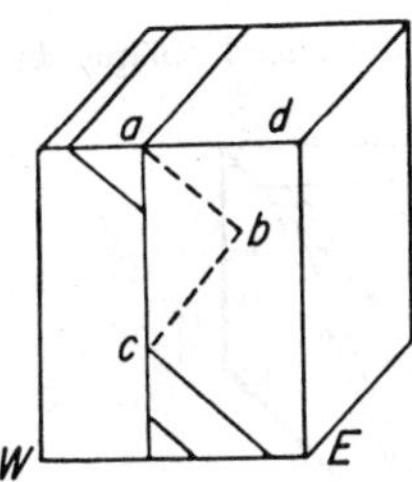

Fig. 590. Diagram for finding the slip of a vertical dip-slip strike fault.

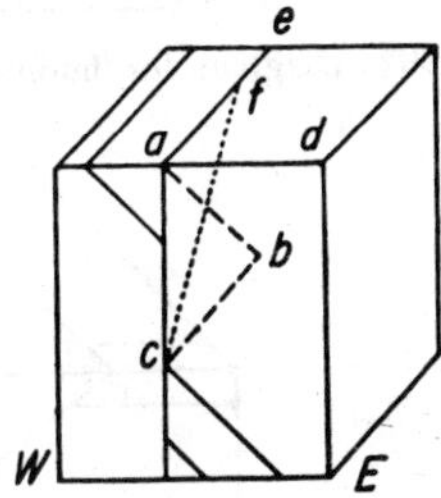

Fig. 591. Diagram for finding the slip of a vertical oblique-slip strike fault.

Let *f*, in the west block, be the point which was once in contact with *c* in the east block. Draw *cf*. Then *cf* represents the amount of actual displacement. Triangle *afc* is a right triangle seen in projection, and $\angle afc = 30°$. *fc* may be obtained from the equation sin $\angle afc$ = sin 30° $= ac/fc$, for *ac* has been found already.

3. *Given:* A strike fault dipping 70° E. and intersecting a series of beds dipping 35° E. Field observations demonstrate repetition of beds in a strip having a breadth, *B*. Movement along the fault was in a direction inclined 20° S.

Required: The net slip (or net shift).

Solution: Having constructed, in cabinet projection, a block diagram showing the relations given (Fig. 592), first determine *ac*, the dip component of the net slip (or net shift), as follows: *a*, in the west block, and *d*, in the east block, are two points at the same horizon in the bedding. The distance between them, *ad*, is the breadth of outcrop, *B*, of the repeated strata. *db*, the thickness of the repeated beds, may be found from the equation $\sin \angle dab = \sin 35° = bd/ad$. Draw *ae* from *a* perpendicular to *gc*, the stratigraphic horizon in the west block that corresponds

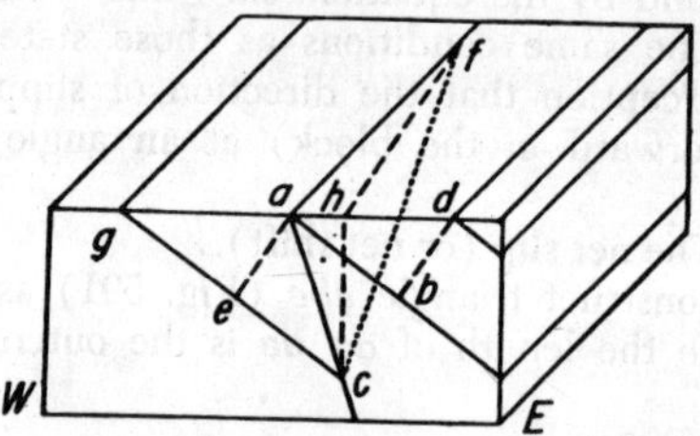

FIG. 592. Diagram for finding the slip of an inclined oblique-slip strike fault.

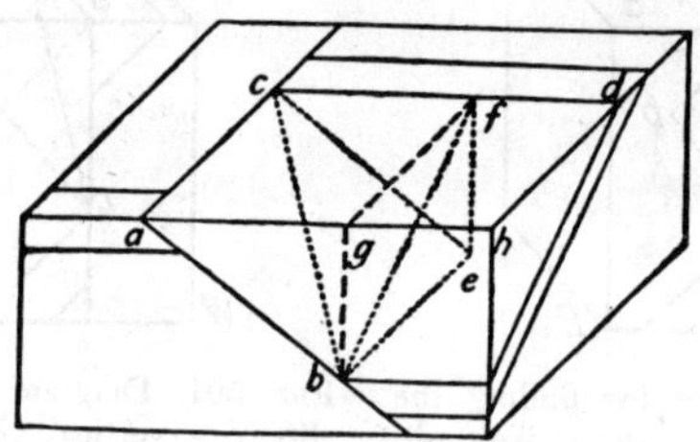

FIG. 593. Diagram for finding the slip of an inclined dip-slip dip fault.

to *ab* in the east block. In triangle *gae* and *abd*, $ae = bd$. Therefore, in triangle *aec*, *ae* is known and

$$\angle ace = \angle bac = \angle dac - \angle dab = 70° - 35° = 35°$$

ac may be found from the equation $\sin \angle ace = \sin 35° = ae/ac$.

Now let *f* be a point in the west block that was formerly in contact with *c* in the east block. Then *cf* lies in the fault and is equal to the net slip (or net shift). Erect the line *ch* from *c* perpendicular to *ad* and draw *hf*. Triangle *hfc* is a right triangle seen in projection and $\angle hfc = 20°$, the inclination of the direction of movement of the faulting. Likewise, triangle *ahc* is a right triangle in the plane of the front face of the block diagram. In triangle *ahc*, $hac = 70°$ and *ac* has been determined. *hc* may be found from the equation sin $\angle hac$ = sin 70° = hc/ac. In triangle hfc, fc may be obtained from the equation,

$$\sin \angle hfc = \sin 20^\circ = hc/fc.$$

4. *Given:* A dip fault dipping 37° E. and intersecting a series of strata which dip 23° S. The fault is a dip-slip fault.

Required: The net slip (or net shift).

Solution: Construct a block diagram (Fig. 593) in cabinet projection as in the previous cases. Let ab be the net slip (or net shift), and let ac be the measurable offset. Draw bc, the trace of the bedding plane, bcd, on the fault plane, abc. Draw ce parallel to ab and draw be parallel to ac. From e draw ef perpendicular to cd, from b draw bg perpendicular to ah. Draw gf and bf. In triangle bef, $be = ac$, which is known, and $\angle ebf = \angle bfg = 23°$, the dip of the beds. $ef = be \cdot \tan \angle ebf$. In triangle cef, $\angle ecf = 37°$, the dip of the fault. Therefore, ce, the net slip (or net shift) $= ef/\sin \angle ecf$.

Chapter 22

PREPARATION OF GEOLOGIC REPORTS

The Report as a Whole

537. General instructions. Not only must the professional geologist be conversant with methods of research, but also he must be able to set forth the results of his work in good, concise English. The practice obtained in writing geologic reports in college courses is seldom long enough to be thorough. The student should therefore make the most of his opportunities while they last. He should plan his theses as if they were intended for publication, even though he may not actually contemplate publishing. The unavoidable differences between course theses and manuscripts for publication are very few indeed. They will be pointed out in the later pages of this chapter where detailed instructions are given for the preparation of reports.

Certain directions of general application may be noted in this place. Endeavor to use clear, idiomatic English. Avoid colloquial and slang phrases. Be heedful of punctuation and spelling. Remember that the words "data," "strata," and "phenomena" are plural forms of which the singular forms are "datum," "stratum," and "phenomenon," respectively. We say "data are," "strata are," "phenomena are"; and "a datum is," "a stratum is," or "a phenomenon is." Avoid repetition of words or phrases, but never at the expense of perspicuity. There are many students who seem to have an idea that these are matters of small moment, and who object to criticism which they think should be confined, in a geologic thesis, to geologic matters. They should realize that solvenly writing is as detrimental to their profession as is careless field or laboratory work.[1] In writing a professional report for a client not too well versed in geology, do not be too booky. Aim to make your report simple and easily intelligible to

[1] Geologists are strongly recommended to peruse Wood's "Suggestions to Authors." Bibliog., Wood, G. M., 4th ed., 1935; 5th ed., 1958. The fourth edition was very much changed and enlarged to make the fifth edition.

him. It will do you no harm if you substitute common words and expressions for more technical terms with which you yourself may have become familiar.

The question is frequently asked, "How long shall I make my report?" This cannot be answered in terms of pages. Treat the theme from all points of view; omit nothing which will serve to elucidate the subject; but be concise. Aim to be brief and thorough. Let there be no mistake in your reader's mind between what is fact and what is theory. Also, be conscientious in acknowledging outside sources of important information, whether these were conversations or published works.

After you have completed your paper, number the pages and see that all page citations in the text are correctly filled in. Never submit the final copy of a thesis or of an article for publication until you have examined it critically for mistakes.

As for the paper, use sheets about 8½ by 11 in. Write on one side only. Leave a margin at least 1 in. wide on all sides. Double space the lines if you typewrite, and use a typewriter whenever possible.

538. Parts of a manuscript report. A finished geologic report, in manuscript form, has a title page, a table of contents, a list of illustrations, the text, the illustrations themselves, and, if the paper is very long, an index, and bibliography. These may be called the "parts" of the report. First, the text is written; then the illustrations, which have already been roughly drawn to assist in composing the text, are completed in final form; and the remaining parts are prepared last.

The Text of a Geologic Report

539. Order of topics. Before beginning to write a paper, one should consider the order of presentation of the subject matter. The topics should be arranged in the sequence of their dependence, that is to say, in a sequence such that each chapter is as little as possible dependent, for its correct understanding, upon the chapters that succeed it. This is difficult to carry out for there is always more or less interdependence of subjects.

Different reports, of course, must be drawn up in different ways. Papers of a specific character, usually those with a purely economic motive, may need individual planning. Papers of a general scientific nature, both course theses and articles for publication, may often be arranged in accordance with a set outline like that given below:

General Outline for a Geologic Report

Abstract (for an article for publication).
Introduction.
  Location of area
  Size of area.
  Purpose of investigation.
  Method of investigation.
  Acknowledgments.
Summary and conclusions.
Recommendations (in a paper with a practical object).
Geography.
  Relief and elevations.
  Topography.
  Drainage.
  Vegetation.
  Rock exposures.
Stratigraphy and petrography.
  Regional, or general.
  Local, or detailed.
Geologic structure.
  Regional.
  Local.
  Structural development.
Geologic history.
Economic considerations.

These headings will now be discussed in order.

540. Abstract. An abstract—that is, a very much condensed presentation of the essential facts and conclusions—should appear immediately following the title of a paper intended for publication. This enables the reader to find out in a very short time just what the paper treats and whether or not, from his standpoint, it warrants his careful study of the main body of the report.

541. Introduction. In the introduction of a geologic essay briefly outline the location of the region to be described and the best ways of reaching it from the nearest cities. State its shape and area, and mention in what manner and to what extent, if at all, the district has been put under culture by man. Add a short explanation of the method in which the field work was conducted. Especially in economic papers, tell the reason for making the investigation and writing the report. Conclude this section with a paragraph acknowledging important sources of information and giving credit to those persons who have furnished assistance in compiling or preparing the report.

542. Summary and conclusions. The usual place for a summary is at the end of a paper, but in scientific literature clearness is gained and time is saved for the reader by putting this section immediately after the introduction. Notwithstanding its position, however, the summary should not be *written* until after the main text is finished. It is in no sense introductory. It should be a very concise review, in outline form, of the principal facts and inferences of the report. The reader should be able to acquire a true perspective of the scope and conclusions of a paper by looking over merely the introduction and the summary.

In economic papers the summary and conclusions should be followed by the recommendations.

543. Geography. Under this head are discussed the relief and drainage of the field area, the nature of the topography, the abundance, shape, and size of outcrops, the relations of outcrop to topography, and the general distribution of surface deposits. Unless these subjects have an important bearing upon the geology proper, they should be briefly treated. In some reports the topography may be taken up with advantage in the introduction.

544. Stratigraphy and petrography. *Stratigraphy* refers particularly to various rock formations (called *map units* if they are shown on a map) in their individual characteristics and in their relations to one another. The description of the rocks themselves belongs under the head *Petrography*.

A brief discussion should first be given of the regional or general stratigraphy and petrography. Then, in chronologic order, each map unit (formation, rock body) should be described in detail and with reference to its local aspects.

In giving the detailed outline of the rock formations, or map units, the following items should receive attention:

A. For sedimentary (and metamorphosed sedimentary) rocks:
   1. Name of rock or formation or map unit.
   2. Areal distribution (may include nature of outcrops and topographic expression).
   3. Lithology (list visible mineral and rock constituents; give such characteristics as texture, color, fresh or weathered; also, describe lithologic structures such as ripple-mark, foliation, etc.).

4. Thickness (state method of measuring thickness and probably accuracy of this measurement) (see **533** also **545**); local and regional changes in thickness.
5. Origin (source of sediment and conditions of deposition).
6. Relations to underlying and overlying rocks (conformable or unconformable; here should be described nature and extent of unconformities).
7. Age and correlation (give method of determining age, and tell how certain the correlation is).

B. For igneous (and metamorphosed igneous) rocks:
1. Name of rock or formation or map unit.
2. Areal distribution (may include nature of outcrops and topographic expression).
3. Lithology (give mineral composition and approximate percentages of different minerals; also texture, internal structure, etc.).
4. Thickness (of flows, dikes, etc.).
5. Origin (intrusive or extrusive; depth at which intruded, or conditions of extrusion; other pertinent data).
6. Relations to underlying and overlying rocks, or to wall rocks.
7. Age and correlation (give method of determining age, and tell how certain the correlation is).

545. Geologic structure. This is the section in which the geologic structure and the mutual field relations of the different rocks are to be described and explained. Consider here the mode of occurrence of the rocks; the contact phenomena of igneous rocks; the spacial relations of magmatic differentiates in an intrusive body; the attitude of dikes, veins, beds, etc.; the nature of folding; joints; faults; cleavage; schistosity; and other like features. In this section, too, measurements of breadth of outcrop and thickness of beds may be taken up in detail, since these are related to folding, etc. Computations for the heave, throw, strike-slip, dip-slip, and other items of fault displacement should be made. Discuss the several topics which relate to your particular problem in some rational order. Whenever appropriate, refer to the geologic maps and sections to illustrate your statements.

In comprehensive reports, discuss the structural development of the area. Explain how the structures originated, giving attention to directions and points of application of forces, role played by competent and incompetent beds, etc. Serial or consecutive maps, sections, and block diagrams are of value in this discussion.

546. Geologic history. For some reason students seem to find it hard to understand just what they should write under the caption, geologic history. There is really no great difficulty in the matter, provided the facts are at hand, if this one important rule is heeded: *describe the events in the natural sequence of their occurrence.* Here is an example: suppose that a certain region is underlain by a folded sedimentary series which is unconformably related to an older body of schists and injected granitic rocks; and suppose, further, that most of the bedrock in the district is covered by glacial deposits, and that the outcrops show evidence of glacial abrasion succeeded by more or less weathering. In the section, geologic history, of a report dealing with this particular area, one should describe the events in the following order: (1) origin of the schists; (2) intrusion of the granitic rocks; (3) erosion of these schists and igneous rocks (the lower unconformity); (4) accumulation of the stratified series; (5) folding of the strata (and probably of the older rocks and structures); (6) erosion culminating in glacial abrasion (the upper unconformity); (7) deposition of glacial materials; (8) postglacial weathering. No doubt other phenomena, such as jointing and veins, would be found in a region of this kind, and these should be mentioned in their proper places in the account.

In the geologic history, then, the mode and conditions of origin of the various rock masses and important structures should receive consideration. Likewise the topographic forms should be described with respect to their origin and in relation to geomorphic cycles (Chap. 12). Some authors include this last subject under *geomorphology* as a separate heading.

Try to determine the geologic age of each event. For this part of your report you will find that the field notes on the relative ages of the different observed phenomena are indispensable.

547. Economic considerations. Geologic facts that have a practical bearing and facts pertaining to economic operations already in progress are reserved for this chapter. Here should be described the pits, quarries, mines, or wells of the district, the product extracted, the values and uses of these products, and the available means for their conveyance to the nearest transportation depot. The subject of the resources not yet touched should also be treated, their nature, distribution, and extent, and the approximate cost of handling them. Recommendations based on these facts are usually presented early in a practical report in order to save the time of the reader, who is likely to be a busy executive.

Parts Other than the Text

548. Quotations and footnotes. Direct quotations from the works of other authors must be identical with the original, except that typographic errors may be corrected.

"Before making a footnote an author should carefully consider whether the matter does not belong in the text. Proper footnotes consist chiefly of references to the literature of the subject discussed."[2] . . . For reference marks superior figures ([1,2,3]) should be used. In the manuscript each footnote should be written immediately below the line in which the reference mark appears and should be separated from the text above and below it by dotted, dashed, or full lines. Footnotes should be arranged according to a standard pattern, as in the following examples:

Geikie, Archibald, Text-book of geology, 4th ed., vol. 1, 1903, p. 49.

Dana, J. D., Volcanic eruptions of Hawaii, Am. Jour. Sci., 2d ser., vol. 10, 1850, p. 235.

Dana, J. D. "Volcanic Eruptions of Hawaii," *Am. Jour. Sci.* (2), X (1850), 235.

Observe the details of capitalization, abbreviation, punctuation, and order in these examples. Notice, also, the differences between the last two. Either way is correct and either way may be adopted; but consistency demands that only one be used for all citations in a given manuscript. If you are preparing an article for some particular journal, adapt your footnotes to the method practiced by this journal.

549. Illustrations.[3] Figures are illustrations which are printed with the text and which are usually smaller than a printed page. Full-page illustrations in the published article are usually printed apart from the text and are then known as plates. All illustrations larger than a printed page are plates in the sense that they are made separately.

With regard to manuscripts, the illustrations should be numbered in the sequence in which they are referred to in the text. The number, name, and description of each *figure* should be

[2] Bibliog., Wood, G. M., 4th ed., 1935, p. 16.

[3] *Idem.*, 4th ed., 1935, p. 45; 5th ed., 1958, p. 122.

given at the place where it is to appear in the text when published. The number, name, and description of each *plate* should be written on a separate sheet of paper, and the place where it is to be found in the publication should be clearly indicated. The original figures and plates themselves are not kept with the text; they are put together in an envelope, and each is properly numbered.

Ordinarily maps and sections should be made in black and white, for the reproduction of colors is expensive. All black line work is to be done with India ink. Put shading in, not by a back-and-forth scratching motion, but by repeated strokes in one direction. The outlines of the illustration may be lightly sketched in pencil before finishing in ink.

If possible, when drawing for publication, make the illustrations larger than they are to appear in print, for their details are often brought into sharper contrast by reduction than by copying in the original size. Lettering must be large enough for the reducing process to make it of proper size. It should never be so small that, when printed, the lower case figures and numbers are less than 1/50 of an inch in height. For easy legibility, they should be a little larger than this minimum size. Illustrations on paper over 8½ by 11 in. may be folded for course theses, but never so for reports to be published. In the latter case they should be sent rolled or flat. *Always be neat.* Do not submit untidy drawings either for publication or for course theses.

Directions for the construction of geologic maps and sections have been given in Chap. 19. A few more suggestions of practical import may be added here. In preparing a geologic map in black and white, only enough of the details of relief, drainage, and culture, need be shown to enable the reader to ascertain from this map the locations of geologic features in the field. Prominent hill crests, rivers, lakes, railroads, town lines, and a few of the more important roads, may be traced from a topographic map and used as a base for plotting the geology. In more accurate work, a finished topographic base map must be employed. It is often a good plan to make two maps on the same scale, one to represent the bedrock and the other, the superficial deposits and outcrops. You should also furnish a small-scale index map of the surrounding country with a small rectangle marked on it to indicate the exact location of the mapped area of investigation (Fig. 594).

Both maps and sections may be drawn on ordinary tracing cloth, from which, if desired, blue print copies can be made. Geologic sections should first be sketched on profile paper so that the measurements can be made accurately and quickly for

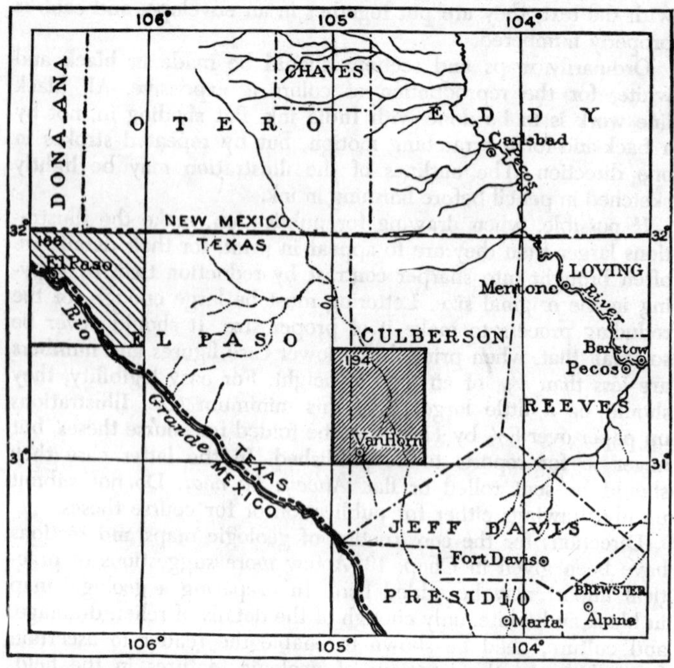

Fig. 594. An index map. The heavily shaded area is the location of the Van Horn quadrangle of which the geology is discussed in the Van Horn Folio. (*Van Horn Folio, No.* 194, *U.S. Geol. Survey,* 1914.)

horizontal and vertical scales. Then they may be traced on the cloth. Line drawings for illustrations, if not traced, should be prepared on the thinnest grade of Bristol board. For photographs, which should always be in sharp focus for scientific purposes, glossy prints should be submitted. Do not fail to assure yourself that each of your illustrations has on it all the data necessary to make it serviceable and comprehensible (**484, 496, 512, 517**).

550. Table of contents, index, etc. There remain for consideration the table of contents, list of illustrations, bibliography, index, title page, and the cover. The *table of contents* is a list of headings and subheadings used in the text. Each division, with the page on which it is to be found, is noted on a separate line. The wording is to be literally identical with that employed in the text. Differences of rank are indicated by indentation, the subordinate sections being set in somewhat to the right of those of next higher degree. The *list of illustrations* has only the names of figures and plates, not the accompanying legends. The pages on which figures appear and the pages facing plates are recorded on the right opposite the appropriate illustrations. *The bibliography,* which is best placed at the end or just before the index, is a catalogue of all books and articles referred to in preparing the report. It may be arranged alphabetically by authors, or chronologically. The utility of a lengthy bibliography may be enhanced by grouping the references according to subject.

An *index* is not necessary except for long articles and books. If one is undertaken, it should be comprehensive and thorough, for a deficient index is far worse than none at all.

After the report is complete it should be securely bound in a cover of some kind either by stitching or by metal fasteners. On the front of the cover are the title of the report and the author's name. In college reports the date on which the paper is due is also on the cover. The title page bears exactly the same information as the cover. Always strive to make the title brief and to the point.

Chapter 23

GEOPHYSICAL SURVEYING[1]

551. Definition and classification. By *geophysical surveying* is meant the making and interpretation of certain physical measurements with the object of furthering the study of subsurface geological conditions of structure or material. Such surveying has been used in the mapping of ore deposits and oil-bearing structures and also in research in pure geology. The measurements are made by sensitive instruments of one kind or another, according to the particular type of geophysical results desired. The more important classes of geophysical work are based on the measurement of variations in: (1) density; (2) magnetic intensity; (3) elasticity; and (4) electrical conductivity. To these may be added (5) measurements of variations in temperature, and (6) measurement of variations in radioactivity. These methods are designated, respectively, as (1) gravimetric; (2) magnetic, or magnetometric; (3) seismic, or seismographic; (4) electric; (5) geothermic; and (6) radioactive. Some of these methods—those that involve measurements in drilled holes, such as electrical logging, geothermic observations, measurements of gamma rays—have been discussed under Subsurface Geologic Surveying (Arts. **468, 470,** and **471**) and under Subsurface Maps (Arts. **500** and **501**). The present chapter concerns the field methods in geophysics, those methods that require field surveying and the collection of data by observations at, or very near, the surface of the ground. These fall mainly under the first four methods listed above. The first two—gravimetric and magnetometric—depend upon naturally occurring fields of force within the earth; the next two—seismic and electric—depend mainly on artificially induced fields of force.[2]

In the following pages no attempt is made to expound the

[1] For valuable suggestions and for some contributed paragraphs in this chapter, the author is greatly indebted to L. G. Ellis, Richard H. Hopkins, W. T. Evans, George McCalpin, and A. G. Winterhalter.

[2] Some electrical methods involve measurement of natural fields.

mathematics of these various geophysical methods, and little is said by way of describing the construction of the instruments used or of explaining the technique of making observations in the field. These are matters of concern for the geophysicist himself. But every geologist should know something as to the nature and differences of these methods, what they can do and what they cannot do for geological interpretation, and the meaning of the maps on which the geophysical data, or geophysical anomalies,[3] are graphically represented.[4] It is for this purpose that we are outlining some of the more significant facts. For detailed information, reference may be had to the writings of others cited herein and to the bibliographies included in many of the citations.[5]

552. Electronic methods of horizontal locations. In all geophysical mapping the horizontal (and usually the vertical) locations of stations or profiles of observation must be determined in order properly to correlate the geophysical data with the subsurface geology. Ordinarily such horizontal location is possible by the common methods of surveying (Chap. 16) or by the use of air photographs or air maps (Chap. 17), but under certain conditions of difficult accessibility and absence of recognizable features in the area to be explored, as in the case of extensive swamps, jungles, and offshore waters, other methods of location have been devised which involve electronics.

For several years after World War II, surveying for geophysical exploration in water-covered areas was accomplished with the aid of slightly modified wartime navigation methods, called Radar and Shoran, but more recently these have been almost wholly replaced by systems capable of greater range and better accuracy.

[3] *Anomalies* are the relative variations in the physical properties determined and mapped by any of the geophysical methods.

[4] See Bibliog., Weaver, Paul, 1934.

[5] For these references, see Bibliog.: Rybar, Stephen, 1923; Ambronn, Richard, 1928; McLaughlin, Donald H. (chairman), 1929; Eve, A. S., and D. A. Keys, 1929; Heiland, C. A., 1929; Fordham, W. H., 1929; Barton, Donald C., 1927, 1929, 1930. Also, volumes on Geophysical Prospecting, published by the A.I.M.M.E. in 1929, 1932, and 1934; *Geophysics*, published periodically by the Society of Exploration Geophysicists; Heiland, C. A., "Geophysical Exploration," Prentice-Hall, Inc., 1940; Nettleton, L. L., "Geophysical Prospecting for Oil," McGraw-Hill Book Company, Inc., 1940; and Dobrin, Milton B., 1952.

Three major services are now available throughout the world for position fixing in offshore geophysical exploration. These are Decca (British), Raydist (United States), and Lorac (United States).[6] The service organization installs and operates stations on shore and provides necessary operators and equipment for the geophysical boats. The operator gives instructions for maintaining the course and position of the boat and records the actual locations of shots or readings made from the boat. A base network of shore stations can handle any number of boats. In areas where there is likely to be considerable work, one or more service organizations may set up semipermanent base installations to cover a long stretch of shore line, as, for instance, the coast of the Gulf of Mexico.

Decca, Raydist, and Lorac, as generally employed, have certain basic technical differences in equipment and in modes of operation, but the same general principles apply to all three methods. Equipment on the boat continuously measures the difference in phase of radio-frequency signals received from two separated transmitters on land. The indication of a phase meter places the boat on one of a family of hyperbolas with the transmitting stations as foci. Signals from a second pair of transmitters place the boat on a second hyperbola, and the point of intersection of the two hyperbolas fixes the position of the boat with regard to the base stations. It is customary to use three stations to generate two families of hyperbolas, the center station being common to both. Knowing the locations of the base stations and the constants for the network, it is possible to convert the position fixes into rectangular coordinates suitable for the reduction of geophysical data.

Since the phase meter makes a complete revolution each time the boat moves a distance, radially from the transmitting station, corresponding to a relative change of one cycle in the transmitted frequency, it is possible to obtain precise measurement of distance from this station. In geophysical work it is customary to maintain the cycle count by means of an automatic counter

[6] The following paragraphs are a somewhat modified version of a description of Decca, Raydist, and Lorac kindly furnished to the author by W. T. Evans and L. G. Ellis. A more complete explanation of all these methods, including Radar and Shoran, may be found in Chap. 20 of Dobrin's "Introduction to Geophysical Prospecting." (Bibliog., Dobrin, Milton B., 1952.)

which is set correctly at some known location and is periodically rechecked.

Charts are made up to a convenient scale with the hyperbolic coordinates and coordinates suitable for the reduction of geophysical data superimposed on sheets of stable transparent drafting material. Work is laid out by plotting proposed lines and stations on the chart or on a print. The meter readings may be read from the chart by interpolating between plotted hyperbolic lines. For sufficient accuracy in most cases, however, it is necessary to make a mathematical transformation of coordinates. This requires the services of an electronic computer for any extensive survey. The table of meter readings obtained by measurement from the chart or by calculation is used by the survey-equipment operator on the boat to guide the boat to successive shot points or station locations. Actual readings are recorded for each station, and the actual positions are plotted on the chart.

The system above described has an advantage over shorter-wave systems, such as Radar and Shoran, in that the signals follow the curvature of the earth and longer ranges are attained. A disadvantage is interference between the ground wave and the wave reflected from the ionosphere, which is troublesome near dawn and twilight so that operation is sometimes unsatisfactory during these hours. The accuracy of the system depends on the precision with which the base stations are located, the frequency employed, and the linearity and resolution of the phase meters.

An important source of error in water work is the difficulty in positioning a boat exactly or pursuing a uniform course under adverse wind and current conditions. This is most critical in seismographic work when the position of the shot in regard to the survey boat must be estimated. Because work is carried on at a considerable distance from the base line, grid distortion in the projection used for mapping is another possible source of appreciable error.

Electronic survey methods such as those described have been applied to precision land and air surveys in which the receiving equipment is carried in a land vehicle or an aircraft. For wide-scale air surveys other electronic methods are available in which all the equipment is installed in the aircraft. The most successful surveys use Doppler radar equipment which may be combined with an inertial navigation system. Electronic computers in the aircraft serve to maintain the flight path and produce position information.[7]

Gravimetric Methods

553. The law of gravitation; gravity. According to Newton's law of gravitation, all bodies in the universe attract one another, no matter what may be their size, or composition, or distance from one another. This force of attraction between any two bodies is in direct proportion to the product of their masses and varies inversely as the square of the distance between them. *Gravity*, as commonly used, refers more particularly to the gravitational attraction of the earth for relatively small objects near its surface. The direction in which the attraction of gravity acts is called the *vertical*. A surface of equal gravitational potential, or a *gravitational equipotential surface* (also called a *level surface*) is everywhere perpendicular to the vertical (Fig. 595). "If the earth were a homogeneous sphere at rest, gravity would be the same everywhere over the surface of the earth and would vary only radially, and the level surfaces would be spherical and concentric with the earth's surface. But the earth is not at rest; it is not a sphere; and its outer crust is in no way homogeneous."[8]

Centrifugal force, due to the earth's rotation, tends slightly to counteract the force of gravity. Because the earth is a spheroid flattened at the poles and because of the rotation of the earth, the value of gravity is at a maximum at the poles and at a minimum at the equator. Certain allowance must be made in all gravity observations to correct for the effect of the centrifugal force of the earth's rotation and the effect of the spheroidal shape of the earth.

The lithosphere, as all geologists know, is very irregular in the distribution and nature of the rock bodies that compose it. These rock bodies are of varying density, and consequently they produce varying amounts of deformation of the level surfaces and lines of force (verticals) that constitute the normal gravitational system. Furthermore, local, relatively shallow variations in

[7] On the applications of electronic surveying to geophysical exploration, see Bibliog., Hawkins, J. E., 1950; Dobrin, Milton B., 1952; and Benson, J. M., and J. E. Swafford, 1953.

[8] Bibliog., Barton, Donald C., 1929 (*a*), p. 417.

density may occur above deeper and often stronger variations which may be regional in their extent.

"As a result of the irregular distribution of mass in the earth's crust the intensity of gravity locally is at a maximum over the areas of excess of mass and at a minimum over the areas of deficiency of mass; the lines of vertical tend to crowd from the bodies deficient in mass into the bodies

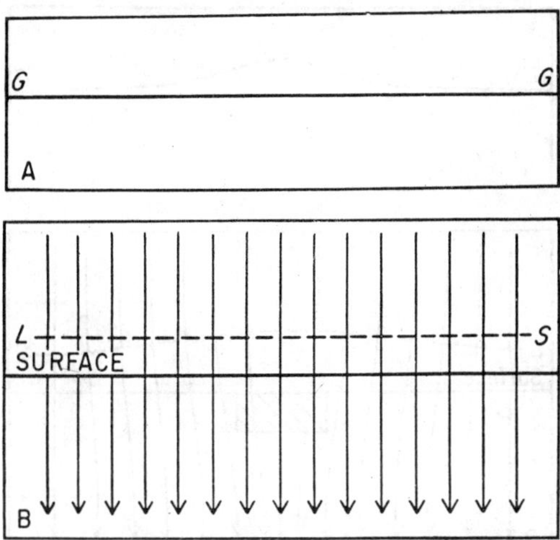

FIG. 595. Diagram of a small section of the earth's crust where there is supposed to be a homogeneous distribution of mass. In A, *GG* is the intensity of gravity, here perfectly uniform. In B, *LS* represents a level surface in section. The arrows represent lines of the vertical. Strictly speaking, the lines *GG* and *LS* should be arcs of circles of large radius, and the arrows should converge slightly downward, toward the earth's center.[9]

with excess of mass—that is, the vertical is deflected toward the excess of mass and away from the deficiency of mass; the level surfaces are warped up, convexly, over the areas of excess of mass and are warped downward, concavely, over the areas of deficiency of mass [Figs. 595–597]."[10]

[9] With Dr. Barton's permission and also permission from the A.I.M.M.E., Figs. 595–597, were copied from Barton's paper "The Eötvös Torsion Balance Method of Mapping Geologic Structure"; and Figs. 610–614 were copied from Barton's "Seismic Method of Mapping Geologic Structure." [Bibliog., Barton, Donald C., 1929 (*a*) and (*b*).]

[10] Bibliog., Barton, Donald C., 1929, pp. 419–420.

554. Quantities measured and instruments used in gravimetric surveying. In some respects the so-called gravitational system may be compared with topography. The "level surfaces," or equipotential surfaces, may be conceived of as being warped, like hills and valleys, with slopes that vary in amount and direction. At any point on such an imaginary warped surface, except

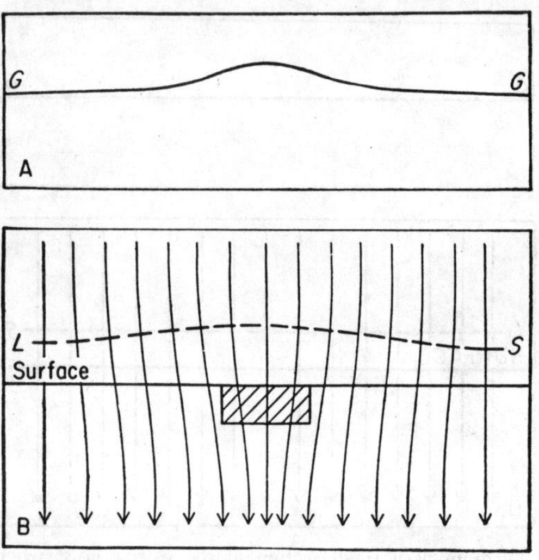

FIG. 596. Diagram of a small section of the earth's crust with a body denser than the surrounding country rock. In A, *GG* is the intensity of gravity, at a maximum above the center of the dense mass, and with steepest gradient over the edges of this mass. In B, *LS* is a level surface, arched up above the dense mass. The arrows represent lines of the vertical. (See footnote to Fig. 595.)

where this surface is locally level, the "vertical" will be somewhat inclined (see Figs. 596 and 597). At this point the inclined line of force, for any satisfactory scale of measurement, may be regarded as the hypotenuse of a right triangle of which one leg is the vertical component and the other leg is the horizontal component of the intensity of gravity. Also, at this point, there will be a direction of maximum slope of the warped surface (equipotential surface), in which direction the intensity of gravity will change a certain amount in a certain measured horizontal distance, an amount which is called the ***horizontal gradient of gravity***.

In gravimetric surveying three principal classes of instrument have been used to measure and map gravity, namely, the torsion balance, the pendulum, and the gravity meter or gravimeter.[11] The torsion balance, now practically obsolete for this kind of surveying, but widely used in the twenties and early thirties of the present century, chiefly measured the horizontal gradient of gravity[12] (see Fig. 598). The pendulum, which has long been used to determine the absolute value of gravity, although employed to a relatively small extent about the same

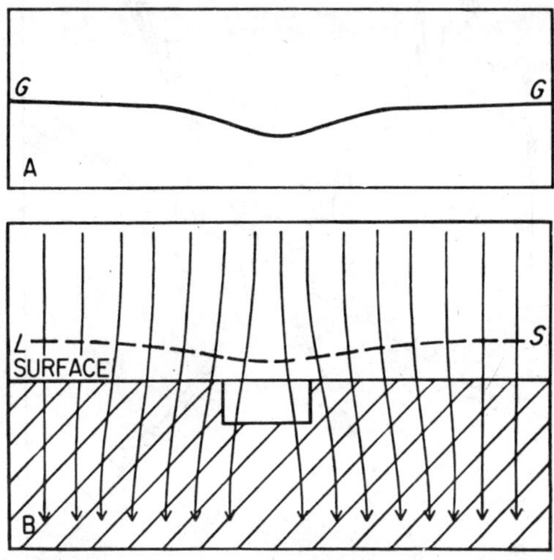

FIG. 597. Diagram of a small section of the earth's crust with a body lighter than the surrounding country rock. Here the gravity profile in A, *GG*, is curved down, with a minimum over the center of the body, and with the steepest gradient over its edges. In B, *LS*, the level surface, is bent down over the light body. The arrows represent lines of the vertical. (See footnote to Fig. 595.)

[11] Pronounced gravim'eter.

[12] The torsion balance also measured the so-called differential curvature, for an explanation of which see Bibliog., Dobrin, Milton B., 1952.

time as the torsion balance for gravimetric surveying, has likewise become practically obsolete for this latter purpose. Both these instruments have been superseded by the gravimeter which directly measures the relative difference of gravity between each

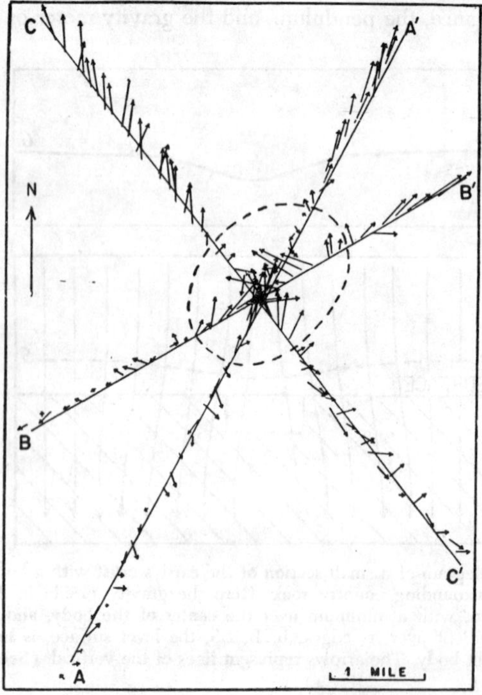

Fig. 598. Gradient arrow map showing results of torsion balance observations along three intersecting traverses (*AA′*, *BB′*, and *CC′*). This map is included here as an example of plotted torsion balance data and for comparison with Figs. 599 and 600.

two observation stations. This measured quantity is called the *relative gravity*, or Δg. Observations are commonly made at the intersections of rectangular grids arranged to cover the area to be surveyed and with a spacing of the cross lines such that anticipated anomalies will not be missed. A spacing of stations ½ mile apart in both directions is frequently used.

555. Correction and plotting of gravity values. Before the observed gravity values can be used for interpretation of the subsurface geology, they must be corrected for station elevation, for the effects of nearby topographic features (terrain correction), for latitude, and for drift,[13] and in highly precise work, for earth tides.[14] When these corrections have been made, the adjusted values, in milligals,[15] are plotted at the proper station points on an *observed gravity map,* and they are then contoured by lines of equal value, called *isogals* (Figs. 599 and 600). For geological purposes the mapped values are relative, not absolute. The case is similar to relative topographic elevations which are not based on sea-level data.

556. Interpretation and application of gravity data. It is obvious from preceding statements that preparation of the *observed gravity map* requires the use of high-precision instruments,[16] the careful recording of the data indicated by these instruments, and correction of these recorded data for several sources of error. When all this has been done, the observed gravity map cannot be used directly to interpret geological conditions from the plotted and contoured data. In the first place, densities of the subsurface rocks must be estimated. In country where no holes have been drilled, assumptions as to the nature of the rocks below the surface must depend on observation of exposed rocks and structures, and therefore, in such regions, conclusions as to the distribution of rock densities underground may be very much in error. If holes have been drilled, and especially deep holes, samples from different depths will give some idea as to subsurface densities, but actually only near the hole. The more holes drilled, the better will be the information available on the distribution of rock densities. In recent years the process of density logging (Art. 472) has provided a means of measuring the density of selected sections of the rocks penetrated

[13] Drift is a change in the gravity reading in a stationary instrument observed at intervals throughout the day.

[14] For discussion of these corrections, see Bibliog., Dobrin, Milton B., 1952.

[15] The common unit employed by geophysicists for the measurement of gravity is the *milligal,* or ¹⁄₁₀₀₀ part of a *gal,* which is the unit of acceleration of gravity, or one centimeter per second per second. Gravimeters can measure gravity differences to a few hundredths of a milligal.

[16] The probable error of an individual station observation with the best gravimeters is in the order of magnitude of a very few hundredths of a milligal, say 0.01 to 0.03 milligal.

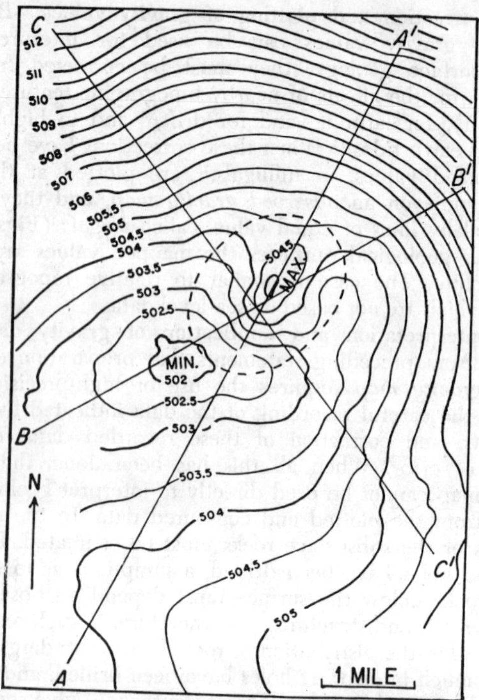

FIG. 599. Isogal map of torsion balance results obtained along lines *AA'*, *BB'*, and *CC'*. The structure here surveyed (the same as represented in Fig. 598) is a shallow salt dome with its cap rock approximately 1,600 ft. below the surface at the shallowest point. The cap rock sloped off moderately to near the position of the dashed line and then plunged off steeply on all sides. This was verified by drilling subsequent to gravity exploration.

in the drilling, but it is still necessary to estimate the density of the prism between holes, or outside the immediate vicinity of a single hole.

In the second place, the data shown on the observed gravity map are resultants of gravity effects of various degrees from various depths, all combined so that they cannot be easily analyzed. Thus, the observed gravity map may combine small local effects with large regional effects in such a way that the local effects, in which we may be particularly interested, are completely masked. To some extent the regional effects may be removed in one way or another to produce a *residual gravity map* (Fig. 601, B), which more clearly reveals the local gravity

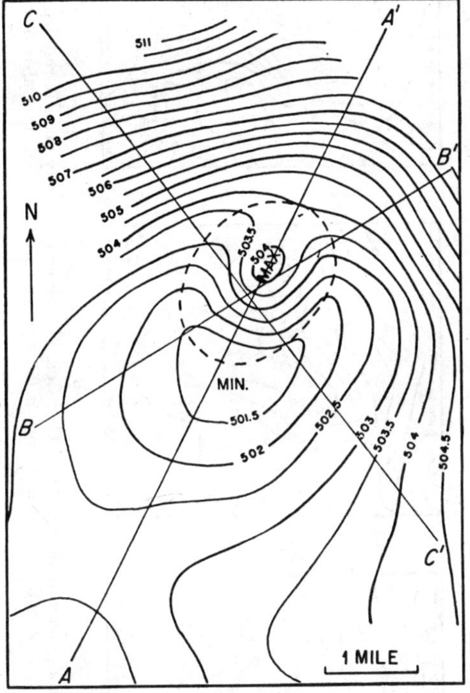

Fig. 600. Isogal map of gravimeter results obtained in the same area as that represented in Figs. 598 and 599.

effects. A special procedure for accomplishing this same object is the construction of what is known as a *second vertical derivative map,* or simply a *second derivative map,* which "tends to emphasize the smaller, shallower anomalies at the expense of larger, regional features. The second derivative picture is therefore often a clearer and better resolved picture of the type of

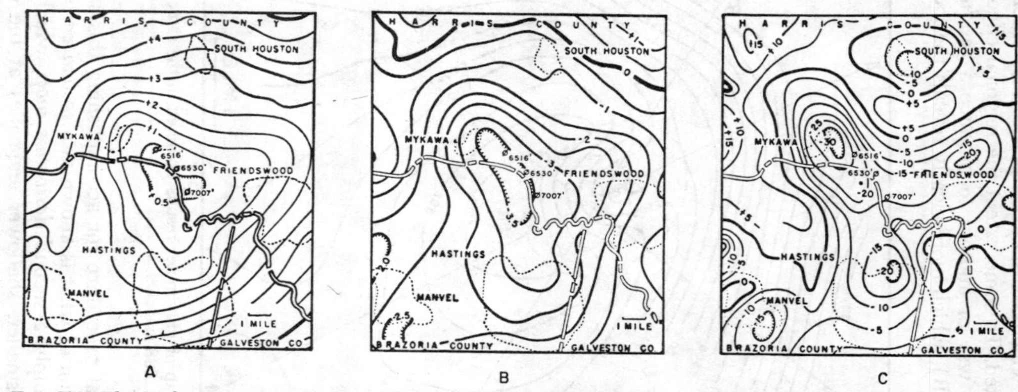

Fig. 601. The Mykawa gravity minimum, Texas Gulf Coast. A, observed gravity map; B, residual gravity map; C, second derivative map. In A and B, contour interval is 0.5 milligal; in C, contour interval is 5×10^{-15} c.g.s. unit. (*After T. A. Elkins.*)

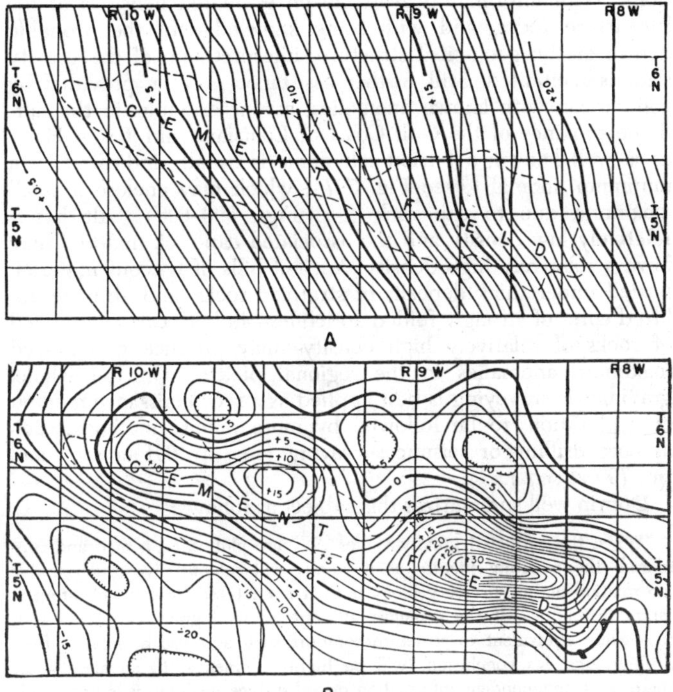

Fig. 602. The Cement Field in southern Oklahoma. A, observed gravity map (contour interval 0.5 milligal); B, second derivative map (contour interval 2.5×10^{-15} c.g.s. unit. This illustrates how different a second derivative map may be from the observed gravity map from which it was derived. (*After T. A. Elkins.*)

anomalies which are important in oil or mineral exploration than is the original gravity picture"[17] (see Figs. 601, 602).

Another difficulty in the geological interpretation of gravity data lies in the fact that the same, or similar, anomalies may result from many different combinations of subsurface condi-

[17] Bibliog., Elkins, Thomas A., 1951. Figures 601 and 602 are reproduced from Elkin's paper with his permission and permission of the Society of Exploration Geophysicists. For further discussion of this subject see Bibliog., Elkins, Thomas A., 1951; and Dobrin, Milton B., 1952.

tions. With information available on estimated densities of the subsurface rocks, and with some knowledge of the probable nature of the geological structure, interpretation of the gravity data is facilitated. Still further assistance may be provided by comparison with known anomalies, as, for example, in the salt-dome province of the Gulf Coast of Louisiana and Texas. Here, as is well known, a buried salt dome is usually indicated by a minimum anomaly (see Fig. 597), which may enclose a small maximum due to cap rock (see Figs. 598–600). Salt has a relatively low density and the associated cap-rock material may have a relatively high density. Ancient hills of igneous material, buried under thick deposits of stratified rocks, and also the uplifted cores of strongly folded anticlines—in both cases composed of rocks of relatively high density—may produce pronounced maximum anomalies in the regional picture. On the whole, gravimetric surveying is best applied as a reconnaissance method of exploration, to be followed by more precise methods, such as core drilling or seismic surveying (see pp. 601 *et seq.*, and pp. 790 *et seq.*).

Dobrin well summarizes this subject as follows:

"When the corrected gravity values . . . are plotted on a map and contoured, the resulting picture as it stands will seldom give much usable information on subsurface geology until it is analyzed by suitable interpretation techniques. If the geologist attempts to read gravity contours as if they were equivalent to structure contours such as those he obtains from drilling logs, his conclusions will be highly erroneous. In an area where there is no independent information on subsurface geology, it is impossible to translate gravity data into reliable estimates of the structure. The more the available data from other sources, the more restricted will be the questions that the gravity information is called upon to answer and the more definite the answers that can be expected. It is important for all who use gravity data—and this means geologists and executives, as well as geophysicists—to realize that interpretation is not a clear-cut process which can be relied on for a unique answer, but is instead subject to numerous limitations which decrease as the independent control increases."[18]

Magnetometric Method

557. The earth's magnetic field. The earth may be described as a large irregular magnet. The intensity of its magnetism varies from place to place. The whole complex system of terrestrial magnetic forces is referred to as the *earth's* magnetic field.

[18] Bibliog., Dobrin, Milton B., 1952, p. 85.

If a small compass needle is suspended at its center of gravity at any point, *P*, in the earth's magnetic field so that it can freely swing in all directions, if undisturbed it will come to rest in a definite position. Except along one particular line (see Fig. 386), it will not lie exactly in a true north-south direction, but will point toward the earth's magnetic pole, which is several miles from the geographic pole; and instead of being level, it will be tilted from the horizontal plane. The horizontal direction of the needle while suspended at rest at *P*, is called the *magnetic meridian* at *P*, and the horizontal angle between this magnetic meridian and the geographic meridian at *P* is the *declination* at this point. The vertical angle between the horizontal plane through *P* and the position occupied by the inclined needle is called the *magnetic dip* or *inclination* at *P*.

In measuring the intensity of the earth's magnetism, a unit called a *gauss* is used. A *gauss* may be defined as the intensity of a magnetic field that will act on a unit magnetic pole with a force of 1 dyne. A *unit magnetic pole* is one that will act on an equal pole with a force of 1 dyne at a distance of 1 cm. In ordinary magnetometric surveying the unit of measurement is the *gamma*, γ, which is 1/100,000 of a gauss.

The force exerted by the earth's magnetic field on a unit pole is the total intensity, *T*, of the earth's magnetism at *P*, any given point. It acts in the direction defined by declination and inclination. In the vertical plane of the magnetic meridian through *P*, *T* can be resolved into two components perpendicular to one another, namely, the vertical intensity, *Z*, and the horizontal intensity, *H*; and *H* can be still further resolved into its geographic north-south and east-west components, known as *X* and *Y*, respectively. The quantities usually measured in magnetometric surveying for geologic structure are *H* and *Z*.

558. Measurement of magnetic anomalies. The instrument most commonly used in field magnetometric work is called a *magnetometer* or *variometer* of the Schmidt type. The magnetometer that registers differences in vertical magnetic intensity, and is therefore called a *vertical magnetometer*, is used more commonly than the *horizontal magnetometer*, which measures differences in horizontal intensity.

For making vertical intensity observations, the instrument is set up at the selected station, properly levelled and oriented in such a way that the vertical plane in which the needle is free to swing will be perpendicular to the magnetic meridian, *i.e.*, to the magnetic north-south line. Usually the needle is unclamped and the scale read two or three times in this position, and then again two or three times after the instrument has been turned 180°, and the average of all these readings is recorded.

In reconnaissance work stations are spaced from 1 to 4 miles apart, whereas for detail work they may be spaced more closely. In reconnaissance field mapping observations may be made at from 20 to 30 stations a day.

559. Correction of magnetic readings. Magnetometric surveying is in many respects similar to barometric surveying. Magnetic readings are subject to errors due to magnetic storms. Furthermore there is a more or less regular diurnal change in the earth's magnetic field at any locality. Experience has shown that it is best to select a "base station" which is visited several times in the course of the day, so that check readings may be made here with the instrument which is used in the field. The use of a stationary instrument at the base station, observed at intervals of from 15 to 30 min., is desirable, especially where accurate results are required. As in barometric surveying, check readings can be made by revisiting any of the field stations. At the end of the day, a diurnal correction curve is constructed and all the station records are adjusted to remove the *storm* and *diurnal* effects. Data observed during a magnetic storm are usually not dependable. Since most magnetometers now in use are compensated for temperature changes, errors due to variations in temperature are small. Correction may be made by reference to a thermometer inside the instrument. Careful calibration and tests for temperature effects are necessary from time to time.

In addition to these short-time fluctuations, there are secular, or long-period changes in the earth's magnetic field. These are sufficiently cared for, in magnetic surveying, by the proper use of isogonic charts and charts of equal magnetic vertical intensity published by the U.S. Coast and Geodetic Survey (see Art. 560).

The magnetic intensity at the base station may be assumed, being chosen somewhere near the values known to be characteristic of the general area; or the value used is that already determined in a network of base stations previously established.[19]

[19] Charts and pamphlets with general information on the earth's magnetic field may be obtained from the Superintendent of Documents, Washington, D.C.

560. Compilation of field data. After the field data, corrected for temperature and diurnal variations, have been assembled, and the stations have been properly located on the base map, correction must be made for the normal or terrestrial regional change in vertical intensity. This is done by reference to the most recently published "Equal Magnetic Vertical Intensity Chart"[20] which shows the broad regional variations in vertical intensity. The lines of regional vertical intensity (vertical isodynamics) for the area in question are laid off on the map in proper position and with proper values.[21] The amount of regional correction to be applied to each station value is then determined from the position of the station with respect to the lines of normal regional change. The correction for the normal variation is added to, or subtracted from, the station value, respectively, as the normal regional value is below, or above, that of the base station or other reference point. The results of this operation are the local anomaly values that are placed on the map. Equal anomalies may be connected by flowing lines called *isonomalies,* or *isanomalies,* which express in gammas the local variations from the average total magnetic intensities in the area. A map so constructed is an anomaly map of vertical magnetic intensity. These anomalies may be caused by geologic structural conditions in the subsurface. They are the values sought in magnetometric surveying for geologic purposes.

561. Application to geology. The application of the magnetic method in geologic work depends upon the fact that rock masses and rock types differ from one another in their magnetic quality, that is, in their magnetic susceptibility. Some ores are highly magnetic; some igneous and metamorphic rocks contain a relatively large proportion of magnetite; and sediments, especially sand and sandstones, may be locally rich in this mineral. It is quite likely that the local anomaly values of magnetic intensity are chiefly to be attributed to the form, size, and distribution of rock bodies (igneous, sedimentary, or metamorphic) of which the constituent rocks are comparatively rich in their content of magnetite. For example, a buried hill (**180**) of granite or schist,

[20] Obtainable from the U.S. Coast and Geodetic Survey.

[21] If 2 or 3 years or more have elapsed between the time of making one survey and the time of surveying an adjoining area, some readjustment of the regional vertical isodynamics may be necessary to make the corrected maps match one another. This is because of the secular changes in the earth's magnetic field.

or an igneous plug or dike, intrusive into sedimentary rocks and covered by alluvium, or a lens of sandstone, may cause abnormally high magnetic intensity values if these rocks carry considerable magnetite.

Interpretation of magnetic anomalies for their geologic meaning, is, however, by no means simple. In some places a distinct relationship has been demonstrated (Figs. 603, 604); but elsewhere very pronounced magnetic anomalies have not been correlated with known lithologic or structural features down to

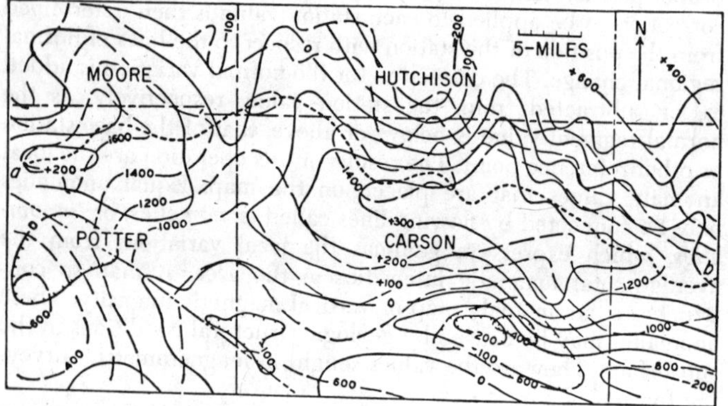

Fig. 603. Map of part of the Panhandle area of Texas, showing lines of equal vertical intensity anomaly (full lines) and structure contours on top of the "Big Lime" (dashed lines). *ab* is the approximate axis of the main anticlinal structure in the "Big Lime."

drilled depths of several thousand feet (Fig. 605). In such cases the effects mapped may be from very deep-lying causes, not reached in the drilling. In wide areas the anomalies are so slight that although unquestionably they reflect definite conditions, they cannot safely be interpreted.

In all magnetometer work, perhaps more than in any other class of geophysical surveying, one must keep firmly in mind that the net intensities measured at individual stations may, and probably do, represent the resultants of many effects, from shallow depths and from greater depths, all combined in a manner to make their correct interpretation difficult. (Compare similar conditions in gravity data, mentioned in Art. 556.) An irregular

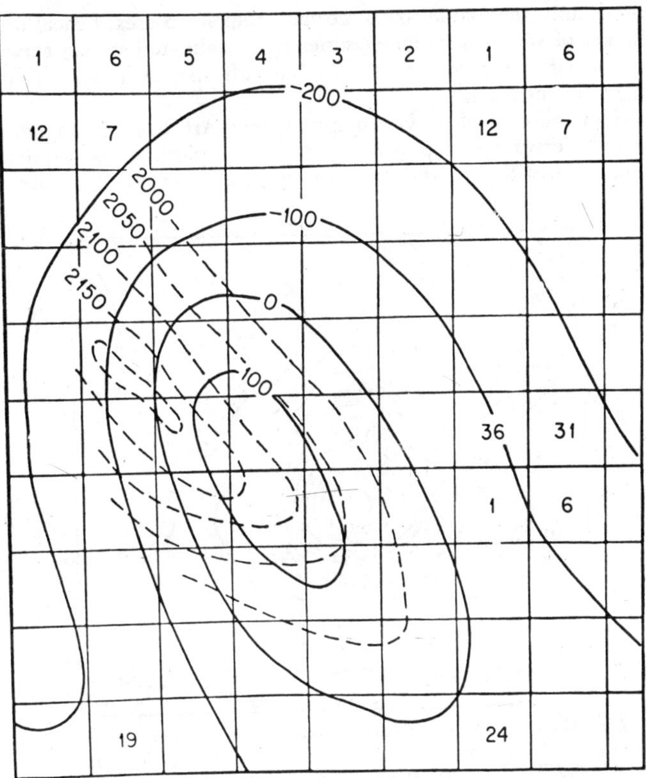

Fig. 604. Sketch map of Hobbs structure in Lea County, N.Mex. The full lines are isanomalies of vertical magnetic intensity; the dashed lines are structure contours on top of the anhydrite. The small squares are square miles. The upright numbers designate the sections. (See Appendix 7.) The only full township on the map is T. 18 S., R. 38 E

distribution of magnetite in a sandstone a few feet, or a few hundred feet, below the surface of the ground may alter or mask the effects of a large deep-seated body. The safest way to apply the magnetometric method is to work from the known to the unknown. Thus, if a geologic feature such as a dike, or a contact between a high-intensity and a low-intensity rock, exposed and mappable in a certain region, passes beneath a blanket of soil or a younger series of consolidated strata, it may be traceable for some distance beneath its cover by careful magnetic surveying

As in the case of gravity mapping (see Art. **556**), a magnetic second derivative map may be made by plotting the vertical second derivative of the magnetic vertical intensity to secure a

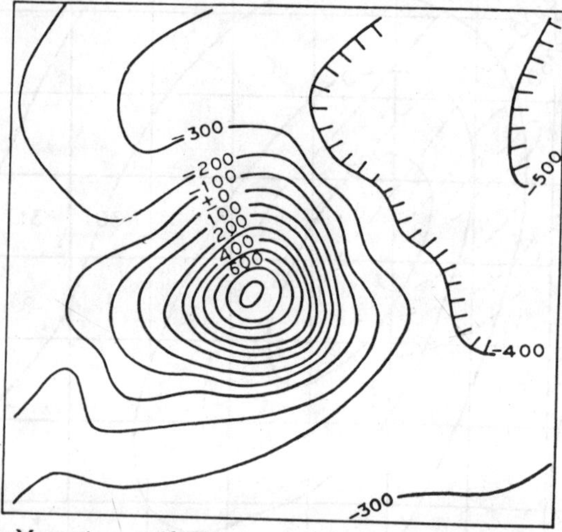

Fig. 605. Magnetic vertical intensity anomaly map of an area in west Texas in which no definite relation to structure was discovered down to a depth of nearly 5,000 ft. The map represents an area of approximately 280 square miles.

better resolution of the magnetic anomaly. While there is fundamentally no unique solution in the interpretation of either magnetic or gravimetric anomalies, a combined study of both, within the same area, may be helpful in arriving at the more probable interpretations as related to their geologic significance. Except in the case of certain magnetic ores, magnetometric surveying is distinctly a reconnaissance method.

562. The airborne magnetometer. In the magnetometric surveying above described, the instrument is stationed on the ground and observations are made at selected *points*. Since the Second World War a technique has been perfected in which the magnetometer is suspended at the end of a cable, usually about 100 ft. long,[22] trailed from an airplane, and readings are automatically and continuously recorded, by wires through the cable, while the "ship" is in flight. The record is therefore a *profile* of magnetic variations along the line of flight.

When an area is to be surveyed, the course is planned to cover it by parallel flight lines which are a certain distance apart, depending on the nature of the terrain and the results desired. Ordinarily these lines are ¼ to 2 miles apart, 1 mile being a commonly adopted spacing. Cross flights at much wider intervals connect the profiles and permit adjustment and correction. The plane is flown as nearly as possible at a constant height above the average land surface (or at a fixed height above an offshore water surface), this height also varying with the nature of the problem from 300 to 1,500 ft., but commonly being about 1,000 ft. The object is to fly high enough to eliminate such disturbing influences as railroads, transmission lines, pipe lines, etc., but nevertheless low enough to be well within reach of the differential magnetic effects of the earth's rock masses.

Knowledge of the correct position of the plane (and magnetometer) along the course is essential. Vertical position is determined by radio altimeter and horizontal position by a continuous strip photograph of the land below the course, where the land features are recognizable, or by electronic survey methods (see Art. **552**) for work offshore or over land areas where there are no easily recognizable features (as in jungles, swamps, etc.). The magnetic profile, the altimeter reading, and the strip photograph for horizontal position are all automatically and continuously recorded, and, for correct correlation of these records, each is similarly and simultaneously marked at frequent regular intervals.[23]

The advantages of the airborne magnetometer over the kind used at station setups on the ground are:

1. Much greater speed of coverage (although it should be noted that office computations of airborne magnetometric readings require much more time than the mere flying of the traverse).
2. Lower cost per unit of area if time is taken into account.

[22] In order to keep the instrument sufficiently far removed from magnetic effects of the plane.

[23] For further details on procedure, see Bibliog., Jensen, Homer, 1946.

3. Ability to survey areas difficult or impossible of access for ground surveying (*i.e.*, swamps, jungles, water).

4. Continuous profiling of magnetic variations instead of point (station) recording.

5. Elimination of effects of local disturbing factors such as magnetic gravels, small volcanic bodies, large buried bowlders, etc., and also, as above cited, pipe lines, transmission lines, railroads, etc.

After a magnetic anomaly map has been made from data obtained by airborne magnetometer, as with the map produced from surveying on the ground, there still remains the problem of interpretation into geological significance.

SEISMIC METHODS

563. Elastic earth waves. The seismic methods of geophysical exploration have been widely used in searching for subsurface structures that might yield oil or gas; in localizing certain types of ore deposits; in mapping the bedrock floor beneath gravel deposits where dams are to be constructed; in measuring the thickness of glacial ice; in studying the configuration of the basement beneath a stratified prism of rocks; and in many other ways. The seismic methods are the most satisfactory of all the geophysical methods for mapping subsurface geological structures. If properly applied they can determine details of structure under many conditions where gravimetric and magnetometric methods can be used only for reconnaissance. In many areas these latter two methods have been applied first, later to be followed by seismic detailed mapping of anomalies which suggest the possibility of underlying structure.

The seismic methods utilize two important characteristics of rock formations: (1) rock materials vary in respect to the speed with which they transmit elastic earth waves, and (2) the sedimentary prisms, in particular, consist of layers that are separated by sharply defined contact surfaces, and these surfaces reflect part of the energy generated as elastic earth waves.

Hard, compact rocks, such as limestone, anhydrite, salt, etc., with relatively high elasticity, transmit shock waves (seismic waves) with greater speed than softer, or less consolidated, rocks. The rate of propagation of seismic waves varies through a wide range, *i.e.*, from about 5,500 ft. per sec. in ordinary clastic sediments to over 23,000 ft. per sec. in some of the plutonic igneous rocks. In general, the rate through a given formation increases with the depth or amount of overburden. Observations in two localities in east Texas revealed an increase from a speed of elastic transmission of 8,800 ft. per sec. in a certain formation at one locality to a speed of 9,200 ft. per sec. in the same formation at a second locality where, 20 miles down the regional dip, it was 1,000 ft. deeper below the surface. It should be noted that average, or over-all, velocity increases with total depth for all localities.

In all areas (except certain offshore areas under relatively deep water) there is a surface layer, called the *weathered layer,* of variable thickness and average velocity. In most instances the thickness of the so-called weathering is less than 100 ft. with an over-all velocity of 2,000 ft. per sec. In special situations, such as parts of southern Louisiana and in the San Joaquin Valley of California, the weathered zone attains a thickness of 300 to 500 ft. in which the velocity may increase to the order of 3,500 ft. per sec. In certain peat or muskeg-covered areas the weathered velocity may be as low as 500 to 600 ft. per sec. The true nature and cause of this layer are not known. It is not strictly a layer of weathered rock materials, geologically speaking. It may be related to the ground water. In any event, there is always a change in elastic properties, usually sharp, in passing down from this weathered zone into the underlying more consolidated rocks.[24]

With regard to the second property mentioned above, seismic waves that travel outward from a point of explosion are reflected back toward the surface of the ground from contact surfaces between strata having distinctly different velocities of wave transmission, *i.e.,* distinctly different elastic properties. There are many such reflecting boundaries (elastic discontinuities) in a prism of strata, but most of the reflections are weak, and only those from the more pronounced contacts are recognizable on the seismographic records. Probably most of these come from the upper surfaces of high-speed beds overlain by low-speed beds, but the reverse is sometimes true; *i.e.,* distinct waves may be recorded from the basal contacts of high-speed strata.

Seismic waves, in their behavior underground, may be compared in many respects with light waves. They undergo transmission, refraction, and reflection. These properties are illustrated

[24] See Art. 568.

in simple and graphic manner in Fig. 606, where *s* is a point, called the *shot point,* at which a charge of dynamite has been exploded. A spherical elastic wave front immediately goes out in all directions from the shot. To simplify the explanation, only lines of travel (*sa, sb, se, sj*) of certain points in the wave front are shown, called rays, and only reflections from the top contacts of the high-speed beds are considered. A point in the wave front will travel directly from *s* along the surface, or close to the surface, of the ground (*stw*). This is called the *surface wave* or

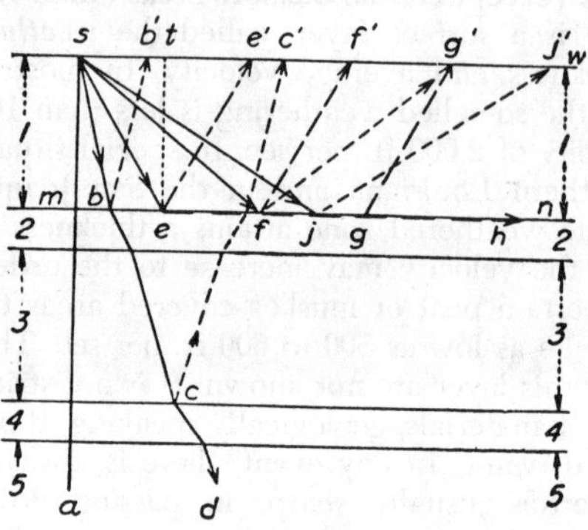

Fig. 606. Paths of earth waves produced by an explosion where the underlying strata are horizontal. The beds marked 1, 3, and 5 have a lower velocity of transmission of these waves than beds 2 and 4. *s*, shot point. (See text for description.) Note that the critical angle, *set*, varies for different formations. It is shown here only with an approximate value, for illustration purposes.

ground roll. The point of the wave front going directly down beneath the explosion will be transmitted in part, vertically downward, and reflected in part, from successive high-speed beds (2, 4, etc.), vertically upward. Other points on the wave front, *e.g.*, point *b*, will partly suffer refraction in passing into bed 2 and will partly be reflected upward from the top surface of 2 at the same angle at which this point in the wave front impinged on 2. Here this part of the wave front will be reflected to *b'*. The energy that travels along *sb* and passes into 2 is again refracted in passing into 3, etc., at each surface that separates two layers having different speeds of elastic transmission; and at each change in velocity, as at *c*, part of this energy is reflected back toward the surface (*cc'*). As the angle *msb* increases, at length a critical angle[25] is reached such that the wave front impinging on the surface *mn* (top of 2) will no longer enter 2 but will be refracted along this contact and upward to the surface of the ground (*ee'*, *ff'*, *gg'*, etc.) along innumerable paths, all of which may be regarded as parallel to *ee'*, *ff'*, *gg'*, etc. These paths will make an angle, *tee'*, equal to *set*, with *mn*. Some of the energy at this angle will be reflected (*ee'*), and, as the angle of incidence (*set*) increases, reflections will become progressively weaker (*sjj'*, etc.). A seismograph located, let us say, at *g'* will receive some vibrations directly from *s* (*sg*), some vibrations reflected from *mn* (*sfg'*), and some vibrations refracted from bed 2 (*segg'*).

From these facts one may conclude, with reference to a given reflecting horizon (*e.g.*, *mn*), that recording instruments (seismographs), made to detect and record the vibrations produced by exploding a charge at a point, such as *s*, (1) do not indicate refracted waves from a given rock body if they (the seismographs) are set up too near the shot point—*i.e.*, in Fig. 606, at a distance less than 2 *st*, which may be roughly stated as equal to, or less than, the depth to the reflecting horizon, *mn*; (2) indicate refraction waves for the most part if the seismographs are set up at a distance on the surface of the ground as much as two or three times the depth, *sm*, from the shot point, *s*, to the reflecting horizon, *mn*.

Further, note that at *c'*, for example, although both reflected and refracted waves would be recorded from the top of 2, only reflected waves would be recorded from 4.[26]

In seismic exploration, both the refracted waves and the reflected waves can be used to study subsurface geology. Thus we have two distinct subdivisions of this work, the refraction method (Art. **565**) that utilizes refracted waves only and the reflection method (Art. **567**) that utilizes mainly reflected waves. The reflection method is used much more widely than the refraction method.

[25] This critical angle is *set*, which equals angle *mse*, where *te* is perpendicular to *mn* at *e*. The critical angle is defined by the equation $\sin i = V_1/V_2$, where i is the angle of incidence (*set* in Fig. 606), V_1 is the velocity of transmission in medium 1, and V_2 is the velocity in medium 2.

[26] An excellent graphical presentation of seismic wave propagation is given by R. H. Thornburgh in "Wave Front Diagrams in Seismic Interpretations," Am. Assoc. Petr. Geols., *Bull.*, vol. 15, 1930.

564. Instruments used in seismographic work. In seismic surveying an instrument known as a seismograph is used to record the ground vibrations caused by an artificial explosion. In practical form, as a rugged mobile exploration unit, it comprises three principal elements, *i.e.*, (1) a detecting device, popularly referred to as seismometer, geophone, detector, or pickup; (2) an electronic amplifier for amplifying the weak electric currents generated by the seismometers; and (3) an oscillograph assembly or camera for recording the amplified electric currents. Modern seismometers are of the moving-coil type, electrically damped, and comprising essentially a spring-supported coil which tends to remain stationary as the supporting system (and outer case) moves in sympathy with the earth movements. The present-day amplifier can be adjusted in sensitivity to reach ground-level disturbances even under quietest ground conditions. Thus amplification greater than 1,000,000 times may be realized without distortion. Separately adjustable high- and low-cut electrical filters are incorporated in the amplifiers to eliminate undesirable components of the amplified signal. The camera comprises a multielement system of coil or string galvanometers whose motions are photographed progressively on a strip of photosensitized paper moving at constant speed past a light beam. One-hundredth-second time-interval lines, as regulated by a device operated by a tuning fork, are photographed on the paper simultaneously with the galvanometer motion. The time of the shot is transmitted either by radio or by wire and is recorded on the same paper with the record of the seismic vibrations from the explosion (Fig. 616, A and B, x). The recording part of the seismograph may be at some distance from, though connected by wire with, the part that receives the vibrations of the ground.

565. The refraction method. The principal object of refraction seismic work is to determine the location and depth of high-speed strata or formations. This is accomplished by plotting the time for transmission of the refracted wave against the distance between the shot point and the recording station. In all field observations this distance must be determined for each recording station, and the exact time at which the charge is exploded must be compared with the exact time at which the impulses are received on the seismographic films.

In the early stages of refraction seismic work, the distance from the shot point to the recording station was determined by the time necessary for the sound wave from the explosion to travel the intervening distance in the air. Because sound waves move more slowly in air (1,100 ft. per sec.) than in the lithosphere, the air waves arrive some time after the earth waves. In long shots, the earth vibrations may have nearly died out before the air wave is recorded. Since the temperature of the atmosphere, and particularly the direction and velocity of the wind, affect the time of the transmission of sound waves in air, allowance must be made for these factors to correct for distance determined in this way. However, on account of the relative inaccuracy of these corrections, it is no longer common practice to compute the distance from the shot point to recording stations by the sound-wave travel time but, instead, to survey these distances by transit or alidade.

Time is communicated by radio. As soon as each instrument man is ready, he signals by radio, at the same time stating his identity by a chosen sign. The chief of the party waits until all the instrument men have signified that they are ready, and then he signals to the shooter to fire. When the explosion occurs, a small cap, electrically discharged at exactly the same moment as the cap that fires the main explosion, also explodes and, in so doing, breaks the continuity of the time record that is being transmitted to the seismographs by radio and thus records the moment of the explosion on the film.

566. Applications of refraction seismic work to geology. In field procedure, the detectors are set up at selected stations (recording stations), *A*, *B*, *C*, etc., and, when the proper time arrives, the charge is exploded at the *shot point*. To reduce the quantity of dynamite needed and to obtain better records, the charge is often placed in holes from 10 to several hundred feet deep, which are drilled for that specific purpose. The object of this practice is to put the charge *below* (preferably *just* below) the base of the weathered layer.

Field work may be conducted according to one of two main plans: (1) *fan shooting* or *fanning;* (2) *profile shooting* or *profiling.*

The shot points and recording stations for both a refraction profile and a refraction fan are shown in Fig. 607. Unless the normal relation of the velocity of transmission to depth is known from previous experience in the region under investigation, a *preliminary profile* may be run to ascertain the *normal.* Such a profile is ordinarily run along, or near, a road in order to facilitate transportation. The road should be as straight as possible. *MN* in Fig. 607 is a line of preliminary profiling for the area in which the fan was later shot.

Fanning is done where the object is to discover such geologic structures as salt plugs, which have a great vertical extent but are of relatively small and approximately equidimensional horizontal cross section. By covering an area by intersecting fans (Fig. 608),

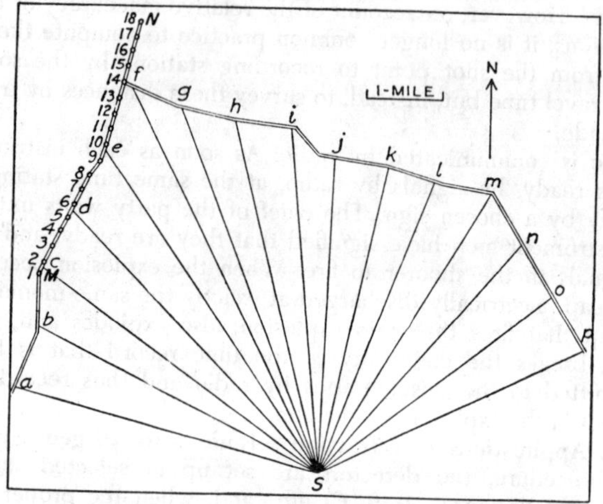

Fig. 607. Fan "shot" across a prospect to locate a salt dome. S, firing station. *a–p*, recording stations. 1–18, stations on preliminary profile, *MN*.

if the radii are close enough, a salt plug of average size and not too deep can hardly be missed, provided the technique of the work is good.

On the other hand, in tracing geologic features of great length as compared with their width in a horizontal plane, like faults or concealed edges of hard strata and the like, or in mapping elongate folds, the refraction method of shooting may be carried out in a series of interconnected profiles laid out essentially at right angles to the direction of elongation of the geologic structure. On each profile, each group of recording stations includes at least one such station from which records were received from two shot points in the line; and, at certain stations in each profile line, records are received from shot points on adjoining lines. In this way all the observations are interrelated. Where indications of abnormal structure have been located and it is desirable to check back, such profiles may be reversed; in other words, the relative positions of the recording stations and the shot point are reversed.

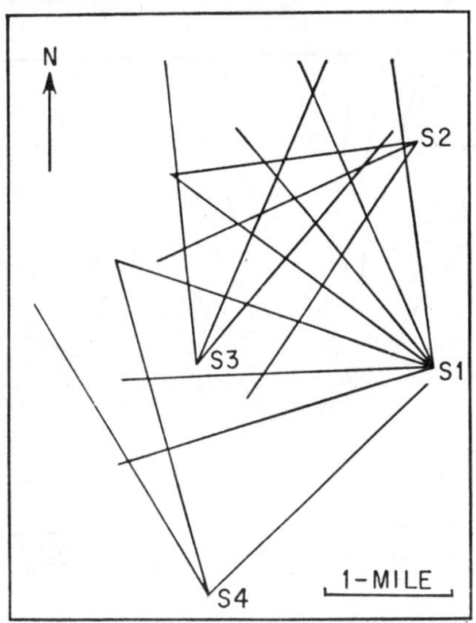

Fig. 608. Group of four intersecting fans, shot in looking for a salt dome in south Texas.

In both refraction methods, final conclusions are based on a comparison of the speed of transmission of refracted waves as they should be under normal conditions with the speed of transmission of refracted waves as actually observed and recorded. If the arrival time of the refracted wave is less than the calculated normal for the area under investigation, the difference obtained by subtracting the shortened arrival time from the normal is spoken of as a "lead" and is expressed in thousandths of a second. These "leads" may indicate the approximate depth and form of high-speed strata or rock bodies in various types of geologic structure.

When the method is fanning, the shot point, on the map, may be taken as the center of a small circle from which, on a chosen scale, the leads noted at the several recording stations are plotted along the respective radii. Thus, in Fig. 609, *s* is the shot point; *a*, *b*, *c*, etc., are the recording seismographs; and *a′*, *c′*, *f′*, etc., respectively, are the leads measured along the radii from the

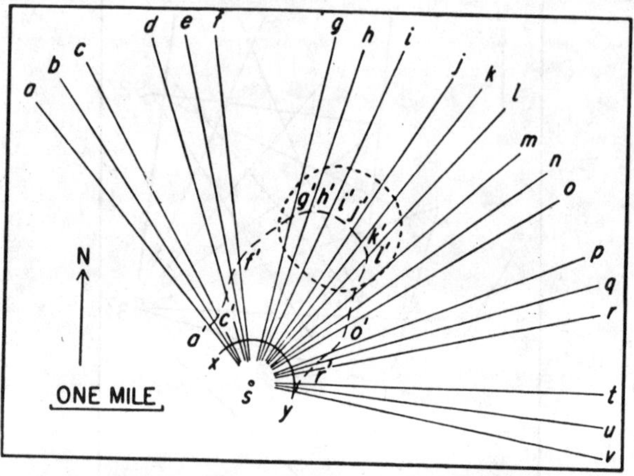

Fig. 609. Plotting of "leads" in fan shooting.

circular base line *xy*. Note that the lead greatly increases in the central area of the fan. This is due to the presence of a salt dome some 2,000 ft. deep, its outline being indicated by the dotted closed line. We may add that other intersecting fans were shot before this dome was exactly located.

Where profiles are shot, time is plotted vertically and distance between shot point and recording stations, horizontally. In Figs. 610–614, taken from Barton,[27] T_1 is the time-distance line plotted for the wave path directly from the shot point to the recording station, through the upper stratum of low velocity of transmission (V_1); and T_2 is the time-distance line plotted for the

[27] Bibliog., Barton, Donald C., 1929 (*b*), pp. 591–593.

wave front that reached the lower, relatively high-speed bed (with velocity V_2), was refracted along its upper contact, and then returned to the surface at the recording station. The course of this point in the wave front corresponds to such lines as *seff′*, *segg′*, etc., in Fig. 606. Quoting from Barton,[28] with reference to certain relations of seismographic records to structure:

"If the higher speed mass is a horizontal stratum of great horizontal extent and if a profile is shot across it, the time distance graph will consist of two intersecting straight lines, T_1 and T_2, and the slopes of T_1 and T_2 will be the same for all azimuths (Fig. 610).[29]

"If the stratum is dipping at a uniform rate, the time-distance graph will consist of the same two straight lines but the slope of T_2 will vary with

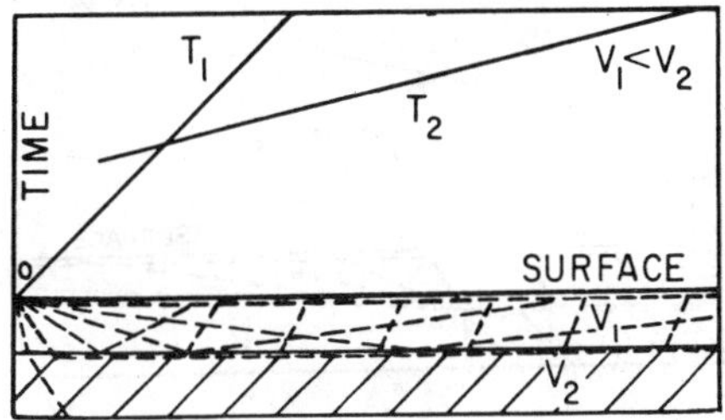

FIG. 610. Figures 610–614 show time-distance curves and paths of waves for a series of types of simple geologic structure. Each formation is assumed to be homogeneous and isotropic. Figure 610 is of an infinitely extensive level flat-topped buried high-speed formation.

the azimuth of the profile and will be at a maximum if the profile is shot down the dip and at a minimum if it is shot up the dip (Fig. 611). The angle of dip and the velocity of the lower formation can be calculated by formulas, from the profiles in which T_2 has the maximum and minimum slope, respectively, and the direction of the dip is the azimuth of the profile in which T_2 has the minimum slope.

"If the stratum is terminated by a scarp (*a*) on a profile shot from a position over the relatively high-speed mass across the scarp, T_2 is straight up to a critical point beyond the scarp and then bends upward to become asymptotic to a line parallel to T_1 (see A, Fig. 612); (*b*) on a profile shot

[28] Bibliog., Barton, Donald C., 1929 (*b*), pp. 591–593. Figures 610 and 614 are reproduced, with permission, from this paper.

[29] T_1 represents time values of transmission of the seismic waves in the formation having the low velocity of transmission, V_1; and T_2, represents time values for the high-speed formation with velocity V_2.

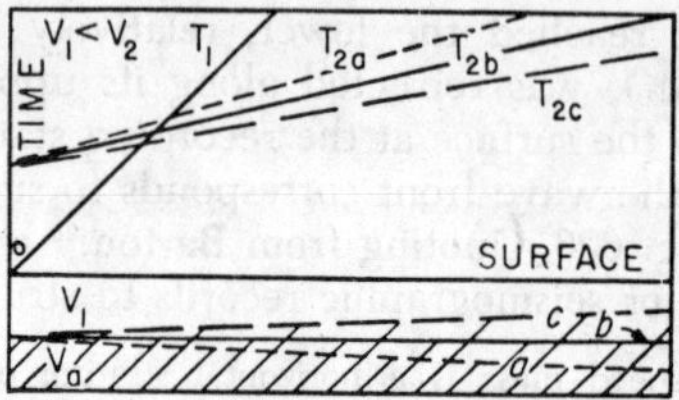

FIG. 611. See legend to Fig. 610. Here, the infinitely extensive buried high-speed formation has a sloping plane surface.

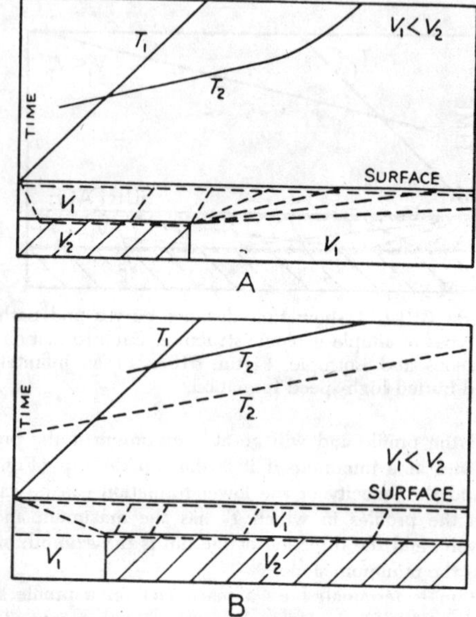

FIG. 612. See legend to Fig. 610. Here, the level flat-topped buried high-speed formation is cut off by a vertical scarp. A, the profile buried is shot from over the high-speed formation across the scarp. B, the profile is shot from off the high-speed formation across the scarp.

in the reverse direction, T_2 is a straight line parallel to, but above, the position which T_2 would have if the V_2 formation extended to the left under the firing point, and the graph is the same as if the V_2 bed were deeper and extended under the firing point.

"If the relatively high-speed stratum is faulted, and is present on both the upthrow and downthrow sides of the fault, T_2 is offset at a critical point

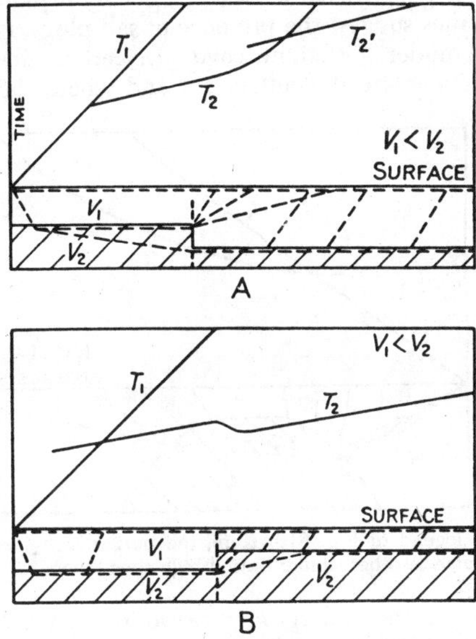

FIG. 613. See legend to Fig. 610. Here, the level flat-topped buried high-speed formation is cut by a vertical fault. The profile is shot from the upthrown side in A, and from the downthrown side in B, in both cases across the fault.

in front of the fault, (*a*) upward if the profile is shot from the upthrown to the downthrown side and (*b*) downward if the profile is shot in the reverse direction. The position of the fault in the high-speed stratum . . . and the throw of the fault" can be calculated (Fig. 613).[30]

Figure 614 shows the time-distance graph for the top of a buried high-speed mass similar to a salt dome.

[30] Bibliog., *Idem*, 1929 (*b*), pp. 592, 593.

Until 1929 or 1930 the refraction method was extensively used, especially in search of salt domes, but since that time it has very largely given place to the reflection method (Art. **567**) in geological exploration. Its main value lies (1) in determining the thickness of the low-velocity weathered layer in connection with reflection exploration and (2) in checking anomalies outlined in other types of geophysical work (*e.g.*, gravity exploration) where these anomalies suggest the presence of salt plugs, igneous plugs, etc., buried under a shallow cover. In certain areas, however, where reflections are difficult to get and where there are dense

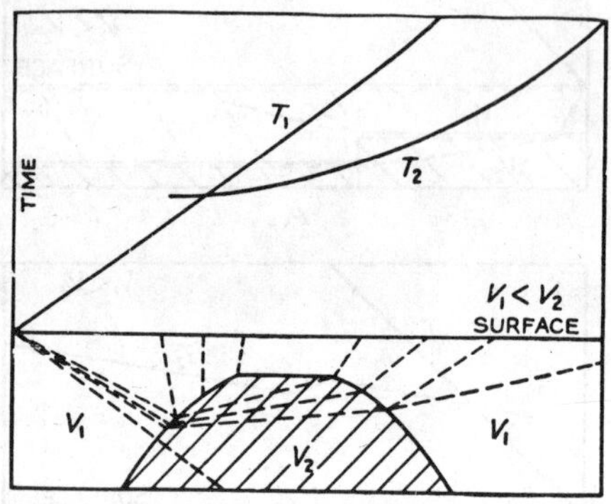

FIG. 614. See legend to Fig. 610. Here, the buried high-speed mass is the top of a salt dome or other similar buried high-speed mass.

strata present in the underground prism, refraction methods may yield more satisfactory results than reflection methods for mapping subsurface structure (*e.g.*, the West Texas Permian Basin).

An important application of the refraction method, developed during the nineteen forties, involves a special technique to outline the flanks of a salt dome.[31] This is particularly valuable where overhang of the salt plug may be expected (see ¶ 6, Art. **180**) and where, therefore, oil and gas accumulations may be present under or against the overhang.

A typical refraction shooting plan for determining the salt profile adjacent to a well bore is diagramed in Fig. 615. Repeated seismic shots are exploded in shallow bore-holes at shot

[31] The following explanation of this technique was kindly furnished by A. C. Winterhalter.

point *A* and shot point *B* as a seismic detector is lowered to successive positions in the deep well bore as indicated by D_1, D_2, etc. The lines emanating from the shot points to the detector locations are approximately the shortest time-distance paths for the seismic waves travelling from the shot points to the detector locations. These times are read off the seismic recordings. The

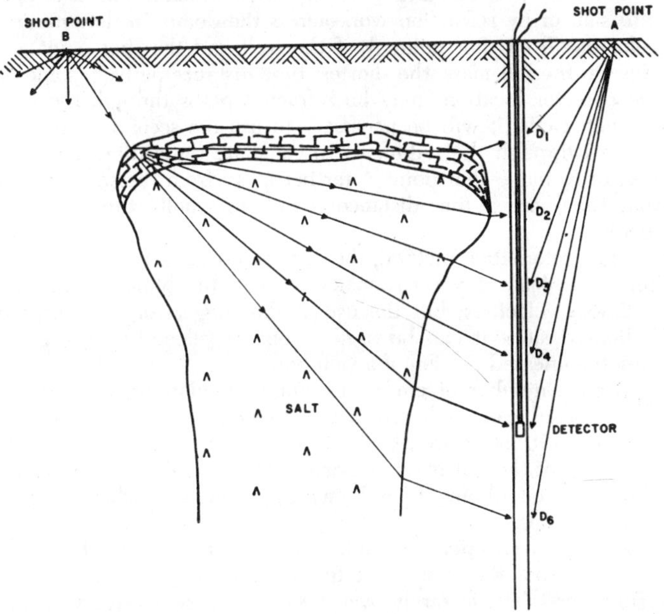

FIG. 615. Seismic surveying of the flank of a salt dome. (*Kindly furnished by A. C. Winterhalter.*)

times from shot point *A* permit calculations of the seismic velocities in the sediments adjacent to the dome flank, and the times from shot point *B* permit calculations of the points of refraction of the seismic waves as they emerge from the salt mass.

The average seismic velocity in the sediments above the dome in the vicinity of shot point *B*, the seismic velocity in salt, and the seismic velocities in the sediments adjacent to the flank are necessary in calculating these emergence points. The velocity on top of the dome is usually obtained by means of shallow refraction work or by means of velocity shooting in shallow wells on top of the dome. The velocity in salt may be assumed to be approximately 15,000 ft. per sec., which is an average value determined by seismic work on several Gulf Coast domes; or, if such a value is considered to be insufficiently precise, a value may be obtained by well shooting, utilizing a well which has been drilled into salt, or by refraction work across the dome. In determining velocities from shot point A, if the well and the shot point are close to the salt mass, the shortest time-distance paths to some of the detector locations may be refracted paths through the salt. In such cases, it will be necessary to use the secondary seismic arrivals through the sediments to calculate the sediment velocities, or to move shot point *A* farther away from the salt mass so that the shortest time-distance paths are wholly through sediments.

As an alternative method, the continuous velocity or sonic logger (Art. **469**) may occasionally be used to obtain the desired sediment velocities; but the use of this logger for this purpose is limited since it can be used to obtain velocities adjacent to only the uncased portion of a well bore.

From a number of emergence-point calculations, a profile of the salt flank can be drawn. If the detector position spacings are 200 to 300 ft. in the well, and if the well bore passes within 1,000 ft. or less of the salt mass, reasonably accurate delineation of the flank can be obtained, and any appreciable mushrooming is made evident.

567. The reflection method. In the reflection method, the distance from the shot point to the recording stations is short (from very short to rarely over 3,000 ft.), as contrasted with the longer distance (commonly from 3 to 7 miles) used in the refraction seismic method. The field instruments for the reflection method, though operating according to the same principles as in the refraction method, differ in their number and arrangement. Consequently, the instrument cannot be used interchangeably in the two methods without suitable adjustments.

In reflection work, as in refraction work, the shot is detonated at the bottom of a hole drilled deep enough to extend through the weathered layer. The detectors are arranged usually in a row along the same line with the shot hole and at equal distances apart. Thus, they may be 50 ft. apart, so that, if there are 12, the outermost 2 will be 550 ft. apart, which distance is known as the *detector spread.* For any setup, there is a single recording station where a single record is made, this record consisting of a number of synchronized *traces*, each one of which is the photographed path of a beam of light from a particular detector or from a compounded company of detectors. Usually there are 6 to 24 traces on a record (see Fig. 616) corresponding to the number of seismometer groups.

There are two objects in arranging the detectors in this way. (1) Reflected waves must be distinguished from refracted and diffracted waves as recorded instrumentally. For practical purposes, a recorded impulse that shows relatively small differences in its time of reception on the various traces is interpreted as the visible resultant of reflected energy. At least two, and preferably six or more, traces are necessary to define a recorded impulse as a reflection. (2) By thus obtaining slightly different recorded time arrivals of a wave reflected from a given rock medium (stratum, etc.), both the depth to and the inclination of the reflecting surface can be calculated (see below).

Interpretation of reflection data may be done in terms of "time" only, but in order to correlate reflecting horizons with stratigraphy, and to make proper corrections for spread length and dip, one must know at least the average velocity to each horizon of interest. Data as to interval velocities are also desirable. These data are usually obtained by surveys in deep wells in the area being investigated. A deep-well geophone is lowered into the well to various depths as determined by local stratigraphy. At each depth of interest, shots fired in shallow holes near the well are recorded by this geophone on a paper or film from which the elapsed time can be read and average velocities can be computed. Modern practice supplements these data by use of one of several acoustic logging tools recently perfected (see Art. 469). These consist of a sound source and one or two receivers, all mounted in a tool which can be lowered into a well on a cable such as used for electrical surveys. These loggers measure travel time in the formation around the hole in microseconds per foot and plot this continuously on a film. Frequently a second trace is recorded, which may be self-potential, gamma ray, or other source of desired information. The travel-time trace can be read for velocity at any point in depth, and can be integrated over all or part of its length to give travel time between

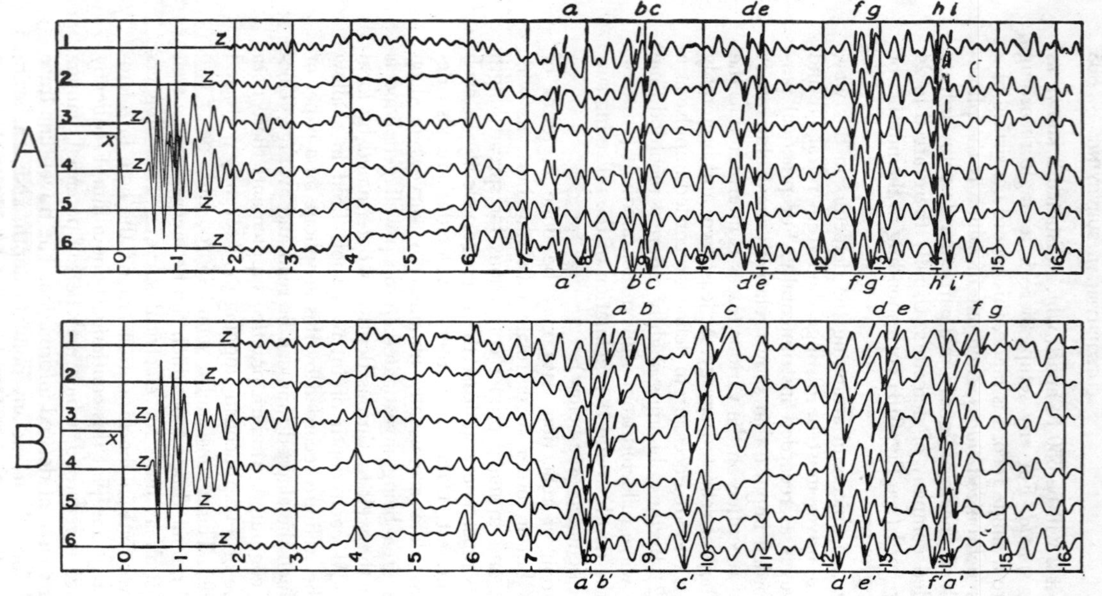

FIG. 616. Two records made in reflection seismic work. In both the mid-spread method was used, *i.e.*, shot point in middle of detector spread. 1–6, at the left, are the traces secured from six detectors, 1 and 6 being the outside detectors of the spread. Figures from 0 to 16, along the lower margin of the record, as here set, are tenths of a second, measured from the instant of discharge (*x*). *z*, on each trace, is the first break, *i.e.*, the beginning of receptions of vibrations by that detector.

In A, horizontal beds (or reflecting surfaces) are indicated by the fact that the end traces show practically simultaneous reception of each reflection (*aa'*, *bb'*, etc.). In B, the beds (or reflection surfaces) dip in the direction from detector 6 toward detector 1, since each reflection (*aa'*, *bb'*, etc.) is recorded on trace 1 considerably later than on trace 6.

various selected points. This log also serves as a correlation tool, especially in areas where the usual logs are affected adversely by salt, anhydrite, etc.

The fundamental conception of the reflection method of seismic surveying is that specific subsurface strata and contacts, down to depths amounting to many thousands of feet, can be detected by their specific reflections on records obtained at different locations in any desired area. It is a method by which these reflections can be identified and studied, and their arrival times can be converted into depths. That is, reflection seismic surveying is a physical method of mapping subsurface structure.[32] The records can be used in two ways: (1) the difference in arrival time of a given wave on the end traces can be noted and converted into differences in depth of the reflecting medium to give its inclination along the line of the detectors; or (2) reflections on a group of records recognizable as coming from the same horizon, can be correlated, and the depth of this horizon below an arbitrary horizontal datum can be plotted at various points on a map, after which contours can be drawn. The first is known as the *dip method* and the second as the *correlation method.* These are more fully described below.

In Figs. 617 and 618 are shown two ways of setting up the detectors in the *dip method.* In Fig. 617 the shot point is midway between the end detectors, which may be from 1,000 to 2,000 ft. apart. In Fig. 618, the shot point is outside the group of detectors and at some distance from the nearest one. The end detectors are usually 1,000 ft. apart. In practice only the travel times from the reflecting horizon (mn), as indicated on the two end traces (from x and y), are used to calculate the dip, the intervening traces serving merely to correlate reflections across the record. As is evident from the figures, the time of travel for an impulse from s to mn and thence to x and y, will differ according to (1) whether the reflecting surface is horizontal or inclined and (2) whether the mid-spread method (Fig. 617) or wide-

[32] Isopach maps may be prepared where the depth interval between two reflecting surfaces is plotted at each station and lines of equal thickness are then drawn. On the assumption that velocity values are essentially constant and that reflecting horizons are continuous over a given area, the differences in arrival time from two such horizons can be plotted at each station and then lines of equal time difference (*isochrons*) can be drawn to produce an *isochron* map, which, in appearance, will be very similar to an isopach map between the same two horizons.

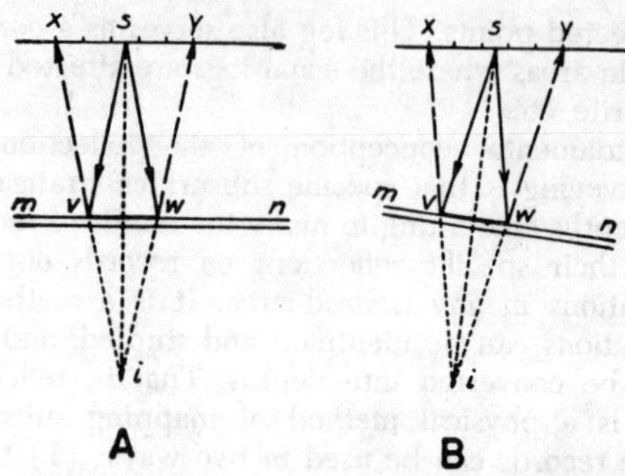

Fig. 617. Diagram to illustrate shot point (s) and detector spread (x to y) in the mid-spread method. i, image point. Reflections from mn to x and y travel along paths svx and swy, respectively. Note that, when the bed is inclined (B), the center of that part (vw) of the reflecting horizon from which the reflections are received at x and y is not vertically below the shot point.

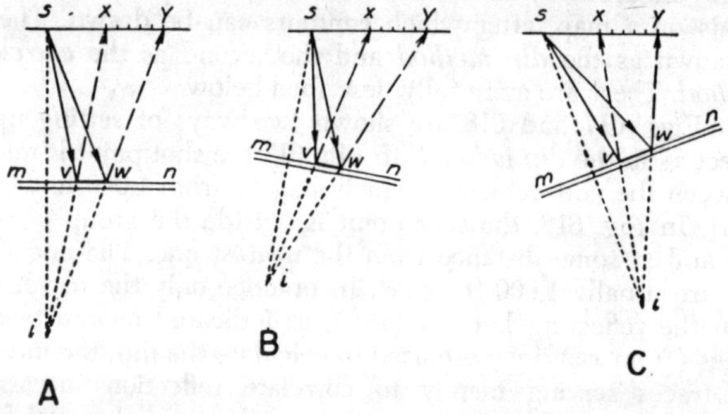

Fig. 618. Diagram to illustrate shot point (s) and detector spread (x to y) in the wide-spread method. A, B, and C, representing three relations, need no special explanation. The lettering in the diagrams corresponds to that in Fig. 617.

spread method (Fig. 618) of dip shooting is followed. The quickest way of translating the time-interval data into distances, and so into dips, is by graphic plotting on cross-section paper. In this manner segments of the reflecting horizon, or horizons, are plotted in their proper positions with reference to all shot points, and a diagram like that in Fig. 619 is constructed.

There are several variations of the dip method. The foregoing description refers to components of true dip unless the row of detectors is at right angles to the strike. Since usually such a position cannot be selected in advance, the instruments may be set up along two lines at right angles to one another, intersecting midway between the end detectors. By this means dip components along these two rectangularly disposed lines can be

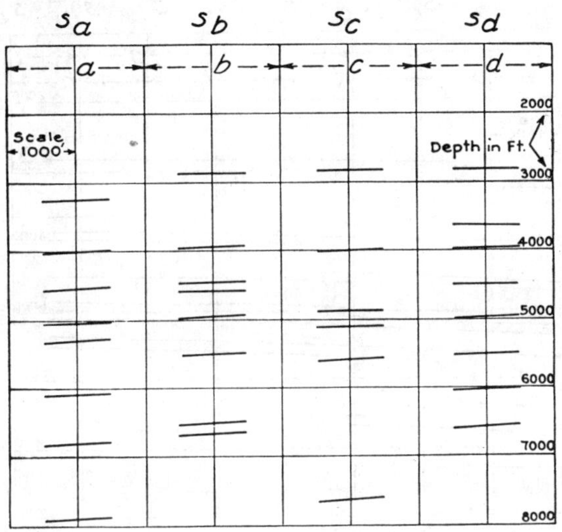

FIG. 619. Section showing dips recorded by mid-spread method with shot points at *Sa, Sb, Sc,* and *Sd.* Note that, although the detector spreads (*a, b, c,* and *d*) are contiguous, end to end, only one-half coverage on reflecting horizons is obtained in this way. (Cf. Fig. 620.)

obtained, and the resultant true dip can be calculated (Fig. 625).

Sometimes the shot points in the mid-spread method are chosen on a line parallel to the line of detectors. Thus, for each setup, the shot point will be at the apex of an isosceles triangle with the two end detectors at the base angles.

In general, the split-dip arrangement, with shot point midway of the recording setup, is used in reconnaissance programs and particularly in regions of appreciable subsurface dip.

From Fig. 619, obviously only one-half the length of any reflecting surface is charted. For greater accuracy, the series of detectors in each setup may be placed to overlap one-half of the adjacent setups; or, to put it in another way, for each setup the shot point may be moved only one-half the length of the spread. In this way the reflecting horizon will be *fully* covered (Fig. 620). This is called the *continuous profile method* of dip shooting.

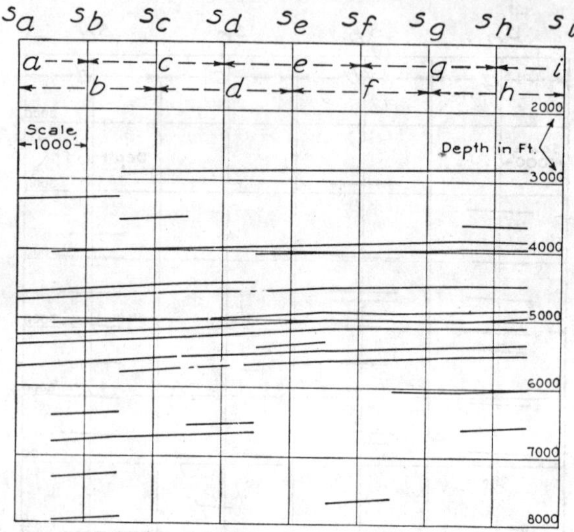

Fig. 620. Section showing dips recorded by mid-spread method with shot points at *Sa*, *Sb*, etc. Here the detector spreads (*a*, *b*, *c*, etc.) overlap by 50 per cent, and therefore complete coverage of reflecting horizons is secured. Discontinuous reflection lines are explained by failure to receive reflections from certain horizons at certain stations.

Continuous profiling is by far the most common method utilized in detail work, as well as for reconnaissance programs whenever required reflections are lacking in character, dominance, continuity, etc.; also where subsurface dips are low. Maximum reliability results when the overlapping half spreads are used to provide continuous subsurface coverage.

The *correlation method* of dip shooting depends, for its success, on the degree of accuracy with which the records, made at different localities within a given district, can be correlated with one another. The reflections from a geologic section consist of a large number of low energy reflections from the many contacts and beds that have nearly the same physical properties and of a smaller number of high energy reflections from the contacts and beds that have outstanding physical properties. From these a record is made that has definite amplitude and frequency relations between the various reflections. The arrival of the reflections, one after another, produces interference patterns and interval relations that are governed by the intervals between the subsurface beds giving the reflections. The result is a photographic record of certain physical properties of the subsurface beds and contacts, at a specific location, a record in which amplitude, frequency, interference pattern, and interval characteristics make possible the identification of certain reflections on the records and their correlation from location to location.

In the correlation method the detectors are usually set up in a row and in line with the shot point, which, as in the wide-spread dip method, is outside the detector spread. The distance between the end detectors may be from 300 to 900 ft., and within this distance there may be from 5 to 40 or more detectors, equally spaced. The shot point may be from 150 to 300 ft. from the nearest detector. Therefore, provided the reflecting horizon is horizontal, the path of the impulses recorded in the detector nearest to the shot point will be almost vertical, and the trace of this detector will indicate reflections from points vertically below a point, called the depth point[33] (Fig. 621), midway between this detector and the shot point. If the reflecting surface is inclined (Fig. 621, B), the depth point will be shifted, depending on the amount and direction of dip of this surface. Not all the traces on a record are used for computations. For certain reasons, either the trace from the detector nearest the shot point or that from the detector farthest from the shot point or that from the detector in the middle of the spread (x, y, and z, respectively, in Fig. 621, A and B), may serve in calculating the depth to the reflecting medium, and, accordingly, this computed depth may be below 1, or 2, or 3, respectively, in these diagrams. In Fig.

[33] The *depth point* is the vertical projection, on the surface of the ground, of the point, in a reflecting surface, from which a recorded impulse is reflected. It is the point, on a map, at which the computed depth to this reflecting horizon is plotted.

622 are shown three records, taken at three different localities in a certain district where shallow correlatable beds are present. Note that certain reflections can be easily correlated across all three of these records.

The correlation method implies widely spaced recording, that is, with a complete lack of continuity between setups. The reflections must exhibit not only a fair-to-good degree of dominance

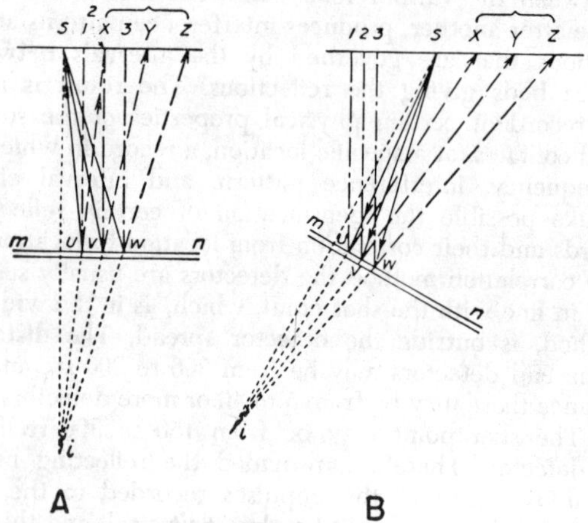

FIG. 621. *s*, shot point; *x*, *z*, end detectors; *y*, middle detector; other detectors between *x* and *z* not shown. *mn*, reflecting horizon (horizontal in A, inclined in B); *i*, image point. The impulses received at *x*, *y*, and *z* were reflected from points *u*, *v*, and *w*, respectively, on *mn*. Vertically above *u*, *v*, and *w* are depth points, 1, 2, and 3, which correspond to the positions on a map, where the depth of *mn*, computed from the traces of *x*, *y*, or *z*, as the case might be, would be plotted.

over background disturbance, but also an inherent character involving persistent frequency changes so that the exact corresponding point can be picked on reflections which are identified as the same for all locations in the area. The method finds favor for quick reconnaissance coverage in regions of good reflection quality. This spot method of recording must of necessity be employed in areas where rough topography or patches of unfavorable surface materials prescribe careful selection of recording positions in order to secure reflection results of usable quality.

FIG. 622. Three records showing correlation of reflections. For study, the records are placed with the top of each record to the left. Tenths of seconds are indicated along the bottom edge of each record. The time of reception of the first "valley" of a correlatable reflection (as *a*), where this is found on the middle trace or two middle traces on each record, is translated into terms of depth below a chosen datum (here 425 ft. above sea level). Thus, on record 1, the depth of *a* is —1,542 ft.; on record 2, *a* is at —1,585 ft.; and, on record 3, this same reflecting horizon, *a*, is at —1.591 ft. Other correlatable reflections are at *b* and *c*.

In each record, *x* is the time at which the shot explodes, and *y* is the "uphole time," *i.e.*, the time at which the impulse is recorded by a detector placed on the surface of the ground close to the mouth of the hole at the bottom of which the shot is exploded.

568. Interpretation of seismic records. Before seismic records can be satisfactorily used for interpretation of subsurface geology, they must be corrected for weathering (page 791), for relative elevation of shot-point and detector stations, and for "step-out,"[34] etc.

For interpretation of seismic records (like those in Fig. 622), several are laid on a table beside one another and in sequence of station positions, for the purpose of selecting those reflections which appear to have continuity across the series and which cover the geologic section of greatest interest. Those reflections which will be used in subsequent interpretations are marked. Some of the records are removed and others are added, and these new ones are then correlated with those remaining from the first group. Thus, a whole series may be correlated—with ease and a fair degree of accuracy if the records are good, but with difficulty in case of poor records and poor continuity.

The next step is to plot the indicated correlations in vertical sections, using wide strips of paper, with the records from successive shot points spaced on a suitable horizontal scale, and with a vertical scale either based on time or on depth (as in Figs. 619 and 620). The correlation lines help the interpreter to visualize the geological structure, as may be seen in the two figures just cited.

These seismic records which are thus examined for their correlation have already been adjusted for the usual corrections and also treated for filtering and mixing.[35] Since about 1950, a special procedure, called *magnetic recording*, has come into wide use. By this method the actual wave motions of the earth, at each of the various instrument stations, are recorded on a magnetic tape which, for study, is run through an analyzer, or "playback system." This analyzer not only provides a means

[34] Step-out may be explained thus: In Fig. 621, A, for example, the first wave impulse reflected from *mn* from a shot detonated at *S* will be received by detector *X* slightly earlier than by detector *Y*, and by detector *Y* slightly earlier than by detector *Z*, because the travel path of *SUX* is shorter than *SVY*, and *SVY* is shorter than *SWZ*. To determine the attitude of bed *mn* (here horizontal), correction has to be made for this so-called "step-out" to calculate the vertical depth of *mn* below *X*, *Y*, and *Z*.

[35] *Filters* are devices used to remove certain classes of wave (such as those due to weathering) for better study of the remaining vibrations.

In order to emphasize certain waves, two or more traces may be combined, or *mixed*, and the combination is then termed a *mix*.

for correcting the *basic record* for weathering, elevation, and step-out, but also permits the geophysicist to apply various filtering and mixing operations in his effort to arrive at the most probable interpretation consistent with the known geological conditions of the area. These magnetic tapes can be played back any number of times for the purpose of trying out various corrections, filters, and mixes. For any such experimental combination of corrections, filters, and mixes, the magnetic records can be played back on to a wide sheet of sensitized paper in such a way that many records, in close juxtaposition and properly placed

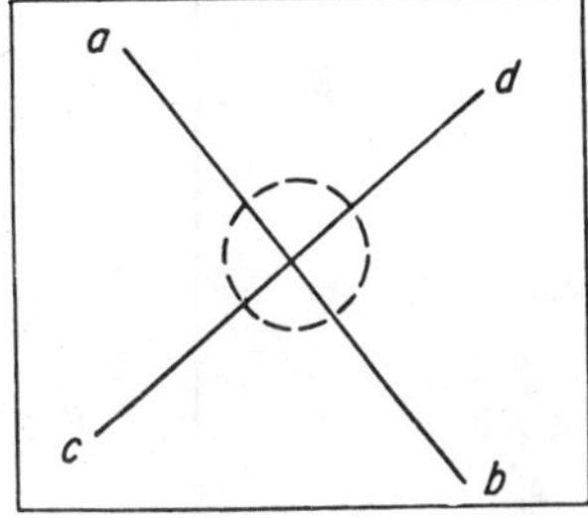

FIG. 623. Sketch map to show preliminary arrangement of lines of seismic exploration (*ab*, *cd*) laid out to check a supposed local structure.

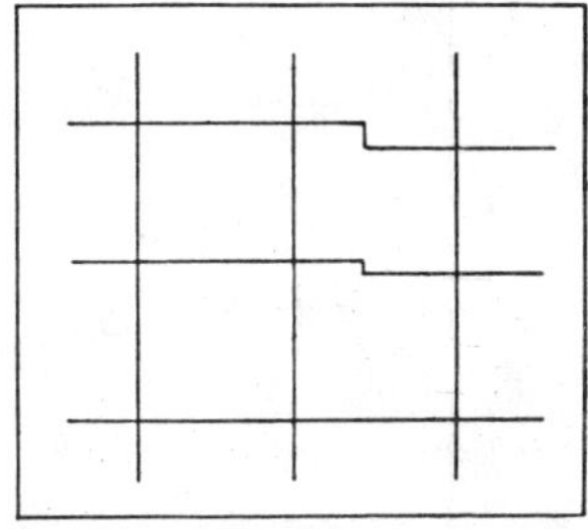

FIG. 624. Grid of lines along which seismic exploration was undertaken in a certain area to investigate a block of land for which subsurface structural conditions were unknown.

as to depth, can be examined for correlation of reflections. The results which seem to be most probable are then compared with the correlated set of corrected seismic records described in the first part of this article.

569. Applications of the reflection method to geology. In planning a program for reflection seismic field exploration, no matter where the area is that is to be investigated, a certain amount of preliminary testing is necessary to ascertain the best arrangement of detectors and shot points for securing data under the existing conditions of subsurface stratigraphy, nature of the weathered zone, and topographic relief. Thus in preparing to survey an area, whether by dip shooting, continuous profiling or correlation shooting, several methods of attack may be followed. If the area is thought to be underlain by a local, more or less equidimensional, structure, two or more lines of observations may be run, intersecting at the center of the supposed anomaly (Fig. 623). If the geologic structures are long and narrow (faults, elongate folds, etc.), parallel lines of observations may be run across their trend. On the other hand, if a large block of land is to be covered, without any previous information as to what structural features may underlie it, observations may be made along intersecting lines laid out as a grid or network (Fig. 624); or, if reasonably good correlatable reflections are obtain-

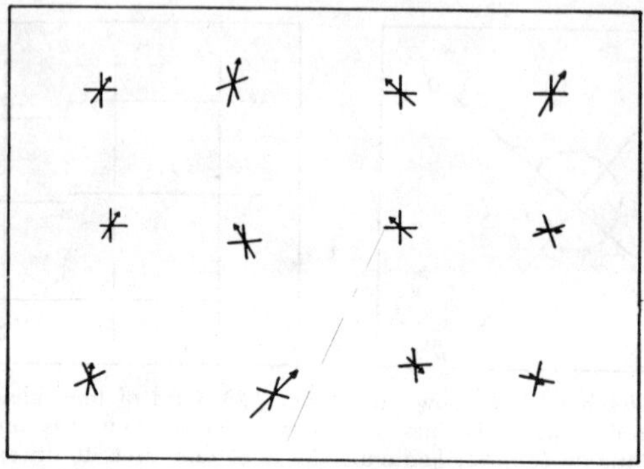

FIG. 625. Map showing locations of isolated observations made by dip method. At each station the true dip was calculated from the dip components measured along the lines that intersect perpendicularly, and was plotted on the map by an arrow the length of which is scaled to represent the amount of the true dip.

able, a number of isolated setups may be made, scattered over the area, and located in the most accessible places along roads, or otherwise (Fig. 625).

In the case where observations are made along intersecting lines in a network, reflecting horizons should be correlated in loops, returning to the starting point; *i.e.*, each polygon should be closed. A definite discrepancy in correlation may thus indicate either an error or the possibility of a fault across the traverse. In this event the records should be carefully reexamined to see if a fault can be located. Where broad reconnaissance is to be done, lines of observation may be far apart, or, in dip shooting, the recording setups may be widely scattered. If more detailed work is required, closer coverage must be planned in the arrangement of detectors and shot points and in the distribution of observation stations.

After the usual corrections of seismic records have been made (Art. **568**), it is important to bear in mind (1) that reflecting surfaces underground are seldom flat (plane), but are more commonly undulating with changing strikes and dips; (2) that even where strikes and dips of subsurface strata are regular, the lines and profiles of seismic observation will often be laid out in directions acute to strike, so that corrections will have to be made to obtain true dips and true strikes from the observed seismic data; and (3) because of the average increase in elastic wave velocities with depth, the *ray*, or direction of travel of any point in the wave front, will be slightly curved, not straight as we have shown it in several of our diagrams (cf. *sb*, *sc*, etc., in Fig. 606), and furthermore these slightly curved rays will be somewhat irregular wherever there are marked differences in the elastic velocities of adjoining lithologic bodies through which the waves have been transmitted.

Electric Methods[36]

570. Electrical conditions within the lithosphere. In speaking of the flow of an electric current through a conductor, we may refer to the relative ease with which the flow of energy occurs as the *relative conductivity* of the material, or we may speak of the degree of resistance offered by the material to the current flow as the *resistivity* of the material. An *ohm* is the resistance against which, or through which, 1 volt can force a current of 1 ampere. The *specific resistivity* of a substance is the resistance offered by a *cube* of the substance, 1 cm. on each edge. Specific resistivity is measured in ohm-centimeters. Conductivity is the reciprocal of resistivity.

Let us imagine a body bounded by a horizontal plane and of infinite thickness and infinite lateral extent, and let us imagine that this body has uniform electrical conductivity (or resistivity). Consider two points, *a* and *b* (Fig. 626), on the horizontal surface, between which there is a potential difference, the

[36] For a discussion of electric methods of surveying see Bibliog., Dobrin, Milton B., 1952, Chap. 16.

potential at *b* being lower than that at *a*. As long as this difference of potential is maintained, an electric current will flow from *a* to *b*. This current from *a* to *b* may be conceived of as flowing along an infinite number of curved lines, or *lines of flow*, throughout the entire body. Along each one of these lines there is a potential drop from *a* to *b*. All points of the *same* potential on the different flow-lines lie in a curved surface, called an

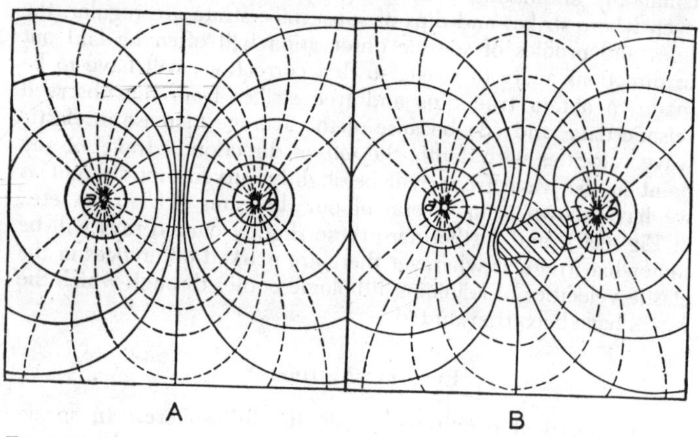

FIG. 626. A, current flow-lines (dashed) and equipotential lines (full) in a field established by two point electrodes in a medium of uniform conductivity. A body of high conductivity (*c*) would distort the field as indicated in B.

equipotential surface. In such an electrical field there is an infinite number of equipotential surfaces. Any equipotential surface is perpendicular to all the lines of flow (Fig. 626, A). Within this ideally uniform body, the point midway between *a* and *b* is the *potential center*.

In the lithosphere there is nowhere a condition of uniform electrical conductivity (or resistivity). Rock masses differ very greatly in respect to this property.[37] Dry rocks are poor conductors. Coal and salt, when dry, are very poor conductors, having a high resistance to the passage of electrical currents through them. However, under natural conditions, rock bodies are more

[37] See discussion of this subject on pp. 621–623, under Art. 468.

or less wet, either on their outer surfaces or within their pore spaces. The result is that the electrical conductivity of a rock body is usually dependent more on its interstitial (pore space) content of water, and particularly on the nature and amount of soluble salts dissolved in this water, than on the mineral characteristics of the rock itself. Fresh water is comparatively resistant to the flow of electrical energy, whereas salt water is an excellent conductor. Clays and shales, having pore spaces too small to permit circulation, and, therefore, containing more or less original connate salt water, may be better conductors than has sands or sandstones in which greater freedom of circulation has diluted and freshened the included water. Sundberg states that

TABLE 15. SPECIFIC RESISTANCE IN OHMS PER CUBIC CENTIMETER[1]

Rock	*Pores filled with surface water or ground water*	*Pores filled with salt water*
Limestone and sandstone	100,000–1,000,000	500–4,000
Sand and clay	40,000–400,000	200–2,200
Marl, loess	2,000–20,000	20–200

[1] See Bibliog., Sundberg, Karl, 1930.

"for practical purposes . . . the specific resistance of a natural water is generally determined by its content of chlorine."[38] He gives the following table of the estimated resistivity of different rock materials when their pore spaces are filled with fresh or nearly fresh water, and when filled with salt water.

The specific resistance of crude petroleum is enormously high as contrasted with most other subsurface materials in sedimentary formation. It amounts to from 10^{10} to 10^{16} ohm-cm.

Because of the diversity of conditions within the lithosphere, the effects of the diurnal heating and cooling of the earth's surface in its rotation, the effects of magnetic storms and variations in the earth's magnetic field, and other causes, there are always local and regional differences of potential within the earth. These differences of potential result in the flow of electrical energy from places of higher potential to places of lower potential. These natural currents are called *ground currents* or

[38] Bibliog., Sundberg, Karl, 1930.

earth currents. They are very irregular and are subject to frequent change. In some localities, as for instance in areas underlain by sulphide ore bodies, they may have considerable strength.

571. Classification of methods of electrical surveying. The many methods which have been practiced or tested in electrical prospecting may be classified in two main groups:

1. Self-potential or electro-chemical methods, which make use of earth currents;
2. Those methods which utilize electrical fields of force artificially produced. These include: (*a*) resistivity methods, (*b*) surface potential methods, (*c*) induction, or electromagnetic methods, (*d*) radiation methods,[39] and (*e*) the electrical transient method.

In all these methods the underlying principle involved is the measurement of the deviation of the observed electrical properties from the values or directions which these properties would have under ideal conditions of uniform conductivity, like those postulated in Art. **570.** In the case of electric currents and fields, we speak of these deviations as the distortion of flow-lines, or the distortion of equipotential lines, or the displacement of the potential center.

The reader will note that all but the self-potential methods may be compared with the seismic method in that the results sought are based on a study of artificially applied fields of force. The self-potential methods in this respect are more like the gravimetric and magnetometric methods, which deal with natural fields of force.

With reference to the second group of methods, which utilize an artificial current, it is customary to balance out any earth currents before taking readings on the artificial field.

In some methods of electrical prospecting the artificial field is established inductively. In others, it is produced by means of ground contacts through which the electric current flows. This is done by means of electrodes which are connected above ground by adequate wire leads to a source of current supply and below ground by the earth itself, thus completing the circuit. One of the difficulties attached to these electrical methods, in using uninterrupted direct current, depends on the fact that ground contacts or electrodes, if not very carefully prepared and used, tend to become polarized through local chemical action,

[39] We shall not discuss the radiation, or high-frequency, methods in this book.

which may cause variable potentials between the electrodes of such magnitude as seriously to modify or mask the current effects to be measured. This polarizing effect can be overcome by certain methods of reversing the energizing current applied to the electrodes.

The self-potential methods have their greatest value in mining districts where some success has been attained. We shall not dwell upon these methods here.[40]

572. Methods which utilize electrical fields of force artificially produced. First among these methods are those which involve the measurement of earth resistivity between selected points. These are the *resistivity methods.* Here belong the Gish-Rooney method, the "Megger" method, the Jakosky method, and others. Four electrodes are staked in the ground at equal distances along a straight line. The distance from each outer electrode, C_1 and C_2, to the nearest inner electrode, and the distance between the two inner electrodes, P_1 and P_2, may be referred to as D. A current (either direct current or alternating current) flows through the ground from C_1 to C_2, the difference in potential between P_1 and P_2 is measured, and the resistance between P_1 and P_2 is calculated. Experience has shown that for practical purposes and at relatively shallow depths, the resistivity of the earth or soil can be measured in this manner to a depth equal to D. Therefore, by starting observations with the distance, D (C_1 *to* $P_1 = P_1$ *to* $P_2 = P_2$ *to* G_2) small, and then successively increasing D by regular stages, it is possible to measure the resistance of the earth to greater and greater depths. Hence, in plotting a curve of resistivity for increasing depth, any marked break in the curve will indicate the presence of a body of either lower or higher resistivity, as the case may be. By making readings of this kind over a wide area, obviously a system of elevation points can be secured for contouring such a body. In this way, it is sometimes possible to map the subsurface configuration of buried river channels, shallow salt domes, ground-water levels, faults, etc.

Details regarding the several resistivity methods may be found in the publications already cited.

The second group of methods utilizing an artificial current, includes the *surface potential methods.* According to one plan, the *linear electrode method,* developed by Hans Lundberg, two

[40] Bibliog., Heiland, C. A., 1929, p. 102; Ambronn, Richard, 1928, pp. 155 *et seq.;* Eve, A. S., and D. A. Keys, pp. 53 *et seq.*

copper wires, 2,000 or 3,000 ft. long, are laid on the ground parallel to one another, and 2,000 ft. or more apart. These wires are connected to the ground by stakes at intervals of 100 ft. One pair of adjacent ends of the wires is connected to a generator which supplies a current (A.C. or D.C.) that flows through one wire, entering the ground at the several electrodes (stakes), passing through the ground and into the other main wire, and so back to the generator. If the subsurface were homogeneous, the current flow lines would be approximately

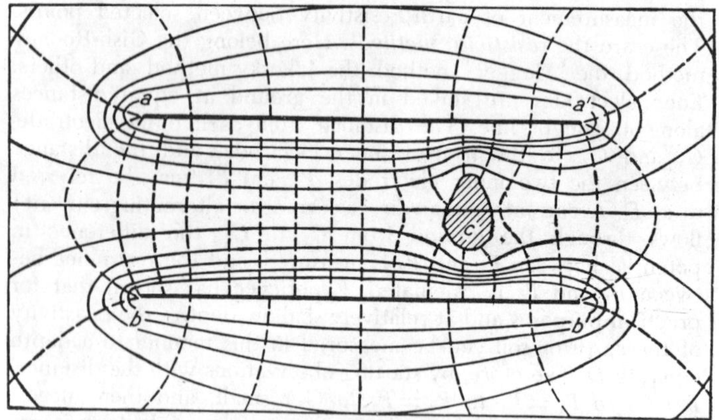

Fig. 627. Current flow-lines (dashed) and equipotential lines (solid) in a field established by two parallel linear electrodes, *aa'* and *bb'*. A body of high conductivity, *c*, would distort the field as indicated in the figure.

perpendicular to the main wires and the equipotential lines would be approximately parallel to these wires. Any relatively highly conducting body within the field will crowd the current flow-lines as observed on the surface and will cause the equipotential lines to bend out around it (Fig. 627). A highly resistant body will have the opposite effect.[41]

In Schlumberger's direct current (D.C.) method, the *point electrode method*, an electric field is produced by supplying an electric current to the ground through two primary point electrodes. With "secondary" or "exploring electrodes," the form

[41] In using alternating current of sufficiently high frequency, capacitive and inductive effects, as well as the conductivity of the body, become of importance.

and distribution of the lines of flow, or the form and distribution of the equipotential lines on the earth's surface, between the two electrodes, can be studied and mapped. Above a good conductor within the depth limits of the method the equipotential

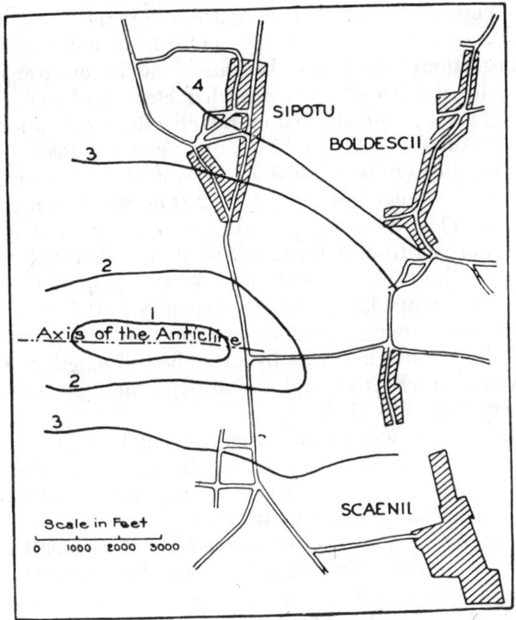

Fig. 628. Map of the region of the Boldeschii anticline in Roumania, showing lines of equal resistivity (1, 2, 3, and 4) as determined by the Schlumberger method. These lines correspond fairly well with contours on the structure (not shown). (*After E. G. Leonardon and S. F. Kelly. From "Geophysical Prospecting:* 1929," *published by the A.I.M.M.E. See Bibliog., McLaughlin, R. P.,* 1929.)

lines will spread apart, and above a bad conductor they will crowd together (Fig. 626). By Schlumberger's method some success has been achieved in mapping buried anticlinal and synclinal structures (Fig. 628), faults concealed beneath alluvium, shallow salt domes, ore bodies, etc.[42]

[42] Bibliog., Leonardon, E. G., and Sherwin F. Kelly, 1929.

A method developed by S. H. Williston and C. R. Nichols, called the *potential center displacement method,* is designed to identify on the ground the potential center of the field artificially created, and to measure the amount and direction of the displacement of this point from the geographic center which it would occupy if the earth had uniform electrical conductivity. The displacement of the potential center is an index of the sum of the distortions which may be caused in the electric field by irregular distribution of resistance characteristics below the surface of the ground and still within the effective exploration depth and radius of the field. Field observations are made along a straight line, carefully surveyed, on which station points are staked out at regular intervals, *I*, of 250 or 500 ft. On this line, the primary electrodes are placed at a much greater distance, *D*, apart, ranging from 3,000 to 10,000 ft. The field is then energized for a short period of time, and the potential center is located and mapped. The whole system is next "stepped" forward, still maintaining *I* and *D* constant, and the procedure is repeated. In this manner, step by step, the full length of the line is surveyed. The effective exploration depth may be regarded as roughly equivalent to $D/2$.

By successive series of observations of this kind, with a different value for *D* in each series, the effective exploration depth may be decreased or increased, thus enabling the observers to study the subsurface conditions at various depths.

The data obtained are plotted in the form of a potential center displacement profile (Fig. 629, A). The displacements are at a maximum approximately over the edges of a relatively highly resistant body with lateral limits. In other words, this method is devised to outline the edges of laterally discontinuous highly resistant bodies. It can be applied in the mapping of subsurface geologic structures, and also in the search for, and mapping of, hidden ore bodies (low resistance), and oil pools (Fig. 629).

In these or other equipotential methods, where direct current is used, the depth of penetration is assumed to be roughly one-half the horizontal distance between the primary electrodes. Within reasonable limits, therefore, the farther apart these electrodes are placed, the deeper can one explore below the earth's surface; but it is to be remembered that this statement does not take into account possible screening effects at the shallower depths, nor the relative strength of the effect being sought or measured at the greater depths. Within a given distance below the surface, other things being equal, a weak conductor or a moderately resistant body might not be detectable, whereas a good conductor or a highly resistant medium might be discovered.

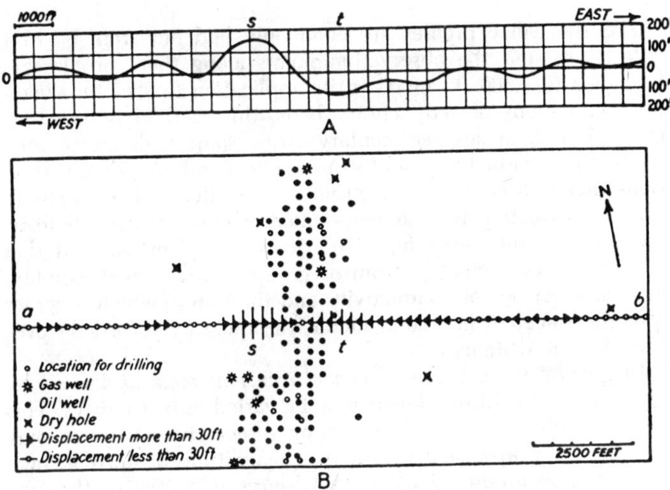

FIG. 629. A, potential center displacement profile. B, map of an oil field, showing line of electrical observations, *ab*. In these figures only the components of displacement along the line *ab* are represented. In A, the amount of this displacement of the potential center is shown in feet, eastward above the zero line, or base line, and westward below the base line. The greatest displacement was found at *s* and *t*. In B, any displacements of more than 30 ft. are shown by a symbol of which the total length of the cross line represents the amount of this displacement and the arrow head indicates the direction. Note that the maximum displacements, *s* and *t* (corresponding to *s* and *t* in A), lie close to the east and west edges of the oil pool.

A third group of electrical methods, founded on artificial electrical fields, includes the *induction* or *electromagnetic* methods. As an example of one of these, we may briefly outline the Swedish-American method. "An insulated copper cable is laid on the ground, usually in the shape of a large rectangle. An alternating electric current of moderate frequency is sent through this cable, and the resulting electromagnetic field," induced in the ground, "is measured . . . along transverse profiles which cross the cable at regular intervals. Usually the electromagnetic field is measured on each transverse line at several different distances from the cable, and both the horizontal and vertical components of the field are measured in regard to amplitude and phase."[43]

The transverse profiles are commonly laid out from ½ to 1 mile apart, and the observation points along these profiles are from 500 to 1,500 ft. apart. In its application to structure mapping in regions of sedimentary beds, this method is based on the fact that, in any sedimentary series, some beds are of relatively high conductivity, and so partially shield underlying strata from penetration of the electromagnetic effects. The depth to such a conducting body is determined at numerous points to be used in structure mapping. Experience has demonstrated that laterally a conducting stratum or group of strata may maintain its characteristics of conductivity and thickness (which together give the so-called induction factor, the quantity recorded) over considerable distances.

In general there is one *electrical transient method*, known by the trade name Eltran, but it may be varied in many ways. This method utilizes "a rapidly changing direct current which may be either a simple sharp change in magnitude of current, or a short intense unidirectional pulse of current."[44] The earth is excited by these short-period electrical impulses introduced at one or more pairs of spaced current electrodes, and the voltage appearing at potential electrodes is passed into an instrument called an *oscilloscope*, where the wave form is photographed. Variations in wave form are presumed to be caused by changes in the electrical properties of the underground mediums investigated. This method is being applied more particularly in trying to localize areas that may be underlain by oil.

Summary on the Geophysical Methods

573. Limitations of methods. In the structure of the lithosphere, rock formations of varying physical character are variously disposed. On the average, rocks are denser with depth;

[43] Bibliog., Sundberg, Karl, 1930.
[44] Bibliog., Rust, W. M., Jr., 1940.

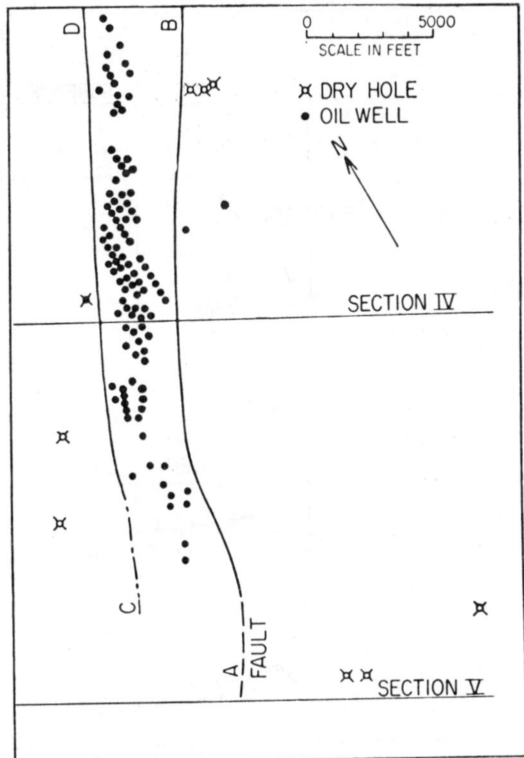

FIG. 630. Map of part of the Bruner or Salt Flat oil field in Caldwell County, Tex. *AB* is the position of a fault determined at a shallow depth by the inductive method of electrical surveying. *CD* is the trace of the same fault (which dips west) where it cuts the top of the Edwards limestone, much lower in the series than the formation cut at *AB*. The section lines (IV and V) are the lines along which electrical observations were made in this part of the field (see Fig. 631). (*Copied from Hedstrom, with modifications. Reproduced with permission of the Am. Assoc. Petr. Geols. See Bibliog., Hedstrom, Helmer, 1930.*)

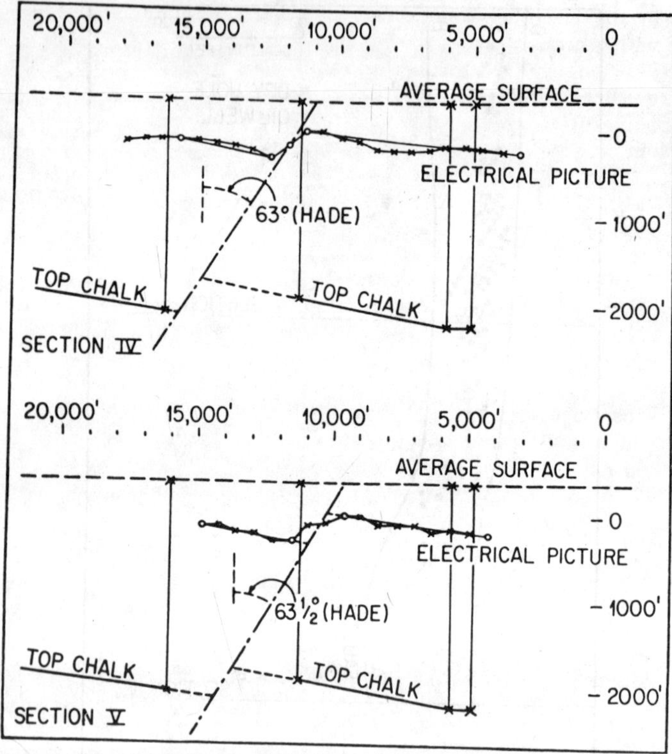

FIG. 631. Sections IV and V showing electrical profiles (through crosses) in relation to Salt Flat structure. (See Fig. 630.) (*After Hedstrom. Reproduced with permission of Am. Assoc. Petr. Geols. See Bibliog., Hedstrom, Helmer,* 1930.)

but in some places formations of relatively low density are buried deeply, and in other places very dense rocks are near the surface. Similarly, from one locality to another there may be wide differences in the elasticity of the underground formations. Or, again, materials of comparatively high magnetic susceptibility may be at slight depths in one district and at great depths in another district. And finally, marked differences may be observed in the electrical conductivity of certain formations contrasted with others.

Theoretically, any subterranean rock body can be distinguished, by geophysical measurements, from adjacent rock bodies from which it differs in respect to any of these properties; but in practice the results of such measurements are distinctly limited, partly because of the inadequate sensitivity of the instruments, partly because of the difficulties of making accurate observations under field conditions, and partly because of the difficulty, and often impossibility, of discriminating between the numerous unknown subsurface effects which together, at any given locality, compose the resultant actually measured.

It is very important that the geologist should recognize: (1) that, in geophysical surveying, methods are available which he may be able to use to advantage in seeking an explanation of subsurface structure; (2) that all these methods have limitations which must be understood and evaluated as far as possible for the most satisfactory interpretation of the results; and (3) that all these methods are not equally suitable for any given area or problem. The best method must be selected after careful consideration of all the factors involved, and these factors are both geological and geophysical.

Of the four groups of geophysical methods which we have briefly described, the seismic methods have yielded the most reliable results. In particular, the reflection method has been widely used for both reconnaissance and detail mapping. The gravimetric and magnetometric methods have their main application in reconnaissance, although the former may be of value in detailing salt domes and the latter in detailing the distribution of magnetic ores. Electric methods have very little use because of their limited subsurface penetration. Locally they have some application in prospecting for certain ores and also in some engineering surveying. All the different classes of geophysical exploration require, for their proper *execution,* men with highly specialized training in mathematics and physics. On the other hand, the *interpretation* of the data obtained by these methods can be satisfactorily accomplished only by the combined efforts of both geophysicist and geologist.

APPENDIX

Appendix 1

GEOLOGIC TIME SCALE[1]

Geologic time is subdivided into eras, periods, epochs, ages, and phases. The corresponding names for the rock bodies are sequences,[2] systems, series, stages, and zones, respectively. Note that the titles under these subdivisions are arranged in the table with oldest at the bottom of the column and youngest at the top, in the stratigraphic sequence of the formations which they represent.

Era or Sequence	*Period or System*	*Epoch or Series*
Cenozoic	Quaternary	Holocene (Recent)
		Pleistocene
	Tertiary	Pliocene
		Miocene
		Oligocene
		Eocene
		Paleocene
Mesozoic	Cretaceous	Late (Upper)
		Early (Comanchean) (Lower)
	Jurassic	Late (Upper)
		Middle (Middle)
		Early (Lower)
	Triassic[3]	
Paleozoic	Permian	
	Pennsylvanian	(together comprising the Carboniferous)
	Mississippian	
	Devonian	
	Silurian	
	Ordovician	
	Cambrian	
Proterozoic	Keweenawan	
	Huronian	
Archeozoic	Temiskamian[4]	
	Keewatinian[4]	

[1] See Bibliog., Krumbein, W. C., and L. L. Sloss, 1958, Chap. 2.

[2] The word "group," although originally proposed for the rock body equivalent of the time division, "era," is now more commonly applied to a much smaller division. Hence some geologists prefer to use "sequence," as recommended in 1933 by R. C. Moore. See a discussion of this and other similar terms in Geol. Soc. Am., *Bull.*, vol. 51, No. 9, pp. 1397–1412, September, 1940.

[3] The Triassic and any of the older periods may be divided into early and late, or early, middle, and late, epochs; and the systems into upper and lower, or upper, middle, and lower, series.

[4] See Bibliog., Moore, Raymond C., 1949.

Appendix 2

IDENTIFICATION TABLE OF COMMON ROCK MINERALS[1]

Group	Hardness/Color	Character	Distinguishing features	Mineral
Nonmetallic light-colored	Hard	Show cleavage	Flesh-colored, stubby	Orthoclase
			Gray-white, lathlike, striated	Plagioclase
			Green columnar	Actinolite
			Gray or red, greasy luster, sol.	Nepheline
		Fracture only	Isometric crystals in dark rocks	Leucite
			Green, glassy, granular	Olivine
			Fine-grained, yellowish green	Epidote
			Glassy, variously colored	Quartz, chert
	Soft	Cleavage	Cubic, salty taste	Halite
			Rhombohedral cleavage, H = 3	Calcite and dolomite
			Flexible plates, etc., H = 2	Gypsum
			Rectangular cleavage, H = 3.5	Anhydrite
			Soapy feel, H = 1	Talc
			Elastic mica	Muscovite
			Fibrous, brittle, H = 2–4	Zeolites
			Fibrous, flexible, H = 2–4	Asbestos
		Fracture	Yellow, burns with blue flame	Sulphur
			Earthy	Kaolinite
			Waxy look, H = 4	Serpentine
			Soapy feel, H = 1	Talc
Nonmetallic dark-colored	Hard	Cleavage	Black: cleavage about 90°	Augite
			Black: cleavage about 60°	Hornblende
			Green, poor cleavage	Epidote
		Fracture	Dirty green	Epidote
			Brown, orthorhombic	Staurolite
			Red, isometric, glassy	Garnet
			Black, hexagonal columns fluted	Tourmaline
			Variously colored, waxy	Jasper, quartz
			Black to red, conchoidal	Obsidian
	Soft	Cleavage	Brown to black, elastic mica	Biotite
			Green to dark blue-gray, H = 1	Chlorite
			Brown rhombohedrons	Siderite
		Fracture	Earthy	Clay
			Green to dark blue-gray, H = 1	Chlorite
			Green, waxy, H = 4	Serpentine
			Green, dark, sandy grains	Glauconite
Metallic-colored	Black	Streak black	Hardness = 6: strongly magnetic	Magnetite
			Hardness = 6: weakly magnetic	Ilmenite
			Hardness = 1 to 3	Graphite and coal
		Streak red		Hematite
		Streak yellow		Limonite
	Red	Metallic		Copper
		Earthy		Hematite
	Yellow	Metallic, black streak, H = 6		Pyrite
		Earthy, yellow streak		Limonite

[1] Reproduced with permission of Prof. Frank F. Grout and D. Van Nostrand Company, Inc., from p. 20 of Grout's revised edition of "Kemp's Handbook of Rocks," published in 1940 by D. Van Nostrand Company, Inc., New York. The sixth edition of this book was published in 1947 by The Macmillan Company.

Appendix 3

CLASSIFICATION OF IGNEOUS ROCKS[1]

Mineral constituents		Dominant feldspars are orthoclase and microcline	Potash feldspar and plagioclase in nearly equal proportions	Dominant feldspars are plagioclase	Little or no feldspar present
Quartz is a principal constituent		(A) Granite (B) Rhyolite (C) Aplite	(A) Granodiorite (B) Dellenite	(A) Quartzdiorite (B) Dacite	
Quartz negligible or absent	Feldspathoids absent	(C) Felsite		(C) Trap	
		(A) Syenite (B) Trachyte	(A) Monzonite (B) Latite	(A) Diorite (B) Andesite — dark minerals, chiefly hornblende or biotite or both (A) Gabbro (B) Basalt — dark minerals, chiefly pyroxene or olivine or both	(A) Peridotite, etc. (B) Limburgite, etc.
		(C) Lamprophyre			
	Feldspathoids present	(A) Nepheline syenite (B) Phonolite	(A) Nepheline monzonite (B) Vicoite	(A) Theralite (essexite) (B) Tephrite and basanite	(A) Missourite, etc. (B) Nephelinite, etc.

In using the table, note that (A) refers to granitoid (even-granular, coarse-grained, or phaneritic) rocks, whereas (B) refers to felsitic (fine-grained or aphanitic) rocks. If rocks under these groups are porphyritic, add the word porphyry to the class. Thus, we may have granite porphyry, rhyolite porphyry, basalt porphyry, etc. In the same manner names preceded by (B) may be used before obsidian to indicate that the aphanitic rock is glassy; thus, rhyolite obsidian; trachyte obsidian; etc. Finally, breccias and tuffs, belonging to the pyroclastic group may be designated as rhyolite breccia or tuff; trachyte breccia or tuff; etc. (C) refers to special rocks that occur as dikes, usually either finely granular or aphanitic.

[1] This classification has been compiled from tables by Pirsson (see Bibliog., Pirsson, L. V., and A. Knopf) and tables prepared by F. M. Van Tuyl and H. T. U. Smith.

Appendix 4

CLASSIFICATION OF SEDIMENTARY ROCKS

A. ROCKS PARTLY OR WHOLLY MECHANICAL IN ORIGIN, CONSISTING OF PARTICLES OR FRAGMENTS OF PREEXISTING ROCKS

(a) Constituent particles or fragments distinctly visible

		Unconsolidated	*Consolidated*
Psephite[1] group	Residual	Residual gravels	Coarse arkose Arkose conglomerate Arkose breccia
	Transported	Talus Landslide débris Till Gravel, pebbles, etc. Volcanic bombs, fragments, etc.	Talus breccia Landslide breccia Tillite Conglomerate Volcanic breccia, agglomerate
Psammite[1] group	Residual, or after short and rapid transportation	Residual sand (grus)	Arkose, consisting largely of feldspar and quartz, derived from granitic rocks. Graywacke, derived from ferromagnesian rocks.
	Transported	Sand (fluviatile, marine, etc.) Volcanic ash	Sandstone Graywacke[2] Tuff

(b) Constituent particles indistinguishable; rock very fine-grained

		Unconsolidated	*Consolidated*
Pelite[1] group	Residual	Residual clays, laterite, terra rossa, etc.	Residual claystones, etc.
	Transported	Clay Mud Loess, adobe Glacial clay (rock flour)	Claystone, argillite Mudstone, shale, slate

B. ROCKS OF CHEMICAL ORIGIN, SOMETIMES INDIRECTLY DUE TO THE ACTION OF ORGANISMS. MORE OR LESS FIRMLY COMPACTED

Calcareous series	Tufa, travertine, oolitic limestone, dolomite
Siliceous series	Siliceous sinter (geyserite), chert, flint
Iron ores	Ferrous carbonate (siderite), greensand, bog iron ore, hematite
Evaporation products	Gypsum, rock salt, alkali, etc.

C. ROCKS DIRECTLY OF ORGANIC ORIGIN

	Unconsolidated	*Consolidated*
Calcareous series	Shells and shell fragments Ooze	Shell limestone Coral limestone Chalk
Carbonaceous series	Peat, etc.	Coal series
Siliceous series	Diatomaceous earth	Tripolite
Phosphates	Guano, etc.	Phosphate rock

[1] These terms are derived from the Greek. The equivalent terms, derived from the Latin and preferred by some geologists, are rudite (from *rudus*, rubble), arenite (*arena*, sand), and lutite (*lutus*, mud).

[2] See Bibliog., American Geological Institute, 1957.

Appendix 5

CLASSIFICATION OF METAMORPHIC ROCKS

A. ROCKS WITH A PARALLEL STRUCTURE WHICH IS OFTEN VERY CONSPICUOUS

Constituents principally silicates and quartz	Gneisses Schists (mica schists, chlorite schists, hornblende schists, talc schists, etc.) Slates Phyllites
Principal constituents carbonates	Impure marbles and dolomites
Principal constituents hematite and quartz	Itabarite
Principal constituent carbon	Graphite

B. ROCKS COMMONLY MASSIVE; SOMETIMES WITH POORLY DEVELOPED PARALLEL STRUCTURE

Constituents principally quartz or (and) silicates	Quartzite Hornfels Serpentine Soapstone Many diverse products of thermal metamorphism
Principal constituents carbonates	Marble Dolomite
Principal constituents magnetite, quartz, etc.	Magnetite rock

Appendix 6

TABLE FOR THE IDENTIFICATION OF CLASTIC SEDIMENTARY ROCKS[1]

This table is applicable to both the unconsolidated and consolidated states. For the sake of brevity, however, a deposit, when referred to, will be given one name and not all the terms which might be applied to it in its different stages of lithification. The primary division of the table is based on texture, for this is perhaps the most striking character of clastic materials. There are three grades, psephites, psammites, and pelites (see Appendix 4). In assigning a deposit to one of these groups difficulty may be experienced because there is sometimes great variation in texture even in small exposures. In such a case, if one grade of coarseness predominates (*e.g.*, gravel), look up the material under that grade. If two or three grades are about equally represented, look up the material under the coarser grade. Remember that all the features noted for a particular kind of rock are seldom present; also, that one characteristic feature is not enough to determine the origin or classification of a rock. Study the deposit carefully and suspend judgment until every possibility has been considered.

Under "Sites of Deposition" are mentioned the principal areas where deposition of the sediment may occur. "Structure" refers to the arrangement of the constituent particles and fragments, and to the nature of the bedding in stratified materials. In the column headed, "Surface Features" (omitted under psephites), are remarks on ripple marks, sun cracks, and other phenomena which form on the original surfaces of sands, muds, and clays. The larger constituents of the psephites (pebbles, etc.) and the finer matrix in which these are embedded receive attention in separate columns which together correspond to "General Characters" in the sections on psammites and pelites. Under "Associated Materials" are mentioned only a few significant associations out of many which might be cited. The student will find it advantageous to look back in the earlier chapters of the book for the more complete descriptions of the features listed in this table.

[1] See Art. **119**.

PSEPHITES (GRAVELS, CONGLOM-

	Sites of deposition	Structure	Matrix
Marine and Littoral	Nearly all littoral, high on beach.	Pebbles usually touch one another. Well sorted. Pebbles may have a definite arrangement. Structure may be pell-mell. Larger stratification good; may not be visible. Local unconformity and cross-bedding occasional. There may be sand lenses which are elongate parallel to the shore line. Rarely over 100 feet thick.	Clear sands, fairly well sorted. Grains angular to rounded.
Lacustrine	On lake beaches, principally above the water line.	Similar to marine.	Similar to marine. Less well sorted and less clean.
Fluviatile	Alluvial cones and piedmont plains; along channels of rapid streams; small deltas.	Frequent textural variation. Sand lenses common; these often cross-bedded and showing contemporaneous erosion at their upper surfaces. They are elongate parallel to the course of the stream. Tendency for materials to accumulate in discontinuous layers. Beds vary greatly in thickness. Sorting may be very poor, like some till. Matrix may be so abundant that pebbles do not touch one another. Cross-bedding and local unconformity frequent. Series may be many hundred feet thick.	Poorly sorted. Grains angular to rounded. More apt to be rounded than lake and marine sand grains.
Aqueoglacial	Typically in kames and eskers and upper layers of sand plains; also upstream part of valley trains and outwash aprons.	Very similar to fluviatile alluvial cone gravels as described above. Stratification may be good, poor, or absent. Structure often pell-mell owing to rapid deposition or to slumping after deposition.	Poorly sorted; angular and subangular grains predominate. Many grains may consist of feldspar and other decomposable minerals.

ERATES, BRECCIAS, ETC.)

Larger fragments (pebbles, etc.)	Associated materials	Relations to subjacent materials
Well-rounded, smooth, with a dull polish. Size pretty uniform.	Sands and sandstones; sometimes limestone which is apt to be of organic origin.	May rest unconformably upon a wave-scoured rock platform. May overlie continental deposits conformably or unconformably. Typically basal.
Similar to marine, but less well rounded and sorted.	Sands and sandstones. Associated limestones apt to be of chemical origin.	May rest unconformably upon an old rock surface or conformably above continental deposits of other kinds.
Of all sizes, up to several tons in weight. Subangular to rounded. Some angular.	Sands and sandstones, usually cross-bedded. Mudstones may be intimately associated, in thin beds.	Usually lie upon an eroded rock floor. If upon finer sediments in the same formation, local unconformity generally separates the two.
Typically subangular. Large striated bowlders may be found, these having been ice-rafted or having dropped in from adjacent ice walls.	Sand or sandstone. May be till.	May rest upon till, wash, or bedrock. Local or regional unconformity may separate these deposits from the underlying materials. If bedrock underlies, it is apt to bear marks of glacial abrasion.

PSEPHITES (GRAVELS, CONGLOM-

	Sites of deposit	Structure	Matrix
Glacial	In the area originally covered by the ice, or as marginal deposits. Till belongs here.	Till and tillite have no true bedding. They may contain isolated nests and small beds of sand, which are often contorted. They consist of an unstratified mass of miscellaneous unsorted rock material.	If arenaceous, sand grains angular. Fresh feldspar and other decomposable minerals may be present. If fine, consists of rock flour which may contain scattered sand grains.
Eolian	Chiefly in deserts. Here belong lag gravels. They are usually in thin accumulations.	No definite structure is found in lag gravels because they are merely residual in the sense that they have been left behind by the wind.	Probably of typical wind-worn sand (*q.v.*).
Volcanic	On or near volcanic vents.	Bedding may be lacking or there may be a rude stratification due to sliding of the materials.	Volcanic sand and dust (*q.v.*).
Gravity	Talus at base of cliffs or on steep hill slopes. Rock glaciers in valleys in cool climates. Various places where mass movements may occur.	Bedding is absent. Talus and similar gravity accumulations are heterogeneous and unsorted, although there is a tendency for the heavier fragments to roll farthest.	Grains commonly angular, ranging in texture to the fineness of powder.
Residual	In regions of disintegration. May be the result of differential weathering of a conglomerate or similar rock or the result of spheroidal weathering.	No true bedding is developed in these materials, for there is no process of mechanical sorting to which they are subjected.	May consist of disintegration sand or eolian sand (*q.v.*).

ERATES, BRECCIAS, ETC.)—*Continued*

Larger fragments	Associated materials	Relations to subjacent materials
Angular or subangular, with snubbed ends and striated facets. Of all sizes. Proportion of pebbles to matrix varies. Pebbles may bear concave fracture scars. If not lithified when handled by the ice, fragments may be very angular and may be distorted.	May be associated with aqueoglacial materials.	If basement was not lithified, the underlying materials are apt to be disrupted and contorted. Striæ are wanting. If basement was consolidated rock, it may bear striæ or grooves of glacial origin. Sometimes it is fractured and the upper parts may be thrust over the lower.
Faceted einkanter, dreikanter, etc. Subangular, and with polished and often pitted faces.	Probably eolian sands.	The basement rock may show evidences of wind abrasion.
Angular, sharp-edged. Broken blocks of all sizes. Often consist of volcanic rocks, but may be fragments of country rock through which lava was ejected. Volcanic bombs may be associated.	Volcanic ash, mud flow, or lava.	No necessary relation.
Angular or subangular. Fragments may have had edges dulled by sliding or by weathering while exposed. Surfaces may be somewhat scratched.	No special association.	In case of landslides, basement rock may be scratched. No important relation for talus. Basement beneath rock glaciers may be striated and grooved by the movement of the materials.
If due to spheroidal weathering, well-rounded and with rough surfaces. If due to differential weathering, characters depend upon original source. (May be pebbles or fragments from any kind of a conglomerate, or they may be concretions.)	Associated with the parent rock.	Bowlders of weathering grade down into the unaffected rock. Residual deposits due to differential weathering lie upon the roughened surface of the parent rock.

PSAMMITES (SANDS

	Sites of deposition	Structure
Marine and Littoral	Sea sands are situated chiefly in the littoral belt. Those which are constantly submerged are usually fine and local. Some sands have been carried far from land, probably by turbidity currents.	Beach sands (not including dunes) have a gentle seaward dip. Their bedding may be fairly regular, but cross-bedding is not uncommon, especially in bars and reefs. Isolated bowlders and "pockets" or "nests" may be found. Graded bedding occurs in turbidity-current deposits.
Lacustrine	Lake sands belong to the shore zone surrounding lakes. They may extend a few rods under water.	Similar to marine sands and sandstones.
Fluviatile	Chiefly in relatively small deltas, along river courses, and in the lower parts of alluvial cones.	Bedding is highly irregular. Numerous gravel or conglomerate lenses. Cross-bedding and local unconformity common. Cross-bedding often due to migration of bars downstream. Length of gravel or conglomerate lenses parallel to course of current.
Aqueoglacial	In valley trains, outwash plains, and some eskers and kames.	Typically cross-bedded. Great irregularity of stratification seen particularly in kames and outwash plains. Frequent local unconformities and current ripple marks. Individual beds vary in thickness. Gravel is often interbedded. Isolated bowlders and gravel pockets may be found.
Eolian	Deserts and beaches.	Typically cross-bedded. Curvature of cross-laminæ often flatter than in water-made cross-bedding. May contain clay galls.
Volcani(	Near volcanoes. (Includes ash and small lapilli.)	Bedding may be absent or it may be well developed. If the ash was wind-laid, eolian features may be seen. If it settled in water, lacustrine structure may be seen.
Residual	Chiefly in dry, hot or cold climates. Locally, in temperate humid climates.	Bedding is absent. The materials may contain structures inherited from the parent rock.

AND SANDSTONES)

Surface markings of the deposit	General characters
Ripple marks and wave marks typical. Rill marks, footprints, and current marks may be found. In general these features are found in littoral deposits, but ripple marks and current marks may occur in deeper-water deposits.	Well-sorted. Sands are cleaner than lake and river sands.
Wave marks and rill marks rare. Ripple marks, current marks, footprints, etc., may be preserved.	Grains less rounded than in marine sands. Less clean.
Current marks common, but wave ripple marks and other beach features are lacking.	Grains rounded to subangular.
No characteristic features. Current marks and ripple marks may be present.	
Rill marks may be found on the lee sides of isolated pebbles.	Grains well-rounded and with a dull polish. There may be some scattered sharp-edged particles. Mica plates may lie at various angles.

PELITES (MUDS, CLAYS, MUDSTONES,

	Sites of deposition	Structure
Marine and Littoral	Continental shelves, especially in front of river mouths (estuarine) Sometimes littoral.	Typically with uniform bedding. May be thinly banded; or if conditions of accumulation were very uniform, bedding may be absent. Cross-bedding and local unconformity rare; if present, made by submarine currents. Isolated, ice-rafted bowlders possible, but not characteristic.
Lacustrine	Lake floors. May be exposed on lake shores. Playa deposits may be listed here.	Thin, uniform lamination common. Evidences of current action rare. Local deformation by slight settling may occur. Isolated, ice-rafted bowlders possible, but, not characteristic.
Fluviatile	Chiefly flood plains and delta flood plains.	Considerable variation. Thin sand layers often interbedded. Local unconformity frequent. Cross-bedding typical, but better developed in sands. Beds not necessarily uniform in thickness.
Aqueoglacial	Principally continental. In glaciated areas. Sometimes many miles beyond extreme limit of ice advance.	Like lake muds and clays, since deposited in standing water. Isolated, ice-rafted pebbles and bowlders, sometimes striated, are not uncommon. Local deformation by the grounding of floating blocks of ice may be observed.
Eolian	Generally far from regions where wind work predominates. Dust accumulates in distant quiet regions.	Bedding often faint or absent. Deposits of loess characteristically homogeneous. Small deposits in the lee of obstructions may show good bedding. Cross-bedding rare.
Volcanic	Usually near volcanoes, but strong winds may blow fine ash far and drop it on land or in water.	Similar to eolian deposits. Particles merely settle down. Cross-bedding rare.
Gravity	Wide distribution in moist climates, on or associated with slopes.	No bedding. Either structureless or with faint tendency toward irregular layering caused by successive mud flows.
Residual	Regions with a moist climate and with poor drainage facilities.	No bedding. Deposit merely accumulates as a residuum, the soluble constituents being gradually leached out.

ARGILLITES, SHALES, SLATES, ETC.)

Original surface features	General characters	Commonly associated beds
None of importance. Current marks and even true wave ripple marks may be made at depths up to 100 fathoms, but these are uncommon. Ripple marks may be well preserved in littoral muds. Rain prints, sun cracks, etc., seldom preserved in littoral muds and not found in marine muds.	Usually consist of certain of the clay minerals[1] and fine quartz grains together with organic matter. Common colors are grays, blues, and greenish grays. Fossils marine.	Fine sandstones or limestones. Where bays were shut off from the sea and rainfall was scant, salt, gypsum, saline muds, and other products of arid conditions may overlie the original marine muds.
Surface markings, such as sun cracks, stand a better chance of preservation than in marine muds, because exposure of the muds may be seasonal.	Usually decomposition products of land waste, as marine muds. Fossils of fresh or brackish-water organisms; occasionally terrestrial animals and plants included.	Coarser clastics overlie. If climate was arid, salt, gypsum, etc., may be interbedded. If climate was warm and moist, coal and bog iron ore may be associated.
Current marks, rain prints, sun cracks characteristic especially of flood-plain deposits in arid and semiarid climates. Sheetflood deposition may be listed here.	Colors: blue, gray, green. Red, maroon, and variegated in dry climates, but other types of mud deposit may have these colors.	Coal or peat beds may alternate with sun-cracked mud beds. In dry climates saline deposits may be associated.
Since the water body is generally temporary and sedimentation is rapid, there is little opportunity for the development and preservation of surface markings.	Largely rock flour, *i.e.*, pulverized rock. Hence a greater proportion of soluble salts than in lake and marine muds and clays. Fossils rare on account of coolness of water.	Possibly coarser aqueoglacial stream or lake deposits; till; or soil beds.
None characteristic.	Soluble constituents abundant. Unusual amounts of lime. Fossils terrestrial.	
None characteristic.	Materials largely volcanic glass. Fossils rare. May belong to any habitat according to the site of deposition.	
Characteristically irregular, with suggestions of slow flow down slope.	Great variety under different conditions. Here belong mud-flow and soil-creep materials.	
None characteristic.	The substance of which the deposit is composed would be found thinly disseminated through the underlying parent rock. Plant remains may be found.	

[1] The clay minerals include the kaolinite, montmorillonite, and illite groups.

Appendix 7

LAND SURVEY DIVISIONS, UNITED STATES AND CANADA

In some of the younger states, including Montana, Wyoming, Kansas, Oklahoma, and others, a system of land division has been adopted, based on measurements from a chosen principal meridian and a chosen standard parallel of latitude called a "base line." The country is laid off in quadrangles, essentially six miles square, known as *townships*. Each township is subdivided into 36 *sections*. The sides of sections are termed *section lines*. Townships are numbered beginning at the intersection of the base line and

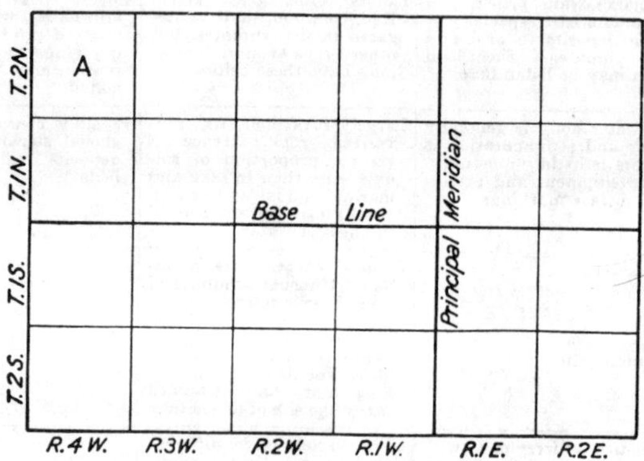

FIG. 632. Method of designating townships and ranges.

the principal meridian, and going east, west, north, and south. It is customary to designate these divisions *ranges* east and west, and *townships* north and south. Thus, in Fig. 632, the township marked *A*, consisting of 36 sections, is described as "township 2 north, range 4 west," or "T. 2 N., R. 4 W."

Sections in the United States are numbered as shown in Fig. 633 A. Parts of sections are described as in Fig. 634, A. Since a section (square mile) consists normally of 640 acres, a quarter section contains 160 acres, ½ of a quarter section contains 80 acres, etc.

On account of the northward convergence of meridians, townships are not always exactly six miles across, nor are sections always just one mile wide. To compensate for this convergence, there is often a slight offset of section and township lines in adjoining townships where they meet along the range lines. In the surveying of sectionized land all excesses and deficiencies due to convergence of meridians are placed, as far as possible, in the northern and western quarter-sections of the township.

A

6	5	4	3	2	1
7	8	9	10	11	12
18	17	16	15	14	13
17	20	21	22	23	24
30	29	28	27	26	25
31	32	33	34	35	36

B

31	32	33	34	35	36
30	29	28	27	26	25
19	20	21	22	23	24
18	17	16	15	14	13
9	8	9	10	11	12
6	5	4	3	2	1

Fig. 633. Methods of numbering sections in a township. A, in United States; B, in Canada.

A

NW 1/4 (160 ac.)

W 1/2 of NE 1/4 (80 ac.)

E 1/2 of NE 1/4 (80 ac.)

SW 1/4 (160 ac.)

NW 1/4 of SE 1/4 (40 ac.)

NE 1/4 of SE 1/4 (40 ac.)

No. 1/2 of SW 1/4 of SE 1/4

SW 1/4 of SW 1/4 of SE 1/4

SE 1/4 of SW 1/4 of SE 1/4

W 1/2 of SE 1/4 of SE 1/4 (20 ac)

E 1/2 of SE 1/4 of SE 1/4 (20 ac)

B

13	14	15	16
12	11	10	9
5	6	7	8
4	3	2	1

Fig. 634. A, method of designating parts of a section in the United States. In Canada (B) the section is divided into 16 "legal subdivisions" of 40 acres each, numbered as shown.

In Canada, townships are numbered north from the International Boundary, and ranges are numbered east and west from the principal meridian. Although these townships, like those in the United States, are 6 miles square and contain 36 sections, each 1 mile square, these sections and their subdivisions are numbered from the southeast corner instead of from the northeast corner (see Figs. 633, B, and 634, B).

Appendix 8

MEASUREMENT AND WEIGHT

Linear Measurement:

1 inch = 2.54 centimeters (cm.).
1 foot = 12 inches = 30.48 centimeters.
1 yard = 3 feet = 91.44 centimeters = 0.9144 meter.
1 rod = 16½ feet = 5½ yards.
1 mile = 5,280 feet = 1.6 kilometers.
1 millimeter = 0.001 meter = 0.03937 inch.
1 centimeter = 10 millimeters = 0.394 inch.
1 meter = 100 centimeters = 3.2809 feet = 39.37 inches.
1 kilometer = 1,000 meters = 0.6214 mile.
1 fathom = 6 feet (for depths).
1 link = 0.66 foot = 7.92 inches.
1 chain = 66 feet.
1 vara { in California = 33 inches.
in Texas = 33⅓ inches.
in Mexico = 32.9931 inches.

Areal Measurement:

1 square inch = 6.452 square centimeters.
1 square foot = 144 square inches = 929.0 square centimeters.
1 square yard = 9 square feet = 0.8360 square meter.
1 square rod = 30.25 square yards = 1/160 acre.
1 acre = 43,560 square feet = 4,840 square yards = 10 square chains (an acre is approximately equivalent to a square 209 feet on a side).
1 acre = 0.4046 hectares.
1 acre = 5,646.5 square varas (Texas value).
1 square centimeter = 0.155 square inch.
1 square meter = 1.1960 square yards.
1 hectare = 10,000 square meters = 2.47 acres.
1 square kilometer = 247.104 acres = 0.3861 square mile.
1 square vara (Texas value) = 7.71 square feet.
1 square mile = 2.5899 square kilometers.

Volumetric Measurement (solid and liquid):

1 cubic inch = 16.387 cubic centimeters.
1 cubic foot = 1,728 cubic inches.
1 cubic yard = 27 cubic feet = 0.7645 cubic meter = 201.96 gallons.
1 acre-foot = 43,560 cubic feet = 7,758.5 barrels of 42 gallons each.
1 cubic meter = 1,000,000 cubic centimeters = 35.316 cubic feet = 1.308 cubic yards.

1 litre (of water weighing 1 kilogram) = 1.0567 quarts.
1 quart = 0.9463 litre.
1 gallon = 8 pints = 4 quarts = 3.7852 litres = 231 cubic inches.
1 barrel (of crude petroleum) = 42 gallons.

Weight:

1 pound = 16 ounces = 0.45359 kilogram.
1 kilogram = 1,000 grams = 2.2046 pounds.
1 metric ton = 1,000 kilograms = 2204.6 pounds.
1 cubic foot of distilled water at 39°F. weighs 62.425 pounds.[1]
1 cubic foot of distilled water at 60°F. weighs 62.36 pounds.
1 barrel of distilled water at 60°F. weighs 349.84 pounds.

[1] The density of water is maximum at 4°C., or 39.2°F.

Appendix 9

SOLUTION OF TRIANGLES

Right Triangle (Fig. 635):

$$\sin A = \frac{a}{b}. \quad \cos A = \frac{c}{b}. \quad \tan A = \frac{a}{c}.$$

$$\sin C = \frac{c}{b}. \quad \cos C = \frac{a}{b}. \quad \tan C = \frac{c}{a}.$$

$$C = 90° - A. \quad b = \sqrt{a^2 + c^2}. \quad c = \sqrt{(b + a)(b - a)}.$$

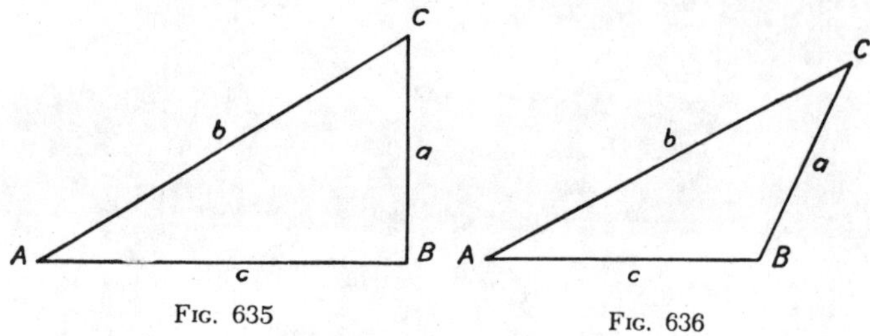

FIG. 635 FIG. 636

Oblique Triangle (Fig. 636):

Given	Required	Formula
A, B, a	b	$b = \frac{a \cdot \sin B}{\sin A}$.
A, a, b	B	$\sin B = \frac{b \cdot \sin A}{a}$.
C, a, b	B	$\tan B = \frac{b \cdot \sin C}{a - b \cdot \cos C}$.
a, b, c	A	If $s = \frac{1}{2}(a + b + c)$, $\sin \frac{1}{2}A = \frac{\sqrt{(s - b)(s - c)}}{bc}$; or $\cos \frac{1}{2}A = \frac{\sqrt{s(s - a)}}{bc}$.
$a, b, c,$	Area	Area $= \sqrt{s(s - a)(s - b)(s - c)}$.
A, B, c	Area	Area $= \frac{1}{2} bc \cdot \sin A$.

Appendix 10

NATURAL CIRCULAR FUNCTIONS[1]

°	Sine	Tang.	Cosine	Cotang.	°
0	0.0000	0.0000	1.0000	Infin.	90
1	0.0175	0.0175	0.9999	57.2900	89
2	0.0349	0.0349	0.9994	28.6363	88
3	0.0523	0.0524	0.9986	19.0811	87
4	0.0698	0.0699	0.9976	14.3007	86
5	0.0872	0.0875	0.9962	11.4301	85
6	0.1045	0.1051	0.9945	9.5144	84
7	0.1219	0.1228	0.9926	8.1444	83
8	0.1392	0.1405	0.9903	7.1154	82
9	0.1564	0.1584	0.9877	6.3138	81
10	0.1737	0.1763	0.9848	5.6713	80
11	0.1908	0.1944	0.9816	5.1446	79
12	0.2079	0.2126	0.9782	4.7046	78
13	0.2250	0.2309	0.9744	4.3315	77
14	0.2419	0.2493	0.9703	4.0108	76
15	0.2588	0.2680	0.9659	3.7321	75
16	0.2756	0.2868	0.9613	3.4874	74
17	0.2924	0.3057	0.9563	3.2709	73
18	0.3090	0.3249	0.9511	3.0777	72
19	0.3256	0.3443	0.9455	2.9042	71
20	0.3420	0.3640	0.9397	2.7475	70
21	0.3584	0.3839	0.9336	2.6051	69
22	0.3746	0.4040	0.9272	2.4751	68
23	0.3907	0.4245	0.9205	2.3559	67
24	0.4067	0.4452	0.9136	2.2460	66
25	0.4226	0.4663	0.9063	2.1445	65
26	0.4384	0.4877	0.8988	2.0503	64
27	0.4540	0.5095	0.8910	1.9626	63
28	0.4695	0.5317	0.8830	1.8807	62
29	0.4848	0.5543	0.8746	1.8041	61
30	0.5000	0.5774	0.8660	1.7321	60
31	0.5150	0.6009	0.8572	1.6643	59
32	0.5300	0.6249	0.8480	1.6003	58
33	0.5446	0.6494	0.8387	1.5399	57
34	0.5592	0.6745	0.8290	1.4826	56
35	0.5736	0.7002	0.8192	1.4282	55
36	0.5878	0.7265	0.8090	1.3764	54
37	0.6018	0.7536	0.7986	1.3270	53
38	0.6157	0.7813	0.7880	1.2799	52
39	0.6293	0.8098	0.7772	1.2349	51
40	0.6428	0.8391	0.7660	1.1918	50
41	0.6560	0.8693	0.7547	1.1504	49
42	0.6691	0.9004	0.7431	1.1106	48
43	0.6820	0.9325	0.7314	1.0724	47
44	0.6947	0.9657	0.7193	1.0355	46
45	0.7071	1.0000	0.7071	1.0000	45
°	Cosine	Cotang.	Sine	Tang.	°

[1] This table has been copied from Dr. C. W. Hayes' "Handbook of Field Geology," 1909, p. 42.

Appendix 11

EQUIVALENT ANGLES OF SLOPE AND PER CENT GRADES[1]

Angle of slope	Per cent grade	Angle of slope	Per cent grade	Angle of slope	Per cent grade	Angle of slope	Per cent grade
35′	1.0	11°	19.4	20° 3′	36.5	33° 49′	67.0
52′	1.5	11° 2′	19.5	20° 18′	37.0	34°	67.4
1° 9′	2.0	11° 19′	20.0	20° 48′	38.0	34° 13′	68.0
1° 26′	2.5	11° 35′	20.5	21°	38.4	34° 36′	69.0
1° 43′	3.0	11° 52′	21.0	21° 18′	39.0	35°	70.0
2°	3.5	12°	21.3	21° 48′	40.0	35° 23′	71.0
2° 17′	4.0	12° 8′	21.5	22°	40.4	35° 45′	72.0
2° 35′	4.5	12° 24′	22.0	22° 18′	41.0	36°	72.6
2° 52′	5.0	12° 41′	22.5	22° 47′	42.0	36° 8′	73.0
3°	5.2	13°	23.0	23°	42.5	36° 30′	74.0
3°	5.5	13° 13′	23.5	23° 16′	43.0	36° 52′	75.0
3° 26′	6.0	13° 30′	24.0	23° 45′	44.0	37°	75.4
3° 43′	6.5	13° 46′	24.5	24°	44.5	37° 14′	76.0
4°	7.0	14°	24.9	24° 14′	45.0	37° 36′	77.0
4° 17′	7.5	14° 2′	25.0	24° 42′	46.0	38°	78.0
4° 34′	8.0	14° 18′	25.5	25°	46.6	38° 19′	79.0
4° 52′	8.5	14° 34′	26.0	25° 10′	47.0	38° 40′	80.0
5°	8.8	14° 51′	26.5	25° 39′	48.0	39°	81.0
5° 9′	9.0	15°	26.8	26°	48.8	39° 21′	82.0
5° 26′	9.5	15° 7′	27.0	26° 6′	49.0	39° 42′	83.0
5° 43′	10.0	15° 23′	27.5	26° 34′	50.0	40°	84.0
6°	10.5	15° 39′	28.0	27°	50.9	40° 22′	85.0
6° 17′	11.0	15° 54′	28.5	27° 1′	51.0	40° 42′	86.0
6° 34′	11.5	16°	28.7	27° 29′	52.0	41°	87.0
6° 51′	12.0	16° 10′	29.0	27° 56′	53.0	41° 21′	88.0
7°	12.3	16° 26′	29.5	28°	53.2	41° 40′	89.0
7° 8′	12.5	16° 42′	30.0	28° 22′	54.0	42°	90.0
7° 24′	13.0	16° 58′	30.5	28° 49′	55.0	42° 18′	91.0
7° 41′	13.5	17°	30.6	29°	55.4	42° 37′	92.0
7° 58′	14.0	17° 13′	31.0	29° 15′	56.0	43°	93.0
8° 15′	14.5	17° 29′	31.5	29° 41′	57.0	43° 14′	94.0
8° 32′	15.0	17° 45′	32.0	30°	57.7	43° 32′	95.0
8° 49′	15.5	18°	32.5	30° 7′	58.0	43° 50′	96.0
9°	15.8	18° 16′	33.0	30° 33′	59.0	44°	96.5
9° 5′	16.0	18° 31′	33.5	31°	60.0	44° 8′	97.0
9° 22′	16.5	18° 47′	34.0	31° 23′	61.0	44° 25′	98.0
9° 39′	17.0	19°	34.4	31° 48′	62.0	44° 43′	99.0
9° 56′	17.5	19° 2′	34.5	32°	62.5	45°	100.0
10°	17.6	19° 17′	35.0	32° 13′	63.0		
10° 12′	18.0	19° 33′	35.5	32° 37′	64.0		
10° 29′	18.5	19° 48′	36.0	33°	65.0		
10° 44′	19.0	20°	36.4	33° 26′	66.0		

[1] See Art. 325.

Appendix 12

EQUIVALENT DIPS EXPRESSED IN ANGLES AND IN FEET PER MILE

Degrees	Minutes	Feet per mile	Degrees	Minutes	Feet per mile	Degrees	Minutes	Feet per mile
0	01	1.54	0	42	64.51	1	46	162.8
..	02	3.07	..	43	66.04	..	48	165.9
..	03	4.61	..	44	67.57	..	50	169.[illegible]
..	04	6.14	..	45	69.11	..	52	172.0
..	05	7.68	..	46	70.64	..	54	175.1
..	06	9.22	..	47	72.18	..	56	178.2
..	07	10.75	..	48	73.72	..	58	181.3
..	08	12.29	..	49	75.26	2	00	184.4
..	09	13.82	..	50	76.80	..	10	199.8
..	10	15.36	..	51	78.33	..	10+	200.0
..	11	16.90	..	52	79.87	..	20	215.1
..	12	18.43	..	53	81.40	..	30	230.5
..	13	19.96	..	54	82.94	..	40	245.9
..	14	21.50	..	55	84.47	..	43	250.0
..	15	23.04	..	56	86.01	..	50	261.3
..	16	24.58	..	57	87.54	3	00	276.7
..	17	26.11	..	58	89.08	..	10	292.1
..	18	27.64	..	59	90.62	..	15	300.0
..	19	29.17	1	00	92.16	..	20	307.5
..	20	30.72	..	02	95.23	..	30	322.9
..	21	32.26	..	04	98.30	..	40	338.4
..	22	33.80	..	05	100.00	..	47+	350.0
..	23	35.33	..	06	101.4	..	50	353.8
..	24	36.86	..	08	104.5	4	00	369.2
..	25	38.40	..	10	107.5	..	10	384.6
..	26	39.94	..	12	110.6	..	20	400.1
..	27	41.47	..	14	113.6	.	30	415.5
..	28	43.01	..	16	116.7	..	40	431.0
..	29	44.54	..	18	119.8	..	50	446.5
..	30	46.08	..	20	122.9	..	52	450.0
..	31	47.62	..	22	126.0	5	00	461.9
..	32	49.16	..	24	129.1	..	10	477.4
..	33	50.69	..	26	132.1	..	20	492.9
..	34	52.23	..	28	135.2	..	25	500.0
..	35	53.76	..	30	138.3	..	30	508.4
..	36	55.30	..	32	141.3	..	40	523.9
..	37	56.83	..	34	144.4	..	50	539.4
..	38	58.37	..	36	147.4	..	57	550.0
..	39	59.90	..	38	150.5	6	00	555.0
..	40	61.44	..	40	153.6	..	..	.....
..	41	62.97	..	42	156.6	..	..	.....
..	..	.....	..	44	159.7	..	..	.....

Appendix 13

CORRECTION FOR DIP IN DIRECTIONS NOT PERPENDICULAR TO STRIKE[1]

Angle of full dip	Angle between strike and direction of section							
	80°	75°	70°	65°	60°	55°	50°	45°
10°	9° 51′	9° 40′	9° 24′	9° 5′	8° 41′	8° 13′	7° 41′	7° 6′
15°	14° 47′	14° 31′	14° 8′	13° 39′	13° 34′	12° 28′	11° 36′	10° 4′
20°	19° 43′	19° 23′	18° 53′	18° 15′	17° 30′	16° 36′	15° 35′	14° 25′
25°	24° 48′	24° 15′	23° 39′	22° 55′	22° 0′	20° 54′	19° 39′	18° 15′
30°	29° 37′	29° 9′	28° 29′	27° 37′	26° 34′	25° 18′	23° 51′	22° 12′
35°	34° 36′	34° 4′	33° 21′	32° 24′	31° 13′	29° 50′	28° 12′	26° 20′
40°	39° 34′	39° 2′	38° 15′	37° 15′	36° 0′	34° 30′	32° 44′	30° 41′
45°	44° 34′	44° 1′	43° 13′	42° 11′	40° 54′	39° 19′	37° 27′	35° 16′
50°	49° 34′	49° 1′	48° 14′	47° 12′	45° 54′	44° 17′	42° 23′	40° 7′
55°	54° 35′	54° 4′	53° 19′	52° 18′	51° 3′	49° 29′	47° 35′	45° 17′
60°	59° 37′	59° 8′	58° 26′	57° 30′	56° 19′	54° 49′	53° 0′	50° 46′
65°	64° 40′	64° 14′	63° 36′	62° 46′	61° 42′	60° 21′	58° 40′	56° 36′
70°	69° 43′	69° 21′	68° 49′	68° 7′	67° 12′	66° 8′	64° 35′	62° 46′
75°	74° 47′	74° 30′	74° 5′	73° 32′	72° 48′	71° 53′	70° 43′	69° 14′
80°	79° 51′	79° 39′	79° 22′	78° 59′	78° 29′	77° 51′	77° 2′	76° 0′
85°	84° 56′	84° 50′	84° 41′	84° 29′	84° 14′	83° 54′	83° 29′	82° 57′
89°	88° 59′	88° 58′	88° 56′	88° 54′	88° 51′	88° 47′	88° 42′	88° 35′

Angle of full dip	Angle between strike and direction of section								
	40°	35°	30°	25°	20°	15°	10°	5°	1°
10°	6° 28′	5° 46′	5° 2′	4° 15′	3° 27′	2° 37′	1° 45′	0° 53′	0° 10′
15°	9° 46′	8° 44′	7° 38′	6° 28′	5° 14′	3° 33′	2° 40′	1° 20′	0° 16′
20°	13° 10′	11° 48′	10° 19′	8° 45′	7° 6′	5° 23′	3° 37′	1° 49′	0° 22′
25°	16° 41′	14° 58′	13° 7′	11° 9′	9° 3′	6° 53′	4° 37′	2° 20′	0° 28′
30°	20° 21′	18° 19′	16° 6′	13° 43′	11° 10′	8° 30′	5° 44′	2° 53′	0° 35′
35°	24° 14′	21° 53′	19° 18′	16° 29′	13° 28′	10° 16′	6° 56′	3° 30′	0° 42′
40°	28° 20′	25° 42′	22° 45′	19° 31′	16° 0′	12° 15′	8° 17′	4° 11′	0° 50′
45°	32° 44′	29° 50′	26° 33′	22° 55′	18° 53′	14° 30′	9° 51′	4° 59′	1° 0′
50°	37° 27′	34° 21′	30° 47′	26° 44′	22° 11′	17° 9′	11° 41′	5° 56′	1° 11′
55°	42° 33′	39° 20′	35° 32′	31° 7′	26° 2′	20° 17′	13° 55′	7° 6′	1° 26′
60°	48° 4′	44° 47′	40° 54′	36° 14′	30° 29′	24° 8′	16° 44′	8° 35′	1° 44′
65°	54° 2′	50° 53′	46° 59′	42° 11′	36° 15′	29° 2′	20° 25′	10° 35′	2° 9′
70°	60° 29′	57° 36′	53° 57′	49° 16′	43° 13′	35° 25′	25° 30′	13° 28′	2° 45′
75°	67° 22′	64° 58′	61° 49′	57° 37′	51° 55′	44° 1′	32° 57′	18° 1′	3° 44′
80°	74° 40′	73° 15′	70° 34′	67° 21′	62° 43′	55° 44′	44° 33′	26° 18′	5° 31′
85°	82° 15′	81° 20′	80° 5′	78° 19′	75° 39′	71° 20′	63° 15′	44° 54′	11° 17′
89°	88° 27′	88° 15′	88° 0′	87° 38′	87° 5′	86° 9′	84° 15′	78° 41′	44° 15′

[1] This table has been adapted from Appendix I, on p. 128, in Dr. A. R. Dwerryhouse's "Geological and Topographical Maps," published by Messrs. Edward Arnold, London.

Appendix 14

PROTRACTOR FOR CORRECTION OF DIP

Professor W. S. Tangier Smith has described a protractor[1] which can be used in place of the foregoing table (Appendix 13). In this protractor, degrees of true dip are represented by the vertical lines (Fig. 637), marked

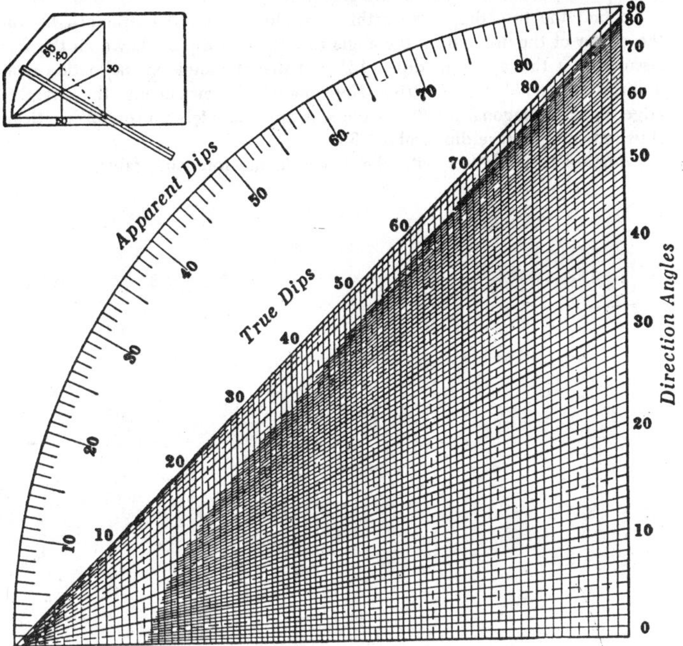

Fig. 637. Chart copyrighted in 1925 by W. S. Tangier Smith, who kindly permitted its reproduction here. (For use of chart, see text.)

along the chord connecting the two ends of the arc; degrees of apparent dip are represented on the arc; and the angle between the strike of the inclined

[1] Copyrighted by Professor Smith. See Bibliog., Smith, W. S. Tangier, 1925.

bed or surface and the direction in which the dip component is measured is shown by the converging lines marked on the right of the diagram.

To illustrate the use of this protractor, assume that a layer is dipping 30° from the horizontal and that we want to find its inclination measured in a direction 60° from its strike. Find the point of intersection of the inclined line marked 60° at the right of the diagram and the vertical line marked 30° for *true dip*. Through this intersection point and the vertex of the protractor (center of the arc at lower right corner) lay a straight-edge, which will then intersect the arc at approximately 26°35′, which is the dip component or *apparent dip* required.

To find the true dip, reverse this procedure. Place the straight-edge on the center of the arc and on the angle for apparent dip as shown on the arc. Assume that this apparent dip is 15° and that the angle of inclination is in a direction at 25° to the strike. Note on which vertical line the straight-edge cuts the diagonal for 25°. Here it is approximately on the 32° vertical, thus indicating a true dip of about 32°.

Compare these figures with the values in the foregoing table.

Appendix 15

GRAPHIC DETERMINATION OF DIP COMPONENTS WHEN DIPS ARE MEASURED IN FEET PER MILE[1]

The accompanying graph may be used to find the inclination of a stratum, or of any relatively flat surface or layer, in directions not perpendicular to strike, when dips are low and are recorded in *feet per mile*. Suppose

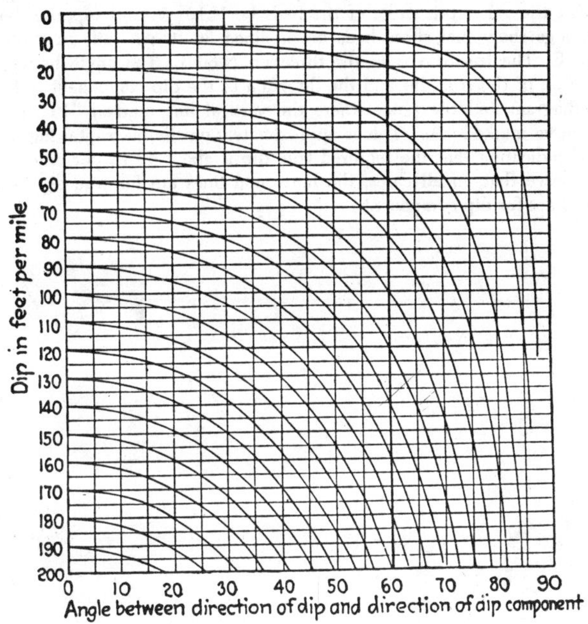

FIG. 638. Curves for the graphic determination of dips and dip components when dips are measured in feet per mile. (Angles recorded at base of figure are in degrees.)

that the strata dip 50 ft. per mile due north and that we want to find their inclination in the direction N.30°E. The latter inclination may be referred

[1] Prepared by F. H. Lahee and printed in *Economic Geology*, vol. 14, pp. 262–263, 1919.

to as the dip component in this direction. The horizontal angle between the true dip and the dip component is here 30°. Find the point on Fig. 638 where the vertical line labelled "30" (bottom of Fig.) interests the horizontal line marked "50" (left of Fig.). This point is between two curves which, if followed up to the left margin of the figure, will be seen to be marked "40" and "50," respectively. Since the point in question lies about one third way from the 40-ft. to the 50-ft. curve, the required dip component is found to be between 43 and 44 ft. per mile in the direction N.30°E.

In like manner, the true dip may be obtained from a known dip component thus: Let the strike of the beds be N.10°W. and suppose that two well logs show that these beds are inclined 30 ft. per mile in a direction N.40°E. The true dip is in the direction N.80°E. The angle between the direction of the true dip and the direction of the dip component is 40°. On the diagram find the point where the vertical line marked "40" intersects the curve marked "30." This is approximately on the horizontal line marked "40," indicating that the required true dip is about 40 ft. per mile.

Observe that, in all cases, the horizontal lines are for true dips and the curves are for dip components.

Appendix 16

DIP, DEPTH, AND THICKNESS OF INCLINED STRATA

This table may be used for determining the thickness of inclined strata or the depth of a point in an inclined stratum provided the dip and the breadth of outcrop on a horizontal surface are known. Divide the breadth of outcrop by 100 and multiply the result by the constant for thickness (or depth for the given dip (see Art. 533).

Dip	Thickness	Depth	Dip	Thickness	Depth	Dip	Thickness	Depth
1°	1.75	1.75	31°	51.50	60.09	61°	87.46	180.40
2°	3.49	3.49	32°	52.99	62.49	62°	88.29	188.07
3°	5.23	5.24	33°	54.46	64.94	63°	89.10	196.26
4°	6.98	6.99	34°	55.92	67.45	64°	89.88	205.03
5°	8.72	8.75	35°	57.36	70.02	65°	90.63	214.45
6°	10.45	10.51	36°	58.78	72.65	66°	91.35	224.60
7°	12.19	12.28	37°	60.18	75.36	67°	92.05	235.59
8°	13.92	14.05	38°	61.57	78.13	68°	92.72	247.51
9°	15.64	15.84	39°	62.93	80.98	69°	93.36	260.51
10°	17.36	17.63	40°	64.28	83.91	70°	93.97	274.75
11°	19.08	19.44	41°	65.61	86.93	71°	94.55	290.42
12°	20.79	21.26	42°	66.91	90.04	72°	95.11	307.77
13°	22.50	23.09	43°	68.20	93.25	73°	95.63	327.09
14°	24.19	24.93	44°	69.47	96.57	74°	96.13	348.74
15°	25.88	26.79	45°	70.71	100.00	75°	96.59	373.21
16°	27.56	28.67	46°	71.93	103.55	76°	97.03	401.08
17°	29.24	30.57	47°	73.14	107.24	77°	97.44	433.15
18°	30.90	32.49	48°	74.31	111.06	78°	97.81	470.46
19°	32.56	34.43	49°	75.47	115.04	79°	98.16	514.46
20°	34.20	36.40	50°	76.60	119.18	80°	98.48	567.13
21°	35.84	38.39	51°	77.71	123.49	81°	98.77	631.38
22°	37.46	40.40	52°	78.80	127.99	82°	99.03	711.54
23°	39.07	42.45	53°	79.86	132.70	83°	99.25	814.43
24°	40.67	44.52	54°	80.90	137.64	84°	99.45	951.44
25°	42.26	46.63	55°	81.92	142.81	85°	99.62	1143.01
26°	43.84	48.77	56°	82.90	148.26	86°	99.76	1430.07
27°	45.40	50.95	57°	83.87	153.99	87°	99.86	1908.11
28°	46.95	53.17	58°	84.80	160.03	88°	99.94	2863.63
29°	48.48	55.43	59°	85.72	166.43	89°	99.98	5729.00
30°	50.00	57.74	60°	86.60	173.21			

Appendix 17

W. S. TANGIER SMITH'S CHART

"This chart[1] (Fig. 639) is intended primarily for the solution of problems which may be expressed in the form

$$\frac{a}{\sin A} = \frac{b}{\sin B} = \frac{c}{\sin C}.$$

"The solution of problems (except the first, below) is accomplished by means of a rotating arm centered at the lower right-hand corner of the figure; or by a fine line drawn on a celluloid strip, or by any convenient form of straight-edge. In solving problems, the line or straight-edge—*index line*—is always set so as to pass through the lower right-hand corner of the chart. This is assumed in most of the solutions given below.

"1. The numerical values of tangents of angles not greater than 45° or the cotangents of the complements of these angles, and conversely, the angles corresponding to the tangent-cotangent values, are given by the intersections of the curved line of the chart with its horizontal and vertical lines.

"2. If the index line is set so as to pass through the upper left and lower right corners of the chart, its intersections with the lines of the chart will give sine-cosine values of angles; also the angles corresponding to sine-cosine values.

"3. Where the true dip does not exceed 10° or where the dip is expressed in terms of grade, the apparent dip, *a*, the true dip, *t*, or the direction angle, *d*, may be determined by means of the chart when the other two of these three factors are known. The determination is made from the relationship

$$\frac{t}{\sin 90°} = \frac{a}{\sin d}.$$

Three of these four terms are known, two of the three giving a known point on the chart. By setting the index line to pass through this point, the intersection of the line with the third known value will then give the fourth term.

"Example: If the true dip is 50 ft. per mile and the direction angle is

[1] This chart and the accompanying description were prepared by Professor W. S. Tangier Smith, who kindly permitted their publication here.

37°, the apparent dip is read from the chart as 30.1 ft. per mile (Fig. 640).

If, in this problem, $t = 5°$ and $d = 37°$ then, $a = 3.01° = 3°0.6'$. (The value calculated from the dip formula is 3°0.84′.) The error involved in using the numerical values of dip angles less than 10° instead of the tangent values is small,—not more than a few minutes at the most.

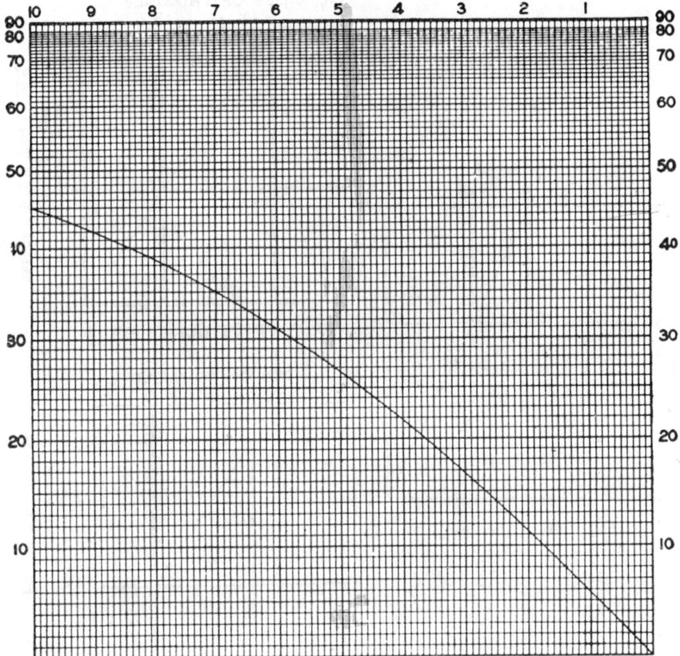

FIG. 639. Two-variable chart prepared by W. S. Tangier Smith for solution of various problems. (See text.)

"4. All cases of right triangles; also, oblique triangles when (*a*) one side and any two angles, or (*b*) two sides and the angle opposite one of them, are given, may be solved by means of the chart. The general method of solution is indicated by Fig. 641. This shows that the three points of intersection of the lines representing the three sides and the lines representing their respective opposite angles all lie in a straight line.

"In that case of the right triangle in which the two sides, *a* and *b*, are given, a being greater than b, the smaller side is first divided by the larger in order to obtain the tangent of the smaller acute angle of the triangle

$$\left(\frac{b}{a} = \tan B\right).$$

From this tangent, the angle B is obtained from the chart (Problem 1). The rest of the solution is as in Fig. 641.

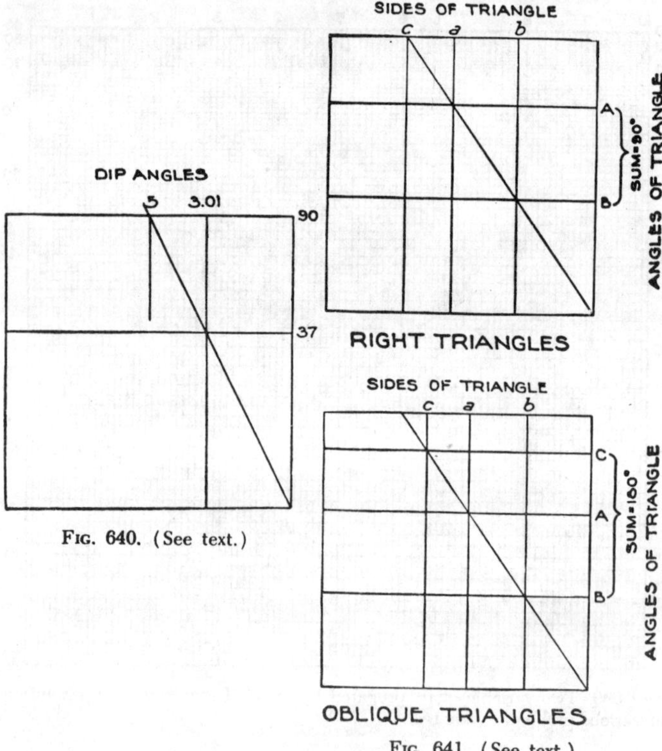

FIG. 640. (See text.)

FIG. 641. (See text.)

"Problems of formation depth and thickness involve triangles and, also, certain angle relationships like those between true dip, apparent dip and direction angle. Any ordinary problem concerning formation depth and thickness may, therefore, be readily worked out by means of this chart and the dip protractor."

Appendix 18

STADIA TABLES[1]

These tables are for use in stadia surveying (**437**) where inclined sights are 19° or less.[2] For vertical angles of more than 3°, a correction should be applied, due to the fact that the inclined sight line is longer than its horizontal (or map) distance by a quantity which becomes larger with increase of the vertical angle (**434**); but for angles of 3° or less, this error may be disregarded in ordinary plane-table surveying.

Example 1. Instrument is set up at *A* and rod is at *B*. Stadia intercept at *B* is 5 ft. as seen from *A*. Therefore, distance from *A* to *B* is $5 \times 100 =$ 500 ft. Vertical angle of inclined line of sight from *A* to *B* is 2°30′. In the table we find that the elevation for a distance of 100 ft. would be 4.36 ft. At 500 ft., the difference in elevation between *A* and *B* would be 5×4.36 ft. $= 21.80$ ft.

Example 2. Instrument is set up at *A* and rod is held at *B*. Observed stadia intercept is 8 ft., which is to be multiplied by 100, the ***stadia constant*** giving a distance value of 800 ft. Vertical angle of inclination of sight line is 12°30′. In the table of "Horizontal Correction for Distances," the correction for 12° and 800 ft. is 34.6 and that for 13° and 800 ft. is 40.5. For 12°30′, it would be $\frac{1}{2}(34.6 + 40.5) = 37.5$ ft., to be subtracted from 800 ft. to give the horizontal distance from *A* to *B*. This is $800 - 37.5 =$ 762.5 ft.

The vertical height for 100 ft. and 12°30′ is 21.13. This multiplied by 8 for the distance 800, is 169.04 ft., which is the difference of elevation between *A* and *B*.

For more refined calculations, a still further correction is applied. This is a quantity, designated $c + f$, which is essentially constant for most alidades, and may be taken as 1. It is the distance, *c*, from the center of the instrument to the center of the objective lens plus the distance, *f*, from the lens to the focal point, a few inches in front of the lens. For all inclined sights, the horizontal projection of this quantity is the correction to be applied. The horizontal values of $c + f$ for different angles are given at the bottom of the accompanying tables.

[1] These tables take care of a very small correction necessitated by the fact that the stadia rod is held vertical instead of perpendicular to the inclined line of sight.

[2] For greater angles, consult Anderson's "Stadia Tables," or tables in handbooks on surveying. Bibliog., Anderson, C. G., 1917.

Example 3. Instrument is set up at A and rod is held at B. Rod intercept at B is 14, indicating distance $AB = 1{,}400$ ft. Vertical angle from A to B is 6°45′. In table for "Horizontal Corrections for Inclined Distances," the correction for 6° and 1,000 ft. is 10.9 ft. and for 7° and 1,000 ft. is 14.9 ft. Interpolating for 45′, the correction for 1,000 ft. and 60°45′ is

$$10.9 + \left(\frac{14.9 - 10.9}{4} \times 3\right) = 10.9 + 3 = 13.9 \text{ ft.}$$

Similarly, for 400 ft. and 6°45′, the correction is

$$4.4 + \left(\frac{6.0 - 4.4}{4} \times 3\right) = 4.4 + 1.2 = 5.6 \text{ ft.}$$

Therefore, for 1,400 ft. the horizontal corrected value is

$$13.9 + 5.6 = 19.5 \text{ ft.}$$
$$1{,}400 - (13.9 + 5.6) = 1{,}400 - 19.5 = 1{,}380.5 \text{ ft.}$$

Under $(c+f)$ corrections for 6° and 7°, the value is 0.99 which for practical purposes may be called 1. Adding this quantity to 1,380.5 ft., we have, for the corrected horizontal projection of $AB + (c+f)$,

$$1{,}380.5 + 1 = 1{,}381.5 \text{ ft.}$$

In the table for Vertical Heights, we find that an angle of 6°45′ subtends a vertical distance of

$$11.64 + \left(\frac{11.70 - 11.64}{2}\right) = 11.64 + .3 = 11.67.$$

For $1{,}400 + (c+f)$ ft. $= 1{,}401$ ft., the vertical difference in elevation would be

$$14.01 \times 11.67 = 163.50 \text{ ft.}$$

Under "$(c+f)$ corrections for vertical heights," the table gives 0.11 for 6° and 0.13 for 7°. For 6°45′, this correction factor would be

$$0.11 + \left(\frac{0.13 - 0.11}{4} \times 3\right) = 0.11 + 0.015 = 0.125,$$

which is to be added to 163.50 ft., giving 163.625 ft., the corrected difference of elevations between A and B.

VERTICAL HEIGHTS FOR INCLINED DISTANCE OF 100

Min.	0°	1°	2°	3°	4°	5°	6°	7°	8°	9°
0	0.00	1.74	3.49	5.23	6.96	8.68	10.40	12.10	13.78	15.45
2	0.06	1.80	3.55	5.28	7.02	8.74	10.45	12.15	13.84	15.51
4	0.12	1.86	3.60	5.34	7.07	8.80	10.51	12.21	13.89	15.56
6	0.17	1.92	3.66	5.40	7.13	8.85	10.57	12.26	13.95	15.62
8	0.23	1.98	3.72	5.46	7.19	8.91	10.62	12.32	14.01	15.67
10	0.29	2.04	3.78	5.52	7.25	8.97	10.68	12.38	14.06	15.73
12	0.35	2.09	3.84	5.57	7.30	9.03	10.74	12.43	14.12	15.78
14	0.41	2.15	3.90	5.63	7.36	9.08	10.79	12.49	14.17	15.84
16	0.47	2.21	3.95	5.69	7.42	9.14	10.85	12.55	14.23	15.89
18	0.52	2.27	4.01	5.75	7.48	9.20	10.91	12.60	14.28	15.95
20	0.58	2.33	4.07	5.80	7.53	9.25	10.96	12.66	14.34	16.00
22	0.64	2.38	4.13	5.86	7.59	9.31	11.02	12.72	14.40	16.06
24	0.70	2.44	4.18	5.92	7.65	9.37	11.08	12.77	14.45	16.11
26	0.76	2.50	4.24	5.98	7.71	9.43	11.13	12.83	14.51	16.17
28	0.81	2.56	4.30	6.04	7.76	9.48	11.19	12.88	14.56	16.22
30	0.87	2.62	4.36	6.09	7.82	9.54	11.25	12.94	14.62	16.28
32	0.93	2.67	4.42	6.15	7.88	9.60	11.30	13.00	14.67	16.33
34	0.99	2.73	4.48	6.21	7.94	9.65	11.36	13.05	14.73	16.39
36	1.05	2.79	4.53	6.27	7.99	9.71	11.42	13.11	14.79	16.44
38	1.11	2.85	4.59	6.33	8.05	9.77	11.47	13.17	14.84	16.50
40	1.16	2.91	4.65	6.38	8.11	9.83	11.53	13.22	14.90	16.55
42	1.22	2.97	4.71	6.44	8.17	9.88	11.59	13.28	14.95	16.61
44	1.28	3.02	4.76	6.50	8.22	9.94	11.64	13.33	15.01	16.66
46	1.34	3.08	4.82	6.56	8.28	10.00	11.70	13.39	15.06	16.72
48	1.40	2.14	4.88	6.61	8.34	10.05	11.76	13.45	15.12	16.77
50	1.45	3.20	4.94	6.67	8.40	10.11	11.81	13.50	15.17	16.83
52	1.51	3.26	4.99	6.73	8.45	10.17	11.87	13.56	15.23	16.88
54	1.57	3.31	5.05	6.79	8.51	10.22	11.93	13.61	15.28	16.94
56	1.63	3.37	5.11	6.84	8.57	10.28	11.98	13.67	15.34	16.99
58	1.69	3.43	5.17	6.90	8.63	10.34	12.04	13.73	15.40	17.05
60	1.74	3.49	5.23	6.96	8.68	10.40	12.10	13.78	15.45	17.10
(c + f) corrections for vertical heights............	0.01	0.03	0.04	0.06	0.08	0.09	0.11	0.13	0.15	0.16

HORIZONTAL CORRECTIONS FOR INCLINED DISTANCES

Dis.	0°	1°	2°	3°	4°	5°	6°	7°	8°	9°
100	0.0	0.0	0.1	0.3	0.5	0.8	1.1	1.5	1.9	2.5
200	0.0	0.1	0.2	0.5	1.0	1.5	2.2	3.0	3.9	4.9
300	0.0	0.1	0.4	0.8	1.5	2.3	3.3	4.5	5.8	7.4
400	0.0	0.1	0.5	1.1	2.0	3.0	4.4	6.0	7.8	9.8
500	0.0	0.2	0.6	1.4	2.5	3.8	5.5	7.5	9.7	12.3
600	0.0	0.2	0.7	1.6	2.9	4.6	6.5	8.9	11.6	14.7
700	0.0	0.2	0.8	1.9	3.4	5.3	7.6	10.4	13.6	17.2
800	0.0	0.2	1.0	2.2	3.9	6.1	8.7	11.9	15.5	19.6
900	0.0	0.3	1.1	2.4	4.4	6.8	9.8	13.4	17.5	22.1
1,000	0.0	0.3	1.2	2.7	4.9	7.6	10.9	14.9	19.4	24.5
(c + f) corrections for horizontal distances.........	1.00	1.00	1.00	1.00	1.00	0.99	0.99	0.99	0.99	0.99

VERTICAL HEIGHTS FOR INCLINED DISTANCE OF 100. *(Continued)*

Min.	10°	11°	12°	13°	14°	15°	16°	17°	18°	19°
0	17.10	18.73	20.34	21.92	23.47	25.00	26.50	27.96	29.39	30.78
2	17.16	18.78	20.39	21.97	23.52	25.05	26.55	28.01	29.44	30.83
4	17.21	18.84	20.44	22.02	23.58	25.10	26.59	28.06	29.48	30.87
6	17.26	18.89	20.50	22.08	23.63	25.15	26.64	28.10	29.53	30.92
8	17.32	18.95	20.55	22.13	23.68	25.20	26.69	28.15	29.58	30.97
10	17.37	19.00	20.60	22.18	23.73	25.25	26.74	28.20	29.62	31.01
12	17.43	19.05	20.66	22.23	23.78	25.30	26.79	28.25	29.67	31.06
14	17.48	19.11	20.71	22.28	23.83	25.35	26.84	28.30	29.72	31.10
16	17.54	19.16	20.76	22.34	23.88	25.40	26.89	28.34	29.76	31.15
18	17.59	19.21	20.81	22.39	23.93	25.45	26.94	28.39	29.81	31.19
20	17.65	19.27	20.87	22.44	23.99	25.50	26.99	28.44	29.86	31.24
22	17.70	19.32	20.92	22.49	24.04	25.55	27.04	28.49	29.90	31.28
24	17.76	19.38	20.97	22.54	24.09	25.60	27.09	28.54	29.95	31.33
26	17.81	19.43	21 03	22.60	24.14	25.65	27.13	28.58	30.00	31.38
28	17.86	19.48	21.08	22.65	24.19	25.70	27.18	28.63	30.04	31.42
30	17.92	19.54	21.13	22.70	24.24	25.75	27.23	28.68	30.09	31.47
32	17.97	19.59	21.18	22.75	24.29	25.80	27.28	28.73	30.14	31.51
34	18.03	19.64	21.24	22.80	24.34	25.85	27.33	28.77	30.19	31.56
36	18.08	19.70	21.29	22.85	24.39	25.90	27.38	28.82	30.23	31.60
38	18.14	19.75	21.34	22.91	24.44	25.95	27.43	28.87	30.28	31.65
40	18.19	19.80	21.39	22.96	24.49	26.00	27.48	28.92	30.32	31.69
42	18.24	19,86	21.45	23.01	24.55	26.05	27.52	28.96	30.37	31.74
44	18.30	19.91	21.50	23.06	24.60	26.10	27.57	29.01	30.41	31.78
46	18.35	19.96	21.55	23.11	24.65	26.15	27.62	29.06	30.46	31.83
48	18.41	20.02	21.60	23.16	24.70	26.20	27.67	29.11	30.51	31.87
50	18.46	20.07	21.66	23.22	24.75	26.25	27.72	29.15	30.55	31.92
52	18.51	20.12	21.71	23.27	24.80	26.30	27.77	29.20	30.60	31.96
54	18.57	20.18	21.76	23.32	24.85	26.35	27.81	29.25	30.65	32.01
56	18.62	20.23	21.81	23.37	24.90	26.40	27.86	29.30	30.69	32.05
58	18.68	20.28	21.87	23.42	24.95	26.45	27.91	29.34	30.74	32.09
60	18.73	20.34	21.92	23.47	25.00	26.50	27.96	29.39	30.78	32.14
$(c + f)$ corrections for vertical heights	0.18	0.20	0.22	0.23	0.25	0.27	0.28	0.30	0.32	0.33

HORIZONTAL CORRECTIONS FOR INCLINED DISTANCES. *(Continued)*

Dis.	10°	11°	12°	13°	14°	15°	16°	17°	18°	19°
100	3.0	3.6	4.3	5.1	5.9	6.7	7.6	8.5	9.5	10.6
200	6.0	7.3	8.6	10.1	11.7	13.4	15.2	17.1	19.1	21.2
300	9.1	10.9	13.0	15.2	17.6	20.1	22.8	25.6	28.6	31.8
400	12.1	14.6	17.3	20.2	23.4	26.8	30.4	34.2	38.2	42.4
500	15.1	18.2	21.6	25.3	29.3	33.5	38.0	42.7	47.7	53.0
600	18.1	21.8	25.9	30.4	35.1	40.2	45.6	51.3	57.3	63.6
700	21.1	25.5	30.2	35.4	41.0	46.9	53.2	59.8	66.8	74.2
800	24.2	29.1	34.6	40.5	46.8	53.6	60.8	68.4	76.4	84.8
900	27.2	32.8	38 9	45.5	52.7	60.3	68.4	76.9	85.9	95.4
1,000	30.2	36.4	43.2	50.6	58.5	67.0	76.0	85.5	95.5	106.0
$(c + f)$ corrections for horizontal distances	0.99	0.98	0.98	0.97	0.97	0.96	0.96	0.95	0.95	0.94

Appendix 19

NATURAL TANGENT TABLE[1]

	100	200	300	400	500	600	700	800	900	
1	0.03	0.06	0.09	0.12	0.15	0.17	0.20	0.23	0.26	1
2	0.06	0.12	0.17	0.23	0.29	0.35	0.41	0.46	0.52	2
3	0.09	0.17	0.26	0.35	0.44	0.52	0.61	0.70	0.79	3
4	0.12	0.23	0.35	0.46	0.58	0.70	0.81	0.93	1.04	4
5	0.15	0.29	0.44	0.58	0.73	0.87	1.02	1.16	1.31	5
6	0.18	0.35	0.53	0.70	0.88	1.05	1.23	1.40	1.58	6
7	0.20	0.41	0.61	0.82	1.02	1.22	1.43	1.63	1.84	7
8	0.23	0.47	0.70	0.93	1.17	1.40	1.63	1.86	2.10	8
9	0.26	0.52	0.79	1.05	1.31	1.57	1.83	2.10	2.36	9
10	0.29	0.58	0.87	1.16	1.46	1.75	2.04	2.33	2.62	10
11	0.32	0.64	0.96	1.28	1.60	1.92	2.24	2.56	2.88	11
12	0.35	0.70	1.05	1.40	1.75	2.09	2.44	2.79	3.14	12
13	0.38	0.76	1.13	1.51	1.89	2.27	2.65	3.02	3.40	13
14	0.41	0.81	1.22	1.63	2.04	2.44	2.85	3.26	3.66	14
15	0.44	0.87	1.31	1.74	2.18	2.62	3.05	3.49	3.92	15
16	0.47	0.93	1.40	1.86	2.33	2.79	3.26	3.72	4.19	16
17	0.50	0.99	1.49	1.98	2.48	2.97	3.47	3.96	4.46	17
18	0.52	1.05	1.57	2.10	2.62	3.14	3.67	4.19	4.72	18
19	0.55	1.11	1.66	2.21	2.77	3.32	3.87	4.42	4.98	19
20	0.58	1.16	1.75	2.33	2.91	3.49	4.07	4.66	5.24	20
21	0.61	1.22	1.83	2.44	3.06	3.67	4.28	4.89	5.50	21
22	0.64	1.28	1.92	2.56	3.20	3.84	4.48	5.12	5.76	22
23	0.67	1.34	2.01	2.68	3.35	4.01	4.68	5.35	6.02	23
24	0.70	1.40	2.09	2.79	3.49	4.19	4.89	5.58	6.28	24
25	0.73	1.45	2.18	2.91	3.64	4.36	5.09	5.82	6.54	25
26	0.76	1.51	2.27	3.02	3.78	4.54	5.29	6.05	6.80	26
27	0.79	1.57	2.36	3.14	3.93	4.71	5.50	6.28	7.07	27
28	0.81	1.63	2.44	3.26	4.07	4.88	5.70	6.51	7.33	28
29	0.84	1.69	2.53	3.38	4.22	5.06	5.91	6.75	7.60	29
30	0.87	1.75	2.62	3.49	4.37	5.24	6.11	6.98	7.86	30
31	0.90	1.80	2.71	3.61	4.51	5.41	6.31	7.22	8.12	31
32	0.93	1.86	2.79	3.72	4.66	5.59	6.52	7.45	8.38	32
33	0.96	1.92	2.88	3.84	4.80	5.76	6.72	7.68	8.64	33
34	0.99	1.98	2.97	3.96	4.95	5.93	6.92	7.91	8.90	34
35	1.02	2.04	3.05	4.07	5.09	6.11	7.13	8.14	9.16	35
36	1.05	2.09	3.14	4.19	5.24	6.28	7.33	8.38	9.42	36
37	1.08	2.15	3.23	4.30	5.38	6.46	7.53	8.61	9.68	37
38	1.11	2.21	3.32	4.42	5.53	6.63	7.74	8.84	9.95	38
39	1.14	2.27	3.41	4.54	5.68	6.81	7.95	9.08	10.22	39
40	1.16	2.33	3.49	4.66	5.82	6.98	8.15	9.31	10.48	40
41	1.19	2.39	3.58	4.77	5.97	7.16	8.35	9.54	10.74	41
42	1.22	2.44	3.67	4.89	6.11	7.33	8.55	9.78	11.00	42
43	1.25	2.50	3.75	5.00	6.26	7.51	8.76	10.01	11.26	43
44	1.28	2.56	3.84	5.12	6.40	7.68	8.96	10.24	11.52	44
45	1.31	2.62	3.93	5.24	6.55	7.85	9.16	10.47	11.78	45
46	1.34	2.68	4.01	5.35	6.69	8.03	9.37	10.70	12.04	46
47	1.37	2.73	4.10	5.47	6.84	8.20	9.57	10.94	12.30	47
48	1.40	2.79	4.19	5.58	6.98	8.38	9.77	11.17	12.56	48
49	1.43	2.85	4.28	5.70	7.13	8.55	9.98	11.40	12.83	49
50	1.46	2.91	4.37	5.82	7.28	8.73	10.19	11.64	13.10	50
51	1.48	2.97	4.45	5.94	7.42	8.90	10.39	11.87	13.36	51
52	1.51	3.03	4.54	6.05	7.57	9.08	10.59	12.01	13.62	52
53	1.54	3.08	4.63	6.17	7.71	9.25	10.79	12.34	13.88	53
54	1.57	3.14	4.71	6.28	7.86	9.43	11.00	12.57	14.14	54
55	1.60	3.20	4.80	6.40	8.00	9.60	11.20	12.80	14.40	55
56	1.63	3.26	4.89	6.52	8.15	9.77	11.40	13.03	14.66	56
57	1.66	3.32	4.97	6.63	8.29	9.95	11.61	13.26	14.92	57
58	1.69	3.37	5.06	6.75	8.44	10.12	11.81	13.50	15.18	58
59	1.72	3.43	5.15	6.86	8.58	10.30	12.01	13.73	15.44	59

[1] See p. 541. Appendices 19 and 20 have been taken from Professor Landes' "Plane Table Notes" with his permission and with permission of George Wahr Publishing Co.

Appendix 19 (*Continued*)

NATURAL TANGENT TABLE

°	100	200	300	400	500	600	700	800	900	
1	1.75	3.49	5.24	6.98	8.73	10.48	12.22	13.97	15.71	1
2	3.49	6.98	10.48	13.97	17.46	20.95	24.44	27.94	31.43	2
3	5.24	10.48	15.72	20.96	26.21	31.45	36.69	41.93	47.17	3
4	6.99	13.99	20.98	27.97	34.97	41.96	48.95	55.94	62.94	4
5	8.75	17.50	26.25	35.00	43.75	52.49	61.24	69.99	78.74	5
6	10.51	21.02	31.53	42.04	52.55	63.06	73.57	84.08	94.59	6
7	12.28	24.56	36.83	49.11	61.39	73.67	85.95	98.22	110.50	7
8	14.05	28.11	42.16	56.22	70.27	84.32	98.38	112.43	126.49	8
9	15.84	31.68	47.51	63.35	79.19	95.03	110.87	126.70	142.54	9
10	17.63	35.27	52.90	70.53	88.17	105.80	123.43	141.06	158.70	10
11	19.44	38.88	58.31	77.75	97.19	116.63	136.07	155.50	174.94	11
12	21.26	42.51	63.77	85.02	106.28	127.54	148.79	170.05	191.30	12
13	23.09	46.17	69.26	92.35	115.44	138.52	161.61	184.70	207.78	13
14	24.93	49.87	74.80	99.73	124.67	149.60	174.53	199.46	224.40	14
15	26.80	53.59	80.39	107.18	133.98	160.77	187.57	214.36	241.16	15
16	28.68	57.35	86.03	114.70	143.48	172.05	200.73	229.40	258.08	16
17	30.57	61.15	91.72	122.29	152.87	183.44	214.01	244.58	275.16	17
18	32.49	64.98	97.48	129.97	162.46	194.95	227.44	259.94	292.43	18
19	34.43	68.87	103.30	137.73	172.17	206.60	241.03	275.46	309.90	19
20	36.40	72.79	109.19	145.59	181.99	218.38	254.78	291.18	327.57	20

Appendix 20

CURVATURE AND REFRACTION TABLE[1]

Distance, ft.	Correction, ft.	Distance, ft.	Correction, ft.
2,000	0.1	16,000	5.1
2,500	0.1	16,500	5.5
3,000	0.2	17,000	5.8
3,500	0.2	17,500	6.1
4,000	0.3	18,000	6.5
4,500	0.4	18,500	6.9
5,000	0.5	19,000	7.2
5,500	0.6	19,500	7.6
6,000	0.7	20,000	8.0
6,500	0.8	20,500	8.4
7,000	1.0	21,000	8.8
7,500	1.1	21,500	9.3
8,000	1.3	22,000	9.7
8,500	1.5	22,500	10.1
9,000	1.6	23,000	10.6
9,500	1.8	23,500	11.1
10,000	2.0	24,000	11.5
10,500	2.2	24,500	12.0
11,000	2.5	25,000	12.5
11,500	2.7	25,500	13.0
12,000	2.9	26,000	13.5
12,500	3.1	26,500	14.1
13,000	3.4	27,000	14.6
13,500	3.7	27,500	15.1
14,000	4.0	28,000	15.7
14,500	4.2	28,500	16.3
15,000	4.5	29,000	16.9
15,500	4.8	29,500	17.5
		30,000	18.0

[1] See footnote to Appendix 19.

Appendix 21

LENGTHS OF DEGREES OF THE PARALLEL[1]

Lat., °	Kilo-meters	Statute miles	Lat., °	Kilo-meters	Statute miles	Lat., °	Kilo-meters	Statute miles
0	111.321	69.172	30	96.488	59.956	60	55.802	34.674
1	111.304	69.162	31	95.506	59.345	61	54.110	33.623
2	111.253	69.130	32	94.495	58.716	62	52.400	32.560
3	111.169	69.078	33	93.455	58.071	63	50.675	31.488
4	111.051	69.005	34	92.387	57.407	64	48.934	30.406
5	110.900	68.911	35	91.290	56.725	65	47.177	29.315
6	110.715	68.795	36	90.166	56.027	66	45.407	28.215
7	110.497	68.660	37	89.014	55.311	67	43.622	27.106
8	110.245	68.504	38	87.835	54.579	68	41.823	25.988
9	109.959	68.326	39	86.629	53.829	69	40.012	24.862
10	109.641	68.129	40	85.396	53.063	70	38.188	23.729
11	109.289	67.910	41	84.137	52.281	71	36.353	22.589
12	108.904	67.670	42	82.853	51.483	72	34.506	21.441
13	108.486	67.410	43	81.543	50.669	73	32.648	20.287
14	108.036	67.131	44	80.208	49.840	74	30.781	19.127
15	107.553	66.830	45	78.849	48.995	75	28.903	17.960
16	107.036	66.510	46	77.466	48.136	76	27.017	16.788
17	106.487	66.169	47	76.058	47.261	77	25.123	15.611
18	105.906	65.808	48	74.628	46.372	78	23.220	14.428
19	105.294	65.427	49	73.174	45.469	79	21.311	13.242
20	104.649	65.026	50	71.698	44.552	80	19.394	12.051
21	103.972	64.606	51	70.200	43.621	81	17.472	10.857
22	103.264	64.166	52	68.680	42.676	82	15.545	9.659
23	102.524	63.706	53	67.140	41.719	83	13.612	8.458
24	101.754	63.228	54	65.578	40.749	84	11.675	7.255
25	100.952	62.729	55	63.996	39.766	85	9.735	6.049
26	100.119	62.212	56	62.395	38.771	86	7.792	4.842
27	99.257	61.676	57	60.774	37.764	87	5.846	3.632
28	98.364	61.122	58	59.135	36.745	88	3.898	2.422
29	97.441	60.548	59	57.478	35.716	89	1.949	1.211
30	96.488	59.956	60	55.802	34.674	90	0	0

[1] From sixth edition of "Tables for a Polyconic Projection of Maps and Lengths of Terrestrial Arcs of Meridian and Parallels," U.S. Department of Commerce, Coast and Geodetic Survey, Special Publication 5, 1946.

Appendix 22

LENGTHS OF DEGREES OF THE MERIDIAN[1]

Lat., °	Kilometers	Statute miles	Lat., °	Kilometers	Statute miles
0– 1	110.5673	68.703	45–46	111.1408	69.060
1– 2	110.5680	68.704	46–47	111.1605	69.072
2– 3	110.5694	68.705	47–48	111.1802	69.084
3– 4	110.5714	68.706	48–49	111.1999	69.096
4– 5	110.5741	68.707	49–50	111.2195	69.108
5– 6	110.5776	68.710	50–51	111.2390	69.121
6– 7	110.5816	68.712	51–52	111.2583	69.133
7– 8	110.5864	68.715	52–53	111.2776	69.145
8– 9	110.5918	68.718	53–54	111.2966	69.156
9–10	110.5978	68.722	54–55	111.3154	69.168
10–11	110.6045	68.726	55–56	111.3340	69.180
11–12	110.6119	68.731	56–57	111.3524	69.191
12–13	110.6198	68.736	57–58	111.3705	69.202
13–14	110.6284	68.741	58–59	111.3884	69.213
14–15	110.6376	68.747	59–60	111.4059	69.224
15–16	110.6475	68.753	60–61	111.4231	69.235
16–17	110.6578	68.759	61–62	111.4399	69.246
17–18	110.6688	68.766	62–63	111.4564	69.256
18–19	110.6804	68.773	63–64	111.4724	69.266
19–20	110.6924	68.781	64–65	111.4881	69.275
20–21	110.7051	68.789	65–66	111.5033	69.285
21–22	110.7182	68.797	66–67	111.5180	69.294
22–23	110.7318	68.805	67–68	111.5323	69.303
23–24	110.7460	68.814	68–69	111.5462	69.311
24–25	110.7606	68.823	69–70	111.5595	69.320
25–26	110.7756	68.833	70–71	111.5722	69.328
26–27	110.7911	68.842	71–72	111.5845	69.335
27–28	110.8070	68.852	72–73	111.5962	69.343
28–29	110.8233	68.862	73–74	111.6073	69.349
29–30	110.8400	68.873	74–75	111.6179	69.356
30–31	110.8570	68.883	75–76	111.6278	69.362
31–32	110.8744	68.894	76–77	111.6371	69.368
32–33	110.8921	68.905	77–78	111.6459	69.373
33–34	110.9101	68.916	78–79	111.6539	69.378
34–35	110.9283	68.928	79–80	111.6614	69.383
35–36	110.9469	68.939	80–81	111.6682	69.387
36–37	110.9656	68.951	81–82	111.6744	69.391
37–38	110.9845	68.962	82–83	111.6799	69.395
38–39	111.0037	68.974	83–84	111.6847	69.398
39–40	111.0230	68.986	84–85	111.6889	69.400
40–41	111.0424	68.998	85–86	111.6923	69.402
41–42	111.0619	69.011	86–87	111.6951	69.404
42–43	111.0816	69.023	87–88	111.6972	69.405
43–44	111.1013	69.035	88–89	111.6986	69.406
44–45	111.1210	69.047	89–90	111.6993	69.407

[1] See footnote to Appendix 21.

BIBLIOGRAPHY

Adams, F. D.: "Experimental Contribution to the Question of the Depth of the Zone of Flow in the Earth's Crust." *Jour. Geol.*, vol. 20, pp. 97–118, 1912.

Alden, W. C.: "Drumlins of Southeastern Wisconsin." U.S. Geol. Survey, *Bull.* 273, 1905.

Ambronn, Richard (translated from the German by Margaret C. Cobb): "Elements of Geophysics." McGraw-Hill Book Company, Inc., New York, 1928.

American Geological Institute: "Glossary of Geology and Related Sciences." Washington, 1957.

American Society of Photogrammetry: "Manual of Photogrammetry." 2d ed., Washington, 1952.

Anderson, C. G.: "Stadia Tables for Obtaining Differences of Elevation." U.S. Geol. Survey, 1917.

Anderson, E. M.: "The Dynamics of Faulting and Dyke Formation with Applications to Britain." London, 1942.

Applin, Esther Richards, Alva E. Ellisor, and Hedwig T. Kniker: "Subsurface Stratigraphy of the Coastal Plain of Texas and Louisiana." Am. Assoc. Petr. Geols., *Bull.*, vol. 9, pp. 79–122, 1925.

Athy, L. F.: "Density, Porosity, and Compaction of Sedimentary Rocks." Am. Assoc. Petr. Geols., *Bull.*, vol. 14, pp. 1–24, 1929 (*a*).

———: "Compaction and Oil Migration." Am. Assoc. Petr. Geols., *Bull.*, vol. 14, pp. 25–35, 1929 (*b*).

Atwood, W. W.: "Glaciation of the Uinta and Wasatch Mountains." U.S. Geol. Survey, *Prof. Paper* 61, 1909.

Bagley, James W.: "Aerophotography and Aerosurveying." McGraw-Hill Book Company, Inc., New York, 1941.

Baker, P. E.: "Density Logging with Gamma Rays." *Jour. Petroleum Technology*, vol. IX, pp. 289–294, 1957.

Balk, Robert: "Structural Behavior of Igneous Rocks." Geol. Soc. Am., *Memoir* 5, 1937.

———: "Structure of Grand Saline Salt Dome, Van Zandt Co., Texas." Am. Assoc. Petr. Geols., *Bull.*, vol. 33, pp. 1791–1829, 1949.

Barrell, J.: "Relative Geological Importance of Continental, Littoral, and Marine Sedimentation." *Jour. Geol.*, vol. 14, pp. 316–356, 430–457, 524–568, 1906.

———: "Geology of the Marysville Mining District, Montana." U.S. Geol. Survey, *Prof. Paper* 57, 1907.

———: "Criteria for the Recognition of Ancient Delta Deposits," Geol. Soc. Am., *Bull.* 23, pp. 377–446, 1921.

———: "Marine and Terrestrial Conglomerates." Geol. Soc. Am., *Bull.*, vol. 36, pp. 279–342, 1925.

Barrow, George: "On an Intrusion of Muscovite-Biotite Gneiss in the Southeast Highlands of Scotland." Geol. Soc. London, *Quart. Jour.*, vol. 49, pp. 330 *et seq.*, 1893.

———: "Lower Dee-Side and the Highland Border." Geologists' Association, *Proc.*, vol. 23, pp. 268–290, 1912.

Barton, Donald C.: "Applied Geophysical Methods in America." *Econ. Geol.*, vol. 22, pp. 649–668, 1927.

———: The Eötvös Torsion Balance Method of Mapping Geologic Structure. "Geophysical Prospecting: 1929," pp. 416–479, 1929 (*a*). (Published by the A.I.M.M.E., New York.)

———: The Seismic Method of Mapping Geologic Structure. "Geophysical Prospecting: 1929," pp. 572–624, 1929 (*b*). (Published by the A.I.M.M.E., New York.)

———: "Geophysical Prospecting for Oil." Am. Assoc. Petr. Geols., *Bull.*, vol. 14, pp. 201–226, 1930 (*a*).

———: "Review of the Geophysical Methods of Prospecting." *Geog. Review*, vol. 20, pp. 288–300, 1930 (*b*).

Bass, N. W.: "Origin of Bartlesville Shoestring Sands, Greenwood and Butler Counties, Kansas." Am. Assoc. Petr. Geols., *Bull.*, vol. 18, pp. 1313–1345, 1934.

Bean, Russell K., and Morris M. Thompson: "Uses of the Orthophotoscope." *Photogrammetric Engineering*, March, 1957.

Beaty, Chester B.: "Landslides and Slope Exposure." *Jour. Geol.*, vol. 64, pp. 70–74, 1956.

Beckwith, R. H.: "Fault Problems in Fault Planes." Geol. Soc. Am., *Bull.*, vol. 58, pp. 79–108, 1947.

Behre, Charles H., Jr., "Talus Behavior above Timber on the Rocky Mountains." *Jour. Geol.*, vol. 41, p. 624, 1933.

Benson, J. M., and J. E. Swafford: "Raydist Systems for Radiolocation and Tracking." *Electrical Engineering*, November, 1953, pp. 983–987.

Bevan, A.: "Rocky Mountain Front in Montana." Geol. Soc. Am., *Bull.*, vol. 40, pp. 427–456, 1929.

Billings, Marland P.: "Structural Geology." 2d ed., Prentice-Hall, Inc., Englewood Cliffs, N.J., 1958.

———: "Stratigraphy and the Study of Metamorphic Rocks." Geol. Soc. Am., *Bull.*, vol. 61, pp. 430–448, 1950.

Birdseye, C. H.: "Topographic Instructions of the United States Geological Survey." U.S. Geol. Survey, *Bull.* 788, 1928.

Black, Robert F., and William L. Barksdale: "Oriented Lakes of Northern Alaska." *Jour. Geol.*, vol. 57, pp. 105–118, 1949.

Blackwelder, Eliot: "The Valuation of Unconformities," *Jour. Geol.*, vol. 17, pp. 289–299, 1909.

———:Mudflow as a Geologic Agent in Semiarid Mountains." Geol. Soc. Am., *Bull.*, vol. 39, pp. 465–484, 1928.

———: "Cavernous Rock Surfaces of the Desert." *Am. Jour. Sci.*, 5th ser., vol. 17, pp. 393–399, 1929.

———: "Desert Plains." *Jour. Geol.*, vol. 39, pp. 133–140, 1931.

Blackwelder, E., and H. H. Barrows: "Elements of Geology." American Book Company, New York, 1911.

Bowen, N. L.: "Crystallization-Differentiation in Igneous Magmas." *Jour. Geol.*, vol. 28, pp. 707–730, 1920; vol. 29, pp. 1–28, 1921.

———: "The Evolution of the Igneous Rocks." Princeton University Press, Princeton, N.J., 1928.

Breck, H. R., S. W. Schoellhorn, and R. B. Baum: "Velocity Logging and Its Geological and Geophysical Applications." Am. Assoc. Petr. Geols., *Bull.*, vol. 41, pp. 1667–1682, 1957.

Broggi, J. A.: " 'Jacob Staff' and Measurements of Stratigraphic Sequences." Am. Assoc. Petr. Geols., *Bull.*, vol. 30, pp. 716–729, 1946.

Brucks, Ernest W.: Luling Oil Field, Caldwell and Guadalupe Counties, Texas. "Structure of Typical American Oil Fields," vol. 1, pp. 256–281, 1929. (Published by the American Association of Petroleum Geologists, Tulsa, Oklahoma.)

Brundall, Laurence, and A. R. Wasem: "Photogeology's Place in Petroleum Exploration." *World Petroleum*, vol. 21, March, pp. 51–54; April, pp. 41–44; 1950.

Bryan, Kirk: "The Papago Country, Arizona." U.S. Geol. Survey, *Water Supply Paper* 499, 1925.

Bucher, Walter H.: "On Ripples and Related Sedimentary Forms and Their Paleogeographic Interpretation." *Am. Jour. Sci.*, vol. 47, pp. 149–210, 241–269, 1919.

———: "The Mechanical Interpretation of Joints." *Jour. Geol.*, vol. 28, pp. 707–730, 1920; and vol. 29, pp. 1–28, 1921.

Cain, Stanley A.: "Palynological Studies at Sodon Lake: I. Size-Frequency Study of Fossil Spruce Pollen." *Science*, vol. 108, no. 2796, p. 115, July 30, 1948.

Campbell, J. D.: "An Echelon Folding." *Econ. Geol.*, vol. 53, pp. 448–472, 1958.

Campbell, John L. P., and John C. Wilson: "Density Logging in the Gulf Coast Area." *Jour. of Petroleum Technology*, vol. 10, pp. 21–25, 1958.

Campbell, M. R.: "Rapid Section Work in Horizontal Rocks." Am. Inst. Min. Eng., *Trans.*, vol. 26, pp. 298–315, 1896.

Chamberlin, T. C.: "Rock-scorings of the Great Ice Invasions.' U.S. Geol. Survey, *Ann. Rept.* 7, pp. 155–248, 1888.

Clapp, F. G.: "Economic Geology of the Amity Quadrangle." U.S. Geol. Survey, *Bull.* 300, 1897.

Clark, Stuart K.: "Classification of Faults." Am. Assoc. Petr. Geols., *Bull.*, vol. 27, pp. 1245–1265, 1943.

Clark, Stuart K., and Jas. I. Daniels: "Logging Rotary Wells from Drill Cuttings." Am. Assoc. Petr. Geols., *Bull.*, vol. 12, pp. 59–76, 1928.

Cloos, Ernst: "Lineation: A Critical Review and Annotated Bibliography." Geol. Soc. Am., *Memoir* 18, 1946.

Coffey, G. N.: "Clay Dunes." *Jour. Geol.*, vol. 17, pp. 754–755, 1909.

Corbett, C. S.: "Method of Projecting Structure through an Angular Unconformity." *Econ. Geol.*, vol. 14, pp. 610–618, 1919.

Cornish, V.: "On the Formation of Sand-dunes." *Geographic Journal* (London), vol. 9, pp. 278–309, 1897.

Crowell, John C.: "Origin of Pebbly Mudstones." Geol. Soc. Am., *Bull.*, vol. 68, pp. 903–1010, 1957.

Cumings, E. R., and R. R. Shrock: "Niagaran Coral Reefs of Indiana and Adjacent States and Their Stratigraphic Relations." Geol. Soc. Am., *Bull.*, vol. 39, pp. 579–620, 1928.

Curray, Joseph R.: "Dimensional Grain Orientation Studies of Recent Coastal Sands." Am. Assoc. Petr. Geols., *Bull.*, vol. 40, pp. 2441–2456, 1956.

Cushman, Joseph A.: "Use of Foraminifera in Geologic Correlation." Am. Assoc. Petr. Geols., *Bull.*, vol. 8, pp. 485–491, 1924.

———: "Foraminifera: Their Classification and Economic Use." Sharon, Mass., 1928. 4th ed., Harvard University Press, Cambridge, Mass., 1948.

Dale, T. N.: "Slate Deposits and Slate Industry of the United States." U.S. Geol. Survey, *Bull.* 275, 1906.

———: "Granites of Maine." U.S. Geol. Survey, *Bull.* 313, 1907.

———: "Slate in the United States." U.S. Geol. Survey, *Bull.* 586, 1914.

Daly, R. A.: "Igneous Rocks and Their Origin." McGraw-Hill Book Company, Inc., New York, 1914.

Dapples, E. C., and J. F. Rominger: "Orientation Analysis of Fine-grained Clastic Sediments: A Report of Progress." *Jour. Geol.*, vol. 53, pp. 246–261, 1945.

Davis, Raymond E., Francis S. Foote, and W. H. Rayner: "Surveying: Theory and Practice." 2d ed., New York, 1934. In 1940, complete revision by Davis and Foote. 6th ed., McGraw-Hill Book Company, Inc., New York, 1953.

Davis, W. M.: "Faults in the Triassic Formation near Meriden, Conn." Mus. Comp. Zool., *Bull.* 16, pp. 61–87, 1889.

———: "Structure and Origin of Glacial Sand Plains." Geol. Soc. Am., *Bull.* 1, pp. 195–202, 1890.

———: "The Triassic Formation of Connecticut." U.S. Geol. Survey, *An. Rept.* 18, Pt. 2, pp. 9–192, 1898.

———: "Geographical Essays." Ginn & Company, Boston, 1909.

———: "Die erklarende Beschreibung der Landformen." Leipzig and Berlin, 1912.

———: "Nomenclature of Surface Forms on Faulted Structures." Geol. Soc. Am., *Bull.* 24, pp. 187–216, 1913.

———: "The Coral Reef Problem." Am. Geog. Soc., *Spec. Publ.* No. 9, 1929.

———: "Rock Floors in Arid and in Humid Climates." *Jour. Geol.*, vol. 38, pp. 1–27, 136–158, 1930.

De Ford, Ronald K.: "Rock Colors." Am. Assoc. Petr. Geols., *Bull.*, vol. 28, pp. 128–137, 1944.

DeGolyer, E., *et al.*: "Geology of Salt Dome Oil Fields." 1926. (Published by American Association of Petroleum Geologists.)

Desjardins, Louis: "Techniques in Photogeology." Am. Assoc. Petr. Geols., *Bull.*, vol. 34, pp. 2284–2317, 1950.

Desjardins, Louis, and S. Grace Hower: "A Technique for Geologic, Topographic, and Structural Mapping." Published in 1938 by the Aero Exploration Company of Tulsa, Okla. The same paper, somewhat modified, was printed on pp. 44 *et seq.* of the *Oil and Gas Journal* for May 11, 1939.

Dobrin, Milton B.: "Introduction to Geophysical Prospecting." 2d ed., McGraw-Hill Book Company, Inc., New York, 1960.

Dodge, John Franklin: "Straight Hole Drilling Practice." Am. Petr. Institute, *Proceedings* of the Tenth Annual Meeting, vol. 11, No. 1, pp. 43–51, Jan. 2, 1930.

Duran S., Luis G.: "Depth Calculations for Structural Maps." Petroleo Interamericano, April, 1948, pp. 82–89.

Dwerryhouse, A. R.: "Geological and Topographical Maps." London, 1911.

Eardley, Armand John.: "Interpretation of Geologic Maps and Aerial Photographs." J. W. Edwards, Publisher, Inc., Ann Arbor, Mich., 1941.

Elkins, Thomas A.: "The Second Derivative Method of Gravity Interpretation." *Geophysics,* vol. 16, pp. 29–50, 1951.

Engel, Celeste G., and Robert P. Sharp: Chemical Data on Desert Varnish." Geol. Soc. Am., *Bull.*, vol. 69, pp. 487–518, 1958.

English, Walter A.: "Some Plane Table Methods." Am. Assoc. Petr. Geols., *Bull.*, vol. 8, pp. 47–54, 1924.

———: "Use of Airplane Photographs in Geologic Mapping." Am. Assoc. Petr. Geols., *Bull.*, vol. 14, pp. 1049–1058, 1930.

Evans, O. F.: "Floating Sand in the Formation of Swash Marks." *Jour. Sedimentary Petrology,* vol. 8, p. 71, August, 1938.

———: "The Classification and Origin of Beach Cusps." *Jour. Geol.*, vol. 46, pp. 615–627, 1938.

———: "The Classification of Wave-formed Ripple Marks." *Jour. Sedimentary Petrology,* vol. 11, pp. 37–41, April, 1941.

———: "Further Observations on the Origin of Beach Cusps." *Jour. Geol.,* vol. 53, pp. 403–404, 1945.

———: "Ripple Marks as an Aid in Determining Depositional Environment and Rock Sequence." *Jour. Sedimentary Petrology,* vol. 19, pp. 82–86, August, 1949.

Eve, A. S., and D. A. Keys: "Applied Geophysics." University Press, Cambridge, London, 1929.

Farrell, J. H.: "Practical Field Geology." McGraw-Hill Book Company, Inc., New York, 1912.

Fath, A. E.: "The Origin of the Faults, Anticlines, and 'Buried Ridge' of the Northern Part of the Mid-continent Oil and Gas Field." U.S. Geol. Survey, *Prof. Paper* 128-C, 1920.

Fay, A. H.: "Glossary of the Mining and Mineral Industry." U.S. Bureau of Mines, *Bull.* 95, 1920.

Fenneman, N. M.: "Lakes of Southeastern Wisconsin." Wisc. Geol. and Nat. His. Survey, *Bull.* 8, 1902.

Foley, Lyndon L.: "Origin of the Faults in Creek and Osage Counties, Oklahoma." Am. Assoc. Petr. Geols., *Bull.* 10, pp. 293–303, 1926.

Fordham, W. H.: "Geophysical Surveying." Inst. Petr. Technologists, *Journal* (London), vol. 15, pp. 35–80, 1929.

Forrester, James Donald: "Principles of Field and Mining Geology." John Wiley & Sons, Inc., New York, 1946.

Fuller, M. L.: "Geology of Long Island, New York." U.S. Geol. Survey, *Prof. Paper* 82, 1914.

———: "Relation of Oil to Carbon Ratios of Pennsylvanian Coals in North Texas." *Econ. Geol.,* vol. 14, pp. 536–542, 1919.

———: "Quick Method of Reconnaissance Mapping." *Econ. Geol.,* vol. 14, pp. 411–423, 1919.

———: "Carbon Ratios in Carboniferous Coals of Oklahoma, and Their Relation to Petroleum." *Econ. Geol.,* vol. 15, pp. 225–235, 1920.

Galloway, J. J.: "Method of Correlation by Means of Foraminifera." Am. Assoc. Petr. Geols., *Bull.,* vol. 10, pp. 562–567, 1926.

Geikie, J.: "Structural and Field Geology." 3d ed., D. Van Nostrand Company, Inc., Princeton, N.J., 1912.

Gilbert, G. K.: "A New Method of Measuring Heights by Means of the Barometer." U.S. Geol. Survey, *An. Rept.* 2, pp. 403–566, 1882.

———: "Lake Bonneville." U.S. Geol. Survey, *Monog.* 1, 1890.

———: "Crescentic Gouges on Glaciated Surfaces." Geol. Soc. Am., *Bull.* 17, pp. 303–316, 1906.

———: "California Earthquake of 1906." *Am. Jour. Sci.,* 4th ser., vol. 27, pp. 48–52, 1909.

Gilluly, James, *et al.:* "Origin of Granite." Geol. Soc. Am., *Memoir* 28, 1948.

Grabau, A. W.: "Principles of Stratigraphy." 1913. 2d ed., A. G. Seiler, New York, 1924.

Grabau, A. W., and H. W. Shimer: "North American Index Fossils." New York, 1909. Revised by Shimer and R. R. Shrock, John Wiley & Sons, Inc., New York, 1944.

Gregory, H. E.: "The Rodadero—A Fault Plane of Unusual Aspect." *Am. Jour. Sci.*, 4th ser., vol. 37, pp. 289–298, 1914.

Grout, Frank F.: "Petrography and Petrology." McGraw-Hill Book Company, Inc., New York, 1932.

———: "Kemp's Handbook of Rocks," D. Van Nostrand Company, Inc., 1940. 6th ed., The Macmillan Company, New York, 1947.

Grubenmann, U.: "Die kristallinen Schiefer." 1904 and 1907.

Gulliver, F. P.: "Shoreline Topography." Am. Acad. Arts and Sci., *Proc.* 34, pp. 149–258, 1899.

Harker, A.: "Natural History of Igneous Rocks." Methuen & Co., Ltd., London, 1909.

Haun, John D., and L. W. LeRoy: "Subsurface Geology in Petroleum Exploration." Colorado School of Mines, Golden, Colo., 1958.

Hawkins, J. E.: "Recent Lorac Developments." National Electronic Conference, *Proc.*, 1950.

Hayes, C. W.: "Handbook for Field Geologists." New York, 1909. 3d ed., John Wiley & Sons, Inc., New York, 1921.

Heald, K. C.: "Determination of Geothermal Gradients in Oil Fields on Anticlinal Structure." Am. Petr. Institute, *Proceedings of the Tenth Annual Meeting*, vol. 11, No. 1 (Drilling and Production Engineering, *Bull.* 204), pp. 102–110, 1930.

Hedberg, Hollis D.: "The Effect of Gravitational Compaction on the Structure of Sedimentary Rocks." Am. Assoc. Petr. Geols., *Bull.*, vol. 10, pp. 1035–1072, 1926.

Hedstrom, Helmer: "Electrical Survey of Structural Conditions in the Salt Flat Field, Caldwell County, Texas." Am. Assoc. Petr. Geols., *Bull.*, September, 1930.

Heiland, C. A.: "Geophysical Methods of Prospecting." Colorado School of Mines, *Quarterly*, vol. 24, March, 1929.

———: "Geophysical Exploration." Prentice-Hall, Inc., Englewood Cliffs, N.J., 1940.

Hemphill, William R.: "Determination of Quantitative Geologic Data with Stereometer-Type Instruments." U.S. Geol. Survey, *Bull.* 1043-C, 1958.

Hewett, D. F.: "Measurements of Folded Beds." *Econ. Geol.*, vol. 15, pp. 367–385, 1920.

Hewett, D. E., and C. T. Lupton: "Anticlines in the Southern Part of the Big Horn Basin, Wyoming, U.S. Geol. Survey, *Bull.* 656, 1917.

Hill, Mason L.: "Graphic Method for Some Geologic Calculations." Am. Assoc. Petr. Geols., *Bull.*, vol. 26, pp. 1155–1159, 1942.

Hill, Raymond A.: "Preliminary Survey Procedure." 1929. (Published by the American Paulin System, Inc., Los Angeles, Calif.)

Hobbs, W. H.: "Examples of Joint-controlled Drainage from Wisconsin and New York." *Jour. Geol.*, vol. 13, pp. 363–374, 1905.

Hodgson, Robert A.: "Precision Altimeter Survey Procedures." American Paulin System, Los Angeles, Calif., 1957.

Hopkins, David Moody: "Thaw Lakes and Thaw Sinks in the Imuruk Lake Area, Seward Peninsula, Alaska." *Jour. Geol.*, vol. 57, pp. 119–131, 1949.

Houston Geological Society Study Group: "Electrical Well Logging." Am. Assoc. Petr. Geols., *Bull.*, vol. 23, pp. 1287–1313, 1939.

Hovey, E. O.: "Striations and U-shaped Valleys Produced by Other Than Glacial Action." Geol. Soc. Am., *Bull.* 20, pp. 409–426, 1909.

Howe, E.: "Landslides in the San Juan Mountains, Colorado." U.S. Geol. Survey, *Prof. Paper* 67, 1909.

Howell, J. V.: See American Geological Institute, 1957.

Huffman, George G., and W. Armstrong Price: "Clay Dune Formation near Corpus Christi, Texas." *Jour. Sedimentary Petrology*, vol. 19, pp. 118–127, 1949.

Huitt, Jim L.: "Three-Dimensional Measurement of Sand Grains." Am. Assoc. Petr. Geols., *Bull.*, vol. 38, pp. 159–160, 1954.

Hume, G. S.: "Fault Structures in the Foothills and Eastern Rocky Mountains of Southern Alberta." Geol. Soc. Am., *Bull.*, vol. 68, pp. 395–412, 1957.

Hyde, H. A.: "Pollen Analysis and the Museums." *Museums Journal*, vol. 44, 1944.

Hyde, J. E.: "Desiccation Conglomerates in the Coal-measures Limestone of Ohio." *Am. Jour. Sci.*, 4th ser., vol. 25, pp. 400–408, 1908.

Irving, J. D., *et al.*: "Field and Office Methods in the Preparation of Geological Reports." *Econ. Geol.*, vol. 8, pp. 66–96, 177–181, 264–297, 373–397, 489–499, 578–597, 691–721, 795–797, 1913; vol. 9, pp. 67–72, 184–189, 1914.

Ives, Ronald L.: "Measurement in Block Diagrams." *Econ. Geol.*, vol. 34, pp. 561–572, 1939.

———: "Glacial Bastions of Northern Colorado." *Jour. Geol.*, vol. 54, pp. 391–397, 1946.

———: "Field Methods: Atemporal Polaris Correction." *Econ. Geol.*, vol. 43, pp. 418–426, 1948.

Jenny, W. P.: "Electric and Electromagnetic Prospecting for Oil." Am. Assoc. Petr. Geols., *Bull.* vol. 14, pp. 1199–1213, September, 1930.

Jensen, Homer: "Operational Procedure for the Airborne Magnetometer." *Oil and Gas Jour.*, July 13, 1946.

Johnson, D. W.: "Beach Cusps." Geol. Soc. Am., *Bull.* 21, pp. 599–624, 1910.

———: "Origin of the Carolina Bays." vol. 11, Columbia University Press, New York, 1942.

Johnson, J. W.: "Dynamics of Nearshore Sediment Movement." Am. Assoc. Petr. Geols., *Bull.*, vol. 40, pp. 2211–2232, 1956.

Johnson, R. H., and L. G. Huntley: "Principles of Oil and Gas Production." John Wiley & Sons, Inc., New York, 1916.

Kay, G. F.: Classification and Duration of the Glacial Period." Geol. Soc. Am., *Bull.*, vol. 42, pp. 425–466, 1931.

Kay, Marshall: "North American Geosynclines." Geol. Soc. Am., *Memoir* 48, 1951.

Kelley, Vincent C.: "Monoclines of the Colorado Plateau." Geol. Soc. Am., *Bull.*, vol. 66, pp. 789–804, 1955.

———: "Primary Structures in Some Recent Sediments." Am. Assoc. Petr. Geols., *Bull.* 41, pp. 1704–1747, 1957.

Keyes, C. R.: "Rock-floor of Intermont Plains of the Arid Region." Geol. Soc. Am., *Bull.* 19, pp. 63–92, 1908.

Kingsley, Louise: "Caldron-subsidence of the Ossipee Mountains." *Am. Jour. Sci.*, 5th series, vol. 22, pp. 139–168, 1931.

Kitson, H. E.: "Graphic Solution of Strike and Dip from Two Angular Components." Am. Assoc. Petr. Geols., *Bull.*, vol. 13, pp. 1211–1213, 1929.

Knechtel, Maxwell M.: "Pimpled Plains of Eastern Oklahoma." Geol. Soc. Am., *Bull.* 63, pp. 689–700, 1952.

Knopf, Eleanora Bliss, and Earl Ingerson: "Structural Petrology." Geol. Soc. Am., *Memoir* 6, 1938.

Kraus, Edgar: "Logging Wells Drilled by the Rotary Method." Am. Assoc. Petr. Geols., *Bull.*, vol. 8, pp. 641–650, 1924.

Krumbein, W. C., and L. L. Sloss: "Stratigraphy and Sedimentation." W. H. Freeman & Co., San Francisco, Calif., 1958.

Krynine, Paul D.: "The Megascopic Study and Field Classification of Sedimentary Rocks." *Jour. Geol.*, vol. 56, pp. 130–165, 1948.

Kuenen, P. H.: "Formation of Beach Cusps." *Jour. Geol.*, vol. 56, pp. 34–40, 1948.

Kuenen, P. H., and C. I. Migliorini: "Turbidity Currents as a Cause of Graded Bedding." *Jour. Geol.*, vol. 58, pp. 91–126, 1950.

Ladd, Harry S.: "Recent Reefs." Am. Assoc. Petr. Geols., *Bull.*, vol. 34, pp. 203–214, 1950.

Lahee, F. H.: "Crystalloblastic Order and Mineral Development in Metamorphism." *Jour. Geol.*, vol. 22, pp. 500–515, 1913.

———: "Graphic Determination of Dip Components Where Dips Are Measured in Feet per Mile." *Econ. Geol.*, vol. 24, pp. 262–263, 1919

———: "The Barometric Method of Geologic Surveying for Petroleum Mapping." *Econ. Geol.*, vol. 25, pp. 150–169, 1920.

———: "Oil and Gas Fields of the Mexia and Tehuacana Fault Zones, Texas." Structure of Typical American Oil Fields, vol. 1, pp. 304–388,

1929 (*a*). (Published by the American Association of Petroleum Geologists.)

———: "Problem of Crooked Holes." Am. Assoc. Petr. Geols., *Bull.*, vol. 13, pp. 1095–1161, 1929 (*b*).

———: "Overlap and Nonconformity." Am. Assoc. Petr. Geols., *Bull.*, vol. 33, p. 1901, 1949.

Landes, Kenneth K.: "Plane Table Notes." Published, together with a very useful notebook, by George Wahr Publishing Co., Ann Arbor, Mich., 1947.

Lange, N. A.: "Handbook of Chemistry." 9th ed., Handbook Publishers, Inc., Sandusky, Ohio, 1956.

Lawson, A. C.: "Geomorphogeny of the Upper Kern Basin." Univ. Calif., Geol., Dept. *Bull.* 3, pp. 291–376, 1902–1904.

Lawson, A. C., *et al.*: "Report of the State Earthquake Investigation Commission on the California Earthquake of April 18, 1906." Carnegie Institution of Washington, 1908.

Lee, Willis T.: "The Face of the Earth as Seen from the Air." Am. Geog. Soc., *Special Bull.*, 1922.

Leith, C. K.: "Rock Cleavage." U.S. Geol. Survey, *Bull.* 239, 1905.

———: "Structural Geology." Holt, Rinehart and Winston, Inc., New York, 1923.

Leonardon, E. G., and Sherwin F. Kelly: Some Applications of Potential Methods to Structural Studies. "Geophysical Prospecting: 1929," pp. 180–198, 1929. Published by the A.I.M.M.E.

LeRoy, Leslie W., and Harry M. Crain: "Subsurface Geologic Methods" (a symposium). Colorado School of Mines, Golden, Colo., 1949.

Levorsen, A. I.: "Convergence Studies in the Mid-continent Region." Am. Assoc. Petr. Geols., *Bull.* 11, pp. 657–682, 1927.

———: "Studies in Paleogeology." Am. Assoc. Petr. Geols., *Bull.*, vol. 17, pp. 1107–1132, 1933.

Lewis, J. V.: "Origin of Pillow Lavas." Geol. Soc. Am., *Bull.* 25, pp. 591–654, 1914.

Lindgren, W.: "Mineral Deposits." 4th ed., McGraw-Hill Book Company, Inc., New York, 1933.

Link, Theodore A.: "En Echelon Tension Fissures and Faults." Am. Assoc. Petr. Geols., *Bull.* 13, pp. 627–644, 1929.

———: "Leduc Field, Alberta, Canada." Geol. Soc. Am., *Bull.*, vol. 60, pp. 381–402, 1949.

Lovely, H. R.: "Onlap and Strike-overlap." Am. Assoc. Petr. Geols., *Bull.* 32, p. 2295, 1948.

Lovering, T. S.: "Field Evidence to Distinguish Overthrusting from Underthrusting." *Jour. Geol.*, vol. 40, pp. 651–663, 1932.

Low, Julian W.: "Plane Table Mapping." Harper & Brothers, New York, 1952.

Lynton, E. D.: "Laboratory Orientation of Well Cores by Their Magnetic Polarity." Am. Assoc. Petr. Geols., *Bull.*, vol. 21, pp. 580–615, 1937.

———: "Recent Developments in Laboratory Orientation of Cores by Their Magnetic Polarity." *Geophys.*, vol. 3, No. 2, 1938.

Mackin, J. Hoover: "Concept of the Graded River." Geol. Soc. Am., *Bull.*, vol. 59, pp. 463–512, 1948.

MacClintock, Paul: "Crescentic Crack, Crescentic Gouge, Friction Crack, and Glacier Movement." *Jour. Geol.*, vol. 61, p. 186, 1953.

Manly, J. M., and J. A. Powell: "Manual for Writers." University of Chicago Press, Chicago, 1913.

Mather, Kirtley F.: "The Manipulation of the Telescopic Alidade in Geologic Mapping." *Bull.* of the Scientific Laboratories of Denison University, Granville, Ohio, vol. 19, pp. 97–142, 1919.

Matthew, G. F.: "Post Glacial Faults at St. John, N.B." *Am. Jour. Sci.*, 3d ser., vol. 48, pp. 501–503, 1894.

McCurdy, P. G.: "Manual of Aerial Photogrammetry." Published by the Hydrographic Office of the U.S. Navy Department, 1940.

McCutchin, John A.: "Determination of Geothermal Gradients in Oklahoma." Am. Assoc. Petr. Geols., *Bull.* 14, pp. 535–558, 1930.

McKee, Edwin D.: "Small-scale Structures in the Coconino Sandstone of Northern Arizona." *Jour. Geol.*, vol. 53, pp. 313–325, 1945.

McKinstry, Hugh Exton: "Mining Geology." Prentice-Hall, Inc., Englewood Cliffs, N.J., 1948.

McLaughlin, R. P. (Chairman): "Geophysical Prospecting: 1929." Published by the A.I.M.M.E., 1929.

McQueen, H. S.: "Insoluble Residues as a Guide in Stratigraphic Studies." Missouri Bureau of Geol. and Mines, 56th *Biennial Rept.* Appendix 1, 1931.

Mead, W. J.: "Notes on the Mechanics of Geologic Structures." *Jour. Geol.*, vol. 28, pp. 505–523, 1920.

———: "Determination of Attitude of Concealed Bedded Formations by Diamond Drilling." *Econ. Geol.*, vol. 16, pp. 37–47, 1921.

Melton, Frank A.: "Preliminary Observations on Geological Use of Aerial Photographs." Am. Assoc. Petr. Geols., *Bull.*, vol. 29, pp. 1756–1765, 1945.

———: "Onlap and Strike-overlap." Am. Assoc. Petr. Geols., *Bull.* 31, pp. 1868–1878, 1947; vol. 32, pp. 2296–2297, 1948.

———: "Aerial Photographs and Structural Geomorphology." *Jour. Geol.*, vol. 67, pp. 351–370, 1959.

Merrill, G. P.: "Rocks, Rock-weathering, and Soils." The Macmillan Company, New York, 1907. (Later edition in 1913.)

Milner, Henry B.: "Sedimentary Petrography." 2d ed., London and New York, 1924; 3d ed., Nordeman Publication Co., New York, 1940.

Moody, J. D., and M. J. Hill: "Wrench-Fault Tectonics." Geol. Soc. Am., *Bull.*, vol. 67, pp. 1207–1246, 1956.

Moon, F. W.: "Field and Office Methods in the Preparation of Geologic Reports." *Econ. Geol.*, vol. 8, pp. 795–797, 1913.

Moore, Raymond C.: "Introduction to Historical Geology." 2d ed., McGraw-Hill Book Company, Inc., New York, 1958.

Moulton, Gail F.: "Some Features of Redbed Bleaching." Am. Assoc. Petr. Geols., *Bull.*, vol. 10, pp. 304–311, 1926. Also discussion of same in same volume, pp. 636–637.

Nettleton, L. L.: "Geophysical Prospecting for Oil." McGraw-Hill Book Company, Inc., New York, 1940.

Nevin, C. M.: "Principles of Structural Geology." 4th ed., John Wiley & Sons, Inc., New York, 1949.

Nevin, C. M., and R. E. Sherrill: "Studies in Differential Compaction." Am. Assoc. Petr. Geols., *Bull.*, vol. 13, pp. 1–22, 1929.

Newsom, J. F.: "Clastic Dikes." Geol. Soc. Am., *Bull.* 14, pp. 227–268, 1903.

Nugent, L. E., Jr.: "Aerial Photographs in Structural Mapping of Sedimentary Formation." Am. Assoc. Petr. Geols., *Bull.*, vol. 31, pp. 478–494, 1947.

Officer, H. G., Glenn C. Clark, and F. L. Aurin: "Core Drilling for Structure in the North Mid-continent Area." Am. Assoc. Petr. Geols., *Bull.*, vol. 10, pp. 513–530, 1926.

Pettijohn, F. J.: "Sedimentary Rocks." 2d ed., Harper & Brothers, New York, 1957.

Pillmore, C. L.: "Application of High-order Stereoscopic Plotting Instruments to Photogeologic Studies." U.S. Geol. Survey, *Bull.* 1043-B, 1957.

Pirsson, L. V., and A. Knopf: "Rocks and Minerals." 3d ed., John Wiley & Sons, Inc., New York, 1947.

Powers, Sidney: "Reflected Buried Hills and Their Importance in Petroleum Geology." *Econ. Geol.*, vol. 17, pp. 233–259, 1922.

———: "Reflected Buried Hills in the Oil Fields of Persia, Egypt, and Mexico." Am. Assoc. Petr. Geols., *Bull.*, vol. 10, pp. 422–442, 1926.

Price, W. Armstrong: The Role of Diastrophism in Topography of Corpus Christi Area, South Texas, in "Gulf Coast Oil Fields." Am. Assoc. Petr. Geols., 1936.

Putnam, W. C.: "Marine Cycle of Erosion for a Steeply Sloping Shore Line of Emergence." *Jour. Geol.*, vol. 45, pp. 844–850, 1937.

Ramberg, Hans: "Origin of Metamorphic and Metasomatic Rocks." University of Chicago Press, Chicago, 1952.

———: "Natural and Experimental Boudinage and Pinch-and-Swell Structures." *Jour. Geol.*, vol. 63, pp. 512–526, 1955.

Rasmussen, W. C.: "Periglacial Frost-Thaw Basins in New Jersey: A Discussion." *Jour. Geol.*, vol. 61, pp. 473, 474, 1953.

Ray, Richard G.: "Photogeologic Procedures in Geologic Interpretation and Mapping." U.S. Geol. Survey, *Bull.* 1043-A, 1956.

Reed, R. D.: "Some Methods of Heavy Mineral Investigations." *Econ. Geol.*, vol. 19, pp. 320–337, 1924.

Reed, R. D., and J. P. Bailey: "Subsurface Correlation by Means of Heavy Minerals." Am. Assoc. Petr. Geols., *Bull.*, vol. 11, pp. 359–368, 1927.

Reid, H. F.: "Geometry of Faults." Geol. Soc. Am., *Bull.* 20, pp. 171–196, 1909.

Reid, H. F., *et al.:* "Report of the Committee on the Nomenclature of Faults," Geol. Soc. Am., *Bull.* 24, pp.163–186, 1913.

Rettger, R. E.: "On Specifying the Type of Subsurface Structural Contouring." Am. Assoc. Petr. Geols., *Bull.* 13, pp. 1559–1561, December, 1929.

Rich, J. L.: "Simple Graphical Methods for Determining True Dip from Two Components." Am. Assoc. Petr. Geols., *Bull.*, vol. 16, pp. 92–94, 1932.

Robinson, G. D.: "Measuring Dipping Beds," *Geotimes,* vol. 4, No. 1, pp. 8 *et seq.*, 1959.

Rogers, G. Sherburne: "Intrusive Origin of the Gulf Coast Salt Domes." *Econ. Geol.*, vol. 13, pp. 447–485, 1918.

Ross, Clarence S.: "Methods of Preparation of Sedimentary Materials for Study." *Econ. Geol.*, vol. 21, pp. 454–468, 1926.

Ross, J. S., and E. A. Swedenborg: Analyses of Waters of the Salt Creek Field Applied to Underground Problems. "Petroleum Development and Technology for 1928–29." Published by the A.I.M.M.E., 1929.

Russell, I. C.: "Hanging Valleys." Geol. Soc. Am., *Bull.* 16, pp. 75–90, 1905.

Rust, William Monroe, Jr.: "Typical Electrical Prospecting Methods." *Geophysics,* vol. 5, pp. 243–249, 1940.

Rybar, Stephen: "The Eötvös Torsion Balance, and Its Application to the Finding of Mineral Deposits." *Econ. Geol.*, vol. 18, pp. 639–662, 1923.

Salisbury, C. L.: "Wind-Induced Stone Tracks, Prince of Wales Island, Alaska." Geol. Soc. Am., *Bull.*, vol. 67, pp. 1659–1660, 1956.

Salisbury, R. D.: "Distinct Glacial Epochs . . . . " *Jour. Geol.*, vol. 1, pp. 61–84, 1893.

———: "Glacial Geology of New Jersey." Geol. Survey of N.J., *Final Rept.*, vol. 5, 1902.

Salisbury, R. D., and W. W. Atwood: "Interpretation of Topographic Maps." U.S. Geol. Survey, *Prof. Paper* 60, 1908.

Schlumberger, C., and M., and E. G. Leonardon: "Electrical Coring; A Method of Determining Bottom-hole Data by Electrical Measurements." A.I.M.M.E., *Trans.*, vol. 110, pp. 237–272, 1934.

Schlumberger Well Surveying Corporation: "Introduction to Schlumberger Well Logging." *Document* 8, Houston, Texas, 1958.

Schuchert, Charles: "Paleogeography of North America." Geol. Soc. Am., *Bull.*, vol. 20, pp. 427–606, 1910.

———: "The Value of Micro-fossils in Petroleum Exploration." Am. Assoc. Petr. Geols., *Bull.*, vol. 8, pp. 539–553, 1924.

Scott, Harold W.: "Solution Sculpturing in Limestone Pebbles." Geol. Soc. Am., *Bull.*, vol. 58, pp. 141–152, 1947.

Secrist, Mark H.: "Perspective Block Diagrams." *Econ. Geol.*, vol. 31, pp. 867–880, 1936.

Shaler, N. S.: "Geology of Cape Anne, Mass." U.S. Geol. Survey, *An. Rept.* 9, pp. 537–610, 1889.

———: "Beaches and Tidal Marshes of the Atlantic Coast." *Nat. Geog. Monographs*, No. 5, 1895.

Sharpe, C. F. Stewart: "Landslides and Related Phenomena." Columbia University Press, New York, 1938.

Sheldon, P.: "Some Observations and Experiments on Joint Planes." *Jour. Geol.*, vol. 20, pp. 53–79, 164–183, 1912.

Shepard, Francis P.: "Submarine Geology." Harper & Brothers, New York, 1948.

Sherrill, R. E.: "Origin of the En Echelon Faults in North-Central Oklahoma." Am. Assoc. Petr. Geols., *Bull.* 13, pp. 31–37, 1929.

Sherzer, W. H.: "Criteria for the Recognition of the Various Types of Sand Grains." Geol. Soc. Am., *Bull.* 21, pp. 625–656, 1910.

Shrock, Robert R.: "Sequence in Layered Rocks." New York, 1948.

Skeels, D.C.: "Structural Geology of the Trail Creek-canyon Mountain Area, Montana." *Jour. Geol.*, vol. 47, pp. 816–840, 1939.

Smith, A. L.: "Delta Experiments." Geog. Soc. Am., *Bull.* 41, pp. 729–742. 1909.

Smith, H. T. U.: "Aerial Photographs and Their Applications." Appleton-Century-Crofts, New York, 1943.

Smith, W. S. Tangier: "An Apparent-dip Protractor." *Econ. Geol.*, vol. 20, pp. 181–184, 1925.

Stanley, Geo. M.: "Origin of Playa Stone Tracks, Racetrack Playa, Inyo County, California." Geol. Soc. Am., *Bull.*, vol. 66, pp. 1329–1360, 1955.

Steidtmann, E.: "The Secondary Structures of the Eastern Part of the Baraboo Quartzite Range, Wisconsin." *Jour. Geol.*, vol. 18, pp. 259–270, 1910.

Straley, H. W., III: "Some Notes on the Nomenclature of Faults." *Jour. Geol.*, vol. 42, pp. 756–763, 1934.

Sundberg, Karl: "Electrical Prospecting for Oil Structure." Am. Assoc. Petr. Geols., *Bull.*, vol. 14, pp. 1145–1163, September, 1930.

Tarr, R. S., and L. Martin: "College Physiography." The Macmillan Company, New York, 1914.

Teas, L. P.: "Differential Compacting the Cause of Certain Claiborne Dips." Am. Assoc. Petr. Geols., *Bull.*, vol. 7, pp. 370–378, 1923.

Terzaghi, Karl, and Ralph B. Peck. "Soil Mechanics in Engineering Practice." John Wiley & Sons, Inc., New York, 1948.

Thom, W. T., Jr.: "Relation of Earth Temperatures to Buried Hills and Anticlinal Folds." *Econ. Geol.* vol. 20, pp. 524–530, 1925.

Thornburgh, R. H.: "Wave-front Diagrams in Seismic Interpretations." Am. Assoc. Petr. Geols., *Bull.*, vol. 15, 1930.

Thornbury, Wm. D.: "Principles of Geomorphology." John Wiley & Sons, Inc., New York, 1954.

Threet, Richard L.: "Horizontal Distance Corrections and Plotting Errors in Stadia Surveying." Am. Assoc. Petr. Geols., *Bull.* 37, pp. 2749–2750, 1953.

Tickell, F. G.: "The Correlative Value of the Heavy Minerals." Am. Assoc. Petr. Geols., *Bull.*, vol. 8, pp. 158–168, 1924.

———: "Examination of Fragmental Rocks." 3d ed., Stanford University Press, Stanford, Calif., 1947.

Tixier, M. P., R. P. Alger, and C. A. Doh: "Sonic Logging." *Jour. Petroleum Technology,* May, 1959, pp. 106–114.

Tracy, John Clayton: "Plane Surveying." John Wiley & Sons, Inc., New York, 1914.

Trueman, J. D.: "The Value of Certain Criteria for the Determination of the Origin of Foliated Crystalline Rocks." *Jour. Geol.*, vol. 20, pp. 228–258, 300–315, 1912.

Turner, F. J.: "Evolution of the Metamorphic Rocks." Geol. Soc. Am., *Memoir* 30, 1948.

Twenhofel, W. H.: "Treatise on Sedimentation." The Williams and Wilkins Company, Baltimore, 1926.

———: "Principles of Sedimentation." 2d ed., McGraw-Hill Book Company, Inc., New York, 1950.

United States Geological Survey: Bibliographies of Geological Literature of North America. See footnote 5, p. 440.

United States Department of the Interior: "Publications of the Geological Survey." Washington, D.C., 1958.

Van Hise, C. R.: "Principles of North American Pre-Cambrian Geology." U.S. Geol. Survey, *An. Rept.* 15, Pt. 1, pp. 581–843, 1896.

———: "A Treatise on Metamorphism." U.S. Geol. Survey, *Monog.* 47, 1904.

Van Orstrand, C. E.: "Apparatus for Measurement of Temperatures in Deep Wells." *Econ. Geol.*, vol. 19, pp. 229–248, 1924.

———: Variation of Temperature with Geologic Structure in California and Wyoming Oil Districts." *Econ. Geol.*, vol. 21, pp. 145–165, 1926.

———: "Temperature Gradients," in "Problems of Petroleum Geology." Am. Assoc. Petr. Geols., pp. 989–1021, 1934.

Vela, Gonzalo Medina: "Notas sobre Fotogrametria." Assoc. Mexicana de Geologos Petroleros, *Boletin,* vol. 11, pp. 177–368, 1959.

Vintanage, P. W.: "Sandstone Dikes in the South Platte Area, Colorado." *Jour. Geol.*, vol. 62, pp. 493–500, 1954.

Walcott, C. D.: "Paleozoic Intra-formational Conglomerates." Geol. Soc. Am., *Bull.* 5, pp. 191–198, 1894.

Wallace, Robert Earl: "Cave-in Lakes in the Nabesna, Chisana, and Tanana River Valleys, Eastern Alaska." *Jour. Geol.,* vol. 56, pp. 171–181, 1948.

Washburn, A. L.: "Classification of Patterned Ground and Review of Suggested Origins." Geol. Soc. Am., *Bull.,* vol. 67, pp. 823–866, 1956.

Weaver, Paul: "Relations of Geophysics to Geology." Am. Assoc. Petr. Geols., *Bull.* vol. 18, pp. 3–12, 1934.

Welex, Inc.: "Fundamentals of Quantitative Analysis of Electric Logs." Welex, Inc., Forth Worth, Texas, 1959.

Wengerd, Sherman A.: "Newer Techniques in Aerial Surveying." *World Oil,* vol. 127, pp. 37–42 in No. 3; pp. 46–54 in No. 4; pp. 49–54 in No. 5; pp. 136–142 in No. 6; pp. 131–136 in No. 8, 1947.

Wentworth, Chester K.: "A Scale of Grade and Class Terms for Clastic Sediments." *Jour. Geol.,* vol. 30, pp. 377–392, 1922.

———: "Striated Cobbles in Southern States." Geol. Soc. Am., *Bull.,* vol. 39, pp. 941–954, 1928.

———: "Plotting and Measurement of Exaggerated Sections." *Econ. Geol.,* vol. 25, pp. 827–831, 1930.

Wheeler, Harry E., and E. Maurice Beesley: "Critique of the Time-stratigraphic Concept." Geol. Soc. Am., *Bull.,* vol. 59, pp. 75–86, 1948.

White, David: "Some Relations in Origin between Coal and Petroleum." Washington Acad. of Sci., *Jour.,* vol. 6, pp. 189–212, 1915.

Willcox, H. Case: Value of Aerial Photographic Surveying and Mapping to Petroleum Companies and Their Geologists, A.I.M.E., "Production of Petroleum in 1924." New York, 1925.

Willis, Bailey: "Mechanics of Appalachian Structure." U.S. Geol. Survey, *An. Rept.* 13, Pt. 2, pp. 213–281, 1892.

———: "Geologic Structures." McGraw-Hill Book Company, Inc., New York, 1923.

———: "The Dead Sea Problem, Rift Valley or Ramp Valley." Geol. Soc. Am., *Bull.,* vol. 39, pp. 490–542, 1928.

Wilson, J. Tuzo: "Some Aspects of Geophysics in Canada with Special Reference to Structural Research in the Canadian Shield." *Trans.* Am. Geophysical Union, vol. 29, pp., 691–726, 1948.

Wolfe, Peter E.: "Periglacial Frost-Thaw Basins in New Jersey." *Jour. Geol.,* vol. 61, pp. 133–141, 1953.

Wood, G. M.: "Suggestions to Authors of Papers Submitted for Publication by the United States Geological Survey." 5th ed., 1958. (Published by the U.S. Department of the Interior.)

Woodward, Louis A.: "Aerial Photogrammetry as Applied to the Petroleum Industry." *Jour. of Petroleum Technology,* vol. 2, No. 1, pp., 9–15, 1950.

Woodworth, J. B.: "Original Micaceous Cross-banding of Strata by Current Action." *Am. Geol.*, vol. 27, pp. 281–283, 1901.

———: "Bowlder Beds of the Caney Shales at Talihina, Oklahoma." Geol. Soc. Am., *Bull.* 23, pp. 457–462, 1912 (*a*).

———: "Geological Expedition to Brazil and Chile." Mus. Comp. Zool., *Bull.* 56, 1912 (*b*).

Zernitz, Emilie R.: Drainage Patterns and Their Significance." *Jour. Geol.*, vol. 40, pp. 498–521, 1932.

Ziegler, V.: "Factors Influencing the Rounding of Sand Grains." *Jour. Geol.*, vol. 19, pp. 645–654, 1911.

INDEX

Numbers in **boldface** type refer to pages on which definitions are given.